LEASHING THE DOGS OF WAR

LEASHING THE DOGS OF WAR
CONFLICT MANAGEMENT IN A DIVIDED WORLD

Edited by Chester A. Crocker,
Fen Osler Hampson,
and Pamela Aall

UNITED STATES INSTITUTE OF PEACE PRESS
Washington, D.C.

UNITED STATES INSTITUTE OF PEACE
1200 17th Street NW
Washington, DC 20036

First published 2007

Printed in the United States of America

The paper used in this publication meets the minimum requirements of American National Standards for Information Science—Permanence of Paper for Printed Library Materials, ANSI Z39.48-1984.

Library of Congress Cataloging-in-Publication Data
　　Leashing the dogs of war : conflict management in a divided world / Chester A. Crocker, Fen Osler Hampson, and Pamela Aall, editors.
　　　　p. cm.
　　Includes bibliographical references and index.
　　ISBN-13: 978-1-929223-97-8 (alk. paper)
　　ISBN-10: 1-929223-97-8 (alk. paper)
　　ISBN-13: 978-1-929223-96-1 (pbk. : alk. paper)
　　ISBN-10: 1-929223-96-X (pbk. : alk. paper)
　　1. Peaceful change (International relations) 2. Conflict management 3. Security, International.
I. Crocker, Chester A. II. Hampson, Fen Osler. III. Aall, Pamela R.
　　JZ5538.L4 2007
　　327.1'72—dc22
　　　　　　　　　　　　　　　　　　　　　　　　　　　　　　　2006027680

CONTENTS

FOREWORD

Richard H. Solomon
President, United States Institute of Peace

For those of us who came of age during the Cold War, the pace and complexity of change in today's world are at best confusing, at worst overwhelming. More than fifteen years after the end of the MAD confrontation between East and West, we find ourselves constantly surprised by new international challenges to our security and economic well-being, uncertain of their causes, and apprehensive of their consequences. Looking back five, ten, or even fifteen years, we now begin to see patterns in the unfolding of events, but those designs that we do see are only beginning to shape the policies and institutions that might help us deal with the post-post–Cold War and post-9/11 era now enveloping the world.

If historians are having a hard time deciphering the course of events since the breakup of the Soviet Union, would-be prognosticators are faced with an impossible task. Back in the early 1990s, talk of the future centered on "the new world order" that would emerge out of the wreckage of the Cold War. We hoped for an international system of multilateral organ-izations that would regulate the constructive interplay of democracies across the globe. By the middle of the 1990s, with the international community learning the meaning of "global chaos" and "ethnic cleansing" and the renewed meaning of "genocide," the future appeared to consist of an unending series of ethnic or religiously fueled conflagrations and of desperate efforts by hastily assembled crews of international firefighters to dampen the flames and—just perhaps—begin to rebuild devastated societies. At the start of the new millennium, the international terrain shifted again, not least in the United States, where intervention in other people's conflicts and nation-building efforts became subordinated to a post-9/11 preoccupation with homeland defense and the war against international terrorism.

The attacks on the Pentagon and World Trade Center, and subsequent terrorist atrocities in Bali, London, and Madrid, profoundly changed the mood and the security agenda not only in Washington but in capitals on five continents. Henceforth, the newly declared "war on terrorism" began to take precedence over all other international concerns and activities. Interventionism gained new legitimacy, justified by the new national security concerns. Nation building, too, gained new relevance in an era of failed states hijacked by religious extremists bent on murderous destruction on a global scale. Furthermore, once the Taliban and their al Qaeda allies had been driven from power in Kabul and chased back into caves and villages in Afghanistan and Pakistan, the U.S. government was emboldened to embark upon a campaign of "preemptive war." Soon, GIs were struggling to stabilize Baghdad. Talk of the future now centered—depending on one's perspective—either on hopes of installing democratic regimes and constitutions across the Middle East or on fears of a widening "imperial overreach."

And today—it is late in 2006 as these words are written—the scene is changing once again: Will the Iraq experience bring on a new period of isolationism (a new type of Vietnam syndrome) or entrap the United States in a "long war" in the tumultuous Muslim world? The only thing that one might safely predict is the warm reception that scholars and students will accord this volume. In an age of chaos and uncertainty, breadth and depth of knowledge are at a premium. If the future must remain shrouded in the fog of current conflicts, it is all the more important that we have a wide-ranging and well-grounded understanding of the recent past and of the present so that we can better adjust to and cope with what seems likely to lie ahead. And such an understanding is exactly what is offered by the editors and authors of *Leashing the Dogs of War: Conflict Management in a Divided World.*

This volume challenges us to reflect deeply on the interplay of war and peace, coercive power, and diplomatic imagination. It provides wide-ranging analyses of the sources of contemporary international conflict and of the means available by which that conflict can be prevented, managed, or resolved. Furthermore,

each chapter is written by an author or authors not only expert in the subject matter but also distinguished by their ability to be both analytically incisive and evenhanded. To be sure, readers will encounter strong arguments and opinions in the pages of this book, but they will not be misled by distortions, nor ensnared by tendentiousness, nor blinded by rhetoric. To the contrary, they will discover reliable facts and figures, revealing interpretations, and readable, unambiguous prose.

Leashing the Dogs of War is the third volume of its kind in recent publications from the United States Institute of Peace Press. And not entirely coincidentally, the other two also appeared at turning points on the road that has led us from the fall of the Berlin Wall to the rise of global terrorism. The first of the trio, *Managing Global Chaos,* appeared in 1996, its title reflecting the humanitarian crises and ethnic violence that sprang forth in the Balkans, Africa, and the Caribbean. Dreams of a new world order were already fading by 1996, and there was a new and acute awareness of the feeble state of many societies and of the daunting complexity of conflicts rooted, as the editors commented, in a "rich brew of ethnonationalism, religion, socioeconomic grievances, environmental degradation, collapsed states, globalized markets, and geopolitical shifts."

The successor to *Managing Global Chaos* was *Turbulent Peace,* which was published five years later, in 2001—but before September 11. Its carefully chosen title reflected a cautious optimism—optimism both that the frequency and intensity of intercommunal conflict were declining and that diplomats and policymakers were learning some useful lessons about conflict management and peacemaking—that is, how third parties have some potential to manage or limit conflict and sometimes to reach negotiated settlements and make them stick. At the same time, however, the volume editors were under no illusions about the fragility of many recent settlements, the vulnerability of many regions to destabilizing shocks, and the lethal intractability of numerous hot conflicts.

The title of the present volume is in many ways the bleakest of the three. Use of the word *War* makes plain that the world is no longer at peace, even a turbulent peace; the dogs of war are now rampant. Yet, despite its title and like its predecessors, *Leashing the Dogs of War* is fundamentally an optimistic book. It recognizes that the global environs are both conflict-ridden and often bloody, and it harbors no illusions that murderous enmity will suddenly give way to universal comity. But it does believe —indeed, its raison d'etre is to advertise—that something can be done to moderate, reduce, and even resolve specific conflicts. In fact, its central message is not that *something* can be done, but that *many things* can be done, and that the test of the skilled peacemaker is to decide which tools will work best on which conflicts and in which combinations. The book also suggests, when taken as a whole, that we can expect to witness war-fighting and peace-making at the same time, sometimes by the same states and other actors.

This same optimism and this same concern —not to predict the future, but to learn from the past about how to bring peace to the present —permeate all the works supported and published by the United States Institute of Peace since its creation in 1984. Given the close associations between the volume's editors and the programs of the Institute, this concurrence

should surprise no one. Chester A. Crocker, the architect while assistant secretary of state of the plan that brought democracy to Namibia, is a member of the Institute's board of directors and was for many years board chairman. Fen Osler Hampson, professor of international affairs at the Norman Paterson School of International Affairs at Carleton University, was a peace fellow at the Institute in 1993-94. Pamela Aall is vice president of the Institute's Education Program. The three of them have jointly edited or authored no fewer than six books published by the Institute's Press.

These books have won many plaudits and a wide readership. *Managing Global Chaos* and *Turbulent Peace* have enjoyed an especially large audience among professors and students of international affairs, conflict resolution, and related disciplines, and *Leashing the Dogs of War* will surely continue the tradition. Indeed, many of the young men and women now building their careers within, for example, diplomatic corps, humanitarian and relief agencies, and intergovernmental organizations will have the opportunity to make practical use of the lessons that can be learned from the experts convened in print by Crocker, Hampson, and Aall. The United States Institute of Peace intends that those lessons will prove useful to the next generation of peacemakers as they work to rein in the dogs of war and constrain the conflicts on which they feed.

ACKNOWLEDGMENTS

The task of creating a book that cuts across disciplines, perspectives, and experiences in order to define the challenges of the current security environment engages many people. Of all of these, Dick Solomon, president of the United States Institute of Peace, deserves special recognition for encouraging us to capture the complex field of conflict management and for giving us the opportunity to do so not just once, but three times, for this volume has two predecessors, *Managing Global Chaos* and *Turbulent Peace*. Thanks also go to the chapter authors, who grappled not only with their own areas of expertise but also with the defining question of this book: Is it possible to be at war and act as a peacemaker at the same time? This is a difficult question and we appreciate their willingness to consider it.

We were wonderfully aided by many people at the United States Institute of Peace, especially Ethan Schechter, Raina Kim, Joseph Sany, Lindsey Ensor, and Jeff Helsing in the Education Program, and Joe Lataille in both Education and Finance. Michael Graham played a critical role, both as head of the Publications Program and as vice president for Management. His unwavering encouragement of this book and the others that the Education Program has produced has been heartening and much appreciated. Many Institute colleagues, including Trish Thomson, Dan Serwer, Paul Stares, Neil Kritz, David Smock, Judy Barsalou, Mike Lekson, and John Crist, have also been very supportive.

Marie Marr, Kay Hechler, and all their colleagues in the Publications Program have performed the miracle of producing a first-class volume from the many worthy but quite diverse chapters that we delivered to them. Once again, Nigel Quinney is at the center of this effort and his superb editorial judgment is reflected throughout the volume. He is an exceptional editor and we are lucky to have him as our collaborator.

CONTRIBUTORS

Chester A. Crocker is the James R. Schlesinger Professor of Strategic Studies, Edmund A. Walsh School of Foreign Service at Georgetown University and former chairman of the board of directors of the United States Institute of Peace. From 1981 to 1989 he was assistant secretary of state for African affairs; as such, he was the principal diplomatic architect and mediator in the prolonged negotiations among Angola, Cuba, and South Africa that led to Namibia's transition to democratic governance and independence, and to the withdrawal of Cuban forces from Angola. He is the author of *High Noon in Southern Africa: Making Peace in a Rough Neighborhood* and coauthor (with Fen Osler Hampson and Pamela Aall) of *Taming Intractable Conflicts: Mediation in the Hardest Cases*. He is also coeditor of *Turbulent Peace: The Challenges of Managing International Conflict; Managing Global Chaos: Sources of and Responses to International Conflict; African Conflict Resolution: The U.S. Role in Peacemaking; Grasping the Nettle: Analyzing Cases of Intractable Conflict;* and *Herding Cats: Multiparty Mediation in a Complex World.* He is an adviser on strategy and negotiation to U.S. and European firms.

Fen Osler Hampson is professor of international affairs at and director of the Norman Paterson School of International Affairs, Carleton University, Ottawa, Canada. He is the author of five books, including *Nurturing Peace: Why Peace Settlements Succeed or Fail,* and coeditor of twenty others, including *Turbulent Peace: The Challenges of Managing International Conflict; Managing Global Chaos: Sources of and Responses to International Conflict; Grasping the Nettle: Analyzing Cases of Intractable Conflict;* and *Herding Cats: Multiparty Mediation in a Complex World.* His recent books include *Madness in the Multitude: Human Security and World Disorder* and *Taming Intractable Conflicts: Mediation in the Hardest Cases* (with Chester A. Crocker and Pamela Aall). Hampson was a senior fellow at the United States Institute of Peace in 1993–94. He is chair of the Human Security Track of the Helsinki Process on Globalization and Democracy, a joint initiative of the governments of Finland and Tanzania.

Pamela Aall is vice president of education at the United States Institute of Peace. Before joining the Institute, she worked for the President's

Committee on the Arts and the Humanities, the Institute of International Education, the Rockefeller Foundation, the European Cultural Foundation, and the International Council for Educational Development. She is also president of Women in International Security. She is coeditor of *Turbulent Peace: The Challenges of Managing International Conflict; Managing Global Chaos: Sources of and Responses to International Conflict; Grasping the Nettle: Analyzing Cases of Intractable Conflict;* and *Herding Cats: Multiparty Mediation in a Complex World.* She is coauthor of *Guide to IGOs, NGOs, and the Military in Peace and Relief Operations* (with Daniel Miltenberger and Thomas G. Weiss) and *Taming Intractable Conflicts: Mediation in the Hardest Cases* (with Chester A. Crocker and Fen Osler Hampson).

◆ ◆ ◆

Mohammed Ayoob is University Distinguished Professor of International Relations, James Madison College and the Department of Political Science, Michigan State University, and coordinator of the Muslim Studies Program, Michigan State University.

Robert J. Art is Christian A. Herter Professor of International Relations, Brandeis University.

Graham Brown is economics research officer for Southeast Asia at the Centre for Research on Inequality, Human Security and Ethnicity (CRISE) at the University of Oxford.

Michael E. Brown is dean of the Elliott School of International Affairs and professor of international affairs and political science at the George Washington University.

Diana Chigas is codirector of the Reflecting on Peace Practice project at CDA-Collaborative Learning Projects, and professor of practice at the Fletcher School at Tufts University.

Paul Collier is professor in the Department of Economics, Oxford University, and direc-

tor of the Centre for the Study of African Economies.

Martha Crenshaw is Colin and Nancy Campbell Professor of Global Issues and Democratic Thought, Department of Government, Wesleyan University.

Patrick M. Cronin is director of Studies at the International Institute for Strategic Studies, London, and a former director of Research at the United States Institute of Peace.

Paul F. Diehl is Henning Larsen Professor of Political Science and University Distinguished Teacher/Scholar at the University of Illinois at Urbana-Champaign.

Sir Lawrence Freedman is professor of war studies and vice principal (Research) at King's College London.

Nils Petter Gleditsch is research professor at the Centre for the Study of Civil War at the International Peace Research Institute, Oslo (PRIO), editor of the *Journal of Peace Research,* and professor of international relations at the Norwegian University of Science and Technology in Trondheim.

Ted Robert Gurr recently retired as Distinguished University Professor at the University of Maryland, College Park, and founding director of the Minorities at Risk Project.

Bruce W. Jentleson is professor of public policy and political science at the Terry Sanford Institute of Public Policy, Duke University.

Margaret P. Karns is professor of political science at the University of Dayton.

Geoffrey Kemp is director of Regional Strategic Programs, The Nixon Center.

Charles King is chairman of the faculty and Ion Ratiu Associate Professor in the School of Foreign Service at Georgetown University.

Stephen D. Krasner is deputy director of the Stanford Institute for International Studies and director of the Policy Planning Staff at the U.S. Department of State.

Louis Kriesberg is Professor Emeritus of Sociology, Maxwell Professor Emeritus of Social Conflict Studies, and founding director of the Program on the Analysis and Resolution of Conflicts at Syracuse University.

Neil Kritz is associate vice president of the United States Institute of Peace and director of its Rule of Law Program.

Jack S. Levy is Board of Governors' Professor, Rutgers University, and president-elect of the International Studies Association.

Andrew Mack is director of the Human Security Centre, Liu Institute for Global Issues, University of British Columbia.

David M. Malone is assistant deputy minister for global issues in the Canadian Foreign Service.

Edward D. Mansfield is Hum Rosen Professor of Political Science and director of the Christopher H. Browne Center for International Politics, University of Pennsylvania.

Kimberly Marten is professor and chair, Department of Political Science, Barnard College, Columbia University.

David Mendeloff is assistant professor of international affairs and director of the Centre for Security and Defence Studies at the Norman Paterson School of International Affairs, Carleton University, Ottawa.

Karen A. Mingst is Lockwood Chair Professor in the Patterson School of Diplomacy and International Commerce and professor in the Department of Political Science at the University of Kentucky.

Joseph S. Nye, Jr. is Distinguished Service Professor, Harvard University.

Michael O'Hanlon is a senior fellow in Foreign Policy Studies at the Brookings Institution and a visiting lecturer at Princeton University.

Marina Ottaway is the director of the Middle East Program at the Carnegie Endowment for International Peace.

Chantal de Jonge Oudraat is senior fellow at the Center for Transatlantic Relations of the Paul H. Nitze School of Advanced Studies of Johns Hopkins University and adjunct professor at the Edmund A. Walsh School of Foreign Service, Georgetown University.

Robert I. Rotberg is director of the Program on Intrastate Conflict and Conflict Resolution, Kennedy School of Government, Harvard University, and president of the World Peace Foundation.

Daniel Serwer is vice president of the Center for Post-Conflict Peace and Stability Operations and the Centers of Innovation at the United States Institute of Peace.

Jake Sherman is a former political affairs officer in the office of the Special Representative of the Secretary-General, United Nations Assistance Mission in Afghanistan.

Jack Snyder is Robert and Renée Belfer Professor of International Relations, Department of Political Science, Columbia University.

Paul B. Stares is vice president of the Center for Conflict Analysis and Prevention at the United States Institute of Peace.

Frances Stewart is professor of development economics and director of the Centre for Research on Inequality, Human Security and Ethnicity (CRISE) at the University of Oxford.

Patricia Thomson is the executive vice president of the United States Institute of Peace.

Saadia Touval is Professorial Lecturer in the Conflict Management Program and a visiting fellow at the Foreign Policy Institute of the Nitze School of Advanced International Studies, Johns Hopkins University.

Sir Brian Urquhart is former under secretary-general of the United Nations.

Ruth Wedgwood is the Edward B. Burling Professor of International Law and Diplomacy, and director of the Program on International Law and Organizations, at the Nitze School of Advanced International Studies, Johns Hopkins University.

Mona Yacoubian is a special adviser to the United States Institute of Peace's Muslim World Initiative and a member of the Council on Foreign Relations.

I. William Zartman is Jacob Blaustein Professor of International Organizations and Conflict Resolution, and director of the Conflict Management Program, at the Nitze School of Advanced International Studies, Johns Hopkins University.

PART I

INTRODUCTION

1

LEASHING THE DOGS OF WAR

Chester A. Crocker, Fen Osler Hampson,
and Pamela Aall

CRY 'HAVOC' AND LET SLIP THE DOGS of war." Shakespeare's Mark Antony issues this call for revenge shortly after Julius Caesar's murder by his erstwhile friends and associates. Antony's vision of revenge includes chaos, "domestic fury and fierce civil strife," and he names "the dogs of war" as the instrument of destruction. What makes the image especially chilling is the knowledge that it is almost impossible to call off the dogs once they have been let slip or unleashed. Over the centuries, these dogs of war have been unleashed on nearly every continent of the world and have directly or indirectly caused the deaths of millions.

Especially in the past century, three hundred years after Shakespeare wrote *Julius Caesar*, the dogs of war roamed freely. The twentieth century has been called a period of "total war" not only because it witnessed two major conflagrations that engulfed much of the planet but also because it saw the dawn of the nuclear age. With the end of the Cold War and the collapse of communist regimes in Eastern

Europe and the former Soviet Union, many hoped for the beginning of a new, more peaceful, chapter in world history. However, the outbreak or continuation of sectarian violence in the Balkans, Africa, the Middle East, and other corners of the globe; the emergence of a more lethal and global brand of terrorism; and a growing cultural divide between Islam and the West dashed many of those hopes. At the same time, there were troubling signs that international norms and institutions, which helped check the proliferation of nuclear weapons and other technologies of mass destruction during the past century, were eroding as a number of states—North Korea, Pakistan, and India—crossed the nuclear threshold. And judging from its early years, the twenty-first century seems—at first glance—no less dangerous or conflict prone than the century it succeeded.

Over the past forty years, however, we have learned much about the sources and nature of conflict as well as the means to prevent or contain war. And over the past decade, scholars, diplomats, nonofficial practitioners, and others

3

have turned their attention to studying and understanding the causes of sectarian violence and its international implications as well as documenting in rich, empirical detail global trends in the frequency, lethality, and implications of different forms of violence. Many of these studies have also discussed the broader policy implications of this research by identifying appropriate strategies, mechanisms, and responses for conflict management and prevention. This volume is intended to capture the best elements of this research and the best policy recommendations and insights that flow from it: in short, to help us leash the dogs of war.

This book differs from its predecessor in a number of ways. *Turbulent Peace: The Challenges of Managing International Conflict* was published in August 2001—before the September 11, 2001, terrorist attacks on New York and Washington, D.C.—and provided comprehensive coverage of the principal issues of the day: the challenges of humanitarian intervention and the difficulties in reaching a sustainable peace. *Leashing the Dogs of War: Conflict Management in a Divided World* starts with the premise that we are in a new security environment. A key consideration in the book is whether powerful states and international organizations can simultaneously conduct a war on terrorism and conflict management policies in zones of conflict. The war on terrorism and the consequences of U.S.-led interventions in Iraq and Afghanistan have changed the global playing field in a serious way. The 1990s dilemmas of humanitarian intervention and peacemaking are now joined by increasingly salient questions about how to effectively pursue nation building and democratization processes in states that are internally divided, capacity deficient, and conflict ridden. U.S.-led interventions to topple unfriendly regimes have also underscored the finite uses of military power and the importance of identifying other instruments to restore political order. There is active discussion and debate about postconflict strategies of conflict management

and what kinds of resources and capacity are required to help states make the transition from war to peace and whether further outbreaks of violence and conflict can be successfully prevented.

All of this has important implications for the teaching of international relations. A lot of contemporary discussion has focused on such questions as, Can we impose democracy in states where we intervene? Can we rebuild wartorn economies? Can outsiders reinstate or create from scratch a strong civil society? Can we quell or prevent the outbreak of sectarian violence? Theoretical questions about the normative and legal legitimacy of humanitarian-driven interventions in a world of "sovereign" states are now joined by more practical questions about how best to mobilize the political will and capacity to intervene, especially when the United States' own power projection abilities are so heavily taxed by its strategic commitments in Iraq and Afghanistan and so few of its allies are willing, or able, to fill the void.

In order to assess these and other questions, this book is organized as follows. Part 2 explores the major causes of contemporary violence in the international system and identifies key trends in the pattern of violence. This part examines the roots, nature, and dynamics of terrorism and the links between terrorism, weapons of mass destruction, rogue states, and conflict. It also assesses the question of whether terrorists are creations or opportunistic beneficiaries of conflict zones. Parts 3 and 4 focus on questions of the diplomacy and tradecraft of conflict management. In addition to identifying the utility of different strategies of conflict management in different conflict settings, these parts explore the question of whether successful conflict management and the peaceful settlement of conflicts in war-torn countries and regions will reduce terrorism in the future. Part 5 examines the roles of different actors and institutions and their capacities, weaknesses, and strengths in different aspects of conflict management. This part looks to the future of international cooperation in addressing the challenges of managing and maintaining international peace and security and examines such questions as, Will coalitions of the willing replace the United Nations in responding to conflicts, and what happens when few are willing? Has the age of international cooperation in meeting complex emergencies ended? What roles will the United Nations, NATO, the Organization for Security and Cooperation in Europe, and other international organizations play? What useful role is there for nongovernmental organizations in the conflict management business? Part 6 looks to the lessons and challenges of state building and nation building and whether we can learn from past successes and failures when the international community has intervened in countries in order to end violence and restore political order.

OLD AND NEW SECURITY CHALLENGES

In addition to changes in the global security environment arising from the increasing threat of terrorism, widening fractures between and among cultures, and the growing threat of nuclear proliferation, there have been changes in the perception of that environment among the leading states of NATO and the European Union and many other societies. This perception includes new attitudes about the hierarchy of interests linked to conflict arenas where these challenges often arise. It also includes a heightened overall sense of insecurity and division in the international system. While recognizing an increase in the number of threats, this volume also points to evidence that all things did not change in 2001 and that many of the conflict sources we became familiar with in the course of the 1990s and from previous epochs—for example, security dilemmas, state failure, economic predation, political transitions—remain as valid and relevant in today's world as in earlier times. Any at-

tempt to draw conclusions about the prospects for international conflict management needs to keep in mind these factors of continuity as well as the drivers of change.

As an example, a number of chapters in part 2 of the volume examine, from one angle or another, the increasingly salient fragmentation within the Islamic world and between it and other cultures and regions. Some contributors explore the roots and different contexts of Islamist militancy, while others examine the uses and limits of physical coercive force in coping with the challenge. While the members of al Qaeda may be unified by a hatred of the United States and the Western values it represents, the societies that they spring from are struggling with much more basic issues: the tensions of modernization, including unequal wealth distribution and unmet expectations; suppressed democracy; internal divisions; and unstable neighborhoods. The anti-Western mobilization is but a new trigger in an already explosive environment, and an example of the combination of old and new security challenges.

There are other developments that also pose a threat to political stability. The "fourth wave" of democracy has witnessed the emergence of democratically elected, populist authoritarian regimes in Latin America and the Middle East—regimes that are distinctly illiberal in the practice of governance and that, in some cases, pose a direct threat to their neighbors. Accompanying this emergence is the rapid growth of paramilitary organizations worldwide. These paramilitary constabularies are typically better armed and equipped than the police and military forces of a country, and they also operate outside normal, legal (and political) constraints. Such organizations are to be found throughout Asia, Africa, and Latin America and are increasingly assuming responsibility for a wide range of so-called internal security functions with the blessing of national or local state authorities. Nor are paramilitary organizations the exclusive prerogative of right-wing governments. The efforts of Venezuela's leader, Hugo Chavez, to begin training a vast army of civilian reserves, allegedly to fight off a U.S. invasion, are consistent with this growing international trend to privatize and decentralize security.

Regional stability continues to be compromised by those conflicts that continue to fester and that largely remain intractable—for example, Israel-Palestine, Sri Lanka, Jammu and Kashmir, Sudan, China-Taiwan, North Korea. Many of these conflicts have refused to succumb to repeated rounds of mediation or third-party efforts to broker some kind of lasting political settlement. They are breeding grounds for terrorism and a major source of international instability because of the obvious risks that an escalation of these conflicts poses to their neighborhoods.

We should also not underestimate the recidivist potential of those states that are no longer at war but have found genuine democracy and economic growth elusive. There is a growing sense that the state-building/nation-building enterprise in countries such as Afghanistan and even some of the earlier success stories from the 1990s, such as Cambodia, is going off the rails for reasons that are still only vaguely understood. The strains of imposing democracy are readily apparent in many countries in transition, and the democratic experiment has been short-lived in some.

Finally, the book also points out the dangers of defining the primary security challenges narrowly as the threat of terrorism. Many contributors focus on other incubators of international conflict and argue for a broader conception of peace and security than is conveyed by the counterterrorism focus. At a minimum, it is clear that the post-9/11 global security environment is a permissive one for violence to emerge, with the political polarization between radical Islamists and their own societies (as well as those of leading non-Islamic states) providing a series of hair triggers for violence.

GLOBAL CONFLICT TRENDS

Several of this volume's authors analyze recent trends in the pattern of global conflict. A somewhat surprising picture emerges from this new research, confirming developments that were first identified in *Turbulent Peace* as well as a number of other major studies that were published at the turn of this century. There is now compelling statistical evidence that the high watermark of global conflicts came just as the Cold War was ending. Since then, there has been a steady decline, not just in the number of intrastate wars, but also in their lethality as measured by the number of victims of these conflicts. These statistics also reveal surprising news about interstate conflict —specifically, that the number of interstate wars has remained at relatively low, if consistent, levels since World War II.

That some countries and regions are much more conflict prone than others is also striking. The locus of regional violence—measured by the number of battle-related war deaths— has shifted over the past five decades. From 1946 to the mid-1970s, East Asia, Southeast Asia, and Oceania accounted for more than half the world's battle deaths, but that region is now one of the world's most peaceful with the ending of conflicts in Vietnam and Cambodia. Sub-Saharan Africa went from being a relatively peaceful area during the final fifteen years of colonial rule that succeeded World War II to being the most violent in the 1980s and 1990s. The Middle East and North Africa have also been important zones of conflict, peaking with the Iran-Iraq War in the late 1970s, which saw the highest sustained level of casualties and deaths in the region. With the exception of the bloody civil wars that erupted in Central America in the late 1970s (and the ongoing civil war in Colombia), the Americas as a whole have generally been quite peaceful for the past half century. So, too, has Western Europe largely escaped the ravages that have torn apart other parts of the world, although it saw conflict in Northern Ireland and the Basque region. Eastern Europe and Central Asia have seen a mix of savage conflict and peaceful transitions over the same period.

The trend, however, is not all toward a reduction in violence and death. Although civilian deaths related to conflict have gone down overall, the recent bloody mayhem in Darfur and massive killings in the Democratic Republic of the Congo show that horrific conflict is still with us. And since 1982, the number of "significant" terrorist attacks—those that have involved "loss of life, serious injury or major property damage"—has risen steadily.

Although terrorists continue to lack the technological capacity to build nuclear weapons —or other weapons of mass destruction— there is little ground for complacency. As a number of essays in part 2 and part 5 argue, the proliferation of such technologies increases the risk that they will fall into the wrong hands. The rise in the number of states in unstable regions such as the Middle East and South Asia who have acquired or seek access to these technologies does not augur well for regional and international stability. Nor does the erosion of long-established norms in the Nuclear Nonproliferation Treaty—norms that are increasingly being challenged by states that have announced their intention to withdraw from the treaty and/or refuse to submit their budding nuclear "research" programs to international inspection and control.

EXPLAINING CONFLICT TRENDS

Explaining these changing trends in the patterns of international conflict is difficult. Although many scholars regard the end of the Cold War—which also saw an end to many of the superpower-instigated "proxy wars" in the Third World—as a major explanatory variable, it is important not to stack the historical deck. The bipolar system also checked and prevented many conflicts from breaking out, and

the Soviet collapse followed by U.S. disengagement coincided with a number of 1990s conflicts that might never have occurred in Cold War times, including wars in Somalia, Sudan, the Democratic Republic of the Congo, Liberia (and its neighbors), Afghanistan (between the mujahideen and Taliban), Aceh/Moluccas/Timor, Tajikistan, Nagorno-Karabakh, Georgia, Moldova, and the Balkans.

As some contributors to this volume argue, another reason why so many armed conflicts —many of which were "long" civil wars that persisted for decades—ended in the 1990s is that the belligerents were deadlocked in a military stalemate in which none of the protagonists could win. This was certainly the case in El Salvador, Mozambique, Namibia, and even Cambodia. Confronted with a "hurting stalemate," many warring parties in different conflict zones looked for a negotiated way out of their impasse. The fact that so many of these conflicts were indeed ripe for resolution made the job of mediation and conflict management both doable and easier.

A third possible explanation for the changing trends in conflict involves outside intervention. The lessons of the peaceful interventions of the past decade point to the conclusion that the international community—both official and nonofficial actors—has played an important role in conflict management and in so doing has had a remarkably good track record, even in conflict zones such as the Balkans and the Horn of Africa, which many have trumpeted as intervention failures.

THE PLACE OF COERCIVE FORCE AND OTHER FORMS OF POWER

A number of chapters in parts 3 and 4 address the merits as well as the limits of coercive and noncoercive forms of power in conflict management. Contributors to part 3 on the role of force in conflict management provide sobering snapshots of the performance of outside actors in dealing with the power dynamics among local parties in civil wars, insurgencies, and terrorist violence. This part looks from various angles at what can be achieved through the use of sanctions, coercive diplomacy, humanitarian intervention, peace operations, and robust applications of power (as well as threats of force) to support negotiated conflict termination and other related goals. Contributors remind us that (a) military and economic power tools may be essential, but they can be blunt instruments, hard to control and harder to translate into desired political outcomes, (b) it is difficult to muster and sustain the political will to deploy coercive instruments to prevent or terminate even in cases of the worst abuse, and (c) the right kinds of coercive power to support conflict management remain in short supply, with their distribution among suppliers lopsided in the extreme.

Some of the challenges reviewed in this volume may respond, under certain conditions, to traditional strategies of deterrence, denial, containment, and prevention (or preemption) of particular threats or conflict-related behavior. Others, however, appear more responsive to a blend of coercive power and political-diplomatic initiatives or to a multilayered set of responses involving a wide range of state, international, and nonofficial actors. Part 4 explores the multidimensional tools of statecraft, diplomacy, and the power of persuasion and attraction. Contributors also evaluate the potential of "nonkinetic" strategies for combating terrorism, multidisciplinary tools for postconflict peace operations, the role of legal tools, mediation initiatives, and nongovernmental conflict resolution approaches for addressing intractable local or regional conflicts. If there is a central message in these varied contributions, it is that power comes in many shapes and forms and that conflict management requires a variety of interventions. This message also reminds us that strategies of engagement based on these varied forms of power may provide an effective means of taming and, ultimately, transforming conflicts.

THE PLACE OF INSTITUTIONS IN CONFLICT MANAGEMENT

During the 1990s, great powers and international organizations such as the United Nations began to play a much greater role in conflict management processes, including the mediation and negotiation of international disputes. The same is true of regional and subregional organizations, which also began to expand their roles in conflict management, sometimes with the support and backing of the international community.

At the same time, a wide variety of small-state and nonstate actors also offered their services in conflict management and resolution processes with positive effect. For example, small and medium-sized powers, such as Australia, New Zealand, Norway, and Switzerland, which had long been active in international peacekeeping operations, began actively to market their negotiation and intermediary services to warring parties. From the Middle East to Central America, Africa, and the Asia-Pacific region, these countries played key roles in instigating negotiations between warring sides, backstopping negotiations once they got under way, and ensuring that the parties remained committed to the peace process after a negotiated settlement was concluded. Nongovernmental organizations—such as the Community of Sant'Egidio, a Catholic lay organization that was a key mediator in Mozambique—also played important roles in bringing parties to the negotiating table and creating much-needed forums for dialogue, discussion, and negotiation, especially at the intercommunal and societal levels.

Part 5, on the uses and limits of institutions in conflict management, suggests that it would be timely to create an inventory of systemic capabilities and gaps for conflict management—for example, gaps by region, gaps in terms of effective institutional "architecture," gaps in terms of political will and the coherence required to have a meaningful impact on conflict zones. A thorough map of current conflict management capacity would portray a picture deficient not only in certain types of capability but also in terms of the structured and coordinated application of those capabilities we do have. This broader look at security would not only suggest what results can be anticipated from the UN system and existing regional security and defense organizations—for example, the African Union, the Association of Southeast Asian Nations, the Organization of American States, and NATO—but also suggest where new capacity is needed and what kinds of institutionalized or ad hoc security mechanisms are most urgently needed.

Just as the international community and its leading actors need to identify best practices in the application of military, legal, and diplomatic instruments in societies emerging from conflict, so also do they need a clearer understanding of how international and nongovernmental institutions fit into the picture. This is especially important in light of the controversies and inevitable frictions that arise when the international security agenda is burdened with new challenges from the proliferation of weapons technologies, new dangers spawned in weak and failing states, and a new wave of asymmetric conflict resulting from nonstate actors using the tool of terrorist violence. The world's leading security institutions, its most effective peacebuilding institutions, and its most powerful and successful societies have a special responsibility to look forward, adapt, or improvise where necessary while retaining coherence and legitimacy among a critical mass of actors. In other words, they must develop the capacity to organize and act for common purposes in managing and supporting conflict management.

Given the central question of who does what, this book underscores the need to broaden and deepen the base of capability for conflict management, and to diversify and strengthen the institutions available for these purposes. It is hard to escape the conclusion that official nonmilitary and nonofficial tools and organizations will play a growing part. The burdens of coercive and noncoercive conflict management are not ideally distributed; some regions participate more fully than others in managing their own security affairs and mobilizing effective conflict prevention and response mechanisms. The sweeping changes facing many parts of the international system are in themselves a source of instability. Modernization, democratization, globalization, and other contemporary dynamics are forces of change and as such potentially destabilizing. For all these reasons, the international system needs capacity that is distributed across institutions and across continents.

THE PLACE OF STATE BUILDING AND DEMOCRATIC GOVERNANCE IN CONFLICT MANAGEMENT

Since the collapse of European empires, the assumption has been that new states emerging in their wake would have whatever time it took to develop effective and legitimate institutions of governance. In the meantime, outside powers pursued their local and regional interests, competed for influence, and engaged —especially after the end of the Cold War— in various forms of capacity building and intervention to contain or help resolve violent conflict. Regional actors in formerly dependent areas have gradually taken control of their own destiny while intensifying linkages to the major world power centers of Europe, Asia, and North America.

Since September 11, 2001, however, new understandings have challenged this assumption. It is no longer accepted that chaotic, ill-governed regions and zones of failed modernization should be allowed to flounder toward an uncertain future, with all the consequences this would imply for people living there and for societies affected by the turmoil they generate. Implicit in many of the dramatic actions and debates in world politics since that time has been the question of urgency. How much time is there for these places to sort themselves out? What is the proper role of outsiders in bringing transformation about? If nation building appears thwarted in societies immersed in or emerging from conflict, what should be done to jump-start the process of building effective sovereign states and democratic polities?

Part 6 revisits themes of governance, nation (or state) building, and state capacity that are posed as sources of conflict earlier in the book. Some of the most challenging issues in world politics and foreign policy arise in this context: What is the proper place of sovereignty and how should it be limited in the interests of human societies living within states? What have we learned about the role of external powers in bringing order, stability, and democratic institutions to societies in conflict? What is the relationship between political and economic governance in building effective states? If in the past war was essential to the state-building exercise and one of the most effective mechanisms for defining state borders and uniting diverse populations within a nation-state, this circumstance has changed dramatically in the late twentieth and early twenty-first centuries. Not only do civil wars strike at the heart of what it means to be a state, but they sometimes—as in the case of the Former Yugoslavia—result in state disintegration. In other cases—Sudan, for example—they yield to a negotiated settlement that puts off to a later date the decision on the nature of the state but does not resolve it. And in many cases—here, Sudan's neighbor Somalia provides a tragic confirmation—the conflict simply eats away at the state's ability to function as a state. A question posed by a number of chapters is how much capacity the state must have in order to make the transition from war to peace. This is an issue that the international community is still grappling with, and the purpose of part 6 is not to provide definitive answers to these questions but rather to outline a few of the really hard choices

facing practitioners and an informed citizenry in the coming period.

Framing the Conflict Management Challenge

Understanding the causes of conflict is critical to developing an effective conflict management strategy, as is understanding the capabilities of various approaches to conflict management and the consequences of using one or another approach. Understanding these elements, however, is only part of designing a successful conflict management strategy. Another critical element is understanding the importance of framing, that is, the way you and others see the problem. These lenses will determine how you define the conflict and grasp the tools in the tool kit of conflict management. Always an important exercise, it becomes ever more important to be cognizant of how the issues are framed at a time when international consensus on these points is declining. For example, the relative emphasis placed on hard power and coercive tools—as compared with political approaches and the use of soft or nonofficial forms of power—depends, at least in part, on how the challenge, or threat, is viewed. Those chapter authors whose focus naturally gravitates toward violent civil conflicts that feature high levels of human suffering and the associated ills of state failure will concentrate on the uses of external power to stop abuses and foster better governance. Their attention centers on the tools, techniques, conditions, and institutions for coercive intervention in conflict-ridden societies. Chapter authors who focus on the political and social bases of violent conflict—within or between states—concentrate on the application of political, diplomatic, economic, normative, social, and legal tools alongside (or in lieu of) physical coercion.

Similarly, observers concerned with the legitimacy of intervention and using force in the service of conflict management will tend to concentrate on the role of norms and institutions and debates about the rights and responsibilities of sovereignty in managing conflict and related security challenges such as terrorism and weapons proliferation. In contrast, contributors concerned with the efficacy and capacity of outsiders to manage other peoples' conflicts are more likely to emphasize the importance of statecraft and skilled coordination as well as the gaps in coercive capacity available to the international community and the inherent limitations of using physical power to influence events. Differences of framing may also emerge from the national interests and circumstances of different societies and their particular histories.

Recognizing the importance of framing also helps in understanding the current security environment. At the present time, Russian leaders may see their country as a victim of terrorism, as a peacebuilder and conflict manager in the "near abroad," and as a country returning to historic patterns of internal stability after the shocks of post-Soviet transformation—in other words, somewhat differently from the way others perceive it. For many Americans, the global security environment appears to pose more threats and dangers than it did during the 1990s or the Cold War, a mind-set that leads to preoccupation with contingencies of direct, physical threat as contrasted with the seemingly indirect security challenges posed by international conflict in other places. European leaders and their counterparts in Asia, Africa, and Latin America have their own perspectives on these issues, shaped by their experience and circumstances.

In this regard, it is apparent that—especially in the post-9/11 period—the global frames of reference have been diverging and the degree of consensus on the priorities for conflict management is declining. When there is declining agreement on what the problems and priorities are, there is reduced likelihood of coherent and effective international responses to security challenges. These include the challenge of

terrorism and weapons proliferation as well as the direct and indirect challenges posed by conflicts that still rage in many societies and that could yet break out in others where states are weak, transitions fail, and societies are fractured by social and economic cleavages. The fragmentation of international consensus has the potential to severely affect the possibilities of conflict management. The same dynamic threatens national consensus on foreign and security issues and also threatens to drive a wedge between the principal institutions that respond to conflict—national governments, the United Nations, militaries, and NGOs. The potential for continued and even increased friction over priorities and responses cannot be ignored.

CONFLICT MANAGEMENT IN A TIME OF TRANSITION

By examining the use and limits of force, diplomatic and nondiplomatic power, and institutional responses in conflict management, this book brings out a number of themes, choices, and trade-offs that face students and practitioners of the field. The volume appears at a moment of transition as the United States, the world's leading power and the one most inclined to view the 2001 terrorist attacks as a basic watershed in world politics, debates and evaluates the external security environment. Friends, allies, rivals, and potential adversaries will all be influenced in some measure by the choices that emerge from the transition. It matters whether—working with its partners and key security institutions such as NATO and the United Nations—the United States is able to isolate and "fix" the direct security challenges and has the energy and the constructive optimism to sustain its long-standing engagement in the search for a more peaceful, and less threatening, world. An alternative scenario in which U.S. policies come to be viewed as exacerbating tension and undercutting U.S. influence could trigger a contrasting mood of isolation, retrenchment, and reduced focus on a narrower, defensive agenda that tolerates or ignores foreign conflicts in order to address direct threats.

The United Nations, too, is struggling with a number of fundamental issues concerning its role in the current security environment and its ability to play that role. Several panels and review boards have undertaken examinations of the United Nations; none have called for an end to the institution, but all have called for changes in the way it functions. Prominent among these recommendations are proposals to strengthen and enlarge the Security Council, institute new normative benchmarks for humanitarian intervention, enhance and streamline the administrative capacities of the organization, provide for greater financial accountability and transparency in its operations, strengthen its role in the promotion and advancement of human rights, and create new mechanisms and capacity so that the organization can play a more effective role in peacebuilding and nation building.

After a decade or more of experience on the front lines of devastating conflict, nongovernmental organizations have adapted to the difficult conditions of delivering humanitarian aid, rebuilding social institutions, and reconstructing societies rent by conflict. The current environment, however, has brought new challenges to this group of institutions as well, not least to their capacity to engage in nation building in the midst of continued civil strife and to their willingness to work alongside institutions—for instance, the coalition forces in Iraq—that are parties to the conflict.

While it is a time of transition for major players in conflict management, it also is a time of transition for conflict itself. As noted earlier, there is evidence that conflict is diminishing in quantity and lethality. It is, however, an open question as to whether the downward trend in armed conflict will continue or begin to turn upward as the many failed or ailing states in the international system find themselves wracked by a host of social, economic, and political problems that they are ill equipped to manage and that feed the fires of social and political discontent. And then there is the ever-present—and perhaps increasing—threat of terrorism.

Can conflict management be effective in this time of transition? Clearly, the so-called war on terrorism will not be won simply by targeting terrorists. Instead, the international community must apply the instruments of conflict management and prevention, which worked so well in the past, to the breeding grounds of terrorism—the conflict zones of so-called failed states and those regions where intractable conflicts endure. If diplomacy, negotiation, and economic development had ended the brutal wars in Sudan and Afghanistan a long time ago, the world might look quite different today. Al Qaeda operatives would have had fewer places to hide and to plan, organize, and prepare for their attacks in New York, Washington, London, Madrid, and elsewhere. Despite powerful arguments supporting the need for sustained engagement in conflict management and peacebuilding/nation building, there is the sobering risk that "intervention fatigue" could set in if such efforts are seen to fail.

In the art of managing conflict, as this volume recognizes, military power and the use of force continue to play a vital role in maintaining global power balances, dealing with regimes that refuse to abide by international norms and/or threaten their neighbors and in some cases providing a measure of response to terrorism. However, events during the past decade have shown that military force alone cannot effectively deal with the myriad problems of failed and ailing states in the international system or with the malaise that grows out of continued conflict in parts of the globe. As many of the essays in this volume underscore, diplomacy—whether official or nonofficial—is important to building effective international coalitions, mobilizing political will, building internal capacity to handle conflict, securing political legitimacy, and promoting the negotiation and mediation of interstate and intrastate disputes. And when it comes to the exercise of nonmilitary political power or the exercise of force for peacemaking purposes, international legitimacy—the consensus and support of the international community, including NGOs—is clearly an important component of effective action.

In effect, the essays in this volume point to a new kind of strategic political resource in international relations, namely, a heightened role for "smart power," which effectively engages the multiple assets and instruments of official and nonofficial diplomacy *and* military power. Smart power involves the strategic use of diplomacy, persuasion, capacity building, and the projection of power and influence in ways that are cost-effective and have political and social legitimacy. Smart power in a conflict management setting is attentive to the timing of mediated/negotiated interventions and the re-

sources, capabilities, and strengths that different actors—including nonstate actors—bring to the multiple tasks of conflict management. Smart power also looks to the lessons of the past decade and a half of conflict management and intervention successes as well as failures. The "war on terrorism" must go hand in hand with the traditional business of diplomacy and conflict management.

This volume began with the question of whether it is possible to fight war and manage conflict at the same time. Our conclusion at the end is that peacemaking and conflict management are central for creating a less divided, less conflicted world—no matter the complexities and, at times, high odds against success. The book provides ample evidence that the international community—both its leading official actors and its nonofficial components—can check hostile adversaries of the international order and make peace at the same time. We are learning to leash the dogs of war.

PART II

SOURCES OF CONFLICT AND CHALLENGES TO GLOBAL SECURITY

2

INTERNATIONAL SOURCES OF INTERSTATE AND INTRASTATE WAR

Jack S. Levy

AS I WRITE THIS ESSAY, IN SPRING 2006, the United States is engaged in its second war in Iraq in fifteen years. Although each war began with a U.S. president named Bush authorizing military operations against Iraqi forces under the leadership of Saddam Hussein, the two wars were very different. The 1990–91 Persian Gulf War was a classic interstate war. Iraq invaded and occupied the sovereign state of Kuwait, and a U.S.-led coalition intervened to expel Iraqi forces and restore Kuwaiti sovereignty. The 2003 Iraq war, which began as an interstate war with the immediate U.S. purpose of defeating the Iraqi Army and overthrowing the repressive regime of Saddam Hussein, quickly evolved into an insurgency against the U.S. occupation and the Iraqi provisional government. The insurgents—primarily Iraqi Sunnis and international fighters associated with the al Qaeda terrorist network—could not match the numbers or firepower of the U.S. military, but they used improvised explosive devices, suicide bombers, political assassinations, kidnappings,

and beheadings against civilian as well as military targets. That insurgency gradually evolved into a low-level sectarian civil war, and after the bombing of a Shiite mosque in February 2006, many feared that the conflict would escalate into a large-scale civil war between Sunnis and Shiites, one that could draw in other states in the region.

During the 1990–91 Persian Gulf War, U.S. president George H. W. Bush and many others spoke of a "new world order." Three years into the 2003 Iraq war, many observers spoke of a "new world disorder." Although old-style interstate wars will undoubtedly continue to occur, and although insurgencies and terrorism are an age-old phenomenon in international politics, few would deny that the nature of warfare has been changing.

The essays in this volume reflect on different aspects of war, peace, and security in the contemporary world. My aim here is to place contemporary warfare in a broader historical and theoretical context. I begin by describing the changing nature of war over time, and ask whether traditional Western conceptualizations of warfare going back to Carl von Clausewitz can adequately capture the "new wars" of the twenty-first century. I raise a number of conceptual issues involved in the analysis of the causes of interstate and intrastate war and suggest certain criteria that any theory of war or explanation for particular wars must satisfy. I then turn to the causes of war between and within states. I focus on international system–level factors, paying particular attention to "realist" theories of interstate war, and I explore the extent to which these theories, or modifications of them, are useful for the analysis of civil wars. I note that weak or failed states are particularly prone to civil war and identify some of the international conditions, both material and ideational, that contribute to state weakness in the contemporary era. After discussing the impact of Cold War bipolarity and then of unipolarity under U.S. dominance on patterns of interstate and intrastate warfare, I end with a discussion of resource scarcity as a condition for internal and external war.

This is not a complete survey of the sources of contemporary violence. I focus on international war and internal war but give little attention to terrorism, insurgency, or genocide. I focus on causal variables at the international level and mention internal variables only when the path leading from system-level factors to war runs through factors internal to states. Domestic variables can also have an important direct effect on interstate as well as intrastate war, and they are analyzed in chapters 6 through 10 and elsewhere in this volume.[1]

THE CHANGING NATURE OF WARFARE

Historians usually identify 1500 as the beginning of the modern world. From that time until the end of World War II, the European great powers played a leading role in shaping the structure and evolution of the international security system and the global political economy, based on their superior military power and wealth. They fought "great-power wars" against each other, including "hegemonic wars" for leadership and control over the system. They fought interstate wars against lesser states in the expanding but European-dominated international system and, in the eighteenth and nineteenth centuries, colonial wars to maintain and expand their worldwide empires. Significant increases in the destructiveness of great-power war over time contributed to a continued decline in the frequency of those wars until an upsurge with the two world wars and related conflicts of the twentieth century. Great-power war has yet to recur in the six decades since World War II, however, making this the longest period of peace between the great powers for at least five centuries. In addition, Europe, which has been the locus of a disproportionate number of modern history's wars, experienced relatively little warfare after World War II.[2]

These trends have led some to characterize the period since World War II as the "long peace."[3] That view is misleading, because this period has been anything but peaceful for most of the world's peoples. We have experienced a long great-power peace, not a general peace. Interstate wars continue to occur, but at a much lower frequency in the period after World War II than during the period before, and with a particularly sharp drop after 1970.[4]

What is new, in addition to the great-power peace and the shift in warfare away from Europe to other regions of the world, is a significant increase in the frequency of civil wars and other forms of intrastate conflict.[5] Civil wars, after fluctuating around a moderate level of frequency for the first seven decades of the twentieth century, exploded in number in the 1970s and have remained fairly frequent despite a modest decline in the 1990s. By one count, between 1816 and 1945, there were 110 intrastate wars and 56 interstate wars. In the half century after 1945, when the number of states in the international system nearly tripled, there were 103 intrastate wars and 22 interstate wars. Thus, before World War II the ratio of internal wars to external wars was about 2 to 1, while after World War II the ratio increased to 4.7 to 1.[6]

Many contemporary intrastate wars pit ethnic or religious groups against each other and are referred to as "ethnic wars" or "identity wars."[7] Many of these take on a transnational dimension, since identity groups straddle state boundaries, and the distinction between interstate wars and civil wars is beginning to blur. The Bosnian wars of the 1990s, for example, were both civil wars within a disintegrating Yugoslavia and interstate wars between Serbia, Bosnia, and Croatia.[8] In addition to civil wars fought for control of the state, or for secession from the state, or for the autonomy and security of an identity group within the state, we see increasing levels of involvement of warlords, private military contractors, and other nonstate actors, driven by their own parochial interests, including control over natural resources.[9]

Thus warfare has shifted away from the great powers, away from Europe, and, increasingly, away from state-to-state conflict toward civil war, insurgency, and terrorism. All of this is still warfare, but it is warfare that is in many respects quite different from the forms of organized violence that have dominated the past five centuries of human history.[10] The typical wars of the past pitted state armies against each other. Particularly for great-power conflicts, but also for many other European interstate conflicts, wars were "symmetric" in the sense that the two sides were of roughly equal strength and fought with the same kinds of weapons. At least by the time that the leading states had consolidated their power internally, a process that occurred gradually and at different times for different states but that had become fairly complete by the seventeenth century, states had a monopoly or near monopoly of force within their borders. This was the basis for Clausewitz's classic formulation of

war as violent conflict fought by state armies, directed by state leaders, waged on behalf of state interests, and settled by decisive battles.

As interstate war has increasingly shifted from state-to-state conflicts to civil wars, and as nonstate actors have played an increasingly prominent role, scholars have begun to question whether the Clausewitzian model accurately captures the nature of contemporary warfare.[11] Most wars are not interstate wars and do not pit state armies against each other. Most recent civil wars, unlike the American one of the nineteenth century, do not involve a single rebel army under the leadership of a single military and political leadership, fighting on roughly equal terms with similar weapons against a state army. Instead, many insurgencies and civil wars involve loose coalitions of different groups fighting for their own purposes.[12] Rebel groups often cannot match the state in organization and advanced weaponry, and consequently they resort to different tactics, including guerrilla war and terrorism, long the "weapons of the weak." Instead of confronting state armies directly, they target civilians in an attempt to weaken morale, demonstrate that the state cannot protect its citizens, and induce a shift in loyalties. Massacre and ethnic cleansing have occurred with increased frequency.

The strategy of decisive battles has been replaced by the strategy of exhaustion, and symmetric war has given way to "asymmetric war." An era in which war and peace were clearly delineated, and war had a well-defined beginning and a well-defined end point,[13] has given way to an intermediary state in which violence "smoulders on."[14] Just as the line between peace and war has blurred, so has the line between war and crime, as criminal networks play a growing role in the funding of civil wars and insurgencies.[15]

While Clausewitz's emphasis on war as a clash between state armies fails to capture a great deal of contemporary combat, there is another aspect of the Clausewitzian model that accurately reflects an enduring core of warfare that transcends the changes noted earlier. That is the idea that war is fundamentally *political*, in the sense that the use of violence is purposeful and intended to advance an actor's political objectives. As Clausewitz phrased it, "[W]ar is a continuation of politics with admixture of other means."[16] True, Clausewitz thought primarily in terms of states, but the idea can easily be applied to other actors. Whether the actor in question is a state, an ethnic group, a rebel organization, or a terrorist group,[17] Clausewitz tells us that we should think of war as one of several instruments or policies (diplomatic, economic, military, etc.) that actors have at their disposal to promote their interests.[18] War involves the coordinated use of violent force, in combination with other instruments, to advance one's interests.

Some might argue that the same idea applies to individuals, that individuals are purposeful in their use of force. Whatever the merits of that argument, we do not think of individual acts of violence as constituting war. War is the coordinated use of force by a political organization or group. A single act of violence by a state or other group would not constitute war. The idea of war also implies that a certain threshold of violence is crossed.[19] Thus war involves intense or sustained violence, though the relevant threshold of intensity varies significantly over the millennia and over different cultural systems. Finally, organized violence is not considered a war unless the other side fights back. The Soviet Union invaded Hungary in 1956 and Czechoslovakia in 1968. The Hungarian army fought back; the Czech army did not. Thus we talk about the Russo-Hungarian War of 1956 and the Soviet invasion of Czechoslovakia in 1968.

Having discussed both elements of continuity and elements of change in the evolution of war over time, we now turn to an analysis of the causes of war. Despite the enormous amount of intellectual energy that has been devoted to the question of war by philosophers, historians, social scientists, biologists, and

others, there is little scholarly consensus on the causes of war, even among scholars within the same discipline. It is important to note also that until recently the scholarly literatures on interstate war, civil war, and terrorism overlapped very little, and scholars of interstate war paid very little attention to research on civil war, and vice versa. This has gradually begun to change, as international relations scholars have shifted their focus and attempted to adapt theories of interstate war and use them to explain civil wars, but the differences are still significant. In the following discussion I attempt to integrate knowledge generated by both interstate and civil war researchers. Before I begin, however, it would be useful to explore some conceptual issues that plague the study of both interstate and intrastate war.

CONCEPTUAL ISSUES

Our earlier discussion of the changes in war over time reminds us that war is a variable, not a constant. It varies in form (interstate, intrastate), regional concentration, frequency, intensity, and other dimensions. This obvious fact has important but often neglected implications for the study of war. Any theory of war must account for variations in war over time and space, and any interpretation of a particular war must explain why that war occurred when it did, and not earlier or later.

With respect to theories of war, the requirement that theories explain variations in war and peace means that any theory that predicts that war is a constant must be rejected, or at least modified to include additional variables that explain observed variation. This means that any explanatory factor that is itself a constant cannot provide a complete explanation for war.[20] For example, while many trace war to human nature (whether in the form of aggressive instincts or other human imperfections) or to the anarchic structure of the international system (the absence of a higher authority to regulate behavior and enforce agreements between states), these factors are basically constants and cannot by themselves explain the enormous variations in war and peace over time and space. They cannot explain the long great-power peace after World War II, the fact that most states are at peace with most other states most of the time, or evidence that humans fought relatively few wars before the development of agriculture and related aspects of civilization.[21]

To take another example, it has become popular to explain the explosion of ethnic violence in the past two decades in terms of "ancient hatreds" between rival ethnic or religious groups.[22] While this factor might contribute to contemporary ethnic conflict, it does not constitute a sufficient explanation of ethnic wars. It fails to explain why wars have broken out between some ethnic communities but not between others, when those violent conflicts occur, and how intensely they are fought. At the level of individual wars, this means that an ancient-hatreds explanation by itself cannot fully explain the outbreak of a particular ethnic war.

To explain the Bosnian wars of the 1990s, for example, it is not sufficient to invoke ethnic rivalries. Serbs and Croats fought each other very little before the twentieth century, so additional factors are necessary to explain why they fought each other during the 1990s. Similarly, while ethnic differences between Persians and Arabs undoubtedly contributed to the outbreak of the Iran-Iraq War (1980–88), those differences led to very little violent conflict between the two peoples over the past two centuries. Moreover, a 1975 treaty resolved most outstanding conflicts of interest between the two states. Thus a satisfactory interpretation of the Iran-Iraq War must explain what happened after 1975 to trigger the war.[23]

Let us now turn to the "levels-of-analysis" framework, which was first developed by Kenneth Waltz and which has been widely used as a framework for the classification of the causes of interstate wars and other forms of state behavior.[24] With some modifications,

this framework can also be applied to intrastate wars. The framework raises some additional conceptual issues in the study of war, which we also consider.[25]

The levels-of-analysis framework classifies the causes of war in terms of whether they are located at the level of the individual, the nation-state, or the international system.[26] The individual level focuses primarily on human nature and predispositions toward aggression and on individual political leaders and their belief systems, personalities, and psychological processes. The national level includes both governmental variables, such as the structure of the political system and the nature of the policymaking process, and societal factors, such as the structure of the economic system, the role of public opinion, economic and noneconomic interest groups, ethnicity and nationalism, and political culture and ideology. System-level causes include the anarchic structure of the international system, the number of major powers in the system, the distribution of military and economic power among them, patterns of military alliances and international trade, systemwide norms influencing their behavior, and other factors that constitute the external environment common to all states. If a state acts on the basis of national-interest calculations, defined in terms of threats and opportunities in its external environment, we say that the state is influenced by system-level factors. It can also be useful to distinguish between global and regional systems and include the dyadic (or bilateral) relations between a particular pair of states.

Let us illustrate the levels-of-analysis framework with respect to various explanations that journalists and scholars have proposed for the U.S. decision to invade Iraq in 2003.[27] Some argue that the U.S. intervention derives from President George W. Bush's worldview and religious beliefs, his determination to finish the job begun by his father, or his disregard for information running contrary to his beliefs and policy preferences. We classify these at the individual level. Individual-level explanations imply that if another individual had been in power, the state probably would have behaved differently.

Others argue that the U.S. decision derives from the traditional U.S. commitment to democracy and the promotion of democracy abroad, from the impact of the September 11 attacks on American political culture, from the hesitancy of members of Congress to argue or vote against the war for fear of possible political repercussions, from the influence of neoconservatives or the U.S. oil industry on the political decision-making process, or from a flawed intelligence apparatus that generated grossly misleading estimates about Iraqi nuclear weapons. These are national-level explanations.

Finally, arguments tracing the war in Iraq to a rational response to the terrorist threat, fears of an Iraqi nuclear weapons capability, or the permissive condition created by the collapse of Soviet power and end of the Cold War over a decade earlier fall at the system level of analysis. The collapse of Soviet power and the permissive condition it created for U.S. intervention relate to the global system, whereas concerns about the impact of a nuclear Iraq on the balance of power in the Middle East is a regional-system factor.

Given the complexity of international politics, many scholars have concluded that no single factor, and no single level of analysis, provides a complete explanation for the causes of war. As a result, many theories of war, and most explanations of individual wars, combine causal variables from different levels of analysis. Most explanations for the 2003 Iraq war, for example, include the rise of international terrorism, the domestic impact of the September 11 attacks, the aim of overthrowing Saddam Hussein's brutal regime and the establishment of democracy in Iraq, the personality and religious beliefs of George W. Bush, the influence of neoconservatives on U.S. foreign policy, and the intelligence failure regarding Iraqi weapons of mass destruction.

Although the levels-of-analysis framework has traditionally been applied to states and to interstate relations, with some modifications it can also be applied to the question of the causes of intrastate war. Consider Michael Brown's classification of the sources of internal war in terms of bad leaders, bad domestic problems, bad neighborhoods, and bad neighbors.[28] We can interpret this typology in terms of levels of analysis. Brown's first factor is an individual-level variable, the second is a domestic-level factor, the third is a regional-system factor, and the fourth refers to the external environment of a particular state.

We can also apply the framework to a wide range of nonstate actors, from international organizations like the United Nations to ethnic groups to transnational terrorist groups. We can ask whether decisions for UN intervention are driven more by the imperatives of the situation, by politics within the United Nations, or by the leadership of the secretary-general; whether the behavior of a particular ethnic group is influenced primarily by the external threats and opportunities it faces, by pressures from subgroups within it (including its military arm), or by the particular beliefs and charisma of an individual leader; or whether the behavior of a terrorist group is driven by the aim of advancing the interests of the group, by internal infighting between competing factions, or by the beliefs and risk-taking propensities of a particular leader.

Although the levels-of-analysis framework can be applied to any actor, the framework assumes that the actor in question is sufficiently coherent that it has a decision-making body that has the authority to act on behalf of the group. If the group is more amorphous, so that we cannot speak of a single group policy with inputs from different levels, it is harder to apply the levels-of-analysis framework. If observers are right that after 9/11 al Qaeda splintered into a loose coalition of distinct terrorist groups, with different but overlapping interests and no single chain of command,[29] it will be difficult to apply the levels-of-analysis framework to a single al Qaeda entity.

The levels-of-analysis framework is useful for organizing the many disparate sources of conflict into categories that help simplify the way we think about war and other aspects of the behavior of states and other actors. Like any framework, however, it is not perfect. Its categories are neither exclusive—in that some factors appear to fit in more than one category —nor exhaustive—in that some factors do not fit easily into any category.[30]

The levels-of-analysis framework highlights some logical problems associated with the analysis of the causes of war. Although analysts often trace the outbreak of a particular war to the beliefs or personalities of a single individual,[31] that does not constitute a logically complete explanation of war. Two problems arise, each involving the definition of war.

First, war is defined in terms of the behavior of political organizations, whether the state, a rebel group, or a terrorist organization. It is not enough to know the preferences, beliefs, and personality of the leader. We have to explain how the leader's preferences, along with the preferences of other decision makers, are translated into a collective decision for the organization (in the case of a state, a foreign policy decision). What this means, for states, is that an individual-level theory of war has to be subsumed within a theory of foreign policy, since it is states, not individuals, that make war.[32] Sometimes political leaders who want war are prevented from implementing that strategy by domestic constituencies. Alternatively (but less frequently), political leaders who believe that war is contrary to the national interest are sometimes pushed into war by a xenophobic public opinion. U.S. president William McKinley hoped to avoid war with Spain in 1898, but because of domestic pressures McKinley "led his country unhesitatingly toward a war which he did not want for a cause in which he did not believe."[33]

Second, war involves violence *between* political organizations. Since it is not a war unless the adversary fights back, a theory of war must explain why both states fight. That is, war is a dyadic or systemic outcome resulting from the interactions of two or more states, and an explanation for war requires the inclusion of dyadic or system-level causal variables.[34] For this reason neither individual- nor societal-level explanations provide a logically complete explanation for the outbreak of war. War is the result of the strategic interaction, or joint actions, of two or more political organizations.[35]

Consider, for example, what we might call the "predatory state hypothesis"—the idea that the primary cause of war is the existence of a predatory or aggressive state or political leader. Such behavior is often a primary cause of war, but the predatory-state argument is not a logically complete explanation for war. Nazi Germany was an aggressive state in the mid-1930s. It violated international treaties by remilitarizing the Rhineland, annexing Austria, and demanding the incorporation into Germany of the Sudetenland, a German-speaking region of Czechoslovakia. For several years, however, none of these actions led to war, because the West chose instead to pursue a policy of appeasement. There is ample evidence that Hitler actually wanted war over Czechoslovakia and was quite angry when the West responded with some concessions.[36] Hitler eventually got the war that he wanted, but only after German armies had invaded Poland, and the West, after some delay, had responded with military force. The point is that showing that a state or leader wants war is not a sufficient explanation for war. We must incorporate the behavior of the adversary into the explanation.

On the other side of the coin, the demonstration that a state pursues a conciliatory policy is not a sufficient explanation for peace. Under some conditions a strategy of extensive concessions does not promote peace but instead induces the adversary to increase its demands in the expectation that further concessions will be forthcoming, which can result in war by miscalculation. The classic example here is the British and French appeasement of Hitler in the 1930s, though many argue that Hitler was bent on war and that consequently the strategy of appeasement, while futile, did not actually make an already likely war any more likely. The larger point is that a theory of war is technically incomplete without a theory of bargaining or strategic interaction that explains how states respond to each other's actions and how they act in anticipation of each other's responses.[37]

We should keep these conceptual considerations in mind as we turn to an analysis of some of the leading theories of war. We begin with realist theories, which have dominated the study of interstate war since the time of Thucydides. Though realist theories were designed to explain interstate relations, they can be useful in explaining some aspects of civil war as well. We then turn to a broader discussion of how system-level factors have contributed to the rise of civil wars in the period since World War II.[38]

INTERNATIONAL SYSTEM–LEVEL CAUSES OF WAR

Balance of Power, Power Transition, and Interstate War

The traditional literature on the causes of interstate war has been dominated by the "realist" paradigm, which subsumes several distinct theories.[39] Traditionally, scholars characterize realism as positing that the key actors are sovereign states that act rationally to advance their security, power, and wealth in an anarchic international system, with anarchy defined in terms of the absence of a legitimate authority to regulate disputes and enforce agreements between states.[40] International anarchy, along with uncertainties regarding the present and future intentions of the adversary, creates a system of insecurity and competition. The system induces political leaders to focus on short-term security needs and on their relative position in the system, adopt worst-case thinking, build up their military strength, and utilize coercive threats to advance their interests, influence the adversary, and maintain their reputations. The core realist hypothesis is that international outcomes are determined by, or at least significantly constrained by, the distribution of power between two or more states. At the dyadic level (between two states), this is captured by Thucydides' argument that "the strong do what they can and the weak suffer what they must."[41]

At the system level, realists argue that the "polarity" of the system (multipolar, bipolar, unipolar), which reflects the distribution of power, shapes patterns of state interaction. During the Cold War, for example, international relations theorists debated whether the bipolarity of the Cold War period was more stable (in terms of minimizing the likelihood of a major war) than the multipolarity of the eighteenth or nineteenth century, when power in the system was distributed more or less equally among at least four or five great powers. With the end of the Cold War, scholars now argue about the relative stability of the unipolar system characterized by U.S. dominance. Many argue that U.S. hegemony is likely to persist, and others argue that U.S. dominance is likely to generate an opposing coalition to limit U.S. power and that a new leading state will invariably arise.[42]

To take a more specific example, many argue that the end of the Cold War and the collapse of bipolarity was a permissive condition for U.S. intervention in the 1990–91 Persian Gulf War and initiation of the 2003 Iraq war. If the Soviet Union had not collapsed and if the Cold War had not ended, intervention in Iraq would have been too risky for the United States, either in 1991 or in 2003.

The distribution of power, and the nature of that power, is also the primary explanation for the declining frequency of great-power war over time and in particular for the great-power peace after World War II. The increasing so-phistication of military technology led to the ever-increasing destructiveness of warfare and consequently to the increasing costs of war and increasing disincentives for states to initi-ate war unless vital national interests were di-rectly threatened. This process culminated in the development of nuclear weapons, the de-terrent effects of which are posited by many to be the primary factor contributing to the ab-sence of great-power war after 1945.[43]

In the realist worldview, wars occur not only because of the actions of states that prefer war to peace but also as a result of the unintended consequences of actions by those who prefer peace to war and who are more interested in preserving their security than in extending their influence.[44] Even defensively motivated ef-forts by states to provide for their own security through armaments, alliances, and deterrent threats are often perceived as threatening by others and lead to counteractions and conflict spirals that become difficult to reverse. This is the "security dilemma"—actions to increase one's security may only decrease the security of others and lead them to respond in ways that decrease one's own security.[45]

Many interpret the U.S.-Soviet Cold War as a conflict spiral between two states that feared each other and that were more inter-ested in security than in domination. Similarly, many interpret the Israeli-Palestinian conflict as a security-driven conflict spiral, in which actions lead to counteractions that are difficult to reverse because of a ratchet effect.

So far, these general realist propositions—that actors behave reasonably rationally to ad-vance their interests, defined primarily in terms of security; that the distribution of power is the primary determinant of international out-comes; and that wars result both as the in-tended consequence of aggressive states that want war to advance their interests and as the unintended consequence of more defensively motivated behavior to provide for security—apply as well to civil wars and other forms of organized violence as they do to interstate war. So do ideas about states forming alliances with other states, and the primacy of security motivations in those alliances. The idea that states have "neither permanent friends nor permanent enemies, just permanent interests" (in the words of Lord Palmerston, a mid-nineteenth-century British leader) applies to coalitions of rebels in civil wars as well as to the great-power politics of earlier centuries.[46]

Other realist propositions are more specific to interstate wars. One of the oldest realist theories is balance-of-power theory, which posits the avoidance of hegemony as the pri-mary goal of states and the maintenance of an equilibrium of power in the system as the pri-mary instrumental goal. The theory predicts that states, and particularly great powers, will build up their arms and form alliances to bal-ance against those who constitute the primary threats to their interests, and particularly against any state that threatens to secure a hegemonic position over the system.[47] Balance-of-power theorists argue that the balancing mechanism almost always works successfully to avoid hege-mony, either because potential hegemons are deterred by their anticipation of a military coalition forming against them or because they are defeated in war after deterrence fails.[48] In this view, the world wars of the twentieth cen-tury and the European war against Napole-onic France a century before were all balance-of-power wars that resulted from the formation of a military coalition to block a threatening state from achieving a position of dominance.

Scholars have also applied balance-of-power theory to regional state systems. One impor-tant difference between great-power systems and regional systems, however, is that the cen-tral assumption of anarchy is less valid for the latter, where, unlike the former case, powerful states outside the system can play a significant role. For example, outside powers can support a regional hegemon against a coalition of other states within the region, a coalition that might otherwise have restored a balance of power in the region. There are no significant powers outside a worldwide great-power system that might play this role. Thus some modifications may be necessary in applying balance-of-power theory to regional systems.

An important alternative to balance-of-power theory is "power transition theory," which shares many realist assumptions but emphasizes the existence of order within a nominally anarchic system. Hegemons commonly arise and use their strength to create a set of political and economic structures and norms of behavior that enhance the stability of the system at the same time that it advances their own security. Differential rates of growth lead to the rise and fall of hegemons, however, and the probability of a major war grows as the hegemon loses its dominant position. The probability of war reaches a maximum at the point at which the declining leader is overtaken by a rising challenger that is dissatisfied with the existing international system. Thus power transition theory appears to make the opposite prediction from balance-of-power theory—an equality of power, not a concentration of power, is most conducive to war.[49]

Power transition theory has direct implications for the contemporary world. It predicts that unipolarity under U.S. leadership contributes to stability in terms of a continuation of the great-power peace.[50] With the inevitable decline of U.S. hegemony, however, new instabilities will arise, particularly in the context of the continued rise of Chinese power. Many believe that the greatest threat to great-power peace will involve the dangers of a Sino-American conflict as the point of power transition approaches, which is estimated to be in about three decades. Although most experts believe that the existence of nuclear weapons will help deter a Sino-American war, most expect an intense rivalry between the two mid-century superpowers. That rivalry might be somewhat mitigated, however, if China abandons its communist ideology and embraces liberal democracy. That would presumably lessen its degree of dissatisfaction with the status quo, as defined by the capitalist international economic system currently led by the United States.[51]

Another prediction of power transition theory, one it shares with balance-of-power theory, is that leading states often act to block the rise of peer competitors. One balance-of-power theorist who explicitly makes this argument is John Mearsheimer, in his influential "offensive realist" theory. Mearsheimer argues, contrary to power transition theorists, that even the strongest states lack the resources to achieve hegemony over the entire world system. These states can sometimes achieve regional hegemony, however, and if they do they will use their power in an attempt to block other great powers from achieving hegemony in other regions.[52]

One of the strategies that states sometimes adopt against rising challengers, in regional as well as great-power systems, is preventive war. The argument is that a state facing a rising adversary may be tempted to initiate a preventive war in order to defeat the adversary while the opportunity is still available—before the adversary achieves a dominant position or crosses a critical threshold of military power.[53] The logic of prevention is reflected in Thucydides' argument that "what made the Peloponnesian War inevitable was the growth of Athenian power and the fear which this caused in Sparta."[54] Preventive logic motivated the Israeli strike against the Iraqi nuclear reactor in 1981, and it was the initial rationale of the second Bush administration for its 2003 war against Iraq.[55] Preventive-war theories have yet to identify the specific conditions under which states take preventive action against rising adversaries, however, and there is considerable uncertainty about whether the United States or possibly others might strike preventively against North Korea or Iran. The former is believed to possess nuclear weapons, and the latter appears determined to develop them.

In power transition theory, it is the combination of equality of power and change in power that is destabilizing in the presence of dissatisfied states. We can separate the static component, which posits that at the dyadic level war is least likely when one state has a preponderance of power over another and most likely when there is an equality of power. This is the "power preponderance hypothesis," which draws strong support from empirical studies of interstate war.[56] It is based on the logic that under conditions of preponderance the strong are satisfied and do not have the incentives for war, and the weak, though dissatisfied, lack the capability for war.

Applications to Civil War and Ethnonational Conflict

Although theorists of civil wars have recently borrowed some ideas from realist theories, balance-of-power theory as a whole is rarely applied directly to civil wars or to domestic political systems more generally. The main problem is that balance-of-power theory is based on the assumption of anarchy—the absence of a legitimate authority to regulate disputes. This assumption is rarely satisfied in domestic political systems with functioning governments.[57] Whereas balance-of-power theory predicts that concentrations of power in the international system are conducive to interstate war, most analysts have concluded that the concentration of power in domestic political systems—in strong centralized states that dominate local influences—minimizes the likelihood for civil war.[58]

Elements of power transition theory, including the power preponderance hypothesis, have some parallels in situations of ethnonational conflict. Just as power transition theorists argue that concentrations of power in the international system are stabilizing and minimize violent conflict, studies of ethnonational conflict generally find that wars that end in decisive victories are far less likely to be followed by renewed violence than are negotiated settlements based on roughly equal power.[59] They also find that a situation characterized by the strong dominance of one ethnic group is less prone to violent conflict than one characterized by an equality of power or a moderate imbalance of power between the two groups.[60]

Arguments about the consequences of a particular distribution of power between ethnonational groups need to be placed within a larger political context. Ethnonational minorities are often secure within stable political systems characterized by strong centralized state or imperial institutions (e.g., the communist political systems in the former Soviet bloc). The collapse of state power, however, leaves ethnonational communities in a condition resembling international anarchy, without any guarantees that their security and rights will be protected. Such ethnonational groups might have no hostile intentions toward other groups but still desire to build up militias for protection. The forces that provide protection might potentially do harm to others, however, and such buildups lead to counteractions, misperceptions, and conflict spirals.

Thus ethnonational groups in a condition of weakening centralized authority lack protection, fear for the future, and face an "ethnic security dilemma" that is quite comparable to the security dilemma facing states in the international system, with many of the same consequences.[61] This ethnic security dilemma is intensified by historical animosities and memories, often exaggerated, of past injustices by the other. This is a realist explanation for ethnonational conflict, with the unit of analysis shifted from states to ethnonational communities or other identity groups. The argument is that much ethnic conflict has less to do with ethnic or religious differences than with security fears in a system that provides no reliable means of protection.

These security-driven insecurities can be exacerbated when the leaders of one group attempt to unify their own people, and to enhance their own standing among them, by rhetorically exaggerating the potential threat posed by the other, acting to rectify past injustices (real or imagined), and generally using other ethnic groups as scapegoats for domestic problems. This is a common interpretation of the Yugoslav wars of the 1990s, with Serbian leader Slobodan Milosevic "playing the ethnic card" as a means of mobilizing his own support. Scapegoating foreigners as a means of enhancing the domestic support of political elites is also a source of interstate wars, as explained by the "diversionary theory of war," which is a national-level theory.[62]

The realist security perspective on ethnic conflict generates a number of propositions about the intensity of the ethnic security dilemma and hence the likelihood of violence. The lower the congruence between state territorial borders and communal boundaries, and the greater the ethnic intermingling, the harder it is to provide security, and the higher the likelihood of violence. Such conditions increase the probability of secessionist wars by captive peoples to withdraw from the territory of a larger state and create their own state, and of irredentist wars by ethnic groups in one state to retrieve ethnically kindred people and their territory from another state.[63]

There are other ways in which weak or failed states create conditions that are ripe for internal violence. These causal paths are explored later in this volume by Rotberg, Ayoob, and others. Part of any explanation for violent outcomes, however, would be why so many contemporary states are weak in the first place, particularly relative to their European counterparts. Standard answers to this question focus on factors internal to states, but the fact that so many contemporary states find themselves in this position suggests that international system–level factors may play a role.

System-Level Sources of State Weakness and Conflict

The states that until recently have done much of the world's fighting but that now do rela-

tively little fighting emerged in early modern Europe. Faced with a highly threatening international environment and internal imperatives to consolidate their power over domestic rivals, states built up their military power, fought frequent wars, and conquered new territories. They constituted the core of an emerging international system in the sixteenth and seventeenth centuries, in which there were no external powers to regulate their behavior and constrain their territorial expansion. The expanded armies needed for external conquest and defense led to expanded administrative and fiscal systems to support those armies, and thus to the increasing centralization of state power. That, plus the new military technologies states had incentives to develop, made wars more destructive.[64] States that lacked the resources, political organization, and military strength to compete on the battlefield were absorbed by their stronger neighbors, and the states that remained were well constituted—in terms of military power, economic resources, and institutional strength—to fight with their external rivals and to maintain internal order. In Charles Tilly's classic formulation, "War made the state, and the state made war."[65]

The political units that emerged from the state-building processes in early modern Europe had the resources and ability to survive the trial by fire of a highly competitive and conflictual international system and were forced by the competition to increase their strength. The same is not true for states formed in the late twentieth century after the collapse of the European colonial empires and then after the collapse of the Soviet empire. These states followed a different developmental trajectory, with different consequences. In the words of Ann Hironaka, in contrast to "strong, battle-scarred states that had proven their capability to withstand both interstate and civil war," former colonies and other new states emerged "not through victory in war, but through the encouragement and support of the international system." The new environment, unlike the one in which European states came of age, was characterized by external superpowers with both incentives and capabilities to maintain a stable international order and by international norms that discouraged both territorial conquest and secession. The competitive pressures that formerly weeded out all but the strongest states no longer operated, leading to the emergence of states that were weak in institutions and resources, vulnerable to internal threats, and less able to contain internal violence. Thus, Hironaka concludes, "the rules and behavior changed," and "the international system after 1945 has encouraged and supported the proliferation of weak states that are susceptible to protracted civil wars."[66]

This argument emphasizes that many of the sources of state weaknesses lie in the international system and the causal paths leading from system-level structures and norms to the military, economic, and administrative strength of states. Moreover, state weakness may even be a source of ethnic differences or at least of the exacerbation of those differences. The absence of strong political institutions in weak states facilitates political mobilization around groups defined in terms of ethnicity or religion, rather than around political parties, and provides leaders with incentives to engage in ethnic scapegoating to bolster their internal support.[67]

This situation has been exacerbated by the legacy of European colonialism. Most civil wars over the past several decades have taken place within the territory of former colonial and imperial empires. The territorial boundaries of these states reflect those of the European colonies they replaced, and European powers drew those borders for their own imperial convenience rather than to reflect ethnic, religious, or economic facts of life. The result is a marked incongruence between the territorial borders of the states and the "natural" boundaries separating various communal groups. Identity groups, cut off from their brethren in other states, were sometimes left too weak to provide for their security, too

small to be economically viable, and incomplete in their identity, and they had strong incentives to attempt to change the status quo.

This incongruence between state boundaries and the distribution of ethnic, religious, and other identity groups has been reinforced by international norms that discourage both territorial conquest and secession. Norms against territorial conquest mean that contemporary states, unlike states in early modern Europe, cannot easily expand to incorporate displaced national minorities and thus to form "natural" boundaries based on the congruence of nation and state. Norms against secession, which deny separatist groups the international recognition and funding that constitute near prerequisites for survival, reinforce the existence of disaffected minorities within states.

The result is a collection of states that have the formal trappings of sovereignty, including international recognition and equal votes in the United Nations, but not the functional capacity required to integrate their disparate parts into an effectively functioning political system. As Robert Jackson argues, "Ramshackle states today . . . are not allowed to disappear juridically—even if for all intents and purposes they have already fallen or been pulled down in fact."[68] The result is the persistence of weak states and of conditions that are conducive to civil wars.

The discrepancy between the boundaries of formal territorial units and communal groups is particularly pronounced in sub-Saharan Africa.[69] This incongruence has been more likely to contribute to civil conflict than to international conflict, as state leaders have hesitated to contest state boundaries for fear that doing so might set a precedent, unleash unpredictable behavior, and undermine the status quo. The normative constraint against challenging existing boundaries may be gradually disintegrating, and if that continues there could be an increase in interstate war in the region. Thus far, however, most wars have remained internal to states.

The legacy of colonialism also contributes to civil conflict through other paths. Imperial powers sometimes promoted internal rivalries in order to enhance their own influence through a divide-and-conquer strategy, and once in place those rivalries tended to persist beyond the collapse of imperial rule.[70] Anticolonial wars often transform into civil wars, as the internal opponents of external armies turn on each other after the external forces have departed.[71]

The institutional structures put in place by the imperial power, and the political cultures that grew up around them, could also have an impact on the strength of new states and their proclivities toward violence. Such institutional structures varied greatly, and this variation—particularly in terms of the strength of the central government—helps to account for the relative ability or inability of the government to withstand centripetal forces from within and possibly also for the extent of government repression. In many cases, the process of state building in new states got off to a particularly difficult start because of the rapid process of decolonialization. The rather abrupt withdrawal of several colonial empires was due in part to traditional U.S. hostility to imperial and colonial rule, U.S. determination to expand its own sphere of influence, and consequently U.S. pressure on European states to withdraw from their colonial empires. Given the politics of Cold War bipolarity and the Soviet threat, European colonial states had little bargaining leverage against U.S. pressure. As a result, many new states emerged from the colonial empires profoundly ill prepared for the tasks of statehood, as illustrated by the new states in the former Belgian and Portuguese empires in Africa and also by the case of Algeria.[72]

From Bipolarity to U.S. Hegemony

Cold War bipolarity had other consequences as well, though how the superpowers and leading regional powers perceived and responded to the distribution of military power and the strategies they adopted were also important.

Within each of the superpower blocs, the hierarchical structure of power, in conjunction with each superpower's incentives and capabilities for maintaining stability, tended to dampen both interstate and intrastate conflicts.

Outside the superpower blocs, however, bipolarity induced a competition between the Soviet Union and the United States for power and influence in the Third World. Given their perceptions of a zero-sum game, the superpowers often had incentives to arm whatever side their adversary was not funding, and governments and rebel groups had incentives to play the superpowers off against each other. The result was that both sides in a civil war often received ample funding from the superpowers, in marked contrast to earlier eras.

In the nineteenth century, for example, European great powers, through the Concert of Europe, often acted together to support governments against domestic rebels. This led to an imbalance in military strength and relatively short civil wars. The funding of both governments and rebels in the Cold War period contributed to a stalemate on the battlefield and thus to longer civil wars. The duration of civil wars during the Cold War was also lengthened by the existence of two rival ideological models that could be used to mobilize recruits and provide additional incentives for fighting.[73] The superpowers also promoted a number of proxy wars to advance their own interests, though they had both the incentives and the ability to keep those wars from escalating out of control.

The erosion of Soviet power and the end of the Cold War had multiple effects. Within the Soviet bloc, the combination of the collapse of hierarchical rule and the movement toward democratization brought new social groups with widely divergent interests into a political process that lacked the institutional capacity and political legitimacy to accommodate those interests. This provided a fertile environment for political entrepreneurs to make nationalist appeals and engage in scapegoating marginalized groups and external enemies, in order to help consolidate their political support.[74] Similar processes could be found elsewhere, as the withdrawal of superpower support for weak authoritarian regimes created power vacuums that facilitated conflict.

The dominant trend, however, was in the other direction. The superpowers no longer had incentives to support proxy wars, and their disengagement from such wars, their efforts to settle some of those wars, and their withdrawal of funding of others both reduced the frequency of new internal wars and helped shorten the duration of ongoing wars. At the same time, however, the increasing globalization of the arms market provided additional opportunities, for both governments and rebels, to find new sources of armaments and economic support. The existence of a global arms market has also generated alliances between rebel groups and international criminal networks, which provide an additional source of funds and arms.[75] The net trend, however, was to suppress conflict, and the end of the Cold War was soon followed by a significant decline in the number of ongoing civil wars.[76]

This discussion has focused primarily on the distribution of power in the global system and the impact of bipolarity and then of unipolarity on internal warfare around the world. A different set of system factors involves resource scarcities in regional systems, which we now consider.

Resource Scarcities and Conflict

The problems confronting weak states are exacerbated by resource scarcities.[77] One of the central themes in the growing literature on environmental scarcity and its implications for international conflict is the neo-Malthusian argument that competition for scarce resources among states with rapidly growing and increasingly urbanized populations, coupled with the degradation of those resources by desertification, deforestation, rising sea levels, pollution, and environmental disasters, will generate famines, economic and social problems, environmental refugees, political instabilities, and serious domestic and international crises.[78] This scenario is most likely to arise in developing countries, which generally lack the wealth and institutional capacity to respond to environmental disruptions.[79]

The combination of population growth, uneven resource distribution, and the environmental degradation of limited resources exacerbates scarcities and contributes to violent conflict in a number of ways. The most direct path is through a "simple-scarcity conflict," or "resource war," in which one state or group uses military force against another for the primary purpose of gaining access to key economic and strategic resources.[80] The primary factor leading Iraqi leader Saddam Hussein to invade Kuwait in 1990, for example, was the goal of gaining control over Kuwait's vast oil supplies as a means of reviving the Iraqi economy, eliminating an oppressive debt, and in doing so further consolidating Saddam's hold on political power.[81] This case is consistent with the argument that conflicts over nonrenewable resources tend to be more destabilizing than disputes over renewable resources. A particularly serious point of conflict in the future, however, may be disputes over fresh water.[82]

Simple-scarcity conflicts are not the only path from environmental scarcity to war. Resource scarcity, sometimes compounded by environmental degradation, droughts, floods, and famines, often leads people to migrate in search of economic security.[83] Population movements can, in turn, contribute to conflict or exacerbate existing conflict through a number of causal paths.[84] Immigrants can generate social conflict within the host or receiving country by putting added strain on scarce resources, particularly in large urban areas. Migrations can change land distribution, economic relations, and the balance of political power among ethnic, religious, or other social groups; undermine state capacity to create markets and other institutions that facilitate adaptation to environmental change; generate a perceived threat to the host country's cultural identity; trigger a social backlash by indigenous people in response to perceived threats to economic security or social identity from migrants; and generally increase communal conflict, political instabilities, and the likelihood of civil strife.[85]

Migrations may also contribute to international conflict by serving as a focal point for relations between home and host countries. Host countries that cannot easily assimilate the new immigrants or deal with the consequent economic problems and social instabilities may attempt to influence the home government to stop or slow the flow of refugees or eliminate the conditions that gave rise to them. If cooperative efforts fail, governments may resort to coercive threats and possible military action to block the flow of refugees, which can trigger a conflict spiral. Political leaders with weak or declining domestic support may under some conditions be tempted to use the migrants or their home government as scapegoats, as a means of bolstering their own internal political support. A good example is the 1979 "Soccer War" between El Salvador and Honduras. While the trigger cause of the war was a dispute emerging from a soccer game, and while an important background cause was a simple-scarcity conflict driven by environmental pressures and famine, scapegoating and other governmental responses to those systemic pressures played a key role in the conflict.[86]

SUMMARY AND CONCLUSION

My aim in this chapter has been to place contemporary warfare in the context of changing patterns of warfare over time and to consider ways in which the changing nature of the international system has shaped interstate and intrastate warfare, with particular attention to the six decades since the end of World War II. We have seen a substantial shift in war away from the great powers and away from Europe, a gradual decline in interstate wars more gen-

erally, and a significant increase in civil wars, particularly in the developing world. I have also raised a number of conceptual issues confronting the study of war and suggested several general criteria that any theory or interpretation of war would have to satisfy. One of the most basic criteria is that any theory of war must be able to account for variations in war and peace. Relatedly, any explanation of a particular war must be able to explain why the war occurred when it did and not earlier or later. I summarized the levels-of-analysis framework, which has been an influential framework for the analysis of interstate war and of other aspects of international relations. I then turned to a survey of some of the leading causes of war associated with the international system–level of analysis. I gave particular attention to realist theories and emphasized how realist theories of interstate war have been modified to explain ethnic wars and other forms of civil war. I emphasized the ethnic security dilemma facing many ethnic groups in the world today and how that security dilemma has been exacerbated by the economic, institutional, and military weakness of states in the developing world. I then explained how the international system has contributed to the weakness of states—and consequently to the incidence of civil war—in the contemporary world. I considered the impact, first of Cold War bipolarity and then of post–Cold War unipolarity, on patterns of interstate and intrastate war, and ended with a discussion of the impact of resource scarcity at the regional level. This survey has left many important causal factors uncovered, but many of these are treated throughout the remainder of this volume.

NOTES

The author thanks the editors of this volume for their helpful comments and suggestions.

1. For a more complete treatment of the causes of interstate war, see Jack S. Levy, "The Causes of War: A Review of Theories and Evidence," in *Behav-*

ior, Society, and Nuclear War, vol. 1, ed. Philip Tetlock, Jo L. Husbands, Robert Jervis, Paul C. Stern, and Charles Tilly (New York: Oxford University Press, 1989), 209–333; and John A. Vasquez, *The War Puzzle* (New York: Cambridge University Press, 1993). On terrorism, see Robert A. Pape, *Dying to Win: The Strategic Logic of Suicide Terrorism* (New York: Random House, 2005); and Mia Bloom, *Dying to Kill: The Allure of Suicide Terror* (New York: Columbia University Press, 2005). On genocide, see Manus I. Midlarsky, *The Killing Trap: Genocide in the Twentieth Century* (New York: Cambridge University Press, 2005).

2. Quincy Wright, *A Study of War* (Chicago: University of Chicago Press, 1965); Jack S. Levy, *War in the Modern Great Power System, 1495–1975* (Lexington: University Press of Kentucky, 1983); and J. David Singer, "Peace in the Global System: Displacement, Interregnum, or Transformation?" in *The Long Postwar Peace,* ed. Charles W. Kegley, Jr. (Glenview, Ill.: Scott, Foresman, 1991), 56–84. If we count China as a great power beginning in 1949, then the Korean War (1950–53) was a great-power war.

3. John Lewis Gaddis, *The Long Peace* (New York: Oxford University Press, 1987).

4. The decline in the frequency of interstate wars is particularly striking in the context of the enormous increase in the number of states in the international system—and hence in the mathematical opportunities for interstate war—in the period after World War II.

5. Kalevi J. Holsti, *The State, War, and the State of War* (New York: Cambridge University Press, 1996).

6. Jack S. Levy and William R. Thompson, "The Arc of War" (unpublished book manuscript, 2006). The decline in the frequency of civil war since the 1990s is well documented. See Monty G. Marshall and Ted R. Gurr, *Peace and Conflict 2005: A Global Survey of Armed Conflicts, Self-Determination Movements, and Democracy* (College Park: Center for International Development and Conflict Management, University of Maryland, 2005); Human Security Centre, *Human Security Report 2005: War and Peace in the Twenty-first Century* (New York: Oxford University Press, 2005), parts 1 and 4; and Lotta Harbom and Peter Wallensteen, "Armed Conflict and Its International Dimensions, 1946–2004," *Journal of Peace Research* 42, no. 5 (September 2005): 623–635.

7. We should not necessarily assume that "ethnic" or "identity" wars are primarily about ethnicity or identity. The primary motivations of key players in some of those wars may be security, economic resources, political power, or private interest. See John Mueller, *The Remnants of War* (Ithaca, N.Y.: Cornell University Press, 2004); V.P. Gagnon Jr., *The Myth Of Ethnic War: Serbia and Croatia in the 1990s* (Ithaca, N.Y.: Cornell University Press, 2004).

8. Susan L. Woodward, *Balkan Tragedy* (Washington, D.C.: Brookings Institution, 1995). Even the U.S. war in Afghanistan is hard to classify. It began as an interstate war against the Taliban regime in 2001 and soon transformed into an "internationalized civil war" with an external power supporting the government against the rebels. Even in the war's early stages, however, the United States basically took sides in an Afghan civil war and paid the Afghan Northern Alliance to conduct a majority of ground operations. Internationalized civil wars are hardly new—the Thirty Years' War (1618–48) began as a civil war within Germany, and the French revolutionary wars soon became internationalized—but they have become much more common.

9. Herfried Münkler, *The New Wars* (Oxford: Oxford University Press, 2004); and Deborah D. Avant, *The Market for Force: The Consequences of Privatizing Security* (New York: Cambridge University Press, 2005).

10. It is still war if we define war broadly as sustained, coordinated violence between political organizations (Levy and Thompson, "The Arc of War"). For a useful survey of definitions of war, see Vasquez, *The War Puzzle,* chap. 2. For discussions about the extent to which the "new wars" differ from "old wars," see Holsti, *The State, War, and the State of War;* Mary Kaldor, *New and Old Wars: Organized Violence in a Global Era* (Stanford, Calif.: Stanford University Press, 1999); Stathis N. Kalyvas, "'New' and 'Old' Civil Wars: A Valid Distinction?" *World Politics* 54, no. 1 (2001): 99–118; and Münkler, *The New Wars.*

11. Martin van Creveld, *The Transformation of War* (New York: Free Press, 1991); Holsti, *The State, War, and the State of War;* and Münkler, *The New Wars.*

12. Donald L. Horowitz, *Ethnic Groups in Conflict* (Berkeley: University of California Press, 1985).

13. For a critique of the Western conception of warfare, see John F. Guilmartin, Jr., "Ideology and Conflict: The Wars of the Ottoman Empire, 1453–1606," *Journal of Interdisciplinary History* 18 (Spring 1988): 721–747.

14. Münkler, *The New Wars.*

15. Mueller, *The Remnants of War.*

16. Clausewitz (*On War*) defines "political" broadly to include diplomatic, strategic, economic, ideological, and related objectives. For a critique of the idea that war is fundamentally political, see John Keegan, *A History of Warfare* (New York: Vintage, 1993), which opens (p. 3) with the provocative statement that "war is not the continuation of policy by other means." See also Holsti, *The State, War, and the State of War;* and Münkler, *The New Wars.*

17. Although scholars continue to debate the motivations of terrorist groups, a growing consensus suggests that the use of terror by terrorist organizations is purposeful and strategic, not nihilistic. See chapter 6, by Martha Crenshaw, in this volume. See also Pape, *Dying to Win;* and Bloom, *Dying to Kill.* With respect to al Qaeda, the standard interpretation is that its immediate aim is to force the withdrawal of U.S. and allied military forces from the Islamic world, in order to facilitate the goal of replacing existing regimes with "true" Muslim regimes.

18. Relatedly, Clausewitz argues that the logic of war itself is fundamentally political, not military. This means that the criterion by which a war is to be evaluated is not whether it results in "victory" or "defeat," which are often hard to define, but rather whether it leaves the actor, or at least its leaders, better off after the war than they were before. A good example of Clausewitzian thinking comes from the Vietnam War. The turning point of the war was the Tet Offensive by the North Vietnamese, which caused American public opinion to turn against the war. In strictly military terms, the Tet Offensive was a U.S. victory. But it was the political consequences that mattered. This is reflected in a conversation between an American colonel and a North Vietnamese colonel after the war. The American said, "You know you never defeated us on the battlefield." His North Vietnamese counterpart replied, "That may be so, but it is also irrelevant." In Harry G. Summers, Jr., *On Strategy* (New York: Dell, 1982), 21. Summers, the American colonel, was himself an admirer of Clausewitz.

19. Political scientists who study warfare in the past two centuries generally use the threshold of one thousand battle-related deaths. J. David Singer and Melvin Small, *The Wages of War, 1816–1965* (New York: Wiley, 1972).

20. In other words, an "independent variable" that is constant cannot explain a "dependent variable" that varies.

21. Robert L. Carneiro, "A Theory of the Origin of the State," *Science* 169 (1970): 733–738.

22. Robert D. Kaplan, *Balkan Ghosts* (New York: Vintage, 1993); and Samuel P. Huntington, *The Clash of Civilizations and the Remaking of World Order* (New York: Simon and Schuster, 1996).

23. One key factor was the Iranian revolution, which brought a fundamentalist Islamic regime to power and threatened the domestic security of the secular Baathist regime of Saddam Hussein in Iraq. Dilip Hiro, *The Longest War: The Iran-Iraq Military Conflict* (New York: Routledge, 1991).

24. Kenneth N. Waltz, *Man, the State, and War* (New York: Columbia University Press, 1959). Waltz spoke of three "images" of war, but it is now common to speak in terms of "levels" of analysis.

25. This discussion builds on my treatment of levels of analysis and theories of war in the earlier edition of this volume: Jack S. Levy, "Theories of Interstate and Intrastate War: A Levels-of-Analysis Approach," in *Turbulent Peace: The Challenges of Managing International Conflict,* ed. Chester A. Crocker, Fen Osler Hampson, and Pamela Aall (Washington, D.C.: United States Institute of Peace Press, 2001), 3–27.

26. Each of the three levels is not in itself a theory but includes a variety of separate theories within it.

27. James Mann, *Rise of the Vulcans: The History of Bush's War Cabinet* (New York: Viking Penguin, 2004); and Michael R. Gordon and General Bernard E. Trainor, *Cobra II: The Inside Story of the Invasion and Occupation of Iraq* (New York: Pantheon Books, 2006).

28. Michael Brown, "Ethnic and Internal Conflicts: Causes and Implications," in Crocker et al., *Turbulent Peace,* 209–226.

29. Rohan Gunaranta, *Inside al-Qaeda: Global Network of Terror,* 3rd ed. (New York: Berkley Publishing Group, 2003).

30. The important factor of misperceptions, for example, can result from system-level uncertainty or adversary strategic deception, national-level ideologies that predispose leaders to interpret the behavior of others in certain ways, and individual-level personalities that contribute to further distortions in incoming information. Economic factors include both national economic interests, such as the stability of a society's economic system, and the influence of private economic groups (e.g., arms manufacturers) on state foreign policies.

31. This argument reflects the "hero-in-history" approach. Sydney Hook, *The Hero in History* (Boston: Beacon Press, 1955).

32. It might seem that in a dictatorship such additional conceptual apparatus might not be necessary, but in fact the dictatorial structure of the regime is part of the explanation. Saddam Hussein's beliefs and personality may be central to an explanation of the origins of the 1990–91 Persian Gulf War, but only in conjunction with the highly centralized structure of the Iraqi regime that allowed Saddam Hussein to make policy in the absence of any significant internal constraints.

33. Ernest May, *Imperial Democracy* (New York: Harper and Row, 1961).

34. This does not necessarily mean that dyadic and system-level variables have a greater causal influence than do individual or domestic variables, only that the former cannot be logically excluded from the analysis.

35. The statement that a state makes a "decision for war" implicitly assumes that the adversary will fight back. On the distinction between war as strategy (of an actor) and war as outcome (of the joint actions of two or more actors), see Vasquez, *The War Puzzle*, chap. 2.

36. A. J. P. Taylor, *The Origins of the Second World War,* 2nd ed. (Greenwich, Conn.: Fawcett, 1961).

37. For hypotheses on the conditions under which threats of force tend to work, see Robert Jervis, *Perception and Misperception in International Politics* (Princeton, N.J.: Princeton University Press, 1976), chap. 3.

38. There are a variety of system-level theories, including realist, liberal, institutionalist, and constructivist theories. We focus here primarily on realist theories emphasizing security interests and power, with some attention to constructivist arguments emphasizing norms. For a survey of international relations theories, see Walter Carlsnaes, Thomas Risse, and Beth A. Simmons, eds., *Handbook of International Relations* (London: Sage, 2002).

39. "Realist" is a nominal label given to the paradigm by its proponents. We should not automatically assume that realist theory provides a more "realistic" or valid portrayal of the world than do alternative theories. That is an empirical question.

40. Anarchy is a structural feature of the international system; it does not equal chaos. Realists hypothesize that anarchy often leads to chaos, which is different.

41. Thucydides, *History of the Peloponnesian War,* in *The Landmark Thucydides,* ed. Robert B. Strassler (New York: Free Press, 1996), 5.89, 352. See also Waltz, *Theory of International Politics.*

42. G. John Ikenberry, ed., *America Unrivaled: The Future of the Balance of Power* (Ithaca, N.Y.: Cornell University Press, 2002).

43. For other explanations of the long great-power peace, see Gaddis, *The Long Peace;* and Kegley, *The Long Postwar Peace.*

44. In the second scenario, states aim to avoid losses rather than make gains. Most people have a tendency to place much greater value on preserving what they have than on acquiring something new and engage in riskier strategies to avoid losses than to make gains. States (and rebel groups) fight to hold on to territory that they might not have fought to acquire in the first place. This is a core insight of "prospect theory." For applications to international relations, see Jack S. Levy, "The Implications of Framing and Loss Aversion for International Conflict," in *Handbook of War Studies II,* ed. Manus I. Midlarsky (Ann Arbor: University of Michigan Press, 2000), 193–221.

45. Jervis, *Perception and Misperception in International Politics,* chap. 3.

46. This is illustrated by the Arab coalition against Iraq in 1991, in which Arab leaders indirectly aligned with their Israeli enemy to counter the more immediate threat posed by Saddam Hussein's Iraq, and also by the constantly shifting coalitions in the civil war in the Democratic Republic of the Congo in the 1990s.

47. Hans J. Morgenthau, *Politics among Nations,* 4th ed. (New York: Alfred A. Knopf, 1967); and John J. Mearsheimer, *The Tragedy of Great Power Politics* (New York: W. W. Norton, 2001).

48. Jack S. Levy, "Balances and Balancing: Concepts, Propositions, and Research Design," in *Realism and the Balancing of Power,* ed. John A. Vasquez and

Colin Elman (Upper Saddle River, N.J.: Prentice-Hall, 2003), 128–153.

49. Robert Gilpin, *War and Change in World Politics* (New York: Cambridge University Press, 1981); and Jacek Kugler and Douglas Lemke, *Parity and War* (Ann Arbor: University of Michigan Press, 1996). An important variation of power transition is long-cycle theory, which emphasizes leadership in the global system based on naval power (and airpower by the mid-twentieth century) and economic power based on dominance in leading sector technologies. See Karen Rasler and William R. Thompson, "Global War and the Political Economy of Structural Change," in *Handbook of War Studies II*, ed. Manus I. Midlarsky (Ann Arbor: University of Michigan Press, 2000), 301–331.

50. While many interpret balance-of-power theory as applicable to all international systems, a new line of argument emphasizes that the theory was based on the experience of five centuries of European history and designed to apply to continental systems like Europe, not to the global maritime system. There is an implicit distinction between land powers and maritime powers. Land powers have large armies that can invade and intimidate and are perceived to be more threatening than are maritime powers. The theory predicts that states will balance against aspiring continental hegemons and that such balancing will be effective in avoiding continental hegemony, but it makes no such predictions about balancing against potential global hegemons. Thus, while it is common to argue that balance-of-power theory incorrectly predicts great-power balancing against U.S. global hegemony, and that the absence of such balancing undermines balance-of-power theory, this alternative perspective suggests that just as British dominance in the nineteenth-century global system did not trigger a countervailing great-power balancing coalition, balance-of-power theory does not necessarily predict a great-power balancing coalition against the United States. See Levy, "Balances and Balancing."

51. The power transition between Britain and the rising United States in the late nineteenth century provides an instructive example. Both were capitalist states and sought a capitalist world economy. This led Britain to anticipate that the United States would not overturn the international political economy, just acquire a dominant position in the existing system, which was acceptable to Britain.

52. Mearsheimer, *The Tragedy of Great Power Politics.*

53. See Jack S. Levy, "Declining Power and the Preventive Motivation for War," *World Politics* 40, no. 1 (October 1987): 82–107.

54. Thucydides, *Peloponnesian War*, 1.23.

55. The Bush administration used the concept of preemption, but that was misleading. Preemption involves attacking an adversary who you believe is about to attack you, whereas prevention involves attacking an adversary before it crosses a critical threshold of military capability. As it turned out, Iraq did not have weapons of mass destruction, and there is growing evidence that Bush and some of his advisors may have known this at the time. Chaim Kaufmann, "Threat Inflation and the Failure of the Marketplace of Ideas: The Selling of the Iraq War," *International Security* 29, no. 1 (Summer 2004): 5–48. On the distinction between prevention and preemption, and on the role of preventive logic in U.S. foreign policy, see Jack S. Levy, "Preventive War and the Bush Doctrine: Theoretical Logic and Historical Roots." In *The Bush Doctrine: Psychology and Strategy in an Age of Terrorism*, ed. Stanley A. Renshon and Peter Suedfeld (London: Routledge, 2007).

56. The evidence is summarized in Kugler and Lemke, *Parity and War*. Note that the stabilizing effects of power preponderance at the dyadic level do not necessarily imply that imbalances of power are stabilizing at the system level, where balancing through alliances can create opportunities for war to restrict concentrations of power.

57. Balance-of-power theory might in principle be applicable in the case of "collapsed" or "failed states," though other theories are more commonly applied to such situations.

58. For discussions of "failed states," see chapters 6 and 7, by Robert Rotberg and Mohammed Ayoob, in this volume.

59. Roy Licklider, "The Consequences of Negotiated Settlements in Civil Wars, 1945–1993," *American Political Science Review* 89, no. 3 (September 1995): 681–690.

60. Chaim Kaufman, "Possible and Impossible Solutions to Ethnic Civil Wars," *International Security* 20, no. 4 (Spring 1996): 136–175.

61. Barry R. Posen, "The Security Dilemma and Ethnic Conflict," *Survival* 35, no. 1 (Spring 1993):

27–47; and Jack Snyder and Robert Jervis, "Civil War and the Security Dilemma," in *Civil Wars, Insecurity, and Intervention,* ed. Barbara F. Walter and Jack Snyder (New York: Columbia University Press, 1999), 15–37.

62. Gagnon, *The Myth of Ethnic War;* and Jack S. Levy, "The Diversionary Theory of War: A Critique," in *Handbook of War Studies,* ed. Manus I. Midlarsky (London: Unwin-Hyman, 1989), 259–288. The fact that students of diversionary war rarely apply their theories to ethnic conflict and that students of ethnic conflict rarely refer to the literature on diversionary war is an unfortunate reflection of the division between the study of interstate war and the study of intrastate war.

63. Stephen Van Evera, "Hypotheses on Nationalism and War," *International Security* 18, no. 4 (Spring 1994): 5–39; and Donald Horowitz, "Irredentas and Secessions," in *Irredentism and International Politics,* ed. Naomi Chazan (Boulder, Colo.: Lynne Rienner, 1991), 9–22.

64. These mutually reinforcing changes in war, military technology and strategy, and political and administrative organization constitute the "military revolution" in early modern Europe. See Michael Roberts, "The Military Revolution, 1560–1660," in *The Military Revolution Debate: Readings on the Military Transformation of Early Modern Europe,* ed. Clifford J. Rogers (Boulder, Colo.: Westview, 1995), 13–35; and Levy and Thompson, "The Arc of War."

65. Charles Tilly, "Reflections on the History of European State Making," in *The Formation of National States in Western Europe,* ed. Charles Tilly (Princeton, N.J.: Princeton University Press, 1975), 42.

66. Ann Hironaka, *Neverending Wars: The International Community, Weak States, and the Perpetuation of Civil War* (Cambridge, Mass.: Harvard University Press, 2005), 7.

67. Ibid., chap. 4; and Gagnon, *The Myth of Ethnic War.* For studies of ethnic conflict wars that give causal primacy to ethnicity, see Kaplan, *Balkan Ghosts;* Walker Connor, *Ethnonationalism: The Quest for Understanding* (Princeton, N.J.: Princeton University Press, 1994); and Stephen M. Saidman, *The Ties That Divide: Ethnic Politics, Foreign Policy, and International Conflict* (New York: Columbia University Press, 2001).

68. Robert H. Jackson, *Quasi-States: Sovereignty, International Relations, and the Third World* (New York: Cambridge University Press, 1990); and Bertrand Badie, *The Imported State: The Westernization of the Political Order* (Stanford, Calif.: Stanford University Press, 2000).

69. Jackson, *Quasi-States.* The problem also applies to the Middle East. For decades before the Iraqi invasion of Kuwait in 1990, Iraqis insisted that part of Kuwaiti territory was historically and rightfully theirs, included in Kuwait only because of British imperial interests.

70. The Azerbaijan-Armenian rivalry, which escalated into war in the 1990s, was influenced in part by Joseph Stalin's deliberate efforts to play one off against the other.

71. This was true of Vietnam, Algeria, and numerous other former colonies.

72. I thank the editors of this volume for bringing this point to my attention.

73. Münkler, *The New Wars;* and Hironaka, *Neverending Wars.*

74. Jack Snyder, *From Voting to Violence: Democratization and Nationalist Conflict* (New York: W. W. Norton, 2000).

75. Mueller, *Remnants of War;* Phil Williams and John T. Picarelli, "Combating Organized Crime in Armed Combat," in *Profiting from Peace: Managing the Resource Dimensions of Civil War,* ed. Karen Ballentine and Heiko Nitzschke (Boulder, Colo.: Lynne Rienner, 2005), 123–152; and Münkler, *New Wars.* For a review of debates about the impact of globalization on civil war, see Katherine Barbieri and Rafael Reuveny, "Economic Globalization and Civil War," *Journal of Politics* 67, no. 4 (November 2005): 1228–1247.

76. Hironaka, *Neverending Wars;* Marshall and Gurr, *Peace and Conflict 2005;* and Human Security Centre, *Human Security Report 2005.*

77. See also the essay by Nils Petter Gleditsch, chap. 11 in this volume. Resource scarcity is another subject that highlights the divergence between the studies of interstate and intrastate conflict. Although the contemporary literature on civil war gives considerable attention to resource scarcities, the traditional literature on interstate war, with its emphasis on power and process but its neglect of specific issues over which states fight (until the recent emphasis on territorial disputes), has given relatively little attention to resource scarcity. The most important exception is Nazli Choucri and Robert North, *Nations in Conflict: National Growth and International Violence* (San Francisco: W. H. Freeman, 1975).

Recent literature on environmental scarcity and its implications for both interstate and intrastate conflict includes Thomas F. Homer-Dixon, *Environment, Scarcity, and Violence* (Princeton, N.J.: Princeton University Press, 1999); "Environmental Conflict," special issue, *Journal of Peace Research* 35, no. 3 (May 1998). On the importance of territorial issues in interstate and intrastate violence, see John A. Vasquez and Marie T. Henehan, "Territorial Disputes and the Probability of War, 1816-1992," *Journal of Peace Research*, 38, no. 2 (2001), 123-138; and Monica Duffy Toft, *The Geography of Ethnic Violence: Identity, Interests, and the Indivisibility of Territory* (Princeton, N.J.: Princeton University Press, 2003).

It is interesting to note that the anthropological literature on the origins of war six to ten millennia ago gives considerable emphasis to resource scarcity. Carneiro, "Theory of the Origin of the State"; Ronald Cohen, "Warfare and State Formation: Wars Make States and States Make War," in *Warfare, Culture, and Environment*, ed. Brian R. Ferguson (Orlando, Fla.: Academic Press, 1984), 329–358; Jonathan Haas, "The Origins of War and Ethnic Violence," in *Ancient Warfare: Archaeological Perspectives*, ed. John Carman and Anthony Harding (Gloucestershire, U.K.: Sutton Publishing, 1999).

78. Robert D. Kaplan, *The Coming Anarchy* (New York: Random House, 2000).

79. This raises the question of whether environmental change is a security issue, and the broader question of whether "human security" should be defined narrowly in terms of violent threats to individuals or broadly to include as well threats from hunger, disease, and natural disasters. For debates, see Daniel Deudney, "The Case against Linking Environmental Degradation and National Security," *Millennium* 19, no. 3 (Winter 1990): 461–476; Marc A. Levy, "Is the Environment a National Security Issue?" *International Security* 20, no. 2 (Fall 1995): 35–62; and Human Security Centre, *Human Security Report 2005*, viii.

80. Homer-Dixon, *Environment, Scarcity, and Violence*.

81. Lawrence Freedman and Efraim Karsh, *The Gulf Conflict, 1990–1991: Diplomacy and War in the New World Order* (Princeton, N.J.: Princeton University Press, 1993). There is also a consensus that Japan's quest for oil and other scarce resources was a primary factor leading to the Pacific War between Japan and the United States in 1941. Michael Barnhart, *Japan Prepares for Total War: The Search for Economic Security, 1919-1941* (Ithaca, N.Y.: Cornell University Press, 1987).

82. Homer-Dixon, *Environment, Scarcity, and Violence;* Miriam R. Lowi, *Water and Power: The Politics of a Scarce Resource in the Jordan River Basin* (New York: Cambridge University Press, 1993); Peter H. Gleick, "Water and Conflict: Fresh Water Resources and International Security," in *Global Dangers: Changing Dimensions of International Security*, ed. Sean M. Lynn-Jones and Steven E. Miller (Cambridge, Mass.: MIT Press, 1995), 84–117.

83. Pressures for migration also come from within states. Communal conflicts, violent secessionist movements, and the political and economic oppression with which they are associated create incentives for ethnic minorities to migrate to find economic security or to join their national homelands. Large-scale population movements may also be the result of deliberate government strategies, which see forced emigration as a strategy of achieving cultural homogeneity or the dominance of one ethnic community over another, eliminating political dissidents, colonizing areas beyond borders, scapegoating a prosperous but unpopular ethnic minority, destabilizing another state, or influencing its policies. Ethnic cleansing in the Balkans during the Yugoslav wars is but one example. Myron Weiner, "Security, Stability, and International Migration," *International Security* 17, no. 3 (Winter 1992–93): 91–126.

84. International migration does not always lead to social conflict. Under some conditions migrants are assimilated into the host country, particularly when they provide needed labor and skills and particularly when population movements take the form of gradual migrations (often in response to gradual changes in demography and economic incentives) rather than sudden displacements arising from ethnic conflicts or environmental disasters.

85. Weiner, "Security, Stability, and International Migration"; Ronald R. Krebs and Jack S. Levy, "Demographic Change and the Sources of International Conflict," in *Demography and National Security*, ed. Myron Weiner and Sharon Stanton Russell (Providence, R.I.: Berghahn Books, 2001).

86. William H. Durham, *Scarcity and Survival in Central America: Ecological Origins of the Soccer War* (Stanford, Calif.: Stanford University Press, 1979).

3

NEW
GLOBAL DANGERS

Michael E. Brown

WHEN THE COLD WAR ENDED, hopes and expectations for a more peaceful world soared. Indeed, the end of the Cold War had tremendously important, positive effects on international security. With the collapse of the Soviet empire in Eastern Europe in 1989 and the disintegration of the Soviet Union in 1991, the Soviet military threat that had loomed over Western Europe for decades vanished. Many of the regional conflicts that had been fueled by superpower patronage began to move toward settlements. Most important, the threat of an all-out nuclear war between the United States and the Soviet Union faded.

At the same time, hopes for a new and predominantly peaceful world—widespread at the beginning of the 1990s—were dashed by the deadly conflicts that followed. International responses to war and slaughter in Bosnia, Somalia, and other lethal trouble spots were appallingly inadequate. Nowhere was this more tragic than in Rwanda, where an estimated eight hundred thousand people were killed in a genocidal slaughter that went on for one hundred days in the spring and summer of 1994. The world watched on CNN.

In the first twelve years of the post–Cold War era (from 1990 to 2001), fifty-seven major armed conflicts took place in forty-five countries. In the first half of this period, the number of conflicts ranged from twenty-eight to thirty-three per year. Although the incidence of conflict dropped as the post–Cold War era stabilized, the number of conflicts has held steady since the late 1990s at around twenty-five conflicts per year.[1] Almost all of the deadly conflicts of the post–Cold War era have been either intrastate conflicts or intrastate conflicts with regional complications. Only four —the Iraqi invasion of Kuwait and the subsequent international intervention, the border war between Ethiopia and Eritrea, the ongoing conflict between India and Pakistan, and the U.S.-led invasion of Iraq in 2003—could be called conventional interstate conflicts.

The prevalence of intrastate conflicts in the post–Cold War era is significant. These conflicts frequently escalate into military campaigns designed to drive out or kill civilians from rival groups. Civilians are consequently subjected to direct, deliberate, systematic attacks. Intimidation, expulsion, rape, assassination, and slaughter are commonly employed instruments. Intrastate conflicts often generate staggering numbers of refugees and internally displaced persons. It is estimated that six million people were killed in armed conflicts in the 1990s alone.[2]

Three things are clear about the prospects for international security in the twenty-first century. First, security problems will continue to be widespread. It would be naive and irresponsible to assume that current problems will simply go away or that new problems will be neutralized by the positive benefits of globalization. Second, the security agenda will be far more complex than it has been in the past. It will include continuing security problems, such as interstate confrontations and intrastate conflicts. It will also include problems that are changing due to the end of the Cold War and the advent of globalization. These problems include the changing dynamics of weapons proliferation and the growing capabilities of transnational actors who operate outside the parameters of the state system. The security agenda of the twenty-first century will also include genuinely new security challenges, such as those posed by advances in information and genetic engineering technologies. All of this will take place in the context of an intense globalization process that no one controls.

Finally, those who have policy responsibilities in the security arena will have to think ahead and work effectively with other international actors. Those who simply react to events will be overtaken by events, and those who try to tackle global problems on their own will simply be overwhelmed. In the complex, increasingly interconnected world of the twenty-first century, multilateralism will not be an option—it will be a necessity.[3]

CONTINUITY AND CHANGE IN SECURITY AFFAIRS

Experts in the field of international relations disagree about the impact of the end of the Cold War and the advent of globalization on international security affairs. Some contend that the fundamental features of the international security landscape have not changed at all, while others insist that everything has changed.

At one end of the spectrum, realists argue that the main features of the international system have not changed, even though the Cold War has ended and globalization has become a growing force in international relations. The international system, they contend, is still anarchic in that states and other actors still have to provide for their own security; there is no international authority capable of providing security for one and all. States, they maintain, are still the dominant actors in the international system, and states are still determined to preserve their survival. The result, they say, is that security competitions and confrontations will still be common features of international relations in the twenty-first century.

For example, Kenneth Waltz argues that the world "has not been transformed" by the end of the Cold War. Rather, "the structure of the system has simply been remade by the disappearance of the Soviet Union." A true transformation in international relations, he says, "awaits the day when the international system is no longer populated by states that have to help themselves." In the meantime, he maintains, "the essential continuity of international politics" is intact.[4] Similarly, John Mearsheimer argues that "international anarchy—the driving force behind great-power behavior—did not change with the end of the Cold War, and there are few signs that such change is likely any time soon. States remain the principal actors in world politics."[5] The future will therefore look much like the past: "The state system is alive and well, and although regrettable, military competition between sovereign states will remain the distinguishing feature of international politics for the foreseeable future."[6]

At the other end of the spectrum, some analysts argue that the nature of the international system is indeed changing. They contend that powerful, technology-driven developments— the advent of the information revolution, the proliferation of global telecommunications systems, and growing economic interdependence —are changing the nature and distribution of power in the international system. States, they say, have lost their information monopolies and control over their economies. They contend that states are therefore becoming less important, while nonstate actors are gaining ground. They predict that increasingly empowered individuals, nongovernmental organizations (NGOs), and multinational corporations will form a new international civil society that will soon supersede the state system.

For example, Jessica Mathews argues, "The end of the Cold War has brought no mere adjustment among states but a novel redistribution of power among states, markets, and civil society. National governments are not simply losing autonomy in a globalizing economy. They are sharing powers—including political, social, and security roles at the core of sovereignty"—with nonstate actors. A power shift—from states to nonstate actors—is taking place: "Increasingly, NGOs are able to push around even the largest governments." In the future, she says, "the relative power of states will continue to decline." The main features of the state-centric system that has dominated the world for centuries "are all dissolving." She concludes, "If current trends continue, the international system 50 years hence will be profoundly different."[7]

Thomas Friedman has a similar but more nuanced view of globalization. He argues that "if you want to understand the post–Cold War world you have to start by understanding that a new international system has succeeded it—globalization." He maintains that globalization is "not just some passing trend. Today it is the overarching international system shaping the domestic politics and foreign relations of virtually every country." Friedman argues that globalization is creating a complex balance of power among states, between states and markets, and between states and individuals, but he does not foresee the demise of states. Friedman concludes that states in general and the United States in particular "are still hugely important today"—but so are markets, individuals, and other nonstate actors.[8]

Instead of adopting a narrow, dogmatic position, it might be more useful to acknowledge that there is both continuity and change in international security affairs in the twenty-first century. The fundamentals of the international system have not yet changed: states are still the dominant actors in international relations, states still seek security, and interstate security competitions and confrontations will continue to be important features of the security landscape. At the same time, globalization is increasingly impinging on state power, nonstate actors are becoming increasingly influential, and the security agenda contains an increasingly complex set of issues. Many of the issues that are on the security agenda today do not fall under the rubric of interstate problems. Some of these problems are entirely new and potentially momentous.

If there is both continuity and change in international security, it is not enough to say that the truth is somewhere in the middle and leave it at that. The challenge for scholars and policymakers is to identify the elements of continuity and change, and to differentiate as sharply as we can between and among different kinds of security problems.

Something Old

Continuing problems include the hardy perennials of international security: competitions and conflicts between states. The names of the players and the arenas of competition of course change over time, but the interstate character of this important set of problems remains the same. These problems have been central features of international relations for centuries, and they will continue to be important in the twenty-first century.

Specific problems include the possibility of armed clashes between states, the proliferation of weapons of mass destruction to dangerous states and unstable regions, and the rise and fall of great powers. Current concerns include the possibility of recurring war between India and Pakistan and armed conflict on the Korean peninsula. The acquisition of nuclear, biological, or chemical weapons by states such as Iran and North Korea is a major worry. The open acquisition of nuclear weapons by India and Pakistan in 1998 has complicated the stability equation in South Asia; the potential consequences of war between these two regional powers are now many times more devastating than they were in the past.

Although the United States currently stands alone as the world's most powerful country, great-power competition will also be an important feature of international relations in the twenty-first century. A key issue will be the evolution of relations between the United States and China as the latter's economic power grows. The continuing rise of China will have profound regional implications as well, as China's neighbors adjust and respond to changing balances of economic, political, and military power.[9] India's emergence as an economic power is another important component of this dynamic equation.[10] In short, interstate problems will continue to be critical security problems in the twenty-first century.

Something New

A second category of contemporary security problems can best be described as *changing problems*. These problems have long-standing roots in national and international security

affairs, but they have changed qualitatively due to the end of the Cold War and the advent of globalization. This large set of problems includes a wide range of interstate problems, intrastate problems, and transnational problems.

Changing interstate security problems include the evolving nature of the nuclear balance between the United States and Russia; the former has reenergized its effort to deploy national missile defenses, and the latter has experienced nuclear command-and-control problems due to the deterioration of the Russian nuclear establishment. More generally, Russia is in the midst of a profound political and economic transformation that has weakened the ability of its military establishment to maintain custody over its nuclear, biological, and chemical weapons stockpiles. It is now a potential source of nuclear, biological, and chemical capabilities for would-be proliferators—including state and nonstate actors.

The international trade in conventional weapons and technologies has also been transformed by the end of the Cold War. The driving forces behind conventional arms transfers are no longer strategic but economic. This makes conventional proliferation substantially harder to control. Although it is not yet clear if technological advances in sensors, information processing, precision guidance, and other advanced conventional weapons systems will constitute a true revolution in military affairs, it is clear that the United States has developed conventional power-projection capabilities that are vastly superior to those of any other country —including its allies. This is affecting the prospects for great-power military intervention as well as alliance relations between the United States and its partners.

Finally, important changes are taking place in nonmilitary arenas, with defense industries becoming more integrated, the global energy market becoming more interconnected, and advances in information technology all having implications for interstate relations in the twenty-first century. New links and new vulnerabilities are being created at the same time.

Intrastate security problems are not new, but they are changing. It is often said that security problems in the developing world were neglected during the Cold War, but the historical record suggests otherwise. The United States and the Soviet Union were deeply concerned about and involved in security problems in what was then called the Third World, but their actions were often destabilizing. The superpowers viewed the Third World through Cold War lenses and sought political advantages wherever they could. Their support for different actors intensified, militarized, and prolonged many armed conflicts in the developing world. Now that the Cold War has ended, the dynamics of conflict in the developing world have changed dramatically. Conflicts that were driven to a large degree by superpower patronage—in Cambodia, El Salvador, Mozambique, Namibia, and Nicaragua, for example—have moved toward settlement. Other conflicts continue to be driven by a wide range of issues, including environmental and demographic pressures, resource competitions, fierce competitions for power, and crises over the political stability and legitimacy of states. Weak, failing, and failed states are increasingly serious concerns. Intrastate violence is facilitated by the changing nature of the conventional arms market: state and corporate suppliers are eager to sell weapons, and the black market in light weapons and small arms has grown substantially.[11] The result is high levels of violent conflict.

A final subset of changing security problems is transnational in character. This includes relatively localized, regional problems as well as transnational problems that transcend any one area. Some of the latter are global in nature.

Many intrastate conflicts have regional dimensions. When intrastate conflicts become violent, refugees often flee across international borders in large numbers. Refugees are not just humanitarian problems; they are also security problems. Fighters often mingle with refugee populations, using refugee camps to rest, recuperate, reorganize, rearm, and relaunch their military campaigns. Large refugee populations can strain economic resources, aggravate ethnic tensions, and generate political instability in host countries. Global refugee populations surged from an average of 11.6 million in the 1980s to an average of 14.7 million in the 1990s; they declined to just over 12 million in the early 2000s.[12]

Intrastate conflicts can also affect neighboring states at a military level. The territory of neighboring states can be used to ship arms and supplies to insurgent groups, which can lead to interdiction campaigns. Outlying regions of neighboring states can also be used as bases from which attacks can be launched. This can lead to hot-pursuit operations across borders and reprisals. Although they may pretend otherwise, neighboring states are not always the innocent victims of turmoil in their regions. On the contrary, they often meddle in these conflicts for self-serving reasons. In short, many intrastate conflicts have regional dimensions that do not fit neatly into either the "interstate" or "intrastate" category. These are complex, hybrid, regional conflicts that can best be thought of as transnational in character.

The expanding capabilities of transnational media organizations, transnational criminal organizations, and transnational terrorist organizations are also growing security concerns. Although media organizations have long played important roles in national and international affairs, the advent of around-the-clock television news in the early 1980s was a watershed development.[13] The impact of the "CNN effect" on policymaking is often overstated, but the growing influence of these organizations is nonetheless real. Transnational criminal organizations pose increasingly grave threats to stability in a growing number of countries. It is estimated that 120 of the more than 190 states in the international system are now challenged by medium-to-strong criminal networks.[14] These networks undermine the rule of law, human rights, economic development, and governance. They are not just crime problems; they are security problems. Many of these networks operate throughout regions; some have global operations.

The threats posed by transnational terrorist organizations—al Qaeda, in particular—have become horrifyingly clear, but the worst may be yet to come. Although al Qaeda's base of operations in Afghanistan has been decimated, al Qaeda's capacities for action have not been eliminated. One possibility might be a physical attack on a target in the West combined with a cyber attack that would disrupt response capacities.[15] Another might be an attack involving nuclear, biological, chemical, or radiological weapons. This is another long-standing security problem that is changing in potentially devastating ways.

Something Out of the Blue

A third and final category of security problems consists of developments that are genuinely new. Since their trajectories and implications are not yet perfectly clear, it might be useful to call these issues *emerging problems*. The driving force in this area is technology: information technology is already changing the world in a multitude of ways, and the implications of genetic engineering are just starting to be appreciated. Some of these developments will have incremental effects on national and international security, while others could bring about truly revolutionary transformations.

The number and the severity of cyber attacks have increased dramatically in recent years, and this trend is likely to continue. Information technology is becoming faster, more powerful, more mobile, and more ubiquitous around the world. According to Dorothy Denning, "There are more perpetrators, more targets, and more opportunities to exploit, disrupt, and sabotage systems."[16] In addition, computer networks are becoming increasingly

integrated with critical infrastructures such as telecommunications, transportation, banking, electrical grids, oil and gas distribution systems, water supply systems, government services, and emergency services. Cyber attacks on these infrastructures have already become common, and deadly attacks on increasingly vulnerable systems could be launched in the future. Terrorists could combine a physical attack with a cyber attack on government response and emergency services systems, for example. "The bottom line," Denning says, "is that we will never have secure systems." In the future, "we can expect to see more attacks, and more mass attacks."[17]

Genetic engineering might have truly cataclysmic security implications. In the near term, genetic engineering could be used to fashion extremely potent biological weapons, or weapons targeted at specific groups of people. Alternatively, genetic engineering might enable people to live decades longer; this, in turn, would have momentous demographic effects. In the long term, according to Loren Thompson, genetic engineering "may change the course of evolution, in the process redefining human nature."[18] For better or worse, many of these technological advances will be socially irresistible and nearly impossible to control for technical reasons. Even if they could be regulated, economic interests would oppose the creation of control mechanisms. Thompson concludes, "Major consequences for world order would appear to be inevitable."[19]

THE NEW SECURITY LANDSCAPE

The debate over the nature of the contemporary security agenda is a debate over parameters and priorities: What exactly is a "security issue"? What are the most important security problems?[20]

Realists tend to answer these questions in narrow terms. Security problems are issues involving states, and they involve the threat, use, or potential use of military force. For realists, the most important issues on the security agenda today are the same issues that have been on the agenda for centuries: the search by states for security; competitions among states for security; and the interstate competitions, confrontations, arms races, and wars that result from these quests.[21] Sophisticated realists understand that there are other conflict problems in the world—at the intrastate level, for example—but they believe that the security landscape is dominated by interstate problems that have prominent military dimensions.

Others have a more expansionist conception of the security agenda.[22] Many argue that intrastate and transnational security problems should be added to the agenda. For example, Michael Klare argues, "Many of the most severe and persistent threats to global peace and security are arising not from conflicts between major political entities but from increased disorder within states, societies, and civilizations along ethnic, racial, religious, linguistic, caste, or class lines."[23] Edward Kolodziej similarly contends that it is misguided to confine the security agenda to "state-centric analysis."[24] Many scholars and analysts have suggested that the security agenda needs to be expanded to consider a wider range of nonmilitary influences on conflict problems. Richard Ullman warns that "defining national security merely (or even primarily) in military terms conveys a profoundly false image of reality." This is dangerous, he says, because "it causes states to concentrate on military threats and to ignore other and perhaps more harmful dangers."[25] Jessica Mathews maintains that global developments call for a broader conception of national security that includes resource, environmental, and demographic issues.[26] Advocates of human security argue that the focus of concern should be redirected from states to groups and individuals, and that a very wide range of issues should be added to the security agenda: economic security, food security, health security, environmental security, and political security.[27] Michael Klare goes so far as to argue

that, given the prevalence of intrastate, nonmilitary security problems, "it is questionable whether there is a role for military power at all."[28]

I believe that each school of thought is half-correct. Realists are correct to point to the fundamentally anarchic nature of the international system and the continued importance of states and interstate problems within it, but they focus too narrowly on traditional, interstate, military security issues. Realism's critics are correct when they argue that intrastate, transnational, and nonmilitary factors must be placed on the security agenda, but they broaden the concept of security to the point where it has no meaning.

Advocates of human security define security as "safety from such chronic threats as hunger, disease, and repression." For them, security "means protections from sudden and hurtful disruptions in patterns of daily life—whether in homes, in jobs, or in communities."[29] If one employs this broad definition, then "security problems" and "public policy problems" become indistinguishable. Barry Buzan, Ole Wæver, and Jaap de Wilde argue that a public policy issue becomes "securitized" when it requires "emergency measures" and "actions outside the normal bounds of political procedure."[30] If one follows this line of thinking, then "security problems" and "public policy emergencies" become indistinguishable. This is unsatisfactory. As Lawrence Freedman convincingly argues, "Once anything that generates anxieties or threatens the quality of life in some respect becomes labeled a 'security problem,' the field risks losing all focus."[31]

The challenge, therefore, is to broaden the agenda to include the full range of factors and actors that can affect the prospects for security while defining meaningful parameters for this set of problems—and, correspondingly, the field of security studies.

I believe that the central issue on the security agenda—and the heart of the field of security studies—is the problem of violent conflict.

Table 1. The New Security Landscape: A Framework with Some Illustrations

	Interstate Problems	**Intrastate Problems**	**Transnational Problems**
Military Challenges	Interstate wars	Military coups	Cross-border insurgencies
	Great-power competitions	Ethnic conflicts	Transnational terrorism
	Weapons proliferation to unstable states or regions	Civil wars	Weapons proliferation via or to nonstate actors
Nonmilitary Challenges	Trade disputes	Population growth	Transnational media
	Resource conflicts	Economic migrations	Transnational crime
	Energy competitions	Resource competitions	Technology proliferation

We should therefore endeavor to understand the full range of military and nonmilitary factors that can contribute to the *causes* of violent conflicts, including the most organized, most intense forms of violence—war and genocide. Nonmilitary factors that can contribute to the outbreak of violent conflicts include historical, political, economic, social, cultural, religious, demographic, environmental, and technological issues and developments. The security agenda should also include all of the issues associated with the *conduct* of violent conflicts, including the dynamics of escalation and de-escalation, as well as the threat and use of military force and other deadly policy instruments. Another set of critical issues involves the challenges of conflict *control,* including efforts aimed at conflict prevention, conflict management, and conflict resolution.

The scope of this agenda is broad; some structure is therefore needed. I argue that it is useful to distinguish the military and nonmilitary challenges that create security problems, on the one hand, and interstate, intrastate, and transnational arenas, on the other. These distinctions can be depicted in the form of a matrix (see table 1).[32]

Interstate security problems include traditional arms races and armed conflicts, as well as weapons proliferation to aggressive regimes or unstable regions. As discussed, these problems will continue to be on the security agenda in the future. Many interstate problems will be driven by nonmilitary disputes; those that have the potential to become violent conflicts qualify as security problems. Some of the possibilities include resource competitions over water, oil, and gas; interstate disputes over cross-border economic migration or refugee populations; and changes in defense industries that have the potential to affect national military capabilities.

Intrastate security problems are often driven by underlying nonmilitary developments that generate social, economic, and political instability, thereby making violent conflict more likely. Particularly important in this regard are demographic developments (population growth and population movements) and environmental developments (resource degradation and depletion) that can combine to produce intrastate resource competitions. The resolution of these competitions frequently depends on the political and administrative capacities of the states in question. Unfortunately, resource competitions in the developing world are common in places where institutional capacities are weak. Violence is often the result.

Many intrastate conflicts are simply the products of elite competitions for power—

between civilian factions, between factions of the military leadership, or between civilian and military leaders. Many of these disputes have ethnic dimensions, but it would be a mistake to categorize all of these problems as "ethnic conflicts." Leaders who are motivated primarily by personal gain—political and economic —often claim to be the champions of their ethnic constituents and they often polarize ethnic relations over the course of their political campaigns, but it is important to distinguish between the parochial motivations that galvanize these conflicts and the ethnic consequences that follow. Many intrastate conflicts are driven primarily by parochial political and criminal agendas.

Finally, transnational security problems can also have either nonmilitary or military dimensions. Transnational media organizations are nonmilitary in character, but they can have effects on the course and conduct of military operations. Transnational criminal organizations are motivated primarily by profit and power, but their operations can undermine state authority and their black market operations often involve the sale and transfer of weapons. Proliferation issues can range from comparatively benign to truly terrifying. The proliferation of information technologies, for example, might not have immediate, direct effects on political conflicts, but they could have powerful, longer-term implications for stability and security. The proliferation of weapons—nuclear, biological, and chemical weapons, in particular— is of course a more immediate and deadly security threat.

Specific policy priorities will of course vary from country to country and region to region, and they will also evolve over time. At this juncture, some parts of the world—Latin America and Southeast Asia, for example —mainly have to contend with intrastate and transnational security problems. Others —Northeast Asia, for example—find interstate security issues higher on the agenda. Some regions have to contend with almost every kind of security problem imaginable; others, with relatively few. This simple framework is most certainly not the final word on a complex and changing set of issues. That said, it provides a starting point for distinguishing between the many security problems that are on the security agenda today.

POLICY LESSONS

In a dynamic and increasingly complex security setting, old policy formulas will quickly become outmoded. Unfortunately, the costs of policy failures will be high because security problems will continue to be deadly. It is imperative, therefore, that policymakers in both the developed and developing worlds prepare themselves for the policy challenges of the future.

Timing Lessons

A good place to start is with timing: When should policymakers begin to tackle security problems? And what planning horizons should they adopt?

First, it is naive and dangerous for policymakers to neglect current and emerging security problems, hoping that they will take care of themselves or go away on their own. Policy problems are rarely self-correcting. On the contrary, if left to themselves, policy problems usually get worse as time goes by. Wishful thinking is not a policy; it is the self-deluding refuge of the shortsighted and the fainthearted. Unfortunately, policy problems are often ignored until they become crises; then and only then do they find their way onto the agendas of busy policymakers. The result is that policy problems are neglected when they are relatively easy to solve, and they are addressed only after they become formidable. In effect, policymakers wait until problems become unsolvable before they try to solve them. This overstates the decision-making dynamic—but not by much. The policy lesson is to engage security problems as soon as possible, even if these problems have not yet become deadly conflicts. Security problems become much more formidable once the violence threshold is crossed.

Second, in a dynamic and increasingly fast-paced world, policymakers no longer have the luxury of waiting for events to unfold before devising policy actions. In the twenty-first century, policymakers must become accustomed to thinking five, ten, and twenty years into the future. This will be inherently difficult for most policymakers; their planning horizons are tied to the daily press of events, legislative calendars, and electoral cycles. Many policymakers do not expect to be in office ten or twenty years down the road; it is difficult for them to expend time, energy, and political capital in the short term when the policy benefits —if any—will be reaped by someone else in the long term. The costs of policy engagement are immediate and often quantifiable; the benefits of far-sighted actions are reaped only in a distant future, and they are often unquantifiable. These incentives and calculations are inherent in the policymaking process, and they will continue to discourage policymakers from strategic thinking. Wise policymakers will work to overcome these structural pressures. The policy lesson is that, in the twenty-first century, those who simply react to events will be overtaken by events.

Third, policymakers generally hope that security problems can be solved quickly and permanently; they hope for quick, permanent fixes to the issues before them. Unfortunately, most security problems are not amenable to quick fixes, and many cannot be solved at all; they can only be managed. Security threats and violent conflicts will be deadly facts of life throughout the twenty-first century. There is no light at the end of this tunnel. The policy lesson is that policymakers must prepare themselves psychologically and politically for the long haul. This means thinking about problems in long-term time frames, as discussed, and it means making long-term and even open-ended policy commitments.

It is generally difficult for policymakers to make long-term and open-ended programmatic commitments. In the United States, for example, presidents are challenged to outline their exit strategies whenever they deploy U.S. military forces abroad. Even so, post–Cold War history suggests that long-term, open-ended commitments can be made at least some of the time. NATO brought three new members into the alliance in 1999, and in 2002 it extended membership invitations to seven additional countries. These were open-ended security commitments to the alliance's new members; these commitments did not come with expiration dates attached. Making long-term and open-ended policy commitments is difficult—not impossible—and in the twenty-first century, it will often be necessary.

Conceptual Lessons

Policymakers also need to reconsider the ways security problems are conceived and how security policies should be framed.

First, many policymakers still define security problems in narrow terms, giving undue weight to interstate conflicts and the military dimensions of security problems. Policymakers should develop broader security agendas that give appropriate weight to the full range of interstate, intrastate, transnational, military, and nonmilitary challenges that are unfolding today. The policy lesson is to think inclusively about the security agenda.

Second, if security problems are complex, multidimensional, and interconnected, it follows that security policies should be multifaceted. Unfortunately, policymakers often favor simple, single-factor policy approaches; they hope that a single silver bullet will solve complex policy problems. This is another example of wishful thinking. The main policy lesson here is that complex, multidimensional security problems do indeed require multifaceted policy responses—often involving a combination of diplomatic, political, economic, and military elements. This is often challenging conceptually and politically, but it is nonetheless necessary.

Third, a related lesson is that many contemporary security problems are not amenable to simple military solutions. Indeed, military responses often turn out to be inappropriate, ineffective, and even counterproductive. The use of military force often appears to be a panacea, but this is all too often illusory. Problems that have nonmilitary roots will almost always require a range of nonmilitary policy responses, even if military actions are part of the equation as well.

International Lessons

Policymakers should keep in mind several general policy lessons about the international dimensions of contemporary security problems and the international dimensions of suitable policy responses.

First, many security problems in the twenty-first century will cross national borders and cut across regions. Some will be truly global in scope. It will be beyond the capability of any one actor—even a superpower such as the United States—to tackle these problems on its own. National leaders who try to tackle these problems unilaterally will fail; national interests will correspondingly suffer. Therefore, one of the most basic principles of security policy in the twenty-first century will be multilateralism: transnational security problems will require multilateral policy responses.

Second, multilateral initiatives will require leadership. Although the United States will not be able to lead on every issue at every juncture, it will continue to be the world's most powerful country for the foreseeable future. U.S. leadership—in identifying problems, devising strategies, forging coalitions, providing resources, and taking actions—will therefore be key. If U.S. political leaders play a more energetic and effective global leadership role, many national, regional, and international security challenges will become more manageable. If U.S. leaders are unwilling, disinclined,

or unable to play this role, a wide array of security problems will become increasingly formidable.

To be more effective, U.S. officials need to develop a better appreciation of what international leadership entails. Since the end of the Cold War and cutting across both Democratic and Republican administrations, the prevailing U.S. approach to international problems has been to set a U.S. course and assume that others will ultimately follow—willingly or grudgingly. Complaints about American presumptuousness and arrogance have consequently become increasingly common. U.S. officials would be wise to appreciate that true leadership is based on true consultation. It is not enough for Washington to inform others of what it intends to do. The United States needs to consult with allies, friends, and others about goals, strategies, and actions. And above all, Washington needs to make a genuine effort to take the views of others into account. The United States clearly has the capacity to undertake unilateral actions in the international arena, but it will be able to lead only if it listens.

This leads to a third set of lessons. Those who seek to forge or sustain multilateral initiatives should keep several operational guidelines in mind.[33] For starters, multilateralism cannot be turned on and off and on again. Building multilateral patterns of cooperation takes steady, sustained engagement. The United States, which often suffers from international attention deficit disorder, will have to pay continual attention to the maintenance of multiple international coalitions. A related guideline is that multilateralism is not an à la carte proposition. The United States cannot champion multilateralism when it is convenient for Washington to do so and slight it the rest of the time. The United States must be prepared to engage on issues across the board. In addition, multilateralism is a two-way street. The United States must be willing to give as much as it gets. Indeed, one would hope that the world's wealthiest and most powerful country would be inclined to give *more* than it gets.

Finally, for multilateralism to endure, it needs a strong institutional foundation—the United Nations. It is certainly true that the United Nations has many structural and political flaws and that it frequently exasperates even its staunchest supporters. It is also true that the United Nations has a unique and important role to play in promoting international peace and security. In the twenty-first century, international actors will have to take coordinated steps to address common threats, and the United Nations provides an indispensable mechanism for facilitating multilateral actions. The United States and the other leading powers in the international system should work to develop the United Nations into a more effective instrument for the promotion of international peace and security. Building a strong, effective, and respected United Nations is in the enlightened self-interest of the world's leading powers—the United States, in particular.

Most of these policy lessons are simple and commonsensical: act early, think ahead, plan for the long haul, avoid simple conceptual schemes and simple policy responses, recognize the limitations of military actions, and recognize the need for multilateral initiatives. They would be banal—but for the fact that policymakers around the world routinely fail to meet even these minimal standards. The first step, therefore, is to master these policy fundamentals.

NOTES

This chapter draws on the author's contributions to Michael E. Brown, ed., *Grave New World: Security Challenges in the Twenty-first Century* (Washington, D.C.: Georgetown University Press, 2003). press.georgetown.edu.

1. See Mikael Eriksson, Margareta Sollenberg, and Peter Wallensteen, "Patterns of Major Armed Conflicts, 1990–2001," in *SIPRI Yearbook 2002: Armaments, Disarmament, and International Security* (Oxford: Oxford University Press, 2002), 63–76. Two recent studies emphasize the positive trend—the decline in conflict since the tumult of the early 1990s. See Monty G. Marshall and Ted Robert Gurr, *Peace and Conflict 2005: A Global Survey of Armed Conflicts, Self-Determination Movements, and Democracy* (College Park: Center for International Development and Conflict Management, University of Maryland, May 2005); and Human Security Centre, *The Human Security Report 2005* (Vancouver: Human Security Centre, University of British Columbia, October 2005).

2. International Institute for Strategic Studies (IISS), Conflict Database Project, London, November 2002.

3. See Chantal de Jonge Oudraat and P. J. Simmons, "From Accord to Action," in *Managing Global Issues: Lessons Learned*, ed. Chantal de Jonge Oudraat and P. J. Simmons (Washington, D.C.: Carnegie Endowment for International Peace, 2001), 722–723.

4. Kenneth N. Waltz, "Structural Realism after the Cold War," *International Security* 25, no. 1 (Summer 2000): 5–41 at 39.

5. John J. Mearsheimer, *The Tragedy of Great Power Politics* (New York: W. W. Norton, 2001), 361.

6. John J. Mearsheimer, "Disorder Restored," in *Rethinking America's Security: Beyond Cold War to New World Order*, ed. Graham Allison and Gregory F. Treverton (New York: W. W. Norton, 1992), 213–237 at 214.

7. Jessica T. Mathews, "Power Shift," *Foreign Affairs* 76, no. 1 (January–February 1997): 50–66 at 50, 53, 65-66.

8. Thomas L. Friedman, *The Lexus and the Olive Tree* (New York: Farrar, Straus and Giroux, 1999), xviii, 7, 11–13.

9. For a provocative analysis of U.S.-China relations in the twenty-first century, see Mearsheimer, *The Tragedy of Great Power Politics*, chap. 10. For a range of views on this issue, see Michael E. Brown, Owen R. Coté, Jr., Sean M. Lynn-Jones, and Steven E. Miller, eds., *The Rise of China* (Cambridge, Mass.: MIT Press, 2000).

10. For a discussion of the rise of India and the international implications of these developments, see U.S. National Intelligence Council, *Mapping the*

Global Future (Washington, D.C.: U.S. National Intelligence Council, December 2004).

11. See Jo L. Husbands, "The Proliferation of Conventional Weapons and Technologies," in *Grave New World: Security Challenges in the Twenty-first Century,* ed. Michael E. Brown (Washington, D.C.: Georgetown University Press, 2003), 62–90.

12. See United Nations High Commissioner for Refugees (UNHCR), *Refugees by Numbers, 2002 Edition,* http://www.unhcr.ch.

13. See Diana Owen, "Transnational Mass Media Organizations and Security," in *Grave New World,* 233–258.

14. See Roy Godson, "Transnational Crime, Corruption, and Security," in ibid., 259–278.

15. See Dorothy E. Denning, "Information Technology and Security," in ibid., 91–112.

16. Ibid., 94.

17. Ibid., 102–103.

18. See Loren B. Thompson, "Emerging Technologies and Security," in ibid., 123.

19. Ibid.

20. For excellent overviews of the evolution of the security agenda and the security studies field, see Joseph S. Nye, Jr., and Sean M. Lynn-Jones, "International Security Studies: A Report of a Conference on the State of the Field," *International Security* 12, no. 4 (Spring 1988): 5–27; and Steven E. Miller, "International Security at Twenty-five: From One World to Another," *International Security* 26, no. 1 (Summer 2001): 5–39.

21. See Waltz, "Structural Realism after the Cold War"; Mearsheimer, *The Tragedy of Great Power Politics;* and Mearsheimer, "Disorder Restored." See also Stephen P. Walt, "The Renaissance of Security Studies," *International Studies Quarterly* 35, no. 2 (June 1991): 211–239.

22. For an excellent overview of these broader issues, see Richard H. Schultz, Jr., Roy Godson, and George H. Quester, eds., *Security Studies for the Twenty-first Century* (Washington, D.C.: Brassey's, 1997).

23. Michael T. Klare, "Redefining Security: The New Global Schisms," in *Globalization and the Challenges of a New Century,* ed. Patrick O'Meara, Howard D. Mehlinger, and Matthew Krain (Bloomington: Indiana University Press, 2000), 131–139 at 133.

24. See Edward A. Kolodziej, "Renaissance in Security Studies? Caveat Lector!" *International Studies Quarterly* 36, no. 4 (December 1992): 421–438 at 422.

25. See Richard H. Ullman, "Redefining Security," *International Security* 8, no. 1 (Summer 1983): 129–153 at 129.

26. See Jessica T. Mathews, "Redefining Security," *Foreign Affairs* 68, no. 2 (Spring 1989): 162–177.

27. For an overview of the human security agenda, see United Nations Development Programme, "New Dimensions of Human Security," in *Human Development Report, 1994* (New York: United Nations, 1994), 22–40. For a thoughtful and balanced assessment of the human security school, see Roland Paris, "Human Security: Paradigm Shift or Hot Air?" *International Security* 26, no. 2 (Fall 2001): 87–102.

28. Klare, "Redefining Security," 139.

29. UN Development Programme, "New Dimensions of Human Security," 23.

30. Barry Buzan, Ole Wæver, and Jaap de Wilde, *Security: A New Framework for Analysis* (Boulder, Colo.: Lynne Rienner, 1998), 23–24.

31. Lawrence Freedman, "International Security: Changing Targets?" *Foreign Policy,* no. 110 (Spring 1998): 48–63 at 53.

32. Many scholars have called for adding nonmilitary factors to the security agenda. See Ullman, "Redefining Security"; Mathews, "Redefining Security." Others have called for adding intrastate and transnational problems to the equation. See Kolodziej, "Renaissance in Security Studies? Caveat Lector!" and Klare, "Redefining Security." An excellent overview of both sets of issues can be found in Schultz, Godson, and Quester, *Security Studies for the Twenty-first Century.* A similar but less elaborate matrix is developed in Paris, "Human Security."

33. These guidelines for multilateralism come from Chantal de Jonge Oudraat.

4

ARMS ACQUISITION AND VIOLENCE
ARE WEAPONS OR PEOPLE THE CAUSE OF CONFLICT?

Geoffrey Kemp

ON SEPTEMBER 11, 2001, NINETEEN young men of Middle Eastern origin hijacked four U.S. airliners and turned two of them into weapons of mass destruction by flying the planes into the twin towers of the World Trade Center in New York City, killing more than twenty-seven hundred people. These terrorist attacks have changed U.S. perceptions of the relationship between military technology and conflict in profound and far-reaching ways. Yet, though we remain mesmerized by the events of that day and fear that another, more spectacular, attack is possible, the next time with even deadlier weapons, it is important not to lose sight of the historic relationship between arms acquisition and warfare and to understand that while terrorism may be the primary concern of U.S. policymakers in the first decade of the twenty-first century, for much of the world, the more traditional linkages between military technology and conflict still have an important resonance and require clear understanding. For this reason the first sections of this essay cover the historical dis-

course on weapons and conflict, concluding with a review of the balance-of-terror doctrines that influenced strategy during the Cold War. The latter part of the essay examines the post–Cold War developments, including the lessons of recent wars, the impact of new technologies on warfare, and the current focus of terrorism and how to contain and defeat it.

BACKGROUND

In the early scenes from Stanley Kubrick's classic 1968 movie, *2001: A Space Odyssey*, the leader of a group of man-apes discovers how to use a dead antelope's bone as a device for killing animals. The group is now able to supplement its primarily vegetarian diet with meat. Soon the group learns that the bone can also kill other man-apes and so the ascendancy of the group possessing the new weapon becomes assured. Primitive weapons, whether bones, rocks, or wooden spears, were infinitely more efficient at killing prey than bare hands. From the earliest times, the human species has found

53

ingenious ways to use new implements to commit acts of violence against each other. While access to weapons does not necessarily make the human species more aggressive, it improves the ability to kill on a large scale.

Thus the relationship between military technology and conflict is definitely a chicken-and-egg affair. The existence of military technology in a conflict region reflects the need for countries to defend themselves against adversaries or to redress grievances, yet arms competition between adversaries can itself become a source of conflict or even a precursor for wars. As a result, there are many different hypotheses concerning this relationship. While many believe that arms races result in wars, it is not easy to demonstrate a simple cause and effect. The real issues are the impact of weapons acquisitions on the stability of military balances and the relationship between these balances and other factors that contribute to conflict.[1]

Likewise, it is difficult to identify specific weapons that contribute to an increase or decrease in the potential for armed conflict. Weapons, including weapons of mass destruction, do not cause wars or assure peace by themselves —any more than handguns alone are responsible for murders or reduced crime in U.S. cities. The critical factor is the politico-military environment into which the weapons are introduced. If the environment is inherently unstable and adversaries have a record of resolving disputes by force, new weaponry may heighten the perceptions of threat, providing a catalyst for war. However, if the environment is stable and the prevailing climate is one of reconciliation and peaceful dialogue or, alternatively, if both adversaries anticipate unacceptable casualties in a war, the impact of new weapons may be less dangerous and could even contribute to stability. Thus, weapons that may be considered destabilizing in one region may be considered stabilizing in another.

This essay argues that there is no general theory of the relationship between arms and conflict, that cases can be found to fit many hypotheses, and that recent dramatic changes in technology have made it increasingly difficult to predict the effects of those changes.[2] Before this essay confronts some of the future issues, some further background is useful.

Throughout history, the possession and production of arms have largely been a monopoly of the dominant political authority in a particular country or region. Until recently, most such authorities were oligopolies, if not outright dictatorships; the right of ordinary citizens to manufacture and own arms is not a universal right.[3] Thus, one of the enduring beliefs of the National Rifle Association is that the constitutional right of U.S. citizens to bear arms is unique and special and is the most reliable way to ensure that the citizenry is not left defenseless against authorities, who traditionally have a monopoly of organized military force at their disposal. While this prerogative is uniquely American and highly controversial, the sentiments it reflects are shared by many of the subject peoples of the world, ancient and modern, who have been systematically denied access to arms and are inherently suspicious of arms control. For instance, during the nineteenth century an international initiative was launched by the European powers to ban the transfer of breech-loading rifles to sub-Saharan Africa on the grounds that such arms in the hands of natives would be a source of instability. If the colonial powers had far superior arms to rule over their subjects, small forces of militia could control vast areas of territory. This line of reasoning was summarized by the British satirist Hilaire Belloc, "Whatever happens / We have got / The Maxim gun / And they have not."

As long as military technology is a monopoly of the state or the colonial power, civil unrest and uprisings are controllable. However, once those who wish to change the status quo gain access to modern military technology—by covert purchase, mutiny, or rebellion—a more even distribution of power results, which often leads to civil war and revolution. Therefore, in considering the long-term perspectives on arms and conflict, it is worth remembering the origins of the American Revolution and the important role that arms, both locally produced and procured from overseas (especially France), played in the course of the Revolution. Without this access to arms, American revolutionaries could not have fought against Britain. As it was, they were able to sustain their confrontation and eventually wear down an initially far superior power.

Since the early 1950s, when thermonuclear weapons entered the inventories of the superpowers, a different set of issues has emerged in the context of arms and international relations. Five are especially important: (1) the relationship between developments in weapons of mass destruction (WMD), including chemical and biological but most especially nuclear technology, and the potential for conflict among the superpowers; (2) the relationship between the transfer of military technology from the great powers, who have traditionally been the major producers of arms, and the propensity of the recipients to engage in armed conflict; (3) the impact on regional security of recent changes in the international system and new developments in military technology; (4) the probability that terrorist organizations—with or without a state sponsor—will get access to weapons of mass destruction, especially nuclear weapons; and (5) the dramatic improvement in modern communication, which means that information on weapons can be more easily shared.

THE COLD WAR, THE CENTRAL ARMS RACE, AND THE BREAKUP OF THE SOVIET UNION

From the late 1940s to the late 1980s, the debate about the impact of military technology on the international system focused on two events: the central arms race between NATO and the Warsaw Pact countries and the proliferation of weapons technology to those conflict regions in the rest of the world that were part of the global Cold War. Throughout this period, ongoing controversy concerned the stability of the central arms race.

There were two very limiting arguments. Pessimists argued that constant changes in nuclear weapons technology and the momentum of the arms race made the balance of power delicate and therefore inherently unstable and dangerous. This group included many of the advocates of unilateral arms control and arms reductions. The Campaign for Nuclear Disarmament (CND), launched in the 1950s, and the nuclear freeze movement that gained momentum in the 1980s are two prominent examples of this line of thinking. Optimists held that the peace in Europe and between the superpowers was secure precisely because the horrors of war were too dreadful to contemplate. This was the view of most Western governments, which subscribed to the principles of deterrence and supported investments in nuclear force modernization as the best way to ensure stability and a balance of power between NATO and the Warsaw Pact forces. Both schools concurred that one effect of the central balance of power, be it delicate or stable, was to export the Cold War to regional conflict areas, which, in turn, led to an accelerated regional arms buildup. However, there was much disagreement about whether regional arms races themselves made local conflict more or less likely.

There is some empirical evidence to suggest that arms transfers during the Cold War exacerbated regional conflicts and in the case of the Middle East contributed to the outbreak of hostilities. Certainly Israel's decision to join Britain and France in attacking Egypt in 1956 was due, in part, to fear that Soviet arms supplies to Egypt, which began in earnest in 1955, would soon put Israel at a major disadvantage in terms of the regional military balance. This was a clear-cut case of preventive war motivated by anticipated asymmetries in weapons capabilities. Notable examples of regional conflicts exacerbated by competitive arms supplies include the Indian-Pakistani war of 1965, the Vietnam War, and many conflicts in Africa, including those in Angola and Ethiopia and Nigeria's civil war.

In terms of whether the huge infusion of NATO and Warsaw Pact weapons into the Third World was stabilizing or destabilizing, what can be said is that while the transfers of weapons technologies may not have triggered specific conflicts, they exacerbated the political antagonism between rivals and raised the stakes for East-West confrontation.

Parallel to the arguments concerning the balance of power, a secondary set of issues concerned the economics of the various arms races. Again, pessimists argued that both the central and regional arms races were spurred by the desire of the military-industrial complex in the advanced countries to promote arms sales. Others made a very different case, namely, that the spread of WMD to regional conflicts was stimulated by the reluctance of the industrial powers to provide adequate conventional arms. Examples of this reaction are the decisions made at different times by Israel, South Africa, and Pakistan to develop nuclear weapons after being subjected to arms embargoes by the key industrial states. It is clear that both the Republic of Korea and Taiwan came close to going nuclear for the same reasons and were persuaded from doing so only by extremely vigorous U.S. diplomatic intervention and increased support for their conventional armed forces.

Most modern theories of the arms race evolved during the Cold War. The primary focus was the impact of thermonuclear weapons on the balance of power and the propensity for conflict. In view of the enormous, quantifiable destruction potential of nuclear weapons, the relatively small number of them in inventories (compared with conventional weapons), and the assumption that an all-out thermonuclear war would be of short duration, it was possible to articulate mathematical models of nuclear war. These models led most observers to believe that as long as there was proximate symmetry between the parties, a balance of terror would deter any side from risking war.

Although it remains unclear whether nuclear deterrence during this era was inherently stable or unstable, there is no doubt that since the 1970s the Warsaw Pact and NATO countries have enjoyed a nominally stable but putatively dangerous relationship. This stability resulted from several conditions:

- The awesome destructive capacity of thermonuclear weapons
- The total integration of nuclear weapons into the force structures and military doctrines of the opposing alliances
- Clearly demarcated and accepted borders separating the forces
- Explicit policies regarding the use of force should either side invade the other
- Virtual consensus that there could be no victor in the event of full-scale war
- An understanding that escalation to nuclear war would be highly likely if conventional war broke out
- Clear lines of communication between adversaries
- Clear acceptance of Soviet and U.S. dominance among the Warsaw Pact and NATO members
- The ability of the adversaries to contain their competition in regional conflicts outside the central theater and to resist military intervention in the conflicts within the alliances
- Stable regimes in both of the opposing camps

The relationship between military technology and the most spectacular event of modern times—the breakup of the Soviet Union—is less clear. Between 1989 and 1991, the largest and possibly the most authoritarian and tightly controlled empire the world has ever seen collapsed. Comparable in scope to the dissolution of the Austro-Hungarian and Ottoman empires at the end of World War I and the defeat of the Axis powers in 1945, that collapse will have a profound impact on the international system for decades to come. However, unlike the situations in 1919 and 1945, when the victorious military powers were able to impose some sort of order on the reemerging political boundaries, the events following the Soviet Union's demise have been anarchic.

The Soviet Union imploded. It was not defeated in a classic military encounter whereby the victors could dictate terms to the vanquished. New countries sprang up so fast that mapmakers could scarcely keep pace with the new names and new boundaries that spread across the Eurasian landmass. The Iron Curtain was shattered, and in its place hundreds of new borders came into being.

Although the breakup did not happen because of war, there is debate about how much the burden of war preparations contributed to the outcome. Some have argued that the United States' decision in the 1980s to deploy the extremely sophisticated Pershing II missile to Europe and to develop a space-based antimissile defense system was the final straw that convinced Mikhail Gorbachev that the Soviet Union had no option but to abandon the arms race with the richer Western countries and to reform the Soviet economy. Once this decision was made, a floodgate of change opened, change that he was unable to control.

There was hope that a new world order reflecting the basic Western ideals that were upheld in the fight against communism would emerge. Peace, democracy, and economic development were to be the triumvirate of the future. The cornerstone of the new world order would be a more cooperative security environment, in which the traditional trappings of power politics—with major military alliances armed and prepared to fight each other—would be replaced by a mutually reinforcing defense concept, an expanded NATO without the Warsaw Pact as an enemy. Each participant would contribute to overall security and the body itself would agree on rules of engagement to resist movement of aggressor countries that deviated from the norm. A new emphasis

on the United Nations and other international organizations would be paralleled by a new focus on economic competition and cooperation as the key ingredients for global growth and political stability. The close relationship between military technology and security would be a thing of the past. But this hope was not to be fulfilled. The breakup of the Soviet Union has undermined one of the key elements of the Cold War balance of power—stable borders and stable regimes—and has encouraged the further proliferation of weapons and the spread of new forms of extremely violent terrorism made more dangerous by the increased use of suicide attacks. The implications of this trend are considered in the latter section of this essay.

THE TRANSFER OF MILITARY TECHNOLOGY AND CONFLICT

Since the late nineteenth century, the transfer (by sale, loan, or gift) of military technology from industrial to less industrial countries has been an important influence on international relations. Today, a revolution in military technology poses a new set of challenges and issues.

Over the decades, most industrial powers have regarded arms transfers as a necessary adjunct of national policy and strategic doctrine. In the case of the United States, it can certainly be argued that, on balance, arms sales and military assistance programs have benefited U.S. strategic interests. U.S. military supplies to allies were instrumental in winning the three critical wars of this century: World War I, World War II, and the Cold War. Other examples can be cited. U.S. arms have been essential to assuring Israel a qualitative edge and denying Arab coalitions any prospect of military victory. U.S. supplies to Saudi Arabia during the 1970s and 1980s permitted the United States and the Saudis to develop one of the most elaborate and modern logistical bases in the world, which was crucial to allied victory in Operation Desert Storm.

Critics of U.S. arms transfers argue that these policies have often led to disastrous, entangling confrontations, including the Vietnam War and the Iran-Contra scandal. Critics also argue that the U.S. supply of certain weapons, especially surface-to-air missiles (SAMs) such as Stingers to Afghan resistance fighters to defeat Soviet troops, is now a threat to the region, including U.S. forces. Thus we shouldn't provide arms to countries battling countries we deem bigger threats because those countries may eventually become threats as well. The fact that Osama bin Laden's first encounters with military operations were in Afghanistan fighting the Russians with weapons provided by the United States and its allies is a case in point. Critics further argue that peacetime arms sales to undemocratic countries strengthen corrupt dictators, promote aggressive behavior, and siphon off scarce economic resources that could be used more productively and humanely on other endeavors.

In the early 1970s, a new phenomenon occurred, namely, the emergence of very rich oil-producing countries of the Middle East that had purchasing power but few skills to produce arms. The rapid buildup of arms in the Middle East and Persian Gulf area strengthened the argument that regional arms races were dangerous and that the recipients would have difficulty in absorbing, maintaining, and operating their advanced equipment without continued intense support from their suppliers. The classic example of this relationship existed between the United States and Iran from 1971 to 1979 and culminated in the deposition of the shah and attempts by the Khomeini government to sell military equipment back to the United States.[4]

Arms transfers are important tests of friendship. Nuclear weapons and their related delivery systems are the most sophisticated weapons. The only recipients of U.S. strategic nuclear delivery systems or support systems and technical knowledge have been Great Britain and France, which have also been the closest U.S. allies. Britain, in particular, has had an extremely close nuclear relationship with the United States. Most recipients of U.S. arms have not been permitted the full array of frontline equipment and key subsystems, even when able to pay full market prices. It may therefore be possible to rank the intimacy of relations between states according to the quality of the arms and other military support that have been provided.

U.S. arms sales to close allies such as Britain are rarely criticized, because they are seen to be part of the NATO alliance and the need to integrate military doctrines and force capabilities to serve common goals. Equally relevant, arms transfers carry important messages in relations between major powers and minor powers. U.S.-Soviet rivalry in the Third World was built around competitive arms supply relationships with a long list of countries, large and small. Soviet arms supplies to Egypt in 1955 opened the way for more assertive Soviet diplomacy in the region. Seventeen years later, the United States used arms aid to bring Egypt back into the Western fold when President Anwar Sadat terminated his military relations with the Russians in 1972. In 1985–86, when Iraq and Iran were desperately fighting for survival in their brutal war, both relied on supplies from the outside to keep them going. The effectiveness of the U.S. arms embargo against Iran was a key reason Ayatollah Khomeini gave instructions to obtain U.S. arms, even if it meant doing business with the United States and the hated Israelis. The White House thought it could use the supply of arms to cajole or tempt Iran into a better relationship and at the same time obtain the release of hostages; the Israelis thought that by supplying arms they could protract the war or, alternatively, ingratiate themselves with those members of the regime who might be favorably disposed to have a relationship with Israel once Khomeini left the scene.

The end of the Cold War has had two profound effects on arms transfers activities. First, it has led to a massive reduction in military aid from the superpowers, which has had the most impact on former Soviet clients. Syria's decision in 1991 to join the Middle East peace process was directly related to Gorbachev's decision to end military aid. Second, the withdrawal of the superpowers from regional rivalries in Africa, Latin America, and South and Southeast Asia has had very different outcomes. In Africa, chaos and conflict continue but with less immediate international interest. South and Southeast Asia are steadily building up their military inventories (India and Pakistan both have nuclear weapons). In Latin America, more democratic regimes have emerged and the arms race is less a burden than it used to be. However, all the major weapons-manufacturing countries still regard arms transfers as a political as well as an economic tool of diplomacy.

Since most recipients of modern arms in the less-developed regions now have to pay for new weapons rather than receiving them as part of an aid package, it has to be asked whether a more free-market environment for arms transfers has encouraged or discouraged weapons proliferation. At the basic level it has meant that the transfer of big-ticket items—jet fighters, tanks, warships, large missiles—has diminished. However, the market for small arms remains extremely lucrative and many of the most violent ongoing conflicts, especially in Africa, are fought primarily with small arms. The conflict in Iraq further demonstrates the lethality of small arms and munitions against even the best-armed and -equipped military force.

Multilateral efforts to control the international conventional arms traffic have gotten nowhere, and it is unlikely there will be any satisfactory regulation of the arms trade anytime soon. Whether various types of weapons and force levels are more likely to promote conflict than others remains an open question. Attempts to classify weapons according to their assumed characteristics (i.e., are some more "offensive" than others?) have clearly failed, because the character of a weapon and its impact on conflict will depend on the unique environment into which it is introduced.[5]

RECENT WARS AND THE IMPACT OF NEW MILITARY TECHNOLOGY

Since the end of the Cold War in the late 1980s there have been a number of regional wars and indigenous conflicts that suggest very different lessons about the evolving relationships between technology and violence. Some conflicts, such as the 1991 Persian Gulf War, the Kosovo war in 1999, the Afghanistan war in 2001, and the first months of the 2003 Iraq war, have demonstrated the awesome capabilities of modern weaponry in the hands of modern military forces. However, the conflicts in Somalia, Rwanda, Kashmir, Gaza and the West Bank, and Iraq after the initial defeat of the Baathist forces point to continuing effectiveness of terrorism, small arms, and explosive munitions.

The 1991 Gulf War had a seminal effect on thinking about modern warfare and the global demand for advanced arms and related technologies.[6] The war revealed the vulnerability of the infrastructure in modern societies to precision bombardment. New technology improved both the precision and survivability of strike aircraft and cruise missiles. The Global Positioning System provided precise navigational information that enabled highly accurate artillery placement, logistical resupply, and battlefield mapping. Thermal sensors and night-vision equipment on U.S. tanks and helicopters enabled them to target the enemy at night and through the thick smoke of oil well fires. The advanced Joint Surveillance and Attack Radar System (JSTARS) enabled U.S. forces to detect and track slow-moving ground targets against a cluttered background. This system, which is orders of magnitude more powerful than the older Airborne Warning and Control System (AWACS), was used to guide missiles in flight.

The industrial states, especially the ones that already possess a nuclear arsenal, saw the war as further proof of the need to restrict the proliferation of weapons of mass destruction, especially in the nuclear field. Yet some weaker states interpreted the U.S.-led nonnuclear technological advances in an entirely different manner. Nuclear weapons (and perhaps other weapons of mass destruction) may be the only tools smaller, less technologically equipped countries can hope to acquire and deploy in the face of U.S. stealth aircraft, precision-guided munitions, and advanced command, control, communications, and intelligence (C3I).

If the first Gulf War provided a new template for conducting rapid modern warfare, the NATO war against Yugoslavia (the Kosovo war) in 1999 was the natural corollary. An air campaign that went on for several months resulted in the downfall of the Milosevic regime in Yugoslavia and the protection of Kosovo from Serbian aggression. The outcome was achieved with no military casualties on the allied side, although several aircraft were destroyed. This was an extraordinary achievement and reinforced the view that small countries have virtually no defense against attack by modern air forces. It was this reality that influenced the view in some U.S. defense circles that large armies of the kind developed during the Cold War were becoming obsolete and that in the future U.S. military power projection could be done predominantly by air- and sea power with small ground-force units to provide backup. This was the model that influenced U.S. planning for the wars in Afghanistan in 2001 and Iraq in 2003.

Following the September 11, 2001, attacks on New York and Washington, the United States went to war with the Taliban regime in Afghanistan because the regime refused to hand over Osama bin Laden, the perpetrator of 9/11, the bombings of U.S. embassies in Kenya and Tanzania in 1998, and the attacks on the USS *Cole* in Yemen in October 2000. The Afghan war was fought in the fall of 2001

and was decisive: the Taliban were ousted and a new interim government installed in Kabul. However, Bin Laden escaped capture. The war demonstrated the remarkable effectiveness of U.S. airpower against the same Taliban fighters who had defeated the Soviet Union following its invasion of Afghanistan in December 1979 and the subsequent nine-year war. Emboldened by this impressive display of U.S. military power, the Bush administration prepared for war against Iraq's Saddam Hussein. In March 2003 the United States, with British help, invaded Iraq. The war commenced with a massive aerial bombardment, the so-called shock-and-awe tactic. The bombings completely disrupted the weakened Iraqi army, and within a matter of weeks Baghdad had fallen to relatively small but highly mobile ground forces. Saddam was on the run and the Bush administration claimed a military victory.

However, the Iraq war was to prove to be much more difficult than anticipated. Defeating the Iraqi army was one thing; fighting an insurgency with well-trained and dedicated terrorists willing to use suicide tactics was quite another. What began as a triumph of U.S. technology, particularly the use of airpower and light ground forces, turned into a bloody ground conflict with high U.S. casualties. As of October 31, 2005, more than two thousand Americans had been killed in combat and more than seven thousand seriously wounded. One weapons category that has been effective against U.S. forces is the improvised explosive device (IED)—there is very little protection against IEDs placed along the road. IEDs are put together with ordinary explosives; very little high technology is involved. After the toppling of Saddam Hussein in 2003, the drive from central Baghdad to Baghdad Airport was for several years a highway of death because of IEDs.

What the Iraq war has shown is that in the absence of good real-time intelligence, the United States' advanced military technology has been unable to destroy an insurgency. While

U.S. military power may eventually prevail over the insurgents, the cost will have been far higher and far bloodier than anyone predicted. It raises serious questions about the nature of modern warfare and whether all the technical advances that have been made since the mid-1980s have changed the balance of power where it counts most—on the ground. Urban warfare remains the bloodiest and most difficult operation to conduct. The Iraq war has forced the United States to rethink the need for a revolutionary new military reorganization that downgrades the importance of ground forces. The Persian Gulf War and the Afghanistan war may have demonstrated the phenomenal superiority of U.S. airpower, but the 2003 Iraq war has proven to be a painful corrective.

Other events occurred during this period that made it clear that modern technology alone cannot stop or contain violence. The disastrous U.S. experience in Somalia in 1993, the genocide in Rwanda, the guerrilla warfare in Kashmir, and, perhaps most important, the failure of Israel to stop Palestinian terrorism despite its overwhelming military superiority showed that in specific arenas, particularly in urban environments, modern military technology has its limitations. This was to become most abundantly clear in the months following the initial U.S. defeat of Saddam Hussein's forces in the spring of 2003.

Following the defeat of the Taliban in 2001, al Qaeda's need for conventional weapons became more limited because with no standing army, an extended procurement network is unnecessary. However, al Qaeda has made attempts to tap into transnational criminal networks to raise money and procure weapons such as SAMs and small arms.[7]

Al Qaeda has also made numerous attempts to become involved in the production and use of unconventional weapons.[8] It has sought and received a fatwa from a Saudi cleric regarding the permissibility of WMD use and, as the UN special monitoring group concluded, "the only restraint they [al Qaeda] are facing

is the technical complexity to operate them [WMD] properly and effectively."[9]

Moreover, al Qaeda has attempted to manufacture its own chemical and biological weapons. Ahmed Ressam, the so-called Millennium Bomber who was apprehended crossing the border between Canada and the United States on New Year's Day 1999, testified in federal court that in al Qaeda training camps in 1998 experiments were performed with chemical and biological weapons. Other al Qaeda–linked groups have also specialized in the development of chemical and biological weapons. In mid-2003 investigators found elements of botulism and ricin toxins at the remains of an Ansar al Islam camp in Sargat, northern Iraq.[10]

TERRORISM, PROLIFERATION, AND ASYMMETRIC WARFARE

The lessons learned from recent wars have prompted greater interest in the development of asymmetric strategies that would allow smaller and poorer countries to deter the major powers. If you cannot afford to match the advanced powers' technology, you must use whatever capabilities you have to threaten the one component of the West's formidable arsenal that is vulnerable—its low tolerance for military casualties.

There are basically two ways to threaten the West's Achilles' heel. These are state-sponsored terrorism and the development of weapons of mass destruction that can be either used directly against Western forces or provided to terrorist groups to conduct covert operations against Western military and civilian targets. This is what 9/11 and the attacks in Madrid in March 2004 and in London in 2005 were all about. While the technical superiority of the Western military forces has gone from strength to strength over the past decade, the parallel concerns about the vulnerability of Western societies to terrorism and WMD have grown. The use of the phrase "rogue states" by the

U.S. government to describe countries capable of this type of strategy became commonplace in the latter half of the 1990s. Concern was motivated by the actions of countries such as North Korea, Iraq, Iran, and Libya and, to a lesser extent, Syria and Cuba. The first four countries demonstrated a willingness to support international terrorism against Western targets as well as a capacity to develop chemical, biological, and nuclear weapons and surface-to-surface missiles as a means of delivery. As a consequence, the United States has developed a number of very elaborate counterproliferation strategies designed to prevent and, if necessary, offset these developments. Some efforts have been more successful than others.

The mass terrorist bombings of the early twenty-first century did not come out of thin air. The World Trade Center bombing on February 26, 1993, was a portent of what was to happen on 9/11. Six people died in the 1993 attack, but, according to the presiding judge at the trial, the attack was meant to topple one tower onto the other tower in a cloud of cyanide gas; tens of thousands of Americans would have died. The gas crystals were supposed to vaporize in the explosion; instead, the gas burned up.[11] In 1995 in Tokyo, fanatics released the nerve gas sarin in the subway. We now know that their plans, too, went astray. Had the gas attack worked as originally planned, thousands of Tokyo citizens would have died, and it is not difficult to anticipate the chaos and horror that would have followed. During the 1990s and in 2002 and 2004 in Russia, Chechen rebels took thousands of hostages and killed hundreds of civilians in their struggle for independence against Moscow.

The vulnerability of modern societies to such terrorist acts may not be new, but the willingness of groups to engage in such acts probably is. While there have been numerous speculations about nuclear terrorists, the control of nuclear weapons has so far proved to be relatively successful. This is not the case with chemical or biological weapons and certainly not

with the Internet and cyberspace. Also, as the Oklahoma terrorist bombing in May 1995 demonstrated, high technology may not be necessary to create devastating results for unwary targets. So far, the radical Palestinian terrorists have killed many Israeli civilians by conducting suicide attacks with conventional explosives strapped to their bodies. It does not take much imagination to see that if the suicide bombers were strapped to a device containing biological or chemical weapons, the effects on Israeli society could be a thousand times worse.

Although 9/11 and the bombings in Madrid and London were devastating, not all attempts at megaterrorism succeed, as the attacks on the World Trade Center and the Tokyo subway indicate. One priority must be to work closely with the countries of the former Soviet Union to prevent the covert export of materials that can be used to fabricate weapons of mass destruction, especially nuclear weapons. The potential danger of "nuclear leakage" is so great that unless more urgent practical steps are taken to help the former Soviet republics, especially Russia, get better control of these resources, a disaster is probable.

CASUALTY AVERSION

The hypothesis that the advanced democratic countries are unwilling to accept significant casualties in event of military conflict is based on mixed empirical data and a number of questionable propositions that have been advanced as a result of interpretation of the data. Four military conflicts are usually cited to make the argument. First, the high casualties suffered by the United States in Southeast Asia during the Vietnam War, including more than fifty thousand deaths of U.S. servicemen, resulted in a national trauma that made a new generation of U.S. military and political leaders unwilling to put American lives on the line absent a crisis that directly threatened vital U.S. interests. The Persian Gulf War was such an occasion, and despite predictions of thousands of U.S. casualties, the net result was fewer than three hundred American deaths (and many of those were attributable to "friendly fire"). As a result, the belief grew that modern wars could be fought with low casualties if correct preparations were made and a strategy of using overwhelming force was applied.

The United States' low tolerance for casualties was reinforced in 1993. The U.S. intervention in Somalia undertaken in late 1992 as a humanitarian mission to save the starving people of that war-torn society turned into a mission designed to remove the key warlords who were fighting each other and the outside forces, including the United States and the United Nations. In one encounter on October 3, 1993, eighteen U.S. servicemen were killed in a clash with Somali warlords, and the body of one airman was dragged through the streets of Mogadishu for all the world to see. All U.S. troops were withdrawn at the end of March 1994 because of the fierce political backlash in the United States against the operation.

The Kosovo case is even more illuminating since no one on the allied side died due to enemy action. It was understood from the beginning of the air war against Yugoslavia that high allied casualties were politically unacceptable. Although the air war was a great success, the sole reliance on airpower put two significant constraints on the operation. The allied leaders ruled out the use of ground forces, thereby encouraging the Yugoslavs to believe they could outlast the allies if they could tolerate the air assaults. Second, it put a premium on caution when flying allied airplanes over Yugoslavia. This led to high-altitude bombing and probably a number of unnecessary civilian casualties due to inaccurate targeting.

Then came the 2003 Iraq war. In the early days of the war U.S. causalities were very low, but by October 2005 the casualty figures were far higher than those anticipated by both the Bush administration and the American public. If the Iraqi insurgency comes to a timely end and U.S. casualties do not significantly increase,

Iraq may yet turn out to be a success. But if the insurgency and new sectarian violence continue and the U.S. casualties continue to rise absent a stable potential settlement, the war will likely be considered a failure and will have a sobering impact on U.S. willingness to engage in future conflicts in the Middle East.

CONCLUSION

The new century will witness a continued debate about the relationship between military technology and conflict. While the prospects for nuclear apocalypse involving the superpowers have receded, the probabilities for the use of weapons of mass destruction in regional wars or acts of terror have increased. This trend, together with new advanced conventional munitions and the willingness of radical groups to resort to megaterrorism, suggests that the subject at hand will continue to be a central and highly dangerous element of international relations.

The horrors of September 11, 2001, and the subsequent terrorist attacks in Madrid in 2004 and London in 2005 have had a profound impact on how the United States and European states view the dangers of the new century. Likewise, Russia, Indonesia, Egypt, and especially Iraq and Israel have experienced the effectiveness of suicide bombings and the difficulties of defending against them. As long as a culture of suicide permeates radical groups, especially in the Muslim world, classical models of deterrence and defense have limited value. Until effective strategies for limiting such acts of violence are developed, the phenomena will dominate debate and discussion about international security. By far the most effective defense against radical terrorism is good, real-time human intelligence. Unfortunately, despite huge sums of money spent on countering terrorism, poor intelligence remains the Achilles' heel.

What conclusions can be drawn today, in the post-9/11 world? Despite the preoccupation with terrorism, one must not lose sight of the continued importance of the classical role of armed forces in influencing power relations between nations. The end of the Cold War did not bring about the "end of history" as the American scholar Francis Fukuyama suggested.[12] Rather, it unleashed a new wave of nationalism as the former states in the Soviet Union asserted their independence. Many of the "new" countries that emerged were in fact old countries, for example, Latvia, Lithuania, and Estonia.[13] Traditional interstate rivalries dominate many of the regions of the world. Europe may have taken steps toward full integration, but devolution remains a powerful force in the Middle East, Asia, and Africa. One of the most-discussed outcomes of the Iraq war is that Iraq will eventually divide into three separate entities, with the Kurds in the north, the Shiites in the south, and the Sunnis in the center.

If one considers the emerging balance of power in Asia, it is likely that the growth of Chinese maritime and nuclear forces and the military countermeasures this will stimulate in Japan and India could look like an old-fashioned arms race. Likewise, how the countries of the Persian Gulf cope with an emerging Iranian nuclear threat and the eventual rebuilding and rearmament of Iraq will have all the elements of a classic regional balance of power. The historical lessons of conflict and its relationship to changing technology remain important even in the age of megaterrorism.

In sum, the political-military environment will continue to be the primary determinant of whether the attributes of particular categories of weapons, including weapons of mass destruction, will increase the danger of war occurring. If a country such as Iran eventually obtains nuclear weapons, the danger of this occurrence will depend on the nature of the country's leadership and the circumstances under which the nuclear bomb was developed. An Iran governed by a moderate leadership willing to have close relations with the West would

pose far less of a threat than an Iranian leadership committed to confrontation. It should be remembered that for decades U.S. decision makers worried about the dangers of India and Pakistan getting nuclear weapons. Stopping the Indian-Pakistani bomb was a priority of U.S. policy, yet today both countries have the bomb and are close U.S. allies. The lesson therefore holds that weapons are neither good nor bad. It all depends on who has them and how they are used.

NOTES

1. For basic readings on the causes of war and conflict, see Konrad Lorenz, *On Aggression* (New York: Free Press, 1988); Kenneth M. Waltz, *Man, the State, and War: A Theoretical Analysis*, rev. ed. (New York: Columbia University Press, 2001); Geoffrey Blainey, *The Causes of War* (New York: Free Press, 1988); and Greg Cashman, *What Causes War? An Introduction to Theories of International Conflict* (Lanham, Md.: Lexington Books, 1993).

2. Some of the themes developed in this essay are examined in more detail in two studies by the author: *The Control of the Middle East Arms Race* (Washington, D.C.: Carnegie Endowment for International Peace, 1991); and "The Continuing Debate over U.S. Arms Sales: Strategic Needs and the Quest for Arms Limitations," in *The Arms Trade: Problems and Prospects in the Post–Cold War World*, ed. Robert E. Harkavy and Stephanie G. Neumann (Thousand Oaks, Calif.: Annals of the American Academy of the Political and Social Science, September 1994).

3. In most Western countries, national laws concerning gun ownership by citizens have been, and remain, very strict. The exception is the United States, where, because of its history as a revolutionary country with an untamed interior and the Second Amendment to the U.S. Constitution, many Americans believe they have a duty and a constitutional right to own firearms. Yet in reality U.S. gun laws vary from state to state. Some states ban handgun ownership without a special permit, and other states condone the purchase and carrying of concealed weapons. For much of America's history, African Americans were denied access to firearms.

4. The Khomeini government canceled $10.6 billion worth of outstanding arms orders. In addition, it wanted to sell back to the United States seventy-eight F-14 aircrafts purchased by the shah. "Proposed Arms Sales for Countries in the Middle East," hearing before the Subcommittee on Europe and the Middle East, 96th Congress, 1st sess., August 1, 1979, 32, 34, cited in Shahram Chubin, *Iran's National Security Policy: Capabilities, Intentions, and Impact* (Washington, D.C.: Carnegie Endowment for International Peace, 1994).

5. For historical discussions of the "offensive" versus "defensive" weapons argument and the difficulties of reaching agreement on the control of the arms traffic, see, among others, Marion William Boggs, "Attempts to Define and Limit 'Aggressive' Armament in Diplomacy and Strategy," *University of Missouri Studies* 16, no. 1 (Columbia: University of Missouri Press, 1941); and Geoffrey Kemp with Steven Miller, "The Arms Transfer Phenomenon," in *Arms Transfers and American Foreign Policy,* ed. Andrew J. Pierre (New York: New York University Press, 1979), 1–97.

6. For more detail, see Patrick J. Garrity, *Why the Gulf War Still Matters: Foreign Perspectives on the War and the Future of International Security,* Report No. 16 (Los Alamos, N.M.: Center for National Security Studies, Los Alamos National Laboratory, July 1993).

7. Ben Venzke and Aimee Ibrahim, *The al-Qaeda Threat: An Analytical Guide to al-Qaeda's Tactics and Targets* (Alexandria, Va.: Tempest Publishing, 2003); Jason Frier, "Arms and the Terrorist," *Journal of International Security Affairs* 1, no. 9 (Fall 2005); and David E. Kaplan, "Paying for Terror," *U.S. News and World Report,* December 5, 2005.

8. See, for example, Anonymous [Michael Scheuer], *Through Our Enemies' Eyes: Osama Bin Laden, Radical Islam, and the Future of America* (Dulles, Va.: Brassey's, 2002); Anonymous [Michael Scheuer], *Imperial Hubris: Why the West Is Losing the War on Terrorism* (Dulles, Va.: Brassey's, 2004); Bruce Hoffman, *Al Qaeda, Trends in Terrorism and Future Potentialities: An Assessment* (Santa Monica, Calif.: RAND Corporation, 2003), 13–16; Reuven Paz, "Global Jihad and WMD: Between Martyrdom and Mass Destruction," in *Current Trends in Islamist Ideology,* vol. 2, ed. Hillel Fradkin et al. (Washington, D.C.: Hudson Institute, 2005), 74–86; and Gary A. Ackerman and Jeffrey M. Bale, *Al Qaeda and Weapons of Mass Destruction* (Monterey, Calif.: Center for Nonproliferation Studies, 2002).

9. Reuven Paz, "Yes to WMD: The First Islamist Fatwa on the Use of Weapons of Mass Destruction," *e-PRISM* (May 2003); and *Second Report of the Monitoring Group, pursuant to resolution 1363 (2001) and as extended by resolutions 1390 (2002) and 1455 (2003) on sanctions against al-Qaida, the Taliban and their associates and associated entities* (New York: United Nations, 2003), 38.

10. Preston Mendenhall, "Positive Tests for Terror Toxins," *MSNBC,* April 4, 2003.

11. See Laurie Mylroie, "The World Trade Center Bomb: Who Is Ramzi Yousef? And Why It Matters," *National Interest* (Winter 1995–96): 3–15.

12. Francis Fukuyama, "The End of History?" *National Interest* (1989).

13. For a more detailed discussion on the impact of the breakup of the Soviet Union on regional conflicts, see Geoffrey Kemp and Robert E. Harkavy, *Strategic Geography and the Changing Middle East* (Washington, D.C.: Brookings Institution Press, 1997).

5

TERRORISM AND GLOBAL SECURITY

Martha Crenshaw

IT HAS BECOME COMMONPLACE TO SAY that September 11, 2001, marked a watershed in international affairs, but the statement is nevertheless true. Previously, few people thought of terrorism as a serious threat to global security. After 9/11, terrorism suddenly became the centerpiece of U.S. national security strategy and a world priority. In 2004 the UN secretary-general's High-Level Panel on Threats, Challenges, and Change concluded that "terrorism attacks the values that lie at the heart of the Charter of the United Nations: respect for human rights; the rule of law; rules of war that protect civilians; tolerance among peoples and nations; and the peaceful resolution of conflict."[1]

This chapter opens with an overview of the nature and origins of the threat of terrorism in the twenty-first century. It then turns to the causes of terrorism. Do the "root causes" lie in conditions such as poverty, inequality, globalization, lack of democracy, or religious doctrines? Do ongoing political conflicts stimulate terrorism? The answers are much more complex than common wisdom would suggest, and focusing exclusively on root causes does not provide a complete explanation of the phenomenon of terrorism. We must also try to understand the intentions and capabilities of the actors using terrorism in specific historical contexts. Why is terrorism attractive to nonstate challengers? This analysis suggests that terrorism serves the purposes of provocation, polarization, mobilization, and compellence. It also contends that such terrorism is not new; post-1990s "jihadist" terrorism and the "old" terrorism of nationalists, revolutionaries, and right-wing extremists have much in common.

The next question the chapter addresses, by way of conclusion, is why terrorism is a threat to international security and how the world community can cope with it. The answer to why terrorism is perceived as a first-level threat lies in its global diffusion, potential destructiveness, and the tenacity and resilience of the jihadist movement. Despite the sharp international differences over how to respond to terrorism raised by the U.S. intervention in Iraq, it is essential that multilateral cooperation be sustained and expanded within the framework of a global consensus that terrorism is not a legitimate form of political struggle.

IDENTIFYING THE CHALLENGE OF TERRORISM

Attempts to define terrorism have been contentious since the phenomenon became an international issue in the 1970s, particularly after the 1972 Munich Olympics attack on Israeli athletes by the Palestinian Black September organization. Since 1973, and despite the passage of twelve antiterrorism conventions, the members of the United Nations have yet to agree on a definition. As the High-Level Panel report explained, disagreement has centered first on whether states should also be considered terrorist when their armed forces or security services attack civilians. The second problem concerns moral justifications for violence. Should the violence of resistance movements confronting foreign occupations be considered terrorism? Overriding these objections, the panel concluded that terrorism is never acceptable, no matter how legitimate or popular the cause it purports to serve. Terrorism should be defined as "any action . . . that is intended to cause death or serious bodily harm to civilians or non-combatants, when the purpose of such act, by its nature or context, is to intimidate a population, or to compel a Government or an international organization to do or to abstain from doing any act."[2]

Since the 1990s, the principal driving force behind terrorism on an international scale has been al Qaeda and its affiliates and offshoots, which together loosely constitute a global Salafist, or jihadi, movement. Al Qaeda is an amorphous type of nonstate actor.[3] It consists of both a remnant of the central core of the organization that ordered the 9/11 attacks and those that preceded it (chiefly, the 1998 East African embassy bombings, the millennium plots, and the 2000 bombing of the USS *Cole* in Yemen)

and local associates and imitators around the world. Their links to what is left of the original conspiracy that was based in Taliban-ruled Afghanistan are hard to trace. The presence of these successor groups is global, including cells within immigrant communities in the West. The most virulent form of al Qaeda–related terrorism persists in Iraq, in conjunction with a Sunni-led insurgency aided by foreign fighters who have provided the majority of suicide bombers since the U.S. intervention in 2003. Since 2001, however, attacks in Indonesia, Morocco, Tunisia, Saudi Arabia, Egypt, Jordan, Iraq, Turkey, Pakistan, Afghanistan, Kenya, Spain, and Great Britain have shown that al Qaeda in the broadest sense, including all aspects of jihadi terrorism, retains both the will and the capacity to conduct operations around the world.

An important source of unity within this diffuse movement is its origin in the anti-Soviet resistance in 1980s Afghanistan. There the links that exist today among individuals and different national groups were forged. These connections are based on shared experiences, socialization, training, and indoctrination in camps in Afghanistan and Pakistan, as well as on ideological affinity. Many of the fighters in Afghanistan returned home with a sense of having fulfilled a transcendental mission, and sometimes with an exalted reputation, to alter the course of local conflicts (e.g., in the Philippines and Indonesia). Others, whether by choice or because their own governments would not permit their repatriation, joined or formed Islamist groups in diasporas in the West.

The convictions driving this movement are vehemently anti-Western and anti-American. The movement is fundamentally antidemocratic and intolerant. Many of its adherents do not shrink from killing Muslims who do not agree with their interpretation of Islam. They are thought to wish not only to overthrow non-Islamist regimes in Muslim countries and reestablish a version of the early Islamic caliphate but to diminish Western influence worldwide, which they see as a threat to Islam. They oppose the presence of "Crusaders and Jews" in Muslim countries and seek a return to a purer form of Islam that would restore the Muslim community to greatness. Scholars and policymakers debate the question of whether al Qaeda is genuinely motivated by the conflicts in Palestine and now Iraq or whether references to these grievances are opportunistic. In either case, conflicts that pit Muslims against non-Muslims, often outside the Middle East, help them to justify their position that Islam is on the defensive and that jihad is a moral obligation for individual Muslims.[4] In providing evidence for these claims, the war in Iraq may have revived a fading movement.

Al Qaeda originated during the U.S.-assisted campaign to drive the Soviet Union out of Afghanistan in the 1980s. Osama bin Laden, a wealthy Saudi Arabian activist, became an energetic supporter of the Afghan mujahideen, raising money and mobilizing recruits from the Muslim world to join the jihad. However, to him it must have seemed that the victory in Afghanistan was short-lived. When Saudi Arabia agreed to allow U.S. troops on Saudi territory after Iraq's invasion of Kuwait, he was apparently infuriated. His opposition to the Saudi regime became sufficiently troubling that he was stripped of his citizenship and removed to Sudan. From there he built an organization that grew out of the contacts he had made in Afghanistan, including links to Egyptian radical groups. When he was expelled from Sudan, he relocated to Afghanistan, conveniently on the eve of the Taliban's takeover. With a sympathetic ally in power, he was able to establish a base of operations and link forces with other radical Islamic groups. Egyptian leader Ayman al-Zawahiri became one of his key lieutenants. Together with other Islamist extremist leaders they issued a fatwa in February 1998, calling for attacks on Americans wherever they might be found. The August 1998 U.S. embassy bombings in Kenya and Tanzania and sub-sequent U.S. retaliation signaled the beginnings of the campaign.

In light of the intense contemporary focus on al Qaeda, it is important to remember that terrorism has been used in the service of a variety of ideologies: nationalism, revolution, religion, and right-wing extremism. Moreover, domestic terrorism has undoubtedly caused more damage than international terrorism, although figures on this are unreliable. Terrorism perpetrated by groups other than al Qaeda continues to threaten democracy and stability. The Revolutionary Armed Forces of Colombia (FARC) and right-wing paramilitaries remain potent forces in Colombia. Both Hezbollah (which retains a capacity for global action although it abandoned attacks on U.S. and other Western targets after the Persian Gulf War) and Hamas are strong and socially rooted Islamic organizations. Both have successfully competed in elections, especially Hamas, which won a majority in Palestinian parliamentary elections in 2006. Palestinian Islamic Jihad and the al-Aqsa Martyrs' Brigade joined Hamas in attempting to block a negotiated settlement between the Palestinian Authority and Israel. India confronts continued terrorism related to the conflict in Kashmir. State-supported terrorism has not disappeared, either, as the United States frequently accuses Iran and Syria of assisting al Qaeda and Hamas, and India holds Pakistan responsible for supporting terrorism in Kashmir.

We should also recognize the fact that campaigns of terrorism can come to an end. After the Good Friday Agreement of 1998, the IRA in Northern Ireland agreed to disarm and abandon violence. Similarly, the Liberation Tigers of Tamil Eelam (LTTE) in Sri Lanka dropped their campaign in 2002, although the subsequent cease-fire was tenuous. ETA remained a problem for Spain into the twenty-first century, although its strength was vastly diminished from its high point in the 1970s. In Germany and Italy, left-wing revolutionary terrorism had largely ended by the mid-1980s.

Peru had defeated Sendero Luminoso by the 1990s. Thus there is precedent for the decline of even very persistent groups.

SOURCES OF CONTEMPORARY TERRORISM

A discussion of the sources of terrorism needs to address two issues: the underlying conditions or structures that facilitate its emergence and encourage its growth, and the specific goals and methods of the actors using terrorism. Risk propensity does not guarantee terrorism; that is, the fact that societies are at risk for terrorism because they have the conditions that might encourage it does not mean that they will necessarily experience it—other things have to happen. The direct causes of terrorism lie in the perceptions and calculations of political actors as they interact with their constituencies and with their opponents in a given historical context.

Several conditions may contribute to the occurrence of terrorism: globalization, democracy, conflict, and ideology or religion.

Globalization

Globalization is associated with terrorism in two senses.[5] One is the possibility that resentment over being left behind fuels terrorism in areas of the world that do not benefit from but feel exploited by the West. The other is that permeability of borders, mobility of persons, and instantaneous worldwide communication through the Internet and the news media provide important resources for terrorist conspiracies. However, the relationship is more complex than one might imagine at first glance.

The first argument is more problematic than the second. It is not clear that the most disadvantaged parts of the world, those that profit least from globalization of the means of production, produce more terrorist conspiracies than those more advantaged. This issue relates to the question of whether poverty and underdevelopment yield terrorism.[6] If they do, then terrorism is a sign of deep conflict between North and South, between haves and have-nots, between the powerful and the powerless. If those who are left out of the process of globalization become terrorists, then terrorism is in effect caused by global inequality.

A variation of this argument takes into account the fact that even in poorer countries most of the individuals who become terrorists are better educated and more prosperous than other members of their societies, that many members of al Qaeda come from Saudi Arabia, and that other jihadist terrorists are citizens of the West. Such individuals are the products of globalization, not those left behind. They seem to be material beneficiaries of the modern world who are socially and politically unassimilated and spiritually adrift. They are caught between traditional families and communities and modernity. Thus they may be left behind by globalization on a psychological rather than a material level.

However, although these propositions may be intuitively plausible, they lack definitive empirical support. If they were valid, we would expect to see much more terrorism than we do, since millions of people live in poverty yet are cognizant of global disparities. Millions of new emigrants live in Western societies. Many people are caught between traditional and modern societies. Few of them turn to terrorism.

The second argument about globalization, that it is a permissive rather than a direct cause, is more convincing. Globalization enables terrorism rather than motivates it. Underground transnational conspiracies can take advantage of all the developments that make the world a smaller place. It is easy to travel, communicate, instruct, and transfer money. Islamist-oriented groups that call for a return to the past, paradoxically, are quite adept in using the tools of the modernity they ostensibly reject. They establish Web sites to promote the cause, talk by cell phone, and jet around the globe. Just as businesses, NGOs, and universities find it easier to integrate their activities and reach consumers and clients on an international scale, so do the users of terrorism. It would be surprising if it were otherwise.

Democracy, or the Lack Thereof

Another condition linked to terrorism is the presence or absence of democracy. Here again the relationship is not simple.[7]

Repression of peaceful means of political dissent may force opposition movements into the underground and encourage their resort to violence, because they lack alternatives and face persecution from the state. Repression fuels perceptions of injustice. Inclinations to use terrorism are thought to be reduced when the political process is open to the expression of diverse viewpoints and when opposition groups are not just heard but represented in the structures of power.

Lack of peaceful means of political expression may sometimes explain terrorism, but the empirical evidence is mixed. At least two caveats are in order before we equate democracy with the absence of terrorism. The first is that the process of democratization, as repressive regimes move toward liberalization, is often violent. The formerly powerful resist loss of power and prestige, and the formerly subjugated lack trust and confidence in the new institutions. If security is not assured during the transition, democracy will be associated with chaos and disorder.

The situation in Iraq after 2003 vividly presents some of these dilemmas. The absence of effective security institutions permits the factions vying for power to use extraordinarily cruel violence to defeat their opponents and exercise vengeance. The case of Algeria is also instructive. The Algerian government in 1990 decided to permit free elections. However, when it appeared that the Front Islamique du Salut (FIS) was poised to win, the military stepped in to halt the process. A deadly civil war ensued, leading to the deaths of possibly as many as one hundred thousand people.

The second caveat is that established liberal democracies have also experienced terrorism,

not only from outside their borders, but from discontented citizens of their own. Before the 2001 attacks on the World Trade Center and the Pentagon, the 1995 bombing of the Murrah Federal Building in Oklahoma City was the most destructive act of terrorism in American history. Timothy McVeigh, who was executed for the crime, was a follower of far-right extremist causes. Spain had to deal with ETA and Britain with the IRA. Germany and Italy faced terrorism from aspiring social revolutionaries. Sendero Luminoso made its appearance just as Peru was making a peaceful transition to democracy. The 2004 and 2005 attacks on public transportation systems in Madrid and London could also be interpreted as internal terrorism, although their goal, apparently, was not to overthrow those governments but to punish them for supporting the U.S. campaign in Iraq.

At the same time, democracies possess real advantages in combating terrorism. They offer peaceful means of expressing dissent. They are also prepared to address economic, social, and political problems that may encourage terrorism. A robust legitimacy means that even if a discontented minority launches a campaign of terrorism, it will not attract mass support. In this regard, the strength of the state also matters. Weak and internally divided democracies are more vulnerable than others. It is also critical that the democratic response to terrorism avoid the excesses of repression and violation of human rights that will trigger more terrorism.

Violent Political Conflict

A third possible condition for terrorism on a global level is violent political conflict, whether civil or international. The logic behind this argument is that if these deep conflicts were resolved, terrorism (as a manifestation of the conflict) would disappear. As often as not, terrorism that accompanies such conflicts is state supported. Thus the conflict between India and Pakistan over Kashmir is presumably the source of Pakistan's support for anti-Indian groups, some of which have lately espoused the cause of radical Islam. The conflict between Israel and the Palestinians is the source of Palestinian radicalism and, to some, even the root of al Qaeda's hatred of the United States. The war in Iraq similarly generates opposition to U.S. policy. Thus conflict resolution would reduce terrorism in the long run.

However, this argument, like that about the effects of globalization, has its weaknesses. Grievances generated by these conflicts are widespread, but terrorism is still a rare occurrence given the numbers of people affected. Also, there are significant anomalies. Al Qaeda launched its jihad before the beginning of the second intifada, when the situation for Palestinians looked considerably brighter than it does now, and well before the war in Iraq. Why are there almost no Palestinians in al Qaeda and no proven links with Hamas or the other Palestinian groups that use terrorism against Israel? Why have no Islamic Palestinian groups attacked U.S. or Western targets?

Furthermore, like the process of democratization, peace processes often attract terrorism from spoilers who do not wish to see a conflict resolved.[8] The use of suicide bombings by Hamas is an excellent example in the context of the Israeli-Palestinian conflict. Obviously, what matters is not the absence of conflict but the terms of the peace. And what constitutes a just peace is subjective and disputed.

Ideology or Religion

A fourth condition is ideology or religion.[9] Although Islam is the focus of the contemporary debate, terrorism has been associated with many religious doctrines. The argument that religion is a source of terrorism is based on the assumption that values and beliefs cause terrorism. It assumes that specific doctrines, particularly those that are millenarian or apocalyptic, motivate terrorism. Because religious terrorists presumably seek only to please a deity, they are oblivious to the human cost of their actions.

The availability of an ideology, secular or religious, that justifies and legitimizes violence is undoubtedly a contributing factor. Normative justification may even be necessary. But the specific doctrines that extremists espouse are typically narrow, inconsistent, and selective interpretations of wider bodies of thought. Furthermore, the decision to use violence may come first, at least on the part of the leadership, which then crafts a borrowed doctrine out of bits and pieces of established ideology or religion in order to support what is in essence a political goal. It is also important to note that adherents of the Islamic party Hizb ut-Tahrir have not resorted to violence despite the party's extreme doctrines and rhetoric (although the party has been officially banned in Germany and Britain).[10]

Three conclusions emerge from this discussion. First, any conditions that generate discontent can provide a pool for terrorist recruiting. Grievances act both as motivation for the individual and as a mobilizing device for the organization. Second, the groups that use or aspire to use terrorism see such actual or potential constituencies as available and accessible and wish to attract their support in order to grow from small underground conspiracies to genuine social movements with political clout. They script their message accordingly. Third, all these conditions lend themselves easily to transnational expansion. Generalized resentment, antiglobalization, and anti-Americanism are attitudes shared across borders. Television conveys emotionally powerful visual images around the globe. Even the presence or absence of democracy has a border-crossing dimension, in that opposition groups that cannot succeed against a repressive local regime may redirect their activities either against local targets outside the country or against outside powers thought to be supporting the local regime. Countries that tolerate dissent may find themselves harboring terrorist conspiracies, as Germany did on the eve of 9/11.

These conclusions also indicate that we cannot explain terrorism exclusively in terms of root causes. Instead, we should turn our attention to the actors using terrorism.[11] They may be motivated by these grievances or combinations of them, but they also see them as opportunities for advancement of their goals. Terrorism is not a spontaneous reaction to circumstances. Groups confronting the same conditions choose different responses.

THE ACTORS USING TERRORISM AND THEIR CHOICE OF STRATEGIES

Terrorism is primarily the province of nonstate actors, although governments can passively and actively support them and occasionally sponsor terrorism directly through official agents.[12] In those cases, intelligence or security agencies perform essentially as underground conspiracies in an attempt to evade detection. For such active state sponsors, terrorism is a means of deception and denial, a way of avoiding accountability, whereas nonstate actors typically claim credit because they seek visibility and recognition. Media coverage is an important part of their communications strategy. Passive sponsors are often failed states, unable to prevent the development of terrorism on their territory. Thus explaining terrorism requires understanding how terrorist conspiracies develop and operate, especially on a transnational scale, and why terrorism is an attractive option for achieving political goals. The answer is not quite as simple as the familiar saying that terrorism is "the weapon of the weak" implies.

THE UTILITY OF TERRORISM

Regardless of overall ideological framework—the structure of beliefs, images, and worldviews that guide action—terrorism has specific tactical purposes that make it attractive. What combination of incentives and opportunities makes terrorism likely? Four main uses of terrorism can be identified: provocation, polarization, mobilization, and compellence. Describing terrorism as useful does not mean that terrorism necessarily succeeds in obtaining its objectives. Nor are these uses mutually exclusive; in fact, they are complementary. Any given attack will likely be motivated by a combination of objectives.

Provocation

Terrorism, especially random attacks on civilian populations, can be used as a means of provoking a government into overreaction. For example, al Qaeda's attacks on the World Trade Center and the Pentagon may have been intended to provoke a massive and indiscriminate U.S. response that would justify the charge that the United States wished to destroy Islam and was an enemy of the Muslim world. ETA's early strategy in Spain was to deliberately provoke the state into repressive acts that would further alienate Basques. The National Liberation Front (FLN) in Algeria followed a similar line. The severe French response to terrorism in Algiers in 1956 and 1957 led to the use of torture during the Battle of Algiers and then as a consequence to public scandal, which helped make the war deeply unpopular in France.

Such strategies are thought to be particularly effective against democracies, the governments of which are both susceptible to public opinion (and thus outrage accompanied by calls for revenge) and simultaneously restrained by human rights norms.[13] A more ruthless regime could respond by crushing all opposition and censoring media coverage of the threat. However, these propositions have not been sufficiently tested.

Polarization

In this sense terrorism resembles communal conflict or civil war, in that it can be used to drive divided societies farther apart and that moderates tend to suffer most. Indiscriminate attacks against representatives of the "other" community, whether ethnic, racial, religious, or linguistic, fragment societies and perpetuate conflict. In Iraq, Sunni terrorism is directed against Shiites, and Shiite militias have infiltrated government security forces to avenge themselves against Sunnis. Indiscriminate and high-casualty attacks on marketplaces, mosques, and even funeral processions have divided the two communities. Similar terrorism has occurred in Pakistan and Kashmir. Sinhalese were targeted by the LTTE in Sri Lanka. Catholics and Protestants attacked each other in Northern Ireland. Currently on both global and national levels, for individuals as well as governments, terrorism generates suspicion and distrust between Muslims and non-Muslims. Many Muslims feel that they are implicated in the crimes of a tiny few who do not represent them. Non-Muslims sometimes charge that Muslims have been hesitant to condemn terrorism. In Europe, anti-immigration sentiment has been strengthened.

Mobilization

Terrorism can do more than alter the behavior of an adversary. It serves importantly to mobilize and invigorate supporters and to develop new constituencies. It demonstrates power, even if striking a blow accomplishes nothing concrete. It satisfies demands for vengeance and overcomes feelings of humiliation and resentment. Terrorism can define issues and put previously ignored grievances on the world agenda by attracting international press coverage. For example, before the Palestinian hijackings of the late 1960s and early 1970s, the issue before the world was "Arab refugees," not Palestinian nationalism. The hijackings and the 1972 attack on the Munich Olympics made it impossible to ignore Palestinian claims, despite the unacceptability of their methods.

Furthermore, carefully targeted terrorism helps frame grievances; the attacks on the World Trade Center and Pentagon defined U.S. economic and military might as the problem. Terrorism is a highly symbolic form of violence, and choice of target conveys a message.

Terrorism can also assist in distinguishing a group from its nonviolent or less violent competitors who seek the same outcome. For this reason, competitiveness among organizations can lead to imitation, as in Israel, where Hamas, Palestinian Islamic Jihad, and the al-Aqsa Martyrs' Brigade competed for public support and recruits in the grim game of suicide bombings during the second intifada. In the 1970s, rivalry among different nationalist factions was common. For example, once the Popular Front for the Liberation of Palestine had inaugurated the tactic of hijacking aircraft in 1968, other groups quickly followed suit. Similar competition may characterize the conflict in Iraq.

Compellence

Terrorism may be perceived as useful in compelling states to withdraw from foreign commitments through a strategy of punishment and attrition.[14] The point is to make the commitment so painful that the government will abandon it. Like provocation, this strategy may work best against democracies, where governments are accountable to the people and where a free press publicizes the effects of terrorism. Such actions may be intended to end a foreign intervention, such as by weakening alliances. To some people, the 2004 Madrid and the 2005 London bombings were meant to force the withdrawal of troops from Iraq. The Madrid bombings appeared to be evidence of this theory, coinciding as they did with national elections lost by an incumbent regime that supported the United States in Iraq. Osama bin Laden pointed to the success of such tactics of compellence elsewhere, particularly in Lebanon in 1983, when the bombing of the U.S. Marine barracks at the Beirut airport led to U.S. withdrawal.[15] He also grandiosely claimed credit for the U.S. withdrawal from Somalia. One purpose of assassinations and kidnappings of Western diplomats in Latin America in the 1960s and 1970s was to compel their governments to withdraw support, both economic and military, for the dictatorships then in power. The hope was that popular revolution could then succeed. Bombings in France in the 1980s were apparently meant to halt French support for Iraq in the Iran-Iraq War. The aim of expelling a foreign occupier is plainly evident in the tactics of the post-2003 insurgents in Iraq. Even the United Nations and humanitarian aid workers, in addition to private contractors, have been targeted in an effort to drive out any stabilizing forces and prevent the restoration of order and prosperity.

The perceived success of such a strategy may be illusory. The U.S. withdrawal from Lebanon may be an exception, not the rule. In most cases, it cannot be shown conclusively that terrorism was the cause of specific government actions (such as the Israeli withdrawal from the Gaza Strip). Furthermore, there are numerous counterexamples. India, for example, has not bowed to terrorist pressure in Kashmir. Russia did not withdraw from Chechnya. The opposite reaction to terrorism may indeed be more common: a reinvigorated determination to resist demands.

OLD VERSUS NEW TERRORISM

A central question regarding actors and strategies is whether al Qaeda represents a transformation of the phenomenon of terrorism or a continuation of existing trends. The terrorism that threatens the post–Cold War world, chiefly al Qaeda and its affiliates, is thought by some analysts to differ profoundly from the terrorism of the past.[16] The difference between "old" and "new," however, may be exaggerated. The differences in question lie along three dimensions: goals, methods, and forms of organization.

Goals

A first dimension concerns goals. Is the global jihadist movement the first nonstate actor to espouse a genuinely international goal, that of reestablishing Muslim domination by driving the West out of Muslim lands and imposing Islamic rule? Is al Qaeda essentially an apocalyptic movement? Or are the goals of such groups basically local and hence part of an old pattern?[17] And how do these goals compare with those of past extremist groups using terrorism?

There is no consensus on what al Qaeda and its attendant groups want. Do their leaders seek to seize power in Iraq, Saudi Arabia, Egypt, Algeria, or Indonesia, in effect replicating the success of the Iranian revolution at the national level; or do they want to challenge the United States and its allies on the global level, in this case repeating the victory over the Soviet Union in Afghanistan? Is the movement driven by religion or politics? An initial casus belli for Osama bin Laden was the U.S. military presence in Saudi Arabia, and after the invasion of Iraq, the war there became a drive to expel the infidel. There is no doubt that the fighting in Iraq fuels a sense of rage and urgency among some Muslims, primarily young men, who see Islam as threatened and rise to its defense (from their perspective) even if they themselves live in the West in countries where Muslims are a minority. The memory of the former greatness of the Islamic empires makes the current perceived state of humiliation and subjugation all the more bitter. Terrorism is a form of punishment of the West. The reality is probably that there are complex combinations of motives, varying from individual to individual and from group to group.

How different are these jihadist goals from those of other groups, past and present? Using terrorism to expel a foreign occupier is a tried-and-true method, familiar to students of the history of nationalism. Nor is there anything new about wanting to seize power, at the level of the state or a portion of its territory, and to implement revolutionary change or establish an autonomous government independent of external control. Numerous revolutionary and nationalist movements have used terrorism, from the Russian revolutionary organizations of the late nineteenth century and the IRA to Sendero Luminoso, ETA, and the LTTE.

If the international ambitions of the jihadist movement are genuine, are they strikingly new? As Olivier Roy has reminded his readers, the left-wing revolutionary movements of the 1960s through the 1980s also conceived of their struggle in global terms.[18] For example, the Red Army Faction in West Germany considered itself the ally of Third World national liberation movements, striking at the heart of the imperialist enemy (the United States and NATO) in Europe. Such groups aimed to promote socialism and defeat imperialism worldwide. And in some cases they were assisted by the Soviet Union and its allies, just as the United States aided the mujahideen in Afghanistan (without foreseeing the consequences). It is possible that the international ambitions of al Qaeda are stronger than those of past groups, which would probably be expected in a world where it is easier to develop and communicate a shared ideology and in which the United States is the sole superpower. In other words, international ambitions may be an effect of changing circumstances as much as changing motivations.

Moreover, using terrorism to retaliate for a government's foreign involvements is not new. Iran and pro-Iranian groups retaliated against France for its support of Iraq during the 1980–88 Iran-Iraq War. German leftists were angered by U.S. support for repressive Third World regimes. The Red Army Faction got its start in demonstrations against the shah of Iran. Opposition to the war in Vietnam was an important component of the ideological anti-imperialist mix, just as opposition to the war in Iraq is for Islamist movements.

Methods

A second dimension of terrorism that is considered new is the desire to cause large numbers of civilian casualties. For this reason, and especially since the 1995 sarin gas attack by the Japanese cult Aum Shinrikyo on the Tokyo subway, there has been a fear that the "new" terrorists would acquire and employ weapons of mass destruction.[19] The "old" terrorists, in contrast, were thought to be inhibited by the shadow of the future, the fact that they expected eventually to become legitimate governments. The prospect of success, however illusory, was a source of restraint. They thus regarded terrorism as a means to a concrete political end, whereas to the new Islamist terrorists, violence and destruction are ends in themselves. To proponents of the "new" terrorism argument, terrorism is no longer instrumental.

Indeed, the numbers killed in the World Trade Center and Pentagon attacks overshadowed anything that had gone before, as the toll of victims rose from the hundreds to the thousands. Subsequent attacks, such as the Bali nightclub bombing and the bombings of train and subway systems in Madrid and London, as well as the bombings of civilian targets in Iraq, reinforce the conclusion that semirandom lethality is the aim.

However, bombings of civilians were scarcely unknown in the past. The film *The Battle of Algiers* dramatizes urban terrorism in 1950s Algeria during the Algerian War, for example. It is also worth noting that the numbers of casualties in single incidents in post-9/11 attacks have not exceeded the bounds of the past.[20] Furthermore, the means of terrorism have so far remained largely low tech, such as homemade explosives delivered by backpack or suicide bombers (improvised explosive devices [IEDs]). Although al Qaeda has apparently shown an interest in acquiring WMD, these means have not been used since the Aum Shinrikyo attack in 1995. The 9/11 attacks were shockingly innovative, as well as destructive, but subsequent attacks have followed a more typical pattern.

Forms of Organization

The third dimension that may distinguish al Qaeda from the past is its form of organization.

Whereas the old terrorists are said to have been organized in centralized and hierarchical underground conspiracies, al Qaeda has progressively become a looser, decentralized, flat network. It is difficult to say whether actions performed in its name are ordered from a central leadership or initiated by local groups acting independently. The original al Qaeda organization was steadily eroded and weakened as the United States prosecuted the "global war on terrorism," starting with the loss of its sanctuary in Afghanistan in 2001. The steady pressure of arrests and killings deprived the organization of key operatives and interrupted its communications. Thus organizational behavior shifted over time as a way of adapting to changing circumstances. The operational autonomy of local groups may have been a response to decline rather than a deliberate choice. It is also worth noting that the concept of "leaderless resistance" originated with the American far right and that it developed as a deliberate and practical way of eluding detection. Louis Beam, an American white supremacist affiliated with the Aryan Nations, conceived of the strategy in 1992, according to Bruce Hoffman.[21] Beam recommended "autonomous leadership units" that would escape government surveillance. Violent resistance could thus be both decentralized and coordinated. He also inaugurated the use of computer bulletin boards and Web sites as means of communication and recruitment.

Thus terrorism associated with Islamic extremist tendencies varies from the past along these three dimensions, but the difference is one of degree rather than kind. The fundamental process of terrorism has not changed.

THE TERRORIST THREAT TO INTERNATIONAL SECURITY

After the shock of 9/11, analysts of international relations called for a new approach to terrorism. Most argued that while in the past terrorism had been a second-order foreign policy issue, it should now be recognized as a major threat to national and international security.[22] The U.S. government had no need of this advice as the attacks immediately propelled terrorism to the top of the president's agenda and led to the launching of the global war on terrorism, the defeat of the Taliban regime in Afghanistan, and the subsequent overthrow of Saddam Hussein. The reaction to 9/11 also stimulated the most comprehensive reorganization of the U.S. government since the aftermath of World War II, including the establishment of a Department of Homeland Security and a reorganization of the nation's intelligence bureaucracy. At the international level, terrorism also became a top priority. The United Nations, NATO, and the European Union moved immediately to recognize the threat and to develop expansive counterterrorism policies based on international cooperation.

What is at stake? Why was and is terrorism perceived as a major threat? States do not face "mutual assured destruction" as they did during the Cold War, despite the gravity of the attacks on the United States in 2001 and the risk that terrorists could acquire WMD. The intensity of the threat does not depend solely on material consequences, such as numbers of killed and injured or infrastructure destroyed. The subjective aspect of the threat is as important as the objective aspect.

For the public, much of what makes terrorism a potent threat lies in the essence of the phenomenon, which has not changed. Terrorism creates uncertainty because it is unpredictable. Terrorism often targets civilians going about their daily lives. They cannot know who among their fellow subway or bus or airplane passengers, among those standing next to them in a crowded spot or sitting next to them in a restaurant, aims to attack. Acts of terrorism themselves, even if relatively minor, are constant reminders of vulnerability. Even threats carry weight. The Cold War was punctuated by the occasional acute and frightening crisis, such as the Cuban missile srisis in 1962, that reminded the world of the precariousness of the "balance of terror," but individuals did not experience a taste of the threat itself, in the sense of a nuclear exchange. Terrorism, in contrast, is visible as a real and present danger, even if residents of Western societies are more likely to die in a household accident than in a terrorist attack. People who normally live in stable societies, whose daily lives are not constantly threatened, are unaccustomed to this risk, although the inhabitants of the many war-torn countries in Africa, Asia, and the Middle East unfortunately are. And the perception of risk is magnified by media coverage, especially television. Americans see terrorism as more of a threat than do Europeans, but sensitivities are generally high.[23]

For governments, terrorism is a threat to sovereignty, reputation, and credibility as well as to the safety of their citizens. National leaders must be sensitive to the challenge to the prestige of the state itself as well as to the security of their territories and populations. The fact that the United States, as the world's sole superpower, not only declared a "war on terrorism" but intervened militarily in both Afghanistan and Iraq probably reinforces the global perception of terrorism as a source of immediate danger and pervasive insecurity.

Today's terrorism appears threatening because of where it happens, how it happens, and why it happens.

Although past waves of terrorism had a transnational dimension (especially the anarchist movement of the late nineteenth and early twentieth centuries), the contemporary threat exhibits a broader and more sustained territorial reach in terms of the geographical diversity of the location of attacks, the sites where the plots are laid, and the nationalities of the individual perpetrators. The threat is both international and local. Terrorism from al Qaeda or groups associated with the ideas behind al Qaeda has occurred in Kenya, Tanzania, Morocco, Tunisia, Saudi Arabia, Egypt, Ye-

men, Jordan, Iraq, Afghanistan, Turkey, Spain, Britain, the United States, Pakistan, Indonesia, and the Philippines, and plots have been foiled in other countries (e.g., in the Balkans and in France). In addition, planning for attacks was undertaken in other locations, including Germany, Italy, and Singapore. The individuals who commit these attacks come from an even broader range of countries, and they include citizens of the countries that are attacked as well as foreigners. A Belgian woman, for example, became a suicide bomber in Iraq in 2005.

In an era of instantaneous mass communication, the audience for terrorism is also global. Nobody who has access to modern communications systems can escape awareness of the danger. Reminders are constant. Terrorism is visible on a daily basis, whether it occurs in Baghdad, London, or Jerusalem. Television, in particular, is a medium well suited to transmitting the information that makes the threat vivid and salient.[24] Terrorists, of course, know this quite well. Over time, audiences might become numb to the terrorism threat. The risk is that terrorists, perceiving this desensitization, will escalate to higher levels of violence in order to shock.

The extreme lethality of the 9/11 attacks may not have been typical, but the horror they caused permanently altered expectations of what terrorists could accomplish. The fear that al Qaeda or those inspired by its message will acquire weapons of mass destruction—chemical, biological, radiological, or nuclear—in order to engage in truly catastrophic terrorism is widespread. The example of Aum Shinrikyo, as well as al Qaeda's apparent aspirations in this regard, cannot be ignored. Some analysts think that such fears are exaggerated and that sufficient harm can be done with "ordinary" weapons at a much-reduced cost to the perpetrators. Coordinated sequences of suicide bombings, for example, have a profound impact on the public. Others think that it is only a matter of time before terrorists take the step.

Finally, in the United States, the image of al Qaeda and jihadist terrorism is that it aims to undermine the values on which Western civilization is built. It is seen as a threat to democracy, tolerance, and freedom. The refrain of the U.S. government is that they hate us because of who we are. Terrorism is seen as a threat to identity rather than interests. Regardless of the accuracy of this portrayal of the motives behind terrorism, the vision is frightening.

Coping with Terrorism: Taking the Offensive

The 9/11 attacks generated an initial burst of international solidarity with the United States and strong support for overturning the Taliban regime and destroying al Qaeda in Afghanistan. However, the decision to invade Iraq introduced a period of bitter disagreement. The war in Iraq divided those who had formerly supported American policy, and other background disagreements related to the war on terrorism came to the fore.

The shock of the attacks on the World Trade Center and the Pentagon, and the distinct possibility that the White House itself might have been struck had the passengers on one flight not rebelled against their hijackers, produced a genuine sense of collective security, in that the attack on the United States was perceived as an attack against all. For the first time in its history, NATO invoked its collective defense provision and then engaged in a process of transforming its conception of security and its post–Cold War mission. The UN Security Council immediately adopted a resolution imposing counterterrorist obligations on its member states. For the first time there appeared to be a solid and comprehensive international consensus against terrorism.

The use of military force to destroy a terrorist organization and overturn the government of the state that supported it was unprecedented, as previous U.S. retaliations had been brief and limited.[25] Nevertheless, the war in Afghanistan was widely approved as a legitimate response since the Taliban had refused repeated requests to surrender Bin Laden and had already been placed under UN sanctions. Even Pakistan abandoned its support for the Taliban and joined the U.S. side. The United States also stepped up military assistance programs for states threatened by al Qaeda–related terrorism, such as the Philippines.

Although U.S. policymakers framed the response as a "war on terrorism" and insisted that the "terrorism as crime" model had been decisively rejected, much of the response to 9/11 consisted of coordinating police and intelligence work around the world. Governments cracked down on terrorist financing, for example, conspiracies were progressively uncovered and dismantled, and hundreds of al Qaeda operatives were arrested in countries around the world.

This aspect of the response to terrorism did have a harder edge than in the past, thus deviating from a strict criminal justice mode. For one thing, the United States was more inclined to use covert operations, including strikes against al Qaeda leaders in Yemen and Pakistan. The United States expanded the practice of rendition rather than extradition or deportation of terrorist suspects. And it introduced the controversial concept of "unlawful combatants" to justify holding suspects in military detention centers in Afghanistan and at Guantánamo Bay in Cuba and then trying them in military rather than civilian courts. These practices were criticized as violations of international law and of human rights from the outset.

The real breakdown of consensus, however, began with the 2003 invasion of Iraq, which isolated the United States from most of its closest allies. Before that move, the United States was viewed as a benevolent superpower; after the intervention in Iraq, the United States appeared assertive and unilateralist. The military offensive followed closely on the adoption of a new security strategy for the United

States, one based on military preemption of threats, including forceful regime change. President George Bush declared that in the war on terrorism, countries were either with the United States or against it. There could be no middle ground.

On grounds of expediency, critics saw the engagement in Iraq as a distraction from the task of securing Afghanistan and dealing with what President Bush had termed the other two axes of evil: North Korea and Iran. The fact that the United Nations had not sanctioned the use of force to overthrow the Iraqi government was detrimental to the legitimacy of American military intervention and subsequent occupation. Turkey refused to allow U.S. forces to use its territory. France and Germany objected strenuously, while Britain remained a staunch U.S. ally. The publics of countries that did support the United States often disapproved of their governments' positions, thus aggravating tensions at home.

The ostensible reason for the invasion, the charge that Iraq possessed chemical, nuclear, and biological weapons, turned out to be false, which further undermined confidence in the U.S. mission. The United States shifted its emphasis to building democracy in Iraq as a stepping-stone to transforming the politics of the Middle East region, but the striking absence of postwar planning for such a task damaged its credibility. So, too, did U.S. support for conspicuously nondemocratic regimes that took the U.S. side in the war on terrorism. Resistance to U.S. occupation only gained strength, as the Sunni minority rejected accommodation with a new Iraqi government dominated by Shiites and Kurds. A "war of ideas" to convince Muslims that the United States was a trustworthy partner and to lay the groundwork for democratization stalled immediately. Instead, Iraq became a magnet for foreign sympathizers prone to suicide bombings. Within two years the conflict had deteriorated into a full-scale insurgency with extensive sectarian violence. To critics, the war in Iraq gave al Qaeda a new life in a second generation of leaders such as Abu Musab al-Zarqawi.

With the efficacy of U.S. policy already in doubt, revelations of mistreatment of prisoners at the Abu Ghraib prison in Iraq propelled human rights issues to the fore. Concern mounted over the use of torture by U.S. forces or by the countries to which suspects were sent, or "rendered." To these concerns were added questions about the defensive side of coping with terrorism: the effect of counterterrorist measures on domestic civil liberties. Even preventive measures were controversial: Britain, for example, was thought before the July bombings of 2005 to be far too tolerant of Islamic extremism. The reaction was then thought to go too far in the other direction, by restricting free speech. Legal coordination of the response to terrorism within the European Union still remained problematic. Asylum and immigration policies came into question.

THE FUTURE

An optimistic projection would foresee a gradual decline of Islamist-inspired militancy, as governments keep up pressure on its networks and constituencies reject the excesses of the movement. As past groups have done, the organization would exceed the bounds of its supporters' tolerance. Its appeal would thus diminish and critical social support would evaporate. Such a scenario would probably depend on a relatively stable Iraq with U.S. forces largely withdrawn. This outcome in turn would depend not just on U.S. policy but on the Iraqis themselves and also on neighboring governments, who would need to support an elected Iraqi government and to prevent infiltration of "volunteers" to assist violent opposition. The precedent of the Lebanese civil war indicates that such a process would be slow. This scenario would also assume that al Qaeda would not regenerate in new failed states.

The task for states and international organizations is to find and implement the policies that will encourage positive developments, particularly the withdrawal of support for al Qaeda or similar groups that might appear in the future. The first requirement is to recognize that terrorism is a political problem, to be solved through political means. Multilateral cooperation in police and intelligence work is the basis of an effective response. This means that counterterrorism must remain a priority at all levels of government. In addition, the sources of popular support for terrorism, even passive support, must be addressed. Otherwise, the terrorist networks that are destroyed will only grow back.

An international consensus on how to deal with terrorism would strengthen the response. UN secretary-general Kofi Annan has identified the main elements of a strategy in terms of five "D's": dissuading those who are dissatisfied from resorting to terrorism, denying them the means to act, deterring state supporters of terrorism, developing the capacity of states to deal with terrorism, and defending human rights.[26] He has called for global recognition of the unacceptability of terrorism under any circumstances and in any culture. At the same time, he has stressed that good governance and respect for human rights are essential to an effective strategy against terrorism.

In the meantime, the world will have to live with the unpredictable threat of terrorism. It can be reduced but not eliminated. And the danger should be put in perspective: terrorism is not an existential threat. Those targeted must resist the terrorists' logic, recalling that terrorists intend to provoke overreaction, polarize communities, mobilize support, and compel the abandonment of commitments. Only a response that respects democratic values and rewards peaceful means of expressing opinion can make terrorism illegitimate.

NOTES

1. United Nations High-Level Panel on Threats, Challenges, and Change, *A More Secure World: Our Shared Responsibility* (New York: United Nations, 2004), 45.

2. Ibid., 52.

3. See *The Far Enemy: Why Jihad Went Global*, by Fawaz A. Gerges (Cambridge: Cambridge University Press, 2005). Gerges explains that Salafism is an ultraconservative Islamic school of thought that "idealizes the time of the Prophet" and "advocates strict adherence to traditional Islamic values, religious orthodoxy, correct ritualistic practice, and moral issues" (pp. 131–132).

4. For some of the debate over al Qaeda's goals, see Quintan Wiktorowicz and John Kaltner, "Killing in the Name of Islam: Al-Qaeda's Justification for September 11," *Middle East Policy* 10, no. 2 (Summer 2003): 76–92; Gilles Kepel, *Jihad: The Trail of Political Islam* (Cambridge, Mass.: Harvard University Press, 2002); and Olivier Roy, *Globalized Islam: The Search for a New Ummah* (New York: Columbia University Press, 2004).

5. On the relationship between globalization and terrorism, see Audrey Kurth Cronin, "Behind the Curve: Globalization and International Terrorism," *International Security* 27, no. 3 (Winter 2002–3): 30–58.

6. For some of the debate, see Michael Mousseau, "Market Civilization and Its Clash with Terror," *International Security* 27, no. 3 (Winter 2002–3): 5–29; C. Knight, M. Murphy, and M. Mousseau, Comments, "The Sources of Terrorism," *International Security* 28, no. 2 (Spring 2003): 192–198; and Alan B. Krueger and Jitka Maleckova, "Education, Poverty and Terrorism: Is There a Causal Connection?" *Journal of Economic Perspectives* 17, no. 4 (November 2003): 119–144.

7. See Martha Crenshaw, "Political Explanations," in *Addressing the Causes of Terrorism: The Club de Madrid Series on Democracy and Terrorism*, vol. 1 (Madrid: Club de Madrid, 2005).

8. See Andrew Kydd and Barbara F. Walter, "Sabotaging the Peace: The Politics of Extremist Violence," *International Organization* 56, no. 2 (Spring 2002): 263–296.

9. On the subject of religion and terrorism, see Mark Juergensmeyer, *Terror in the Mind of God: The Global Rise of Religious Violence* (Berkeley: University of California Press, 2000).

10. See the party's official Web site: http://www.hizb-ut-tahrir.org.

11. For another overview, see Karin von Hippel, "The Roots of Terrorism: Probing the Myths," in *Superterrorism: Policy Responses,* ed. Lawrence Freedman (Oxford: Blackwell, 2002), 25–39.

12. Daniel Byman, *Deadly Connections: States That Sponsor Terrorism* (New York: Cambridge University Press, 2005).

13. Robert Pape suggests that this is the case for suicide terrorism meant to compel withdrawal from occupied territory in *Dying to Win: The Strategic Logic of Suicide Terrorism* (New York: Random House, 2005).

14. Compellence is the companion of deterrence; it is meant to make an adversary do something rather than prevent the adversary from doing something.

15. Translations of Osama bin Laden's speeches can be found in *Messages to the World: The Statements of Osama Bin Laden,* ed. Bruce Lawrence (London: Verso, 2005).

16. See, for example, Daniel Benjamin and Steven Simon, *The Age of Sacred Terror: Radical Islam's War against America* (New York: Random House, 2003).

17. For the view that al Qaeda is motivated by realpolitik rather than zealotry, see Michael Doran, "The Pragmatic Fanaticism of al Qaeda: An Anatomy of Extremism in Middle Eastern Politics," *Political Science Quarterly* 117, no. 2 (2002): 177–190.

18. Roy, *Globalized Islam.*

19. See Richard A. Falkenrath, Robert D. Newman, and Bradley A. Thayer, *America's Achilles' Heel: Nuclear, Biological, and Chemical Terrorism and Covert Attack* (Cambridge, Mass.: MIT Press, 1998); and Jessica Stern, *The Ultimate Terrorists* (Cambridge, Mass.: Harvard University Press, 1999).

20. Walter Enders and Todd Sandler find that although the 9/11 hijackings were unprecedented, transnational terrorism shows little change in its patterns before and after 9/11, other than that terrorists tend increasingly to rely on bombings rather than taking hostages. See "After 9/11: Is It All Different Now?" *Journal of Conflict Resolution* 49, no. 2 (April 2005): 259–277.

21. Hoffman says that the idea came from a novel by William Pierce, *Hunter,* ed. Andrew McDonald (National Vanguard, n.d.). See Bruce Hoffman, *Inside Terrorism* (New York: Columbia University Press, 1998), 117–119.

22. See Martha Crenshaw, "Terrorism, Strategies, and Grand Strategies," in *Attacking Terrorism: Elements of a Grand Strategy,* ed. Audrey Kurth Cronin and James M. Ludes (Washington, D.C.: Georgetown University Press, 2004), 74–93.

23. See the Transatlantic Trends Project of the German Marshall Fund of the United States, http://transatlantictrends.org. In 2005, Americans felt significantly more likely than Europeans to be personally affected by terrorism (71 percent to 53 percent).

24. See Pippa Norris, Montague Kern, and Marion Just, eds., *Framing Terrorism: The News Media, the Government, and the Public* (New York: Routledge, 2003).

25. In 1986 the Reagan administration retaliated against Libya, and in 1998 the Clinton administration used airpower against Sudan and al Qaeda camps in Afghanistan in response to the embassy bombings in East Africa. However, Israel did invade Lebanon in 1982 in order to destroy the PLO.

26. See Kofi Annan, address to the Madrid Summit on Democracy, Terrorism, and Security, March 10, 2005, http://www.un.org.

6

THE CHALLENGE OF WEAK, FAILING, AND COLLAPSED STATES

Robert I. Rotberg

NATION-STATES IN TODAY'S DANGEROUS world are categorized in descending order as strong, weak, failing, or collapsed, depending on their ability or inability to deliver high qualities and quantities of essential political goods. Strong states, primarily the globe's developed, industrial countries, consistently perform well according to that test. Weak states provide only inconsistent or limited qualities and quantities of political goods. Failed states are deficient in these ways. Collapsed states represent extreme and rare cases of failure. Strong states may slide into weakness and then into failure, but it is usually weak states that are susceptible to failing and then failure, over time. Human agency propels all of these failures. In the developing world, as indicated by the cases cited in this chapter, there is a fluid continuum; states can fail and be brought back to weakness. Even a collapsed state can be resuscitated.

This new method of classifying and ranking nation-states is based on an appreciation of the meaning of political goods. Nation-states are largely responsible, especially in the developing world, for creating and supplying political goods. That is the main purpose of states and has been since at least the seventeenth century. The most important political good is security—the projection of state power, the state monopoly of violence, and human security (freedom from criminal attack). Without security, the provision of other political goods becomes difficult, if not impossible. Those other political goods are the instruments and modalities of an effective rule of law, political freedom (including participatory institutions and fundamental human rights and civil liberties), and economic opportunity (including an appropriate regulatory environment and effective fiscal instruments). Other important political goods that nation-states are most often expected to offer include educational training, health services, a commercial and communications infrastructure, and the empowering of civil society.

Of the globe's 193 nation-states, at any one time upward of a dozen are failed or failing.

Another three dozen are weak and intrinsically in danger of slipping into or toward failure. Nepal and Haiti were endemically weak until both poor, fragile polities cascaded into failure and civil strife in 2004. Côte d'Ivoire was regarded as a strong African state until, at the turn of the present century, grievous leadership greed and errors of power produced a rapid rush toward nation-state failure and civil war. At the other end of the African continent, Zimbabwe, also a strong state, descended from 1998 through 2006 to the very brink of failure, with much human misery and state-sponsored brutality, but no all-out civil war.

Sudan and the Democratic Republic of the Congo, enmeshed in one or more enduring conflicts, are classic failed states. They are failed because of their intrinsic insecurities as well as because each is unable to supply necessary political goods to its inhabitants. Afghanistan, with partial security and few political goods; Burundi, with ongoing hostilities and a government unable to provide many political goods; Nepal, without security or many political goods; and Haiti, devoid of an effective national government and riddled with insecurity, are additional failed states. Bolivia, because of its current insecurity and its weakened government, may have been very close to failure in 2005. Kyrgyzstan is another precariously poised failing state. Liberia and Sierra Leone are recovering failed states, moving upward on the scale toward mere weakness.

The sometime geographical expression of Somalia illustrates the stage of full-state failure that approximates collapse. Somalia has only its internationally accepted territorial borders. Nothing else exists, hence its characterization as a collapsed polity. Warlords (nonstate actors) for fifteen years until mid-2006 did provide some security in the cities and districts that they controlled. But the sway of the warlords was removed in mid-2006 when the shadowy Islamic Courts Union gathered sufficient firepower to oust them and began imposing an Islamist, sharia-based fundamentalist order on much of hitherto unruly Somalia. Its rise to power was based on the Union's growing influence over local mosques and Islamic schools throughout the collapsed entity. It had begun providing modest political goods in the late 1990s. In 2006, the Union seemed capable of providing security, Islamic law and education, and rudimentary additional desirable benefits to the inhabitants of much of Somalia (south of Puntland, and not including Somaliland, the de facto nation-state that has carved itself out of the northern section of the larger Somalia). Lebanon, Afghanistan, and Tajikistan were once collapsed states, as well, but all have strengthened thanks to outside intervention and resulting gains in security.

It is important to make clear distinctions among and between nation-states and to classify them in this way: strong, weak, failing, failed, and collapsed. Doing so helps to distinguish the positive and negative qualities of nation-states in the developing world in order to respond to their needs, prevent them from descending from strength to weakness and failure, and rebuild the ones that are eventually overwhelmed by outright failure. Good policy decisions flow from an appreciation of the differences between these kinds of nation-states and especially of how certain kinds of weak nation-states in the developing world are almost always driven by their leaders into the full embrace of failure.

In the post-9/11 world, too, failed and collapsed states bear watching because their very insecurity could potentially create havens for al Qaeda (as in Sudan and Afghanistan in the 1990s) or harbor terrorist cells capable of regrouping, training, and preparing bombing operations (as in Somalia before the car bombings of the U.S. embassies in Nairobi and Dar es Salaam in 1998 and before the missile attacks at the Mombasa airport in 2002).[1]

Moreover, even absent the possibility of terrorist activities, failed states are responsible for most of the intrastate hostility in the world. Nearly all of the hot wars of the world are within states; about fourteen million persons, mostly civilians, have lost their lives since 1990 as a result of civil wars. Another ten million have been driven from their homes, many into camps for refugees or internally displaced persons. Hostilities in the Democratic Republic of the Congo, Sudan, and Angola account for two-thirds of both totals, but the internal wars in Afghanistan, Sri Lanka, Cambodia, Indonesia, and now Nepal, Côte d'Ivoire, and Haiti account for a fair share. Because failure always leads to civil war, if nation-state failure could be reduced or eliminated, much of the globe's civil conflict would vanish, millions of lives would be spared, and people everywhere would live longer and with greater degrees of happiness and satisfaction. Conditions of hunger, in some cases real famine, would also be reduced or eliminated.

The enemy of sustainable economic and political development is conflict, in terms of lives lost or immiserated and in terms of vast expenditures on arms and ammunition. Relief also adds to the accumulated expenses of state failure and collapse. World order never sits idly by when humanitarian crises erupt. It even supplies emergency food rations to populations starved by their own regimes—by despots controlling the food supply to gain power and control, as in North Korea and Zimbabwe.

GOVERNANCE AND POLITICAL GOODS

Nation-states do not stumble into failure. Human agency is always the proximate cause. Even resource-deficient and climatically or physically challenged nation-states, the very weakest of the weak, teeter on the precipice of failure only if and when they cheat their citizens or give unfair preference to one set of elites over another or over ordinary citizens. Corruption precedes and favors failure. So do capital flight, escalating inflation, growing rates of infant mortality and decreasing life expectancy, the harassment of civil society, electoral fraud, the creation of private mili-

tias, small arms races, identity controversies, disenfranchisement of ethnic groups, threats to judicial independence, and the strengthening of state security apparatuses. These institutional and normative breakdowns reflect, but do not cause, the slide within a nation-state from strength and weakness toward incipient failure.

Fortunately for analytical purposes, these slippages can be measured precisely. There need be no reliance on anecdotal or impressionistic calibrations. Strength, weakness, failure, and collapse are categories that describe the extent to which a nation-state delivers appropriately high qualities and appropriately abundant quantities of essential political goods —the critical ingredients of good governance.

Governance is the effective provision of political goods to citizens.[2] Of those political goods, the paramount one is security. There can be no economic growth or social elevation, and no societal strength as opposed to failure, without fundamental security. A nation-state's primary function is to secure the nation and its territory—to prevent cross-border invasions and incursions, to reduce domestic threats to or attacks on the national order, to bolster human security by lowering crime rates, and to enable citizens to resolve their differences with fellow inhabitants or with the state itself without recourse to arms or physical coercion. If a nation-state merely controls its capital city, if it cannot project power to the periphery, if it does not have a monopoly on the use of force within its borders, and if it cannot repress secessionists and potential rebels, then the nation-state has failed or is verging on failure.

In contrast to strong states, failed nation-states cannot control their frontiers. They have lost authority over large swaths of their nominal territory. Often, the expression of official power becomes limited to a capital city (say, Kabul or Kinshasa) and one or a handful of ethnically specific provinces. The extent of a state's failure can indeed be measured by exactly how much of a nation-state's geographical expanse is genuinely subject to the writ (especially after dark) of the official authorities. In 2005, for example, Côte d'Ivoire's government controlled only the southern half of its country. In the 1980s, Mobutu Sese Seko's regime lost authority up-country and progressively thereafter throughout the rest of Zaire/Congo. Nonstate actors appear and gain control as district warlords when the central government no longer can extend its rule effectively across the national patrimony.

Citizens depend on the central governments of nation-states to secure their persons and free them from fear. Thus, when such human security is not provided (and crime rates escalate), the faltering nation-state's failure becomes obvious to its citizens long before rebel groups and other contenders threaten the official government and go to war.

The civil wars that characterize failed states often stem from or have roots in ethnic, religious, linguistic, or other intercommunal enmities. The fear of the other that drives so much ethnic conflict stimulates and fuels hostilities between regimes and subordinate and less-favored groups. Avarice also propels that antagonism, especially when official greed is magnified by dreams of loot from discoveries of new, contested sources of resource wealth—petroleum deposits, diamond fields, gold, or timber. But the outbreak of civil war, whether ostensibly ethnic, linguistic, or religious in character, is almost always a product of leadership decisions that consciously deprive minorities or oppressed majorities of what they consider their human rights, their equal economic opportunities, their appropriate share of official positions, or the social and political goods that they believe they justifiably deserve. For these out-groups, something vital snaps, and the nation-state and its ruling regime decisively forfeit legitimacy. A typical weak state edges toward failure when ruler-led oppression provokes a countervailing reaction on the part of resentful groups (often already termed rebels).

Civil war takes advantage of losses of legitimacy and underlying security weaknesses that have become apparent as the nation-state has been sliding from strength or weakness toward failure.

THE OTHER POLITICAL GOODS

The delivery of other desirable political goods becomes feasible only when reasonable provisions of security are obtained. After security—the prime commodity—good governance requires a predictable, recognizable, systematized method of adjudicating disputes and regulating both the norms and the prevailing mores of the society or societies in question. This political good implies codes and procedures that together compose an enforceable body of law, security of property and the enforceability of contracts, an effective judicial system, and a set of norms that legitimate and validate traditional or new values embodied in what (in shorthand) is called the rule of law. Each of the world's nation-states fashions its own rule of law; the English common law and the Napoleonic systems are but two major jurisprudential methodologies, and most national modalities of adjudicating disputes roughly follow one or other of those outlines. But there are other forms, either ethnically traditional or sharia-like. Without some such formal or formalized body of laws, societal bonds weaken, disputes are settled by violent means rather than peaceful parleys, and commerce cannot proceed smoothly.

Another political good supplied in greater or lesser degrees in the developing world enables citizens to participate freely, openly, and fully in a democratic political process. This good encompasses fundamental freedoms and rights—the right to participate in politics and compete for office; respect and support for national and provincial political institutions, legislatures, and courts; tolerance of dissent and difference; an independent media; and all of the basic civil and human rights. Earnest accountability is provided by the second and fourth of these freedoms. It comes through an independent, well-functioning judicial system, but also because of a fearless, free media. Few state failures have occurred in countries with open media—with privately run television channels and radio stations and a free press. Without such methods of criticism, political freedom and accountability shrink, rulers and ruling regimes can prey on their citizens (as they do in failing and failed states), and nation-state failure can occur without the wider world realizing the full dimension of a nation-state's difficult predicament.

Another critical political good and component of governance is the creation of an enabling environment permissive of and conducive to economic growth and prosperity at national and personal levels. This political good thus encompasses a prudently run money and banking system, usually guided by a central bank and lubricated by a national currency; a fiscal and institutional context within which citizens may pursue individual entrepreneurial goals and potentially prosper; and a regulatory environment appropriate to the economic aspirations and attributes of the nation-state. Where a ruling family or clan arrogates to itself most of the available sources of economic growth, already weak states become weaker and descend toward failure. Likewise, a rapid rise in corruption levels signals the possibility of failure. (The world's failed states all fall near the bottom of Transparency International's annual "Corruption Perceptions Index.")[3] Plummeting GDP figures, both for per capita income and annual growth rates, also are diagnostic, especially in relatively wealthy developing countries such as Côte d'Ivoire and Zimbabwe.

Corruption is fundamental to failed states. Not only does it flourish in failed states, but in them it thrives on an unusually destructive scale. Widespread petty or lubricating corruption exists as a matter of course, but failed states are noted for rising levels of venal corruption: kick-backs on anything that can be put out to fake tender or bid (medical supplies, textbooks, bridge constructions, roads, railways, tourism concessions, new airports, and so on); unnecessarily wasteful construction projects arranged so as to maximize the rents that they are capable of generating; licenses for existing or imaginary enterprises and activities; and a persistent and generalized extortion. Moreover, corrupt ruling elites invest their profits overseas, not at home, thus contributing yet further to the economic attrition of their own states. Rulers of failed states also characteristically dip directly into shrinking state treasuries to pay for external aggressions, lavish residences and palaces (Hasting K. Banda in Malawi constructed thirteen enormous mansions, Robert Gabriel Mugabe in Zimbabwe a mere five), and extensive overseas travel (often to purchase luxury goods) and to ensure the loyalty of their soldiers and security brigades.

Infrastructure (the physical arteries of commerce), education, and medical treatment are three other key political goods, nearly always responsibilities of governments. With rulers and ruling classes siphoning off a country's cash reserves and foreign exchange supplies, with overseas investment drying up, with capital flight, and with inflation rising, governments run out of cash. Official services cease and the delivery of political goods becomes a tertiary priority compared to personal survival.

Metaphorically, the more potholes in main roads (or main roads turned to rutted tracks), the more a state is failing. As there are fewer capital resources for road crews, equipment, and raw materials, so the nation-state's infrastructure slowly erodes or vanishes. Furthermore, maintaining road or rail access to distant districts becomes less and less of a priority. Landline telephone systems (in nearly all developing countries a utility owned and operated by the state) likewise deteriorate and mobile telephones become the only option.

The national educational and health systems suffer similarly from increasing neglect.

Teachers, physicians, nurses, orderlies, and technicians are paid late, if at all. Absenteeism rates naturally increase. Textbooks and medicines become scarce. X-ray and other vital machines break down and are not repaired. In such a situation of impending failure, citizens, especially rural parents, students, and patients, gradually realize that the state is abandoning or has abandoned them to the forces of nature. When the nation-state ceases in this manner to provide basic services, or only provides them at a very low level, it is failing.

The markers for these kinds of lapses, and failure, are declining literacy rates, decreasing levels of educational persistence, rises in infant mortality and (sometimes massive) decreases in life expectancy levels, the spread of HIV/AIDS and other infectious diseases, lowered national health expenditures per person, the loss of physicians, and widespread neglect of hospitals, clinics, and equipment.

The greater Horn of Africa region, including neighboring Yemen, provides a useful comparative example. There, except for Kenya, all of the countries and areas are poor, with underdeveloped road and rail systems, creaky sea and river ports and airports, poor traditional telephone systems and limited teledensity (levels of phone ownership), and low rates of Internet connectivity. Likewise, again except for Kenya and northern Sudan, their health and educational systems are either nearly nonexistent or primitive (even by prevailing limited African standards). In the medical services field, for example, in 2001 there was one physician per 35,000 people in Ethiopia, one per 33,000 in Eritrea, one per 25,000 in Somalia, one per 11,000 in Sudan, one per 7,500 in Kenya, one per 7,100 in Djibouti, and one per 5,000 in Yemen. The Africa-wide average in 2001 was one per about 13,800.

In terms of the number of hospital beds per 1,000 people, Djibouti has more than two, Kenya and Sudan more than one, and all the others a few tenths of a bed. Ethiopia has only 0.24 hospital beds per 1,000. In terms of health expenditures as percentage of GDP, Kenya spends the most (nearly 8 percent), Djibouti and Eritrea follow with 7 percent and 5.7 percent, respectively, and Ethiopia brings up the rear with 1.4 percent.[4] The all-Africa average is about 2.1 percent of GDP.

It comes as no surprise, given these startlingly low health delivery numbers, that infant mortality rates in the region per 1,000 live births range from 133 in Somalia and 114 in Ethiopia down to a comparatively welcome figure of 59 in Eritrea. The all-Africa average is 94.4. Estimated life expectancy at birth in this region ranges from a high of fifty-one years in Eritrea to a low of forty-two in Ethiopia.

What such numbers tell us is that the countries of the greater Horn of Africa region, on average, have delivered poor political goods to their citizens. State failure in a massive territory like Sudan, and total collapse and the lack of most security in Somalia, plus an interstate war between Ethiopia and Eritrea, have contributed to this paucity of political goods. Few of these states have more than rudimentary rules of law, and the canons of political freedom are much honored in the breach. Even so, except for Somalia before 2006, these polities are secure, in some cases oppressively so. Thus, in addition to Somalia, only Sudan (with an ongoing war in Darfur and the provision of few other political goods) is a failed state. But most of the other nation-states of the region (bar Kenya but including Yemen) clearly contain the seeds of failure. The emergence of civil strife in any of them could readily transform weakness into failure.

THE SIGNIFICANCE OF HUMAN AGENCY

Nation-states do not become failed because of structural lapses or global trade issues. Nor do they fail in a fit of absence of mind. Instead, they are failed by the purposeful actions of a leader or leaders. Presidents Mobutu Sese Seko in Zaire/Congo, Siaka Stevens in Sierra

Leone, Samuel Doe and Charles Taylor in Liberia, Gaafar Mohamed el-Nimeiri in Sudan, and Idi Amin in Uganda (to mention only a few of those personally culpable, like General Ne Win in Burma, for nation-state decline and decay) are all tyrants who systematically deprived their constituents of fundamental political goods, ultimately even the overriding political good of security. They each provoked or demanded civil strife in order to profit from the resulting insecurities or otherwise drove their loyal and long-suffering citizens into rebellion by acts of outright discrimination or communal marginalization (as in Côte d'Ivoire and Sri Lanka) or by the wholesale theft or threatened theft of national resources (as in Sierra Leone and Sudan).

A detailed appreciation of the actions of each of those men, year after year, would demonstrate the dynamics of failure and how it is caused. But none is still in office and five are dead. Instead, our analysis of the critical influence of leadership decisions and motivations on state failure is well illustrated by an example of purposeful predation— the case of President Mugabe and failing, but in 2006 not yet fully failed, Zimbabwe.

When Africans finally created a free new nation of Zimbabwe in 1980, Mugabe became first its prime minister and then its president. He gradually gathered all of the reins of power into his own hands. Nevertheless, for much of the country's first eighteen years, nearly all important political goods— security, rule of law, economic opportunity, infrastructure provisions, education, health, and the empowerment of civil society—were delivered in reasonable abundance. Mugabe indeed provided very high levels of educational opportunity, good medical services, strong state security, low rates of crime, and excellent roads and other arteries of commerce. Corruption existed but was held in check. Economic growth was largely positive, based on reasonably solid macroeconomic and microeconomic fundamentals, a well-organized

monetary and banking system, and a comparatively open trading system. Only freedom to campaign politically against Mugabe and the ruling Zimbabwe African National Union–Patriotic Front (ZANU-PF) was curtailed, with increasing severity. (Mugabe also ordered the killing of twenty thousand to thirty thousand of his Sindebele-speaking opponents in 1982–84, but most Zimbabweans and outside observers tended to ignore that ruthless demonstration of a ruler's wrath.) There was freedom of expression in daily life (unlike in, say, Burma), but Mugabe's regime owned or controlled nearly all radio, television, and press outlets. Thus accountability was limited, even though the judicial system remained independent.

This relatively satisfactory and stable arrangement, with Mugabe running a forceful, authoritarian regime and increasingly intimidating or otherwise marginalizing a few brave African opponents, unraveled in the late 1990s. Mugabe started looting the coffers of the state, permitting his relatives and associates to exceed previous levels of greed. Corruption ran rampant; citizens became increasingly cynical where previously they had been loyal and supportive. As Mugabe's legitimacy eroded, he sent thirteen thousand soldiers into Congo to support another dictator. That costly maneuver, coupled with corruption and the movement of cash overseas, bankrupted Zimbabwe. Consumer shortages of fuel and staple commodities followed. The population grew restive and rejected the provisions of a constitutional referendum, favored by Mugabe, early in 2000. He wanted increased powers, which voters denied him after a surprisingly successful grassroots campaign.[5]

Mugabe, never seriously challenged before, grew more threatened and angry. He unleashed a wave of thugs against white (and sometimes black) commercial farmers—the backbone of the national economy. As four thousand white farmers were forced off their farms, production plummeted and four hundred thousand African farmworkers lost their sources of employment. The national economy naturally fell backward, especially after Mugabe rigged or otherwise stole the parliamentary elections of 2000 and 2005 and the presidential poll of 2002, thus denying an emergent opposition any opportunity to propel Zimbabwe back along the path of prosperity and sanity.

FAILING ZIMBABWE

Zimbabwe, a strong state by African and developing world standards until 1998, has since descended rapidly into weakness and to the very brink of failure. Numbers tell the story. Since 1998, thanks to Mugabe's depredations, annual GDP per capita in Zimbabwe has slumped from $800 to $400. A country once growing at a steady 5 percent a year has gone backward by 40 to 50 percent since 2000. A recent study reports that the standard of living of Zimbabweans in 2005 fell in real terms to 1953 levels. About 80 percent of all adult Zimbabweans are unemployed. The local dollar, once stronger than the U.S. dollar, and in 1998 worth about Z$38 to US$1, steadily collapsed to a mid-2006 level of Z$150,000 to US$1. Annual inflation flew well beyond 1,000 percent, the highest rate in the world.

Equally important, by 2000, the country's once-vaunted rule of law was breaking down. Mugabe was reviling and interfering with the courts or refusing to abide by their decisions. Torture of opponents occurred. The presses of the only independent daily newspaper were bombed, and that paper was later banned. Hospitals stopped providing medicines, sutures, and even bandages. Schools lost teachers and textbooks and fell into disuse. A superbly maintained road network decayed. There were periodic shortages of fundamental consumer goods, especially throughout 2005 and 2006, when gasoline, diesel fuel, cooking oil, flour, and many other commodities were unobtainable at almost any price. Indeed, since early

2004, Zimbabwe has experienced serious food scarcities and pockets of extreme hunger and starvation. In 2005, to compound the misery that the regime had inflicted on its citizens, Mugabe unleashed a reign of terror on urban shanty dwellers, most of whom presumably backed the opposition. As many as 1.2 million Zimbabweans lost their homes and small businesses, being forced to flee in the deep cold of winter into rural areas where there was no work and little food. A UN report condemned Mugabe's actions in thus harming his own citizens randomly and arbitrarily, but little international action followed.[6] Possibly the strongest indication of Zimbabwe's near failure is reflected in its alarming emigration statistics. At least two million Zimbabweans (of a nation of twelve million) since 2002 have fled the country for South Africa, Botswana, and Mozambique.

Zimbabwe raced pell-mell toward failure in 2006. The state's delivery of most political goods virtually ceased. All kinds of numbers point to the parlous quality of state services, and to the deep consternation—a typical indication of failure or near failure—of the citizens of Zimbabwe. However, in 2006 the state still controlled the exercise of legitimate and illegitimate sources of violence. Mugabe even felt strong or desperate enough to rebuff Nigerian and South African diplomatic interventions. Although everyone is preyed on, and Mugabe's opponents are pilloried and repressed, in 2006 the state still projected power throughout the entire country and effectively forestalled rebellion. When this situation changes, and if and when civil war breaks out between Mugabe loyalists and regime opponents, then Zimbabwe (like so many other weak and failing states) can be called failed.

MATTERS OF POLICY

These distinctions between types of states are more than arbitrary or academic. As in Zimbabwe, impending failure highlights a serious situation that threatens world order because of the harm that such failure inflicts on a nation-state's people and because the failure that accompanies the rise of anomie and state-sponsored terror, unless checked, can seem internationally sanctioned.

Separating the failed and failing nation-states from those that are merely weak, albeit desperately poor and lacking effective leadership, permits policymakers to focus their preventive energies on weak countries at risk and their reconstruction talents on those that have failed. A careful analysis of nation-state failure and collapse, moreover, permits policymakers to distinguish those failed or near-failed states that are primarily threats only to themselves and their unfortunate inhabitants from those rogue states that possess weapons of mass destruction and for that reason or because of other capabilities pose serious threats to world order. Most rogue nation-states attack their own populations and hold them hostage (as in North Korea), but they are also very secure places and so escape being classified as failed.[7]

A DYNAMIC PROCESS

The failure and collapse of nation-states is a dynamic process. Little is foreordained. No matter how impoverished a state may be, it need not fail. The origins of a state, whether arbitrary or absentminded (as in much of colonialism), again do not predispose to, or fully account for, failure. States born weak and forlorn, such as Botswana, have emerged strong and high performing as a consequence of gifted leadership and not primarily as a result of a subsequent resource bonanza. Wealth must be well managed and distributed genuinely if a nation-state, such as Nigeria or Equatorial Guinea, is to emerge from weakness and become stronger; otherwise there is always the possibility of slippage (as in Nigeria in the 1980s) and failure. In other words, the road to failure is littered with serious mistakes of omission and commission. Where, especially in fragile, isolated states in the developing world, there is little accountability and no political culture of democracy, these errors of commission are almost always made for personal gain by leaders. Human agency (and greed) drives and accounts for failure, or near failure, as in the ongoing cases of Zimbabwe and Côte d'Ivoire, as in Mobutu Sese Seko's Congo, and as in Idi Amin's Uganda. Likewise, nation-states strengthen under positive leadership for good, as in President John Kufuor's Ghana, Nelson Mandela's South Africa, Sir Seretse Khama's Botswana, and Sir Seewoosagur Ramgoolam's Mauritius.[8]

Failure, it should be said, does not creep stealthily into the domain of a body politic. Its pending arrival is there for all to see—if we would but notice. Three kinds of signals—economic, political, and military—provide clear, timely, and actionable warnings. On the economic front, for example, Lebanon in 1972–79, Nigeria in 1993–99, Indonesia in 1997–99, and Zimbabwe in 1998–2005 offered ample early warning signals. In each case, rapid reductions in income and living standards presaged the possibility of failure early enough to have been noted and for preventive measures to have been encouraged from outside or explored from within.

THE DOWNWARD SPIRAL

Once the downward spiral starts in earnest, only a concerted, determined effort slows its momentum. Corrupt autocrats and their equally corrupt associates usually have few incentives to arrest their state's slide. They themselves find clever ways to benefit from impoverishment and misery; they are not the ones to suffer. As foreign and domestic investment dries up, jobs vanish, and per capita incomes fall, the mass of citizens in an imperiled state see their health, educational, and infrastructural entitlements erode. Food and fuel shortages occur. Privation and hunger follow.

Typically, as the poor get poorer, ruling cadres get richer. State treasuries are skimmed, currency perquisites are employed for private gain, illicit gun and narcotics trafficking increase in scale, and secret funds flow out of the country into private structures and nonpublic bank accounts.

In the political realm, too, available indicators are abundant. First, "maximum leaders" and their associates subvert democratic norms, restrict participatory processes of all kinds, coerce civil society, and override institutional checks and balances supposedly secure in legislatures and bureaucracies. Second, they curtail judicial independence, harass the media, and suborn security forces. In other words, rulers show more and more contempt for their own nationals; surround themselves with family, lineage, or ethnic allies; and greatly narrow the focus of their concern and responsibility. Many of these arrogant leaders grandly drive down national boulevards in massive motorcades, commandeer national commercial aircraft for foreign excursions, put their faces prominently on national currencies and on large photographs in private as well as public places, and are seemingly convinced—as was Louis XIV—that the state and the riches of the state are theirs to dispose.

A third indicator is derived directly from levels of violence. If they rise precipitously, the state clearly is crumbling. As national human security levels decline, the probability of failure increases. Not every civil conflict precipitates failure, but each offers a warning sign. Indeed, absolute or relative crime rates and civilian combat death counts cannot prescribe failure conclusively. But they indicate that a society is deteriorating and that the glue that binds a new or an old state is becoming dangerously thin.

There are implicit tipping points. Yet, even as a weak state is becoming a failing state and seemingly plunging rapidly toward failure, desperate descents can be arrested by timely external diplomatic or military intervention.

Usually, however, those interventions are too timid and tepid or much too late. People in the thousands thus die, as in Cambodia, East Timor, Rwanda, Sudan (and Darfur), Congo, Sierra Leone, Liberia, and Lebanon. Many thousands of others flee their homes for sanctuaries or refugee camps.

There is a better way, and the recommendations of the UN secretary-general's High-Level Panel on Threats, Challenges, and Change provided a firm guide to what is needed and should be done. Under guidelines adapted by the UN General Assembly in 2005, a "responsibility to protect" is now officially recognized. Responsibility to protect means that the United Nations and other forces of world order have an obligation, in keeping with Chapter VII of the UN Charter, to enter sovereign territory to prevent the abuse of civilians even if it is a national government that is the attacking party. This new norm supports a strengthened UN security apparatus. Together with an enlarged Department of Peacekeeping Operations, the United Nations now has the moral and logistical tools that could contribute to diplomatic and military interventions if and when nation-states slip toward failure. There thus is a proactive trigger for action that now depends less on individual national initiative than on the United Nations. Serious implementation has still to be tested; whether the importance of sovereignty will trump abuse or be balanced judiciously against the need to protect innocent lives in states that are failing is still to be seen.

In terms of the responsibility-to-protect norm, and because there have been many past examples and several more contemporary cases where presidents willfully destroyed their own states and the livelihoods and social welfare of millions of their own constituents, egregious new infractions rightfully would compel effective regional- or UN-supervised interventions. Given the global failure to intervene in Rwanda and Bosnia until too late, and given the dithering in 2004, 2005, and 2006 over

Darfur, the United Nations' and the globe's major powers would, under the new norm, internalize a moral imperative to intervene—if only to save lives. But political will remains weak, and world order impotent. The United Nations and larger powers usually wait to become involved until intrastate hostilities become too hot, and too many people die, or until foreign nationals are threatened. By then, as in Zimbabwe and Darfur, or earlier in Liberia and Sierra Leone, it is far too late. Recognizing failure early as the threat that it is to world order should encourage timely and more effective responses. Applying an odious label—"failed"—helps.

Preventive diplomacy by the United Nations and world powers is the first line of action in attempting to arrest a slide toward failure. Sanctions are an additional response. Then various kinds of interventions under Chapter VII may be necessary. If, however, as nearly always occurs and may continue to occur even under the new UN arrangements, states do continue to stumble and fail, world order has a responsibility to resuscitate and reconstruct. In postconflict situations there is an urgent humanitarian as well as a security need for conscientious, well-crafted nation building—for a systematic refurbishing of the political, economic, and social fabric of countries that have crumbled, that have failed to perform and provide political goods of quality and in quantity, and that have become threats to themselves and to others. Good governance needs to be reintroduced into polities that have failed. Legal systems need to be re-created. Economies need to be jump-started.[9] Sometimes, as in Haiti, the United Nations needs to take temporary control, as a trustee. This last point is very controversial but is becoming another emerging norm.

The examples of Tajikistan and Lebanon, two failed states that have recovered to the point of weakness and strength, respectively, demonstrate that it can be done—that failure and collapse are not end points but way sta-

tions. In both countries, neighbors—Syria and Russia, respectively—intervened and imposed security, enabling rebuilding to occur.[10] Furthermore, the accomplishments of the UN transitional administrations in Cambodia and East Timor, and of the NATO/EU/UN interim administration in Kosovo, suggest that effective postconflict nation building is possible if there is sufficient political will, if individual outside countries (such as Australia) exert it and take the lead, and if there exists targeted, well-funded, and carefully utilized external aid.

CONTINUING WEAKNESS AND FAILURE

There are always more weak nation-states than failed ones, and in almost any era a handful of the weak ones are at risk for failing. Haiti slipped into this category and failed, after decades of deplorable weakness but little civil strife. Then internal battles began as national security deteriorated, narco-traffickers and nonstate actors took charge, and an interim administration proved dramatically incapable of delivering any of the basic bundles of political goods.

There are more Haitis to follow. Paraguay is always at risk. Bolivia, its neighbor, harbors irreconcilable class conflicts and its regimes are incapable of keeping order, much less providing fundamental political goods. Ecuador and Peru are both weak and capable of floundering further. Guyana is mired in ethnic competition, with few resources and poor leadership. Chad, Guinea, and even oil-rich Nigeria are additional candidates for failure unless their present and future rulers can develop capabilities to satisfy restive citizenries that required political goods will arrive and be well shared. In the Pacific region, Papua New Guinea is very insecure, exhibiting extremely high rates of crime and disorder and limited governance performance, and harboring at least one festering secessionist movement. Indonesia was until recently in a roughly similar situation, but clear-sighted leadership, a successful peace process in Aceh, the moderating of other conflictual situations across the country's vast archipelago, and a strengthening of the delivery of decentralized democracy have greatly improved that once-failing state's prospects.[11]

States falling in the category of odious dictatorship—the worst of the worst among nation-states—fail rapidly once the all-powerful ruler or ruling junta loses its dominance of the local security apparatus. Iraq was one of those places. Now Belarus, Burma, Cuba, Equatorial Guinea, Iran, Libya, North Korea, Syria, Togo, Turkmenistan, Uzbekistan, and Zimbabwe are candidates for failure and even collapse when and if there are effective revolts or the leader's mailed fist atrophies. Each of these cases delivers only security and is held together by oppression and the denial of human rights. Other political goods are largely provided only symbolically, or in limited amounts. Hollow nation-states harboring the incubus of failure they may be, but they cascade into failure only when regimes cease projecting power and start brutalizing their citizens.

Unless the United Nations or the big powers develop an effective series of mechanisms to forestall failure by diplomatic, technical, or military means—a highly unlikely proposition in the modern era—the phenomenon of nation-state failure will remain for years and decades, and the peoples of those deprived and depraved polities will continue to suffer at the hands of avaricious rulers. Their human rights will be abused, their civil liberties curtailed, their economic opportunities foreclosed, and their life expectancies limited until the forces of world order decide that despotism and tyranny are serious, overriding threats to global stability and prosperity. The precariousness of the Congos, Sudans, and Somalias of the current age are, alas, destined to be duplicated elsewhere around the globe in this decade and the next.

NOTES

1. See the detailed discussion of this possibility in Robert I. Rotberg, ed., *Battling Terrorism in the Horn of Africa* (Washington, D.C.: Brookings Institution Press, 2005).

2. For the argument, see Robert I. Rotberg, "The Failure and Collapse of Nation-States: Breakdown, Prevention, and Repair," in *When States Fail: Causes and Consequences,* ed. Robert I. Rotberg (Princeton, N.J.: Princeton University Press, 2004), 3–10; and Robert I. Rotberg and Deborah West, *The Good Governance Problem: Doing Something About It* (Cambridge, Mass.: World Peace Foundation, 2004).

3. See Transparency International, "Corruption Perceptions Index 2005" (Berlin: Transparency International, 2005), http://www.transparency.org/cpi/2005/cpi2004.en.html.

4. Victoria Inez Salinas compiled these figures in 2005 at the Program on Intrastate Conflict and Conflict Resolution, the Kennedy School of Government, Harvard University. She derived them from World Bank and World Health Organization data for various years and from national data.

5. For more details on Mugabe's tyranny, see Robert I. Rotberg, "Africa's Mess, Mugabe's Mayhem," *Foreign Affairs* 79 (July–August 2000): 47–61.

6. Anna Kajumulo Tibaijuka, *Reports of the Fact-Finding Mission to Zimbabwe to Assess the Scope and Impact of Operation Murambatsvina* (United Nations, July 18, 2005). The author was the UN special envoy on human settlements issues in Zimbabwe.

7. For the theory and practice of rogue states, see Robert I. Rotberg, ed., *The Worst of the Worst: Rogue and Repressive States in World Order* (forthcoming).

8. See Robert I. Rotberg, "The Roots of Africa's Leadership Deficit," *Compass* 1 (2003): 28–32.

9. For the method, see Nat J. Colletta, Markus Costner, and Ingo Wiederhofer, "Disarmament, Demobilization, and Reintegration: Lessons and Liabilities in Reconstruction," in *When States Fail,* 170–181.

10. For details, see the relevant country chapters, by Oren Barak and Nasrin Dadmehr, in *State Failure and State Weakness in a Time of Terror,* ed. Robert I. Rotberg (Washington, D.C.: Brookings Institution Press, 2003).

11. For a discussion of Indonesia when failure was more probable, see Michael Malley, "Indonesia: The Erosion of State Capacity," in ibid., 183–218.

7

STATE MAKING, STATE BREAKING, AND STATE FAILURE

Mohammed Ayoob

STATE BREAKING AND STATE FAILURE, both unavoidable accompaniments of the state-making process, lie at the root of most conflicts that the international system has witnessed since the end of World War II. The veracity of this assertion is demonstrated by two generally accepted facts. The first is the incontestable reality that the overwhelming majority of conflicts since the end of World War II have been located in the postcolonial countries that constitute the Third World. The second is the equally incontrovertible fact that most such conflicts either have been primarily intrastate in character or have possessed a substantial intrastate dimension, even if they appear to the outside observer to be interstate conflicts.[1] This means that problems of international and domestic order have become closely intertwined during the current era and are likely to remain so well into the foreseeable future.

The validity of both these assertions, that is to say, the concentration of conflicts in the Third World and the primacy of domestic

sources of conflict, is confirmed by the latest data presented in the *SIPRI Yearbook 2005.* These data demonstrate that all nineteen major armed conflicts that were recorded in 2004 were classified as intrastate in character. However, the report makes clear that "[i]n a reversal of the classic spill-over of conflict from intra- to inter-state, developments in Iraq during 2004 raised the prospect of an international conflict creating a fully fledged civil war."[2] Iraq, therefore, stands out as the exception that proves the rule. In the previous year, 2003, SIPRI (the Stockholm International Peace Research Institute) had identified nineteen major armed conflicts as well, but had noted that two of them, the conflict between India and Pakistan over Kashmir and the invasion of Iraq by the United States and the United Kingdom, were interstate in character.[3] While both Kashmir and Iraq continued to figure in the 2004 list, the basic character of these conflicts was perceived as having been changed by the amelioration of the India-Pakistan dimension of the Kashmir conflict on the one hand and the "success" of the U.S. invasion on the other.

Almost all of the conflicts in 2003 and 2004 were located in the old or new Third World, as had been the case in previous years. The new Third World refers to states in Central Asia, the Caucasus, and the Balkans that emerged out of the disintegration of the Soviet Union and the dismemberment of Yugoslavia. In terms of their colonial background, the arbitrary construction of their boundaries by external powers, the lack of societal cohesion, their recent emergence into juridical statehood, and their stage of economic and political development, the states of the Caucasus and Central Asia and of the Balkans demonstrate political, economic, and social characteristics that are in many ways akin to those of the Asian, African, and Latin American states that have traditionally been considered as constituting the Third World. There are abundant data, therefore, to support the conclusion that the overwhelming majority of conflicts in the international system since 1945 have been "a ubiquitous corollary of the birth, formation, and fracturing of Third World states."[4]

STATE MAKING IN THE THIRD WORLD

The events since the early 1990s, by removing the Second World from the international equation, have helped present the dichotomy between the global core and the global periphery —the First World and the Third World—in very stark terms. By eliminating the Cold War overlay from Third World conflicts and thus exposing their fundamental local dynamics, the end of bipolarity has also demonstrated the close linkage between these conflicts and the dynamics of state making (and its obverse, state breaking and state failure) currently under way in the global periphery. The proliferation of conflicts in the periphery, when compared with the image of relative tranquillity within and amity among the industrialized countries of Western Europe and North America, has

augmented the impression that there are actually two distinct zones in the international system—the zone of peace in the North and the zone of turmoil in the South—and that the two work according to different logics, a Lockean one in the former and a Hobbesian one in the latter.[5]

However, this dichotomous representation of the First and Third Worlds hides the essential similarity in their process of state making, which has been (and is) crucial in determining the political trajectories of states. This point becomes clear if one compares the current situation in the Third World, not with that prevailing within and among the industrial democracies today, but with the situation from the sixteenth to the eighteenth century in Western Europe, when the earliest of the modern sovereign states were at a stage of state making that corresponded with the stage where most Third World states find themselves today.[6]

Youssef Cohen and colleagues have most succinctly defined the process of state making as "primitive central state power accumulation."[7] Thus defined, state making must include the following:

- The expansion and consolidation of the territorial and demographic domain under a political authority, including the imposition of order on contested territorial and demographic space (war)
- The maintenance of order in the territory where, and over the population on whom, such order has already been imposed (policing)
- The extraction of resources from the territory and the population under the control of the state, resources essential not only to support the war-making and policing activities undertaken by the state but also to maintain the apparatuses of state necessary to carry on routine administration, deepen the state's penetration of society, and serve symbolic purposes (taxation)[8]

All three broad categories of activities outlined here, however, depend on the state's success in monopolizing and concentrating the means of coercion in its own hands in the territory and among the population it controls. That is why the accumulation of power becomes so crucial to the state-making enterprise; the more primitive the stage of state building, the more coercive the strategies employed to accumulate and concentrate power in the hands of the agents of the state. Cohen and colleagues stated in a seminal article published in 1981, "The extent to which an expansion of state power will generate collective violence depends on the *level* of state power prior to that expansion. . . . The lower the initial level of state power, the stronger the relationship between the *rate* of state expansion and collective violence."[9] One needs to be reminded that the violence generated during the process of state making is the result of actions undertaken both by the state and by recalcitrant elements within the population that forcefully resist the state's attempt to impose order.

The inherent similarity in the logic of the state-building process provides us explanations for the current replication by Third World states of several dimensions of the early modern European experience of state making. Simultaneously, the difference in the pace at which state building has to be undertaken and completed in the Third World and the dramatically changed international environment in which Third World state making has to proceed explain the divergence in other dimensions from the earlier European model of state building. The similarities and the differences are equally important, as is the bearing they have on problems of authority and governance within Third World states.

It should be noted that in most of Europe, state making usually antedated the emergence of nations and nation-states by a couple of centuries. This is why it is essential not to confuse the building of modern sovereign states with the emergence of nation-states in the nineteenth and twentieth centuries.[10] Sovereign and relatively centralized states that have performed successfully over a long period of time—and have therefore knit their people together in terms of historical memories, legal codes, language, religion, and so forth—may evolve into nation-states or at least provide the necessary conditions for the emergence of nation-states, but they are not synonymous with the latter. Historical evidence has convincingly demonstrated that in almost all cases in Europe, with the exception of the Balkans (an exception that may provide the clue to the current violence and strife in that region), the emergence of the modern sovereign state was the precondition for the formation of the nation.[11]

This generalization applied as much to latecomers such as Germany as it did to the earliest examples of modern states, such as England and France. Without the central role performed by the Prussian state, Germany would probably have remained nothing more than a geographic or cultural expression. The similarity between the German experience on the one hand and the French experience on the other has been summed up well by Cornelia Navari: "When Hegel insisted that it was the state that created the nation, he was looking backwards to the history of France, not forward to the history of Germany. When Germany was unified 'from above' in 1870 and the Reich was formed, this way of proceeding did not appear to most Germans to be at variance with the experience of their Western neighbors—a substitution of Union 'by force' for the 'organic growth' of France and England. It appeared to be a repetition of it, differing only in that it was less bloody. Here, as there, the state was moving outwards into diverse feudal remnants of the old order, dissolving them, making all obedient to the same law."[12]

The chronological sequence of the establishment of the sovereign state and the evolution of nationalism in the Third World bears very close resemblance to that of modern

Europe, with the state taking clear historical precedence over the nation. As Anthony Smith has put it very succinctly, "[T]he western model is essentially a 'state system' rather than a 'nation system'; and this has been its fateful legacy to Africa and Asia." Smith goes on to point out that despite the differences in geopolitical and cultural terms between Europe and the Third World, "the central point . . . of the western experience for contemporary African and Asian social and political change has been the primacy and dominance of the specialized, territorially defined, and coercively monopolistic state, operating within a broader system of similar states bent on fulfilling their dual functions of internal regulation and external defence (or aggression)."[13]

In this context, it is instructive to note Charles Tilly's point that "the building of states in Western Europe cost tremendously in death, suffering, loss of rights, and unwilling surrender of land, goods, or labor. . . . The fundamental reason for the high cost of European state building was its beginning in the midst of a decentralized, largely peasant social structure. Building differentiated, autonomous, centralized organizations with effective control of territories entailed eliminating or subordinating thousands of semiautonomous authorities. . . . Most of the European population resisted each phase of the creation of strong states."[14] Tilly's description of conditions in Europe at the birth of modern sovereign states has an uncanny resemblance to present conditions in many Third World societies. It thus helps to explain why, if one arranges the current state-building strategies employed in the Third World on a continuum ranging from coercion to persuasion (with the two ends representing ideal types), even those states like India that fall relatively close to the persuasive end of the continuum rely on significant amounts of coercion—as witnessed over the past several decades in Punjab, Kashmir, and the northeastern states—to entrench and consolidate the authority of the

state in regions where it faces, or has faced, major challenges.

In order to replicate the process by which relatively centralized modern states are created, Third World state makers need above all two things: lots of time and a relatively free hand to persuade, cajole, and coerce the disparate populations under their nominal rule to accept the legitimacy of state boundaries and institutions; to accept the right of the state to extract resources from them; and to let the state regulate the more important public aspects of their lives. Unfortunately for Third World state elites, neither of these two commodities is available to them in adequate measure. This is because, unlike European states, postcolonial states have to build states and nations within limited time spans, thus forcing them to collapse sequential phases of state and nation construction into one mammoth phase. They have no alternative because their failure to accomplish in decades what European states took centuries to do is likely to hold them up to international ridicule and consign them to permanent peripherality in the international system. Simultaneously, contemporary international norms demand that postcolonial state elites treat their populations humanely and according to codes of civilized behavior, thus restraining their capacity to use force in the pursuit of state making and nation building. The lack of adequate time and normative constraints imposed on state makers make their task very difficult and encourage the emergence of secessionist movements that challenge the state's authority and lay the basis for intrastate conflict.[15]

The point regarding the availability of time becomes clear if one examines the amount of time it took for the states of Western Europe to emerge as full-fledged sovereign states, enjoying the habitual obedience of their populations, basically secure in the legitimacy of their borders and institutions, and, therefore, in a position where they could respond positively to societal demands, since these demands no longer ran counter to the logic of state building and the accumulation of power in the hands of the state. It was not until the beginning of the twentieth century that the states of Western Europe and their offshoots in North America emerged as the responsive and representative modern states that we know them to be today—the end products of the state-making process that had unfolded for at least three or four hundred years. It is instructive to remember that the survival of the American state in its present form hung in the balance in the 1860s, only 150 years ago, and it managed to survive only after a bloody civil war that left millions dead. Although leading historians of state building in Europe differ about the exact dating of the origins, in the sense of beginnings, of the modern sovereign state, there is little argument about the fact that "it took four to five centuries for European states to overcome their weaknesses, to remedy their administrative deficiencies, and to bring lukewarm loyalty up to the white heat of nationalism."[16]

Unfortunately for Third World state makers, their states cannot afford the luxury of prolonging the traumatic and costly experience of state making over hundreds of years à la Europe. The demands of competition with established modern states and the demonstration effect of socially cohesive, politically responsive, and administratively effective states in the industrialized world make it almost obligatory for Third World states to reach their goal within the shortest possible time. The pioneers of European state making (although not the latecomers like Germany and Italy) were remarkably free from systemic pressures and demonstration effects, because all the leading contenders for statehood—England, France, Spain, Holland—were basically in the same boat, trying to navigate the same uncharted sea. Where European states did not have this luxury and had to compress some of the sequential phases that together constituted the process of state building, they suffered from a "cumulation of crises."[17] This

applied particularly to the states of Germany and Italy, which emerged as unified sovereign entities only in the closing decades of the nineteenth century and were immediately faced with the pressures of mass politics. In fact, it can be argued that the emergence of Italian Fascism and German Nazism was a result of the Italian and German state elites' inability in the first two decades of the twentieth century to respond successfully, in a context of mass politics, to the accumulated crises threatening their respective states.[18]

If this was the case with Germany, which had the well-established Prussian state at its core, one can well imagine the enormity of the challenge faced by the postcolonial states of the Third World. The latter's problems have been compounded by the fact that they are under pressure to demonstrate adequate statehood quickly; to perform the task of state making in a humane, civilized, and consensual fashion; and to do all this in an era of mass politics. The inadequacy of the time element and the consequent fact that several sequential phases involved in the state-making process have had to be telescoped together into one mammoth state-building enterprise go a long way toward explaining the problems of authority and governance faced by the Third World states today.[19] Given the short time at the disposal of state makers in the Third World and the consequent acceleration in their state-making efforts necessary to demonstrate that they are moving speedily toward effective statehood, crises erupt simultaneously and become unmanageable as the load they put on the political system outruns the political and military capabilities of the state, thus further eroding the legitimacy of the already fragile postcolonial state.

INTERNATIONAL NORMS OF STATEHOOD AND HUMAN RIGHTS

In addition to these internal factors, the workings of the international system, especially the policies adopted by the superpowers during the Cold War era, have complicated the process of state making in the Third World. With the export of superpower rivalry to the Third World in the form of proxy wars, both interstate and intrastate, and the transfer of weapons to governments and insurgents in fragile polities in volatile regional environments, the bipolar global balance during the Cold War era greatly accentuated the insecurities and instabilities in the Third World. Numerous cases in Africa, Asia, and the Middle East attest to the veracity of this statement.[20]

Equally important, certain international norms that have crystallized relatively recently have also had mixed effects on the security and stability of Third World states. The first of these norms relates to the inalienability of juridical sovereignty or statehood once conferred by international law and symbolized by membership in the United Nations. The sanctity of the borders of postcolonial states forms the logical corollary to this norm. While this international norm has done much to preserve the existence of several Third World states that may have otherwise been unviable, it has also, paradoxically, added to the security predicament of the Third World state. This point can best be understood by recalling that the elimination of states considered unviable, either because of their internal contradictions or because their existence did not suit great-power aspirations, was perfectly acceptable to the European international community virtually through the end of World War I. The Prussian annexation of several Germanic principalities in the 1860s and the periodic disappearance and reappearance of Poland in the eighteenth and nineteenth centuries are prime examples of this phenomenon.

The international consensus on the alienability of juridical statehood began to change during the interwar period and crystallized after World War II in the context of the decolonization of Asia and Africa. Colonies, once granted independence, acquired the right to exist as sovereign entities, even if many of them (especially in Africa) did not possess "much in the way of empirical statehood, disclosed by a capacity for effective and civil government."[21] This change has meant that, while this international norm has protected the legal existence of postcolonial states without regard to their internal cohesiveness or the effectiveness of their domestic control, it has been unable to solve the security problems that such states face as a result of the contradictions present within their boundaries and inherent in their statemaking process.

It is worth noting here that this guarantee encompassing juridical statehood and territorial integrity has begun to weaken in the post–Cold War era. This has been witnessed in a whole host of cases, ranging from northern Iraq to Kosovo, where the international community, led by the major Western powers, has intervened in contravention of the principles of state sovereignty and the territorial integrity of established states. However, this change in international norms, if consolidated, is unlikely to alleviate the Third World's security predicament. In fact, it is likely to worsen that situation considerably and to add to the prevalent instability and disorder in the Third World, because it has become linked to the issue of the right of ethnic groups to self-determination. It appears, therefore, that the Third World is caught in a no-win situation as far as this set of international norms is concerned.

A second set of international norms that has affected the security of the Third World is related to the issue of human rights, with primary emphasis on civil and political rights. While the modern conception of human rights can be traced to the natural law approach developed in eighteenth-century Europe, the recent normative force that human rights have acquired in the international arena is the result of the acceptance by the vast majority of states of the existence and validity of such rights for all human beings, regardless of their status as citizens of particular states.[22]

The changing attitude toward human rights as a legitimate concern of the international community meant that they needed to be brought within the ambit of international law and rescued from their status as the exclusive preserve of sovereign states in relation to their own citizens. This led to their inclusion in the Preamble and Article 1 of the United Nations Charter and to their codification in the Universal Declaration of Human Rights, adopted in 1948, and the two International Covenants on Human Rights, which were opened for signature and ratification in 1966 and became operative in 1976. This was a major development in the evolution of norms that govern the international system, for it acknowledged more clearly than ever before that individuals, as well as states, could now be considered subjects of international law. It also signified the international acceptance of the principle that individuals and groups have rights that are independent of their membership in individual states and that derive not from their national status but from their status as members of the human species.

The major problem with the implementation of human rights in the Third World is that the concept of human rights owes its empirical validity to the existence and successful functioning of the industrialized, representative, and responsive states of Western Europe and North America. These states set the standards for effective statehood, as well as for the humane and civilized treatment of their citizens. They do so by their demonstrated success in simultaneously meeting the basic needs of the large majority of their populations, protecting their human rights, and promoting and guaranteeing political participation. But these states have, by and large, successfully completed their state-building process, are politically satiated and economically affluent, and possess unconditional legitimacy in the eyes of the overwhelming majority of their populations. They can therefore afford to adopt liberal standards of state behavior in relation to their populations, because they are reasonably secure in the knowledge that societal demands will not run counter to state interests and will not put state structures and institutions in any grave jeopardy.

While norms regarding human rights have been a touchstone of civilized behavior on the part of states for almost half a century, a similar status has begun to be accorded to democratic governance since the 1990s. The rhetoric emanating from Washington and other Western capitals and the political conditionalities attached to International Monetary Fund and World Bank loans to developing countries since the 1990s have privileged political participation and encouraged democratic transition in postcolonial countries. One cannot deny that the policy of promoting democratic governance has innate merits. However, in the short run such a policy has the capacity to impede state- and nation-building activities by putting constraints on state elites' pursuit of these goals. This is especially the case in multiethnic societies, where the transition to democracy often accentuates ethnic cleavages and sharpens competition for access to the privileges of power. The danger of systemic breakdown becomes particularly acute when democratization becomes equated merely with procedural or electoral democracy and not much attention is paid to putting in place constitutional and judicial constraints that would prevent majorities from riding roughshod over minority opinions and interests. In divided societies, such as those in the Third World, democracies can easily turn into majoritarian polities where parties engage in competitive chauvinism that widens societal fissures to such an extent that divisions become irreversible. Sri Lanka is the classic case in point, but Iraq seems to be moving in the same direction.[23]

What are currently considered in the West to be norms of civilized state behavior—including those pertaining to the human rights of individuals and groups as well as democratic governance—are, in the Third

World, not infrequently in contradiction with the imperatives of state making. These imperatives, as has been pointed out more than once, not only sanction but also frequently require the use of violent means against recalcitrant domestic groups and individual citizens. Furthermore, the international norm upholding human rights runs directly counter to the norm that prescribes the inalienability of juridical statehood for Third World states.[24] While the latter is uncompromising in upholding the legality of the existence of Third World states within their colonially constructed boundaries, the former undermines the political legitimacy of these same states by prescribing standards and yardsticks in terms that most Third World states, struggling to perform the minimum tasks of maintaining political order, will be incapable of meeting for many decades to come.

Moreover, the simultaneous but contradictory operation of the two norms contributes to the creation and augmentation of internal discontent within Third World states. It does so by, on the one hand, forcing all the diverse and dissatisfied elements within Third World states to remain within their postcolonial boundaries and, on the other, encouraging these very elements to make political, administrative, and economic demands on the states that these states cannot respond to successfully. The states cannot respond either because they lack the capabilities to do so or because doing so could seriously jeopardize their territorial integrity.

One can make the argument on behalf of Third World states, still struggling to translate their juridical statehood into empirical statehood, that the case for human rights (whether of individuals or of groups) and against the state's use of violent means to impose order is not as morally unassailable as it may appear at first sight. This point can be made most effectively in the context of the failed-states phenomenon, where state structures have completely collapsed.[25] In these cases, it can be demonstrated that in the absence of even rudimentarily effective states to provide a min-

imum degree of political order—as in Lebanon for the fifteen years of civil war, or as currently in Somalia, Liberia, Sierra Leone, and, above all, Iraq, where dozens of people are killed every day—the concept of human rights remains nothing more than a pure abstraction. In such a context, the human rights ideal is impossible to implement even minimally, because in the absence of an effective sovereign a truly Hobbesian state of nature prevails, and the very survival of large segments of the population cannot be assured.

These comments should not be taken as an apologia for authoritarian regimes in the Third World that ostensibly emphasize order at the expense of both justice and political participation. Authoritarian regimes quite often contribute a great deal to the creation and augmentation of disorder in Third World states despite paying lip service to the objective of maintaining and promoting order. Iran under the shah, the Philippines under Marcos, Zaire under Mobutu, Nicaragua under Somoza, and Zimbabwe under Mugabe—to cite but a few instances—all provide good examples of this tendency.

It is also true that most regimes in the Third World attempt to portray threats to their regimes as threats to the state. Discerning analysts must, therefore, carefully distinguish between issues of regime security and those of state security. However, in many cases, given the lack of unconditional legitimacy both of the regime and of the state structure in the Third World and the close perceptual connection between regime and state as far as the majority of the state's population is concerned, the line between regime security and state security becomes so thin, and the interplay between the two so dense, that it is virtually impossible to disentangle one from the other. As one perceptive scholar pointed out in connection with the Middle East, "[T]hose who rule must attempt to encourage loyalty to the state, of which they hope themselves to be the chief beneficiaries, while at the same time seeking to disguise the fact that their system of power, and thus the identity of the political structure itself, frequently owes more to the old ties of sectarian and tribal loyalty."[26] In many such countries the fall of the regime is likely to signal the failure of the state as well; any student of Tudor England or Bourbon France will find this phenomenon very familiar. Iraq provides the latest testimony to the veracity of this proposition.

ETHNONATIONAL SELF-DETERMINATION

The human rights issue raises a further problem. Given the multiethnic nature of most Third World states, if human rights are interpreted as group rights and, therefore, are seen to include the right to ethnonational self-determination, they are likely to pose grave threats to the territorial integrity and juridical statehood of postcolonial states, once again pitting one set of international norms against another. The legitimation of the notion of ethnonational self-determination, however partial and selective, following the end of the Cold War—symbolized by the prompt recognition accorded to the successor states to the Soviet Union and Yugoslavia and the separation of Slovakia from the Czech Republic —is likely to have encouraged demands for ethnic separatism in the Third World. Given the latent tensions between ethnicity and state-defined nationalism even in functioning federal polities like India and the clear contradiction between ethnonationalism and state-defined nationalism in much of the Third World, any development anywhere in the international arena that may encourage ethnic separatist demands in the context of state and regime fragilities prevalent in the Third World is bound to add to the great strains already existing within these polities. The effects of such a contagion spreading have been summed up in a Council on Foreign Relations study that concluded that "while the creation of some new states may be necessary or inevitable, the fragmentation of international society into hundreds of independent territorial entities is a recipe for an even more dangerous and anarchic world."[27]

A major problem with ethnonational self-determination relates to the definition of the ethnic self that is seeking to determine its future. The self-perception and self-definition of ethnicity is usually subject to change, depending on the context in which it operates at any point in time. This is what Crawford Young has referred to as "the dynamic and changing character of contemporary ethnicity: Far from representing a fixed and immutable set of static social facts, cultural pluralism is itself evolving in crucial ways and is in major respects contextual, situational, and circumstantial."[28] Therefore, to link such a potent ideology as that of self-determination to a malleable idea like that of ethnicity—and then to legitimize this combination by reference to the principle of human rights of groups—is bound to introduce even greater disorder in the Third World than is already present, because it endows the demands of every disgruntled ethnic group with the legitimacy of the ideal of national self-determination. The danger is that this is exactly what the renewed popularity of the idea of ethnonational self-determination may end up achieving, to the great detriment of both order and justice in the Third World.

The problem is further confounded by the fact that, given the ethnic mixtures of populations in most countries, hardly any pure ethnic homelands still exist. This fact contradicts the ethnonationalists' assumption that "the earth's entire population, or most of it, divides into a finite number of distinct, homogeneous peoples. It follows that the world's ideal condition consists of that finite number of nation-states."[29] Attempts at ethnonational self-determination are, therefore, bound to run into resistance from ethnic minorities in presumed ethnic homelands. As William Pfaff has succinctly put it, "The ethnic state is a product of the political imagination; it does not exist in reality. . . . The idea of the ethnic nation thus is a permanent provocation to war."[30] Such conflict is expected to result either in virulent forms of ethnic cleansing or in the carving out of microstates from the ministates established on the basis of ethnic nationalism, or both.

QUASI STATES AND FAILED STATES

Related to the issue of ethnonational self-determination is the failed-states phenomenon. Jack Snyder has described the link between the two by describing ethnic nationalism as "the default option." According to Snyder, ethnic nationalism "predominates when institutions collapse, when existing institutions are not fulfilling people's basic needs, and when satisfactory alternative structures are not readily available."[31] While this may not provide the total explanation for the revival of ethnonationalism, it does capture a very major ingredient that has contributed to the recent popularity of the ethnonationalist ideology, namely, the lack of effective statehood. This is true not only in the case of the components of the former Soviet Union and of the Former Yugoslavia but also in many parts of the Third World. The lack of effective statehood was responsible for the emergence of what Robert Jackson has termed "quasi-states" in the Third World.[32] These quasi states can now clearly be seen as precursors of failed states in the global South.

The end of the Cold War has had an important impact on the transformation of some of these quasi states into failed states. This is especially true in the case of those states that had witnessed high levels of superpower involvement in the military sphere, including the arena of arms transfers, during the Cold War era. At the height of the Cold War, the superpowers attempted to strengthen client governments in internally fragmented states, each often seeking to maintain a semblance of stability within countries that were allied with itself. One major instrument of such support was the transfer of large quantities of relatively sophisticated arms to friendly regimes. In several instances, such arms transfers led to countervailing transfers of weaponry by the rival superpower to forces opposed to the central authorities. Afghanistan during the 1980s came to epitomize this action-reaction phenomenon.[33]

Past superpower policies of pouring arms into fragmented polities have, however, become a major source of instability and disorder in the post–Cold War period. The presence of large quantities of relatively sophisticated weaponry (ranging from AK-47s to Stinger missiles) and the withdrawal of superpower support to weak and vulnerable regimes— support that was essential to prevent the central authorities from being overwhelmed by domestic rivals who, in turn, were divided among themselves—created near-total anarchy in countries like Afghanistan and Somalia, where central authority completely collapsed, thereby turning these quasi states into failed states.

Furthermore, the failure of the international community, principally the major powers and international organizations, to prevent and control the flow of small arms, which are responsible for the majority of deaths in current conflicts, is exploited by private arms dealers and transnational criminal cartels as well as states interested in making fast money in the murky area of arms trade. This unregulated arms bazaar not only adds to the misery of the populace but also undermines state authority in countries and regions most vulnerable to internal conflicts.[34]

The relationship between state failure and internal conflict is, however, not a one-way street, with the former inevitably leading to the latter. The relationship is in many cases circular, as the two phenomena feed on each other, with state weakness providing the political space for the intensification of conflicts among political factions and/or ethnic groups, and the conflicts in turn further eroding the capacity of the state to maintain order and provide security to its citizens. Suffering from acute insecurity, individuals often turn to political factions, ethnic groups, and even criminal gangs (and sometimes it is difficult to distinguish among the three categories) to provide them with protection in exchange for their loyalty and contribution—financial, physical, or both—to the "war effort."

There is another dimension of state failure that has a major impact on the level of conflict within societies. Alex de Waal has pointed this out with great clarity in relation to Africa. He has argued that economic crisis in Africa has meant that "governments find it more difficult to sustain and control armies, which then turn to local sources of provisioning. These include requisitioning, looting and taxing populations, involvement in commerce, and diverting humanitarian aid. Though the causes of war in Africa and the aims of the combatants are still almost exclusively phrased in terms of achieving state power and affecting constitutional change, the realities on the ground reflect more intense predatory behaviour by soldiers."[35] This search for "survival" on the part of unpaid or poorly paid soldiers, who command great coercive power in relation to the rest of the population, contributes to the reality and perception of state failure while serving a "rational" purpose for those engaged in it.

Finally, state failure, like state making, must be viewed as a process, not an event. In I. William Zartman's words, it is akin to "a long-term degenerative disease"[36] rather than something that occurs at a particular point in time. Such an understanding of state failure will help one comprehend the fact that, as the Lebanese example demonstrates, the process is not irreversible. Furthermore, it will assist one to understand why this process is usually accompanied by long-drawn-out "civil" wars during which political factions fight over what they presume to be the state's carcass and the state attempts to revive itself, drawing on its residual capacity and legitimacy. If and when one faction succeeds in by and large subjugating the others, it usually dons the mantle of the state in order to legitimize the concentration of coercive power in its hands.

Similarly, if one views conflict and war as process and not merely in terms of final outcomes, one can conclude that there are usually groups, factions, and individuals that benefit economically, as well as politically, from the prolongation of such wars. They come to acquire a vested interest in perpetuating such conflicts. This is why "[c]onflict entrepreneurs, as well as conflict victims, must be part of any analytical framework" devised to study what has been termed "complex political emergencies."[37] Such a perspective can help unravel the rationality behind what appear to the outside observer to be totally irrational conflicts.

DEMOCRATIZATION IN THE THIRD WORLD

It may seem obvious to the lay observer that the principal method to prevent state making from being transformed into state failure is to grant greater political participation to those sectors of society—whether ethnic or socioeconomic—that have heretofore been excluded from the exercise of political power. It would be too naive to believe, however, that democratization—defined in terms of increasing guarantees for the exercise of civil and political liberties and in terms of political participation through the medium of competitive electoral politics—by itself, and in all contexts, will succeed in neutralizing ethnic separatism.[38] The success of the democratic experiment in defusing ethnic tensions will, therefore, depend on a number of factors, identified by Renée de Nevers as including "the speed with which ethnic issues are recognized; the level of ethnic tension when the democratization process begins; the size and power of different ethnic groups within the state; the ethnic composition of the previous regime and its opposition; the political positions of the leaders of the main ethnic groups; the presence or absence of external ethnic allies; and the ethnic composition of the military."[39]

There is, however, another side to the democratization coin. The demands of state building and democratization can be reconciled only if the democratizing state in the Third World is credibly able to monopolize the instruments of violence within its territories, thus preventing dissident groups from attempting to change the state's boundaries when political controls are relaxed. This monopoly over instruments of violence is essential because "often the first act of forces liberated by the introduction of democracy is to seek some permanent escape from the state they see as having oppressed them."[40]

This is where the most severe problems are likely to arise, even if democratic political systems become the norm rather than the exception in the Third World. Democratic and (even more important) democratizing regimes cannot afford to be seen as weak when confronted by separatist challenges and cannot, in the final analysis, give up their right to lay down and enforce the rules (even if some of these have been negotiated with the opponents of the state) by which the game of politics is to be played within the boundaries of states over which they preside. Otherwise, the "democratic center may be questioned for its inefficiency in creating or its weakness in handling the secessionist crisis, opening the way for military intervention."[41]

This point is inadequately understood by many proponents of democratization in the Third World, who tend to equate democratic states with weak states on the assumption that strong states are bound to be autocratic by nature. By making this assumption they fail to learn from the European experience that democracy emerged as the final stage of the state-building process and not at the expense of state building. Even in today's context, when democratization cannot wait until state building is completed, it cannot thrive in the absence of

the political order that only a strongly entrenched state can provide. Democratization, therefore, must complement rather than contradict the process of state making; without the political order that can be provided only by effective states, the gains of democratization cannot be sustained. Anarchies—as the examples of Somalia, Liberia, Afghanistan, and Iraq clearly demonstrate—are no respecters of democratic values and human rights.

However, the reconciliation of the two imperatives of the consolidation of state power and democratization is not, and will not be, an easy task even if tremendous goodwill is present on all sides. Major tensions are bound to arise between state elites and their ethnic and political opponents who would like to put significant curbs on the power of the central state. In addition, where separatist insurgencies are already under way, major problems between separatists and democratizing central governments are likely to revolve around two basic questions: What is the guarantee that groups espousing separatism will indeed surrender all arms and reconcile themselves to autonomous or semiautonomous status that will continue to be essentially dependent on the good faith and the continuing political sagacity of the central government? What is the guarantee that central authorities, after persuading separatist ethnic groups to lay down their arms and thus having overcome immediate internal security crises, will continue to abide by their commitment to popular political participation, the constitutional protection of minority rights, and regional autonomy?

The answers provided by the Third World's historical record to these questions do not leave much room for optimism. Furthermore, if one goes by the earlier European experience, one is likely to conclude that the historical juncture at which most Third World states find themselves today is unlikely to permit a great deal of ethnic accommodation and political participation. These two processes usually run counter to the overriding imperative of consolidating state power and fashioning a state that is sovereign, not merely juridically but also empirically. However, one can make an effective argument that the early-twenty-first-century context is so dramatically different from the late-eighteenth- or even the late-nineteenth-century context that radically new solutions must be found for this dilemma.

In other words, the problem of reconciling the demands of state making with those of democratization and human rights—as well as with demands for regional autonomy, devolution of powers, and protection of minority group rights—will have to be addressed much more creatively, and mutually acceptable solutions will have to be found, if the twin specters of failed states and destructive ethnonationalism are to be kept at bay. Above all, this means that the trajectories of democratization (including the preservation of group rights and local autonomy for substate units), on the one hand, and of the consolidation of coercive power and concentration of legitimate authority in the hands of the state, on the other, must not diverge radically. In fact, they should ideally become mutually legitimizing agents, with democratization legitimizing the greater concentration of authority in the hands of the state and the concentration of centralized power legitimizing and facilitating the loosening of political controls and the guaranteeing of political and civil rights to the citizenry.

Most important, the two processes should not be allowed to become the polar opposites of each other. Faced with a stark choice between the territorial integrity of the state and democratization, state elites are invariably bound to opt for territorial integrity over democratization. Where the processes of territorial integrity and democracy collide, democratization cannot prevail without the disintegration of the state. Therefore, in order for the strategy of democratization to work successfully without threatening the disintegration of states, the state elites' decision to democratize must be firmly linked to the negotiated surrender of

separatist groups where they exist. The disarming of such groups should proceed in tandem with the implementation of any plans for autonomy or devolution of powers that may have been negotiated between the parties.

THE ROLE OF THE INTERNATIONAL COMMUNITY IN DEMOCRATIZATION

The international community, working through the United Nations, can play a constructive role in encouraging reconciliation between state building and democratization by adopting a very restrictive approach toward recognizing new political entities that attempt to break away from established states in the Third World. A too-permissive approach to state breaking, as witnessed in the early 1990s in the case of the former Yugoslavia, will add to conflict and anarchy rather than preserving international order. Colonially imposed state boundaries may be an iniquitous way of delineating the borders of Third World states, but every other alternative appears to be infinitely worse.

The United Nations must not fall into the trap of giving legitimacy to demands for secession from member states, unless the terms have been peacefully negotiated with the parent state. Exceptions like Eritrea, East Timor, and Kosovo must not influence, let alone determine, the norms of international behavior. Eritrea was a special case because its separation was negotiated with the post-Mengistu regime in Ethiopia. Furthermore, Eritrea regained the colonially crafted political identity within the colonial boundaries that had been compromised in 1952 by the internationally sponsored merger of the former Italian colony with the Ethiopian empire and the subsequent flagrant violation by Addis Ababa of Eritrean autonomy that had formed an integral part of the merger agreement. However, despite Eritrea's peaceful separation from Ethiopia in the early 1990s, by the late 1990s its relations with Ethiopia had deteriorated once again to such an extent that the two countries fought a bloody border war that has had tremendous adverse consequences for the economies of both states.

East Timor was also not a part of the Indonesian postcolonial state. Unlike the rest of Indonesia, which had been a Dutch colony, East Timor was a Portuguese colony that was forcibly annexed by Indonesia in 1975 when Portugal withdrew from the territory. Although it took twenty-five years for East Timor to regain its independence within its erstwhile colonial borders, the episode demonstrated the deep impact of colonial structures on shaping postcolonial national identities.

Kosovo is unfinished business from the disintegration of Yugoslavia. The division of Yugoslavia into ethnically defined states led on the one hand to major civil conflict in Bosnia and on the other to the assertion of Kosovo's ethnic nationalism. The latter assertion, legitimized by the ethnic division of Yugoslavia, became particularly intense in the context of the Serbian attempt to marginalize politically and economically the large Kosovar Albanian majority by reneging on the province's autonomous status. This forced the Albanians, who formed 90 percent of the population, to live in subordination both to the Serb minority in Kosovo and to the Serbian government in Belgrade. Had the multiethnic Yugoslav federation not been dismantled, the world would not have been faced with the ethnic cleansing in Bosnia, the Serb atrocities on the Kosovar Albanians, and the international intervention to prevent the repetition of ethnic cleansing in Kosovo.

The international community must be especially wary of allowing these precedents to govern its reactions to the situation in Iraq, however dire it may appear in the short term. Encouraging, or even passively acquiescing in, Kurdish demands for secession will open a hornet's nest in the Middle East, reopening questions regarding state borders that have been considered settled and leading to highly negative reactions, not only from the Arab world but from Turkey and Iran as well. Domestic tensions within Iraq, already exacerbated by the U.S. invasion, will be transformed into a regional conflict of major proportions pulling many of Iraq's neighbors into its vortex.

EXTERNALLY INDUCED STATE FAILURE

The case of Iraq, and that of Afghanistan before it, highlights a major cause of, and catalyst for, state failure that has so far been neglected in the analysis of the subject. It has been demonstrated conclusively that great-power involvement in the domestic and regional conflicts afflicting postcolonial states have often had deleterious consequences for state-building efforts in the Third World. Superpower competition during the Cold War era for the loyalties of states, regimes, and factions in developing countries particularly contributed to the intensification of the security predicament faced by Third World states.[42] But Iraq and Afghanistan are unique in the sense that they have clearly shown that external great-power intervention does not merely contribute to state failure but can be its principal cause by setting up the targeted countries for state collapse. They have also thrown into sharper relief earlier cases of great-power intervention that led to state debilitation bordering on state failure. These latter cases include Angola and Mozambique from the mid-1970s until the 1990s. Covert U.S. support to insurgent groups and tribal factions in these sub-Saharan countries played a key role in undermining the effectiveness of postcolonial regimes that were supported by the Soviet Union. This deliberate policy of state debilitation seriously detracted from the capacity of governments in the two countries to maintain order within their domains and provide security to their populations. Mahmood Mamdani argues quite convincingly that the United States applied with great effect the lessons it had learned in Angola and Mozambique, as well as in

Nicaragua, where it armed and equipped the Contras against the socialist Sandinista government, to its venture in Afghanistan, where it once again aimed at destabilizing and incapacitating a regime that was a Soviet ally.[43] In the process, it set up Afghanistan for state failure but this time of a much more dire sort and with enormous unforeseen and unintended consequences.

The Soviet military intervention in Afghanistan began in earnest in December 1979, to save a tottering client regime that had come to power in April 1978 but was riven with discord and was at the same time reeling under the pressure of an insurgency supported by the United States and Pakistan. The United States responded to the direct Soviet intervention by ratcheting up its support to the insurgents and launching what amounted to a full-fledged proxy war in Afghanistan billed as a jihad against godless communism. This jihad not only facilitated the ingathering of transnational jihadi elements in Afghanistan but also launched that country on the slippery slope of state failure. Following the Soviet withdrawal from Afghanistan in 1989, U.S.-armed jihadi factions fought each other brutally, destroying what was left of the state infrastructure. Thus, they succeeded in creating a political vacuum that facilitated the creation by transnational jihadis of a safe haven from which they could launch their global campaign of terror.[44] It is indeed ironic that the terrorist attacks of 9/11 were in large part the direct consequence of the externally induced collapse of the state in Afghanistan, for which the United States bore much of the responsibility. It was the absence of political order in Afghanistan that provided al Qaeda with the opportunity and the space to plan and execute the attacks on the United States.

These terrorist attacks triggered a U.S. response that targeted not only Afghanistan but also Iraq as part of the Bush administration's "war on terror." Iraq was targeted despite the fact that there was little evidence connecting

al Qaeda to the Saddam regime.[45] The U.S. invasion of Iraq created the conditions for the debilitation and potential dismemberment of the Iraqi state by destroying the Iraqi state apparatus and failing to put in place an alternative structure that would be both effective and legitimate. Equally important, according to Robert Malley and Peter Harling, "Washington's conviction that the Ba'athist regime was essentially Sunni (it was not) and that large numbers of Sunni Arabs therefore were inherently opposed to its overthrow (they were not) became a self-fulfilling prophecy. Fearing resistance in Sunni Arab areas before it actually materialised, US forces treated them harshly. This helped heighten hostility from Sunni Arabs who increasingly, albeit reluctantly, identified themselves as such."[46] The consequent alienation of Sunni Arabs from the emerging post-Saddam structure helped create a hospitable environment for the transnational jihadis to operate in.

It would be wrong to equate the Iraqi insurgency merely with transnational jihadi activities.[47] However, faulty U.S. policies provided crucial momentum and operating space to shadowy organizations, such as the al-Zarqawi-led al Qaeda in Iraq, to prepare for and conduct acts of terror both within Iraq and in neighboring countries.[48] The U.S. invasion thus created conditions that not only seemed to be pushing Iraq toward disintegration but also helped provide transnational jihadi terrorists, who had lost their safe haven in Afghanistan following the U.S.-led invasion of that country in 2001–2, with a new base from which they could operate. It is no wonder that President George W. Bush's repeated declaration that Iraq had become the center for international terrorism became a self-fulfilling prophecy.

The blowback for the United States from the Iraq invasion is likely to be far greater than that from the U.S.-supported war against the Soviets in Afghanistan in the 1980s. This will be the case because, as Peter Bergen and Alec Reynolds have pointed out, "Fighters in Iraq are more battle hardened than the Afghan Arabs, who fought demoralized Soviet army conscripts. They are testing themselves against arguably the best army in history, acquiring skills in their battles against coalition forces that will be far more useful for future terrorist operations than those their counterparts learned during the 1980s."[49] Just as many of the leading lights of the current generation of Islamist militants are veterans of the Afghan war, the insurgency in Iraq is likely to produce the leadership for the third generation of jihadis, who are likely to pose major threats to Muslim regimes allied to the United States. According to Bergen and Reynolds, "[T]he blowback from Iraq is likely to be as painful for Saudi Arabia as the blowback from Afghanistan was for Egypt and Algeria during the 1990s."[50]

Afghanistan and Iraq provide grave warnings to major powers and international institutions that they should desist from undue interference, especially of the military kind, in the domestic affairs of developing countries currently in the early stages of state making. Given the fragile and contingent nature of the state-building exercise, such intervention has immense potential to become the proverbial last straw that may break the camel's back, thus leading to state evaporation. Both Afghanistan and Iraq demonstrate that the disintegration or collapse of states, even those initially not considered important actors in the international system, often possesses the capacity to affect the strategic interests of great powers in direct and indirect ways, thus turning such states into major issues of global concern and primary sources of systemic destabilization.

THE INTERNATIONAL COMMUNITY AND HUMANITARIAN INTERVENTION

These warnings are particularly relevant today since humanitarian interventions have come into vogue since the 1990s. The U.S. invasion of Iraq has also been justified post facto as humanitarian. The normative changes regarding human rights mentioned earlier have led from the early 1990s to a dramatic increase in cases of humanitarian intervention undertaken by major powers in the name of the international community. Some of these, such as in Haiti, Bosnia, and East Timor, were authorized by the UN Security Council; others, such as the one in Kosovo, did not receive UN Security Council authorization but were undertaken nonetheless under the aegis of regional organizations such as NATO. Yet others, such as the invasion of Iraq in 2003, were undertaken unilaterally by the lone superpower, the United States, with the token help of allies and camp followers in the teeth of opposition by most states, including the majority of the permanent members of the Security Council.

These multifarious types of interventions have raised critical questions about who has the right to act on behalf of the "international community."[51] The sidelining of the Security Council, as in the cases of Kosovo and Iraq, has detracted enormously from the authority of the United Nations as well as from the legitimacy of the interventions themselves. These latter interventions have also raised the specter of externally assisted state breaking: Kosovo, virtually independent of Yugoslavia, and Iraq, in the throes of a brutal insurgency, are candidates for state failure or dismemberment or both. Such military interventions, even if undertaken for humanitarian reasons, which most people doubt, especially in the case of Iraq, are likely to be counterproductive and end up creating greater disorder in the international system.[52] The invasion of Iraq should, therefore, act as a dire warning that the international community, acting through the Security Council, should prevent the recurrence of unilateral interventionism even if contemplated by the lone superpower.

CONCLUSION

It is in order to conclude with some policy prescriptions. International norms and the policies of international actors—primarily great powers and international institutions—can play a crucial role in preserving international order if they are used sagaciously to persuade domestic protagonists to make deals with one another without violating the sovereignty of existing states. Above all, the international community must strengthen the juridical status and bolster the political authority of Third World states by refusing to countenance secessionist demands while trying to persuade all parties to accept the notion that self-determination must be delinked from secession and should be defined in terms of empowering those segments of the population that have been denied access to political and economic power. In other words, self-determination should be perceived as synonymous with democratization (and its attendant power-sharing arrangements), rather than with the breakup of existing states.

Such an attitude, if adopted by the international community, will send clear signals to all concerned that the sovereign existence of postcolonial states is an essential prerequisite for the creation and maintenance of both domestic and international order. It will also signal that regimes that do not demonstrate a willingness to democratize must be ready to face international opprobrium, pariah status, and even sanctions. Such a stance on the part of the international community is necessary to prevent the Third World from sliding into greater anarchy. For, above all, it must be recognized that the problem of order in the Third World can be tackled, not by trying to transcend the Westphalian model (a world made up of sovereign states), but by attempting to strengthen it. The root cause of disorder in the Third World is linked to the inadequacy of state authority and not to the excessive use of state power. The augmentation of authority usually leads to a decrease in the reliance on force by the state because, as Robert Jackman has argued, power without force is the true measure of the political capacity of states.[53]

Finally, major powers, but especially the United States, must desist from intervening in the domestic affairs of even those states that may have unsavory or hostile regimes unless the latter directly threaten them militarily. The doctrine of preventive assault, as distinct from the preemption of imminent attack, espoused by the current U.S. administration, derogates from international order not merely because it provides a strong justification for many future interventions by many states in many locales. It is very deleterious from the perspective of both political order and political development of targeted states because it ends up creating greater disorder and undermining the legitimacy of established states. Furthermore, it can also be extremely counterproductive and end up creating real threats to the security of the intervenor rather than ameliorating any presumed threats. Iraq provides an eminent example of all these outcomes occurring simultaneously.

The Iraqi state today is in a shambles, and the United States is widely blamed for turning it into a failed state where life is "poor, nasty, brutish, and short." The severe deterioration in state capacity resulting from the U.S. invasion has transformed Iraq into the largest and safest haven for international terrorists whose principal aim is to target the United States and its allies. It has also led to a precipitate increase in hostility in the Muslim world toward the United States, thus helping create a reservoir of potential terrorists that is likely to pose an increasing threat to U.S. interests worldwide if not to the U.S. homeland itself. The major lesson one should draw from Iraq is that, while it is easy to destroy state capacity by the use of overwhelming force, it is next to impossible to resurrect such capacity except over a long period and after great travails. Moreover, there is no assurance that such a revived state will not turn revanchist and revisionist once it has attained appropriate capabilities. State making has to be an indigenous process in order for the final product to be at peace with itself. External intervention, even when undertaken with the best of intentions —and usually it is not—has the distinct potential to lead to state disintegration or state failure with highly negative consequences for both domestic and international order.

NOTES

This chapter is adapted from the author's chapter in *Between Development and Destruction: An Enquiry into the Causes of Conflict in Post-Colonial States,* ed. Luc van de Goor, Kumar Rupesinghe, and Paul Sciarone (London: Macmillan, 1996).

1. Kalevi J. Holsti, *The State, War, and the State of War* (New York: Cambridge University Press, 1996), 22, table 2.1. The table provides data on armed conflicts by type and region from 1945 to 1995. According to Holsti's tabulation, which does not include anticolonial wars of national liberation, 77 percent of the wars during the fifty-year study were internal in character. If one includes anticolonial wars, the proportion is likely to be considerably higher, probably somewhere around 90 percent.

2. Renata Dwan and Caroline Holmqvist, "Major Armed Conflicts," in *SIPRI Yearbook 2005* (New York: Oxford University Press, 2005), chap. 2.

3. Renata Dwan and Micaela Gustavsson, "Major Armed Conflicts," in *SIPRI Yearbook 2004* (New York: Oxford University Press, 2004), chap. 3.

4. Kalevi J. Holsti, "International Theory and War in the Third World," in *The Insecurity Dilemma: National Security of Third World States,* ed. Brian L. Job (Boulder, Colo.: Lynne Rienner, 1992), 38.

5. Max Singer and Aaron Wildavsky, *The Real World Order: Zones of Peace/Zones of Conflict* (New York: Chatham House, 1993). See also James M. Goldgeier and Michael McFaul, "A Tale of Two Worlds: Core and Periphery in the Post-Cold War Era," *International Organization* 46, no. 2 (Spring 1992): 467–491.

6. For greater detail on this argument, see Mohammed Ayoob, "The Security Predicament of the Third World State: Reflections on State Making in a Comparative Perspective," in Holsti, *The Insecurity Dilemma,* 63–80.

7. Youssef Cohen, Brian R. Brown, and A. F. K. Organski, "The Paradoxical Nature of State Making: The Violent Creation of Order," *American Political Science Review* 75, no. 4 (1981): 902.

8. For expanded discussions of the process of state making and its relationship to organized violence, see Keith Jaggers, "War and the Three Faces of Power: War Making and State Making in Europe and the Americas," *Comparative Political Studies* 25, no. 1 (April 1992): 26–62; and Charles Tilly, "War Making and State Making as Organized Crime," in *Bringing the State Back In,* ed. Peter B. Evans, Dietrich Rueschemeyer, and Theda Skocpol (New York: Cambridge University Press, 1985), 169–191.

9. Cohen et al., "The Paradoxical Nature of State Making," 905 (emphasis in the original).

10. The distinction between modern sovereign (or, as Charles Tilly would call them, "national") states and nation-states has been highlighted by Tilly, who has defined the former as "relatively centralized, differentiated, and autonomous organizations successfully claiming priority in the use of force within large, contiguous, and clearly bounded territories." Nation-states, on the other hand, are those "whose peoples share a strong linguistic, religious, and symbolic identity." Charles Tilly, *Coercion, Capital, and European States, AD 990–1990* (Cambridge, Mass.: Basil Blackwell, 1990), 43.

11. For details of this argument and the data on which it is based, see Charles Tilly, ed., *The Formation of National States in Western Europe* (Princeton, N.J.: Princeton University Press, 1975). See also Cornelia Navari, "The Origins of the Nation-State," in *The Nation-State: The Formation of Modern Politics,* ed. Leonard Tivey (Oxford: Martin Robertson, 1981), 13–38.

12. Navari, "The Origins of the Nation-State," 34.

13. Anthony D. Smith, *State and Nation in the Third World* (New York: St. Martin's Press, 1983), 11, 17.

14. Tilly, "Reflections on the History of European State Making," in *The Formation of National States in Western Europe,* 71.

15. For details of this argument, see Mohammed Ayoob, *The Third World Security Predicament: State Making, Regional Conflict, and the International System* (Boulder, Colo.: Lynne Rienner, 1995), especially chap. 2.

16. Joseph R. Strayer, *On the Medieval Origins of the Modern State* (Princeton, N.J.: Princeton University Press, 1970), 57.

17. Stein Rokkan, "Dimensions of State Formation and Nation Building: A Possible Paradigm for Research on Variations within Europe," in *The Formation of National States in Western Europe*, 586.

18. For theoretically informed accounts of the "cumulation of crises" in Italy and Germany, see the chapters on Italy and Germany by Raymond Grew and John R. Gillis, respectively, in *Crises of Political Development in Europe and the United States*, ed. Raymond Grew (Princeton, N.J.: Princeton University Press, 1978).

19. The earliest modern states of Western Europe were able to complete their state-making process in three near-distinct phases: (1) establishing the centralized, "absolutist" state at the expense of a feudal order that had begun to lose much of its economic and political utility, (2) welding together the subjects of the centralized monarchy into a people with a common history, legal system, language, and, quite often, religion (in the sense of Christian schisms), thus leading to the evolution of a national identity and the transformation of the centralized monarchical state into a nation-state, and (3) gradually extending representative institutions (dictated by the necessity to co-opt into the power structure new and powerful social forces that emerged as a result of the industrial revolution), over decades, if not centuries. Above all, as Stein Rokkan has pointed out, "what is important is that the western nation-states were given a chance to solve some of the worst problems of state building before they had to face the ordeals of mass politics." Rokkan, "Dimensions of State Formation and Nation Building," 598.

20. For details of this argument, see Ayoob, *The Third World Security Predicament*, chap. 5.

21. Robert H. Jackson, "Quasi-States, Dual Regimes, and Neoclassical Theory: International Jurisprudence and the Third World," *International Organization* 41, no. 4 (Autumn 1987): 529.

22. R. J. Vincent, *Human Rights and International Relations* (Cambridge: Cambridge University Press, 1986), 19–36.

23. For Sri Lanka, see Neil Devotta, *Blowback: Linguistic Nationalism, Institutional Decay, and Ethnic Conflict in Sri Lanka* (Palo Alto, Calif.: Stanford University Press, 2004); for Iraq, see Larry Diamond, *Squandered Victory: The American Occupation and the Bungled Effort to Bring Democracy to Iraq* (New York: Times Books, 2005).

24. As Seyom Brown has pointed out, the intellectual position that "servicing . . . basic human rights is the principal task of human polities—and that the worth of any polity is a function of how well it performs this task—has put the legitimacy of all extant polities up for grabs, so to speak. Whether particular nation-states, and the prevailing territorial demarcations, do indeed merit the badge of political legitimacy is, according to this view, subject to continuing assessment; accordingly, neither today's governments nor today's borders are sacrosanct." Seyom Brown, *International Relations in a Changing Global System: Toward a Theory of the World Polity* (Boulder, Colo.: Westview Press, 1992), 126.

25. For a discussion of failed states, see I. William Zartman, ed., *Collapsed States: The Disintegration and Restoration of Legitimate Authority* (Boulder, Colo.: Lynne Rienner, 1995).

26. Charles Tripp, "Near East," in *Superpower Competition and Security in the Third World*, ed. Robert S. Litwak and Samuel F. Wells, Jr. (Cambridge, Mass.: Ballinger, 1988), 113.

27. Gideon Gottlieb, *Nation against State: A New Approach to Ethnic Conflicts and the Decline of Sovereignty* (New York: Council on Foreign Relations, 1993), 2.

28. Crawford Young, "The Temple of Ethnicity," *World Politics* 35, no. 4 (July 1983): 659.

29. Charles Tilly, "National Self-Determination as a Problem for All of Us," *Daedalus* 122, no. 3 (Summer 1993): 30.

30. William Pfaff, "Invitation to War," *Foreign Affairs* 72, no. 3 (Summer 1993): 99, 101.

31. Jack Snyder, "Nationalism and the Crisis of the Post-Soviet State," *Survival* 35, no. 1 (Spring 1993): 12.

32. Robert H. Jackson, *Quasi-States: Sovereignty, International Relations and the Third World* (Cambridge: Cambridge University Press, 1990).

33. For details of the situation in Afghanistan in the 1980s during the height of superpower involvement in that country's civil war, see Olivier Roy, *Islam and Resistance in Afghanistan*, 2nd ed. (Cambridge: Cambridge University Press, 1990).

34. Michael Renner, *Small Arms, Big Impact: The Next Challenge of Disarmament* (Washington, D.C.: Worldwatch Institute, 1997). See also British American Security Information Council, *Stopping the Spread of Small Arms: International Initiatives,* report of a seminar held at the United Nations, New York, September 25, 1998.

35. Alex de Waal, "Contemporary Warfare in Africa: Changing Context, Changing Strategies," *IDS Bulletin* 27, no. 3 (1996), 6.

36. I. William Zartman, "Introduction: Posing the Problem of State Collapse," in *Collapsed States,* 8.

37. Jonathan Goodhand and David Hulme, "From Wars to Complex Political Emergencies: Understanding Conflict and Peace-Building in the New World Disorder," *Third World Quarterly* 20, no. 1 (February 1999): 19. The authors provide examples from Sudan, Liberia, and Afghanistan to demonstrate that conflict entrepreneurs benefit from internal war and thus possess a vested interest in their indefinite continuation.

38. Democratization is used in the sense of movement toward democracy; the latter is perceived as the desired goal, while the former is the process through which this goal is achieved or at least approximated.

39. Renée de Nevers, "Democratization and Ethnic Conflict," *Survival* 35, no. 2 (Summer 1993): 31–32.

40. John Chipman, "Managing the Politics of Parochialism," *Survival* 35, no. 1 (Spring 1993): 168.

41. Larry Diamond, Juan J. Linz, and Seymour Martin Lipset, "Introduction: Comparing Experiences with Democracy," in *Politics in Developing Countries: Comparing Experiences with Democracy,* ed. Larry Diamond, Juan J. Linz, and Seymour Martin Lipset (Boulder, Colo.: Lynne Rienner, 1990), 29.

42. Mohammed Ayoob, "Security Problematic of the Third World," *World Politics* 43, no. 2 (January 1991): 257–283.

43. Mahmood Mamdani, *Good Muslim, Bad Muslim: America, the Cold War, and the Roots of Terror* (New York: Pantheon, 2004).

44. Ahmed Rashid, *Taliban: Militant Islam, Oil and Fundamentalism in Central Asia* (New Haven, Conn.: Yale University Press, 2000).

45. Richard A. Clarke, *Against All Enemies: Inside America's War on Terror* (New York: Free Press, 2004); and Scott Ritter, *Iraq Confidential: The Untold Story of the Intelligence Conspiracy to Undermine the UN and Overthrow Saddam Hussein* (New York: Nation Books, 2005).

46. Robert Malley and Peter Harling, "A Counterintuitive Strategy for Iraq," *Financial Times,* November 22, 2005.

47. For the complex nature of the Iraqi insurgency, see Ahmed S. Hashim, "Iraq: From Insurgency to Civil War?" *Current History* 104, no. 678 (January 2005): 10–18; and Ahmed S. Hashim, "Iraq's Chaos: Why the Insurgency Won't Go Away," *Boston Review,* October–November 2004.

48. A number of stringent critiques of the U.S. invasion of Iraq, the subsequent failure in putting together a viable system in the country, and the impact of both these factors on the war against terrorism have been published recently. The following are among the best: George Packer, *The Assassin's Gate: America in Iraq* (New York: Farrar, Straus and Giroux, 2005); Larry Diamond, *Squandered Victory: The American Occupation and the Bungled Effort to Bring Democracy to Iraq* (New York: Times Books, 2005); and Daniel Benjamin and Steven Simon, *The Next Attack: The Failure of the War on Terror and the Strategy of Getting It Right* (New York: Times Books, 2005).

49. Peter Bergen and Alec Reynolds, "Blowback Revisited: Today's Insurgents in Iraq Are Tomorrow's Terrorists," *Foreign Affairs* 84, no. 6 (November–December 2005): 4.

50. Ibid., 6.

51. Mohammed Ayoob, "Humanitarian Intervention and International Society," *Global Governance* 7, no. 3 (July–September 2001): 225–230; and Mohammed Ayoob, "Humanitarian Intervention and State Sovereignty," *International Journal of Human Rights* 6, no. 1 (Spring 2002): 81–102.

52. Mohammed Ayoob, "The War against Iraq: Normative and Strategic Implications," *Middle East Policy* 10, no. 2 (Summer 2003): 27—39.

53. Robert W. Jackman, *Power without Force: The Political Capacity of Nation-States* (Ann Arbor: University of Michigan Press, 1993).

8

POWER, SOCIAL VIOLENCE, AND CIVIL WARS

Charles King

THREE CENTRAL QUESTIONS INFORM the scholarly literature on substate violence. One is why civil wars begin; a second is how they are fought; a third is how they come to an end. The incidence of civil violence has fallen steadily in the past decade, preceded by a serious escalation in the late 1980s and 1990s.[1] But the upsurge in civil wars more than a decade ago has yielded a wealth of studies, some broadly conceptual, others grounded in deep engagement with one or more cases.[2] One important result of the increased attention to the phenomenon has been the development of a more nuanced understanding of the role of power, in its many forms, in the initiation, prosecution, and termination of large-scale organized violence within the boundaries of a single state.

In the early stages of a conflict, potential belligerents size up the power disparities between themselves and the opposite side; beliefs about the possibility of a quick victory, or misperceptions about the relative power of the opponent, can push sides toward war and away from

political management of differences. During a war, assessments of power differences can determine the tactics and modes of military force deployed, or whether to push for an all-out victory or enter into peace negotiations. In a negotiated settlement, power disparities can sometimes nudge the sides toward compromise or, at other times, cement their intransigence.

At each stage of a conflict, "power" means many things: the ability to field fighting forces, the ability to garner international attention and assistance, the ability to determine the conceptual lenses through which outsiders view the violence. This chapter tries to make sense of the varied uses and forms of power by critically surveying recent advances in our understanding of power relationships before, during, and after civil wars. The chapter aims not only to speak to the question of power during the life cycle of fighting but also to link up with the large body of literature on social mobilization and social violence short of war—a literature from which the burgeoning research on civil wars has been largely divorced.

Each section that follows considers power dynamics through the prism of opportunities, organization, and framing—three dimensions that have become central to scholarly discussions about the dynamics of contentious politics in all its forms, from street protests to substate war.[3] The first section examines the role of power issues in the early stages of conflict, at the point where social mobilization morphs into large-scale, organized violence. The second section treats power dynamics during the course of the fighting itself and highlights the ways in which the nature, functions, and goals of violence shift with time. The third section focuses on power relationships during civil war endgames, particularly those whose endings include some form of negotiation. Each of these sections applies the lenses of opportunities, organization, and framing to highlight the multiple uses and forms of power in violent contexts. The conclusion examines the policy implications of the findings in each of the earlier sections. Understanding how power works is critical to crafting effective intervention strategies, even if there is no single magic bullet that can deal with power issues in their various forms. The conclusion also relates the discussion to the question of whether outright victory or negotiated settlement is the more likely outcome in civil wars today. It presents several reasons for believing that we may be witnessing a return to fighting-for-victory as the dominant strategy among belligerents.

POWER AND MOBILIZATION

It is tempting to think about the origins of civil wars metaphorically, as the result of a fateful interaction of sparks and powder kegs. Grievances are amassed on both sides of some social dividing line. A powerful leader gives voice to those grievances. People begin to realize the power of their common cause. A key event—the imprisonment of a popular leader, the government's firing on protesters,

an assassination—crystallizes the discord. Suddenly full-scale war breaks out.

Rarely, however, do things follow this pattern. In the first place, social protest, of whatever form, does not simply "turn violent." Violence is not a stage of social mobilization; it is a wholly different type of social interaction, one with its own causes, dynamics, power relationships, and life cycle.[4] Collective violence is not really about whipping up the masses, the weak targeting the strong, or the setting off of a political powder keg. Instead, as Donald Horowitz has pointed out, the real metaphor is probably closer to a pickup game.[5] Some motivated activists are required to get things moving, but there are other facilitating conditions, too. There must be some social rules governing how the game is to proceed: who can be a player and who a target; how much violence can be visited on the victims; how one determines friend from foe.

In the second place, levels of violence can wax and wane, with little connection to the overall level of social mobilization, the sense of threat perceived by contesting sides, or the feeling of grievance that they harbor. Violent episodes, from riots to all-out war, have a certain life cycle that is often independent of other, cognate forms of social mobilization. They may not be predictable, but they are patterned. There are normally precipitating events, such as rumors or targeted killings. These are usually followed by a quick burst of violence involving relatively few people. Often, a lull comes next, which is in turn followed by deadly attacks that escalate in number and intensity, one incident feeding the fury of the next. De-escalation is brought about by fatigue, the achievement of some overarching aim by one of the contesting sides, or external intervention.[6]

The very complexity of social violence makes it difficult to generalize about its essential qualities and key determinants, but one of the great advances in the field in recent years has been the development of a broad consensus about the areas in which research should be conducted. Through the study of what has come to be known as contentious politics, scholars have highlighted three crucial areas of inquiry. One is the set of opportunities—material, ideological, temporal—that potential entrepreneurs of violence can seize on to get the mobilization game going. Another is the set of organizational structures around which violent mobilization revolves; it is the presence of these organizations that helps distinguish short-term episodes of targeted violence (riots, individual lynchings) from sustained violent conflict (insurgencies, civil wars). A third area of inquiry is the phenomenon of framing, that is, the way in which the goals and objects of mobilization, whether violent or otherwise, are presented to potential adherents, to the designated opponents, and to third parties. Each of these lines of research can provide insights into power dynamics in civil wars.

At first blush, opportunities are perhaps the most easily understandable dimension of violent mobilization. Insurgents who face a weak incumbent government have greater scope for mobilization than those who face a well-armed, disciplined national army. Mobilizers who have the resources to pay people to join their movement—or at least pay for buses to get them to the town square—are predictably more successful than those who can offer little to potential adherents. Mobilizers who can step into the breach and provide food, security, or other goods when government institutions collapse are more successful than those who must operate in environments in which governments are capable and efficient in providing basic services. But the literature on social movements and contentious politics has underscored the essential fungibility of opportunities, that is, the ways in which less powerful groups can use whatever they have at their disposal to overcome the more formidable assets of their opponents.[7] It is perhaps for this reason that the weaker side may "overinvest in ends," compensating for its relative lack of opportunities by highlighting its moral superiority or by substituting intransigent commitment to the cause for firepower.[8] Opportunity structures can also change over time. Authoritarian governments that launch liberalization programs or countries in the throes of democratic transformation often end up opening up political space for contentious, even violent, politics.[9] Violent mobilization can also proceed in cascades, with a set of "early risers"—individuals and groups most inclined to engage in high-risk forms of social protest—making it relatively easier for groups less prone to mobilize.[10]

Organizations, both formal and informal, can also play a key role. Organizations can be seen as patterned and relatively stable forms of interaction within and among social groups, especially those that involve discrete incentive structures that facilitate group action. For any potential mobilizer, engendering collective action is the primary goal. But would-be leaders face an obvious collective action problem: Why would anyone join in a high-risk group activity—engaging in a violent protest or taking up arms in a civil war—when the goods that the protest or war is meant to deliver—more rights for the protesting group, independence, control over the central government—would accrue to him anyway? There are a number of obvious ways of overcoming this problem, from appealing to the moral sensibilities of those people most susceptible to mobilization to forcing members of the group, even at gunpoint, to join the cause. The important point, however, is that it is organizations, not groups, that facilitate collective action (at least in forms of violence that are anything other than short term, episodic, and low casualty). It is never the case that all, or even most, members of a social group—ethnic, racial, class, regional—are mobilized at the same time for some political end; rather, it is usually a smaller organization, claiming to speak in the name of the group, that does the work.[11] The really successful organizations are those that are able to convince significant numbers of people that they are their legitimate representative—and to convince potential outside supporters of the same thing.

Even relatively weak organizations can turn the very fact of their organizational structure into an important mobilizational tool. Consider the role of the agent provocateur. The provocateur is usually understood as someone in the employ of the stronger power—the secret police of a government, for example—and his task is to goad the weaker, insurgent power into engaging in violence, which then provides a pretext for a crackdown by the state. But the provocateur can also work in the opposite direction: as a member of the potential insurgent group himself, he may intentionally provoke a crackdown by the state and then use the resulting oppression as a catalyst for mobilizing insurgents. The logic is that such a reaction will change the calculus of other members of his putative mobilizational group, encouraging them to join the organization as a way of staving off further harsh reactions by the state.

Frames are also critical. It is easy to confuse frames of mobilization—how participants and external observers characterize, label, and categorize a particular episode of collective action —with sources of mobilization. In other words, categories can be mistaken for causes. A conflict that is "framed as ethnic," by belligerent elites or by outsiders, is simply not the same thing as an "ethnic conflict." The former interrogates the label, asking who uses it and for what purpose; the latter simply assumes that there is a natural kind of conflict called "ethnic conflict" and that both analysis and policy should be crafted in such a way as to make a useful distinction between this and other types of organized violence.[12] But as Rogers Brubaker has argued (staking out one of the most radical conceptual positions on this issue), the idea that there is a type of violent conflict that could meaningfully be called "ethnic" should probably be abandoned in favor of research on how social categories (of whatever type) are made, manipulated, and

transformed. For example, many of the conflicts across the postcommunist world might well be considered "ethnicized" conflicts, in the sense that the transformation from mobilization to violence entailed a fundamental reorientation of the lines of contestation from those involving regional affiliations or a particular elite status to putative ethnic identities. That is a rather different thing from claiming that ethnic conflict engulfed the postcommunist world in the 1990s.[13]

To see how all these power processes work, consider the mobilizational strategy of the Kosovo Liberation Army (KLA) in the late 1990s. The KLA was, by any measure, a weak player in the Yugoslav province of Kosovo when the group first began to make its appearance in 1997 and 1998. It lacked international legitimacy, so much so that it was placed on the U.S. government's list of known terrorist organizations. It lacked the support of the local majority Albanian population, which already had a vocal and popular representative in another political formation, the more moderate Democratic League of Kosovo. It was outnumbered and outgunned by Yugoslav police, military, and interior ministry forces.

However, it was this very weakness that determined the KLA's basic modus operandi before the outbreak of full-scale war: staging targeted attacks on Serbian police stations and other representatives of the Yugoslav state in the province. The aim of these attacks was clearly not to convince the Serbs to withdraw from the region; the attacks were far too low intensity to achieve that aim. Rather, their purpose was to provoke a disproportionate response by the Yugoslav government, which in turn would prompt local Albanians to seek protection against government atrocities by joining the ranks of the KLA or otherwise supporting the guerrilla group. The mechanisms were clear: the attacks, and especially the disproportionate counterattacks by Serbs, helped frame the conflict as ethnic; that frame in turn helped convince local Albanians that they needed the KLA to protect them from attack; and, soon, increased resources—men, arms, uniforms, and so on—began to accrue to the organization. In the end, the strategy worked brilliantly, transforming the KLA from a small terrorist organization into the broad representative of mobilized Albanians during the brief Kosovo war—an organization that NATO ended up effectively supporting.

In policy terms, the important point about carefully considering opportunities, organization, and frames is that each one comprises a set of social phenomena that external parties can, in fact, target—and long before large-scale violence has occurred. Believing in the alleged ancient hatreds behind ethnic conflicts or the nihilistic worldviews of terrorist insurgents hardly leads to workable, focused policies for potential third-party intervenors. But examining the precise opportunities available to the mobilizing elites, the formal and informal organizations that allow fights to be sustained, sometimes even across generations, and the frames through which potential violent entrepreneurs understand—and market—a brewing conflict can yield real-world policy prescriptions. The next two sections pick apart power dynamics in the middle of and at the terminal phase of conflicts. The final section examines what an analysis of these dynamics might mean for policy.

POWER AND VIOLENCE

In most instances of large-scale, organized violence, belligerents are widely disparate in terms of their opportunity structures, their organizational strength and sophistication, and their ability to frame the terms of a conflict. Governments have international recognition, the tools of statecraft, and the resources of the state. Insurgents may have popular legitimacy, the ability to disrupt rather than defeat, and the commitment of their followers. They are, in other words, asymmetrical players in a violent game. This simple fact in large

part helps explain why negotiated settlements have been such a historically rare outcome. When opponents share a common perception of the issues at stake, they are more likely to adopt similar strategies for settling the dispute. Symmetrical relations between the contesting parties also encourage conciliatory behavior, since each side possesses an effective veto over the pace and outcome of the negotiating process. Violent conflicts rarely exhibit these traits, however.[14]

To illustrate the dynamics of asymmetry, consider two forms of social violence on either end of the power disparity continuum: suicide terrorism and lynching. The former is asymmetrical in the sense that the perpetrator is singular and the victims are plural—in fact, the set of victims is so plural that it includes the perpetrator himself. The latter is asymmetrical in the opposite sense: the perpetrators are plural and the victim is typically singular. These types of social violence have power issues at their core. Especially after the 9/11 attacks, it is easy to think of suicide terrorism as a nihilistic form of violence motivated in part by religious fervor. But, as Robert Pape has shown, the overwhelming majority of suicide attacks (1) have a discrete political agenda, quite apart from the religious or nationalist ideology of the attacker, at their core and (2) have as their ultimate goal the removal of foreign forces from the perpetrators' territory. From 1983 until 2000, for example, the Liberation Tigers of Tamil Eelam, fighting for Tamil independence from Sri Lanka, staged more suicide attacks than all other major terrorist organizations combined.[15] Even if post-2001 cases are included, suicide strikes—both in number and in lethality—are still overwhelmingly connected with what would normally be labeled secessionist or national liberation struggles, not with a putatively apocalyptic commitment to violence or religion. In other words, suicide terrorism, although a seemingly irrational form of social violence, is by and large an attempt to overcome perceived disparities

between a relatively weak perpetrator and putatively more powerful victims.[16]

Lynchings have a similar dimension. The
popular image of lynchings, particularly in the
American South, is as a form of violence visited upon the weak by the strong—the summary execution of a socially weak black man
by socially stronger white men. But there are
two important caveats to this image. First, the
South's "lynching era," from roughly 1880 to
1930, was associated with a period when power
disparities were being renegotiated. Lynching
as a form of violence emerged as an abhorrent
response to the empowerment of blacks after
the Civil War, an attempt by whites to recoup
some of the social power they perceived as having been lost as a result of the South's defeat.[17]
Second, lynching was also a tool of power
maintenance within both white and black
communities themselves. In the half century
after 1880, about a fifth of all lynchings were
intraracial rather than interracial. Moreover,
most of these within-group incidents occurred
before racial laws had reestablished the clear
social boundaries between racial groups that
had been eroded by the Civil War and Reconstruction.[18] In other words, lynching emerged
not only as a particularly violent tool of power
maintenance between blacks and whites but
also as an instrument wielded by old elites
within both black and white communities to
punish members who had transgressed group
norms or boundaries.

Power asymmetries can exist along a number of different axes during violent conflict.
In the following sections, I briefly examine
how the structure of asymmetry can play itself
out in terms of opportunities, organization,
and framing.

Opportunities, Resources, and Costs

Any form of large-scale violence comes with
opportunity costs, both direct and indirect.
Weapons must be acquired. Fighting forces
must be fed, clothed, and induced to remain
in the field. Civilian populations or other non-

belligerents must be convinced to support the
cause, by forcing them to yield up their own
resources (which, in turn, expends the reservoir
of goodwill and popular support) or by buying
them off.

As conflicts progress, the way in which belligerents analyze the relationship between their
original war aims and the costs that they have
already incurred may begin to change. The
longer a conflict continues, the less its basic
dynamics are reducible to a set of root causes
that can be addressed by negotiations. In instances of prolonged violence, belligerents often
develop two different calculuses, one for past,
or sunk, costs and one for future costs. Sunk
costs come at a psychological markup; future
costs come at a discount. Belligerents come to
see their activity as a kind of investment, so
that future fighting becomes not about achieving some overarching original aim but rather
about justifying the sunk costs—atrocities committed by the adversary, the destruction of
property, the damage done to international
prestige, the death of revered political leaders
—with little concern for the additional costs
that might be incurred.

These calculations exist in many forms of
human activity, from making war to playing a
slot machine. But there seems to be a particular feature of substate violence that encourages
belligerents to think about opportunity costs in
a particular way. Substate conflicts are, almost
by definition, about irreconcilable war aims:
Party A's taking over the government means
that Party B will not; Party A's seceding from
the state means that Party B will no longer
control that bit of territory.[19] This irreconcilable nature of violence also means that civil
wars have historically been particularly fierce,
often accompanied by genocide and other
atrocities; by one calculation, about a quarter
of all civil wars since 1945 have involved the
attempt by one side to liquidate a noncombatant population associated with the adversary.[20]
The entire group represented by one side—
ethnic, religious, regional, ideological—is quite

often seen as the enemy, with little clear distinction between combatants and noncombatants. Taken together, these features in turn mean that the costs analyzed by belligerents are not only the costs of waging war in a narrow sense—expending resources to get the fighting done—but also the derivative grievances of the entire group they claim to represent. Waging a civil war can thus become a reflexive enterprise, with revenge overshadowing the pursuit of those stakes over which the parties originally took up arms. Revenge, an economist might say, is simply an attempt at recouping past losses—the "resources" lost to one belligerent side through the atrocities committed by the other.[21]

Organization

In situations most favorable to negotiations, the opposing sides are relatively well formed, with structures of command and subordination, substantial solidarity among each group's constituents, clear boundaries of group membership, and identifiable spokespeople. This organizational robustness reduces uncertainty and lessens the suspicions of bad faith. It also hedges against the possibility that, once talks have begun, spoilers from either side will seek to wreck the negotiating process.[22]

In civil wars, however, the level of organization among the belligerents varies considerably. On one side, the government is normally able to field a relatively well-provisioned army, composed of professional soldiers, which is able to carry out military operations over much of the state's territory. The government is also able to deploy its nonmilitary organization (such as its foreign relations apparatus) to secure international support. On the other side, forces are often poorly formed and composed of nontraditional combatants: child soldiers, village militias, diaspora returnees, and so on.[23]

The organizational disparity between the sides clearly favors an outcome other than negotiated settlement. The superior organizational power of one side encourages escalation; one more battle, the logic goes, and the weaker side will inevitably collapse. The party with inferior organization may also be divided into a variety of factions, each claiming to speak for the entire group. In such a situation, designating the leadership of one faction as a legitimate bargaining partner provides no guarantee that leaders of rival factions will abide by the terms of a settlement. Simply knowing whom to speak to can be a problem, even if there is a good-faith interest on one side in negotiating. Disparities in organizational power can thus be an important structural impediment to negotiations.

Framing

A critical but often overlooked dimension of violence is the power to manage the way in which the conflict is perceived by outsiders: journalists, policymakers, humanitarian workers, foreign publics. One of the conceits in the study of large-scale violence, particularly research that employs large numerical data sets, is the view that war presents itself as an obvious type, which can then be analytically labeled and studied as a naturally occurring species. Hence, researchers code civil wars as "ethnic," "religious," "ideological," and so on; these terms are then used as a quick shorthand to describe what the wars are essentially about.[24] We speak readily of Hutu and Tutsi in Rwanda, Serb and Muslim in Bosnia, or Arab and African in Darfur as meaningful categories that map the various sides, interests, grievances, and motivations in a particular armed conflict. Research is then conducted along the lines of asking whether types of civil wars—"ethnic" versus "religious," for example —have similar or different causes.[25]

But, as any close observer of conflict—or, indeed, any participant—can attest, the way in which violence is coded and described is itself one of the terrains over which the sides fight. During the Cold War, belligerents in many conflicts routinely came to label their actions in overtly political terms: as a defense of the free market against Soviet- or communist-backed insurgents, for example. In the 1990s, the frames of reference became largely cultural: as national liberation movements, or as the defense of an embattled cultural minority against a majority bent on ethnic cleansing. By the early 2000s, the labels had become rather different: terrorists or insurgents, perhaps even Islamist insurgents, seeking to overthrow a legitimate central government. Conflicts in Angola and El Salvador fall into the first camp; Bosnia, Georgia, and Rwanda, into the second; and Iraq and Afghanistan, into the third.

One could tell a convincing story about the essential change in the nature of substate conflict based on shifts in the international system, from the Cold War, through the brief post–Cold War hiatus, to the post-9/11 world. Data sets on conflict have reflected such a version of events, showing an increase in ethnic conflict in the 1990s and, more recently, a rise in the incidence of terrorist attacks since 2001.[26] These visions of conflict, however, are not merely attempts at analysis; they are, in fact, part of the conflicts themselves.

It is one thing to say that the incidence of something called "ethnic conflict" increased in the 1990s. It is quite another to say that belligerents changed the way they themselves understand what they are doing. There are, of course, real differences among substate conflicts over the past half century; some have involved contestation over control of a central government, while others have had the question of secession and territorial control at their core. But it is simply erroneous to believe that analytical categories through which we view conflict are somehow independent of the political and cultural context in which we are doing the analyzing.

But if we understand categorization as part of the power politics of civil wars, how are we to make sense of who is doing the fighting and how they have come to blows? One of the most creative thinkers in this regard in recent

years has been Stathis Kalyvas, whose work aims to join macrolevel, data set–driven analyses with microlevel, almost anthropological efforts to understand violent conflict from the point of view of those engaged in it.[27]

Kalyvas has argued that the real drivers of violent conflict lie at the intersection of "master narratives" about violence and the everyday concerns of local elites. Master narratives involve a story detailing what the conflict is essentially about: the oppression of one group by another, the treachery of a minority, the past injustices visited on one group by another, the threat posed by one group to another. Rarely, however, are such master narratives enough to prompt large numbers of people to take up arms, much less to continue fighting when the costs of war become apparent. Rather, it is the complex ways in which such narratives intersect with essentially local concerns that can both prompt and sustain violence.

Two important insights follow from Kalyvas's basic model. First, not every master narrative is as good as any other. There are always political figures, both more and less popular, who advocate violence in extremis, but their ability to make their own master narrative of a conflict stick is variable. An entire research program thus suggests itself: studying attempts to create master narratives that did not turn out to produce large-scale violence. While there have been attempts at paired comparisons of violent and nonviolent outcomes, the overwhelming tendency in the literature is to study civil wars, well, by studying civil wars. The alternative—pairing up what Donald Horowitz has called "near misses" with instances of actual large-scale violence—ought to be more central to our thinking about conflict.[28]

Second, narratives are linked not only with microlevel processes but also with international ones. Shifts in the international system are important features of substate violence precisely because they contribute to the quiver of master narratives from which elites can draw. Given a particular global discourse about national self-determination and genocide, master narratives that focus on these themes are likely to gain more traction at the international level than ones that focus, for example, on ideological purity or resource scarcity. Marketing, in other words, is crucial not only to one's own constituents downstream but to one's potential backers upstream as well. To be convinced of this point, one need only examine the numerous insurgent groups that switched from marketing themselves in terms of ideology in the 1980s to espousing ethnic self-determination in the 1990s, or governments that switched from battling Marxist insurgents in the 1980s to doing battle with ethnic separatists in the 1990s and then terrorists in the early 2000s.

POWER AND PEACE

How are power and peace related? Under what conditions do the calculations of belligerents about whether to engage in peace negotiations or continue fighting depend on power relationships among the various sides—or, indeed, within the various sides? One way to think about these questions is to examine the structural dimensions of violence that can inhibit the ability of belligerents to engage in negotiations. The following sections examine these structures, again, through the prism of opportunities, organization, and framing.

Opportunities: Military and Political Objectives

There is often a huge gulf between the battlefield and the negotiating table. What happens on the ground—which side is winning or losing—may be of little relevance to belligerents in their calculations of whether to continue fighting.[29] Part of the problem is the often irreconcilable war aims discussed earlier. But a more important issue concerns the difficulty that each side often has in understanding the resources at its disposal and then making calculations about the deployment of those resources to reach strategic goals.

In civil wars, fighting is often episodic and changeable. Front lines, if they exist at all, shift rapidly. Seasonal weather makes maneuver difficult. Even the number and nature of the fighting forces can change suddenly. Assessing the military costs and benefits, and then correlating those with overall political objectives, can be extremely difficult. Leaders thus have an incentive to make decisions tactically and incrementally, balancing the short-term costs and benefits of a particular move in relation to the decisions that came before it; the highly fluid and uncertain environment in which the fighting occurs, however, makes calculating the costs of any one move in relation to the entire campaign impossible.[30] This logic can go so far that elites may even discount the situation on the battlefield when deciding whether to expend resources on further violence.

Another sense in which resource expenditure is difficult to calculate involves the degree to which war itself is a resource generator. Overall, of course, war is a bad thing for all concerned: crops are destroyed, towns leveled, people killed or made homeless. But for many groups and individuals, the anarchy of civil war can create incentives for personal enrichment. With no effective government control in some areas, business can be conducted free of restraint. Natural resources can be exploited. Trade can be carried on across international frontiers. Illegal crops can be grown and exported. In Eurasia, one of the chief blockages to settlement in four ongoing territorial disputes—Transnistria in Moldova, Abkhazia and South Ossetia in Georgia, and Nagorno-Karabakh in Azerbaijan—has been the degree to which each of the conflict zones has become a revenue generator, both for the secessionist government and for collaborators within central governments.[31] Similar points could be made with respect to the diamond trade in Angola and Sierra Leone, timber in Cambodia, heroin in Myanmar, and opium in Afghanistan.

In recent years, much of the literature on civil wars has been caught up in the debate over "greed" versus "grievance."[32] It is too much to say that the central motivation in all, or even most, civil wars is the greed of unscrupulous elites. But the basic insight that war creates interests—and that those interests grow the longer the fighting rages—cannot be ignored. Negotiated settlements can thus be blocked by the very fact that the resources produced by conflict end up being greater (at least for the decision makers) than the resources expended to keep the conflict going.

Intervention strategies must thus target the array of opportunities available to decision makers. Sanctions and public awareness campaigns, such as the "conflict diamonds" movement, can reduce the scope for profit. Targeted visa bans on key leaders can inhibit their ability to enjoy the benefits of intractable conflict. Greater openness regarding international financial transactions can reveal the channels of war profiteering. It is not enough, however, to block the economic benefits that accrue to elites. The longer conflicts continue, the more likely it is that people at all levels of a war-torn society will find ways of surviving, even thriving, in the midst of uncertainty. Negotiated settlements that do not take account of the new economic incentives and opportunities created by war are doomed to failure. For example, disarmament and demobilization programs must be based on the idea that, in many conflicts, a personal weapon such as an AK-47 is both an economic and a military asset. It can be used as insurance against theft or being cheated in a transaction; it can be sold or bartered for other goods; it can be the basic price of entry for being taken seriously as an economic or political agent.[33] There are opportunity costs to war, but violence also opens up a host of new opportunity agendas for people at every level in a conflict-ridden society.

Organization: Decision-Making and Security Dilemmas

In few civil wars are belligerent sides well organized, with clear command-and-control structures and provisions for punishing spoilers and defectors. Internal battles for defining the goals of the contesting sides, their relations with the enemy, and the point at which they are prepared to accept something less than their ultimate aims are frequent.

In substate conflicts, factionalism is often extremely intense. Belligerent parties break apart and re-form, coalitions appear and dissolve, former allies become, sometimes overnight, sworn enemies, and vice versa. Fighters on the ground may in fact be analogous to bureaucrats in the national security institutions of the modern war-making state: both have specific interests in how a war ends, and their identification of these private concerns with the aims of their own side can create a major barrier to the termination of a conflict. There is thus not only a security dilemma at work across the major divide in a civil war, that is, between the contesting sides. There are often a host of lower-level security dilemmas at work among factions of the same side. With no overarching power available to enforce the implicit contract binding various factions ostensibly on the same side, each has an incentive to hedge against the others' bad faith. The very act of hedging, however, may be taken not only as a sign of reticence but as a signal of bad faith.

External players are therefore often crucial in breaking the security dilemma—both across and within the main lines of contestation.[34] Ending the fighting and laying the groundwork for peace might, over the long haul, enhance the security of all parties, but in the short term the absence of credible security guarantees encourages both sides to stay away from the bargaining table. Hence, because of the organizational weakness of parties in civil wars, belligerents may have little incentive to negotiate. External agents are often thus in the position of providing a kind of surrogate organization for the contesting sides, an organization that is capable of enabling peace and preventing defections, rather than enabling mobilization and conflict.

Framing: The Role of Leaders

Framing processes work at many levels, from the way rival factions on belligerent sides characterize internal disputes all the way up to the norms of the international community. At all levels, however, key leaders are critical. Not only do leaders bring their own interests to bear on how conflicts are framed; they also contribute their particular worldviews—even pathologies—to how a conflict is characterized and marketed, not only to their own sides, but also to potential allies and adversaries outside the conflict zone. This problem, moreover, exists as much during the course of a conflict as after a negotiated settlement has been signed.[35]

As conflicts continue, the distinction between the overarching goals of a particular side and the perceptions of leaders can become fuzzy. Combatants on either side may come to identify their own leaders with the struggle itself, refusing to accept any negotiated settlement that would diminish the status of the wartime leadership—in other words, framing the conflict as essentially about the honor of the leader. External powers may also overinvest in the personality of a particular wartime leadership, in essence framing the conflict as a contest among personalities. One need only consider the dominant discourses about the Yugoslav conflicts—from one of "ancient hatreds" in the early 1990s to one of the treachery of Slobodan Milosevic and his drive for a "Greater Serbia" by the end of the decade—to see how frames of analysis involving key elites can shift over time.

In practice, how leaders choose to frame a conflict—and to frame the possibility of peace—matters a great deal to how the conflict is settled. Disputes that are characterized in all-or-nothing terms, where fundamental differences divide the sides and where no form of settlement within the boundaries of a single state is possible, can be settled only by first shifting the frames through which the conflict is viewed. The role of external players is to present a whole host of alternative ways of seeing the dispute. This is not to say that all conflicts are solvable, but rather that external intervenors must be particularly aware of the way in which the lenses through which they view the conflict can have an impact on how belligerent leaders themselves frame the conflict. Political leaders are born marketers, but in violent conflicts, their target audience is not only their own mobilized populations but also the potential allies and adversaries in the international system.

CONCLUSION: NEGOTIATIONS AND VICTORY

The standard way of thinking about how civil wars end is that they come to a conclusion when one side destroys the other side's will or ability to continue fighting. For at least the past two decades, however, there seems to have been a growing international norm favoring the termination of substate armed conflict through negotiation. Several decades ago, it would have been rare to find an armed conflict in which at least one outside player was not involved as a cobelligerent. Of the 165 civil wars that have arisen since the end of World War II, 36 involved the deployment of troops from another state, and in only one year during that period—1991—were there no internationalized civil wars at all recorded.[36] Today, however, both great powers and international organizations have worked to pressure belligerents into forgoing outright military victory in favor of some sort of mediated settlement. It is rare today to find an ongoing armed conflict in which no outside player is involved as a mediator of some sort.

It is difficult to arrive at conclusions for improving the nature of external intervention and mediation that apply to all cases. While there are key power dynamics that can be identified in a wide range of conflicts, how they play out is dependent on local conditions, local and global interests, and the capacities of potential intervenors. But at least four policy-relevant conclusions suggest themselves from the analysis of opportunities, organization, and frames discussed earlier.

Structuring Opportunities

Opportunities for negotiated settlement do not arise purely because of changes on the battlefield. In fact, what happens militarily may be of little real value in belligerents' calculations. One role of external parties is to convince belligerent parties that the possibility of negotiation really is in their best interest. But success in this regard is hardly guaranteed. It depends on concerted efforts to make continued war unprofitable, to target recalcitrant elites and their sources of enrichment, and to set deadlines and provide incentives for meeting them. In essence, external mediators must be engaged in lowering the opportunity costs of peace, which means not only making continued violence less attractive as an option for key leaders but also raising the attractiveness of negotiation by protecting, to a degree, whatever interests key elites have delivered during the course of the war.

Targeting Organization

It is usually external actors who are responsible for the organizational disparities of civil wars. They provide arms to one side but not the other, or they act as havens for elites and fighters on the run. Targeting these external sources of support is thus often a critical component —in effect, reducing the organizational asymmetries that cause one side to believe that it can win through all-out victory and the other to believe that it has no choice but to avoid destruction by fighting to the finish. The elimination of foreign bases for insurgents, the reduction in arms flows from outside the war zone, the withdrawal of external advisers, and the cessation of foreign aid and support are often critical features of successful settlements. Peace agreements that build in a regional dimension—seeing the organizations

of violence, in effect, as extending well beyond the borders of the state concerned—have now become a critical component of successful war termination.

Manipulating Frames

In all conflicts, belligerents have an incentive to represent what they are doing in ways that not only gain local adherents but also appeal to external intervenors. Human rights, national liberation, pro-communism, antiterrorism: all have, at one time or another, been basic elements of how belligerents market their cause. In the early stages of conflict, especially those in which external parties have a considerable interest, it is difficult to untangle the framing process from the real interests and goals at stake. But over time, learning to distinguish advertising from interests is vital. Not only does it allow a clearer assessment of what belligerent elites might be willing to accept in a peace deal, but it also allows external mediators to manipulate the frames themselves. "National liberation," for example, can be understood in a variety of ways, not only as complete independence but also as substantial autonomy and control over local economies. Shifting the terms of debate will only rarely happen without external assistance, but having the ability to do so depends on being as skillful as the war makers themselves in how one wields conflict frames.

Returning to Victory?

Successful intervention strategies depend on knowing a great deal about the interaction of opportunities, organization, and frames in any violent setting. But there is one final point to consider regarding the nature and efficacy of negotiated settlements today. The emergence of a norm of negotiated settlement has, to a large degree, been the result of the end of superpower competition and the reinvigoration of multilateralism in international politics. Given its origins, this norm may well turn out to be an artifact of the brief post–Cold War era—the long decade stretching from 1989 to 2001. It remains to be seen whether genuine multilateralism, external intervention, and peacemaking will survive the war in Iraq and the global war on terrorism. There are at least three reasons for believing that they will not, that we will see a return to victory as the dominant strategy in the prosecution and termination of substate war.

First, negotiated settlements, while still preferred by the international community, have been the exception, rather than the rule, over the long term. Only about a third of civil wars since 1800 have ended via negotiations (compared with about two-thirds of interstate wars).[37] That figure drops to about a fourth if we consider only those civil wars initiated since the mid-twentieth century.[38] If we further eliminate colonial wars and other conflicts with a substantial international component, the figure for negotiated endings may be as low as 15 percent.[39] The total number of civil wars in the world has declined since the end of the Cold War,[40] but there is no evidence that this is mainly because negotiations have become more successful. On the contrary, the duration and termination of civil wars seem to be correlated with how they begin and are prosecuted: wars arising from revolution or decolonization tend to be brief; those arising out of a land dispute between local populations tend to be longer; and those that are financed through war profiteering, longer still.[41] The preference for negotiation and the assiduous work of international institutions in the 1990s may have been yet another part of the historically unusual nature of international politics during the transition from the Cold War to the war on terrorism. Because of the powerful incentives that are at work in civil wars, the push toward outright victory may well be the natural equilibrium toward which the international system will return.

Second, again over the long term, negotiations tend to produce settlements that are more unstable than the outright victory of one side. Odds are about even that a negotiated settlement will lead, in relatively short order, to renewed war; outright victory by one side produces an outcome in which the chances of stability are better than even.[42] The reasons for this trend are not difficult to see. In civil wars, the winners are rarely magnanimous in victory; the desire to eliminate the enemy, not simply defeat him, has long been a concomitant of large-scale violence within states. With the enemy effectively gone—through the expulsion of populations, ethnic cleansing, and genocide—victors can be far more secure in their victory than those who choose to negotiate. It is for this reason that external interventions, where they succeed, involve a long-term engagement to enable both sides to commit credibly to peace.[43]

Third, the recent historical record offers plenty of examples of outright victory, even if the results of those victories remain unrecognized by the international system. The late 1980s and 1990s are often characterized as a period of peacekeeping and negotiations, and it is certainly true that the size, scope, and intensity of multilateral peacekeeping, particularly that sponsored by the United Nations, increased markedly. But for the civil wars that began then, it was in the main an era of military victory. Secessionists, by and large, defeated central governments and established workable independent states; rebels either ousted established governments or were virtually annihilated, along with their civilian supporters, by recognized regimes. True, those victories did not in all cases lead to outcomes that were generally recognized by the international community. The brief wars for independence in Slovenia and Croatia produced independent governments, yet Somaliland remains unrecognized as a state, as does Kosovo (for the time being) and all the de facto republics that emerged from the conflicts in the former Soviet Union (Abkhazia, Transnistria, South Ossetia, Nagorno-Karabakh). But recognition should not be confused with stability.

More than a decade after the signing of the Dayton peace agreement in Bosnia, few people believe that the country could long survive without the heavy hand of the international community's "high representative," plus a still-sizable peacekeeping force. In contrast, Abkhazia and Nagorno-Karabakh have built relatively stable, functioning, but unrecognized governments in the wake of their military victories over Georgia and Azerbaijan.

Fundamental power dynamics often favor violence over accommodation, continuation over cessation, and victory over negotiation— even if the societies in which violence emerges are ultimately worse off as a result. If the international norm of negotiated settlement is to become more than a slogan, individual states and international institutions will have to work to shift the incentives of both leaders and followers in substate conflicts. The dilemmas of resource disparities have to be understood. The logic of organizational asymmetries has to be addressed. And the power of framing, both by leaders and by potential external intervenors, has to be acknowledged. In the 1990s, the irruption of civil wars, ethnic conflicts, and state-sponsored genocide onto the international agenda gave rise to considerable scholarship and policy thinking about how to deal with these issues. But now that these forms of violence and, indeed, the vocabulary used to speak about them have given way to fighting terrorism, insurgencies, and rebellions, the moment when policymakers worked at quelling civil wars—rather than just taking sides in them—may well have passed.[44]

NOTES

1. Lotta Harbom and Peter Wallensteen, "Armed Conflict and Its International Dimensions, 1946–2004," *Journal of Peace Research* 42, no. 5 (2005): 623–635.

2. For surveys of the state of the field, see Steven R. David, "Internal War: Causes and Cures," *World Politics* 49 (July 1997): 552–576; Ibrahim Elbadawi

and Nicholas Sambanis, "How Much War Will We See? Explaining the Prevalence of Civil War," *Journal of Conflict Resolution* 46, no. 3 (June 2002): 307–334; the special issue of the *Journal of Conflict Resolution* 46, no. 1 (February 2002); Charles King, "The Micropolitics of Social Violence," *World Politics* 56 (April 2004): 431–455; and Havard Hegre, "The Duration and Termination of Civil War," *Journal of Peace Research* 41, no. 3 (2004): 243–252.

3. The field of contentious politics is actually much more extensive than the study of violent forms of social interaction. For overviews, see Sidney Tarrow, *Power in Movement: Social Movements and Contentious Politics*, 2nd ed. (Cambridge: Cambridge University Press, 1998); Ronald Aminzade et al., *Silence and Voice in the Study of Contentious Politics* (Cambridge: Cambridge University Press, 2001); Doug McAdam et al., *Dynamics of Contention* (Cambridge: Cambridge University Press, 2001); and Charles Tilly, *The Politics of Collective Violence* (Cambridge: Cambridge University Press, 2003).

4. Rogers Brubaker and David D. Laitin, "Ethnic and Nationalist Violence," *Annual Review of Sociology* 24 (1998): 423–452.

5. Donald L. Horowitz, *The Deadly Ethnic Riot* (Berkeley: University of California Press, 2001), 266.

6. Ibid., chap. 3.

7. See especially Tarrow, *Power in Movement*, chap. 5.

8. I. William Zartman, "Dynamics and Constraints in Negotiations in Internal Conflicts," in *Elusive Peace: Negotiating an End to Civil Wars*, ed. I. William Zartman (Washington, D.C.: Brookings Institution Press, 1995), 9.

9. Jack Snyder, *From Voting to Violence: Democratization and Nationalist Conflict* (New York: W. W. Norton, 2000).

10. See Mark R. Beissinger, *Nationalist Mobilization and the Collapse of the Soviet State* (Cambridge: Cambridge University Press, 2002).

11. See Rogers Brubaker, *Ethnicity without Groups* (Cambridge, Mass.: Harvard University Press, 2004).

12. The entire literature on the rise of ethnic conflict since the end of the Cold War is in large part built on this view. It is certainly true that more conflicts became framed as ethnic/cultural/religious after the late 1980s, but asking why that was the case is different from asking why there is now more ethnic

conflict in the world than in the past. For works that argue for a fundamental change in the nature of violence, see Daniel P. Moynihan, *Pandaemonium: Ethnicity in International Politics* (Oxford: Oxford University Press, 1993); Mary Kaldor, *New and Old Wars: Organized Violence in a Global Era* (Cambridge: Polity Press, 1999); Nicholas Sambanis, "Do Ethnic and Nonethnic Civil Wars Have the Same Causes? A Theoretical and Empirical Inquiry (Part 1)," *Journal of Conflict Resolution* 45, no. 3 (June 2001): 259–282; and John Mueller, *The Remnants of War* (Ithaca, N.Y.: Cornell University Press, 2004). For critiques, see Stathis Kalyvas, "'New' and 'Old' Civil Wars: A Valid Distinction?" *World Politics* 54, no. 1 (October 2001): 99–118; and Stuart Kaufman, *Modern Hatreds: The Symbolic Politics of Ethnic War* (Ithaca, N.Y.: Cornell University Press, 2001).

13. Brubaker, *Ethnicity without Groups*. For works that challenge the ethnic conflict frame, see Susan L. Woodward, *Balkan Tragedy: Chaos and Dissolution after the Cold War* (Washington, D.C.: Brookings Institution Press, 1995); Stuart Kaufmann, *Modern Hatreds;* V. P. Gagnon, Jr., *The Myth of Ethnic War: Serbia and Croatia in the 1990s* (Ithaca, N.Y.: Cornell University Press, 2004); and Georgi Derluguian, *Bourdieu's Secret Admirer in the Caucasus: A World-System Biography* (Chicago: University of Chicago Press, 2005). For an overview of the way in which scholarship on "nationalism" encouraged a particular view of postcommunist ethnic politics, see Maria Todorova, "The Trap of Backwardness: Modernity, Temporality, and the Study of Eastern European Nationalism," *Slavic Review* 64, no. 1 (Spring 2005): 140–164.

14. Charles King, *Ending Civil Wars*, Adelphi Paper 308 (Oxford: Oxford University Press and IISS, 1997), 40–41.

15. Ehud Sprinzak, "Rational Fanatics," *Foreign Policy* (October 2000): 66–73.

16. Robert A. Pape, "Blowing Up an Assumption," *New York Times*, May 18, 2005; and Pape, "The Strategic Logic of Suicide Terrorism," *American Political Science Review* 97, no. 3 (August 2003): 343–361. See also Pape, *Dying to Win: The Strategic Logic of Suicide Terrorism* (New York: Random House, 2005); Mia Bloom, *Dying to Kill: The Allure of Suicide Terror* (New York: Columbia University Press, 2005); and Diego Gambetta, ed., *Making Sense of Suicide Missions* (Oxford: Oxford University Press, 2005). For a classic statement on the difficulties of studying

terrorist violence, see Walter Laqueur, "Interpretations of Terrorism: Fact, Fiction, and Political Science," *Journal of Contemporary History* 12, no. 1 (January 1977): 1–42.

17. Stewart E. Tolnay and E. M. Beck, *A Festival of Violence: An Analysis of Southern Lynchings, 1882–1930* (Urbana: University of Illinois Press, 1995).

18. E. M. Beck and Stewart E. Tolnay, "When Race Didn't Matter: Black and White Mob Violence against Their Own Color," in *Under Sentence of Death: Lynching in the South* (Chapel Hill: University of North Carolina Press, 1997), 132–154.

19. On the irreconcilability of aims, see Chaim D. Kaufmann, "Possible and Impossible Solutions to Ethnic Civil Wars," *International Security* 20, no. 4 (Spring 1996): 136–175; and Kaufmann, "When All Else Fails: Ethnic Population Transfers and Partitions in the Twentieth Century," *International Security* 23, no. 2 (Autumn 1998): 120–156.

20. Roy Licklider, "The Consequences of Negotiated Settlements in Civil Wars, 1945–1993," *American Political Science Review* 89, no. 3 (1995): 686.

21. For a fascinating study of revenge norms in violent settings short of civil war, see Christopher Boehm, *Blood Revenge: The Anthropology of Feuding in Montenegro and Other Tribal Societies* (Lawrence: University Press of Kansas, 1984).

22. On spoilers, see the classic article by Stephen John Stedman, "Spoiler Problems in Peace Processes," *International Security* 22, no. 2 (Autumn 1997): 5–53.

23. On the key role of diasporas in the Balkan conflicts, see Paul Hockenos, *Homeland Calling: Exile Patriotism and the Balkan Wars* (Ithaca, N.Y.: Cornell University Press, 2003); and Stacy Sullivan, *Be Not Afraid, for You Have Sons in America* (New York: St. Martin's Press, 2004).

24. For overviews of studies that take quantitative approaches, see Roy Licklider, "Early Returns: Results of the First Wave of Statistical Studies of Civil War Termination," *Civil Wars* 1, no. 3 (1998): 121–132; and Nicholas Sambanis, "A Review of Recent Advances and Future Directions in the Literature on Civil War," *Defense and Peace Economics* 13, no. 2 (2002): 215–243. James Fearon, Daniel Posner, and David Laitin have argued for taking the coding of cases more seriously. See Laitin and Posner, "The

Implications of Constructivism for Constructing Ethnic Fractionalization Indices," *APSA-CP: Newsletter of the Organized Section in Comparative Politics of the APSA* 12, no. 1 (Winter 2001): 13–17; and Fearon and Laitin, "Ethnicity, Insurgency, and Civil War," *American Political Science Review* 97, no. 1 (February 2003): 75–90.

25. Nicholas Sambanis, "Do Ethnic and Nonethnic Civil Wars Have the Same Causes? A Theoretical and Empirical Enquiry (Part 1)."

26. Susan B. Glasser, "Global Terrorism Statistics Debated," *Washington Post,* May 1, 2005, A23.

27. Stathis N. Kalyvas, "The Ontology of 'Political Violence': Action and Identity in Civil Wars," *Perspectives on Politics* 1, no. 3 (September 2003): 475–494. See also Kalyvas, *The Logic of Violence in Civil Wars* (Cambridge: Cambridge University Press, forthcoming); Kalyvas, "Wanton and Senseless? The Logic of Massacres in Algeria," *Rationality and Society* 11, no. 3 (1999): 243–285; and Kalyvas, "Red Terror: Leftist Violence during the Occupation," in *After the War Was Over: Reconstructing the Family, Nation, and State in Greece, 1943–1960* (Princeton, N.J.: Princeton University Press), 142–184.

28. Horowitz, *The Deadly Ethnic Riot*, 478.

29. Jane E. Holl, "When War Doesn't Work: Understanding the Relationship between the Battlefield and the Negotiating Table," in *Stopping the Killing: How Civil Wars End*, ed. Roy Licklider (New York: New York University Press, 1993), 269–291.

30. Paul R. Pillar, *Negotiating Peace: War Termination as a Bargaining Process* (Princeton, N.J.: Princeton University Press, 1983), 236.

31. Charles King, "The Uses of Deadlock: Intractability in Eurasia," in *Grasping the Nettle: Analyzing Cases of Intractability,* ed. Chester A. Crocker, Fen Osler Hampson, and Pamela Aall (Washington, D.C.: United States Institute of Peace Press), 269–294.

32. See David Keen, *The Economic Functions of Violence in Civil Wars,* Adelphi Paper 320 (Oxford: Oxford University Press and IISS, 1998); William Reno, *Warlord Politics and African States* (Boulder, Colo.: Lynne Rienner, 1998); Mats Berdal and David M. Malone, eds., *Greed and Grievance: Economic Agendas in Civil Wars* (Boulder, Colo.: Lynne Rienner, 2000); Global Witness, *A Rough Trade: The Role of Companies and Governments in the Angola Conflict*

(London: Global Witness, 1998); and Mats Berdal and Monica Serrano, eds., *Transnational Organized Crime and International Security: Business as Usual?* (Boulder, Colo.: Lynne Rienner, 2002). The debate began with a series of papers by Paul Collier and his colleagues at the World Bank. See, for example, Paul Collier and Anke Hoeffler, *Greed and Grievance in Civil War* (New York: World Bank, January 2001).

33. See Mats Berdal, *Disarmament and Demobilization after Civil Wars,* Adelphi Paper 303 (Oxford: Oxford University Press and IISS, 1996).

34. The classic article on the security dilemma in substate conflict is Barry Posen, "The Security Dilemma and Ethnic Conflict," in *Ethnic Conflict and International Security,* ed. Michael E. Brown (Princeton, N.J.: Princeton University Press, 1993), 103–124.

35. Stephen John Stedman, "Negotiation and Mediation in Internal Conflicts," in *The International Dimensions of Internal Conflict,* ed. Michael E. Brown (Cambridge, Mass.: MIT Press, 1996), 485.

36. Harbom and Wallensteen, "Armed Conflict and Its International Dimensions, 1946–2004."

37. Paul R. Pillar, *Negotiating Peace: War Termination as a Bargaining Process* (Princeton, N.J.: Princeton University Press, 1983), 25.

38. Licklider, "The Consequences of Negotiated Settlements in Civil Wars, 1945–1993," 684.

39. Stephen John Stedman, *Peacemaking in Civil War: International Mediation in Zimbabwe, 1974–1980* (Boulder, Colo.: Lynne Rienner, 1991), 9.

40. Nils Peter Gleditsch, Peter Wallensteen, Mikael Eriksson, Margareta Sollenberg, and Havard Strand, "Armed Conflict, 1946–2001: A New Dataset," *Journal of Peace Research* 39, no. 5 (2002): 615–637.

41. James D. Fearon, "Why Do Some Civil Wars Last So Much Longer Than Others?" *Journal of Peace Research* 41, no. 3 (2004): 275–301.

42. Licklider, "The Consequences of Negotiated Settlements in Civil Wars, 1945–1993," 686.

43. Barbara F. Walter, *Committing to Peace: The Successful Settlement of Civil Wars* (Princeton, N.J.: Princeton University Press, 2001).

44. On the return of taking sides and counterinsurgency as themes in U.S. foreign policy, see Peter Maass, "Professor Nagl's War," *New York Times Magazine,* January 11, 2004; and Maass, "The Salvadorization of Iraq?" *New York Times Magazine,* May 1, 2005.

9

MINORITIES, NATIONALISTS, AND ISLAMISTS
MANAGING COMMUNAL CONFLICT IN THE TWENTY-FIRST CENTURY

Ted Robert Gurr

EFFECTIVE MANAGEMENT OF ETHNIC, separatist, and religious conflicts by civil and international authorities presupposes an understanding of their nature, their causes, and the outcomes of past efforts at management. This chapter surveys some current evidence from and analyses of *communal conflicts*. These are conflicts in which groups such as the Mayans of Chiapas, the Albanians of Kosovo, and the Sunnis of Iraq—groups that define themselves using ethnic, national, or religious criteria—make claims against the state or against other political actors.[1] The actors in these conflicts include many of the 286 groups surveyed in the Minorities at Risk (MAR) project, which provides the basis for many of the comparisons that follow.[2] The following general points need to be kept in mind.

There are many sources of communal group identity. The criteria used by groups to define themselves usually include common descent, shared historical experiences, and valued cultural traits, including shared belief. There is no warrant for assuming that any one basis for

ethnic or cultural identity, such as religion, language, race, or a common homeland, is inherently more important or more likely to cause conflict than others.

Communal groups are motivated by more than greed or power. Most communal groups seek material and political gains, but one cannot explain away the significance of cultural or religious identity by arguing that what "really" motivates such groups is greed or the desire for power. What is important is that communal groups organize around their shared identity to seek gains for members of their group. It is misleading to interpret the Zapatistas as just a militant peasants' movement or the Sunnis of Iraq as the equivalent of a political party. They draw their strength from cultural and historical bonds, not associational ones.

Communal groups are highly diverse. The MAR survey distinguishes between *national* and *minority peoples* (see table 1). National peoples are 156 regionally concentrated, culturally distinct groups that usually have a history of separate political existence and want to protect

Table 1. Minorities at Risk in 2003 by World Region

World Region	Number of Countries with Minorities at Risk	Total Number of Minorities at Risk	Number of National Peoples	Number of Ethnoclasses	Number of Communal Contenders	Number of Religious Sects
Western democracies and Japan	15 of 21	29	16	12	0	1
Postcommunist states of East-Central Europe and Central Asia	23 of 27	62	52	9	0	1
East, Southeast, and South Asia	20 of 24	58	35	4	14	5
North Africa and the Middle East	13 of 20	29	16	1	6	6
Africa south of the Sahara	27 of 45	75	19	6	50	0
Latin America and the Caribbean	18 of 24	33	20	10	2	1
Totals	116 of 161	286	156	42	72	13

Note: Politically significant national and minority peoples greater than one hundred thousand or 1 percent of country population in countries with 1998 populations greater than five hundred thousand. The list is based on current research by the Minorities at Risk Project, Center for International Development and Conflict Management, University of Maryland. Changing political circumstances and new information lead to periodic updates in the inclusion and exclusion of groups under observation. The "numbers of countries" column includes the numbers of countries in the region with minorities at risk, then the numbers of countries in the region above the five-hundred-thousand threshold in 1998.

The Western democracies include Canada, the United States, Australia, New Zealand, and Japan in addition to Western Europe. The Middle East includes North Africa, the Arab states, Turkey, Cyprus, Iran, and Israel. Asia includes Afghanistan, the Indian subcontinent, Southeast Asia, and Pacific Asia. Africa includes South Africa but excludes North Africa. Latin America includes Central America and the Caribbean.

or reestablish some degree of politically separate existence from the states that govern them. The Mayans of Chiapas and the Kosovars illustrate two different subtypes: the Mayans are indigenous peoples, while the Kosovars are ethnonationalists. *Minority peoples* are culturally distinct groups in plural societies who seek equal rights, opportunities, and access to power within existing political communities. African Americans in the United States and Brazil are examples of ethnoclasses, 42 of whom are politically active in the early years of the twenty-first century. The Sunnis of Iraq are communal contenders, one of 72 instances of culturally distinct peoples in heterogeneous societies who hold or seek a share in state power. Muslim and other religious minorities are discussed later in this chapter.

Different kinds of groups choose different strategies. National peoples usually seek *exit,* a goal that often leads to separatist wars and state repression. Minority peoples usually want *access.* In political systems that are open and responsive, the leaders of minority peoples ordinarily pursue such goals by conventional political action and protest campaigns. In states that suppress or ignore such claims, leaders are more likely to choose strategies of violence, which may escalate into protracted communal warfare. The communal contenders of post-invasion Iraq—Shiites, Kurds, and Sunnis—illustrate how struggles for power can lead to civil war. The first two groups formed a coalition, whereas many Sunnis supported armed resistance and terrorism in an effort to regain some of the power they lost when Saddam Hussein was toppled.[3]

The heart of this chapter is a theoretical answer to the question, Why do minorities rebel? Four kinds of factors are examined: why ethnocultural identities become important, the kinds of incentives that motivate ethnopolitical groups, how their leaders build capacity, and the diverse ways in which groups' opportunities and strategies are shaped by states and the international system. To set the stage for this analysis, we look at some evidence about the seriousness of the ethnic challenge to security, how modernization and globalization have driven the rise of ethnopolitical conflict, and —an important new topic—how ethnopolitics is being reshaped by the rise of political Islam. The chapter's last section summarizes the principles of an emerging international regime for managing communal conflict.

HOW SERIOUS IS THE COMMUNAL CHALLENGE TO GLOBAL SECURITY?

Communal conflict has been the world's most common source of warfare, insecurity, and loss of life for several decades.[4] Such conflicts increased throughout the Cold War and in its immediate aftermath, but since the mid-1990s the trend has been reversed.

- One hundred twenty-one national and minority peoples fought guerrilla or civil wars at some time between 1945 and 2003. Of these, sixty were protracted ethnonational conflicts; that is, they were fought over issues of group autonomy and lasted at least a decade.

- In 2002 there were forty-nine serious communal conflicts worldwide, eleven of which were wars and fifteen of which involved low-level rebellion or terror campaigns. Most others were large-scale protest movements punctuated by occasional violent episodes. Some of these have since been settled, but other new communal wars have begun, including the Sunni insurgency in Iraq and the rebellion in Darfur, Sudan, which has prompted a genocidal campaign of ethnic cleansing.[5]

- Since 1955, according to research by Barbara Harff, nearly fifty ethnic and religious minorities have been targeted in forty-one episodes of genocide and mass political murder that killed at least thirteen million and as many as twenty million noncombatants.[6]

- In 2005 there were 11.5 million internationally recognized refugees and an estimated 21.3 million others who were internally displaced. Most of these people were fleeing from civil wars, interethnic rivalries, and campaigns of mass murder and ethnic cleansing.[7]

The alarmist interpretation of these kinds of data is that the world is on the downward slope to anarchy within and among states and to polarization of societies and continents along lines of religious and cultural cleavage. Evidence on trends during the last decade suggests a more optimistic outlook:

- Armed conflicts for self-determination, which include the deadliest and most disruptive of all communal wars, declined from forty at the end of 1990 to twenty-five in early 2005. Most were either stable or de-escalating, because rebels either were defeated militarily or are engaged in a peace process. The latter include a number of long-term and supposedly "intractable" conflicts in which there is a real prospect of enduring settlement, for example, the Israeli-Palestinian conflict and the Aceh rebellion in Indonesia.
- Most new violent communal conflicts of the past fifteen years began near the end of the Cold War, with few commencing since then. More precisely, an average of eight new rebellions began each year between 1989 and 1992; since 1992 the average has fallen to two per year. The main risk in the near future is the breakdown of peace agreements that recently checked communal wars in Sudan, Burundi, Sri Lanka, and elsewhere.
- The number of new campaigns of communal protest traces the same pattern, from an average of twelve per year in the early 1990s to three per year since 1993. This decline foreshadows a continued decline in new communal rebellions. The recent historical record shows that, on average, ten years of nonviolent political action preceded new

communal rebellions. Since the number of new communally based protest campaigns is declining, the pool of potential future rebellions also is shrinking.[8]

- One-sixth, at most, of the world's population identifies with politically active cultural groups. The 286 groups tracked in the Minorities at Risk project include slightly more than one billion people, or one-sixth of the global population. Keep in mind that group boundaries are fuzzy and that only some group members are likely to support political action. The groups are most heavily concentrated in Africa south of the Sahara, the postcommunist states, and Asia. And more than half of these 286 peoples are minorities who seek recognition and rights within existing societies, not a redrawing of international boundaries.[9] Other communal groups may make new claims in the future, but we probably have already heard from most of those that have serious grievances.

MODERNIZATION AND COMMUNAL CONFLICT

The upward trend in communal conflict that captured world attention in the 1990s began in the 1960s. The end of the Cold War made such conflicts more visible. Some were provoked by contention for power in postcommunist states; others were responses to democratic transitions in Africa. But neither the Cold War nor its passing "created" the cultural identities, animosities, or aspirations that have sparked these conflicts. Rather, the long-term trend is best understood as an indirect consequence of global processes of modernization.

Modernization includes four large and interdependent changes that have reshaped the world in the past half century: the growth of the modern state and the state system, economic development, the international movement of peoples, and the communications revolution.[10] The processes of modernization are not new, but their pace and reach since 1950 have no historical precedent, and in combination they have vastly increased interaction and competition among cultural groups and contention between cultural groups and the state.

Expansion of State Powers

Virtually all new and postrevolutionary states of the past half century have been committed to consolidating and expanding their powers, emulating the precedents established by the successful states of the industrial North. This objective dictates, among other things, that states subordinate the special interests and relative autonomy of hundreds of communal groups to state elites' conception of national identity and interest. State building almost everywhere in the Third World has meant policies aimed at assimilating national and minority peoples, restraining their historical autonomy, and extracting their resources, revenues, and labor for the use of the state. The building of new communist states in Eastern Europe after 1945 had the same implications and consequences.

Some minority peoples, including most Chinese communities in Southeast Asia, have been able to share power and prosperity at the center of new states. Others—especially in Africa, where the reach of state power is limited—have been able to hold on to de facto local autonomy and sometimes to regain it when central authority collapsed. Eritrea gained independence after the overthrow of Ethiopia's Marxist military regime in the early 1990s, and Somaliland (northern Somalia) has had an effective government and de facto independence since the early 1990s. But the net effect of state building in most parts of the world has been to substantially increase grievances of most culturally distinct groups, those who have been unable either to protect their autonomy or to participate meaningfully in power at the center.

The Development of a Global Economic System

The worldwide impetus to industrialize and to exploit underutilized human and natural resources has benefited some cultural groups and harmed others. Ethnoclasses in developing societies have often gained from expanding economic opportunities; some also have mobilized in efforts to overcome discriminatory barriers that restricted their access to new wealth. Indigenous peoples have been most adversely affected. Like it or not, their resources and labor are being absorbed into national and international networks of economic activity. They are almost always disadvantaged by the terms of their incorporation. Their reactions have been especially sharp in response to the alienation of the lands, forests, and natural resources on which they are culturally as well as materially dependent.[11]

People in Motion

Many millions of people have crossed international boundaries in the past half century in search of economic opportunity and in flight from privation, repression, and war. Ethnoclasses have proliferated as a result. Attempts to regulate the flow of economic and political migrants have had little effect on the rapid growth of diasporas such as Hispanics in the United States, Muslims in Europe, and migrant workers in the Persian Gulf states and most African countries. Policies designed to speed their incorporation into their host societies, such as requiring the learning of a new language, have mixed results. Most new immigrant groups surveyed in the MAR project are subject to discrimination by resentful members of mainstream society; some face restrictions as a matter of government policy.

Immigrant groups contribute to economic growth while simultaneously posing potential security problems in their home and host states. People of diasporas often carry political grievances in their baggage and send support to one or another faction in communal conflicts in their homelands. Muslim immigrants may come under the influence of jihadists, as they have in Britain, and aim their political anger at host societies. As diasporas become more settled in democratic societies their members enter politics with communal objectives in mind—certainly a better outcome than terrorism, but also a challenge to plural societies that emphasize individual rather than collective rights.[12]

The Communications Revolution

The spread of the mass media and the ready availability of electronic forms of communication facilitate or enhance every stage in the conflict process: rapid communication and dense communication networks make cultural groups more aware of their identities and shared interests; they bring diasporas into close contact with supporters and sources of inspiration elsewhere; and they give leaders powerful means to mobilize mass followings and coordinate their political actions. Virtually every new communication technique has been adapted by communal groups for its own purposes: Islamic activists have used audiocassettes to spread their gospel of renewal and revolution since the 1970s; the Miskito Indians of Nicaragua used the radiophones of Moravian churches to coordinate their resistance to the Sandinistas in the early 1980s; and a great many communal activist organizations now are on the World Wide Web.

THE RISE OF POLITICAL ISLAM

The greatest future risk of communal conflict as of 2005 is not a new wave of ethnonationalism but rather the radicalization of Muslim communal groups. Among them are Shiites in Sunni-majority societies, Muslims in separatist regions, and Muslim minorities in Western democracies and elsewhere. More than 60 of the 286 groups in the MAR survey meet such criteria (see table 2). Their political organizations pursue communal or ethnonational ob-

jectives or, in several instances, are subject to discrimination and repression because they are regarded as heretical by mainstream Islamic groups. If the new ideology of global jihad takes hold among activists in any of these groups, as it has among some Muslims in Britain, Sunnis in Iraq, and Moros in the Philippines, those activists are likely to escalate violence and be more resistant to efforts at conflict management.

In addition, Islamists are active in other countries that have ethnic divisions, for example, in Turkmenistan, Tajikistan, and Malaysia, in ways that can intensify communal rivalries. In Malaysia, for example, Islamists have a limited following among the country's Malay Muslim majority but have alarmed the country's Chinese and Indian minorities with demands for a greater Islamic role in the political system. In Nigeria the problems posed by Islamists are more acute: Muslim activists have fueled communal violence against Christian southerners living in northern Muslim states.

THE POLITICAL MOBILIZATION OF COMMUNAL GRIEVANCES: OR, WHY MINORITIES REBEL

The question here is why culturally distinct groups become engaged in protest and rebellion against the state. Modernization sets the larger context. The specifics of each group's situation determine how it acts within that context. Four general factors determine the nature, intensity, and persistence of the group's actions:

- The *salience of ethnocultural identity* for members and leaders of the group
- The extent to which the group has collective *incentives* for political action
- The extent of the group's *capacities* for collective action
- The availability of *opportunities* in the group's political environment that increase its chances of attaining group objectives through political action

Table 2. Muslim Communal Groups in the Minorities at Risk Survey

Muslim Minorities in Countries with Non-Muslim Majorities	**Muslim Communal Contenders and Minorities in Countries with Muslim Majorities**
United Kingdom: *South Asians*	Afghanistan: Hazaris
France: Muslims	Lebanon: Shiites, Sunni, (Druze)
Germany: Turks	Saudi Arabia: Shiites
Serbia: Kosovar Albanians, Sandzak Muslims	Bahrain: Shiites
Macedonia: Albanians	Iran: Arabs (Baha'i)
Bulgaria: Turks	Iraq: Sunni, Shiites
Greece: Muslims	Pakistan: (Ahmadis)
Cyprus: Turkish Cypriots	Nigeria: Northerners
Israel: *Arabs in Israel proper,* Palestinians in the West Bank and Gaza	
Georgia: Adzhars	**Muslim Ethnonationalists and Indigenous Peoples in Countries with Muslim Majorities**
Russia: Avars, Chechens, Ingush, Karachay, Kumyk, Lezgins, Tatars	Azerbaijan: Lezgins
India: Kashmiris, Muslims	Algeria: Berbers
Thailand: Malay Muslims	Morocco: Berbers, Saharawis
Singapore: Malays	Turkey: Kurds
China: Hui Muslims, Turkmen	Syria: Kurds
Philippines: Moros	Lebanon: Palestinians
Ethiopia: *Oromo,* Afars, Somalis	Jordan: Palestinians
Kenya: Somalis	Iraq: Kurds
Tanzania: Zanzibaris	Iran: Bakhtiari, Baluchis, Kurds
Ghana: Mossi-Dagomba	Pakistan: Baluchi
Côte d'Ivoire: Northerners	Indonesia: Acehnese
Fiji: *East Indians*	Eritrea: Afars
Guyana: *East Indians*	Djibouti: Afars
	Mali: Tuareg
	Niger: Tuareg

Note: Groups in italics include substantial numbers of non-Muslims as well as Muslims. Groups in parentheses are targets of repression because they are regarded as heretical by mainstream Islamic groups.

Groups are listed in the country-by-region sequence of the master roster of Minorities at Risk groups.

Propositions about these four factors are derived from existing theories of collective action and are central to explaining political action by any kind of identity group.[13] The key to analyzing the origins of communal conflict is to show how each factor is activated by the characteristics and circumstances of communal identity groups.

The Salience of Ethnocultural Identity

The first general proposition is that the greater the salience of ethnocultural identity for people who share common descent, cultural traits, and historical experiences, the more likely they are to define their interests in ethnocultural terms and the easier it is for leaders to mobilize them for collective action. I assume that cultural identities—those based on common descent, experience, language, and belief—tend to be stronger and more enduring than most civic and associational identities. Nonetheless, the salience of cultural identity varies widely among and within groups and is subject to change over time. The descriptive question is,

How salient is communal identity at any point in time? The analytic question is, What determines the salience of a group's identity?

Scholars recognize that communal identities are multidimensional, as suggested at the outset of this chapter. Some traits, though, are associated with particularly strong and durable collective identities. In multiracial societies, shared physical attributes ("race") are almost always primary markers of group identity. Religion also is a strong source of group cohesion, not alone in Islamic societies. A group's language is another key marker of identity, a source of group cohesion, and a recurring issue of contention among groups in heterogeneous societies. But I agree with David Laitin that language disputes alone are not a common source of deadly rivalries, because language differences are subject to individual and collective compromises. Individuals in heterogeneous societies can and ordinarily do speak several languages, but they cannot be both black and white or both Hindu and Muslim.[14]

If cultural factors are variable, does salience originate in a people's material interests, as Marxists have argued? It is true enough that claims made by communal groups include material and political demands as well as claims based on their ethnocultural interests. But it is not reasonable to explain away the significance of cultural identity by arguing that what "really" motivates the leaders and members of such groups is greed or the quest for power.[15] The decisive factor is that communal groups organize around their shared identity and seek gains or redress of grievances for the collectivity. It is a commonplace that manipulative leaders, such as Slobodan Milosevic and Franjo Tudjman in postcommunist Yugoslavia, used appeals to nationalism as a means to advance their personal political agendas. It is equally important to recognize that most of those who followed them did so because they thought they were best served by militant nationalists.

The basic argument is that the salience of ethnocultural identity depends on how much

difference it makes in people's lives. If a communal group is treated differently, by denial or privilege, its members will become more self-conscious about their common bonds and interests. Minimize differences, and communal identity becomes less significant as a unifying force.

Three specific principles are suggested. First, the greater a people's dissimilarity from groups with which they interact regularly, the more salient their identity is likely to be. Second, ethnocultural identity is important when it contributes to a group psychology of comparative advantage or disadvantage. Groups in heterogeneous states make comparisons of relative worth based on their collective experiences and myths. Advantaged groups often feel superior because they share a belief that they are the original people of a place (the Malay claim to be "sons of the soil") or that they have exceptional skills (the European claim to a civilizing mission toward colonial peoples) or that they have overcome adversity and hostile challengers (the basis of Afrikaners' sense of superiority over black Africans).[16] The belief in comparative superiority helps to explain ethnic domination and the resistance of advantaged groups to communal challenges. It also motivates some separatist movements by relatively advantaged peoples, for example, the Catalans of Spain.

Comparative superiority is the other side of the coin of what Vamik Volkan calls the "chosen traumas" of disadvantaged peoples, their beliefs about their victimization.[17] The ethnocultural identity of disadvantaged and victimized groups is salient because it is the source of invidious distinctions—the inequalities in status, economic well-being, and access to political power that are maintained by advantaged groups. Insofar as a people's race, culture, or beliefs provide others with grounds for discriminating against them, the salience of their ethnocultural identity is likely to be high.

Third, open conflict with the state and rival groups sharpens the salience of group identity.

Communal leaders often try to increase the salience of group identity by invoking historical memories and symbols of victimization. Serious episodes of conflict leave bitter residues in people's memories and for a long time afterward can be used by leaders to justify political action. Serbian nationalists, for example, made effective use of fifty-year-old memories about atrocities committed by the Croatian Ustashi to mobilize Serbian support for their 1991–92 war with the newly independent state of Croatia. Labeling helps: Serb leaders referred to Croats as Ustashi.

Incentives for Political Action

The second general proposition is that the greater the shared incentives among members of an ethnocultural identity group, the more likely they are to support and participate in communal action. *Communal action* refers to any organized activity in pursuit of the group's objectives, beginning with mobilization, the process by which people are recruited into movements. Once people are mobilized, participation can take diverse forms, depending on the group's political environment and the strategic and tactical decisions of its leaders. The range of actions includes conventional politics, collective action (strikes, demonstrations, nonviolent direct action), and rebellion (terrorism, armed uprisings, guerrilla wars, civil wars).

Three types of incentives prompt political action by identity groups: *resentment about losses suffered in the past, fear of future losses,* and *hopes for relative gains.* The relative importance of each of these factors depends on a group's changing position in relation to other groups and to the state. The proposition builds on familiar arguments about the causes of relative deprivation. People who have lost ground relative to what they had in the past are said to experience decremental deprivation and are motivated to seek redress for what was lost. Those who anticipate losses, especially reversal of an improving trend, experience progres-

sive deprivation that disposes them to support movements that defend and promote the group's present status and attainments. Groups in which nationalist or revolutionary expectations have taken hold are motivated to seek a fundamental change in their political status.

The incentives of communal groups are not inherently nonrational nor do they necessarily dispose people to communal violence. Instead, they constitute a potential for goal-directed political action. They are analogous to what Charles Tilly characterizes as the collective interests that form the basis for group mobilization.[18] But incentives for communal groups are different from Tilly's calculated "collective interests" because of their strong emotional content. Members of identity groups usually resent their disadvantages and seek redress not only, or even necessarily, with self-interest in mind, but with passion, self-righteousness, and solidarity with their kindred.[19] Four general conditions shape group incentives.

Collective Disadvantages. First, the greater a group's collective disadvantages vis-à-vis other groups, the greater the incentives for action. *Disadvantage* means socially derived inequalities in material well-being, political access, or cultural status by comparison with other social groups. Inequalities provide incentives for remedial action. If inequalities are maintained by overtly discriminatory policies, the minorities affected have powerful incentives for action because their resentment is easily focused on the agents of discrimination. All but 50 of the 286 groups in the Minorities at Risk survey were subject to one or several kinds of discrimination in 2003:[20]

Economic discrimination

- One hundred three groups experienced active economic discrimination due to contemporary social practice or public policies.
- Ninety-three groups were economically disadvantaged because of past discrimination or neglect.

- Ninety groups experienced no economic discrimination.

Political discrimination
- One hundred four groups experienced active political discrimination due to contemporary social practice or public policies.
- Ninety groups were politically disadvantaged because of past discrimination or neglect.
- Ninety-five groups experienced no political discrimination.

Cultural discrimination
- Seventy-three groups experienced moderate (fifty-four groups) to substantial (nineteen groups) cultural restrictions due to public policies, for example, with respect to language use, religious practice, practice of group customs, or formation of cultural organizations.
- Forty-eight groups experienced cultural restrictions due to social discrimination.
- One hundred sixty-five groups experienced no cultural restrictions.

The Loss of Political Autonomy. Regaining political autonomy is a second major incentive. Virtually all ethnonationalists, national minorities, and indigenous peoples either were once independent of external control or were part of political entities other than the states that now govern them. The U.S. conspiracy that deposed the last ruling monarch of independent Hawaii in 1893, the fragmentation of the Hungarian nation into a half-dozen segments in 1919, and the conquest of Tibet in 1951 are historical facts that give rise to persistent grievances and hopes for restoration. Such episodes are potent symbols for political entrepreneurs whose projects are to restore indigenous rights or regain national autonomy. The greater the loss of autonomy, and the more recently it occurred, the greater the likely effect of such appeals.

Islamists in the Middle East are promoting a new version of this kind of grievance. They claim that Muslim peoples have the right to be free of Western, Christian, and Jewish influences, invoking the historical memory of the caliphates and the intrusive presence of Israel and its supporters.

Repression. Repressive control of a communal group is a third major incentive for collective action. The general principle is that the use of force against people who think it is unjust may in the short run inspire fear and caution but in the longer run provokes resentment and enduring incentives to resist and retaliate. White supremacy in the American South was maintained until the early 1960s by legal repression and extralegal violence. Long before the Russians' first invasion of secessionist Chechnya in December 1994, Russian governments had used force to establish and maintain control of the region. In both cases repression left enduring legacies of anger and resentment, which in the United States animated a decade of direct action and violent protest by African Americans and in Chechnya motivated widespread, intransigent resistance to Russian attacks in 1994–95 and from 1999 to the present. Despite all Russian strategies—massive security measures, repression, election of tame Chechnyan leaders—the conflict seems impervious to solution.

Frames for Communal Action. Empowering ideas about national self-determination and collective rights of minorities also give impetus to communal movements because they provide justifications for action. Theorists of social movements describe these kinds of orienting ideas as "frames," or cognitive understandings. In Sidney Tarrow's summary, "Inscribing grievances in overall frames that identify an injustice, attribute the responsibility for it to others and propose solutions to it, is a central activity of social movements."[21] The most effective frames for identity groups are those that fit their cultural predispositions and immediate circumstances. Three doctrines that have been widely used as frames by contemporary communal movements are the principle of national self-determination, the doctrine of indigenous rights, and international declarations that guarantee the rights of religious and cultural minorities. The Islamist doctrine of jihad against those who threaten Muslims is the most dramatic new example of frames used to justify political violence. Jihadist doctrine blames Western agents for the humiliation and oppression suffered by marginalized people throughout the Muslim world and in the Muslim diaspora. The doctrine gains plausibility from the United States' long-standing support for Israel and the U.S.-led invasion of Iraq in 2003.[22]

Are frames derived from these empowering doctrines an independent source of incentives for collective action by communal groups? Perhaps they are for intellectuals and aspiring leaders. For collectivities as a whole, though, the effect of these doctrines probably is contingent on other kinds of incentives and on how closely individuals identify with the group. People are more likely to frame their situation and actions as a struggle for group rights or self-determination if they already have a sense of injustice about disadvantages and repression, as many people in the Islamic world do. And group identifiers are more likely to accept these doctrines if they learn of them through networks of communication within the group and from credible leaders like imams.

The Dynamics of Protracted Conflict. The argument to this point incorporates some strong feedback effects. The salience of group identity and incentives for collective action are based partly on repression and disadvantages imposed on the group because they resisted in the past. It is precisely this mutually reinforcing dynamic that generates protracted communal conflicts such as those between Catholics and Protestants in Northern Ireland, Hutu and Tutsi, Palestinians and Israelis, Tamils and Sinhalese. Historical analysis should pinpoint the particular conjunction and sequence of conditions that set off a given episode. Once these conflicts have gone through several cycles, however, they tend to become self-generating. The general approach to the chicken-and-egg question of which came first, grievances or political action, is to examine the consequences of each episode of protracted conflict. If an ethnic group in conflict is subject to repression and its disadvantages persist without any compensatory gains, then we should expect to see a resentful reinforcement of group identity and a disposition (incentives) to wait and work for future opportunities to rebel.

The Capacity for Collective Action

The third general proposition is that the greater the cohesion and mobilization of an ethnocultural identity group, the more frequent and sustained its participation in political action. And, we can add, the more likely it is to gain concessions and greater access to power. Cohesive groups are those held together by dense networks of communication and interaction. *Mobilization as process* refers to the ways in which members of communal organizations are recruited and motivated. *Mobilization as variable* signifies the extent to which group members commit their energies and resources to collective action in pursuit of shared interests.

A sense of collective identity and some awareness of common interests (salience of identity and collective incentives, analyzed earlier) are necessary preconditions for mobilization. A widely used strategy of communal organizations is to build a sense of common interest by employing frames that incorporate symbols of shared identity and grievance. But commitment to communal organizations cannot be constructed from nothing or maintained based on nothing. If a people's cultural identity and incentives for joint action are weak, they seldom can be mobilized by any leaders in response to any new threat or opportunity. On the other hand, the conjunction of shared incentives and a strong sense of group identity—a conjunction found among black opponents of apartheid in South Africa and among Shiites and Kurds in Iraq after the 1991 Persian Gulf War—provides highly combustible material that fuels what may appear to be spontaneous action in response to new opportunities.

Four factors, in addition to shared identity and incentives, shape a group's capacity for sustained and effective political action: its geographic concentration, its prior organization, its formation of coalitions, and the authenticity of its leaders.

Geographic Concentration. Rebellion is feasible for groups that have a territorial base but very difficult to organize for dispersed and urban groups. Recent empirical studies have used large-n comparisons in conjunction with case study materials to test these effects. Monica Duffy Toft examined seventy-two ethnic-based civil wars since 1945 and found that 88 percent involved groups that were regionally concentrated compared with only 6 percent that were dispersed. A reanalysis of the Minorities at Risk data set by James Fearon and David Laitin confirms Toft's results and shows that geographic concentration increases the chances of rebellion in all world regions. In contrast, the groups least likely to rebel are those concentrated in urban areas.[23]

Preexisting Organization. The cohesion of an identity group depends on high and sustained levels of interaction among its members. Speaking a common language and sharing home ground both promote interaction. So does preexisting social organization. Cohesion is high among people who practice a common religion (Shiites in Iraq, Saudi Arabia, and Bahrain), share an economic niche (Chinese entrepreneurs in Southeast Asia), or dominate a political establishment (Hausa-Fulani in the Nigerian officer corps, Mende in Sierra Leone's government ministries). The organizational basis for the U.S. civil rights movement came from black southern churches, colleges, and

the NAACP, all of which expanded rapidly from 1930 to the mid-1950s.[24]

Moreover, established political institutions usually are more cohesive than new political movements and can mobilize members at lower cost. For example, the capacity for collective action is relatively high in groups whose traditional authorities still command respect, as is the case among many Muslim communities. The same is true of groups that control an autonomous regional government. The constituent republics of the USSR provided the institutional framework within which nationalists in the Baltic, the Caucasus, and Ukraine built independence movements in the late 1980s. I am not suggesting that all regional political entities, such as states in India or organized tribes in the United States, are inherently disposed to rebellion. The point is that, given incentives and opportunities, it is easier to build communal political movements among people who have significant cohesion due to frequent and routine interaction as members of an existing institution. In the language of collective action theory, cohesion reduces the costs of organizing collective action.

Overcoming Faction, Forging Coalitions. The capacity for communal action also depends on overcoming narrower loyalties to clans, classes, and communities. Identity groups are heterogeneous and their boundaries fluid. The effective boundaries of a communal group may depend more on coalition formation than on the objective scope of group identity. Palestinians, for example, are dispersed throughout the Middle East, include adherents of two major religions, are stratified by class, and support competing political organizations. The effectiveness of the Palestinian national movement from the 1970s to the 1990s was due to the incorporation of most of these elements into the Palestine Liberation Organization. If the aspiring leaders of communal groups fail to build inclusive coalitions, then mobilization and joint action are impeded, resources are deflected into factional fighting, and it is easier for states to co-opt and deflect communal opponents. Kurdish nationalism offers a counterpoint to the Palestinian example. From the 1920s to the 1990s Kurds in Turkey, Iraq, and Iran fought a series of ethnonational rebellions seeking autonomy or independence. But Kurdish leaders rarely coordinated political action across state boundaries and most of their rebellions were crippled by rifts among the rebels themselves. If the Kurds had coalesced in a coherent and durable transnational movement, they might not now be the Middle East's largest nation—numbering twenty million to thirty million people—without a state. The Kurds of Iraq have overcome their factionalism, but only after the overthrow of Saddam Hussein and in the presence of strong incentives to bargain as a collectivity with their Shiite and Sunni rivals for a share of leadership in a new Iraqi state.

Authenticity of Leadership. Leadership is central to the process of mobilizing and overcoming divisions within groups. *Leadership* refers to a set of skills whose effectiveness in identity groups depends on context, not a manual of organizational behavior or a body of nationalist doctrine. *Authenticity* of leaders may be the most critical factor. The concept is analogous to legitimacy in the arena of conventional politics. Communal leaders are *authentic* if they are seen as representing the most essential values and aspirations of the group and if their actions are thought to be in the common interest.

Authenticity is a matter of degree and can be gained or lost. Established leaders usually have authenticity by virtue of their position. They control resources, command preexisting loyalties, symbolize group identity, articulate group interests and demands, and manage coalitions. Thus they have ample means for overcoming the collective action problem, that is, the reluctance of most individuals to commit to the risky enterprise of protest and rebellion. But they can lose authenticity by wrong words and deeds. Alternative leaders are quick

to capitalize on errors by their established counterparts. Entrepreneurial leaders—those who aim to build new communal movements—face greater obstacles than the leaders of established organizations. They control fewer resources and depend more on symbolic skills and personal example. Entrepreneurial leaders also are more likely to articulate frames that give people a new sense of hope and power. Often they are risk takers who help convince and attract followers by dramatic personal acts of resistance. And they are especially likely to appeal to supporters who are dissatisfied with established leaders and organizations.

To summarize the argument thus far, a communal group's capacity for political action depends, first of all, on the salience of group identity and shared incentives. Capacity is enhanced if the group has preexisting organizational networks and authentic leaders who can bridge internal divisions, whether by coalition building or by other means. And it is easier to build movements and sustain campaigns of political action if most of the group shares a common homeland.

The theory sketched here also incorporates a response to writers who attribute communal violence to "bad leaders" or the self-serving pursuit of money or power. There are many instances of leaders who have led their people into devastating conflicts by playing on communal antagonisms, and sometimes they have done so in the service of personal ambition. Chechens, Serbs, and Rwandan Hutu all suffered grievously in the 1990s from the failed policies of ethnocentric and opportunistic leaders. The counterpoint is that people get the leaders they deserve or, more precisely, they get the leaders they are prepared to follow. Skillful leaders can strengthen existing group ties and provide a greater awareness of shared interests, but they cannot create them. Given the existence of identity and interest, communal entrepreneurs can build militant political movements, but only within the limits of group members' expectations about what objectives and actions are acceptable.[25]

Opportunities and Choices

The ways in which identity, incentives, and capacity are translated into communal action depend on political and cultural context in ways that are difficult to summarize in general principles. Some actions are spontaneous and reactive, such as racially motivated riots in Los Angeles in 1965 and 1992, both of which were provoked directly or indirectly when police used force against individuals resisting arrest. But most communal action, including all sustained campaigns of protest and rebellion, is shaped by strategic assessments and tactical decisions of the leaders and activists of politically mobilized communal groups.

Opportunity Structures. Political opportunity refers to factors external to a group that influence its decisions about how to pursue communal objectives. *Durable* opportunity factors include the political character of the state, its resources, and whether a communal group has long-term alliances with other groups in the domestic political arena. These durable factors shape the ways in which groups organize and affect their long-term choices about strategies. Changes in the structure of a group's political environment are transient opportunity factors. Examples include changes in political institutions, turnover of elites, shifts in government policy, and the emergence of new political allies. Transient factors can give a boost to mobilization and morale, enhance the credibility of some leaders and frames, and lead to shifts in group claims and strategies. They also help determine the targets and timing of political action.[26]

The impact of transnational structures and actions on ethnopolitics has become so pervasive since the 1980s that we need to extend the concept of political opportunities from the domestic to the international level. The role of external support for communal groups has

long been recognized, especially the political and material assistance that external patrons provide for separatist movements. Deepa Khosla has examined the range of political, material, and military support given by foreign states to communal minorities in the Third World in the 1990s. Slightly more than half (95 of 179 minorities in her study) received foreign support. All but 2 of 23 ethnonationalist groups benefited from foreign support, and so did half (32 of 64) of the communal contenders and nearly half (24 of 52) of the indigenous peoples. Communal contenders and ethnonationalists both received more military than non-military support.[27] Other studies point out the crucial importance of diasporas. Gabriel Sheffer observes that of the fifty most active terrorist organizations and groups, twenty-seven either constitute segments of ethnonational and religious diasporas or are supported by such diasporas.[28]

The *international political opportunity structure* encompasses a communal group's international allies and opponents, its kindred groups and diaspora, and regional and international organizations. Recent studies of transnational networks show that they also have patterned effects on political mobilization and strategies of some kinds of communal groups. For example, indigenous groups in Latin America have developed durable transnational links among themselves, with global indigenous movements, and with some environmental NGOs.[29]

The State Context of Communal Action: Effects of State Power and Democracy. The state's political institutions and capabilities structure communal groups' choices about the objectives to pursue and the means used to do so. First, the resources and administrative capabilities of the state set limits on what groups might obtain. Second, the openness of the political system affects group leaders' choices about whether to participate, protest, or rebel. Evidence from the Minorities at Risk study points to the special significance of three factors: *the uses of state power,* the political values and practices of *institutionalized democracy,* and the transient effects of *democratization.*

Uses of state power. State power is a durable opportunity factor. Strong states are those that have ample resources and the administrative and political capacity to control or regulate most economic, social, and political activity. The strongest states in the late twentieth century included most of the advanced industrial democracies plus China and, until the 1980s, some Soviet-bloc states. Postcolonial and postrevolutionary leaders sought to build strong states on the Western or Soviet models. The expansion of state power is likely to have cross-cutting effects on national and minority peoples. State strategies of subordination and assimilation almost invariably increase collective grievances: administrative restraints are imposed, lifeways are altered, traditional cultures are denigrated or marginalized. At the same time, the potential costs of collective action increase because the agents of an expanding state are usually intrusive and vigilant. On the other hand, groups whose leaders have countervailing resources, or low-cost access to decision-making processes, may be able to maintain group autonomy and secure payoffs for cooperating with dominant groups. All such statements are fraught with "maybes" because they depend on the dominant state's ideology and on the abilities of group leaders to obstruct, to adapt, and to acquire and deploy influential allies. In Lenin's USSR the Communist Party recognized the principle of national self-determination for non-Russians, and Stalin accepted the more limited principle of cultural-national autonomy. In Atatürk's Turkey, however, no political or cultural alternatives to Turkish identity were tolerated. One legacy is modern Turkey's exclusive nationalism and difficulty in recognizing Kurdish claims of separate identity. The People's Republic of China follows the principle of cultural autonomy for minority peoples but adamantly opposes

"splittists," such as Tibetan and Muslim Uigher nationalists, who want political autonomy.

The outcomes of minority peoples' resistance to state building are problematic. Strong, resource-rich states have the capacity either to accommodate or to suppress national peoples and minorities at relatively low cost, depending on the preferences of state elites. Gains are most likely to be won by identity-based movements that maintain sustained, nonviolent campaigns for reforms that do not threaten state security. Rulers of weaker states face more stark, zero-sum choices when confronted by communal challenges. They can expand the governing coalition at risk to their own positions, or they can devote scarce resources to all-out warfare against communal rivals. The Tutsi-dominated government of Burundi was under international pressure during the 1980s and early 1990s to incorporate the Hutu majority and, to its credit, attempted to do so by democratic means. The plan foundered in a coup and a welter of killings by militant Tutsi who rejected sharing power with Hutu leaders who won 1993 elections.[30] International support for accommodation has continued to the present and, as of mid-2005, the peace process seems to have worked: the country has a Hutu president, and many Hutu parliamentarians, and, after a lengthy civil war, all rebel factions have agreed to end fighting.

An alternative to incorporation or warfare is to negotiate independence or autonomy with ethnonationalists. The nonviolent deconstruction of the USSR, a powerful but declining state, provided a strong precedent. In 1993 Czechoslovakia fissioned peacefully into two independent republics. Candidates for political fragmentation at the onset of the twenty-first century include Canada, Belgium, South Africa, Russia, Serbia-Montenegro, Iraq, Sri Lanka, Pakistan, Ethiopia, Burma, Sudan, and the Democratic Republic of the Congo (formerly Zaire).

Secession or autonomy is most likely to be gained in either rich democratic states or weak and poor states: in prosperous but fragmented states such as Canada and Belgium because democratic elites may be persuaded that peaceful divorce is less costly than civil war, and in weak states such as Moldova and Somalia because they lack the means to reclaim secessionist regions by force or inducements. Between these extremes are states with enough will and resources to wage war with ethnonational rebels but not the means to bury them or buy them out. These are the states most at risk for protracted communal wars.

Institutionalized democracies. Democratic institutions and elites are the other durable opportunity factor that weighs heavily in the strategic calculus of ethnonationalists. Western European democracies and India afford more than a dozen illustrations in the past twenty-five years of the principle that democratic elites can be persuaded to extend autonomy when enough political resources are brought to bear by communal leaders. Ethnonationalists have used a mix of conventional and violent tactics in these conflicts, but, with a couple of exceptions in India's Assam region—Nagas, Tripuras, Mizos—the winners have been communally based movements that relied on sustained mobilization and participation in conventional politics and protest, not armed rebellion. The practice of *democratic accommodation under pressure* is evident in the ways democratic governments process other kinds of communal demands.

Managing communal conflicts in institutionalized democracies depends most fundamentally on two principles. The first is implementing universalistic norms of equal rights and opportunities for all citizens, including ethnoclasses. The second is pluralistic accommodation of indigenous and regional peoples' desires for separate collective status. Although the application of these norms to national and minority peoples is relatively new and imperfect, empirical comparisons made in the Minorities at Risk study show that national and minority peoples in contemporary industrial democracies face few political barriers to participation and are more likely to use the tactics of protest than of rebellion.[31] The reasons are inherent in the political cultures and policies of modern democratic societies. In the past half century most political leaders of these societies have become more responsive to the interests of politicized communal groups, in particular to groups able to mobilize large constituencies and allies in persistent campaigns of protest—another example of the principle of democratic accommodation under pressure at work. Groups using violent protest and terrorism, in contrast, have risked backlash and loss of public support. Thus, the calculus for communal action in democracies favors protest over rebellion.

Transitions to democracy. The process by which many former autocracies in the Second and Third Worlds have sought to establish more participatory and responsive political systems has problematic consequences for communal mobilization and conflict. Successful democratization means the establishment of regimes in which communal and other interests are accommodated by peaceful means. But the *process* of transition creates threatening uncertainties for some groups and opens up a range of transitory political opportunities for communal entrepreneurs.[32] Postcommunist regimes relaxed coercive restraints on nationalism and intercommunal rivalries at a time when the institutionalized means for their expression and accommodation did not yet exist or were fragile and distrusted. The problem of postrevolutionary communist states was diagnosed by Milovan Djilas, the Yugoslav revolutionary-turned-critic, in an essay written shortly before his death in 1995: "When revolutions occur, communal identities get hammered down, only to bounce back with elemental force unless precisely defined relationships have developed in a society: democratic institutions, a free economy, a middle class. In this regard communism left behind it a desert."[33] The result, in Yugoslavia and elsewhere, was a resurgence of communal activism, both protest and rebellion. Similar consequences can be expected to follow from democratization in multiethnic Third World autocracies. The most dubious expectation of all is that authoritarian states such as Sudan, Iraq, and Burma might be able to defuse communal wars by moving toward democracy.

Recent global studies by the U.S. government–supported Task Force on Political Instability (formerly State Failure) show that democratic reforms in societies riven by communal rivalries are a near-perfect recipe for instability. When factionalism is high, the introduction of democratic reforms is more likely to increase incentives and opportunities for fighting than to provide pathways to peaceful accommodation. More specifically, over the past fifty years the most stable regimes have been full autocracies. Even full democracies, other things being equal, are three to five times more likely to have had internal wars and adverse regime changes. But partial democracies with factional competition along communal, class, or ideological lines are forty to sixty times more likely to experience serious instability than full autocracies. When the preconditions for ethnic wars are studied, partial democracies with factionalism are three to ten times more likely to have ethnic wars than any other type of regime.[34]

To summarize, in established democracies the opportunities for communal mobilization are substantial and so are potential gains—for cohesive groups that rely largely on nonviolent tactics. Institutionalized democracy facilitates nonviolent communal action and inhibits communal rebellion. This tendency is reinforced in strong states, those that have ample power and resources to respond to pluralist interests.

In autocracies that attempt to introduce democratic reforms, in contrast, national and minority peoples ordinarily feel a loss of security simultaneously with a transient increase in opportunities for mobilization and action. New democratic regimes usually lack the resources or institutional means to make and guarantee the kinds of accommodations that typify the established democracies. Therefore, the early stages of democratization in heterogeneous societies facilitate both communally based protest and rebellion. The worst-case scenario is that compromises are rejected by all contenders, leading to civil war and the reimposition of autocratic rule by the strongest faction. But this is an uncommon outcome. Most heterogeneous states that have made transitions to democracy in the past two decades have been relatively successful in managing communal conflict.[35]

It is worth repeating that both the USSR and the Federal Republic of Yugoslavia faced such conditions in 1990–91. The majority of Soviet and Russian leaders chose democracy and minimized the risks of factionalism by decentralization. They accepted the independent statehood of fourteen constituent republics of the USSR and subsequently negotiated autonomy arrangements with a number of regional entities within the Russian Federation whose leaders were toying with secession. Serbian nationalists chose to fight rather than switch, with devastating consequences that persist into the twenty-first century.

THE INTERNATIONAL CONTEXT OF COMMUNAL ACTION

A great many international factors help shape the aspirations, opportunities, and strategies of communal groups. They also affect state policies toward minorities. Moreover, the nature of international engagement is a major determinant of whether communal conflicts are of short duration or long and whether they end in negotiated settlements or humanitarian disasters.

Foreign Support for Contenders

Foreign sympathizers can contribute substantially to a communal group's cohesion and political mobilization by providing material, political, and moral support. Indigenous rights organizations such as the American Indian Movement (in the 1970s) and the World Council of Indigenous Peoples (in the 1980s and 1990s) have promoted the establishment of numerous indigenous peoples' movements, provided strategic guidance for their leaders, and pressured governments to respond positively. In the 1970s and 1980s the Palestine Liberation Organization organized and supported opposition activity by Palestinians in Jordan, Lebanon, and Israel's Occupied Territories. External support for ethnonational groups often provokes responses that offset opportunities. Weak regimes facing communal challengers frequently seek bilateral military assistance and political support that enhance their capacity to counter communal challenges. The most tragic and destructive consequences occur when competing powers support different sides in communal wars. Such proxy wars are usually protracted and very deadly, and they are not likely to end in negotiated settlements unless and until it is in the interest of the external powers.

Withdrawal of external support may open up possibilities for settlement, as happened in Afghanistan and Angola in the early 1990s. In both these instances, however, international efforts at settlement failed, quickly in Afghanistan and slowly in Angola, because one or more contenders could not be persuaded that participation in coalition governments was preferable to fighting for complete victory. In Afghanistan the cessation of Russian and U.S. support in 1991 led to a new phase of civil war, fought this time not between Marxists and Islamists but among communal rivals for power. Despite UN-led support for a succession of coalition governments, the country was rent by another seven years of armed conflict among political movements based on Tadjiks, Uzbeks, Hazaris, and Pashtuns. The Taliban Islamist movement, which consolidated control in 1998, derived its support almost exclusively from the Pashtuns. More exactly, at the

beginning the Taliban represented the political and religious interests of mullahs from Kandahar, in southern Afghanistan. Thus the Taliban was a vehicle by which one element of the Pashtuns reestablished the group's historic hegemony—until it was ousted from power by the United States because it harbored al Qaeda.[36]

The resumption of protracted communal conflict, despite international efforts to broker a political settlement, is another manifestation of what James Fearon analyzes as a commitment problem.[37] Angola affords a clear example. The Angolan government's main challenger after 1975 was the National Union for the Total Independence of Angola (UNITA), based mainly on the Ovimbundu people of southern Angola. During the Cold War the United States and South Africa gave UNITA ample material and political assistance in a proxy war against the Cuban-supported government in Luanda. Near the end of the Cold War, after Cuban troops had withdrawn and the government had shed its Marxist trappings, an internationally brokered peace plan led to multiparty parliamentary and presidential elections in 1992. In the absence of mutual trust and international guarantees, neither party acted in good faith. UNITA rejected the election results, and many UNITA supporters in the capital were massacred. Another round of international pressure led in 1997 to the formation of a coalition government with UNITA's Jonas Savimbi as head of the now-legal opposition. But UNITA did not demobilize its fighters and continued to acquire new arms from old friends. The government expelled some of the UNITA parliamentarians and prompted the others to establish a new, "tame" UNITA. While politicos maneuvered in the capital, UNITA expanded its military control and resumed a full-fledged civil war that ended only after Savimbi's death in early 2002.[38]

A Cold War–era lesson was that military support for contenders in communal wars increases group capacities and opportunities for action but also makes it likely that conflicts will be protracted, deadly, and highly resistant to settlement. During the 1990s the international emphasis shifted to constructive engagement, such as that practiced by the United States toward South Africa (and Namibia) in the 1980s. The essential strategy of constructive engagement in internal wars is the use of political pressure and incentives to push adversaries toward negotiated settlements. Constructive engagement is most likely to succeed when used in a coordinated fashion by major powers and regional and international organizations. In 2003 it seemed that the unilateral use of U.S. military force in Afghanistan and Iraq posed serious risks by fracturing the post–Cold War peace alliance that relied on constructive, multilateral engagement to check local and regional conflicts. The principles and practices proved resilient enough that by 2005 a number of other countries had agreed to support nation-building work in Afghanistan and in postelection Iraq.

International Spillover of Communal Conflict

Group incentives, capacities, and opportunities are amplified by the contagious example of successful political action elsewhere and by diffusion of communal conflict from nearby regions.

Contagion and *communication* refer to the processes by which one group's actions provide inspiration and guidance, both strategic and tactical, for groups elsewhere. Though some observers have argued that civil or communal conflict is in general contagious, a closer reading of the evidence suggests that the strongest contagion effects occur within networks of similar groups. Informal connections and influences have long existed among disadvantaged peoples, so that, for example, one finds Australian Aborigines in the early 1960s organizing freedom rides in rural New South Wales and Dayaks in northern Borneo in the

1980s resisting commercial logging of their forests with rhetoric and tactics like those used by native Canadian peoples in the early 1990s. By the beginning of the twenty-first century, thickening webs of connections among like-minded groups were in place.

More precisely, networks of communication, political support, and material assistance have developed among similar groups that face similar circumstances. The two densest networks now link indigenous peoples and Islamic communities. Their connectivity depends on international meetings, transcontinental travel by activists, and fax, phone, and Internet exchanges. Organizations in these networks gain access to expertise on leadership, ideological appeals, communications, and mobilization. Their appeals gain plausibility because they resonate with sentiments held by similar peoples elsewhere. Equally important, groups in the networks benefit from the inspiration of successful movements anywhere in the world, successes that provide the images and moral incentives that help motivate activists. The links among militant Islamists are threatening in a way that indigenous networks could never be. The indigenous movement asks for local autonomy, while Islamists seek control of Muslim states and call for global jihad against the West and its allies in the Muslim world.

Contagion effects are not automatic. First, as suggested in the discussion of empowering ideas, frames and victories are contagious only for people who have a preexisting sense of collective identity and some notion of common interests. Second, contagion presupposes some degree of leadership and networks of communication within the group, not just images and rhetoric from outside. Stephen M. Saideman makes a persuasive argument that contagion is most likely to affect groups whose economic and political circumstances are similar to those of ethnonational groups that initiate a successful movement, especially other groups in the same country.[39]

Diffusion refers to the direct "spillover" of conflict from one region to another, either within or across international boundaries. The contagion of conflict is indirect; diffusion is direct. For example, more than twenty national peoples in the Caucasus were caught up in communal tumult in the 1990s through the diffusion (and contagion) of proactive and reactive nationalism. The Association of the Peoples of the Caucasus, representing most of the peoples of the North Caucasus, was founded after riots between Georgians and Abkhazians in July 1989 to help Abkhazians and other North Caucasus peoples provide assistance to threatened kindred. Since then activists and fighters have moved fluidly from one regional conflict to another and so have arms and supplies.[40] Governments also are active players. In the early 1990s Russians promoted the Abkhaz war of independence, and North Ossetia (in the Russian Federation) supported autonomy-minded South Ossetians (in Georgia). The most intense and complex spillover effects in communal conflict happen among groups like these that straddle international boundaries—intense and complex, because they draw in a multiplicity of communal and state actors. Of the 286 groups currently in the Minorities at Risk study, nearly two-thirds have kindred in one or more adjacent countries. Political activists in one country often find sanctuary with and get support from their transnational kindred. Generations of Kurdish leaders and *peshmergas* (warriors) in Turkey, Syria, Iraq, and Iran have provided safe havens for one another's political movements.

Diasporas also are a substantial and growing source of external support for ethnonationalists. Since the 1970s Kurdish rebels in Turkey have received substantial funds from Kurdish workers in Western Europe. Chechen communities in the Middle East, descendants of exiles and political refugees from past conflicts, have sent fighters and material support to their rebellious cousins in the Caucasus. Tamil rebels in Sri Lanka were able to maintain

their fight for independence from 1975 to 2001 with a great deal of help, both money and arms, from the Tamil diaspora in Europe and North America as well as Tamils in India. In the aftermath of the 9/11 attacks in the United States, this support began to dry up, which is thought to have been a major factor pushing the Tamil Tigers to begin peace talks with the government.

These observations suggest three principles about contagion and diffusion effects. First, a communal group's incentives for political action are increased by successful mobilization and political action by similar groups elsewhere. Contagion effects are strongest among similar groups (e.g., ethnonationalists) in the same country, weaker in adjoining countries, and weakest for more distant kindred. Contagion is enhanced by the existence of transnational networks linking similar groups. Second, a group's capabilities for political action are increased by political and material support from segments of the group elsewhere, including politically organized diaspora. Political, material, and military assistance from foreign countries also increases capabilities but is likely to prompt the challenged state to seek offsetting support from its own allies. Third, a group's opportunities for rebellion are increased by the number of segments of the group in adjoining countries and by their proximity to open conflict (including civil and interstate war). They also are enhanced by power transitions in regional and global alliance structures.

INTERNATIONAL GOOD PRACTICE FOR MANAGING COMMUNAL CONFLICT

Since the end of the Cold War there has been a distinct shift in international orientations toward communal conflict, away from sponsoring proxy wars and toward promoting the accommodation of contending interests. Efforts at international management of communal conflict have reinforced domestic efforts at reducing communal tensions. The Minorities at Risk study provides two telling bodies of evidence. First is an analysis of the outcomes of seventy-four armed conflicts over self-determination fought between 1960 and 2004, wars such as those of East Timor, Tamil Nadu, southern Sudan, and Nagorno-Karabakh. These wars, whose protagonists claim the right to their own communally based state or autonomous region, are among the most deadly and protracted of all communal conflicts. *Between 1991 and the end of 2004, wars of self-determination have declined by half.* During that time twenty separatist wars were settled by negotiated peace agreements and twenty-three others were checked by cease-fires and ongoing negotiations. Fewer armed separatist conflicts are being fought now—twenty-five by our count—than at any time since the early 1970s. This steep decline helps put the 1997–98 rebellion of Kosovar Albanians in perspective. The armed conflict that began with a few bombings and ambushes by the Kosovo Liberation Army in late 1997 was the only new communal war in Europe after 1994.[41]

Less visible than the shift toward settlement of separatist wars is a parallel trend toward accommodation of communal demands that have not yet escalated into armed conflict. Leaders of communal movements almost always seek support by appealing to minority peoples—resentment about their lack of political participation, material inequality, cultural recognition—and justify such claims by reference to international standards of individual and group rights. Looking past the rhetoric of justice denied, we find substantial evidence of changes in minority group status that undercut the effectiveness of these appeals. Discrimination eased for more than one-third of the groups monitored by the Minorities at Risk project during the 1990s, mainly because governments formally recognized and guaranteed their political and cultural rights.

There was no "invisible hand" guiding the global decline in serious communal conflict or the improvement in minority status during the 1990s. These trends are the result of concerted efforts by a great many people and organizations, including domestic and international peacemakers and some of the protagonists themselves. Relations between communal groups and governments have changed since the early 1990s because of the evolution of a new *doctrine of international good practice* for managing communal conflict that has six essential principles.

1. Recognize and Promote Group Political, Cultural, and Economic Rights

The first and most basic principle is the recognition and active protection of the rights of minority peoples. This means freedom from discrimination based on race, national origin, language, or religion that is complemented by institutional means by which organized communal groups can protect and promote their collective cultural and political interests. Western democracies have taken the lead in articulating, promoting, and implementing such policies. During the early 1990s the emphasis of Western advocates of human rights shifted from individual rights to protection of collective rights of national minorities. The effect of standard-setting texts adopted in 1990–95 by the Organization for Security and Cooperation in Europe (OSCE) and the Council of Europe was to establish principles for protection of minorities in European countries. The texts prohibit forced assimilation and population transfer, endorse autonomy for minority communities within existing states, and acknowledge that national minority questions are legitimate subjects of international relations both at the United Nations and within European regional organizations.[42]

Virtually all European democracies have implemented these principles. In the first stage of democratization in postcommunist Europe, some ethnonational leaders manipulated the democratic process to serve nationalist interests at the expense of minorities such as

Russians in the Baltic states, Hungarians in Slovakia and Romania, and Serbs in Croatia. In most of these countries a combination of diplomatic engagement by European institutions and the democratic electoral process checked the implementation of new discriminatory policies. Similar trends are evident in other world regions. A recent study that tracks economic and political discrimination against 337 groups from 1950 to 2003 shows substantial declines in active discrimination almost everywhere, with improvements being especially pronounced in Third World regions and in the years since 1991.[43]

2. Recognize the Right of Regional Minorities to Substate Autonomy

A corollary principle is the right of national peoples to exercise some degree of autonomy within existing states to govern their own affairs. This is a logical consequence of the first principle. That is, it follows that if minorities who constitute a majority in one region of a heterogeneous democratic state have the right to protect and promote their collective interests, then they should have the right to local or regional self-governance. Federal political systems provide a "one-size-fits-all" approach to regional autonomy. In 1980 the new democratic government of Spain established a countrywide federal system in a largely successful effort to satisfy the separatist ambitions of Basques, Catalans, and Galicians. An alternative is *asymmetrical* federalism, in which some units have greater self-governing powers than others. The United States successfully uses both: federalism with limited powers for the fifty states, quasi sovereignty and more extensive powers to meet the distinctive political interests of organized Native American tribes and the Commonwealth of Puerto Rico.[44]

The principle of substate autonomy for national minorities is difficult to implement in centralized states for several reasons. One is the inherent resistance of most governing elites to devolution of central authority, especially in response to open challenges. Second is the fear that granting autonomy to rebels will lead to outright secession and provide a precedent for other groups. Third is the necessity to negotiate situation-specific arrangements that satisfy both parties. International examples and encouragement can help overcome elite resistance to devolution, especially if it is clear that international actors oppose complete separation and are willing to provide security guarantees to all parties.[45] The second fear is not supported by facts on the ground. There are very few contemporary instances in which negotiated autonomy led to independence. Sometimes an autonomous regional government pushes hard for greater authority, as the Basques have done in Spain, but the ethnic statelets that won de facto independence in the 1990s —Somaliland, Abkhazia, the Transnistria Republic, and the "federated state" of Kurdistan in northern Iraq—did so because states refused to negotiate autonomy arrangements, not because they did so.

With reference to autonomy agreements, there is now a large set of models to draw on. The best-known autonomy agreements have been reached through negotiated settlements of wars of self-determination, such as the Oslo Accords and Northern Ireland's Easter Accords. Less well known but equally effective are conflict-containing agreements that established a federal state for India's Mizos in 1986, an autonomous republic for the Gagauz in Moldova in 1994, and regional autonomy for the Chakma people in Bangladesh's Chittagong Hills in 1997.[46]

3. Democratic Institutions and Power Sharing Are Preferred Means for Protecting Group Rights

The recognition and protection of collective rights are two of the domestic elements of the preferred strategy for managing communal heterogeneity. Political democracy is a third. It provides the institutional means by which national peoples and minorities in most societies secure their rights and pursue collective interests. There are other institutional mechanisms for the protection of communal groups' interests, for example, the hegemonic exchange system (Donald Rothchild's term for communal power-sharing arrangements in which one group dominates) found in many nondemocratic African states. Nonetheless, democracy, in one of its European variants, is widely held to be the most reliable guarantee of minority rights. It is inherent in the logic of democratic politics that all peoples in heterogeneous societies should have equal civil and political rights.

There is near-conclusive evidence that modern democracies rarely fight one another and are tempered in their use of repression against internal opponents. Before-and-after comparisons of national and minority peoples in new democracies, carried out using the Minorities at Risk data, show that their political and cultural status usually improve substantially during democratic transitions. The new democracies of Europe, Asia, and Latin America were especially likely to provide legal and institutional means for protecting and promoting minority rights. Authoritarian governments were not immune to this trend either, especially in Asia.[47] The Vietnamese and Indonesian governments both lifted some restrictions on their Chinese minorities, though for reasons that had more to do with improving relations with the People's Republic and maintaining access to Chinese capital than in response to doctrines of group rights.

Democratization as a solution for communal conflict carries two risks. One is that democratic reforms will be incomplete, by imposing sharp limits on political competition or failing to provide institutional checks on the authority of elected leaders. The other, referred to earlier, is the rise of factional, zero-sum competition among communal contenders (or class or ideological antagonists). If democratization is to work, it is necessary to build parties and institutions that cut across cleavages so that rival groups are encouraged to compromise in the conduct of governance.

4. Mutual Accommodation Is the Preferred Strategy for Managing Civil Conflicts

The fourth principle is that disputes between states and national and minority peoples are best settled by negotiation and mutual accommodation. One remarkable but little-noticed achievement of democratic Russia in the 1990s was its negotiation of power-sharing agreements with Tatarstan, Bashkiria, and some forty other regions in the Russian Federation (only some of which have non-Russian nationalities). The agreement between the federation and Tatarstan went the greatest symbolic distance by treating the parties as equals: it refers to the mutual delegation of power. It could have and should have been a model for settling the dispute between the federation and Chechnya. However much the Russians may have been willing to compromise before embarking on their winter 1994–95 campaign, Chechen nationalists wanted nothing short of total independence, and the conflict continues.

The preference for accommodation is evident in the outcomes of most recent wars of self-determination. Armed conflicts usually begin with demands for complete independence— and end with negotiated or de facto autonomy within the state. There are many reasons why most ethnonational leaders are willing to settle for fifty cents (or less) on the dollar, but it usually comes down to the fact that they are strategically and politically overmatched. Nationalists willing to continue fighting against all odds for total independence, such as rebel leaders in Chechnya, are rare. Governments, on the other hand, tend with increasing frequency to the calculation that it is less costly to negotiate an agreement for regional and cultural autonomy and to redistribute development funds than it is to fight endless insurgencies—all the more so because other states and international organizations are encouraging them to negotiate. The Turkish government's obdurate resistance to organized Kurdish participation in conventional politics has become an anachronism.

If the parties to separatist conflicts recognize that the costs of accommodation are probably less than the costs of prolonged conflict, then it is only a short step to mutual decisions that it is more advantageous to work toward a negotiated settlement early, after an initial show of resolve and force, rather than after prolonged warfare. Gagauz and Moldovan nationalists came to such a conclusion in 1992; so did Tuareg rebels and the governments of Mali and Niger in the mid-1990s.

5. International Engagement to Promote Negotiated Settlements of Communal Conflicts

The principle that serious communal disputes should be settled by mutual accommodation is backed by the active engagement of major powers, the United Nations, and regional organizations such as the European Union, the OSCE, and the Organization for African Unity. Efforts at international management of communal conflict take many forms. The European Union has used the carrot of candidate membership in the European Union to dissuade the Baltic states from imposing draconian restrictions on their Russian residents and to induce Turkey to check human rights abuses against Kurds.

International actors have compelling reasons for seeking the resolution of communal conflicts at an early stage. One is to avoid the regional insecurity that accompanies civil warfare and the breakup of existing states. The scary lessons of regional insecurity in the Balkans and Caucasus in the early 1990s had a galvanizing effect on international opinion and commitment to early and constructive engagement. A second reason is that trade and investment in the burgeoning international economy are dependent on political stability both within and among countries. Humanitarian considerations come in a strong third among the compelling reasons: informed Western publics and activist NGOs lobby ever more effectively for international responses to impending humanitarian crises.

Preventive diplomacy has great current popularity, not only because early engagement is potentially cheaper than belated responses to communal and other internal disputes, but also because it has become the preferred instrument of the new doctrine for managing threats to regional security. The OSCE has relied extensively and effectively on observer missions and discreet diplomacy to help resolve communal disputes. The Organization of the Islamic Conference, not usually recognized as a peacemaker, played a decisive role in promoting negotiations in the 1970s and 1980s aimed at ending hostilities between Moro nationalists and the government of the Philippines. The United States used diplomatic and economic levers throughout the 1990s to prompt the Israeli government and the PLO to engage in meaningful negotiations.[48]

It is important to recognize and encourage the participation of nongovernmental organizations and private individuals as intermediaries and mediators in situations of communal conflict. The World Council of Churches played a crucial role in brokering the 1972 agreement that ended the first phase of Sudan's civil war. Former U.S. president Jimmy Carter, working from the Carter Center at Emory University, helped broker a 1999 agreement by which the governments of Sudan and Uganda agreed to end support for communal insurgents operating in each other's territories. Former U.S. senator George Mitchell played a similar role in securing the implementation of the Easter Accords that ultimately ended violent conflict in Northern Ireland. Such organizations and individuals function effectively in part because they are trusted by parties to conflict—and they are trusted because they are seen to operate independently of big-power political interests.

6. Coercive Intervention Is a Necessary Response to Gross Violations of Human Rights

Most of the United Nations' current peacekeeping operations aim at separating the contenders in communal conflicts. Non-UN operations often have the same purpose. What has happened in the past decade is growing acceptance of the principle that preemptive action —so-called peace enforcement missions— is sometimes necessary and justifiable. Coercive intervention, as in Serbia and East Timor, is the international system's response of last resort to gross violations of human rights and to communal wars whose spillover effects threaten regional security.[49] Nationalist Serbia was the pariah state and bombing range of Europe in 1999 precisely because it had refused throughout the 1990s to make any significant concessions to the Kosovars and, most immediately, because it blatantly violated principles about group rights accepted elsewhere in the region.

A WORK IN PROGRESS

Some parts of the world will continue to experience communal warfare and repression by states and communal movements that reject these six principles for managing conflict in heterogeneous societies. Few states in the Islamic world are prepared to grant full political and cultural rights to religious minorities. The Chinese government adamantly refuses to consider real autonomy as a solution for separatist demands by Tibetans, Uighers, or Mongols. A number of protracted communal conflicts are highly resistant to regional and international influence. The Sudanese government continues to deflect intense international pressures to end genocidal ethnic cleansing in Darfur. Odds are against durable settlements for communal wars between Kurdish nationalists and the Turkish government and between militant Tamils and the Sri Lankan government. Africa poses a great challenge to international practices for containing conflict. A vast conflict zone extends from Sudan and Ethiopia through the Great Lakes region to the Congo basin and the Angola highlands. Interstate rivalries interact in extraordinarily complex ways with

communal rivalries throughout the region. Negotiations and peacekeeping operations have checked most fighting in this region as of late 2005 but observers are not optimistic that peace will continue to hold.

These examples highlight situations of communal conflict that should have the highest priority for remedial and preventive action. By whom and how? The answers depend on which actors have the will, the political leverage, and the resources to act. Kosovo, East Timor, and Chechnya illustrate that the reach of the new doctrine and practice of managing communal conflict depends on whether they are accepted by those whose conflicts are to be managed and equally on the will and ability of regional and international organizations to implement them. International and regional organizations are most likely to pursue effective preventive strategies in areas where the Western powers have vital interests, which means Europe, Latin America, and the Middle East.

African and Asian conflicts are more remote and resistant to external influence. The best strategy here may be to encourage regional organizations, especially the African Union (AU, formerly the OAU) and the Association of Southeast Asian Nations (ASEAN) to use all means at their disposal and assist them in doing so. The AU has employed diplomatic, political, and military strategies on a number of occasions in recent years, but its member states have limited logistical capacity to carry out peacekeeping missions such as the current Nigerian-led AU operation in Darfur. ASEAN for a long time rejected applying its influence to issues other than regional economic policy but late in 2005 for the first time publicly challenged the government of Myanmar to ease repressive policies toward its domestic political and communal opponents.

When preventive strategies fail, or are not pursued in the first place, the international challenges are different: how to provide humanitarian aid and how to contain the regional spillovers of conflict.

Militant Islam poses a new and very different kind of challenge. The threat comes not from states or communal rivals but from jihadists dispersed throughout the Islamic world who would wage war on the West and its agents. It is difficult to see how the six principles for managing conflict in heterogeneous societies could satisfy or deflect their ideologically driven rage. New strategies are needed here. Officials and experts at the International Summit on Democracy, Terrorism and Security, convened by the Club de Madrid in March 2005, proposed a comprehensive response with three dimensions. First is a diagnosis and recommendations for long-term reduction of the root economic and political causes of Islamist and other conflicts that give rise to terrorism. Second is the specification of optimal strategies for policing, intelligence gathering, military responses, and control of terrorist financing. Third is an exploration of how the foundations of democratic governance—the rule of law, human rights, civil society—can be used as assets in the international struggle against extremism.[50]

NOTES

1. A note on terminology: in most previous writing on this subject the groups have been referred to as "minorities" or "ethnopolitical groups." The more general term "communal groups" is used here because politically significant religious communities also are included, such as the Catholics of Northern Ireland, Muslims in India, Baha'is in Iran, and Shiites and Sunnis in Iraq.

2. Much of the information in this chapter comes from the Minorities at Risk (MAR) project, begun by the author in 1986 and since 1988 based at the University of Maryland's Center for International Development and Conflict Management. Funding for work summarized here has been provided by the United States Institute of Peace, the National Science Foundation, the Hewlitt Foundation, and the Carnegie Corporation. For the latest full report on the project's findings, see Ted Robert Gurr, *Peoples versus States: Minorities at Risk in the New Century* (Wash-

ington, D.C.: United States Institute of Peace Press, 2000). Most data for the 2000s used here were prepared by Amy Pate, the MAR project coordinator from 2003 to 2005, who directed the latest update. For documentation on all groups in the study, see http://www.minoritiesatrisk.com.

3. For a useful recent analysis of Sunni factions and objectives, see Amatzia Baram, *Who Are the Insurgents? Sunni Arabs in Iraq,* Special Report 134 (Washington, D.C.: United States Institute of Peace, 2005).

4. In "Armed Conflict, 1989–98," *Journal of Peace Research* 36, no. 5 (1999): 593–606, Peter Wallensteen and Margareta Sollenberg report that during the 1990s about three-quarters of all armed conflicts, including wars between as well as within states, were wars between politically organized communal groups and governments. Of the world's twenty-four major ongoing armed conflicts in early 2005, all but four involved communal groups, according to Monty G. Marshall and Ted Robert Gurr, *Peace and Conflict 2005: A Global Survey of Armed Conflicts, Self-Determination Movements, and Democracy* (College Park: Center for International Development and Conflict Management, University of Maryland, 2005), 79–83, http://www.cidcm.umd.edu.

5. Michael Johns, "Appendix: Serious and Potential Ethnopolitical Conflicts in 2002," in Barbara Harff and Ted Robert Gurr, *Ethnic Conflict in World Politics,* 2nd ed. (Boulder, Colo.: Westview, 2004), 197–204.

6. See Barbara Harff, "Assessing Risks of Genocide and Politicide," in Marshall and Gurr, *Peace and Conflict 2005,* 57–61, and the sources cited there.

7. Estimates are from *World Refugee Survey 2005* (Washington, D.C.: U.S. Commission for Refugees, 2005), http://www.refugees.org. See also the reports of the UN High Commission for Refugees at http://unhcr.ch.

8. For documentation on this and the preceding two points, see Gurr, *Peoples versus States,* chap. 2.

9. The criteria used to identify communal groups are described in ibid., chap. 1, which also discusses differences among such groups by region and type.

10. The foundation of modernization theory was laid by Karl Deutsch, *Nationalism and Social Communication* (Cambridge, Mass.: MIT Press, 1953). For an early reappraisal of what modernization means for ethnic identities, see Walker Connor, "Nation-Building or Nation-Destroying?" *World Politics* 26

(April 1972): 319–355. For important recent assessments, see Jonathan Friedman, *Cultural Identity and Global Process* (London: Sage, 1994); Fred W. Riggs, "The Modernity of Ethnic Identity and Conflict," *International Political Science Review* 19 (July 1998): 269–288; and Susan Olzak, *The Global Dynamics of Racial and Ethnic Mobilization* (Stanford, Calif.: Stanford University Press, 2006).

11. Two important comparative studies are Franke Wilmer, *The Indigenous Voice in World Politics: Since Time Immemorial* (Newbury Park, Calif.: Sage, 1993); and George Psacharopoulos and Harry Anthony Patrinos, eds., *Indigenous People and Poverty in Latin America: An Empirical Analysis* (Washington, D.C.: World Bank, 1994).

12. For a good recent study, see Gabriel Sheffer, *Diaspora Politics: At Home Abroad* (Cambridge and New York: Cambridge University Press, 2003).

13. Evidence about the salience of group identity can be found in many sources; my thinking about the importance of group identities has been especially influenced by Donald L. Horowitz, *Ethnic Groups in Conflict* (Berkeley: University of California Press, 1985). The concept of incentives incorporates arguments about the motivating forces of relative deprivation, from Ted Robert Gurr, *Why Men Rebel* (Princeton, N.J.: Princeton University Press, 1970), and of rational goal seeking. The notion of capacity is analogous to Charles Tilly's concept of mobilization as developed in *From Mobilization to Revolution* (Reading, Mass.: Addison-Wesley, 1978), 69–90. The significance of opportunities external to the group is central to theoretical models developed by Doug McAdam, *Political Process and the Development of Black Insurgency, 1930–1970* (Chicago: University of Chicago Press, 1982); and Sidney Tarrow, *Power in Movement: Social Movements and Contentious Politics,* 2nd ed. (Cambridge and New York: Cambridge University Press, 1998). Milton J. Esman gives political opportunity a prominent role in his comparative analysis of ethnic political movements, *Ethnic Politics* (Ithaca, N.Y.: Cornell University Press, 1994). The process by which groups organize for and sustain collective action is assumed to be fundamentally a rational one, as analyzed by Mark Irving Lichbach in *The Rebel's Dilemma* (Ann Arbor: University of Michigan Press, 1995).

14. Contention about language in heterogeneous societies is the topic of extensive comparative research,

for example, Horowitz, *Ethnic Groups in Conflict;* and the writings of David D. Laitin, most recently, his *Identity in Formation* (Ithaca, N.Y.: Cornell University Press, 1998).

15. World Bank economist Paul Collier and colleagues propose that greed, in the form of predation of scarce natural resources, is a major factor in civil wars. Case studies designed to test their argument show that many other factors also contribute to civil war and suggest that communal wars differ in causation from other civil wars. See Paul Collier and Nicholas Sambanis, eds., *Understanding Civil War: Evidence and Analysis,* 2 vols. (Washington, D.C.: World Bank, 2005).

16. Horowitz, *Ethnic Groups in Conflict,* 141–185. See also articles on Israelis, Afrikaners, and Hindus in "Chosen Peoples," special issue of *Nations and Nationalism* 5, no. 3 (1999): 331–430.

17. See Vamik D. Volkan, "On Chosen Trauma," *Mind and Human Interaction* 4 (1991): 3–19; and Volkan, *Bloodlines: From Ethnic Pride to Ethnic Terrorism* (New York: Farrar, Straus and Giroux, 1997).

18. On patterns of relative deprivation and the conditions under which it leads to political violence, see Gurr, *Why Men Rebel,* chap. 2. On group interests and mobilization, see Tilly, *From Mobilization to Revolution,* 69–90.

19. For a sensitive analysis of minority group members' nonmaterial incentives for taking part in collective action, see Dennis Chong, *Collective Action and the Civil Rights Movement* (Chicago: University of Chicago Press, 1991).

20. Definitions, coding procedures, and a detailed summary of discrimination data for 1998 are given in Gurr, *Peoples versus States,* chap. 4. Data here have been updated for 2003 by Amy Pate. For empirical evidence on the correlation of discrimination with ethnopolitical action, see Ryan Dudley and Ross A. Miller, "Group Rebellion in the 1980s," *Journal of Conflict Resolution* 42 (February 1998): 77–96; and Ted Robert Gurr, "Why Minorities Rebel: A Cross-National Analysis of Communal Mobilization and Conflict since 1945," *International Political Science Review* 14, no. 2 (1993): 161–201.

21. Tarrow, *Power in Movement,* 123. The frame concept is derived from the work of Erving Goffman, *Frame Analysis: An Essay on the Organization of Experience* (Cambridge, Mass.: Harvard University Press, 1974).

22. See, for example, Rik Coolsaet, *Al-Qaeda: The Myth. The Root Causes of International Terrorism and How to Tackle Them* (Ghent, Belgium: Academia, 2005). The Web site of the Middle East Media Research Institute (MEMRI) tracks Islamist doctrine (in English translation): http://www.memri.org.

23. See Monica Duffy Toft, *The Geography of Ethnic Violence: Identity, Interests, and the Indivisibility of Territory* (Princeton, N.J.: Princeton University Press, 2004); and James D. Fearon and David D. Laitin, "Weak States, Rough Terrain and Large-Scale Ethnic Violence since 1945" (paper presented at the annual meeting of the American Political Science Association, Atlanta, September 1999). Similar evidence is reported by Erik Melander, *Anarchy Within: The Security Dilemma between Ethnic Groups in Emerging Anarchy,* Research Report 52 (Uppsala, Sweden: Department of Peace and Conflict Research, Uppsala University, 1999).

24. In *Power in Movement,* Tarrow develops a general argument that social networks and preexisting institutions provide the basis for mobilization for social movements. The institutional origins of civil rights protest are documented by McAdam, *Political Process and the Development of Black Insurgency, 1930–1970.* Jonathan Fox analyzes the role of religious institutions in facilitating political opposition by 105 religiously distinct minorities in "Do Religious Institutions Support Violence or the Status Quo?" *Studies in Conflict and Terrorism* 22, no. 2 (1999): 119–139. He finds that they support opposition only in special circumstances, either when religious institutions are threatened or when the group has a nonreligious political agenda.

25. On the role of leadership rivalries in the Chechen conflict, see Valery Tishkov, *Ethnicity, Nationalism and Conflict in and after the Soviet Union: The Mind Aflame* (London and Thousand Oaks, Calif.: Sage, 1997), 216–219. On the former Yugoslavia, see, for example, V. P. Gagnon, Jr., "Ethnic Nationalism and International Conflict: The Case of Serbia," *International Security* 19, no. 3 (1994–95): 130–166; and Susan Woodward, *Balkan Tragedy: Chaos and Dissolution after the Cold War* (Washington, D.C.: Brookings Institution, 1995). A comparative analysis of the manipulation of communal identities is Human Rights Watch, *Playing the "Communal Card": Communal Violence and Human Rights* (New York: Human Rights Watch, 1995).

26. The concept of political opportunity is widely used in analyses of the origins and dynamics of social movements, for example, by Tilly, *From Mobilization to Revolution;* McAdam, *Political Process and the Development of Black Insurgency;* and Tarrow, *Power in Movement.* The discussion here follows from Tarrow's definition of political opportunity structure as "the dimensions of the political environment that provide incentives for people to undertake collective action by affecting their expectation for success or failure" (p. 85). The distinction between durable and transient opportunity factors is mine.

27. Deepa Khosla, "Third World States as Intervenors in Ethnic Conflict: Implications for Regional and International Security," *Third World Quarterly* 20, no. 6 (1999): 1143–1156. Her analysis uses coded data on international support from the Minorities at Risk project.

28. Gabriel Sheffer, "Diasporas and Terrorism," in *The Roots of Terrorism,* ed. Laura Richardson (New York and London: Routledge, 2006), 117–129.

29. The point is illustrated by a detailed study of the transnational allies of indigenous peoples in the Peruvian Amazon by Pamela L. Martin, *The Globalization of Contentious Politics: The Amazonian Indigenous Rights Movement* (New York and London: Routledge, 2003).

30. See Michael S. Lund, Barnett R. Rubin, and Fabienne Hara, "Learning from Burundi's Failed Democratic Transition, 1993–96: Did International Initiatives Match the Problem?" in *Cases and Strategies for Preventive Action,* Preventive Action Reports, vol. 2, ed. Barnett R. Rubin (New York: Century Foundation, 1998), 47–92.

31. For a detailed analysis of strategies of ethnic political action in established democracies, transitional democracies, and autocracies, see Gurr, *Peoples versus States,* chap. 5.

32. On the problematic consequences of the recent wave of democratization, see Samuel P. Huntington, "Democracy's Third Wave," *Journal of Democracy* 2 (Spring 1991): 12–34. On its implications for communal conflict, see Larry Diamond and Marc F. Plattner, eds., *Nationalism, Ethnic Conflict, and Democracy* (Baltimore: Johns Hopkins University Press, 1994); and Amy L. Chua, "Markets, Democracy, and Ethnicity: Toward a New Paradigm for Law and Development," *Yale Law Journal* 108 (October 1998): 1–107.

33. From Milovan Djilas, *Fall of the New Class: A History of Communism's Self-Destruction* (New York: Alfred A. Knopf, 1998), quoted in Michael Ignatieff, "Prophet in the Ruins," *New York Review*, March 4, 1999, 30.

34. These are among the key results of a ten-year study as reported in two recent papers: Jack A. Goldstone et al., "A Global Forecasting Model of Political Instability," and Ted Robert Gurr, Mark Woodward, and Monty G. Marshall, "Forecasting Instability: Are Ethnic Wars and Muslim Countries Different?" (paper presented at the American Political Science Association Annual Meeting, Washington, D.C., September 1–4, 2005). Both are posted at http://globalpolicy .gmu.edu/pitf, PITF Phase V Papers. According to Goldstone et al., "factionalism can be thought of as a 'pathological' condition arising . . . when lines of authority become unclear, political competition becomes markedly more zero-sum, and alliances are shifting or hardening as groups look for advantages in an unstable constellation of power" (p. 24).

35. Detailed comparative evidence on the impact of democratic transitions in the 1980s and 1990s on minority group rights and conflicts is reported in Gurr, *Peoples versus States,* chap. 5.

36. See also Barnett R. Rubin, *The Fragmentation of Afghanistan* (New Haven, Conn.: Yale University Press, 1995); and Rubin, "Afghanistan under the Taliban," *Current History* 98 (February 1999): 81.

37. James D. Fearon, "Commitment Problems and the Spread of Ethnic Conflict," in *The International Spread of Ethnic Conflict: Fear, Diffusion, and Escalation,* ed. David A. Lake and Donald Rothchild (Princeton, N.J.: Princeton University Press, 1998), 107–126.

38. Donald Rothchild interprets the breakdown of settlements in Angola as a commitment problem in *Managing Ethnic Conflict in Africa: Pressures and Incentives for Cooperation* (Washington, D.C.: Brookings Institution, 1997), chap. 5. A useful comparative analysis of the interplay between warfare and political maneuvering in attempts to settle southern African conflicts, including Angola, is Thomas Ohlson and Stephen John Stedman with Robert Davies, *The New Is Not Yet Born: Conflict Resolution in Southern Africa* (Washington, D.C.: Brookings Institution, 1994).

39. Stephen M. Saideman, "Is Pandora's Box Half-Empty or Half-Full? The Limited Virulence of Secessionism and the Domestic Sources of Disinte-gration," in Lake and Rothchild, eds., *International Spread of Ethnic Conflict,* 127–150.

40. See Paula Garb, "Ethnicity, Alliance Building, and the Limited Spread of Ethnic Conflict in the Caucasus," in Lake and Rothchild, eds., *International Spread of Ethnic Conflict,* 185–199.

41. The separatist conflicts are described and analyzed by Deepa Khosla, "Self-Determination Movements and Their Outcomes," in Marshall and Gurr, *Peace and Conflict 2005,* 21–27, 84–90.

42. See, for example, Hugh Miall, ed., *Minority Rights in Europe: Prospects for a Transnational Regime* (New York: Council on Foreign Relations, 1994); and Jennifer Jackson Preece, "National Minority Rights vs. State Sovereignty in Europe: Changing Norms in International Relations?" *Nations and Nationalism* 3, no. 3 (1997): 345–364.

43. Victor Asal and Amy Pate, "The Decline of Ethnic Political Discrimination, 1950–2003," in Marshall and Gurr, *Peace and Conflict 2005,* 28–38.

44. There are a great many variants of federalism; see, for example, contributions to Günther Bächler, ed., *Federalism against Ethnicity? Institutional, Legal and Democratic Instruments to Prevent Violent Minority Conflicts* (Zürich: Verlag Rügger, for the Swiss Academy of Human and Social Sciences, 1997).

45. On the importance of security guarantees for ensuring that negotiated settlements hold, see Barbara F. Walter, *Negotiating Settlements to Civil Wars* (Princeton, N.J.: Princeton University Press, 2001).

46. For a recent study on how European principles of integration and multitier structures of governance could help settlement of unresolved secessionist conflicts in Cyprus, Serbia, Georgia-Abkhazia, and Moldova-Transnistria, see Bruno Coppieters et al., *Europeanization and Conflict Resolution: Lessons from the European Periphery* (Ghent, Belgium: Academia, 2004).

47. The evidence is reported in Gurr, *Peoples versus States,* 152–163.

48. Representative studies of preventive diplomacy include Kevin M. Cahill, ed., *Preventive Diplomacy: Stopping Wars before They Start,* rev. ed. (New York and London: Routledge, 2000); Bruce W. Jentleson, ed., *Opportunities Missed, Opportunities Seized: Preventive Diplomacy in the Post–Cold War World* (Lanham, Md.: Rowman and Littlefield, 2000); and Fen Osler Hampson and David M. Malone, eds.,

From Reaction to Conflict Prevention: Opportunities for the UN System (Boulder, Colo.: Lynne Rienner, for the International Peace Academy, 2002).

49. For a recent global study that concludes that both UN-led and non-UN-led peacekeeping operations have had similar and substantial levels of success, see Birger Heldt and Peter Wallensteen, *Peacekeeping Operations: Global Patterns of Intervention and Success, 1948–2004* (Uppsala, Sweden: Folke Bernadotte Academy, 2005). A forthcoming study identifies the mix of domestic and international factors that have shaped the success or failure of UN peacekeeping mis-

sions in the post–Cold War period: Darya Pushkina, "A Recipe for Success? Ingredients of a Successful Peacekeeping Mission," *International Peacekeeping* 13, no. 2 (June 2006): 133–149.

50. The strategies are summarized in a three-volume report, the *Club de Madrid Series on Democracy, Terrorism and Security,* available from the Club de Madrid in PDF format at http://clubmadrid.org. Book-length treatments of each set of analyses and strategies are being published, beginning with *The Roots of Terrorism.*

10

TURBULENT TRANSITIONS
WHY EMERGING DEMOCRACIES GO TO WAR

Edward D. Mansfield and Jack Snyder

THE DANGERS OF TRANSITION

The idea that democracies never fight wars against each other has become an axiom for many scholars. It is, as one scholar puts it, "as close as anything we have to an empirical law in international relations."[1] President Bill Clinton invoked this law to explain why promoting democracy abroad was a pillar of his foreign policy. A premise of President George W. Bush's strategic doctrine is that U.S. security may even require preventive wars to unseat dangerous despots so as to build the "infrastructure of democracy" abroad and create a "balance of power that favors freedom."[2] Declaring that U.S. security from terrorism depends on the success of democracy in Iraq and its neighbors, Bush argued that "sixty years of Western nations excusing and accommodating the lack of freedom in the Middle East did nothing to make us safe—because in the long run, stability cannot be purchased at the expense of liberty."[3]

It is probably true that a world in which more countries were mature, stable democracies would be safer and preferable for the United States. But countries do not become mature democracies overnight. They usually go through a rocky transition, where mass politics mixes with authoritarian elite politics in a volatile way. Statistical evidence covering the past two centuries shows that in this transitional phase of democratization, countries become more aggressive and war prone, not less, and they do fight wars with democratic states. This danger is greatest when states embark on a transition prematurely, when they lack the strong political institutions that are needed to make democracy work. Under these conditions, fearful old elites and ambitious new politicians have the motive and the opportunity to use nationalist appeals to rally support from newly empowered masses.

The 1990s bore out this historical pattern of democratization, nationalism, and war. In the decade following the collapse of the Berlin

Wall, armed violence was intense in a number of regions that had just begun to experiment with electoral democracy and increased pluralism of public debate, including such hotbeds of ethnic warfare as the former Yugoslavia, the post-Soviet Caucasus, and Burundi in Central Africa.[4] At the close of the millennium, this trend showed no signs of abating. Ethiopia and Eritrea, both adopting electoral forms of government in the 1990s, fought a bloody border war in 1999–2000.[5] The nuclear-armed, elected regimes of India and Pakistan fought a war in 1999 in the mountainous borderlands of Kashmir. Prime Minister Vladimir Putin ascended to the presidency of Russia's shaky new democracy by riding the popularity of his war in 1999–2000 against the unruly autonomous region of Chechnya.[6] After the fall of the Suharto dictatorship in Indonesia, elections and referenda led quickly to violence and international intervention in the province of East Timor, a former Portuguese colony seeking national independence in 1999, and to ethnic mayhem elsewhere in Indonesia.

The following evidence, which has been updated from an article we published in *Foreign Affairs* in 1995, should raise questions about the U.S. policy of promoting peace by promoting democratization.[7] The expectation that the spread of democracy will probably contribute to peace in the long run, once new democracies mature, provides little comfort to those who may face a heightened risk of war in the short run. Pushing unsettled Islamic societies and a nuclear-armed great power like China to democratize is like spinning a roulette wheel: many of the possible outcomes are undesirable. The roulette wheel is already spinning for Iraq and Iran and perhaps will be soon for other geopolitically significant states. Washington and the international community should be realistic about the dangers of fomenting democratization where conditions are unripe. The building of institutions that are needed to make democracy work should

precede the unleashing of mass electoral politics, or else the risk of violence will increase.

These arguments apply to both external wars and civil wars. In states lacking the institutional infrastructure needed to manage democratization, this process increases the risk of nationalist politics that often stimulates conflict abroad. For many of the same reasons, in ethnically divided countries, nationalist politics occurring during the early stages of a democratic transition can lead to domestic violence. Most of the evidence presented in this chapter centers on external wars during the past two centuries. Nonetheless, we also draw on some cases of ethnic nationalist violence that include civil wars to illustrate our argument, since democratizing regimes are also disproportionately prone to internal conflict, and the underlying causal processes through which democratization encourages external and civil wars have much in common.[8]

THE EVIDENCE

In earlier research, we conducted some preliminary statistical tests of the relationship between democratization and war.[9] Since then, the data and measures of regime type on which we relied have been updated and extended.[10] Here, we use these more recent data and measures to reevaluate the argument that democratic transitions promote war.

Our statistical analysis relies on the classifications of regimes and wars used by most scholars studying the democratic peace. Starting with these standard data, we classify each state as a democracy, an autocracy, or an "anocracy"—that is, a mixed regime with both democratic and autocratic features. Initially, this classification is based on a composite index developed by Keith Jaggers and Ted Robert Gurr that emphasizes the constitutional constraints on the chief executive, the competitiveness of domestic politics, the openness of the process for selecting the chief executive, and the strength of the rules governing participation in politics.[11] However, we also classify each state's regime type based on three of the components that make up this index: the openness of the process for selecting the head of state, the extent of the constraints on the chief executive, and the competitiveness of political participation.[12] In the following tests, we analyze separately Jaggers and Gurr's composite index and each of the three component factors just mentioned.

In these tests, we distinguish between two phases in the process of democratization: the transition from autocracy to a partially democratic regime—which we refer to as incomplete democratization—and the shift to a fully institutionalized democracy—which we refer to as complete democratization. Our argument is that hostilities are more likely to break out when states have made only an incomplete democratic transition. When military, communist, colonial, dynastic, or other authoritarian regimes break down and mass politics begins, democratic procedures are likely to be intermittent, subject to manipulation by both rising and declining elites, and animated by nationalist or other populist ideologies that give rise to international frictions.

Because we view democratization as a gradual process rather than a sudden change, we test whether a transition over a five-year period is associated with the outbreak of an external war in the year following that period. We code each state as democratic, autocratic, or anocratic at the beginning and then again at the end of each five-year period. An incomplete democratic transition occurs if a state changes from an autocracy to a mixed regime during this period. A complete democratic transition occurs if a state shifts from either an autocracy or a mixed regime to a democracy. War is measured in the year immediately after each five-year period. We analyze the outbreak of all external wars, those between nation-states as well as imperial and colonial wars launched by a state against a nonstate actor.[13]

Our argument is that the effects of democratization on war will be stronger and more pronounced in countries having less institutional strength and centralization. Incomplete democratization occurring in the face of weak governmental institutions undermines the state's ability to manage elite interests and newly politicized mass groups. Political institutions are unable to resolve or suppress the conflicts of interest stemming from growing demands for political participation, thereby creating various dynamics that encourage belligerence abroad. Unless the state has the rare luck to inherit fairly strong political institutions at the outset of the transition from autocracy, turbulence is hard to avoid during this first step on the road to democracy.

To measure the extent of institutional strength and centralization, we rely on an eleven-point index—ranging from 0 to 10—created by Gurr and his colleagues.[14] The index takes on higher values where a regime has more clearly established rules regulating political competition and where it enjoys a more centralized grip on the reins of domestic power. Under these conditions, the regime should be better able to manage the rivalry of elite factions and minimize the adverse consequences of interest-group logrolling.

Since our argument is that incomplete democratic transitions are more likely to stimulate the outbreak of war in countries marked by weak and fragmented institutions, we analyze this index of institutional strength as well as its interaction with our measure of incomplete democratization. We also analyze the interaction between this index and our measure of complete democratization to determine whether the effects of all aspects of democratization depend on the strength of domestic institutions.

While our focus is on democratization, it is also important to assess the effects of autocratization on war. It is only through such an analysis that we can determine whether the effects of democratization stem from a more

Figure 1. Predicted Probability of War by Transition Type, Based on the Composite Index

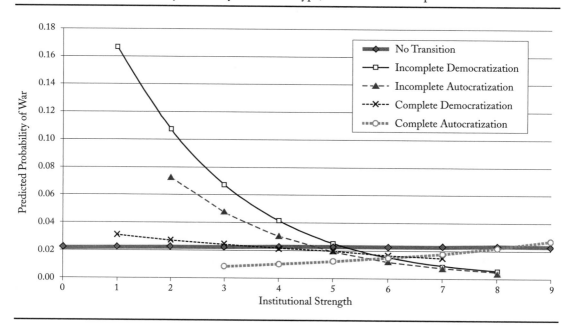

general tendency for regime change of any type to promote conflict. We therefore create two variables, one indicating whether a country underwent a complete autocratic transition (i.e., a transition from either democracy or anocracy to autocracy), and a second indicating whether it underwent an incomplete autocratic transition (i.e., from democracy to anocracy) during each five-year period. Finally, we analyze the interaction between each type of autocratization and our measure of institutional strength and centralization to assess whether the influence of autocratization on war depends on the strength and coherence of domestic institutions.

Our tests span the period from 1816 to 1992, the years that the data sets used to measure regime type and war have in common. We use logistic regression to estimate the effects of democratization and autocratization on war.[15] The results of these tests (which are not presented here to conserve space) strongly support our argument that incomplete democ-

ratization is a potent impetus to war when domestic institutions are weak.[16]

Furthermore, our results refute the view that transitional democracies are simply inviting targets of attack due to their temporary weakness: in fact, they tend to be the initiators of war. We also exclude the possibility that the effect of democratization on war actually reflects the influence of war on democratization: our findings indicate that war has very little bearing on either the occurrence of democratic transitions or whether those transitions that do occur yield coherent democratic institutions.

To illustrate the substantive effects of incomplete democratization on the outbreak of war, figures 1, 2, 3, and 4 show the predicted probability of a given state becoming involved in a war, based on the composite index and the three component measures of regime type. Using the results of the logistic regressions, we calculate the probability of war for each type of regime change analyzed here. For each type, the predicted probability of war is derived

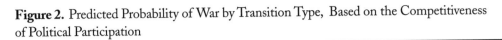

Figure 2. Predicted Probability of War by Transition Type, Based on the Competitiveness of Political Participation

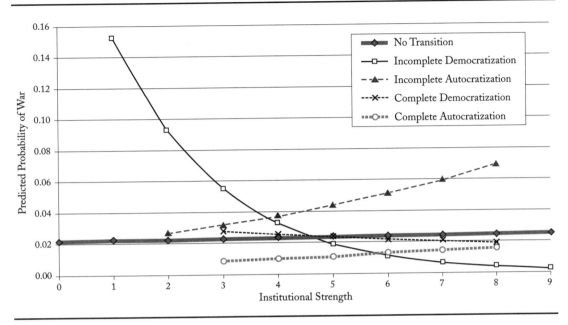

Figure 3. Predicted Probability of War by Transition Type, Based on the Openness of Executive Recruitment

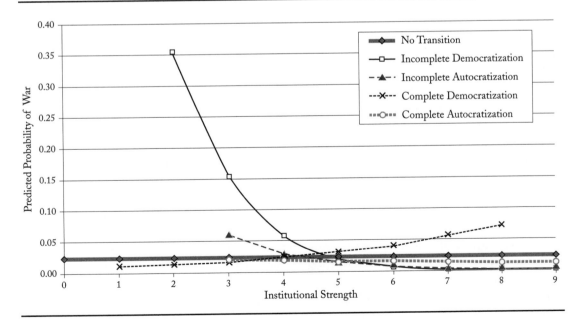

Figure 4. Predicted Probability of War by Transition Type, Based on the Constraints on the Chief Executive

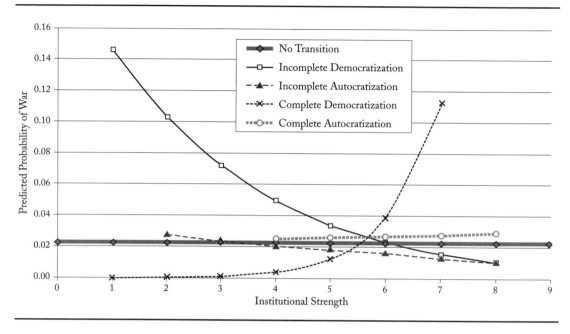

only for the range of values of our measure of institutional strength that actually appears in the data.[17]

These figures show that, regardless of which measure of regime type we analyze, incomplete democratization coupled with weak institutions (i.e., a low score on our measure of institutional strength) is more likely to stimulate war than any other conditions that we consider. Furthermore, these results do not reflect a more general tendency for either all types of democratization (both complete and incomplete) or all types of regime change (both democratization and autocratization) to precipitate hostilities. Although there is some scattered evidence that other kinds of regime change also promote antagonism, the effect of each of these changes is weaker, smaller, and less consistent across our four measures of regime type than is the effect of incomplete democratization. Thus, these findings offer substantial support for our argument.

NATIONALISM AND DEMOCRATIZATION

The connection between democratization and nationalism is striking in both the historical record and today's headlines. Data limitation precluded the direct measurement of nationalism in our statistical tests. Nonetheless, historical and contemporary evidence strongly suggests that rising nationalism often goes hand in hand with the early phases of a transition toward democracy. It is no accident that the end of the Cold War brought both a wave of democratization and a revival of nationalist sentiment in the former communist states.

In eighteenth-century Britain and France, when nationalism first emerged as an explicit political doctrine, it meant self-rule by the people. It was the rallying cry of commoners and rising commercial classes against rule by aristocratic elites, who were charged with the sin of governing in their own interests, rather than those of the nation. Indeed, dynastic rulers and imperial courts had hardly been interested in promoting nationalism as a banner of solidarity in their realms. They typically ruled over a linguistically and culturally diverse conglomeration of subjects and claimed to govern by divine right, not in the interest of the nation. Often, these rulers were more closely tied by kinship, language, or culture to elites in other states than to their own subjects. The position of the communist ruling class was strikingly similar: a transnational elite that ruled over an amalgamation of peoples and claimed legitimacy from the communist party's role as the vanguard of history, not from the consent of the governed. Popular forces challenging either traditional dynastic rulers or communist elites naturally tended to combine demands for national self-determination and democratic rule.

This concoction of nationalism and incipient democratization has been a volatile brew, leading in case after case to ill-conceived wars of expansion. The earliest instance remains one of the most dramatic. In the French Revolution, the radical Brissotin parliamentary faction polarized politics by harping on the king's slow response to the threat of war with other dynastic states. In the ensuing wars of the French Revolution, citizens flocked to join the revolutionary armies to defend popular self-rule and the French nation. Even after the revolution turned profoundly antidemocratic, Napoleon was able to harness this popular nationalism to the task of conquering Europe, substituting the popularity of empire for the substance of democratic rule.

After this experience, Europe's ruling elites decided to band together in 1815 in the Concert of Europe to contain the twin evils of nationalism and democratization. In this scheme, Europe's crowned heads tried to unite in squelching demands for constitutions, electoral and social democracy, and national self-determination. For a time nationalism and democratization were both held back, and Europe enjoyed a period of relative peace.

But in the long run, the strategy failed in the face of the economic changes strengthening popular forces in Western and Central Europe. British and French politicians soon saw that they would have to rule by co-opting nationalist and democratic demands, rather than suppressing them. Once the specter of revolution returned to Europe in 1848, this reversal of political tactics was complete, and it led quickly to the Crimean War. British foreign secretary Palmerston and French emperor Napoleon III both tried to manage the clamor for a broader political arena by giving democrats what they wanted in foreign affairs—a "liberal" war to free imprisoned nations from autocratic rule and, incidentally, to expand commerce.

But this was just the dress rehearsal for history's most potent combination of mass politics and rising nationalism, which occurred in Germany around the turn of the twentieth century. Chancellor Otto von Bismarck, counting on the conservative votes of a docile peasantry, granted universal suffrage in the newly unified Reich after 1870; but in foreign and military affairs, he kept the elected Reichstag subordinate to the cabinet appointed by the kaiser. Like the sorcerer's apprentice, however, Bismarck underestimated the forces he was unleashing. With the rise of an industrial society, Bismarck's successors could not control this truncated democracy, where over 90 percent of the population voted. Every group was highly politicized, yet none could achieve their aims through the limited powers of the Reichstag. As a result, people organized direct pressure groups outside electoral party politics. Some of these clamored for economic benefits, but many of them found it tactically useful to cloak their narrow interests in a broader vision of the nation's interests. This mass nationalist sentiment exerted constant pressure on German diplomacy in the Wilhelmine years before 1914 and pushed its vacillating elites toward war.

Democratization and nationalism also became linked in Japan on the eve of the

Manchurian invasion in 1931. During the 1920s Japan expanded its suffrage and experimented with two-party electoral competition, though a council of military elder statesmen still made the ultimate decisions about who would govern. These semielected governments of the 1920s supported free trade, favored naval arms control, and usually tried to rein in the Japanese army's schemes to undermine the Open Door policy in China. During the 1920s, young radicals in the army developed a populist, nationalist doctrine featuring a centrally planned economy within an autarkic, industrialized, expanded empire, while scapegoating Japan's alleged internal and external enemies, including leftist workers, rich capitalists, liberals, democrats, Americans, and Russians. After the economic crash of the late 1920s, this nationalist formula became persuasive, and the Japanese military had little trouble gaining popular support for imperial expansion and the emasculation of democracy. As in so many previous cases, nationalism proved to be a way for militarist elite groups to appear populist in a democratizing society while obstructing the advance to full democracy.

The interconnection among nationalism, incipient democratization, and war was likewise present among some of the postcommunist states in the 1990s. Shortly after the breakup of the Soviet Union, one-quarter of Russia's voters, disgruntled by economic distress, backed the tough-talking nationalist party of the anti-Semite Vladimir Zhirinovsky in the 1993 parliamentary elections. Before long, more mainstream politicians learned to co-opt popular nationalist issues. Following a series of mysterious terrorist bombings in Moscow, which were attributed to "Chechens," and Chechen bandit raids into Russian territory in the summer of 1999, President Boris Yeltsin's new prime minister, Vladimir Putin, used a highly popular military intervention in Chechnya to position himself as Yeltsin's successor.

The early stages of democratization were also implicated in the violent breakup of communist Yugoslavia. Especially in Serbia, the political and military elites of the old regime, facing pressure for democratization, cynically but successfully created a new basis for popular legitimacy through nationalist propaganda in the mass media they controlled. In the climate of opinion that this manipulation fostered, Serbian elections in the late 1980s and 1990s became contests among different varieties of nationalists, each trying to outbid the others to claim the mantle of the true defenders of Serbdom against its ethnic foes.

THE SORCERER'S APPRENTICE

Although the early stage of democratization increases the likelihood of war in countries with weak political institutions, the average voter in such states does not necessarily want war. Public opinion in democratizing states often starts off highly averse to the costs and risks of war. In that sense, the public opinion polls taken in Russia in early 1994 were typical. Respondents said, for example, that Russian policy should make sure the rights of Russians in neighboring states were protected, but not at the cost of military intervention. Notwithstanding the ambivalence of the Russian public's view of the Chechen problem during the 1990s, by 1999 the Russians had been primed by inflammatory media coverage and the Putin government's military faits accomplis to adopt a more belligerent stance toward the perennially troublesome Chechens.

Numerous historical and recent cases point to the effectiveness of calculated elite efforts to whip up belligerent nationalism among an initially pacific population during the earliest stages of a democratic transition. For example, Napoleon III successfully exploited the domestic prestige from France's share of the victory in the Crimean War to consolidate his rule, despite the popular reluctance and war weariness that had accompanied the war. Having learned this lesson well, Napoleon tried this tactic again in 1859. On the eve of his military intervention in the Italian struggle with Austria, he admitted to his ministers that "on the domestic front, the war will at first awaken great fears; traders and speculators of every stripe will shriek, but national sentiment will [banish] this domestic fright; the nation will be put to the test once more in a struggle that will stir many a heart, recall the memory of heroic times, and bring together under the mantle of glory the parties that are steadily drifting away from one another day after day."[18] Napoleon was trying not just to follow opinion but to make opinion bellicose, in order to stir a national feeling that would enhance the state's ability to govern a split and stalemated political arena.

Much the same has happened in contemporary Serbia. Despite the memories of fascist Ustashi Croatian atrocities in World War II, intermarriage rates between Croats and Serbs living in Croatia were as high as one in three during the 1980s. Opinion was turned warlike by propaganda campaigns in state-controlled media that, for example, carried purely invented reports of rapes of Serbian women in Kosovo, and even more so by the fait accompli of launching the war itself. V. P. Gagnon argues, moreover, that nationalist propaganda served not so much to whip up ethnic hatred as to discredit liberal democratic critiques of the nationalist Croatian and Serbian regimes.[19]

In short, democratizing states are war prone, not because war is popular with the mass public, but because domestic pressures create incentives for elites to drum up nationalist sentiment.

THE CAUSES OF WARS OF DEMOCRATIZATION

Democratization often goes hand in hand with a syndrome of weak central authority, unstable domestic coalitions, and high-energy mass politics. It brings new social groups and classes onto the political stage. Political leaders, finding no way to reconcile incompatible interests, resort to shortsighted bargains or reckless gambles in order to maintain their governing coalitions. Elites need to gain mass allies to defend their weakened positions. Both the newly ambitious elites and the embattled old ruling groups often use appeals to nationalism to stay astride their unmanageable political coalitions.

Needing public support, they rouse the masses with nationalist propaganda but find that their mass allies, once mobilized by passionate appeals, are difficult to control. So are the powerful remnants of the old order—the military, for example—which promote militarism because it strengthens them institutionally. This is particularly true because the early stages of democratization may weaken the central government's ability to keep policy coherent and consistent. Governing a society that is democratizing is like driving a car while throwing away the steering wheel, stepping on the gas, and fighting over which passenger will be in the driver's seat. The result, when political institutions are weak, is often war.

Political Stalemate and Imperialist Coalitions

Democratization creates a wider spectrum of politically significant groups with diverse and incompatible interests. In the period when the great powers were first democratizing, kings, aristocrats, peasants, and artisans shared the historical stage with industrialists, an urban working class, and a middle-class intelligentsia. Similarly, in the postcommunist world, former party apparatchiks, atavistic heavy industrialists, and downwardly mobile military officers share the stage with populist demagogues, free-market entrepreneurs, disgruntled workers, and newly mobilized ethnic groups. In principle, mature democratic institutions can integrate even the widest spectrum of interests through competition for the favor of the average voter. But where political parties and representative institutions are still in their infancy, the diversity of interests may make political coalitions difficult to maintain.

Often the solution is a belligerent nationalist coalition.

In Britain during the period leading up to the Crimean War, neither the Whigs nor the Tories could form a lasting governing coalition because so many groups refused to enter stable political alliances. None of the old elites would coalesce with the parliamentary bloc of radicals elected by urban middle-class and Irish voters. Moreover, protectionist Tories would not unite with free-trading Whigs and Peelite Tories. The social and political mid-Victorian equipoise between traditional and modern Britain created a temporary political stalemate. Lord Palmerston's pseudoliberal imperialism turned out to be the only successful formula for creating a durable ruling coalition during this transitional period of democratization.

The stalemate in Wilhelmine-era electoral politics was even more serious. In principle, coalitions of the left and the right might have formed a two-party system to vie for the favor of the average voter, thus moderating policy. In fact, both the left and the right were too internally divided to mount effective coalitions with internally consistent policies. Progressives dreamed of a bloc extending "from Bassermann to Bebel," from the liberal-democratic middle classes through the Marxist working classes, but the differences between labor and capital chronically barred this development. Conservatives had more success in forging a "marriage of iron and rye," but fundamental differences between military-feudal Junkers and Ruhr industrialists over issues ranging from the distribution of tax burdens to military strategy made their policies incoherent. Germany wound up with plans for a big army and a costly navy, and nobody willing to pay for it.

Inflexible Interests and Short Time Horizons

Groups threatened by social change and democratization, including still-powerful elites, are often compelled to take an inflexible view of their interests, especially when their assets cannot be readily adapted to changing political and economic conditions. In extreme cases, there may be only one solution that will maintain the social position of the group. For Prussian landowners, it was agricultural protection in a nondemocratic state; for the Japanese military, it was organizational autonomy in an autarkic empire; for the Serbian military and party elites, it was a Serbian nationalist state. Since military bureaucracies and imperial interest groups occupied key positions in many authoritarian great powers, whether monarchal or communist, most interests threatened by democratization have been bound up with military programs and the state's international mission. Compromises that may lead down the slippery slope to social extinction or irrelevance have little appeal to such groups. This adds to the difficulty of finding an exit from the domestic political impasse and may make powerful domestic groups impervious to the international risks of their strategies.

Competing for Popular Support

The trouble intensifies when elites in a democratizing society try to recruit mass allies to their cause. Threatened elite groups have an overwhelming incentive to mobilize mass backers on the elites' terms, using whatever special resources they might retain. These resources have included monopolies of information (the Wilhelmine navy's unique "expertise" in making strategic assessments), propaganda assets (the Japanese army's public relations blitz justifying the invasion of Manchuria), patronage (Lord Palmerston's gifts of foreign service postings to the sons of cooperative journalists), wealth (the Krupp steel company's bankrolling of mass nationalist and militarist leagues), organizational skills and networks (the Japanese army's exploitation of rural reservist organizations to build a social base), and the ability to use the control of traditional political institutions to shape the political agenda and structure the terms of political bargains (the Wilhelmine ruling elite's agreement to eliminate anti-Catholic legislation in exchange for Catholic support in the Reichstag on the naval budget).

This elite mobilization of mass groups takes place in a highly competitive setting. Elite groups mobilize mass support to neutralize mass threats (e.g., creating patriotic leagues to counter workers movements) and counter other elite groups' successful efforts at mass mobilization (such as the German Navy League, a political counterweight to the Junker-backed Agrarian League). The elites' resources allow them to influence the direction of mass political participation, but the imperative to compete for mass favor makes it difficult for a single elite group to control the outcome of this process. For example, mass groups that gain access to politics through elite-supported nationalist organizations often try to outbid their erstwhile sponsors. By 1911, German popular nationalist lobbies were in a position to claim that if Germany's foreign foes were really as threatening as the ruling elites had portrayed them, then the government had sold out German interests in reaching a compromise with France over the Moroccan dispute. In this way, elite mobilization of the masses adds to the ungovernability and political impasse of democratizing states.

Ideology takes on particular significance in the competition for mass support. New entrants to the political process, lacking established habits and reliable information, may be uncertain where their political interests lie. Ideology can yield big payoffs, particularly when there is no efficient and free marketplace of ideas to counter false claims with reliable facts. Elites try out all sorts of ideological appeals depending on the social position they are defending, the nature of the mass group they want to recruit, and the kinds of appeals that seem politically plausible. A nearly universal element of these ideological appeals, however, is nationalism, which has the advantage of positing a community of interest uniting elites and masses. This distracts attention from class cleavages that divide elites from the masses they are trying to recruit.

The Weakening of Central Authority

A weakening of the state's authority in the early stages of democratization deepens the political impasse and the recklessness of the ruling elite. The autocrat can no longer dictate to elite interest groups or mass groups. In many such transitions, democratic institutions lack the strength to integrate these contending interests and views. Parties are weak and lack mass loyalty. Elections are rigged or intermittent. Institutions of public political participation are distrusted because they are subject to manipulation by elites and arbitrary constraints imposed by the state, which fears the outcome of unfettered competition.

Among the great powers, the problem was not excessive authoritarian power at the center, but the opposite. The Aberdeen coalition that brought Britain into the Crimean War was a makeshift cabinet headed by a weak leader with no substantial constituency. Likewise, on the eve of the Franco-Prussian War, Napoleon III's regime was in the process of caving in to its liberal opponents, who dominated the parliament elected in 1869. As Europe's armies prepared to hurtle from their starting gates in July 1914, Austrian leaders, perplexed by the contradictions between the German chancellor's policy and that of the German military, asked, "Who rules in Berlin?" Similarly, the 1931 Manchurian incident was a fait accompli by the local Japanese military; Tokyo was not even informed.

In each of these cases, the weak central leadership resorted to the same strategies as did the more parochial elite interests, using nationalist ideological appeals and special-interest payoffs to maintain their short-run viability, despite the long-run risks that these strategies unleashed.

Prestige Strategies

One of the simplest but riskiest strategies for a hard-pressed regime in a democratizing country is to shore up its prestige at home by seeking victories abroad. During Russia's Chechen interventions in the 1990s, newspaper commentators in Moscow and the West were reminded of Russian interior minister Viacheslav Plehve's fateful remark in 1904, on the eve of the disastrous Russo-Japanese War, that what the tsar needed was "a short, victorious war" to boost his prestige. Though this strategy often backfires, it is a perennial temptation as a means for coping with the political strains of democratization. German chancellor Johannes Miquel, who revitalized the imperialist-protectionist "coalition of iron and rye" at the turn of the century, told his colleagues that "successes in foreign policy would make a good impression in the Reichstag debates, and political divisions would thus be moderated."[20] The targets of such strategies often share this analysis. Richard Cobden, for example, argued that military victories abroad would confer enough prestige on the military-feudal landed elite to allow them to raise food tariffs and snuff out democracy: "Let John Bull have a great military triumph, and we shall have to take off our hats as we pass the Horse Guards for the rest of our lives."[21]

Prestige strategies make the country vulnerable to slights to its reputation. Napoleon III, for example, was easily goaded into a full declaration of war in 1870 by Bismarck's insulting editorial work on a leaked telegram from the kaiser. For those who want to avoid such diplomatic provocations, the lesson is to make sure that compromises forced on the leaders of democratizing states do not take away the fig leaves needed to sustain their domestic prestige.

MANAGING THE DANGERS IN TODAY'S WORLD

Though mature democratic states have never fought wars against each other, promoting democracy may not promote peace because states are especially war prone when they start making a transition toward democracy before the requisite institutions are in place. This does not mean, however, that democratization should be squelched in the interests of peace. Rather, it means that proponents of democratization should carefully weigh the timing of their efforts to promote democratization. In particular, they should try to encourage a sequence of transition that begins with institution building and culminates in unfettered electoral competition. This sequence, where it is feasible, is likely to minimize the undesirable side effects of democratization.

Of course, democratization does not always lead to extreme forms of aggressive nationalism, just as it does not always lead to war. But it makes those outcomes more likely. Cases where states democratized without triggering a nationalist mobilization are particularly interesting, since they may hold clues about how to prevent such unwanted side effects. Among the great powers, Great Britain followed the smoothest path toward democracy because it created the necessary institutions—a free press, a legislative body, the rule of law, an effective state apparatus—before opening up electoral competition under wide suffrage. Similarly, South Africa has had a reasonably smooth transition to mass democracy because the institutions needed for effective democracy were created for the white minority under the apartheid regime. They got the sequence right. In contrast, Burundi, where international donors abruptly pressed elections on its ethnic Tutsi minority dictatorship in 1993, had none of these institutions to build on. Within months of the election, more than one hundred thousand people were killed in ethnic strife.

Where the needed institutions are lacking, they can sometimes be built quickly and easily. This has been the case in countries that are relatively rich, where literacy and citizen skills are high, or where past experiments with democracy left a legacy of legal, administrative, or journalistic institutions that could have new life breathed into them. These conditions have facilitated peaceful transitions in much of South America, Northeastern and Central Europe, Korea, and Taiwan.

All too often, however, building the needed institutions has proved exceedingly difficult. Where many citizens are illiterate, per capita income is low, society is ethnically divided, religious sects or other illiberal groups dominate civil society, powerful spoilers fear democracy, nationalist mythmakers control the media, and/or oil revenue makes the state unaccountable to taxpayers, the path of democratization is likely to be neither smooth nor peaceful. In such hard cases, some of the preconditions of effective democracy, including reformed state institutions, need to be put in place before mass electoral politics are unleashed. Premature electoral competition is often an occasion for violence and tends to play into the hands of nationalist demagogues and ethnic or sectarian politicians.

Many of the countries that are still on the "to do" list of democracy promotion are lacking in most of the preconditions for an easy transition. Many Islamic countries that figure prominently in the Bush administration's efforts to promote democracy are particularly hard cases. While we do not claim to be able to foretell the future of democratization in these troubled states, our findings suggest that their path toward electoral politics will be fraught with risk.

Although democratization in the Islamic world might contribute to peace in the very long run, Islamic public opinion in the short run is generally hostile to the United States, reluctant to condemn terrorism, and tolerant of forceful measures in disputed areas. Although much of the belligerence of the Islamic public is fueled by resentment of the U.S.-backed authoritarian regimes under which many of them live, renouncing these authoritarians and pressing for a quick democratic opening is unlikely to lead to peaceful democratic consolidations. On the contrary, unleashing Islamic mass opinion through a sudden democratization might

raise the likelihood of war. All of the risk factors are there: The media and civil society groups are inflammatory, as old elites and rising oppositions try to outbid each other for the mantle of Islamic or nationalist militancy.[22] The rule of law is weak, and existing corrupt bureaucracies cannot serve a democratic administration properly. The boundaries of states are mismatched with those of nations, making any push for national self-determination fraught with peril. Per capita incomes, literacy rates, and citizen skills in most Muslim Middle Eastern states are below the levels normally needed to sustain democracy.[23]

In the Arab world, in particular, states commonly gain their popular legitimacy not through accountability to their own citizens but by acting demagogically in the purported interests of the Arab nation as a whole, which often means taking a belligerent stand on Palestinian issues.[24] When Iraq attempted to make a democratic transition in the late 1940s, the elected leaders of its weak state felt compelled to grant military basing rights to its former colonial ruler, Britain; they then took an inflammatory stance against Israel to try to recoup their diminished nationalist credibility in the eyes of their urban Arab nationalist constituents. This vocal stance by Iraq's flawed democratic regime pushed the more moderate monarchies in the Arab frontline states to reject compromise on the creation of an Israeli state, opening the door to the 1948 Arab-Israeli war and the deepening entrenchment of the Arab-Israeli rivalry.

We do not argue that Islam is culturally unsuited for democracy, but rather that the institutional preparations for democracy are weak in most Islamic states. Thus, sudden increases in mass political participation are likely to be dangerous. Evidence of this is found in the theocratic pseudodemocracy established by the Iranian Revolution; it relentlessly pressed the offensive in a bloody war of attrition with Iraq and supported violent movements abroad. A quarter of a century later, Iranian electoral politics still bears the imprint of incomplete democratization. With liberal democratic reformers barred from running for office, Iranian voters looking for a more responsive government turned in the June 2005 presidential election to the religious fundamentalist populist mayor of Tehran, Mahmoud Ahmadinejad, a staunch proponent of the Iranian nuclear program. The use of nationalism as part of a popular appeal in an electoral system that rules out liberal alternatives is a common tactic.

This does not necessarily mean that all steps toward democracy in the Islamic world would lead to disaster. Etel Solingen argues, for example, that reforms leading toward "democratization from above," combined with economic liberalization, have been consistent with support for peaceful policies in such Arab states as Jordan, Tunisia, Morocco, and Qatar. "The more consolidated democratizing regimes become," she notes, "the less likely they are to experiment with populism and war."[25] Consistent with our argument, these modest success cases indicate that the most promising sequence for democratization in such settings begins with reforms of the state and the economy, together with limited forms of democratic participation, rather than a headlong jump into popular elections before the strengthening of the institutions—such as efficient and evenhanded public administration, the rule of law, professional journalism, and political parties—that are needed to make a democratic system work.

Islamic democratization is hardly the only such danger on the horizon. A future democratic opening in China, though much hoped for by advocates of human rights and democratization, could produce a sobering outcome.[26] China's communist rulers have presided over a commercial expansion that has generated wealth and a potentially powerful constituency for broader political participation. However, given the huge socioeconomic divide between the prosperous coastal areas and the vast impoverished hinterlands, it seems unlikely that

economic development will lead as smoothly to democratic consolidation in China as it has in Taiwan. China's leadership showed its resistance to pressures for democratic liberalization in its 1989 crackdown on the student movement at Tiananmen Square, but party elites know that they need a stronger basis of popular legitimacy to survive the social and ideological changes that economic change has unleashed.

Nationalism is a key element in their strategy. China's demand to incorporate Taiwan in the People's Republic of China, its animosity toward Japan, and its public displays of resentment at U.S. slights are themes that resonate with the Chinese public and can easily be played on to rally national solidarity behind the regime. At the same time, newly rising social forces see that China's leaders permit more latitude to expressions of nationalism than to liberalism. Thus, some of the same intellectuals who played a role in the Tiananmen prodemocracy protests turned up a few years later as authors of a nationalist text, *The China That Can Say No.*[27]

Like many other established elites who have made use of popular nationalist rhetoric, China's party leadership has walked a fine line, allowing only limited expressions of popular nationalist outrage after such perceived provocations as the U.S. bombing of the Chinese embassy in Belgrade, anti-Chinese pogroms in Jakarta, the U.S. spy plane incident of 2001, and the Japanese bid for a permanent seat on the UN Security Council. They realize that criticism of external enemies can quickly become transformed into popular criticism of the government for not being sufficiently diligent in defense of Chinese national interests. It is doubtful that they could maintain a fine-tuned control over an aroused nationalist public opinion if an incompletely democratizing China becomes embroiled in a future crisis with Taiwan.

In short, the Bush administration's efforts to force the pace of democratization in countries that lack the preconditions for it risk playing into the hand of nationalists, ethnic and sectarian politicians, and other populist purveyors of violent political strategies. Instead, democracy promotion should be focused on countries where conditions for it are ripe, or on the patient, properly sequenced construction of the institutional supports that undergird true democracy. In the long run, the enlargement of the zone of stable democracy will probably enhance prospects for peace. In the short run, much work remains to be done to minimize the dangers of the turbulent transition.

NOTES

Adapted from Edward D. Mansfield and Jack Snyder, "Democratization and War," *Foreign Affairs* 74, no. 3 (May-June 1995): 79–97. Copyright © 1995 by the Council on Foreign Relations, Inc. Used by permission. Figures 5.1 through 5.4 are adapted from tables that appeared in Edward D. Mansfield and Jack Snyyder, *Electing to Fight: Why Emerging Democracies Go to War* (Cambridge, Mass.: MIT Press, 2005). Used by permission of MIT Press. © Belfer Center for Science in International Affairs, John F. Kennedy School of Government, Harvard.

1. Jack S. Levy, "Domestic Politics and War," *Journal of Interdisciplinary History* 18, no. 4 (Spring 1988): 662.

2. Executive Office of the President, *National Security Strategy of the United States* (September 2002), 21, 29.

3. George W. Bush, "Remarks by the President at the 20th Anniversary of the National Endowment for Democracy," Washington, D.C., November 6, 2003, reported in David Sanger, "Bush Asks Lands in Mideast to Try Democratic Ways," *New York Times,* November 7, 2003, A1.

4. Jack Snyder, *From Voting to Violence: Democratization and Nationalist Conflict* (New York: W. W. Norton, 2000), chaps. 5 and 6.

5. In *Peoples Versus States* (Washington, D.C.: United States Institute of Peace Press, 2000), 293, Ted Robert Gurr codes Ethiopia as making a transition to "anocracy" (a partially democratic, mixed regime) in 1994. On Eritrea, see Ruth Iyob, "The Eritrean Experiment: A Cautious Pragmatism?" *Journal*

of Modern African Studies 35, no. 4 (December 1997): 647–673.

6. Michael R. Gordon, "Russia Votes, Like It or Not: Chechnya War Fever Gives Pause in the West," *New York Times,* December 21, 1999, A1, A22.

7. Edward D. Mansfield and Jack Snyder, "Democratization and War," *Foreign Affairs* 74, no. 3 (May–June 1995): 79–97. We have updated the statistical findings and added discussions of recent cases, but the historical and conceptual discussion in this chapter remains similar to that article. The fullest statement of our work on the topic is Edward D. Mansfield and Jack Snyder, *Electing to Fight: Why Emerging Democracies Go to War* (Cambridge, Mass.: MIT Press, 2005).

8. For a more extensive analysis of how democratization promotes civil violence, see Snyder, *From Voting to Violence.*

9. See Edward D. Mansfield and Jack Snyder, "Democratization and the Danger of War," *International Security* 20, no. 1 (Summer 1995): 5–38.

10. See Keith Jaggers and Ted Robert Gurr, "Tracking Democracy's Third Wave with the Polity III Data," *Journal of Peace Research* 32, no. 4 (November 1995): 469–482.

11. Ibid.

12. For the procedures used to code these variables, see Mansfield and Snyder, *Electing to Fight,* chap. 4.

13. More specifically, we code each state's regime type in year t-1 and then again in year t-6. We measure incomplete and complete democratic transitions by determining whether the state's regime type changed between years t-6 and t-1. War is measured in year t. On the definition of and data on external wars, see Melvin Small and J. David Singer, *Resort to Arms: International and Civil Wars, 1816–1980* (Beverly Hills, Calif.: Sage Publications, 1982); and Singer and Small, "Correlates of War Project: International and Civil Wars Data, 1816–1992" (data set, stored at the Inter-University Consortium for Political and Social Research, Ann Arbor, Michigan, 1994). Note that the following results are much the same if we focus only on interstate wars rather than all external wars.

14. This variable measures the degree to which domestic authority is concentrated in each state's central government in year t-1. See Ted Robert Gurr,

Keith Jaggers, and Will H. Moore, "Polity II: Political Structures and Regime Change, 1800–1986" (codebook for data set, stored at the Inter-University Consortium for Political and Social Research, Ann Arbor, Michigan, 1989), 39–40. Here, we refer to this variable as "institutional strength." Elsewhere, we have referred to it as the domestic concentration of authority (or "DomConcentration"). See Edward D. Mansfield and Jack Snyder, "Democratic Transitions, Institutional Capacity, and the Onset of War," *International Organization* 56, no. 2 (Spring 2002): 297–337; and Mansfield and Snyder, *Electing to Fight*, especially chaps. 4–6.

15. In conducting these tests, we controlled for whether each state is a major power in year *t*-1, whether each state is involved in a civil war in year *t*-1, the distribution of power throughout the international system, and the length of time since each state last experienced the onset of an external war.

16. These parameter estimates and a more detailed explanation of our tests are presented in Mansfield and Snyder, *Electing to Fight*, chap. 5.

17. Thus, for example, we do not present the predicted probability of war for any type of regime change when our measure of institutional strength equals zero because there is no case in the data where a regime change took place and this measure was equal to zero. We do present the predicted probability of war when no regime change takes place and our measure of institutional strength equals zero, since there are some cases of this sort in the data. Note also that, for the purpose of calculating these probabilities, we hold constant the distribution of power at its mean and assume that the state neither is experiencing a civil war nor is a major power.

18. Alain Plessis, *The Rise and Fall of the Second Empire, 1852–1871* (Cambridge: Cambridge University Press, 1985), 146–147.

19. V. P. Gagnon, *The Myth of Ethnic War: Serbia and Croatia in the 1990s* (Ithaca, N.Y.: Cornell University Press, 2004).

20. J. C. G. Rohl, *Germany without Bismarck* (Berkeley: University of California Press, 1967), 250.

21. Richard Cobden, letter to John Bright, October 1, 1854, quoted in John Morley, *The Life of Richard Cobden,* abridged ed. (London: Thomas Nelson, n.d.), 311–312.

22. In "Islamism, Revolution, and Civil Society," *Perspectives on Politics* 1, no. 2 (June 2003): 257–272, especially 265, Sheri Berman draws parallels to belligerent civil society in the flawed democracy of Weimar Germany and stresses the "Huntingtonian gap" between high demand for political participation and ineffective state institutions.

23. In *Human Development Report 2004* (New York: Oxford University Press, 2004), the United Nations Development Programme reports the following percentage rates of illiteracy among adults over age fifteen: Algeria, 31.1; Bahrain, 11.5; Egypt, 44.4; Iran, 22.9; Jordan, 9.1; Kuwait, 17.1; Lebanon, 13.5; Libya, 18.3; Morocco, 49.3; Oman, 25.6; Saudi Arabia, 22.1; Syria, 17.1; Tunisia, 26.8; United Arab Emirates, 22.7; and Yemen, 51. See also Daniela Donno and Bruce Russett, "Islam, Authoritarianism, and Female Empowerment: What Are the Linkages?" *World Politics* 56, no. 4 (July 2004): 582–607.

24. Michael Barnett, *Dialogues in Arab Politics* (New York: Columbia University Press, 1998).

25. Etel Solingen, *Regional Orders at Century's Dawn: Global and Domestic Influences of Grand Strategy* (Princeton, N.J.: Princeton University Press, 1998), 213.

26. For a balanced view that discusses many of the following points, see David Bachman, "China's Democratization: What Difference Would It Make for U.S.-China Relations," in *What If China Doesn't Democratize?* ed. Edward Friedman and Barrett McCormick (Armonk, N.Y.: M. E. Sharpe, 2000).

27. Song Qiang, Zhang Zangzang, and Qiao Bian, *Zhongguo keyi shuo bu* [The China That Can Say No] (Beijing: Zhonghua gongshang lianhe chubanshe, 1996).

11

ENVIRONMENTAL CHANGE, SECURITY, AND CONFLICT

Nils Petter Gleditsch

AN EXTENDED CONCEPT OF SECURITY?

After the emergence of two totalitarian movements in Europe in the 1920s and repeated defeats for liberal internationalism, the realist school of thought remained dominant in thinking about international relations. Realism emphasizes the struggle for territory and resources, and patterns of conflict and cooperation are seen to form mainly on the basis of the struggle for power—military, economic, and political. A country can strengthen its position through conquest or alliance building and will tend to do so unless checked by countervailing power. The international system is anarchic, with unclear norms and weak institutions that cannot prevent aggression from states that challenge the established order. Security is mainly a zero-sum game in which a gain for one state is a loss for another.

The field of international relations has never universally accepted a purely realist notion of security, and in the past few decades alternative notions of security have gained ground.

After the end of the Cold War, in particular, the notion of security has been subjected to intense scrutiny.

In one of the first challenges to the traditional security concept, the Palme Commission launched the slogan of common security, a positive-sum notion in which the greater security of one state was seen to be mutually reinforcing with that of another.[1] A more radical challenge was put forward with the notion of comprehensive security, which widened the scope of the traditional concerns.[2] Today, human security is the buzzword. Human security focuses on the security of the individual rather than the security of the state. Beyond this, there is little agreement on the scope of the concept. It was very broadly defined by the UN Development Programme as "safety from such chronic threats as hunger, disease and repression" and also "protection from sudden and hurtful disruptions in the patterns of daily life."[3] The *Human Security Report*, on the other hand, focuses on "violent threats to individuals." It reports "a dramatic global decline in

177

political violence since the end of the Cold War."[4] This survey included interstate war and international crises, civil war, genocide, politicide and serious human rights abuses, and military coups. The one ambiguous finding concerns international terrorism: the number of terrorist incidents is down, but the number of casualties is up.

In addition to freedom from violence, a wider notion of security might include

- *Political security*, defined as the freedom from dictatorship and other arbitrary government; tracking political security would involve looking at patterns of democratic governance and respect for human rights[5]
- *Economic and social security*, defined as the freedom from poverty and want[6]
- *Cultural security*, defined as the freedom from ethnic or religious domination[7]
- *Environmental security*, defined as the freedom from environmental destruction and resource scarcity, which is the topic of this chapter

This list corresponds to the wide notion of human rights championed by many human rights activists, in which "the first generation of rights" encompasses political and civil rights, the second generation includes social and economic rights, and the third generation encompasses matters like solidarity and environmental sustainability.

The idea of a wider conception of security was promoted in part by scholars and activists who wanted to undermine the influence of traditional-power political thinking on international relations. After the end of the Cold War, this idea has become more widely accepted, even to the point that it might be seen as the dominant paradigm. Military organizations and national security establishments in the West embraced the idea of a broad concept of security, perhaps as a way of defining a new role for themselves in a world that had robbed them of their main enemy. As early as 1991, NATO acknowledged that "security and sta-

bility have political, economic, social, and environmental elements as well as the indispensable defence dimension."[8] But expanding the concept of security was also seen as an appropriate response to a set of new challenges in the international relations of the post–Cold War period. Moreover, a wide notion of collective security was embraced by the UN secretary-general's High-Level Panel on Threats, Challenges, and Change.[9] The panel identified poverty, infectious disease, and environmental degradation as the three major threats to security, along with armed conflict, terrorism, organized crime, and weapons of mass destruction.

A comprehensive notion of security is not unproblematic. There is a danger of labeling any problem or strain an "insecurity." We might take heed from the discussion about an extended concept of violence in the late 1960s and early 1970s. The concept of "structural violence," originally a precise notion applied to deaths caused by the unequal distribution of resources, became so diluted that almost any perceived injustice could be defined as violence.[10] Structural violence became a political slogan and eventually self-destructed in peace research. The term "insecurity" should be reserved for major threats to human life. With this caveat in mind, we turn to the environmental component of comprehensive security.

ENVIRONMENTAL SECURITY

The concern for how environmental degradation may lead to insecurity is at the core a question of the scarcity of resources. Thomas Malthus suggested that hunger was inevitable because human population grows exponentially, while food production could be made to grow only in linear fashion.[11] Thus, at some point the available food per capita would fall below the minimum needed to sustain the population, and a crisis would be inevitable. Neo-Malthusian thinking follows the same general logic but applies it to a wide range of resources.[12] Thus, numerous writers have commented on anticipated "water stress," based on the idea that finite amounts of available freshwater would have to be shared by an increasing number of people.[13] In the mid-1970s, following the oil embargo organized by Arab oil-producing countries, great concern arose that the supply of minerals and energy sources might soon become deficient. More recently, the "peak oil" movement has predicted skyrocketing oil prices, the crumbling of oil-dependent economies, and exploding resource wars—in short, the end of "civilization as we know it."[14]

Global scarcity is a sufficient but not necessary condition for local scarcities. Thomas Homer-Dixon, one of the most prominent proponents of the view that environmental factors play an important role in generating and exacerbating armed conflict, distinguishes among three forms of resource scarcity:

- *Demand-induced scarcity,* which results from population growth
- *Supply-induced scarcity,* which results from the depletion or degradation of a resource
- *Structural scarcity,* which refers to the distribution of the resource[15]

The classic Malthusian model lies in the intersection of demand-induced and supply-induced scarcity, when the supply of the resource can no longer keep pace with the growth of population. Many neo-Malthusians, particularly those on the political left, put at least equal emphasis on the distributional issues.

Resource scarcity can occur without environmental degradation, simply because a non-renewable source runs dry or demand exceeds what a renewable source can supply. In the event of environmental degradation—usually conceived as a man-made disturbance of the ecosystem—the supply of the resource will become insufficient more quickly. Any form of environmental degradation can be translated into a problem of resource supply. Pollution of freshwater resources reduces the supply of water that can be used for drinking, food

production, and so on. Air pollution reduces the supply of fresh air. Thus, all environmental problems can be interpreted as resource scarcity problems, but not vice versa. I follow standard terminology in talking about "environmental security," but it might have been preferable to talk about "resource security."

An extensive literature has emerged on the conceptual problem of how to define security so that it includes environmental concerns.[16] From this literature, we may distill three particularly important goals:

- To prevent war and armed conflict as a result of resource scarcity and environmental degradation
- To prevent disasters other than war resulting from scarcity and degradation
- To prevent the erosion of the carrying capacity of the earth resulting in the loss of environmental sustainability in the future

All three are deliberately phrased in anthropocentric terms. Even more radical notions of environmental security can be found in the literature. Proponents of "deep ecology" advocate a biocentric view that gives equal weight to the rights of animals, trees, and even inanimate objects of nature, such as mountains.[17] Since none of these can speak for themselves, such rights must be formulated and advocated by human beings.

The first goal of environmental security will be discussed in the next section.[18] This is followed by a briefer discussion of the other two goals.

Environmental Insecurity as Armed Conflict

Despite the recent flurry of interest, the idea that resource constraints may lead to conflict is not a new idea. In fact, it is one of the oldest ideas in research on conflict and peace. Indeed, in one of the modern classics of the scientific study of war and peace, *A Study of War,* Quincy Wright devoted a long chapter to the relationship between war and resource use.[19] Similarly, in *Statistics of Deadly Quarrels* Lewis Richardson discussed economic causes of war, including the desire to acquire territory and the control of "sources of essential commodities."[20]

Above all, the struggle over territory is generally recognized to be the most pervasive form of conflict. Wright noted that "practically all primitive people will fight to defend their territory, if necessary."[21] Michael Klare relates how the Dayaks, an indigenous group in Borneo, have engaged logging companies in armed clashes in order to defend their traditional environment.[22] Kalevi Holsti concluded that among interstate wars in the period 1648–1989, territory was by far the most important issue category.[23] In the first period (1648–1714) such issues played a part in just over half of the wars; this figure declined to about one-quarter during the Cold War. In a reanalysis, John Vasquez found that 80–90 percent of all the wars listed by Holsti involve territory-related issues, with only a slight decline after World War II.[24] Paul Huth in a study of territorial disputes from 1950 to 1990 characterized this issue as "one of the enduring features of international politics."[25] This holds for interstate as well as intrastate conflict. According to the Uppsala/PRIO conflict data, almost 60 percent of the 227 conflicts in the period 1946– 2004 were over territory (the rest were over government).[26] The territorial explanation for war is also consistent with the finding that wars occur most frequently between neighbors[27] or between proximate countries.[28] It is still in dispute whether wars between neighbors occur mainly because the parties fight over territory, because they generate disagreements in their day-to-day interaction, or because they are more easily available for fights. Vasquez presents a credible case for the territorial explanation, but Halvard Buhaug and Gleditsch argue that even if wars are organized on territorial lines, this is not equivalent to saying that the territorial issues were decisive in starting the war.[29]

A variety of territorial conflicts concern the exclusive economic zones on the continental shelf. While the symbolism of underwater territory is not as potent as that of "the soil of our fathers," the value in economic and strategic terms may be enormous. In the 1960s the unilateral declaration of 200-nautical-mile fishery zones by several Latin American coastal states provoked conflict with states with oceangoing fishing vessels. At about the same time, deep-sea drilling for oil and natural gas and the prospects of harvesting minerals on the ocean floor led to increased interest in exploiting the extended coastal zones beyond the fisheries. This further increased the conflict of interest between coastal states and states with a regional or global reach in their commercial activities. After a long-drawn-out process, a compromise was reached in 1982 in the form of the United Nations Convention on the Law of the Sea (UNCLOS). UNCLOS did not enter into force until 1994 and still has not been ratified by the United States, but its provisions are generally respected. One of its results was that an area comprising one-third of the total world ocean surface, almost as much as the world's total land area, was added to the territory of individual nations.[30]

In addition to territory itself, several other resources are commonly seen as worth fighting for. The first is *strategic raw materials*. President Dwight D. Eisenhower—in the statement that made famous the "domino theory" —justified the strategic importance of Indochina in the 1950s by referring to the importance of raw materials such as tin, tungsten, and rubber.[31] Another resource worth fighting for is *sources of energy*, the most obvious example being oil supplies from the Persian Gulf, often mentioned as a factor in the 1990–91 Persian Gulf War and the more recent Iraq war. A third is *shared water resources*, which could give rise to conflicts over water use or navigation rights. There are more than 250 major river systems shared by two or more countries, and many of them are subject to unresolved disputes.[32] A fourth resource arguably worth fighting for is *food*. Disagreements about shared fishery resources have occasioned many confrontations between fishing vessels and armed vessels of coastal states,[33] even in the North Atlantic area, where most conflicts are solved peacefully. Increasing food prices have given rise to violent domestic riots,[34] and in Indonesia in 1998 they were thought to have contributed to the downfall of the Suharto regime. The widespread concern that environmental disruption and resource scarcity might lead to armed conflict was reflected in the awarding of the 2004 Nobel Peace Prize to Wangari Maathai, the first time the prize was awarded to an environmentalist.[35]

Despite the widening concern about the consequences of environmental disruption, there is still limited systematic research about these issues. A number of case studies have linked environmental factors to individual conflicts, built on elaborate theoretical models.[36] It is, however, difficult to generalize from them because of uncertainty about how representative the cases are. The work of Homer-Dixon has been criticized for studying only cases where there is armed conflict as well as environmental destruction.[37] No systematic comparison is provided with cases where armed conflict does not erupt—even though such cases also may suffer from environmental degradation. Thus, it is difficult to draw any conclusions about causes of violence from his work. The case studies may supply persuasive post-facto explanations for why things went wrong in Chiapas or Rwanda, but their value in terms of predicting future conflict is limited.[38]

Wenche Hauge and Tanja Ellingsen integrated soil erosion, deforestation, and lack of clean freshwater into a more general model of civil war data from the 1990s.[39] They concluded that environmental degradation to some extent does stimulate the incidence of conflict, particularly small conflicts, although less so than economic and political factors. Phase II of the State Failure project, on the other hand,

found little evidence for a direct influence of environmental degradation, and neither did Ole Magnus Theisen.[40] Indra de Soysa has questioned the relevance of the results in Hauge and Ellingsen's study since their scarcity variables conflate levels and rates of change.[41] Using World Bank data on the total per capita stock of natural capital as his measure of natural resource availability, de Soysa concluded that resource scarcity has little if any relationship to armed conflict. Helga Binningsbø, de Soysa, and Gleditsch found the ecological footprint—a general and frequently cited indicator of the overall human load on the environment—to be associated with internal peace rather than armed conflict.[42]

Environmental degradation may be seen as an independent cause of conflict, but it can also be interpreted as a symptom of the forms of societal failure, which generate other forms of conflict as well. Authoritarian rule, lack of international cooperation, poverty, excessive consumption in rich countries, and globalization of the economy—these are among the factors that are frequently blamed for environmental problems. The same phenomena are linked to armed conflict, and thus the link between environmental deterioration and conflict may be spurious, at least in part. Possible interaction effects must also be considered. For instance, Günther Bächler concluded that whether an environmental conflict passes over the threshold to violence is dependent on sociopolitical factors.[43]

Some case studies suggest that environmental conflicts arise primarily between different ethnic or national groups. Examples are conflicts between the Hemas and the Lendus in the Democratic Republic of the Congo, the Hutu and the Tutsi in Rwanda and Burundi, and farmers and cattle herders in the Darfur region of Sudan. In particular, states where the government is too weak to maintain a monopoly on violence may be prone to civil war, but also to communal conflict if the authorities are unable to intervene and settle the issue.[44]

Michael Ross suggests that resource-rich states may suffer from lack of governmental control because the easy availability of resource rents makes it unnecessary for the government to develop and enforce a tax-collecting infrastructure.[45] However, using a new data set on "nonstate" conflicts, Theisen is unable to find any direct relationship between environmental scarcity and communal violence. In the three cases mentioned above, the policies of colonial and postindependence governments have played an important role in promoting violence or failing to stop it.[46] In Sudan, Kenya, and elsewhere, authoritarian governments have used divide-and-rule tactics against communal groups in order to prop up the status of their own regimes.

In one of the few studies of similar environmental pressures and interstate conflict, Phillip Stalley tested at the national level whether the depletion of some renewable resources was associated with militarized interstate disputes.[47] He found an effect on conflict of high population density and soil degradation, but no such effect for water scarcity, low fish catch, or land burden. An overall measure of environmental scarcity was also positively associated with interstate conflict. There have been several dyadic studies of the conflict implications of shared freshwater resources. Hans Petter Toset, Gleditsch, and Håvard Hegre found that when two countries share a river (where the river may run along the border or across it) the probability of a militarized interstate dispute between them doubled.[48] This factor is much less conflict inducing (by an order of magnitude) than the neighbor effect itself but is roughly comparable to the effect of standard political and economic predictors to interstate conflict. Kathryn Furlong, Gleditsch, and Hegre found that this effect held up when controlling for the length of the land boundary as a proxy for other shared resources and territorial competition.[49] Gleditsch et al. replicated the earlier findings with an improved data set of shared river basins. They found some limited

support for the neo-Malthusian scenario of river conflict (the upstream-downstream relationship) but little support for an alternative idea that conflicts arise because of fuzzy river boundaries.[50] These studies do not identify the issues involved in conflicts between countries sharing a river basin.

In a series of articles Aaron Wolf and associates have argued that water scarcity is rarely if ever a direct cause of international conflict, based on crisis data from Michael Brecher and Jonathan Wilkenfeld.[51] Many scholars have pointed to the Middle East as an area where water is a source of considerable tension,[52] but the conflict between Israel and its neighbors as well as conflicts between Arab states are motivated by a host of ideological and political issues and by the issue of occupied land territory. Water can, at best, be viewed as one of several conflict issues in the region. In fact, Wolf concludes categorically that "water was neither a cause nor a goal of any Arab-Israeli warfare."[53] Peter Gleick has argued that with growing scarcity water may become "an increasingly salient element of interstate politics, including violent conflict." He has identified fifty-one "events related to water and conflict" over the period 1924–99,[54] but most of them are attacks on water installations as a means of warfare, or threats of such attacks. Thus, these events cannot be used as evidence that the conflicts themselves arose out of disagreements about scarce water resources.

Terrorism, the one indicator of political violence for which the *Human Security Report* did not report a clear decline, has also been linked to environmental degradation. Terrorist activity, such as the events on September 11, 2001, has been interpreted as resulting from deprivation and frustration, among Muslims, among Arabs, and among Third World immigrants in Western countries. However, the kind of frustration that might lead a young person to join a terrorist movement is mainly economic (poverty) or religious (discrimination) rather than environmental. Daniel Schwarz shows that the term "terrorism" has been used to characterize acts of war, such as the deliberate oil spills in Kuwait in the aftermath of the Iraqi invasion in 1990–91.[55] Some radical environmental groups have also engaged in violence, sabotage, and other forms of "ecoterror" in pursuit of their goals,[56] but such terrorist activities have not led to major losses of life. Unlike the end of the Cold War, the introduction of major terrorist events into the heartland of the United States and Western Europe has not led to the sea change in international relations that many expected immediately following September 11.

The greatest challenge to environmental optimism is currently posed by the global warming scenario. A study prepared for the U.S. Department of Defense envisions rapid climate change leading to famine, disease, weather-related disasters, floods of refugees, offensive military aggression, and nuclear proliferation.[57] However, in the most important document defining the agenda for the debate on climate change, the report from the Intergovernmental Panel on Climate Change, the prospects of conflict are hardly featured at all.[58] Jon Barnett accepts that climate change could be an exacerbating factor in conflict in the future but finds that so far the proposed links have been largely speculative.[59]

Environmental Insecurity as Disasters Other than War

Armed conflict is direct violence between two or more organized parties. But environmental stresses and strains can kill in very different ways. Scarcity of freshwater, while not robustly associated with large-scale armed conflict, is certainly a major source of disease in poor countries. Wolf asserts that more than a billion people lack access to safe freshwater, that almost three billion do not have access to adequate sanitation facilities, and that more than five million people die every year from water-related diseases or inadequate sanitation.[60] While these numbers are rough estimates, they do indicate that the current loss of life from such slow environmental disasters is likely to be far greater than that from war. Only very major wars, like the two world wars, can accumulate such death figures. In addition to its direct effects on human health, water shortage is a major threat to food security in dry areas that are too poor to compensate for crop failures by food imports.

While the scarcity of clean freshwater and the lack of proper sanitation facilities may be the biggest environmental problems of our time, many other environmental problems also pose a threat to human security. The chemical spills from an accident at a factory in Bhopal, India, in 1984 are reported to have killed more than two thousand residents in the area and to have permanently disabled even more. The *World Disasters Report* estimates that more than ninety thousand people died in "technological disasters" from 1995 to 2004.[61] In addition to causing direct casualties, such accidents may impair future living conditions.[62] The partial disappearance of the Aral Sea, one of the most dramatic man-made environmental disasters in this century, is seriously degrading the lives of thousands of people. As Murray Feshbach and Albert Friendly have shown, this is just one in a series of environmental catastrophes resulting from Soviet policies that gave priority to rapid industrial development at the expense of the environment and with little regard to human life.[63] Vaclav Smil has reported in similar terms about Chinese environmental policies.[64] Clearly, environmental strains can expose human beings to very serious risks, even in cases where they do not (and are unlikely ever to) result in armed conflict within or between nations. Of course actions of war also have long-term environmental effects that are incidental to the war effort but can claim a large number of lives. The nuclear bombing of Hiroshima and Nagasaki in 1945 provides a clear example.

Various infectious diseases, such as HIV/AIDS, Ebola, and the avian influenza, have raised the specter of major human disasters quite as destructive as major wars. A pandemic —a global outbreak of a new type or subtype of disease—differs from seasonal outbreaks or epidemics of diseases that have been circulating previously. The Spanish flu in 1918–19 may have killed as many as fifty million people worldwide. The Asian flu (1957–58) and the Hong Kong flu (1968–69) were also major killers but at an order of magnitude smaller than with the Spanish flu.[65] Although progress has been made in slowing the effects of the HIV virus, AIDS continues to be a major source of death. For the United States, the cumulative number of AIDS deaths by the end of 2003 approximated the death toll of the Spanish flu.[66] Ignoring various conspiracy theories about the origins of AIDS, there is little hard evidence on the net effect of human activities on such disasters. Globalization of the economy and increased human mobility probably facilitate the rapid spread of pandemics, but the accompanying economic progress and the globalization of health services make for more effective responses to them. There is, however, considerable evidence that war has deleterious effects on health.[67] In this way, traditional security concerns such as armed conflict interact with the broader human security agenda.

Natural disasters can also be as effective at killing as war. The Indian Ocean tsunami in December 2004 killed at least 225,000 people.[68] From 1995 to 2004, natural disasters killed more than 800,000 people. This exceeds by a wide margin the number of battle-related deaths in all wars during the same period, though it is less than the total of war-related deaths.[69] Although extremely serious natural disasters are rare events, large volcanic eruptions or meteor strikes could potentially kill millions. These very large disasters, like pandemics, are part of our hazardous physical environment. The issue for environmental policy is whether human activities, such as human-induced climate change, exacerbate the disaster

rate. The UN High-Level Panel interprets the "dramatic increase in major disasters witnessed in the last 50 years" as evidence of how environmental degradation exacerbates the destructive potential of natural catastrophes, but this remains a very contested issue.[70]

Environmental Insecurity as the Erosion of the Carrying Capacity

Environmental degradation is not a new phenomenon, as is well known to anyone who has read descriptions of streets with running sewers in ancient Rome or of conditions in industrial cities in Britain in the nineteenth century. But environmental concern is much greater today, and there is also a feeling that at the present very high level of general consumption, we are straining the global limits in an unprecedented way.

Examples can clearly be found where environmental damage to nature has long-term—or even more or less permanent—effects. The Central Plateau of Spain and the Highlands of Scotland are unlikely to regain the forests that were destroyed by shipbuilding and overgrazing. If the more pessimistic views of the annual loss of species[71] are anywhere near correct, humankind stands to lose not only the aesthetic value of a variety of exotic species but, much more important, genetic variability that may prove valuable in medical research.

Global warming poses the most serious potential challenge to the future sustainability of human civilization. If the sea level rises by several feet and the Gulf Stream is reversed, to take two of the more dramatic scenarios, life will become virtually impossible in low-lying areas of Bangladesh or the Maldives, as well as in Northern Europe. Cornucopians point to the failure of many past predictions of gloom, such as the periodic warnings of global hunger issued by biologists like Paul Ehrlich and environmentalists like Lester Brown.[72] Negative news, even of future events that may never happen, seems to get more publicity than the slow but steady improvements in agricultural productivity reported by the Food and Agriculture Organization or the encouraging decline in the population growth.[73] Predictions of future disasters cannot be ignored, but neither can they be taken for granted without critical scrutiny.

Conditions of Environmental Insecurity

Resource and environmental factors undoubtedly play some role in human insecurity, although the strength of the relationship is still debated. However, the environmental effect is tempered by other factors that are also associated with insecurity. The resource and environmental factors in conflict must be considered in the context of a multifaceted view of armed conflict. In the next four sections, I look in somewhat greater detail at some of the factors that must be part of such a broader view.[74]

Politics

Democratic politics may influence the relationship between the environment and conflict through its effect on environmental policy and practice, but also through its effect on the way environmental conflicts are handled.

Well-established political democracies are likely, everything else being equal, to demonstrate more enlightened environmental policies.[75] Democracies tend to be more open to trial and error, they are more responsive to the victims of environmental degradation, they participate more in international organizations, and they conclude agreements to alleviate environmental problems. Environmental activists in democratic countries frequently have considerable disagreements with the environmental policies of their own countries. These very complaints form an essential part of the self-adjusting political processes in democracies. This point was brought home with particular force following the exposure of the vast environmental disasters caused by the governments of the Soviet Union and communist China, in complete disregard for the welfare of their citizens and not held in check by any organized opposition. Democracies are much less likely to let environmental problems deteriorate far enough for armed conflict to be a real risk.

The relationship between environmental degradation and conflict is also influenced by the phenomenon known as the democratic peace.[76] Democracies rarely if ever fight one another, even at fairly low levels of violence. Even relatively minor resource conflicts like the "cod wars," the "turbot wars," and other fishery clashes in the North Atlantic are regarded with great embarrassment by the democracies involved. Thus, the parties make great efforts to settle such conflicts before anyone gets killed. Of course, if democracies rarely fight one another for any reason, it is not very likely that they would start fighting each other over resource or environmental matters. Democracies also rarely if ever experience serious levels of violent challenges to their governments for any reason; it is unlikely that domestic resource or environmental conflicts would be dramatically different.[77]

Economics

Economic development may also influence environmental behavior in two ways. First, wealth has a strong effect on environmental sustainability. Early economic progress in general and industrialization in particular are intimately associated with unhealthy working conditions, smog, acid rain, and pollution of freshwater resources. This has led many environmentalists to conclude that economic development, and capitalism in particular, is intrinsically harmful to the environment, following the IPAT formula, in which the environmental impact by definition is set equal to the product of population, affluence, and technology.[78]

But at an advanced stage of industrialization, and even more so in postindustrial societies, the trend may be reversed. An affluent society can afford to invest in new technologies to clean up pollution in industry, agriculture, and waste disposal. In addition, such a society places a higher value on human resources and takes care to avoid death and incapacitation of its highly educated labor force. In an economically advanced economy, a range of traditional indicators of environmental degradation—such as the lack of clean water, inadequate sanitation, deforestation, and air pollution in the cities—have started to decline because economic development has gone beyond a certain level. Many forms of environmental degradation are primarily poverty problems, although the Brundtland Commission report's general identification of environmental unsustainability with poverty elimination is probably more politically than empirically based.[79] The three environmental problems studied by Hauge and Ellingsen—deforestation, soil erosion, and the lack of fresh water—are all closely related to the level of economic development; that is, the higher the economic development, the lower the degree of environmental deterioration.[80] Early industrialization reinforces some of these problems and creates additional forms of environmental degradation, such as urban and industrial pollution, during a period when economic growth takes precedence over all other concerns. This gives rise to an inverted-U-shaped relationship between economic development and environmental degradation, sometimes called an environmental Kuznets curve (EKC).[81] Other environmental problems, such as the emission of CO_2 and other greenhouse gases, keep increasing with economic development. Despite the mounting scientific evidence, these problems have not yet been fully recognized as true environmental concerns. But if the problem of CO_2 extraction and storage is to be solved, a solution is more likely to be promoted by highly developed countries with the application of initially very expensive new technology.

Environmental disasters that at first glance may seem to derive from poor economic conditions are frequently the result of poor economic policy decisions. As Amartya Sen has pointed out, India has not suffered any major famines since independence, in spite of frequent crop failures and endemic starvation.[82] He attributes this to the policies of the Indian government operating under the constraints of political democracy and a free press. These constraints were much weaker under colonial rule, when India experienced several major famines. Similarly, the Chinese government was unable or unwilling to prevent the disaster in the agricultural sector resulting from the Great Leap Forward policy in 1958–60, and as a result tens of millions of people died. The recent North Korean famine is also more a result of economic policy than of environmental misfortune. Economic policy cannot, on the other hand, provide a short-term cure for the poverty that is irrevocably intertwined with large-scale undernourishment and poor health. To root out these problems requires long-term economic growth and technological progress.

Economic development also has a restraining influence on violent behavior in environmental conflict, since wealth is negatively associated with armed conflict, interstate as well as intrastate.[83] Wealthy individuals and groups stand to lose more if war breaks out. If the wealth is widespread, it is likely to act as a general deterrent to participation in major violence. Rich countries trade more, and trade also seems to promote peaceful relations, a phenomenon usually called "the liberal peace."[84]

Cultural Factors

Many countries are seriously divided between ethnic and religious groups fighting for dominance of the state (or for secession from it). Several studies have found ethnic dominance or polarization to be related to internal conflict.[85] Most of the cases studied by Homer-Dixon and his colleagues (Chiapas, South Africa, Rwanda, and Gaza) concern highly divided or even segregated societies. Although environmental factors may have contributed to conflict in South Africa, Valery Percival and Homer-Dixon recognize that it is impossible to overlook the ethnic basis of the conflict; white colonialists treated black Africans and "colored" people as creatures of a lower order.[86] Where ethnic groups cooperate, the prospects of negotiated and cooperative solutions to environmental problems are good. Where they do not, environmental factors will add to the problems created by the cultural conflict.

Conflict History

One of the strongest factors in accounting for current armed conflict, internal as well as external, is a history of armed conflict.[87] Armed conflict can have very destructive effects on the environment, as shown by the wars in Vietnam, Afghanistan, and elsewhere.[88] Human and material destruction of the environment on a vast scale in turn increases the scarcity of resources, possibly to the point where violent conflict over scarce resources is a real possibility. In Vietnam, for instance, intensive bombing and defoliation caused substantial damage to forests and agricultural land. Hard-hit countries may move into a vicious cycle of poverty, authoritarian rule, environmental degradation, and violence. War leads to environmental destruction, which in turn—mixed with poor government and poverty—fuels new conflict.

ENVIRONMENTAL CHANGE AND RESOURCE SCARCITY

Environmental change is always taking place as a result of processes that are still well beyond the control of man. Periods of global warming and cooling have come and gone since long before human activity became so pervasive and widespread that it could influence such basic global processes.

In the environmental debate, neo-Malthusian doomsayers regularly clash with cornucopian prophets of environmental optimism.[89] "The Earth is rich. If there is poverty, it is because of human betrayal," wrote the Norwegian poet Nordahl Grieg in the 1930s, at a time when socialists still held to technological optimism.

Today, radical environmentalists tend to prefer the image of "Spaceship Earth," a repository of limited resources that capitalism is rapidly squandering. The international best-seller *The Limits to Growth* was a prime example, predicting scarcities in a number of strategic minerals and other raw materials.[90] A similar line was taken by Georg Borgström and others who predicted worldwide food shortages.[91] More recently, Brown has pointed to the impending crises that will occur if and when China joins the company of the affluent and its citizens adopt Western-style nutritional habits.[92] On the other hand, writers such as John Maddox, Julian Simon, and Bjørn Lomborg have argued that improved technology and human ingenuity will continue to enable mankind to overcome material scarcity, particularly if we make use of the market mechanism to set appropriate prices for scarce resources.[93] In the mid-1970s the oil crisis was seen as the precursor of a series of similar crises in strategic minerals, such as copper. Today, environmental optimists point out that most of these minerals are available in abundant quantities, raw-material prices have been falling, and developing countries dependent on the exports of raw materials (such as Zambia in the case of copper) have suffered financially. Most international experts in agriculture, whether associated with the Food and Agriculture Organization[94] or with the international agricultural research institutes (such as those gathered in the Consultative Group on International Agricultural Research [CGIAR]), have a more optimistic view of the productive capacity of global agriculture. Current UN projections for world population do not exceed the numbers that can be fed even at the present levels of agricultural technology.

This debate has obvious implications for conflict scenarios. If the optimists are correct, resources are not generally scarce and predictions of increased global strife over resources are unlikely to come true. On the other hand, if the environmental pessimists are correct, we are constantly eroding the carrying capacity of the global environment and our resource use is already beyond sustainable levels. If that is the case, we should expect the competition for resources to get ever fiercer, eventually to the point that it may break the norms of nonviolent behavior, perhaps even within and between democracies.

In the debate about the total volume of global resources, the environmental optimists now appear to have the upper hand. But for the purpose of analyzing conflict behavior, the question of the availability of the resources is more important. While global resources may be abundant, local resources may not be sufficient. In other words, the key to avoiding serious and increasing resource scarcities lies in the question of distribution, within and between nations. This takes us back to the questions of economic and political structure. If people cannot afford to buy food or other basic necessities, or if authoritarian political structures prevent them from making use of available resources, overall abundance will not help. In such cases, we will have starvation amid plenty. Thousands will continue to die from unclean freshwater while others are drinking bottled mineral water at $1,000 per cubic meter.[95]

SCARCITY OR A RESOURCE CURSE?

A perspective adopted by many economists is that civil war is occasioned more by economic and geographical opportunity than by real or perceived grievances.[96] This perspective does see resources as relevant to the conflict but turns the neo-Malthusian perspective on its head: abundant natural resources are likely to hinder rather than stimulate growth and to stimulate authoritarian government. The accumulation through economic development is usually associated with the development of democratic institutions, but countries whose wealth has been built quickly on oil and other raw materials, notably many countries in

North Africa and the Middle East, tend to lag behind other countries at the same level of wealth in the development of their political institutions. Resource abundance may also lead to conflict, partly because politically obsolete structures refuse to give way, but also because control over some or all of the resources can be captured by opposition groups that use them to fund their rebel movements. This is illustrated by the diamond-smuggling rebels in Angola and drug-funded rebels in Colombia and Peru.

The measure of natural resource dependence adopted in the study of economic opportunity in civil war is usually exports of primary product as a share of GDP, but this measure has been criticized because it lumps lootable and nonlootable natural resources.[97] Other studies look at specific lootable resources, such as oil, timber, or diamonds, with more mixed results.[98] Major oil exports seems to be related to the onset of civil war, and the same is true for lootable diamonds after the end of the Cold War.

THE ROLE OF POPULATION PRESSURE

High resource consumption and rapid population growth are the twin pillars of neo-Malthusian scenarios of future resource scarcities. But is population pressure increasing? The 2004 revised medium population projection of the United Nations indicates a world population of nine billion in 2150, down from earlier projections.[99] Even the high-population scenario, which is not widely believed, yields a world population of fewer than seventeen billion in 2150, less than what many food specialists see as the long-run global potential for food production. The main reason that global population projections are being revised downward is that many developing countries have followed industrialized countries in fertility reduction more rapidly and more widely that what had previously been believed. By 1995 no less than 44 percent of the world population lived in countries with fertility below replacement level (2.1 children per woman). While Islamic countries and Africa (despite AIDS) will continue to have high population growth for some time to come, the global specter of overpopulation is largely removed from the debate. Instead, the concern is with particular Third World countries that combine rapid population growth with poor development prospects. In the rest of the world, the greater worry is now the "graying" of the population.

There has been relatively little systematic research on population pressure and violent conflict. Henrik Urdal finds little support for neo-Malthusian hypotheses relating population density and land scarcity to internal conflict, but some limited effect of a high rate of population growth combined with land scarcity.[100] Jaroslav Tir and Paul Diehl found no significant relationship between population density and interstate conflict, but a modest effect of population growth on interstate conflict.[101] There was little or no evidence that population growth increased the probability of states initiating the conflict or escalating it all the way to war. These findings strengthen the notion that population pressure is unlikely to be a significant global factor in conflict in the future, although it may well be an important local factor in certain areas. Urdal finds "youth bulges" to be associated with internal conflict, but this is also more of a distributional problem than one of available resources overall.[102]

Even if population pressure is not likely to have a major influence on armed conflict at the global level, it could be important in stimulating conflict in very poor areas, particularly where there is resource competition between different ethnic groups. Ester Boserup, however, concluded in an influential book that population growth stimulates innovation and reform in agriculture. She argued this thesis in direct contradiction to the neo-Malthusian argument that agricultural productivity deter-

mines the rate of population growth. Boserup's thesis has important implications for economic development and potentially for peace.[103]

Some have extrapolated from studies of rats and other animals in very crowded conditions and have foreseen additional friction and conflict in human beings living under similar conditions. However, in order for such studies to be relevant, population densities would have to be a great deal higher, and the freedom of movement a great deal lower, than what obtains in most human settlements. Indeed, the most crowded states in the world, city-states like Singapore and Hong Kong, are rather peaceful internally and externally, as far as group conflicts are concerned. Individual conflict, such as crime, tends to be higher in urban areas, but this can be accounted for just as easily by greater opportunity and more anonymity as by greater resource conflict. In fact, violent crime would seem to fit the opportunity model of conflict better than the grievance model.[104]

Environmental Cooperation

Environmental insecurity does not as a general rule involve dramatic events such as armed struggle, mass starvation, or extensive and serious degradation. Resource and environmental problems are frequently handled by piecemeal reform and peaceful conflict resolution. Indeed, a conflict of interest may stimulate increased collaboration, in order to regulate the use of the contested resource. The enormous "privatization" of sea territory that was completed with the Law of the Sea Treaty proceeded remarkably peacefully.[105] Wolf argues that while "water wars" are extremely rare, cooperation over shared water resources is quite common. He also records 3,600 water treaties since AD 805, mainly over navigation rights.[106] Several major international rivers, such as the Rhine, the Danube, and the Mekong, have interstate river commissions that provide fora for discussion and resolution of conflicts of interest among the riparian states. Even in the Middle East, countries that were at hot war several times during the Cold War have been able to work out agreements relating to the use of water.[107] In the early 1960s, in the middle of the Cold War, Norway and the Soviet Union were able to agree on a large scheme for the joint exploitation of the Pasvik River for hydroelectric power. Apart from the Soviet-Turkish border, the 200-kilometer border between Norway and the Soviet Union in the High North was the only place where a NATO country bordered directly on the Soviet Union.

ENVIRONMENTAL INSECURITY?

Few, if any, conflicts justify single-issue labels like "environmental conflict" or "ethnic conflict." We can always relate conflict to several issue dimensions, and the influence of one issue is usually modified by the influence of another. Resource and environmental issues do play a role in conflict, but the relationship between these issues and armed conflict is modified by the general political, economic, and cultural factors at work in armed conflict generally. In many cases, environmental degradation may more appropriately be seen as an intervening variable between poverty and poor governance on the one hand and armed conflict on the other. In this sense, environmental degradation may be more appropriately viewed as a symptom that something has gone wrong than as a cause of the world's ills.

For policymakers, as well as NGOs and grass-roots activists, a crucial question is at what point in the causal chain one can intervene to change things for the better. Political institutions may present the most effective short-term intervention points because they can be changed relatively abruptly. In the long term, moving from poverty to wealth is probably the most effective means to improve all forms of human security. In this perspective, the most important function of the environmental indicators is that they can serve very effectively as warning lights, particularly in a world of growing environmental consciousness.

NOTES

My work on these issues has been supported by the United States Institute of Peace and the Research Council of Norway. This chapter draws on some of my earlier work. I am grateful for the help and comments from Jesse Hamner, Naima Mouhleb, Siri Camilla Aas Rustad, Ole Magnus Theisen, Aaron T. Wolf, Arthur Westing, and the editors of this volume, none of whom are responsible for errors in the final version. This publication is associated with the Global Environmental Change and Human Security program (http://www.gechs.org).

1. Olof Palme et al., *Common Security: A Blueprint for Survival* (New York: Simon and Schuster, for Independent Commission on Disarmament and Security Issues, 1982).

2. Arthur Westing, "Environmental Component of Comprehensive Security," *Bulletin of Peace Proposals* 20, no. 2 (1989): 129–134.

3. United Nations Development Programme, *Human Development Report 1994* (Oxford and New York: Oxford University Press, 1994), 23.

4. Andrew Mack, ed., *Human Security Report* (Oxford: Oxford University Press, 2005), viii, http://www.humansecurityreport.info.

5. Standard sources for measuring democratic governance are found in Keith Jaggers and Ted Robert Gurr, "Tracking Democracy's Third Wave with the Polity III Data," *Journal of Peace Research* 32, no. 4 (1995): 469–482; Tatu Vanhanen, "A New Dataset for Measuring Democracy, 1810–1998," *Journal of Peace Research* 37, no. 2 (2000): 251–265; and Freedom House, *Freedom in the World: The Annual Survey of Political Rights and Civil Liberties* (Lanham, Md.: Rowman and Littlefield), http://www.freedomhouse.org.

6. Economic and social security is measured, for instance, by national product per capita (http://pwt.econ.upenn.edu) or life expectancy (http://www.un.org/esa/population/publications/prebank.htm).

7. For a prominent example of work in this area, see Ted Robert Gurr, *Peoples versus States: Minorities* *at Risk in the New Century* (Washington, D.C.: United States Institute of Peace Press, 2000).

8. See point 24 in "The Alliance's New Strategic Concept," agreed on at the North Atlantic Council, Rome, November 7–8, 1991, http://www.nato.int/docu/comm./49-95/c911107a.htm.

9. United Nations High-Level Panel on Threats, Challenges, and Change, *A More Secure World: Our Shared Responsibility* (New York: United Nations, 2004).

10. Johan Galtung, "Violence, Peace, and Peace Research," *Journal of Peace Research* 6, no. 3 (1969): 167–191.

11. Thomas Robert Malthus, *An Essay on the Principle of Population: Or a View of Its Past and Present Effects on Human Happiness: With an Inquiry into Our Prospects Respecting the Future Removal or Mitigation of the Evils which It Occasions* (1798, 1803; repr. Cambridge: Cambridge University Press, 1992).

12. Nils Petter Gleditsch, "Environmental Conflict: Neomalthusians vs. Cornucopians," in *Security and the Environment in the Mediterranean: Conceptualising Security and Environmental Conflicts,* ed. Hans Günter Brauch, P. H. Liotta, Antonio Marquina, Paul F. Rogers, and Mohammad El-Sayed Selim (Berlin: Springer Verlag, 2003), 477–485.

13. Malin Falkenmark, "Global Water Issues Confronting Humanity," *Journal of Peace Research* 27, no. 2 (1990): 177–190.

14. "Life after the Oil Crash," http://www.lifeaftertheoilcrash.net (accessed December 2, 2005).

15. Homer-Dixon specifically refers to scarcity of renewable resources, which he calls "environmental scarcity." But the general argument applies equally to nonrenewable resources. For a critique of Homer-Dixon, see Nils Petter Gleditsch and Henrik Urdal, "Ecoviolence? Links between Population Growth, Environmental Scarcity, and Violent Conflict in Thomas Homer-Dixon's Work," *Journal of International Affairs* 56, no. 1 (2002): 283–302.

16. Barry Buzan, Ole Wæver, and Jaap de Wilde, *Security: A New Framework for Analysis* (Boulder, Colo.: Lynne Rienner, 1998); and Arthur Westing, "Environmental Component of Comprehensive Security."

17. Arne Næss, "A Defense of the Deep Ecology Movement," *Environmental Ethics* 6, no. 3 (1984): 265–270.

18. In this section I deal with interstate as well as intrastate conflict. Resource and environmental issues are relevant to both. As I will argue later, the political, economic, and other factors that mediate between environmental factors and armed conflict are also very similar for the two types of conflict. For these reasons, I have chosen to deal with the two forms of conflict in parallel fashion.

19. Quincy Wright, *A Study of War,* 2nd ed., with a commentary on war since 1942 (Chicago: University of Chicago Press, 1965), 1146–1197.

20. Lewis F. Richardson, *Statistics of Deadly Quarrels,* ed. Quincy Wright and C. C. Lienau (Pittsburgh: Boxwood; Chicago: Quadrangle, 1960), 205–210.

21. Wright, *A Study of War,* 76.

22. Michael Klare, *Resource Wars: The New Landscape of Global Conflict* (New York: Metropolitan, 2001), 202–208.

23. Kalevi Holsti, *Peace and War: Armed Conflicts and International Order 1648–1989* (Cambridge: Cambridge University Press, 1991), 307.

24. John Vasquez, *The War Puzzle* (Cambridge: Cambridge University Press, 1993), 130; and Vasquez, "Why Do Neighbors Fight? Proximity, Interaction or Territoriality?" *Journal of Peace Research* 32, no. 3 (1995): 277–293.

25. Paul K. Huth, *Standing Your Ground: Territorial Disputes and International Conflict* (Ann Arbor: University of Michigan Press, 1996), 5.

26. See Lotta Harbom and Peter Wallensteen, "Armed Conflict and Its International Dimensions, 1946–2004," *Journal of Peace Research* 42, no. 5 (2005): 623–635; and "Armed Conflicts 1946–2004," http://www.prio.no/cscw/armedconflict.

27. Stuart Bremer, "Dangerous Dyads: Conditions Affecting the Likelihood of Interstate War, 1816–1965," *Journal of Conflict Resolution* 36, no. 2 (1992): 309–341.

28. Nils Petter Gleditsch, "Geography, Democracy, and Peace," *International Interactions* 20, no. 4 (1995): 297–323.

29. Vasquez, "Why Do Neighbors Fight?"; and Halvard Buhaug and Nils Petter Gleditsch, "The Death of Distance? The Globalization of Armed Conflict," in *Territoriality and Conflict in an Era of Globalization,* ed. Miles Kahler and Barbara F. Walter (Cambridge: Cambridge University Press, 2006), 187–216.

30. Jennifer Bailey, "States, Stocks, and Sovereignty: High Seas Fishing and the Expansion of State Sovereignty," in *Conflict and the Environment,* ed. Nils Petter Gleditsch (Dordrecht, the Netherlands: Kluwer Academic, 1997), 215–234.

31. For an empirical examination of the relationship between strategic raw material and armed conflict, see Mats Hammarström, "Military Conflict and Mineral Supplies: Results Relevant to Wider Resource Issues," in *Conflict and the Environment,* 127–136.

32. Aaron T. Wolf, Jeffrey A. Natharius, Jeffrey J. Danielson, Brian S. Ward, and Jan K. Pender, "International River Basins of the World," *Water Resources Development* 15, no. 4 (1999): 387–427.

33. Marvin S. Soroos, "The Turbot War: Resolution of an International Fishery Dispute," in *Conflict and the Environment,* 235–252.

34. Indra de Soysa and Nils Petter Gleditsch, with Michael Gibson, Margareta Sollenberg, and Arthur Westing, *To Cultivate Peace: Agriculture in a World of Conflict,* PRIO Report No. 1 (Oslo: International Peace Research Institute; Washington, D.C.: Future Harvest, 1999), http://www.future-harvest.org.

35. See http://www.nobel.no/eng_lec_lau.html. For a critical view of the Nobel Committee's justification for the award, see Nils Petter Gleditsch and Henrik Urdal, "Roots of Conflict: Don't Blame Environmental Decay for the Next War," *International Herald Tribune,* November 22, 2004, http://www.iht .com/articles/2004/11/21/opinion/ednils.html.

36. Thomas Homer-Dixon and Jessica Blitt, eds., *Ecoviolence: Links among Environment, Population, and Security* (Oxford: Rowman and Littlefield, 1998); and Günther Bächler, *Violence through Environmental Discrimination* (Dordrecht, the Netherlands: Kluwer Academic, 1999).

37. Thomas Homer-Dixon, *Environment, Scarcity, and Violence* (Princeton, N.J.: Princeton University Press, 1999).

38. For a more detailed critique along these lines, see Nils Petter Gleditsch, "Armed Conflict and the Environment: A Critique of the Literature," *Journal of Peace Research* 35, no. 3 (1998): 381–400. For a response, see Daniel Schwartz, Tom Deligiannis, and Thomas Homer-Dixon, "The Environment and Violent Conflict," in *Environmental Conflict,* ed. Paul F. Diehl and Nils Petter Gleditsch (Boulder, Colo.: West-

view Press, 2001). For a brief rejoinder, see Gleditsch, "Armed Conflict and the Environment."

39. Wenche Hauge and Tanja Ellingsen, "Beyond Environmental Security: Causal Pathways to Conflict," *Journal of Peace Research* 35, no. 3 (1998): 299–317.

40. Daniel Esty et al., *State Failure Task Force Report: Phase II* (Washington, D.C.: State Failure Task Force, 1998); and Ole Magnus Theisen, "Other Pathways to Conflict" (paper presented at the 47th Annual Convention of the International Studies Association, San Diego, March 22–25, 2006).

41. Indra de Soysa, "Paradise Is a Bazaar? Greed, Creed, and Governance in Civil War, 1989–99," *Journal of Peace Research* 39, no. 4 (2002): 395–416; de Soysa, "Ecoviolence: Shrinking Pie or Honey Pot?" *Global Environmental Politics* 2, no. 4 (2002): 1–27; and Hauge and Ellingsen, "Beyond Environmental Security."

42. Helga Malmin Binningsbø, Indra de Soysa, and Nils Petter Gleditsch, "Green Giant, or Straw Man? Environmental Pressure and Civil Conflict, 1961–99" (paper presented at the 47th Annual Convention of the International Studies Association, San Diego, March 22–25, 2006).

43. Bächler, *Violence through Environmental Discrimination.*

44. James D. Fearon and David Laitin, "Ethnicity, Insurgency, and Civil War," *American Political Science Review* 97, no. 1 (2003): 75–90.

45. Michael Ross, "What Do We Know about Natural Resources and Civil War?" *Journal of Peace Research* 41, no. 3 (2004): 337–356.

46. Theisen, "Other Pathways to Conflict."

47. Phillip Stalley, "Environmental Scarcity and International Conflict," *Conflict Management and Peace Science* 20, no. 2 (2003): 33–58.

48. Hans Petter Wollebæk Toset, Nils Petter Gleditsch, and Håvard Hegre, "Shared Rivers and Interstate Conflict," *Political Geography* 19, no. 6 (2000): 971–996.

49. Kathryn Furlong, Nils Petter Gleditsch, and Håvard Hegre, "Geographic Opportunity and Neomalthusian Willingness: Boundaries, Shared Rivers, and Conflict," *International Interactions* 32, no. 1 (2006): 79–108.

50. Nils Petter Gleditsch, Kathryn Furlong, Håvard Hegre, Bethany Lacina, and Taylor Owen, "Conflicts over Shared Rivers: Resource Scarcity or

Fuzzy Boundaries?" *Political Geography,* no. 4 (2006): 361–382.

51. Michael Brecher and Jonathan Wilkenfeld, *A Study of Crisis* (Ann Arbor: University of Michigan Press, 1997).

52. Miriam R. Lowi, "Bridging the Divide—Transboundary Disputes and the Case of the West-Bank Water," *International Security* 18, no. 1 (1993): 113–138.

53. Aaron T. Wolf, "'Water Wars' and Water Reality: Conflict and Cooperation along International Waterways," in *Environmental Change, Adaptation, and Human Security,* ed. Steve Lonergan (Dordrecht, the Netherlands: Kluwer Academic, 1999), 254.

54. Peter H. Gleick, "Water and Conflict: Fresh Water Resources and International Security," *International Security* 18, no. 1 (1993): 79–112; Peter H. Gleick, *The World's Water 2000–2001: The Biennial Report on Freshwater Resources* (Washington, D.C.: Island Press, 2000); and http://www.worldwater.org/conflictintro.htm.

55. Daniel M. Schwarz, "Environmental Terrorism: Analyzing the Concept," *Journal of Peace Research* 35, no. 4 (1998): 483–496.

56. Edward V. Badolato, "Environmental Terrorism—A Case Study," *Terrorism* 14, no. 4 (1991): 237–239. See the Web sites of the Center for the Defense of Free Enterprise (http://www.cdfe.org/ecoterror.htm) and the Animal Liberation Front, one of the radical groups (http://www.animalliberationfront.com).

57. Peter Schwartz and Doug Randall, *An Abrupt Climate Change Scenario and Its Implications for United States National Security* (Washington, D.C.: Environmental Media Services, 2003), http://www.ems.org/climate/pentagon_climate_change.htm.

58. For a summary and critique of the debate, see Intergovernmental Panel on Climate Change, *IPCC Third Assessment Report: Climate Change 2001* (Geneva: Intergovernmental Panel on Climate Change; Cambridge: Cambridge University Press, 2001), http://www.ipcc.ch; and Ragnhild Nordås and Nils Petter Gleditsch, "Climate Change and Conflict: Common Sense or Nonsense?" (paper presented at the GECHS workshop on human security and climate change, Holmen fjordhotell near Oslo, June 22–23, 2005). For several papers that try to put the debate on a less speculative footing by relating internal conflict to changes in rainfall and other environmental factors

likely to result from climate change, see http://www.cicero.uio.no/humsec.

59. Jon Barnett, "Security and Climate Change," *Global Environmental Change* 13, no. 1 (2003): 7–17.

60. Aaron T. Wolf, "Water and Human Security," *AVISO: An Information Bulletin on Global Environmental Change and Human Security* 3 (1999): 1.

61. International Federation of Red Cross and Red Crescent Societies, *World Disasters Report,* annual (Bloomfield, Conn.: Kumerian; London: Eurospan, 1995), 203.

62. For a discussion of such accidents and how they are exacerbated by war or war preparations, see Arthur Westing, *Environmental Hazards of War: Releasing Dangerous Forces in an Industrialized World* (London: Sage, for PRIO and UNEP, 1990).

63. Murray Feshbach and Albert Friendly, Jr., *Ecocide in the USSR: Health and Nature under Siege* (New York: Basic Books, 1992).

64. Vaclav Smil, *China's Environmental Crisis: An Inquiry into the Limits of National Development* (Armonk, N.Y.: Sharpe, 1993).

65. See Centers for Disease Control and Prevention, U.S. Department of Health and Human Services, http://www.cdc.gov/flu/index.htm.

66. See Centers for Disease Control and Prevention, http://www.cdc.gov/hic/stats.htm#ddaids.

67. Hazem A. Ghobarah, Paul Huth, and Bruce Russett, "Civil Wars Kill and Maim People—Long after the Shooting Stops," *American Political Science Review* 97, no. 2 (2003): 189–202.

68. From the EM-DAT database maintained by the Center for Research on the Epidemiology of Disasters (CRED), http://www/em-dat.et/figures _2004htm. The *World Disasters Report* 2005 reported the same figures. Wikipedia reports 275,000 (http://en.wikipedia.org/wiki/2004_Indian_Ocean_earthquake).

69. Bethany Lacina and Nils Petter Gleditsch, "Monitoring Trends in Global Combat: A New Dataset of Battle Deaths," *European Journal of Population* 21, no. 2 (2005): 145–166. Data on http://www.prio.no/cscw/cross/battledeaths.

70. UN High-Level Panel on Threats, Challenges, and Change, *A More Secure World.*

71. Norman Myers argues that the loss of animal species runs into the thousands every year. On the other hand, Julian Simon and Bjørn Lomborg argue that very few cases of species extinction are documented. Norman Myers and Julian Simon, *Scarcity or Abundance? A Debate on the Environment* (New York and London: W. W. Norton, 1994); and Bjørn Lomborg, *The Skeptical Environmentalist: Measuring the Real State of the World* (Cambridge and New York: Cambridge University Press, 2001).

72. Paul Ehrlich, *The Population Bomb* (New York: Ballantine, 1968); and Lester Brown, *Who Will Feed China? Wake-Up Call for a Small Planet,* Environmental Alert Series (Washington, D.C.: WorldWatch Institute, 1995).

73. Food and Agriculture Organization, *The State of Food and Agriculture* (Rome: Food and Agriculture Organization, annual).

74. The views discussed in the next section are formulated at greater length in Nils Petter Gleditsch, "Environmental Conflict and the Democratic Peace," in *Conflict and the Environment,* 91–106.

75. See Nils Petter Gleditsch and Bjørn Otto Sverdrup, "Democracy and the Environment," in *Human Security and the Environment: International Comparisons,* ed. Edward A. Page and Michael Redclift (Cheltenham, U.K.: Edward Elgar, 2002), 45–79; and Rodger A. Payne, "Freedom and the Environment," *Journal of Democracy* 6, no. 3 (1995): 41–55. For a different view, see Manus Midlarsky, "Democracy and the Environment: An Empirical Assessment," *Journal of Peace Research* 35, no. 3 (1998): 341–361. Eric Neumayer argues that democracies are primarily stronger in their environmental *commitment,* not in environmental *results.* Eric Neumayer, "Do Democracies Exhibit Stronger International Environmental Commitment? A Cross-Country Analysis," *Journal of Peace Research* 39, no. 2 (2002): 101–112.

76. Nils Petter Gleditsch and Håvard Hegre, "Peace and Democracy: Three Levels of Analysis," *Journal of Conflict Resolution* 41, no. 2 (1997): 283–310.

77. Håvard Hegre, Tanja Ellingsen, Nils Petter Gleditsch, and Scott Gates, "Towards a Democratic Civil Peace? Democracy, Political Change, and Civil War, 1816–1992," *American Political Science Review* 95, no. 1 (2001): 17–33.

78. However, if A is operationalized as GDP/cap and T as I/GDP, the IPAT formula is simply a tautology. Jordi Roca, "The IPAT Formula and Its Limitations," *Ecological Economics* 42, nos. 1–2 (2002): 1–2.

79. Gro Harlem Brundtland et al., *Our Common Future* (New York: Oxford University Press, 1988).

80. Hauge and Ellingsen, "Beyond Environmental Security." For empirical illustrations relating to air pollution, see Lomborg, *The Skeptical Environmentalist,* chap. 15.

81. Matthew A. Cole, "Development, Trade, and the Environment: How Robust Is the Environmental Kuznets Curve?" *Environment and Development Economics* 8, no. 4 (2003): 557–580.

82. Amartya Sen, "Liberty and Poverty: Political Rights and Economics," *New Republic,* January 10, 1994, 31–37.

83. Håvard Hegre, "Development and the Liberal Peace: What Does It Take to Be a Trading State?" *Journal of Peace Research* 27, no. 1 (2000): 5–30; and Hegre et al., "Towards a Democratic Peace? Democracy, Political Change, and Civil War, 1816–1992."

84. Bruce M. Russett and John R. Oneal, *Triangulating Peace: Democracy, Interdependence, and International Organizations* (New York: W. W. Norton, 2001).

85. Tanja Ellingsen, "Colorful Community or Ethnic Witches' Brew? Multiethnicity and Domestic Conflict During and After the Cold War," *Journal of Conflict Resolution* 44, no. 2 (2000): 228–249; and Marta Reynal-Querol, "Ethnicity, Political Systems, and Civil Wars," *Journal of Conflict Resolution* 46, no. 1 (2002): 29–54.

86. Valery Percival and Thomas Homer-Dixon, "Environmental Scarcity and Violent Conflict: The Case of South Africa," *Journal of Peace Research* 35, no. 3 (1998): 279–298.

87. Arvid Raknerud and Håvard Hegre, "The Hazard of War: Reassessing the Evidence for the Democratic Peace," *Journal of Peace Research* 34, no. 4 (1997): 385–404; and Hegre et al., "Towards a Democratic Civil Peace? Democracy, Political Change, and Civil War, 1816–1992."

88. Arthur Westing, *Explosive Remnants of War: Mitigating the Environmental Effects* (London: Taylor and Francis, for Stockholm International Peace Research Institute, 1985); and Westing, ed., *Environmental Hazards of War.*

89. For a pointed confrontation, see Myers and Simon, *Scarcity or Abundance?* For a more recent interpretation of the current environmental debate in Malthusian terms, see Leif Ohlsson, "Environment,

Scarcity, and Conflict: A Study of Malthusian Concerns" (Ph.D. diss., Göteborg University, Department of Peace and Development Research, 1999).

90. Donella H. Meadows, Dennis L. Meadows, Jørgen Randers, and William W. Behrens III, *The Limits to Growth: A Report for the Club of Rome's Project on the Predicament of Mankind* (New York: Universe, 1972).

91. Georg Borgström, *The Hungry Planet: The Modern World at the Edge of Famine*, 2nd. ed. (New York: Macmillan, 1972).

92. Brown, *Who Will Feed China?*

93. John Maddox, *The Doomsday Syndrome* (New York: McGraw-Hill, 1972); Julian L. Simon, *The Ultimate Resource 2* (Princeton, N.J.: Princeton University Press, 1996); and Lomborg, *The Skeptical Environmentalist.*

94. FAO, *The State of Food and Agriculture.*

95. Peter Beaumont, "Water and Armed Conflict in the Middle East—Fantasy or Reality?" in *Conflict and the Environment*, 355–374.

96. Paul Collier and Anke Hoeffler, "Greed and Grievance in Civil War?" *Oxford Economic Papers* 56, no. 4 (2004): 563–595; and Ross, "What Do We Know about Natural Resources and Civil War?" 483–496.

97. James D. Fearon, "Primary Commodity Exports and Civil War," *Journal of Conflict Resolution* 49, no. 4 (2005): 483–507.

98. Päivi Lujala, Nils Petter Gleditsch, and Elisabeth Gilmore, "A Diamond Curse? Civil War and a Lootable Resource," *Journal of Conflict Resolution* 49, no. 4 (2005): 538–563. Data on http://www.prio.no/cscw/datasets.

99. United Nations, *World Population to 2300*, ST/ESA/SER.A/236 (New York: United Nations, Population Division, 2004), http://www.un.org/esa/population/publications/longrange2/WorldPop2300final.pdf.

100. Henrik Urdal, "People vs. Malthus: Population Pressure, Environmental Degradation, and Armed Conflict Revisited," *Journal of Peace Research* 42, no. 4 (2005): 417–434.

101. Jaroslav Tir and Paul F. Diehl, "Demographic Pressure and Interstate Conflict: Linking Population Growth and Density to Militarized Disputes and Wars, 1930–89," *Journal of Peace Research* 35, no. 3 (1998): 319–339.

102. Henrik Urdal, "The Devil in the Demographics: The Effect of Youth Bulges on Domestic Armed Conflict, 1950–2000," *International Studies Quarterly* 50 (2006).

103. Ester Boserup, *The Conditions of Agricultural Growth: The Economics of Agrarian Change under Population Pressure* (London: Allen and Unwin, 1965).

104. Eric Neumayer, "Inequality and Violent Crime: Evidence from Data on Robbery and Violent Theft," *Journal of Peace Research* 42, no. 1 (2005): 101–112.

105. Bailey, "States, Stocks, and Sovereignty," 222.

106. Wolf, "'Water Wars' and Water Reality"; and Wolf, "The Transboundary Freshwater Dispute Database Project," *Water International* 24, no. 2 (1999): 160–163. Database from http://terra.geo.orst.edu/users.tfdd.

107. Steve C. Lonergan, "Water Resources and Conflict: Examples from the Middle East," in *Conflict and the Environment*, 375–384.

12

ECONOMIC CAUSES OF CIVIL CONFLICT AND THEIR IMPLICATIONS FOR POLICY

Paul Collier

THIS CHAPTER PRESENTS AN ECONOMIC perspective on the causes of civil war, based on global empirical patterns over the period 1965–99. During this period, the risk of civil war has been systematically related to a few economic conditions, such as dependence on primary commodity exports and low national income. Conversely, and astonishingly, objective measures of social grievance, such as inequality, a lack of democracy, and ethnic and religious divisions, have had little systematic effect on risk. I argue that this is because civil wars occur where rebel organizations are financially viable. The Michigan Militia, which briefly threatened to menace peace in the United States, was unable to grow beyond a handful of part-time volunteers, whereas the Revolutionary Armed Forces of Colombia (FARC) has grown to employ about twelve thousand people. The factors that account for this difference between failure and success are to be found not in the "causes" that these two rebel organizations claimed to espouse, but in their radically different opportu-

nities to raise revenue. The FARC earns around $700 million per year from drugs and kidnapping, whereas the Michigan Militia was probably broke.

The central importance of the financial viability of the rebel organization as the cause of civil war is why civil wars are so unlike international wars. Governments can always finance an army out of taxation, and so governments can always fight one another. The circumstances in which a rebel organization can finance an army are quite unusual. This is why my analysis is entirely confined to civil war: what I have to say has little or no bearing on intergovernment war. Because the results are so counterintuitive, I start by arguing why social scientists should be distrustful of the loud public discourse on conflict. I then turn to the evidence, describing each of the risk factors in civil war. I try to explain the observed pattern, focusing on the circumstances in which rebel organizations are viable. Finally, I turn to the policy implications. I argue that because the economic dimensions of civil war have been largely neglected, both governments and the international community have missed substantial opportunities for promoting peace.

GREED OR GRIEVANCE? WHY WE CAN'T TRUST THE DISCOURSE

There is a profound gap between popular perceptions of the causes of conflict and the results from recent economic analysis. Popular perceptions see rebellion as a protest motivated by genuine and extreme grievance; rebels are public-spirited heroes fighting against injustice. Economic analysis sees rebellion more as a form of organized crime or, more radically, something that is better understood from the distinctive circumstances in which it is feasible, rather than worrying about what might motivate its participants. Either economists are being excessively cynical or popular perceptions are badly misled. I first want to suggest why perceptions might indeed be wrong.

Popular perceptions are shaped by the discourse that conflicts themselves generate. The parties to a civil war do not stay silent: they are not white mice observed by scientists. They offer explanations for their actions. Indeed, both parties to a conflict will make a major effort to have good public relations. The larger rebel organizations will hire professional public relations firms to promote their explanation, and the governments that they are opposing will routinely hire rival public relations firms. Imagine, for a moment, that you are the leader of a rebel organization, needing to offer an explanation of your goals. What are the likely elements? Most surely, they will be a litany of grievances against the government, for its oppression, unfairness, and perhaps victimization of some part of the population that your organization claims to represent. That is, your language will be the language of protest. You will style your rebellion as a protest movement, driven to the extremity of violence by the extremity of the conditions that "your" people face. Almost certainly, the government

will have responded to your insurgency with an incompetent counterinsurgency campaign. "Almost certainly" because counterinsurgency is extremely difficult.

The most obvious difficulty that a government faces in counterinsurgency is getting its army to fight. People prefer not to risk getting killed. Governments try various economic incentives to overcome this problem. For example, in one recent African conflict the government decided to pay its soldiers a premium if they were in a combat zone. Shortly after this incentive was introduced, the war appeared to spread alarmingly. In previously safe areas rebel groups set off explosions near barracks. It turned out that government soldiers were probably planting these explosions themselves. However, the more serious problems occur when the government succeeds in persuading its army to fight but then lacks the means to control the behavior of soldiers on the ground. From Vietnam onward, the result has been atrocities. Rebel groups may even hope for government atrocities because the atrocities then fuel the grievances. This discourse of grievance is how most people understand the causes of conflict. A "thorough" analysis of the causes of a conflict then becomes a matter of tracing back the grievances and countergrievances in the history of protest.

An economist views conflict rather differently. Economists who have studied rebellions tend to think of them not as the ultimate protest movements but as the ultimate manifestation of organized crime. As Herschel I. Grossman states, "in such insurrections the insurgents are indistinguishable from bandits or pirates."[1] Rebellion is large-scale predation of productive economic activities. I will shortly set out why economists see rebellion in this way and the rather powerful evidence for it. However, this view is so at odds with the popular discourse on conflict that there is a temptation to dismiss it as fanciful. The techniques of economics don't help its arguments: compared with the compelling historical detail produced by histories of protest, the economist's approach seems arcane and technocratic. So, before I explain why economists see rebellion as they do, I want to show why the discourse on conflict cannot be taken at face value.

For a few moments, suspend disbelief and suppose that most rebel movements are pretty close to being large-scale variants of organized crime. *The discourse would be exactly the same as if they were protest movements.* Unlike organized crime, rebel movements need good international public relations and they need to motivate their recruits to kill. They need good international public relations because most of them are partially dependent on international financial support. They need to motivate their recruits to kill, because, unlike a mafia, a predatory rebel organization is periodically going to have to fight for its survival against government forces. A rebel organization simply cannot afford to be regarded as criminal: it is not good publicity and it is not sufficiently motivating. Rebel organizations have to develop a discourse of grievance in order to function. Grievance is to a rebel organization what image is to a business. In each case the organization will devote advertising resources to promote it. In the economist's view of conflict, grievance will turn out to be neither a cause of conflict nor an accidental by-product of it. Rather, a sense of grievance is deliberately generated by rebel organizations. The sense of grievance may be based on some objective grounds for complaint, or it may be conjured up by massaging prejudices. However, while this distinction is morally interesting to observers—is the cause *just?*—it is of no practical importance. The organization simply needs to generate a sense of grievance; otherwise, it will fail as an organization and so tend to fade away.

This interpretation of conflict is obviously not shared by rebel organizations or by the people who honestly support them: the justice of the struggle seems central to success. In contrast, the economic theory of conflict argues that the motivation of conflict is unimportant;

what matters is whether the organization can sustain itself financially. It is this, rather than any objective grounds for grievance, that determines whether a country will experience civil war. The rebel organization can be motivated by a whole range of considerations. It might be motivated by perceived grievances, or it might simply want the power conferred by becoming the government. Regardless of why the organization is fighting, it can fight only if it is financially viable during the conflict. War cannot be fought just on hopes or hatreds. Predatory behavior during the conflict may not be the objective of the rebel organization, but it is its means of financing the conflict. By predatory behavior I mean the use of force to extort money or goods from their legitimate owners.

The economic theory of conflict then assumes that perceived grievances and the lust for power are found more or less equally in all societies. Groups are capable of perceiving that they have grievances more or less regardless of their objective circumstances, a social phenomenon known as relative deprivation. Some people will have a lust for power more or less regardless of the objective benefits conferred by power. In this case, *it is the feasibility of predation that determines the risk of conflict.* Predation may be just a regrettable necessity on the road to perceived justice or power, but it is the conditions for predation that are decisive. Whether conflict is motivated by predation, or simply made possible by it, these two accounts come to the same conclusion: rebellion is unrelated to objective circumstances of grievance while being caused by the feasibility of predation.

On the most cynical variant of the theory, rebellion is motivated by greed, so that it occurs when rebels can do well out of war. On the power-seeking variant of the predation theory, rebels are motivated by a lust for power, but rebellion occurs only when rebels can do well out of war. On the subjective grievance variant of the predation theory, rebels are motivated by grievances, imagined or real, but rebellion occurs only when rebels can do well out of war. These three variants have in common the implications that rebels are not necessarily heroes struggling for a particularly worthwhile cause and that the feasibility of predation explains conflict. They can thus be grouped together in contrast to the objective grievance theory of conflict, in which rebels are indeed heroes struggling for a worthwhile cause, with the intensity of objective grievances explaining the occurrence of conflict.

Economists would argue that it is not really necessary to distinguish among the three variants of the predation theory. It does not really matter whether rebels are motivated by greed, by a lust for power, or by grievance, as long as what causes conflict is the feasibility of predation. Indeed, economists tend to attach little credence to the explanations that people give for their behavior, preferring to work by "revealed preference": people gradually reveal their true motivation by the pattern of their behavior, even if they choose to disguise the painful truth from themselves. Rebel leaders may much of the time come to believe their own propaganda, but if their words are decried by their behavior, then their words have little explanatory power.

There is less reason to doubt that those who support rebellion from afar are genuinely committed to the cause of grievance redressal. However, such supporters may simply have been duped. Rebel leaders have always sought outside supporters—"useful idiots" in Lenin's telling phrase. Among the people who are most susceptible to the discourse of grievance are those who care most passionately about oppression, inequality, and injustice. In short, if rebellion presents itself as the ultimate protest movement, it will attract as noncombatant supporters those who normally support protest movements. The economic theory of conflict argues that these people have been taken in by accepting the discourse at face value. As a proposition in social science this theory of conflict is a case of modern economics meeting old Marxism. As in Marx, the underlying cause of conflict is economic: in this case, the rebel organization is predatory on certain parts of the economy. As in Marx, the "superstructure" is a set of beliefs that are false. The difference is simply that it is the *rebel* supporters who have the "false consciousness": they are gulled into believing the discourse that self-interested rebel leaders promote.

So, "greed or grievance"?—we can't tell from the discourse. Occasionally, the discourse is rather blatantly at variance with the behavior. Take the recently settled conflict in Sierra Leone. A rebel organization built itself into around twenty thousand recruits and opposed the government. The rebel organization produced the usual litany of grievances, and its very scale suggested that it had widespread support. Sierra Leone is, however, a major exporter of diamonds, and there was considerable evidence that the rebel organization was involved in this business on a large scale. During peace negotiations the rebel leader was offered and accepted the vice presidency of the country. This, we might imagine, would be a good basis from which to address rebel grievances. However, this was not sufficient to persuade the rebel leader to accept the peace settlement. He had one further demand, which, once conceded, produced (temporary) settlement. His demand was to be the minister of mining. Cases such as this are at least suggestive that something other than grievance may be going on beneath the surface of the discourse. It is to this hidden structure of rebellion that I now turn.

THE EVIDENCE

Modern economics has two powerful tools: statistics and theory. People who are not economists are seldom convinced simply by economic theory so I will begin with the statistical evidence. Together with Anke Hoeffler, I have analyzed the pattern of conflict using a large new database on civil wars during the period 1965–99.[2] Completely independently, two political scientists, James Fearon and David Laitin, followed the same approach, and their results are very similar.[3] I will focus on my own work, simply because I am more familiar with its limitations.

A civil war is classified as an internal conflict with at least one thousand battle-related deaths. During this period there were seventy-three civil wars globally, and, in principle, we analyze the pattern as to why these wars occurred among the 161 countries in our sample. We divide the period into eight five-year subperiods and attempt to predict the occurrence of war during a subperiod by the characteristics at its start. The statistical techniques we use are logit and probit regressions. In practice, some civil wars occur in situations where there is virtually no other data about the country. We know that it had a war, but we do not know enough of its other characteristics to include it in our analysis. This reduces our sample to forty-seven civil wars, listed in the appendix (see page 218). However, this is still sufficient to find some strong patterns. While our published results do not use data beyond 1999, in our more recent work we have revisited our analysis, including data through the end of 2004. The core results remain the same.

In order to get some feel for how important different risk factors are, it is useful to think of a baseline country. I will take as a baseline a country whose characteristics were all at the mean of our sample. By construction, then, this is an extraordinarily ordinary country. These characteristics give it a risk of civil conflict of about 14 percent in any particular five-year period. Now, one by one, I will vary some of the more important risk factors.

One important factor is that countries that have a substantial share of their income (GDP) coming from the export of primary commodities are radically more at risk for conflict. The most dangerous level of primary commodity dependence is 26 percent of GDP. At this level the otherwise ordinary country has a risk of conflict of 23 percent. In contrast, if it had no

primary commodity exports (but was otherwise the same), its risk would fall to only one-half of 1 percent. Thus, without primary commodity exports, ordinary countries are pretty safe from internal conflict, while when such exports are substantial the society is highly dangerous. Primary commodities are thus a major part of our conflict story. Recently, a number of scholars have revisited the issue: the August 2005 issue of the *Journal of Conflict Resolution* was devoted to it. Fearon may be correct in arguing that what we took for an inverted-U relationship between primary commodities and the risk of conflict is no such thing: there is no downturn. Fearon thinks that the risk is largely confined to oil, but other scholars disagree on this point. Rather, beyond a certain point the risk simply levels off. In our current work, Anke and I have updated our analysis by five years to December 2004 and incorporated the latest revisions from political scientists on which events were and were not civil wars. With these new data we still find the same results, but at the time of writing our work is not yet completed. By the time of publication it should be on my Web site.

What else matters? Both geography and history matter. Geography matters because if the population is highly geographically dispersed, then the country is harder for the government to control than if everyone lives in the same small area. The geography of the Democratic Republic of the Congo (the former Zaire) makes the country unusually hard for government forces to control because the population lives around the fringes of a huge area, with the three main cities in the extreme west, extreme southeast, and extreme north. In comparison, Singapore would be a nightmare for a rebellion. In this city-state there is nowhere to hide and government forces could be anywhere in the country within an hour. With Congo-like geographic dispersion our otherwise ordinary country has a risk of conflict of about 50 percent, whereas with Singapore-like concentration its risk falls to about 3 percent.

There is also some evidence that mountainous terrain increases the risk, presumably because it offers greater possibilities of safe haven for rebel forces.

History matters because if a country has recently had a civil war, its risk of further war is much higher. Immediately after the end of hostilities there is a 40 percent chance of further conflict. This risk then falls at around one percentage point for each year of peace. However, how much history matters depends on the size of the diaspora. For example, some countries have very large diasporas in the United States relative to their remaining resident population, whereas others do not. Suppose that our otherwise ordinary country has ended a civil war five years ago and now wants to know what its chances of peace are during the next five years. If the country has an unusually large American diaspora, its chances of conflict are 36 percent. If it has an unusually small diaspora, its chances of conflict are only 6 percent. We focus on diasporas living in the United States because the data are not available for most other countries. Anecdotal evidence points to diasporas based in other countries being a similar problem. For example, finance for explosives used in massacres committed by the Tamil Tigers has been traced to a bank in Canada, and the Albanian diasporas in Europe financed the Kosovo Liberation Army. So, diasporas appear to make life for those left behind much more dangerous in postconflict situations.

Economic opportunities also matter. Conflict is concentrated in countries whose populations have little education. The average country in our sample had only 45 percent of its young males in secondary education. If a country that had 45 percent of its youths in school increased that percentage by 10 percentage points to 55, it would cut its risk of conflict from 14 percent to about 10 percent. Conflict is more likely in countries with fast population growth: each percentage point on the rate of population growth raises the risk

of conflict by about 2.5 percentage points. Conflict is also more likely in countries in economic decline. Each percentage point off the growth rate of per capita income raises the risk of conflict by around 1 percentage point. Conceivably, the apparently adverse effect of slow growth might be spurious, owing to reverse causation. If there was a high risk of civil war, investment might decline and hence growth would slow: the slow growth would appear to cause subsequent conflict, but actually causality would be the other way around. This problem was recently addressed in a valuable contribution by Edward Miguel, Shanker Satyanath, and Ernest Sergenti.[4] They manage to isolate variations in the growth rate that are completely unrelated to the risk of civil war by studying the impact of rainfall shocks on growth, using longtime series on rainfall, country by country, across Africa. Essentially, in a year when rainfall is above its normal level for a given country, growth is also atypically high, and conversely when rainfall is below normal. They show that the growth shocks predicted from rainfall shocks powerfully affect the risk of civil war. By design, these growth shocks are uncontaminated by the risk of war and so the direction of causality is unambiguous; rapid growth really does reduce the risk of civil war.

The ethnic and religious composition of the country matters. If there is one dominant ethnic group that constitutes between 45 percent and 90 percent of the population—enough to give it control but not enough to make discrimination against a minority pointless—the risk of conflict doubles. For example, in Sri Lanka the Tamils are a minority of about 12 percent of the population, and in Rwanda and Burundi the Tutsi are around 10 percent to 15 percent of the population. Of course, in Sri Lanka the Tamils are a weak minority, whereas in Rwanda the Tutsi are a strong minority, controlling the government. However, clearly, in Rwanda the Tutsi minority is too scared of being subject to ethnic dominance to hand over power. While ethnic dominance is a problem, ethnic and religious diversity does not make a society more dangerous—in fact, it makes it safer. A country that is ethnically and religiously homogeneous is surprisingly dangerous—the risk is 23 percent. In comparison, a country with ethnic and religious diversity equal to the maximum we find in our sample has a risk of only about 3 percent. Other than in the fairly unusual case of dominance, diversity makes a society much safer.

Finally, some good news. Since 1990 the world has been significantly safer from civil conflict. If we add a dummy variable for the period since the end of the Cold War, it is statistically significant with quite a large effect. If we hold these causes of conflict constant at the average, the risk of conflict was only half as great during the 1990s as during the Cold War. Of course, some of the other causes of conflict also changed during the 1990s—on average, per capita incomes rose faster than during the 1980s, which also reduced the risk of conflict. However, some countries became more dependent on primary commodity exports or their economies collapsed, and these countries became more prone to conflict. As of 1995, the country with the highest risk of civil conflict according to our analysis was Zaire, with a three-in-four chance of conflict within the ensuing five years. Sadly, our model "predicted" this all too accurately. I should stress, however, that our analysis in not well suited to prediction: firefighters have to look elsewhere. To predict a civil war, it is surely more useful to focus on near-term indicators such as political incidents and rising violence. Rather, our model is useful in pointing to the typical structural risks and so provides some guidance on longer-term policies for prevention.

This has been the statistical pattern of civil conflict since 1960. It is interesting both for what is important and for what is not. Clearly, there are some powerful dangers coming from primary commodities and diasporas, and there used to be risks from the Cold War. However,

equally striking is what does *not* appear to affect conflict risk. Inequality, whether of incomes or of assets, has no discernible effect. Unequal societies are not more prone to conflict, although conflicts in unequal societies do seem to last longer.[5] A lack of democratic rights appears to have no significant effect. Ethnic and religious diversity, as noted, far from increasing the risk of conflict, actually reduces it. These are all obvious proxies for objective grievances. Unequal, ethnically divided societies with few political rights might sound like exactly the sorts of places that would be most prone to rebellion. They are surely the sorts of places most in need of protest. And yet such places, as far as we can tell, have no higher risk of violent conflict than anywhere else— indeed, thanks to their ethnic diversity, they are somewhat safer. The only protest-type variable that matters is ethnic dominance. This may be because we are not measuring objective grievances well enough. However, we have made an honest effort to utilize all the available comparable indices of objective grievance, of which there are now a number. At least as a working hypothesis, civil war is much more strongly related to the economic and geographic variables discussed earlier than it is to objective grievances.

There are thus two surprises to be explained: why rebellion is so unrelated to the objective need for protest, and why it is so strongly related to primary commodities and diasporas.

WHY IS REBELLION NOT LIKE PROTEST?

Economists have studied the dynamics of protest.[6] The first problem with getting a protest going is that it is a "public good." That is, if the protest succeeds in securing justice, everyone will benefit, whether or not they bother to take part in the protest. Public goods always face collective-action problems: it makes more individual sense to free-ride on the efforts of others, and if everyone free-rides, nothing happens. This is a problem in a protest because the government might punish people who take part, unless there are so many people that there is safety in numbers. Further, in order to protest, most people must lose a day of income. This is one reason why such a high proportion of protesters are often students. The temptation to free-ride on a justice-seeking *rebellion* is very much stronger than the temptation to free-ride on a justice-seeking *protest*. A protest costs little, risks little, and offers a sense of citizenship. In effect, protestors are forcing an open election on an issue. Rebellion is a full-time commitment, and it is dangerous. Economists would predict that the collective action problem for a justice-seeking rebellion would usually be insuperable.

Timur Kuran's insight in analyzing the dynamics of protest was to see that a successful protest would be one that escalated, and that this depended on a cascade of participation, drawing in increasingly lukewarm supporters. Suppose the potential supporters of a protest are ranked in order of their willingness to take personal risk. The most ardent supporters join the protest first, at the stage when it is small, because it is easy for the government to victimize participants. Each time an additional supporter joins the protest the risks of punishment for participation go down. The cascade depends on the reduction in this risk inducing enough people to change their minds and join the protest that the risk falls further, inducing another group of people to change their minds. If the cascade works, then when a few committed people create an initial spark it turns into a prairie fire. Could the rebellions we observe be failed protest movements, cases in which a brave few hundred created the spark, but the rest of the society failed to ignite, leaving the brave core to turn into guerrilla fighters against the government? Are rebels just heroes who have been let down by the mass of cowards and so driven into more violent actions to protect themselves? Well, if they are, we should observe a clear pattern in rebellion.

Kuran suggests that the cascade is more likely to work in fairly homogeneous societies, where there is a dense continuum of opinion. Many people will be on the margin of changing their minds and so will be swung into action as the risks of government punishment start to fall. In contrast, if the society is split up into many different groups who see the concerns of other groups as irrelevant to their own, instead of a continuum of opinion there are clusters broken by gaps. As soon as the cascade reaches the first gap it stops. One implication of this insight is that the societies in which protest will get stuck are those that are diverse. That is, if rebellions are the stuff of heroes let down by cowards, we should expect to find more of them in diverse societies. Recall that in fact we find precisely the opposite. Diverse societies have a much lower risk of rebellion than homogeneous societies. Of course, if we scour history sufficiently thoroughly, we will find examples of protest movements that aborted into rebellion. If we scour history, we can find anything. However, the image of the rebel band as that part of the population that is the most dedicated and self-sacrificing is difficult to reconcile with the facts. Rebellion is not generally linked to the objective grievances—such as inequality and political repression—that are repeatedly used in rebel discourse. Nor is its incidence high in societies where we would expect protest movements to face the most difficulties. The sole exception to this is that in situations of ethnic dominance—with or without democracy—minorities (or majorities) may take to the gun. Other than this, the modern rebel appears truly to have been a "rebel without a cause."

A recent analysis of rebel recruitment by Jeremy Weinstein adds an important insight into how rebel motivations may evolve over time.[7] Initially, the rebellion may be motivated by a desire to rectify perceived grievances. However, if there are prospects of gaining control of lucrative revenues, for example, through natural resources or kidnapping, this will gradually affect the composition of recruitment. The volunteers who seek to join the movement will increasingly be drawn from those with criminal rather than altruistic intent, and even an altruistic rebel leader will have difficulties in screening out the criminals. Whatever characteristics the leader demands will be mimicked by criminals wishing to join. Hence, the rebel organization will gradually evolve from being altruistic to being criminal. This may well describe the evolution of the FARC from its origins as a rural protest movement to its present reality as a massive drug operation. Even when rebel recruits are truly dedicated and self-sacrificing, this devotion to a cause is not a reliable indicator that the cause is worthwhile. Probably the largest collective self-sacrificing organization in history was Hitler's SS: toward the end of World War II thousands of men were prepared to die hopelessly for a cause that was despicable beyond measure. Suicide bombers and billionaires who abandon their wealth for the fugitive life are evidently devoted. This does not make their cause remotely worthy of respect. Most societies have a small minority of people seeking meaning in a cause, whatever that might be.

WHAT CONDITIONS MAKE PREDATORY REBELLIONS PROFITABLE?

Empirically, the risk of rebellion is strongly linked to three economic conditions: dependence on primary commodity exports, low average income of the country, and slow growth. I now suggest why this is the case.

Primary commodity exports are the most lootable of all economic activities. An economy that is dependent on them thus offers plenty of opportunities for predatory rebellion.[8] One indication that primary commodity exports are highly lootable is that they are also the most heavily taxed activity—the same characteristics that make it easy for governments to tax them make it easy for rebels to loot them. Indeed, rebel predation is just illegal taxation.

Conversely, in some countries government has been described as legalized predation in which primary commodities are heavily taxed in order to finance the government elite. In the worst cases, those who are the victims of such predation may not discriminate much between the behavior of the rebel organization and that of the government. This does not, however, mean that the rebels are "no worse" than the government. The presence of a rebel organization plunges the society from peace into civil war, and the costs of war are likely to outweigh the costs of government predation.

Primary commodity exports are especially vulnerable to looting and taxation because their production relies heavily on assets that are long-lasting and immobile. Once a mine shaft has been sunk, it is worth exploiting, even if many of the anticipated profits are lost to rebels. Once coffee trees have been planted, they are worth harvesting, even if much of the coffee has to be surrendered. Thus, rebel predation does not kill off the activity or shift it elsewhere, as would happen were manufacturing the target. Further, because the produce is exported, it has to be transported to the port. Along the way there are many geographic "choke points" at which rebels can extract a tribute if they can control them, even if only sporadically. The government can be presumed to control the best choke point of all—the port itself. This behavior makes a rebel group somewhat like organized crime. However, it is organized crime with a difference. The government will try to defend the choke points from rebel attacks—it is, after all, defending its own revenue. Hence, unlike a mafia, the rebel group must expect sometimes to confront substantial government forces and so will need to protect itself. Rebel groups therefore need to be much larger than mafias. Typically, rebel organizations have in the range of five hundred to five thousand fighters, whereas mafia membership is generally in the range of twenty to five hundred. It is because rebel organizations need to be large and to confront government forces in order to function as predators that conflicts can produce cumulative mortality in excess of one thousand and so qualify empirically as civil wars.

Why is the risk of conflict much higher in countries where incomes are low? The explanation that jumps to mind is that when people are poor they have little to lose from joining a rebel group, so that rebel organizations find recruitment cheap. There may be something in this, but if young men can be recruited cheaply for the rebel organization, they can also be recruited cheaply by the government. Hence, low income does not automatically give rebellion an advantage. However, low income does indirectly advantage the rebels. Around the world, the share of income that accrues to the government as tax revenue rises with income. For example, most OECD governments (that is, the rich countries) get about 40 percent of national income as tax revenue. In the really poor economies, the percentage is much lower. For example, in Ghana and Uganda in the early 1980s, the government was raising only about 6 percent of national income as taxation. This reduces the capacity of the government to spend on defense and so makes rebel predation easier. Indeed, in low-income economies, governments will typically derive about half of their revenue from taxes on primary commodity exports (directly or indirectly), so that their revenue base is quite similar to that of the rebels. At higher income levels the government supplements these revenues with revenues from taxes on other economic activities. Thus, poor countries have a high incidence of conflict because governments cannot defend. Of course, there might be other reasons why poverty makes it easier for rebels. Poverty might make people desperate or angry. However, if this was an important effect we would expect to find that inequality made conflict more likely: for a given level of average income, the more unequal income distribution is, the more severe the poverty of the poorest. In fact, inequality does not seem to affect the risk of conflict. Rebellion seems not to be the rage of the poor.

Indeed, if anything, rebellion seems to be the rage of the rich. One way in which rebel groups can lock into predation of primary commodity exports is to secede with the land on which the primary commodities are produced. Such attempted secessions by rich regions are quite common: Katanga, which sought to secede from Zaire, was a copper-mining region; Biafra, which fought to secede from Nigeria, was an oil-producing region; Eritrea, which succeeded in its secessionist ambitions, was a region with double the per capita income of the rest of Ethiopia; and Aceh in Indonesia is an oil-producing region with per capita GDP three times the national average. To the extent that the rebel group is not just benefiting itself through predation but is fighting a political cause, that cause is the grievance of a rich minority at paying taxes to the poor majority. Such rebellions may have more in common with the politics of Staten Island (where a rich suburb tried to secede from the tax jurisdiction of New York) than of Robin Hood. Slow economic growth and rapid population growth both make rebellion more likely. Presumably, both of these assist rebel recruitment. The rebel organization needs to build itself up fairly fast in order to survive against the army. Hence, for a given level of income, the rebel organization has an easier task if there are few job opportunities, few schooling opportunities, and many young people needing work.

So, the observed pattern of rebellion is quite intelligible. High primary commodity exports, low income, and slow growth are a cocktail that makes predatory rebellions more financially viable. In such circumstances rebels can do well out of war.

WHY MIGHT DIVERSITY MAKE A SOCIETY SAFER RATHER THAN MORE DANGEROUS?

One of the most surprising empirical regularities is that societies that are diverse in terms of both ethnicity and religion seem to be significantly safer than societies that are homogeneous. A standard measure of ethnic diversity proxies ethnicity by language and calculates the probability that two people drawn randomly from the country's population will be from different linguistic groups. As part of our work Anke and I constructed an equivalent measure of religious diversity. Unfortunately, there are no global data that combine ethnicity and religion showing us the mosaic, country by country, of ethnoreligious combinations. We approximate such a concept by combining the ethnic diversity and religious diversity measures, investigating the combination both by addition and by multiplication. It is this measure that is significantly negatively related to the risk of conflict. If ethnic and religious hatreds were an important cause of conflict, it might be expected that the pattern would be the reverse, since in homogeneous societies there would be no other group to hate. Conflict seems not to be generated by such hatreds. Indeed, Fearon and Laitin actually investigate a measure of the intensity of intergroup hatred and find it unrelated to the risk of civil war. However, it is less evident why diversity makes a society considerably safer, instead of simply having no effect.

I think that diversity may make a society safer because it can make rebellion more difficult. This is because, first and foremost, a rebel organization is neither a mafia nor a protest movement, but an army. Armies face huge problems of organizational cohesion and motivation. To fight effectively, soldiers must overcome their individual instincts to avoid danger and must take risks to help other members of their team. Military history abounds in stories of small groups defeating larger groups because they were better fighting units. The government army also faces these problems, but it has the advantage of already having had a long time to deal with them. In contrast, the rebel organization cannot usually afford to take years to build up morale before it starts operations: it must recruit from scratch and start fighting

as soon as possible. One simple principle is to keep the recruits as alike as possible. The more social ties there are within the organization—the same kin group, or at least the same ethnic group, language group, and religion—the easier it will be to build a fighting force. This may be especially true of the officer corps. The easiest way for a government to defeat a rebellion may be to buy off some of the officers. The more "social capital" there is within the group, the more cohesive it is likely to be.

This principle implies that in ethnically diverse societies rebellions will tend to be ethnically particular. This has two important corollaries. First, the more that the society is divided into a patchwork of different ethnic and religious groups, the more difficult it will be to recruit a force of a sufficient scale to be viable. For example, in Africa the average ethnolinguistic group has only about 250,000 people, of whom about 25,000 will be young males. Thus, even before we allow for any further divisions of religion, an organization of 5,000 fighters will need to recruit 20 percent of the age group. Diversity in the society thus makes the rebel task more difficult and so makes rebellion less likely.

The second corollary is that where conflict does take place in ethnically diverse societies, it will take the form of some particular ethnic group rebelling against the government. As in any army, recruits will be motivated to kill the enemy by basic indoctrination as to why the enemy deserves to be killed. Indeed, the simple Leninist theory of the rebel organization, which many rebel movements adopt even if they do not adopt Marxist ideology, is that people are initially so oppressed that they do not realize they are oppressed. *It is a key task of the rebel organization to make people realize that they are* the victims of injustice. The economic theory of rebellion accepts this proposition and makes one simple but reasonable extension: the rebel organization can inculcate a subjective sense of injustice whether or not this is objectively justified. The astounding self-sacrifice displayed by SS troops in their loyalty to Hitler is a disturbing indication that passionate commitment to a cause can be inculcated by effective propaganda regardless of the underlying merits of the cause. The rebel organization needs to inculcate a sense of injustice and will work to create it. From this follows a hatred of the enemy and a willingness to fight.

The inculcation of grievance is not a frivolous activity; it is vital for an effective fighting force. Take, for example, the Eritrean People's Liberation Front (EPLF), which was probably the most effective rebellion in recent history. Its recruitment base was barely two million people and it had little foreign government support, yet it defeated an Ethiopian army of more than four hundred thousand men that was supported by Russia. Its success obviously depended on having its much smaller army well motivated. The EPLF deliberately built this motivation by routinely withdrawing its recruits from the front for six months to send them to indoctrination courses. If the society in which the rebellion occurs is ethnically diverse, the rebel organization will nevertheless be ethnically homogeneous to assist cohesion. Since the rebels will therefore be ethnically different from most of the rest of society, the obvious discourse for the rebel leadership to adopt with its recruits is that of ethnic grievance. Hence, ethnic grievance is actively manufactured by the rebel organization as a necessary way of motivating its forces. As a result, where conflicts occur in ethnically diverse societies, they will look and sound as though they were caused by ethnic hatreds.

A more remarkable example is the conflict in Somalia. Somalia is one of the most ethnically homogeneous societies in the world, although, as in all traditional societies, within the single ethnic group are many lineage or kin groups. In the initial postindependence period, political power had been shared reasonably comfortably among these clan groups. However, in the instability following a dictatorship, a political opportunist, Mohammed Farah

Aideed, induced the group living around the national arsenal to seize its considerable contents. The group then proceeded to build an army around these armaments. Building an army fast, Aideed based recruitment on his clan and its proximate lineage groups—in the absence of ethnic distinctions, clan membership was the only basis for creating cohesion in a fighting force. The excluded clans naturally felt threatened by this bid for power and so armed themselves in response. The resulting violent conflict in effect turned what had been a patchwork of closely related clusters of people into large rival groupings that hated each other. The conflict created the equivalent of interethnic hatred in an ethnically unified society.

A surprisingly similar example is the conflict in the Democratic Republic of the Congo. Congo is at the opposite end of the spectrum from Somalia, a society that is highly ethnically diverse. When President Kabila the First fell out with his Tutsi military support, he needed to build an army to oppose them. Because Congo was so ethnically divided, this was difficult. Kabila needed to recruit across ethnic boundaries in order to build a sufficient fighting force. He therefore manufactured an encompassing ethnic grouping, of which all groups other than the Tutsi were members, namely, the Bantu. Just as Aideed had forged several clans in Somalia into a common fighting group distinct from the excluded clans, so Kabila hoped to forge several ethnic groups into a common fighting group. In both cases, the conflict created a need to manufacture intergroup hatred, but the basic conditions for it—a society divided into two large groups—did not exist. In both cases military necessity led to the invention not just of the grievances but of the groupings themselves. Even if conflict is not caused by divisions, it actively needs to create them.

When such conflicts are viewed during or after the event, the observer sees ethnic hatred. The parties to the conflict have used the discourse of group hatred to build fighting organizations, so it is natural for observers to interpret such conflicts as being caused by ethnic hatred. Instead, the conflicts have caused the intergroup hatred and may even, as in Somalia, have created the groups.

If the rebel organization succeeds in generating group grievance, perhaps by manufacturing both the grievance and the group, the resulting civil war becomes defined in terms of political conflict. However, it is the military needs of the rebel organization that have created this political conflict rather than objective grievances. Analysts often reason back from the political discourse during conflict and deduce that the war is the consequence of particularly intense political conflict, based in turn on particularly strong reasons for grievance. Yet the intensity of objective grievance does not predict civil war. Many societies sustain intense political conflict for many years without war developing. Political conflict is universal, whereas civil war is rare. My argument is that where rebellions happen to be financially viable, wars will occur. As part of the process of war, the rebel organization must generate group grievance for military effectiveness. The generation of group grievance politicizes the war. Thus, the war produces the intense political conflict, not the intense political conflict the war.

IF DIVERSITY INCREASES SAFETY, WHY IS ETHNIC DOMINANCE SO DANGEROUS?

The one exception to the rule that homogeneous societies are more dangerous than societies with more than one ethnic group is a society characterized by ethnic dominance. By ethnic dominance I mean a society in which the largest single ethnic group has somewhere between 45 percent and 90 percent of the population. It is not difficult to see why such societies are dangerous. Having 45 percent or more of the population is sufficient in a democracy to give the group permanent control: what political scientists call a stable winning coalition. Having less than 90 percent of the population

suggests that it might be worth exploiting this power by transferring resources from the minority. If the minority is much smaller than 10 percent of the population, there is normally so little to be gained by exploiting it that the gain may be more than swallowed up in the costs of the transfer system.

Thus, in societies characterized by ethnic dominance, the majority probably has both the power to exploit the minority and an interest in doing so. The minority may become sufficiently fearful of permanent exploitation that it decides to fight. This is the exception to the absence-of-objective-grievance effects, and a reason for it may be that democracy can offer no prospect of redress. In diverse societies not characterized by ethnic dominance, small groups that are excluded from power can hope at some stage to bid themselves into a winning coalition. Even dictators do not last forever. Thus, for example, in Kenya, where no tribe has close to a majority, the fifteen years of President Jomo Kenyatta's rule strongly favored his own large tribe, the Kikuyu. However, Kenyatta had chosen as his vice president someone from a very minor tribe. On the death of Kenyatta, the vice president, Daniel arap Moi, succeeded to the presidency and for twenty-five years held together a winning coalition of small tribes, excluding both the Kikuyu and the Luo, the two largest tribal groups. The small tribes in Kenyatta's Kenya were thus right to hope for eventual redress through the political rather than the military process. In contrast, in societies characterized by ethnic dominance, the minority has little to hope for from the political process. Thus, it is possible that rebellion in societies with ethnic dominance is the behavior of despair. Note that it makes little difference whether it is the majority or the minority that is in power. Even if the minority is in power, it dare not trust democracy because it does not trust the majority. This is perhaps the case with the Tutsi-dominated governments of Rwanda and Burundi, and perhaps even of the minority Tigrean-dominated government of Ethiopia. The current acute difficulties in Iraq are thus consistent with what might be expected in a society characterized by ethnic dominance.[9]

WHY ARE DIASPORAS SO DANGEROUS?

Recall that, empirically, if a country that has recently ended a conflict has a large diaspora, its risk that the conflict will resume is sharply increased.

There is little mystery about this effect. Diasporas sometimes harbor rather romanticized attachments to their group of origin and may nurse grievances as a form of asserting continued belonging. They are much richer than the people in their country of origin and so can afford to finance vengeance. Above all, they do not have to suffer any of the awful consequences of renewed conflict because they are not living in the country. Hence, they are a ready market for rebel groups touting vengeance and so are a source of finance for renewed conflict. They are also a source of pressure for secession. For example, the (peaceful) secession of Slovakia from the then Czechoslovakia was initiated not in Czechoslovakia itself but in the Czechoslovak diaspora organizations in North America. City by city, the diaspora organization divorced.[10] The reductio ad absurdum of such a trend would be for immigrant populations of the United States and the European Union to split their countries of origin into tiny "ethnic theme parks" while themselves enjoying the advantages of living in nations with scale and diversity.

Another source of foreign finance is governments that are enemies of the incumbent government. During the Cold War each of the superpowers offered inducements for Third World governments to align with them. Once a government had done this, it became the potential target of destabilization efforts from the other superpower. One means of destabilization was to fund rebel groups. Once the Cold War ended, the need for such destabiliza-

tion ended, and so the external finance for rebel organizations declined, which perhaps explains why the risk of civil conflict was lower during the 1990s. Many governments of low-income countries are on bad terms with their neighbors. Because the international community strongly discourages international war, notably through reductions in aid, warfare with neighbors usually has to be covert. The most straightforward means of such warfare is to arm and finance a rebel group that fights the neighbor. For many years, the government of Uganda covertly supported the Sudan People's Liberation Army, and in response the government of Sudan supported the Lord's Resistance Army in northern Uganda. One problem with such support is that, because the support is covert, it is very difficult to verify if it has ceased, and so it is correspondingly difficult to conclude an effective peace agreement between the two governments: each party has an incentive to sign an agreement but not abide by it.

THE COSTS OF CIVIL WAR

A typical civil war inflicts an immense amount of damage: death, disease, and poverty. Anke and I have attempted to put a cost on this damage and to determine how the cost is divided among different groups of victims.[11] Estimating the cost of conflict is an essential step toward cost-benefit analysis. In turn, cost-benefit analysis has two important applications. The first is to give some broad sense of whether civil war is "worthwhile": is it usually a reasonable "investment" for those societies that embark on it? The second is to guide policies for reducing the incidence of civil war. Most policies cost money, and some cost lives. Are such expenditures warranted in terms of their likely savings?

The costs of civil war are partly directly economic and partly social. By the end of the typical war, the economy is about 15 percent poorer than it would otherwise have been, and mortality is much higher, mainly due to disease triggered by movements of refugees and the collapse of public health systems, rather than to combat deaths. These effects are highly persistent after the end of the war: the typical war lasts about seven years, but it takes over a decade to recover. Hence, much of the cost of a civil war, about half, occurs *after it is over*. Further, a lot of the costs accrue to neighboring countries: both economic decline and disease spread across borders. Because the typical country has about three neighbors, all of whom are affected, the total cost to neighbors is about as large as the cost to the country itself. One implication is that most of the costs of a war accrue either to the future or to neighbors and so are not taken into account by those who start them. Even where rebels initiate conflict with some sense of future benefits to society outweighing future costs, they omit key costs and so their decisions are biased in favor of conflict. Taking all the costs together, we estimate that the typical civil war costs about $60 billion. This is a huge sum, more than double the annual income of the typical civil war country. It dwarfs any likely benefits: most civil wars are terrible investments. It also suggests that it is worth spending large sums to reduce their incidence as long as we can find interventions that are effective.

So What Can Be Done?

I have spent a long time on the diagnosis of the problem because different diagnoses lead to radically different policy solutions.

If you accept the conventional grievance account of conflict, then the appropriate policy interventions are to address the possible objective causes of grievance. On this account, countries should reduce inequality and increase political rights. These noble objectives are desirable on many grounds, but if the objective is civil peace, then by my analysis they will be ineffective.

A further policy, if you accept the grievance account, might be to redraw borders, split countries, and even move populations so as to

achieve greater ethnic homogeneity. In contrast, if you accept that diversity makes countries safer, then this is the road to increased civil conflict and presumably also to increased international conflict. Perhaps an example of such an eventuality is the breakup of Yugoslavia. In the old Yugoslavia there was a sufficiently high degree of diversity that no one group constituted a majority—the society was not characterized by ethnic dominance. First, Slovenia, the richest region of Yugoslavia, seceded in what could be interpreted as an instance of the "rage of the rich," although there were almost surely other motivations. Then Croatia, the next-richest region, also seceded. Owing to these two secessions, the residual Yugoslavia *was* characterized by ethnic dominance. Civil and international war followed.

Hence, the policies that follow from the grievance diagnosis are variously ineffective and counterproductive if you accept the predation diagnosis. What policies will work if this alternative interpretation of conflict is in fact correct? First, we need to distinguish between conflict prevention and postconflict situations. Before conflict, the approach implied by the predation analysis is to work through the major risk factors, identifying how to reduce them. Note that this approach is radically different from the more traditional approach that attempts to identify grievances and redress them. The new approach is basically one of making it harder for rebel organizations to get established, and addressing objective grievances is not usually an effective way of achieving this objective. Postconflict, the problem is rather different. Rebel organizations have forced themselves onto the political landscape and have generated group grievance. Although both the grievances and the groups may be manufactured, they now exist and postconflict policy must address them. Hence, whereas conflict prevention should not be built around the reduction of objective grievances, the construction of sustainable peace in postconflict societies will have to address the subjective grievances of the parties to the conflict. I therefore consider the problems of conflict prevention and postconflict peacebuilding separately.[12]

POLICIES FOR CONFLICT PREVENTION

Each society is different. The overall risk of conflict in a society is built up from a series of risk factors, and the balance of risk factors will differ from one country to another. Hence, the first step in conflict prevention is to decompose the overall risk into its constituent components and then put the most effort into reducing those risks that are the most important and the most amenable to policy. I take the potential risk factors in turn.

Economies with about a quarter of GDP coming from natural resource exports are acutely at risk for civil conflict. There are four strategies that might reduce this risk. First, the government can facilitate diversification of the economy away from dependence on primary commodities. Better economic policy promotes diversification. In a really poor policy environment, the only export activities that survive are those with high location-specific rents. The World Bank's annual measure of policy (the Country Policy and Institutional Assessment) is significant in explaining the extent of primary commodity dependence. Policy improvement, sustained over a five-year period, reduces dependence in the next five-year period.[13]

Second, a government can try to make loot-seeking rebels unpopular by transparently using the revenue from primary commodity exports to fund effective basic service delivery. If the money is seen to be funding primary education and rural health centers, then the population is going to be more hostile to rebels than if they believe that the money is sent off to Swiss banks. There are, however, limits to the effectiveness of this policy. For example, many of the youths who fought for the rebel movement in Sierra Leone are so unpopular that they dare not return to their communities, but this unpopularity did not stop them

from joining a rebellion. The rebels deliberately targeted drug addicts and children for recruitment and so had an unusually dependent labor force.

Third, the international community can make it more difficult for rebel groups to sell the commodities that they loot. Most of the international markets in commodities are, at some point along the marketing chain, fairly narrow, in the sense that there are not many market participants. Although primary commodities are more difficult to identify than branded manufactured goods, they differ in quality, and so markets can usually identify the origin of the commodity in the process of determining its quality. For example, at the stage at which diamonds are cut, their provenance can be established with reasonable accuracy, and diamond cutting is a highly skilled activity that can potentially be subject to a degree of international regulation. Of course, it will never be possible to drive illegal supplies out of the market, but it should be possible to drive them to the fringes of the market, where the goods can be sold only at a deep discount. Rebel predation would then become less lucrative. The Kimberley Process, which is a recent initiative to keep looted diamonds off the market, not only is important for the diamonds trade but also provides a model for other lootable commodities, such as timber and oil.

Low income and economic decline are further risk factors. There is no quick fix to low income. However, within a single generation it is now possible for most poverty-stricken societies to lift themselves out of poverty. In a single generation South Korea managed to grow its per capita income from $300 a year to $10,000 a year. Most very poor countries have poor economic policies. Changing these policies is often politically difficult because in the short term vested interests lose, but many societies have faced down these interests and transformed themselves. In such situations international aid has been shown to be effective in accelerating growth. For example, during the 1990s Uganda transformed its economic policies, and with the help of the international donor community it sustained a 7 percent annual growth rate. It is on track to realize the government objective of overcoming poverty within a generation. Within Uganda, a rebel group called the AFL recruited by offering the unemployed 200,000 shillings per month (about US$150). Rapid growth will gradually make recruitment harder.

A further risk factor is ethnic dominance. If a society has a single ethnic group that is large enough to dominate democratic institutions, then democracy itself is not sufficient to reassure minorities. Ethnic dominance is a difficult problem. The most realistic approach is to entrench minority rights into the constitution. This can be done either by explicitly legislating group rights or through strong individual rights. If all individuals are secure from discrimination, then individuals in minority groups are secure. The scope for this approach depends on the credibility of the checks and balances that the state can erect on government power. Usually, state institutions are not strong enough for this degree of trust, and so they can usefully be reinforced by international or regional commitments. For example, the European Union is requiring that the many Eastern European countries hoping to join it treat their minorities equally. Latvia moderated its policies toward its Russian minority in response to this requirement.

If governments and the international community can defuse the risk from its primary commodity exports, generate rapid growth, and provide credible guarantees to minorities, then the risk of conflict can be radically reduced. Conflict prevention can be achieved through large efforts on a few risk factors.

POLICIES FOR POSTCONFLICT PEACEBUILDING

All the policies that are appropriate for conflict prevention are also appropriate for postconflict peacebuilding. However, they are unlikely to be sufficient. In the first decade of postconflict peace, societies face roughly double the risk of conflict that the preconflict risk factors would predict. Postconflict societies are thus at substantial additional risk because of what has happened to them during conflict.

Several factors may account for this increase in risk. A rebel organization has built an effective military capability, in part by the manufacture of group grievance and in part by the accumulation of armaments, money, and military skills. People have gotten used to violence, so the norms that inhibit political violence in most societies will have been eroded. People's political allegiance may have polarized, so that, as in Somalia, ethnic dominance has been created by the conflict even if the society was initially either diverse or homogeneous.

Many societies have severe objective group grievances that sustain intense political conflict without getting close to civil war. Group grievance and intense political conflict are not in themselves dangerous: they are indeed the normal stuff of democratic politics. However, in postconflict societies, civil war has first built intense political conflict and then conducted that conflict through violence. Whereas most of the societies that have group grievances have no tradition of conducting their political conflict by means of violence, postconflict societies may have no tradition of conducting their political conflict nonviolently.

The rebel organization usually maintains its effectiveness during the postconflict period. Compared with a preconflict society with the same risk factors, the postconflict society is therefore much better prepared for war. The rebel organization has already recruited, motivated, armed, and saved. For example, Jonas Savimbi, the head of the Angolan rebel organization UNITA, was reputed to have accumulated over $4 billion in financial assets during the first war, some of which he then used to finance the start of the second.

Peace requires either that the intense political conflict continue but that the military option of conducting it be made infeasible, or that the political conflict itself be resolved. Each of these is difficult. Removing the military option requires demilitarizing the rebel organization, turning it into a conventional political party. This can happen. For example, Renamo, once a rebel military organization in Mozambique, is now a successful political party. Renamo was willing to demobilize, whereas UNITA was not. Mozambique was a post-conflict success, whereas Angola was a failure, partly because Angola had diamonds, whereas Mozambique did not. Aid donors were able to come up with a moderate financial package for Renamo, which made peaceful political contest an attractive option. Diamonds had made UNITA so rich that nothing donors could offer would matter, while renewed predation offered massive rewards. UNITA is believed to have earned about $2 billion from diamond mining in the first two years of renewed war. The extreme importance of aid donors to the Mozambique economy may also have made the maintenance of a democratic system in which Renamo would have a fair chance more credible. In Angola the government did not need the donors and so had no means of reassuring UNITA that democratic rights of political contest would be maintained. Even when the rebel group demobilizes, the precedent of violent conflict is fresh in people's minds. This is perhaps why time itself improves the prospects of peace: the habits of peaceful conflict replace those of violent conflict.

The alternative to continuing the political contest but making the military option infeasible is to resolve the political contest itself. This requires at a minimum that grievances be addressed, even though on average they are not objectively any more serious than those in peaceful societies. If, indeed, group grievance has been manufactured by rebel indoctrination, it can potentially be deflated by political gestures. While grievances may need to be addressed objectively, the main purpose of addressing them is probably to change people's perceptions.

The task of dealing with conflict that lacks proper boundaries between the political and the violent is difficult whether the approach is to restore boundaries or to resolve the political conflict. However, the attitudes of the domestic population appear not to be the main reason why postconflict societies have a risk of further conflict that is so much greater than implied by their inherited risk factors. Recall that the main risk comes from diasporas living in rich countries. What can be done to reduce this risk? One approach is to build the diaspora into the peace process. For example, in the conflict in Northern Ireland it is evident that the Irish American diaspora played a major part in financing violence. Both the Protestant and Catholic rebel military organizations actively raised funds in North America, and a number of the guns used in shootings turned out to have come (hopefully indirectly) from the Boston police department. When the peace faction within the IRA initiated the peace process, its leader went to Boston, and the British and Irish governments chose an American senator to head the peace negotiations.

An extension of this approach is to target campaigns at the diaspora that emphasize that the domestic population wants to maintain peace because the costs of violence are so high. Diasporas bear none of these costs, and so they need to be reminded that others do. Governments can go much further. Diasporas are potentially major assets for the development process, with skills and business connections. The diaspora organizations can be given explicit tasks in promoting economic recovery, facing them with a choice between a constructive and a destructive role. A complementary policy is for the governments of the countries in which these diasporas are resident to put clear limits on the activities of the diaspora organizations. Political support for violent rebel organizations is legitimate, but supplying material aid is not. For example, U.S. efforts to prevent countries such as Libya, Sudan, and Afghanistan from harboring terrorists who have killed U.S. citizens would have greater prospects of success were they to be set in the context of an international policy to set limits on the conduct of diasporas.

Dependence on primary commodity exports turns out to be even more important as a risk factor in postconflict societies than in preconflict societies: the same level of dependence generates a significantly higher risk. In mitigating the risks from primary commodities, one policy is open to postconflict governments that is not available preconflict: the government might decide to share the revenues peacefully and legally with the rebel organization. The rebels then do not need to fight in order to get what they want. This is, perhaps, what the government of Sierra Leone decided to do by bringing the rebel leader into government as minister of mining. Such a policy attempts to give rebels a greater interest in peace. There are, however, limits to this policy. If it is profitable for one rebel group to be predatory on primary commodity exports, once that group has been bought off, it will probably be profitable for another group to replace it.

While a postconflict government has more options for dealing with primary commodity dependence, it has fewer options for dealing with ethnic dominance. The provision of constitutional guarantees for ethnic minorities is unlikely to cut much ice in the low-trust environment that follows years of mutual hatred and killing. In such situations one option is for the international community to provide reassurance through an extended phase of military presence and its own guarantees. This is the solution currently being attempted in Bosnia and Kosovo. A further possibility is to determine that the country as constituted is unviable. However, rather than ethnic cleansing, a better solution may be federation with a neighboring country in which no ethnic group is dominant.

As in conflict prevention, rapid growth will assist peace. However, the task of achieving rapid growth requires somewhat different policies in postconflict societies. After a long war, economies tend to bounce back; they are so far below their productive potential. For example, in the first five years of peace after a fifteen-year war, economies grow on average at 6 percent a year.[14] Mozambique suffered an even longer war than this and recovered even more rapidly. One of the casualties of civil war is trust. Because life is so uncertain, people shorten their time horizons and are less concerned with building a reputation for honesty. Some people find it more profitable to behave opportunistically. As this behavior becomes more commonplace, the society switches into a low-level equilibrium of mutual suspicion and widespread opportunism. This raises the cost of all sorts of business transactions. For example, in Kampala, Uganda, a manufacturer of mattresses sold them wholesale on credit to agents who went up-country to sell them retail. One of the agents claimed that his entire consignment had been stolen by northern rebels. The manufacturer had to accept this alibi and forfeit the money. On the grapevine, he heard that the agent had invented the story, but he could not be sure what to believe.

Once a society has suffered a collapse into low trust, it takes concerted action to change expectations, and, meanwhile, many functions that other governments rely on simply don't work. The tax collection system, the courts, accountants, and doctors may all have been corrupted by opportunistic behavior. Of course, it is not only societies that have suffered civil war that can experience a breakdown of trust. However, in postconflict situations it is the norm. The government can respond to this problem by creating coordinated changes in expectations, institution by institution. For example, one quite common approach has been to close the old revenue-collecting part of the civil service and establish a new, independent institution to which people are freshly recruited.

In return for better pay they are subjected to more rigorous checks for honest conduct. Being a new institution, it is to some extent able to shed the burden of bad expectations that the old institutions carry.

The combination of primary commodity predation and opportunism implies that some people do well out of war.[15] Although most people lose, others have an interest in war restarting. Hence, when wars do restart, it is not necessarily simply an outpouring of irrational hatred or deep fears. Indeed, both hatreds and fears can be played on by those who expect to gain materially. One way in which a postconflict government can defend the peace against such manipulation is to publicize self-interest for what it is. Society at large needs to recognize that some groups have an interest in a return to conflict.

A corollary of this analysis is that rebel organizations, existing or prospective, can be viewed as rational economic agents. This has both a hopeful and a cautionary implication. The hopeful implication is that rebel organizations are likely to respond to incentives. For example, were the UN Security Council to introduce sanctions that made the economic and military circumstances of rebellion more difficult, the incidence of rebellion would decline. The cautionary implication is that it may be of little avail to buy rebel groups off. In countries where the objective conditions make rebellion financially feasible, if one group is bought off, others are likely to occupy the "market" opportunity for the generation of grievance.

CONCLUSION

Popular perceptions of the causes of civil conflict take at face value the discourse of the rebel organization. Civil war appears to be an intense political contest, fueled by grievances that are so severe as to have burst the banks of normal political channels. Rebellions are thus interpreted as the ultimate protest movements,

their cadres being self-sacrificing heroes struggling against oppression. In fact, most rebellions cannot be like this. When the main grievances—inequality, political repression, and ethnic and religious divisions—are measured objectively, they provide little or no explanatory power in predicting rebellion. In most low-income societies there are many reasons for grievance, but usually these do not give rise to rebellion. Objective grievances and hatreds simply cannot usually be the cause of such a distinctive phenomenon as violent conflict. They may well generate intense *political* conflict, but such conflict does not usually escalate to violent conflict.

In contrast, economic characteristics—dependence on primary commodity exports, low average incomes, slow growth, and large diasporas—are all significant and powerful predictors of civil war. These characteristics all make rebellion more materially feasible: they enable rebel leaders to buy the guns and feed the soldiers, and furthermore to perpetrate large-scale killing without themselves being killed in the process. A viable private army, which is the distinguishing feature of a civil war, is extremely expensive to maintain over the long periods that such wars typically last. Where a private army is viable, the agenda of its leadership could potentially be anything. It may be a public-spirited demand for improved governance. It may be a megalomaniac's agenda of sadism. It may be a mafia-style grab for loot. It may be little more than insanity: Jonestown or Waco with the violence turned outward instead of inward on the devotees. Over the years of a conflict the agenda is likely to evolve, with any political objectives eroding and eliding into rebellion-as-business. Hence, it is these factors that determine viability, rather than objective grievances, that are the true "root causes," which conflict prevention must address if it is to be successful. Since conflict prevention to date has paid scant attention to these causes of conflict, there is probably considerable scope for policy, both domestic and international, to prevent civil conflict more effectively.

While objective grievances do not generate violent conflict, violent conflict generates subjective grievances. This is not just a by-product of conflict but an essential activity of a rebel organization. Rebel military success depends on motivating its soldiers to kill the enemy, and this—as in the classic Leninist theory of rebel organizations—requires indoctrination. Hence, by the end of a civil war, there is intense intergroup hatred based on perceived grievances. A conflict has been generated that has no boundaries between political and violent actions. The task in postconflict societies is partly, as in preconflict societies, to reduce the objective risk factors. However, postconflict societies are much more at risk than is implied by the inherited risk factors, because of this legacy of induced polarizing grievance. Either boundaries must be reestablished between the political contest and violence or the political contest must be resolved. Neither of these is easy, which is why, once a civil war has occurred, the chances of further conflict are so high.

NOTES

1. Herschel I. Grossman, "Kleptocracy and Revolutions," *Oxford Economic Papers* 51 (1999): 269.

2. Paul Collier and Anke Hoeffler, "Greed and Grievance in Civil War," *Oxford Economic Papers* 56 (2004): 563–595.

3. James Fearon and David Laitin, "Ethnicity, Insurgency and Civil War," *American Political Science Review* 97 (2003): 75–90.

4. Edward Miguel, Shanker Satyanath, and Ernest Sergenti, "Economic Shocks and Civil Conflict: An Instrumental Variables Approach," *Journal of Political Economy* 112 (2004): 725–754.

5. Paul Collier, Anke Hoeffler, and Mans Soderbom, "On the Duration of Civil War," *Journal of Peace Research* 41 (2004): 253–273.

6. Timur Kuran, "Sparks and Prairie Fires: A Theory of Unanticipated Political Revolution," *Public Choice* 61 (1989): 41–74.

7. Jeremy Weinstein, "Resources and the Information Problem in Rebel Recruitment," *Journal of Conflict Resolution* 49 (2005): 598–624.

8. For a formal model of loot-seeking rebellion, see Paul Collier, "Rebellion as a Quasi-Criminal Activity," *Journal of Conflict Resolution* 44 (2000): 839–854.

9. Paul Collier, "Iraq: A Perspective from the Economic Analysis of Civil War," *Turkish Political Quarterly* 4 (2005): 71–80.

10. I would like to thank Professor Frederick Prior of Swarthmore College for this information.

11. Paul Collier and Anke Hoeffler, "Conflict," in *Global Crises: Global Solutions,* ed. E. Lomborg (Cambridge: Cambridge University Press, 2004).

12. For a fuller review of policy options, see Paul Collier, Lani Elliot, Harvard Hegre, Anke Hoeffler, Marta Reynol-Querol, and Nicholas Sambanis, *Breaking the Conflict Trap* (New York: Oxford University Press, 2003).

13. Paul Collier and Anke Hoeffler, "Aid, Policy and Peace," *Defence and Peace Economics* 13 (2002): 435–450.

14. Paul Collier, "On the Economic Consequences of Civil War," *Oxford Economic Papers* 51 (1999): 168–183; and Collier and Anke Hoeffler, "Aid, Policy and Growth in Post-Conflict Societies," *European Economic Review* 48 (2004): 1125–1145.

15. Paul Collier, "Doing Well Out of War," in *Greed and Grievance: Economic Agendas in Civil Wars,* ed. Mats Berdal and David Malone (Boulder, Colo.: Lynne Rienner, 2000).

Appendix: Outbreaks of War

Country	Year	Previous War	Country	Year	Previous War
Afghanistan	1975–79	No	Mozambique	1960–64	No
Afghanistan	1990–94	Yes	Mozambique	1975–79	Yes
Algeria	1960–64	Yes	Myanmar/Burma	1965–69	Yes
Algeria	1990–94	Yes	Myanmar/Burma	1980–84	Yes
Angola	1960–64	Yes	Nicaragua	1975–79	No
Angola	1975–79	Yes	Nicaragua	1980–84	Yes
Azerbaijan	1990–94	No	Nigeria	1965–69	No
Bosnia	1990–94	No	Nigeria	1980–84	Yes
Burundi	1970–74	No	Pakistan	1970–74	No
Burundi	1984–89	Yes	Peru	1980–84	No
Burundi	1990–94	Yes	Philippines	1970–74	Yes
Cambodia	1970–74	Yes	Romania	1984–89	No
Chad	1980–84	No	Russia	1990–94	No
China	1965–69	Yes	Russia	1995–99	Yes
Colombia	1980–84	Yes	Rwanda	1960–64	Yes
Dominican Republic	1965–69	No	Rwanda	1990–94	Yes
El Salvador	1975–79	No	Somalia	1980–84	No
Ethiopia	1970–74	Yes	Somalia	1984–89	Yes
Georgia	1990–94	No	Sri Lanka	1970–74	No
Guatemala	1965–69	Yes	Sri Lanka	1980–84	Yes
Guatemala	1970–74	Yes	Sudan	1960–64	No
Guatemala	1975–79	Yes	Sudan	1980–84	Yes
Guinea-Bissau	1960–64	No	Tajikistan	1990–94	No
India	1980–84	Yes	Turkey	1990–94	No
Indonesia	1975–79	Yes	Uganda	1965–69	Yes
Iran	1970–74	Yes	Uganda	1980–84	Yes
Iran	1975–79	Yes	Vietnam	1960–64	Yes
Iran	1980–84	Yes	Yemen	1990–94	No
Iraq	1970–74	Yes	Yemen Arab Republic	1960–64	Yes
Iraq	1984–89	Yes	People's Democratic		
Iraq	1990–94	Yes	Republic of Yemen	1984–89	No
Jordan	1970–74	No	Yugoslavia	1990–94	No
Laos	1960–64	Yes	Yugoslavia	1995–99	Yes
Lebanon	1975–79	Yes	Zaire	1960–64	Yes
Liberia	1984–89	No	Zaire	1990–94	Yes
Liberia	1990–94	Yes	Zaire	1995–99	Yes
Morocco	1975–79	Yes	Zimbabwe	1970–74	No

13

MOTIVATIONS FOR CONFLICT
GROUPS AND INDIVIDUALS

Frances Stewart and
Graham Brown

V IOLENT CONFLICT IS UNDOUBTEDLY a major cause of underdevelopment. Both country studies and cross-country regressions show the heavy economic costs of civil wars. Indeed, twenty-two out of the thirty-two countries with the lowest human development have experienced civil war since 1990.[1] It is also widely accepted that underdevelopment is a major cause of conflict, thus giving rise to a vicious cycle in which poverty begets conflict and conflict begets poverty, summarized in a recent publication as "the conflict trap."[2] Yet the assumption of a straightforward causal relationship between poverty and conflict is oversimple, as indicated by the middle-income or even high-income countries that suffer conflict, such as Northern Ireland, the Balkan countries, and the Basque region of Spain, and by very poor countries that avoid conflict, such as Malawi, Tanzania, and Zambia. This chapter aims to explore the economic causes of contemporary civil wars, asking whether it is simply poverty or more complex situations that cause conflict, with a view to

identifying policies that might help prevent conflict and its recurrence.

The incidence of conflict has changed over time, as figure 1 shows. Between 1945 and the end of the 1980s, there was a steady rise in conflict. Since the end of the Cold War, however, conflict incidence has fallen off sharply, although there was a resurgence of serious conflict in Africa—in 1998 the number of serious conflicts was at the same level as at the peak in the early 1990s. Africa suffered by far the largest number of major conflicts during the 1990s, with over 40 percent of the total. However, lesser conflicts (those with deaths of twenty-five to one thousand annually and more than one thousand cumulatively) were concentrated in Asia. This alone shows that there is no simple equation between poverty and conflict—poverty at a global level has been mostly falling proportionately (although constant or rising in absolute numbers) since 1945. However, the incidence of conflict is undoubtedly heaviest among low-income countries. Thus it is estimated that, from 1960 to 1995,

Figure 1. Global Warfare Trends, 1945–2004

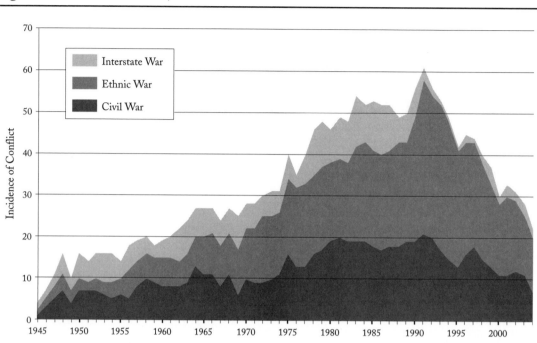

Source: Monty G. Marshall, *Major Episodes of Political Violence, 1946–2004* (Severn, Md.: Center for Systemic Peace, 2005), http://members.aol.com/cspmgm/warlist/htm (accessed July 15, 2005).

0.5 percent of the population of low-income countries died due to conflict, while the proportion was 0.3 percent among lower-middle-income countries and 0.1 percent among upper-middle-income countries.[3] Econometric analysis also shows that low income per capita is a predisposing factor for conflict.[4]

Any review of conflicts shows a considerable variety of types of conflicts, distinguished by their ideology and forms of mobilization, the nature of warfare, and the extent of external intervention or influence. Important types of conflicts over the past decades include

- "Wars by proxy" fought during the Cold War, where East and West supported different sides of a locally fought conflict with funds, arms, and "advisers" in order to capture that country for their own side. Examples are the wars in Central America, Vietnam, Mozambique, and Afghanistan.

Some of these wars ended when the Cold War did, but others gained a life of their own (e.g., Afghanistan). New forms of international intervention are associated with the war against terrorism, such as the current United States military support for the Philippines counterinsurgency operations in the secessionist Muslim south.

- Military "interventions" in domestic conflict by outside powers, usually on the pretext of some alleged abuse committed by the incumbent regime. Since the end of the Cold War particularly, this type of conflict has predominantly been associated with the West; examples are Kosovo, the 2001 invasion of Afghanistan, and the wars in Iraq. But there are other examples that do not involve the West, such as Vietnam's invasion of Cambodia.

- Revolutionary wars, aiming to overturn the established order. Examples are the Khmer

Rouge in Cambodia, the Colombian conflict (especially in its early stages), the Shining Path in Peru, and the rebellion by the Maoists in Nepal.

♦ Wars fought for regional independence or autonomy, such as the wars in Ethiopia (Eritrea), Nigeria (Biafra), Sri Lanka (the Tamils), Russia (Chechnya), southern Sudan, Kosovo, Spain (the Basques), and the southern Philippines (Muslim separatists).

♦ Wars fought to gain (or retain) political supremacy by particular groups representing specific cultures (ethnicities or religion). These include the conflicts in Rwanda, Burundi, Northern Ireland, and Uganda.

♦ Wars fought by coalitions of groups to gain political supremacy—for example, the conflicts in the Democratic Republic of the Congo and Sierra Leone.

Some conflicts fall into more than one of these categories. Besides the first two categories—which quintessentially involve external forces—most conflicts have international or regional dimensions; the Democratic Republic of the Congo is a recent example. These international dimensions can complicate or facilitate peacemaking.

Some wars are initiated by the economically deprived and those without political power, yet others are initiated by the relatively privileged. The variety and complexity of the typology of conflicts suggests that there is no simple single causal explanation. The next section of this chapter will review four alternative economic explanations of conflict and summarize some of the evidence for (and against) each. The third section will consider policy implications emanating from the conclusions of this review.

ECONOMIC EXPLANATIONS OF VIOLENT CONFLICT

While some attribute contemporary conflicts to fundamental differences arising from ethnicity or religion,[5] such differences are evidently an insufficient explanation as many multiethnic or multireligious societies live peacefully —for example, Ghana and Tanzania—while others are at peace for decades before experiencing conflict. In fact, the vast majority of multiethnic societies are at peace.[6] As Abner Cohen succinctly stated three decades ago:

> Men may and do certainly joke about or ridicule the strange and bizarre customs of men from other ethnic groups, because these customs are different from their own. But they do not fight over such differences alone. When men do, on the other hand, fight across ethnic lines it is nearly always the case that they fight over some fundamental issues concerning the distribution and exercise of power, whether economic, political, or both.[7]

Four economic explanations have dominated recent analysis: the first explanation points to group motives and group inequalities as a source of conflict; the second focuses on individual gains from conflict; the third is derived from a failed "social contract"; and the fourth theorizes that environmental pressures are a major source of conflict ("green war").

Group Motivation

Political conflicts, in contrast to most forms of criminality, consist of fighting between groups: groups that wish to gain independence or take over the state, and other groups that resist this, aiming to preserve the integrity of the nation or their own power.[8] The groups that fight are united under a common banner, with broadly common purposes. These common purposes may be termed "group motives" for conflict. While individual motivation is also important, it appears that group motivation and mobilization underlie many political conflicts.

Groups engaged in internal conflict are often united by a common ethnic or religious identity. Since 1945, the proportion of conflicts attributable to ethnic violence has been steadily increasing (figure 2). Such conflicts are generally presented as religious (e.g., in the Philippines and Thailand) or ethnic (as in Rwanda

Figure 2. Trends in Ethnic Conflict, 1945–2004

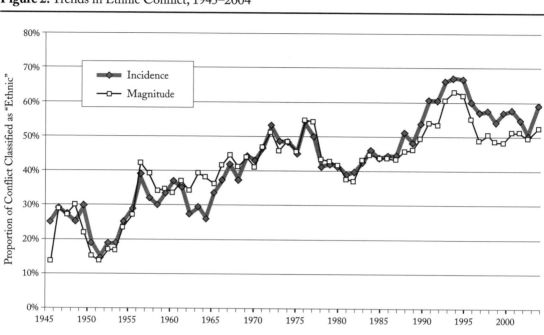

Source: Monty G. Marshall, *Major Episodes of Political Violence, 1946–2004* (Severn, Md.: Center for Systemic Peace, 2005), http://members.aol.com/cspmgm/warlist/htm (accessed July 15, 2005).

and Burundi); such identities provide a powerful source of mobilization and unity. Yet many multiethnic and multireligious societies live relatively peacefully, and in many situations, the majority of people do not perceive ethnic or religious identities as being of overriding importance. Hence we need to look beyond religion or ethnicity, as such, to find the causes of "ethnic" conflict. One plausible hypothesis is that it is where there are significant underlying differences in access to economic or political resources, providing both leaders and followers with a strong motive to fight, that ethnic or religious differences can lead to violent mobilization. Ted Robert Gurr terms such group differences "relative deprivation," and Frances Stewart defines differences in groups' access to economic, social, and political resources as "horizontal inequalities," in contrast to the traditional "vertical inequalities," which rank individuals rather than groups.[9] The horizontal

inequalities explanation of conflict is based on the view that when cultural differences coincide with economic and political differences between groups, this can cause deep resentments that may lead to violent struggles. These inequalities may involve regional differentiation, in which case they often lead to separatist movements (as in Aceh, Indonesia, and the Tamil regions of Sri Lanka), or the different identities may occur within the same geographic space (such as in Rwanda, Northern Ireland, and Uganda), where political participation and economic and political rights are at stake.

Horizontal inequalities (HIs) are multidimensional, involving access to a large variety of resources along economic, social, and political vectors or dimensions. Along the economic vector it is not just income that is important, but also access to employment and to a variety of assets (land, credit, education). Along the social vector, access to services (e.g., health care, water) and to assets (housing) can form relevant HIs. The political vector includes power at the top (presidency, cabinet), at lower levels (parliamentary assemblies, local government), in the bureaucracy at all levels, and in the army and the police. The relevant HIs are those that matter to people, and this varies across societies. For example, in Zimbabwe unequal access to land is important, while in Northern Ireland important differences concern HIs in housing, education, and jobs. HIs seem to be more provocative where they are consistent across dimensions, notably the political and economic dimensions. The evidence seems to suggest that economic and social HIs provide the conditions that lead to dissatisfaction among the general population and, consequently, give rise to the possibilities of political mobilization, but it is political exclusion that is likely to trigger a conflict, by giving group leaders a powerful motive to organize in order to gain support. There is also often a provocative cultural dimension, providing powerful assistance in group mobilization. Examples of cultural issues that give rise to inequalities and resentments are decisions on official languages, religion, or cultural events that favor one group or the other; in the presence of other disposing conditions, such cultural events can provoke violence.[10] The Orange marches in Northern Ireland and the adoption of Sinhalese as the official language in Sri Lanka are examples.

While horizontal inequalities give rise to political movements, these are not necessarily violent. Whether they become violent depends on whether the demands can be accommodated by the political system, or whether they meet resistance. It is important to note that relatively rich groups may instigate conflict, as may relatively poor groups. The relatively rich do so mainly to preserve their riches (and/or power) for themselves, while the relatively poor do so out of a sense of injustice with the intention of achieving some redistribution.

Empirical evidence is accumulating that severe horizontal inequalities constitute a significant cause of violent conflict. In the socioeconomic dimension, cross-sectional quantitative analyses have shown a significant relationship between various dimensions of socioeconomic inequality and conflict. Luca Mancini, for instance, shows that differences in infant mortality rates, which can be taken as a broad proxy for baseline levels of socioeconomic deprivation, between ethnic or religious groups within the districts of Indonesia help explain the location of the wave of communal conflicts that occurred after the fall of Suharto's regime in 1998.[11] Scott Gates and Mansoob Murshed find a significant relationship between "spatial" horizontal inequalities (i.e., differentials between geographical regions) and the intensity of the Maoist insurgency in Nepal.[12] Although multicountry studies have been hampered by a lack of consistent and comparable data, Gudrun Østby found some supporting evidence in a multicountry, multiregional study, while W. L. Barrows found similar evidence across African countries. There is also substantial case study evidence; for example, Stewart's review of the experiences of nine countries shows not only that increasing socioeconomic HIs have preceded the emergence of violent conflict, but that reductions in socioeconomic HIs, such as occurred in Northern Ireland during the 1980s, may contribute to the conditions for a peaceful resolution of such conflicts.[13] However, the connection between HIs and violent conflict is not an automatic one, and some societies show severe HIs without experiencing conflict (e.g., Bolivia, Brazil, and Ghana). Political inclusiveness is one reason that some societies avoid conflict despite severe economic horizontal inequalities; Ghana, for example, has included political representation of all major groups in government. Nigeria has managed an uneasy peace (post-Biafra) by following the federal principle of incorporating people from all regions in government at every level. Moreover, horizontal inequalities were not consistent in Nigeria: most political power was in the hands of northerners, but the southern parts of the country were better off from an economic and social perspective.

Political horizontal inequalities—the exclusion or underrepresentation of groups within the political structure of a state—can provoke violent conflict when they change abruptly. In Côte d'Ivoire, three decades of postindependence rule by Félix Houphouët-Boigny avoided significant conflict, largely due to the policy of balancing representatives of the major groups in positions of importance in the government and bureaucracy. Following Houphouët-Boigny's death and the introduction of multiparty elections in the early 1990s, political leaders sought to mobilize ethnic sentiments to enforce their grip on power and thus undermined Houphouët-Boigny's careful balancing act, leading to a spiral of ethnicization, xenophobia, and, ultimately, civil war.[14]

Private Motivation

People who fight have their own private motivation for doing so as well as loyalty to the group that is fighting. War confers benefits as well as costs on some individuals. Political sociologists such as David Keen and Mark Duffield and economists such as Paul Collier and Anke Hoeffler have emphasized private or individual motivation as the fundamental cause of conflict.[15] The private motivation hypothesis has its basis in rational choice economics, arguing that the net economic advantages of war to some individuals motivate them to fight.[16] In this approach, group identities are regarded not as an independent factor but as instruments, created to help fulfill the private motives of those who fight (especially leaders).

Keen lists many ways in which war confers individual benefit on particular categories of people: it permits people, especially uneducated young men, to gain employment as soldiers; it offers opportunities to loot, to profiteer from shortages and from aid; to trade arms; and to carry out illicit production and trade. Where alternative opportunities are few, because of low incomes and poor employment, and the possibilities of enrichment by war are considerable, wars are likely to be more numerous and last longer. Conflicts may persist because some powerful actors benefit through the manipulation of scarcity, smuggling, and so forth and have no interest in resolving the conflict. An oft-cited case used to support this argument is the role of "conflict diamonds" in the protraction of the civil war in Sierra Leone.[17] Private motivation seems also to be a predominant factor behind the persistent conflict in the Democratic Republic of the Congo, where abundant natural resources offer big rewards to those who control them.

Collier and Hoeffler put forward econometric evidence to support the "greed" hypothesis, arguing that the observation that conflict incidence increases as the share of primary products exports in GDP rises (up to a point) supports the view that conflict is caused by individual greed.[18] However, the share of primary products exports in GDP is a very crude approximation of "greed," and the results have been shown not to be robust to alternative specifications.[19] There is stronger evidence that oil resources are associated with conflict, but this, too, depends on the model specification and exclusions of outliers.[20] Case studies suggest that even where natural resources are abundant, private maximizing motives are rarely the full explanation. As a study of seven countries in conflict concluded: "[V]ery few contemporary conflicts can be adequately captured as pure instance of 'resource wars.' . . . Economic incentives have not been the only or even the primary causes of these conflicts."[21]

It is difficult to accept that rational choice can explain the extreme case of suicide attacks, although Mark Harrison has recently developed a model that attempts to explain these attacks by their appeal to a person's sense of identity and self-worth.[22] However, in so doing, the explanation moves right away from individual aggrandizement to community injustices and community constraints and incentives that influence individuals' perceptions of their own identity. Although suicide attacks account for only a small proportion of violence and can be argued to be unrepresentative, most cases of conflict involve a high risk of death or debilitating injury, which, from a rational choice perspective, would seriously hamper future opportunities for utility, so that "rational" actors might be likely to choose another option before engaging in rebellion. However, while this argument seems relevant to those directly involved in fighting, it may have less force when applied to leaders, who are rarely killed or injured. Hence leaders could be motivated by self-aggrandizement, while their followers may not follow maximizing logic but may be coerced into fighting, or persuaded to fight by leaders playing up religious or ethnic differences and grievances:

> Grievance is to a rebel organization what image is to a business. In the economist's view of conflict, grievance will turn out to be neither a cause of conflict, nor an accidental by-product of it. Rather, a sense of grievance is deliberately generated by rebel organizations . . . [rebel supporters] are gulled into believing the discourse which self-interested rebel leaders promote.[23]

At this point the group explanation and the individual explanation of conflict come together. It is hard to persuade people to risk their lives for grievances that are not genuine (i.e., unless there is some sort of exclusion or economic horizontal inequality), while it seems that leaders may be, at least in part, motivated by personal ambition in both the HI and the individual maximizing paradigms. In both cases, it is argued that they are motivated by political exclusion (i.e., political horizontal inequalities), which denies them access to resources and power.

While generally not a sufficient explanation of conflict, it is clear that the expected rewards sometimes play a role in the decision to rebel. As Collier notes, citing the cases of Aceh (Indonesia), Biafra (Nigeria), and Katanga (Zaire), separatist rebellion often emerges in resource-rich areas of a country, leading him to conclude that rebellion is "the rage of the rich."[24] However, there are also examples of separatist movements in regions with poor resource endowment—for example, the Muslim rebellion in Thailand, the Tamils in Sir Lanka, and Eritrea and Bangladesh. In resource-rich areas, the gains (and motivation) may be individual or group, or both. However, in many cases the leaders of the rebellions left lucrative and safe positions to instigate rebellion. Hassan di Tiro, for example, left a secure position at the United Nations in New York to instigate the Acehnese uprising. In the case of Colombia, often depicted as a "greed"-motivated conflict, interviews with both leaders and those who were mobilized to fight show that generally their economic position worsened as a result of participating in the conflict—most put forward ideological reasons for fighting, including the issue of land reform.[25] Thus short-run self-aggrandizement does not seem to be uppermost as a motive for these leaders. Moreover, the conflicts in the natural resource–rich areas were framed in ethnic terms—the Acehnese in Indonesia, the Igbo in Biafra, and the "authentic" Katanga groups (as opposed to migrant communities) in Zaire. It seems that promoting the objective of political and cultural autonomy for the ethnic group was also an important source of mobilization.

Hence, while individual maximization is certainly part of the story, it is clearly not the whole story. Group identities and group mobilization are also generally present. While leaders undoubtedly often do sell identities as a way of securing support, they cannot create an identity out of nothing: "the [past] acts as a constraint on invention. Though the past can be read in different ways, it is not any past."[26] A common history, language, culture, or religion is generally required to generate felt identities powerful enough to mobilize people for conflict. Nor can leaders expect support unless there are genuine grievances among those who follow them—political, economic, social, or cultural.

Failure of the Social Contract

The third explanation of violent conflict points directly to grievances. It derives from the view that social stability is implicitly premised on a social contract between the people and the government. According to this (hypothetical) contract, people accept state authority as long as the state delivers services and provides reasonable economic conditions in terms of employment and incomes. With economic stagnation or decline, and worsening state services, the social contract breaks down, and violence results. Hence high (and rising) levels of poverty and a decline in state services would be expected to cause conflict.[27] High vertical inequality might also be associated with such a failure, unless accompanied by populist measures to compensate the deprived. Conversely, political institutions that are able to channel and respond to socioeconomic discontents strengthen the social contract and thus reduce the risk of conflict.

Considerable evidence from econometric studies shows that conflict incidence is higher among countries with lower per capita incomes, life expectancy, and economic growth.[28] Many analyses have found an inverted-U-curve relationship between the extent of democratization in a country and the risk of conflict, whereby the incidence of conflict both in consolidated democracies and in extreme authoritarian regimes is lower than in those countries that fall into categories in between. The usual interpretation of this is that "stable" democracies are indeed able to avert violent conflict through a strong social contract, while strongly authoritarian regimes are able to suppress potential conflict.[29] Recent attention, however, has focused on the process of democratization as a time of particular vulnerability to the emergence of conflict, while Marta Reynal-Querol has suggested that it is the particular

type of democracy—whether majoritarian, presidential, or proportional representation—that affects propensity to conflict, rather than the level of "democracy" per se.[30]

"Green War" (Environmental Scarcity)

The fourth explanation of violent conflict, associated with the work of Thomas Homer-Dixon and the Toronto Group, is the "green war," or "environmental scarcity," argument.[31] The essence of this perspective is that contest for control over declining natural resources, often intensified by population pressures, is a major cause of violent conflict around the world. Poorer societies are more at risk because they will be "less able to buffer themselves" from environmental pressures.[32] Three dimensions of environmental scarcity are identified that may lead to conflict: "supply-induced scarcity," linked to the "depletion and degradation of an environmental resource"; "demand-induced scarcity," linked to population growth and the consequent extra pressures on existing resources; and "structural scarcity," which "arises from an unequal distribution of a resource that concentrates it in the hands of a relatively few people."[33] The Toronto Group suggests that there will probably be "an upsurge of violence in the coming decades that will be induced or aggravated by scarcity."[34]

The environmental scarcity hypothesis, in its various manifestations, overlaps substantially with the other hypotheses discussed here. It overlaps with the social contract hypothesis, for instance, in viewing poverty as a root cause of conflict, although it points to specific environmental causes of such poverty. It also often overlaps with the group motivation approach, as proponents emphasize that environmental pressures usually lead to conflict where there are "groups with strong collective identities that can coherently challenge state authority."[35] Indeed, the "structural scarcity" dimension of the green war approach is clearly very similar to the models of relative deprivation and horizontal inequality, albeit restricted to a particular dimension of inequality. In other manifestations, notably Robert Kaplan's prediction of a "coming anarchy" linking environmental degradation with increasing criminality and lawlessness, the environmental scarcity argument has more in common with the private motivation approach.[36]

The environmental scarcity view has been criticized by James Fairhead, who argues that it is environmental riches, not scarcity, that are associated with conflict, interpreting environmental riches as the presence of valuable natural resources such as those found in Congo.[37] The environmental riches hypothesis thus fits into the private motivation/greed hypothesis. In fact, both environmental poverty and environmental riches may cause conflict, for different reasons and in different circumstances.

Other critiques of the green war hypothesis include the accusations of a lack of conceptual clarity and of a somewhat fatalistic approach that leaves few policy options open for conflict prevention and resolution.[38] In addition, the decade that has passed since Homer-Dixon and Kaplan alike predicted an increase in conflict has seen, instead, a significant decline in worldwide conflict. It remains to be seen whether the experience of future decades will validate their predictions. Nonetheless, it is clear that while pressures arising from environmental scarcity may play an important role in many conflicts, the environmental scarcity hypothesis is—and really doesn't claim to be more—a partial theory that contributes toward our understanding of causes of a set of conflicts, but not the general conditions under which conflict is more likely to arise.

◆ ◆ ◆

These theories of conflict causes appear, in their extreme formulations, to be diametrically opposed—the oft-cited "greed versus grievance" debate being a clear example. But, as we have seen, more often than not proponents of one perspective accept or support in part the insights of the others. It seems that some conflicts are neatly explained by one of the explanations, some are explained by others, and some clearly have multiple causes. For example, Keen has explained the long conflict in Sudan as the product of individual greed, as government and soldiers use the war to advance their own economic positions.[39] Yet it can also be seen as an example of sharp HIs, where southerners rebel against their exploitation and seek autonomy, while northerners seek to preserve their privilege.[40] The rebellion in the south can also be seen as an example of a failed social contract: although provision of services for the country as a whole has been improving, service provision in the south is grossly inadequate, there is no physical security, and there is virtually no advantage to being part of the Sudanese state. Finally, the poverty of Sudanese (in both south and west) can be interpreted as due to environmental pressures, and the wars explained as being green wars. Most contemporary conflicts can similarly be explained in terms of more than one of the four explanations just advanced, although in many cases it seems that one (or two) of the explanations is dominant.

Therefore, one rather simple conclusion, which qualitative analysts of conflict are mostly aware of but quantitative analysts tend to overlook, is that each of the broad causal theories discussed involves a degree of oversimplification and excessive generalization. The causes and dynamics of any single conflict are typically complex and sometimes contradictory and involve aspects of many, if not all, of the perspectives discussed. Yet it is important to understand which explanation dominates in a particular case, since this has important implications for appropriate policy prescriptions for the prevention and resolution of the conflict.

Conflict, Poverty, and Underdevelopment

Where does this leave the "poverty and underdevelopment" explanation of conflict? Each of the explanations intersects differently with poverty and underdevelopment. Table 1 illustrates this, showing the main variables associated with conflict, according to the different explanations. As far as group differences and HIs are concerned, it is not absolute poverty but relative poverty that matters. For civil wars, what matters is sharing resources of all kinds across all communities; shared poverty and underdevelopment would not lead to conflict. Where a society is poor but some groups succeed in securing a disproportionate share, there may be a predisposition to conflict: Nepal is an example, where strong caste and geographic inequality have led to acute relative deprivation in the context of a society that is generally quite poor. Moving to the international dimensions of contemporary conflicts, underdevelopment in the South is associated with acute North/South HIs that may be potentially destabilizing. A more specific case is the sharp economic divide between Palestine and Israel, which is a mobilizing factor for Muslims elsewhere—an element in the current terrorist threats.

For those who emphasize individual maximization and rational choice, poverty and underdevelopment lower the opportunity costs of wars. If people, especially young men, lack employment or fruitful income-earning opportunities, even the quite moderate "riches" conferred by war may offer them an attractive alternative. Those who argue for the overwhelming importance of individual motivation of this type point to the empirical correlations of conflict incidence with low average incomes and low levels of education. However, this view of conflict is based on the premise that fighting does offer opportunities for enrichment. This is difficult to argue in very poor societies, such as Afghanistan and Somalia. The general emphasis on "greed" rather than "grievance" in this approach, then, points not so much to poverty and underdevelopment as to natural resource riches (supplemented by aid flows) as the major source of conflict.

The social contract theory incorporates poverty as part of the explanation of conflict. The failed social contract arises because the state fails to deliver—in terms of social services, economic opportunities, and physical security. Poverty and underdevelopment are certainly part of this failure. Afghanistan and Somalia are clear examples. Yet there are poor societies where the state succeeds in providing basic services and sharing the limited opportunities. Low average incomes in a society do not necessarily imply a failed social contract. Some poor states, for example, Tanzania, succeed in delivering sufficient, if minimal, social services and physical security and avoid chronic conflict. Moreover, such countries often experience faster growth rates over the long term, as with Botswana and Malaysia.

The green war hypothesis is certainly in tune with an explanation associated with poverty and underdevelopment, to the extent that the poverty is caused by environmental pressures. However, there are many other causes of poverty and underdevelopment, so this explanation does not provide a general connection between poverty, underdevelopment, and conflict.

While there are many connections between poverty and conflict, then, the view that if we could only eliminate poverty we would also eliminate conflict is not supported by the analysis here. On the one hand, absolute poverty might be eliminated, yet conflict could well persist, as long as HIs continued and some groups were excluded politically as well as economically. On the other hand, a poor society can also be a fair and inclusive one and need not be prone to conflict. Conflict would become less likely if development efforts were successful, leading to a lessening of some sources of conflict—this is shown by the econometric evidence. But policies for the prevention of conflict need to go beyond raising average incomes or reducing poverty if they are to be successful.

Table 1. Summary of Hypotheses and Evidence on Causal Factors in Conflict

Economic Variables Associated with Conflict	Evidence of Association with Conflict	Hypotheses
Decline/stagnation in per capita incomes	Cross-country and case study support	Failure of social contract; environmental degradation; low opportunity costs of war—private motive
Horizontal inequality	Cross-country and case study support	Group motives for conflict (horizontal inequalities)
Vertical inequality	Conflicting evidence	Failure of social contract
High poverty	Same evidence as for per capita incomes	Failure of social contract; green war; private motives
Reduced government revenue and social expenditure	Case study evidence; limited statistical investigation; no evidence for association with IMF programs	Failure of social contract; weak government ability to suppress conflict—failed state
High levels of natural resources	Support for mineral resources only	Private motives (and financing)
Political Factors Associated with Conflict		
History of conflict	Strong statistical and case study evidence	Persistence of economic conditions giving rise to conflict; memory of conflict acting as mobilizing agent
State expenditure as low proportion of national income	Casual evidence	Weak states
Unequal access to political power among groups	Case study and statistical evidence	Horizontal inequalities
Intermediate political regime	Statistical and case study evidence	Inability to negotiate change or suppress violence

ECONOMIC, SOCIAL, AND POLITICAL POLICIES AIMED AT PREVENTING CONFLICT

Economic and social policies may contribute in each of the three stages of conflict: preconflict, conflict, and postconflict. First, in a preconflict situation, where there is no conflict but there is a high probability of one occurring, preventive policies should be aimed at changing the underlying conditions in such a way as to make the outbreak of conflict less likely. Second, when a conflict has broken out, economic and social policies can help protect the economy and people against some of the costs resulting from the conflict, for example, through food distribution.[41] Third, after a conflict has ended, policies are needed to help reconstruct the economy. This section focuses primarily on preventive policies—these are most obviously relevant to the preconflict situation but are also relevant to the other stages, particularly the postconflict situation, since there is generally a high probability of the conflict recurring soon after a conflict has ended and it is therefore vital to introduce preventive policies. Of course, the postconflict stage also requires more straight-forward reconstruction policies, such as investment to replace destroyed facilities, and policies to integrate the combatants into peaceful activities. These are not considered here.

If conflicts are regarded as irrational or caused by unavoidable ethnic clashes, there is little role for policy other than repression or separating people from different groups. But to the extent that conflicts are the outcome of economic causes, preventive policies may be effective in reducing their incidence. Each of the different theories discussed here has implications for preventive policies, which will be considered in this section. The policies should be applied to all countries that are vulnerable to conflict; which policies are relevant will depend on the situation and which theory most closely approximates the situation.

Evidence suggests the following types of countries are clearly vulnerable to conflict:

- All low-income, low-human-development countries, given the fact that at least half of these countries have been in conflict at some time over the past thirty years and that all econometric evidence points to low income as a correlate with conflict
- Any country that has been in conflict over the past thirty years, because the evidence shows that previous conflict is the most significant pointer to further conflict
- Any country with high horizontal inequalities in political or economic dimensions, as such countries are likely to suffer from conflict
- Countries whose political regime is "intermediate," that is, in transition from strong repressive regimes to more democratic regimes

Three types of policies are needed, directed at the main factors responsible for conflict:

- Policies to address horizontal inequalities (policies aimed at group motives)
- Policies to reduce the functionality of conflict (i.e., to address private motives)
- Policies to promote equitable and sustainable development (i.e., to address social contract failures and environmental pressures)

Correcting Horizontal Inequalities

The general direction of policy change to avoid violence must be to reduce group inequalities. To achieve this, it is essential to have politically, economically, and socially inclusive policies. These include policies to achieve geographically balanced benefits, as well as balance between ethnicities, religions, or races. Politically, this means that all major groups in a society participate in political power: the administration, the army, and the police. Inclusive economic outcomes require that horizontal inequality in economic aspects (assets, employment, and incomes) be moderate; inclusive social outcomes require that horizontal inequality in social participation and achieved well-being also be moderate. "Moderate" is a loose term. Group equality would be the ideal. "Horizontal equity" describes a degree of horizontal inequality that is acceptable to major groups in society, and hence such a degree of horizontal inequality would be unlikely to provoke conflict. The importance of any measure of inequality is increased if it occurs systematically over a number of dimensions and grows over time. Hence, such considerations should enter into a judgment of what an acceptable degree of horizontal inequality is. The general objective of inclusivity and moderate horizontal inequality will translate differently into specific policy recommendations in particular cases, depending on the relevant groups in the society, the dimensions of importance in the particular society, and those in which there is substantial horizontal inequality.

Political Inclusivity. The most universal requirement is for political inclusivity because it is monopolization of political power by one group or another that is normally responsible for many of the other inequalities. Yet achieving political inclusivity is among the most difficult changes to bring about. It is not just a matter of democracy, defined as rule with the support of the majority, since majority rule can be consistent with abuse of minorities, as, for example, in the recent history of Rwanda, Cambodia, and Zimbabwe; as long ago as the 1830s, Alexis de Tocqueville had identified the potential problems of the "tyranny of the majority."[42] In a politically inclusive democratic system, particular types of proportional representation are needed to ensure participation by all major groups in the elected bodies. For inclusive government, representation of all such groups is essential not only at the level of the cabinet but also in other organs of government. For political inclusivity, members of major groups also need to be included at all levels of the civil service, the army, and the police. An excellent example of how institutionalization of inclusive politics can avert conflict comes from Switzerland, where the 1848 federal constitution institutionalized a high degree of power sharing, bringing to an end centuries of intermittent fighting between Protestant and Catholic cantons.

It should be emphasized that political participation can occur at many levels (central, regional, local), in different types of decisions (defense, economic, social), and in different institutions (army, police, civil service). Full political participation means that significant groups in the population participate across the board, and that their presence is not just nominal. There are many ways this can be promoted, each of which has been adopted, in some form or another, in divided societies.[43] Here we touch briefly on major aspects:

- A federal constitution. Where groups are mainly separate geographically, a federal constitution can empower different groups, as in the case of Belgium and Switzerland. Nigeria is an example of how the design of the constitution can affect the propensity to conflict. India is an example of a huge developing country that has maintained peace at a national level, probably partly due to its federal constitution.

- The extent and nature of decentralization. Decentralization, like federalism, can contribute to power sharing. This may have been one reason why Bolivia avoided conflict despite deep HIs. But decentralization does not always work in the intended way; it can replace one set of power brokers with another, which may or may not diffuse group domination.[44] Where groups are geographically concentrated, such decentralization may give greater political power to previously underrepresented groups, but it can also lead to continued (or even greater) disempowerment for some (normally minority) groups within the decentralized areas, as is also the case with federalism (e.g., in Nigeria).

- The voting system. A proportional representation (PR) system, or similar voting system, gives more power to minorities, but even with PR a majority can dominate decision making unless a power-sharing system in elected assemblies and other government bodies is also adopted. Such systems are rare in developing countries, although it is worth reporting that no country with PR has had serious internal conflict.[45]

- The nature of the elected assemblies. In a bicameral assembly, it is possible to combine democratic representation in one house of the assembly with geographic (as in the United States) or group representation in the other. The voting system within assemblies can be designed to prevent a single group from dominating (e.g., by requiring a two-thirds majority or by granting veto powers to particular groups).

- Seat reservation in parliament for particular groups. This has been adopted for the unscheduled castes and tribes in India and also for women in a number of countries. It is an important feature of the new Iraqi constitution.

- Employment allocations within government. There can be formal or informal provisions for a fair share of political posts at every level, including the presidency, the cabinet, the senior civil service, the military, and the police. For example, there is provision for three presidents in Bosnia and Herzegovina; postconflict Cambodia had two prime ministers for many years.

- Citizenship rights. These can be comprehensive, covering all who live in an area, or highly restrictive, requiring several generations of residence or extended only to "blood" relatives of some "original" inhabitants. Exclusionary citizenship rights can be highly provocative (as in Côte d'Ivoire), but relatively easy access to citizenship rights can also generate local resentment where this is seen as an attempt to "dilute" a regional minority, as in the Malaysian state of Sabah.

- Constraints on political parties. When there are no constraints, political parties in divided societies tend to become "ethnic."[46] For this reason, multiparty elections often provoke violence.[47] Policies toward political parties range from outlawing them altogether (as in Yoweri Museveni's Uganda) to requiring them to have multiethnic support (e.g., in Nigeria). While such policies can prevent the ethnicization of party politics, they can prove problematic where genuine regional grievances exist. The Indonesian constitution, for instance, bans regional political parties, a ban that was a major sticking point in the recently concluded peace negotiations in the province of Aceh.

- Human rights protection. Strong protection of civil liberties and human rights does not ensure power sharing, but it does limit the abuse of power and clearly has an important role to play. Conversely, some (semi-)authoritarian regimes have used the ethnic diversity of their population to justify limitations on human rights, particularly those relating to freedom of speech and freedom of assembly.

This account has briefly touched on the many policies that can be used to ensure political participation of major groups. There has been considerable experience in designing political systems to achieve inclusive and balanced political participation in sharply divided societies struggling to maintain peace and cohesion. Among developed countries, Belgium and Switzerland are prime examples. Many developing countries initially overcame these problems through authoritarian regimes that suppressed dissent, but the political issues associated with multiethnic societies are coming to the fore with democratization. The widely recommended formula of majoritarian multiparty democracy is inadequate, and postconflict countries have struggled to find alternative, more inclusive models. Nigeria, Fiji, Ethiopia, and Malaysia are examples, having modified their political systems as a consequence of political unrest. It is clear that policies to address political HIs need to accompany economic and social policies if renewed conflict is to be avoided.

Economic and Social Inclusivity. It is not always a straightforward matter to decide what economic and social inclusivity means. Should one aim for equality in opportunities, in access to resources, or in outcomes? Apparent equality of opportunities may lead to very unequal outcomes because of a variety of implicit practices and past disadvantages of some groups relative to others. The liberal philosophy of "equal opportunities" is at best a necessary condition for advancing group equality. Equality in access to resources is likely to get nearer to providing a genuine level playing field, but it may still result in inequalities of outcomes (defined very broadly in terms of health, income per capita, and educational achievements) because the disadvantaged group is likely to be less efficient at using a particular set of assets. For equality of outcomes, inequality in access to targetable assets may be necessary, such as with education, land, and capital.

Policies toward achieving greater group equality in economic entitlements can be divided into three types, although the distinctions are not watertight: first, policies aimed at changing processes that are either directly or indirectly discriminatory can be adopted; second, assistance can be directed to particular groups; and third, targets and quotas can be introduced for education, land distribution, and financial and physical assets.

The first type of policy is not so different from any set of policies to promote competition, although it involves a much more careful search for indirectly discriminatory policies than is usual. It is likely to be a relatively acceptable type of policy and can have a significant impact. For example, this was a major part of the policy set adopted in Northern Ireland. The second type of policy concerns the nature and distribution of public funds, often involving a redirection of expenditure across regions or neighborhoods, as well as groups within them. This is in principle within the control of the government, but it may meet resistance from privileged regions or from the government itself to the extent that it represents privileged groups. This type of policy requires careful review of the implications of all public expenditure (and other relevant policies) for the group distribution of benefits. It is noteworthy that such a review does not form an explicit consideration in the public expenditure reviews supported by the international donors, or that of most governments. The third type of policy, pertaining to quotas and targets, is the most controversial and politically provocative. It is this type of policy that many people mean when they talk of "affirmative action," although affirmative action can be interpreted as including all three types of policies.

If the public sector constitutes a major source of HIs (in education, employment, and infrastructure), a good deal can be achieved through direct action by the government. HIs located in the private sector are more difficult to tackle, though all three types of policies will make a contribution. The growing inequality in South Africa since 1994, despite government action, shows the importance of tackling inequalities that originate in the private sector.[48]

There are many cases where affirmative action has been adopted in one way or another, pointing to a large range of possible policies.[49] Such policies have been adopted in the North (as in the United States, New Zealand, and Northern Ireland) and the South (as in Fiji, India, Malaysia, South Africa, and Sri Lanka). Two sorts of programs can be distinguished: those introduced by disadvantaged majorities, for example, in Fiji (ethnic Fijians), Malaysia (Malays/Bumiputera), Namibia (black population), South Africa (black population), and Sri Lanka (Sinhalese); and those introduced by advantaged majorities for disadvantaged minorities, for example, in Brazil, India, Northern Ireland, and the United States.

Policies that have been introduced to correct group inequalities include

Policies to Correct Asset Distribution
- Policies to improve the group distribution of land through redistribution of government-owned land, forcible eviction, purchases, and restrictions on ownership (Malaysia, Zimbabwe, Fiji, and Namibia)
- Policies concerning the terms of privatization (Fiji and Malaysia)
- Financial assets: bank regulations, subsidizations, and restrictions (Malaysia and South Africa)
- Credit allocation preferences (Fiji and Malaysia)
- Preferential training (Brazil and New Zealand)
- Quotas for education (Malaysia, Sri Lanka, and the United States)

- Public sector infrastructure (South Africa)
- Housing (Northern Ireland)

Policies to Correct Income and Employment Distribution
- Employment policies, including public sector quotas (Malaysia, Sri Lanka, India) and the requirement for balanced employment in the private sector (South Africa)
- Transfer payments: although there are many cases of age-, disability-, and gender-related transfers, transfers according to ethnicity, religion, or race are rare

Reductions in sharp horizontal inequalities may be essential to produce a stable society, but their introduction can be provocative. The most clear-cut example is Sri Lanka, where policies to improve the position of the Sinhalese were a factor stimulating Tamil rebellion. In Zimbabwe, land policies, along with other policies, have been introduced in a highly provocative way and can hardly be taken as a model. In both cases, some action was almost certainly necessary if conflict was to be avoided in the longer run, but such policies clearly have to be introduced with sensitivity. In Malaysia, which has instituted arguably the most extensive and comprehensive policy package in history to reduce horizontal inequalities, the New Economic Policy (NEP), the successful implementation of these policies largely depended on acceptance of their political necessity by all groups, precisely because of the risk of instability associated with the status quo ante. Nonetheless, Chinese discontent with the NEP policies strengthened in the mid-1980s, when the spectacular growth of the previous decade stalled, suggesting that such policies are best implemented in an economic environment that is otherwise favorable.[50]

Reducing Private Incentives

For conflict prevention, it is helpful to introduce policies aimed at reducing the functionality of conflict. One important aspect of such policies is to increase people's peacetime economic opportunities, by extending their access to education and other assets and through a dynamic peacetime economy that offers people employment and earnings opportunities, so the gains that can be made during conflict (through theft, smuggling, looting, etc.) are less attractive.

Much of the profiting from war arises because of general lawlessness—where there is a weak state with little control over criminality. Strengthening the state can be an important aspect of preventive policies, yet the policy agenda today tends to weaken the state through the strong push toward the market, cutbacks in government expenditure, the increasing use of NGOs for service delivery, and moves toward decentralization of government. Governance reforms demanding greater transparency and accountability, aimed at improving the moral character and efficiency of the state, may not strengthen the state in the way required.

Expanding employment opportunities for young men is generally important in preventive policy, and especially for postconflict societies—high male unemployment is frequently associated with outbreaks of conflict, for example, in Sri Lanka and Algeria, while lack of opportunities in general is a common feature of many countries when conflict breaks out, including, for example, in the preconflict situation in Sierra Leone.

Another set of policies commonly recommended to reduce the private incentives for war aim at reducing the "rents" arising from natural resources.[51] These consist partly of domestic reforms, such as greater transparency and competition in the production and marketing of natural resources, and partly of international policies that may reduce trade in war commodities, such as diamonds and drugs. As with the policies discussed earlier, what is appropriate inevitably differs from country to country.

Restoring the Social Contract

Policies to restore the social contract have two important aspects. The more important is to generate equitable and sustainable economic growth. The other, which is closely related to the first, is to ensure that the government provides essential services, including health care and education, economic infrastructure and security—services that form an essential part of the social contract.

While it is universally agreed that equitable and sustainable development would make conflict less likely, this is difficult to achieve in conflict-prone countries. Many such countries have recently experienced conflict, with all the adverse implications for development that conflict entails. Moreover, even in peace, it is difficult to generate sustained development in poor countries with weak human capital, especially those heavily dependent on primary products.

A great deal of analysis has been devoted to delineating the conditions for widely shared growth. Economic growth requires sustained investment in physical and human capital, political stability, and a fair international system, including flows of aid to poor countries, modest debt servicing requirements, and stable terms of trade. It also requires a reasonably responsible and effective government. Equitable growth requires a fair distribution of assets, especially land, a comprehensive educational system, a robust employment situation, and a variety of safety nets for those who are unable to participate fully in the economy. In practice, very few poor countries do meet these requirements, particularly those falling into the "vulnerable to conflict" category.

In addition, the universal and effective provision of basic services is a critical requirement of the social contract, and one that is clearly not being fulfilled in many developing countries.[52] Yet this aspect of the contract is probably the easiest to achieve since the cost of basic services is just a fraction of the national income of even poor countries.

Taken as a whole, these form an ambitious set of policies. Particularly challenging is the aim of achieving equitable and sustainable growth, especially for low-income countries that have recently suffered conflict—the most vulnerable category of countries. One reassuring aspect is that the policies relevant to the different types of causes are in general consistent with one another. Indeed, some are complementary or even the same. For example, policies that promote horizontal equality will also generally promote equity, and the converse is likely to be true. Policies that promote equitable growth are also likely to reduce the incentives for low-income people to become fighters, since they will generate jobs and other income-earning opportunities. Policies that help fulfill the social contract, by extending basic services to everyone, will also help promote economic growth because of the importance of human capital. Policies that improve the physical security of a country are likely to help attract investment and thereby promote growth. Thus the policies reinforce one another. Moreover, they are generally desirable policies even without considering their conflict implications, as they lead to a fair and prospering society.

Policy change, however, is particularly difficult to achieve in the context of a country prone to violence, especially one having a history of conflict. In this context there are inherited memories and grievances, entrenched group identities, and intergroup animosities. The government is rarely broad based, often representing only a subset of the groups potentially involved in conflict. It would often be naive to think that the government even wants to promote peace, given the prevalence of state-instigated violence. In the case of Uganda, for example, the governments of Idi Amin and Milton Obote were themselves responsible for much of the violence. The same is true in Sudan.

Hence the policies suggested here may fall on hostile ears as far as many governments are concerned; the context for introducing policy change must be recognized as structurally unfavorable. Nonetheless, some governments do wish to promote peace (e.g., Nelson Mandela in South Africa and Yoweri Museveni when he first came to power in Uganda) and are willing to promote inclusive policies; in other cases, the majority group constitutes the relatively deprived one and is therefore keen to correct horizontal inequalities (e.g., Malaysia and South Africa).

The role of the international community is therefore important. Yet despite this and the fact that peace-promoting policies would also contribute to development, it is surprising the extent to which such policies are *not* the bread and butter of the international community's policy agenda. A review of policies adopted toward countries that had ended long conflicts and were clearly vulnerable to their renewal illustrates this dissonance:

- IMF insistence on the normal macrobudgetary requirements tended to impede the expenditures needed for infrastructural investment and social sector recovery, for example, in El Salvador and Nicaragua.[53]
- In order to restore or reinforce the social contract, there is a general need to raise revenue and expenditure to extend social services. Yet policies seem to do little toward this aim and often involve reductions in trade taxes, for example, in Rwanda, where government revenue was only 10 percent of GNP, and in Guatemala.[54]
- The objective of correcting horizontal inequalities is rarely an explicit element in policies. The need to have inclusive development is mentioned in World Bank documents, but in most cases no specific policies are recommended for this and the policies are not extended to vulnerable countries generally.[55] Detailed analysis of the postconflict situation in Mozambique shows the limited efforts devoted to correcting HIs—indeed, in Mozambique, economic postconflict policies, including aid distribution, worsened HIs—while the political system virtually disenfranchised major groups.[56] Malaysia is exceptional in this respect,

having introduced explicit affirmative action policies following ethnic rioting in 1969.

This review suggests that the leading economic institutions, the International Monetary Fund (IMF) and the World Bank, put the major focus on recommending responsible macropolicies, market-oriented policies to promote competition and efficiency, and poverty-reduction policies, but largely ignore policies aimed at horizontal equality and, for the most part, vertical inequality. Similarly, the political dialogue conducted by the international community with developing countries stresses the need for multiparty democracy rather than the need for inclusive government. It is important that preventive policies of the types just reviewed become part of development policy toward vulnerable societies.

A notable exception here is Nepal in recent years. Before the insurgency the international community adopted its normal policy-set, but donor policy shifted remarkably following the escalation of the Maoist insurgency in 2001. Whereas previously, the World Bank and other major donors had emphasized macroeconomic reforms, they now address socioeconomic exclusion as an important element of their country assistance strategy. Neither the World Bank nor other donors yet address *political* exclusion, however.[57]

THE NEW INTERNATIONAL SECURITY ENVIRONMENT AND CONFLICT IN POOR COUNTRIES

In the post–Cold War environment, East-West conflicts have been replaced by more location-specific conflicts, yet increasingly these conflicts have an ethnic or religious dimension, making them especially amenable to analysis using a horizontal inequality framework. In addition, the globalized nature of most conflicts has increased in many dimensions —in the nature of the conflicts and the support they get, in military interventions, and in finance and restrictions over finance—although it is easy to exaggerate the change. Almost everything one says about global connections could have been said before, but there has been a change in degree if not in kind. In this section, we consider how each of the four underlying socioeconomic causes of conflict —horizontal inequalities, private motivations, failed social contract, and green war—have played out at the global level, especially in recent years.

For the world as a whole, it seems that inequalities between countries have been falling, mainly due to the rapid growth of China and India.[58] But the politicization of global inequalities has increased. At a general level, this is exemplified by the increasing dissatisfaction with the role of global financial institutions, as evidenced by the wave of protests at World Trade Organization meetings from Seattle to Hong Kong. More serious is that inequalities are high and increasing along the most significant cultural fault line—between Muslims and others—both at a cross-country level and within countries. For example, there are big and growing economic gaps between Israelis and Palestinians, between Western countries and the Middle East, and between Muslim populations within particular countries (e.g., the United Kingdom and France).[59] Each of these inequalities feeds into political mobilization at both local and global levels.

As the horizontal inequalities hypothesis suggests, this dimension of inequality is particularly dangerous because it falls along culturally distinct lines and hence makes mobilization along those lines more likely. Even moderate, broadly pro-Western Muslim leaders such as Malaysian prime minister Abdullah Ahmad Badawi have interpreted the "war on terror" and the associated global insecurity in such terms: "Muslims see ourselves as a collective *ummah* [global community of the faithful]. . . . This is why Muslims who are not affected by poverty or have nothing to do with Palestine feel strongly about this issue. This is

why without addressing the root causes, the war against terrorism will not succeed."[60]

Groups increasingly consider not just their local relative position but their international one—where identities cross nations—and mobilize and provide support for conflicts across borders. This is most evident in Muslim countries, where international connections, finance, and fighters move from one locality to another. For example, fighters from Afghanistan have moved to Algeria and to Iraq; Muslims in the Philippines and Thailand receive support internationally; and British and French Muslims move to Iraq or Afghanistan. The globalization of perceptions of inequality means that the evident inequalities of Muslims in Europe (the United Kingdom, France, the Netherlands) provoke not only conflict in those countries but also support for conflict against the West elsewhere. Similarly, the inequalities between Palestinians and Israelis are used to justify and stimulate conflict in many other places.

Increasing global interventionism feeds into this. Governments in developing countries are able to classify their rebellions as "terrorist" and thus to cash in on the war on terror, gaining military equipment and financing. This extends well beyond conflicts involving Muslim populations; for example, the Philippine, Sri Lankan, Nepalese, and Colombian governments have each gained various types of support for what they now define as their war against terrorists. Governments perceived as being on the "right" side of the war on terrorism are given carte blanche to pursue their agendas, including against their own populations. These are indirect forms of support. Much more serious are the direct military interventions, justified as part of the new security environment—the move into Afghanistan and Iraq—that generate prolonged conflict in these countries.

In terms of the private motivations hypothesis, globalization has extended to the international arena possibilities of gaining financing for conflict and profiting from it. For example, even though empirical evidence suggests that narcotics production has not predisposed regions toward conflict, "conditions of armed conflict boost narcotics production and enable insurgents to become involved in the drug trade to finance their struggle," thereby creating a "crime-terror nexus." This has happened particularly in Afghanistan and Colombia.[61] Nonetheless, the degree to which relatively rich Muslim individuals and groups have involved themselves in such developments as 9/11 and the Iraqi insurgency demonstrates the limitations of the private motivations hypothesis in understanding the new security environment, particularly Muslim perspectives. However, the expectation of massive commercial profits from the "reconstruction" of Iraq for Western companies, which often have political links, as in the case of Halliburton and the Western oil industry, does give credence to the hypothesis that private motivations are playing an important role in the Western motivation underlying the war against terror.

It is perhaps difficult to employ the failed social contract hypothesis to explain the new international security environment, because there is no clear "international social contract," in the absence of global government. This approach, however, would focus attention on the failure of major Western countries and international institutions, such as the United Nations and the Bretton Woods institutions, to provide development and security for all. The resulting poverty in some parts of the world breeds discontent and resentment, makes local conflict and political disintegration more likely, and consequently provides some sort of "haven" for global "terrorists" and a location for the illegal movement of goods and funds to finance global conflicts.

Finally, the relationship between resource scarcity/distribution and the new international security environment is an important area for investigation. Even before the invasion of Iraq, scholars and political commentators were noting that "the determination to ensure US access to overseas supplies of vital resources . . . [and] the protection of global resource flows is becoming an increasingly prominent feature of the American security policy."[62] Oil is not the only global resource that is linked to the international security environment, moreover. Control of water resources has been linked in particular to the Israeli occupation of Palestinian territory, a claim that again long predates the current transformation of international security.[63] Empirical research has found some evidence linking water resources to international conflict, although the causality is not clear.[64]

It was argued earlier that preventive policies toward conflict need to address the underlying causes, including inequality, unemployment, and poverty. This remains true in the new environment, although we now need to consider not just domestic inequality but also global inequality. Yet the global remedies adopted to date have not been of that kind: they have consisted of the provision of military support and aid to improve the repression of rebellion, and support for the interdiction of financial flows that might fund such rebellions. Far from considering the need for inclusive politics at a global level, the one inclusive body—the United Nations—has been weakened and bypassed. Similarly, the dialogue with developing countries facing conflict has focused on repression rather than development.

The new security agenda in some ways has contributed to the reduction of conflict, by strengthening governments' repressive capacities and weakening opportunities and capacities for rebellion. Yet it has maintained and, if anything, increased the underlying incentives for conflict—in the form of inequalities and poverty—so that we cannot be confident that the observed decline in conflict incidence will be sustained.

CONCLUSION

While much contemporary conflict seems to be about ethnic or religious differences, in fact these conflicts generally have an economic and a political basis. HIs form one fundamental economic and political cause. Others include poor economic opportunities and deficient social services leading to a failed social contract, environmental degradation, and the potential enrichment that accompanies some conflicts. These motives have global as well as domestic dimensions.

Appropriate policies depend on the specific situation, notably, which of these underlying causes is applicable. Hence, careful analysis of the local situation is essential. For prevention, it is imperative to address political as well as economic inequalities. It is clear that many of the policies needed for conflict prevention and for the protection of people during war differ from the policies currently advocated (and often required) by the international development community, especially the international financial institutions. The new security environment has increased the global nature of conflicts and has increased the strength of government to repress rebellions, but it has not addressed underlying economic, social, or political causes.

NOTES

We are grateful for extremely helpful comments from the editors of this volume.

1. United Nations Development Programme, *Human Development Report 2005* (New York: United Nations, 2005).

2. Paul Collier et al., *Breaking the Conflict Trap: Civil War and Development Policy* (Washington, D.C.: World Bank, 2003).

3. Frances Stewart and Valpy Fitzgerald, eds., *War and Underdevelopment: The Economic and Social Consequences of Conflict* (Oxford: Oxford University Press, 2001), table 4.3.

4. Juha Auvinen and E. Wayne Nafziger, "The Sources of Humanitarian Emergencies," *Journal of Conflict Resolution* 43, no. 3 (1999): 267–290.

5. For example, see Samuel P. Huntington, "The Clash of Civilizations?" *Foreign Affairs* 72, no. 3 (1993): 22–49.

6. James D. Fearon and David D. Laitin, "Explaining Interethnic Cooperation," *American Political Science Review* 90, no. 4 (1996): 715–735.

7. Abner Cohen, *Two-Dimensional Man: An Essay on the Anthropology of Power and Symbolism in Complex Society* (Berkeley: University of California Press, 1974), 94.

8. Ted Robert Gurr, *Minorities at Risk: A Global View of Ethnopolitical Conflicts* (Washington, D.C.: United States Institute of Peace Press, 1993); and Donald L. Horowitz, *Ethnic Groups in Conflict* (Berkeley: University of California Press, 1985).

9. Ted Robert Gurr, *Why Men Rebel* (Princeton, N.J.: Princeton University Press, 1970); Gurr, *Minorities at Risk;* and Frances Stewart, *Horizontal Inequalities: A Neglected Dimension of Development,* Queen Elizabeth House Working Paper Series, no. 81 (Oxford: University of Oxford, Queen Elizabeth House, Department of International Development, 2002).

10. Anna Dimitrijevics, "Integrating Patterns of Conflict Resolution: A Group-Oriented Approach to the Study of the Genesis and Dynamics of Conflict" (D. Phil. thesis, University of Oxford, Queen Elizabeth House, Department of International Development, 2004).

11. Luca Mancini, *Horizontal Inequality and Communal Violence: Evidence from Indonesian Districts,* CRISE Working Papers Series, no. 22 (Oxford: Centre for Research on Inequality, Human Security and Ethnicity, 2005).

12. Scott Gates and Mansoob S. Murshed, "Spatial-Horizontal Inequality and the Maoist Insurgency in Nepal," *Review of Development Economics* 9, no. 1 (2005).

13. Gudrun Østby, *Do Horizontal Inequalities Matter for Civil Conflict?* (Oslo: Centre for Study of Civil War/International Peace Research Institute, 2004); W. L. Barrows, "Ethnic Diversity and Political Instability in Black Africa," *Comparative Political Studies* 9, no. 2 (1976): 139–170; and Stewart, *Horizontal Inequalities.*

14. Arnim Langer, "Horizontal Inequalities and Violent Group Mobilisation in Côte d'Ivoire," *Oxford Development Studies* 33, no. 1 (2005): 25–45.

15. David Keen, *The Economic Functions of Violence in Civil War* (Oxford: Oxford University Press for the International Institute of Strategic Studies, 1998); Mark R. Duffield, "The Political Economy of

Internal War: Asset Transfer, Complex Emergencies and International Aid," in *War and Hunger: Rethinking International Responses to Complex Emergencies,* ed. Joanna Macrae and Anthony Zwi (London: Zed, 1994); and Paul Collier and Anke Hoeffler, "Greed and Grievance in Civil War," *Oxford Economic Papers* 56 (2004): 563–595.

16. Jack Hirshleifer, "The Dark Side of the Force," *Economic Inquiry* 32, no. 1 (1994): 1–10.

17. Paul Collier, *Economic Causes of Conflict and Their Implications for Policy* (Washington, D.C.: World Bank, 2000), 5.

18. Collier and Hoeffler, "Greed and Grievance in Civil War."

19. James D. Fearon, "Primary Commodity Exports and Civil War," *Journal of Conflict Resolution* 49, no. 4 (2005): 483–507. See also the other papers on the subject in this special issue.

20. James D. Fearon and David D. Laitin, "Ethnicity, Insurgency, and Civil War," *American Political Science Review* 97, no. 1 (2003): 75–90; and Macartan Humphreys and Ashutosh Varshney, *Violence Conflict and the Millennium Development Goals: Diagnosis and Recommendations,* CSGD Working Paper Series (New York: Columbia University, 2004).

21. Karen Ballentine and Jake Sherman, *The Political Economy of Armed Conflict: Beyond Greed and Grievance* (Boulder, Colo.: Lynne Rienner, 2003), 259–260.

22. Mark Harrison, "An Economist Looks at Suicide Terrorism," in *Terrorism: Challenge for the Twenty-first Century? Understandings and Responses,* ed. C. Ankerson (London: Polity, 2005).

23. Collier, *Economic Causes of Conflict and Their Implications for Policy,* 5.

24. Ibid., 10.

25. Francisco Gutiérrez Sanín, "Criminal Rebels? A Discussion of Civil War and Criminality from the Colombian Experience," *Politics and Society* 32, no. 2 (2004): 257–285.

26. Anthony D. Smith, "The Nation: Invented, Imagined, Reconstructed?" *Millennium: Journal of International Studies* 20 (1991): 353–368.

27. Tony Addison and Mansoob S. Murshed, "Post-Conflict Reconstruction in Africa: Some Analytical Issues," in *Post-Conflict Economies in Africa,* ed. Paul Collier and Augustin Kwasi Fosu (London: Palgrave, 2005); and E. Wayne Nafziger and Juha

Auvinen, "The Economic Causes of Humanitarian Emergencies," in *War, Hunger and Displacement: The Origin of Humanitarian Emergencies,* vol. 1, ed. E. Wayne Nafziger, Frances Stewart, and Raimi Väyrynen (Oxford: Oxford University Press, 2000).

28. Collier and Hoeffler, "Greed and Grievance in Civil War"; Ibrahim Elbadawi and Nicholas Sambanis, "How Much War Will We See? Estimating the Incidence of Civil War in 161 Countries," *Journal of Conflict Resolution* 46, no. 3 (2002): 307–334; and Nafziger and Auvinen, "Economic Causes of Humanitarian Emergencies."

29. For example, see Tanja Ellingsen, "Colorful Community or Ethnic Witches' Brew? Multiethnicity and Domestic Conflict during and after the Cold War," *Journal of Conflict Resolution* 44, no. 2 (2000): 228–249.

30. Jack Snyder, *From Voting to Violence* (New York: W. W. Norton, 2000); and Marta Reynal-Querol, "Political Systems, Stability and Civil Wars," *Defence and Peace Economics* 13, no. 6 (2002): 465–483.

31. Thomas Homer-Dixon, "On the Threshold: Environmental Changes as Causes of Acute Conflict," *International Security* 16, no. 2 (1991): 76–116; Homer-Dixon, "Environmental Scarcities and Violent Conflict: Evidence from Cases," *International Security* 19, no. 1 (1994): 5–40; and Val Percival and Thomas Homer-Dixon, "Environmental Scarcity and Violent Conflict: The Case of South Africa," *Journal of Peace Research* 35, no. 3 (1998): 279–298.

32. Homer-Dixon, "Environmental Scarcities and Violent Conflict," 6.

33. Percival and Homer-Dixon, "Environmental Scarcity and Violent Conflict," 280.

34. Homer-Dixon, "Environmental Scarcities and Violent Conflict," 6.

35. Percival and Homer-Dixon, "Environmental Scarcity and Violent Conflict," 280.

36. Robert Kaplan, "The Coming Anarchy: How Scarcity, Crime, Overpopulation, and Disease Are Threatening the Social Fabric of Our Planet," *Atlantic Monthly,* February 1994, 44–74.

37. James Fairhead, "The Conflict over Natural and Environmental Resources," in Nafziger, Stewart, and Väyrynen, *War, Hunger and Displacement.*

38. Nils Petter Gleditsch, "Armed Conflict and the Environment: A Critique of the Literature," *Journal of Peace Research* 35, no. 3 (1998): 381–400; and Marc

Levy, "Is the Environment a National Security Issue?" *International Security* 20, no. 2 (1995): 35–62.

39. David Keen, *The Benefits of Famine: A Political Economy of Famine Relief in Southwestern Sudan, 1883–1989* (Princeton, N.J.: Princeton University Press, 1994).

40. Alex Cobham, "Causes of Conflict in Sudan: Testing the Black Book," *European Journal of Development Research* 17, no. 3 (2005): 462–480.

41. For exploration of policies during the war stage, see Stewart and Fitzgerald, eds., *War and Underdevelopment.*

42. Alexis de Tocqueville, *Democracy in America*, vol. 1 (New York: Vintage, 1954).

43. See Frances Stewart, *Policies towards Horizontal Inequalities in Post-Conflict Reconstruction*, CRISE Working Paper Series, no. 7 (Oxford: University of Oxford, Centre for Research on Inequality, Human Security and Ethnicity, 2005), appendices A2 and A3.

44. Vedi R. Hadiz, "Decentralisation and Democracy in Indonesia: A Critique of Neo-Institutionalist Perspectives," *Development and Change* 35, no. 4 (2004): 697–718.

45. A possible counterexample here is Israel, which practices proportional representation, although the conflict with the Palestinians is not an "internal" conflict per se.

46. Horowitz, *Ethnic Groups in Conflict.*

47. Snyder, *From Voting to Violence;* and Frances Stewart and Meghan O'Sullivan, "Democracy, Conflict and Development: Three Cases," in *The Political Economy of Comparative Development into the Twenty-first Century: Essays in Memory of John C. H. Fei,* vol. 1, ed. Gustav Ranis, Sheng-Cheng Hu, and Yu-Peng Chu (Cheltenham, U.K.: Edward Elgar, 1999).

48. Servaas van den Berg and Megan Louw, "Changing Patterns of South African Income Distribution: Towards Time Series Estimates of Distribution and Poverty," *South African Journal of Economics* 72, no. 3 (2004).

49. Stewart, *Policies towards Horizontal Inequalities in Post-Conflict Reconstruction*, appendix A1.

50. Graham Brown, *Balancing the Risks of Corrective Surgery: The Political Economy of Horizontal Inequalities and the End of the New Economic Policy in Malaysia*, CRISE Working Papers Series, no. 20 (Oxford: University of Oxford, Centre for Research on Inequality, Human Security and Ethnicity, 2005).

51. Collier et al., *Breaking the Conflict Trap;* and United Nations Development Programme, *Human Development Report 2005.*

52. United Nations Development Programme, *Human Development Report 2004* (New York: United Nations, 2004).

53. Tilman Brück, Valpy Fitzgerald, and Arturo Grigsby, *Enhancing the Private Sector Contribution to Post-War Recovery in Poor Countries,* Queen Elizabeth House Working Paper Series, no. 45 (Oxford: University of Oxford, Queen Elizabeth House, Department of International Development, 2000).

54. James K. Boyce, *Investing in Peace: Aid and Conditionality and Civil Wars* (London: International Institute for Strategic Studies, 2002).

55. Collier et al., *Breaking the Conflict Trap.*

56. Stewart, *Policies towards Horizontal Inequalities in Post-Conflict Reconstruction.*

57. Francis Stewart and Graham Brown, "The Implications of Horizontal Inequality for Aid" (paper presented at the WIDER Conference on Aid, World Institute of Development Economics Research, Helsinki, Finland, 16–17 June 2006).

58. Xavier Sala-i-Martin, *The Disturbing "Rise" of Global Income Inequality,* NBER Working Paper 8904 (Cambridge, Mass.: National Bureau of Economic Research, 2002); and Branco Milanovic, *Half a World: Regional Inequality in Five Great Federations,* World Bank Policy Research Working Paper 3699 (Washington, D.C.: World Bank, 2005).

59. Frances Stewart, "Development and Security," *Conflict, Security and Development* 4, no. 3 (2004): 261–288.

60. Abdullah Ahmad Badawi (speech at the Oxford Centre of Islamic Studies, University of Oxford, Magdalen College, 2004).

61. Svante E. Cornell, "The Interaction of Narcotics and Conflict," *Journal of Peace Research* 42, no. 6 (2005): 751–760.

62. Michael T. Klare, *Resource Wars: The New Landscape of Global Conflict* (New York: Henry Holt, 2001), 6.

63. For example, see Sharif S. Elmusa, "The Land-Water Nexus in the Israel-Palestinian Conflict," *Journal of Palestine Studies* 25, no. 3 (1996): 69–78.

64. Nils Petter Gleditsch et al., "Conflict over Shared Rivers: Resource Wars or Fuzzy Boundaries?" *Political Geography* 25, no. 7 (2006).

PART III

USES AND LIMITS OF FORCE IN CONFLICT MANAGEMENT

14

USING FORCE FOR PEACE IN AN AGE OF TERROR

Lawrence Freedman

DURING THE COURSE OF THE 1990S, A view developed that the role of Western armed forces in the post–Cold War world was likely to be essentially altruistic, with the development of a distinct form of military operation, usually described as a "humanitarian intervention."[1] The theory and practice were worked out through the twists and turns of the breakup of the former Yugoslavia and regular turbulence in Africa. These interventions sought to influence the character and course of a developing conflict that was neither taking place on nor directly threatening national territory and that did not relate to any specific obligations to allies. Rather than meeting an existential threat, these operations would instead be intended to do good: looking after the victims of conflict, defending the weak and vulnerable against their oppressors, and creating conditions for peace, stability, and prosperity. Such operations could come in all shapes and sizes. The conflict could be developing within one particular state or involve a number of states; its stage of development

could be early or quite mature; and it could range from sporadic skirmishing to significant battles. Intervention could take a range of forms: from enforcing a blockade to clearing the skies of aircraft engaged in prohibited activities; from providing humanitarian relief to taking and defending territory. The same conflict could include varying types of operations at varying levels of intensity. Elements of high-intensity warfare would be involved whenever there was a possibility of a direct clash involving regular forces. They could also involve a range of risks: entering others' quarrels without paying due care and attention to the nature of the dispute and its likely course might not make things better and could make them worse. One's own forces might be sucked into a messy and apparently interminable conflict. Because it would not always be possible or prudent to act, or hard to summon up any political interest, there was a discretionary aspect to these operations.

The humanitarian trend of the 1990s seemed to be overtaken by the pressing strategic imperatives associated with the traumatic events of the 2000s. In the United States the institutionalized view of the armed forces was that they should be used only for big wars against regular armies. Although susceptible to interventionist inclinations, the Clinton administration was aware of military misgivings and fearful that any casualties would make interventions, and the government that authorized them, unpopular. It was therefore a cautious intervenor, preferring to make its contributions solely through airpower. The administration of George W. Bush promised to be even more reluctant, dubious about getting involved in distant quarrels and acquiring responsibility for nation building. This attitude did not change as a result of the September 11, 2001, terrorist attacks on the United States. The fight against al Qaeda and its associates appeared to be a matter not of choice but of necessity, and one requiring operations of a somewhat old-fashioned variety: invading and occupying other countries against the wishes and resistance of the regime in power, and in one case against the advice and wishes of most of the international community. Yet this was a fateful miscalculation. Once the old order had been overthrown, the problems of establishing a new order led to demands on armed forces similar to those resulting from humanitarian interventions, in particular the need to create conditions for economic and political reconstruction by maintaining security against those who wished to disrupt this process. Not only did the "war on terror" provide more and better reasons to get involved in the problems of distant parts of the Third World, but also the situations in Afghanistan and Iraq required the United States to take operations of the humanitarian type seriously.

This chapter describes the developing theory and practice of humanitarian intervention, including their interaction with the apparently new and unique demands of the war on terror. It argues that the relevance of the former to the latter is substantial, and that the failure

by the Bush administration to appreciate this has added to the stresses and strains of the attempt to bring peace and stability to Afghanistan and Iraq.

INTERVENTIONISM AFTER THE COLD WAR

The shift in focus on the use of force began with the disappearance of core threats rather than the discovery of new ones. Students of the realist school of international relations have challenged the proposition that the end of the Cold War marked the end of the great-power era, when the international system was shaped by competition and rivalry among a set of large states able to project their military strength well beyond their own borders.[2] They argue that the anarchic nature of the system means that great powers cannot really help themselves, whatever their temporary accommodations. The collapse of communism undoubtedly created a unipolar system, as the United States was suddenly transformed from a superpower into a lonely "hyperpower" with no equals. Such power, it is argued, must threaten and inhibit others, who are bound to work separately or in alliance to restrain and constrain the dominant power. To some extent, U.S. behavior in the 2000s encouraged limited countervailing activity of this sort, but in the 1990s it did not.[3] The other great powers mooted as potential challengers either continued to decline in relation to the United States (Russia) or began to do so (Germany and Japan). Only China grew in strength, but China, although taking a robustly realpolitik approach to regional affairs, never exhibited the behavior of a classic great power, taking a somewhat parochial approach to international affairs.[4]

Furthermore, the proposition that the international system encourages insecurity had to be set against the growing economic interdependence resulting from the various processes that came under the heading of "globalization." If insecurity was supposedly a function of assessments of a developing military balance of power, it was hard to see how prospective changes would do anything other than strengthen unipolarity. In the decade after the end of the Cold War, the gap between the United States and all others widened rather than narrowed, reflecting both the growth in the U.S. economy and a persistent focus in its military provision on great-power conflict. This focus had the effect of making it even less likely that the United States would face conventional military challenges. In addition, questions of military balance are irrelevant without a more substantive basis for enmity. Ideological differences were declining, and there was no ascendant state promoting a radical creed. Nor (with the potentially large exception of Taiwan) were there major territorial disputes that could spark conflict between great powers. In fact, the old imperial powers had spent the previous decades divesting themselves of their colonies and had no appetite for new ones. Unlike in earlier times, the entire world's land surface was spoken for, and while many of the boundaries still caused controversy and occasional conflict, there was no reason for great powers to scramble to obtain new territories to gain strategic advantage or to think about influencing trade patterns by controlling sea lines of communication.

Instead, a system dominated by great powers had made way for one marked by a proliferation of states, many of them small and barely viable, yet all prizing their sovereignty. The end of the Cold War could also be seen as the last act of decolonization, as the Soviet Union fragmented and its satellite states in Eastern Europe reasserted themselves. Indeed, at times in the early 1990s any distinctive group that felt its identity lost in a multinational state appeared ready to insist on its own statehood. More states emerged out of the wreckage of Yugoslavia and the more mature division of Czechoslovakia. The number of constitutionally independent entities in the international system grew dramatically.

When the processes of decolonization initially gathered speed in the early decades of the Cold War, opportunities were created for superpower competition. Both the United States and the Soviet Union, each proclaiming its anticolonial credentials, believed that they could draw into their ideological sphere newly independent countries. As struggles for influence developed between the two blocs, questions of bases, arms transfers, and direct military support arose. In this context, otherwise feeble and uninteresting states could attract superpower attention when engaged in local conflicts, often for reasons that had scant actual relevance to the Cold War, by threatening to cross over to the other ideological side. Such games ended with the Cold War. The origins of much conflict were now seen to lie less in great-power struggles than in the inner weakness of so many new states. Poor economic development, profound social cleavages, and feeble political institutions rendered many new states vulnerable to internal conflicts, often ferocious, as well as to predatory neighbors.

Without classical strategic imperatives, and with expectations of a post–Cold War peace dividend, there were, theoretically, fewer reasons than before to intervene in these conflicts. It would not have been surprising if orderly Western countries had viewed disorder elsewhere with sadness or contempt and concluded that it was neither necessary nor possible to do anything about it, beyond extending a certain amount of charity. Yet there were reasons why they might decide to intervene. Partly these motives were altruistic, a straightforward belief that this was the right thing to do. Such attitudes in government might be reinforced by images of suffering, although there is little evidence that governments were unable to resist media pressure when they had good reasons for keeping out.[5] There were also more self-interested motives: expatriate communities were at risk; basic principles of international law, such as nonaggression, were being violated or pernicious and repressive ideologies were taking root; left unregulated, such conflicts could encourage crime and various forms of trafficking, in drugs, arms, or people; or conflicts might spread, so that a whole region might be dragged down, resulting in refugee flows, interrupted trade, and general mayhem. The nearer to home the greater these dangers, which is why countries were more likely to intervene in regional conflicts (Russia in its "near abroad," the United States in Haiti, Western Europeans in the former Yugoslavia, Australia in East Timor). These factors also help explain why, except where there were historic links (as with Britain in Sierra Leone), intervention in Africa proved to be so problematic. While the most vital interests did not prompt these interventions, and the altruistic motives should not be discounted, it was rarely the case that they were wholly disinterested.

Furthermore, interventions created new interests. The reputations of the intervening countries and the sponsoring multilateral organization (if any) would be affected by their performance in the conflict and their ability to get results. It took most of the 1990s, for example, for the idea of an active European foreign policy to recover from the dismal failure of the first attempts to forge one in the context of the breakup of Yugoslavia early in the decade. At the same time, nonintervention could also have an effect on reputation and encourage others to subsequently disregard the nonintervenor's concerns when pursuing their own particular quarrels. Nonetheless, the impact of a decision to admit failure and withdraw was always likely to be far more significant than that of holding back in the first place.[6]

PROBLEMS WITH PEACE SUPPORT

However high-minded the initial motives that prompted intervention, the consequence was engagement in a complex local struggle. Part of the difficulty of coming to terms with the developing class of what came to be seen as "peace support" operations was how different

they were becoming from earlier peacekeeping operations, which involved the insertion of lightly armed troops, geared only to self-defense, along a cease-fire line with the consent of the warring parties and a promise of impartiality. Inserting troops into ongoing, violent conflicts, even with consent, soon challenged attempts at evenhandedness. Not only did some actions (e.g., providing sustenance to a besieged community) make the intervening force appear to be taking sides, but that force soon became a party to the conflict with its own distinctive interests and agendas. The natural tendency was to describe such operations as enforcing, keeping, making, restoring, or supporting "peace." Nor would any peace do: it was also expected to be "just" or "lasting," though even a temporary and unfair peace often proved to be elusive. At a minimum, the aim was to "restore hope" or "provide comfort." Around the mid-1990s, the less inspirational "stability support" was adopted, which had the advantage of not only avoiding exaggerated promises but also of directing attention to the sources of instability, and thus the political context.[7]

This focus on political context also had important implications for force planning. Military officers will naturally yearn for a precise goal against which they can plan and judge success and that, crucially, will tell them when they are allowed to go home. Yet these interventions were unlikely to have clear-cut, let alone happy, endings. Whether the intervenors pushed in the direction of containing the conflict, setting rules for its conduct, easing suffering, or brokering a settlement, there was bound to be a dynamic interaction with the interests of the local parties. Thus intervention had to be recognized not as being directed against a specific end but as being part of a process, though undoubtedly a process with defined stages. Military action could never be sufficient: at best it could create conditions for a more favorable political outcome. Only once the fragility of local institutions, infrastructure, and economic activity had been addressed would it be safe to leave. By definition, a country that can be stabilized only by outside intervention is no longer fully self-governing. The very fact that military means have had to be employed ensures that some parties whose consent may be essential to the viability of a political solution will feel bitter and cheated. By the time military action has become necessary, it must be assumed that satisfactory solutions based on harmony, justice, and consensus are no longer possible, at least in the short term. The uncertain political support for these operations, especially after the Somalia debacle, led the Americans to insist on an exit strategy, even as they entered a conflict. In Bosnia a firm timetable (geared to the 1996 presidential election) had to be abandoned as it became apparent that the early withdrawal of foreign troops would result in instability. Insisting on an exit strategy at the point of entry was something of a giveaway, encouraging the opponent to threaten an interminable conflict, in which the fighting would be long term and mean, even if also spasmodic and at a low level.

Even more important than an exit strategy in building public understanding for intervention was assumed to be force protection. The starting point for this requirement was the presumption of a low tolerance for casualties. Some were prepared to see this as a secular trend, the consequence of a postheroic age.[8] This was a dubious claim. Past ages were not always that heroic, except in an involuntary sense, while in recent years Western countries had been prepared to accept substantial casualties in order to reverse aggression or stop the slaughter of innocents. Few anticipated the modest casualties resulting directly from Desert Storm. What seems to have happened is that during the 1990s, reinforced by the abrupt withdrawal from Somalia in 1994 and harking back to the retreat from Beirut a decade earlier not long after the bombing of the marine barracks,[9] the idea of casualty intolerance took

root in the U.S. political and military establishment. The Triangle Institute for Security Studies, in a study conducted in 1998–99 on the varying attitudes of civilian and military elites, found that in a variety of scenarios the public could actually be quite gung-ho. Military elites were more cautious than their civilian counterparts about intervening in conflicts where national security was not at stake but more insistent on overwhelming force when operations were authorized.[10] The real intolerance was of futility, of sacrifice for no purpose or up to a level completely out of proportion to the stakes in the conflict.

Questions of proportionality raised their own difficulties. The mere act of using military force symbolizes resolve and deep concern and so can convey determination. Symbols without substance, for example, deployments well away from the area of any likely hostilities and with extremely restricted rules of engagement, can simply convey a lack of resolve rather than a readiness to escalate if necessary.

A token action increases the likelihood of futility. Limited measures do not result in limited risks, as they are not necessarily sufficient to support limited interests. Force levels must be set against the level and capabilities of the opponents. Most important, conflicts reflecting a struggle for local political power will be determined by the balance of strength on the ground. Because the critical issues revolve around local territorial control, strategies that ignore this are problematic. For those concerned about casualties, however, it is best to avoid land war. Infantrymen account for about 80 percent of U.S. combat deaths, even though they make up just 4 percent of the total force.[11] This encouraged many U.S. military thinkers to find ways of prevailing on land without putting ground forces at excessive risk, which has naturally led to attempts to rely much more on directed and precise firepower, especially from the air, to influence the course of battle rather than committing ground forces too early in the operation.

The problems this caused were evident in the Bosnian intervention.[12] In early 1992 Serbs began to engage in ethnic cleansing and started to push Muslims into a few urban enclaves. The Bosnian Croats joined in. There was already a UN force being established to monitor a cease-fire in Croatia, site of the first major civil war from the breakup of Yugoslavia. In response to the developing turmoil in Bosnia, the UN force became progressively involved in efforts to alleviate civilian suffering. Many nations were involved, including Canada and the Netherlands, but the British and French, as Western Europe's top military powers, took the lead. They were torn between their reluctance to get too involved and their growing awareness that their humanitarian mission was constantly being undermined by their inability to stop the fighting. Establishing "no-fly" zones, for example, as had been done for the Iraqi Kurds, could have only a limited effect on the main struggle for power going on below as long as "no-artillery" zones and "no-ethnic-cleansing" zones were absent. Putting a few lightly armed troops on the ground to demonstrate an external interest in a conflict and to find practical means of alleviating local distress at best diverted the fighting elsewhere and at worst created a vulnerability that acted as a disincentive when proposals were made to take a more robust stand. For this reason, the UN civilian leadership and military commanders were always nervous when proposals were made by the United States for air strikes, lest their troops be picked on in retaliation.[13] This happened in early 1995 when the Serbs briefly detained UN troops and other international personnel in response to air strikes. The lesson was learned; as soon as the troops were released, they were reorganized into a more coherent force capable of both taking initiatives and defending itself properly. Unfortunately, this was not possible to arrange in time to prevent the massacre of Muslim men at Srebrenica in July 1995. With the risks reduced, air strikes began against Serb posi-

tions; these resulted in the agreement to sort the matter out at talks in Dayton, Ohio, which were successfully concluded in November 1995. This was taken as an example of the coercive impact of airpower, acting independently. In practice, however, Serb calculations were also influenced significantly by the more robust attitude of the UN force and, more important, the fact that Croats and Muslims, now working together rather than against each other, were able to start pushing the Serb units back.

The question of the balance between the land and air elements of a campaign became even more critical during the 1999 Kosovo war,[14] a response by NATO countries to a continuing campaign by the Yugoslav (effectively Serb) government against the Muslim Albanian population in the province of Kosovo. In 1998 the alliance had threatened war if refugees were not allowed to return home, and while President Slobodan Milosevic had initially complied, by early 1999 it was apparent that the agreement was coming apart. From the start of the crisis the alliance had made clear that it intended to rely on airpower for any forceful response. This was in part a matter of logistics, as it was extremely difficult to build up land forces close to the relevant borders, but it was also a matter of politics, in that there was a hope that the coercive impact of airpower would reduce to a minimum the risk of casualties. In the event, the only NATO casualties were in accidents, but this clear choice meant that the campaign would become punitive for Serbian society, rather than just Serb forces. The initial, modest air campaign was large enough to signal an interest but insufficient to compel the target to change behavior. It was reasonable for the Serbs to assume that they would have to face little more than four days of raids on air defense sites and command centers.[15] When it failed to get results, the air campaign was made more extensive and intensive, increasing the reliance on coercion and the risk, not so much of casualty, but of blunder.

Eventually, the damage to Serbia's economic—as much as its military—infrastructure contributed to Belgrade's decision to agree to terms. This was taken as some sort of vindication of airpower acting alone, but it underplayed the critical contribution of activity on the ground. Belgrade may have been influenced by hints that NATO was actually contemplating an eventual land invasion, but as important—if not more so—was the growing strength of the Kosovo Liberation Army (KLA). The whole objective of the Serb campaign had been to defeat the KLA and deprive it of the population base required for sustained operations. But the ability of the KLA to grow in strength and confidence must have indicated to Milosevic that in the end he would lose Kosovo and that there was little point in taking even more pain from NATO airpower. As NATO forces effectively followed it into Kosovo, the KLA acquired far more political clout and prestige than was commensurate with the alliance's prewar political goals. This added to the demands on the postwar peacekeeping force, which soon began a long stay.

LEGITIMACY

The Kosovo case also highlighted issues that had been around for some time but gained prominence because of the controversy with which the Kosovo campaign was soon surrounded. The need to gain support for such operations came to be captured by the concept of "legitimacy," a term implying a mixture of legality and principle. Legality is problematic in international affairs. The "inherent right of self-defence" enshrined in Article 51 of the UN Charter, for example, is so elastic as to cover a multitude of sins. Yet Western governments would still prefer to be endorsed by the UN Security Council and avoid rebukes by the World Court. This was particularly problematic in Kosovo, given that the urge for "humanitarian intervention" involved a reversal of the old norm of "non-interference in internal

affairs" and was established only as a result of regular recourse to the Security Council. This is what an important report called the "responsibility to protect."[16] In a much-publicized speech in Chicago on April 23, 1999, at a delicate period in the Kosovo campaign, Tony Blair pondered the "circumstances in which we should get actively involved in other peoples' conflicts." On the one hand, he argued for the need to qualify the principle of "non-interference in the affairs of other states" when faced with acts of genocide and oppression and with regimes that are so narrowly based as to lack legitimacy. On the other hand, he accepted that it would be impossible to take on all undemocratic regimes engaged in acts of barbarity. He therefore suggested five criteria to use in determining if intervention was warranted: a sure case, the exhaustion of all diplomatic options, available and prudent military operations, preparations for a long-term commitment, and the involvement of some national interests.[17]

The problem—which was self-evident during the Cold War—is that the Security Council has a legitimizing function and its resolutions have legal force, but it is a political and not a judicial body. It has its rules and procedures, but all its considerations of international peace and security are shaped by differing political perspectives and must be resolved, if at all, through bargaining. This is an inevitable consequence of giving veto power to five particular states. The Security Council can perform a legitimizing function only if the permanent members are ready to make it work. The risk for China and Russia, of course, is that if it is clear that they will always veto Western military operations, then the West will seek its legitimacy elsewhere, which is what happened in Kosovo. If the Security Council is unavailable, there is safety in numbers. Doing the necessary work to develop international support takes time—putting together a coalition, arguing points in the UN Security Council, perhaps first trying economic sanctions, and allowing ambassadors of peace to flit hither and thither.

Including allies as a source of legitimacy rather than for additional military strength also has consequences for military operations. In the case of Kosovo, the operation was conducted through NATO. The main contributors expected to control the military operations, yet all countries who signed on to the action were implicated by its conduct and wished to exercise some influence. This affected U.S. views after 1999, when the Americans were reluctant to allow their operations to be subject to the whims of a multinational headquarters and the intervention of anxious governments.[18] It can also be noted that the British and the French had felt similarly irritated by the Clinton administration's commentary on their early operations in Bosnia when it was not prepared to commit forces itself.

Another consequence of the quest for legitimacy is the pressure to demonstrate that Western forces are not engaged in unnecessary slaughter—especially of civilians. The fact that modern weapons are now judged to be extraordinarily precise has rendered attacks on civilian populations even less excusable. Even "collateral damage" is now seen as reflecting a lack of professionalism as much as the "fog of war." A moral preference for avoiding attacks on the innocent is assumed to be matched by available technology, though of course precision strikes still require precision intelligence and that is by no means always available. Moreover, there is a view, with scant empirical basis, that certain types of targets of an essentially political nature—party headquarters and interior ministries—are worth attacking because their destruction could undermine the offending regime.

Serbia saw, as had Iraq earlier, an opportunity in Western promises of low collateral damage: by placing key military assets, such as tanks or aircraft, next to schools, hospitals, and religious sites, it dared attacking air forces to take the risk of causing high civilian casual-ties. Western governments at times appeared caught by the unrealistic expectations they had encouraged. Their own media scrutinized the causes of every civilian casualty and of every evident blunder, of which there were a number. Once exacting standards for precision are set, the routine tragedies of past wars can appear as outrages that threaten to invalidate the whole purpose of a modern war. That being said, given a choice between a principled defeat and a barely legitimate victory, most governments will choose the latter. The public often appeared uncomfortable with the results of NATO's bombing but still recognized that terrible things happen in war, through accident as well as by design, and, critically, took the view that those who initiate violence should not be surprised if it comes to engulf their societies. Kosovo was marked by a battle of narratives as the Serbs sought to demonstrate that NATO was acting outside international law and committing war crimes against civilians, while NATO highlighted the plight of the Kosovar Albanians, large numbers of whom appeared as refugees on the borders with Macedonia and Albania. All this emphasized the extent to which legitimacy would not come easy and that there is a complex interaction between the military and political aspects of any of these discretionary campaigns.

What conclusions might therefore have been drawn by the end of the 1990s? The United Nations was coming to terms with operations, for which it had a notional responsibility, that had come a long way from traditional peacekeeping involving lightly armed collections of moderately trained troops. There were still occasions when no greater force was needed, but it had become apparent that external interventions designed to ease and overcome conflicts could require active and often robust military operations.[19] The military, which had initially inclined to the view that any force trained for proper wars could take such lesser tasks in its stride, was beginning to understand the very special demands of these sorts of operations, which involved combining an ability to gain local trust with the continuing appearance of strength where it mattered. Both effects were likely at some point to require substantial numbers of troops on the ground. The various elements of the package associated with the "revolution in military affairs" (RMA), such as speedy, efficient communications, high-quality sensors, and the ability to attack discrete targets with accuracy over long distances, could all play their part. The full RMA package, however, was unlikely to be needed because the probable opponents were militias rather than regular armies, and even the regulars would be no match for Western forces in conventional battle. The "hearts-and-minds" aspect put special demands on the lowest levels of command, which have the most regular interface with the local population.

All this confirmed the highly political nature of these interventions. They were most likely to succeed when undertaken in a decisive manner, at an early stage in a conflict, although it could be difficult to mobilize political and public opinion in support until after a crisis point was reached. Whatever the humanitarian motives, they could never be politically innocent, as the civilian populations of opposing sides were rarely equally at risk. Furthermore, any success in stabilizing a situation was likely to require a long-term military commitment, since the removal of troops could trigger a recurrence of instability. Last, force alone could not create stable conditions: it required a close connection with a credible political negotiating process. That is, getting an intervention right required getting the politics right.

This pointed to a challenging future. The logic of regular interventions would call for Western states to leave military deposits around the globe, asserting interests in stability and high standards of political behavior and supporting the proconsuls appointed by international organizations. Continuing political influence would depend on sustaining a physical presence. Each deposit would reduce military

capital for future interventions, and at some point, if this process continued, a collection of Western protectorates would have been acquired; however, without further investment or the readiness of other countries to shoulder part of the burden, forces would be stretched so thin that they would be unable to cope with yet another emergency.

THE IMPACT OF THE WAR ON TERROR

Another conclusion that might have been drawn from the 1990s was that it was difficult to conduct any substantial operation without the United States, at least with regard to the provision of intelligence and logistics, if not combat arms.[20] Yet the United States had been a reluctant intervenor. While a British defense review concluded that the military could be a force for good,[21] the U.S. military had resisted any suggestion that they prepare for what Colin Powell, as chairman of the Joint Chiefs of Staff, had derisively called "constabulary duties."[22] The general view as the Bush administration came to power was that the armed forces were to prepare for proper wars against serious threats (with China clearly in mind but also possibly North Korea or Iraq) and not dissipate their energies on activities that seemed closer to social work. In a much-quoted article published during the 2000 campaign, Condoleezza Rice insisted that the military "is not a civilian peace force. It is not a political referee. And it is most certainly not designed to build a civilian society." Her conclusion was that U.S. interventions in "humanitarian" crises would be at best "exceedingly rare." The criteria for getting involved were familiar: the president should ask "whether decisive force is possible and is likely to be effective and must know how and when to get out." Humanitarian interventions were thus largely jobs for allies.[23]

Then came the attacks of September 11, 2001. This led to dramatic changes in the conduct of U.S. foreign policy. President Bush immediately declared a global war on terror.[24]

Secretary of Defense Donald Rumsfeld insisted that this would be a quite new type of war, against a global network of terrorists and their state sponsors. The vocabulary would change:

> When we "invade the enemy's territory," we may well be invading his cyberspace. There may not be as many beachheads stormed as opportunities denied. Forget about "exit strategies"; we're looking at a sustained engagement that carries no deadlines. We have no fixed rules about how to deploy our troops; we'll instead establish guidelines to determine whether military force is the best way to achieve a given objective.[25]

Was this really the break with the past that it claimed to be? The attitude of the United States was certainly different. Now it could not be accused of being a reluctant intervenor. It was in an uncompromising mood, ready to take the military initiative, mobilizing massive forces to do so and accepting the sacrifices that the new campaigns might require. The wars were not presented as discretionary or, initially, as humanitarian in purpose. They reflected the strategic imperatives of the new age of jihadist terror, and so the legitimacy was derived from demands of national security. As the security of all civilized people was at risk from groups such as al Qaeda, all should join the campaign. At the same time, this was a matter of self-defense and there was no absolute requirement to get a sponsoring organization. At most the United Nations could take over occupied countries once the offending regimes had been overthrown. Not even NATO, however, could expect to influence the command and control of the military campaign. The war would be conducted by a coalition of the willing (mainly drawn from the "Anglosphere" of the United States, the United Kingdom, and Australia).

As the source of the 9/11 attacks, Afghanistan was a straightforward and relatively uncontroversial choice for a target. Al Qaeda had developed a symbiotic relationship with the Taliban regime and used the country for training and as a headquarters. The move to dislodge both al Qaeda and the Taliban began in a standard U.S. pattern, with a strategic air campaign. But the infrastructure of Afghanistan was so wretched and primitive that there were few suitable targets to be attacked. What was the point of aiming for power plants in a country where only 6 percent of the population had electricity? Excessive bombing would risk doing no more than "rearranging the sand," said to be the main result of the cruise missile attacks against a supposed al Qaeda enclave in Afghanistan in August 1998 after the attacks on the U.S. embassies in East Africa. Unlike with Kosovo, there was no optimism that such a campaign could by itself achieve the strategic objective, which went beyond coercive demands like those on Milosevic. Yet there was no convenient forward base from which to launch a ground war, and as the limits of the air campaign became apparent, the anti-Taliban Northern Alliance eventually was accepted as the source of the crucial infantry, playing a more substantial and explicit role than the KLA played in Kosovo (and with the same risks of awkward political associations). As close cooperation with the Northern Alliance was forged, the results were impressive; one major stronghold after another fell, and the capital, Kabul, was soon in Northern Alliance hands. After the cities had fallen, attention moved to the Tora Bora caves, where a network of hiding places and passages had been prepared for sturdy defense. Here matters were far less successful. This was not territory in which the Northern Alliance was of much value, and the coalition lacked the troops and local knowledge to hunt down the enemy. Osama bin Laden and his key lieutenants escaped into Pakistan.[26]

In December 2001, before the frustrations at Tora Bora, President Bush suggested that a lesson of more general application had been learned. He spoke enthusiastically about the combination of "real-time intelligence, local allied forces, special forces, and precision air power" that had produced a victory in the first round of the war, adding that this conflict "has taught us more about the future of our military than a decade of blue ribbon panels and think tank symposiums."[27] Apparently, there were few enemies that could not be battered into submission through the application of carefully targeted but also overwhelming airpower, although the technique worked best when used in conjunction with ground forces (preferably someone else's)—to oblige the enemy to occupy open positions, to identify targets, and to follow through after the bombing.

There was nothing particularly exceptional in the combination of the postmodern and the premodern. The most effective irregular forces have always proved to be adept at borrowing the more advanced technologies when it suited them—witness the mujahideen's use of Stinger antiaircraft missiles to blunt Soviet airpower in Afghanistan, Hezbollah's ability to get videos of their ambushes of Israeli units in Lebanon to the news media, or, for that matter, al Qaeda's ability to mount an audacious attack by turning Western technology against itself, with knives acting as the force multiplier at the critical moment as aircraft were hijacked. Moreover, in practice, an important factor in the swift success of the ground campaign was a tried-and-true Afghan way of warfare, depending on coercive diplomacy, with protracted sparring to see who had superior power before the hard bargaining began on the terms of surrender or, as likely, defection. U.S. special forces may have had impressive new gear to help them operate in unfamiliar terrain, and the role played by unmanned aerial vehicles (UAVs) in finding and even attacking targets was impressive, but a critical item in their armory was large wads of dollars that could provide a formidable inducement to waverers. For those with the sense not to fight to the bitter end, defeat became rather like insolvency, with the faction in question soon trading under another name. Trading was often the operative

word, for with territorial control came the opportunity to take a share of all economic activity, including trafficking in guns and drugs. Surrender was conditional: remarkably few Taliban fighters were disarmed and many appear to have drifted back, still armed, to their villages or into banditry. So the Americans were relieved by the speed of the Taliban surrender, but they did not always appreciate its conditional quality.

Also in late 2001, Deputy Secretary of Defense Paul Wolfowitz explained that "one of the lessons of Afghanistan's history, which we've tried to apply in this campaign, is if you're a foreigner, try not to go in. If you do go in, don't stay too long, because they don't tend to like any foreigners who stay too long."[28] In practice, an early departure was impossible. Despite itself, the United States soon learned that it had little choice but to get involved in nation building. Initially, it considered this a job for others, organized into an international force to help the new government secure at least Kabul while a separate force under its own command carried on hunting guerrillas and terrorists. The two had an uneasy coexistence: the continuing counterterrorism operations often undermined the stabilization project. Eventually, more sensible and extensive arrangements were introduced, although valuable time had been lost.

The move against Iraq was far more controversial. It was also described as a war of necessity and part of the war on terror. In building the domestic case for war, the United States constantly asserted direct links between Saddam Hussein's regime and al Qaeda, and even with the 9/11 attacks, although the evidence was flimsy.[29] The international case was based on Iraqi noncompliance with a series of UN resolutions requiring the elimination of all weapons of mass destruction. The evidence here was stronger, but still in vital respects overstated. The humanitarian advantage of getting rid of an evil regime was also cited, but not as the prime purpose for intervention. Only after the regime was overthrown and no WMD or real evidence of links with al Qaeda had been found did this rationale come to the fore.

The initial Iraqi campaign was different from the Afghan campaign. There was no longer seen to be a need for an extended strategic air campaign, nor was there a strong enough local force to take on the Iraqis (other than the Kurds in their semiautonomous northern territories). Coalition armies were engaged from the start. Initial progress was halting and gave some clues as to what was to come (no massive popular enthusiasm for the occupying forces, the use of guerrilla tactics by opponents). The combination of rapid maneuvers and deadly air strikes soon proved irresistible, and the regime's resistance crumbled. Soon Saddam Hussein was in hiding. His sons were killed in an ambush, and by the end of the year Saddam had been dragged from a hole in the ground. The ruthless efficiency of the initial occupation was impressive and confirmed the complete superiority of the United States in conventional warfare. But it also made the contrast with what was to come even starker.

Just as Washington had overstated the threat posed by prewar Iraq, it had understated the problems of postwar Iraq.[30] The experience of Afghanistan at least encouraged some recognition that issues of reconstruction and nation building could not be ducked, yet there was a degree of wishful thinking about the ease with which this deeply divided and brutalized society could settle on a new form of government. Unfortunately, the transition from an invading force to an occupying administration was poorly handled. In part, this was because preparations had been made to cope with the expected problem of hundreds of thousands of refugees, in flight from urban fighting, instead of the actual problem of a breakdown of law and order in the cities. More seriously, there were simply too few troops. With Iraq, Secretary of Defense Rumsfeld wanted to make a point of demonstrating just how much could

be achieved in modern warfare with remarkably few troops on the ground, but this meant ignoring all prewar calculations that suggested that numbers in the region of 500,000 would be needed, rather than the 135,000 actually available. After army chief of staff General Eric Shinseki advised that hundreds of thousands of troops might be needed, Deputy Secretary of Defense Wolfowitz observed that he found it "hard to conceive that it would take more forces to provide stability in a post-Saddam Iraq than it would take to conduct the war itself and to secure the surrender of Saddam's security forces and his army."[31]

This problem was exacerbated by the failure to hold the Iraqi Army together (admittedly difficult as so many had deserted and the barracks had been destroyed). The process of building up competent Iraqi forces for internal security was thereafter slow and difficult. Last, those U.S. troops available were not well trained for a postwar setting. They remained in "force protection" mode and killed too many ordinary Iraqis. The point was made eloquently by a marine serving in central Iraq: "If anyone gets too close to us we f—ing waste them. It's kind of a shame, because it means we've killed a lot of innocent people."[32] This problem grew with the insurgency, as insurgents were able to blend in with civilians and so undermine any hopes of developing trust between the Americans and the local population, especially in Sunni areas. The British, in the relatively more hospitable Shiite south and with more experience in this sort of situation, had fewer problems, although they were unable to exercise much influence on local power struggles.[33]

The perspective of opponents is also important in trying to understand the developing demands on Western forces. Opponents are often not subtle, using extreme and violent means, regularly merging into outright terrorism, to intimidate and coerce. Nor is the jihadist movement a single, homogeneous ideological and political entity: it has its own fault lines that sensible counterterrorist strategies would seek to exploit. The starting point for any insurgent/terrorist group is an understanding that they cannot hope to take and defeat the regular forces of the West and so must play on fears of disproportionate casualties and even direct attacks on alien civil societies. This fear is crystallized in the dread prospect of the development of weapons of mass destruction by rogue states and terrorists, but it is worth noting that the most effective strategies adopted by the West's opponents have been focused and localized, based on making life as uncomfortable as possible for forward-based enemy forces. Thus one of the most successful such groups—Hezbollah—persuaded the United States and, much later, Israel to leave Lebanon. As the West confronts terrorism, it can help to note that the leaders of these terrorist groups are not always strategic geniuses and often squabble among themselves over what can seem to be quite arcane matters to outsiders. Fawaz Gerges has demonstrated how severe the strategic arguments are within the jihadist movement, especially over whether to wage a series of national campaigns or to give their actions a more global focus.[34]

These strategies are debated by people with long historical memories, going back to the days of the Prophet. In more recent times, these disparate groups have emerged from the struggles of the Muslim Brotherhood in secular Arab states and the mujahideen in Afghanistan. Their leaders have interpreted actions that appeared to be almost random matters of choice and humanitarianism in the West as being quite strategic. An anti-Muslim construction can be put on choices not to get involved in Chechnya and Kashmir or to pressure Israel on Palestine, as well as to act only tentatively and belatedly in Bosnia and Kosovo. In East Timor, however, Christians were allowed to secede from a predominantly Muslim country.

The other key strategic issue is the question of the readiness of terrorists to engage in suicidal attacks.[35] In terms of the sheer efficiency of pain infliction, "martyrdom operations" can create a real sense of a security crisis, but they are not necessarily a means of producing the desired political effects in terms of coercing the enemy into major concessions. They have the ability to realize negative objectives, in rendering countries ungovernable, but not positive ones, in allowing the radical groups to seize control. By reaching into their enemy's civil society, they may seize the headlines, but they also create real anger among the victim population. The strategic calculus of the opponent is shifted from the disproportionate costs of trying to control a hostile population to basic self-defense, adding new questions of revenge and reputation, and possibly of appeasing terror. When extreme methods are directly used against national territory, there is pressure for a harsh response, even if this involves the suspension of civil liberties. Israel, for example, coped with the second intifada through setting barriers to movement and engaging in selective assassination.

There may be ways to suppress hostile populations, but they are not the basis for governing them. When harsh action taken against local militants spills over into their families, friends, and local communities, there is always a risk, at least in the short term, of strengthening the links between them rather than undermining them, which should be the basis of a counterinsurgency policy. Such measures tend to be employed, therefore, when much political ground has already been lost, when hearts-and-minds strategies have already failed or possibly never been tried. When the United States found itself in trouble in Iraq, particularly after the Fallujah debacle of April 2004, it almost gave up on local opinion, at least in the Sunni triangle, and adopted tactics closer to Israel's. Unlike with Israel, however, the objective was, not to keep the hostile section of the population behind a wall, but instead to hold the country together and ensure full self-government. Alienating tactics may have been all that were available in the short term, but they are never the basis for a long-term political settlement.

HEARTS AND MINDS

These tensions help explain why the move from humanitarian interventions to the war on terror has more continuity than often assumed, with lessons from earlier periods still relevant. In recent years, military operations have certainly taken on a sharper edge, as the stakes are higher and claims to altruistic motives have less prominence (although these claims are still made). The unifying factor lies in the need to attend to complex interactions between military and political developments. The readiness to accept the importance of such an interaction is often assumed with the adoption of a hearts-and-minds strategy. The term has passed into common parlance since the days when it was first used extensively in Vietnam. It is now invoked whenever there is a need to persuade people through good works and sensitivity to their concerns that the government and the security forces are really on their side. This is believed to be preferable to brute force and fits in with a basic counterinsurgency strategy of cutting the militants off from their potential sources of support, including recruits, intelligence, sustenance, weapons and ammunition, and sanctuaries.

To the extent that the hearts-and-minds strategy failed in Vietnam (some say it was never really given a chance before it was discarded), this was because its purposes were subverted to serve the needs of central government rather than the people. That is, to succeed it has to be passingly democratic, and this may well upset local power structures. In part, it can be a matter of civic action, repairing roads and building schools, or making secure power and sanitation systems, but at some point issues of land reform or ethnic mix may become germane. The alternative approach from Vietnam days—search and destroy—reflects the

traditional military preference for eliminating the enemy faster than its fighting stock can be replenished. This did not fare much better: it was always easier to destroy than to search, and the indiscriminate nature of the destruction served to antagonize the local population and so add to the stock of militants. This approach judged military operations only by their presumed military effects and failed to evaluate their political effects.

But just as search and destroy are not always in harmony, nor are hearts and minds. In other contexts, heart and mind are often put against each other—strong emotions versus cool calculation, appeals to values and symbols versus appeals to the intellect. In strategic discourse, much hearts-and-minds theory seems very hearts oriented, as if showing a human face with a ready smile as desperately needed goods and services are brought to a thankful populace by Sergeant Bountiful backed up by Major Reassurance, can persuade people to forget basic political differences. Such activities can have substantial payoffs, but they require a security situation that allows foreign troops and local people to interact closely and develop trust. A more minds-oriented approach must create that trust by addressing questions of who is likely to win the ongoing political and military conflict and the nature of the long-term agendas of both sides. The insurgent can sow doubts about who among the local population can be trusted, about what is real and what is fake, who is truly on your side and who is pretending. As the insurgents and counterinsurgents play mind games to gain local support, they may be as eager to create impressions of strength as of kindness, to demonstrate a likely victory as well as hand out largesse. In Iraq, for example, much ground may have been lost by delays in setting up electricity supplies and by divisions aggravated by the constitutional provisions and electoral system. But the underlying problem was that the coalition set up a power struggle between and within the Sunni and Shiite communities that they had insufficient strength to control.

A "battle of the narrative" is now creeping into strategic jargon as a way to describe these mind games.[36] The psychological dimensions to counterinsurgency campaigns have long been recognized, although the attempts to address the dimension as "psychological warfare" rarely seemed adequate; they were often presentational rather than substantive. To win a battle of the narrative requires disseminating convincing explanations for events that both pass blame to insurgents and give confidence in the intentions and competence of the security forces, but the best "public affairs" team is not going to be able to compensate for evident blunders and insensitivities. Narratives cannot be conjured up if they bear no relation to the everyday experiences of those to whom they are addressed or if they are insensitive to cultural symbols and misunderstand local references —hence the disaster of the pictures of the gross maltreatment of Iraqi prisoners at Abu Ghraib prison.

In addition, the mind games can be played at a global as well as a local level. Intervening countries have to demonstrate to their home populations that their military efforts are worthwhile and succeeding, and at a tolerable cost. The U.S. withdrawal from Vietnam is normally attributed to the loss of will at home, as casualties grew without any evident progress. Whether or not the North Vietnamese understood what they were doing with the 1968 Tet Offensive, which is now cited as the classic example of a military defeat turning into a political victory, their ability to get into the heart of South Vietnamese cities put an immediate question mark against all the claims that had been made by the U.S. military command over the previous year.[37]

The disillusionment over Vietnam was often attributed to the influence of the media, which certainly picked up on the contradiction between official claims and the realities of the war on the ground and portrayed combat harshly.

The skeptical attitude of journalists and broadcasters was a change from that of the previous generation, which had accepted its role as a patriotic extension of the war effort. After Vietnam, policymakers knew that they could never assume a respectful hearing, especially when events were taking a turn for the worse. In terms of the communication between the combat zone and the home front and on to the wider international audience, the media were very important. The media were less important to those directly caught up in the fighting, who could draw conclusions from their own experiences or word of mouth.

The importance of the media has grown in the intervening years because of the progressive ability to collect and transmit images and words across continents. Governments and armed forces find that they must take this into account in their plans and practices, developing some sensitivity to how past boasts might come back to haunt them or casual cruelty be broadcast around the world. As a result of the Internet, pressure groups and individuals can reach mass audiences more directly than before without the mediating influence of the mass media. Events can be described, discussed, and interpreted within extensive networks of activists and sympathizers. Once the raw material is present in this network, a political critical mass can be created at the press of an Enter key.

Two points of caution are necessary. First, while the new media may make possible new forms of black propaganda, the ability to win a battle of the narrative almost independently of the real battle on the ground should not be overstated. The pictures of torture at Abu Ghraib were undoubtedly a public relations disaster for the United States, because they provided vivid portrayals of matters that had previously only been alluded to in print. This disclosure could have been dealt with had it not soon become evident that the behavior being shown was real, widespread, and the result of a relaxed attitude to tougher interrogation methods sanctioned at the senior levels of government.[38] Second, victory in a narrative battle is not the same as a victory in war unless it leads to comparable political effects. The ability to "swarm" has been described as the form of activism most encouraged by the World Wide Web.[39] It certainly makes it difficult for governments to know quite the arguments they are trying to contest and renders them vulnerable to media ambush. This is not unlike guerrilla warfare. At least in Maoist theory, successful guerrilla groups are those that are able to turn themselves into conventional forces capable of occupying capital cities and installing governments.

Studies of the influence of the media on political decisions about the use of armed force tend to stress the question of whether the government knows its own mind—either resisting what it considers to be imprudent calls for humanitarian intervention or continuing with difficult campaigns even after setbacks. Thus, the more discretionary a campaign already appears, the more likely it will be that bad news from the front will erode public support, while harmful publicity among the local population will make the core task much harder and lead to more bad news. It is thus possible to see how a vicious cycle can be generated, but the starting point will be real events. It therefore needs to be undersood at the start of a counterinsurgency campaign how brutish behavior by one's own side is likely to be interpreted and used by the enemy when constructing its narratives. Such behavior will undermine attempts to construct a counternarrative that portrays your side as more civilized in its approach. It is vital to provide compelling analyses of the developing conflict, as it affects the lives of those you are seeking to influence. The stakes for Western countries engaged in counterterrorist and counterinsurgency operations may be higher than those engaged in humanitarian interventions, but those caught up in vicious cycles of violence on the ground will consider the stakes to be even higher. The

narratives may be different when you are seeking to persuade different communities not to hate each other, as in humanitarian interventions, but the basic need to be sensitive to the cultures and dynamics of the societies in which operations are taking place remains the same.

A much more fundamental lesson may be drawn, however. The experience of recent operations has been frustrating and disillusioning, and also draining. One consequence of this is that there will be a growing reluctance in the future to intervene in situations where the prompts are human distress and unacceptable behavior by repressive or predatory regimes, for example, Sudan. Even with the war on terror it is, ironically, at least for the moment, only in Iraq that a terrorist group might be able to acquire the critical mass to mount attacks against Western countries and their allies that may be contained and eventually defeated only through large-scale combat operations. The more this insurgency prospers, the more it risks creating cadres who will go out and feed into tense situations elsewhere, such as Pakistan, Egypt, or Saudi Arabia, just as the radicalized veterans of the war against Soviet forces in Afghanistan formed the nucleus of al Qaeda. Elsewhere, counterterrorism is more a matter of good intelligence and police work and sensitive community relations.

What may turn out to be more important than the content of new strategic priorities of the 2000s is the mixed experience of their pursuit. The invasion and occupation of Iraq in particular have raised major questions about military methodology and the legitimacy of the use of force and have also left U.S. forces stretched thin and with no evident public appetite for more adventures of this sort. The responsibility to protect as grounds for the exercise of military power may have, at least for a while, less support from those countries that have taken it most seriously. They are feeling bruised and overstretched. This is a consequence not only of the U.S./UK experience in Iraq but also of the French experience in Côte d'Ivoire. The preoccupation with Iraq has resulted in insufficient attention being paid to the dire situation in Sudan. This is not a new phenomenon. It was evident not only post-Vietnam but also after setbacks in other interventions—for example, Beirut in 1983–84 and Somalia and Bosnia a decade later. The setbacks did lead to a reluctance to intervene, thereby creating conditions that led others to act on the assumption that there would be no intervention even if they acted provocatively—as did Iraq in 1990, the *génocidaires* in Rwanda in 1994, and the Serbs in Sarajevo in 1995. In the West for the time being, the use of force may therefore go out of fashion, but it may be that the cycle will turn again and the fear of further quagmires will give way to intolerance of passivity in the face of outrages being committed elsewhere and the emergence of new sanctuaries for terrorists.

Furthermore, it is important to keep in mind that however gloomy the daily headlines may be, the trends are in the right direction. The Canadian Human Security Centre reports that the world is actually getting more peaceful: the number of armed conflicts has declined by more than 40 percent since 1992. There are now fewer international crises than ever before and also fewer military coups and attempted coups, and less money is spent on arms. Armed conflict is now largely confined to the poorest countries in the world, with most taking place in Africa, although even here there is a decline. If these countries can be brought out of poverty, the risk of war will decline. Wars have also become dramatically less deadly over the past five decades. The average number of people reported killed per conflict per year in 1950 was thirty-eight thousand; in 2002 it was just six hundred—a decline of 98 percent. The really deadly ones, of course, cause more deaths through famine and disease than in battle. Only international terrorism is on the rise.[40] The combination of timely intervention and attempts at reconstruction still has much to commend it, what-

ever the frustrations, and, to the extent that it is timely and focused, the opportunities for terrorists to gain recruits and establish bases should be reduced.

NOTES

A number of the arguments in this chapter are developed further in Lawrence Freedman, *The Transformation in Strategic Affairs* (London: Routledge, for the International Institute for Strategic Studies, 2006).

1. For a sample of the literature, see Nigel Rodley, ed., *To Loose the Bands of Wickedness* (London: Brassey's, 1992); Lawrence Freedman, ed., *Military Intervention in European Conflicts* (*Political Quarterly* special issue) (London: Blackwell, 1994); Stephen A. Garrett, *Doing Good and Doing Well: An Examination of Humanitarian Intervention* (Westport, Conn.: Greenwood Press, 1999); Nicholas J. Wheeler, *Saving Strangers: Humanitarian Intervention in International Society* (London: Oxford University Press, 2002); J. L. Holzgrefe and Robert O. Keohane, eds., *Humanitarian Intervention: Ethical, Legal and Political Dilemmas* (Cambridge: Cambridge University Press, 2003); Jennifer Welsh, ed., *Humanitarian Intervention and International Relations* (London: Oxford University Press, 2003); and Andrea Kathryn Talentino, *Military Intervention after the Cold War: The Evolution of Theory and Practice* (Athens: Ohio University Press, 2005).

2. For the best exposition of the strategic assumptions of neorealism, see John Mearsheimer, *The Tragedy of Great Power Politics* (New York: W. W. Norton, 2001). For a discussion of the problems the end of the Cold War posed for neorealism, see William Wohlforth, "Realism and the End of the Cold War," *International Security* (Winter 1994–95): 91–129.

3. The various possible responses to U.S. primacy, and the experience of their adherents (particularly in the 2000s), are assessed in Stephen M. Walt, *Taming American Power: The Global Response to U.S. Primacy* (New York: W. W. Norton, 2005).

4. For a skeptical view, see Gerald Segal, "Does China Matter?" *Foreign Affairs* (September–October 1999). Segal's views were assessed in Barry Buzan and Rosemary Foot, eds., *Does China Matter? A Reassessment* (London: Routledge, 2004). For a more recent assessment of Chinese thinking, see Avery

Goldstein, *Rising to the Challenge: China's Grand Strategy and International Security* (Stanford, Calif.: Stanford University Press, 2005).

5. Piers Robinson, *The CNN Effect: The Myth of News, Foreign Policy and Intervention* (London: Routledge, 2002).

6. It is worth noting that objectives could be set for military intervention as a result of exaggerated expectations for nonmilitary forms of coercion. In the case of the former Yugoslavia, the European Union and the United Nations made demands that could not be enforced through trade embargoes and diplomatic isolation. They had to either abandon their initial position (with a consequent loss of authority) or consider escalation. The prudent military planner, therefore, would start work as soon as an explicit international commitment to a particular outcome for a particular conflict was made, even though the possibility of military enforcement was being excluded at the time.

7. I argued the case for stability support as opposed to peace support in "Bosnia: Does Peace Support Make Any Sense?" *NATO Review* 43, no. 6 (November 1995). I used a comparison with the International Monetary Fund, which, when acting to help countries in desperate economic straits, normally claimed to be stabilizing a situation to enable a government to introduce long-term structural measures that make possible sustainable development. It did not herald its operations as "restoring growth" or "employment support" and recognized that in the short term it would be associated with unpopular policies, at least among some sections of the population (and by no means always the least deserving).

8. Edward Luttwak, "Towards Post-Heroic Warfare," *Foreign Affairs* 74, no. 3 (May–June 1995): 109–122.

9. In both cases there were explanations for withdrawal other than the absolute level of casualties. J. Burk, "Public Support for Peacekeeping in Lebanon and Somalia: Assessing the Casualties Hypothesis," *Political Science Quarterly* 114, no. 1 (1999): 53–78.

10. Peter D. Feaver and Christopher Gelpi, *Choosing Your Battles: American Civil-Military Relations and the Use of Force* (Princeton, N.J.: Princeton University Press, 2004).

11. Robert H. Scales, *Yellow Smoke: The Future of Land Warfare for America's Military* (Lanham, Md.: Rowman and Littlefield, 2003).

12. James Gow, *Triumph of the Lack of Will: International Diplomacy and the Yugoslav War* (London: Hurst, 1997); and Laura Silber and Alan Little, *Yugoslavia: Death of a Nation* (London: Penguin, 1997).

13. For a sharp critique of British policy, see Brendan Simms, *Unfinest Hour: Britain and the Destruction of Bosnia* (London: Penguin, 2002).

14. Albrecht Schnabel and Ramesh Thakur, eds., *Kosovo and the Challenge of Humanitarian Intervention: Selective Indignation, Collective Action, and International Citizenship* (New York: United Nations University Press, 2000); and Ivo Daalder and Michael O'Hanlan, *Winning Ugly: NATO's War to Save Kosovo* (Washington, D.C.: Brookings Institution Press, 2000). On air aspects, see Benjamin Lambeth, *NATO's Air War for Kosovo* (Santa Monica, Calif.: RAND Corporation, 2001). From the commander's perspective, see General Wesley K. Clark, *Waging Modern War: Bosnia, Kosovo and the Future of Conflict* (New York: Public Affairs, 2001).

15. This was especially so in light of the previous December's air raids on Iraq (Operation Desert Fox), which had been of about this intensity and duration and had also had no discernible effect on Saddam Hussein's behavior.

16. International Commission on Intervention, *The Responsibility to Protect: The Report of the International Commission on Intervention and State Sovereignty* (Ottawa: International Development Research Centre [IDRC], November 2002); and Thomas G. Weiss, *Military-Civilian Interactions: Humanitarian Crises and the Responsibility to Protect* (New York: Rowman and Littlefield, 2004).

17. Prime Minister Tony Blair, "The Doctrine of International Community" (speech to the Economic Club, Chicago, April 23, 1999, http://www.number10.gov.uk/output/Page11297.asp). For background, see John Kampfner, *Blair's Wars* (New York: Simon and Schuster, 2003).

18. When the Afghanistan operation began in October 2001, a "senior administration official" was quoted as saying, "The fewer people you have to rely on, the fewer permissions you have to get." Elaine Sciolino and Steven Lee Myers, "Bush Says 'Time Is Running Out,' as U.S. Forces Move into Place," *New York Times*, October 7, 2001.

19. Brahimi Panel, *Report of the Panel on United Nations Peace Operations*, A/55/305-S/2000/809 (New

York: United Nations, August 21, 2000), http://www
.un.org/peace/reports/peace_operations/.

20. One conclusion the key European states drew
from Kosovo was that they really needed to upgrade
their capabilities lest they find themselves in an emergency in which the United States was unable or unwilling to help.

21. "The British are, by instinct, an international-
ist people. We believe that as well as defending our
rights, we should discharge our responsibilities in the
world. We do not want to stand idly by and watch
humanitarian disasters or the aggression of dictators go
unchecked. We want to give a lead, we want to be a
force for good." UK Ministry of Defence, introduction to *United Kingdom Strategic Defence Review
(SDR),* "Modern Forces for a Modern World," par.
15, July 8, 1998.

22. Colin Powell, "U.S. Forces: Challenges Ahead,"
Foreign Affairs (Winter 1992–93).

23. Condoleezza Rice, "Promoting the National
Interest," *Foreign Affairs* 79, no. 1 (January–February
2000): 53.

24. President George W. Bush, *Address to a Joint
Session of Congress and the American People,* United
States Capitol, Washington D.C., September 30, 2001.
Later he described this as "a new and different war,
the first, and we hope the only one, of the twenty-
first century. A war against all those who seek to export terror, and a war against those governments that
support or shelter them." President George W. Bush,
press conference, October 11, 2001.

25. Secretary of Defense Donald H. Rumsfeld,
"A New Kind of War," *New York Times,* September 27, 2001.

26. Anthony Cordesman, *The Lessons of Afghanistan: War Fighting, Intelligence, and Force Transformation* (Washington, D.C.: Center for Strategic and
International Studies, September 6, 2002).

27. President George Bush, remarks at the Cita-
del, Charleston, S.C., December 11, 2001.

28. Paul Wolfowitz, interview on *Face the Nation,*
November 18, 2001.

29. Lawrence Freedman, "War in Iraq: Selling
the Threat," *Survival* 46, no. 2 (Summer 2004): 7–50.

30. George Packer, *The Assassin's Gate: America in
Iraq* (New York: Farrar, Straus and Giroux, 2005).

31. U.S. Congress, Committee on the Budget,
*Department of Defense Budget Priorities for Fiscal Year
2004,* 108th Congress, 1st sess., February 27, 2003.
By 2006 retired military officers were explicitly blaming Rumsfeld. See, for example, Lt. Gen. Greg New-
bold (ret.), "Why Iraq Was a Mistake," *Time,* April 9,
2006.

32. "When Deadly Force Bumps into Hearts and
Minds," *Economist,* December 29, 2004.

33. For a trenchant British critique of U.S. tactics
in Iraq, see Brigadier Nigel Aylwin-Foster, "Changing the Army for Counterinsurgency Operations,"
Military Review (November–December 2005).

34. Fawaz A. Gerges, *The Far Enemy: Why Jihad
Went Global* (Cambridge: Cambridge University Press,
2005). On the various strands of religious and political thought that make up jihadist movements, see
also Olivier Roy's *Globalized Islam: The Search for
a New Ummah* (New York: Columbia University
Press, 2004).

35. Robert A. Pape, *Dying to Win: The Strategic
Logic of Suicide Terrorism* (New York: Random House,
2005); and Mia Blook, *Dying to Kill: The Allure
of Suicide Terror* (New York: Columbia University
Press, 2005).

36. Matt Stoller, "The Narrative as Battlefield,"
December 14, 2003, http://www.bopnews.com/
archives/000084.html.

37. John Mueller, *War, Presidents and Public
Opinion* (New York: Wiley, 1973).

38. Mark Danner, *Torture and Truth: America, Abu
Ghraib, and the War on Terror* (New York: New York
Review of Books, 2004).

39. David Ronfeldt and John Arquilla, *Networks and Netwars: The Future of Terror, Crime, and
Militancy* (Santa Monica, Calif.: RAND Corporation, 2001), http://www.rand.org/publications/MR/
MR1382/.

40. Human Security Centre, *Human Security Report 2005: War and Peace in the Twenty-first Century*
(New York: Oxford University Press, 2006).

15

LIMITS ON THE USE OF FORCE

Brian Urquhart

THE LAST DECADE OF THE TWENTI-
eth century may well go down in history as the time when conventional
battlefield warfare, like the great battleships
of the early part of the century, became an
anachronism. This development has not only
changed the nature of warfare; it has also
changed the way in which military institutions might be used to maintain peace. The
combination of the unimaginable and unacceptable destruction of nuclear weapons at one
end of the scale and the increasing effectiveness of armed insurgency and mass-casualty
terrorism at the other—together with a general spirit of strong national and, in some cases,
religious resistance to foreign powers—is radically changing the concept of insuperable military superiority.

After World War II the UN Charter fore-
saw, as the centerpiece of the new world organization, the full-scale use of collective armed
force to deal with threats to the peace and acts
of aggression such as those that had led up to
World War II. In the political and military

context of the last half of the twentieth century, however, different blends of military technique and new forms of collective diplomacy
and international action would have to be found
to deal with a new combination of threats to
international peace, security, and well-being.
The search for the right combination continues, illuminated from time to time by the practical experience of dealing with real problems
of peace and security.

The unanticipated Cold War and the forty-
year standoff between the Soviet Union and
the West was the first obstacle to the realization of the UN Charter's dream of a collective security system run by the UN Security
Council and based on the military strength of
its five permanent members (Britain, China,
France, the USSR, and the United States). In
addition, the kind of aggression that the writers of the charter were most concerned with,
aggression or the threat of aggression by dictators, became relatively rare in the forty years
of the Cold War. The most common form of
threat to international peace, apart from the

overwhelming threat of the breakdown of the East-West balance of terror, was a series of regional conflicts, starting with Kashmir and Palestine, that were usually the legacy of rapid decolonization. Because it was not possible for the Security Council to agree on who the aggressor was in such regional conflicts, international intervention with major force was out of the question. The Security Council and the Secretariat therefore began to look for a new, nonforceful combination of diplomacy and preventive military force. This came to be called peacekeeping.

As for the Cold War, which involved the veto-bearing five permanent members of the Security Council, it was for the most part outside the practical authority of the Security Council. Nonetheless, the council could sometimes provide a safety net, a place for informal contact, and a face-saver for East and West when the Cold War seemed about to heat up.

During the Cold War the main concern of the so-called international community was to prevent regional conflicts, or any other event, from triggering an East-West confrontation. When the Cold War thawed out in 1990, a profusion of *intra*national conflicts flared up. These situations, in which one or more nongovernmental parties—warlords, rebellious factions, ethnic leaders, thugs, and so on—were usually involved, often proved far harder to resolve than regional conflicts between states. In what may well turn out to be the last conventional case of dealing with aggression by overwhelming force, Iraq's 1990 occupation of Kuwait was successfully reversed by a U.S.-led coalition under a UN Security Council mandate.

The overwhelming success of Desert Storm, the U.S. operational plan to get Iraq out of Kuwait, may also have had a broader, longer-term effect. Potential antagonists finally realized that the conventional battlefield was the last place on earth to confront a U.S.-led coalition or any other powerful conventional force. Instead, armed insurgency and terrorism have become the accepted mode of resistance and

have successfully deprived conventional, overwhelming military force of much of its former effectiveness.

At the same time, the possession of nuclear weapons has seemed to a few governments— such as India and Pakistan—to be the best way to create a local balance of terror. The obvious potential hazards of further nuclear weapons development, for example, in Iran or North Korea, have created much international anxiety, especially among the original nuclear weapons states, who are determined, in the name of nuclear nonproliferation, to limit the possession of nuclear weapons to the present owners.

The search for a practical international security system, in which the appropriate form of limited force must play a part, must be sought within the limits of these recent developments.

THE SEARCH FOR A TWENTIETH-CENTURY INTERNATIONAL SECURITY SYSTEM

World War I was sufficiently atrocious to generate the first attempt at an intergovernmental world organization that was to be an active guardian of the peace. The League of Nations, because of the failure of its creator, the United States, to join it, and the timidity and lack of cohesion of its primarily European membership, proved, after a promising start, to be unable to deal with three aggressive dictatorships: Fascist Italy, Nazi Germany, and imperial/militarist Japan. The seemingly promising disarmament movement of the 1920s evaporated quickly before the totalitarian juggernaut of the 1930s. By 1945 six years of horror, some seventy-five million dead, and staggering devastation once again made the world ready, even desperate, for another try at world organization.

In 1919 Franklin Roosevelt, then assistant secretary of the U.S. Navy, had observed with dismay the dilatory, disorganized, and often wrong-headed proceedings of the Versailles peace conference. In 1944 as president of the

United States, he was determined that the new world organization should be agreed upon before the war was over, so that governments would still be moved by the urgent need to create an organization that could "save succeeding generations from the scourge of war." While tactically effective, this decision also based the new organization on wartime assumptions that soon proved to be at odds with the nature of the ensuing peace and the East-West struggle that dominated it.

The primary goals of the UN Charter were to a large extent dictated by the grim experiences of the previous thirty years. The new world organization was to deal with aggression and threats to the peace, to prevent a new arms race and promote disarmament, and to forestall another worldwide depression. Secondary aims were decolonization, economic and social development, the advancement of human rights, and the promulgation of international law. In these secondary aims the United Nations has had considerable success over the past sixty years. As for the primary aim, the maintenance of international peace and security, the organization was forced, as best it could, to improvise its way around a world not foreseen in the charter and a Security Council often paralyzed by the Cold War.

At the Conference on International Organization, which opened in April 1945 in San Francisco, virtually none of the participants had any inkling either of the existence and imminent use of nuclear weapons or of the future East-West balance of terror. At that time governments and people remembered, and were grateful, that the Soviet Union had played a decisive part in the final defeat of Hitler. At San Francisco, therefore, it seemed obvious that a system of collective security, monitored and, if necessary, enforced by a consortium of the most powerful leaders of the victorious alliance, was the best and most logical arrangement to secure the future peace. This system would, it was believed, also make possible a substantial degree of general disarmament.

Britain, China, France, the USSR, and the United States became, under the UN Charter, the five permanent, veto-bearing members of the Security Council. Much of their armed forces was to be at the disposal of the Security Council to deal with threats to the peace and acts of aggression. The chiefs of staff of their armed forces would constitute the Military Staff Committee (hailed at the time as the "teeth of the charter") and would advise the Security Council on military operations and disarmament. Thus, in a world still at war, the founders of the United Nations designated, to supervise and to police the future peace and security of the world, a group of countries whose mutual hostility would soon become the most likely cause of another world war. This was the first practical postwar limitation on the use of force or of military power in managing international conflict.

THE FREEZING OF THE CHARTER COLLECTIVE SECURITY SYSTEM

By 1948 it was clear that the charter's plan for collective security would be of little relevance to the dramatically worsening relations between East and West, and both sides resorted to military pacts—NATO and the Warsaw Pact—as their first line of defense against each other. This was regarded by many as a crushing defeat for the principles of the UN Charter, but the exigencies of the balance of terror demanded that these two enormous military organizations could ultimately be judged successful only if they maintained a purely preventive function and on no account went to war with each other. Paradoxically, this meant that NATO never heard a shot fired in anger until 2002 in Afghanistan, where some of its troops were on peacekeeping duties. By contrast, after 1948 the United Nations' last-minute, improvised, lightly armed, shoestring peacekeeping operations were often under fire—and under a great deal of patronizing criticism as well—while trying to contain actual conflicts.

In the United Nations' first sixty years there were only two clear-cut cases of what had originally been proclaimed as the United Nations' most important function, its capacity to marshal military power against aggression. When North Korea invaded South Korea in 1950, the Soviet Union was boycotting all UN meetings, including the Security Council, in protest against the People's Republic of China being excluded from China's seat in the United Nations. This allowed President Harry Truman to push through a Security Council resolution under Chapter VII of the charter, authorizing a full military response under the UN flag and under U.S. command to the North Korean attack. (After this, the USSR gave orders that in future the Soviet permanent representative was never to leave the council chamber even for a moment while the council was in session.) In 1990, with Cold War restrictions out of the way, the Security Council unanimously and immediately authorized, again under U.S. command, a coalition to eject Saddam Hussein's forces from Kuwait. The operations in Korea and Iraq achieved their objective, the former with great military sacrifice.

IMPROVISATION AND THE DEVELOPMENT OF PEACEKEEPING

The use of overwhelming military force to preserve the peace clearly could not be the answer to the Cold War situation. In the years after World War II East-West tensions were largely outside the range of possible UN action except for providing a place, usually as a last resort, for confidential and informal consultation between the superpowers. By contrast, the United Nations played an active role in addressing the regional conflicts that sprang from rapid decolonization. The independence process gave rise to all sorts of power vacuums, frictions, and border disputes that sometimes led to open conflict. The Security Council and the Secretariat proved to be very useful in

containing and defusing these situations, some of which—in the Middle East, for example, and later the former Belgian Congo—might otherwise have easily brought the superpowers to a confrontation.

In 1948 wars in the subcontinent and in Palestine produced the first experiments in what later became UN peacekeeping. The 1948 war between India and Pakistan over Kashmir was ended by the negotiation of a cease-fire line in Kashmir, to be monitored by UN military observers. (These observers are still there, generally forgotten but kept on at the insistence of Pakistan, as a reminder that the cease-fire line, or "Line of Control," in Kashmir is still only a temporary line.)

The final surrender by Britain of its League of Nations mandate over Palestine in May 1948 led to the immediate declaration of the State of Israel and, a few hours later, to the invasion of the new state by five Arab nations. The Security Council appointed a mediator, Count Folke Bernadotte, to arrange a cease-fire and to propose a detailed plan for the partition of Palestine. Ralph Bunche, who in 1947 had written the partition plan that had been approved by the UN General Assembly and who was assisting Bernadotte, believed that no cease-fire would last without military observers to monitor and report on it. Bunche therefore set up, and wrote the basic rules for, the UN Truce Supervision Organization (UNTSO still exists). These rules set out the basic principles of objectivity and nonpartisanship that were also the foundation for later peacekeeping operations.

In the Suez crisis of 1956, UN operations progressed from unarmed military observers to armed military units. Lester Pearson, the foreign minister of Canada, suggested to the General Assembly a "police and peace force" to operate between the Egyptian army and the invading forces of Britain, France, and Israel to facilitate their withdrawal from Egyptian territory.[1] Through intensive efforts led by UN secretary-general Dag Hammarskjöld and

Ralph Bunche, the advance units of the force arrived in the Suez Canal zone of Egypt within a week.

The United Nations Emergency Force (UNEF) was the model on which future peacekeeping operations were based. Its immediate task was to provide the pretext on which the British and French, and later the Israeli, forces could withdraw from Egypt with honor and in good order. UNEF I followed up these withdrawals and later provided the pretext for Egypt not to reoccupy the Sinai or the Egyptian gun positions covering the Straits of Tiran, the access to the southern Israeli port of Eilat. It also established buffer zones on the Egyptian side of the armistice line in Gaza and the international boundary in the Sinai. Israel refused to have UNEF troops stationed on the Israel side of the line. For ten years UNEF, the first peacekeeping force, kept peace on what had previously been one of the bloodiest borders in the Middle East.

After much initial skepticism, the UNEF experiment proved highly successful. In 1958 Secretary of State John Foster Dulles suggested to Hammarskjöld that there should be a standing UN peacekeeping force. Knowing the temper of the General Assembly on matters affecting national sovereignty and the inevitable complications of future operations, Hammarskjöld felt strongly that such a move would be premature and that it would be better to be prepared to improvise the next peacekeeping force than to have a standing force that might not be suitable for the new task.

In the end UNEF was too successful for its own good. By 1967, when Egyptian president Gamal Abdel Nasser, in a disastrous gamble, decided to reoccupy the Sinai, UNEF had been reduced to some twelve hundred active soldiers, lightly armed and with the right to use their personal weapons only in self-defense, manning a four-hundred-mile front. Its success had apparently persuaded people in the West that UNEF was as strong as NATO, and had the right, and the military capacity, to

fight Egyptian armed forces on their own territory. In fact, already in 1956, as a condition for allowing the force into Egypt, Nasser had insisted to U Thant's predecessor, Dag Hammarskjöld, that his right to demand UNEF's withdrawal from Egyptian sovereign territory must be respected in the future. When he invoked this understanding in May 1967, the then secretary-general, U Thant, went to Cairo and tried in vain to persuade Nasser to abandon his self-destructive plan. Only after Nasser's refusal did U Thant reluctantly agree to set in motion the lengthy process of withdrawing UNEF.

U Thant was subjected to much abuse and contempt, especially in the United States and Britain, for having failed to "stand up to Nasser"—no other world statesman had had the courage to confront Nasser—or to challenge the Egyptian army on its own sovereign territory. On June 5 Israel, taking advantage of the alleged pretext of an Egyptian threat to Israel, responded with full force, defeating Egypt, Jordan, and Syria within six days and occupying the Sinai, the Golan Heights, and the West Bank, including Arab Jerusalem. Only then did many governments begin to appreciate the importance of a small and lightly armed peacekeeping force accepted by the parties in conflict and deployed on both sides of the line, and how important it was to understand the strengths and the weaknesses of such a force, and, above all, to maintain its position.

The Six Days' War was a disaster for the Arab states, for the Palestinian refugees, and for the fledgling concept of peacekeeping. The concept, however, survived. In 1973 President Anwar Sadat, after his efforts in the Security Council to regain the Sinai by peaceful means had failed, successfully crossed the Suez Canal in an attempt to recapture the Sinai. In the fighting that followed, Egyptian and Israeli troops were engaged on both sides of the Suez Canal. Constant violations made the Security Council–ordered cease-fire unworkable, and there were frightening signs that the war might bring in both superpowers. (The United States went on high nuclear alert, and the Soviet Union was reported to be moving airborne troops toward the Middle East.) The Security Council called urgently for a UN force to pin down the cease-fire on both sides of the canal. This force began to deploy on the ground within seventeen hours of the Security Council decision, and the cease-fire as well as the wider peace were saved.

In the Cold War period, one operation was a precursor of the multifunctional operations of the 1990s operating inside a single country. In the chaos that engulfed the Belgian Congo at its independence in 1960, the Security Council launched a peacekeeping operation, Organization des Nations Unies au Congo (ONUC), whose first objective was to take over security and thus get the Belgian troops withdrawn from the country. ONUC was also to take on most of the administrative functions of the government until Congolese could be trained to take them over, to restore order and parliamentary government, to train the army, and to protect civilians and officials threatened by the ever-widening violence. The operation also had to deal with three secessionist provinces, the most important of which was the mining province of Katanga. Later, after the assassination of the first prime minister, Patrice Lumumba, ONUC was authorized to use force to prevent civil war and to deal with the foreign mercenaries who abounded in the rich mining provinces that had seceded. The secession of Katanga ended in December 1962. By the time the United Nations left the Congo in 1964, the other two secessionist provinces, Kasai and Orientale, had also returned to the authority of the central government, and parliamentary government had, for the time being at least, been restored.

In 1965 the advent of Joseph Mobutu as prime minister and president soon undid these and many of the other achievements of ONUC. In thirty disastrous, kleptocratic years Mobutu, backed for most of the time by the United Sates, reduced the richest country in Africa to poverty and chaos.

UN PEACEKEEPING AND THE COLD WAR

The UNEF model of peacekeeping was very much a Cold War arrangement. During the Cold War, there was a universal and deadly fear of an East-West nuclear confrontation and of the possibility that a regional conflict might trigger such a disaster.

Apart from the intrinsic value of stopping or mitigating regional conflicts, UN peacekeeping operations could, to an important extent, contain and isolate regional conflicts from the East-West struggle. In the Middle East in 1948, 1956, and 1973; in Lebanon in 1958 and 1978; in Cyprus; in the India-Pakistan wars of 1965 and 1971; and in the Congo in 1960, UN peacekeeping operations backed up by skillful diplomacy performed this vital function with some success and with very modest military resources.

Early peacekeeping was very much the child of decolonization, especially British decolonization, in Palestine and the Middle East, the subcontinent, Cyprus, and elsewhere. Residual efforts by European colonial powers to hold on to their colonial possessions by force were doomed to failure. Their resources and authority, weakened by World War II, were no match for the spirit of national independence that surged through the colonial world, and the UN Charter strengthened this spirit. The United Nations provided new possibilities for a peaceful transition to the independence that would still have come about eventually, but certainly with far greater bloodshed and lasting animosity. In general, colonial powers' efforts to stay on, whether in Kenya, Algeria, Aden, Malaya, Singapore, Vietnam, Cyprus, Angola, or Mozambique, served only to evoke armed rebellion, to embitter the indigenous population, and to gain a brief delay in granting independence.

When one or other of the superpowers embarked on a full-scale military expedition outside their sphere of influence and without going through the United Nations, as the United States did in Vietnam and the Soviet Union in Afghanistan, armed insurgency began to prove itself a formidable adversary to conventional military action undertaken without international legitimacy and support.

During the Cold War, except for Korea, Vietnam, and Afghanistan, the most massive military buildups were defensive and preventive. Small, improvised, nonpartisan, peacekeeping forces, with a strictly limited capacity to use force but with the symbolic strength of a Security Council mandate, were a major innovation. In the context of maintaining the East-West balance of terror, peacekeeping operations proved unexpectedly useful.

One major difference between early peacekeeping operations and post–Cold War missions is the speed with which the early operations were deployed—for example, UNEF I was deployed in one week, the first three thousand troops to the Congo in three days, the first contingent of UNEF II to Egypt in 1973 in seventeen hours. East-West hostility and its potentially catastrophic consequences certainly made governments willing to do anything they could, including providing troops, to support UN efforts to contain a regional crisis that might otherwise lead to an East-West military confrontation. Hammarskjöld and Bunche had been determined to respond to the demands of the Security Council or the General Assembly for action with the minimum possible delay, and their example inspired their immediate successors. They were highly respected world figures whose urgent requests for soldiers or other forms of support were taken extremely seriously. Peacekeeping was still a demanding novelty, and governments were prepared to provide contingents for urgent and improvised operations with the minimum of planning and logistical preparation. Interstate peacekeeping operations required mostly military personnel, unlike the complex multifunctional intrastate operations of the 1990s. Now, with sixty years of experience to reflect on, many governments have installed a series of obligatory steps to be taken before a decision on participating in, or even agreeing to, a peacekeeping operation can be taken. Such processes can take up to six months and offer a wide field to domestic opposition.

THE 1990S

With the end of the Cold War and the straitjacket it had imposed on international affairs and international organizations, new problems quickly emerged. In a world with one superpower, the Security Council had a new freedom to launch multifunctional peacekeeping operations for largely humanitarian purposes within the boundaries of a single country. The resulting very large humanitarian problems, as well as the need to deal with various violent nongovernmental groups—for the most part warlords or ethnic leaders who felt no obligation to obey international rules or to respect the decisions of the Security Council or its representatives in the field—provided a challenge that was more confusing and far more complex than that faced by the original peacekeeping operations. This is certainly one of the reasons that the United Nations now has increasing difficulty in mounting operations quickly and securing the services of enough contingents with adequate training.

Of some seventeen multifunctional operations in the 1990s, three in particular—Bosnia, Somalia, and Rwanda—were judged to be failures or worse. The Security Council sometimes, as in Rwanda, refuses to intervene with adequate force at the critical point.[2] The world organization still has no professional, standing rapid deployment force, and this essential spearhead for effective action now seems to be less than ever likely to be agreed on.[3] (A rapid deployment force was not even mentioned in the much-touted summit meeting on UN reform in September 2005.) The Peacekeeping Department of the UN Secretariat is trying to develop substitute rapid deployment possibilities through standby arrangements of various kinds with governments. The weakness of all such arrangements is that they depend on the willingness of governments *at the time of the emergency* to activate the standby arrangement. At the time of the Rwanda genocide there were twenty standby arrangements, but not one could be activated because of the dire and violent nature of the emergency.

The limits on the use of force by peacekeepers in violent conditions within one country have not yet been clearly defined. Early peacekeeping operations were to deal with conflicts between states by offering an honorable alternative to fighting that both sides could willingly agree to. Thus rules for the use of force could be simple—force could be used only in self-defense. In 1978, when the United Nations went into South Lebanon, the provision that force could also be used against efforts to prevent the peacekeepers from carrying out their mandate was added to the rule. In operations within one state, the use of force is a far more complicated issue. As early as 1961, after the assassination of Congo prime minister Patrice Lumumba, the Security Council extended the United Nations' right to use force to preventing civil war and dealing with mercenaries in the secessionist province of Katanga. In the many multifunctional operations of the 1990s, the issue of the use of force was never adequately resolved.

The worst cases were Rwanda and Bosnia. In the first, the Security Council refused to act at all until it was much too late. In the second, the Security Council, unable to agree on who was the aggressor and to mount a forceful operation accordingly, and faced with the unwillingness of the United States to use NATO, put a UN peacekeeping operation with a largely humanitarian mandate into an ongoing, full-scale war and affected to be surprised and

indignant when, in spite of considerable casualties, it turned out not to work very well, although the UN force held the ring until the fighting came to an end and it was safe for the heavily armed troops of NATO to enter Bosnia. Those in the Secretariat who pointed out that, for good reason, one of the basic principles of the use of peacekeeping forces was that they should not be deployed into a full-scale war were strongly disapproved of by the United States.

Coalitions of the willing or the delegation of responsibility in a given crisis to a single government have, on several occasions, gained the approval of the Security Council, something that would not have been possible during the Cold War. For various reasons, governments that take the lead are likely to want to hand over to the United Nations as soon as possible. For example, Australia took the lead in East Timor but, because the action was politically sensitive in Southeast Asia, handed over to the United Nations as soon as it could. Soon after the NATO bombing of Serbia, which, after seventy-nine days, persuaded Milosevic to agree to proposals on Kosovo, the Security Council came out in support of subsequent action in Kosovo. Handing over to the United Nations in Iraq was the dream of some people in Washington after the occupation of Iraq in 2003 turned out to be more difficult than expected. And in fact some vital functions—the putting together of the first interim government and the organization of elections—were assumed by the United Nations.

NEW THREATS

Meanwhile new threats—mass-casualty terrorism, failed states, the proliferation of weapons of mass destruction, and religious fundamentalism and extremism—have arisen to trouble the hoped-for post–Cold War calm. All of these problems are more or less connected, and all call for new forms of collective action and cooperation. Decisive conventional military force, so effective on the traditional battlefield, is not suited to the resolution of most of these problems.

We now have considerable experience in trying to deal with violent insurgency with more or less conventional forces. The British in Malaysia (perhaps the only case where the colonial power was more or less successful), the French in Algeria, France and later the United States in Vietnam, the Soviet Union in Afghanistan, Russia in Chechnya, and, currently, the United States in Iraq are only a few examples of the lesson that conventional forces can seldom finally win in such a struggle. The insurgents usually have the tacit support of large sections of the local population, and they know the country far better than their would-be conquerors. Insurgents are not hampered by the laws of war, by normal scruples about taking life, or by rigidly traditional military tactics. They are expert, flexible, and small enough in number to be independent of any cumbrous logistical system. They are masters of surprise. They can easily vanish into the local scene. Many of these advantages are shared by terrorists, whose fanaticism and willingness, indeed longing, to die make them even more difficult to deal with.

New threats demand new techniques and a new psychological approach, both military and civilian. Postconflict nation building, quite recently condemned in Washington as an unnecessary overexpansion of international action, is now recognized as an essential part of preserving the peace and fighting terrorism, and an essential new role for military forces in some cases. In December 2005, the UN General Assembly agreed to establish a permanent Peace Building Commission to help countries shattered by conflict not to fall back into conflict again.

The concept and the technique of peacekeeping are in a state of constant development, and peacebuilding will require, for its military and police contingents, new rules and methods appropriate to working as part of a multifunc-tional team. As far as terrorism is concerned, a new level both of international intelligence sharing and international police work will be necessary. Clearer and more positive ideas on how to stop the formation and training of terrorists remain to be evolved. Special forces will be in high demand.

Another important question is the authorization and control of peacekeeping operations. During the Cold War, when East and West could agree on very little, peacekeeping was very much a UN monopoly. It represented the maximum action that could be agreed upon in the Security Council, and even then the Soviet Union and France called it illegal and usually refused to pay their share of the costs of peacekeeping operations.

Since the end of the Cold War a much more varied pattern has been possible. NATO, regional organizations such as the African Union and the European Union, and individual states —Russia in Georgia and other parts of the old USSR, Australia in East Timor, Nigeria in various West African disturbances—have undertaken peacekeeping roles, often authorized through Security Council resolutions or involving the participation of UN observers.

As of this writing (May 2006), there are fifteen UN peacekeeping operations totaling some eighty thousand soldiers in the field. A new operation in Darfur is being negotiated. Many governments prefer UN operations to regional or other arrangements as being less likely to be influenced or manipulated by regional interests.

It is hard to see, at present, where the actual use of conventional force belongs in dealing with the new and hellish combination of threats that we now face. It is always possible that a new case of plain, old-fashioned aggression will have to be dealt with, but with the world's population of aggressive dictators in decline, that seems less and less likely. Nonetheless, conventional military strength is one of the main supports of power and influence. It is often most effective when it is present but does not actually use its power. This was true of NATO and the Warsaw Pact for forty years during the Cold War. More recently, it was certainly the buildup of U.S. forces in the Persian Gulf area that persuaded Saddam Hussein to allow the UN inspectors to return to Iraq and to begin to confirm that there was no nuclear or other WMD program. And in 2005, a year of natural disasters, the armed forces of the United States and other leading countries, once again in the forefront of the rescue effort, proved indispensable to rapid relief action in the first, crucial days.

CONCLUSION

I started my adult life with six years in the British army in World War II, where I learned almost as much about what *not* to do with military force as about how to use it to the best effect. I also learned a lot about the essentials of any military enterprise—leadership, intelligent planning, training, discipline, morale, improvisation, communications, logistics, determination, belief that you can win, and good intelligence. As the war dragged on toward its end, I dreamed of how military force, tradition, and discipline might be turned to the service of peace. Much of this experience proved useful when I worked with Dag Hammarskjöld and Ralph Bunche on the setting up and direction of the first UN peacekeeping operations and on trying to develop a guiding tradition and a sounder basis for the later ones.

Service in World War II, however, did *not* prepare one for the political problems that complicate peacekeeping missions at every turn, or the lack of infrastructure at the beginning of any UN operation. These operations, with their different contexts and problems, are still inevitably to some extent of an experimental and improvised nature. They are still open to all sorts of political crosscurrents and they still need strong and persistent political guidance. The smallest and ostensibly most insignificant mistake can still easily grow into a serious international problem. And at the center of each mission there is still the Security Council, no longer frozen into inactivity but still capable of providing an inadequate mandate, of producing a completely irresponsible mandate (as in the "safe areas" in Bosnia), or of failing to take any responsible action at all.

UN peacekeeping operations are still complicated by a basic shortcoming that does not afflict efficient national military forces. Because there is no standing UN peacekeeping force, each operation has to start from scratch and at the last minute, usually well after the crisis has erupted. As Secretary-General Kofi Annan has rightly observed, the United Nations is the only fire brigade in the world that has to acquire a fire engine *after* the fire has actually started. It is true that a number of countries are including rapidly deployable peacekeeping units in their regular armies, but it is by no means certain that those governments will be prepared to commit those units when the crisis comes.

In most emergencies the most rapid possible deployment is even more important than finding competent senior staff and reasonably well-trained contingents and adequately briefing the outgoing troops. In the early days, when governments were enthusiastic and not so aware of the difficulties ahead, we managed to deploy troops remarkably quickly. In 1960 I left for the Congo within twenty-four hours of the Security Council's decision to intervene. I knew practically nothing about the Congo; in fact, I thought it was on the Indian Ocean. But just getting the "blue helmets" there immediately and in large numbers was essential in getting a chaotic situation under control.

In present conditions the delay in deploying a UN peacekeeping force ranges from two to six months. The operation therefore lacks the immediate spearhead impact that establishes from the outset the moral authority of a peacekeeping force. This is a serious problem. Intervening early in a crisis, before the trouble has spread and bloodshed has created a mass desire for revenge, gives a peacekeeping operation an advantage even more important than good planning or briefing.

Regular national or NATO forces are trained, usually have formidable equipment and supporting air and naval forces, and are ready to go when a crisis erupts, provided that the situation demands it and their governments in NATO are willing. UN legitimacy, conferred by a decision of the Security Council, can certainly strengthen non-UN peace operations and help them to command the widest possible cooperation.

National and NATO forces are trained to use force and obviously do it far better than improvised UN forces that are authorized to use force only in self-defense or when they are being prevented from carrying out their mandate. At the same time, governments in trouble are often more willing to accept a UN presence in their countries because of the limitation on the use of force by UN peacekeepers. Being authorized to use only a very limited degree of force can also make it much easier for UN forces to stay above the conflict as objective, nonpartisan peacekeepers. If peacekeepers use force injudiciously, they can very easily become just another combatant.

Since the end of the Cold War efforts have been made to find a way to give UN peace forces more effective guidance on using limited force to carry out their mission.[4] Such guidance is particularly necessary in places such as the Democratic Republic of the Congo, where fighting tribes or warlords have no respect for nonforceful peacekeepers. A new approach still needs to be found, something between enforcement action by large and battle-ready national contingents made available under Chapter VII of the UN Charter and the improvised, more or less symbolic, peacekeeping that served so well during the Cold War but has often proved inadequate since. The rather guarded endorsement by the September 2005 UN summit of the obligation of humanitarian intervention to protect groups being brutally treated needs a lot of imaginative work before it can successfully be translated into practice. Failure to provide a mandate for the necessary use of force in a threatening and chaotic situation may well have worse results than not deploying a peacekeeping operation at all. The continuing failure to stop atrocities in Darfur reveals how many obstacles can stand in the way of fulfilling the obligation to protect.

Another problem for UN peacekeeping has arisen when governments in the Security Council have used peacekeeping forces in an inappropriate way and for their own purposes. The classic example of this unfortunate trend, in Bosnia in the early 1990s, was described earlier. When the Security Council added to UNPROFOR's duties the responsibility to protect six "safe areas" but contemptuously refused to authorize a new mandate and the extra thirty-five thousand troops requested by Secretary-General Boutros Boutros-Ghali to enable UNPROFOR to carry out this new task, the occasional irresponsibility of the council reached a new and lethal level. The results were seen at Srebrenica (one of the safe areas), where Serbs massacred more than seven thousand Muslim men. The Bosnia experience, hotly debated in a divided Security Council, and the source of important disagreements among the Secretariat, the Security Council, and commanders in the field, showed the Security Council at its worst and weakest—unrealistic, confused by different national interests, and unsupportive of the forces and the humanitarian workers in the field.

The successes, mistakes, and failures in the use of the military over the past half century —both in a forceful mode and in a peacekeeping mode—have generated valuable lessons and resulted in international acceptance of various ways of using force in the service of peace. Many national armies, including the armed forces of the United States, are becoming accustomed to forms of action not even dreamed of fifty years ago. Peacekeeping, policing, and monitoring of international agreements, humanitarian emergency action, cease-fire supervision, and even postconflict nation building have now been accepted almost as normal functions of the military.

What is needed now is to get agreement on what type of operation is best suited for which kind of problem, how it can be most rapidly and effectively set up and by whom, and how legitimacy and international cooperation can be assured. There is now much expert discussion of such matters both as a political and as a military problem. Conventional military strength is obviously the starting point for such discussions, even the precondition for them. Subjects such as how best to use the military to deal with terrorism, with the proliferation of WMD, and with failed states require international cooperation, open-minded discussion, and creative experimentation.

We live in a period of rapid flux that demands the development of existing institutions to meet challenges we could scarcely imagine even twenty years ago. Military force and strength must be used constructively and imaginatively if we are to provide peace, security, and hope for the inhabitants of an alarming world.

NOTES

1. The Suez crisis, because of British and French vetoes in the Security Council, had been transferred to the General Assembly under the "Uniting for Peace" Resolution, a U.S.-sponsored plan designed to prevent the Soviet veto from blocking the United Nations from taking action against threats to peace and actions of aggression. It was one of the many ironies of the Suez crisis that this resolution, which the Soviets had vocally opposed, was first invoked to get around the vetoes of Britain and France, normally close allies of the United States.

2. For a fascinating account of the effect of this failing on critical operations in the field, see Sadako Ogata, former UN High Commissioner for Refugees, *The Turbulent Decade: Confronting the Refugee Crises of the 1990s* (New York: W. W. Norton, 2005).

3. There is considerable literature on and around the subject. For an excellent summary of the current state of a UN rapid deployment force, see Peter Langille, *Bridging the Commitment-Capacity Gap: A Review of Existing Arrangements and Options for Enhancing UN Rapid Deployment* (New York: Center for UN Reform Education, 2002). My article "For a UN Volunteer Military Force" in the June 1993 *New York Review of Books*, although on a slightly different topic, provoked a useful series of comments on a UN rapid deployment force in subsequent issues of the publication.

4. Boutros Boutros-Ghali, *An Agenda for Peace* (New York: United Nations, 1992); and Brahimi Panel, *Report of the Panel on United Nations Peace Operations*, A/55/305-S/2000/809 (New York: United Nations, 2000).

16

YET AGAIN

HUMANITARIAN INTERVENTION
AND THE CHALLENGES
OF "NEVER AGAIN"

Bruce W. Jentleson

FOR ALL THE VOWS THAT "never again" would there be another genocide, the reality has been "yet again." The legal and political particulars of the term "genocide" and its application to this or that case can continue to be debated. For accuracy, we may need to speak in some cases "only" of ethnic cleansing, mass killings, deadly conflict, humanitarian emergencies, and the like. The reality remains that millions of people have continued to be killed, maimed, raped, displaced, and otherwise victimized while the international community—the United States, the United Nations, the European Union, and others—has continued too often to do too little too late.

Around the time of publication of *Turbulent Peace*, forerunner to this current volume, there was some hope that we might be moving toward "never again." The United Nations under Secretary-General Kofi Annan's leadership had commissioned its own tough-love self-studies of its role in Rwanda and other key cases and its overall peacekeeping role. The U.S.-NATO intervention in Kosovo, while controversial, on balance succeeded. East Timor generally was considered a success, with Australia stepping forward as the regional leader, working with the United Nations. The United Kingdom led the intervention in Sierra Leone, buttressing the UN presence and helping restore some security and stability. And the problem itself showed signs of diminishing according to some analysts, who forecast declines in the trend lines of ethnic and related conflicts.[1]

There also was much anticipation of a report to be issued by the International Commission on Intervention and State Sovereignty (ICISS). ICISS had been launched on September 14, 2000, at the behest of Secretary-General Annan, with Canada as the sponsor and funding from various governments as well as major foundations, and Gareth Evans, former foreign minister of Australia, and Mohamed Sahnoun, special adviser to Secretary-General Annan, as cochairs. With the one-year deadline approaching, it was just about to issue its report . . . but then came September 11, 2001.[2]

The Bush administration had come into office quite skeptical of humanitarian intervention—"the 82nd airborne escorting kids to kindergarten," as it was cast with aspersion during the 2000 presidential election campaign.[3] This was Clintonian do-goodism that the self-styled realists of the new administration rejected as naive idealism, inconsistent with and even inimical to the national interest.[4] In one sense 9/11 had a helpful impact on this initial strategic disposition. The Bush administration did at least partially rethink its initial rejection of nation building, first in Afghanistan and then in Iraq, insofar as failed and rogue states were not only having egregious effects on their own peoples but also contributing to major threats to U.S. security (albeit disputably in Iraq). Its 2002 National Security Strategy articulated the broader strategic argument of some of the roots of terrorism tracing back to weak states, poverty, and related sufferings.

On balance, though, 9/11 has proved more of a setback than an impetus to humanitarian intervention as a U.S. foreign policy priority. Iraq has been a huge part of this, both in its immediate impact of so deeply splitting the international community and the more indirect effects of exacerbating suspicions about humanitarian justifications for the use of force. More broadly, even with the priority now being given to the global war on terrorism, while some connections are there between humanitarian crises and terrorism, they tend to be insufficiently integral to be main drivers behind decisions on what commitments to make, resources to allocate, and priorities to set. They also can be distorting in working against humanitarian crises that have their own moral imperatives and interest-based rationales but do not link to terrorism—as, for example, in Darfur.

Other international actors have been showing their own ambivalences. The United Nations has taken on some new humanitarian missions, and at its September 2005 World Summit it did adopt some aspects of the "responsibility-to-protect" position that the ICISS report had proposed and the secretary-general's High-Level Panel on Threats, Challenges, and Change had endorsed. On the other hand, it also failed to act decisively in Darfur, in part because of the opposition of Security Council veto-possessing permanent members Russia and China. The compromises made to win adoption of the responsibility to protect leave serious doubt as to whether this will prove to be the basis for more concerted humanitarian action than in the past.

How, then, to assess the progress that has and hasn't been made? And what of future prospects? My view, as argued herein and elsewhere, is that both the United States and the international community would be well served by more effective humanitarian intervention strategies, especially preventive and early-action ones.[5] Interests would be defended; principles would be lived up to.

This chapter proceeds in three parts. First, the lessons of the 1990s are reviewed. Second, the impact of 9/11 and other recent developments are assessed, with a particular focus on the Darfur case. Third, strategies are proposed to meet the challenges of getting to "never again."

LESSONS OF THE 1990S

Humanitarian intervention was one of the dominant issues of the 1990s. Ethnic cleansing in the Balkans, genocide in Rwanda, and all too many other deadly conflicts made it clear that the end of the Cold War had not meant the end of war. While there was plenty of contention about who within the international community bore what share of the blame, there was plenty of blame to go around.

Five sets of issues defined the policy debate across the cases: (1) What are the driving forces of these conflicts? (2) When should military force be used? (3) Why is intervention justified? (4) Who decides on intervention? and

(5) How to intervene effectively? What follows is a brief review of lessons of the 1990s based on the policy experiences and what has become a rich and extensive literature on humanitarian intervention.[6]

What Are the Driving Forces?

Many policymakers took the "primordialist" view of these conflicts as the playing out of histories of fixed, inherited, deeply antagonistic group identities. In this analysis the end of the Cold War stripped away the constraining effects of the strategic overlay of bipolar geopolitics, releasing the "Balkan ghosts" and other historical hatreds to their "natural" states of conflict.[7]

A number of studies have shown, though, that ethnic identities are much less fixed over time, and the frequency and intensity of ethnic conflict more varying than primordialist theory would have it. The sources and dynamics have tended to be much more purposive in nature, historically shaped but not historically determined, following more of a *political causality* resulting from deliberate and conscious calculations made by leaders and groups of the purposes to be served by political violence.[8] Conflict, yes: few if any of these places were going to go through the transitions they faced without some violence. But there is a huge difference between "some" and "so much." Indeed, there is ample empirical and analytic evidence in many of these cases of missed opportunities for the international community to have limited if not prevented these conflicts from becoming as bad as they did.[9] These include the "warning-response gap" identified by Alexander George and Jane Holl: "In many ethnic and religious conflicts, humanitarian crises or severe human rights abuses, *timely or accurate warning may not be the problem at all.* Rather, for one reason or another, as noted, *no* serious response is likely to be taken."[10] George and Holl cite bureaucratic, political, analytic, and other reasons for the lack of response despite early warning, all of which pose their own policy problems but ones that speak to missed more than unforeseeable opportunities.

When Should Military Force Be Used?

Noninterventionism had largely served the post–World War II international system well. The constraints on the major powers had helped maintain order and security. The protection for small countries and newly independent states emerging from colonialism had buttressed (albeit not guaranteed) self-determination, freedom, and justice. Force was to be a last resort and a highly restricted one at that. But Bosnia, Rwanda, and related conflicts exposed deep and disturbing contradictions between the limits of the traditional noninterventionist regime and the very norms and values of peace, justice, and humanitarianism on which the UN system claimed to rest.

The 2001 ICISS report made cautious but nevertheless significant acknowledgment that from a humanitarian perspective military force may need to be something other than an absolute last resort:

> [M]ilitary action can be legitimate as an *anticipatory* measure in response to clear evidence of likely large scale killing. Without this possibility of anticipatory action, the international community would be placed in the morally untenable position of being required to wait until genocide begins, before being able to take action to stop it.

> Every diplomatic and non-military avenue for the prevention or peaceful resolution of the humanitarian crisis must have been *explored.* . . . This does not necessarily mean that every such option must literally have been tried and failed: often there will simply not be the time for that process to work itself out. But it does mean that there must be *reasonable grounds for believing that, in all the circumstances, if the measure had been attempted it would not have succeeded.*[11]

While couched in diplomatic language, the thrust was that although force should not become a first resort, its threat or use did need to possibly be an early and not just a last resort.

This manifested a logic of deterrence strategy, as befits this type of conflict. As long as the Milosevics of the world know that they do not have to worry about external intervention until some late stage of the conflict, they will feel free to exploit their military advantages at least until that late stage draws closer and the external threat becomes credible. The argument for force as an early resort also has been made by liberal internationalists such as Stanley Hoffmann, who wrote that "there are situations in which a quick, early use of force may well be the best method, and the only one capable of preventing a further aggravation of the [humanitarian] crisis."[12] In my own work I have argued strongly for "coercive prevention" to act early and prevent mass killings, not just respond to them, as both more realist and more humanitarian.[13] If the threshold for intervention is that the bodies already have started to pile up, this is hardly humanitarian—perhaps less inhumanitarian than not acting at all, but that is not exactly a high standard.

Why Is Intervention Justified?

Relatedly, the issue of sovereignty was homed in on in a debate over the rights versus the responsibilities of states. The traditional conception of sovereignty as rights attributes to states jurisdictional exclusivity within their own borders and grants very limited and narrowly construed bases of legitimacy for other actors, whether another state or an international institution, to intervene in any form in what in their territorial locus are considered domestic affairs. "No agency exists above the individual states," as Robert Art and Robert Jervis write, "with authority and power to make laws and settle disputes." The strong emphasis is on the rights that come with sovereignty, "the complete autonomy of the state to act as it chooses," as Abram and Antonia Handler Chayes put it.[14] But in an era in which intrastate conflict had become the dominant and most lethal form, the international community could not continue to readily accept the invocation of

state sovereignty as a normative barrier behind which aggression could hide. The UN Charter, stressed Secretary-General Kofi Annan, "was issued in the name of 'the people,' not the governments. . . . It was never meant as a license for governments to trample on human rights and human dignity."[15] States have the responsibility "at the very least," as Francis Deng, I. William Zartman, Donald Rothchild, and colleagues argued, "of ensuring a certain level of protection for and providing for the basic needs of the people."[16]

The ICISS report's core conception of the responsibility to protect tilts toward sovereignty as responsibilities of states and not just their rights:

> [T]he responsibility to protect its people from killing and other grave harm was the most basic and fundamental of all the responsibilities that sovereignty imposes—and if a state cannot or will not protect its people from such harm, then coercive intervention for human protection purposes, including ultimately military intervention, by others in the international community may be warranted in extreme cases.[17]

To answer the concern that this ends up opening the way for big powers to go on doing what they want to do, the commission was careful to distinguish its conception of the responsibility to protect from a "right to intervene." While understanding the historical roots of some such trepidations during colonialism and the Cold War, the commission was unwilling to allow such arguments to be too easily invoked as rationalizations distracting from its core concern about ethnic cleansings, genocides, and other mass killings: "What is at stake here is not making the world safe for big powers, or trampling over the sovereign rights of small ones, but delivering practical protection for ordinary people at risk of their lives, because their states are unwilling or unable to protect them."[18]

Especially if sovereignty were to be less sacrosanct, establishing criteria for justifiable intervention was all the more important. These efforts tapped heavily into the just-war tradition and, while differing in some of their particulars, generally stressed four factors: just cause, in terms of an "extreme humanitarian emergency" or comparably dire situation and a credible claim that the intervenor is acting for these humanitarian motivations more than particularistic self-interest; proportionality of the military means—that is, using just enough force to achieve the humanitarian objective; strong probability of success, including a net sense of collateral damage, civilian casualties, and the proverbial not-destroying-the-village-in-order-to-save-it; and force as a last resort, although with more willingness to set this threshold with anticipatory flexibility, as in the ICISS formulation cited earlier.[19] These criteria left obvious room for interpretation and contestation. Thomas Weiss, who served as ICISS research director, observes that "the 'just cause threshold' is higher than many would have hoped."[20] Others still bristled at any sovereignty-abridging justification. The debate thus hardly was settled, but it was advanced.

Who Decides on Intervention?

The crucial question here has been how vested humanitarian intervention decisions are in the UN Security Council. The Kosovo case brought this to a head when Chinese and Russian opposition prevented Security Council action. While not endorsing the U.S.-NATO intervention, Secretary-General Annan did speak out against Security Council inaction when faced with these "crimes against humanity" and thereby "betray[ing] the very ideals that inspired the founding of the United Nations." For all the invocations of Serbian sovereignty and claims of principle Russia and China made, their positions were based more on their concerns about precedents with Chechnya, on the one hand, and Taiwan and Tibet, on the other.[21] Kosovo also led to the unusual distinction of the U.S.-NATO intervention being illegal in the sense of not having followed the letter of the UN Charter but legitimate in

the sense of being consistent with the norms and principles that the charter embodies.[22] The ICISS report recognized that military interventions outside UN auspices "do not—it would be an understatement to say—find wide favour." But it then continued with its own ambivalence: "But that may still leave circumstances when the Security Council fails to discharge what this Commission would regard as its responsibility to protect, in a conscience-shocking situation crying out for action. It is a real question in these circumstances where lies the most harm: in the damage to international order if the Security Council is bypassed or in the damage to that order if human beings are slaughtered while the Security Council stands by."[23]

A study conducted by the Fund for Peace of regional views on humanitarian intervention found a general consensus on the United Nations as "the preferred authorizing body" but also on "the UN's limits in both addressing conflicts before they become emergencies and coming to the rescue once a humanitarian crisis is clear." The balance proposed was that regional and subregional organizations "be seen as having legitimacy both to authorize and organize a response with the provision that UN approval be sought, ex post facto if necessary."[24] This was an interestingly flexible formulation both in allowing for regional action prior to UN authorization and only requiring that that authorization be "sought." This fits with the track record of at least eleven non-UN-authorized interventions or peace operations other than Kosovo done on a regional basis, including by the Russia-led Commonwealth of Independent States in Georgia-Abkhazia, NATO in Macedonia, France in Côte d'Ivoire, the African Union (AU) in Burundi, the Economic Community of West African States (ECOWAS) in Liberia, and Australia in the Solomon Islands. While none of these cases had the kind of opposition within the United Nations that the U.S. invasion of Iraq had, some raised greater concerns of decision-making authority and legitimacy than others.[25]

How to Intervene Effectively?
This was an issue for the United Nations, for the United States, and for those taking on lead regional roles, particularly the European Union and the Organization of African States/African Union.

The United Nations entered the 1990s having just won the Nobel Peace Prize (1988) for its peace*keeping* forces, hailed for their role in having "contributed to reducing tensions where an armistice has been negotiated but a peace treaty has yet to be established."[26] This was a statement of the classic definition of peacekeeping in that the UN forces were brought in after the warring parties had agreed to the terms of that peace and with the largely third-party reassurance mission of ensuring and facilitating the keeping of that peace. The United Nations had further successes over the next few years in Namibia, Mozambique, El Salvador, and Cambodia in "second-generation peacekeeping" cases that were more intrastate and involved elections and other aspects of nation building. Cases such as Croatia and Bosnia, however, were much more in the nature of peace*making* and peace *enforcing* in that the conflicts were still raging or at best under tenuous cease-fires, conditions in which traditional stratagems of impartiality and limited mission were not sufficient. There also was the problem of having taken on too many missions, for example, increasing from five in 1988 to seventeen in 1994, with a concomitant eightfold increase in the number of blue-helmeted troops from 9,570 to 73,393 and an exponential soaring in the peace operations budget from $230 million to $3.6 billion. With an eye to institutional learning, Secretary-General Annan established a high-level review commission led by Under-Secretary-General Lakhdar Brahimi. The UN *Report of the Panel on United Nations Peace Operations* (the Brahimi Report), issued in August 2000,

laid out a series of recommendations, including greater permanent peacekeeping capacity, more rapid deployment, more robust rules of engagement beyond largely self-defensive force protection, and better-equipped and better-trained forces.[27]

The U.S. track record also was mixed. The Somalia intervention, while having achieved some of its initial humanitarian crisis goals in late 1992–early 1993, ended in the debacle of withdrawal under political pressure. In Rwanda, "the fastest, most efficient killing spree of the twentieth century . . . the United States again stood on the sidelines."[28] The U.S. role in Bosnia ultimately was a crucial peace broker one, but only after years of inaction and indecisiveness. The United States exerted leadership in Kosovo and won, but "won ugly."[29] Some saw an emerging "Clinton Doctrine" in the president's June 1999 speech asserting that "if somebody comes after innocent civilians and tries to kill them, en masse, because of their race, ethnic background, or religion, and it's within our power to stop it, we will stop it."[30] But this wasn't really tested during the remainder of Clinton's term. Major studies were initiated, such as the interagency Managing Complex Contingency Operations (PDD [Presidential Decision Directive] 56), seeking to more effectively coordinate the range of actors involved (civilian, military, NGO). But these were principally about after-the-fact interventions and postconflict reconstruction and were still not taking on the even tougher issues of prevention and deterrence.

The European Union had its stops and starts with efforts to develop its Common Foreign and Security Policy, distinct from NATO's and more subsuming of individual national policies, as well as greater military capacity through a rapid-reaction force. EU efforts remained focused more on the diplomatic, political, and socioeconomic aspects of conflict prevention.[31] In some instances Britain and France individually took on lead military roles in conflicts in their respective former colonial spheres, such as Britain in Sierra Leone and France in Côte d'Ivoire.

The most substantial regional initiatives were in Africa. The Clinton administration's African Crisis Response Initiative sought to provide training, resources, and some logistical support for African efforts to develop regional humanitarian intervention capacity through the Organization of African Unity and its successor, the African Union. The European Union and the Group of Eight (G-8) had similar programs.

Doctrinally, the fundamental dilemma for effective intervention was garnering a strong and broad enough political mandate and fielding forces capable of a robust, proactive presence that could do more as needed than manifest impartiality or only provide limited force protection. In many of the 1990s peacemaking and peace-enforcing conflicts, impartiality was a "delusion."[32] In classic peacekeeping, when the strategy is reassurance of parties that have already agreed to peace, impartiality works well. But when the parties are still in conflict, impartiality can be quite dysfunctional, meaning not coercing either side irrespective of which one is doing more killing, seizing more territory, and committing more war crimes. Mandates limited to self-protection do little to provide security to the populaces facing the humanitarian threats. Along these lines, one recent study of major 1990s cases showed that "interventions that directly challenge the perpetrator or aid the target of the brutal policy are the only effective type of military responses, increasing the probability that the magnitude of the slaughter can be slowed or stopped."[33]

◆ ◆ ◆

In sum, the 1990s were marked by horrendous death and destruction in conflicts driven largely by the politics of identity: who I am, who you are, and why this is a basis for mass killings. Things no doubt could have been worse, and the interventions in Bosnia, Kosovo,

East Timor, and a few other places were better late than never. In other cases, the interventions were so late, limited, and otherwise flawed that they exacerbated the conflicts. In still others, success was proclaimed but on the basis of such weak truces and other agreements that the conflicts reignited quickly and sometimes even more intensively.[34]

All told, there was some sense of collective lesson learning, with a number of initiatives for entering the next decade and new century with a strengthened commitment and capacity for humanitarian intervention.

IMPACT OF 9/11

The Bush administration came into office very critical of the Clinton humanitarian intervention record. Its criticism was especially about priorities, as in the derisive comment made during the 2000 presidential campaign about the 82nd Airborne being used to escort kids to kindergarten. The new administration was going to focus on major powers, such as Russia and China, and on major regional conflicts, such as the Arab-Israeli conflict, the one involving India-Pakistan, and that on the Korean peninsula. Much less priority was to be given to small countries and isolated trouble spots that, whatever the humanitarian impulse, just were not that strategically important. Take Afghanistan, for example: with the Soviets long gone, however offensive the Taliban's repressive rule, what strategic importance could this failed state and its caves really have?

A lot, as was all too tragically demonstrated on September 11, 2001. One of the lessons of 9/11 thus was that there was no failed state or trouble spot anywhere whose effects could assuredly be assumed to be localized. This couldn't mean that the United States would intervene everywhere, but it did mean that there was nowhere that could be automatically ignored. Some proponents of humanitarian intervention were hopeful that, as Tom Farer put it, 9/11 would "stiffen humanitarianism with the iron of national security and thus make it interesting to the parochial, narrowly compassionate figures who predominate in the councils of the leading states."[35] Some shift in strategic thinking did come through, as in the statement in the 2002 Bush *National Security Strategy* report that "weak states, like Afghanistan, can pose as great a danger to our national interests as strong states. Poverty does not make poor people into terrorists and murderers. Yet poverty, weak institutions and corruption can make weak states vulnerable to terrorist networks and drug cartels within their borders."[36]

On balance, though, 9/11 has proven a major setback for humanitarian intervention. It put "hard" security issues back at the top of the U.S. and international agenda—the global war on terrorism (GWOT) has been trumping all other security issues. While there are some connections between humanitarian crises and terrorism, they tend to be insufficiently integral to be main drivers behind decisions on what commitments to make, resources to allocate, and priorities to set. The terrorism link also can be distorting in working against humanitarian crises that have their own moral imperatives and interest-based rationales but do not link to terrorism.

The main problem has been Iraq, in both immediate and indirect senses. The immediate impact was in how deeply the Iraq war split the international community. No conflict in recent memory has generated such widespread and intensive animosities among countries that were otherwise friends and allies. The Bush administration derogated many of the same European countries that had gone to war with the United States in Kosovo and the 1990–91 Persian Gulf War as the "old Europe." Europeans in turn were biting and caustic in their positions and anti-American rhetoric. The more indirect impact was a discrediting of the use of force, particularly in a preventive or preemptive mode, which derailed the flexible definition of last resort that ICISS and others had been pushing toward. The Bush

administration's decision to go to war against Iraq, made on a largely unilateral basis in the face of significant international opposition and based on a very weak preventive and even weaker preemptive case, was seen by many as confirming concerns about loosening up strict constructionist noninterventionism. It "had the effect," observes Adam Roberts, "of reinforcing fears both of US dominance and of the chaos that could ensue if what is sauce for the US goose were to become sauce for many other would-be interventionist ganders."[37] Moreover, the fact that humanitarian rationales were invoked as part of the potpourri of casus belli made it even worse, demonstrating "the danger of abuse":

> If all wars can be "humanitarian," then the humanitarian exception itself ceases to have meaning. . . . The danger with accepting the legal and moral arguments for war with Iraq is that it will undermine the veracity of those arguments: Security Council resolutions can be interpreted so broadly as to mean anything and nothing; pre-emptive self-defense blurs into aggression; humanitarian wars become the norm, but selectivity on the basis of the "national interests" of the interveners remains.[38]

For these and other reasons Thomas Weiss concluded that "the blowback from Iraq precludes serious discussion [of guidelines for humanitarian intervention] for the foreseeable future."[39]

The 2004–5 UN reform process belied some of these concerns but bore out others. The report of the secretary-general's High-Level Panel (HLP) on Threats, Challenges, and Change did endorse the responsibility to protect as an "emerging norm" and did make a strong statement that "the principle of non-intervention in internal affairs cannot be used to protect genocidal acts or other atrocities." It also carried forward ICISS's flexibly anticipatory conception of force as a last resort: "Has every non-military option been explored, with reasonable grounds for believing that other measures will not succeed?"[40] But on the who decides question it came down much more unequivocally on the UN Security Council as the sole source of legitimacy for the use of force other than in Article 51 national self-defense cases (and these it defined very restrictively): "The task is not to find alternatives to the Security Council as a source of authority but to make the Council work better than it has."[41]

The 2005 UN World Summit did adopt the responsibility-to-protect norm.[42] The official World Summit *Fact Sheet* claims that there was

> clear and unambiguous acceptance by all governments of the collective international responsibility to protect populations from genocide, war crimes, ethnic cleansing and crimes against humanity. . . .
>
> Willingness to take timely and decisive collective action for this purpose, through the Security Council, when peaceful means prove inadequate and national authorities are manifestly failing to do so.[43]

The actual final document, though, does not seem to live up to its billing. It does mention responsibility to protect, but as the responsibility of "each individual state," and with the role of the international community no more than to "encourage and help States to exercise this responsibility."[44] And if states don't exercise that responsibility, and international encouragement and help are not enough? In the elaboration of means that follow there is no mention of the use of force. Indeed, the section explicitly on use of force reads a lot like classic noninterventionism. It urges "further development of proposals for enhanced rapidly deployable capacities to reinforce peacekeeping operations" but leaves anything more substantive for the future. It "endorses the creation of an initial operating capability for a standing police capacity," but here, too, endorsing is not acting even for that initial capability.[45] A new Peacebuilding Commission has been created with a mix of preventive and postconflict reconstruction responsibilities, but these are defined largely in political and economic terms. I find myself less bullish than others on just how much change this represents, seeing watering down from the HLP report and especially the ICISS report much more than anything clear, unambiguous, or assertive. To the extent that it can now be said that the responsibility to protect is a norm of the international system, it is what scholars call a "soft norm."[46]

As for actual policy and events on the ground, the signs were mixed. Some positive signs: The *2005 Human Security Report* showed declines in both the number and the lethality of armed conflicts.[47] Macedonia came close to unraveling in 2001, but the conflict was contained, with the European Union, NATO, and the Organization for Security and Cooperation in Europe (OSCE) taking lead roles.[48] Kosovo has teetered but was deemed ready in late 2005 to move to the next phases of negotiations on its permanent status. Liberia held its first elections since its civil war had started in 1989, indeed, the first truly free election in its 158-year history. Sierra Leone was emerging from its own decade-long civil war.

There were also negative signs, however. The death toll in the Democratic Republic of the Congo exceeded four million people. Conflict in Côte d'Ivoire intensified. Conflict resolution processes in Rwanda and Burundi moved ever so slowly. In Liberia, the success of the elections notwithstanding, the tasks of postconflict reconstruction amid the devastated economy and deeply torn social fabric (more than two hundred thousand dead and one-third of the population displaced) were formidable. So, too, in Kosovo, where estimates of unemployment ranged from 30 percent to 70 percent, the economy was expected to shrink by 2 percent, and the government was near bankruptcy.[49] Indeed, in an October 2004 report taking a broad global view, the International Peace Academy concluded that "a full decade after it became a high-profile international commitment, post-conflict peacebuilding remains a fragile undertaking with mixed results."[50]

The major test was in Darfur—and the international community failed yet again.

DARFUR

As many as four hundred thousand dead. More than two million in internal refugee camps and across the border in Chad. Countless villages burnt or otherwise decimated. As one telling indication that the crisis was growing even worse, the World Food Programme had to raise its appeal from its January 2005 level of food for 2.8 million people to food for 3.5 million in June—which amounted to more than half of Darfur's preconflict population.[51] There were some glimmers of hope later in 2005, with a cease-fire, peace talks, and a seeming decline in the violence. But those hopes proved false. To the extent the death toll was down, it was because there were few Darfurians outside the protected refugee camps left to kill— although the Janjaweed soon took to attacking the camps, making even these locales unsafe.[52] By early 2006 the conflict had spread to Chad, interacting with the Chadian civil war in another deadly mix. Meanwhile, the World Food Programme was forced by budget shortfalls to cut by half the amount of food distributed to the Darfurian refugees.[53] Hopes were raised by the May 2006 peace agreement, but not for long as commitments were breached and killings spiked. Time will tell how enduring this agreement proves to be. Even if it does provide a durable basis for peace, it will end but not erase the genocide.

As with so many other cases, the Darfur conflict had deep historical roots.[54] The main conflict in Sudan, sparking numerous civil wars since independence in 1956, most especially the twenty-year-plus one that raged until recently, has been between the Muslim north and the Christian south. Darfur had been an autonomous sultanate prior to 1916, when Britain as the colonial power merged it with Sudan. While largely Muslim, its main division has been between "Arabs" and "Africans," differentiated by skin color as well as economically, with the Arab Darfurians more nomadic herders in need of grazing land and the Africans more village-based farmers.[55] Tensions were intensified by the devastating 1980s drought, which left the various tribal and religious groups competing for shrinking resources of water, grassland, and arable soil. While most accounts do attribute the initial attacks to Darfurian rebel groups, what began the transformation from limited conflict with economic-ecological roots into mass killings were the Arabization policies of the Khartoum government that, along with the targeting of the Christians in the south as non-Muslims, targeted Darfurians as Africans. These policies intensified and radicalized parts of the antigovernment insurgency, which did pose a threat. Mostly, though, the insurgency provided an excuse for the government to team up with Arab tribesmen whose dubbing as Janjaweed was taken from an old epithet of "devils on horseback." Documents captured by the African Union peacekeeping force showed the direct complicity of the Sudanese government. As reported by Nicholas Kristof, one document directed to regional commanders and security officials calls for the "execution of all directives from the president of the republic. . . . Change the demography of Darfur and make it void of African tribes . . . [by] killing, burning villages and farms, terrorizing people, confiscating property from members of African tribes and forcing them from Darfur."[56]

While not fully preventable, the conflict in Darfur was containable well short of the tragic dimensions it reached. Key signs of another missed opportunity were there. While some details came only over time, early warning went back to early 2003, when Darfur refugees escaping to Chad reported the scorched-earth attacks of the Sudanese army and Janjaweed.[57] By December 2003 close to one hundred thousand refugees were in Chad. When UN agencies, NGOs, and journalists finally were able to get into Darfur in early 2004, the scope and scale of the conflict was very heavily reported.[58] After coming to see for themselves, both Secretary-General Annan and Secretary of State Colin Powell used the "g-word" (genocide). So, too, did President Bush in his own statement and the U.S. Congress in a condemnatory resolution. But the Janjaweed militias continued to kill, rape, and destroy with the Sudanese government's support and complicity.

The international community did little, and what it did was too weak to be credible. The opportunity existed through various negotiations, including the Abeche process led by Chad in 2003, to apply pressure on Khartoum for an immediate workable cease-fire and to begin linkage of the Darfur and the southern Sudan conflicts. To the extent that attention was paid to Darfur, it was focused almost entirely on humanitarian relief and not the underlying political issues fueling the crisis.[59] The UN Security Council did pass a number of resolutions, but they were weak and their deadlines were not enforced. UN Security Council Resolution 1547 (June 11, 2004) focused mostly on southern Sudan, with only brief mention of Darfur. UNSC Resolution 1556 (July 30) was tough in its rhetoric, giving Khartoum thirty days to disarm the Janjaweed and invoking a Chapter VII mandate to intervene based on the threat to international peace and security. But it was more words than action. The United Nations was more than happy to let the African Union, which was pushing for an "African solution to an African problem," take the lead on a peacekeeping force. The Security Council authorized the African Union Mission in Sudan (AMIS), but with the kind of limited mandate that the United Nations' own Brahimi Panel had counseled against. Nor did the Security Council invoke economic sanctions, saying only that it would "consider further actions." When the thirty-day deadline was not met, the UN special envoy signed on to a "plan of action" with Khartoum that lacked solid benchmarks and to some observers looked "more like an escape route than a discipline upon the government."[60]

UNSC Resolution 1564 (September 18) established a commission of inquiry but once again did little more than reiterate possible future action. UNSC Resolution 1574 (November 19) authorized an increase in the size of AMIS and some extension of its mandate but again failed to demand specific actions, imposed no deadlines, and made no explicit and specific threats of consequences. UNSC Resolutions 1588 (March 17, 2005), 1590 (March 24), and 1591 (March 29) again deplored and again demanded but again took limited action. UNSC 1593 (March 31) did take the significant step of referring the Darfur case to the International Criminal Court (ICC) based on violations of international humanitarian law and human rights law as documented in the report of the International Commission of Inquiry. Another flurry of resolutions came a year later, including one (1672, April 25, 2006) imposing targeted economic sanctions against four Sudanese government officials and militia leaders deemed among the most egregious perpetrators.

None of these actions in themselves or even cumulatively qualify as concerted, priority efforts. Sanctions against four people? All those resolutions using language about the UN Security Council being "seized with the matter," yet actions that hardly lived up to the words? The message to aggressors is in the limits, not the scope, of such actions. They know what they are doing, what conditions they are not complying with, what deadlines they are not meeting. Far from complying with UNSC resolutions, the Sudanese government continued financing the Janjaweed. Sudanese armed forces and law enforcement agencies themselves were joining in individual and gang rapes.[61] Claims may have been made of sending a tough or toughening message, but the message as received was devoid of serious credibility. Instead, "the looming threat of complete lawlessness and anarchy draws nearer," Secretary-General Annan acknowledged in early 2006; "the international response has been so ineffectual that 'people on the ground are just laughing,'" UN special envoy Jan Pronk was quoted as saying.[62]

Opposition from Russia and China was a main reason for the limits and weaknesses of UN action. Their positions reflected in part strict sovereignty constructionism, as over Kosovo, and in part their economic interests. Russia actually completed a sale of military aircraft, the same aircraft being used to bomb villages in Darfur, "even as Security Council members deliberated over how to address the crisis."[63] For China, the issue was especially about Sudanese oil. Sudan was part of China's "global hunt for energy."[64] As of 2004 Sudan was supplying 6 percent of China's oil needs, with projections very much on an upward curve. China also had approximately $3 billion invested in Sudan's oil sector, had been awarded hundreds of millions of dollars in additional contracts for the construction of pipelines and port facilities, and was the principal financer of a $200 million hydroelectric plant.[65] "China has even established three arms factories in Sudan," Nicholas Kristof reported, "and you see Chinese-made AK-47s, rocket-propelled grenades and machine guns all over Darfur."[66] To get China even to abstain, the UNSC resolutions had to be watered down.

Even the limited pledges of humanitarian assistance that had been made were going unfulfilled. The UN appeal for $693 million for the first half of 2005 brought in only $358 million. The United States was the largest donor at $252 million, plus another $100 million for relief efforts elsewhere in Sudan. Britain was second at $36 million, plus another $50 million for the rest of Sudan. Japan gave only $7.9 million, Germany $4.2 million, France $1.8 million. Only two fellow Muslim countries even made the list of the top eighteen donors.[67] The Arab League saw fit to hold its March 2006 summit in Khartoum, at which it once again showed more support for, than outrage with, the Sudanese government.[68] Osama bin Laden called for jihadists to go to Sudan to fight any effort the West might make to stop this mass killing of Muslims. By this "logic," the jihadists would be killing other

Muslims—based on other UN peace operations, most of the troops likely would be from Bangladesh, Pakistan, India, and Jordan—who are seeking to protect Muslim people who've already suffered over 400,000 deaths.[69]

While the African Union is to be credited for taking on the humanitarian mission, its role has reflected three of the major dilemmas in many humanitarian intervention cases. First is the discrepancy between the nature of the mission and the mandate and resources for achieving it. AMIS started in April 2004 as only a cease-fire-monitoring mission, not an enforcement one, with only 120 monitors spread across a vast territory. It became a troop presence later that year, building up to about 7,700 by October 2005, with a goal of 12,300 by spring 2006. But it just wasn't able to expand capacity to this level. Moreover, its mandate remained largely one of monitoring and force self-protection, and the aid, training, and support the United States, Western Europe, and others pledged have been slow to materialize, and then only partially. Sensing this weakness, and calculating that aggression against the existing AMIS forces would deter more than foster expanded deployments, the Sudanese government and Janjaweed forces ambushed AMIS forces on October 8, 2005, killing six. The next day an entire AMIS patrol of eighteen was kidnapped, and then a rescue mission of twenty was also captured.

Second has been the African Union's own ambivalence about fully stepping up to its own charter's Article 4(h) commitment to collective intervention. The final communiqué of its October 2004 minisummit reaffirmed support for Sudan's sovereignty, rejecting "any foreign intervention by any country, whatsoever."[70] This tension grew even more problematic when Sudan was scheduled to rotate to the AU presidency in 2006. This move was blocked, but the tacit quid pro quo included an AU resolution that leaned much more toward the traditional intervention-restrictive conception of sovereignty than toward responsibility to protect.

Third has been the ways in which deferring to regional initiatives allows the international community to pass the buck. While there are many benefits from and rationales for regional leadership, it can have a perverse dynamic, making for what former assistant secretary of state for Africa Susan Rice has called "a conspiracy of absolution" in which "the African Union has absolved reluctant Western countries of any responsibility to consider sending their own troops," for which the United States, the United Nations, and the European Union are "undoubtedly grateful."[71] The regional actor, the African Union in this case, ends up being put in a position far beyond its feasible capacity and political will. By early 2006 efforts were increasing for a hand-off to a UN peacekeeping force, with NATO support for AMIS as a possible bridge. Yet even then the dialogue at the United Nations referred to almost a year delay at minimum between authorization and actual deployment of a peacekeeping force.

U.S. policy has shown some signs of focus and leadership but has been uneven at best in its follow-through and substance. The United States has been doing more than its share as a donor. The g-word has been invoked, although with the caveat of a restrictive interpretation of the 1948 Genocide Convention that did not require concerted action.[72] Secretary of State Condoleezza Rice made a dramatic visit in July 2005, making a point to meet with rape victims. Deputy Secretary of State Robert Zoellick became the administration's point man, making numerous trips of his own, including one breaking out of diplomatic niceties and pushing back (literally and figuratively) against Sudanese government obstructionism and disingenuousness.[73] Zoellick also played a key role in the important peace agreement reached in May 2006. Back home, though, the administration was slow to break the congressional deadlock over the Darfur Peace and Accountability Act. The delay was due partly to internal congressional issues, partly to administration priorities. Bipartisan alliances, such as that between Senators Barack Obama (D-Ill.) and Sam Brownback (R-Kans.), helped move the legislation.[74] The bill that finally passed included targeted sanctions, additional funding and other support (e.g., logistics, training) for AMIS, and urgings for NATO involvement in support of AMIS or a UN peacekeeping force. But the bill worked its way through conference committee and other congressional procedures with no real sense of urgency. Similarly, in the executive branch the issue attracted attention but was not accorded marked priority.

The Darfur issue was less of a U.S. domestic political problem than often is the case for humanitarian intervention. The Christian Right, which had been very involved in the southern Sudan conflict in defense of the Sudanese Christians, also was weighing in on Darfur. "Just because you've signed a peace deal with the South," Franklin Graham (son of Billy) told a White House aide, "doesn't mean you can wash your hands of Darfur."[75] On the left, various NGOs were generating at least a degree of attention and action, including the Genocide Intervention Network, started by socially entrepreneurial college students, which had raised $250,000 by late 2005.[76] A June 2005 public opinion poll showed strong and broad support for more U.S. leadership and tougher policies, albeit short of sending U.S. ground forces.[77] The Rally to Stop Genocide held April 30, 2006, in Washington, D.C., featured a range of speakers rarely found on the same podium, including Richard Land, president of the Southern Baptist Convention, actor George Clooney, Holocaust survivor Elie Wiesel, and Paul Rusesabagina, made famous by the movie *Hotel Rwanda*. While overall media attention was typically lacking, *New York Times* columnist Nicholas Kristof made Darfur a recurring focus, creatively blending his newspaper column and Internet resources, for which he received a 2006 Pulitzer Prize.

Nor has the problem been a shortage of ideas and alternatives. Numerous viable proposals for international action have been put forward at various junctures of the crisis, but time and again little was done. Even when there is early warning and a strong rationale for action, the missed-opportunity argument also requires that the commitments entailed be measured and proportional and that the alternatives be available at the time and not just in hindsight. Both conditions have been met in the Darfur case. Indeed, just from one NGO, the International Crisis Group (ICG), have come a whole series of proposals: in March 2004 the ICG laid out a number of tangible, focused, doable measures to toughen diplomacy; in August it laid out an "international action plan"; in April, July, and October 2005, updated versions; in March 2006, a plan for a hand-off from AMIS to a UN peacekeeping force of double the size and with a more robust mission and mandate.[78] These and other proposals were measured, although as each opportunity was missed the next proposal had to scale up, in the dynamic we have seen so many other times, in which the problems grow worse over time and the scope and nature of the options needed become greater.

A peace agreement was reached in early May 2006 (just before this book went to press). Its key provisions included rapid disarmament of the Janjaweed, some military and political integration of the rebel movements, and funds for economic reconstruction and refugee resettlement. Time will tell how enduring this agreement has been. Even at the time it was greeted with a note of caution. With some groups outside the agreement and the will of the parties that did sign still untested, the situation seemed susceptible to the spoiler problem as well as other factors that have undermined similar agreements.[79] "Unless the right spirit is there, the right attitude," said Nigerian president Olusegun Obasanjo, who had been playing a key role in the negotiations, "this document will not be worth the paper it's written on."[80] One can hope that the deeply discouraging conclusion drawn

by former assistant secretary of state Princeton Lyman and Council on Foreign Relations scholar Cheryl Igiri in a November 2005 study might be dispelled: "The crisis in Darfur reveals that, despite all the promises since Rwanda that such a catastrophe would not be allowed to happen again, the international community still lacks the institutions, procedures and political unity to respond in a timely way. The global response to rapidly developing conflicts is still the same: painfully and tragically slow."[81] One can hope, but not count on. Indeed, with the ink barely dry the Sudanese government reinvoked the sovereignty rationale to try to keep UN peacekeepers out, and some rebel groups that had not signed the agreement escalated their attacks.

THE CHALLENGES OF GETTING TO "NEVER AGAIN"

We need to do better. We still too often do too little too late to prevent or limit mass killings —too little genuinely humanitarian intervention and too much of what Thomas Weiss calls "inhumanitarian nonintervention."[82] Prevention of all mass killings is unrealistic. But prevention of more than in the past is not.

September 11 helped demonstrate how ostensibly low-priority failed-state and humanitarian issues could have highest-priority security effects. Beyond such instrumental linkages, though, is the subtler but in many respects more penetratingly undermining effect tolerance of genocide, ethnic cleansing, and comparable mass killings has on the international system. Two of the five key functions identified by noted scholar Robert Keohane for there to be any semblance of effective global governance are "limit the use of large-scale violence" and "provide a guarantee against the worst forms of abuse, particularly involving violence and deprivation. . . . Tyrants who murder their own people may need to be restrained or removed by outsiders."[83] This grows truer as globalization grows more extensive and intensive, for reasons that trace back to Immanuel Kant's assertion that rights violations "in one place in the world [are] felt everywhere."[84] Zbigniew Brzezinski shows that this is a concern not just of liberal internationalists but also of more traditional realists in his emphasis that even for the United States, with all its military strength, security "must be reinforced by systematic efforts to enlarge the zones of global stability, to eliminate some of the most egregious causes of political violence, and to promote political systems that place central value on human rights and constitutional procedures."[85]

With many, albeit not all, political humanitarian crises, Africa has been the place that "continues to test the resolve of the international community and the United States to prevent mass killings and genocide." Africa's increasing strategic importance is a further factor stressing the interests and not just the ideals at stake. As a Council on Foreign Relations task force observed, "2005 was the year for Africa, but we missed the point. . . . Africa is becoming steadily more central to the United States and to the rest of the world in ways that transcend humanitarian interests. Africa now plays an increasingly significant role in supplying energy, preventing the spread of terrorism, and halting the devastation of HIV/AIDS. Africa's growing importance is reflected in the intensifying competition with China and other countries for both access to African resources and influence in the region."[86]

The five sets of issues laid out earlier provide a framework for pursuing strategies that can get us closer to "never again." First, political causality rather than historical determinism needs to be the analytic starting point for what drives these conflicts. Of course, they are historically shaped: "The past is never dead," as William Faulkner once wrote. "It's not even past."[87] But historical shaping is one thing, fixed determinism positing few, if any, options for international actors quite another. So much of the scholarly and policy literature shows the

purposive nature of ethnic and related conflicts, driven by demagogic and other aggressive leaders and factions in ways and to extremes that were not inevitable. Moreover, because part of this calculus is how free a hand there is to play the ethnic or other identity-based hatred card based on the likelihood of international intervention, there really is no nonimpact option for international actors. The missed-opportunities findings show that in case after case there have been viable options knowable at the time and doable within realistic and pragmatic parameters. It is thus more than time that questions like "Can anything be done?" be left behind and full focus be given to "What is to be done?"

Second, the norm of the responsibility to protect needs to be further strengthened as a legitimate basis for abridging state sovereignty and intervening in intrastate conflicts that cross the just-cause threshold. The Darfur case was the first major opportunity since adoption at the 2005 UN World Summit of the responsibility-to-protect principle, but instead we got excessive deference to strict sovereignty constructionism. Deputy Secretary of State Zoellick stressed the difficulties and dangers as a practical matter of sending a peacekeeping force in when the host government opposes it. Even aid workers were being blocked and attacked by Sudanese government forces and their allies. Yet given that over 95 percent of contemporary armed conflicts are intrastate, shifts away from classical noninterventionism are crucial to international peace, security, and justice.[88] The risks, both immediate and as precedent for abridging sovereignty, are not to be discounted, but the risks of not acting need to be weighed against those of acting. This requires the United States and other major and regional powers to be conscious of concerns about high-minded humanitarian rationales being manipulated as cover for classical self-interested interventions. Those with power have a responsibility to protect the legitimacy of the responsibility to protect. At the same time, those who would tightly restrict interventions in the name of broad principles such as sovereignty, yet are acting much more out of their own self-interest in being free to be repressive and murderous within their own borders, also need to be stripped of their cover story. As cited earlier from Secretary-General Annan, the UN Charter "was issued in the name of 'the people,' not the governments. . . . It was never meant as a license for governments to trample on human rights and human dignity."[89]

Third, force cannot just be a last resort; it may need to be an early resort. Unless force can be used as something more than a last resort, we will consign ourselves to continuing to pick up the pieces of societies torn asunder by mass deaths and other devastation and destruction. As hard as conflict prevention is, postconflict reconstruction is so much harder. One study after another has shown the profound effects these conflicts have on economies, intercommunal relations, and virtually all societal institutions. Take a look at Somalia, which as of early 2006 was on its fourteenth attempt to reestablish central government since 1991. Or Rwanda, which more than a decade after the genocide was still in the earliest phases of judicial and reconciliation processes for war crimes. Failing states are enough of a problem, failed ones much worse. To be sure, any and all debates about the use of force other than as a last resort have been further complicated by fallout from the Iraq case.[90] But as stressed earlier, the debate about the threat of force having to be more than just a last resort for humanitarian interventions already was engaged pre-Iraq. There is a peace-through-strength logic here that is consistent with deterrence strategy as adapted to today's realities.

Fourth, on the "Who decides?" question, the UN Security Council is to be the preferred but not the exclusive source of legitimate authority. The Darfur case again demonstrated the Security Council's limited functionality, both in major powers trumping collective commitments with national interests (China and Russia, in this case) and in other members (the United States, France, Britain) not exerting anything close to the political will necessary for concerted action. Roles shift in other cases (Iraq as the obvious example), but the net effect is the same: a Security Council still not worthy of being the sole depository of authority over humanitarian interventions.[91] Yet we also know from Iraq the dangers of largely unilateral use-of-force decision making. Regional organizations provide a viable intermediate basis with potentially stronger claims to legitimacy than largely unilateral actors or ad hoc coalitions of the willing. This also can be complicated, especially if the Security Council explicitly opposes an action, as distinct from not acting. But it is worth bearing in mind ICISS's challenge as to which is worse for the international community, "if the Security Council is bypassed or in the damage to that order if human beings are slaughtered while the Security Council stands by."[92]

Fifth, greater humanitarian intervention capacity must be created. Here there is real progress on which to build. The 2005 *Human Security Report* heavily attributes the decline in the numbers and intensity of wars to UN preventive diplomacy and peace operations.[93] Recent studies show the United Nations has been more successful than it often is given credit for and by some comparisons has been more successful than the United States.[94] But Mats Berdal's point about UN capacity varying according to the nature of the mission also is true, that "the UN is both structurally ill-equipped and unlikely to ever obtain the requisite political support to undertake—that is, to plan, mount, direct and sustain—enforcement operations."[95] Concern has also been mounting of late about overextension in the sheer number of missions on the UN docket, with the lessons of the early 1990s overload in numbers as well as types of missions in mind.[96] The new Peacebuilding Commission can help, but as noted earlier, its approach and tools are largely political, diplomatic, and economic. The United Nations still also needs greater military intervention credibility and capacity —and this aspect of strategy remains to be seriously addressed.

Humanitarian intervention capacity building also has to entail stepped-up national and regional efforts. The United States was headed in this direction in the late Clinton administration, only to be reversed at the beginning of the Bush administration. Even with the lessons of Iraq about how ill-equipped U.S. forces were and how deficient U.S. strategy has been, the 2006 Bush National Security Strategy and Pentagon Quadrennial Defense Review shows that the administration still has neither significantly elevated the priority of, nor seriously re-thought the strategy for, peacekeeping and conflict prevention.

Europe also has a vital role to play. Some of this is through NATO, some through the European Union. Humanitarian intervention is one of the areas in which a common European foreign and security policy draws on some inherent strengths and global comparative advantages. One recent report concluded that "much has changed for the better," crediting substantial progress both structurally and in some key cases while also expressing concern that many changes were "as yet mostly words on paper."[97] Among the other regional multilateral organizations, the African Union is to be credited for its Darfur role, although this also has shown how far it has to go.

Meeting these five sets of challenges is a tall order. It will be difficult to achieve. But it is possible—and, most of all, necessary if we are to have any chance of making the "never again" pledge reality and not just rhetoric.

NOTES

Thanks to Kurt Wise for research assistance and to Alexander George, David Hamburg, Princeton Lyman, Donald Rothchild, and David Lake and participants in the Duke conference Delegating Sovereignty: Constitutional and Political Perspectives (March 2–4, 2006) for insightful comments.

1. Ted Robert Gurr, *People versus States: Minorities at Risk in the New Century* (Washington, D.C.: United States Institute of Peace Press, 2000); and Gurr, "Minorities and Nationalists: Managing Ethnopolitical Conflict in the New Century," in *Turbulent Peace: The Challenges of Managing International Conflict*, ed. Chester A. Crocker, Fen Osler Hampson, and Pamela Aall (Washington, D.C.: United States Institute of Peace Press, 2001), 163–188.

2. Publication of this report was delayed by 9/11, but only by a few weeks until September 30, 2001. Attention, though, was not nearly what it might have been.

3. Michael R. Gordon, "The 2000 Campaign: The Military: Bush Would Stop U.S. Peacekeeping in Balkan Fights," *New York Times*, October 21, 2000, p. A1. The 82nd Airborne is widely considered one of the top units of the American military.

4. See, for example, Condoleezza Rice, "Promoting the National Interest," *Foreign Affairs* 79, no. 1 (January–February 2000): 45–62.

5. Bruce W. Jentleson, ed., *Opportunities Missed, Opportunities Seized: Preventive Diplomacy in the Post–Cold War World* (Boulder, Colo.: Rowman and Littlefield, 2000); Jentleson, *Coercive Prevention: Normative, Political and Policy Dilemmas*, Peaceworks No. 35 (Washington, D.C.: United States Institute of Peace, 1999); and Jentleson, "The Realism of Preventive Statecraft," in *Conflict Prevention: Path to Peace or Grand Illusion?* ed. David Carment and Albrecht Schnabel (New York: United Nations University Press, 2003), 26–46.

6. See, for example, Carnegie Commission on Preventing Deadly Conflict (CCPDC), *Preventing Deadly Conflict* (New York: Carnegie Corporation of New York, 1997); David A. Lake and Donald Rothchild, eds., *The International Spread of Ethnic Conflict: Fear, Diffusion and Escalation* (Princeton, N.J.: Princeton University Press, 1998); Samantha Power, *"A Problem from Hell": America and the Age of Genocide* (New York: Basic Books, 2002); Nicholas J. Wheeler, *Saving Strangers: Humanitarian Intervention in International Society* (New York: Oxford University Press, 2000); Simon Chesterman, *Just War or Just Peace? Humanitarian Intervention and International Law* (New York: Oxford University Press, 2001); J. L.

Holzgrefe and Robert O. Keohane, eds., *Humanitarian Intervention: Ethical, Legal and Political Dilemmas* (New York: Cambridge University Press, 2003); and Martha Finnemore, *The Purpose of Intervention: Changing Beliefs about the Use of Force* (Ithaca, N.Y.: Cornell University Press, 2003). I structure a broader discussion of U.S. foreign policy and the use of force within a similar set of analytic questions in "Who, What, Why and How: Debates over Post–Cold War Military Intervention," in *Eagle Adrift: American Foreign Policy at the End of the Century*, ed. Robert J. Lieber (New York: Longman, 1997), 39–70.

7. Robert D. Kaplan, *Balkan Ghosts: A Journey through History* (New York: St. Martin's Press, 1993).

8. Lake and Rothchild, *The International Sources of Ethnic Conflict*; Power, *"A Problem from Hell"*; CCPDC, *Preventing Deadly Conflict*; and Jentleson, *Opportunities Missed, Opportunities Seized.*

9. Jentleson, *Opportunities Missed, Opportunities Seized.*

10. Alexander L. George and Jane E. Holl, "The Warning-Response Problem and Missed Opportunities in Preventive Diplomacy," in *Opportunities Missed, Opportunities Seized*, 29 (emphasis in the original).

11. International Commission on Intervention and State Sovereignty (ICISS), *The Responsibility to Protect* (Ottawa: International Development Research Centre, 2001), 33, 36 (emphasis added).

12. Stanley Hoffmann, *World Disorders: Troubled Peace in the Post–Cold War Era* (Lanham, Md.: Rowman and Littlefield, 1998), 170.

13. Jentleson, *Coercive Prevention.*

14. Robert J. Art and Robert Jervis, *International Politics: Enduring Concepts and Contemporary Issues* (New York: HarperCollins, 1992), 2; and Abram Chayes and Antonia Handler Chayes, eds., *Preventing Conflict in the Post–Cold War World: Mobilizing International and Regional Organizations* (Washington, D.C.: Brookings Institution Press, 1996), 60.

15. Kofi Annan, "Secretary-General Reflects on 'Intervention' in Thirty-fifth Annual Ditchley Foundation Lecture," press release SG/SM/6613, June 26, 1998, http://www.un.org/News/Press/docs/1998/19980626.sgsm6613.html (accessed October 16, 2003). See United Nations General Assembly, *Report of the Secretary-General on the Work of the Organization*, 54th sess., Supplement No. 1 (A/54/1),

August 31, 1999, 4, http://www.un.org/Docs/SG/Report99/toc.htm (accessed October 16, 2003).

16. Francis M. Deng, Sadikei Kimaro, Terence Lyons, Donald Rothchild, and I. William Zartman, *Sovereignty as Responsibility: Conflict Management in Africa* (Washington, D.C.: Brookings Institution Press, 1996), 28.

17. ICISS, *The Responsibility to Protect*, 69.

18. Ibid., 11.

19. Michael Walzer, *Just and Unjust Wars: A Moral Argument with Historical Illustrations* (New York: Basic Books, 1977); ICISS, *The Responsibility to Protect*; and Chesterman, *Just War or Just Peace?*

20. Thomas G. Weiss, "The Sunset of Humanitarian Intervention? The Responsibility to Protect in a Unipolar Era," *Security Dialogue* 35, no. 2 (June 2004): 139.

21. H. E. Mr. Tang Jiaxuan, minister of foreign affairs of the People's Republic of China, statement to the 54th Session of the UN General Assembly, September 22, 1999, http://www.undp.org/missions/china/unga.htm (accessed September 24, 1999); and Bates Gill and James Reilly, "Sovereignty, Intervention and Peacekeeping: The View from Beijing," *Survival* 42, no. 3 (Autumn 2000): 41–59.

22. Independent International Commission on Kosovo, *The Kosovo Report: Conflict, International Response, Lessons Learned* (Oxford: Oxford University Press, 2000).

23. ICISS, *The Responsibility to Protect*, 54–55.

24. Fund for Peace, *Neighbors on Alert: Regional Views on Humanitarian Action*, Summary Report of the Regional Response to Internal War Program (Washington, D.C.: Fund for Peace, October 2003).

25. Alex J. Bellamy and Paul D. Williams, "Who's Keeping the Peace? Regionalization and Contemporary Peace Operations," *International Security* 29, no. 4 (Spring 2005): 166. There also have been cases in which the United Nations was the authorizing body, but operational command was exercised by non-UN forces: for example, NATO in Bosnia and later the International Security Assistance Force (ISAF) in Afghanistan.

26. Norwegian Nobel Committee, "The Nobel Peace Prize 1988," press release, http://nobelprize.org/peace/laureates/1988/press.html.

27. William J. Durch, Victoria K. Holt, Caroline R. Earle, and Moira K. Shanahan, *The Brahimi Re-*

port and the Future of UN Peace Operations (Washington, D.C.: Henry L. Stimson Center, 2003).

28. Power, *"A Problem from Hell,"* 334–335.

29. Ivo H. Daalder and Michael E. O'Hanlon, *Winning Ugly: NATO's War to Save Kosovo* (Washington, D.C.: Brookings Institution Press, 2000).

30. Seyom Brown, *The Illusion of Control: Force and Foreign Policy in the Twenty-first Century* (Washington, D.C.: Brookings Institution Press, 2003), 36.

31. See, for example, Peter Cross, ed., *Contributing to Preventive Action,* Conflict Prevention Network of the Stiftung Wissenschaft und Politik (SWP), CPN Yearbook 1997–98 (Baden-Baden: Nomos, 1998); and International Crisis Group, *EU Crisis Response Capability: Institutions and Processes for Conflict Prevention and Management,* ICG Issues Report No. 2 (Brussels: International Crisis Group, June 26, 2001). See also *G8 Miyazaki Initiatives for Conflict Prevention,* Kyushu-Okinawa Summit Meeting 2000, http://www.g8kyushu-okinawa.go.jp/e/documents/html/initiative.html.

32. Richard R. Betts, "The Delusion of Impartial Intervention," *Foreign Affairs* 6, no. 73 (November–December 1994): 20–33.

33. Matthew Krain, "International Intervention and the Severity of Genocides and Policides," *International Studies Quarterly* 49, no. 3 (September 2005): 363.

34. Stephen Ellis, "How to Rebuild Africa," *Foreign Affairs* 84, no. 5 (September–October 2005): 135–148; and Philip G. Roeder and Donald Rothchild, eds., *Sustainable Peace: Power and Democracy after Civil Wars* (Ithaca, N.Y.: Cornell University Press, 2005).

35. Tom J. Farer, "Humanitarian Intervention before and after 9/11: Legality and Legitimacy," in *Humanitarian Intervention,* 88–89. See also Tom J. Farer et al., "Roundtable: Humanitarian Intervention after 9/11," *International Relations* 19, no. 2 (June 2005): 211–250.

36. President George W. Bush, *National Security Strategy of the United States,* September 2, 2002, http://www.whitehouse.gov/nsc/print/nssa11.html (accessed October 24, 2002).

37. Cited in Weiss, "The Sunset of Humanitarian Intervention?" 143.

38. Alex J. Bellamy, "Ethics and Intervention: The 'Humanitarian Exception' and the Problem of

Abuse in the Case of Iraq," *Journal of Peace Research* 41, no. 2 (March 2004): 145.

39. Thomas Weiss, "Cosmopolitan Force and the Responsibility to Protect," in Farer et al., "Roundtable: Humanitarian Intervention," 234.

40. United Nations High-Level Panel on Threats, Challenges, and Change, *A More Secure World: Our Shared Responsibility* (New York: United Nations, 2004), 65, 67.

41. Ibid., 63.

42. This norm has come to have its own acronym: R2P.

43. United Nations Department of Public Information, *Fact Sheet: 2005 World Summit,* September 2005, http://www.un.org/summit2005/presskit/fact_sheet.pdf.

44. United Nations General Assembly, *2005 World Summit Outcome,* A/60/150, September 20, 2005, pars. 138–139, http://www.un.org/summit2005/documents.html.

45. Ibid., pars. 77–80, 92–105.

46. Thanks to Michael Barnett on this point.

47. Human Security Centre, *Human Security Report 2005: War and Peace in the Twenty-first Century* (New York: Oxford University Press, 2005), 1–2 and passim.

48. Henryk J. Sokalski, *An Ounce of Prevention: Macedonia and the UN Experience in Preventive Diplomacy* (Washington, D.C.: United States Institute of Peace Press, 2003).

49. Nicholas Wood, "Ambitious Experiment Leads Kosovo to a Crossroads," *New York Times,* October 3, 2005.

50. Necla Tschirgi, *Post-Conflict Peacebuilding Revisited: Achievements, Limitations, Challenges* (New York: International Peace Academy, 2004), i.

51. "The Donors and Darfur," editorial, *Washington Post,* June 20, 2005, A14.

52. Joel Brinkley, "Violence and Refugee Numbers Grow in Sudan, U.S. Official Finds," *New York Times,* November 11, 2005.

53. Lydia Polgreen, "UN Agency Cuts Food Rations for Sudan Victims," *New York Times,* April 29, 2006.

54. See, for example, Gerard Prunier, *Darfur: The Ambiguous Genocide* (Ithaca, N.Y.: Cornell University Press, 2005); Francis M. Deng, *War of Visions: Con-*

flicts of Identities in the Sudan (Washington, D.C.: Brookings Institution Press, 1995).

55. Samantha Power, "Dying in Darfur," *New Yorker,* August 30, 2004.

56. Nicholas Kristof, "The Secret Genocide Archive," *New York Times,* February 23, 2005, http://select.nytimes.com/search/restricted/article?rs=F50810FF3D590C708EDDAB0894DD404482. See also Human Rights Watch, *Entrenching Impunity: Government Responsibility for International Crimes in Darfur,* December 2005, http://hrw.org/reports/2005/darfur1205.

57. Scott Anderson, "How Did Darfur Happen?" *New York Times Magazine,* October 17, 2004; International Crisis Group, *Darfur Rising: Sudan's New Crisis,* ICG Africa Report No. 76 (Brussels: International Crisis Group, March 25, 2004); Amnesty International, "Sudan: Crisis in Darfur; Urgent Need for International Commission of Inquiry and Monitoring," press release, April 28, 2003, http://web.amnesty.org/library/Index/ENGAFR540262003?open&of=ENG-SDN.

58. See, for example, the numerous columns by Nicholas Kristof, at http://topics.nytimes.com/top/opinion/editorialsandoped/oped/columnists/nicholasdkristof/index.html.

59. ICG, *Darfur Rising,* 23.

60. International Crisis Group, *Darfur Deadline: A New International Action Plan,* ICG Africa Report No. 83 (Brussels: International Crisis Group, August 23, 2004), 4.

61. Joel Brinkley, "Sudan Still Paying Militias Harassing Darfur, U.S. Says," *New York Times,* July 21, 2005; and Warren Hoge, "UN Charges Sudan Ignores Rapes in Darfur by Military and Police," *New York Times,* July 30, 2005.

62. Joel Brinkley, "Plan to End Darfur Violence Is Failing, Officials Say," *New York Times,* January 28, 2006.

63. Cheryl O. Negri and Princeton Lyman, *Giving Meaning to "Never Again": Seeking an Effective Response to the Crisis in Darfur and Beyond,* CSR No. 5 (New York: Council on Foreign Relations, September 2004), 24.

64. David Zweig and Bi Jianhi, "China's Global Hunt for Energy," *Foreign Affairs* 84, no. 5 (September–October 2005): 25–38.

65. Gerald Butt, "Thirst for Crude Pulling China into Sudan," *Daily Star,* August 17, 2004; and U.S. Department of Energy, Energy Information Administration, *Sudan: Country Analysis Brief,* March 2005, http://www.eia.doe.gov/emeu/cabs/sudan.html.

66. Nicholas D. Kristof, "China and Sudan, Blood and Oil," *New York Times,* April 23, 2006.

67. "The Donors and Darfur," editorial, *Washington Post,* June 20, 2005, A14.

68. "Shameful and hypocritical," wrote one Muslim commentator in the Lebanese *Daily Star;* Fatema Abdul Rasul, "Arab, Muslim Silence on Darfur Conflict Is Deafening," *Daily Star,* April 10, 2006, http://www.dailystar.com.1b/article.asp?edition_id=10&categ_id=2&article_id=23635.

69. Bruce W. Jentleson, "Bin Laden Supports Genocide against Muslims," America Abroad, April 24, 2006, http://americaabroad.tpmcafe.com/node/29153.

70. Paul D. Williams and Alex J. Bellamy, "The Responsibility to Protect and the Crisis in Darfur," *Security Dialogue* 36, no. 1 (March 2005): 43. See also International Crisis Group, *The AU's Mission in Darfur: Bridging the Gaps,* Africa Briefing No. 28 (Brussels: International Crisis Group, July 6, 2005), http://www.crisisgroup.org/home/index.cfm?id=3547&l=1.

71. Susan E. Rice, "Why Darfur Can't Be Left to Africa," *Washington Post,* August 7, 2005.

72. Williams and Bellamy, "The Responsibility to Protect and the Crisis in Darfur," 31.

73. Brinkley, "Violence and Refugee Numbers Grow in Sudan."

74. Barack Obama and Sam Brownback, "Policy Adrift on Darfur," *Washington Post,* December 27, 2005.

75. Power, "Dying in Darfur."

76. Nicholas Kristof, "Walking the Talk," *New York Times,* October 9, 2005, http://www.genocideinterventionfund.org.

77. International Crisis Group, *Do Americans Care about Darfur? An International Crisis Group/Zogby International Opinion Survey,* Africa Briefing No. 26 (Brussels: International Crisis Group, June 1, 2005).

78. International Crisis Group, *Darfur Rising; Darfur Deadline; A New Sudan Action Plan,* Africa Briefing No. 24 (Brussels: Internatonal Crisis Group, April 26, 2005); *The AU's Mission in Darfur; Unifying Darfur's Rebels: A Prerequisite for Peace,* Africa Briefing No. 32 (Brussels: International Crisis Group, October 6, 2005); and *To Save Darfur,* Africa Report No. 105, (Brussels: International Crisis Group, March 17, 2006).

79. Stephen J. Stedman, "Spoiler Problems in Peace Processes," *International Security* 2, no. 2 (Fall 1997): 5–53; Roeder and Rothchild, eds., *Sustainable Peace.*

80. Glenn Kessler and Emily Wax, "Sudan, Main Rebel Groups Sign Peace Deal," *Washington Post,* May 5, 2006, http://www.washingtonpost.com/wpdyn/content/article/2006/05/05/AR2006050500305_pf.html.

81. Negri and Lyman, *Giving Meaning to "Never Again,"* 23. See also Refugees International, *No Power to Protect: The African Union Mission in Sudan,* November 19, 2005, http://www.refugeesinternational.org/content/publication/detail/7222/.

82. Weiss, "The Sunset of Humanitarian Intervention?" 149.

83. Robert O. Keohane, "Governance in a Partially Globalized World," *American Political Science Review* 95, no. 1 (March 2001): 23. See also John D. Steinbruner, *Principles of Global Security* (Washington, D.C.: Brookings Institution Press, 2000).

84. Cited in Wheeler, *Saving Strangers,* 308.

85. Zbigniew Brzezinski, *The Choice: Global Domination or Global Leadership* (New York: Basic Books, 2004), 25.

86. Council on Foreign Relations, *More than Humanitarianism: A Strategic U.S. Approach towards Africa,* Report of an Independent Task Force (New York: Council on Foreign Relations, December 2005), http://www.cfr.org/content/publications/attachments/Africa%20Task%20Force%20Web.pdf.

87. William Faulkner, *Requiem for a Nun,* http://www.mcsr.olemiss.edu/~egjbp/faulkner/faulkner.html.

88. Human Security Centre, *Human Security Report,* 23.

89. "Secretary-General, 'Intervention,' Ditchley Lecture," 1998.

90. See also James Steinberg, "Preventive Force in U.S. National Security Strategy," *Survival* 47, no. 4

(Winter 2005–6): 55–72; and Ivo Daalder and James Steinberg, "The Future of Pre-emption," *American Interest* 1, no. 2 (Winter 2005).

91. Security Council expansion, kicked down the road again at the 2005 World Summit, could have effects in either direction. As with any organizational group, more members can mean more problems in achieving action-oriented consensus, especially given that the increase would not be just in size but of perspectives and interests. On the other hand, given the sensitivities military intervention inherently carries in the historical contexts of colonialism and superpower Cold War interventionism, greater Third World participation could enhance the legitimacy of Security Council authorizations of intervention. Bruce W. Jentleson, "Tough Love Multilateralism," *Washington Quarterly* 27, no. 1 (Winter 2003–4): 17.

92. ICISS, *The Responsibility to Protect,* 54–55.

93. Human Security Centre, *Human Security Report.*

94. James Dobbins et al., *The UN's Role in Nation-Building: From the Congo to Iraq* (Santa Monica, Calif.: RAND Corporation, 2005); and Dobbins et al., *America's Role in Nation-Building: From Germany to Iraq* (Santa Monica, Calif.: RAND Corporation, 2003). See also Michael W. Doyle and Nicholas Sambanis, *Making War and Building Peace: United Nations Peace Operations* (Princeton: Princeton University Press, 2006).

95. Mats Berdal, "The UN Security Council: Ineffective but Indispensable," *Survival* 45, no. 2 (Summer 2003): 24.

96. As of June 2004 the number of UN peacekeeping forces authorized was 74,478, but only 56,261 had been provided by member states. Williams and Bellamy, "The Responsibility to Protect and the Crisis in Darfur," 43.

97. International Crisis Group, *EU Crisis Response Capability Revisited,* Europe Report No. 160 (Brussels: International Crisis Group, January 17, 2005), http://www.crisisgroup.org/library/documents/europe/160_eu_crisis_response_capability_revisited_edit.pdf.

17

COERCIVE DIPLOMACY

Robert J. Art and Patrick M. Cronin

COERCIVE DIPLOMACY IS A TECHNIQUE of statecraft that involves what Alexander George aptly termed "forceful persuasion."[1] It is an attempt to get a target—be it a state, groups within a state, or a nonstate actor—to change its behavior through the threat to use force or through the actual use of limited force. Coercive diplomacy can include, but need not include, the use of positive inducements, and it generally involves a mix of both negotiation and coercion. Coercive diplomacy therefore stakes out a middle ground in statecraft between the wholesale resort to force, on the one hand, and the use only of diplomacy, on the other. Coercive diplomacy is attractive to decision makers because it promises the achievement of their objectives "on the cheap": it holds out hope of big results with small costs (to the coercer). If the record of the United States is indicative, however, coercive diplomacy is hard to execute successfully.

This chapter provides an overview of coercive diplomacy as it has been practiced by the United States since the end of the Cold War. We concentrate on the United States because there is a dearth of studies on how other states have used coercive diplomacy, but a relative abundance of them on how the United States has employed it, especially since 1990.[2] We proceed as follows. First, we examine the nature of coercive diplomacy. Second, we analyze how the United States used this technique in eleven instances from 1990 to 2003 and why it was successful in some cases and unsuccessful in others. Third, we examine the protracted and ongoing cases of North Korea and Iran and U.S. attempts, unsuccessful so far, to apply coercive diplomacy in order to get the former to give up its nuclear weapons and the latter its quest for them. Finally, from these cases we draw some general conclusions about the exercise of coercive diplomacy.

So, what is coercive diplomacy, what is its track record, and why does it work in some cases but fail in others? These are the questions this chapter addresses.

THE NATURE OF
COERCIVE DIPLOMACY

Alexander George of Stanford University was the first to theorize systematically about coercive diplomacy.[3] Beginning in the early 1970s, he asked a simple question: How could a global nuclear power like the United States successfully use a limited amount of force or simply the threat of force to compel a much weaker adversary to retreat from territory that it had occupied, or to halt its military aggression, or in some cases even to relinquish its hold on governmental power? The crux of the challenge for the user of coercive diplomacy, thought George, was how to persuade, not bludgeon, an opponent into seeing a situation the user's way. The philosophy associated with President Teddy Roosevelt—"speak softly and carry a big stick"—embodies the spirit of coercive diplomacy: it is a means of signaling to an opponent the merits of settling disputes without having to wage war. Thus, what separates coercive diplomacy from mere diplomacy is the use of some force so as to convince a target of the coercer's willingness and capacity to resort to full-scale military action should the target not give way.

George studied seven cases of coercive diplomacy, all of which but the first took place during the Cold War: U.S. opposition to Japanese expansion in the 1930s, the 1961–62 crisis in Laos, the 1962 Cuban missile crisis, the 1965 confrontation with North Vietnam, confrontations with Nicaragua and Libya in the early 1980s, and the 1990 Persian Gulf crisis precipitated by Iraq's invasion of Kuwait. By his reckoning, the United States clearly achieved its objectives only in the Cuban and Laotian cases and failed in the Japanese, Vietnam, and Persian Gulf cases. George found the Nicaraguan and Libyan cases sufficiently ambiguous that they were hard to classify as either a success or a failure because he could not determine whether U.S. actions helped to produce the outcomes.[4]

From these cases George derived some general lessons. First, he emphasized that the coercer had to be crystal clear about what it sought from the target and to communicate clearly to the target what was wanted. If the coercer was vague about what it wanted, or if the target did not understand what was wanted of it, then coercive diplomacy was not likely to work. Second, George underlined the importance of creating in the target a sense of urgency about complying with the demands; otherwise, the target would find little incentive to comply. Third, the coercer had to find a way to convey to the target a sufficiently credible threat of punishment for noncompliance; otherwise, there would be no reason for the target to comply. Fourth, the coercer had to decide whether to couple the threatened punishment with positive inducements, something that George had found to be pivotal in his two successful cases. Fifth, the coercer had to be strongly motivated to accept the costs and risks of engaging in coercive diplomacy, to provide strong leadership, and to garner sufficient domestic and international support for its actions.[5]

Finally, from the cases that he examined, George derived a typology of three strategies for implementing coercive diplomacy.[6] In the first instance, the coercer issues an ultimatum, whether explicit or tacit, by drawing a red line, setting a deadline for action, and threatening punishment for noncompliance. In the second instance, the coercer resorts to a "try-and-see" strategy: the coercer issues an ultimatum, follows this up with a coercive action or threat, but does not communicate a sense of urgency about compliance to the target and waits to see how the target responds before deciding whether to issue more threats or take other coercive actions. Or, in the third instance, the coercer adopts a strategy that George called "turning the screw," which involves communicating at the outset to the target that pressure and punishment will be gradually ratcheted up if the target does not comply. The first is the starkest form of coercive diplomacy; the second and third are softer forms.

All but one of George's cases occurred during the Cold War, when the superpower rivalry between the United States and the Soviet Union dominated world politics. With the end of the Cold War and the breakup of the Soviet Union, the nature of conflict changed. Instead of proxy wars between the two superpowers, there arose a wave of ethnic, political, and religious wars, exemplified by the dissolution of Yugoslavia, conflicts with Saddam Hussein, confrontations with transnational terrorists, and a confrontation with China. If the Cold War had been a time when survival itself seemed at stake for the superpowers, the 1990s for the United States became a series of more limited uses of force for more limited aims: containing Iraq in the aftermath of the 1991 Gulf War throughout the 1990s, confronting warlords in the midst of humanitarian operations in Somalia in 1992–93, reinstalling order in Haiti in 1994, averting war with North Korea while attempting to freeze its nuclear weapons program in 1993–94, suppressing aggression and human rights abuses in Bosnia in 1995 and Kosovo in 1999, staring down the Chinese across the Taiwan Strait in 1996, and dealing with nonstate terrorist organizations in the late 1990s.

These cases became the subject of a second group effort to develop further George's insights about the U.S. exercise of coercive diplomacy.[7] In analyzing these cases, we tried to determine, in particular, why coercive diplomacy proved so difficult for the United States to execute successfully (the United States achieved unqualified success only in the Haiti and Bosnia cases) during a period when the United States was the only global superpower. Why did a state as strong as the United States, no longer restrained by the existence of another superpower, find it so difficult to bend to its will actors so much weaker than itself? This was our puzzle, and from the cases we examined, we drew four fundamental reasons

why we believe coercive diplomacy is so difficult, even for powerful states.[8]

First, coercive diplomacy is a form of compellence, and compellence is intrinsically difficult. Unlike deterrence, which seeks to dissuade a target from changing its behavior, compellence tries to get a target to change its objectionable behavior.[9] Affecting changes in the behavior of a target is difficult because there is greater humiliation for the target if it changes its behavior in the face of a compellent action than if it does not change its behavior in the face of a deterrent threat. In the former case, the target cannot claim that its actions were taken freely; in the latter case, it can. Compellent threats also engage the passions of a target more directly than do deterrent threats. Finally, compellent threats bring about changes in the status quo, while deterrent threats maintain the status quo, and changing the status quo requires more effort than preserving it.

Second, as Robert Pape has pointed out, threats of force and demonstrative uses of force are less effective than significant amounts of force in denying an adversary a goal, in punishing it, or in posing it with the risk of further punishment.[10] Denial is a strategy that seeks to prevent a target from achieving its aims by undercutting its military capability and strategy. Punishment is a strategy that attempts to get the target to change its behavior by raising the costs of its continuing resistance. Risk is a strategy that promises punishment if the target does not comply. A risk strategy is difficult to apply because the infliction of actual pain is more effective than the promise of pain. Coercive diplomacy either poses risk through threats to use force or else administers only a small amount of punishment because the force used is limited. Because of this fact, coercive diplomacy cannot produce as much punishment or pose as great a risk as can larger amounts of force. Similarly, because it uses only threats or quite limited amounts of force, denial is difficult for coercive diplomacy.

In fact, strictly speaking, coercive diplomacy cannot undercut a target's military capability and strategy; it can only threaten to do so or demonstrate that it could do so. For all these reasons, coercive diplomacy has a harder time with denial, punishment, and risk than the use of larger amounts of force.

Third, coercive diplomacy is directed at a target's resolve—the intensity and strength of the target's will to prevail in a contest of wills. Resolve, however, is notoriously difficult to estimate before a coercive contest begins, and it can change during that contest. Coercive diplomacy contests are equivalent to games-of-chicken crises in which the strength of the respective resolves of the coercer and the target are in play. If the relative strength of these wills were known before the crisis, there would be no crisis because the party with the weaker will would give way, or if the wills were equal in strength, both parties would simply muster all their capabilities and fight until the party with the greater strength won. Crises are ways to measure the relative strength of wills; consequently, mistakes are easy to make in situations where resolve is hard to estimate. In such situations, the coercer too often underestimates the target's will to resist because, more often than not, the target cares more about the matter at issue than the coercer. Consequently, the coercer has to apply larger amounts of force, but then it has entered the realm of war, not coercive diplomacy.

Fourth, a target finds it difficult to give in to a coercer because both its credibility and its power are at stake. By bending to a coercer's will, a target not only loses some of its reputation for resolve, it also loses some of its capabilities. It not only appears to be weaker than thought; it can actually become weaker. A target must worry not only about the present, but also about the future. It has to ask itself, "If I give way on this issue, will the coercer be emboldened to demand even more again shortly and will I be able to resist when I will

have become weaker by complying now?" Because power stakes are also at issue, a target is less willing to comply with the coercer, making coercive diplomacy more difficult to execute.

These four factors operate in nearly every coercive diplomatic situation. In addition, two more factors can be present, depending on the particular circumstances in a given situation. Sometimes, there can be either multiple coercers or multiple targets, or both. Multiple coercers mean that a coalition of coercers is operating, raising the difficult problem of holding a coalition together. Multiple targets can complicate coercive diplomacy because different targets require different strategies for coercion, but also because actions taken to coerce one target may actually embolden another target not to give way, especially in situations where the two targets are at loggerheads with one another. Another factor that can sometimes be present is the target's calculation that it has the wherewithal to counter the coercer's measures. To the extent that the target believes it can do so, it is not likely to give way. Even more vexing are those situations where a target believes it can counter the coercer's measures but cannot say so publicly because doing so would undercut its countercoercion capabilities. In that situation coercive diplomacy is even more likely to fail.

For all these reasons, coercive diplomacy is a difficult tool of statecraft to employ. If it fails, the coercer has two choices: back down or up the ante. Backing down will affect the coercer's reputation in future situations; upping the ante usually means crossing the line from coercive diplomacy to war. Neither outcome is a good one from the coercer's standpoint, and for that reason coercive diplomatic gambits should never be undertaken lightly. A brief overview of the instances in which the United States has employed coercive diplomacy since the end of the Cold War in 1990 illustrates the points developed thus far.

CASE STUDIES IN COERCIVE DIPLOMACY, 1990–2003

From 1990 to 2006, the United States resorted to coercive diplomacy thirteen times: in Somalia in 1992–93 against the warlords, in Bosnia in 1995 and Kosovo in 1999 against the Serbs, in Haiti in 1994 against the military government, against Iraq from 1990 to 1998, against the North Korean government in 1994, against China over Taiwan in 1996, against al Qaeda and against the Sudanese and Taliban governments to combat terrorism in 1998 and again in 2001, against Iraq in 2002–3, against Libya in 2003, against North Korea from 2001 to 2006, and against Iran from 2001 to 2006.[11] The last two cases are ongoing; consequently, we deal with the first eleven in this section and the last two in the next. [12]

Somalia in 1992–93

The United States' intervention in Somalia in 1992–93 was only partly successful. Somalia had remained one of the world's poorest countries throughout two decades of rule under the military dictator, Mohammed Siad Barre, who once told then assistant secretary of state Chester Crocker, "We are not Americans, and I am not Lincoln." Two years of civil war created further deterioration to the point that the government collapsed in January 1991. Initially, the U.S. goal was aimed at forestalling widespread famine, which threatened perhaps two million people. Through a threat to react with overwhelming military force should they oppose U.S. intervention, the Bush administration persuaded the Somali warlords to stop using starvation of civilians as a means of waging war and to allow the United States to bring food to the population.

Once that phase of the intervention proved successful, however, the United Nations, with the Clinton administration's backing, undertook a much broader mandate—the reconstruction of the Somali government and the disarming of the warlords' militias—but with a force far smaller than the one used to stop the starvation. Paradoxically, the United Nations approved a more ambitious goal with a much smaller force, and the nation-building exercise proved a disaster after the United States made a halfhearted attempt to disarm one of the most powerful warlords in Mogadishu. That attempt led to U.S. casualties that, while relatively few in number, prompted the evacuation of the U.S. military force. The U.S. government had failed to fully calculate the potential costs of trying to coerce a warlord out of power. The warlords had acquiesced in the humanitarian mission partly due to U.S. threats, partly due to their calculation that the U.S. intervention was only temporary, and partly due to the fact that the United States would not contest their military might as long as they did not oppose the feeding of civilians. Disarming the warlords and reconstructing the country were entirely different matters: these would undercut the bases of warlord power. The warlords agreed to a temporary humanitarian intervention but not to actions that would end their power. The United States succeeded in the first phase of the Somalia intervention because it correctly matched means to ends; it did not succeed in the second phase because it failed to match means and ends.

Bosnia in 1995 and Kosovo in 1999

Bosnia and Kosovo became flashpoints after the Yugoslav Federation dissolved in the early 1990s and unleashed competing claims of national self-determination. In 1992, Bosnian Muslims sought to follow the lead of Slovenia and Croatia and establish their own independent state. Meanwhile, Bosnian Croats and Bosnian Serbs sought to take "their" parts of Bosnia and incorporate them, respectively, into the newly independent states of Croatia and Serbia. As the Bosnian tragedy unfolded, the West resisted forceful intervention for a time, but the strangulation of Sarajevo in the summer of 1993, the massacre of civilians in the Markala market in February 1994, and the assault on Gorazde in April underscored the price of feckless diplomacy. In 1995, the North Atlantic Treaty Organization (NATO), galvanized into action under strong U.S. leadership, finally acted to end the Bosnian war by coercing Serbs and Muslims to cease fighting and sign a peace agreement. A few weeks of air strikes and heavy artillery bombardment brought the Serbs to the bargaining table, while the threat to end air strikes coerced the Muslims to do likewise. Bosnia might be judged a borderline success for coercive diplomacy—borderline because the Serbs were facing pressure not simply from U.S. and NATO military action, but also from the Croats who had launched a lightning ground offensive in the Krajina and were threatening to bring on the collapse of the entire Serbian military position in western Bosnia. In addition, several years of economic sanctions also had an effect on Slobodan Milosevic, president of Serbia, and made him willing to put pressure on the Bosnian Serbs to settle.

The settlement reached at Dayton in December 1995 ended the Bosnian war, and NATO troops dispatched to Bosnia to enforce the accord stabilized the country. Kosovo was not so lucky, and it was largely ignored by the great powers after the breakup of Yugoslavia. To be sure, there had been an early threat, the so-called Christmas warning by President George H. W. Bush in December 1992, to use force against the Serbs should they attack the Kosovars; but to achieve success in Bosnia, the United States and Europe had to secure Milosevic's cooperation, and they largely ignored the persecution that Milosevic was inflicting on the Kosovars. In time, peaceful resistance by Albanian Kosovars gave way to the Kosovo Liberation Army's (KLA) violent tactics to secure the independence of Kosovo from Serbia. NATO sought to protect the Kosovars' minority rights within the Serbian federation (leaving aside the more controversial

demand for secession), but in the summer of 1998 a successful KLA offensive prompted a Serbian counteroffensive. Nearly a quarter of a million Kosovar Albanians were displaced. United Nations Security Council Resolution 1199 was followed by a NATO activation warning. U.S. statesman Richard Holbrooke negotiated an accord with Milosevic in October 1998 in Belgrade. But in 1999, an attempt to end Serb repression of Albanian Kosovars was rebuffed by Milosevic, who was willing to risk NATO bombing rather than sign an agreement not to his liking. The NATO threat was undercut in part by Russian and Chinese diplomatic opposition at the UN Security Council, but the NATO threat was also undermined by NATO's own failure to take decisive action after numerous previous threats went unheeded. In particular, there was a conscious decision to avoid making the threat of a ground assault if demands were not met. When Milosevic refused to negotiate any further, NATO initiated some limited air assaults in March 1999, but when Milosevic did not back down, the alliance was compelled to escalate the air attack into an extended campaign. Eventually, Milosevic capitulated, especially when NATO, under U.S. pressure, began to direct its air assault away from Serbian positions in Kosovo and toward Serbia proper. Because the air campaign against Serbia was extensive and sustained, coercive diplomacy failed in this case. In the end, Milosevic's compliance required a fully mobilized war effort.

Haiti in 1994

In Haiti the United States had to deploy more coercion than diplomacy. Haiti held its first free election in December 1990, and a young priest—but by no means a saint—named Jean-Bertrand Aristide won and took office in February 1991. Seven months later, the Haitian military overthrew the democratically elected Aristide. For the next three years the United States issued empty threats in various diplomatic démarches. Finally, in 1994, President

William Clinton dispatched a high-level, bipartisan team comprising former president Jimmy Carter, Senator Sam Nunn, and former chairman of the Joint Chiefs of Staff Colin Powell, who in turn had twenty-four thousand troops behind them. The goal of the United States was clear: Raoul Cedras, the leader of the military junta, had to relinquish power so that the freely elected government of Aristide could be reinstated. Equally clear was the threat of punishment: an invading army. Although negotiations came within a knife-edge of collapse, a deal was struck. However, Haiti cannot be considered an unqualified success, because the premature deployment of force nearly scuttled delicate talks with General Philippe Biamby, number two in the Haitian military chain of command, who called off negotiations believing that the Americans were attacking rather than bargaining. Ultimately, his decision was reversed and U.S. troops invaded, although the invasion was bloodless and the deal with the Haitian military was consummated. Haiti is a borderline success for coercive diplomacy because an invasion was required to get the military junta to resign, even though it was a bloodless invasion. Subsequent difficulties with security and development in Haiti have been legion, but they cannot be blamed on coercive diplomacy but rather on the failed efforts at nation building in Haiti by both the United Nations and the United States.

Iraq from 1990 to 1998

The case of Iraq from 1990 to 1998 is complicated and instructive. During this period, coercive diplomacy was but one of several strategies, which also included engagement, containment, and deterrence used by the United States from the time of Saddam Hussein's invasion of neighboring Kuwait in 1990 until 1998, when the United States embraced the goal of regime change in Iraq and when Saddam in retaliation expelled UN weapons inspectors from Iraq. The U.S. goals during this period included evicting Saddam from Iraq, keeping his military weak, deterring him from attacking Kuwait again, preventing him from invading the Kurdish area of Iraq, destroying his weapons of mass destruction (WMD), and making certain that he did not acquire the wherewithal to reconstruct his WMD programs. The United States had mixed results in using coercive diplomacy against Iraq during this period, even though it was generally successful in containing him and preventing him from reconstituting his WMD programs. For starters, in the autumn of 1990, the United States launched Operation Desert Shield—a massive military mobilization and deployment to the Persian Gulf—while it attempted to negotiate a reversal of Iraq's invasion of Kuwait. The buildup of U.S. military forces in Kuwait and Saudi Arabia, and the clear threat to go to war to evict Iraqi forces from Kuwait, did not compel Saddam to leave. Coercive diplomacy failed, and the United States had to go to war in early 1991 to evict him from Kuwait.

After the war was won in 1991, the United States then used the threat of air strikes and limited precision strikes to coerce Saddam into stopping assaults on the Kurds and the Shiite communities (it was more successful in the former case than in the latter), as well as to stop his interference with international weapons inspectors that were helping to enforce UN Security Council resolutions imposed on the Iraqi government. One early success of coercive diplomacy was Operation Provide Comfort, which protected a safe haven for the Kurds in the north of Iraq and prevented a tide of Kurdish refugees from streaming into Turkey and Iran. At least until August 1996, the Iraqis stood down large-scale attacks because of the strong diplomatic warnings backed by limited force, both on the ground and by air assault. The success of coercive diplomacy in shoring up the no-fly zones and inspections in the two years after the war had more mixed results. Having accepted the arms control inspections under duress as a condition of the 1991 cease-fire, Saddam soon ordered his soldiers to intimidate the inspectors, who were sprayed with warning shots as early as July 1991. When inspectors discovered a cache of documents indicating that the Iraqis were developing a clandestine nuclear program, Saddam denied them permission to leave a parking lot for four days. The UN Security Council threatened enforcement, the United States dispatched forces, and the Iraqis relented. Saddam also backed down in February 1992, when the UN Security Council declared Iraq to be in material breach of its resolutions and threatened serious consequences. After Iraqi military forces encroached on the southern no-fly zone and restricted United Nations Special Commission (UNSCOM) inspectors' travel in late 1992, Iraq soon announced a unilateral cease-fire in January 1993 in the face of unified Western pressure and UN support. Perhaps the most successful coercive diplomacy gambit toward Iraq was Operation Vigilant Warrior in 1994, which was a swift U.S. military troop deployment in response to Iraq's massing of some fifty thousand troops near the Kuwait border in October 1994. Stern diplomatic warning backed by deployed U.S. troops convinced the Iraqi regime to retreat.

In many ways, the mid-1990s marked a turning point in the battle to contain Saddam Hussein. At this point, Western powers were losing their enthusiasm for military action, Saddam was slowly rebuilding and learning to adapt his countercoercive diplomacy tactics, and the international community was becoming more concerned with the deprivations of many Iraqi people rather than the prevarications of their leader. Specifically, one can look at an assault by forty thousand Iraqi troops into northern Iraq in 1996, in which Kurdish troops were killed, members of the Iraqi National Council were arrested, and a covert operation run by the Central Intelligence Agency in Irbl was reportedly smashed. In a situation that some likened to the famous Bay of Pigs

fiasco against Cuba, the United States did not provide air cover for the Kurdish fighters. Although Iraqi troops quickly withdrew, they had already accomplished their objectives. An emboldened Saddam Hussein then went after the UNSCOM weapons inspectors with renewed determination, even as the corrupt Oil-for-Food Programme was providing the Iraqi regime with hidden streams of money. In 1997–98, in defiance of UNSCOM, Saddam issued an eviction notice in October 1998. The U.S.-led response was Operation Desert Fox in December 1998. Alas, Saddam had gained the upper hand, a hand he would play until the U.S.-led coalition would topple him from power just over four years later. In sum, coercive diplomacy had some successes and some failures against Iraq under Saddam in the 1990s, but eventually Iraq became inured to limited threats of force, and Saddam became more adroit at seeking tailored approaches to finite goals against a sagging international coalition.

North Korea in 1994

The United States has engaged in coercive diplomacy twice against North Korea, first in 1994 with mixed success and then again from 2001 until the present, with the outcome still to be decided. (The second instance is treated in the next section.) In both instances, the U.S. goal has been to stop North Korea from developing nuclear weapons and to give up any that it had developed. In the 1994 case, U.S. actions were designed to convince the Kim Il Sung government to halt its program to acquire the fissile material—plutonium—necessary to produce nuclear weapons. To achieve this objective, the United States threatened to impose economic sanctions and then made threats to use force if North Korea did not comply with its demands. U.S. actions were centered on stopping North Korea from reprocessing the plutonium embedded in the spent fuel rods that it had extracted from its 30-megawatt experimental nuclear reactor at

Yongbyon. The crisis began in March 1993, when North Korea, in response to a demand by Hans Blix, director general of the International Atomic Energy Agency (IAEA), to inspect two suspected nuclear waste sites, announced that it intended to withdraw from the Nuclear Nonproliferation Treaty (NPT) after three months. By June 1994, the United States and North Korea were on the verge of war. North Korea was not budging from its refusal of the full cooperation with the IAEA that was necessary to account for whether it had already reprocessed plutonium, while the United States had issued threats, both publicly and privately, that it would not permit North Korea to develop nuclear weapons and was prepared to use force if diplomacy failed.

The crisis turned from the path of war toward resolution when former president Jimmy Carter, on his own initiative, went to Pyongyang in June, committed the United States to a resumption of talks with the North and told Kim Il Sung that the United States would not go to the Security Council to seek the imposition of sanctions, an action that North Korea had declared would be equivalent to an act of war. In return, Kim agreed to freeze North Korea's nuclear program under IAEA monitoring and to begin talks again with the United States. Even though the Clinton administration had not sanctioned Carter's actions, it ended up essentially agreeing with them. On October 21, 1994, the United States and North Korea reached agreement on what came to be known as the Agreed Framework. Each got something that it wanted. The United States obtained North Korea's agreement on a verifiable freeze on its known nuclear activity, a commitment to resolve its nuclear past through special inspections (to see how much plutonium it had reprocessed), and an agreement to dismantle its nuclear weapons program. North Korea got direct engagement and negotiations with the United States, heavy oil to solve its immediate energy needs, the promise of future provision of new light-water reactors, the lifting of economic sanctions, and increased aid and trade.[13]

On the face of it, the North Korean case appears to be a success for the exercise of coercive diplomacy. Such a judgment, however, is complicated by two factors: Jimmy Carter's unauthorized intervention and North Korea's subsequent cheating on the Agreed Framework. Carter's intervention, especially his unilateral and unauthorized announcement about sanctions, appears to have turned the two states away from war in the early summer of 1994 and toward negotiations. Had he not intervened, war might well have occurred. Second, although the North Koreans adhered to the Agreed Framework's provisions regarding the reprocessing of plutonium for nearly ten years, it secretly began work on uranium enrichment several years later, violating the spirit if not also the terms of the agreement.[14]

In addition to these two factors, there are two more that render a final judgment on this case difficult. Although North Korea cheated, a case could be made that the United States and its allies were not as forthcoming on the provision of light-water reactors as the agreement called for. Whether this caused the North Koreans to believe that the United States had no intention of meeting its commitments at all, or whether they would have cheated anyway, is not clear. Furthermore, although the North Koreans began a covert uranium enrichment program, they did cease their reprocessing program for nearly ten years, which means that they had far less fissile material, and therefore far fewer nuclear weapons, ten years later than would have been the case had there been no 1994 agreement. For all these reasons, a final judgment about the degree of success of coercive diplomacy in the North Korean case remains problematical. At best, it is a highly qualified success; at worst, a clear failure.

China in 1996

The crisis between the United States and China in 1996 over Taiwan is also an ambiguous one for coercive diplomacy, in part because both the United States and China were engaging in coercive actions against each other. Both China and the United States were taking coercive actions in order to shore up their respective red lines regarding Taiwan: China opposes the independence of Taiwan, and the United States opposes the mainland's use of force to resolve the status of Taiwan. In 1996, both states engaged in coercive diplomacy to strengthen the deterrent power of these respective red lines.

From China's perspective, Taiwan in the 1990s appeared to be moving toward independence, and the United States appeared, even if indirectly, to be increasing its support for it. In order to stop this creeping independence and U.S. support for it, China resorted to a display of force by firing missiles around Taiwanese waters. In response, the United States sent two aircraft carrier battle groups into the Taiwan Strait. China's missiles were meant to show its willingness to escalate to the use of force to stop the independence creep if necessary. The U.S. action was meant to show that it, too, was willing to make good on its commitment to prevent the forceful resolution of Taiwan's status by using its air and naval power if necessary. By engaging in displays of force, none of which involved direct combat, both China and the United States signaled to each other the seriousness of their respective intents. The result of these displays of force was an outcome that achieved the objectives that both the United States and China wanted, although not what Taiwan's leadership wanted. China affected Taiwan's calculations about the costs of independence and succeeded in curtailing U.S. support of Taiwan's moves toward independence. For its part, the United States shored up its reputation in the region by demonstrating that it remained committed to the defense of Taiwan should China take military action against it.

From the U.S. standpoint, was the 1996 crisis an example of the successful exercise of coercive diplomacy? The answer is not clear. To date, China has not resorted to forceful displays to rein in the Taiwanese government, but there also has been less need for it to do so, in part because the United States has exerted pressure on that government to avoid steps that could be interpreted by the mainland as provocative or to retract actions to which the mainland has objected. China's actions made the United States more aware of the risks of unconstrained Taiwanese behavior, thus causing the United States to put Taiwan on a tighter leash. U.S. actions made China more aware of the United States' determination to match the mainland's use of force, thus causing the mainland to be more restrained in its use of force. The best that can be said about this case is that the United States and China both had a vested interest in preventing Taiwan from unilaterally declaring independence when they were dramatically reminded what the costs for them both would be if that happened.

The 1998 and 2001 Strikes against Terrorism

Before the 9/11 attack on the United States and immediately after it occurred, the United States resorted overtly to coercive diplomacy to deal with terrorism, and al Qaeda was its target. The first attempt occurred in August 1998, and the second in September 2001.

The first consisted of two cruise missile strikes—one against a pharmaceutical plant in Khartoum and the other against training camps in Afghanistan used by Osama bin Laden. The purpose of the strikes was to retaliate against al Qaeda in response to the terrorist bombings of the U.S. embassies in Kenya and Tanzania. These two strikes were examples of coercive diplomacy because they were designed not simply to retaliate but also, in the case of the Afghanistan attack, to kill Bin Laden. Retaliation is a form of revenge, but also of disruption, destruction, and coercion. To the extent that the air strikes were coercive, they partook of this logic: "Do not strike me again because this is what I will do to you." They are akin to the China case: an attempt to deter future attacks by engaging in coercive measures.

The second attempt is classic case of coercive diplomacy. It came in September 2001, after the 9/11 attacks, and was directed at the Taliban regime in Afghanistan. In this case the United States demanded that the Taliban turn over Bin Laden for trial and threatened military attack if it did not, and backed up the threat by the movement of heavy bombers and other forces to within striking distance of Afghanistan.

Neither of these attempts at coercive diplomacy worked. The 1998 Sudan and Afghanistan strikes did not coerce al Qaeda into ceasing its attacks against U.S. targets; the 2000 attack against the U.S. destroyer *Cole* that was docked in port in Yemen for refueling and the 9/11 attacks in New York and Washington, D.C., are concrete proof of that. The 2001 coercive threat also failed to work because the Taliban regime refused to turn Bin Laden over, and the United States had to go war with it to overthrow the regime. (War signals a failure of coercive diplomacy.) Coercive diplomacy failed in both cases because terrorist groups are, by definition, highly determined and are prepared to lose their lives for their cause. In fact, trying to coerce terrorists may be the most challenging test for coercive diplomacy, not only because terrorists are so highly motivated, but also because one of the goals of their actions is to provoke a response from a government, hopefully an overreaction. What the government views as coercive diplomacy, therefore, may be exactly what the terrorist is trying to bring about.

Iraq in 2002–3

The Iraqi case is especially interesting because, unlike in the Afghanistan case, coercive diplomacy worked. Saddam Hussein, under threat of attack, allowed UN inspectors back into Iraq to look for weapons of mass destruction.

He ultimately gave way to assure the survival of his regime, but the Bush administration was not interested simply in defanging Iraq of any weapons of mass destruction it may have harbored; it also wanted to remove Saddam from power. For the United States, regime change was the ultimate guarantee that Iraq would not harbor, nor acquire, such weapons.

From various accounts of his decision to go to war, it seems clear that President George W. Bush had made up his mind by the spring of 2002 to wage war against Iraq in order to remove Saddam from power.[15] In his UN speech of September 2002, he threatened military action if Iraq did not comply with the Security Council resolutions. According to the Duelfer Report, this speech "unsettled Saddam and the former Regime's leadership," especially the threat inherent in Bush's words that "the purposes of the United States should not be doubted."[16] On October 10, the U.S. Congress backed the president by authorizing him to use force against Iraq as he "determines to be necessary and appropriate."[17] Saddam continued to resist inspections. On November 8, 2002, the Security Council unanimously adopted Resolution 1441, finding Iraq in "material breach of all its obligations under relevant resolutions."[18] Resolution 1441 required that Iraq provide the UN inspection team (the United Nations Monitoring, Verification, and Inspection Commission, UNMOVIC) and the IAEA "immediate, unimpeded, unconditional, and unrestricted access" to all buildings, records, and persons whom UNMOVIC and the IAEA wanted to see or talk with.[19] Iraq then allowed UNMOVIC and the IAEA into the country to resume inspections but still did not cooperate fully. Under tremendous pressure from both the Russians and the French, and fearing looming U.S. military action, Saddam called together his senior officials in December and told them to cooperate completely with the inspectors, "stating that all Iraqi organizations should open themselves entirely to UNMOVIC inspections."[20] This even included the Republican

Guard, the military mainstay of Saddam's tenacious hold on power.

According to the Duelfer Report, Saddam evidently hoped that full cooperation would not only avert a U.S. attack but also lead to the lifting of UN sanctions once the UN inspectors found no evidence of weapons of mass destruction.[21] Although Hans Blix, head of UNMOVIC, reported on January 27, 2003, that Saddam "appears not to have come to a genuine acceptance . . . of the disarmament which was demanded of it," nonetheless, the inspectors failed to find any evidence of biological, chemical, or nuclear weapons and continued their work.[22] Three weeks later, Blix reported that "the situation has improved" and that the inspections "are effectively helping to bridge the gap in knowledge that arose due to the absence of inspections between December 1998 and November 2002."[23] However, the Bush administration was not interested in allowing inspections to go on for several more months, something that its European allies favored.[24] Having failed to get a second resolution out of the Security Council authorizing the use of force, the United States, together with its British ally, attacked Iraq on March 20.

In this case, coercive diplomacy had worked to obtain Iraq's full cooperation with inspectors. Saddam agreed to inspections and then to full cooperation to save his regime and to obtain the lifting of sanctions. The threat of military action, combined with Saddam's hope that sanctions would be lifted with full cooperation, produced compliance. The Bush administration, however, refused to take yes for an answer. It wanted regime change, something that Saddam would not willingly agree to. As a consequence, coercive diplomacy failed in this case to meet the administration's full objectives, although it did work to meet the terms of UN Resolution 1441.

Libya in 2003

Libya is a clear success for coercive diplomacy. The United States got Mu'ammar al-Gadhafi to abandon his quest for nuclear weapons and to yield up his chemical weapons capability and restricted classes of ballistic missiles.[25] What is at dispute in the Libyan case is not the fact that coercive diplomacy succeeded, but how important to its success was Bush's overthrow of Saddam Hussein's regime and the implied threat to do the same to Gadhafi if he did not yield up his weapons of mass destruction.

Gadhafi took steps to approach the United States before the Bush administration came to power. In fact, according to Martin Indyk, who handled Middle Eastern affairs under Clinton as assistant secretary of state, Gadhafi had tried to open back channels with the Clinton administration through various Arab interlocutors as soon as Clinton came into office, all to little avail. In May 1999 at Geneva, Indyk and Libyan representatives first met to discuss outstanding issues, and, at that meeting, the Libyan representatives officially conveyed the offer to surrender Libya's weapons of mass destruction. At the time the Clinton administration was more concerned about settling the Pan Am 103 issues (getting Libya to admit culpability and compensating the families of the victims) and stopping Libya's support of terrorism than it was about Libya's WMD programs. Libya's clandestine chemical weapons program was not believed to be an imminent threat, and its nuclear program had barely begun. As a consequence, the Clinton administration did not follow up on Libya's offer to surrender its chemical weapons program, an offer Libya repeated in October 1999, and chose to concentrate on the Pan Am issues instead.[26] In all, there were five meetings between May 1999 and early 2000.[27] The significance of these contacts with the Clinton administration is that Gadhafi had made a decision "to come out of the cold" and reach an accommodation with the United States before the Bush administration came to power and certainly before it launched the Iraqi war of 2003.

The Bush administration followed up on these initial contacts. It, too, put settling the outstanding issues of Pan Am 103 before dealing with Libya's weapons of mass destruction. It told the Libyan representatives that once Libya dealt with the Pan Am issues, the United States would allow UN sanctions to be lifted. By early 2003 Libya had done so, and the UN sanctions were lifted. However, the Bush administration told the Libyans that U.S. sanctions would not be lifted until Libya addressed other U.S. concerns, particularly its WMD programs.[28] This is the context in which the Libyan decision of December 2003—to give up its chemical weapons capability and its nuclear weapons quest— must be understood.

Viewed from the perspective of nearly six years of U.S.-Libyan contacts, negotiations, and bargaining, what stands out is not Gadhafi's decision to give up his WMD programs, but his initial decision to approach the United States with the objective of normalizing relations, together with his continued willingness to meet the various terms that the United States set for such a normalization. Domestic factors loom large in Gadhafi's decision. Libya's economy was in a shambles by the 1990s owing to disastrous economic policies, and UN and U.S. sanctions made it impossible for Libya to import the oil technology necessary to expand oil production. As a consequence, Gadhafi was facing increasing unrest at home and became increasingly concerned about his hold on power. Regime survival appears to be the key reason that Gadhafi decided to do what was necessary to reach a rapprochement with the United States, and the key to regime survival was getting the multilateral and unilateral U.S. sanctions lifted.[29]

What effect did the U.S. overthrow of Saddam Hussein have on Gadhafi? No definitive answer is possible. One view is that regime change in Iraq concentrated Gadhafi's mind, and this view points to a phone conversation in which Gadhafi said to Italian prime minister Silvio Berlusconi, "I will do whatever the Americans want, because I saw what happened in Iraq, and I was afraid."[30] The other view is that it was the implicit assurances of regime survival that Bush gave to Gadhafi that finally persuaded him to come in from the cold. Rather than seeking regime change, the Bush administration, in Robert Litwak's words, accepted "behavior change."[31] The truth probably lies somewhere between these two views. The Iraqi war had an effect on Gadhafi, making him fear for his survival, but he already had good domestic reasons for worrying about his regime's survival, and it was these that had impelled him to seek normalization of relations with the United States in the first place. Had the Bush administration not provided assurances that it was not seeking regime change in Libya, Gadhafi could just as easily have been repelled from normalization by the Iraqi invasion and accelerated his WMD programs. The invasion increased Gadhafi's already-present concern about his hold on power, but the Bush administration's assurances that it did not seek regime change were necessary for Gadhafi to continue on the rapprochement path. In short, the threat of regime overthrow could work only if assurances of regime survival were also given.

Summary

The analysis of these eleven cases, spanning the period from 1990 to 2003, supports the argument made at the outset: coercive diplomacy is difficult to execute successfully. Measured by the ability of the U.S. government to achieve its objectives through its own use of force short of war, only Libya in 2003 was an unequivocal success for coercive diplomacy. Iraq in 2002–3 was a success for coercive diplomacy if measured by Saddam Hussein's willingness to agree to UN inspections of his WMD capabilities, but not if measured by the goals of the Bush administration: to remove him from power. Bosnia in 1995, Haiti in 1994, and North Korea in 1994 were borderline successes. The United States succeeded in achieving its objectives in Bosnia only with the help of the Croats who had launched a highly effective ground offensive against Serbian forces before NATO undertook the bombing of Bosnian Serb forces. It took a U.S. military invasion of Haiti to bring the Cedras government to heel, even though no shots were fired in that operation. North Korea cheated by beginning a uranium enrichment program while it suspended its plutonium reprocessing program. Somalia in 1992–93 and Iraq from 1990 to 1998 had as many elements, if not more, of failure than of success and thus constitute highly mixed cases of success and failure. Kosovo in 1999 and the 1998 and 2001 terrorism cases are clear failures. China in 1996 is too ambiguous to call. This is a record that supports a success rate of 10 percent to 50 percent, depending on how the cases are coded. Coercive diplomacy is not impossible to bring off, but it is difficult, even for a state as powerful as the United States.

What accounts for the differences in the outcomes of these cases? Many factors are involved in making for success or failure in coercive diplomacy. Among them are the price of what is being asked of the target, the coercer's ability to create a sense of urgency in the target, the target's fear of the costs of escalation, the clarity of the objectives being sought in the target's mind, and the intensity of the target's attachment to the issue in dispute. Generally, the coercer is more likely to be successful if its will to prevail is stronger than that of the target's.

In these cases, however, another factor appears to be at work. In nearly every case where the United States had a clear or partial success, inducements and reassurance, either tacit or explicit, were as important as threats. In the Libyan case, Gadhafi was offered a return to the international community, the lifting of sanctions and, most important, the security of the regime, while the coercive threat was, depending on one's interpretation of the case, his overthrow through internal unrest or through the implicit exercise of U.S. military force. In the case of Iraq in 2002–3, the inducements were Saddam's hope of staying in power if he agreed to UN inspections and the lifting of sanctions, while the coercive threat was the use of U.S. power to remove him from office if he did not agree. In Bosnia, Ambassador Holbrooke made verbal promises to Milosevic that sanctions on Serbia would be lifted, while the coercive threat was more force used against the Bosnian Serbs that would reverse their military gains in the war. In Haiti, Cedras and his officers were promised a U.S.-Haitian military agreement to bring about the renewal and modernization of Haitian military forces, as well as a safe haven outside the country, while the coercive threat was the use of the invasion force that had occupied the capital to fight the junta. In the 1994 North Korean case, the offer to build light-water reactors and the promise of eventual normalization of relations with the United States were the inducements, while the threat to go to war and unseat the regime was the coercion.

In these cases of success or borderline success, the United States appeared to have found the correct balance between threat and inducement. In the cases of failure, the United States offered little or no inducement to the target to comply. In the Somalia case, the United States offered Mohammed Farah Aideed, the most powerful Somalia warlord, nothing by way of inducement, and instead, sought to capture or kill him. There were no inducements that the United States offered Saddam Hussein between 1990 and 1998, only containment, deterrence, and coercion. In Kosovo, the United States gave Milosevic no assurance that Serbia would retain control over Kosovo, offered him no other inducements, and presented him only with the threat of NATO force. In the terrorism cases, the United States offered nothing by way of inducement to Bin Laden to stop his attacks, and the demand made of the Taliban to give up Bin Laden would have been suicidal for the regime because of the central role that al Qaeda played in propping it up. In the cases of failure, then, no positive inducements were offered, either because the situation did not merit it or because the United States chose, for whatever reason, not to offer any. One possible conclusion from these cases, then, is that coercive diplomacy has a better chance of working when threats and limited uses of force are combined with reassurances and inducements.

NORTH KOREA AND IRAN, 2001–6

Negotiations with North Korea and Iran during the first decade of the twenty-first century reveal the limits of compellence in general and coercive diplomacy in particular. Both these cases, moreover, demonstrate how difficult coercive diplomacy can be when issues of core security are involved and when the balance between threat and inducement is weighted more heavily toward the former.[32]

North Korea, 2001–6

President George W. Bush entered office in 2001 determined to prevent Iraq and Iran from acquiring nuclear weapons and to pressure North Korea to give them up. These were the three countries he dubbed the "axis of evil" in his second State of the Union address in January 2002. The most immediate impact of the new Bush administration's policy, and it was almost surely inadvertent, was to end the common negotiating strategy between South Korea and the United States. One of the achievements of the Clinton administration's handling of North Korea was the concerted attempt by Secretary of Defense William Perry to align the United States, Japan, and South Korea in a common negotiating strategy. That strategy, in effect, was nullified when South Korean president Kim Dae-jung visited President Bush in the early weeks of the new U.S. administration. Japan's concern about the status of its citizens that North Korea had abducted in previous years further complicated the administration's attempts to realign external pressure against North Korea. Diplomacy was fro-

zen, and the subsequent terrorist strikes on the United States pushed North Korea further down the U.S. agenda.

After it had ousted the Taliban regime in Afghanistan and removed Saddam Hussein from power in Iraq, the Bush administration dispatched Assistant Secretary of State James Kelly to confront the North Koreans with the basic choice of disarm or pay the price. Kelly was not authorized to offer new incentives, and, in a meeting in Pyongyang in October 2002, he thought he heard the North Koreans confirm his accusation that they were engaged in a covert highly enriched uranium program —one quite independent of the earlier plutonium reactor that had been frozen under the 1994 Agreed Framework. Washington sought to slap what further sanctions it could find on North Korea, but the key act was the administration's decision to stop oil shipments, which had been part of the Agreed Framework bargain. The abrupt end to the Agreed Framework was something not entirely unexpected, because the prospect of completing the two light-water nuclear reactors agreed to in 1994 was less palatable to the Bush administration than it had been to the Clinton White House. (The Korean Energy Development Organization that was building the reactors would officially suspend activity in November 2003.) North Korea responded by removing IAEA seals at the Yongbyon facilities, expelling the inspectors, removing the fuel rods from their storage tanks, and then later reprocessing them. North-South talks and a planned joint railroad also fell victim to rising tensions and mutual recriminations between Pyongyang and Washington.

The search for what in effect would be a new framework for diplomacy—one that would try to dismantle both the plutonium and enrichment programs—proved to be quite elusive for the next three years. By the spring of 2003, North Korea was hinting at a nuclear deal after quiet talks were established in Beijing with China's help. Yet later that year North

Korea was reported to be back at reprocessing fuel rods at the Yongbyon reactor. President Bush insisted that North Korea submit to a comprehensive and verifiable end to all its nuclear programs before the United States would consider steps to improve relations between the two, whereas President Kim Jong Il insisted on a host of demands if it froze its nuclear program, not the least of which were direct talks with the United States. The Bush administration sought to "front-load" its proposals with North Korea, while the North Koreans demanded "rewards for freeze"—and, even so, it was never apparent that North Korea was placing its highly enriched uranium on the bargaining table.[33] Washington tried to ratchet up the pressure on Kim Jong Il by establishing the Proliferation Security Initiative (PSI), which provided a coalition of the willing to stop any WMD contraband. The PSI was not limited to North Korea, but it was aimed primarily at it and Iran. Washington also took quiet steps to try to close down the foreign bank havens for North Korean assets. If these steps yielded major dividends, they were not readily apparent.

North Korea eventually agreed to participate in a new multilateral negotiation process, which was dubbed the Six Party Talks, and these negotiations included the United States, South Korea, China, Japan, and Russia.[34] The talks became effectively stalemated in 2005 when the United States applied financial sanctions over North Korean currency counterfeiting and other illicit activity. In the meantime, North Korea continued to increase the size of its nuclear arsenal. The best available intelligence estimate had been that the North could have built one or two nuclear weapons based on the fissile material it had produced at Yongbyon in the 1990s; now estimates suggested the North might have quadrupled its small arsenal based on additional reprocessing in 2003–5. In 2006, North Korea continued to be secondary to security concerns in the Middle East, a fact that may have prompted

Pyongyang's missile launches in July. North Korea remained surprisingly stable and stubborn. Whether the Six Party Talks and the pressure put on North Korea through the Proliferation Security Initiative and the financial controls would eventually yield results, only time could tell. However, the exertion of coercive diplomacy in this second trial must be judged thus far a provisional failure.

Iran, 2001–6

Unlike North Korea, Iran is a large power with enormous natural resources critical to the global energy supply. Moreover, the government of Iran tended to maintain cooperation with the West and with the IAEA and to adhere to the Nuclear Nonproliferation Treaty —notwithstanding being found in violation of its safeguards agreement with the IAEA. The Bush administration focused initially on providing more intelligence and information on Iran's nuclear program, supporting the IAEA to expose Iran's safeguards violations. The United States kept the threat of military force on the table—something that in 2003 seemed more than just an idle bluff, given the intervention in Iraq and the 2002 National Security Strategy's emphasis on preemption. Even so, the Bush administration kept diplomacy in the forefront by giving Britain, France, and Germany (the so-called EU-3) a chance to try to secure a deal with Iran to suspend and ultimately forgo its enrichment and reprocessing programs.

In the fall of 2003 and then again in 2004, Iran would seemingly back down and accept negotiations and a voluntary suspension of enrichment-related activity when faced with the threat of IAEA censure and referral of Iran to the UN Security Council. In the fall of 2005, however, Iran unilaterally opted to resume this activity. The IAEA eventually did vote to refer Iran to the UN Security Council, although it postponed the time before debate over possible sanctions would begin. In the meantime, in April 2006, Iran declared that it had achieved success in its experimental enrichment program. Heightened concerns about possible military action, including leaked reports that the Pentagon was being told to keep the possible use of tactical nuclear weapons on the table, seemed to strengthen, not weaken, Tehran's resolve to proceed with its nuclear ambitions.[35]

From the outset of the Bush administration until June 2006, diplomacy backed by threats of force against Iran had done little to stem the Islamic Republic's push to master nuclear technology and, most observers assume, to build nuclear weapons. Indeed, the culmination of this five-year effort of dealing with the nuclear threat from Iran was the announcement in Tehran that it had successfully experimented with enriched uranium and thereby "joined the nuclear club."

In June 2006, the Bush administration sharply changed course. It announced its conditional willingness to open direct talks with Iran for the first time in a quarter century if Iran verifiably suspended its uranium enrichment program.[36] This concession was, in the first instance, a bid to strengthen U.S. leverage with the EU-3 in their ongoing negotiations with Iran, as well as to make a common approach more palatable to China and Russia, whose support in the UN Security Council would be necessary for any forceful actions against Iran. The EU-3 had consistently been urging the United States to be more forthcoming toward Iran and to join the direct negotiations, while the Chinese and Russians were resisting the imposition of sanctions against Iran and were opposed to even more forceful measures. The Bush administration reversed its position, much as it had done earlier with regard to North Korea, and agreed to direct negotiations because it had no choice. The EU-3–Russian–Chinese coalition would not have supported sanctions, much less military action, against Iran unless the United States took every diplomatic step possible to engage it.[37] Whether this radical change of course will

bear fruit is not clear at the time of this writing (June 2006), but if the Iraqi and Libyan cases are any guide to the Iranian one, the Bush administration will not make significant headway with Iran unless it is prepared to give security assurances to the Iranian regime.

Summary

The United States made little progress between 2001 and late spring 2006 in getting either North Korea to give up its nuclear program or Iran to stop its program. Three factors were responsible for these stalemates.

First, each state believed that a nuclear program was essential to its security, and where security—the most vital of a state's national interests—is at issue, compromise is hard. Coercive diplomacy is difficult to pull off successfully when a state believes that what it is being asked to give up makes it vulnerable to the actions of the coercing state.

Second, the Bush administration tended to follow a hard line in its negotiations with both states. It offered little in the way of reassurance and inducement to either one, and mostly demanded concessions from both. For example, with regard to North Korea, in the fall of 2005, after nearly five years of a hard-line, no-compromise policy, the Bush administration finally offered an inducement—providing North Korea with a civilian power plant, but only "well after North Korea had dismantled all its nuclear facilities and allowed highly intrusive inspections of the country." North Korea promptly stated that the United States "should not dream" that it would dismantle its program until after it received the new nuclear plant.[38] With regard to Iran, in May 2003, the Bush administration passed up an opportunity either to achieve a normalization of relations or to test the Iranian's sincerity about doing so. The Iranian foreign ministry proposed a grand bargain in which Tehran would deal with U.S. concerns about terrorism and proliferation among other issues, while the United States would lift its economic sanctions and provide security assurances and drop "regime change" from its vocabulary. The Bush administration did not respond and instead castigated the Swiss diplomats (Switzerland represents U.S. interests in Iran) who passed on the proposal.[39] Coercive diplomacy is difficult when there is primarily coercion and little diplomacy.

Third, the Bush administration was as much if not more interested in regime change as it was in stopping the nuclear programs of both states. The administration alternated between the goals of changing the regimes and getting the regimes to change their policy, thereby further increasing the insecurity of both.[40] Coercive diplomacy is difficult when the coercer communicates to the regime it is trying to coerce that it wants regime change, as the case of Iraq in 2002–3 also demonstrated.

In sum, attempts to get states to give up programs that they believe are vital to their security are difficult enterprises. It becomes even more difficult when little is offered in return and when the states concerned are made to feel even more insecure.

CONCLUSIONS

The case studies of U.S. resort to coercive diplomacy since 1990 reveal the numerous difficulties that are encountered in applying this technique. These difficulties can all too easily undermine the target state's willingness to comply with the coercer's demands. The cases also show that success at coercive diplomacy is more difficult when several states are employing the strategy together against more than one target. In addition, targets of coercion develop countercoercion techniques that constrain the coercing power's ability to pursue strong action. Coercive diplomacy is also difficult to employ on behalf of humanitarian goals because what the coercer may consider to be humanitarian the target state considers vital. Moreover, in general, positive inducements should not be offered until coercive threats or limited force is used in order to make

clear that there will be punishment for noncompliance. Finally, it can be difficult to determine whether coercive diplomacy has succeeded. Coercive diplomacy is a seductive tool of statecraft because it promises "success on the cheap," but the cases surveyed in this chapter demonstrate that U.S. decision makers should not be easily seduced because coercive diplomacy too often fails.

Three other general points are in order. First, coercive diplomacy works best when the goal sought is limited. Regime change has proved difficult to effect through coercive diplomacy, but so, too, has the goal of denying a state a nuclear program that it believes vital to its survival. Indeed, some would question whether it is at all realistic to expect either a large middle power such as Iran or a survival-seeking regime such as North Korea to respond to coercive diplomatic attempts to get rid of its nuclear program. Second, if coercive diplomacy is to have a good chance of success, then methods of reassurance and forms of positive inducements must also accompany the coercion. Third, coercive diplomacy often involves an element of bluff. If the threat of limited action proves futile, a state may well find its resort to coercive diplomacy in the future undercut if it does not follow through on its current threats. Consequently, a state should not utilize this technique unless it is prepared to go down the path of war should coercive diplomacy fail.

Coercive diplomacy has the best chance of succeeding when the coercer's objective is focused, when the target regime's survival is not threatened, when threats are mixed with incentives to effect a face-saving element for the target, when there is a united front from the international community against the target rather than escape valves offered by other states or actors that make it unnecessary for the target to comply, and when the coercing state is persistent in pursuit of its objectives. However, because coercive diplomacy is about particular actors pursuing particular goals at a particular time, it is difficult before the fact to state with certainty whether any given coercive diplomatic gambit that meets these ideal conditions will succeed.

NOTES

1. Alexander L. George, *Forceful Persuasion: Coercive Diplomacy as an Alternative to War* (Washington, D.C.: United States Institute of Peace Press, 1991).

2. Todd Sechser will rectify this situation when his study of coercive diplomacy in the twentieth century is completed. See Todd S. Sechser, "Winning without a Fight: Power, Appeasement, and Compellent Threats" (PhD diss., Stanford University, forthcoming). For a preliminary version of his investigations, see Todd Sechser, "Why Can the United States Deter but Not Compel? How Military Power Makes Compellence More Difficult" (paper prepared for the 101st American Political Science Association Convention, September 1, 2005). Sechser finds that the overall success rate of coercive diplomacy is higher than what we have found for the U.S. experience with it since 1990, but he does confirm the lower success rate for the United States.

3. See Alexander L. George, David K. Hall, and William E. Simons, *The Limits of Coercive Diplomacy —Laos, Cuba, Vietnam* (Boston: Little, Brown, 1971); and Alexander L. George and William Simons, *The Limits of Coercive Diplomacy*, 2nd ed. (Boulder, Colo.: Westview Press, 1994). Subsequent theoretical studies on coercive diplomacy include Lawrence Freedman, ed., *Strategic Coercion: Concepts and Cases* (Oxford: Oxford University Press, 1998); Peter Jakobsen, *Western Use of Coercive Diplomacy after the Cold War: A Challenge for Theory and Practice*; and Daniel L. Byman and Matthew C. Waxman, *The Dynamic of Coercion: American Foreign Policy and the Limits of Military Might* (Cambridge: Cambridge University Press, 2002).

4. See the chart in George et al., *The Limits of Coercive Diplomacy*, 2nd ed., 270. See also the abbreviated discussion of each case in George, *Forceful Persuasion*.

5. See *Forceful Persuasion*, 27, 35, and 75–80; and *The Limits of Coercive Diplomacy*, 2nd ed., 288.

6. *Forceful Persuasion*, 7–9.

7. See Robert J. Art and Patrick M. Cronin, eds., *The United States and Coercive Diplomacy* (Washington, D.C.: United States Institute of Peace Press, 2003).

8. The following discussion draws from ibid., 361–370.

9. Thomas Schelling coined the term "compellence." See Thomas C. Schelling, *Arms and Influence* (New Haven, Conn.: Yale University Press, 1966), 69–86.

10. See Robert A. Pape, *Bombing to Win: Airpower and Coercion* (Ithaca, N.Y.: Cornell University Press, 1996), 18–19.

11. Several cases can be broken down into multiple cases, but here we treat them as one case. To see how some can be broken up into multiple cases, see Art and Cronin, *The United States and Coercive Diplomacy*, 378, 386.

12. The discussion of the first eight cases in this section draws primarily from the case studies in ibid.

13. For the definitive account of the negotiations with North Korea by members of the Clinton administration most directly involved in them, see Joel S. Wit, Daniel B. Poneman, and Robert L. Gallucci, *Going Critical: The First North Korean Nuclear Crisis* (Washington, D.C.: Brookings Institution Press, 2004).

14. In the Agreed Framework was a provision committing North Korea to implement the North-South Joint Declaration on the Denuclearization of the Korean peninsula, which explicitly states that neither North nor South Korea will possess nuclear reprocessing and uranium enrichment facilities.

15. See, for example, Ivo H. Daalder and James M. Lindsay, *America Unbound: The Bush Revolution in Foreign Policy* (Washington, D.C.: Brookings Institution Press, 2003), chap. 9.

16. Central Intelligence Agency, *Comprehensive Report of the Special Advisor to the DCI on Iraq's WDM* (known as the Duelfer Report), vol. 1, 62, September 30, 2004, http://www.cia.gov/cia/reports/iraq_wmd_2004/contents.htm.

17. Quoted in Robert S. Litwak, *Strategies of Regime Change* (forthcoming), chap. 4. We are indebted to Rob for sharing with us his book manuscript before publication.

18. Quoted in ibid.

19. Ibid.

20. Ibid., 62–63.

21. Ibid., 63.

22. Quoted in ibid., chap. 5, 31.

23. Quoted in Philip H. Gordon and Jeremy Shapiro, *Allies at War: America, Europe, and the Crisis over Iraq* (New York: McGraw-Hill, 2004), 143.

24. For the transatlantic differences over inspections and the general differences in approach between the Americans and the British, on the one hand, and the Germans and the French, on the other, see ibid.

25. We have found especially helpful these two sources for the Libyan case: Bruce W. Jentleson and Christopher A. Whytock, "Who Won Libya? The Force-Diplomacy Debate and Its Implications for Theory and Policy," *International Security* 30, no. 3 (Winter 2005–6): 47–87; and Litwak, *Strategies of Regime Change*, chap. 5.

26. This account is based on Martin Indyk, "Iraq Did Not Force Qaddafi's Hand," *Financial Times*, March 9, 2004, 11. Flynt Leverett, who served on the Policy Planning Staff of the State Department under Bush and then became senior director for Middle Eastern affairs on the National Security Council in 2002–3, confirms that these talks took place in 1999. See Flynt Leverett, "Why Libya Gave Up on the Bomb," *New York Times*, January 23, 2004, A25.

27. Litwak, *Strategies of Regime Change*, chap. 5, 18.

28. Leverett, "Why Libya Gave Up on the Bomb."

29. Indyk, "Iraq Did Not Force Qaddafi's Hand"; and Litwak, *Strategies of Regime Change*, chap. 5, 37.

30. Quoted in Litwak, *Strategies of Regime Change*, 34.

31. Ibid., 40. Jentleson and Whytock make the same point. See Jentleson and Whytock, "Who Won Libya?" 81–82.

32. For a comprehensive analysis of U.S. policy toward North Korea and Iran, see Litwak, *Strategies of Regime Change*, chaps. 6 and 7. For particulars on the North Korean and Iranian nuclear programs, see *Iran's Strategic Weapons Programs: A Net Assessment* (London: International Institute of Strategic Studies, 2005); and Larry A. Niksch, *Iran's Program to Produce Plutonium and Enriched Uranium*, CRS Issue Brief (Washington, D.C.: U.S. Department of State, March 25, 2005).

33. The phrases are taken from Litwak, *Strategies of Regime Change*, chap. 6, 36.

34. See Nautilus Institute, *Full Text of Six-Nation Statement on North Korea*, September 20, 2005, http://www.nautilus.org/napset/sr/2005/0577Agreement.html.

35. See Seymour M. Hersh, "The Iran Plans," *New Yorker*, April 17, 2006, 30–37.

36. See Steven R. Weisman, "U.S. Now Ready to Meet Iranians on Nuclear Plan," *New York Times*, June 1, 2006, A1.

37. See the analysis by David E. Sanger, "Bush's Realization on Iran: No Good Choice Left Except Talks," *New York Times*, June 1, 2006, A8.

38. Joseph Kahn and David E. Sanger, "U.S.-Korean Deal on Arms Leaves Key Points Open," *New York Times*, September 20, 2005, A1.

39. Flynt Leverett, "The Gulf between Us," *New York Times*, January 24, 2006, A25; and Litwak, *Strategies for Regime Change*, chap. 6, 32.

40. Litwak makes this crystal clear in his chapters on Iran and North Korea. See Litwak, *Strategies for Regime Change*, chaps. 6 and 7.

18

EXPANDING GLOBAL MILITARY CAPACITY TO SAVE LIVES WITH FORCE

Michael O'Hanlon

HUNDREDS OF THOUSANDS OF PEOPLE a year lose their lives from the direct effects of war as well as war-related famine and disease. At present, several countries suffer badly from ongoing serious conflicts or the aftermath of those conflicts and would benefit greatly from more extensive international efforts at peacekeeping and/or nation building—the Democratic Republic of the Congo (formerly Zaire) and Sudan are only the most obvious examples. These wars exact an obvious and extremely tragic toll in lost human lives.[1] They have other costs as well. They can provide terrorist groups with havens, as in Afghanistan, and with motivating causes, as in much of the Middle East. They keep much of Africa mired in misery, economic stagnation, and disease—with implications not just for Africans but for humans around the globe. As Sandy Berger and Brent Scowcroft recently wrote, "Thus, action to stabilize and rebuild states emerging from conflict is not 'foreign policy as social work' . . . It is equally a national security priority."[2] So is stopping conflict in the first place.

The international community should be able to deploy up to 200,000 troops at a time for such peacekeeping and stabilization missions (independent of, and extending beyond the duration of, the Iraq deployment and independent of other possible "traditional wars," such as a conflict scenario in Korea). This number is based on fifteen years of post–Cold War experience with civil conflict around the world, an assessment of current conditions, and projections about the future. Since some countries will choose not to participate in any given operation, and since troops will need to be rotated to avoid exhaustion and burnout, a total pool of perhaps 600,000 personnel would be desirable. While these numbers are large, they pale in comparison with the world's total of 20 million individuals under arms. There is no need to enlarge militaries to reach the 600,000-troop goal; in fact, in many cases, it will be more appropriate to shrink them, in order to free up defense funds for improving the equipment, training, and transportability of the peace operations forces.

The international community already has about that number of military personnel who can be rapidly deployed and then sustained in overseas theaters. The problem, however, is that two-thirds of the total number now come from the United States. That fact may not be a major problem for traditional military missions such as the Iraq operation. However, the situation is not nearly so good in regard to humanitarian intervention and muscular peace operations, since the United States is unwilling to accept such a disproportionate burden for these types of missions.

The world's lack of response is partly due to the fact that the United States is unwilling to provide most of the necessary forces and that other countries generally cannot provide enough. At present, the United States is unwilling to participate in most humanitarian missions because of the severe strain being placed on its force structure by the Afghanistan and Iraq missions; at other times, it is politics rather than lack of available capacity that stands in the way of a more muscular U.S. response. U.S. resistance to involvement often goes too far. Its unwillingness, for example, to intervene to help stop the Rwanda genocide remains a serious failure in the country's history, and its unwillingness to intercede in the brutal wars of West Africa in the past decade was also tragic and wrong. But while they should do more at times, there is no reason to think that Americans, who already shoulder a dominant share of the global military burden for handling traditional interstate conflict, should be expected to do far more than their share for humanitarian purposes. They should participate, and contribute—partly because the moral authority of the United States and the legitimacy of U.S. global leadership are reinforced when U.S. security policy has a generous character. But Americans should not have to be the world's policemen for civil conflicts. Nor is there any realistic chance that they will agree to play that role. That means that, while the U.S. armed forces should prepare for such missions, too, it

is principally other countries that need to improve their capacities. Washington is hardly off the hook, however; improving capacity in developing countries will often require substantial economic and technical support from the major powers.

Possessing more military capacity does not mean always having to use it. Individual nation-states will continue to make their own sovereign decisions about when and how they put their national prestige, and the lives of their military personnel, at risk. Not all possible interventions are good ideas; not all conceivable missions are well enough designed that one can be confident they will do more good than harm; sometimes the involvement of a given country in a given conflict is too sensitive a matter politically. So creating more military capability should not lead to a world in which countries are automatically expected to use it. But without the capacity, intervention is clearly not possible even in situations where it would be appropriate and beneficial.

Governments and international institutions have made numerous efforts to mitigate civil conflicts since the Cold War ended. The world's handling of a number of African civil wars, notably Rwanda's and Angola's as well as Liberia's throughout much of the 1990s, was on the whole unsuccessful. But other efforts have been successes—or at least partial successes—in the sense that intervention made conditions better than they would otherwise have likely been. Specifically, missions in Cambodia, Mozambique, Albania, Kosovo, and East Timor all probably made a significant difference for the better. The NATO-led mission in Bosnia ultimately helped matters as well, even if NATO's and the UN Protection Force's roles in the first three years of the war were less impressive.[3] Even the aborted mission in Somalia mitigated the famine there, saving tens of thousands of lives. NATO's International Security Assistance Force (ISAF) mission in Afghanistan has not prevented that country from depending on illegal drugs as its main source of income and depending on warlords for much regional security. But it has nonetheless helped usher in impressive progress in education, health, women's rights, and political rights more generally.[4]

But these tasks are far from easy. Doing the job right requires substantial numbers of well-trained and well-equipped troops. Proponents often cite a goal of 5,000 troops, motivated in large part by the claim of Canadian general Romeo Dallaire that such a capability, if added to his small UN force in Rwanda in 1994, could have stopped the genocide there. However, first, Rwanda is a small country. Second, although there is little doubt that General Dallaire would have used 5,000 more troops bravely and with some effectiveness, it appears a low estimate even for Rwanda based on standard criteria for sizing intervention forces.[5] Third, in the event of two or more simultaneous conflicts requiring rapid attention, such a force would certainly be much too small.

The international community should develop the capacity to deploy and sustain at least 100,000 troops abroad, above and beyond those forces it possesses today.[6] Smaller numbers of elite or even private soldiers can sometimes handle discrete and difficult tasks, but the broader problem of stabilizing a country requires significant numbers of troops.[7] Once a decision on intervention is reached, moreover, it is generally preferable to send forces promptly and in decisive quantities. Such an approach conveys resolve, discourages resistance, and improves the odds of success—especially in the most difficult of conflicts.[8] It also offers the greatest hope of ending a conflict with minimum loss of life to intervening soldiers as well as to local populations.[9]

Raising a dedicated UN force of this size would be very expensive. Given the poor starting point, enormous progress and effort would be needed to change this situation. U.S. political leaders, at least, would be unlikely to support such a goal. Most Republicans are inherently skeptical of the United Nations. Most Democrats, whatever their substantive views, remember from the early to mid-1990s the domestic political danger of supporting the United Nations in jobs it lacks the capacity to perform (recall Bill Clinton's change of heart after his initial 1992 endorsement of a UN army and his willingness to entrust the United Nations with very difficult tasks in Somalia and the Balkans).[10] Moreover, none of the major reviews of the UN system and its role in international security in recent years—the United Nations' 2000 Brahimi Report (compiled by the Brahimi Panel on UN Peace Operations), the 2004 High-Level Panel on Threats, Challenges, and Change (convened by the secretary-general), the 2005 Gingrich-Mitchell report done for the U.S. Congress—favored creation of dedicated UN combat units. (Some did call for stronger UN planning and headquarters staffs, as well as some standing police capability and larger standing inventories of equipment for peacekeepers.)[11]

Moreover, while some situations are so extreme as to create consensus about the need for intervention, deciding on when to deploy forces is generally an extremely contentious matter, especially for forcible humanitarian interventions. In light of this fact, it is more practical to keep peace operations forces under the control of the governments that will be making the inherently subjective political decisions about whether to ask their soldiers to participate in a given mission. UN action will still generally be appropriate for authorizing intervention, but in matters of military operations, it makes better sense to recognize the limits of the United Nations and defer to individual states or organizations of states.

Fortunately, it is not necessary to create a UN army. National armies around the world are already paid and equipped, so building on their existing capacities rather than creating a new one from scratch is almost surely a more efficient way to spend resources. They also provide a much more appropriate and realistic basis for improved intervention capabilities than do private contractors—though the latter do have important roles, even if generally not in direct combat, and could contribute somewhat more than they do now.[12] Some efforts are required at the level of multilateral organizations, to be sure, for planning staffs, command-and-control assets, some logistics, and equipment stockpiles. But as for physical capacity for intervention, the case is strong that it should remain primarily at the level of the nation-state.

There are limits to what robust and timely military interventions can accomplish. For example, in the case of the Rwanda genocide, so much killing happened so quickly that even a U.S.-led operation to stop it could have taken several weeks to complete its deployment and hence might not have saved many of the victims.[13]

But even in Rwanda, the robust and prompt deployment of force could have made a major difference. Before the genocide began, a robust preventive force of the type requested by the commander on the scene in early 1994 could have been effective. After the genocide began, the very act of beginning a deployment might have affected the behavior of the locals and convinced them to desist or scatter out of fear of retribution. Even if a preventive deployment had not been tried, and a prompt deployment after the genocide began had not caused the pace of killing to slow, intervention could have physically saved 200,000 or more victims.[14] Moreover, given the extreme pace of the genocide, Rwanda was very much the exception and not the rule, so the international community should hardly be discouraged by this one example. In recent wars that have also been characterized by enormous (in some cases, even greater) death tolls, such as those in Somalia, Sudan, Angola, and Congo, the dying has been far more gradual.

This chapter lays out an agenda for increasing the international community's military capacity to stop deadly conflict. It estimates how many troops and police might be needed if

the international community took a more comprehensive and rigorous approach to stopping conflict in cases where the prospects for restoring peace were good. It also suggests a plan for sharing the military burden of doing so among key countries and regions, and to a lesser extent the private sector as well. Most of the focus is not on the U.S. military, already overstressed by its present workload and already too frequently perceived as an arm of an imperialist America. The primary emphasis is on suggesting how countries in Western Europe, Africa, South Asia, East Asia, and elsewhere can make greater contributions. The goal is to show how a global military pool of at least 100,000 fully deployable soldiers, above and beyond those available today, might be created—and to estimate what equipment and training would be needed to make such a force effective and rapidly deployable.

What are the policy implications of this concept for the United States in particular? In regard to major U.S. allies, political encouragement may suffice. Washington needs to accept that its allies will expect greater influence in humanitarian and peace operations if they provide more capabilities—but that trade-off is one that the United States should be more than willing to accept. In the case of poorer countries, the United States and other Western states should provide economic aid and technical assistance to help those countries improve their own national capabilities. Existing efforts along such lines, including the U.S. Global Peace Operations Initiative, should be gradually expanded severalfold.

ESTIMATING REQUIREMENTS FOR INTERVENTION FORCES

There is no way to reach a definitive judgment on how much intervention and peacekeeping capacity the world needs. Every case must be assessed on its own terms and in light of its own local and international politics. It will sometimes not be possible to stop wars if the likely cost in blood is too high or if the prospects for success are poor. Nonetheless, policymakers need some basis for knowing when to consider intervention seriously.

A baseline from present operations is that about 70,000 UN peacekeepers were deployed around the world as of mid-2005. This tally includes 1,350 troops and 70 police in Sudan; 5,500 troops and 120 police in Burundi; 6,250 troops and 210 police in Côte d'Ivoire, 14,900 troops and 1,100 police in Liberia; 16,100 troops and 325 police in Congo; 3,300 troops in Ethiopia/Eritrea; 3,350 troops and 70 police in Sierra Leone; 6,300 troops and 1,400 police in Haiti; 1,000 troops in the Golan Heights; 2,000 troops in Lebanon; and smaller numbers in the Western Sahara, Georgia, Cyprus, the India-Pakistan border area, and the Palestine region.[15] Adding in the ISAF mission in Afghanistan, the EU-led mission in Bosnia, and the NATO-run Kosovo operation pushes the total up to almost exactly 100,000 (not counting the Iraq mission).

This figure of 100,000 troops devoted to stabilization missions and peace operations is typical of the post–Cold War era. In the 1990s, the international community averaged deploying 50,000 UN peacekeepers around the world, and by the second half of the decade it also typically had a comparable additional number in the Balkans.[16] In the early years of this decade, the UN-run peacekeeping mission in Sierra Leone as well as operations in East Timor and elsewhere kept numbers of blue-helmet peacekeepers in the vicinity of 40,000.[17] The international community also deployed some 40,000 troops in the Balkans under NATO auspices during this time period. So while numbers were down slightly, they were not down dramatically. In broad strokes, the post–Cold War baseline has clearly been established—about 100,000 military personnel and police have at any time been deployed to address the world's conflicts and to stabilize postconflict environments.

But the broader point is that this historical baseline of deployed troops has been inadequate for the tasks at hand. Over the past fifteen years, the world community has failed to include more substantial and timely intervention forces in Rwanda, Liberia, Sudan, and elsewhere. Today, the deficit remains. International forces in Afghanistan are almost certainly short by at least 10,000 troops. Even more notably, a major possible mission in Congo has not been seriously contemplated, despite the severity of that nation's war.[18] A serious mission in Congo could easily require 100,000 troops itself, using standard force-sizing criteria—two to five troops per thousand local inhabitants—and making reference as well to the sheer enormity and challenging topography of that country.[19] As of 2005, therefore, the combination of ongoing missions in the Balkans, Sierra Leone, and elsewhere, together with the desirability of a much larger peacekeeping force in Congo than is now being contemplated, suggests a need for nearly 200,000 peacekeepers; that is roughly double the number who are now actually in the field.

Demands are unlikely to decline in the future. As the National Intelligence Council (NIC) put it in late 2004, after interviewing large numbers of experts around the world and performing its own analyses, "Lagging economies, ethnic affiliations, intense religious convictions, and youth bulges will align to create a 'perfect storm,' creating conditions likely to spawn internal conflict." The NIC noted that the number of internal conflicts in 2004 was down considerably from the late 1980s–early 1990s period, but then wrote, "Although a leveling off point has been reached, the continued prevalence of troubled and institutionally weak states creates conditions for such conflicts to occur in the future." Its report further noted the potential for internal conflicts to spread into interstate war, create sanctuaries for terrorists, or permit criminal syndicates to operate in weakly governed territories.[20]

It is hardly inconceivable that there could be future operations in places such as Angola, Burundi, Sudan, and Indonesia, were political circumstances to change somewhat in any of these countries. Indeed, in Sudan, the case for large-scale outside intervention is already rather compelling. The case of Burundi may be particularly plausible in the near future, given the international community's guilt stemming from the 1994 Rwanda genocide and Burundi's proven potential for a similar type of violence.[21] It is at least remotely possible that the international community could find itself in places that now seem unthinkable—such as Kashmir. If political dynamics in those regions evolved to the point where local parties decided to invite international forces into their neighborhoods to help stabilize them, missions that seem unthinkable today could become not only possible but even likely. Even if operations were limited to smaller countries or localized regions of larger ones, such as Aceh in Indonesia, serious efforts would generally each require at least 10,000 to 20,000 troops.[22] Since an operation, once begun, would typically last at least two years and often longer, it is plausible that several large missions could go on at once. Indeed, referring back to the 1990s experience, the typical mission did last anywhere from eighteen months to several years.

In summary, current UN and related stabilization missions and peace operations involve nearly 100,000 troops. Taking the Congo mission seriously, and perhaps intervening to stop the genocide in Darfur, Sudan, could double that. Additional hypothetical missions in Burundi or elsewhere could drive numbers above 200,000.

The preponderance of the total of 200,000 personnel should be soldiers, since establishing basic control and order is the first order of business in countries wracked by extreme conflict. But subsequent efforts to arrest war criminals, restore criminal justice systems, and generally institute a rule of law that will make possible the safe departure of intervening forces ultimately require some type of policing, be it military or civilian. Such policing is difficult, particularly for a multinational force drawn from various policing and legal traditions. Preparations are therefore needed to develop a sufficiently large and well-trained pool of police officers from which personnel can be drawn when needed.[23] Police have often made up about 20 percent of all deployed forces, though they make up less than 10 percent today.[24] This would suggest that a pool of 200,000 security personnel might appropriately include 30,000 to 40,000 police officers.

PROJECTABLE MILITARY FORCES IN THE WORLD TODAY

The global community spends about $1 trillion a year on military forces and keeps more than 20 million men and women under arms in active-duty forces.[25] But only modest numbers of those dollars, and only a very small fraction of those troops, translate into military force that can be projected over substantial distances. Leaving aside the United States, with a $400 billion-plus defense budget and hundreds of thousands of troops that can be deployed overseas within months and sustained abroad indefinitely, the rest of the world combined cannot muster more than a couple hundred thousand military personnel for such purposes. The United Kingdom has considerable capabilities, particularly in light of its size. But most countries do not.

My methodology for estimating countries' projectable military capabilities focuses on three elements: strategic lift, logistics assets that allow units to operate in austere foreign regions, and legally deployable military personnel. Focusing on these three issues reveals many constraints on most countries' capabilities. Many countries do not have long-range airlift and sealift (even if they may have some limited tactical transport capabilities for moving over short distances). Most

Table 1. Estimates of Forces Available for Rapid Deployment

Country	Total Active-Duty Ground Strength (in thousands)	Ground Forces Deployable in 1–3 Months, Sustainable for a Year (in thousands)	Percent of Total Quickly Deployable
United States	649	400	62
United Kingdom	121	25	21
France	152	15	10
Germany	212	10	5
Italy	138	5	4
Canada	19	4	21
Netherlands	15	4	27
Denmark	13	1	8
Other NATO	949.2	20	2
Other Europe	95.4	5	1
Australia	24	5	21
New Zealand	4	0.75	19
Japan	149	5	3
South Korea	560	5	1
India	1,100	10	1
Pakistan	550	2	0.3
Bangladesh	120	0.3	0.3
Sri Lanka	95	1	1
Malaysia	80	2	3
Singapore	50	2	4
Russia	329	35	11
China	1,610	20	1
African states	398.6	10	3
Argentina, Brazil, Chile	300	12	4
Non-U.S. Total	7,084.2	about 200	about 3%

Source: Michael O'Hanlon, *Expanding Global Military Capacity for Humanitarian Intervention* (Washington, D.C.: Brookings Institution Press, 2003), 56–57.

Note: The first column shows total active-duty army (and, where they exist, marine) forces in a country's military. The second and third columns indicate what fraction of this total has the proper equipment, logistics support, transport capacity, and legal authority to be quickly deployable with its full suite of equipment abroad.

depend on their national economies and civilian infrastructures to provide logistics support—ranging from equipment repair to provisions of fuel and ammunition to medical care to food and water for troops. If troops are taken away from their home territories, these countries are often unable to support them. Finally, many countries still depend on conscripts to fill out their force structures—and frequently impose legal or political restrictions on deploying such troops abroad. Typically, whatever is the weakest of these three requirements—strategic lift, deployable logistics, and deployable troops—determines a country's capacity.

The estimates in table 1 focus on forces available for rapid deployment. As a rough rule of thumb, the standard is that forces should be deployable within two to three months and then supportable in a foreign theater for an indefinite period—at least a year—thereafter. These criteria are similar to those associated with the EU Headline Goals initiative, a 1999 European decision after the Kosovo experience to create a rapid-response capacity to deploy up to 60,000 forces abroad for various types of military missions and sustain them in the field for up to a year. Many countries could rent sealift, call up reserves, obtain special legal authority to deploy conscripts, and take other such measures if time were not a constraint. Given the nature of most humanitarian missions, however, delays of many months are generally unacceptable. Countries are also usually reluctant to take the extreme steps mentioned earlier for peace and humanitarian operations in any event. For these reasons, this chapter focuses on promptly deployable and sustainable forces.

AN AGENDA FOR IMPROVING INTERVENTION CAPACITY

As argued earlier, it would be desirable that the international community be able to deploy up to 200,000 troops at a time for humanitarian intervention and peace operations, from a total pool of 600,000. With the United States unwilling to assume most of the responsibility for these operations, other countries will have to take up the slack. That means that of the desired pool of 600,000 deployable military personnel, non-U.S. countries should provide about 500,000 of the troops. In other words, countries besides the United States should more than double their aggregate power-projection capabilities. The United States should, under normal circumstances at least, be willing to deploy 25,000 to 50,000 forces at a time for peace operations and related missions, as in fact it did in the latter half of the 1990s (principally in the Balkans). But other countries should have the capacity to deploy and sustain at least 150,000 more.

These estimates are sobering for those who consider humanitarian military operations to require only relatively modest amounts of force. But it should be within reach for the international community, if not right away, then over time. To begin with, not all troops need be equally well trained and equipped. Some missions will be less demanding than others. Some will not require rapid response or long-range transport. Either the peace accords that precede them will be negotiated over an extended period, allowing ample time for preparations, or the operations will be close to home for countries contributing troops. Even if 200,000 forces might be needed at a time, it is unlikely that it would be necessary to deploy more than 50,000 urgently, and unlikely that more than half to two-thirds would need to operate in extremely austere surroundings.

The division of labor for a greater global effort to develop adequate capacity for humanitarian intervention and difficult peace operations might look something like this: The United States would make modest improvements in parts of its force structure, to facilitate the types of deployments it has carried out over the past decade and make possible a slightly greater level of effort in the future (most of these efforts are now under way owing to the U.S. Army's restructuring efforts, but for the foreseeable future they are, of course, focused on sustaining coalition efforts in Iraq and Afghanistan). European Union nations would more than double their Headline Goal aims for rapid-force deployment from the stated 60,000 to 150,000, committing to buy the strategic lift and logistics needed to make those numbers meaningful.[26] (These forces could also be useful for other missions, such as defeating aggression in the Persian Gulf, if the EU countries so desired.) African countries, with help from the United States and Western Europe, would seek to develop the capacity for deploying at least 50,000 fully equipped troops abroad—as well as another 50,000 proficient in infantry skills and peace operations, even if not fully outfitted for autonomous military operations in austere environments. In this regard, the G-8 goal of 75,000 well-prepared African troops, espoused at the 2004 summit on Sea Island, Georgia, is in the right ballpark if delivered on. South and Southeast Asia would collectively adopt comparable goals. South American states would be somewhat less ambitious but would pursue an aggregate capacity of close to 50,000 deployable and sustainable troops. Japan might aim only half as high in terms of troops but would also purchase strategic lift to transport its own self-defense forces as well as other militaries. Countries such as Canada and New Zealand would make at least modest improvements in their capabilities as well. However, countries such as Turkey and South Korea are unlikely to be able to play a greater role in the near term given more immediate security concerns, and Russia and China are unlikely to be willing to contribute meaningfully to such missions given their ideological reservations as well as their own more immediate security concerns.

Taken together, achieving these goals would provide some 500,000 non-American troops for humanitarian and peace operations, together with adequate lift and logistics for rapid and sustained operations. They would give the international community the resources it needs to make a serious and fairly systematic effort at reducing the human tolls associated with the world's most violent wars.

Major Western Democracies

In light of their wealth, military proficiency, and commitment to human rights, democracies other than the United States have a crucial role to play in any global initiative to improve military capacity for humanitarian intervention and for difficult peace operations.

Europe

Most European members of NATO as well as Canada should be able to increase defense spending. Few of the major powers devote more than 2 percent of their GDPs to their militaries; even Britain and France devote no more than about 2.5 percent, in contrast to a U.S. level of about 4 percent. Political realities and budgetary constraints being what they are, however, such desirable steps may prove infeasible. Even so, European countries in general could also develop adequate power-projection capabilities without increasing their defense budgets if they cut forces further and used the resultant savings to purchase the necessary strategic transport and deployable logistics assets. Those that have not yet done so could also create all-volunteer units for deployment.

Eight countries in Europe have, for reasons of geography and available resources, the greatest latent military potential. These countries include three countries with high defense spending—Germany, France, and the United Kingdom—as well as another, Italy, in an intermediate category. Four more—Belgium, Denmark, the Netherlands, and Norway—are of limited size yet notable capacity. With the exception of Britain and the partial exception of France, however, they have not yet exploited their potential in this area.

A reasonable goal for the "elite eight" European members of NATO might be to further reduce the sizes of their armed forces, preserving their most modern equipment and units but otherwise scaling back to about 1.1 to 1.2 million total troops. That would essentially entail having the other European countries follow Britain's model of keeping a smaller but better-equipped and more professional military. In addition, the major NATO European countries could purchase more strategic lift and more logistics equipment. Were this group of eight countries to organize its armed forces in the way Britain does today, they would be able to field 125,000 deployable troops on their own. Other EU countries could then make more modest contributions, together attaining the aggregate goal of 150,000 deployable soldiers and police.

Put in terms of major military units, this initiative might aim to develop eight to ten deployable and sustainable ground combat divisions. Breaking down the total country by country, each of the three major states might aim for two such divisions (a goal that Britain has already realized), Italy would aim for at least one, and the smaller key countries of northern Europe would each properly train and equip one or two brigades. The initiative would involve a comparable number of air wings. However, here the need for change would be less onerous because the weapons themselves are largely self-transportable and because the transport requirements for supplies are much less. Other NATO and EU members would ideally make modest contributions as well.

How much would this cost? The price tag would be significant but not astronomical. That is to say, costs would be too large to be found easily within the normal framework and assumptions of yearly defense budgeting. But they are quite modest when placed in broader perspective: the $50 billion or so of investments that would be needed to make these forces deployable could easily triple the long-distance war-fighting capabilities of countries that are already spending in the range of $200 billion each and every year on their defense establishments. A reasonable approach would be to devote $10 billion a year over five years for the necessary equipment and organizational changes, beyond what is already being spent. Annual operating costs thereafter, again dominated by the airlift fleet, would approach $750 million.[27]

Japan

More than half a century after World War II, and more than a decade after the fall of the Berlin Wall, it is time for Japan to do more in the international security sphere. It need not and should not mimic the United States, or even Great Britain. Unilateral power-projection capabilities would unsettle some neighbors and

displease many Japanese themselves. Nor need it even increase defense spending very much. But Japan should reexamine the basic way in which it structures and equips its military, a view with which Japan's leader, Prime Minister Junichiro Koizumi, appears to agree.[28] It should also regain the momentum it began to establish in the early 1990s—when it sent about 700 personnel to Cambodia in 1992–93 for peace-keeping and then 400 to Zaire in 1994 for humanitarian relief after the Rwanda genocide —but lost in subsequent years.[29] As of this writing it has several hundred troops in Iraq. But the restrictive rules of engagement it applies for its forces there make one question if they might better be sent to a less controversial mission, such as in Africa.

Many other Asian countries would oppose such a Japanese security policy out of fear of latent Japanese militarism. Within Japan, that worry exists, too. But the alternative force structure outlined here would involve far too few troops to threaten a country such as China, Korea, the Philippines, or Vietnam. Yet the new capabilities would be quite substantial when measured against the demands of global humanitarian, peacekeeping, and peace enforcement missions.

The basic idea of this proposal for Japan would be to expand the country's physical capacities for operations abroad, but keep legal, diplomatic, and military checks on these new capacities so as to reassure Japan's neighbors and the Japanese people about the nature of the effort. The goal would expressly *not* be that Japan become an independent, global military power. Under such a framework, Japan would consider projecting power only in the context of multilateral security missions, preferably if not exclusively those approved by the UN Security Council. It would not develop the physical capacity for doing more than that.

Japan's home islands are now much more secure against possible invasion than was the case during the Cold War. That means that active-duty ground forces for territorial defense may not be needed in the numbers currently maintained. Reservists could be used in greater numbers for this purpose if necessary, as in the cases of countries such as Switzerland and the Scandinavian nations. The Japanese army could reorient itself to a smaller, more mobile organization, including an expeditionary ground capability of at least 25,000 individuals. That would allow sustained deployment of at least two brigades, as well as numerous other capabilities such as military police and translators. Soldiers would be equipped for sustained operations abroad and trained for missions ranging from humanitarian relief to armed, forcible intervention to stop genocides and other civil conflicts to hostage rescue and counterterrorism operations. The Japanese navy and air force could acquire the long-range transport assets needed to move the ground self-defense forces about.

Under this plan, Japan would make changes to its airlift and sealift capabilities proportionate to those recommended above for Europe. New mobile logistics support capabilities for combat units would also be needed. Notable on the list of required assets are mobile equipment repair depots and hospitals, transport trucks, mobile bridging and other engineering equipment, water purification and distribution systems, mobile fuel storage containers and dispensing equipment, and more mundane requirements such as food distribution and preparation facilities. About $5 billion might be needed for this hardware acquisition, using the cost factors assumed in the analysis for NATO countries—averaging out to $500 million a year over ten years.

DEVELOPING COUNTRIES

Developing countries would face many budgetary challenges in any effort to expand military capabilities. The costs would follow from the need for more rigorous training and for better equipment.

In Africa, a continent facing many acute economic problems to accompany its widespread wars, the Western powers will need to provide many of the resources required to expand and improve regional military capabilities. Programs now under way, such as the U.S. Global Peace Operations Initiative, are important steps in the right direction. But they do not involve nearly enough troops or provide sufficiently rigorous training and sufficiently capable equipment.

Under current assistance programs, exercises and classes typically take no more than a few weeks, or at most a couple of months. Yet creating a highly ready military, competent across a broad spectrum of operations including combat, typically takes many months, if not longer.[30] As a U.S. Army field manual puts it, "The most important training for peace operations remains training for essential combat and basic soldier skills"—underscoring the scope of the challenge for preparing good troops for such missions.[31] Moreover, troops conducting peace and humanitarian interventions must work with nongovernmental organizations that provide relief and other services, adding further complexities to any mission.[32] The United States and other foreign militaries cannot be expected to build other countries' armed forces up from the ground level; nor would such offers necessarily be well received even if voiced. But months of specialized training, as opposed to weeks, are needed. So are refresher courses every one to two years.

To estimate costs, one approach is to examine the U.S. Marine Corps budget. Since the marines are very sustainable abroad, their budget does cover the costs of deployable logistics (though not the costs of strategic transport, which are provided for them by the air force and especially the navy). Cost estimates produced in that way may wind up high, however, given the more costly equipment usually purchased even by the most frugal of the U.S. military services.

Over the past twenty years the Marine Corps has typically spent $1.5 billion to $2 billion on procurement for nearly 200,000 Marines. Allowing for the fact that some of those funds have gone to aircraft, it has acquired $25 billion to $30 billion in equipment for 150,000 Marines focused on ground combat.[33] These numbers suggest a cost of $15 billion to $20 billion per 100,000 ground troops.

In all, the donor community might therefore spend up to $20 billion to make such an arrangement work. The U.S. share might be $7 billion to $8 billion, assuming that Europe would provide an equal amount and that countries such as Japan would contribute significant assistance as well. If provided during a ten-year initiative, annual aid would be about $750 million for this purpose; operating and training costs could drive the total close to $1 billion.

At present, European countries are collectively spending about $50 million a year helping African militaries improve their equipment and training for peacekeeping, and if the Bush administration is successful in obtaining its budget goals, the United States will soon be providing about $100 million annually.[34] So a tenfold increase would be needed to fully reach the goal. That said, these costs may be somewhat higher than actual circumstances would require. And lesser amounts of money could still fund a substantial program. A great deal could be accomplished even with $300 million to $500 million a year from the donor community. But it will be essential to keep pushing and ensure that recent increases do not become one-time events that, driven by Darfur or the proximity of the 2004 G-8 summit, quickly evaporate when political focus is lost.

There would also be nonbudgetary costs for such an initiative. Specifically, substantial numbers of U.S. military personnel might be needed to carry out the associated training. For example, 150 special-forces personnel were involved in Operation Focus Relief in 2001, for a program focused on training just 4,000 troops.[35] Were that program increased by a factor of ten, more than 1,000 special-forces troops might be needed, out of a total of only 30,000 active-duty special forces in the U.S. inventory. However, were such requirements deemed too great, private contractors would probably be willing to carry out the requisite functions, with only a modest level of oversight necessary by active-duty U.S. troops. This problem should be solvable.

CONCLUSION

When viewing individual crises and conflicts, those planning peacekeeping missions and humanitarian interventions have an extremely hard job deciding what to do and how to do it in specific cases. This is inherent to the nature of the enterprise and unlikely ever to change.

But when viewed in aggregate, trends are clear, and the world's capacity deficits are fairly obvious. The international community needs several hundred thousand more deployable, and sustainable, troops to handle the world's worst conflicts as well as the aftermaths of those conflicts. That is a daunting number. But when one takes account of the fact that 20 million active-duty troops are under arms in the world today, it should seem more attainable. Different groups of states will need different policies to reach appropriate goals, but in all cases the task should be doable.

NOTES

1. There may be 200,000 child soldiers in Africa alone; see United Kingdom, Ministry of Defence, *The Causes of Conflict in Africa* (London: Ministry of Defence, 2000), http://www.mod.uk/index.php3?page=2526, part I, 6.

2. Samuel R. Berger and Brent Scowcroft, "In the Wake of War: Getting Serious about Nation-Building," *National Interest*, no. 81 (Fall 2005): 50.

3. See William J. Durch, "Keeping the Peace: Politics and Lessons of the 1990s," in *U.N. Peacekeeping,*

American Policy, and the Uncivil Wars of the 1990s, ed. William J. Durch (New York: St. Martin's Press, 1996), 1–34.

4. See Adriana Lins de Albuquerque, Nina Kamp, and Michael O'Hanlon, "The Afghanistan Index," http://www.brookings.edu.

5. There are various ways of estimating force requirements using generic, standardized rules of thumb. Some link necessary forces to the size of opposing forces and suggest that outside troops be at least as numerous as the largest indigenous army. Others tie requirements to the size of the civilian population base needing protection and assume that two to ten troops are generally needed for every 1,000 inhabitants of a troubled region or country. By the first metric, an intervening force in Rwanda might not have had to exceed 5,000 in strength, since that was the size of the Rwandan military at the time (not counting irregular forces). By the second, however, at least 15,000 troops would have been needed to protect a population of 8 million. See James T. Quinlivan, "Force Requirements in Stability Operations," *Parameters* 25, no. 4 (Winter 1995–96): 59–69; and Michael O'Hanlon, *Saving Lives with Force: Military Criteria for Humanitarian Intervention* (Washington, D.C.: Brookings Institution Press, 1997), 38–42.

6. For another argument in favor of building up the capacities of states, rather than international organizations, for humanitarian interventions, see S. Neil MacFarlane and Thomas Weiss, "Political Interest and Humanitarian Action," *Security Studies* 10, no. 1 (Autumn 2000): 115.

7. For a good discussion of some of the potential, but also the limits, of private security forces in civil conflicts, see Greg Mills and John Stremlau, eds., *The Privatisation of Security in Africa* (Johannesburg: South African Institute of International Affairs, 1999).

8. See Richard N. Haass, *Intervention: The Use of American Military Force in the Post–Cold War World,* rev. ed. (Washington, D.C.: Brookings Institution Press, 1999), 87–94; see also, Annika S. Hansen, "Lines in the Sand: The Limits and Boundaries of Peace Support Operations," in *Boundaries of Peace Support Operations: The African Dimension,* ISS Monograph No. 44, ed. Mark Malan (Pretoria: Institute for Security Studies, 2000), 23.

Characteristics of conflicts that make them particularly difficult to terminate include the involvement of multiple parties with access to resources and arms and with fundamentally divergent aims. See Brahimi Panel, *Report of the Panel on United Nations Peace Operations,* A/55/305-S/2000/809 (New York: United Nations, 2000), 4, 9.

9. See Michael Walzer, *Just and Unjust Wars* (New York: Basic Books, 1977); and Andrew S. Natsios, *U.S. Foreign Policy and the Four Horsemen of the Apocalypse: Humanitarian Relief in Complex Emergencies* (Westport, Conn.: Praeger, 1997), 119–120.

10. John F. Harris, *The Survivor: Bill Clinton in the White House* (New York: Random House, 2005), 125–126.

11. Report of the Task Force on the United Nations, *American Interests and UN Reform* (Washington, D.C.: United States Institute of Peace Press, 2005), 16, 89–93; Victoria K. Holt with Moira K. Shanahan, *African Capacity-Building for Peace Operations: U.N. Collaboration with the African Union and ECOWAS* (Washington, D.C.: Henry L. Stimson Center, 2005), 27–36; and United Nations High-Level Panel on Threats, Challenges, and Change, *A More Secure World: Our Shared Responsibility* (New York: United Nations, 2004), 107.

12. See P. W. Singer, *Corporate Warriors: The Rise of the Privatized Military Industry* (Ithaca, N.Y.: Cornell University Press, 2003); and Michael O'Hanlon and P. W. Singer, "The Humanitarian Transformation: Expanding Global Intervention Capacity," *Survival* 46, no. 1 (Spring 2004): 91–96.

13. An important work on this subject is Alan J. Kuperman, *The Limits of Humanitarian Intervention: Genocide in Rwanda* (Washington, D.C.: Brookings Institution Press, 2001). Kuperman appears somewhat too pessimistic about the number of air deployment corridors and regional airfields that intervening forces could have used had they attempted to be creative and maximized the urgency of their response, but his overall message is persuasive and the care of his military analysis is exemplary.

14. Alison L. Des Forges, "Alas, We Knew," *Foreign Affairs* 79, no. 3 (May–June 2000): 141–142. For an analysis that may be somewhat too optimistic about the capacity of the international community to stop the genocide early, but which is nonetheless valuable as a counterweight to Kuperman, see also Scott R. Feil, *How the Early Use of Force Might Have Succeeded in Rwanda* (New York: Carnegie Corporation, 1998).

15. See United Nations Peacekeeping Factsheets, July 31, 2005, http://www.un.org/Depts/dpko/missions/unmis/mandate.html (accessed August 26, 2005).

16. Peace and Security Section of the Department of Public Information in cooperation with the Department of Peacekeeping Operations, United Nations, 2002, http://www.un.org/depts/dpko/dpko/contributors/30042002.pdf; and Michael O'Hanlon, *Expanding Global Military Capacity for Humanitarian Intervention* (Washington, D.C.: Brookings Institution Press, 2003), 32–33.

17. The Sierra Leone mission is likely to continue and in fact may need to become more ambitious in order to establish lasting stability—since doing so may require defeating RUF forces. If the war continues to fester, not only Sierra Leone, but also neighboring Guinea, where hundreds of thousands of refugees have fled the war, may suffer serious consequences. See International Crisis Group, *Sierra Leone: Time for a New Military and Political Strategy,* ICG Africa Report No. 28 (Brussels: International Crisis Group, April 11, 2001).

18. See International Crisis Group, *From Kabila to Kabila: Prospects for Peace in the Congo,* ICG Africa Report No. 27 (Brussels: International Crisis Group, March 16, 2001), 5–6.

19. Some estimates have suggested that the total military manpower involved in Congo's recent civil war has totaled as many as 150,000 fighters. However, more recent estimates put the size of the two largest rebel groups, Rwandan Hutu (largely the *interahamwe* who led that country's 1994 genocide) and Burundian Hutu, at 15,000 and 10,000, respectively. See International Crisis Group, *Scramble for the Congo: Anatomy of an Ugly War,* ICG Africa Report No. 26 (Brussels: International Crisis Group, December 20, 2000), 4; and *Disarmament in the Congo: Investing in Conflict Prevention,* Africa Briefing (Brussels: International Crisis Group, June 12, 2001), 2–3. Those latter estimates suggest that, if governments agreed to a cease-fire or peace plan but rebels did not, roughly 25,000 intervening forces might suffice. However, the enormity of Congo's territory and the size of its population—now roughly 50 million—point to much higher numbers, with 100,000 troops being a conservative estimate based on the rule that it is usually necessary to deploy at least 2 security personnel for every 1,000 indigenous civilians.

20. National Intelligence Council, *Mapping the Global Future: Report of the National Intelligence Council's 2020 Project Based on Consultations with Nongovernmental Experts around the World* (Washington, D.C.: December 2004), 97–98.

21. For a sobering assessment of Burundi's potential for violence, see International Crisis Group, *Burundi: Breaking the Deadlock,* Africa Report No. 29 (Brussels: International Crisis Group, May 14, 2001).

22. For example, the secessionist conflict in Aceh, a small and troubled province of Indonesia, involves some 3,000 guerrillas against a population base of 4.3 million. Sizing an intervention force to the guerrilla force would suggest deploying at least 3,000 troops; sizing it relative to the population base would suggest at least 10,000. In Burundi, similar force-sizing criteria would suggest that at least 25,000 intervening troops might be needed. In Afghanistan, where the Taliban commands perhaps 40,000 troops and the United Front resistance some 10,000–12,000, any intervention (as unlikely as it may be) would surely need to include at least 10,000 troops, even under relatively benign political circumstances. See Kelly M. Greenhill, "On Intervention to Deter Deadly Conflict: A Cautionary Prospective Analysis," *Breakthroughs* 10, no. 1 (Spring 2001): 36–44; Rohan Gunaratna, "The Structure and Nature of GAM," *Jane's Intelligence Review* (April 2001): 33–35; Ali A. Jalali, "Afghanistan: The Anatomy of an Ongoing Conflict," *Parameters* (Spring 2001): 92; James T. Quinlivan, "Force Requirements in Stability Operations," *Parameters* 25, no. 4 (Winter 1995–96): 59–69; and O'Hanlon, *Saving Lives with Force,* 38–42.

23. United States Institute of Peace, *American Civilian Police in UN Peace Operations,* Special Report No. 71 (Washington, D.C.: United States Institute of Peace, July 6, 2001).

24. Brahimi Panel, *Report of the Panel on United Nations Peace Operations,* 20.

25. International Institute for Strategic Studies, *The Military Balance 2004–2005* (London: Oxford University Press, 2004), 358.

26. For an even more ambitious goal from a group of European scholars, see Julian Lindley-French and Franco Algieri, *A European Defence Strategy* (Guetersloh, Germany: Bertelsmann Foundation, 2004), 10.

27. Rachel Schmidt, *Moving U.S. Forces: Options for Strategic Mobility* (Washington, D.C.: Congressional Budget Office, February 1997), 11, 62.

28. National Institute for Research Advancement, *Japan's Proactive Peace and Security Strategies,* NIRA Research Report No. 20000005 (Tokyo: National Institute for Research Advancement, 2001), 15–17.

29. National Institute for Research Advancement, *Japan's Proactive Peace and Security Strategies,* 39.

30. For a good explanation of how hard the U.S. military needed to work to improve its own standards after Vietnam, see Robert H. Scales, Jr., *Certain Victory: The U.S. Army in the Gulf War* (Washington, D.C.: Brassey's, 1994), 1–38.

31. U.S. Army, *Field Manual 100-23: Peace Operations* (Washington, D.C.: U.S. Army, 1994), chaps. 3, 8, http://www.adtdl.army.mil/cgi-bin/atdl.dll/fm/100-23/fm100-23.htm.

32. See, for example, Chris Seiple, *The U.S. Military/NGO Relationship in Humanitarian Interventions* (Carlisle Barracks, Pa.: U.S. Army War College Peacekeeping Institute, 1996).

33. O'Hanlon, *Expanding Global Military Capacity for Humanitarian Intervention.*

34. Adriana Lins de Albuquerque, Brookings Institution, and Amadeu Altafaj-Tardio, spokesman for the European Commission, e-mail communication, March 13, 2005; and Office of Management and Budget, *Budget of the United States Government 2006* (February 2005), http://www.omb.gov and http://www.state.gov/documents/organization/42247.pdf (accessed March 31, 2005).

35. Segun Adeyemi, "Special Forces Teach Peace Support Skills," *Jane's Defence Weekly,* May 23, 2001.

19

ECONOMIC SANCTIONS AND INTERNATIONAL PEACE AND SECURITY

Chantal de Jonge Oudraat

UNITED NATIONS SECRETARY-GENERAL Kofi Annan has called economic sanctions a "vital tool" in dealing with threats to international peace and security— "a necessary middle ground between war and words."[1] Sanctions are also favored by most UN member states.

Since the end of the Cold War, the UN Security Council has imposed economic sanctions more than two dozen times to deal with violent conflicts and terrorism (see table 1). The use of sanctions has undergone dramatic changes over the course of this period. Two phases can be distinguished.

The first phase dates from the end of the Cold War to the mid-1990s. The sanctions regimes of this period were directed primarily at intrastate and interstate conflicts. These sanction efforts had ambitious goals: their strategic objective was compellence—the reversal of policies that provoked or sustained violent conflict. In addition, they were comprehensive in scope and encompassed the totality of the target's economy. The effectiveness of these sanctions regimes was poor. They led to tremendous economic costs for the target countries but often not to changes in the political behavior of the leaders of those countries. The economic impacts on the countries in question also had damaging social and humanitarian effects, leading many commentators to question the morality of economic sanctions as policy instruments.[2] These sanctions often hurt innocent neighboring countries as well.

The second phase started in the mid-1990s. Policymakers recognized that the adverse humanitarian effects of comprehensive sanctions regimes undermined political support for these actions. They also acknowledged the poor track record of comprehensive sanctions regimes. In the search for more effective policy instruments, they increasingly turned to targeted sanctions—measures that target specific people, resources, or services and that would reduce harmful humanitarian effects.[3] The shift to targeted sanctions was accompanied by more modest and achievable goals. Starting in the mid-1990s the strategic objective of most

Table 1. UN Security Council Sanctions Imposed under Chapter VII of the UN Charter (1945–2005)

Country/Groups	Date Imposed	Date Lifted	Arms Embargo	Targeted Sanctions	Comprehensive Economic Sanctions	Enabling UNSC Resolution
Southern Rhodesia	Dec. 1966	Dec. 1979			✓	232 (1966) 460 (1979)
South Africa	Nov. 1977	May 1994	✓			418 (1977) 919 (1994)
Iraq	Aug. 1990	May 2003			✓	661 (1990)[a]
	May 2003		✓			1483 (2003)[b]
Republics of the Former Yugoslavia	Sept. 1991	June 1996	✓			713 (1991)[c] 1021 (1995)
Federal Republic of Yugoslavia	May 1992	Nov. 1995			✓	757 (1992)[d] 1022 (1995)[e]
	Mar. 1998	Sept. 2001	✓			1160 (1998) 1367 (2001)[f]
Bosnian Serbs	Sept. 1994	Oct. 1996			✓	942 (1994) 1074 (1996)
Somalia	Jan. 1992		✓			733 (1992) 1425 (2002)[g]
Libya	Mar. 1992	Apr. 1999 (suspension) Sept. 2003 (lifted)	✓	✓		748 (1992)[h] S/PRST/1999/10 1506 (2003)
Liberia	Nov. 1992	Mar. 2001	✓			788 (1992)
	Mar. 2001		✓	✓		1343 (2001)[i]
Haiti	June 1993	Aug. 1993	✓	✓		841 (1993) 861 (1993)
	Oct. 1993		✓	✓		873 (1993)
	May 1994	Oct. 1994			✓	917 (1994)[j] 944 (1994)
UNITA (Angola)	Sept. 1993	Dec. 2002	✓	✓		864 (1993)[k]
Rwanda	May 1994	Aug. 1995	✓			918 (1994)[l] 1011 (1995)[m]
Sudan	May 1996	Sept. 2001		✓		1054 (1996)[n] 1372 (2001)
	July 2004		✓			1556 (2004)
	Mar. 2005		✓	✓		1591 (2005)[o]
Sierra Leone	Oct. 1997		✓	✓		1132 (1997)[p]
Taliban (Afghanistan)	Nov. 1999		✓	✓		1267 (1999)[q]
Eritrea/Ethiopia	May 2000	May 2001 (expiration)	✓			1298 (2000)
Terrorists/States/ Nonstate actors UNSC 1373	Sept. 2001		✓	✓		1373 (2001)[r]
Democratic Republic of the Congo	July 2003		✓			1493 (2003)[s]
Terrorists/ Nonstate actors	Apr. 2004		✓			1540 (2004)[t]
Côte d'Ivoire	Dec. 2004		✓	✓		1572 (2004)[u] 1584 (2005)

Table 1. *(cont.)*

Source: United Nations, Office of the Spokesman for the Secretary-General, *Use of Sanctions under Chapter VII of the UN Charter,* March 31, 2000, http://www.un.org/News/ossg/sanction.htm.

Notes

a. For subsequent resolutions on Iraq, see Office of the Spokesman for the Secretary-General (OSSG), *Use of Sanctions under Chapter VII of the UN Charter,* http://www.un.org/News/ossg/sanction.htm.

b. UNSC Resolution 1483 (2003) of May 22, 2003, ended all sanctions established by UNSC Resolution 661 (1990) of August 6, 1990, with the exception of sale or supply of arms and related materiel, other than those required by the occupying power to serve the purposes of Security Council resolutions.

c. See also UNSC Resolution 727 (1992) of January 8, 1992, which reaffirmed that the arms embargo applied to all republics of the former Yugoslavia.

d. See also UNSC Resolution 787 (1992) of November 16, 1992, and UNSC Resolution 820 (1993) of April 17, 1993, which strengthened the sanctions regime. UNSC Resolution 943 (1994) of September 23, 1994, suspended certain sanctions on the Federal Republic of Yugoslavia.

e. Sanctions were suspended in November 1995. They were lifted on October 1, 1996. See UNSC Resolution 1074 of October 1, 1996.

f. This resolution, passed by a unanimous vote, lifted the remaining sanctions on the Federal Republic of Yugoslavia and ended the work of its sanctions committee.

g. UNSC Resolution 1425 (2002) of July 22, 2002, established a panel of experts to study the violations of the arms embargo imposed in 1992. See also UNSC Resolution 1474 (2003) of April 8, 2003, and UNSC Resolution 1558 (2004) of August 17, 2004, which extended the panel's mandate.

h. Targeted sanctions included a reduction of Libyan diplomatic personnel serving abroad. See also UNSC Resolution 883 (1993) of November 11, 1993, which tightened sanctions on Libya, including freezing funds and financial resources in other countries and banning provision of equipment for oil refining and transportation. On September 12, 2003, UNSC Resolution 1506 (2003) formally lifted all sanctions against Libya and terminated the mandate of the sanctions committee.

i. Additional measures in this resolution included a ban on the direct or indirect import of all rough diamonds from Liberia and travel restrictions on senior members of the government and their spouses as well as any other individuals who provide financial and military support of armed rebel groups in countries neighboring Liberia.

j. UNSC Resolution 917 transformed the sanctions regime into a comprehensive regime.

k. See also UNSC Resolution 1127 (1997) of August 28, 1997, and UNSC Resolution 1130 (1997) of September 29, 1997, which strengthened the sanctions regime.

l. See also UNSC Resolution 997 (1995) of June 9, 1995, which affirmed that the prohibition on the sale and supply of arms for use in Rwanda also applied to persons in the states neighboring Rwanda.

m. The sale and supply of arms to nongovernmental forces for use in Rwanda remained prohibited.

n. See also UNSC Resolution 1070 (1996) of August 16, 1996, which foreshadowed an air embargo on Sudan. This embargo never went into effect because of the expected humanitarian consequences.

o. In January 2006 the Panel of Experts on Sudan submitted to the Security Council a confidential list of names the panel believed should be designated for sanctions. See S/2006/65, January 2006.

p. UNSC Resolution 1306 (2000) of July 5, 2000, prohibited the direct or indirect import of all rough diamonds from Sierra Leone. UNSC Resolution 1385 (2001) of December 19, 2001, extended the ban for a period of eleven months, to be further extended by UNSC Resolution 1446 (2002) of December 4, 2002, for an additional period of six months.

q. See also UNSC Resolution 1333 (2000) of December 19, 2000, which established an arms embargo, targeted financial sanctions (Bin Laden and associates), and a flight ban; UNSC Resolution 1390 (2002) of January 16, 2002, and UNSC Resolution 1455 (2003) of January 17, 2003, maintained sanctions measures in UNSC Resolution 1267 (1999).

r. Resolution 1373 also established a Counter-Terrorism Committee (CTC) to monitor implementation of the resolution. In March 2004 the Security Council established a Counter-Terrorism Executive Directorate (CTED) to assist the CTC.

s. UNSC Resolution 1493 (2003) of July 28, 2003, imposed a ban on all arms, related materiel, and assistance, advice, or training related to military activities. See also UNSC Resolution 1553 (2004) of March 12, 2004, establishing a sanctions committee and UNSC Resolution 1596 (2005) of April 18, 2005, which added a travel ban and an assets freeze to those violating the embargo.

t. UNSC Resolution 1540 decided that all states shall act to prevent the proliferation of WMD, particularly to nonstate actors.

u. See also UNSC Resolution 1584 (2005). In February 2006, three individuals were put on the sanctions list.

sanctions regimes shifted from compellence to denial—withholding the means that could lead to threatening policies or behavior—and to deterrence—discouraging the adoption of threatening policies or behavior. In addition, sanctions were increasingly used to fight terrorism. This fight became a top priority for the United Nations after the September 11, 2001, terrorist attacks in the United States.

The mid- to late 1990s saw a fundamental shift in the use of sanctions along three dimensions: strategic objectives, instruments, and focus. The change in the strategic objectives of sanctions to deterrence and denial, combined with the shift to targeted sanctions and an increased focus on terrorism, improved the sanctions record in this second phase from poor to fair.

First, the new strategic objectives helped improve the record. For starters, compellence is inherently difficult.[4] Deterrence is easier for several reasons. First, deterrence does not require immediate action from those who are deterring. In addition, deterrence requires no public action by the one being deterred. Finally, deterrence aims to maintain the status quo, which is generally easier than challenging the status quo.[5]

Denial is also easier than compellence. When the goal is denial, actors seek to isolate the offending party and limit its ability to threaten international peace and security. The key to successful denial action is third-party compliance, especially from neighboring states —international assistance can bolster third-party compliance.

Second, the shift to targeted sanctions also helped to improve the track record of sanctions efforts. Targeted sanctions, by virtue of their limited nature, are easier to implement than comprehensive sanctions. In addition, political support for targeted sanctions is easier to mobilize since these sanctions target only those directly responsible for dangerous behavior.

Third, the improved track record of sanctions was brought about because sanctions ef-

forts were redirected from the problems of violent conflicts to terrorism. Violent conflicts are inherently difficult policy problems. Those who are involved in these conflicts are highly motivated and difficult to influence. International actors usually have weaker motivations. Coordinated international actions are difficult to organize and sustain. Mobilizing international support for counterterrorist actions is much easier. All of the permanent members of the UN Security Council have an interest in this issue, and all have been the object of terrorist attacks. The Security Council has recognized terrorism as an unlawful activity and a threat to international peace and security. It is consequently easier for the United Nations to organize sanctions efforts with respect to the threat of international terrorism.

The scholarly literature on sanctions is abundant.[6] However, most scholars have failed to recognize the fundamental changes that have taken place in sanctions efforts since the mid-1990s. They have failed to recognize how the shift in strategic goals (from compellence to deterrence and denial), the shift in sanctions instruments (from comprehensive to targeted sanctions), and the shift in focus (from violent conflicts to terrorism) changed the sanctions equation.[7] Most assessments of post–Cold War sanctions are based on the track record of the early 1990s and are consequently negative. Scholars have not given adequate consideration to developments that have taken place since the mid-1990s. This has led to misguided policy recommendations about the use of economic sanctions.

This chapter does four things. First, it reviews the mechanics of UN sanctions. Second, it examines UN sanctions regimes in the early 1990s, the first phase of post–Cold War sanctions, focusing on the sanctions regimes imposed on Iraq, the Federal Republic of Yugoslavia (FRY), and Haiti. Third, the chapter examines UN sanctions regimes imposed since the mid- to late 1990s, focusing on sanctions efforts to combat terrorism. Fourth, the chapter defines the parameters of a successful sanctions strategy.

THE MECHANICS OF UN SANCTIONS

Economic sanctions are nonmilitary measures that restrict or stop normal international economic exchanges with a state or a nongovernmental group, for the purpose of compelling, denying, or deterring political or military behavior by the targeted government or group.[8] Economic sanctions are different from trade wars, in which governments restrict or stop international economic exchanges in order to gain more favorable terms of trade.

Underlying the theory of sanctions is the expectation that economic costs will translate into political effects—that economic deprivation will produce public anger and politically significant protest. It is expected that this, in turn, will lead to changes in the behavior of troublemaking elites or to their removal from power.

UN sanctions are coercive measures intended to restore or maintain international peace and security. They are elements of a bargaining strategy that includes measures ranging from the severance of diplomatic ties to interruption of economic relations to the threat and use of military force.[9]

Chapter VII of the UN Charter provides the legal authority for the imposition of UN economic sanctions. It outlines the actions the UN Security Council can take to deal with threats to international peace and security. The charter gives the council tremendous latitude in defining threats to international peace and security, and the council has shown great creativity in the post–Cold War era in defining these threats. Indeed, it has increasingly identified internal conflicts, gross violations of human rights, and terrorism as justifications for international action and the imposition of sanctions.

A decision to impose mandatory sanctions needs affirmative votes of nine members of the UN Security Council, including the votes of China, France, Russia, the United Kingdom, and the United States—the five permanent members (P-5) of the council. Once the council has decided to impose economic sanctions under Chapter VII of the charter, all UN member states are required to implement them.[10] The Security Council usually establishes a sanctions committee to facilitate implementation of a new sanctions regime.[11] In recognition of the importance of implementation, the council may also establish panels of experts to monitor implementation of the regimes. It has done so increasingly since the end of the 1990s.

PHASE I: SANCTIONS AND VIOLENT CONFLICTS

Sanctions regimes tended to be ambitious and broad in scope in the early 1990s. Three sanctions regimes defined this phase: the comprehensive sanctions imposed on Iraq in 1990, because of its invasion and illegal occupation of Kuwait and, subsequently, to ensure compliance with the cease-fire resolution and disarmament provisions; on the FRY in 1992, in response to the FRY's involvement in the war in Bosnia and Herzegovina (and in 1994 on the Bosnian Serbs); and on the military junta in Haiti in 1994, because of its reversal of the 1991 elections.[12]

In all three cases, sanctions quickly led to deterioration in the economic and social conditions in the countries concerned. However, they did not lead to changes in the behavior of the political leaderships. On the contrary, these leaders generally became more repressive. Iraqi president Saddam Hussein managed to convince large segments of the Iraqi population that the United Nations and other outside powers were responsible for the humanitarian consequences of the sanctions regime.[13] Profound differences among UN Security Council members developed by the late 1990s. Some believed that sanctions should be lifted because of their dire humanitarian consequences. Others argued that sanctions could contain

Iraq, prevent it from becoming a threat to the region, and keep it from developing new weapons programs. Sanctions, they believed, had an important denial function. A third group, composed of the United States and the United Kingdom, had hoped that sanctions would lead to the overthrow of Saddam Hussein. Once it became clear that sanctions reinforced rather than weakened the Saddam Hussein regime, this group concluded that sanctions had run their course and that forceful removal of the regime was the only viable option. The debate in the UN Security Council over this issue resulted in a rift among UN Security Council members. In March 2003 the United States and the United Kingdom brought the debate to an end when they invaded Iraq without UN Security Council imprimatur.

Despite the comprehensive sanctions that were imposed on the FRY in 1992 and extended to the Bosnian Serbs in 1994, a lack of clear strategic objectives and disagreements among the Western allies undercut the sanctions effort. Ultimately, it was direct military action in 1995 that ended the war in Bosnia.

The UN Security Council imposed comprehensive sanctions on Haiti after the military ousted the democratically elected president of Haiti, Jean-Bertrand Aristide. Here, too, divisions among UN Security Council members undercut the effectiveness of the coercive strategy to restore Aristide to power. The junta, bolstered by a weak and disjointed adversary, believed it could weather the storm even when the Security Council imposed a total trade ban on Haiti in May 1994. By this time, the council had lost much of its credibility. Only the threat of military force, delivered in person by Chairman of the U.S. Joint Chiefs of Staff Colin Powell, U.S. senator Sam Nunn, and former U.S. president Jimmy Carter and backed up by U.S. forces on high alert, persuaded the junta to budge.

The poor sanctions record of the early 1990s generated four policy lessons. First, broad international support for sanctions is a key to their success. Unfortunately, such support was often lacking during this period, either because of disagreement over the objectives to be achieved or because there was no country that would take the lead and provide a sharp focus to UN Security Council action.

Second, many sanctions regimes were hindered because they were stand-alone measures that were not integrated into comprehensive coercive strategies that included the threat or use of force. This is one of the main reasons why sanctions were ineffective as instruments of compellence during this period.

Third, the comprehensive sanctions regimes of the early 1990s produced great social and human costs that were politically difficult to sustain over a long period. This fueled the search for targeted sanctions. Starting in the mid-1990s, several international workshops were organized to assess and refine the notion and scope of targeted sanctions.[14] The use of targeted sanctions shifted the focus of sanctions from compellence to deterrence and denial—from ambitious to more limited goals. The new objective was to deny ruling and warring elites access to resources and thereby reduce their ability to wage war.

Fourth, for targeted sanctions to work, third-party compliance and implementation are key. This lesson spurred the creation of monitoring groups and investigative expert panels.[15] These groups developed important insights into sanction-busting behavior. This led the Security Council to pay greater attention to the behavior of third parties and neighboring countries and to focus on the deterrence and denial functions of sanctions. "Naming and shaming" and the imposition of secondary sanctions were part of this effort.

PHASE II: SANCTIONS AND THE CAMPAIGN AGAINST TERRORISM

The sanctions imposed against Libya in 1992, accused of involvement in the terrorist attacks in 1988 and 1989 on U.S. (Pan Am) and French

(UTA) airliners, respectively, spearheaded the UN Security Council concern with terrorism.[16] The council went on to impose mandatory Chapter VII sanctions to fight terrorism on two other occasions in the 1990s—in 1996 against Sudan and in 1999 against the Taliban regime in Afghanistan.

The Security Council had two main counterterrorism objectives in imposing sanctions against these three countries: to compel—to change the behavior of state sponsors of terrorism and make sure that individuals believed to be responsible for specific terrorist attacks were extradited; and to deter—to discourage states from providing support to terrorist groups.[17]

In the case of Libya, UN sanctions were fairly effective. Even before sanctions took effect, Libya offered to surrender the suspects of the UTA bombing to a French court and those responsible for the Pan Am explosion to an international court. However, the broader security objective—weakening Libya's support for terrorist groups—required the continuation of sanctions. By the late 1990s, this broader objective had been largely achieved. In 1996, the U.S. State Department noted that Libya's support for terrorism had been sharply reduced.[18] Maintaining UN sanctions consequently became difficult to justify. In addition, international support for the sanctions regime was crumbling. These developments led the United States and the United Kingdom to develop a proposal whereby the two Libyan suspects would be tried under Scottish law in a court in the Netherlands. The Libyan government accepted the plan in early 1999, and sanctions were suspended on April 8, 1999—three days after the two Libyan suspects had arrived in the Netherlands.

In the case of Sudan, travel sanctions were imposed on Sudanese government officials in April 1996, after Khartoum refused to extradite three suspects in the assassination attempt of Egyptian president Hosni Mubarak. Although Sudan subsequently expelled a number of Egyptians, Palestinians, and "Arab Afghans"

—including Osama bin Laden—sanctions were kept in place. The United States argued that Sudan continued to be used as a safe haven by terrorist groups such as al Qaeda. The Security Council agreed and imposed an air embargo on Sudan. However, the embargo was never implemented because council members feared the humanitarian consequences of such an embargo, particularly on a country already ravaged by civil war. Even so, the adoption of the air embargo sent a message—that support of terrorist activities was not acceptable and could provoke a reaction by the international community.[19]

Members of the Security Council—the United States, in particular—became increasingly concerned about the changing nature of the terrorist threat in the 1990s. Terrorist groups seemed to be operating more and more as part of a global network. In addition, the 1995 sarin nerve gas attack in the Tokyo subway by Aum Shinrikyo increased fears that terrorists might one day use chemical, biological, or nuclear weapons.

The September 2001 attacks showed how difficult it was to compel regimes such as the Taliban and transnational groups such as al Qaeda.[20] UN sanctions had no noticeable effect on the Taliban, mainly because of its isolated economic position.[21]

Although the UN sanctions regimes of the 1990s failed to stop worldwide terrorist activities, they helped to change at least the declared attitudes of states toward terrorist groups, particularly the attitudes of state sponsors of terrorism.[22]

Sanctions since September 11, 2001

The terrorist attacks of September 11, 2001, made terrorism a top priority for the UN Security Council. Two weeks after the attacks, the council adopted UN Security Council (UNSC) Resolution 1373 (2001), obligating all 191 UN member states to take far-reaching domestic legislative and executive actions in order to prevent and suppress future terrorist activities.[23] To monitor implementation, the Security Council established the Counter-Terrorism Committee (CTC), whose goal was "to help the world system to upgrade its capability, to deny space, money, support, haven to terrorism."[24] In 2004 the CTC's capacity was increased by the establishment of a small, dedicated secretariat—the Counter-Terrorism Executive Directorate (CTED).

Five problems have hindered the council's effort to deny and deter terrorist activities.[25] Some of these problems were familiar in that they had been encountered in previous sanctions regimes.

First, states often have different interpretations of key terms and sanctions provisions. For example, the financing of terrorist activities and groups is frequently equated with money laundering and dealt with in that context. However, money used to finance terrorism is not necessarily generated by illegal business transactions; much of this money is legal and is acquired by legitimate means. Similarly, there is confusion about freezing, seizing, confiscating, and suspending bank accounts.

Second, many states lack the legislative and administrative capacity to implement Resolution 1373 (2001). An informal analysis conducted in the fall of 2003 revealed that seventy states were willing to comply with Resolution 1373 (2001) but were unable to do so.[26] Denying terrorists access to financial resources has proved to be very difficult.[27] The UN group monitoring sanctions on the Taliban and al Qaeda noted serious shortcomings in identifying and blocking al Qaeda assets other than bank accounts.[28] A further complication is that many terrorist attacks since September 11 have involved relatively small amounts of money.

Travel bans were similarly hampered by implementation problems. Border controls are weak in many countries; many governments do not have the capacity to effectively police the territories under their jurisdiction. In addition, the travel bans imposed on members of al Qaeda, the Taliban, and associated groups are difficult to implement because of the widespread use of forged travel documents and a lack of information regarding the individuals concerned.[29]

Third, UN Security Council actions lacked coordination. In 2005 the Security Council had four main bodies dealing with counterterrorism and overseeing various sanctions regimes:

- The CTC, which had a broad counterterrorism mandate and was assisted by the CTED
- The 1267 Al Qaeda/Taliban Committee, which was created in 1999 to monitor implementation by states of sanctions against the Taliban, al Qaeda, and their associates and was assisted by an Analytical Support and Sanction Monitoring Team
- The 1540 Committee, which was created in 2004 to monitor measures put into place by UN member states to prevent terrorists from obtaining nuclear, chemical, or biological weapons
- The 1566 Working Group, established in 2004 to examine measures against people or groups associated with terrorist activities not covered under the al Qaeda/Taliban resolutions[30]

Other UN departments and organizations, such as the Terrorism Prevention Branch of the UN Office on Drugs and Crime, not to mention the more than fifty-seven regional and functional international organizations, also had counterterrorism responsibilities.[31] All of these organizations and committees asked states for information on counterterrorism efforts—often in different formats. As a result, many states developed "reporting fatigue."[32] Overlapping mandates and duplication of efforts were inevitable and, without a central coordinating body, international efforts lost their sharp focus. Recognizing this problem, the UN secretary-general announced in March 2005 the creation of an implementation task force.[33]

Fourth, no consensus existed within the United Nations about the problem of non-compliant states. With the adoption of UNSC Resolution 1373 (2001), the Security Council ordered states to adopt and implement a wide range of measures, but it had neither formal standards for nor the material capacity to evaluate compliance. In addition, there was no agreement among members of the Security Council on the appropriate responses when faced with noncompliance, or on the question of who was authorized to act.

Fifth, the nature of the terrorist threat has evolved considerably since the 1990s. In 2005, the members of the Al Qaeda/Taliban Monitoring Team identified three distinct but related groups: the established al Qaeda leadership, the fighters who had attended training camps in Afghanistan and had graduated as experienced terrorists, and the growing number of supporters who had never left their countries of residence but had embraced core elements of the al Qaeda message. This third group is growing, is mostly unknown to the international community, and presents a great challenge.[34] The terrorist attacks in Madrid (March 2004) and in London (July 2005) were manifestations of these homegrown terrorist challenges.

International coercive measures, such as financial sanctions and travel bans, are of limited value against this third group. First, it is difficult to compile lists of people who do not have terrorist track records. Second, many of these terrorists do not have to travel, because they already live in their target countries. Third, the attacks carried out by this type of terrorist involve small amounts of money that are hard to track.

In sum, sanctions are not panaceas and formidable challenges remain. That said, the international opprobrium on terrorist activities is firmly established. Sanctions helped to bring about this change. Second, the international sanctions machinery established to deny terrorists access to resources and deny them safe havens is now also accepted and likely to be reinforced. Third, national capacities to monitor borders and financial flows are being strengthened. This will have important collateral benefits that might help UN Security Council efforts to deal with violent conflicts and other threats to international peace and security.

SUCCESSFUL SANCTIONS STRATEGY

The track record of sanctions since the end of the Cold War has shown that sanctions are complex policy instruments. The use of sanctions to deal with violent conflicts had limited success in the early to mid-1990s. The Security Council has increasingly used sanctions to combat terrorism since the end of the 1990s. At the same time, it has started to pay greater attention to sanctions implementation. The sanctions machinery it has put into place, particularly after September 2001, may also be useful if sanctions are employed in the future to deal with other threats to international peace and security.

An effective sanctions strategy should contain five elements. First, it must assess the target's strengths and weaknesses. Second, it must define an objective. Third, it must determine which tactics to follow. Fourth, it must evaluate and ensure implementation. Fifth, it must subject sanctions regimes to periodic review.

Assessing the Target

The effectiveness of coercive efforts, including sanctions, depends on the economic and political characteristics of the target. These characteristics will determine whether the target is able to withstand economic pressures and devise counteractions that could neutralize the effects of sanctions. Knowledge about the target is particularly important in the case of targeted sanctions.

Sanctions designers should start by examining the general characteristics of the target economy. For example, labor-intensive economies tend to be less vulnerable to sanctions.

Imposing sanctions on developing or troubled economies may not be advised, because sanctions aggravate existing problems and can result in humanitarian crises. Knowledge about export and import dependencies and the target's main trading partners is key. Sanctions designers should also be able to evaluate the volume of overseas assets and the nature of international banking contacts, including the volume and nature of the financial portfolios of the elites to be targeted. When dealing with nonstate actors—rebels or terrorists—it is important to know the source of their financial assets and the extent of their international financial and economic networks. Identification of specific target individuals is key but may be difficult.

Social and political characteristics of the target must also be assessed. The level of group cohesion—the willingness to withstand outside pressures—tends to be stronger in rural and ethnically and religiously homogeneous societies. Similarly, authoritarian regimes are generally less vulnerable to sanctions than democratic governments because the former are usually better able to control their political opponents. The effectiveness of travel bans depends on knowledge about the social, cultural, and political behavior of the ruling elites, rebels, or terrorists one is trying to target. Finally, the existence of a political opposition is often cited as one of the critical conditions for the success of sanctions, since one of the principal aims of sanctions is to bolster political opposition to a regime. However, imposing sanctions when the opposition is weak may be counterproductive. Ruling elites may depict their domestic opponents as traitors and thus amplify existing jingoistic attitudes. This in turn insulates the political leadership from criticism and allows it to draw strength from its defiance of outside forces.

When a country is in the midst of a civil war, sanctions will often have asymmetric effects, because different groups will almost always have different vulnerabilities. Identifying the different strengths and weaknesses of these groups, including the different effects sanctions may have on them, is essential to avoid hurting innocents or the "good guys."

Defining Objectives

Sanctions can be used to compel, to deny, or to deter political actors. Compellence is particularly difficult in cases of violent conflict. Indeed, the parties engaged in many of these conflicts have become engaged in violent behavior because of perceived threats to the survival of a group, or because of a belief that violent behavior will produce considerable political gain. In intrastate and interstate conflicts, the stakes are very high.[35] Compelling terrorists is also difficult because they, too, believe that vital interests are at stake.[36]

Compellence within a multilateral—UN—context is particularly difficult. It requires the members of the UN Security Council to clearly define and agree on what needs to be reversed, and it requires international actors to maintain this consensus over time.[37] Whether they are able to do so will depend on how their interests are affected. The position of the P-5 is particularly important in this regard.

Denial is easier to achieve. However, for denial to be effective outside powers need to effectively implement embargoes of the singled-out goods and/or services. The longer an embargo is in effect, and the more parties are involved, the more difficult that will become. Long-lasting embargoes also tend to lose their effectiveness because the embargoed party will often develop alternative supply sources.

Deterrence is relatively easy. Deterrence means discouraging certain behavior through fear of the consequences. It "involves setting the stage—by announcement . . . —and waiting."[38] This makes deterrence easier to achieve, particularly in a multilateral setting, where it is not necessary for all outside powers to be able to make that threat credible—it suffices if there is one leader who can. The onus for breaking the deterrent threat is on the other side. Engaging in such an action will not be an easy step to take since retaliation will follow. Deterrence has been particularly effective in reducing state support for terrorist activities.

Sanctions cases have shown that the threat of sanctions is often more effective than their actual imposition.[39] There is also some evidence to suggest that UN sanctions regimes have served as a deterrent to states considering supporting terrorist groups.

In sum, sanctions are most effective when they aim to deter political actors—states, in particular—from engaging in behavior that threatens international peace and security. Sanctions are somewhat effective when they aim to deny actors access to resources and services that would make dangerous behavior more difficult. Sanctions are least effective when they are used to compel actors to change or reverse behavior. That said, the threat to impose sanctions has been very effective when embedded in a comprehensive coercive strategy that included the use of force.

Determining Tactics

Once the target's strengths and weaknesses are properly assessed, sanctions designers must decide which tactics are most likely to be effective: a swift and crushing blow, or a gradual tightening of the screws.

Two schools of thought dominate the debate on sanctions tactics. One school maintains that sanctions are most effective when they are imposed immediately and comprehensively. Those who subscribe to this line of thinking argue that sanctions should be imposed early in a crisis, since gradual action gives the target time to adjust by, for example, stockpiling supplies, finding alternative trade routes and partners, and moving financial assets.[40]

The other school of thought contends that sanctions are most effective when imposed gradually and incrementally. Proponents argue that swift and crushing blows are the equivalent of wars by attrition, which will almost always cause people to rally behind the regime

and solidify the target's position. They argue that sanctions are instruments that should bring parties to the negotiating table.[41]

Both schools of thought are right some of the time. The objectives to be achieved, the political and economic characteristics of a target, and the target's environment, including implementation capacity, are the keys to determining which approach to choose. In determining whether to strike quickly and bluntly or slowly and softly, outside powers should consider the seriousness of the situation at hand. Sanctions should be proportionate to the objective: the more ambitious the goal, the stronger the sanctions regime. When outside powers are faced with trying to reverse gross violations of human rights or genocide, they may want to forgo the imposition of sanctions altogether and intervene militarily. In almost all cases, the threat of the use of force should remain on the table. It greatly enhances the deterrent threat of sanctions, as seen in Haiti and the FRY.

Evaluating and Ensuring Implementation

Sanctions strategists also must evaluate the target's environment—in particular, the economic and political characteristics of neighbors. Third-party compliance with sanctions regimes is critical. Four problems stand out.

First, interpretation problems interfere with the effectiveness of sanctions. Once a UN sanctions resolution is adopted, most states have to adopt national legislation to implement the UN measures. However, the language of UN sanctions resolutions is often the result of compromise formulations with vague and ambiguous wording.[42] The interpretation of such resolutions will thus often vary from state to state. In addition, interpretation problems may lead to acrimonious discussions within UN sanctions committees. This undermines political unity and may lead targets to doubt the resolve of outside powers. Building a strong political consensus is key and may help overcome some of these issues.

Second, the uneven distribution of sanctions costs is a problem. The costs of sanctions are almost always distributed unequally across states. Sanctions often have unintended negative effects on third states, and some states are harder hit than others. Moreover, targeted states may engage in countermeasures and make the cost of compliance too high for third parties.[43] Without assistance from the international community, these states may not be sufficiently motivated to implement and enforce the sanctions regime in question.[44]

Third, capacity problems must be addressed. Few states have the expertise or resources needed to establish or maintain efficient monitoring and enforcement mechanisms. Sanctions regimes that do not investigate violations and consequently deal with violators are regimes that ultimately lose their credibility. Since the late 1990s state capacity to monitor and regulate financial services and physical borders has improved, but more needs to be done. Improving state capacity would also help to stabilize regions as a whole—an important collateral benefit. Finally, building up state capacity has potential strong deterrent effects.

Fourth, outside actors need to deal with noncompliant third parties. A regime that does not deal with violations will quickly lose its effectiveness. The use of investigative panels and naming and shaming has produced good results.[45] Similarly, the threat and use of secondary sanctions against noncompliant states seem effective.[46]

Implementation—third-party compliance—is essential for the effectiveness of sanctions efforts. They require the building of an international political consensus, the provision of financial resources to address burden-sharing problems, capacity building, and the establishment of monitoring and enforcement mechanisms. Contrary to popular belief, economic sanctions are not cost-free.

Reviewing Sanctions Regimes

All sanctions regimes should be subject to periodic review. Time limits in sanctions resolutions force states to periodically question whether sanctions should be maintained.[47] Those imposing sanctions should also formulate the conditions under which sanctions should be lifted, either because the behavior that led to their imposition has changed or because they have failed to bring the desired results.[48] If the imposition of sanctions has no political effect, two alternatives should be considered. First, outside powers can promise to lift some elements of a sanctions regime if the target starts to engage in "good" behavior. That said, a carrot-and-stick approach requires accurate and timely assessments of the target's aspirations and intentions. Outside powers should be careful that the target doesn't use this opportunity to strengthen its forces so that it can resume its deviant behavior later on. The second alternative is to increase pressure on the target by threatening the use of military force. The threat may have to be made early if the target is not vulnerable economically or politically. The threat to use force often makes sanctions more effective by giving credibility to the coercive effort.

CONCLUSION

The UN Security Council has used economic sanctions to maintain and restore international peace and security on many occasions since the end of the Cold War. The use of sanctions has changed dramatically over this period. In the early 1990s sanctions were comprehensive in scope, had ambitious objectives, and focused on violent conflicts. Their track record was poor. In the mid- and late 1990s the Security Council increasingly turned to targeted sanctions. It also scaled down the strategic objectives it sought to achieve and became increasingly focused on terrorism. Together, these developments improved the sanctions track record.

Economic sanctions are complex policy instruments. Although formidable challenges remain, the international community has steadily improved its understanding of economic sanctions—and hence their effectiveness.

NOTES

The author would like to thank Lori Gronich and the editors of this volume for their comments on an earlier draft. Very special thanks go to Michael E. Brown.

1. See Kofi Annan, *In Larger Freedom: Towards Development, Security and Human Rights for All* (New York: United Nations, 2005), par. 109.

2. See, for example, Joy Gordon, "A Peaceful, Silent, Deadly Remedy: The Ethics of Economic Sanctions," *Ethics and International Affairs* 13 (1999): 123–150; John Mueller and Karl Mueller, "Sanctions of Mass Destruction," *Foreign Affairs* 78, no. 3 (May–June 1999): 43–53; and Thomas G. Weiss, David Cortright, George Lopez, and Larry Minear, *Political Gain and Civilian Pain: Humanitarian Impacts of Economic Sanctions* (Lanham, Md.: Rowman and Littlefield, 1997). On how sanctions criminalize societies, see also Peter Andreas, "Criminalizing Consequences of Sanctions: Embargo Busting and Its Legacy," *International Studies Quarterly* 49, no. 2 (June 2005): 335–360.

3. Targeted sanctions are sometimes also called smart sanctions. They usually consist of travel bans, asset freezes, and embargoes or regulations on strategic goods such as diamonds and timber. Targeted sanctions are not panaceas and they can also hit innocent people hard. To reduce this collateral damage, the UN Security Council started to request that the UN Secretariat draw up humanitarian assessment reports either before or shortly after the imposition of sanctions. A first report of this nature was prepared in 1997 and concerned the proposed sanctions regime on Sudan. It led to the decision by the Security Council not to impose an aviation ban.

4. See Thomas C. Schelling, *Arms and Influence* (New Haven, Conn.: Yale University Press, 1966); Alexander L. George, *Forceful Persuasion: Coercive Diplomacy as an Alternative to War* (Washington, D.C.: United States Institute of Peace Press, 1991); and Robert J. Art and Patrick M. Cronin, *The United States and Coercive Diplomacy* (Washington, D.C.: United States Institute of Peace Press, 2003).

5. Given these strategic dynamics, it is not surprising that the threat to impose sanctions has had a relatively good track record.

6. For a very critical view, see, for example, Robert Pape, "Why Economic Sanctions Do Not Work," *International Security* 22, no. 2 (Fall 1997): 90–136; and Pape, "Why Economic Sanctions Still Do Not Work," *International Security* 23, no. 1 (Summer 1998): 5–65. For a more nuanced view, see Kimberly Ann Elliot, "The Sanctions Glass: Half Full or Completely Empty?" *International Security* 23, no. 1 (Summer 1998): 66–77. See also Gary Clyde Hufbauer, Jeffrey J. Schott, and Kimberly Ann Elliot, *Economic Sanctions Reconsidered,* rev. ed., 2 vols. (Washington, D.C.: Institute for International Economics, 1990); and David Baldwin, "The Sanctions Debate and the Logic of Choice," *International Security* 24, no. 3 (Winter 1999–2000): 80–107.

7. Notable exceptions in this regard are David Cortright and George Lopez. See David Cortright and George A. Lopez, *Sanctions and the Search for Security: Challenges for UN Action* (Boulder, Colo.: Lynne Rienner, 2002); and Cortright, Lopez, et al., *The Sanctions Decade: Assessing UN Strategies in the 1990s* (Boulder, Colo.: Lynne Rienner, 2000). Targeted sanctions have been the object of three main policy seminars. See the proceedings of the Interlaken seminars organized by the Swiss government at http://www.smartsanctions.ch/start.html; the proceedings of the first expert seminar on smart sanctions organized by the Bonn International Center for Conversion and the Foreign Office of the Federal Republic of Germany, Bonn, November 21–23, 1999, http://www.bicc.de./general/events/unsanc/papers.html; and the proceedings of the Stockholm process in Peter Wallensteen, Carina Staibano, and Mikael Eriksson, *Making Targeted Sanctions Effective: Guidelines for the Implementation of UN Policy Options* (Stockholm: Uppsala University, 2003), http://www.smartsanctions.se.

8. Embargoes and export controls limit and ban exports. Boycotts limit and ban imports. Arms embargoes are not to be confused with export controls. An arms embargo generally has a triggering event, such as the outbreak of violent conflict, and tends to be of a temporary nature—it will be lifted once the armed conflict has stopped. Arms embargoes may have unintended effects. In internal conflicts, they tend to favor the warring factions that have access to governmental stockpiles and industries. In such cases, arms embargoes can undermine the ability of others to organize and defend themselves. Arms embargoes can thus favor one side over the other and may permit one side to win, rather than pushing both sides toward a military stalemate and political settlement. See Joanna Spear, "Arms Limitations, Confidence

Building Measures, and Internal Conflict," in *The International Dimensions of Internal Conflict,* ed. Michael E. Brown (Cambridge, Mass.: MIT Press, 1996), 377–410.

9. See the United Nations Charter, Chapter VII, Articles 39, 40, 41, and 42. UN sanctions are not intended to punish targets. Sanctions imposed by the Security Council are political, not legal, instruments. They are discretionary measures decided on by the council outside any legal or disciplinary context and as such are unlike sanctions to enforce international or national law. See Serge Sur, *Security Council Resolution 687 of 3 April 1991 in the Gulf Affair: Problems of Restoring and Safeguarding Peace,* UNIDIR Research Papers, No. 12 (New York: United Nations, 1992), 15–16. See also Vera Gowlland-Debbas, *Collective Responses to Illegal Acts in International Law: United Nations Action in the Question of Southern Rhodesia* (Dordrecht: Martinus Nijhoff, 1990), 461–485.

10. Indeed, when states join the United Nations they pledge to carry out the decisions of the Security Council. See UN Charter Articles 41, 25, and 27.

11. It may be recalled that the interpretive guidance of the sanctions committees is not binding on UN members.

12. In addition to these comprehensive regimes, the Security Council imposed in this first phase stand-alone arms embargoes on Somalia, Liberia, and Rwanda. An arms embargo and targeted sanctions were imposed on the National Union for the Total Independence of Angola (UNITA). All these sanctions regimes were poorly implemented. It was only in the late 1990s that the council started paying serious attention to these regimes. For details, see Chantal de Jonge Oudraat, "UN Sanction Regimes and Violent Conflict," in *Turbulent Peace: The Challenges of Managing International Conflict,* ed. Chester Crocker, Fen Osler Hampson, and Pamela Aall (Washington, D.C.: United States Institute of Peace Press, 2001), 323–351.

13. UN Security Council members had tried to mitigate the humanitarian consequences of the sanctions regime by adopting the Oil-for-Food Programme. Under the terms of this program, adopted in 1991, revenues from the sale of Iraqi oil could be used to pay for food and medicine. However, it was not until 1996 that Baghdad accepted the conditions of the program, and even then it would frequently order insufficient food and medicines, hoard them in ware-

houses, illegally reexport humanitarian supplies, or simply stop oil exports. The strategy was apparently to increase the misery of the Iraqi people, thereby putting pressure on the Security Council to lift sanctions altogether. In 2000, UN secretary-general Kofi Annan warned the members of the council that they were losing the propaganda war about who was responsible for the situation in Iraq—Iraqi president Saddam Hussein or the United Nations. Annan also acknowledged that the program established to mitigate the humanitarian effects—the Oil-for-Food Programme—had not met its objectives. See United Nations, press release SC/6833, New York, March 24, 2000; and UN Security Council document S/2000/208, March 10, 2000.

14. See note 8.

15. See Alex Vines, "Monitoring UN Sanctions in Africa: The Role of Panels of Experts," in *Verification Yearbook 2003* (London: Vertic, 2003), 247–263. The March 2000 Security Council report on violations of the Angola/UNITA sanctions regime was a first in this regard. See UN Security Council document S/2000/203, March 10, 2000.

16. For details, see Chantal de Jonge Oudraat, "The Role of the UN Security Council," in *Terrorism and the UN: Before and After September 11,* ed. Jane Boulden and Thomas G. Weiss (Bloomington: Indiana University Press, 2004), 151–172.

17. Washington recognized "this type of concerted multilateral response to terrorism . . . as an important deterrent to states considering support for terrorist acts or groups." See UN General Assembly document A/48/267/Add. 1, September 21, 1993, par. 6.

18. See Anna Sabasteanski, ed., *Patterns of Global Terrorism 1996* (Washington, D.C.: U.S. Department of State, 1996).

19. UN sanctions were lifted in September 2001 after Sudan pledged its full support for the global antiterrorist campaign

20. The Taliban had been struck by financial and aviation sanctions in October 1999 when they refused to hand over Osama bin Laden, who was accused of involvement in the bombings of the U.S. embassies in East Africa. Bin Laden had been indicted by the United States, in November 1998, for his involvement in the bombings of the U.S. embassies in East Africa and had found refuge in Afghanistan, after having been expelled by Sudan.

21. The Taliban had limited funds abroad, and the extent of Taliban-controlled air traffic was negligible. The Taliban, moreover, was not active in the above-board global economy; much of its money came from the illegal opium and heroin trade. A strengthened sanctions package adopted in December 2000 did not change these economic fundamentals. An additional sign of the Taliban's intransigence was that the prospect of a U.S.-led attack, which grew in the wake of September 11, 2001, did not change the regime's policy. The Taliban still refused to hand over Bin Laden.

22. The U.S. State Department recognized this transformation in the late 1990s and again in 2001 when it noted the continuation of a slow trend away from state sponsorship of terrorism. See Anna Sabasteanski, ed., *Patterns of Global Terrorism 2001* (Washington, D.C.: U.S. Department of State, 2001).

23. UNSC Resolution 1373 (2001) globalized the ban against terrorism and required states to change and/or adopt domestic legislation to criminalize terrorist acts, including the support and financing of such acts; deny safe haven to terrorists and prohibit any other support for terrorists, such as the provision of arms; and cooperate with other states in the implementation of these measures.

24. Chairman of the UN Counter-Terrorism Committee, press briefing, New York, October 19, 2001.

25. See, for example, Walter Gehr, "Recurrent Issues: Briefing for Member States on 4 April 2002," http://www.un.org/Docs/sc/committees/1373/rc.htm.

26. Some sixty states were very gradually moving into compliance, and among the thirty states considered to have achieved "a considerable degree of compliance," inadequacies remained—particularly with respect to the prevention of illegal financial transfers. The study identified twenty states as "inactive"—that is, countries "that for a variety of reasons have chosen not to comply with resolution 1373." Cited in David Cortright, George Lopez, Alistair Millar, and Linda Gerber, *An Action Agenda for Enhancing the United Nations Program on Counter-Terrorism* (Goshen and Notre Dame, Ind.: Fourth Freedom Forum and Joan B. Kroc Institute for International Peace Studies, September 2004), 7–8.

27. For example, while $112 million was frozen in the first three months after the September 11, 2001, attacks, only $24 million was blocked in the following two years—a small fraction of the total

funds believed to be available to terrorist organizations. See United Nations High-Level Panel on Threats, Challenges, and Change, *A More Secure World: Our Shared Responsibility* (New York: United Nations, 2004), par. 149.

28. See report of the UN Monitoring Group, UN Security Council document S/2003/669, July 8, 2003, 10–18; and the Report of the Analytical Support and Sanctions Monitoring Team, UN Security Council document S/2004/679, August 25, 2004. See also Edward Alden and Mark Turner, "UN Says Lack of Cooperation Is Aiding Al Qaeda," *Financial Times,* November 14, 2003, 1.

29. Many states have pointed to the deficiencies of the "consolidated list"—that is, the list maintained by the Al Qaeda/Taliban Committee and containing the names of individuals and entities associated with al Qaeda. Problems have ranged from uncertain spellings of names to lack of details on birth dates, addresses, or other identifying information.

30. See UNSC Resolution 1566 (2004) of October 8, 2004. Russia introduced this resolution after the terror attack in Beslan, Ossetia, in which hundreds of students and teachers were killed by Chechnyan separatists.

31. In 2003 the CTC organized a special meeting with these organizations, but it was not given a central coordinating role.

32. For example, by September 30, 2003, forty-eight states were late in submitting their reports to the CTC. All were mentioned in a report to the UN Security Council (see UN Security Council document S/2003/1056 of October 31, 2003) and except for Sweden were developing countries. The UN Sanctions Committee overseeing sanctions on the Taliban and al Qaeda operatives (also known as the 1267 Committee) also complained about the small number of states reporting. See UN Security Council Document S/2003/669 of July 8, 2003.

33. See the statement made by Kofi Annan at the international summit Democracy, Terrorism, and Security in March 2005 in Madrid. Kofi Annan, press release SG/SM/9757, March 10, 2005. The task force met for the first time in the fall of 2005.

34. See the Report of the Monitoring Team, UN Security Council document S/2005/572 of September 9, 2005, par. 8–16. See also the statement by the chair of the 1267 Committee to the UN Security

Council on July 20, 2005 (5,229th meeting), press release SC/8454.

35. Similarly, asking states to forgo nuclear weapons or stop the development of a nuclear weapons program is extremely difficult. Again, political leaders will embark on such courses only if they believe that vital interests are at stake. They will consequently invest a considerable amount of political capital and resources in the policy. Reversal of the policy could lead to their removal from office. See Scott D. Sagan, "Why Do States Build Nuclear Weapons: Three Models in Search of a Bomb." *International Security* 21, no. 3 (Winter 1996–97): 54–86.

36. Making states stop supporting terrorist groups is a question more of deterrence than of compellence. State sponsors of terrorism have generally complied with demands to hand over suspected terrorists because few states are willing to publicly support terrorist activities.

37. As Schelling reminds us, "Compellence . . . usually involves *initiating* an action (or an irrevocable commitment to action [such as the adoption of a UN Security Council resolution under Chapter VII] that can cease, or become harmless, only if the opponent responds." See Schelling, *Arms and Influence,* 72.

38. Ibid., *Arms and Influence,* 71.

39. See, for example, the histories of the sanctions regimes against the FRY, Somalia, Libya, Haiti, Sudan, Sierra Leone, and Liberia. Simon Chesterman and Beatrice Pouligny have suggested that "the threat of sanctions may serve to focus the minds of local elites in the context of a bargaining model, with a clear economic choice. Once sanctions are imposed, the clarity of this choice becomes dissipated among the competing economic incentives that emerge." See Simon Chesterman and Beatrice Pouligny, "Are Sanctions Meant to Work? The Politics of Creating and Implementing Sanctions through the United Nations," *Global Governance* 9 (2003): 512. See also David Cortright and George A. Lopez, *Sanctions and the Search for Security: Challenges for UN Action* (Boulder, Colo.: Lynne Rienner, 2002), 13–15; and de Jonge Oudraat, "UN Sanction Regimes and Violent Conflict."

40. See, for example, Kimberly Ann Elliot, "Factors Affecting the Success of Sanctions," in *Economic Sanctions: Panacea or Peacebuilding in a Post-Cold War World?* ed. David Cortright and George Lopez (Boulder, Colo.: Westview Press, 1995), 51–60; Carnegie Commission on Preventing Deadly Conflict, *Prevent-*

ing Deadly Conflict: Final Report (New York: Carnegie Corporation of New York, December 1997), 54; and U.S. Department of State, Inter-Agency Task Force on Serbian Sanctions, "UN Sanctions against Belgrade: Lessons Learned for Future Regimes," in *The Report of the Copenhagen Round Table on UN Sanctions: The Case of the Former Yugoslavia, Copenhagen, 24–25 June 1996, and Annexes* (Brussels: SAMCOMM, European Commission, 1996), 327.

41. See, for example, Ivan Eland, "Economic Sanctions as Tools of Foreign Policy," in *Economic Sanctions,* 29–42; and James McDermott, Ivan Eland, and Bruce Kutnick, *Economic Sanctions Effectiveness as Tools of Foreign Policy* (Washington, D.C.: U.S. General Accounting Office, February 1992, GAO/NSIAD-92-106).

42. Many authors have argued that the UN Security Council should adopt standardized texts for its sanctions resolutions. This would also facilitate efforts to develop national legislation for sanctions regimes. See Cortright and Lopez, *The Sanctions Decade,* 234.

43. Indeed, the enforcement of a sanctions regime may entail the use of force. Naval blockades are the most common sanctions enforcement mechanism.

44. Article 50 of the UN Charter gives states the right to consult with the Security Council if they suffer unduly from sanctions imposed on other countries.

45. Sanctions imposed on the UNITA rebels in Angola led to good results. According to one observer, those sanctions were among the best observed and most effective in Africa. See Vines, "Monitoring UN Sanctions in Africa," 253. Vines also notes that compliance was so good because of the political will in the Security Council and an aggressive advocate—the Angolan government.

46. In 2001, the Security Council imposed secondary sanctions on Liberia and on key individuals in Liberia responsible for undermining the peace process in Sierra Leone. This was the first time that the council imposed secondary sanctions.

47. Since 2000, all UN sanctions regimes have included time limits. That said, the issue of time limits remains very controversial and was triggered by the debate over the Iraq sanctions. In the late 1990s France and Russia had been advocating a change in the sanctions regime on Iraq. However, the United States and the United Kingdom opposed this and were able to block such a decision by the Security Council. The

United Kingdom and the United States are in principle opposed to time limits, even though they have voted in favor of council resolutions that have imposed such limits. They have argued that time limits take the bite out of sanctions. France and Russia, on the contrary, have argued that periodic renewal of a sanctions regime shows resolve by UN Security Council members. These issues have been discussed at length in the UN Informal Working Group on General Issues of Sanctions. See the statement of the chairman of the UN Informal Working Group, UN Security Council document S/2003/1197, January 22, 2004.

48. The importance of exit or termination strategies has been recognized within the UN community. However, in practice, such strategies have not been adopted. See, for example, *United Nations Sanctions as a Toll of Peaceful Settlement of Disputes: Non-paper submitted by Australia and the Netherlands*, UN General Assembly document A/50/322, August 3, 1995.

PART IV

USES AND LIMITS OF STATECRAFT, DIPLOMACY, AND SOFT POWER IN CONFLICT MANAGEMENT

20

THE PLACE OF GRAND STRATEGY, STATECRAFT, AND POWER IN CONFLICT MANAGEMENT

Chester A. Crocker

DURING MUCH OF THE 1990S, FOREIGN policy debates in Washington and other major capitals were conducted in something of a strategic vacuum. What should replace the familiar adversarial bipolarity we had taken for granted for decades? The very quality of the debate suggested that there were plenty of available options from which American and other world leaders could make their selection. We stopped thinking strategically because we perceived that there was (a) no unifying challenge or threat, (b) no self-evident basis for establishing priorities among objectives, (c) no focus for mobilizing resources, and (d) no discipline for deciding on where and how to deploy them. The process of selecting a grand strategy[1] was treated at times with the gravitas of a visit to the shopping mall. This was the golden age of discretionary foreign policy, an age apparently free of imperatives and full of available options.

In this environment, the very meaning of security expanded beyond national or regional levels to notions of global security. The tra-ditional focus on the security of states began to be challenged by concepts of "human security," examining ways to protect and secure the overall well-being of individuals and substate groups.[2] Without the discipline required when confronting an adversary intellect, leaders and elites in the United States acted as if the conduct of foreign policy was a discretionary matter where one was literally free to choose what to care about, what to engage in, where to intervene, and which humanitarian disasters mattered, or whether they mattered at all.

The events of September 11, 2001, could have changed all that, becoming a decisive turning point akin to the great decisions of the late 1940s. But that did not happen. Perhaps the most striking characteristic of post-9/11 American foreign policy has been the Bush administration's continuation of its predecessor's tradition of engaging in discretionary foreign policymaking. To be sure, militant Islamist terrorists attacked the U.S. homeland, and it was both necessary and entirely correct to go after them, rip them up, and take them down.

But this did not require the United States to dignify them and their dirty attacks by declaring a "global war on terrorism." American leaders—with a measure of coalition support—made a conscious choice to occupy and remake Afghanistan, without fully understanding the enormity of that undertaking. Further, they chose to go to war in an unrelated Muslim land, Iraq, to settle an old score, to take down a criminally abusive regime in the name of stopping WMD proliferation, and to mount a massive effort to occupy and remake the Iraqi nation. The last of these rationales was viewed as the cutting edge of a breathtakingly ambitious program to democratize the world of Islam.

While it is essential to check, if not defeat, the phenomenon of Islamist terror, these additional undertakings represent discretionary choices rather than strategic imperatives. Moreover, the choices have not provided a strong basis for the world's leading power—and its closest partners and allies—to conduct their affairs. As a result, fifteen years after the end of the Cold War and five years after the terrorist attacks of 2001, the search for a new strategic framework continues.

First, this chapter illustrates why the notion of a global war on terrorism (GWOT)—by itself—is a dubious strategic template for the security challenges of the early twenty-first century. Second, the chapter illustrates why it is so important for practitioners of conflict management to evaluate military instruments in the context of good old-fashioned statecraft based on the smart application of all forms of power. Third, the chapter looks at the underlying and more basic challenges of managing international conflict and coping with state failure. The analysis rests on the premise that even the globe's most powerful state cannot afford a discretionary grand strategy as the basis for its foreign policy. Precisely because it is the leading world power, the United States has a strategic imperative to contain, manage, and wind down violent conflict and create the building blocks of regional and global security.

WHAT'S WRONG WITH A GWOT?

The basic problem with the global war on terrorism as a strategic concept is that it grossly oversimplifies the challenges facing Western societies, creating a severe distortion of focus among policymakers because it is based on a false strategic premise. As a result, it is over-reliant on physical force as an instrument of policy, and it discounts the contribution of the nonmilitary dimensions of statecraft that are essential for addressing the dangerous security environments flourishing in much of the world. In the process, some of the political and diplomatic legitimacy needed for the achievement of American purposes has been forfeited. The real problems with the GWOT are much broader than the intelligence failures that have bedeviled Washington's Iraq project, the tactical miscues that have magnified the threat to coalition forward-deployed forces, or the shortcomings of U.S. occupation and state-building strategy.[3]

There are three conceptual problems with the GWOT as a strategy. First, terrorism is not an adversary. It is a tactic in which violent means are used indiscriminately to kill innocent, noncombatant civilians. As such, terrorism is a weapon of the weak in an asymmetrical struggle against the powerful. The impossibility of "defeating terrorism," especially when it is so broadly defined as to include local and regional as well as genuinely global terrorist actors, means that the concept of GWOT is a formula for permanent war or struggle. This characteristic of a permanent struggle may confer political advantages on those waging the war, but it brings significant strategic costs in terms of diverting attention and political capital away from other, more fundamental and potentially longer-lasting, strategic challenges. Moreover, in some circumstances, the GWOT can become a liability; those who define themselves as GWOT leaders will likely sink or swim with its perceived success. Unless they see evidence of significant ongoing threats, Western publics may tire of sustaining a permanent state of heightened readiness and the accompanying military and budgetary implications.

Second, the GWOT struggles to come up with a strategically meaningful definition of who is the terrorist adversary against whom to wage a global war. Clearly, it is not all terrorists and all forms of terrorism. Equally clearly, the adversary is not the Muslim world. It is not possible to argue that the Western nations face a monolithic, centrally controlled totalitarian adversary—a functional equivalent of the Nazis or the Soviets; the actuality is something quite different: a diffuse, loosely structured series of networks, something tellingly described by U.S. Central Command (CENTCOM) combatant commander General John Abizaid as an Islamist movement of Salafist jihadis (literally, holy warriors adhering to a fundamentalist Islam inspired by the original men of the Prophet's time) drawing support from a variety of social and political contexts in both Islamic and Western societies.

Unless the adversary is identified with considerable care and precision, the strategic consequences of "waging war" will be perverse in the extreme. Neutralizing this vanguard movement of Islamic "puritans" cannot be accomplished by direct, physical measures alone.[4] The global struggle against militant Islamist terror will be a long one, requiring a sustained campaign to "drain the swamp," transforming regions of failed modernization, endemic conflict, and authoritarian politics. It is these bad conditions and poor security environments that deserve the lion's share of our strategic focus. Western policymakers increasingly must recognize that the challenge is considerably more complex and long term than is implied by the catchphrase "waging war on terrorism." A grand strategy for the age cannot rest primarily on the notion that it is possible to "take out" a specific set of bad guys and thereby make the world safe for democracy, free markets, and Western values. Waging physical war against militant jihadis—unless accompanied by a comprehensive and more broadly focused political strategy to manage international conflict—will only enhance their recruitment efforts and legitimize their cause.

The key ingredient in the struggle against Islamist militants is to understand and act on the social, religious, and political context in which they operate. That context includes militant extremists seeking to purify Islam and return it to its roots, a civil war within Islam and a war of ideas among Muslims, a pattern of failed modernization in many Islamic nations that is a source of anguish and humiliation to Muslims everywhere in an age of globalization and instant communications, and a perception among many Muslim elites that their problems and weaknesses owe something to Western perfidy, occupation, and domination. Accordingly, Western strategy needs to avoid elevating extremist Islamic insurgents; it should work to marginalize them and separate them from their surrounding social context.

The third problem with the GWOT is that policymakers readily succumb to the temptation to conflate terrorism with the dangers posed by weapons of mass destruction (WMD) in the hands of rogue regimes. To be sure, just as it is essential to check Islamist terrorists, it is also critical to prevent the threat of further proliferation of such weapons, including their potential diversion into the hands of nonstate actors. But there is a twin fallacy in conflating the threats of terrorism and weapons proliferation. Terrorists and rogue state leaders do not have an automatic harmony of interest and strategic intent. The effort to link Saddam Hussein to al Qaeda failed, just as the claim that Saddam Hussein succeeded in his drive to acquire WMD during the late 1990s was shown to be hollow. Moreover, a strategy for our age cannot rest on waging war against the spread of military technology, any more than it can on defeating terrorism. WMD—like terrorism—are a tactic, a tool—not an adversary.

STATECRAFT AND SMART POWER

To secure world order against the threat posed by WMD proliferation, it will be necessary to target the apparently intractable political tensions and unresolved or frozen geopolitical divisions where the quest for mass-destruction weaponry typically arises. It is not an accident that the most worrisome threat of WMD proliferation arises in specific kinds of insecure environments: (a) empires or societies undergoing a profound political transformation (e.g., South Africa and the four nuclear successors of the Soviet Union in the early 1990s), raising serious doubts about their ability to control or dismantle dangerous technologies, (b) intractable regional conflict patterns (such as the Korean peninsula and the South Asian subcontinent) rooted in contested sovereignty conflicts or internationalized civil wars, and (c) unstable regions such as the Middle East featuring unresolved conflicts and powerful states determined to ward off dangers of encirclement, isolation, or abandonment. These environments cry out for sophisticated multidimensional and multinational strategies. Tough counterproliferation policies have their place, but a far broader diplomatic strategy is the essential underpinning for success, as the termination of the Libyan WMD program in 2003–4 clearly demonstrates.

To start with, it is important that policymakers carefully examine the shadowy political circumstances in which rogue state leaders and weapons proliferation networks thrive—in autocratic political systems and unaccountable bureaucracies—to understand why specific regimes pursue WMD. The Libyan case was notorious, and its roots go back many years—as, indeed, do the beginnings of the eventual solution. Its quixotic leader, Mu'ammar Gadhafi, spent much of his first three decades

in office attempting to escape the narrow confines of his modest power base and to project himself as a leading pan-Arab, anti-imperial champion of insurgent and terrorist causes across the Third World. A series of campaigns to assert leadership of Arab and African regional politics ensued in the 1970s, 1980s, and early 1990s. Libya used state support of numerous rebel and terror organizations, subversion and intervention in neighboring states, and direct engagement in a range of terrorist actions against Western targets to advance Gadhafi's vision. Oil revenues fueled these efforts and permitted a conventional military buildup as well as serious programs to acquire chemical and nuclear weapons capabilities, with the clandestine cooperation of the network headed by Pakistani nuclear scientist A. Q. Khan.

The latter efforts had achieved real traction by late 2003 when observers were startled to learn of a stunning Anglo-American diplomatic breakthrough with Gadhafi. The turnabout was announced on December 19 of that year: Gadhafi agreed to declare and dismantle all of his WMD programs, allow immediate on-site inspections by the International Atomic Energy Agency (IAEA), accede to the Chemical Weapons Convention, and permit British and American experts to dismantle and remove a vast array of sensitive components, equipment, weapons materials, and design documents.[5]

These dramatic developments did not occur in a vacuum. Gadhafi came in from the cold due to several factors. First, his bizarre, personalized leadership had repeatedly failed to bring him the recognition and role he craved; on the contrary, he found himself isolated in the Arab world, contained if not totally checked in African regional affairs, and internationally ostracized for his support of terrorism. Libya's role in the downing of Pan-Am 103 over Lockerbie, Scotland, in December 1988 placed Gadhafi squarely under a wide range of UN and U.S. sanctions. As a result, he began responding to Arab and African intermediaries and sending feelers out to Washington and London in 1999. The maverick Libyan wanted to explore a way out of the international doghouse he had been consigned to for his support of terrorism and began dropping his connection to terrorist movements and activities at that time.

Second, the leading Western powers picked up on the opening created by third-party diplomacy and Gadhafi's own signals. The next four years of carefully coordinated American and British efforts produced a mutually understood script, or road map, of steps to be taken by Libya and corresponding quid pro quos Washington and London would undertake. By 2003, Libyan intelligence agents had been convicted in a Scottish court, and Libya had accepted official responsibility for Lockerbie and offered substantial financial compensation to the victims' families, while the two Western powers allowed UN sanctions to lapse. This enabled Libya to begin reconnecting itself to the world economy.

Third, Western diplomacy on terrorism was complemented by tough counter-proliferation measures and the backdrop of the American-led wars in Afghanistan and Iraq. Libyan emissaries approached Washington and London for talks on WMD as coalition forces were entering Iraq. A short while later, in October 2003, intelligence cooperation and joint action by U.S., UK, German, and Italian authorities resulted in the high-seas interception of a German freighter loaded with sensitive nuclear enrichment components destined for Libya. The WMD game was nearly over. Nonstop diplomacy exploited the fruits of direct, coercive action to bring a halt to the Libyan effort within weeks while also enabling the Western powers to take down the Pakistan-centered nuclear trafficking ring that lay behind it. Gadhafi essentially surrendered his weapons effort in the face of mounting pressures but also in the certain knowledge (guaranteed by both London and Washington) that there could be an end to U.S. sanctions

and normalization of economic and, perhaps, political relations if he did so. This was a classic instance of creative diplomacy backed by a demonstrated readiness to use all elements of national power to achieve a negotiated result.

The Libya case demonstrates the value of an integrated strategy for coping with troublesome, isolated leaders. To be sure, each case is unique and the approaches used with Tripoli cannot simply be duplicated in reference to North Korea, Iran, Syria, or other places. Libya, in the words of one commentator, may have been "low hanging fruit" that was easier to manage as a matter of policy and strategy than these other examples.[6] A number of factors need to be considered—the international situation, regime coherence and orientation, the range of issues at stake, and available trade-offs to be considered in organizing incentives and pressures. But the real point is not whether Libya can be replicated. It is the need for the leading Western nations to decide whether they are prepared to take yes for an answer when dealing with pariah regimes over the issues of the day. Or, to put it another way, the challenge is to prioritize the objectives of strategy so that troubled and recalcitrant regimes can figure out whether to bargain seriously or to hunker down because they cannot see the outlines of soft landing for themselves. If they perceive that the leading powers will accept nothing less than regime change in the name of a generalized quest for freedom and democracy, then diplomacy is relegated to the sidelines and there is little left but bluff, bluster, and the episodic use of force.

The real choice, then, is not between unilateralism and multilateralism; nor is it between hard-power and soft-power approaches for coping with challenges to international security. The real issue—so clearly evident in the Libya case—is the presence or absence of good old-fashioned statecraft based on the smart application of power: when wits, wallets, and muscle all pull together so that statecraft uses all of the available assets and resources of a society and assures effective coordination between all the arms of foreign policy. Statecraft uses power intelligently, providing a strategic context for it. That context will include long-standing bilateral relationships, regional organizations, alliance systems, international regimes, and institutions. It may also entail creating special-purpose instruments such as the Proliferation Security Initiative, launched in 2003, that organize activities and capabilities among participating countries concerned about the WMD challenge.[7]

As professional soldiers are the first to recognize, successful military action can defeat enemy forces, topple regimes, seize and occupy territory, or deter immediate threats. But military action by itself creates only brief moments of opportunity, not lasting political results. To exploit these opportunities, you need agile and innovative diplomacy, actively maintained relationships with partners and allies, expert knowledge of regional politics and cultures, adept familiarity with the workings of key global and regional institutions, effective assistance and training resources, and carefully husbanded legitimacy to make possible the persuasive advocacy of one's goals. The United States and its liberal democratic allies still possess massive amounts of such smart power, including leadership roles in all the major international institutions, outright command of the "global commons" in military as well as nonmilitary terms, and a dominant share of the world's diplomatic, communications, and intelligence capabilities. The challenge lies in the conscious harnessing of all this potential leverage in the pursuit of common purposes among the leading powers to tackle the global security agenda.

The Iran case provides eloquent testimony to the central importance of statecraft and the smart application of Western influence. The potential U.S. agenda with Iran ranges from human rights and Iranian behavior with regard to the Middle East peace process and support of terrorist movements, to the terms

for freezing or terminating the Iranian nuclear program, Iran's quest for security assurances and an end to its economic isolation, U.S. and UK worries over Iranian meddling in Iraq, and the search for a framework for regional security in the Persian Gulf. Making sense of this inventory of issues, getting the sequence right, and establishing the trade-offs would be a herculean task in the best of circumstances. Ideally, the United States should strive for a truly global consensus with its principal allies and other leading powers and present it to the Iranians, backed by the threat of sharply increased international isolation and pressure and by the prospect of meaningful security, economic, and diplomatic incentives.

Sadly, the war in Iraq hampered American capacity to line up such support and handed Tehran fresh influence over American (and, to a degree, European) freedom of action, by giving the Iranians' "Iraqi cards" to play. Admittedly, the U.S. refusal to engage Iran in direct bilateral negotiation over nuclear and other issues is not altogether surprising, given the deeply troubled history of U.S.-Iranian relations.[8] There are few good options for checking Iran's pursuit of nuclear technology.[9] But standing back and leaving it to the European Union's troika of Britain, France, and Germany to try its hand—as Washington did for a period until mid-2004—could not produce positive results: the European diplomatic quest for a permanent, comprehensive nonproliferation deal required the active engagement of Washington, the support of Russia in containing Iranian nuclear aims, and the help of both Russia and China in the Security Council.

Western statecraft improved significantly after the June 2004 Group of Eight (G-8) summit, as the leading Western nations worked together to shape some elements of joint approach, and Washington publicly committed itself to support the EU-led talks in early 2005. But leadership changes in Tehran and continued divisions over Iran among the Permanent Five of the UN Security Council continued to hamper effective action. The Western nations will face continuing frustration over Iran until they find the necessary concepts and elements to regain the strategic initiative and are able to place the ball squarely in the Iranian court. Whether this should take the form of a step-by-step road map, a gradual series of confidence-building measures and dialogue in separate fields, or some form of "grand bargain"—building on the U.S.-European proposals of 2006—will depend on a host of variables. The point for our discussion here is that smart statecraft confronts difficult international actors with tough choices, not just threats; it uses the potential leverage and leadership of other powerful actors even when this entails some sharing of decision-making control; and it works within frameworks and institutions that the most important nations accept and recognize.

TOWARD A BROADENED GLOBAL SECURITY AGENDA

There are three patterns of insecurity that warrant sustained attention, using the statecraft and smart-power tools at the disposal of the major powers. Success in dealing with them will serve to drain the swamp that sustains bad actors while also advancing a range of other critical goals and values essential to building a more secure world order. The three patterns are (1) unresolved or frozen geopolitical divisions in regions where the quest for mass-destruction weaponry typically arises, (2) apparently intractable political tensions and hot conflicts that continue to fester within societies wracked by civil strife, and (3) the challenge of failed and failing states, where so many of today's ills breed and then spill across borders and whole regions. These patterns of insecurity, often flowing into and reinforcing each other, are the dominant challenges of our age. That is partly because they are sometimes capable of breeding the very specific "hard" security challenges we associate with the war on terrorism. Beyond terror and the WMD

threat, however, the central argument is that the bulk of the world's troubles are generated in its least successful and most turbulent neighborhoods, where civil wars, regional conflicts, and failed states are commonplace.

Regional Conflict Systems

Many of the toughest security challenges have developed within regional or subregional conflict systems in which poisoned, distrustful interstate relationships interact with troubled, often authoritarian-ruled states. Conflicts within one society become the hostage of a neighboring country's policies on refugee flows, diaspora support, and weapons trafficking. Under the classic principle of "the enemy of my enemy is my friend," regional conflict systems tend to feature reciprocal, cross-border support of rebels or warlords. In regions, such as Central Asia and sub-Saharan Africa, where arms are plentiful and borders are porous, it is almost axiomatic that one country's internal struggle will spill into neighboring lands, as the cases of Afghanistan, Liberia, and Rwanda so clearly demonstrate. Often, a regional patchwork of ethnic or communal minorities adds crucial tinder to the mix, as in the Balkans and the south Caucasus.

These regional patterns are resistant to a one-country approach focused exclusively, for example, on ending an individual civil war. They also resist a single-track approach focused on fixing the external symptoms of the problem—for example, arms races or dangerous weapons programs. Counterproliferation initiatives, while useful, will not fix them because the underlying pattern of conflict is not addressed. Expensive peace operations run the risk of becoming long-term commitments; alternatively, the "solution" they offer is likely to collapse when foreign forces leave. Antiterrorism campaigns may roll up one set of bad guys, but they also train local rulers and rogues on how to game the international system, for example, by defining their local adversaries as terrorists in order to solicit support from powerful states and to entrench further their hold on power.

The security architecture of some twelve subregional conflict zones needs sustained attention and additional linkage building.[10] A natural division of effort and sharing of roles (and credit) can be effective, especially if external powers operate on the premise that their goal is to work themselves out of a job by successfully shepherding the emergence of legitimate, self-dependent security structures and mechanisms. The quality and contribution of such linkages vary widely depending on such factors as local security capabilities, regional tensions, and external rivalries. There are roles for both official and nonofficial initiatives.

Part of the answer to these embedded regional conflict patterns lies in developing regional (or subregional) security dialogue mechanisms, paralleled by regional partnerships with external states or groups of states. Where such mechanisms already exist, they can be upgraded and deepened through external support. But conflict-torn regions are likely to remain mired in their bad security environments until they find, through one means or another, a basis of connectedness to an external source of security support, interest, and engagement. This need is the genesis of "groups of friends," typically donors and historic partners of regional conflict parties that agree to sponsor and support regional peace processes with negotiation assistance (such as offering observers or facilitators) and general political support activities such as diplomatic backstopping in the United Nations and confidence-building initiatives linked to regional organizations.[11]

In some cases, regional security initiatives are mounted for a pragmatic mix of purposes by stronger states that seek to dominate regional affairs by shaping the security affairs of weaker ones. One such effort is the Shanghai Cooperation Organization (SCO), grouping Russia, China, Uzbekistan, Tajikistan, Kazakhstan, and Kyrgyzstan, created in June 2001. Part political alliance and part collective security vehicle for Central Asia, the SCO emerged on the basis of the Shanghai Five, an earlier initiative aimed at checking Western influence in Central Asia's new states and offering a forum for cooperation on boundary issues. In the post–September 11, 2001, environment, China and Russia have pushed the concept of the SCO as a recognized regional security forum. While members have focused on border controls and combating terrorism and militant Islamic movements, a clear subtext has been the Chinese-Russian desire to curb U.S. influence and counter the spread of domestic democracy movements patterned on Ukraine and Georgia.[12] These goals are matched by the weaker states' quest for help from strong partners in quelling local dissidents. The SCO can be viewed as a by-product of the war on terrorism, and a predictable form of soft balancing against American global power. Whether constructive regional cooperation actually flows from this particular initiative remains to be seen.

An example of a very different sort focuses on the security sector of Africa, one of the world's most conflict-prone regions. The United States, the European Union, and individual European states have mounted significant capacity-building efforts, such as training and equipping as well as general financial support for the African Union's embryonic African Standby Force and individual national units.[13] This "adopt-a-region" approach can be useful in pulling a regional conflict system toward political solutions, including support of demobilization and reintegration of combatants, especially where each party or group of parties maintains separate links to diverse external states.

One of the most noteworthy examples of linking regional security organs to the broader international system is the ASEAN group's 1993 decision to create a minimally institutionalized ASEAN Regional Forum (ARF) to enhance official dialogue on political and security cooperation in the East Asia–Pacific region. The twenty-five-member ARF has achieved modest but important results as it evolves—slowly and consensually—along a trajectory notionally including confidence building, information sharing, interaction with other regional and international organizations and track-two organizations, preventive diplomacy, counterterrorism cooperation, and even conflict management. The ARF's natural partner is the nonofficial Council on Security Cooperation in the Asia Pacific (CSCAP), launched in 1992 by some two dozen strategic studies centers from ten countries in the Asia-Pacific region (Australia, Canada, Indonesia, Japan, South Korea, Malaysia, the Philippines, Singapore, Thailand, and the United States). Now a vast network of twenty national or regional member committees from around the globe, CSCAP has seen its original goal of providing a structured regional process linking nongovernmental security experts expand to include interaction with the ARF member governments via the ASEAN secretariat.

When governments prove unable to build their own regional security architecture, the task may fall to nonofficial security initiatives such as those of the London-based International Institute of Strategic Studies. Its series of "regional security summits" (dubbed "the Gulf Dialogue") promote security dialogue among governments of the Gulf Cooperation Council, Iran, Iraq, and Yemen; regional participants are joined at these privately convened but officially hosted conferences by nonregional government representatives from the United States, Russia, China, India, Britain, France, Germany, Singapore, Australia, and Japan. Gulf "summit" meetings debate such sensitive questions as Arab state concern over growing Iranian influence, what form possible regional security architecture should take, military and nonmilitary approaches to combating terrorism, and the proper role of external powers in Gulf security. This is one of the few forums where Iranian officials interact on critical regional issues with their neighbors.[14]

Intractable Civil Wars

Violent disputes that fester into protracted struggles, often over decades, acquire fresh layers of complexity and additional obstacles to settlement. The intractable cases deserve consideration in any grand strategy because they, like regional conflict systems, may spawn terrorism and promote a form of "struggle politics" that justifies the quest for the most destructive weapons. Intractable conflicts breed leaders who depend on adversaries and wartime conditions to justify and sustain their hold on power. The most salient current cases define our age, shaping the battle of ideas and values at stake in a number of regions—the Koreas, Kashmir, Colombia, Israel and Palestine, the Balkans, Sri Lanka, Cyprus, and within such African states as Côte d'Ivoire, the Democratic Republic of the Congo, Sudan, Uganda, and Somalia.

In intractable cases, the passage of time adds to the sides' sense of grievance, elevating sunk costs and making compromise less attractive. The calculus facing leaders is perverse: continued conflict hurts them too little for their cost-benefit analysis to shift toward settling; entrenched interests in the war economy grow as time passes, while the economic and political cost of settling grows apace. Peace could, in some cases, become a threat to their place in history, to their political careers, their personal wealth and safety. Intractable conflicts feature leaders who are relatively unconstrained by their domestic political base and can command the resources required to keep on fighting. In other cases, one or both sides are too weak or divided to make peace, an inherently divisive process.

This brief portrait illustrates the obstacles to terminating such conflicts, but it also points the way toward methods and circumstances that can favor settlements.[15] A smart grand strategy would give a central place to the possibilities of diplomacy, negotiation, and mediation—backed by all relevant forms of power and influence—deployed in the service of winding down these festering conflicts and thereby helping to drain the global swamps. This is not to say that every intractable case can be successfully mediated. But measures of conflict management and conflict ripening are within reach in most cases. If conflict management is skillfully orchestrated by well-prepared and sustained third-party initiatives, it may be possible to place the conflict parties under fresh pressures to make tough choices and to review their options. At certain points, the so-called intractable cases do, in fact, become amenable to settlement, typically with the assistance of determined and creative third-party efforts. Cyprus came close before the failure of the April 2004 referendum to approve the so-called Annan plan and will in time no doubt return to the parameters of this UN-led negotiation. As a result of sustained and purposeful peacemaking efforts led by the United States, the United Kingdom, Kenya, and Norway from 2002 to 2005, Sudan's north-south conflict reached the point of settlement with the adoption of a comprehensive peace agreement. The Sudanese case shows an awareness of the link between conflict, peacemaking, failed states, and terrorism. Northern Ireland is a case of conflict being resolved in drawn-out stages; the Balkans have also witnessed piecemeal peacemaking. Cambodia, Angola, and Mozambique all moved—eventually, after sometimes long interludes of war and negotiation—from war to peace.

Some breakthroughs occur at times of basic systemic change in the surrounding environment. Others emerge with a change in leadership in one of the parties, a change in the military balance, the introduction of new external relationships, or the entry of a powerful or especially persuasive mediator. Smart strategy cannot count on—or wait for—such conditions to emerge and must focus on those things that can be controlled, or at least influenced. These include reinforcing local military stalemates and blocking the parties' search for unilateral military advantages, helping to define and legitimize the zone of negotiability in long-festering conflicts so that the parties are gradually sobered into more realistic settlement terms, creating coherent negotiating mechanisms so that parties are effectively encircled by a unified game plan for settlement talks and not able to go "forum shopping," cultivating the emergence of more imaginative leaders, and constraining or threatening the more recalcitrant ones.

A smarter strategy for the leading democracies would recognize that every intractable conflict is in one sense unique and that formal mediation may not be appropriate in certain instances where pride is too great or power asymmetry too large. But it would give conflict management a central place at the top table, where statecraft is developed and strategies for shaping events are defined.

Weak and Failing States

A panoply of interests and values of concern to the international community are placed in jeopardy in the fifty to sixty potential weak states identified in one study.[16] Failing states can (a) breed terror and extremist or fundamentalist politics when a hollowed-out state abdicates its role or is pushed aside by the social welfare arm of religious parties (a serious risk in many Muslim states), (b) lead to massive humanitarian disasters, (c) host criminal networks, drug mafias, and warlord economies, (d) spawn regionwide warfare, (e) promote horrendous practices such as child soldiering and human trafficking, (f) produce health pandemics and eco-disasters, and (g) be taken over by rogue leaders who may go for WMD.

In sum, it is not difficult to make the case that weak and failed states are a problem—one increasingly recognized at the most senior levels of powerful governments.[17] They occupy a vast zone stretching across large parts of developing Asia, the Middle East, Africa, and pockets of Latin America. The strategic issues are how to select among the host of candidates to address and what tools offer the best chances for positive effect. One study of counterterrorism makes the case that weak states may be more attractive hosts to foreign terrorists and dangerous criminals than states that have failed outright due to the advantages of having a corruptible buffer of ineffective governance in such porous, easily penetrated places.[18] The basic criteria for selection would seem to include (a) states caught up in the intra-Islamic ferment taking place in parts of Africa, the Middle East, and Central, South, and Southeast Asia, (b) states whose agonies have the greatest likelihood of spreading regionally to bring whole subregions into turmoil, and (c) states whose failures have the greatest potential for enabling rogues, tyrants, and terrorists to become firmly established.

There is much debate about state building in the context of declining state viability, outright state collapse, or the aftermath of a fundamental political transformation or violent regime change. But the core of the problem is to replace the rule of men and guns by the rule of law and institutions. Some view the challenge as essentially one of economic development. In reality, the development gap is political and institutional, as well as economic. A central concern is getting the sequence of modernization processes right. If the first priority is to strengthen state institutions, this could have profound implications for both democracy promotion and development assistance policies. Similarly, the institution-building approach requires careful examination of what roles outside actors can play that successfully enhance state capacity and fit the local cultural context while avoiding measures and programs that ironically undercut local capacity.[19]

After the experience of state failure in Somalia, Afghanistan, and Rwanda—and the risk of a similar trajectory in Pakistan and Nigeria —leading democracies have focused increasing attention on remedies. Some mixture of the following have drawn particular attention: expanded support of capacity building to upgrade local and regional resources for peace operations, enhanced techniques of transitional administration or de facto trusteeship for societies moving from one status or political dispensation to another, greater reliance on de facto measures of shared sovereignty in selected fields of endeavor where "stateness" is especially undeveloped and the capacity to behave in a sovereign manner is lacking.[20]

Beyond these general programs, discrete policy sectors such as customs and tax collection, oil revenue management and distribution, port and maritime security, air traffic control, central banking, commercial law, and police and judiciary reform all lend themselves to focused cooperation between local and external authorities. The tools and techniques of counterproliferation and counterterrorism could make significant contributions to broader, concerted state-building initiatives—for example, vulnerable areas such as immigration control, corruption, and criminal business activity can—potentially— be systematically addressed through upgraded intelligence sharing and strengthened multilateral cooperation on forensic accounting and asset tracing.

There is no shortage of tools and resources for tackling the weak state challenge. A brief visit to any recent G-8 summit Web site will reveal a veritable cornucopia of individual programs and commitments of engagement between G-8 members and developing areas such as Africa. Some of these inventories bear closer resemblance to a laundry list than a strategy. The need is for joint planning that produces decisions on a country or regional focus, sequencing, and burden sharing. The challenge of state failure is not a U.S. project, and it certainly is not a short-term undertaking. Choices must be made, priorities set, burdens shared internationally. A good starting place is to obtain a clearer understanding of which manifestations of state failure produce which consequences,[21] and what is the sequence for repairing a weak or weakening state.

CONCLUSION

Since the Berlin Wall came down in 1989, the United States and its leading allies have been exploring a new basis for grand strategy. That historic watershed ended the age when Western democracies faced monolithic totalitarian adversaries. It also began a period of experimentation, an age of discretionary foreign policy where political elites, interest groups, and nongovernmental organizations openly debated which challenges and threats to focus on. After September 11, 2001, one might have expected that this period of strategic disorientation would end. Instead, the opportunity for considered reappraisal was taken over by the "global war on terrorism." While it is essential to contain and defeat terror networks and to stop WMD proliferation, this has been in many respects a "war of choice" that overlooks the broader context of the age.

The examples discussed here confirm that the ideas and instruments exist not only for prosecuting the campaign against terrorism and weapons proliferation but for a comprehensive grand strategy capable of building stronger states, more stable regions, and more peaceful societies. The world's leading nations will inexorably come to recognize the need for this broadened strategy and to appreciate the limits of a narrow strategic focus on terror and proliferation. No single power can address the range and depth of conflict management challenges outlined in this chapter. To develop the necessary traction, the United States requires the assets, insights, hard- and soft-power resources, diplomatic reach, broad-based ownership, and legitimacy that are available only through effective multilateral diplomacy. Smart statecraft would concentrate on how best to strengthen existing institutions and structures while laying the basis for new ones that, over time, will produce an international system less conflicted and less dependent on a few powerful actors. In the meantime, however, much will depend on the United States—in league with its closest European and Asian part-

ners—being able to generate the vision and coherence to show the way.

NOTES

1. The term "grand strategy" is used in various ways by scholars and others. As used here, it encompasses the deployment of the full range of national assets and resources toward the advancement/defense of a nation's primary purposes. In this sense, it is consistent with the elaboration in Edward N. Luttwak, *Strategy: The Logic of War and Peace* (Cambridge, Mass.: Harvard University Press, 2001), 209ff. See also Philip Windsor, *Strategic Thinking* (Boulder, Colo.: Lynne Rienner, 2002). An example of grand strategic analysis is John Lewis Gaddis, "Grand Strategy in the Second Term," *Foreign Affairs* (January–February 2005). For an assessment of grand strategy choices in the mid-1990s, see Barry R. Posen and Andrew L. Ross, "Competing Visions for U.S. Grand Strategy," *International Security* 21, no. 3 (Winter 1996–97).

2. For further readings on this debate, see Fen Osler Hampson, *Madness in the Multitude: Human Security and World Disorder* (Oxford: Oxford University Press, 2002); S. Neil MacFarlane and Yuen Foong Khong, eds., *Human Security and the UN: A Critical Perspective* (Bloomington: Indiana University Press, 2006); and Roland Paris, "Human Security: Paradigm Shift or Hot Air?" *International Security* 26, no. 2 (2001): 87–102.

3. See Francis Fukuyama, ed., *Nation-Building beyond Afghanistan and Iraq* (Baltimore, Md.: Johns Hopkins University Press, 2006).

4. See interview with General Abizaid in David Ignatius, "Achieving Real Victory Could Take Decades," *Washington Post*, December 26, 2004.

5. Some details of the breakthrough are available in "The Libyan Disarmament Model: Aberration or Precedent?" *Strategic Comments* 10, no. 4 (London: IISS, May 2004). On the political background and diplomatic context prior to the breakthrough, see *U.S.-Libyan Relations: Toward Cautious Reengagement*, Atlantic Council of the United States Policy Paper (Washington, D.C.: Atlantic Council of the United States, April 2003). For other views of how it occurred and the significance of the Libyan case, see Jon B. Alterman, "Libya and the U.S.: The Unique Libyan Case," *Middle East Quarterly* (Winter

2006); Flynt L. Leverett, "Why Libya Gave Up the Bomb," *New York Times*, January 23, 2004; and Thomas Donnelly and Vance Serchuk, *Beware the "Libyan Model,"* (Washington, D.C.: American Enterprise Institute, March 2004).

6. See Alterman, "Libya and the U.S."

7. Official U.S. information about this program can be located at http://usinfo.state.gov/products/pubs/proliferation/.

8. Geoffrey Kemp, *US and Iran: The Nuclear Dilemma: Next Steps* (Washington, D.C.: Nixon Center, 2004).

9. For a discussion of the more coercive options, see Richard N. Haass, "Regime Change and Its Limits," *Foreign Affairs* (July–August 2005).

10. These are the Balkans, the north and south Caucasus, the Israel-Syria-Palestine nexus, the Central Asian republics, India-Pakistan, the Andean nations, the Korean peninsula, the Persian Gulf, the Horn of Africa, West Africa's troubled zone (Sierra Leone, Guinea, Liberia, Côte d'Ivoire), the Great Lakes region of Central Africa, and the Sudan conflict zone (spilling into Eritrea, Ethiopia, Uganda, Chad, and the Democratic Republic of the Congo).

11. An insightful discussion of the uses and limits of "friends" groups is by Theresa Whitfield, *A Crowded Field: Groups of Friends, the United Nations and the Resolution of Conflict*, occasional paper of the Center on International Cooperation (New York: New York University, June 2005).

12. Benjamin Goldsmith, *Here There Be Dragons: The Shanghai Cooperation Organization* (Washington, D.C.: Center for Defense Information, September 26, 2005).

13. Nina M. Serafino, *The Global Peace Operations Initiative: Background and Issues for Congress*, CRS Report for Congress (Washington, D.C.: U.S. Department of State, February 16, 2005), http://www.fas.org/sgp/crs/misc/RL32773.pdf.

14. *IISS News* (Winter 2005).

15. This discussion is drawn from Chester A. Crocker, Fen Osler Hampson, and Pamela Aall, *Taming Intractable Conflicts: Mediation in the Hardest Cases* (Washington, D.C.: United States Institute of Peace Press, 2004). A number of the cases mentioned in *Taming Intractable Conflicts* are discussed in detail in the editors' companion volume, *Grasping the Nettle: Analyzing Cases of Intractable Conflict* (Washington, D.C.: United States Institute of Peace Press, 2005).

16. Jeremy Weinstein, John Edward Porter, and Stuart E. Eizenstat, *On the Brink: Weak States and US National Security; A Report of the Commission on Weak States and US National Security* (Washington, D.C.: Center for Global Development, 2004). See also Robert Rotberg, "The Challenge of Weak, Failing, and Collapsed States," chapter 6 in this volume; Stewart Patrick, "Weak States and Global Threats: Assessing Evidence of 'Spillovers,'" Working Paper No. 73 (Washington, D.C.: Center for Global Development, January 2006); and Chester A. Crocker, "Engaging Failed States," *Foreign Affairs* (September–October 2003).

17. Works that indicate such an awareness include *The National Security Strategy of the United States of America* (Washington, D.C.: White House, September 17, 2002); and Condoleezza Rice, "Transformational Diplomacy: Remarks at Georgetown School of Foreign Service" (Washington, D.C.: U.S. Department of State, January 18, 2006).

18. Jonathan Stevenson, *Counterterrorism: Containment and Beyond*, Adelphi Paper 367 (Oxford: Oxford University Press for the IISS, 2004).

19. Francis Fukuyama, *State-Building: Governance and World Order in the 21st Century* (Ithaca, N.Y.: Cornell University Press, 2004). For critical essays on U.S. policy and the need for institutional memory and a capacity to learn from experience, see also Fukuyama, ed., *Nation-Building: Beyond Afghanistan and Iraq* (Baltimore, Md.: Johns Hopkins University Press, 2006).

20. See Stephen D. Krasner, "Sharing Sovereignty," chapter 36 in this volume; and James D. Fearon and David D. Laitin, "Neotrusteeship and the Problem of Weak States," *International Security* (Spring 2004).

21. See Patrick, "Weak States and Global Threats."

21

A FRAMEWORK
FOR SUCCESS
INTERNATIONAL INTERVENTION
IN SOCIETIES EMERGING
FROM CONFLICT

Daniel Serwer and Patricia Thomson

SINCE THE END OF THE COLD WAR, THE United States and the international community have repeatedly intervened in societies emerging from conflict. Multinational interventions in Cambodia, Somalia, Haiti, Bosnia, Kosovo, Sierra Leone, Liberia, the Democratic Republic of the Congo, Afghanistan, and Iraq have cost thousands of lives and hundreds of billions of dollars. None of these operations has been an unqualified success, and many have faced costly and at times deadly obstacles. It is hardly necessary to argue how important it is for the United States and the international community to improve their capacity and effectiveness in what is euphemistically termed "postconflict reconstruction and stabilization."[1]

"Peacefare" is not as developed as warfare. Military organizations worldwide organize, plan, train, and fight within clearly established objectives, doctrine, and even internationally established laws of war. But once major fighting ends—and what the U.S. military calls "stability operations" begin—the civilians and their military counterparts operate without common doctrine, shared frameworks for planning, or joint training. Just as military forces systematically plan and train, so too should the civilians who undertake an international intervention. And they should do it together with the military, or at least on the basis of a common framework.

The number and variety of international civilians involved are themselves bewildering. A typical international intervention might include officials and diplomats of numerous foreign governments and intergovernmental organizations (IGOs) such as the United Nations, the World Bank, the UN Development Programme (UNDP), and the World Health Organization; regional organizations such as the African Union and the Organization for Security and Cooperation in Europe (OSCE); well-known nongovernmental organizations (NGOs) such as Mercy Corps and World Vision, as well as hundreds of other, smaller organizations; and private-sector employees, including contractors and private security firms.

369

The military and police forces, which typically include former warring parties, as well as international peacekeepers and police from several (and sometimes dozens of) countries, are also likely to feature among the actors in the intervention. This creates a truly confusing mix of personnel, organizational objectives, and command-and-control relationships.

In 2005, the U.S. Defense Department issued a directive putting stability operations on an equal footing with warfighting as a military function.[2] Shortly thereafter, President George Bush signed a directive that established an overall U.S. government policy for reconstruction and stabilization, designating the State Department as the lead agency.[3] As a result, key U.S. government agencies are now tasked with giving stability operations the priority and attention they deserve. Yet the civilians remain far behind in virtually every aspect. The State Department's Office of the Coordinator for Reconstruction and Stabilization (S/CRS) is making progress but does not have the personnel or resources required to lead the U.S. contribution to extraordinarily complex and challenging operations.

Other countries and intergovernmental organizations are also beefing up their civilian capacities, though they remain thinly staffed and poorly financed. Germany, the United Kingdom, France, Australia, Denmark, Norway, and Canada have designated advisers or established units to coordinate some aspects of civilian operations in societies emerging from conflict. The United Nations, in addition to enhancing the capabilities of its Secretariat, is mobilizing a Peacebuilding Commission that will eventually oversee international interventions in their later stages.[4] UNDP, the World Bank, and other specialized UN agencies are likewise building up their stabilization and reconstruction capabilities. The European Union has created a multifunctional civilian reserve for deployment in international interventions.

While their military counterparts may have prepared for years for war, the civilians who manage an international intervention in a society emerging from conflict often first learn of their role after the signing of the peace agreement, or at best shortly before. Each mission is operated according to its own design (or lack thereof). The high representative in Bosnia (the senior civilian implementer of the Dayton Peace Accords) for years had no publicly available organizational chart because of the difficulties of determining the relationships among different parts of his mission. The United Nations discovered that it would lead the civilian intervention in Kosovo only after the military-technical agreement ending the warfare was signed. Even UN missions have not been standardized, though the secretary-general is now trying to enforce an "integrated" structure in which his special representative is the senior coordinator in-country for the UN "family." But the United Nations is often a small part of an international intervention; in Iraq, for instance, it has not been clear how it and many other international organizations fit into a structure led by the United States.

This kind of "ad hocery" has the great advantage of flexibility, which we do not want to lose. One size will not fit all. However, it does not allow the civilian side of an international intervention to come together quickly in a structure whose goals are clear. Nor does it allow military personnel and civilians to figure out with whom they need to collaborate. Moreover, it makes evaluation of progress difficult: if the goals are not defined, success and failure are hard to gauge.

A STANDARDIZED FRAMEWORK

In an effort to clarify what is required for success, we set forth a framework (see figure 1) to be shared by military, government, NGO, IGO, and even private-sector leaders, as well as by domestic leaders in societies emerging from conflict. While this framework should be used in predeployment planning and training, it is designed to guide operations and ensure

Figure 1. United States Institute of Peace Framework for Success: Societies Emerging from Conflict

	Safe and Secure Environment	Rule of Law	Stable Democracy	Sustainable Economy	Social Well-Being
DESIRED END-STATES					
CRITICAL LEADERSHIP RESPONSIBILITIES	• Build unity of purpose among the military, NGOs, IGOs, government authorities, and the private sector • Develop and execute integrated plans that are based on the peace agreement or mission mandate • Ensure involved players have the authority they need to succeed and adequate financial and staff resources • Build and maintain legitimacy • Engage the international community; establish peaceful relations with neighboring countries • Build constituencies for peace; deploy effective strategic communications and public awareness campaigns • Identify and address original and emerging drivers of conflict; manage spoilers • Collect and use intelligence; manage information effectively • Manage transitions from military to civilian and from international to local control				
KEY OBJECTIVES	• Prevent renewal of fighting (e.g., enforce cease-fire; secure weapons/stockpiles; disarm, demobilize, and reintegrate former fighters) • Protect civilians (e.g., counter organized crime, de-mine) • Ensure freedom of movement (e.g., for civilians, relief workers, peace monitors) • Protect key historical, cultural, and religious sites, as well as important buildings, property, and infrastructure • Protect witnesses and evidence of atrocities • Protect international borders, airspace, and ports of entry • Build effective security forces, under civilian control	• Establish coherent, legitimate, and just legal frameworks (e.g., constitution, criminal and civil frameworks) • Build effective and independent courts • Build effective police, customs, immigration, and border control forces • Build effective corrections system • Build effective legal profession/bar • Protect human rights • Ensure equal access to justice and equal application of the law • Promote public awareness and legal empowerment	• Develop legitimate systems of political representation at national, regional, and local levels (e.g., legislatures) • Build effective and legitimate executive institutions at national, regional and local levels (e.g., ministries, civil service) • Promote free and responsible media • Promote the creation of political parties • Promote robust civil society and civic participation (including minorities and marginalized groups)	• Reconstruct infrastructure (e.g., electricity, communications, transportation) • Promote sound fiscal/economic policy • Build effective and predictable regulatory and legal environment • Build effective financial and economic institutions (e.g., banks) • Create a viable workforce • Promote business development and sustainable employment; increase access to capital • Protect, manage, and equitably distribute natural resources/revenues • Limit/contain corruption and illicit economy	• Ensure the population is fed • Ensure the population has water • Ensure the population has shelter • Meet basic sanitation needs • Meet basic health needs • Build an effective education system • Enable displaced persons and refugees to return or relocate • Address legacy of past abuses (e.g., truth commissions) • Promote peaceful coexistence (e.g., interethnic, interfaith)

• The end-states, leadership responsibilities, and objectives included above and are not presented in any particular order. There is no "one-size-fits-all" solution, and the above framework will need to be tailored as circumstances warrant.
• This framework was developed drawing on the expertise of USIP staff and external advisors. It also draws upon the *Post-Conflict Reconstruction Task Framework* developed by the Association of the U.S. Army and CSIS, as well as the *U.S. Government Draft Planning Framework for Reconstruction, Stabilization, and Conflict Transformation*, prepared by S/CRS and the Joint Warfighting Center of JFCOM, with support from USIP. The framework also incorporates input from leaders of international intervention (collected during discussions at USIP on March 22 and 23, 2005).

interoperability in the time frame between when major combat ends and "sustainable peace" begins, meaning a peace that can be expected to persist without extraordinary international intervention.

The framework we set forth is based on both accumulated experience and extensive scholarly work since the end of the Cold War, which marked an important break in international objectives.[5] Particularly important is the research and expertise of the United States Institute of Peace (USIP), synthesized through a series of working sessions at USIP. Also of great importance is the work of the Center for Strategic and International Studies (CSIS) and the Association of the U.S. Army (AUSA), as well as two RAND volumes that provide indepth analysis of specific international interventions. We also drew on the *U.S. Government Draft Planning Framework for Reconstruction, Stabilization, and Conflict Transformation,* prepared by the State Department's Office of the Coordinator for Reconstruction and Stabilization and the Joint Warfighting Center of the Joint Forces Command, with support from USIP.[6] In addition, this chapter builds on the input from leaders of international interventions collected during discussions at USIP on March 22 and 23, 2005, as well as on publications by USIP's researchers and practitioners.[7]

FOCUS ON END-STATES AND OBJECTIVES

While the framework presented here builds on the work of others, it is different in several important ways. Unlike earlier frameworks, this framework starts with end-states—the ultimate goals of a society emerging from conflict. While particular circumstances vary dramatically, there is a remarkable degree of consensus in the post–Cold War period on the end-states desired, even though there may be a good deal of debate on how best to achieve them. We believe that all societies emerging from conflict should aspire, explicitly or implicitly, to five end-states: a safe and secure environment, the rule of law, a stable democracy, a sustainable economy, and social well-being. For the purposes of this framework, the end-states describe the place a society emerging from conflict ultimately wishes to be. For those familiar with strategic planning, they are the strategic goals—the ultimate ambitions that anchor a plan.

The five end-states are not mutually exclusive. One of the challenges when developing a framework of this sort is to ensure that it is useful and substantive, but also not burdensomely complicated. When balancing these demands, it is necessary to divide interrelated components. For example, a safe and secure environment is important in and of itself, but it is also an important condition for a sustainable economy. Similarly, rule of law is an important goal on its own, but it is also important to the other four end-states. The end-states of this framework should not be treated as distinct and independent "pillars," but rather as interconnected components that influence one another.

Within each end-state is a series of objectives. These represent some of the key things that need to be accomplished in order to achieve the desired end-state and serve as an added level of specificity that further defines the end-state. We have tried to focus on "ends," not "means," but in some cases this distinction is a tenuous one—a matter of definition, not substance. Moreover, the objectives within each end-state are often interrelated. For example, free and responsible media help ensure effective and legitimate executive institutions that in turn contribute to a stable democracy. Or consider economic development: building effective financial and economic institutions contributes to a regulatory and legal environment that promotes business development, which contributes to a sustainable economy. Ultimately, we included objectives that are (1) relatively easy to define, (2) at least partly within the control of those engaged in international intervention, and (3) measurable (i.e., corresponding metrics can be identified and used to gauge success).

One of the important merits of building the framework around end-states and corresponding objectives is that such a framework can more readily be standardized across missions than one based on specific tasks. There is no one-size-fits-all approach for peacebuilding in societies emerging from conflict, and the tasks of an intervention change—but end-states and objectives do not. A framework that starts at this strategic level can be used in a standardized fashion from operation to operation. High-order standardization of this sort, while still allowing for a great deal of flexibility to adapt to particular circumstances, greatly facilitates strategic planning and operational coordination among different organizations: international and local, civilian and military, official and private.

More importantly, by creating a strategic framework, we not only enhance our ability to plan for, train for, and coordinate these complex missions but also keep our efforts focused on the ultimate results we hope to achieve.

CRITICAL LEADERSHIP RESPONSIBILITIES

This framework also includes "critical leadership responsibilities." We know that without several critical components—from resources and authority to international support and legitimacy—a mission will falter or fail. Earlier frameworks tend to embed these types of responsibilities within mission activities, thereby disguising or even entirely hiding the responsibilities. By highlighting critical leadership responsibilities, which cut across all five end-states, the USIP framework presents a more accurate picture of the elements required for mission success.

UNDOING LINEARITY: ALLOWING CUSTOMIZATION

Articulating a framework, whether in words or graphically, necessitates that the content

be presented in some order. Such sequencing can be misinterpreted as implying a linear progression of mutually exclusive phases. This framework should not be used this way. The end-states, objectives, and leadership responsibilities included are not presented in any particular order—neither in terms of priority nor as regards sequencing. In a society emerging from conflict, instability on the ground consistently thwarts linear progression. Moreover, a particular mission's resources and challenges will in large part dictate which activities are undertaken and, perhaps more important, in which order. In many cases, only some parts of the framework will apply. This framework will need to be tailored as circumstance warrant.

THE END RESULT: EMPOWERING STRATEGIC PLANNING AND COORDINATION

In sum, the framework presented herein has several important features. First, it is crafted to be useful to (and ideally shared by) all the actors involved in postconflict situations, civilian and military, enhancing interoperability. Second, it is organized around end-states, ensuring a focus on the ultimate goals of societies emerging from conflict. Third, it recognizes that there are critical leadership responsibilities that have a crosscutting impact crucial to mission success. Fourth, it is designed to allow for easy customization, recognizing that each postconflict mission will be unique. Fifth, the framework reflects the fact that international interventions are multifaceted, synchronous, and dynamic: soldiers, government officials, NGOs, IGOs, local populations, aid workers, and others are all working at the same time on different aspects of a problem whose relevance changes over time. Sixth and last, while this framework is most valuable in planning and operations, it also has great value as an underlying structure from which training programs, monitoring efforts, and coordination mechanisms should cascade.

END-STATE I: A SAFE AND SECURE ENVIRONMENT

A safe and secure environment is one in which citizens and intervenors can go about their business without fear of being caught up in fighting. This is the intervening military's, and often the local population's, most immediate concern in a society emerging from conflict, but getting to this end-state requires extensive collaboration with civilian authorities. This is especially true as time passes: *the role of intervening military forces is much stronger at the beginning of a successful international intervention than it will be toward the end.* For example, in Bosnia NATO began in 1996 with an intervention force of about sixty thousand troops, reduced to twenty thousand a few years later. NATO in 2004 turned the military responsibility over to the European Union, which in 2005 had only about two thousand soldiers in Bosnia. At the same time, the belligerents of the Bosnian war were being demobilized and Bosnia's civilian police force was being vetted and retrained, so that threats to the peace were sharply reduced and the civilian role in preventing violence was sharply increased.

The most immediate threat to a safe and secure environment is generally a return to fighting by the former warring parties. Cease-fires are not self-enforcing—it can take months after a peace agreement is signed for a cease-fire to become fully effective, and reversion to warfare can remain a serious risk for a long time. Angola's lengthy guerrilla war saw numerous cease-fires that broke down, as has Sri Lanka's. Even when belligerents are demobilized, as in Iraq, the fighters may still represent a serious threat to public order, as the U.S.-led coalition that deposed Saddam Hussein discovered during the Baghdad looting that followed its victory.

What to do with the former fighters and their weapons is a major challenge in many societies emerging from conflict. Their heavy weapons can be placed in cantonments, but the fighters will often keep their small arms and

> **Safe and Secure Environment**
>
> - Prevent renewal of fighting (e.g., enforce cease-fire; secure weapons/stockpiles; disarm, demobilize, and reintegrate former fighters)
> - Protect civilians (e.g., counter organized crime, de-mine)
> - Ensure freedom of movement (e.g., for civilians, relief workers, peace monitors)
> - Protect key historical, cultural, and religious sites, as well as important buildings, property, and infrastructure
> - Protect witnesses and evidence of atrocities
> - Protect international borders, airspace, and ports of entry
> - Build effective defense forces, under civilian control

it may take decades to map and remove the land mines they use to mark territory under their control. It took years after the Northern Ireland peace agreement was signed for the Irish Republican Army to agree to give up its arms. The fighters often include not only professional and citizen soldiers in uniform but also others more difficult to identify: child soldiers, local or ethnic militias, paramilitary police, intelligence services, and criminal organizations. Some of these can be brought into the police or newly organized defense forces, but many may be unacceptable in those roles, either because of their previous behavior toward the local population or because they lack qualifications.

No intervention can afford to focus exclusively on military issues, even initially. Protection of civilians is vital. They face a wide spectrum of security threats: land mines may dot their fields, former soldiers may seize their property, and organized criminals may extract protection money. The civilian population will not see the benefits of peace unless these threats are countered: at the very least, land mines need to be marked and thugs signaled that they will not be allowed to take what is not theirs.

Freedom of movement is often highly restricted in the immediate aftermath of conflict, especially when military forces remain on territory that they feel is not entirely secure. After the Dayton agreements ended the Bosnian war, it took months for the NATO implementation force to take down the checkpoints that the former warring parties believed were necessary to protect the territory they controlled. Real freedom of movement for civilians, however, was not established until several years later, when the international civilian authorities imposed ethnically neutral license plates throughout the country, thus enabling people to drive wherever they wanted without being readily identifiable as Serb, Croat, or Bosniak. Seven years after the NATO-Yugoslavia war, freedom of movement is still not firmly established in Kosovo, in part because Serbs use Belgrade-issued license plates that are readily distinguishable from the UN-issued license plates that Albanians use.

The need for accountability for previous behavior puts complex and weighty burdens on international intervenors, many of whom will not be able to tell one competing group from another and will not know much about the prior conflict. Protection of mass grave sites and witnesses to massacres is not something they expect to have to do—but they may be the only ones available to do it. Similarly, with long-term relationships and reconstruction in mind, involved forces must protect key historical, cultural, and religious sites, as well as important buildings, property, and infrastructure. It is generally agreed that the failure to protect key institutions from Saddam Hussein's "stay-behind" operation severely hampered subsequent stabilization and reconstruction efforts in Iraq.

Borders, airspace, and ports of entry must also be protected in short order. In the long term, a safe and secure environment requires creating fully vetted local defense forces under civilian control. Also, customs, immigration, and border patrol forces must be part of either the military or law enforcement institutions. This effort takes years, not months, and until it is accomplished international intervenors will have to carry at least some of the burden. In Liberia, Sierra Leone, and the Democratic Republic of the Congo, it will be many years before newly constituted institutions can defend the borders; in the meantime, UN forces do their best to assist.

END-STATE II: RULE OF LAW

While military forces aim to establish a safe and secure environment, the rule of law requires much more: security of individuals and accountability for crimes committed against them. This requires the full spectrum of civilian law-and-order capabilities—from criminal intelligence and investigation to arrest, prosecution, and defense, through to sentencing and incarceration. All too often, some element of this spectrum is missing, causing systemic

---

Rule of Law

- Establish coherent, legitimate, and just legal frameworks (e.g., constitution; criminal and civil frameworks)
- Build effective and independent courts
- Build effective police, customs, immigration, and border control forces
- Build effective corrections system
- Build effective legal profession/bar
- Protect human rights
- Ensure equal access to justice and equal application of the law
- Promote public awareness and legal empowerment

failure. *Establishing the full spectrum of rule-of-law capabilities is a major, immediate challenge.* The management of the transition from military responsibility for rule of law to international civilian (eventually local civilian) institutions is one of the most difficult problems confronting mission leadership.

The first step in international interventions is often determining applicable law. Once the Taliban had fallen in Afghanistan, it made no sense for the international intervention to continue to apply the Taliban's draconian version of sharia. But there were literally no copies left in Afghanistan of the pre-Taliban laws, which the Taliban had systematically destroyed. These had to be painstakingly reassembled from foreign sources and translated, so that internationals as well as Afghans would know what was in them. In Kosovo, many months were lost when the United Nations tried to insist on application of Serbian laws, which it thought were still valid. The 90 percent of the population that was Albanian (including all the Albanian judges) refused to acknowledge Serbian laws and insisted on application of laws from the period of Kosovo's autonomy.

Beyond a determination of initially applicable law, societies emerging from conflict will likely require a legal reform agenda, either because the previous regime was abusive or because the country is divided into distinct legal regimes, which somehow have to be reconciled with one another. In Sudan, decades of civil war have left the north with avowedly sharia laws determined by the government in Khartoum, laws that are not accepted in the largely non-Muslim south. Moreover, in much of rural Sudan the formal legal system is rarely applied; instead, tribal chieftains administer justice according to a customary system. Although widely accepted, the customary system does not appear to meet international human rights standards. This problem also exists in Afghanistan, where the formal system barely extends beyond Kabul and the customary system prevails elsewhere.

Many societies emerging from conflict will also require a new constitution. In Sudan, the south has a new constitution, and the peace agreement is incorporated by reference into the existing national constitution, which will need to be changed. In Kosovo, the constitutional framework was written by internationals and imposed. In Iraq, Ayatollah Ali al-Sistani, the most revered of the Shiite clerics, refused to allow this to happen and insisted that the constitution be prepared on the authority of an elected assembly and approved in a popular referendum.

Laws and constitutions mean little without the rest of the justice system, which includes institutions (e.g., police, customs, immigration, border patrol, courts, corrections); processes (e.g., investigation, arrest, indictment, trial, incarceration); and people (e.g., police, prosecutors, defenders, judges, civil lawyers, corrections officers, clerks, prison guards). All of these may already exist, but few may meet the standards that long-term success requires. Vetting, training and retraining, and eventually reforming educational systems will all likely be required. Building up these institutions, processes, and personnel takes years and even decades, not months. Moreover, it has to be an iterative process: the police used in the immediate aftermath of an intervention will look sorely inadequate a year or two later. The Bosnian police had to be vetted half a dozen times in the decade after the war, and the Iraqi police will no doubt require several rounds of vetting before those who are loyal to militias rather than the state are removed.

All of this cannot be done at once, and the question of priorities therefore arises. While ordinary citizens may worry more about petty crime and theft, serious crimes (including organized crime and illicit networks) and property claims are often more important from the perspective of building peace. Former belligerents and their secret services, skilled in sanctions busting and smuggling, readily develop into organized-crime networks that finance "spoilers" (who oppose peacebuilding efforts) and become a major obstacle to reaching all the end-states. Property claims are important because they are so often a driver of conflict. Seven years after the war in Kosovo, unsettled Serbian church property claims generated Albanian demonstrations that could easily have turned violent. The return of property to displaced people and refugees in Bosnia and Croatia was a vital step in the peacebuilding process, since people cannot return to their homes if they are unable to regain possession.

It is impossible to eliminate all major criminals from the scene instantaneously (though that is often what many people in a society emerging from conflict want). Peace agreements are made between competitors for power, by definition competitors willing to use violence. Therefore, those who make them will seek to capture and hold on to the resources required to keep them in power during peacetime. This was especially apparent in Afghanistan, where warlords who had fought for decades held on to power, becoming governors of their regions, members of parliament, and government ministers. While many may complain that peace benefited mainly the former belligerents, others would argue that it is better to have them inside the tent playing politics rather than outside playing war games.

It follows that protection of human rights, as well as equal access to and application of justice, will be far from satisfactory in the immediate aftermath of many conflicts. This is frustrating to locals, who have often spent years being abused and expect immediate improvements, as do international intervenors, who do not want to preside over continuing abuses. Afghan women, prevented even from going to school under the Taliban, have seen dramatic improvements in their lives but still face obstacles to their full participation in political and social life, including access to justice. Often the best that can be done early in an intervention is to promote public awareness of rights, while building the kind of judicial system that will eventually ensure full access and equal application of justice. Only with a well-informed and empowered public will the longer-term goal be reached.

END-STATE III: STABLE DEMOCRACY

All international interventions since the end of the Cold War have aimed at establishing democracies, some sooner and some later. Legitimate systems of political representation at the national, regional, and local levels are defining components of democracy.

Eventually power, which during war comes from the barrel of a gun, needs to come from a ballot box. A stable democracy is one that regularly elects a representative legislature in accordance with established rules and in a manner recognized as "free and fair." But there is much more to establishing legitimate systems of political representation than holding elections. Legislatures must be designed consistent with a legal framework and/or constitution. Officials must be trained, processes created, and rules established.

It is important to recognize that early national elections in a highly polarized society often empower hard-liners and criminals, who

---

Stable Democracy

- Develop legitimate systems of political representation at national, regional, and local levels (e.g., legislatures)

- Build effective and legitimate executive institutions at national, regional, and local levels (e.g., ministries, civil service)

- Promote free and responsible media

- Promote the creation of political parties

- Promote robust civil society and civic participation (including minorities and marginalized groups) may quickly institutionalize politics as a zero-sum game. It is generally far better to hold provincial or local elections first, thus minimizing the degree of national polarization and allowing leaders to emerge who win election on the grounds of being able to deliver services or meet the demands of their constituents. One of the difficulties in focusing early attention on local political processes is the lack of intervenor capacity at the local level. Military units too often find themselves tasked to convene local councils or administer local government because there are no civilians available to take on the task. This is unfortunate. As is the case with all five end-states, there is a compelling need for deployment of civilian capacity to assist with local governance along with the troops as soon as possible after an intervention commences.

In Bosnia, the United States demanded a national election within one year of the deployment of NATO forces in order to fulfill a presidential promise to Congress. Nationalists, taking advantage of a constitution negotiated at Dayton that gave them much of what they wanted, won those elections and have dominated the political scene in Bosnia ever since. This mistake was avoided in Kosovo, where municipal elections were held first, displacing local governments that had been appointed by the Kosovo Liberation Army and opening political opportunities for more moderate forces. In Afghanistan, repeatedly delayed national elections put a relatively moderate president in place. In Iraq, two rounds of elections held under still difficult security conditions polarized the population and political parties along ethnic lines. Thus, while it is vitally important to build legitimate and representative legislatures at all levels, it may often be wiser to postpone elections than to hold them under grossly undemocratic conditions.

Stable democracies require not only legitimate systems of political representation but also effective executive institutions. It takes years, not months, to repair the damage of war

and to build effective ministries and an effective civil service at all levels of governance. In the meantime, elements of the old regime or rebel forces may suffice, or it may be necessary for the international intervention to take on governing responsibilities itself or to appoint executives. In Kosovo, the United Nations actually administered, whereas in Bosnia the so-called high representative was eventually given virtually dictatorial powers to remove officials and to impose laws. In Afghanistan, the overall political process was negotiated at a conference in Bonn, but the United Nations insisted on playing a more behind-the-scenes implementation role inside Afghanistan. This worked well. In Iraq, the Americans initially planned to decapitate the Iraqi ministries and quickly turn governing authority over to those who had opposed Saddam Hussein, but in the end they had to establish a coalition occupation authority to govern the country directly for the better part of a year.

Stable democracies also require free and responsible media, multiple political parties, and a robust civil society. Free media often crop up quickly in the aftermath of conflict and there are well-established international organizations committed to training and professionalizing journalism (the Institute for War and Peace Reporting, Internews, and IREX, to name just a few). Responsible media are a separate question. Media in societies emerging from conflict are all too often sensationalist and highly partisan. In Kosovo, one newspaper chose to publish the names of Serbs alleged to have committed atrocities under Milosevic; murders of the alleged perpetrators followed. Media commissions or voluntary agreements to restrain media may be necessary to prevent abuse. Likewise, political parties and civil society organizations grow quickly in societies emerging from conflict, but all too often those parties and organizations are based on ethnic identity or association with one of the warring sides rather than on serious political programs. Veterans' groups and political parties focused on protecting narrow ethnic interests are not the kind of robust civil society democracy requires.

END-STATE IV: A SUSTAINABLE ECONOMY

Economies generally react well to the end of war. All sorts of licit and illicit commerce previously inhibited by hostilities break out quickly. Ordinary citizens who have lived with enormous uncertainty during war may have surprisingly large stashes of cash, gold, food, gasoline, and other valuables, all of which suddenly become available in the marketplace. Add to this the billions of dollars in international assistance money as well as the presence of tens of thousands—or even hundreds of thousands—of foreign soldiers and civilians, many willing to pay premium prices for translators, drivers, and other services. It is common to see extremely rapid economic growth of the local economy, from a very depressed base, in the first year or two after war.

Much of this is, however, a temporary bubble, one that creates its own share of problems by sharply increasing income inequalities, denuding local government and organizations of their educated and capable cadres, and opening opportunities for corruption. *What an international intervention needs to do in the immediate aftermath of war is not to worry about growth per se but to focus on those elements that will enable the economy to become self-sustaining.* These elements include physical infrastructure, sound fiscal and economic policy, an effective and predictable regulatory and legal environment, effective financial and economic institutions, a viable workforce, business development and increased access to capital, and husbanding of natural resources—things that do not necessarily produce immediate economic benefits but will enable sustained growth in the future.

The most important players in many of these areas are the private sector and the World Bank, with the International Monetary Fund and bilateral assistance playing secondary but

---

Sustainable Economy

- Reconstruct infrastructure (e.g., electricity, communications, transportation)
- Promote sound fiscal/economic policy
- Build effective and predictable regulatory and legal environment
- Build effective financial and economic institutions (e.g., banks)
- Create a viable workforce
- Promote business development and sustainable employment; increase access to capital
- Protect, manage, and equitably distribute natural resources/revenues
- Limit/contain corruption and illicit economy

---

important roles. A number of societies emerging from conflict have also benefited enormously from the return of diaspora economic experts: Serbia after the fall of Milosevic brought back internationally trained economists in key positions, as did Afghanistan after the fall of the Taliban. Bringing back economic experts is often less controversial than bringing back experts to help shape policy in more politically sensitive areas.

As the threat of violence fades in a society emerging from conflict, the threat of corruption and illicit activities grows, or, more accurately, the perception of the threat grows. During conflict, smuggling of gasoline or the use of secret funds to buy arms is common. But the people who make a living from these activities do not like to abandon them when the conflict ends. Moreover, new opportunities arise as government regulation and taxation take hold. Societies emerging from conflict need mechanisms for accountability and control of finances that do not come naturally and often need to be built up from next to nothing. Even three years after the fall of Saddam Hussein, a significant percentage of Iraq's oil is disappearing into the black market, often to be reimported at great profit into a market where domestic oil products are sold at artificially low prices. In the oil-poor countries of the Balkans, sale of state assets at preferred prices to political favorites was common. Transparency and accountability are vital.

None of the efforts so far outlined is likely to quickly satisfy the biggest demand of the local population: jobs. While informal employment is likely to increase rapidly, formal employment for less educated people, including former combatants, may remain difficult to find; what constitutes "formal" employment may even be unclear. While there may be good reasons in particular circumstances to employ large numbers of people in nonsustainable jobs such as cleaning the streets, the main focus should be on creating the conditions for a self-sustaining economy.

END-STATE V: SOCIAL WELL-BEING

The most immediate needs of a society emerging from conflict are often all too clear: food, water, shelter, basic sanitation, and health care. Elaborate and tested international mechanisms exist for delivering these basic needs: the World Food Programme, the World Health Organization, UNICEF, and international NGOs such as the International Rescue Committee and Mercy Corps, as well as bilateral assistance programs. They move remarkably quickly and agilely in most postwar situations, often because they were already present during the conflict. They also handle, albeit after a delay to allow the situation to settle, the return of displaced people and refugees who want to return to their homes.

Often less attention is paid to longer-term needs: developing educational systems (particularly ones that do not feed historic grievances), addressing past abuses, and promoting peaceful coexistence between parties to the conflict.

Social Well-Being

◆ Ensure the population is fed

◆ Ensure the population has water

◆ Ensure the population has shelter

◆ Meet basic sanitation needs

◆ Meet basic health needs

◆ Build an effective education system

◆ Enable displaced persons and refugees to return or relocate

◆ Address legacy of past abuses (e.g., truth commission)

◆ Promote peaceful coexistence (e.g., interethnic, interfaith, intercommunal)

The failure in many international interventions to fix the educational system is particularly harmful and risks laying the basis for future warfare. It was many years after the Dayton agreements that the internationals in Bosnia finally turned their attention to the fact that Muslims, Croats, and Serbs were being taught to continue to hate one another in their history classes. Local private initiative, not internationals or the education ministry, took on the task of curricular reform in Macedonia after the 2001 Albanian insurgency. While concern about "successor generations" is common in international interventions, the international resources flowing to primary and secondary curricula that will help determine students' attitudes on war and peace issues are often minimal.

The question of compensation for past damage is also one the internationals shy away from. Not so the locals. Bosnia is pursuing its genocide case at the World Court in The Hague against Serbia in part to establish a basis for compensation. Iraq's constitution provides for oil money to go preferentially to communities damaged under the Saddam Hussein regime. One of the main issues in the negotiations over Kosovo's final status will be compensation.

No amount of compensation is sufficient for many of those who suffered during war. In addition to justice, they demand acknowledgment of truth: what was done and why. This is not an easy demand to satisfy, especially when there is no outright victory or externally imposed regime change. Getting the truth out in South Africa after the fall of apartheid required amnesty for perpetrators, but that is not generally regarded as possible in instances of crimes against humanity or genocide. Various mechanisms have been used to satisfy the desire for an accounting of the facts of past wars and abusive regimes: truth commissions, judicial prosecution, reparations proceedings, property claim mechanisms, amnesty, communal or tribal justice, and lustration, to name a few. The specific circumstances determine what is appropriate.

The issue of reconciliation is even more difficult to address than are the issues of truth and justice. Many people in societies emerging from conflict care little to be reconciled with those who killed, tortured, or maimed their families and friends or who tolerated or supported the cruelty. At the same time, it is hard to see how a country such as Rwanda, for example, can move ahead unless it combines some degree of reconciliation with its mechanisms for justice, since there were so many people involved in its mass killings. The International Criminal Tribunal for Rwanda and the country's national courts can handle only a small percentage of the crimes committed. Most cases are handled, controversially, through a locally administered justice process that establishes wrongdoing but allows certain perpetrators (those who did not plan or organize the genocide or commit particularly heinous crimes) to be reintegrated into society quickly. At the same time, letting off perpetrators can create an environment of impunity, thus increasing the chances of a return to past behavior.

While opinions differ on if—and how—to promote reconciliation, there is widespread agreement about the need to promote peaceful coexistence between parties to a previous conflict. Sustained interreligious, interethnic, and intercommunal dialogues are essential tools in the process of discovering and mitigating lingering drivers of conflict. So, too, are efforts to strengthen civil society organizations, professional organizations, and other groups that integrate and build relationships between former enemies. Within a year after the NATO-Yugoslavia war, the U.S. Army in a town in Kosovo asked USIP to train local Serb and Albanian leaders in negotiation techniques so that they could begin to talk with one another again. A former Serbian policeman and a former Kosovo Liberation Army fighter were among the trainees, some of whom subsequently established an NGO called the Council of Professionals, which organized interethnic cooperation along professional lines (e.g., among doctors, among lawyers, and among teachers). The council remained for years a mainstay of interethnic comity in a town that now prides itself on relatively good relations between Serbs and Albanians.

CRITICAL LEADERSHIP RESPONSIBILITIES

The five standard end-states and corresponding objectives are vital elements of the framework we propose. Leadership is also vital. Whether transformation efforts are led by an international body, a coalition of nations, or the domestic leaders of the country emerging from conflict, the success of those efforts depends on leaders shouldering a particular set of responsibilities. Based on extensive discussions with leaders of international interventions, we have identified nine leadership responsibilities that are critical to success.

Build unity of purpose among the military, NGOs, IGOs, government authorities, and the private sector

The military has long recognized that unity of command is critical to success in warfare, but

Critical Leadership Responsibilities

- Build unity of purpose among the military, NGOs, IGOs, government authorities, and the private sector

- Develop and execute integrated plans that are based on the peace agreement or mission mandate

- Ensure involved players have the authority they need to succeed and adequate financial and staff resources

- Build and maintain legitimacy

- Engage the international community; establish peaceful relations with neighboring countries

- Build constituencies for peace; deploy effective strategic communications and public awareness campaigns

- Identify and address original and emerging drivers of conflict; manage "spoilers"

- Collect and use intelligence; manage information effectively

- Manage transitions from military to civilian and from international to local control

unity of command is rare in peacefare. While UN-led interventions will often have a single civilian special representative of the secretary-general (SRSG) who in principle commands both civilian and military UN assets, many other interventions do not. In any event, an SRSG does not generally command non-UN assets, and many NGOs answer only to their own governing bodies, even though they may be operating with funding from governments or IGOs. The best that can be hoped for on the civilian side of an international intervention is unity of purpose.

Focusing on end-states, which are outcomes all involved parties can generally support, is

one way of ensuring unity of purpose. But much more is needed: people involved in pursuing each of the end-states need to understand what the others are doing and why. In the aftermath of the Bosnian war, military forces under NATO command tried to prevent Muslims from returning to their homes in Serb-controlled areas, because of the likelihood that they would be attacked. But returns were, from the civilian perspective, an essential part of the peace process decided at Dayton. It took several years before the military and civilians worked out the modalities of returns so that the process could be done safely.

Some NGOs will resist efforts to ensure unity of purpose, especially those undertaken by a belligerent. In both Iraq and Afghanistan, NGOs resisted being viewed as "force multipliers" or partners of the intervening military forces. They preferred to maintain their independence, for both philosophical and practical reasons: association with belligerent forces may be viewed as inconsistent with their humanitarian purposes as well as dangerous to their personnel. This does not preclude some coordination between NGOs and the military, especially in assessing humanitarian needs and in identifying security threats. In fact, USIP is currently engaged in a civilian-military dialogue whose purpose is to develop the "business practices" governing cooperation between NGOs and the U.S. military in nonpermissive environments.

Develop and execute integrated plans that are based on the peace agreement or mission mandate

It is no accident that many of the most difficult issues in international intervention arise at the interface between military and civilian functions (e.g., dealing with serious crimes, returning refugees and internally displaced people, and demilitarizing, demobilizing, and reintegrating former warring parties). Meeting the needs in these areas generally requires thorough and immediate coordination of military and civilian capacities, as well as government and nongovernment actors. Achieving any of the five end-states requires similar long-term coordination.

Whether the effort is led by an international body, a coalition of nations, or the domestic leaders of the country emerging from conflict, the players of any postconflict effort should work together to develop a shared strategic plan that is based on the peace agreement or mission mandate. This plan should be the basis from which individual operational plans cascade. At a minimum, it should detail the ultimate outcomes desired, high-level strategies, roles and responsibilities, and agreed-on coordination mechanisms (e.g., regular meetings, shared reporting, and vehicles for escalating and solving shared problems). The plan should also identify key metrics that will be used to gauge progress and, ultimately, success, as well as monitoring mechanisms.

Ensure involved players have the authority they need to succeed and adequate financial and staff resources

The authority required in international interventions varies dramatically. Sudan's Comprehensive Peace Agreement between the Khartoum government and the Sudan People's Liberation Movement is being implemented —so far with some success—without strong authority being vested in internationals, who are acting as observers and monitors. Few believe that an agreement concerning the Darfur conflict in the west of Sudan could be implemented without a UN mission with the power to detain and even incarcerate. It is often difficult to know precisely what will be required: the "Bonn powers" that the high representative used in Bosnia were granted only three years after the war had ended, after many bitter disappointments in the way the peace was being implemented by local authorities.

It is clearly preferable to start with more authority than needed. Excess authority can always be given up; gaining additional authority requires difficult negotiations that are best completed well before an international intervention sets foot in-country. Authority is often bestowed by a UN Security Council resolution or a formal act by a regional body, though it may also be created through an agreement with a country previously at war.

It is common for the military and official civilian agencies involved in an international intervention to number in the dozens, with even more IGOs and NGOs involved. Some of these organizations may have mandates or authorities at variance with the overall effort, or they may operate with caveats about the kinds of cooperation they may undertake with other organizations, particularly military ones. Moreover, each NGO will generally have its own operational procedures, and even among official agencies belonging to the same government or international organization, operational authority and procedures may vary greatly. Understanding and respecting these variations, while continuing to focus on the desired end-states, is a key function of mission leadership.

Just as the authority granted to an organization involved in postconflict peacebuilding should be consistent with its mandate, so too should the resources allocated. The combination of ambitious mandates and inadequate resources will lead to failure. The kinds of resources required include not just financial resources but also trained and experienced staff with the specialized skills necessary to accomplish an operation's objectives. In Haiti, repeated international interventions have failed in part because of inadequate salaries for the local police and insufficient commitment among international intervenors to training and monitoring police performance.

Resources should come not only from outside. While many societies emerging from conflict are desperately poor, those societies always possess some indigenous resources, which those responsible for prior violence or an abusive regime will seek to hold on to so that they can perpetuate their hold on power. International intervenors need a robust capacity to assess financial flows, including the ability to obtain and interpret detailed information about revenue flows from natural resources, public utilities, and customs duties. They also need to understand smuggling networks (especially in countries previously subjected to international sanctions) and the disposition of state assets, which even in seemingly poor countries can be an important source of illegitimate wealth and power if left in the hands of belligerents, and an important contribution to peacebuilding if put in the right hands.

Build and maintain legitimacy

Legitimacy is in the eye of the beholder, and many of the beholders may not be friendly to an international intervention. There is no magic formula for acquiring and preserving legitimacy, but some ingredients of legitimacy are clear: concurrence by as broad a spectrum of the international community as possible (including, when possible, Security Council permanent members), respect from a broad cross section of the population in the country in which the intervention occurs, proper behavior by intervening military personnel and civilians, and fair treatment of all segments of the society emerging from conflict. Legitimacy is less a question of what is written on a piece of paper in New York and more a question of whether a warlord in Afghanistan feels constrained by the local population to give an American lieutenant the cooperation she is asking for in rebuilding a local school. Legitimacy is acquired in the field, not given by outsiders.

The NATO intervention in Kosovo had legitimacy with the Kosovo Albanian population, even though it lacked approval in the Security Council. Legitimacy is what the U.S. intervention in Afghanistan has generally had but the intervention in Iraq has generally lacked, especially among the Sunni Arab community. It is arguable that the United States has all the authority it requires in Iraq enshrined in carefully crafted UN Security Council resolutions. That authority has proven

insufficient, however, because some Sunnis have continued to view the intervention as illegitimate, a view that has gained enough adherents to slow progress toward the defined end-states.

Engage the international community; establish peaceful relations with neighboring countries

The support of the international community is important not only to grant authority and support legitimacy but also to enable cost and risk sharing. The United States intervened in Haiti in 1994, but less than a year later turned over the effort to the United Nations, thus sharing costs with other countries. Strong international support also allows more flexibility in dealing with emerging obstacles, as multinational coalitions can often bring to bear diplomatic, political, and economic pressure that exceeds the capacity of a single country. *At a minimum, efforts to build international support should target major donors or troop contributors, members of the Security Council, and pertinent regional powers or organizations.*

Neighboring states also have a particularly important role. If they are prepared to cooperate with the intervention, it becomes far more difficult for spoilers to find refuge or supplies. Both Iran and Syria appear to have aided resistance to the U.S.-led coalition in Iraq, while other neighbors have not done all they could to discourage the flow of arms and money to insurgents. Moreover, uncooperative neighbors can destabilize a multiethnic country such as Bosnia through political support to their co-nationals across the border. Progress in building peace in Bosnia has depended greatly on attitudes in Zagreb and Belgrade. There is serious doubt about whether Pakistan has done all it could to discourage Taliban and neo-Taliban resistance among Pashtuns in Afghanistan. Informal "friends of . . ." arrangements have often proved effective among neighboring states, provided the intervening powers are involved and provided the state in which the intervention takes place is also included in the deliberations.

Build constituencies for peace; deploy effective strategic communications and public awareness campaigns

An international intervention will initially find itself dealing primarily with the former warring parties, whose cooperation is needed in the early stages. *Attention needs to shift quickly to identifying and building relationships with political, ethnic, civic, business, and religious leaders looking to build a lasting peace.* It is also vital to engage women, minority and marginalized groups, and in some cases diaspora populations. If the intervention is successful, these people will be far more important in the longer term than the people who dominate the political and military landscape in the initial period. For example, the engagement of women in the peacebuilding process in Rwanda has contributed substantially to keeping the peace there.

A proactive strategic communication strategy and corresponding public awareness campaigns need to be developed and regularly refined. It cannot be assumed, as it often is by intervenors, that the local population will understand that foreign soldiers are there for the good of ordinary people. On the contrary, the intervening military forces and civilians will often be painted in a negative light or will even be seen as favoring one side. *An international intervention is not neutral—it favors those who support peace and opposes those who fail to cooperate—but it must be seen as fair and working toward goals that are supported by citizens who have an interest in peace.*

Identify and address original and emerging drivers of conflict; manage spoilers

Surprisingly, many international interventions do not seek to address drivers of conflict, either those that operated in the past or new ones that emerge after a peace agreement of some sort is reached. Nor do they necessarily target the spoilers who resist peacebuilding. It is as if the intervenors expect both warring parties and the underlying drivers of conflict to evaporate with the promise of peace and prosperity.

Rarely does this happen. *Conflicts that drove people to war continue after a peace agreement, and new ones emerge.* Unless this is recognized and countered, a return to violence becomes more likely. International interventions need to understand how power is redistributed in the peacebuilding process and anticipate that the losers are likely to resist. The Americans failed to recognize how Sunni Arabs in Iraq would react to democracy, which necessarily deprived them of their position as a privileged minority. The insurgency is at least in part an attempt to keep the Shiite Arabs in check despite their numerical superiority.

In general, organized criminal enterprises that are closely allied with the intelligence and security services of the former regime and extremist or corrupt politicians are also a serious threat to international interventions. Managing these spoilers is a critical leadership responsibility.

Ultimately, success requires a transformation —the development of institutions and processes (described in this framework) that parties can use to deal with conflicts via nonviolent means.

Collect and use intelligence; manage information effectively

For a long time, the United Nations and other international organizations resisted the need to collect and use intelligence effectively. National governments do not talk about their intelligence capacities, but they certainly have them, as do belligerents. *It is untenable for an international intervention that is less than 100 percent welcome to carry out its mission in an environment where spoilers are reading its communications but it is not reading theirs.* This was an important reason for UN failure in Bosnia in the early 1990s, and it came close to causing UN failure in Kosovo as well. Serbs, Muslims, Croats, and Albanians were all collecting intelligence on UN operations, which were rarely kept secret and thus surprised nobody. Only when the high representative in Bosnia learned to keep a planned bank raid secret was he able to collect the evidence needed to accuse top Croat politicians of stealing from the electrical utility. The UN Mission in Kosovo markedly improved its effectiveness against major criminals once it had the capability to tap telephone conversations.

There is also a broader information management issue: with dozens of organizations engaged, an international intervention has a hard time telling its left hand what its right hand is doing. Both informal networks and more formal information-sharing systems help to improve communication.

Finally, people deployed in international interventions find it difficult to learn about what has been done in similar situations elsewhere. The UN Best Practices Unit and USIP are aiming to make lessons learned and effective practices readily available to those engaged in international interventions, but there is still a long way to go.

Manage transitions from military to civilian and from international to local control

Ultimately, the objective in all international interventions today is to turn responsibility over to locals. Rarely will it be possible to start with leadership in local hands. More likely, intervenors will lead, with the intervening military forces serving as the default organization until adequate international civilian capacity is deployed. In the immediate aftermath of violent conflict, an intervening military will inevitably find itself with far more responsibilities than it wants to have. Both soldiers and civilians want to see the effort led by civilians as early in the intervention as feasible.

There is thus a need to manage the transition from a major international military role to a major international civilian role and eventually to full empowerment of locals. Many military organi-

zations would be content to separate warring parties or disband a defeated army and sit on the situation or, even better, withdraw. This will not, however, lead to success. The military needs to hand off to civilians, as all of the end-states are ultimately civilian rather than military responsibilities. Even where it proves possible to deploy civilian capabilities along with fighting forces, however, a society emerging from conflict knows that it is the people with the guns who hold ultimate power. Civilians can often do no better in the immediate aftermath of conflict than function as advisers to military commanders. It is the leadership—both military and civilian—that needs to plan and implement a transition, so that in due course the military will be advising the civilians rather than the other way around.

The most difficult part of the process is transition to local control. All too often, local authorities find it convenient to leave responsibility with an international mission, thus ducking difficult decisions and having someone else to blame for failures. Lack of local technical capacity and financial resources exacerbates the problem. Moreover, internationals may be enjoying their roles—and their perks. Few international interventions have found it easy to get out completely; in many countries, some remnant of the intervention organization may remain for a long time. It is important, however, for the leadership to have its eye from the beginning on building capacity that will ultimately enable locals to take over.

CONCLUSION

While the difficulties of dealing with societies emerging from conflict (whether internal or international) are so great that intervention should always be undertaken with caution, there is often no real choice in a world where failed states can become havens for international terrorism, sources of massive population movements, and threats to the entire international community.

We must wage peace as we wage war—with shared goals and corresponding strategies, with trained professionals and common doctrine, and with a focus on results. We hope that the framework presented here will facilitate training, planning, monitoring, interoperability, and coordination. Ultimately, we hope it will help societies emerging from conflict enjoy sustained peace.

NOTES

1. "Postconflict reconstruction and stabilization" implies that the conflict has stopped. But some violence often continues, and even when it does not, the original drivers of conflict often continue to exist and must be addressed. Also, rarely, if ever, is the aim of reconstruction something that existed previously or stabilization of the status quo—transformation rather than stabilization is the overall aim. "Democratic and economic transformation in societies emerging from conflict" would more accurately describe what is meant, but the phrase is admittedly an awkward one.

2. United States Department of Defense, "Military Support for Stability, Security, Transition, and Reconstruction (SSTR) Operations," Directive Number 3000.05, November 28, 2005, http://www.dtic.mil/whs/directives/corres/pdf/d300005_112805/d300005p.pdf (accessed June 20, 2006).

3. White House, "National Security Presidential Directive 44: Management of Interagency Efforts Concerning Reconstruction and Stabilization," December 7, 2005, http://www.fas.org/irp/offdocs/nspd/nspd-44pdf (accessed June 20, 2006).

4. United Nations General Assembly, "Resolution 60/180: The Peacebuilding Commission," Sixtieth Session, December 30, 2005, http://daccessdds.un.org/doc/UNDOC/GEN/N05/498/40/PDF/N0549840.pdf?OpenElement (accessed June 21, 2006); and United Nations Security Council, "Resolution 1645," December 20, 2005, http://daccessdds.un.org/doc/UNDOC/GEN/N05/654/17/PDF/N0565417.pdf?OpenElement (accessed June 21, 2006).

5. During the Cold War, it was accepted international practice to freeze conflicts using peacekeepers or other means, including dictatorship. Since the end of the Cold War, the international community has increasingly set as its explicit or implicit goal helping to ensure that societies emerging from conflict are free.

6. Robert C. Orr, ed., "Appendix One: Center for Strategic and International Studies and the Association of the United States Army Post-conflict Reconstruction Task Framework," *Winning the Peace: An American Strategy for Post-conflict Reconstruction* (Washington, D.C.: Center for Strategic and International Studies Press, 2004); United States Department of State, Office of the Coordinator of Reconstruction and Stabilization, "Post-conflict Reconstruction Essential Tasks," April 2005, http://www.state.gov/documents/organization/53464.pdf (accessed June 20, 2006); United States Joint Forces Command, *U.S. Government Draft Planning Framework for Reconstruction, Stabilization, and Conflict Transformation*, J7 Pamphlet, Version 1.0, December 2005, http://www.dtic.mil/doctrine/training/crs_pam051205.pdf (accessed June 20, 2006); James Dobbins, Seth G. Jones, Keith Crane, Andrew Rathmell, Brett Steele, Richard Teltschik, and Anga Timilsina, *The UN's Role in Nation-Building: From the Congo to Iraq* (Santa Monica, Calif.: RAND Corporation, 2005); and James Dobbins, John G. McGinn, Keith Crane, Seth G. Jones, Rollie Lal, Andrew Rathmell, Rachel Swanger, and Anga Timilsina, *America's Role in Nation-Building: From Germany to Iraq* (Santa Monica, Calif.: RAND Corporation, 2003).

7. United States Institute of Peace, "Reconstructing and Stabilizing War-Torn States: The Challenge before Us," March 22 and 23, 2005, http://www.usip.org/events/2005/0323_reconstructing.html (accessed June 20, 2006). See also Jock Covey, Michael J. Dziedzic, and Leonard R. Hawley, eds., *The Quest for Viable Peace: International Intervention and Strategies for Conflict Transformation* (Washington, D.C.: United States Institute of Peace Press, 2005).

22

THE PLACE OF SOFT POWER IN STATE-BASED CONFLICT MANAGEMENT

Joseph S. Nye, Jr.

POWER AND CONTEXT

Conflicts are struggles over power, but what is power? Traditional analysis is often too mechanical, treating power as wealth, resources, and military assets, and proponents of traditional analysis often assume that conflicts will be won by those who possess the most assets. But having the most resources of power does not guarantee that you will always get the outcome you want. For example, in terms of resources, the United States was far more powerful than Vietnam, yet it lost the Vietnam War. And the United States was the world's only superpower in 2001, but it failed to prevent the transnational terrorist attack on September 11. Converting resources into realized power in the sense of obtaining desired outcomes requires well-designed strategies and skillful leadership. Yet strategies are often inadequate and leaders frequently misjudge—witness Adolf Hitler's invasion of Russia in 1941 or Saddam Hussein's invasion of Kuwait in 1990.

It is more useful think of power in terms of behavior. Power is the ability to affect the behavior of others to get the outcomes one wants. Both the parties to a conflict and would-be mediators try to influence the behavior of the others. Often this is seen in terms of threats or payments, but these are not the only means to influence a conflict. There are several ways to affect the behavior of others. You can coerce them with threats. You can induce them with payments. Or you can attract or co-opt them to want the outcomes that you want. This ability to influence others by attraction rather than coercion or payments is soft power.[1]

Sometimes I can affect your behavior without commanding it. If you believe that my objectives are legitimate, I may be able to persuade you without using threats or inducements. For example, loyal Catholics may follow the pope's teaching on capital punishment not because of a threat of excommunication but out of respect for his moral authority. Or some radical Muslims may be attracted to support Osama bin Laden's actions not because of payments or threats but because they believe in the legitimacy of his objectives. In other words, perceptions of legitimacy are a power reality. They create attractiveness, or soft power. They help to influence others to produce desired outcomes.

I have defined power in terms of the behavior of producing desired outcomes, but this is often difficult to measure in advance of actions. As mentioned, practical politicians and ordinary people turn to a shortcut definition of power: the resources that can influence outcomes. Someone who has strength, wealth, or an attractive personality is called powerful. Power defined in terms of resources seems concrete and measurable, but it can also be misleading. Sometimes the measured resources do not produce the expected behavior. Resources that produce power behavior in one context may not in another. A boy who gets what he wants because of his physical strength on the playground may find that those power resources count for little when he returns to a disciplined classroom. Muscle may be the key power resource for winning a conflict on the playground, but brains may be more important in solving a conflict in the schoolhouse.

In international politics, by this second definition of power as resources, analysts consider a country powerful if it has a relatively large population, territory, abundant natural resources, economic strength, military force, and social stability. The virtue of this second definition in terms of resources is that it makes power appear concrete, measurable, and predictable in world affairs. In assessing the probable outcomes of a conflict, this shorthand can be useful. Power in this sense is like holding the high cards in a card game; it is a good place to start. But this definition has problems on the international stage, just as on the school playground. Power is very context dependent. When people define power as synonymous with the resources that produce it, they sometimes encounter the paradox that those best endowed with power in one context do not always get the outcomes they want in another context.[2] Power resources that may seem overwhelming in one conflict may be less determining in a conflict that occurs in another context.

If you show the highest cards in a poker game, others are likely to fold their hands rather than challenge you. But power resources are not as fungible as money. What wins in one game may not help at all in another. Holding a winning poker hand does not help if the game is bridge. Even if the game is poker, if you play your high hand poorly, or if you fall victim to bluff and deception, you can still lose.

Measuring power in terms of resources is an imperfect but useful shorthand. As a first approximation in any game, it helps to figure out who is holding the high cards. But it is equally important to understand which resources provide the best basis for power behavior in a particular context or you may make the wrong assessment of a conflict. Tanks are a great military power resource when a battle is on an open plain, but not when the battles are fought in swamps. Oil was not an impressive power resource before the industrial age, nor was uranium significant before the nuclear age. Power resources cannot be judged without knowing the context. Before you judge who is holding the high cards, you need to understand what game you are playing and how the value of the cards may be changing. In some situations, those who hold high office, command force, or possess wealth are not the most powerful parties in the conflict.

SOFT POWER

Everyone is familiar with hard power. We know that military and economic might often get others to change their position. As mentioned earlier, hard power can rest on inducements ("carrots") or threats ("sticks"). But sometimes you can get the outcomes you want without tangible threats or payoffs. The indirect way to get what you want has sometimes been called "the second face of power."[3] A country may obtain the outcomes it wants in world politics because other countries want to follow it, admiring its values, emulating its example, aspiring to its level of prosperity and openness, and seeing its goals as legitimate. In this sense, it is important to set the agenda and attract others, and not only to force them to change by threatening coercive measures. This soft power—getting others to want the outcomes that you want—co-opts people rather than coercing them. Effective mediators often require (and acquire) a considerable degree of soft power.

Soft power rests on the ability to shape the preferences of others. At the personal level, we are all familiar with the power of attraction and seduction. In a relationship or a marriage, for example, power resides not necessarily with the larger partner but in the mysterious chemistry of attraction. And in the business world, smart executives know that leadership is not just a matter of issuing commands but also involves leading by example and attracting others to do what you want. It is difficult to run a large organization by commands alone unless you can get others to buy in to your values. Similarly, contemporary practices of community-based policing rely on making the police sufficiently friendly and attractive that a community wants to help them achieve shared objectives.[4]

Political leaders have long understood the power that comes from attraction. If I can get you to want to do what I want, then I do not have to use carrots or sticks to make you do it. And while leaders in authoritarian countries can use coercion and issue commands, politicians in democracies have to rely more on a combination of inducement and attraction. Soft power is a staple of daily democratic politics. The ability to establish preferences tends to be associated with intangible assets such as an attractive personality, culture, political values and institutions, and policies that are seen as legitimate or having moral authority.

As mentioned earlier, legitimacy is a power reality, and it is particularly important for soft power. But legitimacy, or rightful authority, is in the eye of the beholder. It is not enough for a leader or country to merely assert the morality of its cause. If a leader represents moral values that others want to follow, it will cost less to lead. But that requires a leader to listen to and understand his or her possible followers. What are their values, needs, and desires? How can they be influenced? What strategies and approaches will be most effective? Soft power often involves two-way communication. For example, in the struggle against terrorism since 9/11, it is very unlikely that jihadist extremists will be attracted by American values and policies and thus the United States has little soft power to influence them. But the larger moderate majority in the Muslim world is attracted to some values that Americans represent, and listening to and understanding their values and needs can improve our capacity to attract them away from the extremists. In this conflict, the democracies cannot win unless the moderates prevail in the Muslim world. Hard power may be important for dealing with the irreconcilable jihadists, but soft power will be essential for determining the larger outcome of the conflict.

Soft power is not the same as influence. After all, influence can also rest on the hard power of threats or payments. And soft power is more than just persuasion or the ability to move people by argument, though that is an important part of it. It is also the ability to attract, and attraction often leads to acquiescence. Simply put, in behavioral terms, soft power is attractive power. In terms of resources, soft-power resources are the assets that produce such attraction. Whether a particular asset is a soft-power resource that produces attraction can be measured by asking people through polls or focus groups. Whether that attraction in turn produces desired policy outcomes has to be judged in particular cases. Attraction does not always determine others' preferences.

But the gap between power measured as resources and power judged as the outcomes of behavior is not unique to soft power. It occurs with all forms of power.

One way to think about the difference between hard power and soft power is to consider the variety of ways you can obtain the outcomes you want:

- You can command me to change my preferences and do what you want by threatening me with force or economic sanctions.
- You can induce me to do what you want by using your economic power to pay me.
- You can restrict my preferences by setting the agenda in such a way that my more extravagant wishes seem too unrealistic to pursue.
- Or you can appeal to my sense of attraction, love, or duty in our relationship and appeal to our shared values about the justness or legitimacy of contributing to those shared values and purposes.

If I am persuaded to go along with your purposes without any explicit threat or exchange taking place—in short, if my behavior is determined by an observable but intangible attraction—soft power is at work. Soft power uses a different type of currency—not force, not money—to engender cooperation, an attraction to shared values and the justness and duty of contributing to the achievement of those values. It is often a crucial component of crisis management.

THE INTERPLAY BETWEEN HARD POWER AND SOFT POWER

Hard power and soft power are related because they are both aspects of the ability to achieve one's purpose by affecting the behavior of others. The distinction between them is one of degree, both in the nature of the behavior and in the tangibility of the resources. Command power—the ability to change what others do—can rest on coercion or inducement. Co-optive

power—the ability to shape what others want—can rest on the attractiveness of one's culture and values or the ability to manipulate the agenda of political choices in a manner that makes others fail to express some preferences because they seem to be too unrealistic.

The types of behaviors between command and co-option range along a spectrum from coercion to economic inducement to agenda setting to pure attraction. Soft-power resources tend to be associated with the co-optive end of the spectrum of behavior, whereas hard-power resources are usually associated with command behavior. But the relationship is imperfect. For example, sometimes people are attracted to others with command power by myths of invincibility. As Osama bin Laden put it in one of his videos, "When people see a strong horse and a weak horse, by nature, they will like the strong horse." And even physical coercion can sometimes have psychological effects that produce attraction—witness the so-called Stockholm syndrome, in which some hostages eventually become attracted to their captors.

As Machiavelli pointed out four centuries ago, a prince can gain power from the careful use of force. In Machiavelli's words, if a prince must choose, it is better for him to be feared than loved. But Machiavelli also warned that constant coercion alone can be counterproductive by producing a hatred that becomes dangerous to the prince. Sometimes it may be better to be feared than loved, but the opposite of love is not fear; it is hatred. To cite an example from modern U.S. history, President John F. Kennedy went ahead with nuclear testing in 1961 despite negative polls, because he worried about global perceptions of Soviet gains in the arms race. Kennedy "was willing to sacrifice some of America's 'soft' prestige in return for gains in the harder currency of military prestige."[5] But he also pursued policies such as arms control negotiations and the creation of the Peace Corps and the Alliance for Progress, which were investments in soft power.

Hard power and soft power sometimes re-inforce and sometimes interfere with each other. A leader who courts popularity may be loath to exercise hard power when he should, but a leader who throws his weight around without regard to the effects on his soft power may find others placing obstacles in the way of his hard power. Nobody likes to feel manipulated, even by soft power. And soft power is not good or bad per se.[6] Like any form of power, it can be used by bad leaders as a weapon for bad purposes. Both Hitler and Bin Laden exercised soft power.

Sometimes the same power resources can affect the entire spectrum of behavior from coercion to attraction. And in many real-world situations, people's motives are mixed. Moreover, the distinction between hard power and soft power is one of degree, as mentioned earlier. Both are aspects of the ability to achieve one's purposes by affecting the behavior of others.

Hard power and soft power can complement each other. The ability to combine them effectively might be termed "smart power." For example, in the Cold War, Western military power served to deter possible Soviet aggression, but Western soft power in the form of political ideas such as democracy and human rights and popular culture ranging from the Hollywood movies to the Beatles' music helped to erode the attraction to communist governments. When the Berlin Wall finally fell in 1989, it went down under hammers wielded by citizens, not an enemy artillery barrage.

THE LIMITS OF SOFT POWER

Some skeptics object to the idea of soft power because they think of power narrowly, in terms of commands or active control. In their view, imitation or attraction does not add up to power. Some imitation or attraction does not produce much power over policy outcomes, and neither does imitation always produce desirable outcomes.

For example, in the 1980s Japan was widely admired for its innovative industrial processes, but imitation by companies in other countries came back to haunt the Japanese when it reduced their market power. Similarly, armies frequently imitate and therefore nullify the successful tactics of their opponents and make it more difficult for them to achieve the outcomes they want. Such observations are correct, but they miss the point that attraction often does allow you to get what you want. The skeptics who want to define power only as deliberate acts of command and control are ignoring the second, or "structural," face of power—the ability to get the outcomes you want without having to force people to change their behavior through threats or payments.

At the same time, it is important to specify the conditions under which attraction is more likely to lead to desired outcomes, and those when it will not. As we saw earlier, all power depends on context—who relates to whom under what circumstances—but soft power depends more than hard power on the existence of willing interpreters and receivers. For example, the United States enjoys more soft power in Central Europe than in the Middle East today. American values of liberalism and women's rights, which attract Europeans, often offend and repel conservative Muslims. The same cultural resources that produce soft power in one cultural context can produce its opposite in another. But one must be careful not to overgeneralize. In Iran, for example, the ruling mullahs regard Hollywood films as an instrument of the "great Satan," but Iranian teenagers in the privacy of their homes are attracted to the same videos played by U.S. teens.

Where it works, attraction often has a diffuse effect of creating general influence, rather than producing an easily observable specific action. Just as money can be invested, politicians speak of storing up political capital to be drawn on in future circumstances. Of course, such goodwill may not ultimately be honored, and diffuse reciprocity is less tangible than an immediate exchange. Nonetheless, the indirect effects of attraction and a diffuse influence can make a significant difference in obtaining favorable outcomes in bargaining situations. Otherwise, leaders would insist only on immediate payoffs and specific reciprocity, and we know that is not always the way they behave.

Soft power is also likely to be more important when power is dispersed, as it is in democracies. A dictatorial leader cannot be totally indifferent to the views of the people under his rule, but he can often ignore popularity when he calculates his interests. In settings where public opinion matters, leaders have less leeway to adopt tactics and strike deals than in autocracies. Even though the Turkish government seemed willing to strike a deal to permit the transport of U.S. troops across the country in 2003, the Turkish parliament resisted because U.S. policies had greatly reduced American popularity in public opinion and in the parliament. In contrast, it was far easier for the United States to obtain the use of bases in authoritarian Uzbekistan for operations in Afghanistan.

Finally, while soft power sometimes has direct effects on specific goals, it is more likely to have an impact on general goals. For example, it is easier to attract people to democracy than to coerce them to be democratic. Both specific and general goals are important, but soft power is particularly relevant to the latter. The fact that the impact of attraction on achieving preferred outcomes varies by context and type of goal does not make it irrelevant, any more than the fact that bombs and bayonets do not produce desired outcomes when we seek to prevent the spread of infectious diseases, slow global warming, or create democracy. Soft power may play little role, for example, in settling the conflict between the United States and North Korea over the latter's nuclear weapons program, but it has everything to do with the Bush administration's interest in spreading democracy as a means of preventing future conflicts.

THE INFORMATION REVOLUTION

The conditions for projecting soft power have changed dramatically in recent decades. The information revolution and globalization are transforming and shrinking the world. At the beginning of the twenty-first century, these two forces have enhanced U.S. power. But with time, technology will spread to other countries and peoples, and the United States' relative preeminence will diminish. For example, today the American one-twentieth of the global population represents almost half of the Internet. In a decade or two, English may remain a lingua franca, as Latin did after the ebb of Rome's might, but at some point in the future, the Asian cyber-community and economy may loom larger than the American. Already, India's Bollywood film industry produces more movies than Hollywood, albeit with less universal distribution. And as we have seen, American popular culture is not uniformly popular in all parts of the world, particularly in conservative Muslim countries.

Even more important, the information revolution is creating virtual communities and networks that cut across national borders. Transnational corporations and nongovernmental actors will play larger roles. Many of these organizations will have soft power of their own as they attract citizens into coalitions that cut across national boundaries. Political leadership becomes in part a competition for attractiveness, legitimacy, and credibility. The ability to share information—and to be believed—becomes an important source of attraction and power. And such credibility is an important dimension both of conflict management and of mediation.

This political game in a global information age suggests that the role of soft power relative to hard power will likely increase, but soft-power resources are difficult to control. Indeed, a government that tries too hard to control them may actually damage its credibility. When information is perceived to be propaganda, it often loses its attraction. Soft power is also difficult to control because many of its crucial resources are outside the sway of governments, and their effects depend heavily on acceptance by the receiving audiences. Moreover, soft-power resources often work indirectly by shaping the environment for policy and sometimes take years to produce the desired outcomes.

Of course, these differences are matters of degree. Not all hard-power actions promptly produce desired outcomes to conflicts—witness the length and ultimate failure of the Vietnam War, or the fact that economic sanctions have historically failed to produce their intended outcomes in more than half the cases where they were tried.[7] In Iraq, Saddam Hussein survived sanctions for more than a decade, and although the four-week military campaign of 2003 broke his regime, it was only a first step toward achieving U.S. objectives in Iraq. In fact, it has turned out to be much more difficult to win the peace in Iraq than to win the war. As one former military officer has observed, the mark of a great campaign is not what it destroys, but what it creates.[8] Moreover, sometimes dissemination of information can quickly produce or prevent a desired outcome. But generally, soft-power resources are slower, more diffuse, and more cumbersome to wield than hard-power resources.

Information is power, and today a much larger part of the world's population has access to that power. Technological advances have led to a dramatic reduction in the cost of processing and transmitting information. The result is an explosion of information that has produced a "paradox of plenty."[9] Plenty of information leads to scarcity—of attention. When people are overwhelmed with the volume of information confronting them, it is hard for them to know what to focus on. Attention rather than information becomes the scarce resource, and those who can distinguish valuable information from background clutter gain power. Editors and cue givers become more in demand, and this is a source of power

for those who can tell us where to focus our attention.

Among editors and cue givers, credibility is the crucial resource and an important source of soft power. Reputation becomes even more important than in the past, and political struggles occur over the creation and destruction of credibility. Governments compete for credibility not only with other governments but with a broad range of alternative actors, including news media, corporations, nongovernmental organizations, intergovernmental organizations, and networks of scientific communities.

Politics has become a contest of competitive credibility. The world of traditional power politics is typically about whose military or economy wins. Politics in an information age "may ultimately be about whose story wins."[10] Governments compete with each other and with other organizations to enhance their own credibility and weaken that of their opponents. Those with more credibility are more likely to be effective in bargaining, managing, and mediating conflicts.

Reputation has always mattered in political leadership, but the role of credibility becomes an even more important power resource because of the "paradox of plenty." As mentioned earlier, information that appears to be propaganda may not only be scorned but also turn out to be counterproductive if it undermines a reputation for credibility. Under the new conditions more than ever, the soft sell may prove more effective than a hard sell. It is a mistake to discount soft power as just a question of image, public relations, and ephemeral popularity. It is a form of power—a means of obtaining desired outcomes. When we discount the importance of our attractiveness, we will be likely to pay a price in the outcomes of conflicts.

Finally, power in an information age will come not just from strong hard power but from sharing. But in an information age, such sharing not only enhances the ability of others to cooperate with us but also increases their inclination to do so.[11] As we share with others, we develop common outlooks and approaches that improve our ability to deal with the new challenges. Power flows from that attraction. Dismissing the importance of attraction as merely ephemeral popularity ignores key insights from new theories of leadership as well as the new realities of the information age. Both the parties to a conflict and the mediators must be attentive to their soft as well as their hard power if they want to get their desired outcomes.

SOFT POWER AND CONFLICT MANAGEMENT

Soft power can play an important role in managing conflicts, but one must not oversell it. For one thing, as mentioned earlier, soft power is often difficult for governments to use directly. Much of it is produced and controlled by civil society outside the control of government. To some extent, national soft power in the form of values is almost an inadvertent by-product of domestic political life, and American popular cultural exports are controlled more by Hollywood than by Washington. Even in countries with more central political control than in the United States, the importance of credibility limits the extent to which governments can manipulate their soft power in an information age. Moreover, as mentioned, setting an example does not provide power unless others choose to follow it. Sometimes examples are ignored; and sometimes, when cultural values differ dramatically, examples can be counterproductive. Thus soft power is not simply another "tool" to be added to the peacekeeper's "tool kit" like an additional battalion of troops. But attraction to the values for which peacekeepers stand can facilitate their tasks.

At the same time, there are aspects of a country's soft power that governments can control. The substance and style of foreign policy is clearly within government control, and the implementation of political values such as democracy and human rights is subject to government influence. Even with culture, while democratic governments cannot control it, effective public diplomacy programs can promote it. For example, educational and cultural exchange programs, libraries and publications, and international broadcasting are all aspects of public diplomacy.

The United States spends over a billion dollars a year on its public diplomacy (about the same as Britain or France, though the United States is five times larger), but it spends 450 times more on its hard military power. The U.S. Information Agency was abolished during the Clinton administration. Proponents argued that placing its functions under an undersecretary in the State Department would integrate them more closely with overall diplomacy, but this neglected the low value attributed to public diplomacy in the traditional culture of the State Department, and the undersecretary's job was vacant for nearly half of the four years of the first Bush administration. By 2004, a report by the Pentagon's Defense Science Board said, U.S. public diplomacy was in "crisis." Although the United States started new broadcasting outlets like Radio Sawa and al Hurra television for the Arab world, better broadcasting is not enough. As former assistant secretary of state for near eastern affairs William Burns once pointed out, public diplomacy must be accompanied by "a wider positive agenda for the region, alongside rebuilding Iraq; achieving the President's two state vision for Israelis and Palestinians; and modernizing Arab economies."[12]

To accomplish its professed objective of promoting democracy in the Middle East, the United States must develop a long-term strategy of cultural and educational exchanges aimed at creating a richer and more open civil society in Middle Eastern countries. Democracy will not come simply out of the barrel of a gun. The most effective spokespeople for the United States are not Americans but local people who understand America's virtues as well as its faults. Visa policies that have cut back on the number of Muslim students in the United States do us more harm than good.

Much of the work of developing an open civil society can be promoted by corporations, foundations, universities, and other nonprofit organizations, as well as by governments. Companies and foundations can offer technology to help modernize Arab educational systems. U.S. universities can establish more exchange programs for students and faculty. Foundations can support the development of institutions of American studies in Muslim countries, or programs that enhance the professionalism of journalists. Government can help, such as by supporting the teaching of the English language and financing student exchanges, but its contributions are not sufficient.

As mentioned earlier, hard power and soft power should not be seen as opposed to each other in policy contexts or conflict management. They work best when they reinforce each other and create "smart power." At the beginning of the twenty-first century, the position of the United States is a stronger version of that occupied by Britain in the late nineteenth century. The United States is preponderant, but not an empire able to control the world. At best it can hope to shape the environment of global politics, including by not only protecting its national interests narrowly defined but also realizing that if the largest country in the system does not attend to the production of public goods such as international order, no smaller country will be able to do so. Thus the U.S. national interest must include systemic values as well as more particular concerns. An approach to national interest that includes the interests of others will enhance U.S. legitimacy and soft power. This approach can diminish the prospects of conflict by shaping the environment.

For nineteenth-century Britain, such an approach meant maintaining the balance of power so there were no temptations to wage

Table 1. How a Leading Power Can Shape the Context of Conflict

1. Maintain the balance of power among major states (most notably, Russia, China, India, Japan, and the European Union).

2. Promote an open international economy (in areas such as money, trade, services, and energy).

3. Keep international commons open (e.g., oceans, outer space, global climate, species, cyberspace).

4. Support international rules and institutions (in such areas as nonproliferation, peacekeeping, economic cooperation, environmental protection, humanitarian issues, and human rights).

5. Act as convenor and mediator (as, for instance, in the cases of coalitions of the willing, the Middle East, Northern Ireland, and Greece and Turkey).

aggressive war, promoting an open international economy so that all countries could prosper, and maintaining access for all to the international commons (which in that period meant freedom of the seas). As updated and added to in table 1, these systemic goals are appropriate for the United States. To the extent that the largest country pursues such systemic goals, it will prevent crisis situations and reduce the prospects of conflict—indirectly through the first four roles and directly in the case of the fifth role listed in the table. A combination of hard power and soft power is the best means to accomplish these systemic goals. Obviously, the hard-power resources of military and economic clout are essential, but to the extent that U.S. military and economic presence is welcome because the United States stands for attractive values and lives up to them in its domestic and international behavior, the U.S. presence will be more effective. And the acceptability of that presence will help when the United States turns to the direct role of convenor and mediator.

From this analysis, one can derive five maxims, or rules of thumb, for policymakers to follow in using soft power to avoid and manage conflicts. First, and perhaps most important, is to use hard power to structure situations so that soft power can be more effective. Europe provides a good example. With the collapse of the Soviet empire at the end of the Cold War, there were a number of paths that Eastern European nations could take. Some, such as Yugoslavia, collapsed into bitter ethnic conflicts. Others, such as Romania, Hungary, and Slovakia, might have succumbed to such tensions. One of the reasons that they did not was the attraction of Brussels, headquarters of both NATO and the European Union. Those two institutions acted as magnets of attraction and enhanced Europe's soft power by providing a vision of a positive future that had a powerful effect in dampening conflict well in advance of the dates on which any of the Eastern European countries might hope to enter the Western clubs. In doing so, they provided incentives in Eastern European domestic politics to eschew the easy path of arousing and riding ethnic hatred. U.S. and Western European officials made clear that such a path would preclude entry into those organizations and the attractive future that they represented. Today, Turkey and others are finding themselves drawn by the soft power of the European Union.

At a broader level, the promotion of democracy and human rights is an important part of a foreign policy that tries to shape a less conflictual future environment. Democracy can rarely be imposed by force, and values such as democracy and humans rights cannot be the sole goal of a foreign policy. Survival is a logically prior value, and strategic stability is thus a vital interest. Moreover, it is not clear that we know how to promote democracy where economic and social preconditions do not yet exist. There is considerable evidence, however, that liberal democratic countries are less likely to fight each other and that countries that respect the rights of their citizens are less likely to fight other liberal societies. Thus the use by the United States of soft power to foster democracy and human rights can be an important part of conflict prevention.

A second maxim is to invest in soft power when possible. Even though much soft power is an inadvertent societal by-product, policy decisions can have some effect. But equally important will be to follow policies that protect civil liberties and democracy even in the face of a terrorist threat. Americans should be clear when their policies weaken the power of their attractive example, as racial segregation did in the past and accusations of mistreatment of prisoners have done in recent years. Promoting racial and other forms of social justice remains crucial for the United States. Immigration policy is also important, both as a symbol of a multiethnic society and because many immigrants provide crucial avenues of communication with their former countries. Visa policies and education exchange programs are important in maintaining the flow of international students into our educational institutions. And while most U.S. broadcast and communications exports will be in the private sector, it remains important to invest in government cultural centers and radio programs. Some areas will be too small or conversely too powerful to be left to the market alone—for instance, Bosnia and China (where market considerations have led some companies to self-censor). Investment in public diplomacy should be increased.

Third, it will be important for Western policymakers to find ways to include the right nongovernmental organizations in their planning. NGOs today provide more aid than the entire UN system. Some, such as the Red Cross and Médecins Sans Frontières, have unique access to areas of conflict. Often they can provide crucial information. Many are effective observers and promoters of human rights. Some organizations, such as the International Crisis Group, are explicitly devoted to conflict prevention and resolution. By engaging new institutions, we can spread the risks and resource base. We can benefit from, and reinforce, the soft power of these institutions of civil society. Conversely, it will be important not to reinforce the soft power of the wrong type of nongovernmental actors. In some areas, terrorist networks such as that of Osama bin Laden are seen as attractive. If we act in ways that increase their ability to recruit, we build up their heroic stature and ironically increase *their* malevolent soft power.

Fourth, the United States should use its position in the world to play the role of peacemaker and conciliator for the systemic reasons stated earlier, but also because it is an investment in soft power (which in turn can increase our effectiveness as a conflict manager). When the United States helps to mediate conflicts in the Middle East, Northern Ireland, or the Aegean, it develops a reputation for being an attractive nation. This role is not available to the United States alone. Norway, for example, has increased its soft power and weight in international politics through its development assistance and its mediation in areas such as Sri Lanka and the Middle East. But the United States is involved globally.

The capacity to mediate works better in some situations and regions than in others. It helps when the mediator is attractive and has soft power. In Ulster, both Ireland and Britain had strong ties to the United States, and Senator George Mitchell was seen as an impartial arbiter. In the Israeli-Palestinian conflict, the United States was clearly more aligned with Israel, but its influence in Israel and it efforts to play an evenhanded role made it an indispensable part of the negotiating process in the 1990s. In the Aegean, the United States was an attractive interlocutor to both its Greek and Turkish NATO allies and managed to stave off a number of dangerous incidents. On the other hand, in South Asia, India has mistrusted the United States (and eveyone else) on the difficult issue of Kashmir, and on the Russia-Japan dispute over the Kuril Islands, the United States is allied with Japan and not able to solve the problem with Russia. A reputation for evenhanded-

ness, for possession of intelligence in all senses of the word, and for generally attractive values can enhance conflict mediation. In turn, a reputation for success in conflict mediation contributes to future attractiveness in that domain. Successful mediation is not only good per se but also a wise investment in soft power.

Finally, it will be important for U.S. policymakers (and congressional leaders) to resist unilateralist temptations. The United States may not need a permission slip to protect its vital interests, but it does need the help of others to deal with many of the transnational challenges that it faces, including the threat of terrorism. The United States has a general interest in multilateral regimes of laws and institutions to organize international actions to deal with issues such as trade, finance, the environment, proliferation, peacekeeping, human rights, and a number of other relevant concerns. Americans give up some portion of their freedom of action in order to constrain others. That is the price of living with global interdependence. Those who denigrate the importance of multilateral laws and institutions forget that legitimacy is a power reality. When the United States acts as a bully that extends its laws (e.g., on trade with Iran or Cuba) into the jurisdiction of other countries, or when it gratuitously rejects a multilateral framework (such as the Geneva Conventions), its soft power is diminished. The German journalist Josef Joffe points out that historically, when one country is preponderant, the desire of others to balance its power leads them to team up against it. He asks why this has not yet happened to the United States. One of the reasons he cites is U.S. soft power. Most others see the United States not as a threat but rather as an attraction. Succumbing to unilateralism would be a rapid way to squander this soft power.[13]

CONCLUSION

Soft power has always been a key element of conflict, its management, and its mediation.

The power to attract—to get others to want what you want, to frame the issues, to set the agenda—has its roots in thousands of years of human experience. Skillful leaders have always understood that attractiveness stems from credibility and legitimacy. Power has never flowed solely from the barrel of a gun; even the most brutal dictators have relied on attraction as well as fear. Globalization and the communications revolution pose new leadership challenges that will increase the importance of credibility, legitimacy, and accountability. In an age when it is necessary to win the battle of the story as well as the battle on the field, leaders need to pay more attention than ever to soft power.

When the United States paid insufficient attention to issues of legitimacy and credibility in the way it went about its policy on Iraq, worldwide polls showed a dramatic drop in U.S. soft power. That did not prevent the United States from entering Iraq, but it meant that the United States had to pay higher costs in blood and treasure than would otherwise have been the case. Or to take a different example, if Yasir Arafat had chosen the soft-power model of Mahatma Gandhi or Martin Luther King rather than the hard power of terrorism, he would have attracted moderate Israelis and he might have been able to create a Palestinian state. Neglecting soft power is expensive.

Conflict management is a complex process. Success depends on a range of choices that leaders and countries make. But whether large or small states, the most effective conflict managers are those who learn to combine hard power and soft power into smart power.

NOTES

1. This section draws on my book *Soft Power: The Means to Success in World Politics* (New York: Public Affairs, 2004).

2. See David Baldwin, "Power Analysis and World Politics," *World Politics* 31 (January 1979): 161–194.

3. Peter Bachrach and Morton Baratz, "Decisions and Non-decisions: An Analytical Famework," *American Political Science Review* (September 1963): 632–642.

4. I am indebted to Mark Moore for pointing this out to me.

5. Mark Haefele, "John F. Kennedy, USIA, and World Public Opinion," *Diplomatic History* (Winter 2001): 78.

6. See the interesting critique by Janice Bially Mattern, "On Why 'Soft Power' Isn't So Soft," *Millennium* 33, no. 3 (2005): 583–612.

7. Gary Hufbauer, Jeffrey J. Schott, and Kimberly Ann Elliott, *Economic Sanctions Reconsidered*, 2nd ed. (Washington, D.C.: Institute for International Economics, 1990).

8. Jane Holl Lute (remarks at the Aspen Strategy Group, August 2003).

9. Herbert A. Simon, "Information 101: It's Not What You Know, It's How You Know It," *Journal for Quality and Participation* (July–August 1998): 30–33.

10. John Arquila and D. Ronfeldt, *The Emergence of Neopolitik: Toward an American Information Strategy* (Santa Monica, Calif.: RAND Corporation, 1999).

11. Ibid., 52.

12. William Burns, "Democratic Change and American Policy in the Middle East" (remarks to the Center for the Study of Islam and Democracy, Washington, D.C., May 16, 2003).

13. Josef Joffe, "How America Does It," *Foreign Affairs* (September–October 1997): 13–27.

23

THE RULE OF LAW
IN CONFLICT MANAGEMENT

Neil J. Kritz

THE CHANGED NATURE OF WAR AT THE beginning of the twenty-first century requires a fresh perspective on the methods of managing conflict on the one hand and of making and maintaining peace on the other. Today, the overwhelming majority of wars around the world are intranational rather than international. Wars fought between the military forces of two sovereign countries are increasingly the exception to the norm. In their stead, ethnic and religious conflicts, disputes over self-determination or secession, and violent power struggles between opposing domestic political factions account for 93 percent of the major armed conflicts recorded in recent years worldwide. In 2004, in fact, all nineteen major armed conflicts were intrastate.[1] This statistic has profound ramifications for the processes of conflict prevention, conflict resolution, and postconflict peacebuilding. Tools and techniques that may be appropriate for resolving "classical" wars between state actors are often inadequate for achieving a meaningful accommodation and

reconciliation between domestic adversaries, who together must build a durable national union. One element that assumes far greater importance in this changed context of war is the development of the rule of law.

It is essential at the outset to distinguish between the rule of law and simply rule *by* law. Broad concepts like democracy and the rule of law can easily be distorted. Even totalitarian regimes frequently use law as a tool in their arsenal of mechanisms for social control. The Nazis clothed much of their atrocities with a veneer of legality. The Soviet constitution of 1936 reads like a litany of legal entitlements, yet it served Stalin well with its wide loopholes for contortion.[2] Repressive states from Romania to Zimbabwe have invoked the law even while attacking their own citizens. These are each examples of rule *by* law, in which courts, statutes, and regulations are manipulated in the service of tyranny. In contrast, the rule of law does not simply provide yet one more vehicle by which government can wield and abuse its awesome power; to the contrary, it establishes principles that constrain the power of government, oblige it to conduct itself according to a series of prescribed and publicly known rules, and, in the postconflict setting, enable wary former adversaries to all play a vital role in keeping the new order honest and trustworthy.

Adherence to the rule of law entails far more than the mechanical application of static legal technicalities; it involves an evolutionary search for those institutions and processes that will best facilitate authentic stability through justice. Beyond its focus on limited government, the rule of law protects the rights of all members of society. It establishes rules and procedures that constrain the power of all parties, hold all parties accountable for their actions, and prohibit the accumulation of autocratic or oligarchic power. It also provides a variety of means for the nonviolent resolution of disputes, whether between private individuals, between groups, or between these actors and the government. In this way it is integrally related to the attempt to secure a stable peace. At a historic meeting in Copenhagen in 1990, the thirty-five nations then composing the Conference on Security and Cooperation in Europe (CSCE) affirmed this linkage, declaring that "societies based on . . . the rule of law are prerequisites for . . . the lasting order of peace, security, justice, and cooperation."[3]

The shift from international to intranational conflict engages the rule of law in two significant ways. First, international law is tracking and adapting to these new circumstances through evolutionary changes in the rules of warfare. Many of the normative standards that had previously governed only wars between states, proscribing a variety of wartime abuses as violations of international law, are increasingly applicable to intrastate conflicts as well.[4] Sixty years ago, when the world held individuals to account for war crimes and crimes against humanity at Nuremberg, those crimes were generally understood in international law as engendering liability only when perpetrated

in the context of battles between states. By November 1994, when the United Nations Security Council established an international criminal tribunal to prosecute the genocide in Rwanda, that understanding had changed. As approved by the Security Council, the charter of the Rwanda tribunal severed any nexus requirement between the international prosecution and punishment of crimes against humanity, on the one hand, and the international or noninternational character of the conflict in which they were committed, on the other, applying these international prohibitions to purely domestic conflict.[5] The statute of the recently established International Criminal Court similarly incorporates this approach, defining genocide, crimes against humanity, and a range of war crimes as international offenses over which the court will have jurisdiction even when committed in conflicts of a noninternational character.[6]

A second example of the evolution in international law is the expanded acceptance of the principle of universal jurisdiction over these crimes, resulting in some countries asserting the jurisdiction of their national courts to prosecute genocide, war crimes, or crimes against humanity even when committed in an internal armed conflict in a second country. In the past decade, more than a dozen countries have undertaken investigation or prosecution of foreign nationals for such crimes allegedly committed in their home countries.

The shift from international to internal conflict also introduces a new problem in enforcing the law vis-à-vis those who may commit these grave crimes. As required by the Geneva Conventions (to which almost every country is a party), regular military forces in many countries receive basic instruction in the international rules that govern their conduct and their treatment of combatants and citizens even during times of war. In contrast, irregular forces and insurgent groups engaged in civil wars, to whom these international rules of conduct now apply, do not generally receive any training in the laws of war. What are often ragtag, young illiterate militia members in many countries need to be exposed to the norms by which they will now be held accountable. Exacerbating the problem, the governments against which they are fighting are often reluctant to have such insurgent groups sign an agreement to adhere to the Geneva Conventions or receive such training, lest such steps be perceived as legitimizing the rebels. A challenge in the coming years is the need to more effectively disseminate and enforce these rules vis-à-vis such nonstate actors.

Yet another sense in which law is pertinent to the changed nature of war—and the principal focus of the present essay—is the central role played by the rule of law in establishing stability and a durable peace following an intranational conflict. It is completely plausible —and often the case—that a classical war between two independent states can be resolved and a durable peace developed without any modification to the internal rules, structures, or institutions of either party to the conflict. The 1980–88 war between Iran and Iraq could end and leave tyrannies firmly in place on both sides. The border conflict between Peru and Ecuador and the Ethiopia-Eritrea war demonstrate the same proposition. In none of these six combatant countries did conclusion of the conflict necessitate any significant degree of internal reorganization. On the other hand, resolving violent conflicts between groups within a state and preventing their recurrence require the nurturing of societal structures and institutions to assure each combatant group that its interests will be protected through nonviolent means. This is rarely, if ever, possible without attention to the establishment of the rule of law. As stated by then UN secretary-general Boutros Boutros-Ghali in his description of peacebuilding, "Peacemaking and peacekeeping operations, to be truly successful, must come to include comprehensive efforts to identify and support structures which

will tend to consolidate peace and advance a sense of confidence and well-being among people. . . . There is an obvious connection between . . . the rule of law and . . . the achievement of true peace and security in any new and stable political order."[7]

EMERGING INTERNATIONAL STANDARDS AND INTERNATIONAL ASSISTANCE

In recent years, international standards have evolved to define the meaning of the rule of law with ever-greater detail, providing an increasingly nuanced road map for those engaged in peacebuilding efforts. This articulation of explicit standards results primarily from the convergence of trends in two areas—democracy and human rights—each of which is closely related to, but distinct from, the rule of law.

During the latter half of the twentieth century, one school of thought focused on democratic systems as the best guarantor not only of freedom, but also of peace. (This school was largely, but not exclusively, the domain of Western political conservatives who advocated democracy in a Cold War context.) Extensive research demonstrated what was to some an obvious postulate: democracies are less likely to go to war with one another than are totalitarian or authoritarian regimes.[8] But promoting democracy as a paradigm for the organization of society invites further inquiry. How does one create and ensure a democratic polity? Answering this question requires a shift from democracy as a macro concept to an examination of those specific institutional structures and mechanisms that are essential to democracy and that distinguish it from a nondemocratic system. The result is a recognition and articulation of the basic elements of the rule of law, which is the ultimate guarantor of democracy.

The human rights stimulus followed an opposite path of analysis, moving from the specific to the general. Prompted in part by the atrocities of World War II, international law, as defined by the United Nations and various regional organizations, provided guarantees for an ever-widening catalog of human rights. Over time, however, the international human rights movement (dominated to some degree by more liberal perspectives) increasingly recognized a basic fact: while an international campaign could often free a political prisoner from detention, he or she could quickly be replaced by many new victims unless the system and the structures that permitted their abuse were changed. Stated differently, fundamental guarantees of individual human rights, already provided in international law, could most effectively be secured by more detailed guidelines on the institutions and procedures through which these rights should be enforced. The result once again was a recognition of the need to elaborate on the meaning of the rule of law.

As a consequence, a growing corpus of UN conventions, resolutions, declarations, and reports today elaborates standards on the rule of law. Various regional organizations have similarly contributed to the articulation of these guidelines. The Organization for Security and Cooperation in Europe (OSCE) has produced a detailed definition of the institutional and procedural elements of the rule of law—the most comprehensive catalog of this sort ever adopted by an international organization—which serves as a standard for its fifty-five member states.[9] The Council of Europe long ago made adherence to the rule of law an explicit requisite of membership in the organization and has similarly developed a sophisticated series of standards. Both the Organization of American States and the Council of Europe have developed and enforced their rule-of-law standards in part through the jurisprudence of a regional commission and court on human rights. (In the case of the Council of Europe, these two bodies were recently merged into one.) Although there are variations in emphasis in the definitions articulated by different sources,[10] the obligations imposed by the rule

of law are generally understood to include the following:

- A representative government in which the executive is accountable to the elected legislature or to the electorate
- The duty of the government and security forces to act in compliance with the constitution and the law
- A clear separation between the state and political parties
- Accountability of the military and the police to civilian authorities
- Consideration and adoption of legislation by public procedure
- Publication of administrative regulations as the condition for their validity
- Effective means of redress against administrative decisions and provision of information to the person affected on the remedies available
- An independent judiciary
- Protection of the independence of legal practitioners
- Detailed guarantees in the area of criminal procedure
- Compensation of victims of official abuse
- Free and fair elections at regular intervals
- Comprehensive rights of political participation
- Equal access and equal protection of the law

In elaborating the principle of the rule of law, some of these documents reiterate and expand on traditional human rights commitments, including freedoms of association, religion, expression, and movement, and protection against torture.

Beyond the articulation of standards on the rule of law, there has been a vast expansion in recent years of assistance programs to facilitate their implementation, particularly in countries emerging from conflict. Assessments, technical assistance, training, expert consultations on drafting of legislative and regulatory reforms, observer and advisory missions, and donation of resources and materials for the enhancement of the rule of law are now increasingly standard features of the postconflict scene. Those providing such assistance routinely include various agencies of the United Nations (including in particular the United Nations Development Programme, the Department of Peacekeeping Operations, and the Office of the High Commissioner for Human Rights), regional organizations, the World Bank, several bilateral governmental donors, and an assortment of foreign nongovernmental organizations.[11] Lawyers in military peacekeeping units have at times played an active role, and there is an emerging recognition that peacekeeping forces may need to fill important rule-of-law functions until the civilian contingents are able to be deployed to assume those functions; in various peacekeeping operations, this has included detaining suspected criminals, gathering evidence, surveying the needs of the courts and the justice system overall, and disseminating legal codes. There are so many providers of rule-of-law assistance that it has become common in many postconflict locations to convene rule-of-law donor coordination meetings on a regular basis to share information, avoid duplication, and attempt to provide sequenced assistance in keeping with the often-limited absorption capacity of postconflict local legal institutions. (Even with this heightened level of activity, the aggregate level of resources available for postconflict legal rebuilding has generally been much less than the amount needed, and donors often still pursue differing agendas.)

It must be kept in mind that the standards outlined here provide an important road map for development of the rule of law in a postconflict society but are seldom maintained to perfection in circumstances that are so far from perfect. In a country emerging from a protracted and bloody civil war, the justice system is generally in severe disrepair. Even if the courts had once been credible, the institutions and personnel of the system have typically been destroyed or corrupted. Notwithstanding significant foreign assistance, rebuilding an effective justice system (or, in the case of some countries, constructing one for the first time) will not occur overnight. The need to recruit and train investigators, prosecutors, judges, court administrators, police, and corrections personnel; adopt needed legislative and regulatory reforms; develop a robust independent legal profession; put in place the material resources and equipment necessary to the operation of the system; and create a culture of respect for the law will generally take several years at best. Postconflict evolution of the rule of law, like many other postconflict processes, may be somewhat messy and slow; it has to be nurtured intelligently with a view to the long term and a strategy that extends well beyond the funding cycle of many foreign donors.

Even when the international community intervenes so thoroughly as to take over the task of local judicial administration, it has been unable to satisfy all of its own rule-of-law standards. A telling case in point is that of postwar Kosovo, where the UN mission was vested with all executive and legislative powers, and foreign experts imported by the United Nations were given the mandate to administer the system of justice. Even in this case, an October 2000 report by the OSCE Kosovo office complained of common practices in the UN-run courts, and provisions of UN-imposed regulations, that fell short of these international standards.[12]

Meaningful postconflict rule-of-law reform, as implied earlier, requires attention to more than the number of laws passed or courthouses built. To be effective, there is a need for country- and context-specific strategies that are informed by political, economic, and social realities and by local legal tradition. It requires engaging both the personnel of the justice system and the general public over an extended period. It also requires a recognition that serious rule-of-law reform will impinge on the interests of various powerful interests in the postwar setting; this may include warlords, organized-crime syndicates, tribal elders, and others whose influence will be affected by a transition to a more robust, transparent, and nondiscriminatory system of justice. A program of technical tinkering by those providing rule-of-law assistance will be inadequate to meet such challenges, which require sustained political will as well.

The international capacity to provide timely legal assistance in such countries still has a ways to go but is developing in significant new directions. It has often taken months to recruit, train, and place on the ground the small number of foreign personnel who will actually design and implement justice sector assistance. (In Afghanistan, for example, the primary rule-of-law post within the UN mission remained vacant for over two years.) Recently, the European Union and the OSCE have each begun to put in place rapidly deployable civilian response capacity for rule-of-law needs. The United Nations and the U.S. government are exploring the development of, respectively, a ready roster and a pretrained civilian reserve corps to fill postconflict rule-of-law functions.

SOME MAJOR STRUCTURAL AND PROCEDURAL ELEMENTS

The rule of law incorporates many of the elements necessary to ease tension and lessen the likelihood of further conflict. While a comprehensive review of all aspects of the rule of law is far beyond the scope of this essay, an examination of some of the major elements is warranted to understand their vital role in postconflict peacebuilding and conflict prevention.

An Independent Judiciary

A primary requisite for the functioning of the rule of law, of course, is an independent judiciary. At the most fundamental level, the principal purpose of the courts in virtually any system is to serve as a forum for the peaceful resolution of disputes. Conflict and disagreement are inevitable in any human system; it would be foolhardy to construct an idyllic

model that did not assume disagreements between individuals and between groups. To forge a durable peace, it is necessary to channel those conflicts into a routinized and accepted mode of amelioration before they become violent and less tractable.[13]

In any country emerging from armed conflict, numerous claims and grievances will remain. These may include demands for punishing the perpetrators of war crimes and other atrocities. Wars frequently displace large numbers of people, and the subsequent return of refugees or prisoners will often result in competing claims to property. In the postconflict context, courts are also often called upon to resolve disputes regarding the use of minority languages or the eligibility of various factions to participate in elections. Each of these is a highly volatile issue, and it is imperative to avoid a scenario in which vigilantism raises the risk of new cycles of violence. An independent judiciary can provide a peaceful and trustworthy means of addressing such claims. The judiciary also addresses, of course, the normal, everyday disputes between people, hopefully contributing to an overall culture that resolves its conflicts through such nonviolent means.

It is important to note that not every dispute is amenable to judicial resolution. Some points of conflict are purely political, not addressed by any law that the courts might apply. To make the courts the arbiter of such disputes—particularly if the judiciary is still a fragile institution—risks politicizing the very institution that must be blind to politics, undermining the credibility and independence of the judicial system. Several analysts have suggested that this sort of politicization characterized the Russian constitutional court in the early 1990s, rendering it a more high profile but less effective institution for facilitating Russia's difficult democratic transition.

Finally, it is important to avoid being too mechanistic or narrow when considering postconflict judiciaries. In the postconflict phase, the formal justice system is generally weak and, even with international aid and personnel, has the capacity to handle only a relatively small number of the most important cases. Experience has shown that it will often take several years to significantly expand that capacity. On the other hand, various tribal, religious, or other traditional systems of justice often survive a prolonged conflict far more intact than the formal courts, and may be in a position to play a vital complementary role in providing justice and a nonviolent means for resolving disputes during the postconflict phase. These systems are routinely more accessible to the local population (both physically and financially) than the formal courts. In many countries, they also predate the formal system and may have deep roots in local culture. To resolve land disputes or matters of family law, for example, local people may view customary bodies as the appropriate and traditional redress. In evaluating and assisting postconflict justice, however, international actors have tended to ignore these customary systems, in part because they do not necessarily comport with international rule-of-law standards. This is beginning to change, and aid providers and policymakers are exploring how to shape more holistic rule-of-law strategies that integrate and perhaps adapt these customary systems of justice.

Law Enforcement and Criminal Justice

The rule of law requires a system of criminal justice that deters and punishes banditry and acts of violence, allowing the citizenry to live with a sense of security. At the same time, the criminal justice system must be immune from abuse for political purposes and must adhere to a lengthy list of internationally recognized rights of criminal procedure.[14] In other words, if societal tensions and the likelihood of further conflict are to be minimized, people must become confident that they will not be abused either by private sector criminals or by the authorities.

A problem confronting many countries emerging from war or from a repressive regime to a democracy is the hiatus in law enforcement capabilities. A transitional period unfolds during which the old police and security forces (as well as the system of authority in general) are eliminated or weakened, but the new order has yet to take hold. Retaining the old police and judiciary, many of whom were part of the problem rather than of the solution, undercuts the credibility of the new order and could threaten the ability of the new government to manage the transition. At the same time, as the recent experience in Iraq has vividly demonstrated, the dissolution of an effective police force can result in a dramatic deterioration of the security environment and render the rule of law a far more distant goal. This is a delicate balance, requiring a careful process of vetting and reprofessionalizing the police and related forces.

Under the best of circumstances, it takes at least a couple of years to train new personnel, establish new lines of command, and build a new and credible criminal justice system. In Russia, Haiti, South Africa, and El Salvador, to cite a few examples, this time lag has resulted in a security vacuum readily capitalized upon by criminal elements. In each of these four countries, the transition has produced a soaring crime rate; the same pattern occurs in many other states in the postconflict phase. While people's daily fear of being caught in the crossfire of war, or of being persecuted by the authorities because of their political views, has dramatically receded, it has been partially replaced by a new fear of the thieves, gangs, and mafias that operate with relative impunity in the interim period. In some cases these new criminals are demobilized combatants and commanders of the conflict just ended, still possessing their weapons but no new livelihood. In El Salvador, for example, an official inquiry determined that the death squads that killed thousands of leftists and moderates during the war transformed themselves into new criminal bands following the conflict, unchecked and undaunted by an ineffective criminal justice system. Organized-crime gangs similarly emerged out of former combatant units in the Balkans and Iraq. Uncontrolled, this dramatic rise in crime poses a very real threat to the stability of the new peace.

Because of this vacuum of effective law enforcement, postconflict settings also provide fertile ground for the growth of transnational criminal operations. Once established, these organizations then become difficult to uproot and can undermine the stability not only of the country in question but of other nations as well. The postconflict absence of an effectively functioning government in Kosovo provides a poignant recent example. In January 2001, the British government was obliged to send a special criminal intelligence squad to Kosovo to focus on the entrenchment of criminal gangs involved in smuggling illegal immigrants, prostitutes, and drugs to Western Europe.[15] More recently, transnational criminal activities crisscrossing the borders of Sierra Leone, Liberia, and Côte d'Ivoire undermine efforts to build stability and the rule of law in these three countries. The void in law enforcement capacity can also provide a handy environment for exploitation by international terrorist groups, as occurred in Somalia and Afghanistan. Further compounding this problem, the postconflict government's incapacity to deal effectively with this threat may be viewed by outsiders as complacency toward transnational crime, which may in turn put at risk some of the international assistance and investment it badly needs.

To address these problems, postconflict reconstruction has to move quickly to establish courts that are above corruption and intimidation by criminal elements; police forces need to be supported, and individual officers must be held accountable for violations of the rule of law; and training and cleansing of the law enforcement and criminal justice systems need to begin promptly following the conflict. The 1995 Dayton Peace Accords to end the war in Bosnia and Herzegovina, for example, at-

tempted to integrate this lesson, addressing each of these points explicitly in the terms for the postconflict phase.[16]

In addition, to confront some of the more serious and complex criminal threats, including in particular those posed by transnational and domestic organized-crime groups, it may be necessary to create specialized units, capacity, and legal tools within the justice system. Development of such targeted concentrations of expertise and resources focused on these more challenging categories of crimes may be warranted with respect to all components of the criminal justice apparatus, including investigations, enforcement, prosecution, the courts, and prisons, in order to track and pursue these crimes more effectively. At the same time, safeguards need to be in place to ensure that specialized units and tools to confront serious crimes stay within the bounds of the rule of law.

Finally, international police operations have expanded significantly in the last few years, becoming commonplace in postconflict scenarios to help fill this void in law enforcement. In 2006, nearly 7,500 UN civilian police were authorized for deployment in nine postwar countries. The organization and fielding of such police operations is gradually becoming more professionalized, but numerous challenges remain with respect to the recruitment, training, coordination, and accountability of these forces in the future, as well as clarification of the law to be applied by them.

Transparency and Predictability

It is accepted and proven that transparency and predictability of action by adversaries reduce the likelihood of international conflict. Confidence-building measures have been instituted to reduce tensions in a variety of regions, under which certain actions that might agitate an opposing party (e.g., troop movements or missile testing) can be taken only according to prescribed procedures that facilitate communication and reduce suspicion.

Traditionally, diplomats and those involved in conflict resolution and conflict prevention have applied this principle primarily to conflicts between states. As conflicts have become increasingly intranational, however, the principle is equally valid. Confidence and trust will be increased—and the potential for suspicion, surprise, and tension reduced—when parties are required to conduct their activities in the open. The rule of law requires that governments adhere to principles of transparency and predictability, and it establishes several mechanisms to ensure that this is so. These include requirements that laws be adopted through an open and public process by a representative body, all regulations be published, no rules be applied retroactively, government agencies conduct their affairs according to prescribed rules, and the whole system be subject to judicial scrutiny to ensure compliance with these rules. As articulated by the conservative Austrian-born economist Friedrich von Hayek:

> Nothing distinguishes more clearly conditions in a free country from those in a country under arbitrary government than observance in the former of the great principles known as the Rule of Law. Stripped of all its technicalities, this means that government in all its actions is bound by rules fixed and announced beforehand—rules which make it possible to foresee with fair certainty how the authority will use its coercive powers in given circumstances and to plan one's individual affairs on the basis of this knowledge.[17]

Controlling the Bureaucracy

Even when the relationship between securing the rule of law and avoiding further conflict is recognized, attention and foreign assistance tend to focus fairly exclusively on the courts and the legislature. These may be the primary institutions, but as technology advances and as society becomes more complex, parliaments are able to address a decreasing proportion of the issues with which governments must deal. Legislative bodies can generally paint only with broad brushstrokes, leaving more and more of

the details, as well as the implementation, to be provided by the administrative bureaucracy of the modern state.

In many countries, the average citizen will most frequently experience the presence or absence of the rule of law (and will accordingly feel less or more alienated from the system) not through any interaction with the legislative or judicial process, not through any involvement in broad constitutional questions, but through encounters with the administrative state. Resolving a problem with their social security benefits, obtaining a license to run a business and support their family, getting a permit to build a house or a church or register a political party, obtaining state certification and funding for an ethnic language school—these are the sorts of events that bring most people into contact with the state, and they are not generally in the purview of the legislative branch. Unless the rule of law is extended to administrative decision making, these interactions are unlikely to be subject to public scrutiny and thus are open to corruption, manipulation, and discrimination. For most nationals and foreign advisers engaged in reconstructing war-torn societies, administrative procedure is hardly as glamorous as constitution writing or elections, but they are ill advised to neglect it, for it is in this realm that, unnoticed, the seeds of grievance and confrontation may quietly, even unwittingly, be sown.

In Peru in 1984, some correlation was believed to exist between the level of public confidence in the government on the one hand and the effectiveness of the violent opposition on the other. Peru had a functioning democratic legislature, with laws adopted and published following public debate; to the casual observer, the system adhered to the rule of law. Despite this appearance, economist Hernando de Soto found that 99 percent of the rules governing daily life in the country never went through the legislative process. They were, instead, the result of regulations issued by executive branch agencies, a process that was not subject to public participation, procedural controls, or any oversight, and that was consequently highly corrupt.[18] At the start of the twenty-first century, this kind of situation is not unique to Peru. Insofar as the power of these administrative bureaucracies continues unchecked in the postconflict period, it makes it more likely that individuals and groups will feel disenfranchised from the system, individual and national economic growth will be hampered by corruption, and administrative regulations or decisions may discriminate on the basis of political affiliation, ethnicity, religion, race, or geography.

Other Institutional Elements

Although it is beyond the scope of the present essay to discuss all the structural components required for a justice system to function, an important lesson to emerge from postconflict experience over the past two decades is that the rule of law will not be viable if any one of its core components lacks adequate capacity. To establish an effective criminal justice system— always a priority in the postconflict period— assistance to the courts will be wasted unless efforts are also taken to ensure a professional and law-abiding police force, prison system, and criminal defense bar, all governed by a coherent legal framework. While the link to basic security concerns makes criminal justice a top priority, mechanisms to deal with adjudication of financial claims, property disputes, and administrative law challenges are also needed for postconflict progress. In addition, assistance to these various components should be provided in a coordinated manner, and the various institutional components need to understand their respective functions as part of a holistic system. Whether in Afghanistan or the Palestinian Authority, for example, turf battles between the Ministry of Justice, the attorney general's office, and the Supreme Court have had severely dysfunctional consequences for efforts to strengthen the rule of law, diluting the value of international aid.

◆ ◆ ◆

Those involved in postconflict peacebuilding and the rule of law will often need to confront two challenges of particular urgency for the process of societal reconstruction: accountability for past abuses and construction of a new constitutional order.

RECKONING WITH WAR CRIMES AND OTHER PAST ABUSES

A basic question confronting many societies in the postconflict phase is how to deal with the legacy of massive abuses that may have been inflicted by those on each side of the conflict. The worst of these offenses are those classified by international law as war crimes, crimes against humanity, and genocide. Nations also need to come to terms with the question of accountability for those abuses that, while not constituting such international crimes, still give rise to deeply felt resentment and antagonism in the postconflict phase. Some of these abuses may have been perpetrated in the heat of the conflict; others may have taken place earlier, fanning the resentments that led to the conflict. A variety of approaches need to be considered in contemplating the issue.

Criminal Accountability

Some argue that not only are the trial and punishment of these offenses essential to achieve some degree of justice, but that a public airing and condemnation of the crimes are the best way to draw a line between times past and present, lest the public perceive the new order as simply more of the same. A minority claim that these are simply show trials unbefitting a search for peace and democracy, that a public review of wartime atrocities will inflame passions rather than calm them, and that the best way to rebuild and reconcile the nation is to leave the past behind by forgiving and forgetting the sins of all parties to the conflict. As noted earlier, the latter argument has been rejected by international law.

In many countries, prosecutions for abuses committed during the conflict can serve several functions. They provide victims with a sense of justice and catharsis—a sense that their grievances have been addressed and can more easily be put to rest rather than smoldering in anticipation of the next round of conflict. In addition, they can establish a new dynamic in society, an understanding that aggressors and those who attempt to abuse the rights of others will be held accountable.

Because these trials tend to receive much attention from both the local population and foreign observers, they often provide an important focus for rebuilding the judiciary and the criminal justice system in accordance with rule-of-law principles. Perhaps most important for purposes of long-term reconciliation, this approach underscores that specific individuals— not entire ethnic or religious or political groups —committed atrocities for which they need to be held accountable. In so doing, it rejects the dangerous culture of collective guilt and retribution that too often produces further cycles of resentment and violence.

The issue of accountability versus impunity not only is relevant to the resolution of conflict within a war-torn country; it also may have grave consequences for future, seemingly unrelated conflicts in other parts of the world. In explaining his confidence that he could proceed with his diabolical campaign of genocide without fear of retribution by the international community, Adolf Hitler is infamously alleged to have scoffed, "Who remembers the Armenians?"—referring to the victims of a genocide twenty-five years earlier for which no one had been brought to account. Recent evidence suggests that the Bosnian Serb leadership, in pursuing a campaign of ethnic cleansing and genocide in the 1990s, was emboldened by the fact that the Khmer Rouge leadership had never been prosecuted or punished for the atrocities it committed in Cam-

bodia in the 1970s. (Nearly thirty years after the killing fields, a special tribunal is now being put in place in Phnom Penh to prosecute some of those cases.)

When prosecutions are undertaken, how widely should the net be cast in imposing sanctions on those who committed war crimes or similar abuses? How high up the chain of command should superiors be responsible for wrongs committed by their underlings? Conversely, how far down the chain should soldiers or bureaucrats be held liable for following the orders of their superiors in facilitating these abuses?

International legal standards are evolving that help address these questions; at least for the most heinous violations of human rights and international humanitarian law, a sweeping amnesty is now understood to be impermissible.[19] On the other hand, offenses like genocide or crimes against humanity generally require the participation of a vast number of people, and international law does not demand the prosecution of every individual implicated in the atrocities. Putting all of the hundreds and sometimes thousands of such individuals on trial, whether before a local or international court, would be financially, politically, and logistically untenable. A symbolic or representative number of prosecutions of those most culpable may satisfy international obligations, especially if an overly extensive trial program would threaten the stability of the country. The Special Court for Sierra Leone, for example, is limited to prosecution of those "who bear the greatest responsibility for serious violations of international humanitarian law" and specified crimes under Sierra Leonean law; accordingly, even though large numbers of combatants participated in gruesome atrocities, the Special Court has issued indictments against just thirteen people. Often, the challenge of numbers is addressed by using different mechanisms to deal with (1) the leaders, those who gave the orders to commit war crimes, and those who actually carried out the worst offenses (inevitably the smallest category numerically) and (2) those who perpetrated serious abuses but do not rise to the first category. In East Timor, perpetrators of minor crimes (generally property offenses) could apply to participate in a "community reconciliation process" in which they confessed to their offense in a local public hearing, and the local community decided on an appropriate form of community service for the applicant, ranging from an apology to a fine to rebuilding a property he had burned down during the 1999 violence in East Timor. Perpetrators of war crimes, crimes against humanity, murder torture, or rape, on the other hand, were ineligible for this process and were subject to the jurisdiction of a "Serious Crimes Unit" established to investigate and prosecute these major abuses.

The Rwandan case demonstrates the need for pragmatism to temper an absolutist approach to prosecution. For decades, elites maneuvering for power manipulated ethnic rivalries between Hutu majorities and Tutsi minorities for political ends, without any fear of being called to account for their actions. This culminated in 1994 in one of the most horrific genocidal massacres in recent memory, as between 800,000 and 1 million Tutsis and moderate Hutus were brutally slaughtered in just fourteen weeks.

To break this cycle of violence, the new Rwandan government correctly insisted that it was necessary to replace the endemic culture of impunity with a sense of accountability. To achieve this, many senior members of the new government insisted throughout their first year in office that every person who participated in the atrocities should be prosecuted and punished. The result was the multiyear pretrial detention of some 125,000 alleged *génocidaires* in prisons built to house a small fraction of that number—far fewer than the total number of potential defendants but vastly more than the number of genocide cases that could be handled by the most robust criminal

justice system in a reasonable amount of time. To compound the problem, Rwanda's criminal justice system was decimated during the genocide, as most lawyers and judges were killed, in exile, or in prison. By 2004, the Rwandan courts had actually processed more than 7,000 genocide cases—a herculean feat matched by virtually no society in history, let alone one still reeling from destruction—in proceedings that were evaluated as generally fair by independent observers, including those representing the defense. As impressive a record as this is, however, and notwithstanding the importance of a rhetorical commitment to put every perpetrator of gross abuses in the dock, 125,000 genocide defendants were never going to be tried in Rwanda, and during the several years it was attempted, this task largely monopolized the justice system and delayed progress on other matters crucial to social reconstruction.

The Rwandan solution has been to move the overwhelming majority of the caseload to a new village-level system called *gacaca*, loosely based on an indigenous model of traditional justice. The program does not satisfy all the criteria set by international standards relating to criminal defense rights and fair trials; defense lawyers are not permitted, the judges of the more than 12,000 gacaca courts lack legal training, and there have been allegations of witness intimidation. On the other hand, most Rwandans in the justice system feel they have no alternative: the caseload cannot be handled by the courts in any timely manner; it is politically not an option to simply throw open the prisons and release more than 100,000 alleged génocidaires; and it is not acceptable to continue to keep people locked up for years without trial. Although it will be controversial, Rwandans argue that the gacaca program will engage local villages in the process of justice (attendance is actually compulsory), return and reintegrate perpetrators into their home communities, and empty the prisons of untried cases within a relatively short time. Perhaps of most concern are the staggering projections by some senior government and gacaca system officials that rather than reducing the caseload, the gacaca process will ultimately identify and process some 750,000 genocide defendants—a tenth of the Rwandan population—compounding rather than relieving the challenge of numbers.[20]

Given the complexity of the imperative to deliver adequate criminal justice for past grave abuses, reasonably clear objectives need to be established early on. Although the answer to "How much is enough?" may change during the course of a nation's transition, and although the question will continue to be a point of debate both in the international community and within countries where massive atrocities have occurred, experience over the past few decades in several transitional countries suggests the need for flexibility and realism in the quest for criminal accountability for such horrific offenses. Concern for the needs of victims is not best served by encouraging them to mistakenly assume that every perpetrator will be brought to trial when this is clearly not possible. Similarly, the interest in quickly establishing an effective justice system will not be best served by overwhelming the entire system for years with nothing but atrocity cases. Exempting all perpetrators from justice is morally, and now legally, unacceptable, but subjecting every participant in an extended campaign of mass abuses to trial will usually be impossible. A careful balance will be needed in each case, based on the crimes committed and numbers involved, the capacity of the criminal justice system, local culture and priorities, and available resources.

Cleansing the Structures of Government

Holding individuals accountable will usually entail more than criminal trials. In many countries, limitations may be placed on participation in the public sector by those associated with past abuses. A durable peace requires the establishment of public confidence in the institutions of the new order. That confidence can be seriously undercut if these institutions are staffed by the same personnel who gave rise to old resentments. Those who kept the engine of a now-ousted government running may be perceived as of uncertain loyalty. Even though they are not liable in a criminal sense, those who facilitated past abuses should not be permitted to infect or represent the new governmental structures. On the other hand, if people have not personally been involved in past abuses, then some of these people may be vital to national reconstruction in the immediate postconflict phase, with knowledge and experience that will be useful in making the new order function.

In El Salvador, the peace agreement provided for a special commission, which identified one hundred senior military officers for retirement due to their implication in past human rights abuses. In Bosnia, the International Police Task Force was tasked with excluding from the newly reconstituted local police any candidate who had previously engaged in abuse of ethnic minorities. Even if such individuals are not prosecuted for their crimes, permitting them to occupy positions in which their presence would be cause for a sense of insecurity among their former victims would be unjust and would detract from peacebuilding efforts.

Administrative purges do not, however, provide the same level of due process protection as does a criminal proceeding. Because they involve a large number of people, purges tend to be conducted in summary fashion. In stressing the importance of individual responsibility and accountability, the rule of law rejects any notion of collective guilt. When large numbers of people are removed from their places of employment solely because they had worked there during the conflict or because of their membership in a particular political party, without any demonstration of individual wrongdoing, they may legitimately cry foul and question the democratic underpinnings of the new government. Rather than contributing to reconciliation and rebuilding, such purges may create a substantial ostracized opposition that threatens the stability of the new system. In Iraq, a major controversy has been ongoing over precisely this point for more than three years, often pitting Sunni against Shiite constituencies, in the context of the appropriate scope of exclusion from public positions through "de-Ba'athification." In some cases, the dislocational effects of such a measure have been tempered by limiting any ban on public service by implicated individuals to a cooling-off period of a few years, permitting their reentry only after the initial postconflict phase and after stable and trustworthy public institutions are in place. In other instances, people are appointed or reinstated on a probationary basis, to monitor and verify their adherence to the norms of the new democratic order.

Although they vary from country to country, such vetting efforts, sometimes referred to as "lustration," routinely target a far larger number of offenders than do most programs of criminal trials, but they have not received adequate attention. In the next few years, significant work will be needed to develop guidelines on how best to strike the right balance and design vetting programs that do not constitute simple political purge programs but that instead legitimately cleanse the structures of government and contribute to the establishment of the rule of law.

Establishing a Historical Record

In the transitional period after an intranational conflict, history is always controversial. Each side will still have its defenders who will deny that the abuses of which it is accused ever took place, will claim that they were actually perpetrated by others, or will suggest that they were justified by exigent circumstances. Left uncontested, these competing claims may undermine the new order and the effort at peacebuilding; they may also add insult to the injury already inflicted on the victims, deeply

sowing seeds of resentment that can result in a new round of violence. The Bosnian war displayed unresolved issues of history and resentment dating back some seven centuries; a decade after the war, the country's next generation is being socialized into one of three competing Bosniak, Serb, or Croat realities identifying their own ethnic group as victims and the other two as perpetrators of atrocities during the conflict in the 1990s.

As a consequence, in addition to the focus on individual perpetrators, establishing an official overall accounting of the past is often an important element to a successful transition, providing a sense of national justice, reckoning, and catharsis. Fairly conducted criminal trials are one way to establish the facts and figures of past abuses; the formation of a "truth commission" is another. While the two processes can complement each other, a truth commission may be all the more useful for healing and reconciliation if the country is not equipped to conduct fair and credible trials. Long-term reconciliation requires a careful examination of the mix that will best fit the society in question.

In El Salvador, the twelve-year civil war between the government and the Farabundo Martí National Liberation Front (FMLN) left some 75,000 people dead. "As the peace negotiations advanced, the charges and countercharges relating to [atrocities committed by each side] threatened to become serious obstacles to any peaceful resolution of the conflict. It was soon recognized, therefore, that the hate and mistrust built up over the years required . . . some mechanism permitting an honest accounting of these terrible deeds."[21] At the war's conclusion in 1992, the judiciary was intact, but it was highly politicized and compromised and incapable of credibly addressing the difficult issue of accountability for war crimes or egregious violations of human rights in an objective manner. The three-member United Nations Commission on the Truth, established by the peace agreement between the warring parties, was seen as an alternative vehicle through which to attain some sense of justice and accountability.[22]

Although not a court, the commission—like similar entities that have been created in several countries facing a legacy of abuses on a mass scale—investigated and reported on abuses that had been committed by both sides during the war, giving both victims and perpetrators an opportunity to make their testimony part of the official record. Because of the absence of a credible criminal justice system, the commission also felt obliged to render certain judgments in its 1993 report that would otherwise have been left to the Salvadoran judiciary. A prime example was the commission's decision to publicly name those individuals it determined were guilty of particularly egregious abuses, even though the commission process had not afforded these individuals all the due process protections to which they would be entitled in a judicial proceeding. Had a credible national justice system been functioning, the commission might have kept all such names confidential in its report and instead turned them over to the authorities for prosecution.[23] In its report, the commission analyzed the ways in which the militarization of Salvadoran society had eviscerated all three branches of government; it also made recommendations to enhance the prospects for each of these institutions and the military to function in accord with the precepts of the rule of law.

Truth commissions have provided a forum and voice for the hundreds or thousands of victims who will never be called to testify at trial. More than 20,000 victims in South Africa, 22,000 in Morocco, 17,000 in Peru have provided their accounts to the truth commissions in those countries, ensuring that what happened to them or their relatives or colleagues is acknowledged and woven into the fabric of the nation's official history. Truth commissions have been used in several countries to look not simply at individual cases, but also at the systemic problems that made abuses pos-

sible, at the role of various sectors, through acts of omission and commission, in engendering the environment for these offenses to occur —be it the security forces, religious leadership, the media, the educational system, the judiciary, and so on. Based on their analysis, they have been tasked with developing detailed recommendations for appropriate governmental and societal reforms. Truth commissions established or contemplated in postconflict settings have recently been charged with developing ways to contribute to the process of reconciliation. In Guatemala, where a civil war raged for thirty-five years and cost more than one hundred thousand lives, the peace agreement provided for appointment of a truth commission and stressed the importance of establishing the "whole truth" about past abuses by all parties, presenting this as part of a process that "will help lay the basis for a peaceful coexistence" and that "will eliminate all forms of retaliation or revenge as a prerequisite for a firm and lasting peace."[24] In Bosnia, if a truth commission is established, all stakeholders have agreed that its mandate will include a requirement, in the context of documenting the atrocities that occurred, to also expose the positive stories of individuals on all sides of the conflict who took risks to protect fellow citizens from other ethnic groups from abuse.

The Need for an Integrated Approach

Massive and systemic atrocities are often an outgrowth of complex problems in a society, or they contribute to the creation of the same. They are not generally amenable to simplistic solutions. It has become increasingly clear that effective postconflict peacebuilding generally requires not one of the mechanisms outlined here, but a nuanced and integrated approach that combines and sequences various approaches to address the particular case. For more than two years in postwar Bosnia, many argued that a truth and reconciliation commission should be created, as a complementary process to the work of the International Criminal Tribunal in the The Hague, to provide a forum for thousands of victims, to develop recommendations for systemic reforms, and to undertake other tasks. The effort was stymied by those who insisted that no such body should be established until conclusion of the tribunal's work. The result would have been an implicit statement that, if a postconflict society is determined to be incapable of conducting its own credible war crimes trials and the function is assumed by the international community, that society should then be blocked for several years from pursuing any other program to deal with its own troubled past. Similarly, in Sierra Leone, the 1999 Lomé peace agreement provided for establishment of a truth and reconciliation commission. Subsequently, the UN Security Council mandated the establishment of a special war crimes court in Sierra Leone—at which point many international actors suggested that the commission effort could be abandoned. Ultimately, both bodies were established.

Increasingly, however, while truth commissions may precede prosecutions as they did in Argentina and Chile, function concurrently with trials as in Sierra Leone and East Timor, or follow initial trials as may occur in Bosnia, they are understood to be not alternatives but complements to criminal trials, serving a different but often vital function for societies in transition.

THE CONSTITUTION-MAKING PROCESS

In many countries in transition from civil war to a new government, one of the first important tasks is drafting a new constitution. The constitution is, of course, the foundational legal document from which the entire national system of rules will derive; it is the cornerstone for the rule of law. In addition, insofar as the constitution enshrines the vision of a new society, articulates the fundamental principles by which the political system will be reorganized,

and redistributes power within the country, both its substantive provisions and the process by which it is created can play a significant role in the consolidation of peace.

When a constitution is drafted and imposed by a small group of elites from the victorious party, a foundation may result that is not only less democratic but also less stable. While powerful elite factions will play a dominant role in any postconflict constitution-making process, it is important to reduce their monopolization of that process and to avoid a final constitution that simply reflects a division of the spoils between such factions. If the constitution and the process of its adoption are to play a positive role in transforming society, then constraints on such monopoly of power need to be built into the process.

In an alternative scenario to such closed-door division of spoils, constitution making can involve a process of national dialogue, allowing competing perspectives and claims within the postwar society to be aired and incorporated, thus facilitating reconciliation among these groups. It can also be a process of national education with respect to concepts of government, the problems and concerns of different groups within the country, the development of civil society and citizen responsibility, and international norms of human rights, nondiscrimination, and tolerance that have been incorporated into recent constitutions. In short, the process of constitution making can contribute to peace and stability.[25]

To provide the best chance of success in this vital endeavor, there should be broad national agreement on the constitutional process. This is frequently characterized by two elements, as seen with increasing regularity in the constitutional processes of a variety of postconflict or transitional countries. The first element is an articulation of the rules, details, and timetable of the constitutional process. Having such a framework from the outset facilitates greater transparency and public credibility with respect to the steps in the constitutional process. It enables all actors—including not only the members of a constituent assembly or constitutional commission, but also civil society organizations, the media, and the general public—to know what to expect, how to monitor the process, and how and when they can provide input to the constitution-making process. The second element is a set of fundamental principles to which the new constitution must adhere. These principles typically include human rights such as freedom of religion and expression; freedom of assembly; nondiscrimination on the basis of gender, religion, nationality, or belief; and the guarantee of a range of rights in the criminal justice system. They may also include the organization of the state and the relationship between the branches of government, or other substantive bargains that have been agreed to by the parties at the outset. In some cases, such as South Africa, the new draft constitution may be made subject to judicial review by a constitutional court to ensure that it in fact comports with these fundamental principles. These interim arrangements can establish adequate political space to enable all stakeholders to participate in the process and debate even hotly contentious constitutional issues in an atmosphere that safeguards their rights and interests during the development of a final constitution and permanently thereafter.

This initial package of temporary rules, whether in the form of an interim constitution or otherwise, will typically be the product of negotiations between key factions (in contrast to the more broadly based and open constitutional process to follow). As a consequence, pressure from outside groups, including international institutions and donors, is important to producing a set of rules that will enable a robust and democratic process to follow.

Meaningful public participation is increasingly regarded as an essential ingredient to ensure the legitimacy of the constitution-making process and to ensure real public ownership of the process and of the resulting constitu-

tion. Such an approach, however, has consequences for the duration of the process. A rapidly adopted constitution will generally only reflect a deal between the powerful. A more open and extended process that provides an opportunity for other groups and civil society in general to challenge and debate and influence the process is far less efficient in the short run. It takes longer and costs more. For this reason, the international community has frequently sought to expedite the process, at times to the detriment of the constitutional result. In Cambodia, for example, the Paris Peace Accords of 1991 provided that the constitution-making process should be completed in a period of ninety days. Although a very limited effort at national dialogue and input from certain groups occurred during this time, analysts of this process have unanimously taken the view that this period was clearly too short, particularly given the lack of human resources resulting from the Cambodian genocide and the impossibility generally of conducting an effective constitution-making process under such time constraints even in the most ideal of circumstances. Some have suggested that the rushed nature of the process contributed to the weakness of the system created under the constitution, and the coup d'état of 1997 has lent credence to that view. In East Timor, only one month was allocated to the public consultation component of the constitutional process; several months later when the process was seen to have failed, a new round of public consultation was conducted.

Developing a constitution through this process of national dialogue, however, is far less efficient than the alternative model, in which the terms of this crucial social compact are determined by a small group behind relatively closed doors and handed down to the people like contemporary tablets from Mount Sinai. A drawn-out process of constitution making could be destabilizing, for example, if it means a lengthy transition governed by no basic rules or a transition still governed by an old constitutional system that had exacerbated the conflict. In such situations interim arrangements may first be needed for the consolidation of peace. Such was the case in South Africa, where a negotiated interim constitution established the basis for transition, and a lengthier process then followed to debate the tough issues and develop the final document.

Constitution making in South Africa provides an example of the usefulness of this approach. During one session in the spring of 1995, for instance, the Constitutional Assembly spent hours deliberating over provisions in the new draft constitution concerning the security forces in the new South Africa, hardly a minor or noncontroversial topic for opponents emerging from years of conflict. A variety of sensitive issues—such as emergency powers and their limits, the authorization of soldiers to disobey orders that violate international law, and civilian control of the security forces —were all respectfully discussed and debated by former enemies now in parliament, ranging from Pan-African Congress members on the left of the political spectrum to those of the Freedom Front on the right. Several participants subsequently acknowledged that as little as a year earlier, such a discussion would have been inconceivable.[26] In the context of the transition, however, the lengthy Constitutional Assembly process (made possible by an interim constitution and rules for the process) provided an important avenue for previously violent adversaries to negotiate and collaborate in constructing each piece of their new order.

In Albania, broad-based civic education and public consultation regarding the constitution included radio and television programs and telephone call-ins, dissemination of pamphlets and newspaper serials on constitutional issues, essay contests, and public forums throughout the country that focused on various constitutional questions. As a result of extensive comments from members of the public on a draft constitutional text published by the Albanian constitutional commission, the commission amended no less than 25 percent of the articles in the draft before finalizing the text and submitting to parliament and then to public referendum.

In country after country, the public has demonstrated that, when given an opportunity to participate in the shaping of the supreme law and social compact by which their nation will be governed, they will seize the opportunity. An informed and engaged citizenry is a requisite for the rule of law. In South Africa, those organizing the constitutional process embraced the principle of public participation and thought they might need to process as many as a couple thousand inputs; instead, the consultation process resulted in an astounding two million public submissions. In Iraq, notwithstanding the high level of violence that restricted the possibilities for public forums and outreach, the constitutional commission received some 400,000 public submissions. Owing to the overly brief time line allotted for the constitutional process and the insufficient capacity of the commission staff, however, there was no opportunity to review these submissions or in any way have them taken into consideration by the constitution drafters.

While robust public participation will strengthen the constitutional system that follows, a lesson of past cases is that the constitutional process also needs to build in institutional and political mechanisms to ensure constitutional implementation. In Eritrea, following a thirty-year war for independence, the constitution-making process was intentionally structured to facilitate the consolidation of peace—a two-year effort that was proclaimed "a historic process of a coming together of Eritreans for a creative national discourse."[27] The Constitutional Commission included a variety of religious, ethnic, and regional constituencies. Offices were established in five regions of the country, with an additional office responsible for involving the estimated 750,000 Eritreans living abroad in the process. The Constitutional Commission adopted a strategy "which involves the widest possible public consultation, a strategy which eschews the top-down approach."[28] Discussions were initiated through an extensive series of civic education seminars, debates, and town and village meetings reaching more than a hundred thousand people. Pamphlets, newspapers, television, and radio were used to facilitate public education and dialogue. Articulation of basic principles and of a draft constitution was the subject of further public debate and input. Nine years after its adoption, although the resulting national charter has deep public support, an authoritarian government has not yet implemented the constitution.

Finally, it is essential to recognize that not all of society's problems can be resolved through the constitution. As was suggested earlier with respect to the courts, viewing constitution making as a means of redressing all group grievances may force onto the plate issues that are not appropriate to this process. This can result either in rejection of the process by disgruntled factions or inclusion of promises in the new document that cannot be fulfilled, either of which would damage the credibility of the process and of the new constitution.

Enabling a broad spectrum of society to participate in shaping the compact means that the process will take longer to complete, entail higher administrative costs and greater debate, and possibly result in some compromises that might otherwise be avoided. On the other hand, it can also produce a constitutional system that is more widely understood and accepted, more stable, and more supportive of peace.

HOW LARGE A FOREIGN ROLE?

As noted, while the challenge of demonstrating a new beginning founded on justice and the rule of law will present itself very early in the postconflict phase, constructing new institutions and training new lawyers, judges, police, and other personnel can take years. This a recurring quandary.

In some instances, the solution has been to pursue justice through the medium of an international entity. In El Salvador, for example, the country's relatively small population was felt to be too polarized to achieve any consensus on the abuses committed during the conflict. As a consequence, the UN truth commission was composed entirely of non-Salvadorans in order to achieve a degree of neutrality, objectivity, and acceptability that could not be garnered by any domestic body at that early stage in the transition from war.

The United Nations Security Council created two international criminal tribunals to respond to civil war and genocide in Rwanda and the former Yugoslavia—the first such bodies established since the Nuremberg tribunal a half-century earlier. Several factors militated in favor of internationalizing the response in these cases:

- The crimes were so horrific and so great a challenge to basic precepts of international law
- The need for justice as an essential ingredient in achieving reconciliation and breaking the cycle of violence was so apparent
- The domestic justice systems (particularly in Rwanda) were so thoroughly decimated

In addition, an international tribunal was better positioned than a domestic court to (1) convey a clear message that the international community will not tolerate such atrocities, hopefully deterring future carnage of this sort, not only in Rwanda and Bosnia but worldwide; (2) be staffed by experts able to apply and interpret evolving international law standards; (3) be more likely to have the necessary human and material resources at its disposal; (4) function—and be perceived as functioning —on the basis of independence and impartiality rather than retribution; (5) advance the development and enforcement of international criminal norms; and (6) obtain jurisdiction over many of the worst perpetrators who were no longer in the country. The two tribunals have produced several important advances in the understanding and treatment of war crimes, crimes against humanity, and genocide.

In rare circumstances such as these, creating an international entity to provide a sense of justice has served vital goals. In the vast majority of instances, however, this should only be the second choice. Even in cases such as Rwanda and Bosnia, where the establishment of international criminal tribunals was appropriate, durable peace requires that robust domestic institutions be established, developing within the states in question the capacity to undertake efforts at justice and reconciliation. Although it is hardly a zero-sum equation, the relative allocation of resources makes a statement regarding international priorities in the area of postwar justice and the rule of law: total contributions to the two international tribunals has been more than $2 billion; at some $250 million per year, they represent more than 15 percent of the ordinary UN budget. Allocations during this same period to develop the legal institutions within the countries in question have been a small fraction of that amount.

Whether accountability and justice are achieved through a court or through a truth commission, they are generally best achieved through a domestic process managed by the country in question. If it can be conducted in accord with the protections afforded by the rule of law, prosecution before domestic courts can enhance the legitimacy of the new post-conflict government and of the judiciary, be more sensitive than outsiders to nuances of the local community, emphasize that the nation will henceforth hold all individuals accountable for their crimes, and stress a viable alternative to vigilante justice. In addition, the state and the body politic will generally be most likely to integrate these lessons of justice, accountability, and reconciliation following a cathartic *domestic* process that includes representatives of all parties. This internalization is extremely important to building peace. Conversely, if the state is relieved of the need to face these issues, leaving them to be handled and concluded by outsiders (and therefore easily disowned by local leaders if that becomes politically expedient), then the experience may contribute less to a durable peace and the entrenchment of the rule of law.

A UN Commission of Experts that preceded creation of the Rwanda tribunal acknowledged this point, noting that domestic courts could be more sensitive to individual cases and that resulting decisions "could be of greater and more immediate symbolic force, because verdicts would be rendered by courts familiar to the local community."[29]

Two developments suggest a gradual acknowledgment of the priority to be given to domestic ownership of the process. First, since 1995, there has been no purely international body established, à la the El Salvador commission or the Yugoslavia and Rwanda tribunals. Instead, where an international role (beyond support and assistance) is deemed necessary, the trend has been toward creation of hybrid international-domestic bodies, with local members generally forming the majority. Examples include the truth commissions in Guatemala and Sierra Leone, and hybrid courts in Cambodia, Sierra Leone, and Bosnia. Second, unlike the international tribunals for the former Yugoslavia and Rwanda, which were given primacy of jurisdiction that trumps the ability of any domestic court to pursue a prosecution, the statute of the new International Criminal Court (ICC) correctly shifted that primacy. The ICC is complementary to national justice systems and can assert its jurisdiction only over a case of genocide, war crimes, or crimes against humanity when the national system is incapable of or unwilling to do so.[30]

Similarly, there is a growing recognition that the rule of law requires local ownership. Outsiders can and should provide substantial levels of assistance, but they cannot descend upon a country for a year or two and magically impose a viable system and culture of respect for the rule of law. "While the international community is obliged to act directly for the protection of human rights and human security where conflict has eroded or frustrated the domestic rule of law, in the long term, no ad hoc, temporary or external measures can ever replace a functioning *national* justice system."[31] As noted earlier, meaningful reforms related to the rule of law will require the development of significant local capacity and political will. This is often a painstaking and drawn-out process that does not jibe with the funding and program cycles and political attention span of international donors. As a consequence, while the rhetoric of "the importance of local ownership" is on the rise, these other factors often still result in the imposition of foreign-driven priorities and timetables for rule-of-law reform efforts. In various countries, after an international postconflict mission spends a few years directing affairs or deciding priorities, well-meaning international staff depart the country, leaving little in place in the way of changed capacity or attitudes and wondering why their efforts have not produced more significant results. Part of the answer lies in the degree of real local dissemination and local ownership of rule-of-law reform.

Practice, however, seems to be moving in the direction of rhetoric. The role of the international community in building the rule of law in postconflict societies is expanding, as noted earlier. As our collective understanding grows, however, of the relationship between the rule of law and postconflict stabilization and of how to facilitate the sustainable entrenchment of the rule of law, the place of local ownership is becoming more central, meaning that different approaches will be adopted based on local decisions informed by outside advice.

CONCLUSION

New challenges to peace require new tools. As war in all parts of the globe changes its complexion, becoming preponderantly intra-national, establishing the rule of law plays an increasingly critical role, particularly in the immediate postconflict construction of peace.

There are those who, even today, imply that emphasis on the establishment of the rule of law is irrelevant, or at best tangential, to the real work of conflict resolution and postconflict peacebuilding—an exercise naively engaged in by those who believe that the simple imposition of legal regulations and institutions will promptly erase deep-seated resentments, hatreds, and power struggles. Nothing could be less accurate. The rule of law has at its core a hard-nosed and not particularly optimistic assessment of human nature and the prospects for conflict. It assumes that pacific pledges and conciliatory rhetoric are obviously important to peacebuilding but can be too tenuous. In the worst case, the rule of law imposes a network of institutions, mechanisms, and procedures that check sources of tension at an early phase, constrain the ability of any party to engage in violent or abusive action, and force an open process and a relatively level playing field. In the best case, when diligently nurtured, this system of accountability, conflict resolution, limits on power, and the airing and processing of opposing views—all undertaken through nonviolent channels—becomes habit forming, reducing the likelihood of another civil war.

NOTES

1. Lotta Harbom and Peter Wallensteen, "Patterns of Major Armed Conflicts, 1990—2004" in *SIPRI Yearbook 2005: Armaments, Disarmament and International Security* (Oxford: Oxford University Press, 2005), 121. The SIPRI study defines a major armed conflict as "the use of armed force between the military forces of two or more governments, or of one government and at least one organized armed group, resulting in the battle-related deaths of at least 1,000 people in any single year and in which the incompatibility concerns control of government and/or territory." The study found that during the period

1990–2004, only four of fifty-seven conflicts (7 percent) were wars of the classical interstate variety.

2. "The proclamation of this constitution . . . not only did not stop lawless and arbitrary rule, but also served to camouflage it, allowing the torture and killing of innocent people while praising Stalin's law for all the people." Aleksandr Iakovlev, "Constitutional Socialist Democracy: Dream or Reality," *Columbia Journal of Transnational Law* 28 (1990): 117.

3. "Concluding Document of the CSCE Copenhagen Conference on the Human Dimension, June 29, 1990," *International Legal Materials* 29 (1990): 1305, 1306. The CSCE member states explained that "the rule of law does not mean merely a formal legality which assumes regularity and consistency in the achievement and enforcement of democratic order, but justice based on the recognition and full acceptance of the supreme value of the human personality and guaranteed by institutions providing a framework for its fullest expression."

4. See, for example, Theodor Meron, "International Criminalization of Internal Atrocities," *American Journal of International Law* 89 (1995): 554.

5. United Nations, "Statute of the International Tribunal for the Prosecution of Persons Responsible for Genocide and Other Serious Violations of International Humanitarian Law Committed in the Territory of Rwanda and Rwandan Citizens Responsible for Genocide and Other Such Violations Committed in the Territory of Neighboring States, between 1 January 1994 and 31 December 1994," UN Doc. S/RES/955, annex (New York: United Nations, 1994). Even though the war in the former Yugoslavia was treated as international in nature, the international criminal tribunal created to address the abuses of that conflict stated its conviction that its jurisdiction also extends to crimes perpetrated in both internal and international conflicts. United Nations, *Annual Report,* UN Doc. A/49/342-S/1994/ 1007, par. 19 (New York: United Nations, 1994).

6. Rome Statute of the International Criminal Court, UN Doc. A/CONF.183/9, Articles 6–8.

7. Boutros Boutros-Ghali, *An Agenda for Peace* (New York: United Nations, 1992), 32–34.

8. See, for example, Melvin Small and J. David Singer, "The War-proneness of Democratic Regimes," *Jerusalem Journal of International Relations* 1, no. 4 (Summer 1976): 50–69; Rudolph J. Rummel, *War, Power, Peace,* vol. 4 of *Understanding Conflict and War*

(Newbury Park, Calif.: Sage Publications, 1979); Rudolph J. Rummel, "Libertarianism and International Violence," *Journal of Conflict Resolution* 27, no. 1 (March 1983): 27–71; Bruce Russett, *Grasping the Democratic Peace: Principles for a Post–Cold War World* (Princeton, N.J.: Princeton University Press, 1993); Zeev Maoz and Nasrin Abdolali, "Regime Types and International Conflict, 1815–1976," *Journal of Conflict Resolution* 3 (1989): 3–35; and William J. Dixon, "Democracy and the Peaceful Settlement of International Conflict," *American Political Science Review* 88, no. 1 (March 1994): 14–32. Much of the research on the "democratic peace" finds its roots in the theory propounded nearly two hundred years ago by Immanuel Kant. But see, for example, Edward D. Mansfield and Jack Snyder, "Democratization and War," *Foreign Affairs* 74, no. 3 (May–June 1995): 79–97. They suggest that although fully democratized nations are less likely to go to war with one another, the process of transition to democracy exacerbates instability and thereby enhances the possibility of entry into conflict in the short term.

9. "Concluding Document of the CSCE Copenhagen Conference on the Human Dimension." In 1994, to reflect a series of structural changes as the Helsinki process moved from a series of periodic meetings to a permanent organization with several institutional components and full-time staff, the name of the Conference on Security and Cooperation in Europe was formally changed to the Organization for Security and Cooperation in Europe.

10. See, for example, Rachel Kleinfeld, "Competing Definitions of the Rule of Law," in *Promoting the Rule of Law Abroad,* ed. Thomas Carothers (Washington, D.C.: Carnegie Endowment for International Peace, 2006).

11. As one observer of rule-of law-assistance has noted:

> Assistance in this field has mushroomed in recent years, becoming a major category of international aid. . . . Russia's legal and judicial reforms, for example, have been supported by a variety of U.S. assistance projects, extensive German aid, a $58 million World Bank loan, and numerous smaller World Bank and European Bank for Reconstruction and Development initiatives, as well as many efforts sponsored by Great Britain, the Netherlands, Denmark, and the European Union. . . .
>
> Almost every major bilateral donor, a wide range of multilateral organizations—especially

development banks—and countless foundations, universities, and human rights groups are getting into the act. In most countries, U.S. rule-of-law assistance is a small part of the aid pool, although Americans frequently assume it is of paramount importance. They mistakenly believe that rule-of-law promotion is their special province, although they are not alone in that. German and French jurists also tend to view their country as the keeper of the flame of civil code reform. British lawyers and judges point to the distinguished history of the British approach. Transitional countries are bombarded with fervent but contradictory advice on judicial and legal reform.

Thomas Carothers, "The Rule of Law Revival," *Foreign Affairs* 77, no. 2 (March–April 1998): 95, 103–104.

12. Organization for Security and Cooperation in Europe, *Kosovo: A Review of the Criminal Justice System* (Vienna: Organization for Security and Cooperation in Europe, October 18, 2000).

13. As UN secretary-general Kofi Annan has noted, "experience in the past decade has demonstrated clearly that the consolidation of peace in the immediate post-conflict period, as well as the maintenance of peace in the long term, cannot be achieved unless the population is confident that redress for grievances can be obtained through legitimate structures for peaceful settlement of disputes and the fair administration of justice." Kofi Annan, *The Rule of Law and Transitional Justice in Conflict and Post-Conflict Societies*, UN Doc. No. S/2004/616 (New York: United Nations, August 23, 2004), 3, par. 2.

14. For a comprehensive review of this category of rights, see Stanislav Chernichenko and William Treat, *The Administration of Justice and the Human Rights of Detainees: The Right to a Fair Trial—Current Recognition and Measures Necessary for Its Strengthening*, UN Doc. No. E/CN.4/Sub.2/1994/24 (New York: United Nations, June 3, 1994); and William M. Cohen, "Principles for Establishment of a Rule of Law Criminal Justice System," *Georgia Journal of International and Comparative Law* 23 (Summer 1993): 269–287.

15. Radio Free Europe/Radio Liberty, "Britain Sends Special Crime Squad to Kosovo," *Balkan Report* 5, no. 3 (January 12, 2001).

16. "General Framework Agreement for Peace in Bosnia and Herzegovina," annex 7, article I, par. 3, and annex 11, November 21, 1995.

17. Friedrich A. von Hayek, *The Road to Serfdom* (Chicago: University of Chicago Press, 1944), 72.

18. Hernando de Soto, *The Other Path: The Invisible Revolution in the Third World* (New York: Harper and Row, 1989), 253.

19. See, for example, Diane F. Orentlicher, "Settling Accounts: The Duty to Prosecute Human Rights Violations of a Prior Regime," *Yale Law Journal* 100 (June 1991): 2537–2615.

20. Adding to the concern that the gacaca approach will not quickly calm the situation, between April 2005 and March 2006, some 19,000 Rwandans sought asylum in neighboring Burundi, reportedly fleeing persecution under the gacaca system. "Burundi-Rwanda: Thousands More Asylum Seekers Repatriated," IRINnews.org, June 13, 2006; and UN Office for the Coordination of Humanitarian Affairs, http://www.irinnews.org/print.asp?reportid=53896, June 23, 2006.

21. Thomas Buergenthal, "The United Nations Truth Commission for El Salvador," *Vanderbilt Journal of Transnational Law* 27, no. 3 (October 1994): 503.

22. As Thomas Buergenthal, one of the three members of the commission, has noted, the "establishment of the Truth Commission marks the first time that the parties to an internal armed conflict, in negotiating a peace agreement, conferred on a commission composed of foreign nationals designated by the United Nations the power to investigate human rights violations committed during the conflict and to make binding recommendations. . . . National reconciliation is often difficult to achieve in countries trying to overcome the consequences of a bloody, internal armed conflict or an especially repressive regime without an appropriate accounting for or acknowledgment of past human rights violations. To the extent that the Truth Commission as an institution met the demands of the Salvadoran peace process, it has become a model the international community is likely to draw upon in the years to come." Ibid., 501–502. In his article, Professor Buergenthal provides an insightful firsthand description and analysis of the Truth Commission and its relationship to the peace process.

23. United Nations, *Report of the Commission on the Truth for El Salvador: From Madness to Hope*, UN Doc. S/25500, annex (New York: United Nations,

1993), 25; and Buergenthal, "The United Nations Truth Commission for El Salvador," 522.

24. "Agreement between the Government of Guatemala and the Guatemalan National Revolutionary Unity on the Establishment of the Commission for Historical Clarification," June 23, 1994.

25. A multiyear interdisciplinary project on constitution making, peacebuilding, and national reconciliation, organized by the United States Institute of Peace in cooperation with the United Nations Development Programme, conducted case studies of the constitution-making processes of eighteen countries in transition to derive a series of lessons for application in postconflict environments. The analyses developed through the project inform this section of the present essay.

26. Interviews by the author.

27. Government of Eritrea, Proclamation No. 55/1994, March 15, 1994.

28. Bereket Habte Selassie, "Constitution Making as a Historic Moment" (keynote speech to the International Symposium on the Making of the Eritrean Constitution, Asmara, Eritrea, January 7, 1995).

29. "Preliminary Report of the Independent Commission of Experts Established in Accordance with Security Council Resolution 935," 1994, 31.

30. Rome Statute of the International Criminal Court, UN Doc. A/CONF.183/9, Preamble and Article 17.

31. Annan, *The Rule of Law and Transitional Justice in Conflict and Post-Conflict Societies*, 12, par. 34 (emphasis added). A UN-sponsored study on postconflict reconstruction proceeds from the same premise: "Wartorn societies inevitably depend to a large degree on external assistance for reconstruction. . . . The question of the relative role, responsibility and authority of external donors and actors, as opposed to local ones, in bringing about and maintaining peace and in rebuilding the country is one of the most important and most delicate questions. . . . External assistance, rather than being subsidiary to local efforts, tends to become a substitute, and worse, destroys local coping and resistance mechanisms and controls emerging local institutions and solutions. A large-scale foreign presence . . . is obviously not sustainable in the long term, neither politically for the local actors nor financially for the external ones. A policy of 'betting on the local' may in the short term be more laborious, less spectacular, and take more time, but in the long term may be the only realistic option." *Rebuilding Wartorn Societies: Problems of International Assistance in Conflict and Postconflict Situations* (Geneva: United Nations Research Institute for Social Development and the Programme for Strategic and International Security Studies of the Geneva Graduate Institute of International Studies, August 1994), 17.

24

RETHINKING THE "WAR ON TERROR"
NEW APPROACHES TO CONFLICT PREVENTION AND MANAGEMENT IN THE POST-9/11 WORLD

Paul B. Stares and Mona Yacoubian

THE NEW STRATEGIC CHALLENGE FAC-
ing the United States in the wake of
9/11 is often compared with the great
"generational" struggles of the twentieth century against fascism and communism. While
the contest likely will be as prolonged and require a comparable mobilization of national
and international resources if the United States
is to prevail, the comparison should not be
pushed too far. The struggle we now find ourselves in is like neither World War II nor the
Cold War, with their clearly defined combatants, "front lines," and rules of engagement.
The perpetrators of the September 11 attacks
represent a transnational, highly dynamic, increasingly decentralized, religiously inspired
movement propelled for the most part by a diverse collection of nonstate actors. They operate
in some instances openly but more often clan-
destinely, using unorthodox tactics and weapons. The challenge posed by what we define as
"Islamist militancy" is fundamentally different, therefore, from traditional "state-centric"
threats to international peace and security.

As such, Islamist militancy has more in common with other so-called new security challenges that transcend national borders and are
driven by nonstate actors and processes. This
does not mean that the traditional toolbox of
national security responses is now irrelevant or
renders obsolete the standard menu of conflict
prevention and management techniques—on
the contrary. But these techniques must be
adapted and complemented with new approaches that acknowledge unconventional
attributes of these new security challenges. In
the case of Islamist militancy, the nature of the
evolving challenge is still poorly understood.
Thus, before describing an alternative, and
what we believe to be a more effective strategy
for responding to Islamist militancy than the
approach currently favored in the "global war
on terror," this chapter will first lay out a different way of thinking about the new strategic
challenge confronting the United States.

THE NEW STRATEGIC CHALLENGE

Despite a plethora of studies and policy prescriptions since the September 11 attacks, we
are still trying to grasp the nature of the new
strategic challenge we face and how best to

Figure 1. Islamist Militancy, c. 2006

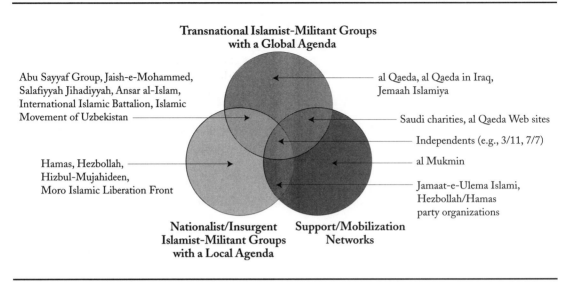

Transnational Islamist-Militant Groups with a Global Agenda

Abu Sayyaf Group, Jaish-e-Mohammed, Salafiyyah Jihadiyyah, Ansar al-Islam, International Islamic Battalion, Islamic Movement of Uzbekistan

al Qaeda, al Qaeda in Iraq, Jemaah Islamiya

Saudi charities, al Qaeda Web sites

Independents (e.g., 3/11, 7/7)

Hamas, Hezbollah, Hizbul-Mujahideen, Moro Islamic Liberation Front

al Mukmin

Jamaat-e-Ulema Islami, Hezbollah/Hamas party organizations

Nationalist/Insurgent Islamist-Militant Groups with a Local Agenda

Support/Mobilization Networks

counter it. There is no better indication of this than the complete lack of consensus or common lexicon about what to call the threat. Is it "global terrorism," "Islamic terrorism," "al Qaeda and its affiliates," "Sunni jihadists," "Islamist radicals," or "terrorist extremism"? This is not just a semantics issue; words and names have vital operational import. Without clarity on who, precisely, is our adversary, we are unlikely to ever develop a clear and comprehensive understanding of its objectives, strategy, and operational character. And without such a common understanding, it will be difficult, if not impossible, to conceive of an effective and sustainable response. Yet it is our assessment that there is neither a broadly accepted understanding of the challenge we face nor a comprehensive long-term strategy to counter it.

Our preference is to classify this broader challenge as "Islamist militancy." Like the 9/11 Commission, we feel it important to use the modifier "Islamist"—a politico-religious movement within the Muslim world—rather than "Islamic"—the culture and religion of Islam.[1] Unlike the 9/11 Commission, however, we prefer the simpler, less loaded term "militancy"

to "terrorism." Using the term "militants" to refer to those who either employ or espouse violent means in pursuit of political ends not only avoids the notoriously slippery definitional problems associated with terrorism but also serves to underscore that the challenge is both multidimensional and broad based, involving more actors than just those who actually carry out terrorist attacks.[2] Indeed, Islamist militancy has three main constituent groups whose memberships are constantly evolving and overlap in significant ways.

There are, first, the transnational jihadist groups that have a global agenda (principally al Qaeda and its affiliates); second, the nationalist insurgent groups that have essentially a local agenda (e.g., Hamas, Hezbollah, and some of the Kashmiri groups); and, third, the miscellaneous organizations and networks that directly and indirectly support these militant groups. Distinctions among these groups are difficult to discern. Indeed, more and more new organizations and groups are emerging that share common traits with overlapping agendas. Figure 1 provides a general snapshot of the principal actors in 2006. The diagram is not meant to be exhaustive and is merely illustrative of the phenomenon and its key constituent elements.

Islamist militancy does not represent a conventional national security threat—that much is clear and generally understood. Neither does it represent a conventional terrorist threat, which typically has a distinctive—often singular—identity with reasonably clear political goals, organizational structure, and area of operations. Conventional counterterrorist responses, with their emphasis on apprehending an organization's leaders and rolling up networks or cells of activists and supporters through improved intelligence gathering and sharing, are usually effective therefore. Although such methods remain just as necessary to any campaign against Islamist militancy, it is also becoming clear that they will not be sufficient. The growing trend, exhibited in attacks such as those in Madrid (March 2004), London (July 2005), and elsewhere, toward the emergence of localized, self-organizing militant groups acting largely independently of higher operational direction underscores the limits of conventional counterterrorism responses.

Not surprisingly, an increasing number of experts now advocate drawing on the strategies and tactics of unconventional, or "irregular," warfare to meet the challenge.[3] The threat is portrayed as a global insurgency that requires a commensurate global counterinsurgency (COIN) campaign. There is some logic to this as elements of the challenge reflect characteristics of a classic insurgency. Certainly, al Qaeda's stated goals of expelling "Jews and crusaders" from the Muslim world and cleansing it of apostate regimes—all with the objective of reestablishing a purified caliphate—can be viewed as an insurgency of sorts. The recognition that success ultimately hinges on winning "hearts and minds" in the Muslim world is also a critically important attribute of a counterinsurgency response.

Yet just as classic counterterrorism measures have their limits, so a strictly counter-insurgency approach has its shortcomings and even liabilities. Describing the phenomenon as a global insurgency dangerously exaggerates the threat by assuming a degree of organization and unity among its various actors that currently does not exist. The COIN approach also risks conflating many kinds of Islamist struggles and perversely even serving to legitimize them. Unless suitably adapted, the standard COIN framework with its simplistic distinctions between "enemies," "friends," and "uncommitted" could make matters worse, especially if military or "kinetic" responses come to dominate.

With these concerns in mind, we propose an alternative strategy to countering Islamist militancy that views the challenge as one would a global public health threat or epidemic. The conceptual leap required by this approach is not as far as it first appears. Social scientists increasingly have looked to epidemiology to understand a variety of social contagions, and here Islamist militancy is no different. Specifically, our approach draws on the scientific principles and practices of epidemiology as well as the insights from a growing body of research on "social contagion phenomena" such as fashions, fads, rumors, civil violence, and revolutionary ideas.[4] Moreover, many commentators and even U.S. officials have employed disease metaphors to describe the challenge of Islamist militancy.[5] Thus references to terrorism being a "virus" or to al Qaeda "mutating" or "metastasizing" are common. Similarly, the image of madrassas and mosques being "incubators" of a "virulent ideology" is frequently invoked. Such metaphors have a visceral appeal in that they help to convey a dangerous and, moreover, darkly insidious threat. For some, the disease metaphor also sets—implicitly, at least—a more realistic goal for what can be practically achieved to eliminate this scourge. Just as very few diseases have been completely eradicated, so the likelihood that terrorism or political violence will be rendered extinct is remote. The best that can be hoped for is for it to become a manage-able, low-probability, albeit sometimes deadly, nuisance much like many other social ills.

Beyond its metaphorical appeal there are more practical attractions to an epidemiological/ public health approach. Three stand out:

• First, epidemiologists observe rigorous stan-dards of inquiry and analysis to understand the derivation, dynamics, and propagation of a specific disease. In particular, they seek clarity on the origins and geographical and social contours of an outbreak: where the disease is concentrated, how it is transmit-ted, who is most at risk or "susceptible" to infection, and why some portions of society may be less susceptible or, for all intents and purposes, immune. Applying the same methodological approach to mapping and understanding Islamist militancy can yield immediately useful guidance on where and how to counter it.

• Second, epidemiologists recognize that dis-eases neither arise nor spread in a vacuum. They emerge and evolve as a result of a complex dynamic interactive process be-tween people, pathogens, and the environ-ment in which they live. Indeed, the epi-demiologic concept of "cause" is rarely if ever singular or linear but is more akin to a "web" of direct and indirect factors that play a lesser or greater role in differing cir-cumstances. To make sense of this com-plexity, epidemiologists typically employ a standard analytical device that "deconstructs" the key constituent elements of a disease. This model helps not only to understand the phenomenon in its entirety but also to anticipate how it might evolve in the fu-ture. As will be discussed, the same systemic conception of disease can be adapted to un-derstand the constituent elements of Is-lamist militancy and their evolution.

• Third, just as epidemiologists view disease as a complex, multifaceted phenomenon, so public health officials have come to recog-

Figure 2. The Epidemic Model

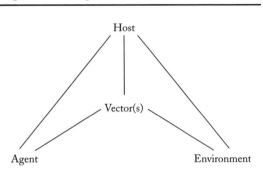

nize that success in controlling and rolling back an epidemic typically results from a carefully orchestrated, systematic, priori-tized, multipronged effort to address each of its constituent elements. At the same time, however, it is also recognized that signifi-cant progress or major advances can some-times be precipitated by relatively minor interventions—or "tipping points."[6] Again, there are lessons and insights to be learned here for orchestrating a global counter-terrorism campaign.

Before turning to what such a campaign to defeat Islamist militancy might look like were it to follow a public health or counterepidemic approach, it is necessary to understand how epi-demiologists typically try to understand dis-ease and how this can help us understand the challenge we face.

THE EPIDEMIC MODEL

As indicated, epidemiologists employ a stan-dard approach, or model, to study epidemics that deconstructs an outbreak into four key components, recognizing that in reality they are all dynamically interconnected, as shown in figure 2.[7]

In simple terms, the agent refers to the pathogen (e.g., a virus or bacterium) that causes disease. The host is the person infected by the disease (the "infective"), while the environment

Figure 3. The Epidemic Model Applied to Islamist Militancy

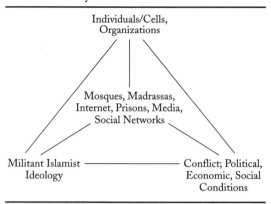

refers to a variety of external factors that affect both agent and host. At the center of the triad are the vectors, the key pathways, or conduits, that help propagate the disease.

Islamist militancy is clearly not a disease in a comparably clinical fashion. Whereas those who fall victim to disease are typically passive and unwitting receptors of the pathogen, Islamist militants to a lesser or greater extent willingly decide to play an active role of some kind. Yet their actions are clearly driven by a core set of ideas and beliefs—an ideology—that has an "infectious" appeal. In this and other respects Islamist militancy can be seen as having epidemic-like qualities. It, too, therefore, can be deconstructed using the classic epidemic model, as shown in figure 3.

Thus, so applied, the agent is Islamist militant ideology. Specifically, two primary "strains" can be identified: (1) a transnational Salafist/jihadist ideology as espoused by al Qaeda[8] and (2) a nationalist/insurgent Islamist militant ideology as espoused by groups such as Hezbollah, Hamas, and some of the militant Kashmiri groups. Each of these ideological strains is characterized by a specific set of underlying assumptions, motivations, and goals.

The host is the group or person "infected" by the agent. More specifically, the host refers to a group or individual who becomes to a

lesser or greater extent an adherent of militant Islamist ideology. As defined, Islamist militants are those who employ or espouse the use of violence in pursuit of political goals.

The environment refers to key factors specific to the Muslim world that promote exposure to Islamist militancy—conflict, political repression, economic stagnation, and social alienation being the leading influences. Vectors in this case refer to a variety of known conduits that are used to propagate the ideology and associated action agendas, such as mosques, prisons, madrassas, the Internet, satellite television, and diasporic networks.

It is important to understand that the epidemic model of Islamist militancy acknowledges that the vast majority of Muslims find the core elements of Islamist militant ideology to be both aberrant and abhorrent. In this respect they are effectively "immunized" to its appeal. However, some unknown, yet critical, proportion of the population is clearly "susceptible" to becoming not only an adherent of the ideology but actively motivated by it.

Several policy-relevant benefits accrue from conceiving of Islamist militancy in this fashion. First, it captures the key elements of the challenge in a *systemic* manner rather than in the disaggregated, unconnected way that so often bedevils analysis and understanding. Second, it is a *dynamic* model that acknowledges that the phenomenon is not static but constantly evolving with the emergence of new strains, new hosts, new vectors, and changing environmental conditions. Third, it provides insights into how Islamist militancy may evolve in the future.

However, unlike with an outbreak of disease, in which those infected typically (though not always) are motivated to report their condition to seek treatment, the size and spread of Islamist militancy are clearly more difficult to assess. A combination of indicators (e.g., the number of attacks conducted or thwarted and militants killed or incarcerated, the influence of jihadist Web sites, the dissemination

Figure 4. Growth of the "Epidemic"

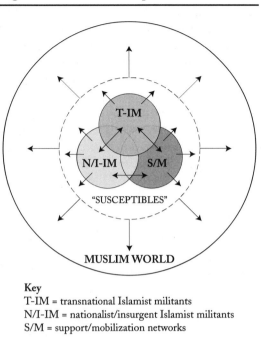

Key
T-IM = transnational Islamist militants
N/I-IM = nationalist/insurgent Islamist militants
S/M = support/mobilization networks

of training materials, etc.) suggests that the phenomenon is expanding as well as mutating in the ways indicated earlier. Surveys within the Muslim world of people's attitudes toward the United States and the West more generally would also suggest that the pool of "susceptibles"—those at risk for becoming Islamist militants—is large and expanding in certain countries. Figure 4 depicts the overall growth of Islamist militancy.

THE COUNTEREPIDEMIC APPROACH

Faced with the outbreak of an infectious disease, public health officials typically employ a three-pronged strategy to counter the threat.

First, *contain* the most threatening outbreaks to prevent them from gaining enough mass and momentum to overwhelm public health responders and threaten public order. Standard measures include quarantining specific areas to contain the movement of infectious

individuals, eliminating or decontaminating identifiable vectors of transmission, and, if an antidote exists, treating and rehabilitating individuals who have succumbed to the disease. Containing and contracting the number of infectives can effectively eradicate the pathogen, though such a success is rare, as indicated earlier.

Second, *protect* those who are most vulnerable or susceptible to the disease (the high-risk groups) as well as those who are most critical to a functioning society (high-value groups). The most effective countermeasure is selective or targeted immunization programs. Interestingly, not everyone needs to be inoculated to achieve what is known as "herd immunity"—essentially, the level at which the probability of an infected person being in contact with a nonimmunized person is very low, if not zero. If an effective vaccine is not available, other protective strategies are employed, including encouraging "safe practices" through public education to reduce the probability of exposure and the rate of new infection.

Third, *remedy* the environmental conditions that fostered the emergence of the disease in specific areas and its subsequent spread. Many types of interventions are conceivable, from the local to the global, depending on the nature of the threat.

Adapting the same basic strategic imperatives of a counterepidemic campaign to the threat posed by Islamist militancy would immediately translate into the following operational priorities:

◆ Containing and contracting the activities of the most "virulent" Islamist militant organizations—the transnational jihadist groups with global reach and apocalyptic agendas—as well as those who could gain a meaningful operational presence in areas of significant strategic interest. These areas would include most notably Iraq, Pakistan, Afghanistan, Saudi Arabia, Egypt, Palestine, the Caucasus, and the Muslim diaspora communities of Western Europe, as well as areas in the vicinity of key global financial/ economic infrastructure assets.

- Protecting the high-risk/high-value communities of the Muslim world. According to open-source—unclassified—accounts, a disproportionate number of the officers and foot soldiers in the transnational jihadist cause come from a few countries—Saudi Arabia, Egypt, Morocco, Algeria, Yemen, Pakistan—and from the European diaspora communities. The high-value communities consist of the educational, religious, political, and security sectors of countries where Islamist militant organizations could make the greatest inroads and the growing number of transnational cultural, business, and media networks that affect the lives of many millions of Muslims throughout the larger *Ummah* (Islamic community).

- Remedying the key environmental factors that foster Islamist militancy. The most important would appear to be the ongoing conflicts or insurgencies involving Muslims and non-Muslims that help validate the central jihadist argument that Islam is under attack and that also serve as recruiting magnets and training grounds—notably, Iraq, Palestine, Kashmir, Afghanistan, Chechnya, and several smaller conflicts in Central and Southeast Asia. Social alienation within the European diaspora communities and public corruption, political repression, and economic stagnation in key areas of the Muslim world are widely viewed as additional factors.

These strategic imperatives can be further translated into specific containment, protective, and remedial programs or initiatives that, again, draw on the principles and practices of a counterepidemic campaign.

Containment Measures

In addition to limiting the operational reach and capabilities of the most threatening Islamist militant organizations by using standard counterterrorism measures and discrete special intelligence/military operations, containment initiatives would extend to placing greater emphasis on disrupting and restricting the untrammeled use of key vectors—the Internet, satellite TV, prisons, schools, mosques, and so on—by Islamist militant organizations. Some vectors can be physically shut down, others "decontaminated" of unwanted infectious agents.[9] Containment measures appear to be a largely haphazard, after-the-fact effort at the present, rather than a systematically planned, internationally executed campaign.

Because of the practical limits to such efforts in an open society, greater attention should also be given to nurturing and propagating what can be termed an "ideological antidote" to the key tenets of Islamist militant ideology. This can involve a broad-gauged campaign to denounce and delegitimize jihadist propaganda and practices such as beheadings and the killing of innocent civilians, including fellow Muslims, as well as more discrete efforts aimed toward a specific group or community. The former includes mobilizing moderate religious figures to issue fatwas condemning the ideology and tactics used as a perversion of Islam and encouraging key opinion makers, cultural leaders, and mass media figures to do the same.[10] Such efforts have been made, but apparently not in an extensive or concerted way.[11] More targeted activities include exploiting the ideological contradictions or schisms within the transnational jihadist movement to foment internal dissension and possible defection. There are reports, for example, of successful counterideological efforts in Yemen that in turn yielded operational success in rolling up a local al Qaeda network.[12]

Although many Islamist militants are beyond such intellectual suasion—essentially the health care equivalent of treatment and rehabilitation—this may not be the case with some groups and organizations. Local national-insurgent movements, in particular, may be susceptible to a "rehabilitative" process in much the way that other terrorist organizations have abandoned armed struggle. The evolving role of groups such as Hamas and Hezbollah, for example, suggests the possibility of their integration into their respective political systems. The provision of amnesties to insurgents willing to lay down arms, as in Afghanistan, constitutes another element of rehabilitation. And in Iraq, reports suggest a growing rift between the nationalist Iraqi elements of the insurgency and foreign jihadists, in part as a result of the latter's indiscriminate targeting of civilians.[13]

Protective Measures

Whereas the containment measures are directed primarily at those already infected, protective measures are aimed at those who are most at risk and those who play important societal functions. It is conceivable that with better understanding of why certain groups and individuals become first sympathetic to, then supportive of, and, finally, actively engaged in Islamist militant causes, targeted programs to effectively immunize at-risk groups could be designed. There are many cases where key populations have been targeted in ways designed to turn off their receptiveness to specific ideas, messages, and unhealthy or antisocial practices, including by appealing to people's common sense, their personal safety, their peer group standing, religious edicts, and societal norms, among other approaches. In some cases the tactics used are not unlike real vaccination programs that work on the principle of exposing uninfected populations to a weakened or attenuated version of the virus so that the body learns to identify and reject the real thing. Political campaigns, for example, often expose key undecided voters to the arguments of opposing candidates, in some cases to ridicule the candidates, but more often to "arm" the voters with convincing reasons to be skeptical when they hear the same arguments from those candidates.[14]

Similar public programs aimed at undermining the appeal of militant Islamist ideology could be designed and implemented in many different arenas, from schools to mosques to mass media outlets. Unless they are undertaken in the Muslim communities of Western Europe, however, these are clearly not initiatives that the United States (and the West more generally) should lead or be openly associated with. Western states can, however, prod allies and partners in the Muslim world and provide discreet assistance.

Such "ideological immunization" efforts aimed at high-risk communities should not just provide a negative image of militant Islamism, however. Ideally, they should also offer a positive and compelling alternative vision for the future. Indeed, efforts to undermine militant Islamism and provide a positive counterideology can be mutually reinforcing. Again, the same arenas and conduits—schools, mosques, mass media outlets—have a critical role to play, and thus efforts designed to mobilize and strengthen moderate voices in these sectors should be an indispensable component of the overall effort.[15]

Remedial Measures

Many of the previous initiatives will be harder to accomplish or will likely fail if parallel efforts are not also taken to remedy some of the key environmental conditions that promote Islamist militancy in the Muslim world. For reasons discussed earlier, an intensified effort should be made to resolve or at least tamp down the violent conflicts that have a particularly strong resonance within the Muslim world. Indeed, successful conflict management and prevention strategies will play a key role in impeding the spread of Islamist militancy. Besides reducing the direct role of the presence of violent conflict in jihadist recruitment and training, conflict resolution efforts will help invalidate jihadist propaganda and buttress moderate support.

The implementation of political reforms focused on good governance, particularly greater transparency, accountability, and the

Figure 5. Countering the "Epidemic"

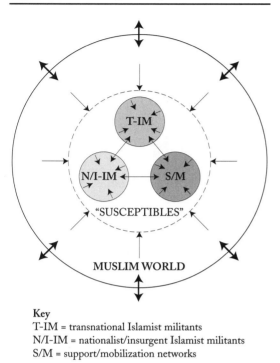

Key
T-IM = transnational Islamist militants
N/I-IM = nationalist/insurgent Islamist militants
S/M = support/mobilization networks

rule of law, will also play a key role in neutralizing Islamist militant ideology that calls for the overthrow of corrupt regimes. Likewise, greater civil liberties, including broader freedoms of assembly and expression as well as the freedom to form political parties and other associations, will help to level the political playing field and allow "healthy" outlets for dissent. Particular emphasis should be placed on institution building so as to prevent democratic gains from being undermined by autocratic regimes or exploited by nondemocratic opposition forces. Facilitating the political participation of peaceful, moderate Islamists can also help to develop an effective counterweight to Islamist militants and their violent tactics.

The implementation of economic reforms designed to spur growth and bolster job creation will likewise help to ease popular disaffection, particularly among the region's disproportion-

ately young population. In addition, economic reforms that create an environment that is more appealing to foreign investors will help the Muslim world to integrate more effectively into the broader global economic system and help bridge the gap in relative performance between the Muslim world, particularly the Arab world, and the global economy.

◆ ◆ ◆

The combined effect of these containment, protective, and remedial measures will be to reverse over time the negative trends discussed earlier. As figure 5 depicts, the effect will be to divide, isolate, and weaken the Islamist militant organizations and marginalize their operational impact. The pool of susceptibles will also shrink in relation to the rest of the Muslim world, which through the various remedial efforts will become a more "healthy" and integrated part of the larger, globalizing world.

As with a global health campaign, success in countering the challenge of Islamist militancy will depend on a sustained commitment over many years, if not decades, by a broad coalition of like-minded states acting in partnership with a multitude of nongovernmental actors. Simply stated, there is no single or easy cure.

CONCLUDING OBSERVATIONS

The counterepidemic approach to meeting the challenge of Islamist militancy follows in fundamental respects the basic tenets of effective conflict prevention and management. These tenets can be summarized as follows using common admonitions from the world of public health care:

◆ *Prevention is better than cure.* Reducing the momentum of a conflict, especially after passions have become inflamed and blood spilt, is clearly more difficult than taking early preventive measures to forestall violence;

positions harden, options narrow, and the costs rise. Early warning and early response can therefore make all the difference.

- *Diagnose before treating.* Knowing thy ailment is just as important as knowing thy enemy. While it doesn't guarantee success, understanding clearly the source(s) and dynamics of a conflict before taking action obviously improves the chances of applying the right tools in the right place with the right outcomes.
- *Do no harm.* The Hippocratic Oath is no less relevant to conflict management. As countless examples attest, poorly timed or calibrated interventions can make a problem worse, not better. Knowing what to do and when to do it in conflict management is as much an art as a science, but again, experience provides a rich set of guidelines, particularly when it comes to balancing incentives and disincentives, force with diplomacy, and so on.
- *Address the source, not the symptoms.* Resolving the root cause of a conflict typically raises the bar in terms of what is required to secure peace, but as many long-festering disputes attest, the "Band-Aid" approach to conflict management at best delays and in many instances complicates the task of finding a sustainable solution.
- *Palliate what you cannot cure.* Sometimes, however, a solution is beyond practical reach. Just as some diseases are—for the time being, at least—incurable, so some conflicts become, for all intents and purposes, intractable. Under such circumstances the best that can be achieved is to limit the consequences and not make a bad situation worse.

As indicated at the outset, however, the task of conflict prevention and management must adapt to the emerging realities of the twenty-first century. As a consequence of the forces of globalization, the world has clearly become a smaller, more interconnected place. Threats to

international peace and stability that may have previously been considered distant and inconsequential can now resonate more widely, more quickly, and with greater impact. For similar reasons, nonstate actors can now wield unprecedented power for good and bad while also having much greater latitude to operate across borders—again with positive and negative consequences, as al Qaeda and numerous warlords around the world have demonstrated.

At the same time, states seeking to prevent and manage conflict, whether it be within their borders or in areas both adjacent and far away from them, find themselves in a changed operating environment. Besides the interdependencies of a globalizing world, emerging legal rules and norms affect their freedom much more than was ever previously the case. Their actions, furthermore, are subject to greater scrutiny and accountability by virtue of not only the constant 24/7 gaze of the global media but also an expanding network of intergovernmental and nongovernmental organizations.

As a consequence of these new realities, states can rarely, if ever, address threats to peace and stability as singular actors. The task is likely to be too big to solve alone, while important advantages—not least in terms of generating international legitimacy—can be derived from acting collectively. This imperative to cooperate may seem too high a price to pay to those concerned about national sovereignty, but such concerns are arguably becoming redundant in an increasingly interdependent world if they haven't already become so. Indeed, giving up some de jure sovereignty may be the only way for states to regain some de facto sovereignty, especially when it comes to nonstate-based threats such as transnational terrorism.

The growing imperative to cooperate internationally is matched by the comparable need for states to partner with nongovernmental actors and civil society in general. The benefits are mutual. States need the cooperation of NGOs to manage those who would exploit the business and commerce sectors, among others, for nefarious ends. NGOs likewise need the support of governments to operate effectively and relatively freely. Again, such partnerships can confer legitimacy on both sides.

Finally, states must adapt their internal political and bureaucratic structures and processes to these new imperatives. What were largely vestiges of the Cold War and earlier eras have to be reformed or replaced with new mechanisms for governmental decision making, coordination, and implementation. Without such changes, effective conflict prevention and management will only become more difficult to achieve.

NOTES

An earlier version of this chapter was presented to the Aspen Strategy Group Workshop "Mapping the Jihadist Threat: The War on Terror since 9/11," Aspen, Colorado, August 5–10, 2005. It also draws on a larger body of USIP-sponsored research reported in "Rethinking the War on Terror: A Counter-Epidemic Strategy," *Peace Watch* (Washington, D.C.: United States Institute of Peace, April-May 2006), http://www.usip. org/peacewatch/2006/april_may/war_on_terror.html.

1. See National Commission on Terrorist Attacks, *The 9/11 Commission Report: Final Report of the National Commission on Terrorist Attacks upon the United States* (New York: W. W. Norton, 2004), 362n3.

2. We recognize, therefore, that there are also peaceful Islamist organizations, including legal Islamist political parties such as the Party for Justice and Development in Morocco and charitable organizations such as the Red Crescent.

3. See, for example, David J. Kilcullen, "Countering Global Insurgency," in *Journal of Strategic Studies* 28, no. 4 (August 2005): 597–617; and Bruce Hoffman, testimony to the House Armed Services Committee: Subcommittee on Terrorism, Unconventional Threats and Capabilities, 109th Cong., 2nd sess., February 16, 2006.

4. See, for example, Malcolm Gladwell, *The Tipping Point: How Little Things Can Make a Big Differ-*

ence (Boston: First Back Bay, 2002); Joshua M. Epstein, "Modeling Civil Violence: An Agent-Based Computational Approach," *Proceedings of the National Academy of Sciences,* vol. 99, suppl. 3 (May 14, 2003): 7243–7250; Luis M. A. Bettancourt, Ariel Cintron-Arias, David I. Kaiser, and Carlos Castillo-Chavez, "The Power of a Good Idea: Quantitative Modeling of the Spread of Ideas from Epidemiological Models," Santa Fe Institute Working Paper (Santa Fe, N.M.: Santa Fe Institute, February 6, 2005).

5. For example, Richard N. Haass, former director of policy planning, U.S. State Department, went further in drawing the analogy in a major speech: "The challenge of terrorism is . . . akin to fighting a virus in that we can accomplish a great deal but not eradicate the problem. We can take steps to prevent it, protect ourselves from it, and when an attack occurs, quarantine it, minimize the damage it inflicts, and attack it with all our power." Richard N. Haass, speech to the Council on Foreign Relations, New York, October 15, 2001. Likewise, France's top counterterrorism official, Judge Jean-Louis Bruguière, has often compared the terrorist threat posed by groups such as al Qaeda to a mutating virus. See, for example, "Frontline: Al Qaeda's New Front," October 12, 2004, http://www.pbs.org/wgbh/pages/frontline/shows/front/map/bruguiere.html.

6. Numerous examples of "tipping points" exist in nearly every realm of life, from fashion to politics. The reversal of New York City's burgeoning crime wave in the 1980s stands as a classic example of identifying and successfully exploiting a tipping point. In that case, the New York police embarked on a strategy of cracking down on relatively minor "quality-of-life" crimes. They went after panhandlers on the street and subway fare-beaters, as well as employing a concerted effort to clean the graffiti from subway cars and ensure that they stay clean. These relatively minor measures constituted a key tipping point that apparently contributed to a significant downturn in serious crime.

7. Two key references were consulted for this section: B. Burt Gerstman, *Epidemiology Kept Simple: An Introduction to Traditional and Modern Epidemiology* (Hoboken, N.J.: Wiley Liss, 2003); and Leon Gordis, *Epidemiology,* 3rd ed. (Philadelphia: Elsevier Saunders, 2004).

8. The modern Salafi movement traces its roots to the nineteenth-century Egyptian religious figure

Muhammad Abduh and his disciple Rashid Rida, who denounced the innovations and schisms (notably the Sunni-Shiite divide) within the Muslim community as perversions of Islam. Salafists demand a return to the pure form of Islam as practiced by the prophet Muhammad and his immediate successors. Over the past two centuries, the Salafi movement has evolved, split, and adapted to differing circumstances throughout the Muslim world. Salafists do not necessarily call for the use of violence; some focus almost exclusively on social behavior, calling for an ultraconservative moral code to direct dress and other social practices. However, a violent/extremist branch of the movement combines the missionary zeal associated with the call to purge Islam of its impure elements with the violent anti-Western extremism incubated among jihadists in Afghanistan in the 1980s and 1990s. Sources on the Salafist/jihadist ideology include Quintan Wiktorowicz, "The New Global Threat: Transnational Salafis and Jihad," *Middle East Policy* 8, no. 4 (December 2001): 18–38; Christopher M. Blanchard, *Al Qaeda: Statements and Evolving Ideology,* CRS Report for Congress (Washington, D.C.: U.S. Department of State, February 4, 2005); Anonymous, *Through Our Enemies' Eyes: Osama Bin Laden, Radical Islam, and the Future of America* (Washington, D.C.: Brassey's, 2002); and Gilles Kepel, *The War for Muslim Minds* (Cambridge, Mass.: Harvard University Press, 2004).

9. For example, in February 2005, London's Finsbury Park mosque, once a bastion of radicalism, was reclaimed. A new board of directors ousted the mosque's radical cleric, Abu Hamza al-Masri, and literally changed the locks. See Lizette Alvarez,

"Britain's Mainstream Muslims Find Voice," *New York Times,* March 6, 2005. Similarly, measures must be taken within prison systems to curtail and ultimately cease recruitment. See Ian Cuthbertson, "Prisons and the Education of Terrorists," *World Policy Journal* 21, no. 3 (Fall 2004): 20, for specific recommendations.

10. Alvarez, "Britain's Mainstream Muslims Find Voice." Mainstream Muslims in Britain have also taken steps to isolate Islamist militants and strengthen ties between moderates and the British establishment.

11. See David E. Kaplan, "Hearts, Minds, and Dollars," *U.S. News and World Report,* April 25, 2005.

12. See James Brandon, "Koranic Duel Eases Terror," *Christian Science Monitor,* February 4, 2005.

13. Sabrina Tavernise, "Marines See Signs Iraq Rebels Are Battling Foreign Fighters," *New York Times,* June 21, 2005.

14. See Matt Bai, "The Framing Wars," *New York Times Magazine,* July 12, 2005. See also Bettancourt et al., "The Power of a Good Idea," 10.

15. In Jordan, for example, a broad curriculum review is taking place that emphasizes more moderate and progressive interpretations of Islam. See Hassan M. Fattah, "Jordan Is Preparing to Tone Down the Islamic Bombast in Textbooks," *New York Times,* June 12, 2005. A number of European governments are also exploring options for having greater influence over the training of imams who preach in European mosques. See Elaine Sciolino, "Europe Struggling to Train New Breed of Muslim Clerics," *New York Times,* October 18, 2004.

25

INTERNATIONAL MEDIATION

I. William Zartman
and Saadia Touval

INTERNATIONAL CONFLICTS ARE FRE-
quently the subject of third-party mediation. Mediation is as old as history (the
earliest recorded occurrence comes from some
thirty-five hundred years ago); it was practiced in *Romeo and Juliet* with catastrophic effects and has been part of diplomacy since the
establishment of the state system in 1648.[1] It
remains crucial in the present post–Cold War,
post-9/11 era. Although the terror attacks on
September 11, 2001, had a major impact on international relations, half a decade later no significant changes are discernible in the nature
and practice of international mediation.

"Conflict" here refers to politico-security
issues. Typically, in international economic or
environmental disputes, rival parties are not as
forcefully competitive nor are the means of
conducting the dispute as violent as in politico-
security conflicts. Conflicts over politico-
security issues take place within a context of
power politics, which has a major effect on international mediation. This premise provides
the conceptual underpinning of our analysis

of the participants' motives in mediation, the
conditions that affect the performance and
roles of mediators, and the keys to effective
mediation of international conflicts. The term
"international conflict" refers here both to interstate conflicts and to domestic ones where
external parties are involved through political,
economic, or military assistance or asylum and
bases for the domestic actors.

Mediation is a form of third-party intervention in a conflict. It differs from other
forms of third-party intervention in conflicts
in that it is not based on the direct use of force
and it is not aimed at helping one of the participants to win. Its purpose is to bring the conflict to a settlement that is acceptable to both
sides and consistent with the third party's interests. Mediation is a political process with
no advance commitment from the parties to
accept the mediator's ideas. In this respect,
it differs from arbitration, which employs judicial procedure and issues a verdict that the
parties have committed themselves before-
hand to accept. Mediation is best thought of

as a mode of negotiation in which a third party helps the parties find a solution that they cannot find by themselves. To accomplish its purposes, mediation must be made acceptable to the adversaries in the conflict, who must in turn cooperate diplomatically with the intervenor. But mediators often meet initial rejection from the conflicting parties; thus their first diplomatic effort must be to convince the parties of the value of their services before the mediation process can get started.

While mediation is designed to help conflicting parties find their own solutions, not all conflicts can be mediated, any more than are all conflicts negotiable. Parties who demand the suicide of their opponent as the necessary ingredient of a solution are unlikely subjects of mediation. Thus total absolute terrorists (e.g., suicide bombers), as opposed to contingent terrorists (e.g., hostage takers), can be considered beyond mediation, as well as negotiation.[2] On the other hand, the mediator's (and negotiator's) challenge is to turn nonnegotiable positions into something negotiable, and many demands that start as absolutes turn out to be flexible under negotiation (and mediation).

THE MEDIATOR'S MOTIVES

States use mediation as a foreign policy instrument. Their intervention as mediators is legitimized by the goal of conflict reduction, which they typically proclaim. The desire to make peace, however, is intertwined with other motives best described within the context of competitive politics. To understand these motives, it is most helpful to employ a rational-actor approach, using cost-benefit considerations. Mediators are players in the plot of relations surrounding a conflict, and so they have an interest in its outcome; otherwise, they would not mediate. In view of the considerable investment of political, moral, and material resources that mediation requires and the risks to which mediators expose themselves, motives for mediation must be found as much

in domestic and international self-interest as in humanitarian impulses. Mediators are seldom indifferent to the terms being negotiated. Not surprisingly, they try to avoid terms not in accord with their own interests, even though mediators' interests usually allow for a wider range of acceptable outcomes than the interests of the parties. Self-interested motivation holds for states and intergovernmental organizations, as well as for many nongovernmental actors.

Mediation by States

Mediating states are likely to seek terms that will increase the prospects of stability, deny their rivals opportunities for intervention, earn them the gratitude of one or both parties, or enable them to continue to have a role in future relations in the region. Both defensive and influence enhancing goals can be promoted through mediation, and they often blend together.[3] A mediator acts defensively when a continuing conflict between others threatens its interests. An end to the conflict is therefore important to the mediator because of the conflict's effects on its relations with the disputing parties or with other international actors. For example, if two of the mediator's allies engage in a conflict, the dispute can disrupt and weaken the alliance or strain the parties' relations with the third-party mediator. A conflict between two states may also upset a regional balance or provide opportunities for a rival power to increase its influence by intervening on one side of the conflict.

In some situations, a conflict may threaten to escalate and draw in additional parties. Actors who fear such escalation and expansion may seek to reduce the conflict to avoid becoming involved in hostilities. Mediation in such cases may involve a single intervenor or it may be a collective endeavor by two or more states acting within or outside the framework of an international organization. For example, the efforts to mediate the various conflicts arising out of the dissolution of Yugoslavia involved the

European Union, the Organization for Security and Cooperation in Europe, NATO, the United Nations, the informal "Contact Group," Russia, and the United States. Even rival powers, protecting their turf, are known to have cooperated and engaged in joint mediation when they feared that continuation of a particular conflict might endanger their security (e.g., U.S.-Soviet/Russian cooperation on Laos in 1961–62, on the Arab-Israeli war in 1973, and even on Kosovo in 1999).

Domestic political needs of governments also often motivate mediation. Public opinion and influential domestic groups often call for intervention to stop atrocities or alleviate suffering that accompanies conflicts. Mediation is a low-risk form of intervention in such situations, helping to protect a government from domestic critics, while also serving its foreign policy goals.

The second self-interested motive for mediation is the desire to extend and increase influence. In this case, mediation is mainly a vehicle for enhancing a state's international status and influence, or for improving relations with one or both parties. A third party may hope to win the gratitude of one or both parties in a conflict, either by helping them out of the conflict or by aiding one of them to achieve better terms in a solution than would otherwise be obtainable. Although the mediator cannot throw its full weight behind one party, it can increase its influence by making the success of the negotiations depend on its involvement and by making each party depend on it to garner concessions from the other party. Mediators can also increase their presence and influence in a region by becoming guarantors of any agreement, which necessarily includes risks and responsibilities.

Mediation by Major Powers

The United States has been the most active mediator of international conflicts since 1945.[4] This involvement is consistent with an interest-based explanation of mediators' motives. That Americans were involved in mediation more often than the Soviets can easily be understood if we remember the unequal extent of the two powers' spheres of influence. The Soviet sphere was limited to Eastern Europe, China, and a few additional countries that became dependent on Soviet military aid (while at the same time China broke away from the Soviet sphere). The remainder of the world, sometimes called the Free World, was considered by the United States as part of its own sphere (notwithstanding that some states in this group proclaimed themselves to be non-aligned). Although actual U.S. influence varied among these Free World states, the Soviet Union carried less influence there than did the United States. The claim made in 1971 by Andrei Gromyko, then Soviet foreign minister, that Soviet interests extend to every corner of the globe and that "there is no question of any significance that can be decided without the Soviet Union or in opposition to it" reflected ambition rather than reality. Thus, the wider sphere of U.S. influence explains why the United States mediated so many more conflicts than did the Soviets. Because the United States feared during the Cold War that conflicts would provide the Soviet Union with opportunities to intervene and expand its influence, the United States often sought to dampen conflict within the non-Soviet sphere, and mediation was an appropriate instrument to that end. As a result, U.S. diplomats and policymakers gained experience and skill in mediation, and so were increasingly solicited to play the role.

In addition, mediation appeared to be the best policy for the United States when smaller states engaged in conflict called for its support in their conflict. Fearful that support for one side in a local conflict would throw the other side into the Soviet embrace, the United States offered mediation as the least risky course. A number of historical examples illustrate these interests. U.S. mediation in the Rhodesia/

Zimbabwe conflict in 1976–79 and the Soviet mediation between India and Pakistan in 1966 were inspired by a mixture of defensive and influence-extending motives. From a defensive vantage, the United States feared that the Rhodesian conflict would provide opportunities for the Soviet Union to gain influence by supporting the African nationalists. But because the African groups concerned were already politically close to the Soviet Union and China, the U.S. mediation was also an attempt to improve relations with these groups and thus extend U.S. influence.

On occasion, Soviet actions followed the same motives. Its mediation between India and Pakistan was partly inspired by its desire to improve relations with Pakistan, a country that had hitherto been on better terms with the United States and China than with the Soviet Union. It also sought to build its prestige and establish a precedent that would justify future involvement in the affairs of the region. At the same time, there were important defensive motives for its intervention. The Indian-Pakistani conflict provided China an opportunity to extend its influence into Pakistan and thus establish a presence close to the southern borders of the Soviet Union. By reducing the conflict, this expansion would become more difficult for China.

The same pattern continues. The United States has continued to play a leading mediatory role in numerous conflicts since the end of the Cold War, despite some notable contributions by other countries in specific cases and despite its (as it became) preoccupation with fighting terrorism and its loss of some of its popularity because of the war in Iraq. The continued frequency of U.S. involvement can be attributed not only to the motives already discussed but also to the need to support mediation initiatives of other actors. Because of the United States' preeminent standing as the sole remaining superpower, parties to conflicts look to the United States as the power that can determine the outcome of the struggle

that they are engaged in by supporting them, opposing them, or being indifferent. This sometimes produces situations in which mediation efforts by other actors cannot come to closure until the United States demonstrates its support for those mediation efforts by active involvement. U.S. support (and sometimes eventual supplanting) of others' efforts in Bosnia, Sudan, Jordan, and Mozambique, among others, are examples.

The patterns of interest prompting states to mediate have not changed since the end of the Cold War and the current rise in terrorism, although the readiness of third parties to become involved and the political geography of mediatory interventions have been modified. A notable shift has been taking place in Western countries, where humanitarian concerns of public opinion have come to play a more important role in shaping foreign policies than in the past. The need to respond to domestic public opinion has sometimes led a government to intervene in foreign conflicts, including civil wars, even when they are not perceived as impinging on its security interests. Since mediation carries fewer costs for intervenors than military action, especially if pursued through international organizations, collective mediation (i.e., coordinated multiparty mediation) seems to be on the increase. Examples of such mediation include the mediations in Afghanistan, Angola, Burundi, Haiti, Liberia, Mozambique, Rwanda, Sierra Leone, Somalia, Sudan, and the former Yugoslavia.

Mediation by Small and Medium-Sized Powers

Mediation by small- and medium-sized powers is also motivated by the same concerns of self-interest, some of which are also related to domestic concerns. Such interests include the possibility that a conflict may spill over into the mediator's territory; the fear that the local conflict may expand and draw in powerful external actors (India's mediation in Sri Lanka in 1986 before its military intervention is an example of both these concerns); the reluctance to take sides in a conflict between other nations (Saudi Arabia in many inter-Arab conflicts); and the attempt to promote norms that tend to enhance the mediator's own security (the 1963 Ethiopian mediation between Algeria and Morocco and the 2000 Algerian mediation between Ethiopia and Eritrea concerning the validity of established borders).

Small- and medium-sized powers may also wish to enhance their influence and prestige through mediation. Egypt and Algeria's mediation between Iran and Iraq in 1975 was motivated by the desire to prove their usefulness to both belligerents, as well as to reduce intra-Islamic conflict. Algerian mediation between the United States and Iran in 1979 on the issue of American hostages seems to have been inspired by the hope that mediation would generate goodwill from the U.S. public toward Algeria and thus help improve relations between Algeria and the United States. This hope was related to U.S. support for Algeria's adversary, Morocco, in the Western Sahara war against the Algerian-supported Polisario movement. Other cases in which states sought to enhance their international standing through mediation stretch from India's attempt to mediate between the United States and the Soviet Union and China in the 1950s to Libya's efforts to mediate in the War of the Zairean Succession in Congo in 1998–99, the Eritrean-Ethiopian war in 1998–2000, and the Darfur conflict in Sudan in 2003–04.

Small and medium states have few alternative foreign policy instruments at their disposal, and mediation increases their usefulness and independence in relation to their stronger allies. Moreover, when pressed to take sides in a conflict, they, like great powers, may seek to escape their predicament by assuming the role of a mediator. In the post–Cold War era, small and medium states continue to have a role as mediator. Kenya and Zimbabwe attempted to mediate the Mozambique conflict, Zaire (the Democratic Republic of the Congo) the

Angolan conflict, South Africa the conflicts in Nigeria and Swaziland, the Association of Southeast Asian Nations (ASEAN) the conflict in Cambodia, Norway the Israeli-Palestinian conflict and the civil war in Sri Lanka, and Saudi Arabia the conflicts in Yemen and Lebanon. Many states—including South Africa, Togo, Tunisia, Algeria, Saudi Arabia, Costa Rica, and Colombia—consider mediation of the conflicts in their regions to be a major element of their foreign policy.

Mediation by International Organizations and NGOs

The motives of international organizations are somewhat more complex than those of states. Peacemaking is the raison d'être of several international organizations and is thus enshrined in their charters. Yet intergovernmental organizations are also subject to the particular policies and interests of their member states. Accordingly, the United Nations was frequently paralyzed by the Cold War and engaged in peacemaking much less than its charter suggested it should. Some of the mediation efforts that it undertook were often smoke screens to conceal the intensity of U.S. involvement (e.g., in the Arab-Israeli conflict). Regional organizations were not hindered by the Cold War to the same extent as the United Nations, although they had their own similar concerns. Because mediation requires agreement among the organizations' most influential members, as well as acceptance by the parties directly involved, regional organizations were not as active in peacemaking as they might have been.

The end of the Cold War freed international organizations from their bipolar constraints, and they rushed into mediation and conflict management. As a result, their reputations and resources became overextended and their efforts were not rewarded with the expected quick success. But the UN experiences in Somalia, Rwanda, and Cambodia have shown both the great possibilities for mediation by the world organization and the difficulty in separating its role from the specific—indeed, narrow—interests and concerns of leading member states in the Security Council.

Mediation activities by regional organizations are similarly affected by state interests. The European Union's mediation efforts in the Balkans and between Israel and the Palestinians were shaped in significant measure by the desire to establish and assert a role for itself in international security matters. The Organization for Security and Cooperation in Europe (OSCE) has been utilized for mediation in Europe and the Caucasus in fulfillment of its raison d'être of accommodating the security interests of Russia and the West; its High Commissioner on National Minorities has been subtly active in informal mediation. ASEAN took on new mediation roles in part to prevent conflicts in the region from becoming entangled in great-power rivalries. Some African states utilized the African Union (AU) as well as subregional organizations such as the Economic Community of West African States (ECOWAS), the Intergovernmental Authority on Development (IGAD) and the Inter-Governmental Agency on Drought and Development (IGADD) in East Africa, and the Southern African Development Community (SADC) to assert their aspirations for leadership and protect their interests in regional conflicts, but also to use the mediation challenge to reinvigorate the organizations and assert their relevance in the continent.

Nonstate mediators, whose interests are not as apparent or suspect as the primary players of power politics, nevertheless share motives of self-interest. At the very least nonstate mediators have a role and a reputation to establish or defend and thus an interest in appearing as good and successful mediators. (The concerns of the World Council of Churches and the All-Africa Conference of Churches in launching their mediation of the Sudanese civil war in 1971 is an interesting example, as is the highly motivated work of the Vatican in 1978–84 in mediating the Beagle Channel

dispute and of the Community of Sant'Egidio in mediating in Mozambique and Algeria.[5] Often this role extends beyond mediation to become an organizational interest in establishing a presence and in keeping the organization clean and ready for other functions. In this regard, nonstate mediators come very close to state mediators in the nature of their interests.

Concern for peace as a value in and of itself, suspicion of interested mediators' motives, and perception of the inherent limitations on states' mediating roles have led a variety of nonstate actors to propose themselves as international mediators. Many of these are interested in a particular outcome, not because it affects them directly, but because they believe in its inherent desirability. Thus, the several private agencies striving for usefulness in the Rhodesian and Liberian civil wars were working to find an acceptable path to Zimbabwean independence and to a new political system in Liberia, respectively, not some other outcome. All nonstate actors have an interest in enhancing their positions as useful third parties, not out of any venal egotism but because they believe they have something to offer; furthermore, a reinforcement of their standing and reputation helps them do their job.

THE PARTIES' MOTIVES IN ACCEPTING MEDIATION

Opponents in a conflict face two interrelated questions: whether to accept mediation and, if so, whose offer of mediation to accept. Parties accept intervention because they, like mediators, expect it to work in favor of their interests.[6] The most obvious motive is the expectation that mediation will gain an outcome more favorable than the outcome gained by continued conflict—that is, a way out. The parties also hope that mediation will produce a settlement when direct negotiation is not possible or will provide a more favorable settlement than can be achieved by direct negotiation. Although the adversary may not have a similar assessment, it may accept and cooperate with the mediator if it feels that rejection might cause even greater harm—for example, damaging relations with the would-be mediator, decreasing the chances for an acceptable negotiated outcome, or prolonging a costly conflict. Such considerations sometimes help to induce states to accept intervention even in domestic conflicts (e.g., Sri Lanka's acceptance of India's and then Norway's mediation, Angola's acceptance of U.S. mediation, and Sudan's acceptance of external mediation to end the insurgency in the South). The parties may also accept mediation in the hope that the intermediary will reduce some of the risks entailed in making concessions and the costs incurred in conflict, protecting their image and reputation as they move toward a compromise. They may also believe a mediator's involvement implies a guarantee for the final agreement, thus reducing the danger of violation by the adversary.

The acceptance of mediation by international organizations can also be premised on the ability of these organizations to bestow normative approval, rather than on their capacity to influence the adversary or arrange for a satisfactory compromise. This factor is present in the case of the United Nations but is perhaps clearest in the case of the International Committee of the Red Cross (ICRC). The ICRC's ability to offer an improved image to a fighting or detaining authority can be a powerful incentive for the parties to accept its presence and services and to accede to its proposals.

Partiality and Acceptability

If the acceptance of mediation is based on a cost-benefit calculation, then the assumption that mediators must be perceived as impartial needs to be revised.[7] The mediator's impartiality is not as important to the adversaries' decision to accept mediation as is their consideration of the consequences of accepting or rejecting mediation: How will their decision affect the prospects of achieving a favorable outcome? And how will it affect their future relations with the would-be mediator?

Initially, third parties are accepted as mediators only to the extent that they are seen as capable of bringing about acceptable outcomes; then, their subsequent meddling is tolerated because they are already part of the relationship. Although there is no necessary relationship between a mediator's past partiality and its future usefulness, good relations between it and one of the adversaries may in fact be an aid to communicating, to developing creative proposals, and to helping the two parties' positions to converge. Closeness to one party implies the possibility of "delivering" it. The party closer to the mediator may soften its stand for the sake of preserving its favored relationship with the would-be mediator. The other side, which does not enjoy close relations with the mediator (and especially if it is the weaker side), sometimes perceives the potential advantages of accepting a "biased" third party as mediator: such a mediator is more likely to be able to extract concessions from its friend than an impartial mediator who carries no particular influence with the adversary, and the other side may actually be able to ingratiate itself into the good graces of the mediator by being reasonable in making an agreement with the mediator's friend.

Several examples illustrate these points. In the Rhodesia/Zimbabwe mediation in 1976–79, the Africans' belief that British and U.S. sympathies were with the white Rhodesians rendered British and U.S. mediation promising and stimulated African cooperation. In several mediations between Arab parties and Israel, the Arabs' belief that the close U.S.-Israeli ties would enable the United States to deliver Israeli concessions made U.S. mediation attractive to them. In the Tashkent mediation in 1966, the Soviet Union was accepted as a mediator by Pakistan, despite its close relationship with India. Pakistan perceived the Soviet Union as concerned enough about Pakistan's growing cooperation with China to want to improve its own relationship with Pakistan and as close enough to India to bring it into an agreement. Algeria was accepted by the United States as a mediator with Iran in 1979 not because it was considered impartial, but because its ability to gain access to and facilitate the agreement of people close to Ayatollah Ruholla Khomeini held promise that it might help to release the hostages. Viktor Chernomyrdin was effective as a mediator with Slobodan Milosevic in 1999 because of Russia's earlier support of the Serbs.

Although they cannot fully side with one party, mediators can allow themselves some latitude in their degree of partiality. This latitude may allow them to express their preference regarding the outcome of the negotiation. In the Zimbabwe and Namibia negotiations, the United States was not indifferent to the nature of the settlement: the outcome had to open the way for majority rule. Although this meant that the United States supported the essence of the African position and, by implication, sought to eliminate the white settlers as a sovereign political actor, the white settlers nevertheless accepted U.S. mediation as a means to get them out of a no-win situation.

An interest in specific outcomes is quite common in the mediations of international organizations. The United Nations, the OAU, the ICRC, and the Organization of American States (OAS) all have some general norms that they wish to uphold beyond the principle of peaceful settlement. They try to promote solutions that can be interpreted as compatible with the standards of the Geneva Conventions and of their charters and that protect their image as guardians of these standards. Indeed, they can formally condemn parties for deviating from these standards as a means to enforce them. The European Union, trying to mediate a settlement of the disputes arising out of the dissolution of Yugoslavia in 1991, and concerned about the impending dissolution of the Soviet Union, enunciated the principle of the inviolability of internal borders within states, equating their status to that of international borders. On the other hand, the OAU was so strongly attached to the principle of successor state integrity that it was incapable of mediating the Biafran or Namibian conflict, so strongly attached to the principle of *uti possidetis* (legitimacy of inherited boundaries) that it was unable to mediate the Ogaden war, and so strongly attached to the principle of noninterference in internal affairs that it was unable even to constitute a commission to mediate the Sudanese and Rwandan civil wars.

Independent nonstate agencies, such as the ICRC or the Community of Sant'Egidio, do not have the same kind of partiality or composition problems. Nevertheless, their acceptance as a mediator is still not automatic. Conflicting parties are not concerned whether the ICRC or Sant'Egidio will perform humanitarian functions objectively, but whether the framework of its involvement will further their interests. Thus, states may deny that an armed conflict that would justify an ICRC intervention is occurring or has occurred or that a Sant'Egidio venue for dialogue is appropriate. Yet the legal framework is sometimes subject to negotiation, and the terms of involvement can be influenced by their perceived effect on the interests of the parties, rather than by the latter's perception of the mediator's impartiality. Mediators must be perceived as having an interest in achieving an outcome acceptable to both sides and as being not so partial as to preclude such an achievement. Again, the question for the parties is not whether the mediator is objective, but whether it can provide an acceptable outcome.

TIMING OF MEDIATION

Since mediators are motivated by self-interest, they will not intervene automatically, but only when they believe a conflict threatens their interests or when they perceive an opportunity to advance their interests. Such threats and opportunities are unlikely to be noticed when there is a mild disagreement between parties. Usually, it is only after the conflict escalates that its implications are perceived. By then, the parties are likely to have become committed to their positions and to a confrontational policy, ever reducing the common grounds on which mediation must proceed. For that mediation to succeed, the parties must be disposed to reevaluate their policies.

Two conditions for such ripeness for mediation are especially conducive to such reevaluation: mutually hurting stalemates and crises bounded by a deadline or, to use a metaphor, plateaus and precipices.[8] A mutually hurting stalemate begins when one side realizes that it is unable to achieve its aims, resolve the problem, or win the conflict by itself; the stalemate is completed when the other side reaches a similar conclusion. Each party must begin to feel uncomfortable in the costly dead end that it has reached. Both sides must see this plateau not as a momentary resting ground, but as a flat, unpleasant terrain stretching into the future, providing no later possibilities for decisive escalation or graceful escape.

Mediation plays upon the parties' perceptions of having reached an intolerable situation. Without this perception, the mediator must depend on persuading the parties that breaking out of their deadlock is impossible. Indeed, the mediator may even be required to make it impossible. Thus, deadlock cannot be seen as a temporary stalemate, to be easily resolved in one's favor by a little effort, a big offensive, a gamble, or foreign assistance. Rather, each party must recognize its opponent's strength and its own inability to overcome that strength, as well as the cost of staying in the stalemate.

For the mediator, this means cultivating each side's perception that its unilateral policy option—to take action without negotiation—is a more expensive, less likely way of achieving an acceptable outcome than the policy of negotiation. A plateau is therefore as much a matter of perception as of reality for the parties and as much a subject of persuasion as of timing for the mediator. Successful exploitation of a plateau shifts both sides from a combative mentality to a conciliatory mentality.

A crisis, or precipice, represents the realization that matters are swiftly becoming worse. It implies impending catastrophe, such as probable military defeat or economic collapse. It may be accompanied by a policy dilemma that involves engaging in a major escalation, the outcome of which is unpredictable, or seeking a desperate compromise that threatens one side as much as the other. It may also be a catastrophe that has already taken place or has been narrowly avoided. Whatever its tense (because parties are bound to disagree about the inevitability of an impending event), it marks a time limit to the judgment that "things can't go on like this."[9]

For the mediator, the crisis as precipice should reinforce the dangers of the plateau, lest the parties become accustomed to their uncomfortable deadlock. Mediators can manipulate stalemates and crises: they can use them and they can make them. If there is a recognized impending danger, mediators can use it as a warning and as an unpleasant alternative to a negotiated settlement. And if they do not agree that a crisis exists, mediators can work to implant a common perception that it or a mutually hurting stalemate does exist. In its most manipulative role, a mediator may have to create a plateau or a precipice, usually citing pressure from a fourth party. That is what the United States did in 1977 to get the Namibia negotiations started, citing irresistible pressure for sanctions if the sides did not start talking, or in 2002 to get the Sudanese negotiations restarted, citing pressure from domestic Christian groups in the United States and antiterrorist policy needs that would force it to adopt a harsher policy if serious negotiations did not begin.

Plateau and precipice are precise but perceptional conditions, and they have governed the timing of successful mediation in most cases. They are not self-implementing: they must be seen and seized. Unfortunately, they depend on conflict and its escalation. It would be preferable if the need for a ripe moment could be combined with the desirability of treating conflict early, as sought in preventive diplomacy. To do this, mediators need to develop a perception of stalemate at a low level of conflict, or to develop a sense of responsibility on the part of a government to head off an impending conflict, or to develop an awareness of an opportunity for a better outcome made available through mediation. There are few examples, as yet, of mediators using such tactics successfully.

MODES OF MEDIATORS

Mediators use three modes to marshal the interests of all the involved parties toward a mutually acceptable solution to the conflict—communication, formulation, and manipulation, in that order. Since mediation is helping the parties to do what they cannot do by themselves, each of these three modes refers to a different level of obstacle to the conduct of direct negotiations.

The mediator can serve as communicator when conflict has made direct contact between parties impossible, thereby preventing the parties from talking to each other and from making concessions without appearing weak or losing face. In this situation, mediators simply act as a conduit, opening contacts and carrying messages. They may be required to help the parties understand the meaning of messages through the distorting dust thrown up by the conflict or to gather the parties' concessions together into a package, without adding to the content. This role is completely procedural, with no substantive contribution by the mediator, and in its simplest form it is completely passive, only carrying out the parties' orders for the delivery of messages. Tact, wording, and sympathy, mixed in equal doses with accuracy and confidentiality, are necessary character traits of the mediator as communicator. Norwegians in Oslo rarely exceeded the role of communicator if they took any part in the Israeli-Palestinian negotiations in 1993.

The second mode of mediation requires the mediator to enter into the substance of the negotiation. Since a conflict may not only impede communications between parties, but be so encompassing that it prevents them from conceiving ways out of the dispute, the parties need a mediator as formulator. Formulas are the key to a negotiated solution to a conflict; they provide a common understanding of the problem and its solution or a shared notion of justice to govern an outcome. Just as the conflict often prevents the parties from finding imaginative ways out, it may also prevent them from seeing the value of the mediator's suggestions at first hearing. Therefore, the mediator as a formulator often needs to persuade the parties, as well as to suggest solutions to their disputes. Persuasion involves power and therefore requires greater involvement than mere communication. Not only does the mediator get involved in the substance of the issue, but it must also lean on the parties—albeit in the subtlest ways—to adopt its perceptions of a way out. Mediators as successful formulators must be capable of thinking of ways to unblock the thinking of the conflicting parties and to work out imaginative ways to skirt those commitments that constrain the parties.

The third mode requires the mediator to act as a manipulator. This is the maximum degree of involvement, requiring the mediator to become a party to the solution if not to the dispute. As a manipulator, the mediator uses its power to bring the parties to an agreement, pushing and pulling them away from conflict and into resolution. When the obstacle to agreement is the seemingly paltry size of the outcome, the mediator must persuade the parties of its vision of a solution; it must then take measures to make that solution attractive, enhancing its value by adding benefits to its outcome and presenting it in such a way as to overcome imbalances that may have prevented one of the parties from subscribing to it. The mediator may have to go so far as to improve the absolute attractiveness of the resolution by increasing the unattractiveness of continued conflict, which may mean shoring up one side or condemning another, either of which actions strains the appearance of its own neutrality. This is the role of the "full participant," such as U.S. diplomats played in the 1970s' Middle East peace process, in the 1980s' Namibian-Angolan negotiations, and in 1995 in ending the Bosnian war.

Mediation is a triangular relationship. When the mediator operates as a communicator, it operates as a bridge between two contestants, or as a pump on the conduit between them. As a formulator, the mediator assumes a position of greater activity, one from which pressures and messages emanate as well as pass through. As a manipulator, the mediator becomes so active that it calls into question the triangular relationship. It may even unite the two adversaries in opposition to the mediator; for example, in the Yemen civil war (1962–70) the two sides resolved their differences in order to oppose Egyptian interference, when Egypt was acting more as an intervenor than as a mediator. But the mediator, by throwing its weight around, threatens and is threatened by the possibility of turning the triangle into a dyad. The mediator's threat to side with one party may bring the other party around, for fear that mediation might end and with it any possibilities for a solution. As a threat to the mediator, each party may try to win the mediator over to its own side to increase its chances of winning rather than of having to come to terms. At the same time, of course, each party may regard the mediator with high suspicion as a potential ally of the other side. Although it makes the mediator's job more difficult, suspicion is good because it keeps the mediator honest and aware of the disputants' concerns

POWER IN MEDIATION

Power—the ability to move a party in an intended direction—is often referred to in mediation as "leverage." Although leverage is the ticket to mediation, mediators tend to remain relatively powerless throughout the exercise. The extent of the mediator's power depends entirely on the parties, whose acceptance of a mediator depends on its likelihood (potential power) of producing an outcome agreeable to both sides. This circular relationship plagues every mediation exercise. Contrary to a common misperception, mediators are rarely "hired" by the parties; instead, they have to sell their services, based on the prospect of their usefulness and success. From the beginning, the mediator's leverage is at the mercy of the contestants. The parties, whose interest is in winning, view mediation as meddling, unless it produces an outcome favorable to each of them. They welcome mediation only to the extent that the mediator has leverage over the other party, and they berate the mediator for trying to exert leverage over them.

A mediator has five sources of leverage: first, persuasion, the ability to portray an alternative future as more favorable than the continuing conflict; second, extraction, the ability to produce an attractive position from each party; third, termination, the ability to withdraw from the mediation; fourth, deprivation, the ability to withhold resources from one side or to shift them to the other; and fifth, gratification, the ability to add resources to the outcome. In every case the effectiveness of the mediator's leverage lies with the parties themselves, a characteristic that makes leverage in mediation difficult to obtain.

The first source of leverage is persuasion. The mediator in any mode must be able to point out the attractiveness of conciliation on available terms and the unattractiveness of continued conflict, a purely communicative exercise independent of any resources. Secretary of State Henry Kissinger, whose country was not devoid of resources or the willingness to use them, nevertheless spent long hours painting verbal pictures of the future with and without an agreement for Egyptian, Syrian, and Israeli audiences. President Jimmy Carter's mediation at Camp David in September 1978 and in Cairo and Jerusalem in March 1979 bore the same characteristics of the power and limitations of persuasion.

Mediation is unwelcome until it can extract a proposal from each party that is viewed as favorable by the other. This second source of leverage, extraction, is the most problematic, yet it is the basis of all mediation. The crucial moment in mediation comes when the mediator asks a party's permission to try for the other's agreement to a proposal; this exchange is the heart of the formulation mode. But its success depends on the parties' need for a way out of the impasse of conflict—demonstrating the importance of the mutually hurting stalemate and the absence of attractive alternatives as elements of the ripe moment. Assistant Secretary of State Chester A. Crocker and his team shuttled back and forth between Angola and South Africa in search of attractive proposals to carry to each side, but that exchange was not forthcoming until the military conditions of 1988 made the stalemate intolerable to both sides.

The third source of leverage, termination, lies in the mediator's ability to withdraw and leave the parties to their own devices and their continuing conflict. Again, the impact of withdrawal is entirely in the hands of the disputing parties; they may be happy to see the mediator leave, but if the mutually hurting stalemate is present, they will be sensitive to the threat of leaving. However, if the mediator needs a solution more than the parties, it will be unable to threaten termination credibly. Secretary Kissinger brandished the threat in mediating the Golan Heights withdrawal in 1974 and activated it at the second Sinai withdrawal the following year. Another example comes from the 1995 Bosnia Peace Conference at Dayton.

It was only after Secretary of State Warren Christopher told the delegations on November 20, the twentieth day of the conference, that in a few hours he would announce that the conference had failed, that the parties finally resolved their remaining differences, bringing the conference to a successful conclusion.

The remaining sources of leverage use the conflict and the proposed solution as their fulcrums, thus making manipulation their primary mode of mediation. Leverage derives from the mediator's ability to tilt toward (gratification) or away from (deprivation) a party and thereby to affect the conditions of a stalemate or of movement out of it. The activity may be verbal, such as a vote of condemnation, or more tangible, such as visits, food aid, or arms shipments. The point of this leverage is to worsen the dilemma of parties rejecting mediation and to keep them in search of a solution.

The mediator might shift weight in order to prevent one party from losing the conflict because the other's victory would produce a less stable and hence less desirable situation. Such activity clearly brings the mediator very close to being a party in the conflict. Arms to Israel and Morocco, down payments on better relations with South Africa, and abstentions on UN votes are examples of U.S. shifts-in-weight during various mediation processes. The Soviet Union threatened to shift weight away from India in the Security Council debate on the Indian-Pakistani war, and Britain threatened to shift weight against the Patriotic Front in Rhodesia. Threats of this kind are effective only to the degree that they are believed.

The last source of the mediator's leverage is the side payment, the subject to which the term "leverage" is usually applied. As weight shifts affect the continuing conflict, side payments may be needed to augment or enhance the outcome to one or more parties. Side payments require considerable resources and engagement from the mediators, thus they are rarely made and are certainly not the key to successful mediation. Yet when the outcome is not large enough to provide sufficient benefits for both parties or to outweigh the present or anticipated advantages of continued conflict, some source of additional benefits is needed. Side payments may be attached to the outcomes themselves, such as third-party guarantees of financial aid for accomplishing changes required by the agreement, or they may be unrelated to the outcome itself, simply additional benefits that make agreement more attractive. The graduated aid package attached to the Israeli and Egyptian agreement to disengage in the Sinai and then to sign a peace treaty is *one* example. The promise to train and equip the Bosnian Federation army as an incentive to the Muslims to accept the Dayton Peace Accords is another. Sometimes the demand for side payments by the parties may be as extraneous to agreement as is their supply.

Of all these, the principal element of leverage is persuasion—the ability of the mediator to reorient the parties' perceptions. Like any kind of persuasion, the mediator's ability depends on many different referents that are skillfully employed to make conciliation more attractive and continuing conflict less so. These referents may include matters of domestic welfare and political fortunes, risks and costs, prospects of continuing conflict and of moving out of it, reputations, solidity of allies' support, world opinion, and the verdict of history.

The other basic element in leverage is need —the parties' need—for a solution that they cannot achieve by themselves, for additional support in regional or global relations, and for a larger package of payoffs to make a conciliatory outcome more attractive. Perception of this need can be enhanced by the mediator, but it cannot be created out of nothing. Side payments with no relation to the outcome of the conflict are effective only insofar as they respond to an overriding need that outweighs the deprivation of concessions on the issues of the conflict itself. Parties can be made aware of needs that they did not recognize before,

particularly when the chances of assuaging these needs seem out of reach. The provision of Cuban troop withdrawal from Angola, which met South Africa's need for a countervailing reward, led to the South African troop and administration withdrawal from Namibia, yet this need was not formulated during the 1970s' rounds of the mediation. Persuasion often depends on need, but then need often depends on persuasion.

What do these characteristics say about "powerful" and "powerless" mediators? The common distinction between "interested" and "disinterested" mediators is less solid than might appear. All mediators have interests, most mediators are interested in the conflict situation in some way, and "biased" mediators may even have an advantage in access to one or both of the parties. If mediation were only persuasion, or "pure" persuasion, it would not matter who practiced it, and entry into the practice would be equally open to any silver-tongued orator. But mediation is more than simple persuasion, and the basis of effective persuasion is the ability to fulfill both tangible and intangible needs of the parties. The mediator's leverage is based therefore on the parties' need for the solution it is able to produce and on its ability to produce attractive solutions from each party.

Although official mediators are usually needed to help conclude agreements between disputing parties, unofficial (i.e., nonstate) mediators may be effective persuaders and may be useful in helping to reorient the perceptions of the parties' values and opportunities. If the required mode of mediation is low— limited to communication—and the felt need for a solution is high in both parties, informal mediation may be all that is necessary to bring the parties to negotiation. However, the higher the required mode, the lower the felt needs, the more structural interests involving a third party, and the more the conflict involves states rather than nonstate actors, the less likely informal mediation can be an effective substitute for the official attention of states. Statesmen are not necessarily better mediators, but they can provide interest- and need-related services that informal mediators cannot handle.

Unofficial mediation in Africa provides a good illustration. Textbook cases of mediation were effected by the World Council of Churches and the All-Africa Conference of Churches in the southern Sudanese civil war in 1972, and the Community of Sant'Egidio in Mozambique in 1990–92 and Algeria after 1994. The church bodies widened the perceptions of opportunity among the parties and persuaded them to move to resolution. The mediators were not unbiased, having closer ties with the southern Sudanese and Mozambican rebels than with the government, and they were not without means of leverage, being able to threaten a resumption of supplies if the government broke off talks; in Algeria, all they could offer was a venue and encouragement. The stalemates that had been building over the years were reinforced by a mediator-induced perception of an attractive way out for the parties. The nonstate mediator played a major role and deserves credit for the operations; the subsequent collapse of the Sudanese agreement a decade later and the incompleteness of the Algerian démarche were due to other causes, not to a failed mediation. But behind the nonstate mediator in Sudan stood an international organization—the assistant secretary-general of the OAU, Mohamed Sahnoun—and behind him stood a mediator of last resort—the emperor of Ethiopia, Haile Selassie; and around the nonstate mediator in Mozambique stood an array of interested states—the United States, Russia, Italy, Portugal, Kenya, Zimbabwe, and South Africa. At a number of telling points in the operation, state actors were needed because guarantees that only a state could provide were required. The loneliness of the nonstate mediator in Algeria in 1995 goes far to explain its limited success.

Nearly two decades after the Sudanese venture, another private mediation was attempted in 1990 in a related conflict between the Eritrean rebels and the Ethiopian government. The private mediator was a former head of state, Jimmy Carter, who was perceived in the field as carrying official backing. The démarche responded to an appeal elicited from the parties and was carried out with dedication and skill. It failed because there was no mutually hurting stalemate and because the nature of the conflict changed during the mediation. The success of the Tigrean rebellion caused any ripeness in the previous moment to dissipate. The mediator was unable to persuade the parties of their deadlock or of their need to find a way out or to respond to any of the parties' needs for solutions, support, or side payments. Carter was in contact with heads of state in the region and obtained their sympathy and interest, even their benevolent neutrality during the mediation. But only states could have supplied the missing elements of support and side payments, and even then there was no guarantee that they would have been any more successful than Carter was, given the absence of a ripe moment.

An example of a private mediation backed by a state was Carter's intervention in Haiti in 1994. When the ruling junta refused to give up power and transfer it to the elected president, Jean-Bertrand Aristide, as demanded by the United Nations, Carter went to Haiti, persuaded the junta leaders to withdraw, and negotiated the terms of their withdrawal. Carter succeeded this time mainly because his mediation took place hours before the scheduled launch of a U.S. military invasion intended to remove the junta by force and because political credibility was added by the participation of Senator Sam Nunn, chairman of the Senate Armed Services Committee, and General Colin Powell, former chairman of the Joint Chiefs of Staff.

Many other mediations have benefited from a reversal of the roles portrayed in the Horn and in Haiti, that is, from informal support and assistance in a mediation performed by a state actor. In Zimbabwe, and more broadly in the Arab-Israeli dispute, many private efforts have helped strengthen the context and prepare the terrain for official mediation. Although any efforts to improve premediatory conditions make a contribution, private efforts actually to mediate in the Northern Irish, Falklands, Cyprus, and current Arab-Israeli conflicts have been notorious failures. Ripe moments and leveraged buy-offs by state mediators are the necessary ingredients, and even they may not be sufficient.

ETHICAL DILEMMAS

Mediators often pursue the double goal of stopping a war and settling the issues in dispute. They will pursue both aims, trying to end the bloodshed and to devise a settlement that is perceived to be fair by the parties involved, and thus be acceptable and durable. However, in trying to achieve these goals, mediators are often confronted with the realization that settling the conflict in a manner that is considered fair by the disputants is likely to take a long time. Mediators may therefore face a dilemma of whether or not to give priority to a cease-fire and postpone the settlement of the conflict for later. Viewed somewhat differently, the choice may be seen as one between peace (order) and justice.[10] To be sure, the two objectives are closely related. A durable cessation of hostilities requires a peace settlement. Justice requires order, and order, to endure, must be just. But these are long-term historical perspectives. For mediators, the choice is immediate: What should they do next? Should they pursue both objectives simultaneously, or should they give priority to a cease-fire?

Such a dilemma has been faced by the international community seeking to mediate the conflict in Bosnia. The choice there has been perceived as one between separating the warring parties through a partition, or pursuing a settlement that will preserve the integrity of a multiethnic Republic of Bosnia and Herze-

govina. Partition has been criticized as tantamount to legitimizing territorial conquests and the consequences of ethnic cleansing, and thus rewarding aggression. Insistence on a settlement respectful of the norm of preserving the integrity of the Bosnian state has been criticized for prolonging the war and thus costing tens of thousands of additional casualties (besides the argument that it is inconsistent with the reluctance of the international community to protect the integrity of the pre-1991 multiethnic Yugoslav state).

The dilemma facing mediators in such situations is stark. What comes first—striving to protect the norm of respect for the integrity of states, trying to teach members of warring ethnic groups (Serbs, Croats, and Bosnian Muslims; Greeks and Turks in Cyprus; southern, western, and northern Sudanese; Armenians and Azeris in Afghanistan) to coexist in peace, or saving lives by separating the groups and postponing the search for justice until later?

The sequencing has consequences. As we have seen, warring parties are more likely to settle when the continuing confrontation hurts badly and produces grave risks. A cease-fire, ending the bloodshed, is likely to ease the pain and reduce the risks. It will create a tolerable stalemate, a situation that the disputants might find preferable to the alternative of granting the concessions necessary for a compromise settlement. But cease-fires tend to be unstable and are often punctuated by wars and additional bloodshed, for example, the cease-fires between Israel and various Arab parties, between India and Pakistan, between Greeks and Turks in Cyprus, and between the warring parties in the former Yugoslavia. Such a condition can be termed an S5 situation—a soft, stable, self-serving stalemate, the hallmark of intractable conflicts whose long history makes them so impervious to mediators' efforts.[11] Such stalemates and their consequences are the strongest reasons for mediating and resolving conflicts early, with sustained robust mediation where necessary.

Unfortunately, it is impossible to predict reliably which course of action will ultimately cost more—an early cease-fire that may collapse and be followed by more fighting because the conflict remains unresolved, or a continuation of a war while the search goes on for a definitive settlement of the conflict. An argument for giving priority to a cease-fire is that predictions of the near term are generally more reliable than those of the more distant future. The mediator can be certain that an ongoing war will produce casualties. The proposition that cease-fires break down, leading to the renewal of war and producing higher casualties over the long term, is far less certain. Nevertheless, the dilemma exists. To escape the dilemma, it needs to be clearly understood by all that the cease-fire or conflict management effort will be followed by equal efforts to deal with the causes of the conflict or a conflict resolution effort. In this case, the danger of falling back into conflict if the cease-fire breaks can work to perpetuate the necessary sense of ripeness.

Another dilemma is whether to facilitate an attainable settlement that violates international norms or to hold out for one that is consistent with principles of justice adopted by the international community. One might argue that mediators of international conflicts should pursue terms that are attainable, even if they are attainable mainly because they reflect the balance of power between the adversaries, rather than jointly held notions of justice. There are two important arguments against such a course of action. One is that such a settlement is unlikely to endure. One of the parties (sometimes both) will resent terms that it considers unjust and will seek to overturn them at the earliest opportunity. The other argument concerns the wider ramifications of such settlements for world order. A settlement that is inconsistent with international principles may tend to undermine their validity, creating uncertainties about the norms and thus weakening constraints on international conduct. In other words, such settlements, while appearing to settle a particular conflict, may cause wider long-term damage by undermining the foundations of international peace and security. This was the dilemma repeatedly facing peacemakers in Sierra Leone in the 1990s, where horrendously brutal violence could be stopped, it appeared, but only at the cost of bringing the perpetrators into positions of power in the government. In the penultimate move, in the Lomé Agreements of 1999, that is what happened, but in the end, the perpetrators—the Revolutionary United Front (RUF)—betrayed themselves by not holding to even those agreements and had to be defeated by British shock troops.

Good answers to such dilemmas would require prescience. It is possible that promoting a settlement that is perhaps attainable, but inconsistent with international norms, might cause serious long-term injury to international peace and security. Should mediators work for terms that seem attainable, provided they promise to stabilize a cease-fire, despite their corrosive long-term effects? Viewing norms as merely tentative and conditional propositions is destructive to order. But eschewing settlements that do not conform to established norms, even if doing so allows mutual slaughter to continue, is also destructive to peace and order. Such dilemmas are not new. But these and other ethical issues have become pressing for international mediators in recent years. Guidelines for resolving such dilemmas are not easy to come by.

CONCLUSION

More interest and less leverage is involved in third-party mediation than is commonly assumed. Adversarial parties and potential mediators each make an interest calculation that involves much more than the simple settlement of the dispute. Their calculations include relations among the conflicting parties and third parties and the costs and benefits of all of them in both conflict and conciliation. Leverage comes from harnessing those interests and from the third party's ability to play on perceptions of needs, above all on needs for a solution.

Mediation acts as a catalyst to negotiation. It facilitates the settlement of disputes that parties ought to be able to accomplish on their own, if they were not so absorbed in their conflict. Mediation becomes necessary when the conflict is twice dominant: providing the elements of the dispute and preventing parties from seeking and finding a way out together. Even when it is successful, mediation can cut through only some of those layers, providing a means for the parties to live together despite their dispute—it does not provide deep reconciliation or cancel the causes of the conflict. Left again to their own instincts, the parties may well fall out of their mediated settlement, and there are plenty of cases—such as the Sudanese Addis Ababa Agreement of 1972, or the Haitian Governors Island Agreement of 1993, or the Mideast Oslo Agreement of 1993, among many others often unstudied by analysts and practitioners focusing on the moment of mediation—in which the hard-bargained agreement has subsequently fallen apart under changed conditions or revived enmities. For this reason, although the mediator is often tempted to start a process and then slip away as it develops its own momentum, it may in fact be required to be more involved in the regional structure of relations after its mediation than before. Early satisfaction with superficial results and premature disengagement by the mediator is one of the most frequent causes of failure in peacemaking. Yet the mediator must not be a crutch forever, lest it become a party to the conflict. This is the final challenge and dilemma for mediators: How to disengage from a mediating role without endangering the carefully brokered settlement.

NOTES

Adapted from "Mediation: The Role of Third-Party Diplomacy and Informal Peacemaking," in *Resolving*

Third World Conflict, ed. Sheryl Brown and Kimber M. Schraub (Washington, D.C.: United States Institute of Peace Press, 1992), 239–261. It draws on the authors' previous work, especially the chapter in *Mediation Research,* ed. Kenneth Kressel, Dean G. Pruitt, and Associates (San Francisco: Jossey-Bass, 1989).

1. Jacob Bercovitch, ed., *Studies in International Mediation* (New York: Palgrave, 2002).

2. I. William Zartman, ed., *Negotiating with Terrorists,* special issue of *International Negotiation* 8, no. 3 (2003; repr., Boston: Nijhoff, 2005).

3. For further discussion of states' interest in managing conflict, see Vadim Udalov, "National Interests and Conflict Reduction," and I. William Zartman, "Systems of World Order and Regional Conflict Reduction," in *Cooperative Security: Reducing Third World Wars,* ed. I. William Zartman and Victor Kremenyuk (Syracuse, N.Y.: Syracuse University Press, 1995).

4. Saadia Touval, "The Superpowers as Mediators," in *Mediation in International Relations: Multiple Approaches to Conflict Management,* ed. Jacob Bercovitch and Jeffrey Z. Rubin (New York: Macmillan/St. Martin's Press, 1992).

5. Hizkias Assefa, *Mediation of Civil Wars* (Boulder, Colo.: Westview Press, 1987); Thomas Princen, *Intermediaries in International Conflict* (Princeton, N.J.: Princeton University Press, 1992); Douglas Johnston and Cynthia Sampson, eds., *Religion: The Missing Dimension of Statecraft* (New York: Oxford University Press, 1994); and I. William Zartman, ed., *Elusive Peace: Negotiating an End to Civil Wars* (Washington, D.C.: Brookings Institution, 1995).

6. Chester A. Crocker, Fen Osler Hampson, and Pamela Aall, eds., *Herding Cats: Multiparty Mediation in a Complex World* (Washington, D.C.: United States Institute of Peace Press, 1999); and Mohammed Maundi et al., *Getting In: Mediators' Entry into African Conflicts* (Washington, D.C.: United States Institute of Peace Press, 2005).

7. Saadia Touval, *The Peace Brokers* (Princeton, N.J.: Princeton University Press, 1982).

8. I. William Zartman, *Ripe for Resolution,* 2nd ed. (New York: Oxford University Press, 1989); and Zartman, "Ripeness: The Hunting Stalemate and Beyond," in *International Conflict Resolution after the*

Cold War (Washington, D.C.: National Academy Press, 2000).

   9. I. William Zartman, "The Middle East: Ripe Moment?" in *Conflict Management in the Middle East*, ed. G. Ben-Dor and D. Dewitt (Lexington, Mass.: D. C. Heath, 1987), 285ff.

   10. Saadia Touval, *Mediation in the Yugoslav Wars: The Critical Years, 1990–95* (New York: Palgrave, 2002); and I. William Zartman and Victor Kremenyuk, eds., *Peace vs. Justice: Negotiating Forward- and Backward-Looking Outcomes* (Lanham, Md.: Rowman and Littlefield, 2005).

   11. Chester A. Crocker, Fen Osler Hampson, and Pamela Aall, *Taming Intractable Conflicts: Mediation in the Hardest Cases* (Washington, D.C.: United States Institute of Peace Press, 2005).

26

CONTEMPORARY CONFLICT RESOLUTION APPLICATIONS

Louis Kriesberg

IT MIGHT SEEM OBVIOUS THAT THE FIELD of conflict resolution, at least for Americans, has little to contribute to countering terrorist attacks against the United States or to waging other international wars. It seems wrong to negotiate with terrorists and evildoers, with or without mediators. Indeed, people working in the conflict resolution field generally do not regard negotiation or mediation to be appropriate between perpetrators of a crime and their victims. Furthermore, it is true that conflict resolution practitioners, advocates, and theorists tend to take a broader approach than they would as militant partisans of one side, which would seem to minimize their role in working with the U.S. government in a state of war.

In actuality, however, as the conflict resolution (CR) field has developed, it offers many strategies and methods that are relevant for partisans in a fight as well as for intermediaries seeking to mitigate destructive conflicts. The new developments in CR are largely responses to the changing international environment. However, they also build on ideas from the early years of the field, as well as innovations within the field, developed as CR workers elaborate and differentiate their areas of endeavor. Furthermore, those new developments themselves actually affect the way conflicts are waged in societies and in the international system. In this chapter, the expanding and evolving CR field is depicted, then its current basic features are presented, after which the applications of CR ideas and practices to contemporary large-scale conflicts are examined, and finally, major current issues are discussed. Throughout this chapter, CR workers include academics, diplomats, workshop organizers, and heads of adversarial organizations when they analyze the CR approach or wittingly or unwittingly employ elements of it.

DEVELOPMENT OF THE CONFLICT RESOLUTION FIELD

Conflict resolution has many sources in practice, theory, and research, resulting in ongoing diversity and controversy within the field. Some of these sources are identified, along with re-lated public events, in chronological order in table 1. The authors noted are from many areas of study, including anthropology, sociology, psychology, economics, peace studies, interna-tional relations, mathematics, law, and political science. The applications are also to be found in many settings, including industrial relations, international diplomacy, judicial proceedings, military affairs, and national struggles against injustice.

Although this examination relates particu-larly to developments in North America and Europe since the 1950s, the analysts and prac-titioners in this field have drawn from cen-turies of religious thought, social scientific analyses, and innovative as well as traditional practices in societies around the world. For ex-ample, nonviolent methods of struggle were used by Mohandas Gandhi in South Africa to oppose discrimination against Indians there, and later in India against British rule. Further-more, as the CR developments in North Amer-ica and Europe diffused into other regions, those ideas were modified and adapted to local conditions. Those adaptations and the knowl-edge of various traditional conflict resolution approaches in other societies also influenced the evolving CR approach in North America and Europe. For example, they helped raise recognition of the importance of relations be-tween adversaries and community assistance in mending ruptures in those relations.[1]

The term "conflict resolution" began to be widely used in the mid-1950s, referring to mutually acceptable ways of ending conflicts. An early site for academic work that contrib-uted significantly to the field's emergence was the University of Michigan, where the *Journal of Conflict Resolution* began publication in 1957 and the Center for Research on Conflict Reso-lution was founded in 1959.[2] Members of these organizations recognized that many conflicts were not to be resolved and hence thought the term "conflict resolution" was a misnomer, but some disliked the term "conflict management,"

with its connotations of manipulation, even more. In recent years, the terms "conflict trans-formation," "problem-solving conflict resolu-tion," "conflict mitigation," "dispute settlement," and "principled negotiation" have also been used, often referring to particular arenas within the CR field.

The diverse sources of CR theory and prac-tice have had varying importance at different periods of CR's development, as its areas of analysis and application expanded. At the out-set of the rapid growth of the field, in the 1980s, mediation and negotiation were the primary foci of activity. Subsequently, earlier stages in the conflict cycle became additional matters of attention, particularly de-escalation and prepa-ration to enter negotiations. Soon, attention also began to be given to CR at even earlier conflict stages: preventing destructive escala-tion and fostering constructive escalation. Most recently, a great deal of attention in the field has been given to postcombat and postsettle-ment concerns, to implementing peace agree-ments and building institutions to sustain peace. The discussion here takes up each arena of at-tention in that sequence, noting some of the many sources that contributed to them.

Utilizing Negotiation and Mediation

In the late 1970s and early 1980s, work in the field began to gather momentum, in many ways appearing to be a social movement.[3] The field was then highly focused on negotiation and mediation, and their utilization in every-day domestic disputes.[4] Training and practice grew, particularly in what came to be called al-ternative dispute resolution (ADR). Operating in the shadow of the law, community dispute resolution centers were established across the United States to handle interpersonal disputes. Practitioners and theorists also applied the CR approach to a variety of organizational, com-munity, and national conflicts, for example, re-lating to the environment and other public disputes.[5] Workers in the field drew on formal theories about maximizing mutually beneficial

Table 1. Chronology of Publications, Developments, and Events Relevant to Conflict Resolution

Year	Publications Pertaining to Conflict Resolution	Institutional Developments in Conflict Resolution and Global Political Events
1942	M. P. Follett, *Dynamic Administration* Q. Wright, *A Study of War*	National War Labor Board established in United States
1945	M. K. Gandhi, *Teachings of Mahatma Gandhi*	World War II ends
1947		U.S. Federal Mediation and Conciliation Service established British sovereignty over India ends
1948		Universal Declaration of Human Rights adopted by the General Assembly of the United Nations signed
1956	L. Coser, *The Functions of Social Conflict*	Successful ending of civil rights bus boycott in Montgomery, Alabama
1957	K. Deutsch et al., *Political Community and the North Atlantic Area*	*Journal of Conflict Resolution* begins publishing, University of Michigan Pugwash Conferences begin, in Canada
1959		Center for Research on Conflict Resolution established, University of Michigan International Peace Research Institute (PRIO) founded, Oslo, Norway
1960	L. Richardson, *Statistics of Deadly Quarrels* T. Schelling, *The Strategy of Conflict*	Dartmouth Conferences begin
1961	T. F. Lentz, *Towards a Science of Peace*	
1962	K. Boulding, *Conflict and Defense* C. E. Osgood, *An Alternative to War or Surrender*	Cuban missile crisis
1964		*Journal of Peace Research* begins publishing, based at PRIO International Peace Research Association founded
1965	A. Rapoport and A. Chammah, *The Prisoner's Dilemma*	J. W. Burton and others organize problem-solving workshop with representatives from Malaysia, Indonesia, and Singapore
1966	M. Sherif, *In Common Predicament*	

Continued

Table 1. Chronology of Publications, Developments, and Events Relevant to Conflict Resolution (*continued*)

Year	Publications Pertaining to Conflict Resolution	Institutional Developments in Conflict Resolution and Global Political Events
1968		Centre for Intergroup Studies established in Capetown, South Africa
1969	J. W. Burton, *Conflict and Communication*	
1970		Peace Research Institute Frankfurt established in Germany
1971	A. Curle, *Making Peace*	Department of Peace and Conflict Research established at Uppsala Universitet, Sweden
1972	J. D. Singer and M. Small, *The Wages of War, 1816–1965*	Détente reached between Soviet Union and United States Treaty on the Limitation of Anti-ballistic Missile Systems signed
1973	M. Deutsch, *The Resolution of Conflict* Gene Sharp, *The Politics of Nonviolent Action*	Department of Peace Studies established, University of Bradford, United Kingdom Society of Professionals in Dispute Resolution (SPIDR) initiates conference
1975		Helsinki Final Act signed, product of the Conference on Security and Cooperation in Europe
1979	P. H. Gulliver, *Disputes and Negotiations: A Cross–Cultural Perspective*	Egyptian-Israeli Treaty, mediated by President J. Carter Iranian revolution
1981	R. Fisher and W. Ury, *Getting to YES*	
1982		Carter Center established in Atlanta, Georgia National Conference on Peacemaking and Conflict Resolution (NCPCR) initiated in United States Search for Common Ground established in Washington, D.C. United Nations Convention on the Law of the Sea adopted

Year	Events	Publications
1984	United States Institute of Peace founded in Washington, D.C. The William and Flora Hewlett Foundation initiates grant program supporting conflict resolution theory and practice International Association for Conflict Management founded	R. Axelrod, *The Evolution of Cooperation*
1985	The Network for Community Justice and Conflict Resolution established in Canada	S. Touval and I. W. Zartman, eds., *International Mediation in Theory and Practice* I. W. Zartman, *Ripe for Resolution: Conflict and Intervention in Africa*
1986	International Alert founded in London	C. W. Moore, *The Mediation Process* (1st ed.)
1987		L. Susskind and J. Cruikshank, *Breaking the Impasse: Consensual Approaches to Resolving Public Disputes*
1989	Berlin Wall falls Partners for Democratic Change founded, linking university-based centers in Sofia, Prague, Bratislava, Budapest, Warsaw, and Moscow	K. Kressel and D. G. Pruitt, eds., *Mediation Research* H. W. van der Merwe, *Pursuing Justice and Peace in South Africa* L. Kriesberg, T. A. Northrup, and S. J. Thorson, eds., *Intractable Conflicts and Their Transformation*
1990	Organization for Security and Cooperation in Europe, 55-state institution, originated with the Charter of Paris for a New Europe Association of Southeast Asian Nations (ASEAN) begins informal workshops	
1992	Instituto Peruano de Resolución de Conflictos, Negociación, y Mediación (IPRECONM) established in Peru	
1993	PLO and Israel sign Declaration of Principles European Union established	M. H. Ross, *The Management of Conflict*
1994	Nelson Mandela elected president of South Africa UN Security Council creates the International Criminal Tribunal for Rwanda	D. Johnston and C. Sampson, eds., *Religion, the Missing Dimension of Statecraft* A. Taylor and J. B. Miller, eds., *Conflict and Gender*
1995	U.S. brokers end of war in Bosnia International Crisis Group established in Brussels	J. P. Lederach, *Preparing for Peace*
1996	South African Truth and Reconciliation Commission established	F. O. Hampson, *Nurturing Peace* Michael S. Lund, *Preventing Violent Conflicts*

Continued

Table 1. Chronology of Publications, Developments, and Events Relevant to Conflict Resolution *(continued)*

Year	Publications Pertaining to Conflict Resolution	Institutional Developments in Conflict Resolution and Global Political Events
1997	P. Salem, ed., *Conflict Resolution in the Arab World*	
1998	E. Weiner, ed., *The Handbook of Interethnic Coexistence*	U.S. Federal Alternative Dispute Resolution Act enacted Good Friday Agreement reached for Northern Ireland International Criminal Court established by Rome statute; entered into force in 2002
1999	H. H. Saunders, *A Public Peace Process* B. F. Walter and J. Snyder, eds., *Civil Wars, Insecurity, and Intervention*	People of East Timor vote for independence from Indonesia
2000	E. Boulding, *Cultures of Peace* J. Galtung et al., *Searching for Peace* T. R. Gurr, *Peoples versus States*	Second intifada begins between Palestinians and Israelis
2001		September 11 terror attacks on United States
2002	D. Cortright and G. A. Lopez, *Sanctions and the Search for Security* D. R. Smock, ed., *Interfaith Dialogue and Peacebuilding*	
2003	R. O'Leary and L. Bingham, eds., *The Promise and Performance of Environmental Conflict Resolution* E. Uwazie, ed., *Conflict Resolution and Peace Education in Africa*	U.S. and allied forces invade Iraq
2004	Y. Bar-Siman-Tov, ed., *From Conflict Resolution to Reconciliation*	Australian Centre for Peace and Conflict Studies founded at University of Queensland, Brisbane Peace agreement between government of Sudan and Sudan People's Liberation Army
2005	C. A. Crocker, F. O. Hampson, and P. Aall, eds., *Grasping the Nettle* D. Druckman, *Doing Research: Methods of Inquiry for Conflict Analysis*	PhD program in peace and conflict studies established at University of Manitoba, Canada

negotiation outcomes as well as experimental and field research about ways of negotiating.[6] They also drew on the long experience with collective bargaining, government mediation services, and international diplomacy to develop effective ways of negotiating and mediating.

Some of the methods and reasoning developed in relation to everyday domestic disputes were adapted and applied to large-scale international and intranational conflicts.[7] The negotiation principles include separating persons from positions, discovering and responding to interests and not simply to stated positions, and developing new options, often entailing packaging trade-offs. More general strategies also were developed, such as reframing issues, substantively as well as symbolically. Another principle is to consider what is the best alternative to a negotiated agreement (BATNA), thereby knowing when breaking off negotiations may be worthwhile. This suggests the value of improving one's BATNA to strengthen one's bargaining position, without raising threats. In any conflict, furthermore, improving one's options independently of the opponent reduces vulnerability to the opponent's threats.

Mediation includes a wide range of services that help adversaries reach a mutually acceptable agreement,[8] including helping arrange meetings by providing a safe place to meet, helping formulate the agenda, and even helping decide who shall attend the negotiation sessions. In addition, services include facilitating the meeting by assisting the adversaries' communication with each other so that each side can better hear what the other is saying, by shifting procedures when negotiations are stuck, and by meeting with each side to allow for safe venting of emotions. Mediators can also contribute to reaching an agreement by adding resources, proposing options, building trust, and gaining constituency support for the negotiators' agreement.

Mediation is conducted by persons in a wide variety of roles, which vary in their capacity to provide specific services. Officials generally have recognized legitimacy to foster and channel negotiations; they also may have access to positive as well as negative sanctions to help reach and sustain agreements. Persons in nonofficial roles, however, may be able to explore possible negotiation options without necessitating great commitment by the adversaries. In addition, they are often involved in fostering and facilitating informal interactions between people of various levels from the opposing sides.

De-escalating and Preparing for Negotiation

As CR workers turned to civil and international wars and other large-scale conflicts, they gave increasing attention to ways intermediaries as well as partisans can reduce the intensity of a conflict and move it toward negotiations for an agreement acceptable to the adversaries.[9] CR analysts and practitioners drew from many academic and practitioner sources to develop methods and strategies that contribute to that change in the course of a conflict. They began to map out a variety of possible de-escalating strategies and assess their suitability for specific times and circumstances.[10]

Two often-noted de-escalation strategies are the graduated reciprocation in tension-reduction (GRIT) strategy and the tit-for-tat (TFT) strategy.[11] According to the GRIT strategy, one of the antagonists announces and unilaterally initiates a series of cooperative moves; reciprocity is invited, but the conciliatory moves continue, whether or not there is immediate reciprocity. The TFT strategy was derived from game theory, experimental research, computer simulations, and historical practice. Such evidence indicates that the strategy most likely to result in cooperative relations and the one yielding the highest overall payoff is simply for one player to begin a series of games cooperatively and afterward consistently reciprocate the other player's actions, whether cooperative or noncooperative.

The GRIT and TFT explanations were compared in an empirical analysis of reciprocity in relations between the United States and the Soviet Union, between the United States and the People's Republic of China (PRC), and between the Soviet Union and the PRC, for the period 1948–89.[12] The Soviet leader Mikhail Gorbachev announced a change in policy toward the United States and Western Europe and made many conciliatory moves, conducting what the analysts call super-GRIT. It transformed relations with the United States and also led to normalized relations with China.

Several methods involving nongovernmental interventions have become features of many de-escalating efforts that help prepare for or that expedite negotiations. These occur at various levels, including between high officials, elites and professionals, and relatively grassroots members of the opposing sides. Such initiatives may be intended to foster mutual understanding between the adversaries or to develop possible solutions to the issues of contention between them. They include various forms of track-two or multitrack diplomacy.[13] Track-one diplomacy consists of mediation, negotiation, and other official exchanges between governmental representatives. Among the many unofficial, or track-two, channels are transnational organizations within which members of adversarial parties meet and discuss matters pertaining to the work of their common organizations. Another form of track-two diplomacy is ongoing dialogue groups, in which members from the adversary parties discuss contentious issues among their respective countries, communities, or organizations.[14]

Some forms of unofficial diplomacy began in the Cold War era and contributed to its de-escalation and ultimate transformation. For example, in 1957 nuclear physicists and others from the United States, Great Britain, and the Soviet Union who were engaged in analyzing the possible use of nuclear weapons began meeting to exchange ideas about reducing the chances that nuclear weapons would be used

again.[15] From the 1950s through the 1970s, the discussions at these meetings of what came to be called the Pugwash Conferences on Science and World Affairs contributed to the signing of many arms control agreements. Another important example of such ongoing meetings during the Cold War is the Dartmouth Conference, which began in 1960.[16] At the urging of President Dwight D. Eisenhower, a group of prominent U.S. and Soviet citizens, many having held senior official positions, were brought together as another communications channel when official relations were especially strained.

With the support of the Association of Southeast Asian Nations (ASEAN), a series of informal workshops were initiated in 1990 to develop habits of cooperation in managing the many potential conflicts in the South China Sea,[17] including regarding conflicting territorial claims, access to resources, and many other matters. Senior officials primarily from governments in the region were participants in their personal capacities, not as representatives of their governments. That nonofficial characterization enabled participants to meet and discuss issues that could not be touched when only official positions could be presented. The workshops helped achieve the 1992 ASEAN Declaration on the South China Sea, committing the signatory states to settle conflicts peacefully, and the workshops helped establish many cooperative projects, relating to exchanging data, marine environmental protection, confidence-building measures, and using resources of the South China Sea.

Another important form of track-two diplomacy is the interactive problem-solving workshops, which involve conveners (often academics) who bring together a few members from opposing sides and guide their discussions about the conflict.[18] The workshops usually go on for several days. Participants typically have ties to the leadership of their respective sides or have the potential to become members of the leadership in the future, and workshops have usually been held in relation to protracted societal and international conflicts, such as those in Northern Ireland, Cyprus, and the Middle East. Participants themselves sometimes become quasi mediators on returning to their adversary group, but as workshop participants, they do not attempt to negotiate agreements.[19] Some workshop members later become negotiators, as was the case in the negotiations between the Palestine Liberation Organization (PLO) and the Israeli government in the early 1990s.[20] They also may generate ideas that help solve a negotiating problem.

As the CR approach has gained more recognition and acceptance, its practitioners have found increasing interest among members of one side in a conflict in learning how to negotiate better (among themselves and then with the adversary when the time for that comes). Such training helps build the capacity of the side with less initial negotiating capability, reducing the asymmetry in the conflict relationship.

These various unofficial, or track-two, methods, however, do not assure the transformation of destructive conflicts. They are often undertaken on too small a scale and are not always employed most appropriately; furthermore, at any given time, groups acting destructively can overwhelm them. Nevertheless, in the right circumstances, they can make important contributions to conflict transformation. Thus, during the 1990s many governmental and nongovernmental parties engaged in mediating a transformation of the seemingly intractable conflict in Northern Ireland. A series of track-two workshops brought together persons representing the several adversarial parties of Northern Ireland, acting as midwives for the formal negotiations.[21] The culmination of this multiparty mediation was the 1998 Good Friday Agreement, which included establishing a power-sharing executive, north-south bodies, and an elected assembly, as well as scheduling the decommissioning of arms.

Avoiding Destructive Escalation

Some CR workers give attention to conflict stages that precede de-escalation, including interrupting and avoiding destructive escalation and advancing constructive escalation. Important work in averting unwanted escalation was undertaken during the later years of the Cold War between the Western bloc and the Communist bloc. This type of work has drawn from many sources, including traditional diplomacy, the work of international governmental and nongovernmental organizations, and peace research, to be relevant to conflict stages before negotiating a conflict settlement, melding them into the overall CR approach.

There actually are numerous ways to limit destructive escalation, many of which can and are undertaken unilaterally by one of the adversaries. These include enhancing crisis management systems to foster good deliberations and planning for many contingencies. They also include avoiding provocation by conducting coercive actions very precisely and by restructuring military forces to be nonprovocatively defensive. Coercive escalation often is counterproductive, arousing intense resistance and creating enemies from groups that had not been engaged in the conflict. The risks of coercive escalation are compounded by the tendency of the winning side to overreach; having scored great advances, it senses even greater triumphs and expands its goals. Therefore, simply being careful and avoiding overreaching is a way to reduce the chances of self-defeating escalation.

Another strategy that limits destructive escalation is avoiding entrapment, the process of committing more and more time or other resources because so much has already been devoted to a course of action.[22] Entrapment contributed to the U.S. difficulty in extricating itself from the war in Vietnam. President George W. Bush and his advisers experienced some of this difficulty after invading Iraq, as suggested by the speech the president gave on

August 22, 2005, to the convention of the Veterans of Foreign Wars. Recognizing the members of the U.S. armed forces lost in military operations in Afghanistan and Iraq, he said: "We owe them something. We will finish the task that they gave their lives for. We will honor their sacrifice by staying on the offensive against the terrorists, and building strong allies in Afghanistan and Iraq that will help us . . . fight and win the war on terror."

More proactive strategies can also help avoid destructive escalation. These include agreements between adversaries to institute confidence-building measures (CBMs), such as exchanging information about military training exercises and installing direct communication lines between leaders of each side.[23]

Although some external interventions instigate and prolong destructive conflicts by providing support to one side resorting to destructive methods, many other kinds of interventions help prevent a conflict from escalating destructively. Diverse international governmental and nongovernmental organizations are increasingly proactive in providing mediating and other services at an early stage in a conflict. An important action is using various forms of media to alert the international community that conditions in a particular locality are deteriorating and may soon result in a grave conflict. In addition to expanding media and Internet coverage, particular NGOs issue reports and undertake intermediary activities to foster conciliation; for example, see the International Crisis Group (http://www.crisisgroup.org), International Alert (http://www.internationalalert.org), and the Carter Center (http://www.cartercenter.org). The United Nations and other international governmental organizations provide CR services to alleviate burgeoning conflicts. For example, the Organization for Security and Cooperation in Europe (OSCE), with fifty-five member countries, has a High Commissioner on National Minorities, which has been instrumental in helping to limit the interethnic conflicts that have

erupted in countries that were part of the former Soviet Union, such as Latvia. When Latvia gained its independence, the government announced that naturalization of non-Latvians would be based on proficiency in Latvian and residency or descent from residents in Latvia before 1940. Because a third of the population—Soviet-era settlers and their families—spoke Russian, this policy would have made nearly a quarter of the country stateless. Over an extended period of consultation, mediation, and negotiation, an accommodation was reached that was in accordance with fundamental human rights standards.

Coercive interventions to stop gross human rights violations and other destructive escalations are also increasingly frequently undertaken. Sometimes this entails the use of military force or the threat of it. In many cases, this is coupled with negotiations about subsequent relations among the antagonistic parties and their leaders. The terms of those subsequent relations and the continuing involvement of external intervenors are often matters of dispute and require good judgment, broad engagement, and persistence to minimize adverse consequences. Coercive interventions may also be more indirect and nonviolent, as in the application of various forms of sanctions and boycotts. When it results in particular alterations of conduct by the targeted groups, such escalation can prove constructive.

Fostering Constructive Escalation and Conflict Transformation

For many years, analysts and practitioners in peace studies and nonviolence studies have examined how conflicts can be waged constructively and how they can be transformed.[24] In recent years, these long-noted possibilities and actualities have drawn much greater attention within the CR field.[25]

One form nonviolent action has taken entails recourse to massive public demonstrations to oust an authoritarian government. Outraged by fraudulent elections, corrupt regimes, and failed government policies, widespread non-violent protests, for example, in the Philippines, Serbia, and Ukraine, have succeeded in bringing about a change in government and sometimes installed a more benign and legitimate one. The new information technologies help mobilize demonstrators and gain widespread attention, which then may produce external support.

Other governments often aid such popular movements. For example, the U.S. Congress established the National Endowment for Democracy (NED) in 1983. This nonprofit organization, governed by an independent, nonpartisan board of directors, is funded by annual congressional appropriations and also contributions from foundations, corporations, and individuals. It awards hundreds of grants each year to NGOs working to develop civil society in various countries. In addition, the U.S. government directly and publicly provides assistance to NGOs and projects abroad that foster democracy, particularly in countries that have suffered violent conflict and authoritarian rule.

Many transnational NGOs, notably the Albert Einstein Institution (http://www. aeinstein.org) and the Fellowship of Reconciliation (http://www.forusa.org), working as advocacy and service organizations, provide training in nonviolent action and help local NGOs to function more effectively. This help may include mediation, consultation, and auditing elections; for example, these functions were served by the Carter Center, in cooperation with the Organization of American States and the United Nations Development Programme, when it helped to manage the 2002–4 crises relating to the demonstrations demanding the recall of Hugo Chávez as president of Venezuela.

Diverse members of one adversary group can choose from several constructive strategies that may induce an opponent to behave more in accordance with their preferences. One widely recognized strategy is to try to define

the antagonist narrowly, as a small core of a small group, separating the penumbra of sympathizers and supporters from the core combatants. Widely shared norms may be called on to rally international support, which can help lessen the opponent's legitimacy. Another general strategy is for members of one side to increase their independence from the opponent, reducing the threats it might use against them.

Whatever strategy may be selected, implementing it effectively is often difficult in large-scale conflicts. On each side, spoilers, opposing moving toward an accommodation, may try to undermine appropriate strategies. The strategies may also be hampered by poor coordination among different agencies, between different levels of government, and between governmental and nongovernmental organizations. CR work encompasses the growing attention to collaborative problem-solving methods and training in order to increase the capacity of conflicting parties to act constructively.

Implementing and Sustaining Peace Agreements

Most recently, considerable attention has been given to postcombat and postsettlement circumstances and possible CR applications.[26] Governments have not been prepared to handle the tasks involved and therefore have relied to a great extent on outsourcing to NGOs tasks to help strengthen local institutions. In addition, various nongovernmental organizations provide independent assistance in establishing and monitoring domestic arrangements for elections and other civic and economic development projects.

One major area of CR expansion and contribution during the postsettlement or post-accommodation stage of a conflict is aiding reconciliation between former enemies.[27] Reconciliation is multidimensional and occurs, insofar as it does, through many processes over an extended period of time; it occurs at different speeds and in different degrees for various members of the opposing sides. The processes relate to four major dimensions of reconciliation: truth, justice, regard, and security.

Disagreements about the truth regarding past and current relations are a fundamental barrier to reconciliation. Reconciliation may be minimally indicated when people on the two sides openly recognize that they have different views of reality. They may go further and acknowledge the possible validity of part of what members of the other community believe. At a deeper level of reconciliation, members of the different communities develop a shared and more comprehensive truth. Progress toward agreed-on truths may arise from truth commissions and other official investigations, judicial proceedings, literary and mass media reporting, educational experiences, and dialogue circles and workshops.

The second major dimension, justice, also has manifold qualities. One is redress for oppression and atrocities members of one or more parties experienced, which may be in the form of restitution or compensation for what was lost, usually mandated by a government. Justice also may take the form of punishment for those who committed injustices, adjudicated by a domestic or international tribunal, or it may be manifested in policies and institutions that provide protection against future discrimination or harm.

The third dimension in reconciliation involves overcoming the hatred and resentment felt by those who suffered harm inflicted by the opponent. This may arise from differentiating the other side's members in terms of their personal engagement in the wrongdoing, or it may result from acknowledging the humanity of those who committed the injuries. Most profoundly, the acknowledgment may convey mercy and forgiveness, stressed by some advocates of reconciliation.[28]

The fourth dimension, security, pertains to overcoming fears regarding injuries that the former enemy may inflict in the future. The adversaries feel secure if they believe they can look forward to living together without threatening each other, perhaps even in harmony. This may be in the context of high levels of integration or of separation with little regular interaction. Developing such institutional arrangements is best done through negotiations among the stakeholders. Such negotiations can be aided by external official or unofficial consultants and facilitators, for example, by staff members of the United Nations or the United States Institute of Peace.

All these aspects of reconciliation are rarely fully realized. Some may even be contradictory at a given time. Thus, forgiveness and justice often cannot be achieved at the same time, although they may be attained, in good measure, sequentially or by different segments of the population in the opposing camps.

Although these various CR methods have been linked to different conflict phases, to some degree they can be applied at every stage. This is so in part because these stages do not neatly move in sequence during the course of a conflict. Furthermore, in large-scale conflicts different groups on each side may be at different conflict stages, and those differences vary with the particular issues in contention.

THE CONTEMPORARY CONFLICT RESOLUTION ORIENTATION

Given the great variety of sources and experiences, a clear consensus about CR ideas and practices among the people engaged in CR is not to be expected. Nevertheless, there are some shared understandings about analyzing conflicts and about how to wage or to intervene in them so as to minimize their adverse consequences and maximize their benefits.

General Premises

Three premises deserve special attention. First, there is widespread agreement in the field, not only that conflicts are inevitable in social life, but that conflicts often serve to advance and to sustain important human values, including security, freedom, and economic well-being. The issue is how to avoid conducting conflicts in ways that contribute to their becoming destructive of the very values that are being pursued. Unfortunately, fighting for security can often generate insecurities, not only for an adversary, but also for the party fighting to win and protect its own.

The second CR premise is that a conflict is a kind of social interaction in which each side affects the other. Partisans tend to blame the opponent for all the bad things that happen in a fight, and they even tend to regard their own bad conduct as forced on them by the opponent. From a CR perspective, such self-victimization reduces the possible ways to resist and counter the antagonists' attacks. As discussed elsewhere in this chapter, each side is able to affect its opponent by its own conduct. Furthermore, it can strengthen its position in various ways, besides trying to destroy or harm the antagonist. Of course, relationships are never entirely symmetric, but they are varyingly unequal.

Third, given the destructive as well as constructive courses that conflicts may traverse, understanding the forces and policies that shape a trajectory is crucial in CR. A conflict needs to be carefully analyzed to improve the chances that particular policies chosen by partisans or by intermediaries will be effective and not turn out to be counterproductive. The analysis should include gathering as much good information as possible about the various stakeholders' interests and their views of each other. That knowledge should be coupled with theoretical understanding of conflicts generally, based on experience and research, which can suggest a wide range of possible options for action and indicate the probabilities of different outcomes for various options. Such an analysis can help parties avoid policies that seem attractive based on internal considerations but are unsuitable for contending with the external adversary. The analysis can also help

parties avoid setting unrealistically grandiose goals, unattainable by any available means.

Specific Ideas

The CR field incorporates numerous specific ideas about methods and strategies that are relevant for reducing the destructiveness of conflicts, although persons engaged in CR differ to some degree about them.

Human Interests and Needs. Some CR theorists and practitioners argue that all humans have a few basic needs in common and that the failure to satisfy those needs is unjust and an important source of conflicts, while fulfilling them adequately is critical to justly resolving a conflict.[29] Other CR workers, however, doubt that a particular fixed set of needs is universal and stress the cultural variability in needs and how they are defined.[30] Thus, all humans may wish to be respected and not be humiliated, but how important that wish is and how it is defined and manifested vary widely among cultures and subcultures. One way to bridge these differences is to draw on the consensus that is widely shared and expressed in various international declarations and conventions about universal human rights, as shown in the earlier discussion of the OSCE's mediation in Latvia.[31]

Social Construction of Conflict Parties. Members of each party in a conflict have some sense of who they are and who the adversaries are; they have a collective identity and attribute one to the adversary. However, a conflict often involves some measure of dispute about these characterizations. The identities may seem to be immutable, but of course they actually change, in part as the parties interact with each other. Moreover, every person has numerous identities associated with membership in many collectivities, such as a country, a religious community, an ethnicity, and an occupational organization. The understanding of the changing primacy of different collective identities is particularly well studied in the creation of an ethnicity.[32] Conventional thinking often reifies an enemy, viewing its members as a single organism and so giving it a singularity that it does not possess. Actually, no large entity is unitary and homogeneous; the members of every large-scale entity differ in hierarchical ranks and in ways of thinking, whether in a country or an organization. They tend to have different degrees and kinds of commitment for the struggles in which their collectivity is engaged. A simplified image of one adversary in a conflict is depicted in figure 1, incorporating three sets of concentric circles. One set shows the dominating segment of the adversary in regard to a particular conflict, consisting of a small circle of leaders and commanders, a somewhat larger circle of fighters and major contributors, a larger circle of publicly committed supporters, and finally a circle of private supporters. In addition, however, some people in each collectivity dissent and disagree with the way the conflict is being conducted by the dominant leaders. They may disagree about the goals and the methods being used, favoring a variety of alternative policies. Some dissenters may prefer that a harder line be taken, with more extreme goals and methods of struggle, while others prefer a softer line, with more modest goals and less severe means of struggle. Two such dissenting groups are also depicted, one more hard-line and the other less hard-line than the dominant group. Finally, one large oval encloses the dominating and dissenting groupings and also numerous persons who have little interest in and are not engaged in the external conflict. Obviously, the relative sizes of these various circles vary greatly from case to case over time. For example, in the war between the United States and Iraq, which began in 2003, American dissenters differed widely in the goals and methods they favored and they increased in number as the military operations continued. More persons became engaged, and private dissenters became more public and vocal in their dissent. People

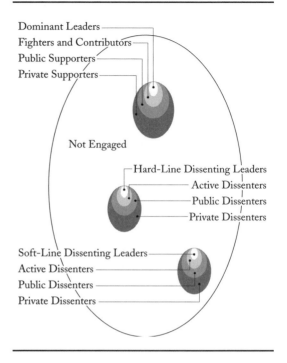

Figure 1. Components of an Adversary

Dominant Leaders
Fighters and Contributors
Public Supporters
Private Supporters

Not Engaged

Hard-Line Dissenting Leaders
Active Dissenters
Public Dissenters
Private Dissenters

Soft-Line Dissenting Leaders
Active Dissenters
Public Dissenters
Private Dissenters

who had been strong supporters of the prevailing policies weakened their support and some of them became dissenters.

Another related insight is that no conflict is wholly isolated; rather, each is linked to many others. Each adversary has various internal conflicts that impinge on its external adversaries, and each has a set of external conflicts, some linked over time and others subordinated to even larger conflicts. One particular pair of adversaries may give the highest importance to their fight with each other, but its salience may lessen when another conflict escalates and becomes more significant.[33]

Alternatives to Violence. The word "conflict" is often used interchangeably with "war" or other words denoting violent confrontations; or, if it is defined independently, it includes one party harming another to obtain what it wants from that other.[34] In the CR field, however, conflict is generally defined in terms of persons or groups who manifest incompatible goals.[35] That manifestation, moreover, may not be violent; indeed, each contending party uses various mixtures of nonviolent coercion, promised benefits, or persuasive arguments to achieve its contested goals. Conflicts are waged using a changing blend of coercive and noncoercive inducements. Analysts and practitioners of CR often note that great reliance on violence and coercion is risky and can be counterproductive.[36]

Intermediaries and NGOs. Adversaries wage a conflict against each other within a larger social context. Some of the people and groups not engaged as partisans in the conflict may be drawn in as supporters or allies of one side; that possibility can influence the partisans on each side to act in ways that do not spur the outsiders to help their opponent. CR workers generally stress the direct and indirect roles that outsiders exercise in channeling the course of conflicts, particularly as intervenors who mediate and otherwise seek to mitigate and settle destructive conflicts.[37] As may be envisaged in figure 2, intermediary efforts can be initiated between many different subgroups from each adversary, including official (track-one) mediation between the dominant leaders of the antagonistic sides, track-two meetings of persons from the core groups on each side, and dialogue meetings between grassroots supporters or dissenters on each side.

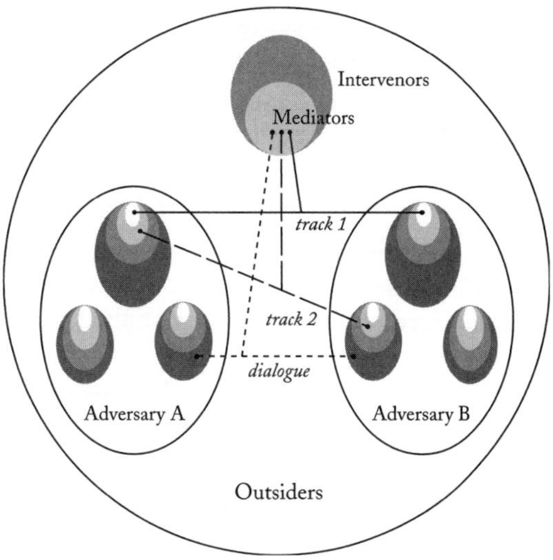

APPLICATIONS IN THE POST-9/11 WORLD

As the editors of this book note, some contemporary conflicts are like many past ones in most regards, while some exhibit quite new features. This discussion of contemporary conflicts focuses on conflicts that are especially affected by recent global developments, including the end of the Cold War and the decline in the influence of Marxist ideologies and the increased preeminence of the United States. They also include the increasing impacts of technologies

Figure 2. Adversaries and Intervenors

relating to communication and to war making; the increasing roles of nonstate transnational actors, both corporate and not-for-profit organizations; and the growing roles of religious faiths and of norms relating to human rights. Possible CR applications in these circumstances are noted for different conflict stages, undertaken by partisans and by outsiders.

Preventing Destructive Conflicts

Partisans in any conflict, using CR conceptions, can pursue diverse policies that tend to avoid destructive escalation. A general admonition is to carry out coercive escalations as precisely targeted as possible to minimize provocations that arouse support for the core leadership of the adversary. Another general caution is not to overreach when advancing toward victory; the tendency to expand goals after some success is treacherous. This may have contributed to the American readiness to attack Iraq in 2003, following the seemingly swift victory in Afghanistan in 2001.

More specific CR strategies have relevance for avoiding new eruptions of destructive conflicts resulting, for example, from al Qaeda–related attacks. Al Qaeda is a transnational nonstate network with a small core and associated groups of varyingly committed supporters, whose leaders inspire other persons to strike at the United States and its allies. Constructively countering such attacks is certainly challenging, so any means that may help in that effort deserve attention.

Some Muslims in many countries agree with al Qaeda leaders and other Salafists that returning Islam to the faith and practice of the Prophet Muhammad will result in recapturing the greatness of Islam's Golden Age.[38] Furthermore, some of the Salafists endorse the particular violent jihad strategy adopted by al Qaeda. The presence of large Islamic communities in the United States and in Western Europe threatens to provide financial and other support for continuing attacks around the world. However, these communities also provide the opportunity to further isolate al Qaeda and related groups, draining them of sympathy and support. The U.S. government's strategic communication campaigns to win support from the Muslim world, initiated soon after the September 11, 2001, attacks, were widely recognized as ineffective;[39] the intended audiences often dismissed U.S. media programs celebrating the United States. Consequently, in 2005 President Bush appointed a longtime close adviser, Karen P. Hughes, to serve as under secretary of state for public diplomacy and public affairs, and oversee the government's public diplomacy, particularly with regard to Muslims overseas. Despite some new endeavors, the problems of fashioning an effective comprehensive strategy were not overcome.[40]

Many nongovernmental organizations play important roles in helping local Muslims in U.S. cities feel more secure and integrated into American society. Some of these are long-standing organizations such as interreligious councils and American Civil Liberties Union (ACLU) chapters, while others are new organizations, focusing on Muslim–non-Muslim

relations. In addition, American Arab and Muslim groups, such as the American-Arab Anti Discrimination Committee (http://www.adc.org) and the Council on American-Islamic Relations (http://www.cair-net.org), act to protect their constituents' rights, to counter discrimination, and to reject terrorist acts in the name of Islam.

Engagement by external actors is often crucial in averting destructive conflicts. The engagement is particularly likely to be effective insofar as the intervention is regarded as legitimate. Collective engagement by many parties tends to be seen as legitimate and is also more likely to be successful in marshaling effective inducements. Thus, in international and in societal interventions, multilateral sanctions are more likely to succeed than are sanctions imposed by a single power. This was true for the UN sanctions directed against Libya, led by Mu'ammar al-Gadhafi, which followed the clear evidence linking Libyan agents with the bombing of Pan Am Flight 103 on December 21, 1988.[41] The sanctions contributed to the step-by-step transformation of Gadhafi's policies and of U.S. relations with Libya.

More multilateral agreements to reduce the availability of highly destructive weapons to groups who might employ them in societal and international wars are needed. Overt and covert arms sales and the development of weapons of mass destruction are grave threats requiring the strongest collective action. The defensive reasons that governments may have for evading such agreements should be addressed, which may entail universal bans and controls. Those efforts should go hand in hand with fostering nonviolent methods of waging a struggle.

Interrupting and Stopping Destructive Conflicts

One adversary, or some groups within it, can act unilaterally to help stop and transform a destructive conflict in which it is engaged. At the grassroots level, such action may be efforts to place in power new leaders who will undertake to de-escalate the fighting. It may also take the form of opposing provocative policies that contribute to destructive escalation, as was visible in the resistance to the U.S. government policy in Nicaragua and El Salvador by Americans in the early 1980s and to the Soviet invasion of Afghanistan by the families of Soviet soldiers. At the elite level, some persons and groups may begin to challenge policies that are evidently costly and unproductive, compelling changes in policies and ultimately in the core leadership. These developments within the United States and the Soviet Union contributed greatly to the end of the Cold War between them.[42]

The actions that members of one side take toward their adversary certainly are primary ways to interrupt destructively escalating conflicts. This can occur at the popular level with people-to-people diplomacy, which may help prepare the ground for significant changes at the leadership level, or the actions may be conducted at the elite level and signal readiness to change directions. In confrontations as broad as those relating to the advancement of democracy, the renewal of Islam, or the countering of terrorism, engagement at all levels is extremely important. Demonizing the enemy may seem useful to mobilize constituents, but it often creates problems for the inevitable changes in relations.

Acts by leaders of one side directed at leaders on the other side or to their various constituent groups are particularly important in the context of rapidly expanding channels of mass and interpersonal communication. These channels convey a huge volume of information about how friends and foes think and intend to behave. Attention to that information and responding to it should be given very high priority.

Forceful interventions by external actors to halt disastrous escalations have become more frequent in recent decades. These include increasingly sophisticated and targeted sanctions, which require a high degree of multilateral cooperation to be effective. This is also true for police work to locate and bring to justice perpetrators of gross human rights violations, as well as to control the flow of money and weapons that sustain destructive conflicts.

De-escalating and Reaching Agreements

To bring a destructive conflict to an agreed-on end, it is important for the adversaries to believe that an option exists that is better than continuing the fight. Members of one side, whether officials, intellectuals, or popular dissidents, may envision such an option and so help transform the conflict. Communicating such possible solutions in a way that is credible to the other side requires skill and sensibility, given the suspicions naturally aroused by intense struggles; overcoming such obstacles may be aided by knowledge of how this has been accomplished in the past.[43]

Intermediaries can be critical in constructing new options by mediation, which may entail shuttling between adversaries to discover what trade-offs can yield a generally acceptable agreement or resolve a seemingly intractable issue. For example, in the 1980s, during the civil wars in Lebanon, groups associated with Hezbollah took hostage fifteen Americans as well as thirty-nine other Westerners. When George H. W. Bush took office as president of the United States in 1989, following President Ronald Reagan, he signaled an opening for negotiations to free the hostages.[44] UN diplomatic operations then did bring about the release of the remaining hostages. In particular, Giandomenico Picco, assistant secretary-general to UN secretary-general Javier Pérez de Cuéllar, conducted intensive mediation, shuttling from one country to another in the region.

Implementing and Sustaining Agreements

The tasks to be undertaken after an accommodation has been reached, whether largely by imposition or by negotiation, are manifold.

Importantly, institutions should be established that provide legitimate ways to handle conflicts. This may entail power sharing among major stakeholders, which helps provide them with security. The CR orientation provides a repertoire of ways to constructively settle disputes and generate ideas about systems to mitigate conflicts. CR ideas also provide insights about ways to advance reconciliation among people who have been gravely harmed by others.

CURRENT ISSUES

The preceding discussion has revealed differences within the CR field and between CR workers and members of related fields of endeavor. Five contentious issues warrant discussion here.

Goals and Means

CR analysts and practitioners differ in their emphasis on the process used in waging and settling conflicts and their emphasis on the goals sought and realized. Thus, regarding the role of the mediator, some workers in CR, in theory and in practice, stress the neutrality of the mediator and the mediator's focus on the process to reach an agreement, while others argue that a mediator either should avoid mediating when the parties are so unequal that equity is not likely to be achieved or should act in ways that will help the parties reach an equitable outcome. The reliance on the general consensus embodied in the UN declarations and conventions about human rights offers CR analysts and practitioners standards that can help produce equitable and enduring settlements.

Violence and Nonviolence

Analysts and practitioners of CR generally believe that violence is too often used when nonviolent alternatives might be more effective, particularly when the choice of violence serves internal needs rather than resulting from consideration of its effects on an adversary,

when it is used in an unduly broad and imprecise manner, and when it is not used in conjunction with other means to achieve broad constructive goals. However, CR workers differ in the salience they give these ideas and which remedies they believe would be appropriate. These differences are becoming more important with increased military interventions to stop destructively escalating domestic and international conflicts. More analysis is needed of how various violent and nonviolent policies are combined and with what consequences under different circumstances.

Short- and Long-Term Perspectives

CR analysts tend to stress long-term changes and strategies, while CR practitioners tend to focus on short-term policies. Theoretical work tends to give attention to major factors that affect the course of conflicts, which often do not seem amenable to change by acts of any single person or group. Persons engaged in ameliorating a conflict feel pressures to act with urgency, which dictates short-term considerations; these pressures include fund-raising concerns for NGOs and electoral concerns for government officials driven by elections and short-term calculations. More recognition of these different circumstances may help foster useful syntheses of strategies and better sequencing of strategies.

Coordination and Autonomy

As more and more governmental and nongovernmental organizations appear at the scene of most major conflicts, the relations among them and the impact of those relations expand and demand attention. The engagement of many organizations allows for specialized and complementary programs but also produces problems of competition, redundancy, and confusion. To enhance the possible benefits and minimize the difficulties, a wide range of measures may be taken, from informal ad hoc exchanges of information to regular meetings among organizations in the field to having one organization be the "lead" agency. As more NGOs are financially dependent on funding by national governments and international organizations, new issues regarding autonomy and co-optation arise.

Orientation, Discipline, Profession

The character of the CR field is a many-sided matter of contention. One issue is the degree to which the field is a single discipline, a multidisciplinary endeavor, or a general approach that should contribute to many disciplines and professions. A related issue is the relative emphasis on core topics that are crucial in training and education or on specialized knowledge and training for particular specialties within the broad CR field. Another contentious issue is the degree to which the field is an area of academic study or a profession, with the academic work focused on providing training for practitioners. Finally, there are debates about certification and codes of conduct and who might accord them over what domains of practice.

These contentions are manifested on the academic side by the great proliferation of MA programs, certificate programs, courses, and tracks within university graduate schools, law schools, and other professional schools in the United States and around the world (http://www.campusadr.org/Classroom_Building/degreeoprograms.html. About eighty graduate programs of some kind function in the United States, but PhD programs remain few.[45] The first PhD program in conflict resolution was begun at George Mason University in 1987, but since then only one other PhD program has been established in the United States, at Nova Southeastern University.

On the applied side, the issues of establishing certificates and codes of ethics and the frequently changing set of professional associations bespeak the unsettled nature of issues relating to the CR field's discipline and professional character. An important development, linking theory and applied work, is the assessment of practitioner undertakings. A growing body of empirically grounded assessments examines which kinds of interventions, by various groups, have what consequences.[46]

CONCLUSION

The CR field continues to grow and evolve. It is not yet highly institutionalized and is likely to greatly expand in the future, become more differentiated, and change in many unforeseen ways. In the immediate future, much more research assessing various CR methods and projects is needed. This is beginning to occur and is often required by foundations and other funders of NGO activities.[47] This work needs to be supplemented by research about the effects of the complex mixture of governmental and nongovernmental programs of action, and of the various combinations of coercive and noncoercive components in transforming conflicts constructively. Past military campaigns are carefully analyzed and plans for future war fighting are carefully examined and tested in war games. Comparable research and attention are needed for diplomatic and nongovernmental engagement in conflicts. So far only a little work has been done on coordination between governmental and nongovernmental organizations engaged in peacebuilding and peacemaking.[48]

The fundamental ideas of the CR approach are diffusing throughout American society and around the world. Admittedly, this is happening selectively, and often the ideas are corrupted and misused when taken over by people profoundly committed to traditional coercive unilateralism in waging conflicts. The CR ideas and practices, nevertheless, are not to be dismissed; they are increasingly influential and great numbers of people use them with benefit. Ideas and ideologies can have great impact, as demonstrated by the effect of past racist, communist, and nationalist views and those of contemporary Islamic militants, American neoconservatives, and advocates of political democracy. Although gaining recognition,

CR ideas are still insufficiently understood and utilized. Perhaps if more use were made of them, some of the miscalculations relating to resorting to terrorist campaigns, to countering them, and to forcefully overthrowing governments would be curtailed.

It should be evident that to reduce a large-scale conflict to an explosion of violence, as in a war or a revolution, is disastrously unrealistic. A war or a revolution does not mark the beginning or the end of a conflict. In reality, large-scale conflicts occur over a very long time, taking different shapes and with different kinds of conduct. The CR orientation locates eruptions of violence in a larger context, which can help enable adversaries to contend with each other in effective ways that help them achieve more equitable, mutually acceptable relations and avoid violent explosions. It also can help adversaries themselves to recover from disastrous violence when that occurs. Finally, the CR approach can help all kinds of intermediaries to act more effectively to mitigate conflicts, so that they are handled more constructively and less destructively.

Many changes in the world since the end of the Cold War help explain the empirical finding that the incidence of civil wars has declined steeply since 1992 and interstate wars have declined somewhat since the late 1980s.[49] The breakup of the Soviet Union contributed to a short-lived spurt in societal wars, but the end of U.S.-Soviet rivalry around the world enabled many such wars to be ended. International governmental and nongovernmental organizations grew in effectiveness as they adhered to strengthened international norms regarding human rights. On the basis of the analysis in this chapter, it is reasonable to believe that the increasing applications of the ideas and practices of CR have also contributed to the decline in the incidence of wars.

NOTES

I wish to thank the editors for their many helpful suggestions and comments, and I also thank my colleagues for their comments about these issues, particularly Neil Katz, Bruce W. Dayton, Renee deNevers, and F. William Smullen.

1. John Paul Lederach, *Preparing for Peace: Conflict Transformation across Cultures* (Syracuse, N.Y.: Syracuse University Press, 1995); Paul Salem, ed., *Conflict Resolution in the Arab World: Selected Essays* (Beirut: American University of Beirut, 1997); and Ernest Uwazie, ed., *Conflict Resolution and Peace Education in Africa* (Lanham, Md.: Lexington, 2003).

2. Martha Harty and John Modell, "The First Conflict Resolution Movement, 1956–1971: An Attempt to Institutionalize Applied Disciplinary Social Science," *Journal of Conflict Resolution* 35 (1991): 720–758.

3. Peter S. Adler, "Is ADR a Social Movement?" *Negotiation Journal* 3, no. 1 (1987): 59–66; and Joseph A. Scimecca, "Conflict Resolution in the United States: The Emergence of a Profession?" in *Conflict Resolution: Cross-Cultural Perspectives,* ed. Peter W. Black, Kevin Avruch, and Joseph A. Scimecca (New York: Greenwood, 1991).

4. Roger Fisher and William Ury, *Getting to YES* (Boston: Houghton Mifflin, 1981).

5. Lawrence Susskind and Jeffrey Cruikshank, *Breaking the Impasse: Consensual Approaches to Resolving Public Disputes* (New York: Basic, 1987).

6. Howard Raiffa, *The Art and Science of Negotiation* (Cambridge, Mass.: Harvard University Press, 1982).

7. Roger Fisher, Elizabeth Kopelman, and Andrea Kupfer Schneider, *Beyond Machiavelli: Tools for Coping with Conflict* (New York: Penguin, 1994).

8. Christopher W. Moore, *The Mediation Process: Practical Strategies for Resolving Conflict,* 3rd ed. (San Francisco: Jossey-Bass, 2003).

9. Janice Gross Stein, ed., *Getting to the Table: The Process of International Prenegotiation* (Baltimore and London: Johns Hopkins University Press, 1989).

10. Loraleigh Keashly and Ronald J. Fisher, "Complementarity and Coordination of Conflict Interventions: Taking a Contingency Perspective," in *Resolving International Conflicts,* ed. Jacob Bercovitch (Boulder, Colo.: Lynne Rienner, 1996), 235–261; and Louis Kriesberg and Stuart J. Thorson, eds., *Timing the De-Escalation of International Conflicts* (Syracuse, N.Y.: Syracuse University Press, 1991).

11. Charles E. Osgood, *An Alternative to War or Surrender* (Urbana: University of Illinois Press, 1962); and Robert Axelrod, *The Evolution of Cooperation* (New York: Basic, 1984).

12. Joshua S. Goldstein and John R. Freeman, *Three-Way Street: Strategic Reciprocity in World Politics* (Chicago: University of Chicago Press, 1990).

13. John W. McDonald, "Further Explorations in Track Two Diplomacy," in Kriesberg and Thorson, eds., *Timing the De-Escalation of International Conflicts*, 201–220; and Joseph V. Montville, "Transnationalism and the Role of Track-Two Diplomacy," in *Approaches to Peace: An Intellectual Map*, ed. W. Scott Thompson and Kenneth M. Jensen (Washington, D.C.: United States Institute of Peace Press, 1991).

14. David R. Smock, ed., *Interfaith Dialogue and Peacebuilding* (Washington, D.C.: United States Institute of Peace Press, 2002); and Eugene Weiner, ed., *The Handbook of Interethnic Coexistence* (New York: Continuum, 1998). See also http://coexistence.net.

15. Michael J. Pentz and Gillian Slovo, "The Political Significance of Pugwash," in *Knowledge and Power in a Global Society*, ed. William M. Evan (Beverly Hills, Calif.: Sage, 1981), 175–203.

16. Gennady I. Chufrin and Harold H. Saunders, "A Public Peace Process," *Negotiation Journal* 9 (1993): 155–177.

17. Hasjim Djalal and Ian Townsend-Gault, "Managing Potential Conflicts in the South China Sea," in *Herding Cats: Multiparty Mediation in a Complex World*, ed. Chester A. Crocker, Fen Osler Hampson, and Pamela Aall (Washington, D.C.: United States Institute of Peace Press, 1999), 109–133.

18. Ronald Fisher, *Interactive Conflict Resolution* (Syracuse, N.Y.: Syracuse University Press, 1997); and Herbert C. Kelman, "Informal Mediation by the Scholar Practitioner," in *Mediation in International Relations*, ed. Jacob Bercovitch and Jeffrey Z. Rubin (New York: St. Martin's, 1992).

19. Louis Kriesberg, "Varieties of Mediating Activities and of Mediators," in *Resolving International Conflicts*, ed. Jacob Bercovitch (Boulder, Colo.: Lynne Rienner, 1995), 219–233.

20. Herbert C. Kelman, "Contributions of an Unofficial Conflict Resolution Effort to the Israeli-Palestinian Breakthrough," *Negotiation Journal* 11 (January 1995): 19–27.

21. Paul Arthur, "Multiparty Mediation in Northern Ireland," in Crocker, Hampson, and Aall, eds., *Herding Cats*, 478.

22. Joel Brockner and Jeffrey Z. Rubin, *Entrapment in Escalating Conflicts: A Social Psychological Analysis* (New York: Springer, 1985).

23. Shai Feldman, ed., *Confidence Building and Verification: Prospects in the Middle East* (Jerusalem: Jerusalem Post; Boulder, Colo.: Westview, 1994).

24. Johan Galtung, *Peace by Peaceful Means: Peace and Conflict, Development and Civilization* (Thousand Oaks, Calif.: Sage, 1996); Lester Kurtz, *Encyclopedia of Violence, Peace, and Conflict* (San Diego: Academic, 1999); Roger S. Powers and William B. Vogele, eds., with Christopher Kruegler and Ronald M. McCarthy, *Protest, Power, and Change: An Encyclopedia of Nonviolent Action from ACT-Up to Women's Suffrage* (New York and London: Garland, 1997); Gene Sharp, *The Politics of Nonviolent Action* (Boston: Porter Sargent, 1973); and Carolyn M. Stephenson, "Peace Studies: Overview," in *Encyclopedia of Violence, Peace, and Conflict*, 809–820.

25. Louis Kriesberg, *Constructive Conflicts: From Escalation to Resolution*, 3rd ed. (Lanham, Md.: Rowman and Littlefield, 2006); Lederach, *Preparing for Peace*; and John Paul Lederach, *Building Peace: Sustainable Reconciliation in Divided Societies* (Washington, D.C.: United States Institute of Peace Press, 1997).

26. Stephen John Stedman, Donald Rothchild, and Elizabeth Cousens, eds., *Ending Civil Wars: The Implementation of Peace Agreements* (Boulder, Colo.: Lynne Rienner, 2002).

27. Yaacov Bar-Siman-Tov, ed., *From Conflict Resolution to Reconciliation* (Oxford: Oxford University Press, 2004).

28. Michael Henderson, *The Forgiveness Factor* (London: Grosvenor, 1996).

29. John Burton, *Conflict: Resolution and Prevention* (New York: St. Martin's, 1990); and James Laue and Gerald Cormick, "The Ethics of Intervention in Community Disputes," in *The Ethics of Social Intervention*, ed. Gordon Bermant, Herbert C. Kelman, and Donald P. Warwick (Washington, D.C.: Halstead, 1978).

30. Kevin Avruch, *Culture and Conflict Resolution* (Washington, D.C.: United States Institute of Peace Press, 1998).

31. Eileen F. Babbitt, *Principled Peace: Conflict Resolution and Human Rights in Intra-state Conflicts* (Ann Arbor: University of Michigan Press, forthcoming).

32. Benedict Anderson, *Imagined Communities: Reflections on the Origin and Spread of Nationalism* (London: Verso, 1991); and Franke Wilmer, *The Social Construction of Man, the State, and War: Identity, Conflict, and Violence in the Former Yugoslavia* (New York and London: Routledge, 2002).

33. Bar-Siman-Tov, *From Conflict Resolution to Reconciliation.*

34. Lewis A. Coser, *The Functions of Social Conflict* (New York: Free Press, 1956).

35. Paul Wehr, *Conflict Regulation* (Boulder, Colo.: Westview, 1979).

36. Chalmers Johnson, *Blowback: The Costs and Consequences of American Empire* (New York: Henry Holt, 2000).

37. William Ury, *The Third Side* (New York: Penguin, 2000).

38. Marc Sageman, *Understanding Terror Networks* (Philadelphia: University of Pennsylvania Press, 2004).

39. Report of the Defense Science Board Task Force on Strategic Communication, 2004, available online at http://www.publicdiplomacy.org/37.htm. United States Government Accountability Office, "U.S. Public Diplomacy: Interagency Coordination Efforts Hampered by the Lack of a National Communication Strategy," GAO-05-323 April 2005; available at www.gao.gov.

40. Steven R. Weisman, "Diplomatic Memo: On Mideast 'Listening Tour,' the Question Is Who's Listening," *New York Times,* September 30, 2005, A3.

41. David Cortright and George Lopez, with Richard W. Conroy, Jaleh Dashti-Gibson, and Julia Wagler, *The Sanctions Decade: Assessing UN Strategies in the 1990s* (Boulder, Colo.: Lynne Rienner, 2000).

42. Richard K. Herrmann and Richard Ned Lebow, *Ending the Cold War: Interpretations, Causation, and the Study of International Relations* (New York: Palgrave Macmillan, 2004); Louis Kriesberg, *International Conflict Resolution: The U.S.-USSR and Middle East Cases* (New Haven, Conn.: Yale University Press, 1992); and Jeremi Suri, *Power and Protest: Global Resolution and the Rise of Detente* (Cambridge, Mass.: Harvard University Press, 2003).

43. Christopher Mitchell, *Gestures of Conciliation: Factors Contributing to Successful Olive Branches* (New York: St. Martin's, 2000).

44. Giandomenico Picco, *Man without a Gun* (New York: Times Books, 1999).

45. Johannes Botes, "Graduate Peace and Conflict Studies Programs: Reconsidering Their Problems and Prospects," *Conflict Management in Higher Education Report* 5, no. 1 (2004): 1–10.

46. Mary B. Anderson and Lara Olson, *Confronting War: Critical Lessons for Peace Practitioners* (Cambridge, Mass.: Collaborative for Development Action, 2003), 1–98; and Rosemary O'Leary and Lisa Bingham, eds., *The Promise and Performance of Environmental Conflict Resolution* (Washington, D.C.: Resources for the Future, 2003).

47. Anderson and Olson, *Confronting War.*

48. Susan H. Allen Nan, "Complementarity and Coordination of Conflict Resolution in Eurasia," in *Conflict Analysis and Resolution* (Fairfax, Va.: George Mason University, 1999).

49. Monty G. Marshall and Ted Robert Gurr, *Peace and Conflict, 2005* (College Park: Center for International Development and Conflict Management, University of Maryland, May 2005). See also Human Security Centre, *Human Security Report 2005* (New York: Oxford University Press, 2006), 151. Wars are defined to have more than 1,000 deaths. The report is accessible at http://www.cidcm.umd.edu/inscr; see also Mikael Eriksson and Peter Wallensteen, "Armed Conflict, 1989–2003," *Journal of Peace Research* 41, 5 (September 2004): 625–636.

27

THE POWER OF NONOFFICIAL ACTORS IN CONFLICT MANAGEMENT

Pamela Aall

IT HAS BEEN A COMMON OBSERVATION since the end of the Cold War that peacemaking has opened up to a variety of new actors. Powerful states have been joined by smaller states willing to commit time and resources to promoting peace in South Asia, the Middle East, and Central America. The United Nations has been joined by a growing number of regional organizations that undertake specific missions in their geographical area—the Organization for Security and Cooperation in Europe (OSCE), the Africa Union, the Intergovernmental Authority on Development (IGAD), the Southern African Development Community (SADC), the Organization of the Islamic Conference (OIC), the Organization of American States (OAS), and even NATO, historically a collective defense organization that has lately taken on the role of securing peace in Afghanistan. In terms of numbers, however, the greatest growth of new actors has been in the nonofficial field. Organizations as diverse as Catholic Relief Services—a multimillion-dollar relief and development NGO—and the Carter Center, a specialized agency devoted to conflict resolution, have taken on activities that range from preventing conflict to postconflict reconciliation and are active at all phases of the conflict cycle.[1]

Nonofficial organizations that engage in third-party peacemaking are very different in size, resources, capacity, and flexibility. Counting the number of unofficial organizations that have entered the peacemaking field is daunting, because one is immediately confronted by definitional issues: What is a nonofficial organization? Is it the same as a nongovernmental organization? What is peacemaking and what activities does it encompass? Are these activities similar to those undertaken by the official institutions or are they specific to the nonofficial world? This chapter takes a broad view of the nonofficial world and includes examples from international and local organizations, both large and small. It also includes organizations with strong ties to the official world as well as those that operate entirely in and through civil society. The chapter considers peacemaking and how it encompasses mediation as well as many peacebuilding activities that precede, follow, and surround peace talks, from negotiation training to building a constituency for peace in the wider society.

When the activities of official and nonofficial organizations are compared, a distinction is often made about their ability, or lack thereof, to employ the tools of power in mediation to persuade parties to a conflict to talk rather than fight. In this regard, governments, especially large governments, have quite a lot of power, international organizations have less, and the general perception is that nonofficial organizations have next to none. And in most conflicts, the general perception continues, a "mediator with muscle" is necessary to close the deal. As Saadia Touval and I. William Zartman note in chapter 25 of this volume, in the difficult work of bringing parties to an agreement, "ripe moments and leveraged buy-offs by state mediators are the necessary ingredients" and, they add realistically, "even they may not be sufficient."[2]

However, since states are not always available or willing to engage in peacemaking efforts in other people's conflicts, or capable of doing so, a strategic approach to expanding capacity in conflict management would suggest a better understanding of the objectives, resources, and capabilities of nonofficial organizations whose mission is to respond to conflict. A closer look at how official and nonofficial organizations function—their sources of power, the way that they apply leverage, and the ways that they interact with peace processes—does not support the common perception that NGOs are powerless. Not only are they not powerless, but their sources of power and the way they employ it are similar to the way that recognizably powerful institutions use their resources to promote peace. These similarities can provide a basis for collaborating in the business of peacemaking and may produce a product with more staying

power than many negotiated peace agreements of the past had.

This chapter examines the issue of the power of nonofficial actors, starting off by looking at a particular case—the role that two nonofficial organizations played in talks between the government of Indonesia and Acehnese rebels—in order to illustrate both opportunities and pitfalls awaiting nonofficial intermediaries who take on a peacemaking role. The chapter then examines the nature of power available to "powerless" nonofficial organizations that engage in peacemaking, making the argument that these powers are similar to those employed by more powerful organizations. It then moves on to examine how nonofficial organizations use their powers to gain their objectives and concludes with a recommendation for closer official and nonofficial collaboration in the pursuit of peace.

NONOFFICIAL MEDIATION IN ACEH: HENRI DUNANT CENTRE FOR HUMANITARIAN DIALOGUE AND THE CONFLICT MANAGEMENT INITIATIVE

In 2000 the Henri Dunant Centre for Humanitarian Dialogue (HDC), a Geneva-based nongovernmental organization, facilitated negotiations between the Indonesian government and the Free Aceh Movement (GAM). The fact that there were negotiations was itself unexpected. The conflict between the government and GAM dated back to 1976 and centered around GAM's adamant desire for Acehnese independence and the equally adamant Indonesian government insistence that Aceh was an integral part of Indonesia. In addition, despite the long war, the government of Indonesia had been openly hostile to the idea of third-party involvement in what it viewed as an illegal internal rebellion. And although GAM was not on the U.S. terrorist list, there had been over the years enough rumor and accusations of terrorist links to discourage outsiders from taking up the cause of this remote, orphaned conflict.

The HDC was created in late 1998 to "prevent human suffering in war" through promoting and facilitating dialogue between belligerents.[3] Its first challenge as a new organization with virtually no track record was to gain entry as a legitimate intermediary in a serious conflict. An HDC representative visiting East Timor sent back word that a conflict over independence between the national government and a province was ongoing in Aceh, and the organization decided to engage.[4] Despite—or perhaps because of—its lack of history and relationships in the area, the Indonesian government agreed to allow the HDC to host talks between itself and GAM. Over the next three years, talks continued. The first concrete achievement was the negotiation of a cease-fire in 2000, a "humanitarian pause" that brought hope for a permanent settlement to the people of Aceh even though it was regularly breached over the next two years. Finally, in December 2002, the parties signed a more robust document, the Cessation of Hostilities Agreement, a framework agreement that mapped out the steps to peace from full cease-fire and demilitarization to autonomy talks and eventual provincial elections in Aceh.[5] In a period of just under three years, a nonofficial organization from Geneva managed to put an obscure and forgotten conflict on the international map and to broker a peace agreement.

The cease-fire, however, broke down within six months. The Indonesian government and military accused GAM of using the cease-fire to regroup and rearm, and in May 2003 the government claimed that a "military emergency" would force it to end the conflict by destroying GAM through compellence. The hard fighting over the next two years taxed the GAM's leadership and militia and ate away at support in the broader Acehnese society for continued armed struggle. An election in Indonesia in 2004 produced a new administration

with a desire to end the conflict and an Indonesian president who showed a readiness to enter into negotiations. It seemed that both parties, exhausted by the fight, recognized that they might be able to settle their issues at the negotiating table. The opening for negotiation was widened dramatically by the 2004 tsunami that devastated Aceh and brought an unprecedented amount of international attention to the province and the conflict.

In the new move toward a negotiated agreement, the parties once again turned to a nonofficial organization. The Conflict Management Initiative, located in Helsinki and headed by former Finnish president Martti Ahtisaari, hosted five rounds of talks in the first half of 2005. As a result of these talks, the parties signed the Helsinki Memorandum of Understanding, which went far beyond the earlier Cessation of Hostilities Agreement. Like the earlier agreement, it contained clauses on cease-fire and demobilization, but it also covered the political relationship between Aceh and the Indonesian government, political participation, human rights, economic matters, and provisions for monitoring the postsettlement process by the European Union and the Association of Southeast Asian Nations (ASEAN).[6]

It is too early to predict whether the memorandum of understanding will lead to a sustainable peace, but even without that outcome, there are lessons to be learned from the cases of two nonofficial interventions in the Acehnese conflict. How, for instance, did the HDC, a small and heretofore unknown NGO, manage to gain the trust and cooperation of the parties in 2000? How did it muster the strength, skill, and legitimacy to act as a mediator in a seemingly intractable conflict that had endured for twenty-five years? And was the failure of the peacemaking effort an indication of its lack of power to keep the cease-fire on track? If so, did the Helsinki-based Conflict Management Initiative bring a different set of powers to the table that allowed it to help the parties move beyond a cease-fire agreement to a comprehensive peace settlement? The following sections of this chapter will consider these and other questions in its examination of the power of nonofficial peacemakers.

UNDERSTANDING THE NATURE OF NONOFFICIAL POWER

Talking about power and mediation in the same breath may strike many as odd. Power, or rather the deployment of power, is usually associated with imposing your will on another entity or preventing another entity from imposing its will on you. Mediation, on the other hand, is an attempt to help opposing parties settle differences without resorting to violence. Although the mediating institution may have interests in the outcome, it is not a party to the conflict. It is also not attempting to impose a resolution on the parties, as would be the case with arbitration and adjudication. A mediator exercises his or her power as a way of focusing the attention of the parties on the costs of continuing to fight versus the benefits of a negotiated agreement. In pursuit of this, a major power such as the United States, France, Russia, or China has a number of tools at its disposal. It can use trade, aid, or promises of a special relationship to induce one or all parties to the conflict to pay attention. It can also use threats of withdrawal of special privileges, the prospect of sanctions, or even the threat of force to change the behavior of the belligerents.

It is a bit harder to understand the nature of power that the United Nations and other international organizations bring to a peacemaking effort. The United Nations, for example, cannot threaten force against a country or nonstate actor without the consent and active involvement of the Security Council—a rare circumstance, given the different national interests of the Security Council members. Even political or economic sanctions can be beyond the capacity of the United Nations to impose and enforce, as members with interests in continuing diplomatic or economic ties find ways to skirt punitive measures. The body also has fewer means at its disposal to promise the types of direct incentives available to individual powers.

The United Nations can, however, offer a stable of diplomatic expertise in mediation and has been very active in applying this expertise to conflict resolution and peacemaking in conflicts ranging from Angola and Afghanistan to East Timor and Haiti. The secretary-general appoints special representatives of the secretary-general (SRSGs) to nearly every ongoing conflict; in early 2006, approximately fifty SRSGs were active in thirty conflicts around the world. The United Nations can also offer legitimacy to the parties to the conflict through recognition of the conflict by the international community—that amorphous entity comprising both international organizations and individual powers—and acknowledgment that the outcome of the conflict is important. This attention can be worth a great deal to a weak government struggling to keep its country from disintegrating into conflict, as has been the case in Burundi. And, as the eventual independence of East Timor shows, it can be worth a great deal to a rebel group struggling to gain support for its side of the issues.

Whether they come in the form of tangible promises or threats, or as intangible prospects of recognition (or rejection) as a member in good standing of the international community, these incentives and disincentives give individual states and international organizations some tools to help convince parties to a conflict that they may wish to abandon violence and turn to negotiation as a means of settling their dispute. The widely held view of nonofficial organizations is that they lack these tools. They cannot threaten a country with the use of force or the imposition of sanctions; they also cannot offer the international legitimacy that UN or regional organizations can. How, then, have they been able to affect conflicts at all?

In order to answer this question, it is necessary to examine a bit more closely the nature of power as it relates generally to mediation. In a 1992 essay on the topic, Jeffrey Z. Rubin identified six bases of power in mediation:

- *Informational power* depends on the mediator's access to information that the parties want or need; in using this power, the mediator might act as a go-between, transmitting messages from one side to the other.
- *Expert power* is based on making the parties believe that the mediator has greater knowledge and experience with certain issues.
- *Referent power* reflects the value that the parties to the conflict place on their relationship with the mediator; if parties place a high value on the relationship, they are more likely to listen to the mediator, thus increasing the mediator's referent power.
- *Legitimate power* arises from the parties' perception that the mediator has the right to act as a third party and to ask for changes in behavior or compliance.
- *Reward power* is the ability to use incentives to offer the parties something that they want—aid, trade, or side payments—in exchange for changes in behavior.
- *Coercive power* involves the ability to threaten or use force in order to change the behavior or perceptions of the parties.[7]

The following sections look at each of these powers in more detail, examining how both official and nonofficial mediators use these powers to help parties to a conflict reach a settlement or at least some sort of mutual accommodation.

Informational Power

Informational power stems from the mediator's ability to act as an agent of communication, to bring the parties information that they need—such as messages from one another or messages from the outer world—as well as to help them recognize, define, and articulate their needs and possible areas for negotiation.

Parties to a conflict often lack the means to communicate with one another. Protracted conflict can result in a "taboo on direct talks," as former secretary of state James A. Baker III noted in his account of the shuttle diplomacy he undertook in preparation for the Madrid talks in 1991. As Baker traveled to Tel Aviv, Jerusalem, Riyadh, Cairo, Amman, and Damascus, he carried messages from one party to the next, but he was also an active participant in shaping these messages. He suggested, for instance, to King Fahd of Saudi Arabia that the Saudis drop the economic boycott of Israel in exchange for U.S. pressure on the Israelis to withdraw the Israeli army from parts of the West Bank and Gaza. By carefully stitching together a quilt of contingent options, he used informational power to bring the parties on board.[8]

Nonofficial organizations have used informational power creatively to establish relationships and bring parties together. The Workshops on Managing Potential Conflicts in the South China Sea—a nonofficial effort hosted by a Canadian academic and a former Indonesian government minister (Ian Townsend-Gault and Hasjim Djalal) to discuss common problems like piracy in the South China Sea—developed into a multilateral negotiating forum for the countries involved. The organizers used the parties' interest in and need for information to gather them together. The resulting agreements were relatively low level and functional, but the process allowed the small states in the area to develop a pattern of multilateral negotiation with China, their big neighbor to the north, and allowed participants to develop relationships that proved useful in future negotiations.[9]

Betty Bigombe's work with the Lord's Resistance Army offers a more direct example of a nonofficial entity—in this case an individual—using the power of communication. Bigombe, a former government minister in Uganda, left her job at the World Bank in 2004 to attempt to restart negotiations between the northern Uganda rebel group the Lord's Resistance Army (LRA) and the government of Uganda. Although she had ties with the Ugandan government, she came as a private person who had built up trust with both parties when she had been involved in Ugandan government–LRA negotiations in 1994. As a private person, she had few resources to help with the mediation. She noted in 2005 that she had spent thousands of her own dollars on calls to the rebels' satellite phones and on food for the rebels.[10] Most of her effort was spent in facilitating communication—she passed messages between the rebels and the government and talked both sides through options for action. She also used silence as a means of communication. As reported by the *Christian Science Monitor*, "Rebel commanders also call Bigombe from their satellite phones in fits of rage, she says. They demand, for instance, that Uganda's Army withdraw fully from the north. Bigombe goes quiet. After a while the commander often asks, 'Are you still there?' Eventually he barks, 'I'll call you back in 30 minutes.' When he does, she says with a knowing smile, he's 'much more reasonable. . . . When I go silent, they know I'm not pleased,' she explains. It sends a simple message: 'Do you want to blow it all up—or move toward peace?'"[11]

As this example shows, employing informational power requires that the mediator already possess both legitimate power and referent power: that is, be legitimate in the eyes of both parties and have a strong enough relationship with both to be viewed as an honest broker. If these conditions are present, informational power can be effective in helping parties to recognize realities, see beyond their current situation, and change their perceptions of the costs of beginning or continuing to fight versus the benefits of negotiating.

Expert Power

Expert power—power drawn from the mediator knowing, or at least appearing to know,

more than parties do—may incorporate several elements, ranging from analytic insights and current intelligence on the conflict to expertise in designing formulas that can resolve the parties' dispute. In some cases, mediators may have had prior experience and relationships that lead parties to believe that they have a unique understanding of some part of the mediation process. As High Commissioner on National Minorities for the Organization for Security and Cooperation in Europe, Max van der Stoel exploited his status as an expert by arranging seminars on federalism and other responses to minority concerns for governments facing possible conflict. In some meetings, his intermediatory efforts seemed closer to graduate-school classes than mediation.[12]

Nonofficial organizations have used similar types of expert power in efforts to prepare parties for negotiation.[13] The South China Sea process brought in expertise on common problems as part of the formula for relationship building in Southeast Asia. As another example, former Canadian officials, acting in their private capacities, have introduced Tamil Tigers to the Canadian model of federalism. These engagements are efforts not to determine the outcomes of peace negotiations but rather to develop the parties' understanding that political solutions—whether negotiations over common problems, as in the South China Sea, or negotiations over governance arrangements, as in Sri Lanka—are viable alternatives to political violence.

At times, expert power may come from sharing similar experiences with the conflict parties. For several years, the United States Institute of Peace (USIP) has assisted Israeli and Palestinian educators in their efforts to develop relationships, exchange ideas, and create a joint curriculum. The USIP team included a professor of education from Northern Ireland and a professor of psychology from Macedonia. Both professors had firsthand experience of the tension, distrust, and strong resistance to change in their own countries' education system. In explaining how they and their colleagues had coped with these challenges in Northern Ireland and Macedonia, they provided the opportunity for the Israeli and Palestinian educators to see their situation in a comparative framework and to develop some options to try in their own school systems. Similarly, Father Alex Reid (who played a mediator's role in his own conflict in Northern Ireland) deployed expertise gained in helping to bring about an IRA cease-fire in Northern Ireland to push both the Spanish government and ETA, the Basque separatist movement, toward negotiations. Before his engagement in this conflict, he had no connection with the Spanish government or ETA, but, based on his expertise in Northern Ireland, he was able to establish the necessary relationships and credibility to be an effective go-between in the Basque conflict.

Expert power is, however, a complicated resource that can work both for and against a mediator. When former senator George Mitchell accepted the invitation to chair the International Body that eventually mediated the Good Friday Agreement in Northern Ireland, he had fourteen years of experience in the U.S. Senate, including six years as Senate majority leader. He also had been the special adviser to the president and the secretary of state for economic initiatives in Ireland. In addition to a relationship with the U.S. president, he brought with him deep knowledge of protracted negotiations, gained in his long years in the U.S. Senate. This expert power appealed to the British government and the Irish government, as well as to a number of the direct parties to the conflict. It did not, however, appeal to the Unionists, who felt that he and the International Body were being thrust on them by the British, Irish, and U.S. governments without consultation. In their eyes, his expert power was to be put to use to further a larger agenda that they did not share. Their objections to Mitchell did not last—shortly thereafter, the Unionists changed their minds

and withdrew their objections, and negotiations about the negotiations started in earnest.[14] This example shows, however, that expert powers can lead parties to embrace the mediator but can also lead them to repudiate him or her.[15]

Referent Power

Referent power—the power to influence one or both sides because the parties to the conflict value the relationship with the third party —is often associated with a powerful state: the parties to the conflict value the relationship because the powerful state can use its resources to protect or support the interests of both parties. A classic example is the U.S. role as mediator of choice in the Israeli-Palestinian conflict. Over the years, both sides have valued the relationship, Israel because the United States is its staunchest ally and the Palestinians because the United States provides much-needed aid and can use its power to nudge the Israeli government toward peace. There are examples from the nonofficial world as well. Former president Jimmy Carter used referent power to engage the parties when he mediated the cease-fire in Bosnia in 1994 (although, as the cease-fire did not hold, his accomplishment can be contested) and the agreement in 1999 between the Sudanese and Ugandan governments. The Vatican used a great deal of referent power when it facilitated negotiations in 1984 in the century-old dispute between Argentina and Chile over territorial rights to three islands in the eastern part of the Beagle Channel.[16] As a result of its intervention, Argentina and Chile signed a treaty assigning the islands to Chile, an agreement that holds to this day.

Many may argue that Jimmy Carter owed his referent power to his status as former U.S. president and to the possibility (usually unconfirmed) that he may have had the backing of the sitting U.S. administration as part of his mediator's kit. Equally, the Vatican's moral authority and prestige allowed it to exert far more pressure on Chile and Argentina than any other nonofficial organization could. These observations raise the question of whether these two examples are sui generis—in a class of their own—and therefore should not be seen as evidence that nonofficial mediators can develop referent power. There are, however, many other cases in which a nonofficial mediator derives power from the relationship he or she has with the conflict parties. Paul Wehr and John Paul Lederach have written about the "insider-partials" as mediators in internal disputes.[17] An insider-partial is a "'mediator from within the conflict,' whose acceptability to the conflictants is rooted not in distance from the conflict or objectivity regarding the issues, but rather in connectedness and trusted relationships with the conflict parties. The trust comes partly from the fact that the mediators do not leave the postnegotiation situation."[18] In other words, insider-partials derive their influence from their relationship with the parties to the conflict and are accepted as mediators precisely because they have an interest in the outcome and will be personally affected by the agreement.

The Muslim-Christian Dialogue Forum provides an example of the use of referent power as an insider-partial. The Muslim-Christian Dialogue Forum was founded by Nigerian religious leaders Pastor James Wuye and Imam Muhammed Nurayn Ashafa, who had been militants in their country's interreligious conflicts. Their interest in dialogue grew from their religious beliefs, but their early attempts to talk to each other were marked by mutual suspicion and distrust. Nevertheless, they continued to pursue—often in public settings—the goal of understanding each other's perspectives and of identifying the common elements of Christianity and Islam, and in the end they coauthored a book on the topic.[19] Well respected within their own communities, they were able to use their relationships with their communities and with each other to encourage Muslim-Christian dialogue

in the highly charged intercommunal conflict in central Nigeria's Plateau State. Their efforts resulted in the Kaduna Peace Declaration, signed on December 18, 2002, by twenty senior religious leaders, who continued to collaborate on reducing conflict and increasing local capacity for conflict resolution.[20]

A valuable relationship does not necessarily mean a public one. At times, parties to a conflict do not want a strong relationship with the third party or close identification with a peace process. This is particularly true when the parties to a conflict run the risk of repudiation by their own constituencies because they meet or even consider meeting the other side. A low-key mediator who can be dismissed as unimportant if the early moves toward peace fail is an advantage in these circumstances. Paul Arthur, a professor at the University of Ulster, used this "deniability" as he and his university-based colleagues organized workshops for Northern Irish politicians in the period leading up to the 1998 Good Friday Agreement. In his account of these workshops, Arthur recognized the benefits of operating below the radar. "That the workshops took place in a scholarly setting was advantageous because journalists were inclined to dismiss them as being merely 'academic' and not newsworthy."[21] This approach protected the Unionist and Nationalist politicians who took sizable risks in terms of their own constituencies' support in agreeing to talk with each other. The workshops—and the seminar-like atmosphere they encouraged—also provided an opportunity for these officials (acting in a nonofficial capacity) to test some ideas and gauge the reactions of the other side. In this case, the value of the third-party relationship was in its informal and nonbinding nature. As this example makes clear, relationships do count for a great deal, but the nature of the referent power that results from relationships varies from one case to the next. At times a relationship is valued precisely because it can be repudiated with credibility.

Legitimate Power

In Rubin's typology, power also comes from the mediator's legitimacy, or the mediator's "*right* to make a request." He notes that "almost any third party, in almost any setting, is likely to rely on some measure of legitimate power in exercising influence. After all, simply by virtue of being a mediator, it is probably assumed that this individual or group is legitimately positioned to make certain kinds of requests."[22] This power may derive from the fact that the mediator represents a powerful institution that the parties find difficult to ignore —the United States, the Vatican, a "group of friends" of the process who are determined to keep pressure on the parties. The power may also stem from a longtime relationship or a satisfactory peacemaking partnership in the past.

This power may be easier to recognize when the mediator does not have it—or ceases to have it—in the eyes of one or more of the parties. The involvement of the Norwegian government as mediator in the Sri Lankan conflict between the Sri Lankan government and the Tamil Tigers seems to be a case in which the mediator gained and lost legitimate power on a number of occasions. In 2005 the mediator's legitimacy became a national political issue in the campaign for Sri Lanka's presidency. Although both parties had accepted Norway as mediator, there was among the Sinhalese majority a perception that Norway had closer ties to the Tamil Tigers than to the official government. In addition, stories appeared in the press speculating about Norway's motivation, claiming that Norway's seemingly disinterested mediation was actually motivated by its desire for fishing rights off the Sri Lankan coast. In the 2005 election, presidential candidate Mahinda Rajapakse campaigned on an anti–peace talks platform, criticizing the ceasefire that was negotiated with Norwegian assistance and threatening to fire the Norwegians as mediators if he won. Whether his preelection opposition to the Norwegians was based on an assessment of their shortcomings or on a desire to make political hay, he tapped into a strong popular doubt among Sinhalese about Norway's legitimacy as mediator. After his election, the Norwegians had no choice but to withdraw until Rajapakse asked them to reengage, perhaps in response to the growing levels of violence in the country.[23]

As this example shows, the issue of legitimacy has its complexities for all types of mediators, as each side to the conflict will have different reasons for finding the mediator legitimate. All sides will want the mediator to understand (and favor, even if secretly) their position and will attempt to win the mediator over. If the mediator holds firm, one or occasionally all parties will be tempted to repudiate the third party or to seek out a more sympathetic one. Legitimacy is a power that can evaporate quickly under the stress of negotiations.

For nonofficial actors, taking hold of and retaining this power is just as complex, as they are usually involved in the talks only because the parties want them to be. This is a weak position from which to make requests, to use Rubin's term. But it is worth noting that requests are not demands. Nongovernmental organizations have often played a role in reframing, in persuading parties to a conflict to rethink their positions, objectives, and attitudes so that they can identify some issues that might yield to negotiation. Roger Fisher popularized this notion of structuring negotiations toward a "win-win" solution, a solution in which both parties reach a satisfactory agreement on issues critical to all.[24] Herbert Kelman developed the problem-solving workshop approach that brings together in a neutral setting influential—although not official —individuals who represent differing parties to a conflict. The objective of the workshop is to increase understanding of each party's position and circumstances and to identify acceptable solutions to the conflict. As the participants return to their own communities, they take their new insights and suggestions for action and feed these into the political process.[25]

While Kelman does not make direct requests, the expectation behind the problem-solving workshops is that parties will change their thinking and convey these changes back to their communities. Kelman used the problem-solving workshops to promote dialogue among Israeli and Palestinian "influentials"; ten years later, Coventry Cathedral's International Centre for Reconciliation used similar methods to promote dialogue among religious leaders in the Middle East.[26]

In the case of Aceh, the Conflict Management Initiative's Martti Ahtisaari had a great deal of legitimacy in the eyes of the parties as a senior statesman and former president. In the 2005 negotiations, he used this legitimacy to keep the parties focused on a comprehensive agreement rather than a step-by-step approach to the issues, insisting that "nothing is agreed until everything is agreed."[27] In an examination of these cases, it may be appropriate to expand Rubin's definition of legitimacy as "the right to make a request or to ask them to reframe the terms of the conflict." Viewed in this way, nonofficial mediators frequently exercise legitimate power.

Reward and Coercive Powers

Finally, we come to the deployment of reward and coercive powers, the "mediator with muscle" that Touval and Zartman consider essential for third-party political intervention to succeed. Offering rewards and making credible threats are relatively concrete powers and are generally linked to state-based mediators who can marshal the will to use resources and political capital to settle someone else's dispute. The promise and delivery of massive amounts of U.S. military and economic assistance to Israel and Egypt that accompanied the signing of their peace agreement in 1979 illustrates well the reward capacity of a major power. Equally, the economic sanctions imposed on the Milosevic regime in 1992 and the NATO threat and the use of force against Belgrade over Kosovo in 1999 are

examples of using coercive power in the attempt to raise the costs associated with continued fighting.

Without question, nonofficial organizations are weak with regard to these two powers. They lack sufficient material resources to offer incentives and at the same time they have little or no access to the tools of coercion such as arms, control over funds, and ability to establish blockades. There is little they can do to force changes in behavior on war-hardened parties. However, their willingness to engage in a dialogue process, and to pressure the international community on behalf of such a process, may be valuable to combatants who are exhausted by the conflict but cannot take the first steps toward negotiation without outside help. By exercising their other powers—informational, expert, referent, and legitimate—nonofficial organizations do provide incentives for parties to change their behavior, if only because they provide a moment in which change may be possible. Once rejected, the moment may not recur for a long time. Equally, an NGO's threat to withdraw from the role of third-party peacemaker—as insignificant as it may seem to the larger parties—might be enough to make parties reconsider their hard-line positions. Closing the door on negotiations, no matter how quietly, can leave parties isolated and diminish international patience for their positions. Although these are not robust powers, nonofficial organizations should recognize them as elements that they can use in the attempt to focus antagonists' attention on the benefits of negotiation and the costs of its collapse.

LEVERAGING POWERS

Understanding the nature of mediators' influence on the parties is only part of the story. It is also important to understand how they can apply their resources in order to increase their influence. Much has been written on the topic of leverage—where it comes from and how to deploy it—but most of this work has focused on the leverage that powerful states possess by virtue of their ability to dangle carrots and brandish sticks in front of reluctant parties.[28] "Leverage" has also often been used as a synonym for "power." In the practice of mediation, however, power—and especially the use of force—is rarely applied directly. Instead the mediator or third party attempts to persuade the participants in the conflict to refrain from using violence or to abandon the battlefield for the negotiating table. The meaning of "leverage" in this sense is similar to its meaning in physics: a factor by which a lever multiplies a force or, translated into social relations, the "power to produce an effect by indirect means: influence, sway, weight."[29] Seen this way, sources of leverage have been and are being used by organizations that do not have large caches of power.

Zartman and Touval explain the complicated relationship between power and leverage in mediation: "The extent of the mediator's power depends entirely on the parties, whose acceptance of a mediator depends on its likelihood (potential power) of producing an outcome agreeable to both sides."[30] In other words, leverage results from a combination of powers, the skillful use of powers, and the confidence that the principals have that the mediators know what they are doing and can produce results. This is not a question of smoke and mirrors; it is rather a question of having a strategic approach to the mediation, understanding the nature of the obstacles and the power that the mediator has to move or remove them, and building up alliances with other official and nonofficial organizations that can help. All mediators have sources of leverage, including the ability to influence the parties' costs and benefits as well as their fears and insecurities, the ability to keep both parties under pressure to move toward settlement, and the ability to get other third parties involved in order to encourage the peace process and keep the parties moving forward.[31]

It is important to note that a critical ingredient in allowing mediators—whether official or nonofficial—to leverage their powers so that they produce a more significant result does not reside in the mediators' character, background, international support, or resources. It lies instead in the environment of the conflict—specifically in how ripe the conflict is for resolution.[32] Ripeness is a contested theoretical concept, because critics claim it can be identified only by its result—if a conflict is settled, it must have been ripe; if it failed to settle, then it was not ripe.[33] Regardless of the theoretical disputes, the notion of ripeness is one that practitioners seem to recognize. The condition of ripeness may be momentary, reflecting an alignment of factors that might include exhaustion on the part of the parties—a realization that they will not be able to win militarily—and the leadership necessary to make the move from war to peace. An official mediator can cultivate ripeness through manipulating incentives and disincentives, in other words, by raising the cost of continued warfare or the benefits of negotiation. A nonofficial mediator can also cultivate ripeness by using the other powers discussed here—the power to persuade, to reframe issues, to present different options, to communicate.

Through its work in Aceh, the HDC mediators thought that they had recognized a moment of ripeness and took advantage of that set of circumstances to help the parties negotiate the initial agreement. As it turned out, the state of ripeness that the HDC identified may have been a moment when the parties paused to catch their breath, and the HDC did not have sufficient powers to transform this moment of apparent ripeness into a more permanent state. The absence of ripeness became apparent as the two parties spent the next two years in vicious fighting. By the time the Conflict Management Initiative became involved, the conflict had chipped away at the parties' commitment to continued fighting, and the tsunami had changed the facts on the ground for the Acehnese rebels. In addition, a new set of actors and a changed attitude toward the conflict in the Indonesian government created a negotiating partner for the Acehnese leaders. Given these circumstances, there was far less need for the Conflict Management Initiative to create ripeness; instead, it could focus its efforts on preserving the ripeness that had developed in the two years of continued violence and keeping up the momentum of the negotiation workshops. By fostering the existing ripeness, the Conflict Management Initiative added to its leverage over the parties, as they were reluctant to lose the advantages they perceived they had gained through negotiation.

DEPLOYING POWERS

If nonofficial organizations have access to powers similar to those available to official organizations when it comes to preventing or ending conflict, do they use them in the same way? In the broadest sense, they do: as Diana Chigas points out, there are cases in which NGOs have served as principal mediators in developing agreements, helped to implement agreements, built up support for peace processes in the international community, and promoted policy change to create a better environment for peace and political transformation.[34] However, most of the time, NGOs have been effective in conflicts and in activities in which the more powerful mediators do not engage: for instance, in putting issues and conflicts on the international agenda and in building the capacity for change within a conflict.

Putting Issues and Conflicts on the International Agenda

One of the most potent mechanisms that NGOs have at their disposal is their ability to bring an issue to the attention of policymakers and the general public. From the earliest days of Amnesty International's first letter-writing campaigns, human rights NGOs have em-

ployed this power effectively to shine a spotlight on human rights abuses within states and put pressure on the international community to respond. In the process, international human rights NGOs have formed alliances with local, in-country NGOs whose ability to investigate and report has given credence to the human rights community's charges. In the face of evidence produced by local organizations, leaders accused of human rights abuses find it harder to claim that the NGOs or the international community or both are fabricating stories for their own political ends. International human rights NGOs have also developed strong relationships with lawmakers in various capitals who are sympathetic to their causes and with journalists who are capable of giving their perspective broad exposure. Using all these channels—direct campaigns, pressure on law- and opinion makers, and media exposure—human rights organizations have worked to change the international agenda. Thirty years ago, notions of the sanctity of national sovereignty kept local human rights abuses hidden from outsiders or, equally common, ignored and unacknowledged by the international community. Today, as we have seen in Rwanda, Bosnia, and Darfur, the international community may still fail to respond adequately to human rights violations. The failure, however, is explained away no longer in terms of the inviolable nature of national sovereignty but rather in terms of intervention fatigue. Human rights NGOs did not change these norms by themselves; they were, however, important players in the growing international appreciation that human rights abuses can be—and in many eyes should be—addressed by outside governments and international organizations to protect individuals from their own leaders.

In recent years, a few nonofficial organizations devoted to preventing and resolving conflict have adopted some of the same techniques as human rights NGOs to alert decision makers and influential individuals to conditions that may provoke an outbreak of violence or promote its spread. Through on-the-ground investigations and resulting reports, they draw attention to deteriorating conditions or changing circumstances that affect peace and conflict. Using the Internet and news media, they distribute their analysis to the engaged public, and, through their considerable political connections, they press policymakers to take action. The International Crisis Group (ICG), an NGO based in Washington and Brussels, is an example of a conflict-monitoring organization. It not only keeps a watching brief on conflicts in various countries around the world but often reports on the conflict's effect on domestic conditions. For instance, it has long followed the military and political situation in Pakistan as part of its effort to alert the international community about the prospects for further conflict in the South Asia area. But besides its focus on traditional security concerns, it has investigated the role that the Pakistani education system plays in the conflict and in turn the impact that the conflict has on the education system. This ability to focus on specific sectors and targets of opportunity allows the ICG to recommend appropriate policies to address conflicts at many levels.[35]

Through these sorts of activities, NGOs have also played an important role in drawing international attention to conflicts forgotten by the rest of the world. These conflicts—which have included at times Nepal, Sri Lanka, Aceh, East Timor, Afghanistan, Rwanda, Uganda, Myanmar, Burundi, and Somalia, among others—are often labeled intractable conflicts, in recognition of their long duration. Powerful third parties are reluctant to engage with them for a number of reasons, ranging from the fact that they take place in remote areas of the world to the judgment that these conflicts cannot be negotiated but will have to burn themselves out. However, it has been argued that the lack of purposeful, sustained third-party engagement is an element of these conflicts' intractability. Forgetting these con-

flicts may make it more likely that they will burn on rather than burning out.[36] The example of the Community of Sant'Egidio's mediation of the Mozambican conflict in 1992 has been used to prove that, given the right relationships and circumstances, even a charitable organization can mediate a conflict. In fact, it is just as important to recognize that without Sant'Egidio's involvement, the Mozambican conflict could have burned on for some time, threatening its region with instability and destroying the little that remains of the country. Sant'Egidio prevented the Mozambican conflict from being forgotten, just as the HDC reminded the international community of the persistent conflict between Aceh and the government of Indonesia.

Building the Capacity for Change within a Conflict

As civil-society members themselves, nonofficial organizations are well situated to promote capacity building within conflicted societies. This capacity building might take the form of encouraging the growth of civil society, building local capacity for peacemaking by improving mediation and negotiation skills, training local officials in management and problem solving, strengthening support for the rule of law and democratic institutions, and working with educational authorities and others to reform education.[37] In carrying out these tasks, nonofficial organizations deploy all sorts of expert, legitimate, and informational powers. Through their own example, they also employ a "soft power" not dissimilar from Joseph Nye's notion of the soft power exercised by governments, persuading their local partners to adopt ideas or change behaviors through attraction rather than through coercion.[38]

Using a capacity-building approach, Harold Saunders and his colleagues from the Dartmouth Conference Regional Conflicts Task Force not only worked to establish a dialogue among influential leaders in Tajikistan but also used the mechanism of the informal workshops to strengthen negotiation skills. In this case, the task force identified important members of the pro-government and opposition groups in Tajikistan and gathered them in an informal series of meetings called the Inter-Tajik Dialogue. Starting in 1993, this dialogue process provided the first occasion for the antagonists to talk, develop an agenda for discussion—return of refugees was identified early on as a common concern of all parties—and build capacity for the UN-sponsored negotiation that started in 1994.[39] Another example is provided by the London organization International Alert, which operated in West Africa, the Great Lakes region, the former Soviet Union, and Sri Lanka to support peacemaking and peacebuilding efforts, working with official and nonofficial groups to increase institutional capacity and offer adversaries a chance to discuss issues and develop relationships in an informal setting.

A quite different strategy for building the capacity for change within a society is the development of civil opposition to repression. This strategy consists of well-planned, orchestrated deployment of such tools as protests, refusal to cooperate, and direct action aimed specifically against repressive leaders or institutions. In 2000 a strategic nonviolent campaign spearheaded by a student group known as Otpor successfully overthrew former Yugoslavian president Slobodan Milosevic. This campaign was not the result of a spontaneous civil revolt. Rather, it was the result of intensive training sessions run by the quasi-governmental NGOs the National Democratic Institute and the International Republican Institute for the members of Otpor.[40] The training was based on theories of power and nonviolence developed by Gene Sharp, as well as a hands-on introduction to the tools of nonviolent change.[41] In applying these lessons, Otpor mobilized support from all elements of society and formed alliances with the police, the very security forces that Milosevic needed in order to remain as head of government. Through nonviolent

means, the youth galvanized the power of the people and neutralized the power of the state.[42] Several years later, Otpor leaders transferred this knowledge to Georgian student activists. These student activists became the core of the Rose Revolution, which brought down then president Eduard Shevardnadze.[43] Deploying informational and expert powers, the nonofficial student organization from Serbia helped the nascent student organization in Georgia to understand how to gather its noncoercive powers—communication, co-optation, attraction, and legitimacy—and apply them strategically to force change in their own society.

While overthrowing a government through nonviolent protest is by no means the same as third-party engagement in peacemaking, it does give an example of what nonofficial organizations can accomplish in terms of creating an altered environment and changing attitudes and behaviors among a wider population.[44]

Conclusion

Returning to the account of the roles that the HDC and the Conflict Management Initiative played in mediating the talks between the Acehnese rebels and the government of Indonesia, it is possible to identify some of the powers that each organization had. In its efforts, the HDC deployed a full set of powers—informational, expert, legitimate—to get the parties to an agreement. It also managed to draw in a number of more powerful actors as international donors to lend the process reward power. Despite the HDC's efforts, however, the peace agreement broke down. Many reasons lay behind this turn of events—the dissipation of the moment of ripeness, the disparity between the goals of the two conflict parties, the unrealistic implementation timetable established by the government, the narrow focus in the implementation talks on demilitarization rather than on an all-inclusive dialogue. Another reason, however, was the HDC's own limitations as a third party, especially its inability to convince the government of Indonesia to accept a more powerful mediator to take on the implementation phase or to convince the donor nations to accept responsibility for the implementation. As a consequence, the HDC was left on its own to help drive the implementation, a task that far exceeded its mediatory powers.[45]

Like the HDC, the Conflict Management Initiative had informational, expert, and legitimate powers, but it had three additional advantages that allowed it to push the parties to a more comprehensive agreement. The first grew out of the years of continued violent conflict that followed the HDC cease-fire, violence that exhausted Acehnese society and changed its perception of the costs and benefits of negotiations. The second was a change of Indonesian leadership and an increased willingness to take a chance on peace. The third was an advantage that grew out of a tragedy—the tsunami's devastating effects on Aceh, its society, and its culture—and produced pressure on the Indonesian government, the GAM, and the international community to resolve the conflict. In short, the conflict was much riper for resolution than it had been in the early years of the decade. In addition to ripeness, the Conflict Management Initiative had another advantage in its leadership. Martti Ahtisaari, the former Finnish president, combined experience developed through years of exposure to negotiations as a former diplomat and government official with the freedom of action of a nonofficial person. Like former president Jimmy Carter, he represented a new actor in conflict management: an individual who understood the nature of both official and nonofficial power and used this knowledge to urge parties along the rough road to peace.

One question that this book tries to answer is whether we need new institutions to meet the conflict management and resolution challenges that we face today. This is the impetus behind many efforts at reform of the United Nations, the changing missions of regional or-

ganizations such as NATO and the African Union, and the establishment of nongovernmental organizations that combine elements of official and nonofficial institutions. It is possible that a new, overarching conflict management organization will emerge—a streamlined and empowered United Nations, a global state-based "group of friends" whose mission is to respond to threats to peace, or another institution as yet unimagined. Until the time when there is consensus on the new institution or sets of institutions, it is critical—following the Conflict Management Initiative example—that official and nonofficial actors develop closer working relationships in the difficult business of making and securing peace.

In designing an effective approach to third-party assistance to peacemaking, Rob Rocigliano has proposed a chaordic approach. "Chaordic" is a composite word, combining "chaos" and "order," capturing the chaotic, multilevel nature of conflict and the resultant need for both order and flexibility in the response, that is, a multilevel, multi-institutional strategy of peacemaking based on shared principles and objectives. "Rather than trying to make conflict resolution more tractable by organizing it into a linear, top-down process, today's processes need to reflect the chaotic nature of the conflict. In short, they need to be 'chaordic,' a mixture of de-centralized, flexible, adaptable, and multi-pronged efforts loosely organized in the pursuit of a common goal."[46] This is a lesson that both official organizations and NGOs should take to heart. The powers that third-party nonofficial actors have in the complicated task of preventing and resolving conflict, or of helping postconflict societies reach reconciliation, are fairly considerable, from providing information to acting as a primary mediator. Official organizations should recognize and support these powers. At the same time, nonofficial organizations should recognize when they can deploy their powers in support of an official process.

Only by adding these powers together can third parties—official and nonofficial—hope to counteract the strong, pervasive destructive powers that propel conflict.

NOTES

1. For a fuller discussion of NGO activity in conflict, see Diana Chigas, "Negotiating Intractable Conflicts: The Contribution of Unofficial Intermediaries," in *Grasping the Nettle: Analyzing Cases of Intractable Conflict*, ed. Chester A. Crocker, Fen Osler Hampson, and Pamela Aall (Washington, D.C.: United States Institute of Peace Press, 2005), 123–158.

2. For a critical view of efficacy of state mediation, see Marieke Kleiboer, "Great Power Mediation: Using Leverage to Make Peace?" in *Studies in International Mediation: Essays in Honor of Jeffrey Z. Rubin* (Basingstoke, UK, and New York: Palgrave Macmillan, 2002), 127–140.

3. Henri Dunant Centre for Humanitarian Dialogue, mission statement, http://www.hdcentre.org/Mission+Statement.

4. Kira Kay, *The "New Humanitarianism": The Henry Dunant Center and the Aceh Peace Negotiations*, WWS Case Study 02/03 (Princeton, N.J.: Woodrow Wilson School of Public and International Affairs, 2004), http://www.wws.princeton.edu/cases/papers/newhumanit.htm (accessed January 7, 2006).

5. Konrad Huber, *The HDC in Aceh: Promises and Pitfalls of NGO Mediation and Implementation*, Policy Studies, No. 9 (Washington, D.C.: East-West Center Washington, 2004).

6. Edward Aspinall, *The Helsinki Agreement: A More Promising Basis for Peace in Aceh?* Policy Studies, No. 20 (Washington, D.C.: East-West Center Washington, 2005).

7. Jeffrey Z. Rubin, "International Mediation in Context," in *Mediation in International Relations*, ed. Jacob Bercovitch and Jeffrey Z. Rubin (New York: St. Martin's Press, 1992), 254–256.

8. James A. Baker III, "The Road to Madrid," in *Herding Cats: Multiparty Mediation in a Complex World*, ed. Chester A. Crocker, Fen Osler Hampson, and Pamela Aall (Washington. D.C.: United States Institute of Peace Press, 1999), 183–205.

9. Hasjim Djalal and Ian Townsend-Gault, "Managing Potential Conflicts in the South China Sea: Informal Diplomacy for Conflict Prevention," in *Herding Cats*, 109–133.

10. Abraham McLaughlin, "Africa's Peace Seekers: Betty Bigombe," *Christian Science Monitor*, September 13, 2005.

11. Ibid.

12. Max van der Stoel, "The Role of the OSCE High Commissioner in Conflict Prevention," in *Herding Cats*, 72.

13. For an example of using expert knowledge about transitional justice and constitution making as a peacemaking tool, see Neil Kritz, "Rule of Law in Conflict Management," chapter 23 in this book.

14. Mark Durcan, "The Negotiations in Practice," in *Striking a Balance: The Northern Ireland Peace Process*, ed. Clem McCartney (London: Conciliation Resources, 2003).

15. It is important to recognize that the other members of the International Body, former Finnish prime minister Harri Holkeri and former chief of the Canadian Defence Staff John de Chastelain, brought a considerable amount of expert power to the task, which gave the International Body widespread credibility and aided the mediation and postagreement implementation efforts.

16. Thomas Princen, *Beagle Channel Negotiations*, Pew Case Studies in International Affairs, Case 401 (Washington, D.C.: Institute for the Study of Diplomacy, Georgetown University, 1988).

17. Paul Wehr and John Paul Lederach, "Mediating Conflict in Central America," *Journal of Peace Research* 28, no. 1 (1991): 85–98; and Wehr, "The Citizen Intervenor," *Peace Review* 8, no. 4 (1996): 555–561.

18. Wehr and Lederach, "Mediating Conflict in Central America," 87.

19. James Wuye and Muhammed Nurayn Ashafa, *The Pastor and the Imam: Responding to Conflict* (Lagos, Nigeria: Ibrash Publications, 1999).

20. David R. Smock, "Mediating between Christians and Muslims in Plateau State, Nigeria," in *Religious Contributions to Peacemaking: When Religion Brings Peace, Not War*, ed. David R. Smock, Peaceworks No. 55 (Washington, D.C.: United States Institute of Peace, 2006), 17–24; and "The Pastor and the Imam: The Muslim-Christian Dialogue Forum in Nigeria," in *People Building Peace II: Successful Stories*

of Civil Society, ed. Paul van Tongeren, Malin Brenk, Marte Hellema, and Juliette Verhoeven (Boulder, Colo., and London: Lynne Rienner, 2005), 226–232.

21. Paul Arthur, "Multiparty Mediation in Northern Ireland," in *Herding Cats*, 487.

22. Rubin, "International Mediation in Context," 255.

23. "Tigers and a Hawk: A New President Faces Old Dilemmas in Pursuing Peace," *Economist*, U.S. ed., November 24, 2005, http://www.economist.com/displaystory.cfm?story_id=5220582; and BBC News, December 7, 2005, http//news.bbc.co.uk/go/pr/fr/-/2/hi/south_asia/4506856.stm.

24. Roger Fisher and William Ury, *Getting to Yes: Negotiating Agreement without Giving In* (New York and London: Penguin Books, 1981).

25. Herbert C. Kelman, "The Interactive Problem-Solving Approach," in *Managing Global Chaos: Sources of and Responses to International Conflict*, ed. Chester A. Crocker and Fen Osler Hampson with Pamela Aall (Washington, D.C.: United States Institute of Peace Press, 1996), 501–519.

26. Smock, *Religious Contributions to Peacemaking*.

27. Aspinall, *The Helsinki Agreement*.

28. Kleiboer, "Great Power Mediation."

29. *Roget's II: The New Thesaurus*, s.v. "leverage."

30. I. William Zartman and Saadia Touval, "International Mediation in the Post–Cold War Era," in *Managing Global Chaos*, 455.

31. Chester A. Crocker, Fen Osler Hampson, and Pamela Aall, eds., *Taming Intractable Conflicts: Mediation in the Hardest Cases* (Washington, D.C.: United States Institute of Peace Press, 2004), 94–95.

32. I. William Zartman, *Ripe for Resolution* (New York: Oxford University Press, 1989).

33. Marieke Kleiboer, "Ripeness of Conflict: A Fruitful Notion?" *Journal of Peace Research* 31, no. 1 (February 1994): 109–116.

34. See chapter 31 in this volume.

35. *Pakistan: Reforming the Education Sector*, Asia Report No. 84 (October 7, 2004).

36. For a fuller treatment of this theme, see Crocker, Hampson, and Aall, *Taming Intractable Conflicts*, 45–72.

37. For examples of these activities, see the Web sites of the United States Institute of Peace, http://www.usip.org; the Open Society Institute, http://www.soros.org; and the National Endowment for Democracy, http://www.ned.org.

38. See chapter 22 in this volume.

39. See Harold H. Saunders, "The Multilevel Peace Process in Tajikistan," in *Herding Cats*, 159–179.

40. Michael Dobbs, "U.S. Advice Guided Milosevic Opposition," *Washington Post*, December 11, 2000.

41. Gene Sharp, *From Dictatorship to Democracy: A Conceptual Framework for Liberation* (Boston: Albert Einstein Institution, 1993).

42. See Peter Ackerman and Jack DuVall, *A Force More Powerful: A Century of Non-violent Conflict* (New York: Palgrave, 2000); Peter Ackerman and Christopher Kruegler, *Strategic Nonviolent Conflict: The Dynamics of People Power in the Twentieth Century* (Westport, Conn.: Praeger, 1994); *Passing the Baton: Challenges of Statecraft for the New Administration*, Peaceworks No. 40 (Washington, D.C.: United States Institute of Peace, 2001), 34–36; Steve York, director, *A Force More Powerful*, video recording (Washington, D.C.: York Zimmerman, 2000); and York, director, *Bringing Down a Dictator*, video recording (Washington, D.C.: York Zimmerman, 2001–2).

43. Natalia Antelava, "How to Stage a Revolution," BBC News, December 4, 2003.

44. Does it work? is a critical question for the nonofficial field to answer. Not only are these organizations spending money—funded by individual donations, government contracts, foundation grants, UN programs—based on the assumption that it does work, but they and others also undertake serious risks in the work. There is a growing amount of interest in determining whether these unofficial, or track-two, activities work. However, when Mary Anderson, a pioneer in the field of evaluation of humanitarian work, turned her attention to evaluating peacemaking and peacebuilding, she found reluctance within the field to look at the question. Correspondents claimed it was too soon to evaluate results or too complicated to assess outcomes when so many actors were involved. They also noted that peacemaking involved encouraging attitude and behavior changes that were not measurable. See Mary Anderson and Lara Olson, *Confronting War: Critical Lessons for Peace Practitioners* (Cambridge, Mass.: Collaborative for Development Action, 2003), 8–9.

These objections are not insignificant. The transformation of individual and social attitudes and behavior necessary for long-term peacemaking stretches out over years, if not decades. Short-term assessments will have difficulty capturing the total effect of these programs, much less whether any one program had an impact that was measurably distinct from those of the many other institutions engaged in these "good efforts." However, despite the resistance, there are assessment projects that have tried to grapple with these issues. Anderson's Reflecting on Peace Practice interacted with more than two hundred agencies and practitioners, drawing significant lessons from the exercise. Jay Rothman of the Action Evaluation Project has developed methodology for evaluation that engages all participants from the beginning of a project in defining and measuring the objectives. Cheyanne Church at Search for Common Ground has also contributed to this area. It is hoped that their results will shed more light on how and when nonofficial peacemaking works.

45. Huber, *The HDC in Aceh;* and Edward Aspinall and Harold Crouch, *The Aceh Peace Process: Why It Failed,* Policy Studies, No. 1 (Washington, D.C.: East-West Center Washington, 2003).

46. Rob Rocigliano, "The Chaordic Peace Process," *Journal for the Study of Peace and Conflict,* annual edition (2003–4): 1–11.

PART V

USES AND LIMITS OF INSTITUTIONS IN CONFLICT MANAGEMENT

28

THE UNITED NATIONS AND CONFLICT MANAGEMENT
RELEVANT OR IRRELEVANT?

Karen A. Mingst and Margaret P. Karns

W AR WAS THE CHIEF MOTIVATING factor for the creation of the United Nations in 1945, as it had been for the League of Nations in 1919 and the Concert of Europe in 1815. Despite the fact that the twentieth century was the most destructive century in human history, it was also the century of building multilateral institutions for preventing war. A central issue for this chapter is whether the United Nations remains relevant for managing conflict in the early twenty-first century, given the changing nature of security threats and the United Nations' own mixed record in responding to those threats.[1]

Over the past fifty years, there has been a sharp decrease in the incidence of interstate war, that is, wars between two or more states. Since 1992, the number has declined by more than 40 percent, with the deadliest (1,000-plus battle deaths) dropping by 80 percent. The number of intrastate conflicts, or conflicts within states resulting from the collapse of an already weak state, increased dramatically to over 95 percent of all armed conflicts but has

leveled off in recent years.[2] Civil wars that become internationalized with the intervention of other states or groups represent another problem. These developments are the result of three major political changes: the end of colonialism, the end of the Cold War, and increased international activities, especially by the United Nations in the 1990s, to stop ongoing wars and prevent new ones.

Thus, although the United Nations Charter was designed to deal with interstate conflicts and most countries remain jealous of their sovereignty, and hence are wary of international interventions that compromise the principle of nonintervention in states' domestic affairs, UN member states have empowered the body in the post–Cold War era to play a much more active role in dealing with conflicts within states. Many of these conflicts have also involved humanitarian crises resulting from fighting, from ethnic cleansing or genocide, from the collapse of governmental authority, and from famine, natural disasters, and disease. These have provoked debates about the legitimacy of international armed intervention under UN auspices to protect human beings. As a result of the growth of international human rights norms in the second half of the twentieth century, the balance between the rights of states and the rights of people began to shift in these debates to an emerging norm of responsibility to protect human beings.

Two other types of security threats have posed additional challenges to the United Nations' conflict management role. These are, first, the increase in international terrorism since the 1970s, with the dramatic escalation in the nature of the threat from networks of Islamic extremists signified by the September 11, 2001, attacks on the World Trade Center and Pentagon, the July 2005 attacks on London's transport system, the 2002 and 2005 attacks on tourist sites in Bali, and the 2004 Madrid train bombings. Second, the problem of "rogue" states seeking to acquire nuclear weapons has put a new face on the long-standing issue of nuclear proliferation, adding to the complexity of this security threat.

THE UNITED NATIONS' CONFLICT MANAGEMENT ROLE

The United Nations' conflict management role is defined by three sections of the United Nations Charter as well as by practice over the past sixty years. Article 2 (Sections 3, 4, and 5) of the charter obligates all members to settle disputes by peaceful means, to refrain from the threat or use of force, and to cooperate with UN-sponsored actions. The Security Council has primary responsibility for maintenance of international peace and security (Article 24). Chapter VI specifies the variety of ways in which the Security Council, in collaboration with the secretary-general, can promote peaceful settlement of disputes, including investigating and mediating disputes. For the most part, peaceful settlement mechanisms have provided a useful alternative to coercive measures

and been used extensively over the years. Chapter VII specifies actions the United Nations can take with respect to threats to the peace, breaches of the peace, and acts of aggression. The Security Council can identify aggressors (Articles 39 and 40), decide what enforcement measures should be taken (Articles 41, 42, 48, and 49), and call on members to make military forces available, subject to special agreements (Articles 43–45). Chapter VIII recognizes the roles of regional organizations in peaceful settlement of disputes, but it requires Security Council authorization for the use of force, thus maintaining the United Nations' primacy with respect to enforcement.

Over time, the United Nations has addressed security threats in ways that reinforced Chapters VI and VII of the charter. During the Cold War these included the development of preventive diplomacy, mediation by the secretary-general, and peacekeeping. Before the Cold War's end, however, the Security Council had invoked Chapter VII's provisions on enforcement only three times. Following Iraq's invasion of Kuwait in 1990, it began to use those provisions extensively throughout the 1990s to authorize the use of force and various types of sanctions. Innovations have included not only peacekeeping operations that involve the use of lightly armed military personnel to help maintain or restore international peace following a cease-fire but also humanitarian interventions to protect innocent civilians from famine, natural disaster, ethnic cleansing, or genocide; peacebuilding or nation building involving diverse tasks by civilian and military personnel to rebuild a stable state; targeted sanctions; enhanced monitoring procedures for disarmament, demobilization, and sanctions; ad hoc criminal tribunals to prosecute war crimes and crimes against humanity; and various counterterrorism measures. Inevitably, as the United Nations was called on to undertake more and more peace and security activities after the Cold War's end, there were sharp questions raised about its capacity to act, its limitations, and hence its credibility. The rancorous debate over Iraq in 2002–3, the U.S. decision to launch a war without Security Council authorization, and the limited UN role in postwar Iraq were particularly damaging to UN credibility. These developments renewed interest in UN reform to enhance both its legitimacy and its effectiveness.

FROM COLLECTIVE SECURITY TO ENHANCED ENFORCEMENT MEASURES

Writers of the UN Charter had assumed great-power unity since concurrence of the five permanent members (P-5)—the United States, Russia, China, France, and Great Britain—is required for Security Council action. Yet their veto power ensured from the outset that the United Nations' capacity as a collective security organization was limited. Indeed, only two situations—Korea in 1950 and Iraq's invasion of Kuwait in 1990—resemble collective security actions, where the international community acted collectively against an aggressor.

The Cold War's end and the UN response to Iraq's invasion of Kuwait marked a turning point, when, at least for a short time, there was unprecedented cooperation among the P-5. Security Council members agreed to the passage of twelve successive resolutions activating Chapter VII of the charter, including authorizing member states to use all necessary means to reverse the occupation of Kuwait. The military operation was a successful U.S.-led multinational effort—a subcontract on behalf of the United Nations. Since 1990, Chapter VII has been invoked on many other occasions to authorize the use of force or various types of sanctions. In Bosnia, Haiti, East Timor, Rwanda, and Sierra Leone, the Security Council authorized the use of force either by a regional organization such as NATO (Bosnia) or by a "coalition of the willing" led by a country willing to commit military forces to the effort, such as the United States (Haiti), Aus-

tralia (East Timor), France (Rwanda), and Great Britain (Sierra Leone).

The "Sanctions Decade"

In addition, beginning with the Iraq crisis in 1990, the Security Council extensively utilized the Chapter VII provisions for economic, diplomatic, and financial sanctions to prevent or deter threats to international peace or counter acts of aggression. During the Cold War, these Chapter VII provisions were used only twice: to impose economic sanctions on the white minority regime in Southern Rhodesia after it unilaterally declared its independence from Great Britain in 1965 and to impose an arms embargo on South Africa in 1977. Enforcement actions have included arms embargoes against Yugoslavia (1991–96; 1998–2001), Angola (1993–2002), Rwanda (1992–95), and Afghanistan (1990–2000), as well as comprehensive sanctions against Iraq (1990–2003) and Haiti (1993–94), among others. In an effort to hurt those most responsible for conflicts rather than ordinary people, the Security Council imposed targeted sanctions such as freezing assets of governments or individuals (Libya and Afghanistan), travel bans for government and rebel leaders and their families (Sudan, Sierra Leone, Liberia, and Afghanistan), and import/export bans for specific commodities, such as oil, tropical timber, and diamonds (Liberia, Sierra Leone, Angola, and Haiti). The purposes of these sanctions have broadened, not only to counter aggression (Iraq), but also to restore a democratically elected government (Haiti), curb massive human rights violations (Yugoslavia, Rwanda, and Somalia), end wars (Angola, Sierra Leone, Ethiopia, and Eritrea), and bring suspected terrorists to justice (Libya).[3]

The most extensive enforcement undertaking was the effort to get Iraq to comply with the complex terms of the April 1991 cease-fire agreement. These were embodied in Security Council Resolution 687, which enumerated the terms of the cease-fire agreement and a far-reaching plan for dismantling Iraq's weapons of mass destruction programs. The sanctions initiated after Iraq's invasion of Kuwait were to continue until all the provisions were carried out to the Security Council's satisfaction. The only exception was oil sales authorized under the 1995 Oil-for-Food Programme to pay for food and medical supplies.

The comprehensive sanctions on Iraq in the 1990s became highly controversial, however, as they contributed to a mounting humanitarian crisis among ordinary Iraqis. Many critics also pointed to the Iraqi government's manipulation of the Oil-for-Food Programme, diverting revenues and, hence, deepening the suffering of Iraqi citizens. Over time, sanctions fatigue among neighboring and other nations that had traditionally relied on trade with Iraq grew and compliance eroded.

The disarmament sanctions regime involved the most intrusive international inspections ever established, with the United Nations Special Commission (UNSCOM) overseeing the destruction of Iraq's chemical and biological weapons, along with production and storage facilities, and the International Atomic Energy Agency (IAEA) responsible for inspecting and destroying Iraq's nuclear weapons program. Between 1991 and 1998, inspectors moved all over Iraq, carrying out surprise inspections of suspected storage and production facilities, destroying stocks of materials, and checking documents. Iraq, however, continually thwarted UNSCOM and IAEA inspectors, eventually ending all cooperation in November 1998. In late 2002 the United Nations Monitoring, Verification, and Inspection Commission (UNMOVIC) was established and new inspections began in Iraq, to be terminated only when the United States, in coalition with the United Kingdom and others, launched the war in March 2003.

Although the IAEA succeeded in destroying Iraq's existing nuclear weapons materials and production facilities, UNSCOM was unable to certify that it knew the full extent of Iraq's chemical and biological weapons production

facilities. Destroying stocks and facilities did not destroy the knowledge base that Iraq had developed or its access to alternative technologies. Yet no weapons of mass destruction or active programs have been found in Iraq despite massive search efforts following the U.S. invasion in 2003.

Two key lessons the Security Council drew from the experience with comprehensive sanctions on both Iraq and Haiti were the importance of tailoring what and who is sanctioned to the specific situation to reduce ambiguity, close loopholes, and avoid unacceptable humanitarian costs, and the importance of monitoring compliance. For example, sanctions were among several approaches used by the United Nations in efforts to end the civil war in Angola during the 1990s, but they had little impact until 1999, when an independent panel of experts was created to investigate sanctions violations and recommend ways to enhance compliance. Lessons learned in Angola have been applied to the conflicts in Sierra Leone and elsewhere and to counterterrorism efforts following September 11, with independent expert panels gathering data on violators, supply routes, networks, and transactions and the Security Council naming and shaming violators by publicly identifying them. In addition, regional and nongovernmental organizations as well as private corporations have been recruited as partners in implementing and monitoring sanctions. Thus, sanctions continue to be a major tool in UN enforcement efforts.

Legitimizing Enforcement Actions: Afghanistan and Iraq

A major issue relating to the United Nations' conflict management role concerns the debate over whether and when states, including the world's only superpower—the United States —must get authorization from the Security Council to use force. In the post–Cold War era, the issue was first joined in the debate over the legitimacy of NATO-led action in Kosovo in 1999, as discussed later. It arose again after 9/11 when the United States intervened in Afghanistan on the grounds of self-defense to bring down the Taliban government that had harbored al Qaeda training camps for terrorists. The issue was most sharply debated in 2002–3 when the United States pushed for Security Council endorsement of military action to bring down the government of Saddam Hussein in Iraq on the grounds that Iraq had repeatedly failed to implement Security Council resolutions, ousted UN weapons inspectors, and was developing weapons of mass destruction. In short, the United States argued that Iraq constituted a threat to regional and global peace and security and that it (the United States) would act with or without Security Council approval.

The United States expended a great deal of diplomatic effort during the fall and winter of 2002–3 in trying to muster Security Council support for action against Iraq. Following President George W. Bush's address to the General Assembly on September 12, 2002, in which he warned Iraq that force would be used to uphold the objectives set by the Security Council unless it accepted being peacefully disarmed of all weapons of mass destruction (WMD), the Iraqi government accepted the immediate and unconditional return of weapons inspectors. In October 2002, the U.S. Congress authorized the president to use armed force if necessary. In November the Security Council unanimously passed a new resolution (1441) reinforcing the inspections regime and giving Iraq a last opportunity to disclose full information on its WMD and missile programs. Although Security Council members were unwilling to authorize states in advance to use force against Iraq in case of noncompliance, they did agree that lack of cooperation, lies, or omissions would constitute a material breach that could lead to action. Despite IAEA and UNMOVIC reports showing Iraq was cooperating with the strengthened inspections regime, the United States and the United Kingdom sought Security Council authorization in February and March 2003 for military action to disarm Iraq. They were forced to withdraw their draft resolution in the face of opposition from the other three P-5 members (France, Russia, and China), as well as most nonpermanent members, including Germany. As one analyst has noted, this opposition was "not surprising, given their different interests, their different views of war, their different assessments of any threat posed by Iraq, and their stated concerns about U.S. dominance."[4]

By deciding to go to war in Iraq in March 2003 in clear defiance of the majority of the Security Council, however, the United States, the United Kingdom, and their coalition allies posed a serious challenge to the authority of the council to authorize the use of force in situations other than self-defense. And because a major argument for military action involved what has been called "anticipatory self-defense" —or preventive action—the question was one of whether military action can be taken unilaterally in response to nonimminent threats. In short, the war in Iraq raised a host of questions of principle and practice concerning the UN role in conflict management, including the fundamental question of the United Nations' relevance. Did the Security Council's failure to support the U.S. action in Iraq illustrate the United Nations' ineffectiveness and confirm its waning legitimacy, especially in the face of a superpower with overwhelming military power and a willingness to pursue its own agenda without Security Council authority, as some have argued? Or did the Security Council work as its founders envisioned, not supporting UN involvement unless all of the P-5 and a majority of nonpermanent council members concurred? The debate has taken on a new intensity, with supporters of the U.S. position deriding the United Nations for its lack of follow-up to the sanctions, and opponents of the U.S.-led war applauding the UN stance, appreciative of the UN role in postconflict peacebuilding.[5]

As one observer, however, has noted, "The suggestion . . . that the UN was on the verge of irrelevance and political bankruptcy, has turned out to be profoundly misplaced . . . [as] the occupying powers soon realized . . . that *some* form of UN involvement was essential to help overcome the difficulties created by the occupation's lack of legitimacy and public support."[6] The United Nations' assistance in both Iraq and Afghanistan is best seen in the context of peacebuilding activities, which have been more extensive in Afghanistan.

Coalitions of the Willing and Subcontracting

A major lesson of sixty years of UN efforts to provide collective security and enforcement is that while international military action (in contrast to sanctions) should be authorized by the United Nations, the actual work of applying force has to be subcontracted to what has become known as a "coalition of the willing" led by one or more major powers with sufficient military capabilities. States never have and never will empower the United Nations with the means to exercise coercion. This becomes still clearer as we look at peacekeeping operations where the line between peacekeeping and enforcement is blurred and the situation requires use of military force. In addition, as the Iraq War makes clear, although international legitimacy matters, a sole superpower determined to take action will not be deterred by the absence of Security Council authorization.

Finally, although the United Nations has used the enforcement powers embodied in Chapter VII far more extensively since 1990 than in the forty-five previous years, its conflict management role both before and after 1990 has been most notable in the evolution of peacekeeping and the complex activities related to peacebuilding. Despite all of the debate over the United Nations' continuing relevance and effectiveness, there has been a dramatic increase in UN peacekeeping and peacebuilding operations since 2003. This illustrates the

continuing vitality of these innovative approaches to conflict management that evolved during and after the Cold War.

FROM TRADITIONAL TO COMPLEX PEACEKEEPING

Traditional Peacekeeping

The United Nations first used unarmed observers for monitoring cease-fires in Kashmir and Palestine in the late 1940s. That practice evolved into an idea formally proposed by Canadian secretary of state for external affairs Lester B. Pearson at the height of the Suez crisis in 1956 to secure a cease-fire pending a political settlement by deploying small numbers of lightly armed troops. Labeled peacekeeping, it has come to be defined as "an operation involving military personnel, but without enforcement powers, undertaken by the United Nations to help maintain or restore international peace and security in areas of conflict."[7] Since there is no UN Charter provision for peacekeeping, it lies in a gray zone between the peaceful settlement provisions of Chapter VI and the military enforcement provisions of Chapter VII and is sometimes referred to as Chapter VI and a half. Its development demonstrates that the members did not allow the Cold War to block efforts to use the United Nations to promote and maintain international security. The activity enabled the United Nations to play a positive role in dealing with regional conflicts at a time when hostility between East and West prevented the use of the charter provisions for collective security and enforcement.

Peacekeeping has taken different forms and evolved over time. Operations have relied on ad hoc military, civilian, or police units voluntarily contributed by states to the United Nations or on subcontracting to a coalition of states or a regional organization. During the Cold War, peacekeepers were drawn almost exclusively from the armed forces of nonpermanent members of the Security Council (often small, neutral, nonaligned, or middle-power members such as Canada, India, Sweden, Ghana, and Nepal) to keep the superpowers out of regional conflicts or, in the case of postcolonial problems, to keep former colonial powers from returning. The size of peacekeeping forces has varied widely, from small monitoring missions numbering fewer than one hundred to major operations in Congo in the 1960s and Cambodia, Somalia, and Bosnia in the early 1990s, requiring more than twenty thousand troops. Since the end of the Cold War, and especially with the undertaking of complex operations requiring greater "muscle," major powers, including the United States, Great Britain, France, and Russia, have also contributed forces. Still, the majority of peacekeeping contingents continue to come from countries other than the P-5.

During the Cold War, peacekeeping forces were used most extensively in the Middle East and in conflicts arising out of the decolonization process in Africa and Asia when the interests of the United States and the Soviet Union were not directly at stake. Participants were either unarmed or lightly armed, often stationed between hostile forces to monitor truces and troop withdrawals or to provide a buffer zone between belligerents' forces. These "first-generation" peacekeeping operations provided impartial and neutral assurance to the parties desiring at least a cease-fire and a guarantee that the United States and the Soviet Union would not directly intervene. In the late 1980s, traditional peacekeepers facilitated the withdrawal of Soviet troops from Afghanistan and supervised the cease-fire in the war between Iran and Iraq. These actions were possible because of increasing consensus among the P-5 following dramatic changes in Soviet foreign policy beginning in 1987.

Traditional peacekeeping continues to be useful in interstate conflicts where there is a cease-fire agreement and limited mandate. In 2000, for example, after two years of fighting, Eritrea and Ethiopia signed a peace agreement, although Ethiopia subsequently refused to accept the decision of the independent commission created to demarcate the boundary between the two countries. The United Nations Mission in Ethiopia and Eritrea (UNMEE), with up to four thousand personnel, was created to monitor a buffer zone between the two countries and the deployment of their troops. Several long-standing, traditional peacekeeping missions continue, such as in Kashmir (1949–present), Cyprus (1964–present), and the Golan Heights (1974–present). Most peacekeeping operations since the Cold War's end, however, have been complex ones with broader mandates, often involving Chapter VII authorization to use force, and a variety of tasks intended to lay the foundations for long-term stability in internal or civil conflicts (see table 1).

Complex Peacekeeping and Peacebuilding

The successful experience with UN peacekeeping in the late 1980s and the United Nations' active role in responding to Iraq's invasion of Kuwait increased world leaders' enthusiasm for employing UN peacekeepers in still more missions in the emerging post–Cold War era. Indeed, many observers believed that the new international climate provided the United Nations with opportunities for ending persistent civil conflicts in Central America, Southern Africa, and Southeast Asia. In addition, collapsing state institutions, violent civil conflicts, and complex humanitarian emergencies in the former Yugoslavia, Angola, Mozambique, Somalia, Rwanda, the Democratic Republic of the Congo, and Sierra Leone demanded new approaches. This often meant committing peacekeepers in intrastate conflicts before warring parties had reached agreement, with authorization to use greater force and involvement in complex peacebuilding efforts after fighting ceased.

In post–Cold War conflicts where UN peacekeepers have been deployed without a cease-fire in place, there has been no consent from all parties, and operations have been

Table 1. Tasks in Selected UN Complex Peacekeeping Missions

Country	Namibia	Somalia	Somalia	Mozambique	Rwanda	El Salvador	Cambodia	Cambodia	East Timor	Bosnia/ Croatia	Croatia/ Slavonia	Kosovo	Afghanistan
Mission	UNTAG	UNOSOM I	UNOSOM II	ONUMOZ	UNAMIR	ONUSAL	UNAMIC	UNTAC	UNTAET	UNPROFOR	UNTAES	UNMIK	UNAMA
Dates	4/89–5/90	4/92–5/93	5/93–5/95	12/92–2/94	10/93–5/96	7/91–4/95	10/91–3/92	2/92–9/93	10/99–5/02	2/92–12/95	1/96–1/97	9/99–	1/02–
Military Tasks													
Monitoring cease-fire	X	X	X	X	X	X	X	X	X	X	X		
Peace enforcement			X					X	X	X	X		
Securing humanitarian corridor			X		X				X				
Disarmament	X		X	X	X			X			X		
Observing troop withdrawal	X			X					X	X	X		
Demining	X		X		X		X	X			X		
Securing safe areas					X					X			
Collecting weapons			X	X							X		
Refugee Tasks													
Overseeing refugee return	X		X	X	X		X	X	X	X	X	X	
Overseeing IDP return					X			X		X	X		
Protecting refugees					X				X			X	
Humanitarian Assistance Tasks													
Assisting civilians	X	X	X	X	X			X	X	X	X	X	
Protecting international workers		X	X	X							X	X	

Task	1	2	3	4	5	6	7	8	9	10	11	12	13
Civil Policing Tasks													
General monitoring of police	X	X				X	X				X	X	
Retraining police	X	X	X			X	X	X			X	X	X
Electoral Assistance Tasks													
Conducting elections						X			X				
Monitoring elections	X	X				X	X		X		X	X	X
Overseeing elections	X												
Providing technical assistance	X							X					
Legal Affairs Tasks													
Reforming constitution/judiciary	X	X	X			X	X	X	X		X	X	X
Promoting national reconciliation	X	X	X			X	X	X			X		X
Establishing war crimes tribunal		X	X					X	X	X	X		
Overseeing human rights		X	X			X	X	X	X		X	X	X
Administrative authority	X					X	X	X	X		X	X	

expected to protect refugees and civilians from attack or genocide and perhaps to compel parties to end fighting. Thus, these operations have cost more and had a greater probability of casualties for peacekeepers. Some have required the major powers' logistical capability, personnel, heavy equipment, and even airpower. They have often been controversial because they blur the line between peacekeeping and enforcement actions under Chapter VII, with the result that the requisite muscle was not always readily forthcoming because states were reluctant to provide sufficient military forces to back up a Security Council mandate. The UN operations in Somalia and Yugoslavia in the 1990s illustrated the difficulties of these more complex operations.

In the case of Somalia in 1992 and 1993, the United Nations confronted a situation in which civil order had totally collapsed and warring clans had seized control of the country. Widespread famine and chaos accompanied the fighting and, with control of food a vital political resource for the Somali warlords, hundreds of thousands of civilians were pushed to the brink of starvation. The Security Council was initially slow to act, assuming that it needed consent from the warlords to provide humanitarian assistance, consistent with the norms of traditional peacekeeping. In August 1992 a small contingent of lightly armed Pakistani troops was deployed (United Nations Operation in Somalia [UNOSOM I]) to protect relief workers, but it was inadequate to the task at hand. Finally, in December 1992, the Security Council authorized a large U.S.-led military-humanitarian intervention (Unified Task Force [UNITAF], known to the U.S. public as Operation Restore Hope). The UN secretary-general wanted U.S. forces to impose a cease-fire and disarm factions, but U.S. leaders who had signed on to the humanitarian mission were reluctant to enlarge the objectives. That disagreement complicated relations among the participants. When U.S. soldiers were killed in October 1993, the United States

announced that all its forces would be withdrawn by March 1994 and undertook a major reevaluation of its participation in UN peacekeeping operations. UN operations in Somalia ceased in 1995, having succeeded in ending the humanitarian emergency (famine), but not in helping the Somalis establish an effective government or end their internal strife.

In the case of the disintegration of Yugoslavia in the early 1990s into five separate states and war, especially in Bosnia and Herzegovina, the Security Council devoted a record number of meetings between 1991 and 1996 to debate whether to intervene, to what end, and with what means. The mission of UN peacekeepers sent in 1992 was broadened from maintaining a cease-fire in Croatia and delivering humanitarian assistance to creating safe areas for refugees, protecting basic human rights, and using NATO to enforce sanctions and a no-fly zone and to conduct air strikes. Security Council resolutions alone did not produce the manpower, logistical, financial, or military resources needed to fulfill the mandate, however. All sides interfered with relief efforts and targeted UN peacekeepers and international aid workers. UN personnel were reluctant to use the authority given them to employ NATO air strikes. The UN safe areas were anything but safe for the civilians who had taken refuge in them and, in the case of Srebrenica, UN peacekeepers were humiliated when they failed to prevent the massacre of more than seven thousand Muslim men and boys by Bosnian Serbs in July 1995.[8] The United Nations' peacekeeping role in Bosnia and Croatia ended when the United States brokered the Dayton Peace Accords in November 1995 and NATO troops replaced UN blue helmets. The United Nations' role in the subsequent peacebuilding process focused on reforming Bosnia's police forces, resettling refugees, and aiding economic development.

The United Nations has confronted similar challenges where the line between the need for enforcement and traditional peacekeeping was blurred in a number of conflicts since the late 1990s. These include Liberia, Sierra Leone, Côte d'Ivoire, Sudan, the Democratic Republic of the Congo, Burundi, and Haiti. For example, in Sudan, a UN peacekeeping force (United Nations Mission in Sudan [UNMIS]) authorized in 2005 is charged with supporting the Comprehensive Peace Agreement between the government and the Sudan People's Liberation Movement/Army. It has authority under Chapter VII to take necessary actions involving use of force and a range of peacebuilding responsibilities.

More complex peacekeeping operations involve both civilian and military activities. While troop contingents may be engaged in observer activities characteristic of traditional missions, other military personnel and civilians, along with humanitarian NGOs and personnel from different UN agencies, may be involved in organizing elections, reorganizing police forces, delivering relief, and carrying out other activities aimed at creating viable states. This is the essence of peacebuilding.

Namibia—a former German colony administered by South Africa from the end of World War I until 1989 and the object of intense international efforts to secure its independence—represented the first experiment with peacebuilding. The United Nations Transition Assistance Group in Namibia (UNTAG), deployed in April 1989, had the most ambitious, diverse mandate of any UN mission to that time. It included supervision of the cease-fire between South African and South West Africa People's Organization (SWAPO) forces, monitoring the withdrawal of South African forces from Namibia and the confinement of SWAPO forces to a series of bases, supervising the civil police force, securing the repeal of discriminatory and restrictive legislation, arranging for the release of political prisoners and the return of exiles, and creating conditions for free and fair elections, which were subsequently conducted by South Africa under UN supervision. With military and civilian personnel provided by 109 countries, UNTAG played a vital role in managing the process by which Namibia moved step-by-step from war to a cease-fire and then to full independence. The United Nations' success in Namibia led it to undertake a number of other complex missions, not all of which enjoyed the same success.

The agreements ending the twenty-year civil war in Cambodia in 1991 "charged the UN—for the first time in its history—with the political and economic restructuring of a member state as part of the building of peace under which the parties were to institutionalize their reconciliation."[9] The United Nations Transition Authority in Cambodia's (UNTAC) tasks called for up to twenty-two thousand military and civilian personnel. The military component was charged with supervising the cease-fire and disarming and demobilizing forces. Civilian personnel assumed full responsibility for administering the country for an eighteen-month transition period. The United Nations also monitored the return of 370,000 refugees from camps in Thailand, organized the 1993 elections that returned civil authority to Cambodians, and rehabilitated basic infrastructure. As then UN secretary-general Boutros Boutros-Ghali observed, "Nothing the UN has ever done can match this operation."[10] The United Nations' presence helped end the civil war and bring peace of sorts to most of the country. UNTAC was unable, however, to achieve a complete cease-fire, demobilize all forces, or complete its civil mission. Cambodia, therefore, illustrates the difficulty of carrying out all aspects of a complex peacekeeping and peacebuilding mission. Although the peacekeeping mission itself largely accomplished its goals and the United Nations conducted a successful election in 1993, Cambodia was not a stable state, as UNTAC's mandate had not included building an effective legal system and constitutional process or promoting economic development.

Two more recent complex peacekeeping and peacebuilding operations—Kosovo and

East Timor—further illustrate the challenges the United Nations faces in such situations. Following NATO bombing of Serbia and intervention to protect Kosovar Albanians in 1999, the United Nations Mission in Kosovo (UNMIK) was authorized to establish an interim administration with all executive, legislative, and judicial powers and wide-ranging functions, including maintaining civil law and order, aiding the return of refugees, coordinating humanitarian relief, and reconstructing key infrastructure. In addition, UNMIK has key political tasks of promoting autonomy and self-government and helping to determine Kosovo's future legal status. The head of UNMIK, a special representative of the UN secretary-general, coordinates the work of several non-UN international organizations among whom various functions are divided, the United Nations having chief responsibility for police and justice and civil administration.

The Kosovo mission is pathbreaking in its nature and scope but also has critical problems. Its mandate is both vague and potentially contradictory; the Albanian Kosovars want independence, but the United Nations is committed to promoting self-government without undermining Serbia's sovereignty and territorial integrity. Security is provided by NATO troops under KFOR, yet the division of responsibility between NATO and the United Nations, the European Union, and the Organization for Security and Cooperation in Europe is not entirely clear. When and how the United Nations' interim administration could end is likewise uncertain, even if UN-mediated talks on Kosovo's future status yield an agreement on independent statehood.[11]

Skepticism about the long-term outcome of peacebuilding in Kosovo has been reinforced by the experience in East Timor, where the transition to independence under UN auspices was successful, but the new government has little capacity beyond its capital, the economy is weak, and critical issues remain unresolved. This mission was undertaken in 1999

after almost fifteen years of UN-mediated efforts to resolve the status of East Timor—a former Portuguese colony seized by Indonesia in the mid-1970s—when violence broke out, Indonesian troops failed to restore order, and almost a half million East Timorese were displaced from their homes. The Security Council initially authorized Australia to lead a multilateral force to restore order and then created the United Nations Transitional Administration in East Timor (UNTAET) with an ambitious and extensive mission, ranging from exercising all judicial, legislative, and executive powers to assisting in developing civil and social services, providing security, ensuring the delivery of humanitarian aid, promoting sustainable development, and building the foundation for stable liberal democracy. Renewed violence led to the return of peacekeepers in 2006, raising doubts about East Timor's future.

Ambitious peacebuilding missions such as in Cambodia, Kosovo, and East Timor are only beginning to be subjected to careful analysis. Although the length of interim administration was circumscribed in Cambodia and East Timor, that is not the case in Kosovo (nor in Bosnia, where an EU-appointed high representative remains in overall control). The missions have been variously described as forms of international trusteeship, protectorates, and even neoimperialism.[12] What is evident, however, is that peacebuilding is a long process where success may not be seen for years or even decades. Recognizing the need for greater coherence in supporting the multiple dimensions of long-term assistance to ensure that countries recovering from war do not relapse into conflict, the 2005 World Summit of government leaders, convened at the beginning of the sixtieth annual General Assembly session, approved creation of a new intergovernmental Peacebuilding Commission (PBC), backed by a Peace Support Office and Peacebuilding Fund. The PBC is intended to "bring together all relevant actors to marshal resources and to advise on and propose integrated strategies" for the needs of particular countries in developing public institutions and economic recovery.[13] It is also expected to have a role in preventing a relapse into violent conflict by alerting the international community if adequate progress is not being made.[14]

Evaluating the United Nations' Record in Peacekeeping and Peacebuilding

What defines success in peacekeeping and peacebuilding? An end to fighting? A political solution in the form of a peace agreement? A period of years (two, five, ten?) without renewed violence? The establishment of a viable state that endures for a period of time? In reality, different types of missions should be evaluated with different criteria. Traditional peacekeeping missions, therefore, can be assessed in terms of their ability to prevent the resumption of interstate war, and here the evidence is strong that the presence of peacekeepers reduces the risk of another war. The first United Nations Emergency Force (UNEF I) averted war between the Arab states and Israel for eleven years (1956–67), while the United Nations Disengagement Observer Force (UNDOF) has kept peace between Israel and Syria on the Golan Heights since 1974. The United Nations Force in Cyprus (UNFICYP) has averted overt hostilities between the Greek and Turkish communities for forty years, although it could not prevent the Turkish invasion of northern Cyprus in 1974. There has been no renewal of hostilities either between Iraq and Iran or between Iraq and Kuwait, and UN monitors' presence has helped India and Pakistan to contain intermittent hostilities along the line of control in disputed Kashmir for more than fifty years.

Yet fifty years of experience also demonstrates that having international monitors for a truce does not lead to resolution of the underlying conflict and that fighting may resume, even with UN monitors in place, especially since the United Nations has historically been reluctant to condemn states for violations for fear of jeopardizing its impartiality. As one scholar notes, "This unfortunately undermined the organization's ability to use the spotlight of international attention to help maintain peace."[15] Closer examination also shows that peacekeepers are most likely to be deployed in the most difficult cases, where the military outcome has been indecisive, where belligerents have a long history of conflict, and, hence, where peace is most fragile. The tension, however, between credibility and impartiality is a dilemma for the United Nations, one that has changed somewhat since the Cold War's end, with greater willingness to condemn belligerents and even to take military action against those who threaten peace as we discussed earlier under enforcement.

UN missions involving arms control verification, human rights monitoring, and election supervision tend to be successful because they are most similar to traditional peacekeeping; that is, they involve unarmed observers. They are generally linked to a peace agreement and, hence, involve consent of the parties to a peacekeeping operation. Thus, UN peacekeepers have compiled an excellent record in facilitating elections in Namibia, Cambodia, Mozambique, Eastern Slavonia, East Timor, and elsewhere.

Those missions that differ most from traditional peacekeeping operations tend to have the greatest difficulties, often because the forces are shorthanded, inadequately equipped, and not well designed to carry out multiple functions. The United Nations has had particular difficulty recruiting sufficient numbers of civilian police for peacebuilding missions. Mandates for complex operations are also frequently unclear. Precisely because they combine different types of tasks as well as civilian and military components, the assessment of such operations may be mixed. In Somalia, as noted, UN and U.S. forces were successful in achieving the humanitarian tasks, but they failed in the pacification and nation-building tasks. Cambodia is now regarded as a short-term success with longer-term mixed reviews. Likewise, East Timor was a relative success as far as achieving independence, but the long-term prognosis is uncertain. In Kosovo, the outcome remains in doubt, as it does in the several African conflicts in which the United Nations has most recently been involved—Sierra Leone, Liberia, Côte d'Ivoire, the Democratic Republic of the Congo, and Sudan.

Factors that can facilitate success in these complex operations include the parties' desire for peace; the political will of member states to make necessary resources available (including sufficient forces, equipment, and authority to use them); wide deployment of police monitors along with police and judicial reform; extensive training of election monitors; the energy, skill, and improvisation of the secretary-general's special representative in the country; even-handed treatment of the parties; and, most critically, continual political support. The United Nations itself does not have the capability to ensure all of these factors are in place but depends on the commitments of states and, most especially, the major powers. Wars with an ethnic or religious component and a large number of factions are less likely to be resolved and less susceptible to peacebuilding efforts. Where parties, such as in Angola and Sierra Leone, depend on exports of primary products such as diamonds or oil for buying arms and personal enrichment, peacebuilding is also less likely to be successful because there is too much temptation to renew war to loot resources.[16] One study concludes that learning and adaptation by UN personnel make a critical difference.[17] Another found that turning warring parties into political parties through demobilization and demilitarization of soldiers was critical.[18]

Finally, the cases that come to the United Nations tend to be the very hard ones, from the Israeli-Palestinian conflict, Cyprus, and Kashmir to Liberia, Darfur, and the Democratic Republic of the Congo. Almost half of the UN peacekeeping operations of any type

both before and since the Cold War's end have been in Africa, showing, as one observer notes, that "conflicts and problems of governance continue to haunt Africa more than ever."[19] Yet ever since the debacle in Somalia in 1993, the United Nations has had notable difficulty mustering adequate resources—especially military forces—for African operations, leaving them woefully shorthanded and susceptible to charges of racism. At the end of 2005, of sixteen peacekeeping operations deployed, eight were in Africa and five of those had begun since 2000. Seventy-six percent of the sixty-eight thousand peacekeepers in the field were in African operations, yet these troops were still inadequate to deal with a number of difficult situations. As a result, the Economic Community of West African States (ECOWAS) and the African Union (AU) have mounted peacekeeping efforts authorized by the Security Council. Yet African troops need significant outside support.

Many peacekeeping operations since the Cold War's end, including several in Africa, have also faced major humanitarian crises. These crises have called for international responses to human suffering, despite the long-standing norm of noninterference in states' domestic affairs.

FROM NONINTERFERENCE IN DOMESTIC AFFAIRS TO HUMANITARIAN INTERVENTION

The UN Charter specifically precludes the United Nations from intervening "in matters which are essentially within the domestic jurisdiction of any state" (Article 2, Section 7). During the Cold War, not one Security Council resolution mentioned humanitarian intervention. Yet over the life of the United Nations, the once-rigid distinction between domestic and international issues has weakened. Civil war was not under the traditional purview of the United Nations, but because human rights are often abrogated, refugees displaced, and weapons moved across borders, such conflicts have increasingly been viewed as international, justifying UN action. In April 1991, after the Gulf War's end, Western allies created safe havens and no-fly zones to protect Iraqi Kurds in northern Iraq and Shiites in the south. The United Nations' intervention in Somalia was initiated for humanitarian reasons, as was NATO's in Kosovo.

Yet the United Nations is known more for its failures than for its successes in humanitarian intervention. Rwanda offers the most striking example. In 1993 the United Nations had authorized a traditional peacekeeping operation to monitor a peace agreement between the Hutu-dominated government and Tutsi rebels in the Rwandan Patriotic Front (RPF). In April 1994, following the death of Rwandan president Juvénal Habyarimana (a Hutu) in a mysterious plane crash, Hutu extremists in the Rwandan military and police began slaughtering the minority Tutsi as well as moderate Hutu. Despite reports of the growing violence by UN personnel on the ground, the Security Council voted to reduce UNAMIR's personnel initially, then reversed that decision a month later in the name of humanitarianism. It took almost four months to get states to provide forces, and, by that time, the genocide had left 750,000 Rwandans dead and two million displaced. The United Nations' own Department of Peacekeeping Operations, then headed by Kofi Annan, was later faulted for not communicating the urgency of the crisis to the Security Council, and members of the council were criticized for their failure to take action to prevent the human tragedy.[20] All agreed "never again" would they fail to respond to genocide.

The 1999 NATO action in Kosovo marked another watershed in the debate over humanitarian intervention. The issue was not inaction but legitimacy and effectiveness. The crisis was triggered by Yugoslav (Serbian) rejection of a political settlement for Kosovo and growing evidence of ethnic cleansing that led NATO to initiate military action without Security Council authorization. Two key questions emerged: First, could the use of force be justified without a UN Security Council resolution? Although Russia, China, and other countries protested the illegality, a Security Council resolution condemning the NATO action failed, suggesting that many felt there was a legitimate case to be made for intervention. Months of diplomacy had preceded NATO's intervention and failed to change Serbian policy; all other means short of force had been used. Second, did NATO bombing alleviate or worsen the humanitarian crisis by accelerating the flight of refugees and humanitarian suffering, civilian casualties, and destruction of major infrastructure? Although the evidence on this question is mixed, an independent commission concluded that intervention in Kosovo was "illegal but legitimate."[21]

Beginning in 2003, the western region of Darfur in Sudan presented yet another horrific humanitarian disaster. Thousands of refugees fled their homes after attacks from government-backed Arab militias (Janjaweed), and many sought shelter in neighboring Chad. Over the next year, the humanitarian disaster grew to one hundred thousand refugees and more than one million internally displaced persons, with various estimates of those killed ranging from ten thousand and up. Although various UN agencies were active in providing food, establishing refugee camps, and initiating a massive vaccination program, their efforts were frequently blocked by the Sudanese government. It was May 2004, however, before the Security Council addressed the issue, and then only with weak words to Sudan, followed by promises to aid the African Union's deployment of cease-fire monitors. A subsequent resolution suggested possible action if Sudan failed to curb the violence, but four members, including two of the P-5 (China and Russia) abstained. Secretary-General Annan pushed for more concerted action, supported by U.S. secretary of state Colin Powell, who labeled Darfur a clear case of genocide in mid-

2004.[22] In March 2005 the Security Council, acting under Chapter VII, referred the Darfur crisis to the International Criminal Court (ICC) for action against those responsible for the genocide. By that time, between 180,000 and 300,000 people had died, 2.4 million people had been displaced, and the Sudanese government announced it would not cooperate with the ICC. The AU had some seven thousand military and police personnel deployed in Darfur by fall 2005, but they were too few in number and poorly equipped for the job, and it was not clear enough whether their mandate was only to monitor a cease-fire or to protect civilians.[23] The "never again" promise following Rwanda's genocide again looked hollow.

The Darfur case highlights three essential problems that the United Nations (and the international community) confronted with humanitarian intervention. The first is selectivity. Why did the United Nations intervene in Somalia but ignore Sudan and Liberia, where large-scale loss of life due to deliberate starvation, forced migrations, and massive human rights abuses were also occurring in the early 1990s? Why did the United Nations and NATO focus on Kosovo but ignore the war in Chechnya? More recently, why did the international community mobilize so rapidly to aid the victims of the 2004 Indian Ocean tsunami but fail to respond to the humanitarian crises in the Democratic Republic of the Congo and Darfur? The experience with Darfur has led many to conclude that the United Nations no longer is prepared to act in Africa because of racism and/or donor fatigue. The second problem is one of timely action and the difficulties of intervening given the remoteness and sheer size of the Darfur region, which is ten times the size of Bosnia, for example, where 60,000 NATO troops were deployed in 1995. International action was too little and too late to save thousands of human lives in Somalia, Srebrenica, Rwanda, Sierra Leone, and now Darfur. Mobilizing a force takes time and significant resources—unless one or more major

powers deem it in their national interest to act. In February 2006, the Security Council began discussion of replacing the African Union force in Darfur with a much larger, better-equipped UN force with a broader mandate, yet those discussions were expected to be lengthy because no major power, including the United States, was prepared to lead a Darfur mission. That is one of the reasons why there have been proposals for a small rapid-reaction force at the disposal of the secretary-general. Still, learning from peacekeepers' experience, the best such a force could do is draw international attention to a crisis and hope that a larger response would be forthcoming. The third problem Darfur represents is the problem of political will for humanitarian intervention. The P-5 states have conflicting interests in many situations; Russia and China have economic interests in Sudan and both states have traditionally opposed using enforcement measures for internal disputes. The Europeans and the United States have put priority on the peace accord ending the long civil war in southern Sudan. Also, the United States does not want to jeopardize the Sudanese government's cooperation in the war against terrorism, nor does it want to commit U.S. troops to intervene.

Regardless of selectivity, egregious errors, and continuing controversy, the very fact that debate is taking place over the legitimacy of humanitarian intervention marks a change. Following the report of the International Commission on Intervention and State Sovereignty[24] and extensive debate, the 2005 World Summit Outcome endorsed the emerging norm of international responsibility to protect civilians from large-scale violence when states cannot protect their own.[25] In so doing, it recognized that state sovereignty and the principle of nonintervention in internal affairs cannot be used to bar the United Nations or regional organizations from intervening if states fail to prevent large-scale humanitarian violations. Yet the case of Darfur illustrates that the political will to stop, let alone prevent, humanitarian disasters is still lacking.

THE UNITED NATIONS' ROLE IN COMBATING TERRORISM

Terrorism is an old threat to individual, state, and regional security that has taken on a number of new guises, making it a much greater threat to international peace and security. The Middle East conflict spawned a cycle of terror following the 1967 Arab-Israeli war and Israeli occupation of the West Bank, Gaza, and the Golan Heights when Palestinian groups began using terrorism to draw attention to their cause of establishing a homeland (or destroying Israel). Contemporary terrorism frequently targets innocent civilians. The goals are not limited to overthrowing a government or leader, or gaining an independent Tamil, Palestinian, or Basque homeland, but include eliminating a Western, and especially an American, presence in Islamic holy lands. The increased ease of international travel and telecommunications have made transnational terrorism less confined to a particular geographic place and enabled terrorist groups to form global networks and to move money, weapons, and people easily from one area to another—thus creating a global problem. The possibility that terrorists might acquire biological, chemical, nuclear, or miniaturized weapons has also raised the dangers of terrorist attacks.

International efforts to address terrorism have long been hobbled by the inability to agree on a definition. The problem is "how to formulate the term without criminalizing all armed resistance to oppressive regimes. . . . how to distinguish legitimate armed struggle from terrorism and how much emphasis to place on identifying root causes of grievances that lead individuals and groups to adopt terrorist methods."[26]

The UN General Assembly first began to address the general issue of terrorism in 1972 in the wake of several incidents and worked to develop a normative framework defining terrorism as a common problem (without agreeing on a definition of terrorism itself) and to conclude a series of international treaties. Hijackings, so prevalent in the 1970s, led to three treaties on airline and airport safety that declared terrorist acts against civil aviation illegal and sought to ensure the safety of the flying public. Concern about similar problems at sea led to the conclusion in the late 1980s of several conventions that guarantee safety of maritime navigation and fixed platforms on the continental shelf (i.e., drilling rigs). A 1979 convention addressed the problem of hostage taking. One approved in 1980 established a legal framework to protect nuclear material during transport. In 1996 the UN General Assembly drafted the Comprehensive International Convention on Terrorism, but differences over how to define terrorism held up adoption. The struggle over definition was avoided in treaties on specific issues by avoiding language on terrorism's causes.

The Security Council began to address the question of terrorism only in the 1990s in response to specific events, particularly the downing of Pan Am and UTA flights, the assassination attempt against Egyptian president Hosni Mubarek, and the 1998 bombings of U.S. embassies in Africa. These led the United States to push the council into an activist stance on terrorism and to impose targeted sanctions against three countries—Libya, Sudan, and Afghanistan—for their roles in supporting terrorism. While broader concerns were also at work in the council's increased attention to terrorism—such as evidence of growth in global networks of terrorists and fears that terrorists might acquire more powerful weapons—it took the attacks on September 11, 2001, to make terrorism a key priority for the United Nations and especially for the Security Council.

The United Nations and Post-9/11 Responses to Terrorism

The September 11, 2001, attacks on the World Trade Center and Pentagon elicited immediate and general condemnation by the international community. A day after the attacks, the UN Security Council passed Resolution 1368, condemning the heinous acts of terrorism and calling for international cooperation to punish those responsible. Most important, the resolution affirmed that the terrorist attacks were a breach of international peace under Chapter VII and recognized "the inherent right of individual or collective self-defense" as a legitimate response. This was the first time that the use of force in self-defense was authorized in response to terrorism and it was completely open-ended, allowing wide latitude for interpretation.

Two weeks later, on September 28, 2001, the Security Council adopted Resolution 1373, obliging all states to clamp down on the financing, training, and movement of terrorists and to cooperate in a campaign against them, even with force if necessary. The resolution called on states to take a number of measures, including suppressing the financing of terrorist groups, freezing their assets, blocking the recruitment of terrorists, and denying them safe haven. Under Chapter VII, the measures outlined in Resolution 1373 are binding on all 192 UN member states in contrast to the twelve treaties that bind only those states that accede to them. The resolution also established the Counter Terrorism Committee (CTC), which comprises all fifteen Security Council members and is designed to monitor states' capability to deny funding and/or haven to terrorists. The committee has been hobbled by the lack of resources to undertake comprehensive monitoring and follow-up and many states lack the capabilities to carry out the requirements; others are reluctant to do so for other reasons. In 2004 the Security Council took steps to revitalize the CTC by creating a Counter Terrorism Executive Directorate (CTED), responsible for carrying out technical assistance programs to bolster states' capacity for compliance as well as engaging in proactive dialogue with states and cooperating with international, regional, and subregional organizations. While the Security Council appeared ready to impose intrusive measures in Resolution 1373, its choice to exercise no control or oversight on the use of military force in response to terrorism is troubling and may erode the United Nations' authority.[27]

In 2004 the secretary-general's High-Level Panel on Threats, Challenges, and Change recommended a broad-ranging strategy to address root causes of terrorism and more immediate measures such as intelligence sharing and controlling dangerous materials. The UN General Assembly in adopting the 2005 World Summit Outcome took a major step by condemning terrorism "in all its forms and manifestations, committed by whomever, wherever and for whatever purposes, as it constitutes one of the most serious threats to international peace and security." It also stressed the need to conclude a comprehensive convention on terrorism and called for steps to adopt and implement a comprehensive and coordinated strategy to counter terrorism.[28] Yet defining terrorism may be insufficient and conflict prevention efforts alone ineffective in preventing terrorism, whose causes lie in the structure of the global system itself. While those issues have not yet been addressed, they are linked to fundamental questions of the United Nations' legitimacy in today's world and of the need for major UN reform, on the one hand, and broad global changes, on the other.

UN LEGITIMACY IN QUESTION AND THE DILEMMAS OF REFORM

The U.S. invasion and occupation of Iraq in 2003 in the face of clear opposition from a majority of the Security Council brought to the fore a sharp debate over the effectiveness and legitimacy of the United Nations, as discussed earlier. The debate was fueled by continuing controversy over the failures of several UN peacekeeping operations in the 1990s, along with a seemingly widening gap between ambitious Security Council resolutions and the political will of member states to provide the necessary resources to carry out the resolutions they approved. Just as that debate was intensifying, the UN Secretariat itself was rocked by a series of scandals that raised the issue of UN accountability and, hence, legitimacy. No scandal was more publicized than that over the United Nations' management of the Oil-for-Food Programme.

The Oil-for-Food Scandal

Initiated in 1996, the Oil-for-Food Programme (OFFP) was an exception to the comprehensive sanctions imposed in 1990 that permitted limited sales of Iraqi oil to finance food supplies and medicine as humanitarian relief. About $67 billion was transferred through the program. In 2004 sources revealed that Saddam Hussein's government had pocketed more than $10 billion from smuggling and kickbacks. Both control of smuggling and approval of contracts were responsibilities of the P-5, but administration of the contracts was a UN Secretariat task. Among those ultimately identified as receiving kickbacks were some two thousand companies and individuals, including European politicians, the Palestine Liberation Organization, and the UN director of the OFFP. An independent investigation led by former U.S. Federal Reserve chairman Paul Volcker found contractor overcharges, violations of bidding rules, and insufficiently monitored contractors.[29] Although Secretary-General Kofi Annan was not found guilty, he, along with the Security Council and member states, was faulted for the corruption and poor administration of the program. Annan's own son was implicated, and others at the United Nations resigned or were fired. Clearly, the scandal provided fuel for UN critics in the United States and elsewhere. It raised major questions about the United Nations' ability to manage large, long-term projects and, hence, the wisdom of ambitious Security Council actions. Among the suggestions that have been put forward to remedy the Secretariat's short-

comings is the establishment of a senior post in charge of daily UN operations—a chief operating officer.[30] Various proposals have also been made to reform other aspects of the United Nations' conflict management structure.

UN Reform

Interwoven in the debate over the United Nations' legitimacy and effectiveness were long-standing issues about the need for UN reforms, especially in the makeup of the Security Council. This is not a new debate. Over the United Nations' sixty-year history, there have been periodic calls for reform of the institution, including charter revision. In the 1970s the thrust was on improving coordination of economic and social programs in the UN system; in the 1980s calls for financial reforms dominated the agenda. In the 1990s the increase in peacekeeping and enforcement activities led to several efforts to reform the United Nations' security apparatus, while U.S. congressional pressures led to extensive reductions of UN staff and the introduction of management reforms.

Among the notable reform efforts relating to the United Nations' conflict management role was the 1992 *An Agenda for Peace,* commissioned by the Security Council.[31] This led to major changes in the Department of Peacekeeping Operations (DPKO), including the addition of military staff from member states and of experts in demining, training, and civilian policing. In 2000 the Brahimi Report, commissioned by the secretary-general, called for strengthening the planning and management of complex peace operations, increasing the Secretariat's information-gathering and analysis capacity to improve conflict prevention, and further changes in the DPKO to increase its size and competence. The report also signaled doctrinal changes, namely, the need to prepare for more robust peacekeeping—a clear lesson from the experiences in Somalia, Bosnia, and elsewhere in the 1990s.[32] Many of that report's recommendations have been implemented, including the creation of strategic deployment stocks and rapid-deployment teams. The most recent security reform initiative was the report of the High-Level Panel on Threats, Challenges, and Change submitted in December 2004. Titled *A More Secure World: Our Shared Responsibility*, the report called for "getting serious about prevention." Among other things, it called for making the Security Council's composition better reflect today's realities (by no means a new idea), creating a Peacebuilding Commission to coordinate international efforts to rebuild states (a new idea), and strengthening the secretary-general's role in mediation and peacebuilding.[33]

As stated earlier, the 2005 World Summit approved the proposed Peacebuilding Commission, but, in other respects, the summit was a disappointment to most observers. As one noted, "The optimists had hoped for a 'San Francisco moment' in New York, as decisive and momentous as the signing of the UN Charter 60 years earlier. . . . Critics might well conclude that instead the United Nations had an Einstein moment, recalling his definition of madness as doing something over and over again and expecting a different result each time." Among the explanations is that "all sides pushed their own interests, blocked items not of interest to them, and criticized others for not elevating the common interest." South Africa's President Thabo Mbeki, for example, criticized "rich and powerful nations" for blocking expansion of the Security Council to include more developing countries. Another explanation is that "the shared values and solidarity that makes up an international community may have frayed a thread too far" with the diversity of interests and perspectives of the United Nations' much larger membership today than in 1945. Ultimately, one must recognize that UN reform is not just about process and management but embodies fundamental questions of policy, values, and legitimate behavior that pose clear dilemmas.[34]

Dilemma 1: Strengthening the UN Secretariat versus the Political Will of States. Managing large, complex peacekeeping and peacebuilding operations requires capacities that the UN Secretariat has never had. Thus, many of the problems and shortcomings that arose in the 1990s were not surprising, given the increased demand for peacekeeping operations and sanctions. Nevertheless, the Secretariat has now taken steps to limit the damages arising from the scandals that have rocked the organization and to prevent recurrence. For example, the Secretariat has instituted a zero-tolerance policy in dealing with problems of sexual exploitation by UN peacekeepers in Congo and elsewhere, fired several UN personnel with oversight responsibilities, and pressured offending states to punish those individuals responsible. In response to the OFFP scandal, the Secretariat introduced measures to improve the performance of senior management, including a better selection system for senior officials, monitoring of individual performance, and a new Office of Internal Oversight Services. With the adoption of policies covering antifraud and corruption, whistleblower protection, financial disclosure, conflict of interest, and procurement contracts, the Secretariat is being reorganized to prevent the types of personnel abuses found in the oil-for-food scandal. Finally, a Department of Safety and Security has been established in direct response to the bombing of UN Headquarters in Baghdad in August 2003 that took the lives of twenty-two UN staff members and underlined the need for increased security for UN personnel working in conflict environments. In short, the UN Secretariat has needed to grow in capacity, adapt its management and working procedures, and introduce efficiency measures to maintain its effectiveness, security, and legitimacy.

Yet there are clear limits to what reforms of the Secretariat can accomplish. It will always be subject to the political will of states, for such is the nature of intergovernmental organizations—they exist and operate because states wish them to. Even if the DPKO had recognized the pending genocides in both Rwanda and Darfur, it could not act without the approval of powerful states. Although the United Nations could have prevented contract abuses in the Oil-for-Food Programme, it was states that were responsible for enforcing the sanctions by monitoring Iraq's borders, and they failed to do so. Even if the Secretariat were perfectly organized to coordinate peacebuilding in Kosovo or East Timor, states still control the financing of reconstruction efforts and seconding of troops, civilian police, and other personnel. Relatively little has been done to end the problem of sexual abuse by peacekeepers because the Secretariat cannot force member states to prosecute offenders or to impose discipline on their troops. In short, the Secretariat has only limited independent capability and any reforms must be designed to better utilize that capability. The United Nations' 2005 summit failed to strengthen that capability significantly because developing countries in particular fear that Westerners would dominate the senior staff positions even more than at present if the General Assembly gave the secretary-general more authority over hiring and firing personnel.

Dilemma 2: Reforming the Security Council versus the Power of the United States. Security Council reform has been discussed for decades (and achieved once, in 1965, with an expansion from ten to fifteen members). Many have argued that if the United Nations is to remain relevant, the council's structure cannot remain rooted in the post–World War II outcome, with the victors as permanent members with veto power over substantive issues. Most reform initiatives have agreed on the need to enlarge the council to accommodate the increased number of underrepresented developing countries and unrepresented regions. There is general agreement on the need to add more permanent members to reflect the importance of

countries such as Japan, Brazil, and India in financing or other contributions to peace and security. The key to Security Council reform is to increase the number of members for geographic representation and, hence, enhance its capacity and legitimacy while maintaining a small enough size to ensure efficiency. Unresolved are therefore three issues: how much to enlarge the council, whom to add as new permanent members, and the status of the veto— whether new permanent members would be given veto power or not and whether the use of the veto should be limited to certain situations. Disagreement over who should be the new permanent members is intense: Germany, Japan, or Italy as major donors? The European Union as a single entity? From Latin America, Argentina, Mexico, or Brazil? For Africa, South Africa, Egypt, or Nigeria? The 2004 High-Level Panel report suggested that selection criteria include not only geographic representation but also financial, military, and diplomatic contributions. The 2005 World Summit failed to act on the issue of Security Council reform despite intensive efforts, especially by Secretary-General Kofi Annan, India, Brazil, Japan, and Germany, to promote the need for change. Almost every potential candidate has an opponent, and the current permanent members are hardly prepared to give up their own privileged status. The best members could do at the 2005 summit was to commit to "continuing . . . efforts to achieve a decision."[35] Whatever proposal is ultimately (if ever) adopted requires charter revision to take effect, but it is hard to predict what set of circumstances will produce the necessary urgency and impetus for action on the issue of Security Council membership.

Lack of transparency in Security Council proceedings has been an issue particularly since the Cold War's end, when secret meetings became the norm. Yet some improvements have already been made and others have been proposed that do not require charter revision. Draft agendas are now circulated, "private" meetings open, and consultations with troop-contributing countries and NGOs occurring.

The real dilemma is that as security threats have required more complex and more coercive responses, the only state with the capability to undertake enforcement actions is the United States, perhaps in cooperation with a few other states. Thus, if the Security Council is to enforce its decisions, the United States must participate. Or, if the United States identifies a security threat and others do not concur, then the United Nations is threatened with irrelevance if the United States acts alone, as it did in Iraq. As Thomas Weiss explains, "The choice is not between the UN as a rubber stamp and a cipher —between the axis of subservience and the axis of irrelevance." The test is "Can the council engage the United States, moderate its exercise of power, and restrain its impulses?"[36]

CONCLUSION

For more than sixty years, the United Nations has shown its ability to adapt to changing security needs and, hence, to retain a major role in global conflict management. To be sure, there have been periods when it seemed less relevant, such as during the height of the Cold War, and relevance depends somewhat on perspective. To the United States, the United Nations was a hostile, irrelevant place during the 1970s, when the General Assembly and other bodies were caught up in endless debates over the proposed New International Economic Order and Zionism as a form of racism. To developing countries, the United Nations in those years was a valuable tool for promoting their interests as the new majority. The Cold War's end and the terrorist attacks of September 11, 2001, demonstrated how the United Nations can gain new relevance even for its most powerful members and be called on to meet new demands.

Collective security—the concept that threats in any region of the world are threats to all—is even more applicable today than when the United Nations was founded in 1945, given the nature of global terrorism and the renewed threat of nuclear proliferation, to name just two global problems. Still, there is agreement that the United Nations needs to strengthen its preventive diplomacy and mediation capacity for preventing wars between and within states. When prevention fails, there is a need for earlier decisive action by the Security Council and for steps to protect civilians, using force if necessary to avert humanitarian disasters. If the United Nations is going to be asked to undertake peacekeeping missions, especially those requiring more muscle, and to play a major role in rebuilding societies shattered by war, then its member states, especially the United States and other major powers, will have to provide adequate resources in the form of peacekeepers, willingness to incur casualties, standby capacity for rapid action, transport, financing, and logistical support. Likewise, the United Nations and member states need new tools for dealing with terrorism, including coercive measures when necessary and tools for helping states enhance their own capacity to combat the threat domestically.

Debates over the United Nations' legitimacy and effectiveness have come and gone over the years. Current concerns regarding the United Nations' continuing relevance, including those relating to U.S. unilateralism, need to be taken seriously. Nonetheless, there is a striking cyclical pattern wherein states ignore the United Nations for a period of time, challenge its legitimacy, and then turn to it again for conflict management and dealing with new security threats. The United Nations remains the only truly global security institution—a valuable tool for states and many nonstate actors to manage conflicts and address global security threats—and has shown that it *can* work.

NOTES

1. This chapter draws on material in the chapters on peace and security in two of our recent books,

International Organizations: The Politics and Processes of Global Governance (Boulder, Colo.: Lynne Rienner, 2004); and *The United Nations in the Twenty-First Century*, 3rd ed. (Boulder, Colo.: Westview Press, 2007), © copyright 2007, reprinted with permission.

2. The data are from *The Human Security Report 2005* (New York: Oxford University Press, 2005), http://www.humansecurityreport.info.

3. There is an extensive literature on sanctions. For a set of excellent studies of the "sanctions decade," however, see David Cortright and George A. Lopez, *The Sanctions Decade: Assessing UN Strategies in the 1990s* (Boulder, Colo.: Lynne Rienner, 2000), and *Sanctions and the Search for Security: Challenges to UN Action* (Boulder, Colo.: Lynne Rienner, 2002).

4. Adam Roberts, "The Use of Force," in *The UN Security Council: From the Cold War to the 21st Century*, ed. David M. Malone (Boulder, Colo.: Lynne Rienner, 2004), 141.

5. See Michael J. Glennon, "Why the Security Council Failed," *Foreign Affairs* 82, no. 3 (May–June 2003): 16–35; and responses from Edward C. Luck, "The End of an Illusion," Anne-Marie Slaughter, "Misreading the Record," and Ian Hurd, "Too Legit to Quit," all published in *Foreign Affairs* 82, no. 4 (July–August 2003): 201–205. See also the debate, "The United Nations Has Become Irrelevant," *Foreign Policy*, no. 138 (September–October 2003): 16–24.

6. Mats Berdal, "The UN after Iraq," *Survival* 46, no. 3 (Autumn 2004): 82.

7. United Nations, *The Blue Helmets: A Review of United Nations Peace-Keeping*, 3rd ed. (New York: UN Department of Public Information, 1996), 4.

8. United Nations, *Report of the Secretary-General Pursuant to General Assembly Resolution 53/35: The Fall of Srebrenica*, UN Doc. No. A/54/549, November 15, 1999, http://www.unorg/peacesrebrenica.pdf.

9. Michael W. Doyle, *UN Peacekeeping in Cambodia: UNTAC's Civil Mandate* (Boulder, Colo.: Lynne Rienner, 1995), 26.

10. United Nations, "The 'Second Generation': Cambodia Elections 'Free and Fair,' but Challenges Remain," *Chronicle* 30, no. 5 (November–December 1993), 26.

11. Alexandros Yannis, "The UN as Government in Kosovo," *Global Governance* 10, no. 1 (January–March 2004): 67–81.

12. For extended discussion of the issues of international administration, see Richard Caplan, *International Governance of War-Torn Territories: Rule and Reconstruction* (New York: Oxford University Press, 2005), and the special issue of *Global Governance* (January–March 2004).

13. 2005 World Summit Outcome, UN General Assembly A/60/L.1, Section 98.

14. Tim Murithi, "The UN Peacebuilding Commission and the Implications for Africa" (unpublished paper presented at the Conference on the UN at 60: Towards a New Reform Agenda, sponsored by the Institute for Global Dialogue, South African Office of the Friedrich Ebert Stiftung, and the University of Pretoria, Pretoria, South Africa, October 27–28, 2005).

15. Virginia Page Fortna, "Interstate Peacekeeping: Causal Mechanisms and Empirical Effects," *World Politics* 56 (July 2004): 510.

16. Among recent assessments, see, for example, Michael J. Doyle and Nicholas Sambanis, "International Peacebuilding: A Theoretical and Quantitative Analysis," *American Political Science Review* 94, no. 4 (December 2000): 779–801.

17. Lise Morjé Howard, "Learning to Keep the Peace? United Nations Multidimensional Peacekeeping in Civil Wars" (Ph.D. diss., University of California, Berkeley, 2001).

18. Stephen John Stedman, "International Implementation of Peace Agreements in Civil Wars: Findings from a Study of Sixteen Cases," in *Turbulent Peace: The Challenges of Managing International Conflict*, ed. Chester A. Crocker, Fen Osler Hampson, and Pamela Aall (Washington, D.C.: United States Institute of Peace Press, 2001), 737–752.

19. Assefaw Bariagaber, "Africa," in *Global Agenda: Issues before the 59th General Assembly of the United Nations*, ed. Angela Drakulich (New York: UNA/USA, 2004), 109.

20. United Nations, *Report of the Independent Inquiry into the Actions of the United Nations during the 1994 Genocide in Rwanda*, S/1999/1257, December 15, 1999.

21. Independent International Commission on Kosovo, *The Kosovo Report: Conflict, International Response, Lessons Learned* (Oxford: Oxford University Press, 2000).

22. Powell's remarks were contained in testimony before the Senate Foreign Relations Committee and

reported in the news. See http://www.washington-post.com/wp-dyn/articles/A8364-2004Se9.html.

23. Ophera McDoom, "AU Darfur Force Needs Stronger Mandate," Reuters, http://www.defensenews.com/story.php?F=1301625&C=mideast.

24. Commission on Intervention and State Sovereignty, *The Responsibility to Protect: Report of the International Commission on Intervention and State Sovereignty* (Ottawa: International Development Research Centre for ICISS, 2001), http://www.iciss-cisse.gc.ca. On the subject of changing norms on intervention, see also Martha Finnemore, *The Purpose of Intervention: Changing Beliefs about the Use of Force* (Ithaca, N.Y.: Cornell University Press, 2003), particularly chap. 4.

25. 2005 World Summit Outcome, Sections 138–140.

26. M. J. Peterson, "Using the General Assembly," in *Terrorism and the UN: Before and After September 11,* ed. Jane Boulden and Thomas G. Weiss (Bloomington: Indiana University Press, 2004), 178.

27. Jane Boulden and Thomas G. Weiss, "Whither Terrorism and the United Nations?" in ibid., 11.

28. See the 2005 World Summit Outcome, Sections 81–90.

29. For reports and documents of the Independent Inquiry Committee into the United Nations Oil-for-Food Programme, see http://www.iic-offp.org/.

30. See United States Institute of Peace, *Report of the Task Force on the United Nations: American Interests and UN Reform* (Washington, D.C.: United States Institute of Peace, June 2005), http://www.usip.org/un/report/index/html.

31. Boutros Boutros-Ghali, *An Agenda for Peace: Preventive Diplomacy, Peacemaking, and Peacekeeping* (New York: United Nations, 1992).

32. United Nations, *Report of the Panel on United Nations Peace Operations* [Brahimi Report], A/55/305-S/2000/809 (New York: United Nations, August 21, 2000), http://www.un.org/peace/reports/peace_operations/.

33. See United Nations High-Level Panel on Threats, Challenges, and Change, *A More Secure World: Our Shared Responsibility* (New York: United Nations, 2004), http://www.un.org/secureworld/.

34. Ramesh Thakur, "U.N.'s 'Einstein' Moment," *Japan Times,* October 3, 2005, http://www.japantimes.co.jp/cgi-bin/makeprfy.p15?eo20051003a2.htm.

35. 2005 World Summit Outcome, Section 153.

36. Thomas G. Weiss, "Security Council Reform: Problems and Prospects in September 2005," UNA-USA Policy Brief No. 9, June 23, 2005, 4.

29

SUCCESSES AND CHALLENGES IN CONFLICT MANAGEMENT

Andrew Mack

INTRODUCTION

Is there more political violence in the world today than during the Cold War era? This is certainly the view conveyed by the mainstream media, voiced by many policymakers, and even advanced by some scholars. But the evidence tells a very different story. The Cold War years were characterized by ever-escalating warfare. In their aftermath global security has improved dramatically.

It is true that the Cold War was the longest period without armed conflict between major powers in hundreds of years. But while international relations scholars were celebrating the so-called Long Peace and the stability of the Cold War years, the rest of the world was experiencing an ever-increasing number of wars. Indeed, from 1946 to 1992, the number of armed conflicts being waged around the world increased threefold.

Then, at the beginning of the 1990s, at precisely the point that commentators in the West began to fret about an "explosion" of ethnonationalist warfare around the world, the number of armed conflicts and other forms of political violence began to drop. The decline continued throughout the decade and into the new millennium.

The full extent of this shift was revealed with the publication by Oxford University Press of the *Human Security Report* late in 2005.[1] (Previously, only the relatively small conflict research community had paid much attention to the decline.)[2] Drawing on a wide variety of academic resources and specially commissioned research, the *Human Security Report*'s findings generated considerable publicity around the world precisely because they ran so contrary to the prevailing conventional wisdom of the day. They included the following:

• The number of armed conflicts worldwide has declined by more than 40 percent since 1992.[3] The number of the deadliest conflicts (those with one thousand or more battle deaths) has dropped even more dramatically—by 80 percent.

• The number of international crises, often harbingers of war, fell by more than 70 percent between 1981 and 2001.

Figure 1. Number of Worldwide Armed Conflicts, 1946–2002

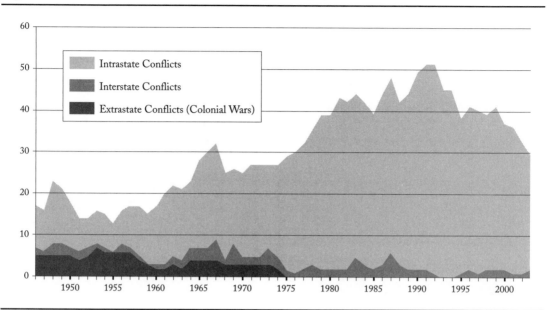

Sources: Uppsala Conflict Data Program, Uppsala University, Uppsala, Sweden; and Centre for the Study of Civil War, International Peace Research Institute, Oslo.

• Wars between states, the traditional focus of security scholars, are more rare than in previous eras and now constitute less than 5 percent of all armed conflicts.

• The number of military coups and attempted coups has declined by some 60 percent since 1963. In 1963, there were twenty-five coups or attempted coups; in 2004, there were ten. All failed.

• The period since the end of World War II is the longest interval without wars between the major powers in hundreds of years.

• Most of the world's conflicts are now concentrated in Africa. But even here there are signs of hope. (A new data set created by Uppsala University's Conflict Data Program for the *Human Security Report* found that in 2002–3 the number of armed conflicts in Africa dropped from forty-one to thirty-five.)

• The drop in armed conflicts in the 1990s was associated with a worldwide decline in arms transfers, military spending, and troop numbers. (Global military expenditures rose

again in the new millennium, but the rise was mostly driven by major increases in the U.S. defense budget.)

• Wars have also become dramatically less deadly over the past five decades. The average number of people reported killed (combatants, plus civilians caught in the cross fire) per conflict per year in 1950 was thirty-eight thousand; in 2002, it was just six hundred —a decline of 98 percent.

• In the 1950s, 1960s, and 1970s, by far the highest battle death tolls in the world were in the wars in East and Southeast Asia. In the 1970s and 1980s, most of the killing took place in the Middle East, Central and South Asia, and sub-Saharan Africa. But by the end of the 1990s, more people were being killed in sub-Saharan Africa's wars than in the rest of the world put together. But even here the battle-related death toll declined in the new millennium.

• The new data set compiled for the *Human Security Report* found that in 2002–3 the number of reported deaths from all forms of political violence fell by 62 percent in the Americas, 32 percent in Europe, 35 percent in Asia, and 24 percent in Africa.[4] A two-year period is obviously too short to determine trends, but the data provide further evidence that the world is *not* becoming ever more violent.

- Notwithstanding the horrors of Rwanda and Srebrenica, Bosnia, the number of genocides and other mass killings plummeted by 80 percent between the 1989 high point and 2001—following the same trend as the most violent armed conflicts.

- Note that violent conflict deaths, usually called battle-related deaths, are usually only a minority of total war deaths. In poor countries the biggest death tolls are not from those killed in the actual fighting but from war-exacerbated disease and malnutrition. These "indirect" deaths can account for as much as 90 percent or more of the total war-related death toll. Some argue that while battle deaths may have declined recently, "indirect" deaths have increased. In fact, there is no evidence to support such a contention. Currently, there are insufficient data to make even rough estimations of global or regional "indirect" death toll trends. But, as explained later, there are firm grounds for believing that these deaths have declined, too.

- The data on trends in international terrorism are contested—not least because definitions of what counts as an international terrorist incident are rarely consistent. Some data sets have shown an overall decline in international terrorist incidents of all types since the early 1980s but an increase in the number of high-casualty attacks over the past decade. But whatever the definition, it is clear that the death toll from annual international terrorist attacks is only a tiny fraction of the annual war death toll.

- Core human rights abuses (e.g., torture, extrajudicial executions, and killings by officially backed death squads) appear to have declined modestly in five out of six regions in the developing world since the mid-1990s.[5] Here again the data are contested, however.

Data on political violence are not very reliable—collecting statistics in war zones is difficult if not impossible, for example—and just about every figure can be queried. But a decade after the end of the Cold War there is no longer any doubt about the direction and scope of the trends—even though they remain largely unknown to most people.

WHY THE WORLDWIDE DECLINE IN POLITICAL VIOLENCE IS SO LITTLE KNOWN

The trend data on political violence around the world presented in the *Human Security Report* refute the conventional wisdom that we live in an ever-more violent age. But why should the dramatic changes that the report identifies be so little known or understood? There are several reasons.

First, most people get their information about world events from the media, where the "if-it-bleeds-it-leads" imperative drives news reporting. So dramatic outbreaks of political violence always get far greater coverage than the wars that end in quietly negotiated peace agreements, or simply fizzle out.

Second, part of the mandate of human rights and humanitarian NGOs such as Amnesty International, Human Rights Watch, and Médicins Sans Frontières is to "speak truth to power"—to bring the plight of the oppressed and the victims of war to the attention of the international community. They do this to great effect and in the process add to the impression that we live in an ever more dangerous world. But there are no NGOs that have the reporting of *good* news as a central part of their mandate. The picture is again unbalanced.

Third, there are no *official* statistics on the numbers of wars, war casualties, genocides, mass killings of civilians, military coups, terrorist attacks, or core human rights abuses that can be used as a reality check.[6] Without access to reliable trend data, the United Nations, other international agencies, donor governments, and NGOs have had no way of determining whether things are getting better or worse. This in turn means that security planners have had no way of determining whether or not their conflict prevention, postconflict peace-building, or human rights abuses are effective.

The dearth of official data on security issues stands in stark contrast to the vast amount of government data (on development, health, education, etc.) that track progress (or lack thereof) toward meeting the 2015 Millennium Development Goals (MDGs)—the range of development targets the international community has pledged to reach by 2015. There are no Millennium Security Goals to complement the MDGs because there are no official data with which to track them. There are no data in part because statistics are rarely collected in states at war, in part because many governments see security information as too sensitive to share even when it is collected, and in part because there is often no consensus on definitions. The United Nations General Assembly, for example, has never been able to agree on what constitutes terrorism, while some repressive governments refer to armed resistance against their rule as "violent crime." Without agreed-on definitions, data collection is impossible. There are useful sources of information in the scholarly community that, to a degree, make up for the lack of official data, but much of the academic material is highly technical, inaccessible to nonspecialists, and thus not widely known.

The net effect of these factors is that popular assumptions about trends in global security tend to be very much at odds with reality.

WHY WE HAVE FEWER WARS

Remarkably few attempts have been made to explain the decline in political violence since the end of the Cold War. There are a number of possible, indeed plausible, explanations, but most can—at best—explain only a small part of the decline.

The End of Colonialism

From the early 1950s to the early 1980s, wars of liberation from colonial rule made up 60 percent to 100 percent of all international conflicts, depending on the year. Today there are no such wars—the demise of colonialism has removed a major source of conflict from the international system.

But this security-enhancing change had less impact than might have been expected. Civil war numbers continued to rise rapidly throughout the 1980s well after the last violent anticolonial wars had come to an end. This was in part because in many newly independent countries the struggle against colonial rule was replaced by armed conflicts over who should control the postcolonial state, and in part because the Cold War was now driving—or at least sustaining—much of the warfare in the developing world.

Democratization

The number of democracies increased by nearly half between 1990 and 2003, while the number of civil conflicts declined sharply over the same period (see figure 2). At first glance the surge in democratization might appear to be a plausible explanation for the decline in warfare. Established and inclusive democratic states not only, almost, never go to war against each other, but they also have a very low risk of succumbing to civil war. But while the risk of civil war is indeed very low in stable and inclusive democracies, countries with governments that are partly democratic and partly authoritarian—sometimes called "anocracies" by political scientists—are more prone to civil war than either inclusive democracies or autocracies. This matters because, while the number of democratic regimes increased dramatically in the early 1990s, so, too, did number of anocracies.

Figure 2. The Rising Tide of Democratization, 1946–2002

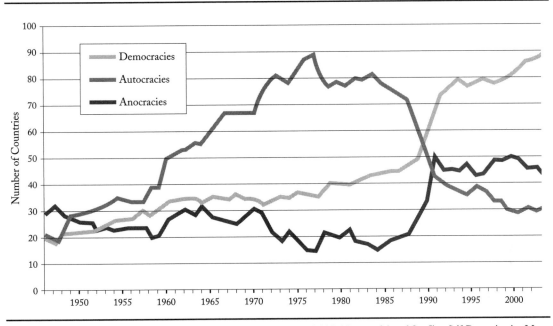

Source: Monty G. Marshall and Ted Robert Gurr, *Peace and Conflict 2005: A Global Survey of Armed Conflicts, Self-Determination Movements, and Democracy* (College Park: Center for International Development and Conflict Management, University of Maryland, 2005).

Hence it seems likely that the positive impact of the increase in the number of inclusive democracies was largely offset by the negative impact of the comparable increase in more war-prone anocracies.

War, Poverty, and State Capacity

Levels of economic development and the risk of war are very strongly associated (see figure 3). Indeed, one of the most striking findings to emerge from conflict research is that most of today's wars take place in very poor countries and that as per capita gross domestic product increases, the risk of war declines.[7] Indeed, as figure 3 shows, the risk of war in countries with a $5,000 per capita income is some thirty times less than in those with an income of $250.

This does not, of course, mean that the poor are inherently more violent than the rich. Indeed, the key factor here does not appear to be income at all but rather state capacity, for which income per capita is simply a useful

"proxy" measure. Other things being equal, the higher the per capita income a country has, the stronger and more capable its government. This in turn means more state resources to crush rebels and to redress grievances. The pursuit of equitable economic growth—and hence state capacity—would, therefore, appear to be a highly effective long-term conflict prevention strategy, in addition to being a necessary condition for sustainable human development. But while there is no doubt that growth in state income and capacity is associated with a reduced risk of armed conflict *in the long term,* neither factor can explain the major decline in civil wars since the early 1990s. The rate of economic growth in this period is simply too slow to account for such a rapid drop in conflict numbers.[8]

Ethnic Discrimination and Conflict

Determining what drives so-called ethnic conflict has been the subject of intense scholarly

Figure 3. The Association between War and Poverty

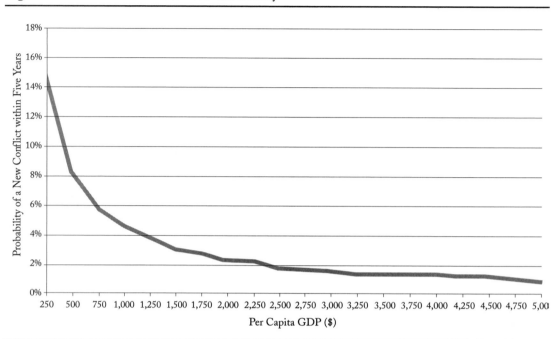

Source: Macartan Humphreys and Ashutosh Varshney, "Violent Conflict and the Millennium Development Goals: Diagnosis and Recommendations" (paper prepared for the Millennium Development Goals Poverty Task Force Workshop, Bangkok, June 2004), http://www.columbia.edu/~mh2245/papers1/HV.pdf (accessed May 6, 2006).

interest in recent years. According to the Minorities at Risk project at the University of Maryland, "high levels of political discrimination are a key cause of violent ethnic conflict."[9] The significance of this finding lies in the fact that there has been a steady decline in political discrimination by governments around the world since 1950. In 1950, some 45 percent of governments around the world actively discriminated against ethnic groups, according to Minorities at Risk researchers; by 2003, that share had shrunk to 25 percent. Economic discrimination by governments followed a similar trend.[10] But while this is again a trend that enhances security in the long term, it, too, fails as an explanation for the sharp decline in armed conflict in the 1990s.

The security-enhancing effect of the steady reduction of political and economic discrimination was not strong enough to offset the inexorable decade-by-decade increase in civil

wars from the 1950s to the early 1990s. And there is no evidence to suggest that, after the end of the Cold War, the reduction in discrimination suddenly became a powerful enough force to account for the decline in conflict numbers.

The explanation for the dramatic drop in political violence in the 1990s has to be found in other changes that took place during, or immediately preceding, this period.

The End of the Cold War

The most persuasive explanation for the decline in civil conflict is found in the far-reaching political changes wrought by the end of the Cold War. First, the end of the Cold War removed a major driver of ideological hostility from the international system—a change that affected civil wars as well as international wars. Second, the end of the Cold War meant that the two superpowers ceased supporting their erstwhile clients in proxy wars in the developing world. Denied this support, many of these conflicts simply petered out, or the parties sued for peace. But less than 20 percent of the post–Cold War decline in conflict numbers appears to be attributable to this factor. Third, and most important, the end of the Cold War liberated the United Nations, freeing the Security Council from the paralysis that had gripped it throughout most of the East-West confrontation and allowing it for the first time to play an effective global security role —and, indeed, to do far more than its founders had originally envisaged. The impact of this wave of post–Cold War activism on political violence around the world has been both profound and the subject of extraordinarily little study.

The Upsurge in International Activism

Since the end of the 1980s, the United Nations has spearheaded a remarkable, if often inchoate, upsurge in conflict management, conflict prevention, and postconflict peacebuilding activities. The World Bank, donor states, and a number of regional security organizations, as well as literally thousands of NGOs, have both complemented United Nations activities and played independent prevention and peacebuilding roles of their own.

Despite the United Nations' many flaws, its charter and universal membership—and hence its legitimacy—give the world body a unique mandate as a security actor. But other institutions play more important roles in specific regional contexts. The United States is clearly a more important security actor in the Middle East and East Asia than the United Nations, for example, while the Organization for Security and Cooperation in Europe (OSCE) has played a more important security role in Eastern Europe and the former Soviet Union.

The extent of the changes that have taken place over the last fifteen years is as remarkable as it has been underreported. The following list is far from exhaustive.

Preventive Diplomacy and Peacemaking. There has been a striking increase in preventive diplomacy and peacemaking activities since the end of the 1980s. UN preventive diplomacy missions (i.e., those that seek to prevent wars from breaking out in the first place) increased sixfold between 1990 and 2002. UN peacemaking activities (those that seek to stop ongoing conflicts) also increased nearly fourfold —from four in 1990 to fifteen in 2002. There were comparable increases in the OSCE's conflict prevention and peacebuilding activities over the same period and a sharp upsurge in activism among other regional security organizations.

The increase in preventive diplomacy activity helped prevent a number of latent conflicts from crossing the threshold into warfare, while the rise in peacemaking activities has been associated with a major increase in negotiated peace settlements. Approximately half of all the peace settlements negotiated between 1946 and 2003 have been signed since the end of the Cold War.

International Support for Peacemaking and Peacebuilding. There has also been an extraordinary increase in international support—political as well as economic—for UN peacemaking and postconflict peacebuilding missions. The number of Friends of the Secretary-General, contact groups, and other mechanisms created by governments to support UN peacemaking activities and peace operations in countries in —or emerging from—conflict increased from four in 1990 to more than twenty-eight in 2003, a sevenfold increase. Regional organizations also benefited from increased support in *their* security-building efforts during this period.

Postconflict Peace Operations. There has been a major increase in postconflict peace operations, not just UN missions but those of regional organizations as well. One major goal of the ever-growing range of peacebuilding activities that these missions pursue is the prevention of any

Figure 4. Number of UN Peacemaking Activities, 1989–2002

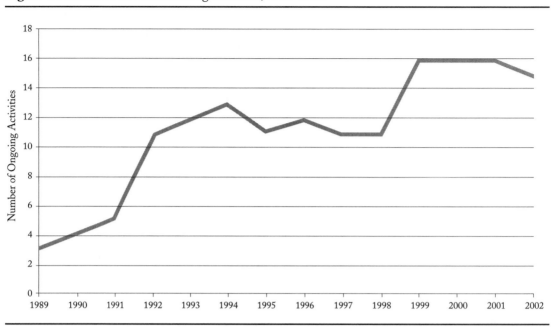

Source: Data provided by the United Nations Department of Political Affairs.

recurrence of conflict. Since some 40 percent to 50 percent of postconflict countries relapse into political violence within five years of a war ending, any policy initiatives that can minimize this risk will in turn reduce the risk of future wars.

The number of UN peacekeeping operations more than doubled between 1988 and 2005—from seven to seventeen (see figure 5).

The peace operations of the post–Cold War era are not merely larger and more numerous than Cold War peacekeeping missions, they are also far more ambitious. Whereas the Cold War missions typically involved little more than monitoring cease-fires with relatively small numbers of soldiers, many of today's operations are more akin to nation building. And despite the much-publicized failures, a recent RAND Corporation study found that two-thirds of UN nation-building missions that it examined had been successful.[11] Comparable U.S. missions enjoyed a success rate of only 50 percent.

The Use of Force—and Sanctions. The United Nations Security Council has been increasingly willing to authorize the use of force to deter "spoilers" from undermining peace agreements and in so doing to restart old conflicts. And UN peace operations are now routinely mandated to use force to protect the peace, not just their own personnel. Sanctions are the other coercive instrument in the United Nations' armory, and the number of sanctions regimes imposed by the Security Council increased more than fivefold between 1990 and 2000. While many sanctions regimes have been ineffectual and/or have imposed great harm on civilians, they can help deny warring parties access to arms and can pressure recalcitrant regimes—and rebel groups—to enter peace negotiations.

Attacking the Culture of Impunity. In addition to the establishment of the International Criminal Court and the various UN and ad hoc tribunals, the number of governments

Figure 5. Number of UN Peacekeeping Missions, 1948–2004

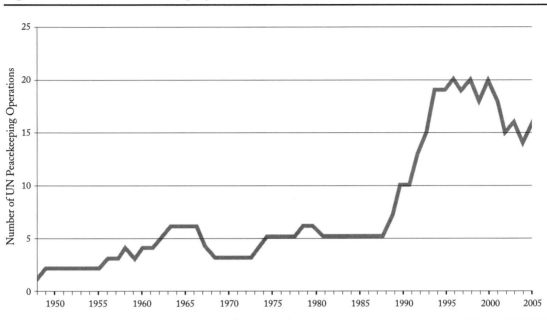

Source: Based on data from the United Nations Department of Peacekeeping Operations, http://www.un.org/Depts/dpko/dpko/index.asp (accessed July 22, 2005).

prosecuting agents of former regimes for grave human rights abuses increased from one to eleven between 1990 and 2004. If would-be perpetrators of gross human rights abuses believe there is some prospect that they will be brought to justice for the crimes they commit, they may be deterred from acting in the first place.

A Greater Emphasis on Reconciliation. The number of truth and reconciliation commissions in operation in any one year has more than doubled since the end of the Cold War —from one in 1989 to seven in 2003. The effective pursuit of reconciliation in postconflict environments reduces the risk of renewed violence. Reconciliation is also a major aim of most peacebuilding programs.

Addressing the Root Causes of Conflict. The United Nations, the World Bank along with other international agencies, and donor governments are increasingly designing development and aid policies to address what are perceived to be the "root causes" of political violence. Individually, none of these initiatives has had a great impact on global security. Indeed, most have achieved only modest success in terms of their own goals. But even where the success rate is very low—say, 30 percent to 40 percent—which is quite common, these are still successes that simply were not happening before the 1990s because so little was being attempted then.

The case argued here is simple. Despite inappropriate mandates, inadequate resources, lack of coordination, and multiple inefficiencies, international activism aimed at stopping wars and preventing their reccurrence has had a real impact. But a lot more research is required to determine which specific activities and mechanisms have been most effective.

Figure 6. Attacking the Culture of Impunity, 1970–2004

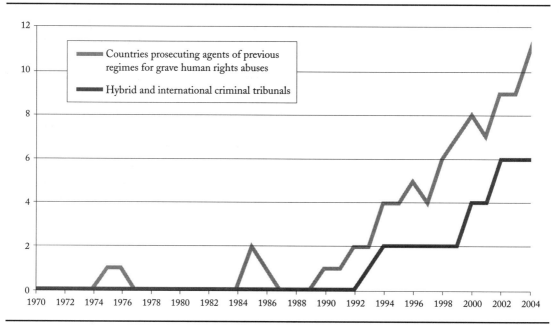

Source: Data compiled by the Human Security Centre from a wide variety of print and online sources.

WHY TODAY'S WARS KILL FEWER PEOPLE

The explosion of international activism after the Cold War helps explain the subsequent decline in the *number* of armed conflicts, but it doesn't tell us why warfare has also become progressively—though unevenly—less *deadly* since the 1950s. There was an average of thirty-seven thousand battle-related deaths for each conflict waged in 1950; in 2002, there were just six hundred—an extraordinary decline.

Here the key explanatory factors are quite different from those relating to the post–Cold War decline in *incidence* of conflict.

- The major wars of the Cold War era typically involved huge armies, heavy conventional weapons, air bombardment, and massive external intervention. They killed hundreds of thousands—sometimes millions.
- The overwhelming majority of today's wars are low-intensity conflicts fought primarily with small arms and light weapons. They

typically pit government forces that are weak and relatively few in number against small bands of ill-trained rebels. They rarely involve major engagements, with civilians rather than combatants often being the targeted. Although often brutal, they kill relatively few people compared with the major wars of the Cold War era—typically hundreds or thousands of battle-related deaths rather than hundreds of thousands.

- The decline in the battle-death toll may also be related to the huge increase in the number of refugees and internally displaced persons (IDPs) in the 1980s. By 1992, the peak year, the worldwide total of displaced people exceeded forty million—up from a little over ten million at the end of the 1970s. (The data from the 1970s and earlier are suspect, but there is no doubt that there was a huge increase from the 1970s to the 1990s.) Displacement is a humanitarian tragedy, but had these millions *not* fled their homes, hundreds of thousands—possibly far more—could have been killed. So the increase in displacement is likely one of the reasons for the decline in battle deaths.

WHAT ABOUT INDIRECT DEATHS?

The death toll from combat is a critically important measure of the human cost of war. But, as noted earlier, it measures only the tip of the iceberg of total war deaths. In poor countries war-exacerbated disease and malnutrition cause far more death and disability than bombs and bullets.

In the Democratic Republic of the Congo a series of epidemiological studies by the International Rescue Committee (IRC) has estimated that some 3.9 million people have died as a consequence of the fighting since 1998.[12] These so-called excess deaths are people who would not have died had it not been for the war. According to the IRC, less than 2 percent of these deaths resulted from violence. As noted earlier, there are no global data on excess deaths, just a series of individual country case studies of very uneven quality. But all the studies indicate a similar causal pattern: the poorer the country and the more destructive the war, the greater the number of excess deaths caused by disease and malnutrition.

These findings raise an obvious question. We know that in poor countries war-related disease and malnutrition are far greater killers than combat, but we have no data to tell us whether deaths from these causes are increasing or decreasing. So how is it possible to claim that the world is more secure?

Some NGOs have pointed to the extraordinarily high death rates in the Democratic Republic of the Congo and Darfur in Sudan and argued that, even though the numbers of wars and battle-related deaths may be dramatically down, the number of indirect deaths has risen. This is highly unlikely. The main drivers of excess deaths are the scope and intensity of fighting (for which combat deaths are the best measure), the numbers of people

displaced, the preexisting levels of nutrition and access to health care, and the timeliness, degree, and efficacy of humanitarian intervention. Since war numbers, combat deaths per conflict, and the numbers of people displaced have all declined in the past fifteen years, while funding for humanitarian assistance has more than doubled over the same period, we have every reason to expect that indirect deaths should have declined as well.

What is clear is that we have more data on indirect deaths today than in any previous period. Levels of indirect deaths comparable to those in the Democratic Republic of the Congo and Darfur almost certainly occurred in earlier wars, but because they were never measured, they went largely unnoticed.

NO GROUNDS FOR COMPLACENCY

Despite the positive changes in the global security climate that the *Human Security Report* has described, there are no grounds for complacency. Although wars and war deaths are down, some sixty armed conflicts are still being waged around the globe, many of which have defied resolution for decades. There are still gross abuses of human rights, widespread war crimes, and ever-deadlier acts of terrorism. Moreover, because the underlying causes of conflict are too rarely addressed, the risk of new wars breaking out and old ones starting again remains very real. And as the many failures of the past—and numerous recent reports —have made clear, the United Nations remains in urgent need of reform if it is truly to fulfill its charter mandate to "save succeeding generations from the scourge of war."

UN reform is critical if the present ad hoc system of managing global conflict is to become less dysfunctional. An important start was made in 2000 with the launch of the Brahimi Report—a widely praised package of recommendations for reform aimed at making UN peacekeeping operations more effective.[13]

The Brahimi Report pointed out that the UN Secretariat had been unprepared, under-staffed, and underfunded to undertake the spate of new missions that were authorized in 1999 and subsequently. In sharp contrast to many UN reports, it eschewed empty rhetoric in favor of pragmatic and highly specific recommendations on how to improve UN peace operations. Many—not all—of these recommendations have been implemented. This, plus the commitment of the current under-secretary-general for peacekeeping to promoting a "lessons-learned" culture and an evidence-based approach to mission planning, has made the Department of Peacekeeping Operations (DPKO) a far more effective body than it was in the 1990s.

But no amount of internal reform in the DPKO can overcome the more pervasive problems that confront UN operations in the field, namely, the lack of adequate resources, problems with inadequately trained and equipped peacekeeping personnel, and—above all—the lack of effective coordination and collaboration among agencies, donors, and NGOs on the ground and between the field and headquarters.

It was in large part to address the last issue that the new Peacebuilding Commission—a recommendation from Secretary-General Annan's 2004 High-Level Panel on Threats, Challenges, and Change[14]—was finally approved at the United Nations' September 2005 World Summit. The Peacebuilding Commission is an intergovernmental body with a membership of thirty-one states that is supposed to guide overall peacebuilding policy, plan missions for postconflict environments, set standards, help ensure adequate funding, and bring a degree of coherence to field operations that has too often been lacking. But while widely welcomed both within the UN Secretariat and among member states, the new commission and its critically important Secretariat–based Peacebuilding Support Office (PBSO)—which will do most of the work—face daunting challenges.

One of the major arguments for creating the Peacebuilding Commission has been the widely agreed-on need to address the endlessly-on discussed, but never resolved, "coordination problem" that all humanitarian and peacebuilding missions confront to a greater or lesser degree. But the commission is essentially a consultative body that has no executive authority. So it is by no means clear that it will be able to resolve the endless turf battles between UN agencies, the intense competition between NGOs, and the mutual suspicion that so often characterizes relationships between donors and those working in the field. It is these organizational pathologies that so often have prevented effective coordination and collaboration in the past. Moreover, it is already clear that the Peacebuilding Commission is confronting exactly the same problem that in the past has stymied so many other UN security initiatives—namely, lack of adequate funding. The staff numbers and budgets for the PBSO recommended by the secretary-general have both been cut—an extraordinary exercise in penny-pinching by member states given that the total annual funding originally requested for the PBSO was less than one-tenth of 1 percent of current peacekeeping expenditure.[15]

Notwithstanding the very real problems it confronts, the creation of the new Peacebuilding Commission is further evidence of an emerging system of global governance that seeks to address human security issues. The birthing process is messy, funding is inadequate, and disagreements are pervasive. But the effort is not in vain. The evidence clearly indicates that the actions of an engaged international community *can* make a difference. Wars can be prevented, sustainable peace agreements negotiated, war-torn societies rebuilt, and hundreds of thousands of lives saved. The combined cost of the efforts that create these changes is little more than one-half of 1 percent of global military expenditure.

NOTES

Much of this chapter, including all the statistics and graphs, is drawn from Human Security Center, *Human Security Report 2005: War and Peace in the Twenty-first Century* (New York: Oxford University Press, 2005). By permission of Oxford University Press, Inc.

1. See Human Security Centre, *Human Security Report 2005: War and Peace in the Twenty-first Century* (New York: Oxford University Press, 2005).

2. Among the first to draw attention to the decline were Monty Marshall and Ted Gurr, then of the University of Maryland, and researchers at the International Peace Research Institute, Oslo, and the Conflict Data Program at Uppsala University in Sweden.

3. Armed conflicts are here defined as violent armed political confrontations that have at least twenty-five battle-related deaths a year and that involve a government as one of the belligerents. Wars are armed conflicts with one thousand or more battle-related deaths a year. Most data sets count only conflicts between states or between a state and a rebel group, but a new data set created by Uppsala University's Conflict Data Program for the Human Security Report project also counts conflicts between nonstate groups in which a government is not one of the warring parties.

4. The new data set includes deaths from intercommunal violence and "one-sided" attacks on civilians that had not been counted previously.

5. There is a clear association between states that are major abusers of core human rights and international conflict (see Mary Caprioli and Peter F. Trumbore, "Human Rights Rogues in Interstate Conflicts, 1980–2001," *Journal of Peace Research* 43, no. 2 [March 2006]). The relationship between human rights abuse and civil wars is more complex. The econometric literature on the causes of armed conflict indicates that moves from autocracy toward greater political rights are associated with increased risks of armed conflict. But it is also clear that effective repression can repress human rights and the risk of war at the same time. For example, the decline in armed conflict in the Middle East and North Africa that began in the early 1980s has been associated with an increase in political repression.

6. One rare exception is the collection of terrorism and human rights data by the U.S. government. But these data sets—particularly those dealing with terrorism—have been subject to considerable criticism with respect to methodology and bias.

7. Association is not the same as cause, of course. War has aptly been described as "development in reverse," and it is clear that in many countries low incomes are a consequence of war. In fact, the causal relationships run in both directions

8. Suggestive evidence for the long-term impact of economic growth in reducing the risk of armed conflict comes from East and Southeast Asia, where the number of armed conflicts declined as economic growth in the region accelerated from the mid-1970s. In contrast, in sub-Saharan Africa conflicts rose throughout much of the 1990s while GDP per capita fell.

9. Victor Asal and Amy Pate, "The Decline of Ethnic Political Discrimination, 1950–2003," in *Peace and Conflict 2005: A Global Survey of Armed Conflicts, Self-Determination Movements, and Democracy,* ed. Monty G. Marshall and Ted Robert Gurr (College Park: Center for International Development and Conflict Management, University of Maryland, 2005), 28–38.

10. Ibid.

11. RAND Corporation, "RAND Study Says UN Nation Building Record Compares Favorably with the US in Some Respects," press release, February 18, 2005, http://www.rand.org/news/press.05/02.18.html (accessed July 26, 2005).

12. See International Rescue Committee, "The Lancet Publishes IRC Mortality Study from DR Congo; 3.9 Million Have Died: 38,000 Die per Month," January 6, 2006, http://www.theirc.org/news/page.jsp?itemID=27819067.

13. The Brahimi Report took its name from its chairman, former Algerian foreign minister Lakhdar Brahimi. Its official title is *Report of the Panel on United Nations Peace Operations.* For a brief description, see http://www.un.org/peace/reports/peace_operations/docs/pr1.htm.

14. See United Nations High-Level Panel on Threats, Challenges, and Change, *A More Secure World: Our Shared Responsibility* (New York: United Nations, 2004), http://www.un.org/secureworld.

15. As is so often the case in the United Nations, the success—or failure—of the exercise will depend less on formal structures than on the caliber of the people appointed to the key posts.

30

NEW ROLES FOR REGIONAL ORGANIZATIONS

Paul F. Diehl

ARTICLE 52 OF THE UN CHARTER explicitly recognizes certain roles for regional organizations in the promotion of international peace and security. Yet that same document makes it clear that such roles are to be inherently limited. First, regional organizations are confined to geographically narrow ("regional" or "local") disputes, as opposed to those with broader scope and potential impact. Second, regional organizations are clearly to be subordinate to the United Nations Security Council, which retains supervisory authority over regional actions as well as the right to supersede regional efforts if necessary. For much of the Cold War era, regional organizations performed those limited roles in conflict management, more likely because of their underdevelopment rather than for reasons of strict adherence to UN Charter norms.

With the end of the Cold War, regional organizations have assumed increasingly varied, and in some cases primary, roles in conflict management. The contention in this chapter is that regional organizations have increased,

in some cases dramatically, their conflict management activities, but that (1) there is tremendous variation across organizations and (2) this increase has not come at the expense of the United Nations but is parallel to the trend toward general increases in global conflict management. Furthermore, regional organization efforts have some advantages and disadvantages relative to those global activities, making the former less than clear substitutes for the latter.

REGIONAL ORGANIZATIONS AND CONFLICT MANAGEMENT

The range of conflict management options open to regional organizations is essentially the same as that available to the United Nations.[1] Conflict management encompasses a range of actions, all designed to promote the prevention, mitigation, and ultimately resolution of conflict. One can conceive of a continuum of conflict management activities that vary according to the level of commitment (resources and political) required and the operational level of the activity.[2]

At the lower end of the continuum, regional organizations create norms on a variety of subjects, several of which may promote peace and security in the region. For example, there is a strong norm of democratization in the Western Hemisphere, fostered by the Organization of American States (OAS).[3] This norm not only discourages extraconstitutional regime change, which could promote regional instability, but also may promote peaceful conflict management indirectly, given that democratic states are less likely to fight one another and more likely to adopt peaceful dispute resolution mechanisms.[4]

More directly, regional organizations pass normative resolutions or issue statements on particular threats to regional order. The Association of Southeast Asian Nations (ASEAN) issued a declaration in 1992 calling for the peaceful resolution of disputes surrounding the Spratly Islands and the South China Sea. More specific to a given event, the North Atlantic Treaty Organization (NATO) issued a declaration on terrorism following the Madrid train bombings in 2004. Such actions serve to promote the interests of a region's members broadly and consequently are not necessarily expected to have an immediate impact. In contrast, other normative actions are designed to promote immediate changes in behavior by member states. For example, following a military coup in Ecuador in 2000, the OAS passed resolutions denouncing this action and called for the restoration of the democratically elected president.[5]

Moving along a continuum indicating greater commitment and more operational activities, regional organizations undertake a variety of diplomatic efforts to advance peace and security. Diplomatic efforts, such as mediation, assume that conflicts cannot ultimately be managed or resolved except by the disputants themselves. Diplomatic efforts are able to achieve conflict management in a number of different ways, most notably by bringing the parties in dispute together when they otherwise might not negotiate with one another. Political pressure and the prospect of legitimacy and prestige are elements that allow the regional organization to bring warring parties to the bargaining table. Regional organizations and their representatives may also play an active role in the negotiations themselves. They may clarify the positions of the parties, redefine the issues,[6] serve as conduits for negotiation, pressure each side to make concessions, and formulate alternative proposals. Regional organizations may also play a role in providing additional incentives for the parties to come to an agreement, such as economic or political aid. Regional groups or their members might also offer themselves as guarantors of any conflict management agreement, undertaking an ongoing role in the implementation of the peace agreement.

There are several conditions under which regional organizations develop norms and promote cooperation. One is in response to ongoing crises and war. The European Union (EU) was among the first actors to respond to the internationalized civil war in Bosnia, dispatching a peace mission led by former NATO secretary-general Lord Carrington. Similarly, the Southern African Development Community (SADC) was instrumental in the negotiations of the 1999 Lusaka Accords dealing with the war in the Democratic Republic of the Congo (formerly Zaire).[7] Regional organizations also respond to long-term threats to peace and security, sometimes by constructing norms on weapons or by facilitating arms control cooperation. For example, the Arms Control and Regional Security (ACRS) initiative in the Middle East was a (failed) effort to achieve arms control in that region.[8] Finally, some regions have moved beyond traditional security concerns to emerging topics on the security agenda, with the goal of establishing joint rules and norms. Such concerns include drug trafficking, terrorism, and "human security" problems, with Latin American organizations being the most involved in these areas.[9]

Regional organizations may also initiate sanctions against a state, an action requiring considerable political commitment from the organizations' members and potentially incurring some economic costs. Sanctions include, most commonly, restrictions on trading certain goods with a given state as well as arms embargoes directed against an entire region. The Organization of African Unity (OAU) maintained sanctions for years against the apartheid regime in South Africa. Similarly, the OAS has excluded Cuba from its membership. Of course, the imposition of economic sanctions may be done as much (or more so) for normative reasons as for inducing a change in behavior.

Moving toward the other end of the continuum, regional organizations also participate in a range of activities that fall under the peacekeeping rubric; one might include a series of related operational activities (e.g., election supervision) in this category as well. Traditional peacekeeping refers to the deployment of lightly armed troops in response to threats to regional security or in response to ongoing wars, as in Congo. Peacekeeping may entail a variety of functions, including cease-fire monitoring, humanitarian assistance, postconflict reconstruction, and arms control verification. An example of a regional peacekeeping effort is the operation in Liberia authorized by the Economic Community of West African States (ECOWAS), referred to as ECOMOG (ECOWAS Monitoring Group). Regional organizations might also promote conflict resolution and democratic institutions in ethnically divided states, a role taken on by the Organization for Security and Cooperation in Europe (OSCE).

The most coercive set of options, requiring the greatest political and resource commitments, can be categorized as enforcement. Traditionally, enforcement refers to large-scale military operations designed to defend the victims of aggression and restore peace and security by the defeat of aggressor forces; enforcement may also be designed to impose a particular solution in a given conflict.[10] This strategy relies on the deterrent value of collective military action; if deterrence fails, however, states need to carry out the threatened military action and restore peace and security in the region. A recent example of this is NATO's actions against the former Yugoslavia in Kosovo. Enforcement actions can be roughly subdivided into two types. The first is *collective security*, in which a coalition of states, generally acting through an international organization, seeks to deter or defeat (if necessary) any coalition member(s) that uses military force to alter the status quo. A second type is what has been referred to as *collective defense*. This also involves deterrence or military action against an aggressor but is more often the product of a traditional military alliance rather than an international governmental organization. The original role of the NATO alliance in Europe is the prototypical example.

PATTERNS OF REGIONAL ORGANIZATION INVOLVEMENT

During the Cold War, regional organizations played limited roles in conflict management. At the diplomatic level, some regional groups responded to crises in their regions, but such a response was far from assured. The OAS actually handled eleven cases during the 1960s, largely on a consensual basis with respect to the normative actions taken. This level of cooperation disintegrated, however, in the following two decades, and the organization became considerably less active in security affairs.[11] In several cases (e.g., Panama), U.S. unilateral action replaced collective policy in the region. Similarly, the League of Arab States (LAS) convened to discuss the first crisis between Iraq and Kuwait in 1961, but the organization was largely paralyzed in handling disputes among its other members in the following decades; only with respect to policy toward Israel did there seem to be broad, although not universal, consensus on joint action.[12]

Regional organizations partook in peacekeeping operations during the Cold War era, but only in a very limited fashion. The OAU launched an operation in Chad in the early 1980s, but with largely disastrous results.[13] Other operations seemed to resemble enforcement operations as opposed to conventional peacekeeping, serving the interests of leading states in the region as much as, or more than, the region members as a whole. For example, the Inter-American Peace Force, which followed the U.S. invasion of the Dominican Republic in 1965, and the Syrian intervention in Lebanon in the mid-1970s, sanctioned by the League of Arab States, were largely multilateral actions in name only. With respect to enforcement actions, no regional organization carried out a true collective security military action. NATO and the Warsaw Pact were active military alliances, pursuing deterrent strategies against each other; except for the use of Warsaw Pact troops in putting down dissent in Czechoslovakia, however, neither alliance carried out missions on the battlefield and indeed had no need to do so.

From the late 1980s and early 1990s to the present time, there has been a dramatic upsurge in regional conflict management activities of all forms. Regional organizations dramatically increased their mediation attempts; before 1975, regional organizations conducted only an average of two mediation attempts per year, whereas after 1989, these averaged almost twenty per year.[14] African organizations have become more involved diplomatically, reflecting a change in norms on that continent. The OAU was a historically weak organization that took little direct action in the region, adhering to a strict interpretation of national sovereignty. Its successor, the African Union (AU), has attempted to play a much more activist role.[15] Normatively, the OAU/AU passed

several resolutions on the Ethiopian-Eritrean conflict as well as the dispute over the disposition of the Comorian island of Mayotte. It also drafted a treaty on a nuclear weapons–free zone and one on preventing and combating terrorism, the latter several years before the 9/11 attacks.

The European Union has also expanded its security role and has been extensively involved in mediation, especially during the Bosnian war. In its formative decades, the European Union concentrated on cooperation in economic and social areas. In the past decade, it has attempted to form common defense and foreign policies, allowing the organization to take collective action when regional threats to security arise, as was the case in Macedonia and Kosovo. The European Union also devoted attention to old problems (e.g., Cyprus) that had been largely ignored previously, because they had implications for membership expansion. The OSCE as well has played the role of mediator, most visibly in the Nagorno-Karabakh conflict between Armenia and Azerbaijan. Furthermore, NATO also adopted normative positions, passing resolutions and issuing statements on, among other subjects, Albania, nuclear tests in Pakistan, Georgia, and Iraq (note that each of these situations would have been considered "out of area" during the Cold War and therefore not within NATO purview).[16]

There has been perhaps no more visible expansion of regional organization efforts than in the area of peacekeeping.[17] The total number of regional peacekeeping operations increased dramatically from nine before 1989 to thirty-one begun thereafter.[18] In Africa alone since 1990, regional organizations have conducted ten peace operations. ECOWAS has carried out half of these operations, most prominently in Liberia. The AU deployment in the Sudan also received considerable attention. Although regional peacekeeping has grown most in Africa, that continent is not alone in seeing more peace operations carried out by regional groupings. NATO has transformed itself from a purely military alliance to an organization that now carries out various peace operations, as in Bosnia, Kosovo, and Afghanistan. The European Union has also begun operational activities, taking over for NATO in Bosnia and carrying out missions in Kosovo. The Commonwealth of Independent States (CIS) has also sent troops to Moldova, Georgia, and Tajikistan, although as with Cold War peacekeeping, these operations were largely national efforts (here by Russia) with the imprimatur of a regional association.

The increase in regional conflict management has not come at the expense of global efforts. UN-sponsored mediation has increased at a faster rate than that of regional organizations. Furthermore, the United Nations has conducted more than three times as many peace operations since 1988 than it did in the previous forty-three years, with an accompanying expansion of mission scope as well. Peace operations overall have increased since the end of the Cold War, with regional organizations dramatically expanding the number of operations, but the ratio of regional to global operations has stayed about the same.[19] Also, regional organizations have partnered with the United Nations in carrying out some missions, making the global-regional distinction somewhat misleading; for example, CIS peacekeeping forces cooperated with the UN mission in Tajikistan (UNMOT).

Finally, regional organizations have conducted some enforcement operations as well. NATO's bombing of Kosovo, as well as its subsequent occupation, was the closest to being a traditional military operation. ECOWAS has also carried out missions with some enforcement elements to them, including in Sierra Leone and Côte d'Ivoire. This is not to say that regional organizations have not approved military action taken by their members—for example, the Organization of East Caribbean States sanctioned the U.S. invasion of Grenada in 1983—yet such instances provide what Inis Claude referred to as "collective legitimatization"[20] to national actions rather than evidence of regional action per se.

REASONS FOR GREATER REGIONALISM

There are a number of reasons for a greater emphasis on conflict management at the regional level. Most obvious is that the demand for conflict management has increased as well, evidenced by an increase in armed conflicts over the past two decades.[21] Interstate war has remained constant or even declined since the end of the Cold War. Intrastate or civil conflict has increased both in number and variety. The international system has seen an increase in the number of civil wars over the past two decades, many with significant negative externalities, including fighting and refugees streaming across the borders.[22] Beyond traditional civil wars, the world has experienced a relatively new phenomenon—"failed" or "disrupted" states. Such entities also foster instability in regions as well as carrying a human toll that may exceed that from civil wars. Global organizations and their members have been overburdened with these challenges, resulting in limited attention to some areas as well as donor fatigue. The United Nations and leading states have also chosen to ignore certain wars or failed states. This leaves gaps that have been filled by regional organizations, many of which cannot afford to ignore the conflicts and problems at their doorsteps. Yet any increase in armed conflict cannot alone account for the magnitude of the upsurge in regional conflict management.[23] Other factors are at work as well.

The end of the Cold War has had some ancillary effects beyond establishing U.S. unipolarity. During the Cold War, the superpowers often assumed primary roles in regional conflicts. Within their respective spheres of influence, the United States and the Soviet Union were able to suppress most violent conflict, through either direct military intervention or at least the threat of it. To the extent that regional organizations and efforts existed, they were largely subordinate to the interests and directions of the leading states. Beyond the Western Hemisphere and Eastern Europe, the superpowers were as frequently involved in exacerbating conflict as they were in mitigating it. Most notably in Africa and the Middle East, the superpowers supplied arms and political support to client groups and states. When the superpowers did "cooperate"[24] to manage conflict, it was frequently to prevent escalation of those conflicts that might have drawn themselves into the fray. Rare were the instances in which the two leading states sought to resolve a conflict fully with joint action. The end of the Cold War created a vacuum in some regions and new opportunities for regional efforts to fill the gaps.

The end of the Cold War also led to a change in the international security environment and the interests of the leading states. With a few exceptions, such as the Iraqi invasion of Kuwait, regional conflicts no longer directly affected the economic and security interests of Western states. Furthermore, domestic political support in those same states for intervention into regional conflicts has also declined (and strategic doctrines have been adjusted accordingly).[25] Leading states may seek regional arrangements as alternatives to bilateral alliances and unilateral actions.[26] This is not to say that such states will wholly abandon such initiatives (indeed one might suggest that unilateral actions have increased in recent decades), but merely that some conflicts will be dumped or subcontracted to regional groupings.

The movement toward regional conflict management, however, is not solely a function of the Cold War's demise. Some of the recent regional efforts follow on the heels of failed global efforts, especially by the United Nations. In the early 1990s, there was optimism that the United Nations would play a major role in addressing threats to international peace and security. These hopes were only enhanced by the global cooperation in redressing Iraq's invasion of Kuwait. Yet the limits of a new world order were quickly apparent as failed peacekeeping in Somalia, genocide in Rwanda, and war in Bosnia exposed flaws in global efforts. As optimism faded by the middle of the 1990s, regional alternatives to UN-sponsored efforts began to emerge.

REGIONAL ADVANTAGES AND DISADVANTAGES

Possible Advantages

Overall, regional organizations have no record of performance superior (or indeed inferior) to that of the United Nations in conflict management.[27] Nevertheless, there are differences between the two kinds of organizations. Although one might expect regional conflict management efforts to experience success and failure for many of the same reasons as UN efforts, the former may have some unique advantages, including greater consensus in the organization, greater support from the disputants, heightened chances for conflict resolution, and more control over third-party states.

Greater Consensus in the Organization. One might expect regional organizations to have an advantage over the United Nations because their membership is more homogeneous.[28] States in a regional organization are more likely to be at the same development level; share historical, ethnic, or tribal roots; and have similar political outlooks stemming from facing common regional problems. These commonalities are supposed to provide greater consensus among the members and make authorization of conflict management easier, as there will be fewer disagreements blocking strong action. Regional organizations are also not constrained, as is the United Nations, by the veto power of leading members.[29] Indeed, some regional organizations have adopted procedures to avoid such a deadlock; the OSCE rule on "consensus minus one" allows it to take action against any one of its members.[30]

In practice, these expectations have often gone unfulfilled. One often finds great splits among members of regional organizations when dealing with regional conflicts. For example, the LAS was virtually paralyzed during the Iran-Iraq War and the Iraqi invasion of Kuwait because its members were strongly divided in their loyalties to the protagonists. Regional animosities also tend to hamper regional organizations' actions. Unity from homogeneity comes in response to threats to security external to the organization, such as Arab unity against Israel or African support for decolonization in Angola. The most common threats to regional peace, however— internal threats—are exactly those least likely to generate consensus. It is of course conceivable that, for certain conflicts, regional organizations may be able to achieve greater consensus and act more swiftly than the United Nations. Nevertheless, regional groupings have no inherent advantage on this point, and one might suggest that a disinterested global organization in a post–Cold War world may actually be better able to limit local conflict.[31]

Greater Support from the Disputants. A second possible advantage for regional organizations is that the support given them by the disputants and the local population will be greater than for comparable UN efforts. This argument relies on the notion that the people and governments in a region have a natural affinity with those in that geographic area and an inherent suspicion of what they perceive as outside intervention. Thus, there are frequently calls for "Arab" or "African" solutions to regional conflicts before international forces intervene. Disputants may be more accepting of actions by a regional organization, but, just as important, subnational groups and others in the conflicting states may see such actions as more legitimate.[32]

To the extent that regional actions can generate more support than UN missions, they have an important advantage. Yet they must clear two hurdles that may frequently trip up such attempts. First, the organization must reach sufficient consensus to authorize the mission, in order to give it legitimacy, far from a foregone conclusion in most cases. Second, and more directly to this point, a regional organization must be accepted as an honest broker in the conflict. This again may be difficult to achieve. For example, an OAS operation that is led by the United States and that may serve U.S. interests will have less legitimacy than a UN force. A Nigerian-led force in West Africa would encounter similar difficulties. If the conflict at hand causes divisions in the region as a whole, then any action is unlikely to receive authorization and, even if approved, may not be perceived as impartial or fair by all parties. Thus, while the advantage of greater support is true in theory, it is less likely to be manifest in practice.

Heightened Chances for Conflict Resolution. Regional efforts may also be better at promoting conflict resolution than is the United Nations, which has tended to respond to crises with Band-Aid solutions to security problems, with limited follow-up diplomatic efforts. The United Nations has often helped negotiate cease-fires and/or deployed peacekeeping troops *prior to* conflict resolution (e.g., in Cyprus), but it has not often facilitated a final peace settlement once those peacekeepers are in place. The net effect is that the international community and the protagonists themselves may be discouraged from pursuing further diplomacy to resolve the disputes and from reaching a settlement if negotiations do occur.[33] At best, the United Nations has waited until a settlement was reached to deploy peacekeepers and carry out peacebuilding activities, but such a settlement may never occur or take place too late to save hundreds or thousands of lives. Regional organizations may be more concerned with resolving the underlying conflict because the implications are much greater for the states in the area. Furthermore, they may more closely tie passing resolutions and the stationing of peacekeeping troops to a mechanism, such as negotiations, or to an actual settlement plan, such as elections for resolving the dispute. In this way, there is hope that regional organizations can not only promote conflict management but facilitate final conflict resolution as well.

In theory, this contention offers little with which to quibble. In practice, much depends on the success of those regional diplomatic efforts and the form that they take. Regional organizations such as the OAU and the Arab League have followed peacekeeping efforts with extensive diplomatic initiatives, yet reconciliation attempts in Lebanon and Chad, for example, have not always been successful in the long run. Intervention by regional organizations is not necessarily any more successful than global efforts, even though it may be more frequent. Indeed, the formulation of the Vance-Owen plan for Bosnia, a joint effort of the European Union and the United Nations, was a failure; the Dayton Peace Accords, largely a U.S. initiative, came about after multiple failures by both organizations.

More Control over Third-Party States. A final possible advantage of regional conflict management efforts is that they may be better able to secure the support of the interested third-party states, who will almost certainly participate in the debate and authorization of any action, whereas they may not in a UN forum. Interested third parties are those that border the affected area and/or have significant economic and security interests in the conflict (e.g., Syria in Lebanon, Vietnam in Cambodia). In this way, the third-party state has a better chance of modifying the operation according to its views and is more likely to support it. More important, it is less likely to sabotage the organization's efforts, a major

cause of the failure of UN peacekeeping operations[34] and economic sanctions.

Although this advantage is by no means guaranteed, the support of third-party states is a definite benefit for regional efforts and constitutes the primary advantage over activities run by global organizations or multinational configurations. Yet one must recognize that there may be instances in which a third-party state is not cooperative with a regional effort (e.g., Israel in any LAS action), and regional groups still have to contend with potential opposition from subnational actors, much as the United Nations does. Third-party opposition might also prevent the regional organization from taking any action.

Possible Disadvantages

Regional organizations may also face situational constraints when dealing with external threats to regional peace and the involvement of regional powers.

Little Control over External Threats. An inclusive global organization by definition has no limitations on the geographic scope of its actions (except those set by national sovereignty) or on its theoretical capability to deal with threats to international peace and security. Regional organizations, in contrast, may have problems with conflicts that involve external intervention. On the one hand, there may be greater consensus in the organization when external threats are present. The OAU was created, in part, to eliminate colonialism and extraregional interference in African affairs. The OAS is in some ways an extension of the Monroe Doctrine and its solidarity against external attack. One might anticipate fewer problems with internal consensus in such cases.

Effective conflict management, however, depends on more than consensus in the authorizing organization. All disputants and relevant third parties must acquiesce or cooperate if the mission is to be successful. Unfortunately, regional organizations do not have the political influence, moral suasion, or means of coercion to convince external powers to cooperate in conflict management efforts. The United Nations had enough difficulties convincing Belgium to refrain from hostile acts during the Congo operation in the 1960s. Similarly, the Gulf Cooperation Council (GCC) can do little to ensure Israeli or Iraqi cooperation in any conflict in the area. Only a global organization can deal effectively with threats from states external to the region or organization. The advantage that regional organizations have in bringing in interested third-party states disappears if those states are at the heart of the conflict and are external to the region.

The Inability to Restrain Regional Powers. A consistent theme in the analysis of regional organizations is their inability to take concerted action against their most powerful members.[35] Regional operations are unlikely to be authorized in conflicts that directly involve the global powers or regional powers. The organization has neither the political clout nor the resources to mount an operation opposed or not actively supported by those states. A regionally powerful state would be able to resist pressure to support any action, and even were one authorized, the hegemon could effectively sabotage the mission through direct action or covertly through intermediate actors. This condition necessarily confines strong regional responses to conflicts between or within smaller states.

The problem of dealing with a hegemon is most evident in the Western Hemisphere. The OAS has been unable to mount any effective operational action that is not supported by the United States. Although the United Nations might also face difficulties in gaining U.S. cooperation for a peacekeeping operation in Panama, for example, the possibility seems foreclosed in the case of the OAS. Other regions may have fewer problems, at least given current power configurations. Any regional arrangement in Asia would have difficulty restraining Chinese or Japanese behavior.

Similarly, a variety of regional and subregional organizations in Africa probably could not compel South Africa to halt any transgression it might commit.

In general, only the United Nations offers the potential to restrain a regional power, although perhaps not a superpower. The United Nations has the resources, even without the cooperation of some states, and it has the political power to pressure states to accede to its peacekeeping operations. The inability to restrain regional hegemons is a major disadvantage to regional initiatives.

VARIATIONS ACROSS REGIONAL ORGANIZATIONS

To this point, we have juxtaposed regional organizations against the United Nations, treating the former as a homogeneous grouping for analytical purposes. In fact, there is tremendous variation across regional organizations with respect to conflict management. Such differences include the frequency and type of involvement as well as the organizations' likely capacity for playing important future roles in their regions.[36] A number of significant differences in characteristics account for such wide variation in performance.

Threats

To some extent, international organizations tend to handle the most serious conflicts. Lesser disputes either are resolved with outside intervention or are not considered worthy of international organizations, which are primarily reactive and crisis driven in terms of what kinds of conflicts appear on agendas. Yet no single configuration of threats fits all regions. Accordingly, some regions must deal with more intractable conflicts, and therefore regional associations in those areas may be less likely to take action and less likely to succeed when they do.[37]

Perhaps not surprisingly, the most successful regional organizations have been those dealing with the least serious threats, ceteris paribus.[38] South America has had little need for collective conflict management since 1990 and correspondingly has been quite effective in dealing with lower-level threats to security.[39] Similarly, Western Europe has been largely free of the most dangerous and protracted forms of conflict, allowing its institutions to concentrate on newer security issues and to direct attention to security problems in the eastern part of the continent.

The most notable variation in threats has been with respect to ethnic conflict and "weak states." These problems have been prevalent in Africa,[40] but almost nonexistent in the Western Hemisphere (with the exception of Haiti). The reason that ethnic conflicts and weak states are key problems for regional conflict management is that these conflicts have significant negative externalities. Historically, internal conflicts were not considered to be in the purview of regional organizations but rather were something to be dealt with solely by the state itself. This represented a "hard-shell" view of state sovereignty. Many members of the African Union have objected to any military intervention in Darfur, Sudan, on sovereignty grounds. At the same time, ethnic conflicts and weak states have contributed to greater prospects for intervention by neighboring states, independent of regional organizations. The recent Congo conflict is the most egregious case of direct intervention in a civil war; there, a number of neighboring states sent troops to fight for and against various Congolese factions. This makes it almost impossible for a regional organization to reach consensus on taking action.

Another problematic threat to regional peace and security comes from territorial disputes, in which states fight over the possession of a piece of land, usually geographically contiguous to both sides. Especially dangerous are those disputes that involve territory that is valued for its intangible rather than tangible qualities; that is, religious, ethnic, and historical claims

to a territory make it more difficult to find compromise positions than do those territorial disputes over resources or defense concerns.[41] Some boundary disputes persist in Latin America, but most of these are of the less salient variety. One of the reasons that Latin America is alleged to be a "zone of peace" is that it had largely settled its borders by the end of the nineteenth century.[42] The same cannot be said for all the other regions of the world, and this has significant implications for the effectiveness of regional organization efforts. Africa still suffers from the results of the 1885 Berlin Conference, in which its colonial borders were drawn without reference to historical delineation or the groups living within various territories. This has been somewhat mitigated, however, by the agreement among African leaders around the time of independence that state borders would not be altered by military force. South Asia also must deal with territorial disputes, most notably the dispute over Kashmir and the problems along the Indian-Chinese border. Most border issues have been settled in Europe, although some disputes (e.g., in Cyprus and the Balkans) have proved intractable for European institutions.

Internal Rivalries

Related to the kinds of threats that a region faces is the presence of internal rivalries between its members. Such rivalries not only may present conflicts that are difficult to manage but also may paralyze attempts at collective action by the regional association. Regional wars and other serious threats to peace seem to coalesce around these rivalries.[43] We know that such rivalries, often labeled "enduring rivalries" in the scholarly literature, are the greatest threats to peace.[44] Similarly, the multifaceted Arab-Israeli rivalry (in actuality, several intertwined rivalries) represents the greatest threat to peace in that region. Other regions of the world are less defined by one or more central rivalries. Europe traditionally revolved around the U.S.-Soviet rivalry but no longer has its security arrangements organized around that competition. Latin America certainly has had traditional rivalries (e.g., Argentina-Chile), but these had more limited negative externalities.

A comparison of Asia and Europe reveals how rivalries affect regional conflict management efforts.[45] ASEAN+3 states (ten members plus China, Japan, and South Korea) are involved in nineteen rivalries, as of 2001, with a number of patterns relevant for regional conflict management. First, several of the rivalries reflect a common external enemy—North Korea. Nevertheless, a closer inspection reveals that although China, Japan, and South Korea share some interests with respect to North Korea (e.g., limiting nuclear proliferation), their preferences and policies with respect to that country are by no means convergent. Furthermore, each of those three states has rivalries *with the other two*. Thus, although some cooperation with respect to foreign policy might be forthcoming, there is certainly not a broad basis for regional cooperation centered on North Korea. The lack of a common external enemy has long been a limiting factor in furthering Asian security cooperation.[46]

Second, and related to the previous point, eleven of the rivalries are internal to the ASEAN+3 grouping; that is, these states are more likely to fight one another than an external enemy. Most notable are the rivalries between three of the largest economic forces in the grouping—China, Japan, and South Korea (the +3 states). Indeed, the presumed leading states in the coalition—China and Japan—are involved in eleven rivalries, including against each other. Yet there are several crosscutting rivalries as well, most critically the disagreement over the Spratly Islands, which involves China, the Philippines, Malaysia, Vietnam, and Brunei. Until the major-power rivalries and to a lesser extent the controversy surrounding the Spratlys are resolved, there will be limits to how far the ASEAN+3 states can cooperate on regional security matters.

EU states stand in marked contrast to those in Asia. Although there are seventeen rivalries involving European states, most of them concern a common external opponent—the former Yugoslavia. These military confrontations with Yugoslavia stem from the Bosnian war, and many involve joint NATO actions in Kosovo. If anything, they reveal a common approach to regional security. Importantly, none of the rivalries is internal to the organization; of course, that could change if and when Turkey joins the European Union. Still, it appears that European states have largely resolved internal squabbles, as a consequence of past integration efforts, but also as a pathway to further cooperative efforts in the security area.

Mandate/Authority and Institutions

The ability of regional organizations to play significant roles in conflict management is largely conditioned by the authority granted to them by their members.[47] In some cases, no security institution at all exists in a region. For example, the north Asian region has no regional organization to handle conflict management.[48] In other parts of Asia, the institutions are relatively weak. The South Asian Association for Regional Cooperation (SAARC) provides for cooperation only in the social and economic issue areas. By definition then, it is unable to exercise any significant role in the Indo-Pakistani conflict, except very indirectly and then only through a functionalist approach to peace.[49] Other regional organizations, such as ASEAN, are similarly handicapped by limited mandates for security action. ASEAN action, in particular, has been limited to normative declarations. ASEAN has taken some recent steps[50] to clarify its decision rules, but the organization has not committed itself to the use of military force and has reaffirmed its principle of noninterference in the internal affairs of members.

In other regions, the mandates of organizations and the level of institutionalization vary widely. Until recently, the African Union was structurally weak, often little more than a forum for yearly meetings of heads of state on that continent. Much of this may be a backlash against UN involvement in Congo during the 1960s and a preference for nonintervention of any variety by outside actors. Indeed, the predecessor OAU prohibited alliances among its members, effectively foreclosing collective security options. Accordingly, to the extent that it was involved in peacemaking activities, the organization operated through ad hoc committees.[51] The AU has expanded its activities to include election monitoring and peacekeeping. It also made provisions in 2005 for a nonaggression and common defense agreement, although it is not clear that this addresses some of the main security threats there, including civil war and failed states.

Several regional organizations have the legal provisions to undertake a variety of different kinds of actions. The Organization of American States has collective security provisions contained in its charter (Article 28) as well as provisions for other kinds of actions, although most of these are directed against extraregional threats or interstate aggression, rather than being internal matters. Similarly, the GCC and the LAS also have collective security provisions at their disposal. Some regional entities also contain conflict management provisions, even if their primary purposes are in the economic realm. For example, several regional trade associations in Africa include mechanisms for conflict management when disputes arise over resources.[52]

At the other extreme of the continuum is the European region, which has multiple institutions for dealing with security. These have overlapping memberships and complementary roles. Of longest-standing import is NATO, which traditionally handled the duties for collective security and collective defense. Since the end of the Cold War, its missions have been modified and it now functions as a peacekeeper in Bosnia and Afghanistan. The European Union has extended its authority in the security realm with a common defense policy and various diplomatic initiatives. NATO and the European Union are supplemented by the West European Union (WEU) and the Organization for Security and Cooperation in Europe, the latter of which has been involved in ethnic conflicts and election supervision.

Thus, to a large extent, the roles of regional organizations will be determined by the mandates given to them and the extant institutional arrangements to give them effect. Yet authority for action does not guarantee action, as resources and hegemony limitations will affect when and how action is taken by the regional organization.

Resources

Merely having the authority to carry out a conflict management activity is not enough if the organization lacks the requisite resources to take effective action. "Resources" in this context refers to the financial, political, and in some cases military/logistical capacity to take action. Organizations are not inherently endowed with such capacities but must rely on members for their provision for operational activities. The alternative is that conflict management actions will be confined to normative and diplomatic initiatives, which require few tangible resources.

Some operations, specifically peacekeeping, collective security, and humanitarian assistance, require large amounts of money to pay for supplies and personnel. A number of regional organizations (e.g., SADC) are composed of less developed states that lack the capacity for adequately constructing such operations, much less sustaining them. Increasingly, such organizations have appealed for support (i.e., financial, logistical, training) from the United Nations, NGOs, or leading states in the world system to carry out missions; to a limited extent, this has mitigated some of the problems encountered. This may be more common in the future as global actors "subcontract" activities they are unwilling to perform to regional organizations and others.[53] In contrast, wealthier institutions, such as the European Union, have the financial ability to run peacekeeping operations, for example, for long periods of time; this is not to say that financial concerns are absent, but rather that the reluctance of those organizations to allocate funds comes from political motivations rather than financial exigencies.

The presence of financial resources alone is not a guarantee of effectiveness for a regional organization. The organization and its members must also have political capital to influence regional activities. There is little doubt that the GCC, made up of six oil-rich Arab states, has the financial resources to fund almost any operation, but its members (save perhaps Saudi Arabia) are weak politically and militarily and are unable to broadly affect policy in the Middle East.[54] One might speculate that any subregional organization with small membership would encounter this problem.

Military resources are the third component distinguishing effective regional organizations from their less effective counterparts elsewhere. NATO clearly has the military training, logistics, and personnel to carry out a broad range of operations, even beyond the immediate European theater. Other regional organizations must draw on poorly trained and equipped military personnel from their member states, and those militaries often lack long-force projection capabilities. The net effect is that some coercive options are foreclosed for those regional institutions. When such operations are authorized, they may have suboptimal numbers of personnel, and soldiers and other organizational staff may be especially prone to commit abuses (e.g., rape, looting).

Hegemony

Two aspects of hegemony account for variations in regional conflict management effectiveness. First, competition for regional influence among association members is a source of conflict and one difficult to resolve. In the European theater, this was a major source of war for centuries. Such competition has been largely muted there; to the extent that such competition still exists, it is largely played out in the economic and political institutions of the European Union. In contrast, in the Middle East, Arab states (traditionally Iran, Iraq, Egypt, and Syria) may be somewhat united in their support of the Palestinian cause, but they still see one another as competitors for pan-Arab influence or leadership. These competitions are difficult for regional associations to handle because members may have allied with different sides in the competition. Even absent that, the association may be unable to broker an agreement and take action when the leading members of the organization are directly involved.

Second, even when one state has clearly established itself as a regional hegemon, the consequences for regional conflict management efforts are not necessarily promising. Regional organizations will largely be incapable of stopping regional hegemons, if those states are the source of regional instability. Thus, the OAS can do little to restrain U.S. unilateral efforts,[55] and ECOWAS has not been able to regulate the abuses committed by Nigeria in organization missions. One might hypothesize that were Asia to have stronger regional organizations, it is unlikely that they could rein in China or India. Thus, when regional groupings include a hegemon, they will be less effective than associations with a more equal balance of capabilities among the membership.

SUMMARY AND CONCLUSION

Although regional organizations are referenced in the UN Charter, their importance in international relations only became evident several decades after the United Nations was founded. Much of the growth in regional associations is a recent phenomenon, and most of that growth has been in the economic rather than in the security area.[56] Nevertheless, the end of the Cold War marks a turning point, with an upsurge in regional conflict management activities, including peacekeeping and mediation, as well as an expansion of organization roles into areas such as election supervision. The increase in regional conflict management is not a function of the devolution of global governance from the United Nations to regional entities; indeed, UN conflict management actions have increased at least as much as those of regional associations. Rather, regional organizations have responded to increases in conflict demand in the post–Cold War era, a demand that has been generated by the end of the superpower competition and the failure of the United Nations in some key conflicts.

Projecting into the future, one might speculate that any future increases in regional conflict management are unlikely to come from the same sources as in the past. There is no linear trend toward more conflict in the international system, and some studies suggest that the most violent conflict is abating.[57] This is not to say that organizations in some regions may not experience heightened activity in response to certain wars (note the extensive involvement of different European organizations in the Bosnian war), but only that there is unlikely to be a uniform pattern of rising conflict. Instead, increased regional involvement will come from organizations that choose to involve themselves in a greater proportion of conflicts that occur. Such actions may come from members who decide to expand their organizations' mandates, paving the way for greater involvement in the internal affairs of members or in operational activities such as peacekeeping. Economic associations may also adopt conflict management provisions for the security realm (much as the European Union has done) as a logical extension of integration efforts or simply because such provisions become essential for increased economic cooperation (e.g., management of common pool resources such as water rights). Furthermore,

regional organizations may also increasingly promote democratic processes in a variety of ways[58] and thus directly (e.g., by supervising elections) and indirectly (democracies are less war prone) contribute to regional peace and stability.

Ultimately, one must question whether increased regional conflict management activity matters. The record of effectiveness for these associations remains mixed. Regional associations are not inherently superior (or inferior) to the United Nations in conflict management efforts. Still, it is hard to argue that regional actions are not at least as beneficial as, or superior to, inaction in most cases. Nevertheless, there is considerable variation among regional groupings with respect to institutional development, resources, security challenges, and membership, and therefore effectiveness. Given the gradual evolution of international organizations, one should not expect a global network of fully developed regional conflict management institutions anytime soon.

NOTES

The author would like to thank Tze Kwang Teo and Matthew Shafter for their research assistance.

1. See, for example, Connie Peck, *Sustainable Peace: The Role of the United Nations and Regional Organizations in Preventing Conflict* (Lanham, Md.: Rowman and Littlefield, 1998).

2. Robert Cox and Harold Jacobson, "The Framework for Inquiry," in *The Anatomy of Influence,* ed. Robert Cox and Harold Jacobson (New Haven, Conn.: Yale University Press, 1971), 1–36.

3. See Randall Parish and Mark Peceny, "Kantian Liberalism and the Collective Defense of Democracy in Latin America," *Journal of Peace Research* 39 (2002): 229–250. See also Dexter Boniface, "Is There a Democratic Norm in the Americas? An Analysis of the Organization of American States," *Global Governance* 8 (2002): 365–381.

4. Bruce Russett, *Grasping the Democratic Peace* (Princeton, N.J.: Princeton University Press, 1994);

and William Dixon, "Democracy and the Peaceful Settlement of International Conflict," *American Political Science Review* 88 (1994): 14–32.

5. Andrew Cooper and Thomas Legler, "The OAS Democratic Solidarity Paradigm: Questions of Collective and National Leadership," *Latin American Politics and Society* 43 (2001): 103–126.

6. P. Terrence Hopmann, *The Negotiation Process and the Resolution of International Conflicts* (Columbia: University of South Carolina Press, 1996).

7. I. William Zartman, "Regional Conflict Management in Africa," in *Regional Conflict Management*, ed. Paul F. Diehl and Joseph Lepgold (Lanham, Md.: Rowman and Littlefield, 2003), 81–103.

8. Peter Jones, "Negotiating Regional Security and Arms Control in the Middle East: The ACRS Experience and Beyond," *Journal of Strategic Studies* 26 (2003): 137–154.

9. See Carolyn Shaw, "Conflict Management in Latin America," in *Regional Conflict Management*, 123–152. Human security refers to protecting human freedoms and fulfillment and includes issues related to organized crime, poverty, disease, environmental degradation, and civil violence, among others.

10. Joseph Lepgold and Thomas Weiss, eds., *Collective Conflict Management and Changing World Politics* (Albany: State University of New York Press, 1998).

11. Carolyn Shaw, *Cooperation, Conflict, and Consensus in the Organization of American States* (New York: Palgrave, 2004).

12. Hussein Hassouna, *The League of Arab States and Regional Disputes* (New York: Oceana Publications, 1975).

13. Terry Mays, *Africa's First Peacekeeping Operation: The OAU in Chad, 1981–1982* (London: Praeger, 2002).

14. Paul F. Diehl and Young-Im Cho, "Passing the Buck? Regional Organizations and Conflict Management in the Post–Cold War Era," *Brown Journal of World Affairs* 12, no. 2 (2006): 191–202.

15. Ahmed Ali Salem, "Collective Security Action in the OAU: Did the OAU Need a Replacement?" in *African Regional Integration: Perspectives and Prospects—The Proceedings of the First AFRISP International Conference for Young Researchers on African Affairs,* Mohamed Ashour and Ahmed Ali Salem (Cairo: Cairo University African Regional Integration Support Project, 2005), 35–58.

16. For some discussion of NATO's adaptation to post–Cold War roles, see Patrick Morgan, "NATO and European Security: The Creative Use of an International Organization," *Journal of Strategic Studies* 26 (2003): 49–74.

17. For an overview of these regional organization efforts, see Alex Bellamy and Paul Williams, "Who's Keeping the Peace? Regionalization and Contemporary Peace Operations," *International Security* 29 (2005): 157–195.

18. Diehl and Cho, "Passing the Buck?" 14n.

19. Ibid.

20. Inis Claude, "Collective Legitimization as a Political Function of the United Nations," *International Organization* 20 (1966): 367–379.

21. Paul Hensel, "The More Things Change . . . : Recognizing and Responding to Trends in Armed Conflict," *Conflict Management and Peace Science* 19 (2002): 27–52.

22. In "Armed Conflict and Its International Dimensions, 1946–2004," *Journal of Peace Research* 42 (2005): 623–635, Lotta Harbom and Peter Wallensteen point to an increase in armed conflict, especially intrastate conflict, over the past decade and a half. See also Hensel, "The More Things Change . . . ," 22n. Yet other sources suggest a diminution of armed conflict in recent times. Much depends, however, on the baseline for comparison chosen. For example, in *Peace and Conflict 2005* (College Park, Md.: Center for International Development and Conflict Management, 2005), Monty Marshall and Ted Robert Gurr report a key finding on decreased conflict, but this refers only to conflicts with at least one thousand related deaths and therefore is better understood as a reflection of a decline in conflict magnitude rather than frequency. *The Human Security Report 2005: War and Peace in the 21st Century* (Oxford: Oxford University Press, 2005), by the Human Security Centre, also reports a decline in wars. However, because one of the report's key baselines is 1992, it is not clear whether altering that baseline would produce similar conclusions.

23. Diehl and Cho, "Passing the Buck?" 14n.

24. Edward Kolodziej and Roger Kanet, eds., *The Cold War as Cooperation: Superpower Cooperation in Regional Conflict Management* (Baltimore: Johns Hopkins University Press, 1991).

25. Edward Kolodziej, "Modeling International Security," in *Resolving Regional Conflicts*, ed. Roger Kanet (Urbana: University of Illinois Press, 1998), 11–40.

26. Good illustrations are U.S. efforts in Asia. See Galia Press-Barnathan, "The Lure of Regional Security Arrangements: The United States and Regional Security Cooperation in Asia and Europe," *Strategic Studies* 10 (2000–2001): 49–97; and Donald Blair and John Hanley, "From Wheels to Webs: Reconstructing Asia-Pacific Security Arrangements," *Washington Quarterly* 24 (2001): 7–17.

27. Robert Butterworth, *Moderation from Management: International Organizations and Peace* (Pittsburgh: University Center for International Studies, 1976); and Charles Boehmer, Erik Gartzke, and Timothy Nordstrom, "Do Intergovernmental Organizations Promote Peace?" *World Politics* 57 (2005): 1–38.

28. A. Leroy Bennett, *International Organizations: Principles and Issues*, 5th ed. (Englewood Cliffs, N.J.: Prentice-Hall, 1991).

29. This key point is made by Connie Peck, "The Role of Regional Organizations in Preventing and Resolving Conflict," in *Turbulent Peace: The Challenges of Managing International Conflict*, ed. Chester Crocker, Fen Osler Hampson, and Pamela Aall (Washington, D.C.: United States Institute of Peace Press, 2001), 561–583.

30. John Duffield, "Regional Conflict Management in Europe," in *Regional Conflict Management*, 239–268.

31. An opposite view is expressed in Peck, *Sustainable Peace*, 1n.

32. Ibid., 30n. Again, Peck argues for the opposite position: the United Nations may have more legitimacy.

33. See J. Michael Greig and Paul F. Diehl, "The Peacekeeping-Peacemaking Dilemma," *International Studies Quarterly* 49 (2005): 621–625.

34. Paul F. Diehl, *International Peacekeeping*, rev. ed. (Baltimore: Johns Hopkins University Press, 1994).

35. Jessica Byron, "Regional Security in Latin America and Africa: The OAS and OAU in Light of Contemporary Security Issues," PSIS Occasional Papers 1/84 (Geneva: Graduate Institute of International Studies, 1984).

36. Boehmer et al., "Do Intergovernmental Organizations Promote Peace?" 27n.

37. In the parlance of scholarly research, this is known as a "selection effect." That is, how and which conflicts are chosen for international organization action have downstream consequences for the outcomes of those actions. Failing to account for selection effects can lead to invalid conclusions about the effectiveness of international organizations.

38. Indeed, regional organizations have been more inclined to address such lower-level threats, as compared with the United Nations, which has intervened more often in high-level disputes. See Jacob Bercovitch, Scott Gartner, and Molly Melin, "The Method in the Madness of Mediation: Some Lessons for Mediators from Quantitative Studies of Mediation" (paper presented at the annual meeting of the American Political Science Association, Washington, D.C., 2005).

39. Joseph Lepgold, "Regionalism in the Post–Cold War Era: Incentives for Conflict Management," in *Regional Conflict Management*, 9–40.

40. Zartman, "Regional Conflict Management in Africa," 7n.

41. Paul Hensel, "Territory: Theory and Evidence on Geography and Conflict," in *What Do We Know about War?* ed. John Vasquez (Lanham, Md.: Rowman and Littlefield, 2000), 57–84.

42. Arie Kacowicz, *Zones of Peace in the Third World: South America and West Africa in Comparative Perspective* (Albany: State University of New York Press, 1998).

43. See Paul F. Diehl and Gary Goertz, *War and Peace in International Rivalry* (Ann Arbor: University of Michigan Press, 2000).

44. Ibid.

45. Data are taken from James Klein, Gary Goertz, and Paul F. Diehl, "The New Rivalry Dataset: Procedures and Patterns," *Journal of Peace Research* 43 (2006): 331–348. Data are available at ftp://128.196 .23.212/rivalry/riv500web.zip.

46. Rosemary Foot, "Pacific Asia: The Development of Regional Dialogue," in *Regionalism in World Politics*, ed. Louise Fawcett and Andrew Hurrell (Oxford: Oxford University Press, 1995), 228–249.

47. Boehmer et al., "Do Intergovernmental Organizations Promote Peace?" 27n.

48. Christopher Hemmer and Peter Katzenstein, "Why Is There No NATO in Asia? Collective Identity, Regionalism, and the Origins of Multilateralism," *International Organization* 56 (2002): 575–607.

49. Kanti Bajpai, "Managing Conflict in South Asia," in *Regional Conflict Management*, 209–238.

50. See ASEAN Troika (http://www.aseansec.org/3701.htm) and the ASEAN Regional Forum (http://www.aseansec.org/3742.htm).

51. Zartman, "Regional Conflict Management in Africa," 7n.

52. Kathy Powers, "International Institutions: Formal Mechanisms for Dealing with Resource Conflict" (paper presented at the conference "Territorial Conflict Management," Urbana, Ill., 2004).

53. Thomas G. Weiss, ed., *Beyond UN Subcontracting: Task-Sharing with Regional Security Arrangements and Service-Providing NGOs* (New York: St. Martin's Press, 1997).

54. Benjamin Miller, "Conflict Management in the Middle East: Between the 'Old' and the 'New,'" in *Regional Conflict Management*, 153–208.

55. Shaw, "Conflict Management in Latin America," 9n.

56. Edward Mansfield and Helen Milner, eds., *The Political Economy of Regionalism* (New York: Columbia University Press, 1997).

57. Marshall and Gurr, *Peace and Conflict 2005*, 23n; and Human Security Centre, *The Human Security Report*, 22n.

58. For the role of regional organizations in democratization, see Jon Pevehouse, *Democracy from Above: Regional Organizations and Democratization* (Cambridge: Cambridge University Press, 2005).

31

CAPACITIES AND LIMITS OF NGOS AS CONFLICT MANAGERS

Diana Chigas

BECAUSE INTERNATIONAL INTERVENTION in conflicts has gained new significance and scope since the Cold War, nongovernmental organizations (NGOs) have emerged as a vital player in conflict management. The new agendas for peacebuilding —beginning with the 1992 *Agenda for Peace*— entail a multiplicity of roles and tasks, often carried out at different levels, and deep intervention in governance, humanitarian aid, and development. Conflict management is no longer seen solely in terms of peacemaking —mediation, good offices, and intermediary functions to bring about agreements—and traditional peacekeeping. "Direct prevention," supplemented by the notion of "structural prevention," which includes a wide range of activities, such as human rights education, development assistance, and support for democratic institutions and the rule of law, has emerged as part and parcel of the peacebuilding and conflict management agenda. The result has been an increase in the range of NGOs involved in conflict management, from conflict resolution NGOs to humanitarian, human rights, development, and other NGOs, and in the range of ways NGOs can and do contribute to conflict management.

There has been great debate about the contributions of nongovernmental third parties. Many praise them, noting their potential for developing a broader set of ideas and approaches to address what are today more complex conflicts involving relationships among whole bodies politic, based not on state interests, and across permeable boundaries diluted more and more by globalization.[1] NGOs are said to offer flexibility, expertise, rapid responses, and commitment to local environments to meet the challenges of the new generation of peace operations and to make connections to civil society and the grassroots, now seen as essential components of democracy and peacebuilding.[2] Others warn of the dangers inherent in multiple agendas, the lack of accountability of NGOs, and their potential for diverting needed funds from the United Nations and other responsible intergovernmental organizations.[3]

With more than thirty-six thousand NGOs working internationally, and countless more grassroots organizations in areas of conflict, with different methods, different populations, and different goals, it is almost impossible to draw general conclusions about the value of NGOs.[4]

This chapter proposes a framework for considering the roles that NGOs are playing in conflict management and explores the contributions, as well as the limitations, of the various forms of NGO activities in the transformation of intractable conflict.[5]

ROLES OF NGOS IN CONFLICT MANAGEMENT

Unofficial third-party intervention is a concept that means different things to different people.[6] The range of unofficial intervenors is broad, including religious institutions, academics, former government officials, nongovernmental organizations, humanitarian organizations, and think tanks, among others. The range of interventions is equally broad, going far beyond traditional notions of NGOs acting as intermediaries, go-betweens, facilitators, or mediators between the sides of a conflict to include empowerment, advocacy, and economic and social development activities.

NGO activity is almost always positioned in contrast to official peacemaking and peacebuilding efforts but also as a complement to them. A brief word about official third-party intervention is therefore warranted in order to situate NGO efforts within a context of intervention. NGO interventions are designed to supplement and plug the gaps in high-level, official third-party conflict management efforts and are often contrasted with official diplomacy to emphasize the different methods and tools that are used by unofficial third parties. Official diplomacy, or mediation by governments or intergovernmental organizations (such as the United Nations, the Organization for Security and Cooperation in Europe [OSCE],

and the African Union), is commonly referred to as "track-one diplomacy." The term was coined by Joseph Montville, a former diplomat, who distinguished traditional diplomatic activities (track-one diplomacy) from "unofficial, informal interaction between members of adversarial groups or nations with the goals of developing strategies, influencing public opinions, and organizing human and material resources in ways that might help resolve the conflict," which he called "track two."[7] Louise Diamond and John McDonald later refined the concept of track-two diplomacy to describe multiple (nine) "tracks" of diplomacy needed for sustainable peacebuilding, only one of them taking place among decision makers or delegated negotiators.[8]

In track-one diplomacy, the intervenor is almost always official—a government, such as the United States in the Israeli-Palestinian conflict and Norway in Sri Lanka, or an intergovernmental organization, such as the Intergovernmental Authority on Development (IGAD) in Sudan, the United Nations in Cyprus, and the OSCE in the Georgian–South Ossetian conflict. Track-one diplomacy entails a broad range of possible activities, from the relatively nonforceful activity of facilitating communication between adversaries to proposing solutions and applying pressure or coercion to recalcitrant parties to come to a resolution. Peace operations mounted by international organizations or coalitions of governments—for instance, the United Nations in Kosovo and East Timor, NATO in Afghanistan, the "coalition of the willing" in Iraq— have expanded the domain of track-one intervention greatly, bringing it into the day-to-day governance of postwar societies. The intended product of these track-one interventions is an agreement or a decision, whether to support a cease-fire to end violence or to accept a more comprehensive settlement of the underlying conflict.

In contrast to governments and international organizations, NGOs have few political resources and little leverage to bring to the table and therefore generally take on a more facilitative, educational, or persuasive role. There are many ways of categorizing NGO roles and activities. Figure 1 represents one typology, dividing NGO intervention into three tracks, or levels, of third-party activity. The typology is based on the level at which the intervention occurs, the type of activity that NGOs typically pursue during the intervention, and the broad products of the intervention. In each track, the third party works with a different class of participants (from top decision makers in track one and a half to grassroots communities in track three) and generally engages in a different type of activity with different anticipated products (from mediation or premediation dialogue with officials aimed directly at furthering official negotiation processes in track one and a half to a broader range of training, education, and empowerment activities to promote grassroots involvement in peace processes and develop cooperative attitudes and actions at the grassroots level to promote sustainability of peace in track three).

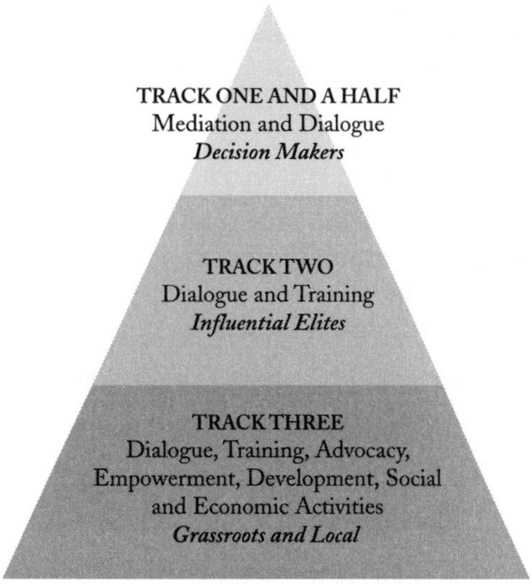

This typology is designed to highlight a fundamental characteristic of peacebuilding in intractable conflicts: namely, that it cannot occur solely at the elite level, nor aim only at settlements or agreements. At the same time, a general caveat concerning the roles and significance of NGOs is appropriate in light of the explosion of NGO activity that has occurred since the 1990s. The fact that there are many efforts taking place at all the levels of NGO activity does not guarantee that they will reinforce one another and make a cumulative contribution to the peace process. Although, as this chapter suggests, NGOs have the potential to make a significant contribution to conflict management, they have often not realized that potential. There are several reasons for this failure: lack of skill or competence, as humanitarian, development, and other NGOs have entered a field that, in the words of many practitioners, is "not an area for amateurs;"[9] gaps in strategic thinking and program design;

Figure 1. Three Tracks of Unofficial Third-Party Intervention

TRACK ONE AND A HALF
Mediation and Dialogue
Decision Makers

TRACK TWO
Dialogue and Training
Influential Elites

TRACK THREE
Dialogue, Training, Advocacy,
Empowerment, Development, Social
and Economic Activities
Grassroots and Local

and inherent limitations on what NGOs can do. The remainder of this chapter elaborates on the roles NGOs can play—and have played—at each level of intervention. It then analyzes how NGO activities have contributed to the transformation of conflicts, identifies a number of limitations within which NGOs must operate, and concludes with a summary of strengths and weaknesses of NGOs in conflict management.

UNOFFICIAL INTERVENTIONS WITH DECISION MAKERS: TRACK-ONE-AND-A-HALF DIPLOMACY

In track-one-and-a-half diplomacy, unofficial actors (former government officials and religious or social organizations such as the Catholic Church or Quaker organizations) intervene with official government representatives to promote a peaceful resolution of conflict. Track-one-and-a-half diplomacy typically takes two forms: direct mediation, in which the unofficial intermediary tries to mediate a settlement to the conflict or specific issues in dispute, or consultation, in which the unofficial third party acts as an impartial facilitator of informal problem-solving dialogue among decision makers or negotiators trying to "assist the parties in analyzing and dealing with their antagonistic attitudes and the basic issues in their relationship."[10]

Unofficial Direct Mediation and Conciliation

Unofficial actors have acted directly as mediators or conciliators between conflicting parties either by hosting and facilitating talks or by providing unofficial shuttle diplomacy. The latter is exemplified by the role of Quaker peacemaker Adam Curle in the Nigerian conflict of 1967–70. Curle shuttled between the Nigerian government and the Biafran rebel leaders delivering messages and engaging in bilateral discussions with both sides to help them develop a clearer picture of the issues, ideas for solution, and possibilities for progress.

The Community of Sant'Egidio, a private, voluntary Catholic organization based in Rome and with contacts in the Vatican, has acted as a host and facilitator of direct negotiations. It has been able to play this mediation role based on its mission, its close association with the Vatican, and its extensive network of contacts and relationships.[11] Building on fourteen years of establishing relationships and providing humanitarian aid in Mozambique, the Community of Sant'Egidio assumed the role of primary mediator there in 1990. Bringing the main parties to its home in Rome, Sant'Egidio mediators facilitated, with the support of the international community, the agreement that ended the civil war in that country. Building on a similar extensive network of contacts among all parties and its widely acknowledged motivation for caring for the less fortunate, Sant'Egidio mediated one of the only agreements between the Serbian government and the Albanian community in Kosovo: the September 1, 1996,

Educational Agreement for Kosovo.[12] Although this agreement was never implemented and was overtaken by the events that led to the NATO bombing in 1999, it did represent a significant achievement in that context.

Former U.S. president Jimmy Carter and the Conflict Resolution Program at the Carter Center at Emory University in Atlanta are another example. The Conflict Resolution Program operates with six permanent staff members supporting the mediation efforts of Carter and his wife, Rosalynn, who undertake most missions at the request of the parties. Carter consults with governments, as well as relevant governmental and intergovernmental organizations.[13] However, he acts in an unofficial capacity, albeit with official blessing. His status as a former president of the United States gives him legitimacy and entry at the highest levels. Yet, acting as an unofficial mediator, he is free to initiate discussions, facilitate communication, and explore new ideas. Moreover, because as a neutral mediator he does "not have constituents that demand success on each involvement," he is "less reluctant than principal mediators to become engaged."[14]

In this role, Carter undertook a mission to North Korea in 1994 to defuse escalating tensions between that country and the United States.[15] Alarmed by the lack of direct contact between North Korea and the United States amid a growing crisis over North Korea's refusal to allow the International Atomic Energy Agency (IAEA) to inspect one of its nuclear plants, Carter took the initiative to meet with North Korean leader Kim Il Sung. The White House had declined direct contact until its conditions were met but did not object to Carter's acceptance of an invitation to go to North Korea, provided he made it clear that he was going as a private citizen and not with any authority from the U.S. government to negotiate. Explaining that he had come as a private citizen, but with the knowledge and support of his government, Carter succeeded in developing a deal that defused the crisis. He had no authority, of course, to commit the White House to the option he had developed with Kim Il Sung. But his announcement on CNN of North Korean readiness to agree to the deal just as he left North Korea made it difficult for the administration to reject it. Carter succeeded in providing a face-saving way for the administration to back down from a rigid position that was contributing to rapid escalation of tensions. Still, however, he was not greeted enthusiastically in Washington as his CNN announcement had forced a divided administration to make a decision it had not yet been ready to make about how to deal with North Korea.

Direct mediation by unofficial third parties is not common. As the chilly reception given to Jimmy Carter on his return to Washington from Pyongyang demonstrates, unofficial intermediaries can be seen as interfering with policies of interested governmental parties or mediators. There are also few individuals or organizations with sufficient stature or moral authority and/or sufficient connections within interested governments to play such a role.

Unofficial Consultation

More often NGOs play what Ron Fisher has called a consultant's role.[16] In this model, key individuals from the parties are brought together in their *personal* capacities, rather than as representatives of their side, for direct, private interaction. The meetings are low key, closed to the public, and nonbinding. Participants share their perceptions and concerns, focusing on the interests and basic needs underlying their positions, jointly analyze the underlying issues and their relationship, and jointly develop ideas for resolution. The setting, ground rules, agenda, and third-party role facilitate a different kind of interaction than that normally occurring between the parties and thus change perceptions, bring new information into the discussion, and promote openness and creativity. The workshops are designed to promote relationship and trust building across conflict lines, develop lines of communication,

and explore options that could meet both sides' interests and needs.

Negotiation and conflict resolution training has also been used as both a method and a forum for track-one-and-a-half dialogue. Generally, such training brings participants from conflicting parties for a common learning experience in which they are introduced to concepts and skills and use them to focus on their own conflict.[17] At times, unofficial intermediaries work separately (in parallel) with the parties to develop analytic and operational skills and a common vocabulary that can assist them when they do come together to negotiate.[18] While sharing characteristics and goals with "consultation" and dialogue, joint training also seeks to provide an opportunity for participants to reflect on process, learn about common negotiation dynamics, and develop broadly applicable new skills.

The Conflict Management Group's (CMG) initiative in the Georgian–South Ossetian peace process is an example of a track-one-and-a-half intervention that combined both problem-solving dialogue and training methods. The Georgia–South Ossetia Dialogue Project, undertaken by CMG from 1994 to 2002 in partnership with the Norwegian Refugee Council (NRC), comprised a series of facilitated joint brainstorming meetings over five years. "Facilitated joint brainstorming" is a method devised by Roger Fisher of Harvard Law School and CMG to develop settlement options for negotiation. The meeting agendas included exercises and skill building in negotiation, designed to stimulate reflection on participants' assumptions about negotiation and future possibilities for mutual gains negotiation. In structured communication processes, participants were asked to talk about their own experiences, interests, needs, and fears and listen to and explore those of the other side. Participants brainstormed ideas related to the Georgian–South Ossetian negotiation process, particularly on issues they discovered to be of common concern, such as cultural and economic ties, refugees, and development. A significant amount of formal and informal time for relationship building was incorporated into the program. Following the last overseas meeting, a core group of Georgian and South Ossetian high-level officials formed a steering committee, which met on a regular basis closer to home, especially before official negotiating sessions mediated by Russia and the OSCE, to informally share perspectives, correct misunderstandings, and develop ideas relevant to the negotiation process. Like the brainstorming meetings, the steering committee sessions were designed to develop deeper understanding of the core issues of concern to both parties and explore new approaches to resolving them, *not* to negotiate or agree on a single idea.

The Woodrow Wilson Center for International Scholars' Burundi Leadership Training Program (BLTP) is another example of a track-one-and-a-half training effort. The project began in late 2002 to aid the fragile transition to peace begun with the Arusha and later with the Pretoria accords. Its main objective is to "build a cohesive, sustainable network of leaders who could work together across all ethnic and political divides in order to advance Burundi's reconstruction" through training in interest-based negotiation, communication, mediation, conflict analysis, strategic planning, and organizational change.[19] BLTP conducted several intensive six-day workshops initially for close to one hundred key individuals from political parties, the military, and civil society.[20] These workshops catalyzed profound personal transformation in the way participants saw and related to each other. Follow-up workshops were conducted to deepen and reinforce skills and relationships developed in the initial workshops. While the general follow-up workshops had limited broader impact, targeted workshops for key security sector actors led to significant breakthroughs in negotiations after the workshops; drawing on the trust, communication, and confidence in their ability to resolve differences that had been developed

during the workshops, participants were able to resolve issues on which the parties had previously been deeply divided.[21]

UNOFFICIAL INTERVENTIONS WITH UNOFFICIAL ACTORS: TRACK-TWO DIPLOMACY

The consultant's role described earlier originated with the development of track-two interventions. In track-two diplomacy, unofficial intermediaries work with nonofficial yet influential people from the conflict sides to improve communication, understanding, and relationships and to develop new ideas for resolving the conflict. The Kashmir Study Group is a good example. Founded by a Kashmiri-American businessman, the Kashmir Study Group (KSG) has brought together academics, retired diplomats, NGO leaders, and members of the U.S. Congress for dialogue. The KSG has developed new ideas for resolving the Kashmir problem that have generated serious discussion in both India and Pakistan. The social stature and networks of the participants, the range of perspectives they represent, and the creativity of the KSG's ideas have earned the group a reputation for nonpartisanship and a measure of influence in both countries.[22]

A number of methodologies for conducting track-two diplomacy have been developed and well documented since the 1970s. The best known and most developed of the track-two models is the interactive problem-solving workshop originated by John Burton, Herbert Kelman, Ronald Fisher, and others.[23] The workshop brings together nonofficial but influential members of the parties for direct, private interaction, joint analysis of the conflict, and joint problem solving. The identity and the role of third parties are similar: they are knowledgeable and skilled scholar/practitioners who are impartial and whose training and expertise enable them to facilitate productive dialogue and problem solving between the parties.[24] Participants in these efforts, however, are not officials or members of negotiating teams but rather "politically involved and often politically influential members" of conflicting societies.[25] They may be parliamentarians, leaders, and activists of political movements, journalists, members of think tanks, and academics: people who are within the mainstream of their societies and close to the political center. Their unofficial position, along with the academic setting in which the meetings are conducted, permits them greater freedom to explore alternative perspectives and formulate new (joint) ideas.[26]

Kelman and his colleagues have applied this approach to workshops primarily between Israelis and Palestinians since the 1970s. The workshops have been credited with contributing to the breakthrough achieved in the Oslo Accords of September 1993 by preparing cadres to negotiate productively, by providing substantive inputs (in terms of both ideas and awareness of sensitivities and perspectives of the other side), and by creating a better political atmosphere for negotiation.[27]

Another model for track-two diplomacy, developed by former U.S. diplomat Harold Saunders, seeks to "engage representative citizens from the conflicting parties in designing steps to be taken in the political arena to change perceptions and stereotypes, to create a sense that peace might be possible, and to involve more and more of their compatriots." This "public peace process" has been applied in the Inter-Tajik Dialogue, begun in 1993 under the auspices of the Dartmouth Conference Regional Conflicts Task Force.[28] In this model, dialogue proceeds through a five-phase process. In the first phase, defining the problem and deciding to engage with the other side, the organizers contacted more than one hundred people in Tajikistan, seeking broad representation of the different factions in conflict, at a second or third tier of authority to ensure their ability to explore ideas freely.[29] The second phase, involving mapping issues and relationships and identifying possibilities for working

together, began with the first meeting in 1993, during which participants "were absorbed with unloading their feelings about the origins and conduct of the civil war."[30] The third phase, analyzing the problem through dialogue and designing ways of changing the relationship, was ushered in by participants' emerging desire to focus on starting a negotiation to create conditions for refugee return. In this phase, participants explored approaches to each key issue and came to broad conclusions about desirable ways to address problems. The fourth phase, building scenarios of interacting steps that can be taken in the political arena to change the relationships, and the fifth phase, acting together, have resulted in at least eighteen joint memoranda to convey ideas to the negotiating teams and the larger body politic. Dialogue participants shared these ideas with decision makers and international actors. They also held public events abroad and in Tajikistan. Some participants became delegates to the official negotiations and were able to transmit the ideas to their teams. The dialogue continued after negotiations started, focusing not only on the issues under negotiation but also on preparing citizens to implement the agreements that would follow.[31]

NGO ROLES AT THE GRASS ROOTS: TRACK-THREE DIPLOMACY

This area of activity has seen the greatest growth since the beginning of the 1990s, as identity, representation, governance, and human security issues have assumed greater importance on the peacebuilding agenda. In track-three diplomacy, NGOs work with people from all walks of life and sectors of a society to find ways to promote peace in settings of conflict. These efforts "aim at overcoming revealed forms of direct, cultural and structural violence, transforming unjust social relationships and promoting conditions that can help to create cooperative relationships."[32] Many track-three activities operate at the local, or community, level. Most involve longer-term relationship building among ordinary citizens across conflict lines and capacity-building endeavors. The underlying theory is that conflict is experienced most by people at the grass roots, and that sustainable peace requires *transformation*, not merely resolution, of the conflict, involving changed relationships and conditions throughout society.[33] Conflict transformation is

> a process of engaging with and transforming the relationships, interests, discourses and, if necessary, the very constitution of society that supports the continuation of violent conflict. Constructive conflict is seen as a vital agent or catalyst change. People within the conflict parties, within the society or region affected, and outsiders with relevant human and material resources all have complementary roles to play in the long-term process of peacebuilding. This suggests a comprehensive and wide-ranging approach, emphasising support for groups within the society in conflict rather than for the mediation of outsiders. It also recognizes that conflicts are transformed gradually, through a series of smaller or larger change as well as specific steps by means of which a variety of actors may play important roles.[34]

The range of NGO activities at this level is broad. In addition to dialogue, training, and other mediatory activities that bring people together across conflict lines, track-three interventions include psychosocial work to help communities deal with trauma that violent conflict has produced; joint social, sports, and arts events; joint business or economic projects; peace education; social mobilization; economic and social development projects that establish concrete incentives for peace; and work with the media, religious organizations, and other shapers of public opinion, among others.

In Sudan, for example, the People-to-People process undertaken by the New Sudan Council of Churches in 1997 had some success in promoting Dinka-Nuer reconciliation in Southern Sudan, achieving some concrete results in opening paths for humanitarian assistance, providing for reconstruction of homes and accommodation of internally displaced people, and ending violence.[35] While some people have criticized this church process as fostering political parties, it has achieved significant results in mitigating ethnic and factional fighting within the South. Studio Ijambo, an independent radio station established in Burundi in 1995 by the U.S.-based NGO Search for Common Ground, produces programs dedicated to peace and national reconciliation and dialogue among polarized groups. Studio Ijambo was a response to the need for balanced and anti-inflammatory media programming in a country where radio reaches an estimated 85 percent of the population and has been used to promote hatred and fear and manipulate listeners into committing unspeakable acts of violence.[36]

Much work is done with youth. Seeds of Peace, a U.S.-based nongovernmental organization, is one example. This NGO works with the next generation of leaders from the Middle East and other conflict areas at its 150-acre International Camp for Conflict Resolution along the shores of Pleasant Lake in Otisfield, Maine. The Seeds of Peace goal is to create a safe place where teenagers who have grown up perceiving the "other" as a permanent enemy can begin to feel comfortable with their adversary, if not to form lasting friendships. Through the participation of the Israeli and Palestinian ministries of education in selecting who will attend the camps, governments help send the signal that the involvement of ordinary people in the peace process is as vital as that of the governments.[37]

Finally, humanitarian and development agencies have engaged in track-three activities by adjusting traditional programs—in health, education, agriculture, and income generation, among others—to include a conflict management perspective. The Medical Network for Social Reconstruction in the Former Yugoslavia, as an example, brings together health professionals from the entire region. Network members are trained extensively in conflict management and reconciliation concepts and skills. The organization now convenes conferences to promote professional exchange and engages in health care delivery and social reconstruction. It has developed a training program for other health care professionals in psychosocial assistance and trauma recovery.[38]

In the economic development domain, NGOs are promoting community-driven reconstruction processes in which they help communities form broad-based local councils that decide democratically the community's reconstruction needs; they provide block funds to implement their reconstruction priorities. These projects are widely implemented in a variety of forms in places as diverse as Rwanda, Serbia, Afghanistan, East Timor, and Iraq. NGOs aim not only to deliver reconstruction assistance quickly and efficiently but also to create alternative forms of organization that foster cooperation and reconciliation.[39]

The premise of these track-three activities is that peace can and must be built from the bottom up as well as from the top down. Post–Cold War conflicts affect a broad spectrum of people and pervade many aspects of a community's life. For any peace process to be successful, a "peace constituency" must exist. Track-three interventions are therefore generally directed at rebuilding "social capital" in communities that have been fractured by conflict.[40] In many instances, the local level is a microcosm of the larger conflict; lines of identity in the conflict are often drawn through local communities, dividing them into hostile groups, and people at this level experience the day-to-day consequences of those divisions and of the decisions of the political elite. Track-three projects offer an opportunity for people to work at the community or local level, away from the political negotiation, on issues of peace and conflict resolution.[41] As Louise Diamond, originator of the concept of multitrack diplomacy, notes:

> The forces of war have an existing infrastructure that enables them to mobilize and actualize their aims—they have armies and arms suppli-

ers; transportation, commerce and communication systems; banking, taxing and other funding methods; media, education and propaganda systems; and government ministries, clans, villages, political parties and other entities capable of taking action. The forces of peace have little of this. . . . Much more needs to be done to create both a human and an institutional infrastructure for peace-building, in order to concretize these methods and approaches in social, political and economic systems that can both stand on their own and work together toward a shared goal.[42]

IMPACT OF NGO INTERVENTIONS

As Oliver Richmond has pointed out, "it is the space between officialdom, state and human security, which NGOs have begun to fill; no other actor has this potential in world politics."[43] NGOs have a number of qualities that have catapulted them into a significant role in post–Cold War multidimensional peacebuilding efforts.

First, they are flexible. As nonstate actors with little or no coercive power, they have greater flexibility than official actors to initiate and conduct discussions with the parties in a conflict area, including "illegitimate" actors with whom governments or international organizations do not want to speak because that might legitimize them or their behavior. NGOs' unofficial status also creates lower stakes for parties in conflict to engage in their conflict management activities. In the case of track-one-and-a-half and track-two activities, parties can maintain their incompatible positions while exploring whether there may be any possibilities for achieving their goals through negotiation. Any ideas generated in an unofficial mediation are later deniable. The political costs of noncooperation with unofficial third parties are also lower than those of noncooperation with official initiatives. Ironically, this may lower resistance to and open space for exploration of negotiation possibilities when the parties still are committed to unilateral action. In track-three activities,

NGOs frequently provide the only safe space where people from the two sides of a conflict can meet. For example, Mercy Corps' humanitarian program in Ambon, Indonesia, established fifteen months after Christian-Muslim conflict began there, was the first on the scene to have a mixed (Muslim-Christian) staff working out of a single office in a neutral area of segregated Ambon town. It later enlarged the neutral space by opening an NGO resource center in which Christians and Muslims from local organizations could gather.[44] The neutral space created by Mercy Corps was again expanded by other NGOs locating their offices in the area and creating a safe zone where local residents could meet and engage in market activity.[45]

Second, NGOs are often on the ground and committed to local environments for long periods of time. They understand the communities. They are able to identify and respond quickly to opportunities to strengthen connections or mitigate the impact of negative developments. Moreover, as the scope of peacebuilding expands and encompasses many areas of governance—from rule of law to transitional justice to economic policy, corruption, and refugee return—the need for specialized expertise has increased. NGOs are also able to mobilize and provide this expertise quickly.

Third, NGOs are able to deal with more subjective, social-psychological aspects of conflict that official diplomatic processes cannot. Traditional instruments of negotiation, mediation, and conflict management are not adequate to address these aspects of conflict. They tend to be well suited to resolving resource-based issues (e.g., control over land, poverty, power sharing, distribution of economic opportunities) that may indeed serve as instrumental modalities for the protection of identity and human needs. But issues of identity, survival, and demonization of the other require a process that works directly to change the underlying human relationship and deals with perceptions, trust, and fears that fuel the institutionalization and self-reinforcing dynamic that sustains intractability.

Yet while the gaps in the official processes and the potential contributions of NGOs are clear, assessing the real impact of NGOs in conflict management is not easy. In the case of track-one-and-a-half mediation or conciliation by unofficial third parties, impact can be determined clearly by virtue of the achievement and maintenance of agreements. As Jimmy Carter's success in North Korea and Sant'Egidio's successes in Mozambique and Kosovo demonstrate, unofficial intermediaries can play valuable roles where official mediators are unavailable, uninterested, or seen as biased, or when any acceptance of mediation is perceived by the parties as a sign of weakness or legitimation of the enemy. Nonetheless, as Jimmy Carter's chilly reception in Washington on his return from Pyongyang and the unraveling of the Sant'Egidio–mediated Educational Agreement for Kosovo also demonstrate, NGO mediation is fraught with difficulties. Nongovernmental organizations do not have the resources or the authority to bring parties who are not ready or willing to the negotiating table, and there is a great risk of their being manipulated by the parties for their own initial (and incompatible) strategic objectives. While there is some evidence of NGO mediation and conciliation contributing directly to the prevention of further escalation and deepening of a protracted conflict, as former President Carter's intervention in North Korea did, these kinds of NGO interventions are uncommon and do not touch on the underlying divisions.

For track-three and some track-two NGO activities, assessing impact is more difficult. These forms are generally not designed to achieve the goals of traditional diplomacy; they are not designed to produce agreements, nor to effect major shifts in policy in the short term. Rather, they seek to affect more intangible factors driving conflict, such as attitudes and relationships, that are more difficult to measure and whose contribution to change in the broader conflict environment is difficult to assess. Where "concrete" results are achieved —in the form of joint projects, infrastructure development, refugee return, and so forth—it is still not clear that these products truly reflect the improved relationships and interdependence the processes hoped to create.

Moreover, even when the impact of the interventions on participants' attitudes and relationships can be measured, the significance of these "microlevel" achievements for the larger conflict resolution process is often not clear. Attribution of impact among the myriad independent and interdependent variables is difficult.[46] It can be hard to identify NGO contributions where, despite large investments of time and resources in NGO conflict management activities, there is no movement in overcoming intergroup divides in places as diverse as Kosovo, Bosnia, Afghanistan, and Kashmir, or where progress made—in Cyprus, Israel, and Palestine, Georgia–South Ossetia, for example—is easily reversed by political developments at the "track-one" level. And when there is movement—as there was in the Israeli-Palestinian conflict following Oslo, in South Africa, and in Northern Ireland—the most direct and visible causal links relate to changes in "objective" or structural factors in the conflict— changes in leadership, the regional environment, or the domestic political environment, often achieved through application of the resources and leverage of traditional (state and intergovernmental) third parties to change the cost-benefit calculus of key people in the conflict.

Nonetheless, some real, substantiated contributions of unofficial third parties can be identified. While less direct and dramatic, they are an important part in conflict management. All forms of unofficial conflict management —from track-one-and-a-half consultation to track-three activities—have shown demonstrable successes in dealing with the psychological, cultural, perceptual, and relationship aspects of conflict, at least with respect to the participants they engage: in particular, chang-

ing attitudes and relationships among participants and building their capacity to work together cooperatively to develop peaceful means for resolution. In the words of Swedish diplomat Jan Eliasson, "the parties themselves— not just the conflict—must be 'ripe.'"[47] The attitude and relationship transformations facilitated by NGOs help the parties break out of the adversarial dynamic that characterizes their intractable relationship and help them recognize and seize ripe opportunities for negotiation as well as overcome hurdles to resolution at the table. The most significant impacts of NGOs can be grouped into four categories: (1) changes in attitudes and psychology of the parties, (2) improved communication and relationships across conflict lines, (3) development of new options to bridge the polarization or competition of solutions, and (4) contributions to de-institutionalization of the conflict. The first three relate to changes in the participants in the NGO programs themselves. The fourth relates to the impact of NGO programming on the broader peace. Here the evidence of impact is much weaker, even while the potential for NGO contribution in this area remains strong.

Changed Attitudes about the Other and about the Conflict

The most commonly observed change resulting from NGO conflict management is the breaking down of negative stereotypes and generalizations of the other side. These enemy images serve both as tools for mobilizing public resources in support of policy and as psychological constructs that enable leaders to justify violence and confrontation against another group.[48] Some programs, such as nationwide media programs, have had broad impact on public attitudes about the "other" and conflict, for example, a children's television series created by Search for Common Ground helped children in Macedonia (and their parents, with whom it was found 45 percent of the child viewers discussed the show) learn more about the other communities in their country and about alternative ways of managing conflict. Although the program did not influence children's opinions and behavior vis-à-vis the "other" in everyday life, it did help establish the vision of cooperative interethnic relationships portrayed in the series as the ideal they and their parents wished for Macedonia.[49]

Dialogue-based activities can deepen this kind of attitude change at a small-group level by helping participants develop a deep understanding of the other's intentions and rationale for policies and behavior, their political culture, and the decision-making context.[50] Merely getting to know the other in an informal context can change conceptions of them, especially where there is little contact other than exchange of positions in official fora or the media. In many cases, participants note that workshops clarify misinformation about the other side and help them understand that the other community, like their own, has suffered in the conflict.[51] The development of an empathetic understanding of the other side's experiences, perspectives, and needs can form an initial basis for trust.

Myths that the other is not interested in dialogue are often broken, and a working trust can begin to develop as the other's motivations become clarified and human connections develop. In CMG and NRC's track-one-and-a-half initiative in Georgia–South Ossetia, for example, one South Ossetian reported that he realized in a way that he had not before that the Georgians also genuinely wanted to get something out of the conflict resolution process. This deep realization allowed him to really listen to the Georgian perspectives for the first time since the war began.[52] Similar stories emerge from Cypriot, Israeli-Palestinian, and other unofficial processes: the Greek Cypriot nationalist who became an activist for bicommunal rapprochement, or the Greek Cypriot journalist who participated in a workshop for political, economic, and media leaders from both sides, first locked his door in fear of what his counterpart from the other side would do

to him then was later suspended from his job for refusing to use language the other community found offensive.[53] The structure and content of the dialogue allow participants to see a more differentiated and less negative image of the "enemy" and its "intentions." Participants learn that there is a diversity of views on both sides, including views that cut across conflict lines, and identify "coalition partners" on the other side with whom they might work to open a path to negotiation.

NGO dialogue processes also can help participants transform their perceptions of the conflict in ways that open space for negotiation by facilitating mutual understanding and acceptance of these concerns about survival and identity and a transformating win-lose, survive or perish framing of the conflict.[54] These processes engage the social-psychological dimensions of the definition of the conflict directly. Participants identify underlying needs, values, and interests that are compatible and that can form the basis for a new definition of a common problem that the two sides share an interest in solving. They develop, as a result of deeper understanding of the other side's needs, a greater openness to abandoning previous nonnegotiable positions.[55] Participants also report a greater hope and confidence that joint solutions can be found and a greater willingness to engage with the other side.[56] For example, participants in the Inter-Tajik Dialogue report that the dialogue helped them gain a new understanding of the sources of conflict in Tajikistan and helped them moderate their own positions.[57] Even where "nonnegotiable" gaps persist, the empathy and mutual understanding that unofficial processes facilitate lessen the emotional reactivity and make it easier for the parties to work together to find compromise solutions.[58]

Improved Communication, Relationships, and Trust

Negative perceptions, and the distrust and confrontation they breed, are perpetuated by lack of communication. In some cases, the barrier is physical. Until recently, for example, the UN-patrolled Green Line in Cyprus dividing the two communities was difficult to cross, and telephone connections were limited to three United Nations lines. In other cases, where such physical restrictions are not imposed, political, social, and psychological constraints limit possibilities for communication in an equally powerful way. The communication vacuum "provides a greenhouse in which rumors flourish. Facts are embellished or distorted."[59] Interpretation and conjecture are taken as fact.

NGOs have made a significant contribution in opening channels of communication between parties who otherwise would find it difficult to meet or acknowledge any contact and in improving the quality of communication —and consequently of understanding across conflict lines. This is particularly important in hot conflicts, where violence and heightened tensions usually lead to interruption of lines of communication, at both elite and grassroots levels.

At a time when there were no official contacts between the United States and the Palestine Liberation Organization, Landrum Bolling, former president of Earlham College in Richmond, Indiana, and a Quaker peacemaker, served as an unofficial liaison between Yasir Arafat and President Jimmy Carter. Track-two dialogues have constituted one of the few fora in which Israelis and Iranians could meet. Likewise, owing to political constraints on official contacts, track-two dialogues have offered a unique opportunity for Israeli-Syrian dialogue.[60] In times of increasing tensions, these fora may be a significant channel for parties to clarify misperceptions and correct miscommunication that could lead to further escalation. The parties' concerns about legitimizing the status of the enemy, looking weak, or prejudicing their positions can be lessened by the unofficial identity and the facilitative, diagnostic role of the intermediary.

At the grassroots level, NGOs have convened youth camps, common sports and cultural events, and joint technical training sessions and have facilitated economic cooperation projects that in some cases provide the only forum and venue for safe cross-conflict contact and communication. In Kosovo, for example, even in 2006, because of intragroup intimidation and security concerns, people do not readily meet each other for anything other than the most official transactions on their own initiative. As one participant in youth dialogues in eastern Kosovo notes, "if there were no NGOs, things would be very different in Gjilan town. There would be no communication and people would not be as close as they are now."[61]

The common ground rules, structure, and venue for unofficial discussions also make possible a kind of communication that is generally not feasible among parties in intractable conflicts. Extreme polarization of communication, characterized by blaming, accusation, and use of language that is provocative or threatening to the other side, occurs at all levels of society. This dynamic perpetuates confrontation, mistrust, and hopelessness about the possibilities for change. Negotiation and problem solving under these conditions become impossible.

Unofficial dialogue processes can help to close this gap in communication by changing the nature of the discussion. Participants exchange personal stories about their experiences in the conflict. In the more systematic track-two processes, participants begin to analyze the conflict in a structured way, delving beneath positions and arguments to understand interests, needs, fears, concerns, priorities, constraints, and values.[62] Participants become aware of the ways their language reinforces mutual mistrust because it is experienced as offensive, disrespectful, or threatening by the other side. They begin to develop a de-escalatory language that contributes to creating an environment in which they can communicate and solve problems more effectively. This is the basis for development of a working trust between the sides that permits joint analysis and joint problem solving to overcome barriers to settlement.[63]

The transformation of attitudes and communication is often inextricably tied to the establishment of deep relationships of mutual trust among participants in unofficial processes. Being with the "enemy" at breakfast, in the meetings themselves, and at the bar at night rehumanizes the conflict and helps participants recognize that they share many fears, needs, and concerns. The track-two diplomacy initiatives on Kashmir have helped participants develop greater rapport and overcome suspicions of the Indian and Pakistani governments.[64] While this newfound trust, and in some cases friendship, do not always extend beyond the boundaries of the workshop to the other side as a whole, these personal relationships can be critical to the capacity of parties to develop a process for coming to the table and to deal with the hurdles in negotiation.[65] In this context, unofficial intermediation can be seen as "attempts to strengthen the hands of the pro-negotiation elements on each side in their internal struggle" against the hawks.[66]

The impacts of improved relationships could be seen in the Georgian–South Ossetian negotiations in 2002. Participants in CMG's workshops reported that improved relationships brought with them the ability to talk informally on breaks from intense official negotiating sessions and to call each other when hot issues erupted. This, they concluded, significantly improved the official negotiations.[67] OSCE mediators also noted these shifts in relationship and attributed the improved tone of negotiations to the relationship building achieved in the unofficial workshops.[68] Similarly, personal relationships developed during unofficial regional dialogues in the Middle East positively affected official interactions. For example, one Israeli participant associated with the Likud party used his track-two contacts to arrange meetings between then Likud leader Benjamin Netanyahu and Jordanian

officials. Egyptian and Israeli track-two participants commented that negotiation at the official level was easier because of the contacts and relationships they had made when working on a global arms control agreement.[69]

New Options for Productive Negotiation

Many unofficial initiatives have gone beyond understanding and dialogue to Saunders's fifth phase of public dialogue—that of "acting together"—to have a concrete impact on changing the relationship between the parties.[70] Unofficial processes can generate creative ideas for settlement that cannot be raised in official negotiations, as well as cadres of people with experience working with the other and capable of conducting productive negotiations.

A number of track-one-and-a-half and track-two initiatives have developed new ideas for de-escalation and settlement. The Kashmir Study Group developed novel and useful ideas about resolving the Kashmir conflict and has influenced high-level decision makers to think about options outside their normal policy framework.[71] The Dartmouth Conference's Inter-Tajik Dialogue produced eighteen joint memoranda with recommendations on organization of the negotiation process, and several participants in Kelman's problem-solving workshops have published joint papers discussing potential directions for resolution of the thorniest issues in the Israeli-Palestinian conflict. In the Inter-Tajik negotiations specifically, the Commission on National Reconciliation (CNR)—the central implementation mechanism of the 1997 General Agreement, which included several dialogue members—later organized its work program through four subcommissions, echoing the model discussed in that first memorandum.[72] The Harvard Study Group, a two-year initiative conducted under the auspices of Harvard's World Peace Foundation, produced a range of ideas for settlement of the Cyprus conflict that were shared with the leaders on both sides and the main official third parties involved (e.g., the United

Nations and the United States); the ideas had some influence on the 2002 United Nations proposal (the Annan Plan). Similarly, CMG's Georgia–South Ossetia Dialogue project resulted in a number of ideas for joint projects in education, culture, science, and economics, and ideas for confidence-building steps, options for cooperation in law enforcement, and steps toward normalization of life in the conflict zone.[73] In the Georgia-South Ossetia case, many of these ideas were adopted in the formal negotiations, and although settlement of the conflict is still far away,[74] tensions between the parties de-escalated significantly for a period of time before changes in the Georgian government brought new attempts to coerce a resolution of the conflict. The informal and unofficial nature of the meetings and the intermediary made it possible to present, explore, and discuss ideas openly, including ideas that may have been too bold or too sensitive to bring up in official negotiations.

Impacts on Conflict Institutionalization: Changed Conflict Dynamics

To have impact on the broader peace process, most track-one-and-a-half and track-two processes rely on transfer of the learning, changed attitudes, and new insights described thus far to the negotiation or political process. NGO processes at the track-two and track-three levels also aim to have macrolevel impact by affecting the structure of conflict in ways that can facilitate transformation of intractability by strengthening pro-negotiation forces, changing public discourse and opinion about the conflict, and building peace constituencies at all levels of society. Yet, as Mary Anderson and Lara Olson note, "All of the good peace work being done should be adding up to more than it is. The potential of these multiple efforts is not fully realized. Practitioners know that, so long as people continue to suffer the consequences of unresolved conflicts, there is urgency for everyone to do better."[75] In this area especially, NGO efforts seem to have made

little impact. Nonetheless, the *potential* contributions of NGOs are clear, even if performance is not always as great as it could be.

Creating Cadres for Negotiation and Problem Solving. In addition to generating useful ideas, unofficial, citizen-based intermediation can be a forum for nurturing cadres able to negotiate effectively with the other and resolve intractable issues when the window of opportunity opens. In South Africa key players in the negotiations between the African National Congress and the National Party, including the chief negotiators on both sides, were veterans of previous informal discussions.[76] The Oslo process that led to the 1993 Declaration of Principles between Israelis and Palestinians similarly involved negotiators who had long experience with unofficial dialogue processes. In Ecuador and Peru, participants in both a CMG-Harvard-led "facilitated joint brainstorming" process and a University of Maryland–facilitated "Innovative Problem Solving Workshop" process later were brought directly into the track-one peace process and drew on their experience in those sessions in negotiating the agreements that ended more than forty years of conflict over their border.[77] Armed with both strong working relationships with counterparts on the other side and a deep understanding of the other side's perceptions, interests, and needs, these people were able to work together to overcome obstacles to resolution at the table.

Strengthening Forces for Moderation. Citizen-based track-two and track-three processes can help create space for voices of moderation that have been silenced or marginalized as a result of the polarization of the parties. In intractable conflicts it is difficult for moderates on either side to have a voice in policy or public debate. They are often driven into exile, intimidated into silence by political oppression, or threatened by their authorities or extremist groups. Even those who do take a pro-negotiation stance find themselves isolated or marginalized within their own groups because there appears to be no responsive voice on the other side. As Herbert Kelman notes, "[b]ecause of the psychological and political constraints under which they labor, [pro-negotiation elements on both sides] are likely to undermine each other's efforts to promote negotiations. . . . [I]n contrast to the hawks, when the doves on the two sides do what comes naturally, they work at cross-purposes: They tend to communicate to the other side less moderation and willingness to negotiate than they actually represent, and thus undermine each other's argument that there is someone to talk to on the other side and something to talk about."[78]

Unofficial processes can facilitate the formation of "coalitions across conflict lines" that can help organize and strengthen the "negotiating middle" and give a public platform to previously silenced voices for moderation. For example, a July 1997 workshop organized by American University among East Timorese who fell into the "negotiating middle" helped reinforce the position of political moderates and facilitated the formulation of joint negotiation options.[79] In South Africa a 1987 conference brought together sixty-one predominantly Afrikaans-speaking intellectuals to the left of the governing National Party and seventeen African National Congress (ANC) representatives in Dakar, Senegal. The success of this conference reinforced the influence of "diplomats," such as Thabo Mbeki, within the ANC over those who supported insurrection and mass mobilization.[80]

In addition to bolstering the influence of pro-negotiation elements within each side, unofficial processes can give voice to silenced or marginalized moderate perspectives in the public discourse. The Dakar Conference contributed to changes in white public opinion and increased public discussion of possibilities of negotiation with the ANC as white participants engaged in public speaking, "debriefings and house meetings" and even created an alternative Afrikaans newspaper. Daniel Lieberfeld

concludes that Dakar "desensitized" whites to talks with the ANC, as evidenced by the comparative lack of media controversy over a follow-up meeting a year later.[81]

Similar impacts on public opinion can be seen in other conflicts. In Cyprus, where powerful norms of group loyalty and cohesiveness have made taboo the expression of views that the enemy may not be as bad, aggressive, or inflexible as assumed, opening public discussion to previously silenced voices for negotiation and rapprochement has occurred. Bicommunal meetings have become uncontroversial, and "bicommunal rapprochement" has now become part of the public vocabulary and public debate in the mainstream media and political circles. Even a fledgling capacity for organization and preemptive action against extremist-provoked escalation of the conflict developed. Following violent incidents at the buffer zone separating the two communities in 1996, the Bicommunal Trainers Group was able to bring together participants in a counterdemonstration to a belligerent nationalist demonstration. This led UN officials to organize a UN Day event that attracted several thousand people and prevented a potentially explosive border clash from escalating further.[82] These activities may also have contributed to the emergence of a more active peace constituency on the island. Driven by the dismal economic situation in Turkey and northern Cyprus, and the prospect of membership in the European Union, tens of thousands of Turkish Cypriots demonstrated in 2003 in favor of the United Nations' "Annan Plan." This pro-negotiation movement was enhanced by a decade-long history of bicommunal dialogue, and most of its leaders were veterans of track-two and track-three initiatives. While the unofficial contacts did not bring about changes in the negotiation positions of the parties and, as the later Greek Cypriot rejection of the Annan Plan demonstrated, were not sufficient to overcome obstacles to settlement, they did soften the rigidly confrontational nature of the relationship between adversaries and have created public openness to a negotiated resolution.

Social Networks: An Infrastructure for Peace. Because intractable conflicts involve "continuous interaction among significant elements of whole bodies politic across permeable boundaries," it is important to build a political environment—a peace constituency—and a *capacity* to support and sustain peacemaking efforts at the top levels, and to resist repolarization of the conflict when inevitable setbacks occur.[83] Broad participation by civil society actors of the opposing sides can help in preparing adversaries for taking de-escalating steps and negotiating and implementing a settlement. These peace constituencies and social networks across conflict lines help to open space for negotiations to occur and postconflict peacebuilding to progress and minimize rejectionist impacts in both camps.[84]

The experience of "community relations" work in Northern Ireland provides a powerful example of the importance and potential impact of this work. Community relations work, as cross-community intermediation is called, long preceded the start of the negotiations between the main political actors that resulted in the Good Friday Agreement. Such work at the grassroots level established dense social networks and interdependencies across conflict lines and institutionalized a number of practices, including common history texts and curricula, that effectively restrain repolarization and return to violence.[85] The strong community-based networks developed through track-two and track-three processes have contributed significantly to a common sentiment that the difficulties encountered in the political process in resolving intractable issues such as decommissioning of weapons and police reform cannot (and should not) lead to a resurgence of violence.

Research on the role of bridging social capital, defined as the "connections among individuals—social networks and the norms

of reciprocity and trustworthiness that arise from them," has reinforced notions of the importance of peace constituencies.[86] Ashutosh Varshney's research on violence prevention in India, in particular, has suggested that networks of joint activity and cooperation, on both an institutional and an everyday level, can play a major role in mitigating conflict and has led to increased NGO support for joint activities and cooperative projects across conflict lines.[87] Most track-two and track-three processes result in concrete, constructive joint actions intended to influence the political environment in which negotiations might take place. In Cyprus numerous joint projects— from a bicommunal choir to an EU study group and a lawyers' group identifying areas of divergence between the two communities' legal developments since the division of the island—provided practical experience and a model of cross-conflict cooperation. In Tajikistan dialogue participants have founded and become active in new civil society organizations. The Tajikistan Centre for Citizenship Education produces materials and organizes roundtable seminars on subjects important for peacebuilding. The Public Committee for Promoting Democratic Processes, also in Tajikistan, is working on a range of projects that help to (a) foster economic development benefiting all members of strife-torn communities, (b) develop university programs and courses in conflict resolution, (c) foster dialogue in public fora at the regional level on issues of national importance, and (d) create a second national-level inter-Tajik dialogue.[88] Mercy Corps's Eastern Kosovo Stabilization Program developed interethnic agricultural market linkages that provided new business possibilities to both Serbs and Albanians when they worked together.[89] In Georgia and South Ossetia, joint business ventures and other cross-conflict projects promote interdependence and the development of substantive interests for peace. Radio Macedonia (Search for Common Ground's project in Macedonia) runs

programming depicting interethnic cooperation and dialogue.[90]

The idea is that by promoting public education, by offering opportunities for people at all
levels of society to engage in dialogue, and by
creating tangible benefits of cooperation across
conflict lines these projects will contribute to
the development of a peace constituency to support negotiation. As yet, however, these activities have not led to broad, conflict-preventive
civic engagement—either the cross-group associational networks (e.g., business or trade
associations) or the everyday social networks
(e.g., book clubs) described by Varshney—
because of the "projectization" of the work, the
emphasis of donors and NGOs on the concrete results of the activities, and the short time
frames within which they must work.[91]

Nonetheless, they can build strong relationships among participants.[92] In the words of
one Greek Cypriot leader in the bicommunal
movement on Cyprus, "these activities disclose in many significant ways the outlines of
the anticipated society, the society of a federated Cyprus. Greek Cypriots and Turkish
Cypriots gathering together, reflecting together, planning together, building together,
even dreaming together, on equal terms, with
their differences and similarities. . . . Among
other things, the top-level agreements for a
federal solution to the Cyprus problem require
a serious follow-up of corresponding citizen
activities, gestures, symbols, holidays, events,
projects, which reflect the mentality and values of federation." In this sense, unofficial processes create a model or a metaphor for the
possibility of a different relationship.[93] They
also establish links across fault lines that form
the basis for a societal capacity to resist extremist images and rhetoric, as well as an infrastructure for negotiating and implementing a
settlement. Indeed, some analysts hypothesize
that greater "significant social movement action" and greater density of social links between
Israeli Jews and Palestinians might have helped
the Oslo process continue.[94]

LIMITATIONS OF NGO CONTRIBUTIONS

Many NGO projects are small and, in the case
of track-three interventions, very localized.
Their impact often depends on personal participation and experience of a different kind of
relationship with the "other." While this can
lead to profound changes in mind-set not generally achievable through large-scale policy-
oriented initiatives, they can reach only a limited number of people. And the experience in
these programs represents only a limited part
of the daily experience of participants or beneficiaries. Yet funders and NGOs themselves
expect (or hope) that these conflict management programs will build a negotiation or peace
constituency at either the elite or grassroots
level that will produce breakthroughs in negotiations or help strengthen or implement a
fragile peace.

This is a tall order for NGOs. Three broad
factors constrain NGOs' ability to have the
macro level impact they hope or are expected to
have: the political environment, donor agendas
and time lines, and NGOs' own strategies and
priorities.

Hostile Political Environment

NGO contributions are limited, and sometimes undermined, by the very political forces
they are trying to affect. Because of their independent and unofficial character, NGOs are
often able to bring people together across conflict lines in interaction that is less politicized
than that which occurs at governmental and
intergovernmental levels. However, they cannot completely insulate themselves from the
political environment in which they are acting.
As Dalia Kaye remarks about the effectiveness
of track-two regional security dialogues in the
Middle East, "It is an ironic aspect of track two
that when such dialogue is most needed, it is
often most difficult to bring about" or to sustain.[95] Participants in NGO efforts are always
responsive to the political developments in

their own communities and evaluate their joint work in the context of official activities, media coverage, and public opinion. In hot conflict and postconflict situations, this context is invariably hostile. "Spoilers" actively try to undermine and marginalize efforts to build bridges across conflict lines. Participants are subject to direct harassment, intimidation, and sometimes violence from rejectionists, hardliners, and their own governments. Other, less overtly rejectionist but still hostile, bureaucratic actions by political authorities—including failure to grant visas and permissions, and enforcement of laws forbidding contact—make participation difficult.[96] And while NGO activities are generally designed to be nonpartisan, low key, and private, they are vulnerable to negative media exposure caused by leaks or media commentary.[97] These constant and unrelenting attacks on the political space for dialogue can have a harsh effect on morale and deter all but the most intrepid participants.

The hostile context also makes maintenance of attitude changes difficult owing to the "reentry problem."[98] Participants in unofficial intermediation efforts must preserve a delicate balance between forging coalitions across conflict lines and preserving their status, social networks, and effectiveness on their own side. A new and meaningful social identity, or definition of "us" and "them," may have been activated in unofficial processes, but many other social contexts reinforce participants' identity as a member of their group or side—with all the attendant prejudices, stereotypes, and fears. Economic and infrastructure projects implemented by development and humanitarian agencies seek to avoid this problem by offering an incentive—economic rewards for cooperation—for maintenance of cooperation and development of a sense of commonality based on shared interests. However, these programs too (contrary to the assumptions of both donors and NGOs) have not led automatically to changes in perceptions, stereotypes, or enemy images.[99] Participants can be and often

are influenced by new information about and experiences of the other that may lead to private internalization and acceptance of new images of the other and new possibilities for intergroup relations. But they are also subject to pressures from their own communities to conform to prevailing attitudes and norms about the "other" that exercise a contrary pull and lead them to question the new attitudes or not act upon them.[100] If not reinforced by ongoing and frequent dialogue and cooperation, and in some cases *intragroup* work, attitude change and cooperation itself can quickly dissipate as people fall back into old habits.

A different but equally significant way in which politics can undermine unofficial intermediation is related to asymmetries in the relationships between the parties. Differences in power or resources between the parties are often reflected in the views of the participants and their attitudes toward unofficial processes. In the Israeli-Palestinian conflict, for example, Mohammed Abu-Nimer notes, Palestinians often come to groups with the express purpose of fostering changes in Israeli political views, while Jewish participants tend to be more concerned with establishing lines of communication and building social connections.[101] While unofficial intermediaries try to redress this imbalance by equalizing numbers and balancing participants' contributions, they often do not have the resources to equalize the relationship and may inadvertently reinforce the asymmetry in the agenda and structure of the meetings.[102] As a consequence, weaker parties sometimes view these processes as denying the asymmetries and not addressing the central problems in the conflict.

Donor Agendas and Time Lines

The NGO-donor relationship creates problems for NGOs, which often do not, or cannot, make adequate investment (in terms of resources, time, and effort) in processes and structures that allow participants to maintain their cross-conflict coalition and develop strategies and activities that have a meaningful impact in their societies. Bronwyn Evans-Ken and Roland Breiker note that donors sometimes require fulfillment of political or economic conditions before delivery of aid.[103] In Bosnia and Herzegovina, for example, U.S. assistance was conditional on elections, which in the end were held at a time when, according to OSCE observers, the process could not be free or fair. Similarly, in 2004 the United States suspended aid to Serbia because of Serbia's failure to cooperate adequately with the criminal tribunal at The Hague.[104] Such conditionality often results in programming favoring the priorities and political preferences of the donors rather than the needs of the communities. The policy preferences of donors also make it difficult for NGOs that focus on different but equally urgent issues to secure funding. Finally, short time lines limit the impact of programs such as the Eastern Kosovo Stabilization Program described earlier. Although this program achieved promising results in terms of cross-ethnic cooperation, relationships, and communication, the NGO was unable to deepen what it had started, as it was forced to move on to other geographic areas after the one-year grant ended. As a result, its impact on the broader peace was not great.[105] For international, governmental, or private donors, funding cycles are frequently short, resources limited, and agendas and theories of change often in conflict with the agendas of NGOs or participants themselves.[106] In this context, it is difficult to have a significant macrolevel impact in a conflict.

NGO Strategies and Practices

There is one area where NGOs have limited their own effectiveness: in project planning and implementation that do not foresee negative conflict impacts and that do not consider how the individual programs fit into the larger peacebuilding picture.

Negative Impacts of Aid. All NGO programming can be considered a form of aid, whether the programs transfer tangible resources such as money, infrastructure, and jobs or softer resources such as skills training, status for participation in events, trips abroad, and so forth. Mary Anderson's and Peter Uvin's groundbreaking works on the impact of humanitarian and development assistance on conflict underlined the reality that all assistance, at all times, affects conflict by increasing or decreasing tensions or, in Uvin's formulation, providing incentives or disincentives for peace or war.[107] Standard programming decisions—about participants or beneficiaries (and who will not participate), about hiring local staff, about local partners, and about where and what aid is provided—can increase divisions or strengthen connectors across conflict lines. For example, targeting a particular class of people (internally displaced persons [IDPs], returnees, excombatants, or the neediest, those with housing most damaged by war, farmers, etc.) may exacerbate divisions when the targeted class overlaps with one of the groups in conflict.[108] An NGO's criteria for hiring, such as English language or a certain level of formal education, may similarly exacerbate conflict by inadvertently limiting access to employment because education or language skills are unevenly spread across the population and coincide with intergroup lines of division. Anderson presents several agencies' reflections on this impact in Central Africa: "After the war, refugees who had resided in exile in neighboring English-speaking countries returned to their home country, which was francophone. When agencies required English language skills for local staff this favored this ethnic group over others."[109]

The way in which NGOs behave and interact with participants can also inadvertently escalate conflict or promote cynicism that undermines the impact of conflict management. In one dialogue program, for example, in which a U.S. agency brought together very influential people from both sides of a conflict in South America, the leader of the U.S. facilitation team, who spoke no Spanish, invited the only English-speaking member of the group (from one side of the conflict) to his home after the session to continue to develop the promising ideas that had emerged from the session. The dialogue almost fell apart. Although the facilitator had invited the participant because he could communicate, participants from the other side felt this action was biased, and the dialogue effort risked worsening divisions between the sides.

Even the way NGOs interact with each other can create negative impacts that reduce the effectiveness of their work collectively. It is noteworthy that in Cyprus, the period of greatest growth and influence of the bicommunal movement for rapprochement was a time when NGOs coordinated well, informed each other and included each other in activities, and promoted collaboration and networking among participants by demonstrating the same collaboration among themselves. By the end of the 1990s, agencies competed with each other, did not know about each other's work, and "bad-mouthed" each other. The level of cooperation among bicommunal groups also decreased, and for several years, they were increasingly marginalized. Their influence on the public discourse decreased.

Of course, NGO aid will not determine the dynamics of conflict. But given that in some cases NGOs can provide up to 90 percent of paid employment in a region or can represent a large proportion of resources coming into a region, especially in poor countries, the negative impacts can be significant. At the same time, these programmatic limitations on NGO impact are not inherent in the role; there are always options for avoiding or mitigating these negative impacts, and for designing and implementing projects in ways that strengthen local capacities for peace.[110]

Planning for Macrolevel Impact. NGO programmatic approaches typically reflect underlying assumptions and beliefs about what needs

to be done to achieve peace. These are rarely articulated or discussed. As a result, NGOs engaged in conflict management have typically assumed that they are contributing building blocks of peace and that the efforts will "add up" some day. Yet Mary Anderson and Lara Olson, in a multiyear, multiagency collaborative learning effort, Reflecting on Peace Practice, conclude that, in fact, "the evidence is that, without explicit efforts to add it up, this does not automatically or inevitably occur."[111] The Reflecting on Peace Practice project points to NGOs' limiting of their own impact on the broader, or macrolevel, peace in several ways. First, by failing to do a macrolevel conflict analysis to identify what the driving factors of conflict (or peace) are, they often "miss the mark" and do not address those elements most important for resolving conflict or building peace. NGOs typically focus their analysis on where, in a given context, the things they know how to do can be useful and on whether their approach to change fits the context.[112] They do not do a broad conflict analysis that identifies where the priority areas for intervention are in terms of the driving factors of the conflict. Humanitarian NGOs have an additional difficulty, as "it is the very nature of humanitarianism to be reactive," and staff turnover impedes organizational learning.[113] Second, NGOs typically assume that the impacts of their activities will automatically either "spill over" into other domains of their lives—for example, that the profound personal and relationship changes catalyzed by NGO activities will lead to changes in political attitudes and actions—or "trickle up" to influence key decision makers. The evidence gathered by the Reflecting on Peace Practice project and others suggests that this does not happen—at least not automatically.[114] Reflecting on Peace Practice found that all activities are based essentially on one of two approaches related to *who* needs to be engaged for peace and one of two approaches related to the *level* at which change needs to occur (figure 2).

Figure 2. Matrix of Programming Approaches

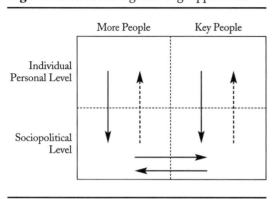

The Reflecting on Peace Practice initiative found that programming that focuses on change at the individual/personal level—in attitudes, relationships, feelings, perceptions, the "hearts and minds" of people—but is never linked to or translated into action at the sociopolitical level has *no discernible effect* on peace. Peacebuilding efforts that focus on building relationships and trust across conflict lines, increasing tolerance, building skills in conflict management, increasing hope that peace is possible—in other words, a significant proportion of NGO conflict management activity—often produce dramatic transformations in attitudes, perceptions, and trust of individuals participating. But evidence shows that impacts for the broader peace are significant only if these personal transformations are translated into actions at the sociopolitical level—the public, political, and institutional sphere of activity. Many NGO programs do not make these linkages. A recent study of the effectiveness of peacebuilding work in Kosovo, for example, found that although agencies assumed that participants in programs would spread their experience to others and take their own initiatives, participants themselves reported feeling powerless to change anything; "feelings of hatred are too strong."[115]

Reflecting on Peace Practice also found that approaches that concentrate on more people—the grassroots and middle-level elites, cre-

ating a "peace constituency"—fall short of their potential and indeed risk becoming marginally relevant if they do nothing to link to or affect key people, decision makers, and other groups or individuals without whom peace is not achievable. The inverse was found also to be true; strategies that focus on key people but do not include or affect more people can quickly become stuck or unsustainable. Indeed, in the CMG-NRC program in Georgia–South Ossetia described earlier, after several years of dialogue in which progress was made on a number of important issues, including convergence of thinking on a political resolution, leaders on both sides claimed they were blocked from making more progress. Public opinion was "not ready." The effort was stuck at "key-people" and unable to affect "more-people."

This "adding up" of activities seems to be one important area in which NGOs have potential for expanding their own effectiveness by planning how to connect their work to activities that produce impacts in other quadrants, and by supporting participants in their programs in connecting to other quadrants. This does not mean that NGOs need to have programming in all quadrants of the matrix depicted above, but they do need to connect to other activities across the two approaches —more people and key people—and across the two levels—individual/personal and sociopolitical—for maximum effectiveness

CONCLUSION

This chapter has suggested that while NGOs have made limited and generally indirect contributions to conflict management that are often difficult to assess and attribute, the contributions are important and should not be assessed solely by visible influences on track-one negotiations or policymaking processes. NGOs can and sometimes do play an important role in bringing parties to the table, in changing negotiation and conflict dynamics, in dealing with the psychological and perceptual factors of conflict, and in changing the political cultures on both sides to make the parties more receptive to negotiation and problem solving.

While NGOs bring special capacities to conflict management that official (track-one) third parties do not have, the contributions of unofficial third parties should not be overestimated. NGOs cannot substitute for coherent political action at the track-one level. Their impact depends as much or more on the "receptivity" of conflicts to conflict management and NGOs' contributions as to the quality of the intervention itself, even if NGOs, especially local NGOs, can affect public opinion over time.[116] NGOs generally do not have the capacity to change political incentives; they have few resources to offer as "carrots" and have even fewer "sticks" to wield to bring parties to the table or to encourage resolution.[117] Often, the people who could benefit most from such interaction with the other side are unwilling to participate; unofficial processes often attract those who have more moderate views, do not involve those more supportive of the conflict, and consequently do not reach those whose participation would be most necessary for the resolution of the conflict.

In the final analysis, no single conflict management process—from big-power mediation to track-three civil society bridge building—is adequate to deal with conflict. All are needed to address the complex web of factors that perpetuate intractability. NGO conflict management activity is most effective when linked, even if not formally, with official (track-one) efforts and is able to draw on the resources of track-one actors—both to attract the right participants to these efforts and provide needed follow-up and to create the windows of opportunity that unofficial intermediation prepares participants to seize. At the same time, there is evidence that some track-one efforts benefit greatly from parallel, independent (or quasi-independent) unofficial efforts to help prepare the ground for effective negotiation, post-settlement peacebuilding, and open space for

the parties to explore how to break deadlocks. Unofficial and official methods must take place alongside each other, in a complementary manner in order to achieve de-escalation, settlement, and peacebuilding.

Yet the need for synergy with track-one efforts poses increasingly difficult dilemmas for NGOs after September 11. The relationship between NGOs and governments and intergovernmental organizations, already growing muddy in the 1990s, is even muddier. In the extreme, the "nongovernmental" character of NGOs may be coming under question. The trend in governmental aid is to channel more and more assistance through NGOs and to contract tasks out to them. This privatization of conflict management (and humanitarian and development) work, it is argued, also makes all but the purest track-one-and-a-half and track-two mediatory processes technical. The increasing framing of NGO and donor strategies as apolitical approaches to managing conflict risks focusing on technical rather than political solutions and thereby undermining the impact of NGOs generally on the broader peace.[118]

At the same time, the increased government funding for NGOs and the post-9/11 reformulation of security strategy in light of the "war on terror" may compromise the political impartiality of NGOs and make it more difficult for them to perform one of their traditionally valuable roles: informally "mediating" between parties and points of view. NGOs, especially those from the United States, are increasingly seen as "part of the Western 'crusade.'"[119] Greater synchronization and linkage (direct or otherwise) of all tracks of NGO work to track one could, in the post-9/11 context, risk undermining the advantages NGOs bring to conflict management. In coordinating or subordinating their work to the new security agenda of the "war on terror," NGOs may well find that they are undermining their flexibility to deal with a wide range of actors and their ability to work with parties when official processes are stalemated. As the focus of peacebuilding shifts to "weak states" and nation building, peacebuilding activity is increasingly organized around democracy-building and sectoral work, "stabilization," and harder aspects of security in the broader "war on terror"; meanwhile, the importance of dealing with the social-psychological and relationship aspects of conflict dynamics between the parties is becoming obscured. While these new policies appear to foresee a greater role for NGOs working in closer concert with governments, intergovernmental organizations, and the military, NGOs may well find that the space within which they can operate is shrinking, that the range of contributions they can make is narrowing, and that their comparative advantage in conflict management is reducing.

NOTES

1. Connie Peck, *Sustainable Peace: The Role of the United Nations and Regional Organizations in Preventing Conflict* (Lanham, Md.: Rowman and Littlefield, 1998); and Harold Saunders, "Possibilities and Challenges: Another Way to Consider Unofficial Third-Party Intervention," *Negotiation Journal* 11 (1995): 271–275.

2. Henry Carey and Oliver Richmond, *Mitigating Conflict: The Role of NGOs* (London: Frank Cass, 2003); and Oliver Richmond, "Post-Westphalian Peace-Building: The Role of NGOs," *Martin Journal of Conflict Resolution* (Moscow: University of Idaho, 2001), http://www.class.uidaho.edu/martin_archives/conflict_journal/conflict2.html.

3. Peck, *Sustainable Peace.*

4. Ibid.

5. Like "unofficial third-party intervention," the term "conflict management" means different things to different people. Here I use the term in a general sense to describe the full range of nonviolent processes for dealing with conflict. This includes what in the literature is referred to as conflict settlement (outcome- or agreement-oriented processes), conflict resolution (process-oriented activities that aim to address the underlying causes of conflict), and conflict transformation processes (long-term peacebuilding efforts oriented toward outcomes, processes, *and* structural change to transform unjust social relationships). These terms roughly correspond to what John Paul Lederach describes as top-level, middle-level, and grassroots approaches to peacebuilding. Cordula Reimann, "Assessing the State of the Art on Conflict Transformation," in *Berghof Handbook for Conflict Transformation,* ed. David Bloomfield, Martina Fischer, and Beatrix Schmelzle (Berlin: Berghof Centre, 2005), http://www.berghof-handbook.net/articles/reimann_handbook.pdf; Christine Bigdon and Benedikt Korf, "The Role of Development Aid in Conflict Transformation: Facilitating Empowerment Processes and Community Building," in *Berghof Handbook for Conflict Transformation,* ed. Bloomfield, Fischer, and Schmelzle; and John Paul Lederach, *Building Peace: Sustainable Reconciliation in Divided Societies* (Washington, D.C.: United States Institute of Peace Press, 1997), 44–55.

6. Nadim Rouhana, "Unofficial Third Party Intervention in International Conflict: Between Legitimacy and Disarray," *Negotiation Journal* 11 (1995): 225–270.

7. J. Montville, "Transnationalism and the Role of Track-Two Diplomacy," in *Approaches to Peace: An Intellectual Map,* ed. W. Scott Thompson and Kenneth M. Jensen, with R. N. Smith and K. M. Schraub (Washington, D.C.: United States Institute of Peace Press, 1991), 262.

8. Louise Diamond and John McDonald, *Multitrack Diplomacy: A Systems Approach to Peace,* 3rd ed. (West Hartford, Conn.: Kumarian Press, 1996).

9. Mary B. Anderson and Lara Olson, *Confronting War* (Cambridge, Mass.: CDA Collaborative Learning Projects, 2003), 89.

10. Ronald J. Fisher and Loraleigh Keashly, "Distinguishing Third Party Interventions in Intergroup Conflict: Consultation Is *Not* Mediation," *Negotiation Journal* 4 (1988): 383.

11. Andrea Bartoli describes Sant'Egidio's relationships with the parties as "long-term, open, transparent, respectful and allow[ing] for the exploration of political options not otherwise available. While the quality of some personal contacts, especially with Bishop Jaime Goncalves, was an essential component of the lasting effect of Sant'Egidio's involvement, it is without a doubt that the availability of these relationships to explore alternatives to specific constraints of the Mozambique political scene contributed greatly

to the success of the peace process." Andrea Bartoli, "Learning from the Mozambique Process: The Role of the Community of Sant'Egidio," in *Paving the Way: Contributions of Interactive Conflict Resolution to Peacemaking,* ed. Ronald Fisher (Lanham, Md.: Lexington, 2005), 90.

12. Roberto Morozzo della Rocca, "Community of Sant'Egidio in Kosovo," in *Private Peacemaking: USIP-Assisted Peacemaking Projects of Nonprofit Organizations,* ed. David Smock, Peaceworks no. 20 (Washington, D.C.: United States Institute of Peace, 1998).

13. James Taulbee and Marion Creekmore, "NGO Mediation: The Carter Centre," in *Mitigating Conflict: The Role of NGOs,* ed. Henry Carey and Oliver Richmond (London: Frank Cass, 2003); and Peck, *Sustainable Peace.*

14. Taulbee and Creekmore, "NGO Mediation," 158.

15. For a detailed account of the 1994 North Korean nuclear crisis and Carter's mediatory role, see Michael Watkins and Susan Rosegrant, *Carrots, Sticks, and Question Marks: Negotiating the North Korean Nuclear Crisis* (Cambridge, Mass.: John F. Kennedy School of Government Case Program, Harvard University, 1995); and Taulbee and Creekmore, "NGO Mediation."

16. Ronald J. Fisher, "Third Party Consultation: A Method for the Study and Resolution of Conflict," *Journal of Conflict Resolution* 16 (1972): 67–94; and Fisher and Keashly, "Distinguishing Third Party Interventions in Intergroup Conflict."

17. Ronald J. Fisher and Louise Diamond, "Integrating Conflict Resolution Training and Consultation: A Cyprus Example," *Negotiation Journal* 11, no. 3 (1995): 287–301.

18. Diana Chigas, "Unofficial Interventions with Official Actors: Parallel Negotiation Training in Violent Intrastate Conflicts," *International Negotiation* 2 (1997): 409–436.

19. Howard Wolpe and Steve McDonald, "Training Leaders for Peace," *Journal of Democracy* 17, no. 1 (2006): 132–138.

20. The workshops were designed to "address the four political imperatives for the reconstruction of war-torn societies: a shift from a zero-sum paradigm to one that affirms interdependence and common ground; the development of a modicum of trust among the decision makers; moving from confrontational to co-operative rhetoric; and a consensus on how power will be organized and decisions will be made, i.e., on the rules of the game." Howard Wolpe, with Steve McDonald, Eugene Nindorera, Elizabeth McClintock, Alain Lempereur, Nicole Rumeau, and Allie Blair, "Building Peace and State Capacity in War-Torn Burundi," *Round Table* 93, no. 375 (2004): 464.

21. Peter Uvin and Susanna Campbell, "The Burundi Leadership Training Program," Case Study for the Project on Leadership and State Capacity (Washington, D.C.: Woodrow Wilson Center for International Scholars, forthcoming). The nontargeted follow-up training for participants in the initial workshops was less effective than the targeted workshops. While participants interacted more outside the workshops, the impact was limited, according to Uvin and Campbell: contact was primarily social and not very widespread, and there was little observable professional or political change attributed to the project.

22. Howard Schaffer and Teresita Schaffer, "Kashmir: Fifty Years of Running in Place," in *Grasping the Nettle: Analyzing Cases of Intractable Conflict,* ed. Chester A. Crocker, Fen Osler Hampson, and Pamela Aall (Washington, D.C.: United States Institute of Peace Press, 2005).

23. Herbert C. Kelman, "The Role of the Scholar-Practitioner in International Conflict Resolution," *International Studies Quarterly* 1, no. 3 (2000): 273–288; Nadim Rouhana and Herbert C. Kelman, "Promoting Joint Thinking in International Conflicts: An Israeli-Palestinian Continuing Workshop," *Journal of Social Issues* 50, no. 1 (1994): 157–178; Christopher R. Mitchell, *Peacemaking and the Consultant's Role* (Westmead, UK: Gower Press, 1981); Fisher, "Third Party Consultation"; Herbert C. Kelman, "The Problem-Solving Workshop in Conflict Resolution," in *Communication in International Politics,* ed. Richard L. Merritt (Urbana: University of Illinois Press, 1972); and John Burton, *Conflict and Communication: The Use of Controlled Communication in International Relations* (London: Macmillan, 1969).

24. Ronald J. Fisher and Loraleigh Keashly, "The Potential Complementarity of Mediation and Consultation within a Contingency Model of Third Party Intervention," *Journal of Peace Research* 28, no. 1, special issue on international mediation (1991): 29–42; and Rouhana and Kelman, "Promoting Joint Thinking in International Conflicts."

25. Kelman, "The Role of the Scholar-Practitioner in International Conflict Resolution"; and Rouhana and Kelman, "Promoting Joint Thinking in International Conflicts."

26. Kelman, "The Role of the Scholar-Practitioner in International Conflict Resolution."

27. Ibid.

28. Gennady Chufrin and Harold H. Saunders, "A Public Peace Process," *Negotiation Journal* 9, no. 3 (1993): 155–177.

29. Harold H. Saunders, "Sustained Dialogue in Tajikistan: Transferring Learning from the Public to the Official Peace Process," in *Paving the Way: Contributions of Interactive Conflict Resolution to Peacemaking*, ed. Ronald J. Fisher (Lanham, Md.: Lexington, 2005); and Randa Slim and Harold H. Saunders, "The Inter-Tajik Dialogue: From Civil War towards Civil Society," *Politics of Compromise: The Tajikistan Peace Process*, ed. Kamoludin Abdullaev and Catherine Barnes, ACCORD Series (London: Conciliation Resources, 2001).

30. Slim and Saunders, "The Inter-Tajik Dialogue."

31. Ibid; and Saunders, "Sustained Dialogue in Tajikistan."

32. Bigdon and Korf, "The Role of Development Aid in Conflict Transformation," 2.

33. Lederach, *Building Peace.*

34. Hugh Miall, "Conflict Transformation: A Multi-Dimensional Task" in *Berghof Handbook for Conflict Transformation*, ed. Bloomfield, Fischer, and Schmelzle, 4, http://www.berghof-handbook.net/articles/miall_handbook.pdf.

35. Hadley Jenner, '*When the Truth Is Denied, Peace Will Not Come': The People-to-People Process of the New Sudan Council of Churches* (Cambridge, Mass.: Collaborative for Development Action, 2000), http://www.cdainc.com.

36. For more information, see Search for Common Ground's Web site, http://www.sfcg.org/actdetail .cfm?locus=CGP&name=programs&prgramid =424.

37. John Wallach, *The Enemy Has a Face: The Seeds of Peace Experience* (Washington, D.C.: United States Institute of Peace Press, 2000).

38. Paula Gutlove and Gordon Thompson, "Human Security: Expanding the Scope of Public Health,"

Medicine, Conflict, and Survival 19, no. 1 (2003): 17–34.

39. Arne Strand, Hege Toje, Ingrid Samset, Alf Morten Jerve, and Inge Tvedten, *Community-Driven Development in Contexts of Conflict,* concept paper commissioned by ESSD and the World Bank (Bergen: Chr. Michelsen Institute, 2003).

40. Robert Putnam, *Bowling Alone: The Collapse and Revival of American Community* (New York: Simon and Schuster, 2000).

41. Lederach, *Building Peace.*

42. Louise Diamond, *The Courage for Peace: Daring to Create Harmony in Ourselves and the World* (York Beach, Maine: Conari Press, 1999).

43. Richmond, "Post-Westphalian Peace-Building."

44. Mercy Corps, *Maluku Case Study, Mercy Corps Indonesia: Integrating Relief, Recovery, and Civil Society in a Conflict-Affected Environment* (Portland, Ore.: Mercy Corps, 2002).

45. Mercy Corps also selected a Muslim and a Christian partner for its emergency warehouses for food distribution. The partners agreed to work together even though they had had no contact since the war began. Their relationship developed over the two years they worked together on procurement and in mixed communities, until they joined forces to create a consortium of Muslim and Christian organizations to advocate for the rights of conflict-affected people. Mercy Corps, "Maluku Case Study."

46. Marc H. Ross, "Evaluation in Conflict Resolution Training and Practice" (paper presented at a United States Institute of Peace symposium, Washington, D.C., June 27–28, 2000); and Daniel Lieberfeld, "Evaluating the Contributions of Track-Two Diplomacy to Conflict Termination in South Africa, 1984–90," *Journal of Peace Research* 39, no. 3 (2002): 355–372.

47. Jan Eliasson, "Perspectives on Managing Intractable Conflict," *Negotiation Journal* 20 (2002): 371–375.

48. R. William Ayres, "Mediating International Conflicts: Is Image Change Necessary?" *Journal of Peace Research* 34, no. 4 (1997): 431–447.

49. Emery Brusset and Ralf Otto, "Evaluation of Nashe Maalo: Design, Implementation, Outcomes, and Social Transformation through the Media (On Behalf of Search for Common Ground)" (Ohain,

Belgium: Channel Research, 2004), http://www.sfcg
.org/sfcg/evaluations/nash2004.pdf.

50. Indeed, one suggestion of the evaluators for the *Nashe Maalo* program was to develop or promote follow-up activities that help incorporate the *Nashe Maalo* model and thinking into everyday interethnic relations. Ibid., 69.

51. Marion Angelica, "Evaluation of Conflict Resolution Training Efforts Sponsored by Cyprus Fulbright Commission, 1993–1998" (Nicosia: Cyprus Fulbright Commission, 1999), http://www.Cyprus-conflict.net.

52. Susan Allen-Nan, "Unofficial Conflict Resolution as a Complement to Diplomacy: A Case Study of Georgian–South Ossetian Peace Process Highlighting Track One and a Half Diplomacy" (paper presented at the International Studies Association Convention, New Orleans, Louisiana, March 24, 2002).

53. Dalia D. Kaye, "Track Two Diplomacy and Regional Security in the Middle East," *International Negotiation* 6 (2001): 49–77; Kendra Kenyon, "The Development of a Comprehensive Interdisciplinary Learning Model for International Peacebuilding: The Case of Cyprus" (PhD. Diss., University of Idaho, 1999); and Conflict Management Group, "Final Report to AMIDEAST: Cyprus Conflict Management Project" (unpublished report, Conflict Management Group, Cambridge, Mass., 1994).

54. Jay Rothman and Marie Olson, "From Interests to Identities: Towards a New Emphasis in Interactive Conflict Resolution," *Journal of Peace Research* 38, no. 3 (2001): 289–305; and R. Frederic Pearson, "Dimensions of Conflict Resolution in Ethnopolitical Disputes," *Journal of Peace Research* 38, no. 3 (2001): 275–287.

55. Harold H. Saunders, "We Need a Larger Theory of Negotiation: The Importance of Prenegotiating Phases," *Negotiation Journal* 1, no. 3 (1985); Roelf Meyer, "Paradigm Shift—the Essence of Successful Change?" (Derry/Londonderry, UK: INCORE Occasional Papers, 2002), http://incore.ulst.ac.uk/home/publication/occasional; and Kaye, "Track Two Diplomacy and Regional Security in the Middle East."

56. Conflict Management Group, "Final Report to AMIDEAST: Cyprus Conflict Management Project" (unpublished reports, 1994, 1996).

57. Slim and Saunders, "The Inter-Tajik Dialogue."

58. Morton Deutsch, "Commentary: On Negotiating the Non-negotiable," in *Leadership and Negoti-*

ation in the Middle East, ed. Barbara Kellerman and Jeffrey Z. Rubin (New York: Praeger, 1988), 248–263.

59. Dean Pruitt and Sun Hee Kim, *Social Conflict: Escalation, Stalemate, and Settlement,* 3rd ed. (New York: McGraw-Hill, 2004), 108.

60. Kaye, "Track Two Diplomacy and Regional Security in the Middle East."

61. Diana Chigas, with Cheyanne Church, Jos De La Haye, Monica Llamazares, Olivera Markovic, and Artan Venhari, "What Difference Has Peacebuilding Made? Peacebuilding and the March '04 Riots in Kosovo" (Cambridge, Mass.: CDA-Collaborative Learning Projects, forthcoming).

62. Kelman, "The Role of the Scholar-Practitioner in International Conflict Resolution."

63. Meyer, "Paradigm Shift—the Essence of Successful Change?"; and Kelman, "The Role of the Scholar-Practitioner in International Conflict Resolution."

64. Schaffer and Schaffer, "Kashmir."

65. Angelica, "Evaluation of Conflict Resolution Training Efforts Sponsored by the Cyprus Fulbright Commission, 1993–1998."

66. Herbert C. Kelman, "Coalitions across Conflict Lines: The Interplay of Conflicts within and between the Israeli and Palestinian Communities," in *Conflict between People and Groups,* ed. Jeffrey Simpson and Steven Worchel (Chicago: Nelson-Hall, 1993), 240.

67. Nan, "Unofficial Conflict Resolutions as a Complement to Diplomacy."

68. Allen Nan, "Track-One-and-a-Half Diplomacy: Contributions to Georgian–South Ossetian Peacemaking," in *Paving the Way: Contributions of Interactive Conflict Resolution to Peacemaking,* ed. Ronald J. Fisher (Lanham, Md.: Lexington, 2005), 171; and "Unofficial Conflict Resolutions as a Complement to Diplomacy."

69. Kaye, "Track Two Diplomacy and Regional Security in the Middle East."

70. Chufrin and Saunders, "A Public Peace Process."

71. Schaffer and Schaffer, "Kashmir."

72. Slim and Saunders, "The Inter-Tajik Dialogue."

73. Lara Olson, *The Georgia–South Ossetia Dialogue: A View from the Inside,* Case Study, Reflecting

on Peace Practice Project (Cambridge, Mass.: Collaborative for Development Action, 2000).

74. For example, the informal meetings were partially responsible for a shift in Georgian policy of withholding from South Ossetia international aid for reconstruction. In addition, protocols signed by the leaders of the two sides on refugee return and on mutually acceptable identity documents, the installation of telephone lines, the reduction of peacekeeping posts, and assistance to Georgian–South Ossetian joint business ventures had their origins in the unofficial dialogue meetings. Ibid.

75. Mary B. Anderson and Lara Olson, *Confronting War: Critical Lessons for Peace Practitioners* (Cambridge, Mass.: CDA-Collaborative Learning Projects, 2003), 10.

76. Lieberfeld, "Evaluating the Contributions of Track-Two Diplomacy to Conflict Termination in South Africa, 1984–90."

77. Edy Kaufman and Saul Sosnowski, "The Peru-Ecuador Peace Process: The Contribution of Track-Two Diplomacy," in *Paving the Way: Contributions of Interactive Conflict Resolution to Peacemaking,* ed. Ronald Fisher (Lanham, Md.: Lexington, 2005).

78. Kelman, "Coalitions across Conflict Lines," 237–238.

79. Michael Salla, "East Timor," in *Private Peacemaking,* ed. Smock.

80. Lieberfeld, "Evaluating the Contributions of Track-Two Diplomacy to Conflict Termination in South Africa."

81. Ibid.

82. Oliver Wolleh, *Local Peace Constituencies in Cyprus: The Bicommunal Trainers' Group,* Berghof Report No. 8 (Berlin: Berghof Research Center, 2001).

83. Saunders, "Possibilities and Challenges," 272.

84. Louis Kriesberg, "Mediation and the Transformation of the Israeli-Palestinian Conflict," *Journal of Peace Research* 38, no. 3 (2001): 373–392; and Norbert Ropers, *Roles and Functions of Third Parties in the Constructive Management of Ethnopolitical Conflicts,* Berghof Occasional Paper 14 (Berlin: Berghof Research Centre for Constructive Conflict Management, 1997).

85. Mari Fitzduff, *Beyond Violence: Conflict Resolution Processes in Northern Ireland* (Washington, D.C.: Brookings Institution, 2002).

86. Putnam, *Bowling Alone.*

87. Ashutosh Varshney, *Ethnic Conflict and Civic Life: Hindus and Muslims in India,* 2nd ed. (New Haven, Conn.: Yale University Press, 2003); and Ashutosh Varshney, "Ethnic Conflict and Civil Society: India and Beyond" *World Politics* 53, no. 3 (2001): 362–398.

88. Slim and Saunders, "The Inter-Tajik Dialogue."

89. Diana Chigas and Brian Ganson, "Grand Visions and Small Projects: Coexistence Efforts in Southeastern Europe," in *Imagine Coexistence: Restoring Humanity after Violent Ethnic Conflict,* ed. Martha Minow and Antonia H. Chayes (San Francisco: Jossey-Bass, 2003); and Gavin Preuss, "Dialogical Development: A Kosovo Case Study," *Journal of Peacebuilding and Development* 1, no. 2 (2003): 36–48.

90. More information is available at Search for Common Ground's Web site, www.sfcg.org/actdetail.cfm?locus=CGP&name=programs&programid=64.

91. See, for example, Chigas, *What Difference Has Peacebuilding Made?;* Anderson and Olson, *Confronting War;* and Eileen Babbitt, "Imagine Coexistence: Assisting Refugee Reintegration Efforts in Divided Communities," Research Study Prepared for the UN High Commissioner for Refugees (Medford, Mass.: Fletcher School, 2002), available at http://fletcher .tufts.edu/chrcr/pdf/imagine.pdf.

92. Douglas Schlemmer, "Building Peace in Kosovo: An Assessment of Mercy Corps's PRM Refugee Assistance Programs," Policy Analysis Exercise (Cambridge, Mass.: John F. Kennedy School of Government, Harvard University, 2005).

93. Kelman, "The Role of the Scholar-Practitioner in International Conflict Resolution."

94. Kriesberg, "Mediation and the Transformation of the Israeli-Palestinian Conflict," 388.

95. Kaye, "Track Two Diplomacy and Regional Security in the Middle East," 68.

96. In Cyprus, for example, the Greek Cypriot government refused to protect participants in bicommunal activities from physical harassment by demonstrating nationalists at the buffer zone, while after 1997 the Turkish Cypriot government prosecuted civil servants participating in bicommunal activities under a law forbidding such contact.

97. Regional dialogues in the Middle East, for example, have suffered from negative media exposure.

98. Kelman, "Coalitions across Conflict Lines."

99. Michael Lund and Natasha Wanchek, *Effectiveness of Participatory Community Development in Managing Conflicts: Local Democracy, Social Capital, and Peace,* Report to USAID (Washington, D.C.: Management Systems International, 2004); and Chigas and Ganson, "Grand Visions and Small Projects."

100. Chigas and Ganson, "Grand Visions and Small Projects:" and John C. Turner, *Social Influence* (Pacific Grove, Calif.: Brooks/Cole, 1991).

101. Mohammed Abu-Nimer, *Dialogue, Conflict Resolution, and Change: Arab-Jewish Encounters in Israel* (New York: State University of New York Press, 1999).

102. Kriesberg, "Mediation and the Transformation of the Israeli-Palestinian Conflict."

103. Bronwyn Evans-Ken and Roland Breiker, "Peace Beyond the State? NGOs in Bosnia and Herzegovina," in *Paving the Way: Contributions of Interactive Conflict Resolution to Peacemaking,* ed. Ronald J. Fisher (Lanham, Md.: Lexington, 2005).

104. BBC News, "Washington Cuts Off Aid to Serbia," March 31, 2004, http://www.bbc.co.uk/l/hi/world/Europe/3586919.stm.

105. Douglas Schlemmer, "Building Peace in Kosovo."

106. Chigas and Ganson, "Grand Visions and Small Projects"; and Rothman and Olson, "From Interests to Identities."

107. Mary Anderson, *Do No Harm: How Aid Can Support Peace—or War* (Boulder, Colo.: Lynne Rienner, 1999); and Peter Uvin, *Aiding Violence: The Development Enterprise in Rwanda* (Hartford, Conn.: Kumarian Press, 1999).

108. Mary Anderson, *Options for Aid in Conflict: Lessons from Field Experience* (Cambridge, Mass.: CDA-Collaborative Learning Projects, 2000).

109. Ibid., 32.

110. Anderson has collected the experiences of a wide range of NGOs that have avoided or overcome these kinds of negative impacts. Ibid., 7.

111. Anderson and Olson, *Confronting War,* 64.

112. Ibid., 9, 46, 54.

113. Michael Schloms, "Humanitarian NGOs in Peace Processes," in *Mitigating Conflict: The Role of NGOs,* ed. Henry Carey and Oliver Richmond (London: Frank Cass, 2003).

114. Anderson and Olson, *Confronting War;* and Chigas and Ganson, "Grand Visions and Small Projects."

115. Chigas, "What Difference Has Peacebuilding Made?"

116. Ronald J. Fisher, "Conclusion: Evidence for the Essential Contributions of Interactive Conflict Resolution," in *Paving the Way: Contributions of Interactive Conflict Resolution to Peacemaking,* ed. Ronald J. Fisher (Lanham, Md.: Lexington 2005), 203–230.

117. This is changing as nongovernmental organizations involved in development and humanitarian assistance in conflict areas are becoming more concerned with their impact on conflict. The commitment of these agencies, however, to neutrality—and to maintaining the apolitical nature of their work—means that they have rarely become involved in activities with an overtly political dimension. (The Norwegian Refugee Council in Georgia–South Ossetia is an exception.)

118. Karin Aggestam, "Conflict Prevention: Old Wine in New Bottles?" in *Mitigating Conflict: The Role of NGOs,* ed. Henry Carey and Oliver Richmond (London: Frank Cass, 2003), 12-23.

119. Antonio Donini, Larry Minear, and Peter Walker, "The Future of Humanitarian Action: Mapping the Implications of Iraq and Other Recent Crises," *Disasters* 28, no. 2 (2004): 194.

32

WAR AND LAW
THE DILEMMAS OF
INTERNATIONAL LAW AND
COERCIVE ENFORCEMENT

Ruth Wedgwood

THE LIMITS OF LAW

International law is based on a gamble about reciprocity: that the articulation of fundamental values and operational rules of the road will assist states and free peoples in their mutual relations within an international system. It is, in part, a trading system of tit for tat. Each participant hopes to be rewarded for its contribution and self-restraint through similar behavior by others and expects some form of sanction for broad deviations. Law can contribute to the constructed identity and conceived self-interest of the players. And values of legitimacy and honor may constrain and impel the behavior of democratic states and their publics. Universal rules are valued as a sign of impartiality, granting equal respect for the claims of all human beings and political communities.

Yet law's high aspirations should not be mistaken for simplicity. The application of international law reflects the harried circumstances of an international system frequently dominated by regional rivalries, internal conflicts, resource constraints, and a narrower account of self-interest.

In the real world of international politics, states faced with security problems are commonly left to survive on their own. Regardless of the pretense, international organizations do not provide any automatic security guarantees or an international police force.[1] International law has not removed the desperate dilemmas faced by states or populations in unraveling situations. The law does not substitute for strategic deterrence or have a formula for avoiding conflict escalation. It does not oblate the fact that war is a daunting and unpredictable enterprise and that few countries will volunteer to fight on another's behalf unless they see their own safety at stake.

In framing the place of law, one must also acknowledge that traumatic events and historical tides often transform the structure of the international community, in ways that can make law's power seem modest in comparison. The granting of self-governance to colonial peoples was propelled by the exhaustion of Europe after World War II as well as by the moral worthiness of the claim. The extension of public international law to protect the rights of individuals against gross mistreatment grew from the moral abyss of the Holocaust, in which no other country took the part of European Jews. International human rights law now asserts that the rights of individuals are of cogent interest, regardless of citizenship. Yet alongside the law's extension, World War II brought a moral and physical exhaustion that has not yet spent its force. Europe pledged to abolish the use of military force within Europe's own community, but this same reticence about the past has engendered a reluctance to invest in the military infrastructure needed to play a global role. The "responsibility to protect" is now a familiar refrain in the language of the United Nations community,[2] but there are few countries interested in contributing the combat forces, or even peacekeeping personnel, needed to make good on the moral pledge of protection in situations of genocidal conflict or international threat. Japan and Germany are the second and third largest economies of the world, but have hesitated to invest in the force structure, transport, and logistics needed to deal with humanitarian and security crises outside their immediate areas. The several countries that are reliable sources of peacekeepers, such as Pakistan, India, and Bangladesh, do not have logistical capabilities for long-range power projection.

And then, of course, there is the classic problem of "collective action" described several decades ago by economist Mancur Olson and lately detailed by rational choice and game theory.[3] It would be pleasing if this were only a theoretician's construct, but its effect is seen again and again in international crises. A state may benefit from the "public good" of international security and yet see little reason to bear the immediate costs of its provision. If there is another state likely to confront a common foe, or if a threat is distant in time or geography, a state may gamble that it does not

need to volunteer to meet the challenge. It may hope to buy a "separate peace" from an adversary or just enjoy the positive effects of security efforts by others. Indeed, at times, some have worried that the growth of international criminal law and penalties imposed after an event is complete may become a convenient excuse for inaction at the time of a crisis. Promising accountability for war crimes after the fact may divert attention from the failure to take the needed measures of prevention and assistance on behalf of a beleaguered population.

There is also the normative problem of "catching up." International legal rules are typically defined by treaty, by customary law (consisting of state practice and legal consensus), or by a slender category of fundamental norms that do not depend directly on consent, called *jus cogens*. But treaties are hard to revise and may survive only through reinterpretation in light of changed circumstances. The negotiation of new rules through treaty amendments or new regimes is rarely available until long after a crisis has passed. Customary law is equally stolid, with no obvious means for change other than the emergence of new state practice that may initially be disputed. And the idea of a binding peremptory norm is too delicate to be turned into an all-purpose gap filler when consensus is hard to achieve, although international lawyers have traditionally taken some account of the idea of natural law and moral limits as in the famous Martens formula.[4]

The halting sources of law and adaptation may not matter much when there is normative consensus around a problem. But the intractability of the law, and the obvious investment in its observance because it *is* law, may actually inhibit the international community's willingness to respond to a crisis. Differences in legal tradition, style, and language may influence the willingness to adapt international law to new problems. Continental lawyers from the civil tradition suppose that the law can and should be codified and specified in advance.

The propriety of equitable exceptions to an absolute rule is not openly acknowledged, though some argue that the delegation of enforcement to official authority provides a source of adaptation.[5] In contrast, Anglo-American common law has supposed that the law is necessarily incomplete, and is built and changed through the accretion of individual cases and incidents, rather than through codification. The common-law view of the normative power of accumulated practice fits within the philosophical traditions of pragmatism and skepticism, doubting that abstractions could ever suffice to resolve all real-life dilemmas, and draws implicitly on a philosophy of language that doubts the determinacy of words and phrases. In addition, the common-law view of an open-ended law may reflect the sense that codification is bound to be premature in any rapidly changing situation. Certainly in the portion of international law that deals with armed conflict, one discovers that new technologies and strategic dilemmas have pushed the law, at least in operational aspects.

International law also faces the constant problem of balancing aspiration against a realist's prediction of what states will be willing to accept. The high stakes of war and conflict require a hardheaded calculation about compliance and defiance. A state responsible for the protection of its society and population will ultimately recall that the law is not self-executing, and an observant party must calculate the costs if the other party abandons the law for immediate strategic advantage.

In addition, one must face the politics of law creation. Negotiating security matters has been more difficult for the United States in the post–Cold War environment. The welcome end of the Cold War gave Europe a new independence, and some Continental governments proved eager to define their differences from the United States. The European Union no longer expects to fight wars and has not sought a broad "out-of-area" role in security policy. It entertains different views on the role of military strength in international politics, whether as a source of deterrence or enforcement. Indeed, Europe's stance at times seems a resumption of the peace movement of the mid-nineteenth century, with the optimistic assumption that simple persuasion and economic sanctions will suffice as sources of containment against spoilers in the international system. Europe's stated aspiration for an "ethical" foreign policy has also driven issues with immediate operational consequences for countries that must deploy forces in the field, even in international peace enforcement operations. In the United Nations and its venues of negotiation, international treaty texts are most often delivered at the conclusion of large multilateral conferences, where nongovernmental organizations take an active role. This also can make it harder for interested states, including major democracies, to arrive at stable and common negotiating positions that weigh the practical concerns of statecraft. The responsibilities of sovereignty are, strange to say, sometimes underrepresented in public settings in showcase conferences.

Finally, in preliminary measure, one should acknowledge that opinions delivered on the law are not always immune from the effect of political considerations. This is a temptation for all sides. The same values and challenges animate the positions taken by a state both in international law and in international diplomacy. If a state does not wish to contribute to a peace operation, it is easy to say that the operation is unlawful rather than to acknowledge a self-regarding protective judgment. And in some societies, the prestige of the law is such that critics may choose to frame political, moral, and prudential disagreements in the imperative language of the law. Conversely, if a state believes that an intervention is morally compelled, such as humanitarian intervention against genocide, it is tempting to assert that what is legitimate, and indeed morally imperative, may also be legal.

COERCION AND INTERNATIONAL REGIMES

With these preliminaries, we may turn to the question of the international legal framework for regulating the use of armed force. We will look at the anxious issues of *jus ad bellum* (when a state can resort to armed force) rather than issues of *jus in bello* (how a war is fought), though both are sources of controversy and difficulty. One discovers the full run of problems in adapting an international legal framework to political and security situations that have worked out differently than earlier draftsmen supposed.

The framers of the United Nations Charter, working in San Francisco in June 1945, gambled that member states would create a collective security mechanism sufficient to meet any major threats to international peace and security. This was an improbable assumption, after the manifest failure of the League of Nations in the 1920s and 1930s. The League, after all, did not thwart the rearmament of Germany, the invasion of Ethiopia, the invasion of Manchuria, or Hitler's designs on the Sudetenland. It was clear, from the League, that a collective security organization is no more robust than the will of its members. The fatal consequences of interwar disarmament by England and France should have taught that dwindling military budgets and declining military capacity can be an invitation to adventure by other rising powers. Yet even in 1945, it was possible for allies to overlook the hazards of disarmament, because the United States' absence from the League of Nations seemed by itself a sufficient explanation for the organization's failure. The belief that an American presence would make a difference in the capacity of the United Nations was there from the beginning, even if the current asymmetric power enjoyed by the United States was hard to imagine at the time.

The United Nations at its start was not a formal organization. Rather, the name derives from the wartime alliance against the fascist powers. The Atlantic Charter of 1941 declared that the United States and United Kingdom would seek the final destruction of the Nazi tyranny.[6] This was followed by the United Nations Declaration of 1942, pledging the twenty-six allied states to the goal of unconditional victory against Germany and Japan.[7] A realist might have wondered about the durability of a wartime alliance, even under an inspiring name. Moscow's history did not mark it as a natural ally. Russia's nonaggression pact with Hitler and historic ambitions in the Balkans and Central Asia pointed to future sources of conflict. The Russian footprint in Central Europe was foreseeable, in light of the Yalta and Potsdam Agreements. The Comintern agenda for Western Europe warned of additional dangers. Some diplomatic historians have read the United Nations Charter as an attempt to keep the United States involved abroad in the postwar period, beating back a return to U.S. isolationism by building on the architecture of the original alliance of World War II.[8] Franklin Roosevelt and Harry Truman were not naive, in this view. Rather they thought that the entanglement of legal alliances was the only way to break the American habit of returning home.

The United Nations Charter was negotiated after the end of the fighting in Europe, but before the surrender of Japan. The June 1945 charter signing was punctuated two months later by the explosion of atomic bombs over Hiroshima and Nagasaki, shocking the leadership of Japan into surrender. That startling juxtaposition, of pacific aspiration and bellicose fact, may be a useful tonic to any readers who are inclined to think of the UN Charter as an automatic machine of conflict resolution. Soon after the war concluded, Soviet ambitions in Turkey and Greece became apparent, and President Harry Truman announced a U.S. commitment to the region. The Berlin blockade in 1948 and the founding of the North Atlantic Treaty Organization in 1949 made plain that the wartime alliance with Russia was over. The 1950 North Korean invasion of the southern Korean peninsula was countered by the first official police action of the United Nations. With a commitment to conjoint decision making that may now seem distant, U.S. secretary of state Dean Acheson felt obliged to invoke the powers of the General Assembly to authorize the use of force, stepping outside the charter through the "Uniting for Peace" resolution to circumvent an anticipated Soviet veto in the Security Council. The United States did not rely simply on a theory of collective self-defense under Article 51 of the charter.

It is well to start with the plain text of the UN Charter for a sense of how the system was supposed to work. The charter invokes the "scourge of war" as a harm to be avoided and seeks to limit armed force as a casual instrument of national ambition. Clausewitz's instrumental view of war as an available extension of politics was eschewed by the UN Charter. A state could no longer embark on a campaign of conquest seeking booty or territory. Rather, Article 2(4) of the UN Charter enjoins that "[a]ll Members shall refrain in their international relations from the threat or use of force against the territorial integrity or political independence of any state, or in any other manner inconsistent with the Purposes of the United Nations."

Article 2(4) was anything but straightforward, nonetheless. It may be a simple or a complex injunction. It can be read as a prohibition on any threat or use of force, *tout simple,* even for an end that enforces the norms of international law. Or instead it may be read as a more limited bar, only condemning the deployment of armed force for the illicit purposes of prejudicing the territorial integrity or political independence of another state or otherwise traducing the purposes of the United Nations pact.

The complications in reading Article 2(4) are enhanced when considered against the background of the Kellogg-Briand Pact of 1928. This celebrated Pact of Paris sought to abolish the use of war. The agreement between U.S. secretary of state Frank Kellogg and French foreign minister Aristide Briand was then extended to other states, and its terms were explained in a U.S. circular letter. The circular letter states that the right of self-defense is not limited by the agreement and even intimates that this exception might be self-judging.[9] One interpretive question is thus whether the UN Charter should be read in light of the Kellogg-Briand assurances, and what those assurances meant in practice.

But the UN Charter is also different, for it proposes a collective security scheme seeking to bypass the need for self-help. Article 24 of the charter announces that the Security Council is to have "primary responsibility for the maintenance of international peace and security," in order to "ensure prompt and effective action by the United Nations." This includes the power to investigate international disputes and to recommend procedures and methods of peaceful resolution, per Articles 33 and 34. Added to this are the famous provisions of Chapter VII of the charter, allowing the Security Council to install mandatory measures against the parties to a dispute, including economic sanctions, the severance of diplomatic relations, and, ultimately, the use of armed force.[10] To gain these powers, the council must agree on an assessment that there is a "threat to the peace, breach of the peace, or act of aggression," and that measures must be undertaken "to maintain or restore international peace and security." Chapter VII allows an escalatory ladder. The Security Council may recommend mediation, negotiation, or arbitration to adversaries, in the attempt to avoid the use of force. But should peaceful methods of crisis resolution fail, then the council has the power to mandate coercive measures.

There are evident problems with this device. A decision by the Security Council requires the affirmative vote of at least nine of the fifteen members of the council, and requires the concurrence of the five permanent members. Only by a bit of legal legerdemain was the charter interpreted to allow abstentions by the permanent members to count as concurring votes.[11]

And then there is the question of an effective remedy. Under Article 41 of the charter, the Security Council has frequently resorted to economic sanctions, of wide or narrow scope, in the attempt to dissuade a state from provocative action. The multilateral basis of a sanctions regime is important, if one wishes to avoid opportunistic market penetration and frustration of the sanctions by commercial rivals. Sanctions were at the center of the League of Nations enforcement scheme, and despite their inefficacy in that setting, the framers of the UN Charter clearly hoped that they would be workable in the postwar world.

But sanctions have not met their advance billing. Several empirical studies have argued persuasively that sanctions have little chance of compelling a change of policy to which an adversary is strongly committed and, in any event, will achieve such a result only over a long period of time.[12] Broad sanctions have the unfortunate effect of imposing serious hardship on a civilian population and may allow an autocratic regime to strengthen its power by controlling the distribution of scarce goods. Ethicists are bound to note that the idea of "targeting" civilians in order to induce a change of government policy is seen, in the parallel setting of law of war, as legally impermissible. The question is thus put, why sanctions deliberately targeting a civilian population to work a political change might not be subject to the same challenge.[13] In practical terms, a regime of sanctions can create serious problems in postconflict reconstruction, by disrupting the economy and running down the national infrastructure. Sanctions often inflict damage on neighboring countries, as seen in the effect of the sanctions against Serbia on the economy of Macedonia to the south, and the effect of sanctions against Iraq on the

neighboring states of Turkey and Jordan. The neighbor of a targeted country may have structured much of its economy around its role as a trading partner or entrepôt. The UN Charter allows such an injured third-party state to seek assistance from the Security Council, but in fact that portion of Chapter VII has been a dead letter.

The mitigation of the hardship of sanctions on a civilian population, by drilling a hole in a sanctions program to provide humanitarian goods, can also create complications, as seen in the Oil-for-Food Programme in Iraq. Saddam Hussein collected a kickback from the suppliers of humanitarian goods and imposed a surcharge on Iraqi oil exports, correctly gauging that the international community would not have the capacity or the energy to counter these misdeeds. The distribution of oil allotments to international political supporters of the Iraqi regime in the course of the sanctions debate sought to influence the politics of Security Council members themselves.

The design of "smart" sanctions has been championed as a way to get past these difficulties, by targeting regime elites and their personal finances rather than general populations. In addition, sanctions have been directed against civil war combatants and their local resources, by seeking to bar the world-market distribution of valuable minerals such as "conflict diamonds."[14] One may entertain a measure of skepticism about the practical effect of this, yet diamonds can be marked with holographs and sanctions still serve as political markers of public disapproval and political disgust.

RESORTING TO FORCE

Where sanctions are ineffective, the Security Council is authorized to take the profound step of using deadly force—mounting "such action by air, sea, or land forces as may be necessary to maintain or restore international peace and security." This power under Article 42 of the UN charter does not require the formal exhaustion of alternatives, although in the political world such exhaustion is often wise.

It is well to remember that the charter's original conception of collective force was a very different model than the patchwork system that later evolved. The charter text presumes that armed forces will be ready at hand for missions framed by the Security Council. Article 43 recites that "[a]ll Members of the United Nations . . . undertake to make available to the Security Council . . . armed forces, assistance and facilities," pursuant to negotiated cooperation agreements. In addition, Article 45 anticipates the availability of air power. Member states were to "hold immediately available national air-force contingents for combined international enforcement action." In turn, a "military staff committee" was to be assigned the task, under Article 47, of dispensing advice on military questions, and was to include the "Chiefs of Staff of the permanent members of the Security Council or their representatives." The military staff committee was seen as a venue for "strategic direction of any armed forces placed at the disposal of the Security Council," with issues of operational command worked out thereafter.

Standing forces were, of course, never provided. The UN military staff committee has convened for decades only for a nominal meeting, adjourned *sine die*, by its low-level members. In 1945, the United States Congress authorized President Truman to provide a discrete number of troops at the United Nations' disposal, through an Article 43 agreement, reflected in the United Nations Participation Act of 1945. But the Cold War intervened, and such an agreement was never completed. In retrospect, it may seem naïve to suppose that any country would have been willing to send troops around the globe, at the United Nations' call, without exercising a choice of yea or nay on each particular proposal. In peacekeeping and in peace enforcement, the willingness of countries to contribute forces depends crucially on the type of conflict and the identities of the parties. Sentimental ties, perceived self-interest, and the political views of democratic publics all limit the willingness of states to commit their troops for a purpose yet to be named.

The UN Charter's security scheme has also been rewritten by practical problems as much as by politics. The limits of a loose political organization in providing operational command are plain. At the time of the 1994 Rwanda massacre, the secretary-general said he lacked any ability to communicate directly with the force commander of UN troops in the field. The "operations center" of UN Headquarters in New York still lacks any secure or encrypted line to transmit communications to the field. And even in more benign circumstances, in light-duty peacekeeping, few states are willing to place their troops under international operational command. A UN peacekeeping force commander soon discovers that his orders will be obeyed only after each contingent clears the proposal with its national capital, and this holds true for democracies where the disposition of troops is of keen interest to the public and the legislature.

In addition, one cannot forget that in modern war fighting, joint forces pose a daunting challenge. Forces cannot be intermarried a few days before a particular crisis. A joint war-fighting force requires a shared conception of operations, extensive training and exercises, compatible communications, and a practiced sense of specific capabilities. The willingness to rely on a partner requires a track record of past performance. It is thus a conceit to suppose that standby military forces can be married into a joint force on short notice. Few states would commit troops to an operation where they had not been intimately involved in the planning.

And then there is the problem of intelligence. Military operations depend crucially on both strategic and tactical intelligence. The United Nations has traditionally been uncomfortable with the very idea of intelligence, since collection presupposes limited transparency and surreptitious operations. As an all-inclusive organization, the United Nations has been loath to discriminate among its members on access to information. Even if intelligence were distributed only to Security Council members, belligerent states can seek a friend in that setting.

The idea of operational UN combat forces was thus quickly tabled in the real-life application of the charter. The allied defense of South Korea in 1950 was described as a UN police operation, but it consisted of troops volunteered by interested parties under a joint U.S. command. In a radical transformation of the "common law" UN Charter, the exercise of authority by the Security Council has been limited to the authorization of the use of force by volunteer states, rather than the actual mustering of needed military forces. In its practice, the Security Council has never suggested that any particular states have a legal obligation to contribute forces, either for enforcement operations or for peacekeeping. A state faced with the threat of aggression may appeal to the Security Council for aid and assistance, but in practice, rescue will depend on the affiliation and support of interested and friendly allies. One might thus style the operative UN Charter as "Version 2.0." Under its aegis, international law provides no guarantee of protection against aggression of the rankest kind.

After the fall of the Berlin Wall, some observers hoped that the Security Council could gain a new efficacy. Indeed, after Iraqi forces invaded Kuwait, the council voted economic sanctions and then approved the use of force by the allies. But the formal UN role was limited to authorization, with no suggestion that any country in particular must contribute armed forces to the effort. After the successful coalition effort, UN Secretary-General Boutros Boutros-Ghali fielded a major white paper, styled "An Agenda for Peace," seeking to project a future role for the United Nations. The secretary-general briefly supposed that formal

Article 43 agreements might have a future, but then retreated to the practical position that the United Nations should simply solicit states to see what forces might be available for future peacekeeping efforts.[15]

One should not deride the Security Council's normative role. An authorizing vote by the council has political and legal advantages for any coalition of the willing assembled in defense of a victim state. The force of a council resolution under Chapter VII will largely quiet issues about the legality, if not the prudence, of using force. But it is crucial to remember that a resolution is not a summons or call to arms; it is no more than permission. Indeed, when the major powers anticipate difficulty in finding countries willing to contribute forces, they are often reluctant to vote authorization in the first place.

A parallel roadblock that challenges multilateral action is political. The Security Council is, at root, a political organ. Although it is charged with meeting threats to international peace, its members may take positions that involve an individual calculation of advantage and hazard. This is not always a matter open to public inspection. Security Council members can be influenced by the views of the regional group to which they belong. Though the UN Charter speaks of universal ideals, votes often fracture along regional lines. Member states are organized and vote in regional slates when they seek political positions in the larger UN structure, acting through such little known regional groups as GRULAC (the Latin and Caribbean states) and WEOG (West European and others), as well as the African and Asian groups. Countries of the South often reach common positions in closed-door meetings of the 115-member "Non-Aligned Movement," the 132-member so-called Group of 77, and the 56-member "Organization of the Islamic Conference." The need of a state for cooperation on other issues in its regional group may affect its vote on security matters in formal organs of the

United Nations. In addition, bilateral relationships and bilateral disputes between states can affect Security Council votes. China, for example, notoriously refused to extend the UN preventative deployment in Macedonia when that small state recognized Taiwan. The Haitian peacekeeping mission was interrupted for a similar reason. Some problems are never reflected on the council's agenda, because of the influence of permanent members of the council and other large powers. The influence of India and the veto of China mean that the disputes in Sri Lanka and Tibet are not likely to be seen on the council's agenda. This brand of politics affects the substance of council decisions as well. The Security Council can vote a mandate only with the assent of the five permanent members and four of the ten rotating nonpermanent members. Thus, any superpower in the council can veto or recast an enforcement action.

The Security Council also has organizational preoccupations that can affect the reaction to new crises. In the 1990s, at the high point of peacekeeping, with crises in Cambodia, Bosnia, Somalia, and Haiti, it was hard for the council to take on new business. The fatigue of peacekeeping contributors may exhaust the likely sources of new troops and, in turn, affect the willingness of the Security Council to engage a crisis. The efforts of a West African regional organization in Sierra Leone and Liberia in the early 1990s reflected the council's distraction. The Economic Community of West African States, led by Nigeria and Ghana, mounted peacekeeping missions in Liberia and Sierra Leone at a time when the UN council did not wish to engage new commitments. The council later applauded the regional efforts. But this example of gaining Security Council approval after the fact rewrote the practical understanding of Chapter VIII of the UN Charter. Article 53 was classically read to require prior authorization by the council of any regional enforcement action,[16] but the ECOWAS episode was taken to constitute an effective reworking of this rule.[17]

There is nothing in the UN Charter that need celebrate passivity. The United Nations was originally conceived as a war-fighting alliance against the aggression of Germany and Japan, and the purpose of the United Nations Declaration of 1942 was to pledge that the allies would continue to fight. But the discordant nature of international politics, the need for volunteers in troop provision, and the requirement of gaining the assent of a supermajority of the Security Council mean in practice that there is often no action. Especially in the Bosnian crisis, it was observed that the council was more inclined to rely on rhetoric than on enforcement. When the secretary-general proposed the creation of "safe areas" to protect civilians in Bosnia, the council approved the idea but could not muster more than seven thousand troops—falling far short of the thirty-four thousand troops estimated to be necessary. In a sense, this shortfall foretold the Srebrenica massacre, when UN forces did not resist a Serb offensive. Fidelity to the United Nations system thus can create a dilemma. The use of collective action in resorting to force has normative prestige. But there are occasions when the timely use of force is necessary to prevent catastrophe. The Security Council may choose not to act, tethered by its disparate membership, by the rivalries among major powers, or simply by differing views on what the situation requires. The moral and, in a larger sense, legal dilemma is whether inaction is always an acceptable price, in order to respect the supermajority decision rule of the council and the force of the veto permitted to the permanent members.

COERCION AND STABILITY

One is thus put to hard questions about the relationship between the UN Charter and effective international security. One view of the international system is that the use of force and indeed the threat of force must be exceptional and extraordinary and that the Security Council's frequent inclination to defer decision is a caution that should be respected. Waiting for the Security Council is the cost of preserving an impartial arbiter of international crises. A scattered regime of self-judging actors would lead to a proliferation of conflicts, in this view. Forbidding unilateral state decisions to intervene is the necessary cost of preventing anarchy. In any event, it is argued, the council's political split is a likely sign that the merits of intervention are doubtful.

But a competing view argues that the Security Council may be paralyzed for reasons far removed from the merits of the dispute and the human values at stake. The deliberative role of the council is important, but may be worth truncating in a particular case in order to take the action needed to save human life and avoid catastrophe.

This may be a setting in which interpretive ambiguity has some virtues. The Security Council may be more inclined to take action if it supposes that a respected coalition of the willing or regional organization can intervene in the event of its abdication. In addition, there are varied forms of council action. Other decisions by the council may contribute indirectly to the legitimacy of an intervention by an *ad hoc* coalition, even where there is no specific mandate for the use of force. In the Kosovo crisis, for example, NATO's military intervention to protect the Muslim population against abuse by Belgrade was mounted without a Chapter VII resolution. But the Security Council had earlier concluded that Milosevic was exercising indiscriminate violence against the Kosovar Albanian community.[18] And after the military campaign was completed, the Security Council concluded that a transitional administration should displace Serbia's governance of the province until the ultimate fate of Kosovo was determined by referendum.[19] Thus, the predicate for NATO's intervention depended on the United Nations' diagnosis of the crisis, and the suspension of Serbian administration after the military intervention was imposed by the authority of the United Nations.

The common-sense reader may wonder why the idea of self-defense is not broad enough to accommodate the emergencies where the Security Council has abdicated. But the UN Charter's language is less helpful. The charter speaks in Article 51 of an inherent right of self-defense in a single situation, without clarifying whether this is an example or the limit. Article 51 recognizes and acknowledges the "inherent right" of individual and collective self-defense where "an armed attack occurs against a Member of the United Nations." But this leaves a number of contested areas that are obviously of great concern in the present state of the international community, where a security threat seems urgent but there has not yet been an armed attack by one state against another state.

First, what should happen when a state attacks its own population in a genocidal campaign? Such a depredation may not launch an interstate war, yet the human harm can be as profound. In recent years, the Security Council has concluded that threats to international peace and security can be read broadly to include internal conflicts. Large-scale pogroms and massacres generate cross-border refugee flows and cause regional destabilization, harming human security in the same fashion as a cross-border war. But these second-order effects are in truth an attempt to extend the normative reach of Chapter VII. The rereading of "international peace and security" expands the occasions when the council can authorize the use of force under a multilateral mandate to protect human security.

If the council is justified in taking an expanded view of its own authority, there may be an argument based on coherence to suppose that Article 51 itself should be read more broadly. Perhaps an armed attack on a population should "count" in the same way that an attack against a member state is counted—

justifying the use of force to protect innocent lives, allowing intervention by an ad hoc coalition even in the absence of a Security Council decision. Indeed, Secretary-General Kofi Annan has offered an opinion close to this view. In an eloquent address to the General Assembly in September 1999, titled "Sovereignty and Intervention," he recalled the Rwandan genocide.[20] His backward glance came a few months after NATO had intervened in Kosovo lacking a specific authorizing resolution from the Security Council.

The secretary-general recalled the international community's utter abdication in the midst of the Rwanda genocide. Faced with a crescendo of attacks by Hutu militia against Tutsi civilians, the United Nations unaccountably withdrew its peacekeeping force from Rwanda in April 1994, and the Security Council declined to authorize any new and more robust intervention force. The secretary-general asked with evident chagrin whether that was a satisfactory moral history. If an international ad hoc coalition were willing and able to intervene in Rwanda to interrupt and stem the genocide, should that assemblage of countries have refrained from acting in the absence of a Security Council resolution? The secretary-general mused plaintively: "If, in those dark days and hours leading up to the genocide, a coalition of States had been prepared to act in defence of the Tutsi population, but did not receive prompt Council authorization, should such a coalition have stood aside and allowed the horror to unfold?"[21] Annan did not answer the question, but left the plangent conclusion to the listener.

Allowing intervention against genocide even without the immediate approval of the Security Council would credit the substantive purposes of the charter alongside its procedures. The foundational nature of the Genocide Convention may also deserve special weight in the construction of the UN Charter. Procedural perfectionism would not then drain the charter of its normative commitments.

A second challenge to the regulation of force stems from the problem of weapons of mass destruction in the hands of irresponsible regimes or non-state actors. How should one handle the problem of warning and anticipation, where the impact of an attack will be devastating? International law scholars in the United States generally hold that Article 51 of the UN Charter allows so-called anticipatory self-defense when an armed attack is imminent. The classic formulation of anticipatory defense derives from a British and American incident of 1837, the *Caroline* case, in which a group of Irish-American revolutionaries embarked on a cross-border invasion of Canada. The British sank the insurgents' ship on the American side of the Niagara River, and this was accepted by U.S. secretary of state Daniel Webster as a permissible action of defense. The standard, Webster said, was whether a hostile threat was "instant, overwhelming, leaving no choice of means, and no moment for deliberation."[22] The UN secretary-general has acknowledged the propriety of anticipatory self-defense in some circumstances,[23] though the doctrine is less congenial to European public international law scholars. The problem remains whether even the *Caroline* test and its required demonstration of "instant" threat will suffice in a world of WMD where a single blow can be devastating and the signs of an impending attack may be nonexistent. With weapons of mass destruction, there may be no sign of armies mobilizing on a border or other manifest signals. Intelligence collection is a delicate craft, and one may apprehend the general attitude of an adversary but remain unable to characterize a foe's immediate specific intent.

This problem did not come to crisis in the Cold War's fifty-year confrontation with the Soviet Union because of the sheer fact of deterrence. The strategic nuclear doctrine of "mutually assured destructive capability" was grim in its contemplation, but the ability to strike back effectively against any first attack meant that an adversary had to contemplate the loss of his own society in any nuclear exchange.[24] In an age of nonstate actors, the logic of deterrence is absent. Terror groups can be mobile. They lack the broader linkages and commitments of a state. And with no return address, there is no second-strike capability. This could also be a fateful dilemma where a state regime has decided to quietly hand off weaponry to such an agent.[25]

Deterrence may also be lacking because of the nature of the weapons. Biological weapons cannot be used even in a retaliatory stike, because of the disastrous effect on innocent civilians and future generations. The source of a biological attack may also be obscure, limiting even conventional retaliation.

Thus, a strategist is newly brought to the question of whether it is ever licit to use defensive force to eliminate a weapons capability, even before an adversary has demonstrable intent to mount an attack. In the case of nonstate actors, there is no recognized right to accumulate any military capability. The Security Council has mandated in Resolution 1373, passed under Chapter VII authority, that states cannot give any direct or de facto assistance to international terror groups, whether through the provision of logistics, weapons, intelligence, or even territorial asylum.[26] A state's unwillingness or inability to control such actors in "ungoverned areas" may justify a more direct response.

The United Nations has recognized the strategic abyss created by weapons of mass destruction and the potential collaboration between reckless regimes and international terror groups. In December 2004, the secretary-general's High-Level Panel on Threats, Challenges, and Change warned that the association of "irresponsible states" and international terror groups could pose an extraordinary danger. Even if a state is the only actor likely to have the capability of assembling certain weapons, their delivery to nonstate actors could lead to an attack whose source was disguised. De-

terrence would then fail. There is a hope that the fissile elements of a nuclear or radiological weapon could give a sufficient telltale concerning place of manufacture, to deter complicit state actors. But the UN High Level Panel reached a dire conclusion about this kind of state-nonstate collaboration. This somber view was taken by some extraordinary "formers"— a retired Russian prime minister, a Chinese vice premier, a French constitutional council president, a British ambassador to the United Nations, an Australian foreign minister, and a U.S. national security adviser. There was unanimity that WMD capacity in the hands of an "irresponsible state" would pose a grave and lively threat to international peace and security.

The High-Level Panel's conclusion was historic, asserting that state acquisition of weapons capacity could be actionable by the international community, even against states that stand outside or exit from treaty-based arms control regimes. To be sure, the acquisition and use of biological and chemical weapons are already banned by *treaty* law for participating states. Customary law bans the *first use* of chemical weapons and *any use* of biological weapons. But acquistion of these deadly agents was not limited by customary law. Even now, states that have not joined the Nuclear Nonproliferation Treaty still claim the right to acquire nuclear weapons. The High-Level Panel's doctrine suggests, for the first time, that the acquisition of mere capacity might be countered as a threat to international peace and security. The panel soberly warns that "[i]n the world of the twenty-first century, the international community does have to be concerned about nightmare scenarios combining terrorists, weapons of mass destruction and irresponsible States, and much more besides, which may conceivably justify the use of force, not just reactively but preventively and before a latent threat becomes imminent."[27] Indeed, UN Secretary-General Kofi Annan similarly noted that "[w]here threats are not imminent but latent, the Charter gives full authority to the

Security Council to use military force, including preventively, to preserve international peace and security."[28] Former National Security Advisor Brent Scowcroft has taken a similar view.[29]

To be sure, the High-Level Panel assumes that it is the Security Council that will confront the challenge of "irresponsible states." The United Nations, says the panel, no longer is mired in a Cold War where the Security Council was "manifestly not operating as an effective collective security system."[30] The end of ideological confrontation between East and West may indeed strengthen the relative capacity of the Security Council to address common threats. And catastrophic terrorism, including the threat posed by radical Islamist terror groups, remains a first-tier concern of the world's major powers. But it may be too much to assume, as the panel does, that the council will be able to act. The temptations of national self-interest, including economic relationships with countries that combine oil and radical regimes, may stand in the way. Even Voltaire's Dr. Pangloss would be hard put, in a post–September 11 world, to suppose that the absence of collective action shows the absence of a problem.[31] Indeed, in discussing the work of the High-Level Panel, UN secretary-general Kofi Annan and former national security adviser Brent Scowcroft seemed to acknowledge just this point.[32]

It has been a matter of controversy whether the military intervention against Iraq in March 2003 was intended to advance such a new paradigm of preventive action. After September 11, 2001, there was renewed concern that Iraqi programs to develop weapons of mass destruction could lead to a handoff of matériel to nonstate actors, including Islamist terror groups. But the Security Council had set the ground rules for Iraq more than a decade before, in the aftermath of the invasion of Kuwait. In March 1991, Security Resolution 687 declared imperative conditions to the cease-fire after allied forces expelled Iraq's invasion force from Kuwait. Prime among these conditions was that Iraq would refrain, in perpetuity, from any research, development, manufacture, stockpiling, or use of weapons of mass destruction, as well as missiles with a range beyond 150 kilometers.

This was a unique legal regime, at the time of the council's action. It was not based on speculation about intention but rather was seen as a necessary response to limit a regime that was already dangerous, as shown by the invasion of Kuwait. The March 2003 intervention in Iraq was undertaken by an allied coalition without the availability of a new Security Council resolution authorizing the use of force. But it is at least arguable that the original council authorization for the use of force, meeting the 1991 invasion of Kuwait, was still valid and available, in light of Iraq's deliberate breach of the cease-fire conditions. Thus, the 2003 allied intervention in Iraq need not be seen as a harbinger of a larger doctrine.

Nonetheless, the Iraqi intervention has been interpreted by some as an example of preventive response. The U.S. *National Security Strategy* issued in 2002 spoke of the possibility of preventive intervention under extraordinary circumstances.[33]

Even apart from these quandaries regarding unilateral versus multilateral action, and imminence versus capacity, there is a separate emerging debate about the power of the council itself. In supposing that Security Council authorization can quell all controversies, some proponents of charter classicism may have overlooked a separate flank of attack. The council is admitted to have compulsory power. It can impose binding obligations on member states by taking a "decision" under chapter 7 of the UN Charter, and member states are legally obliged to comply under Article 25 of the charter. Article 103 further announces that the UN Charter is binding even in the face of other treaty obligations.

But some states take a more confined view of the competence of the Security Council to authorize intervention, even under Chapter VII authority. There may be an attempt to use other political and legal organs, even within the United Nations, to challenge the competence of the Security Council to address new forms of international threats. This means that the distance between the 1945 charter and the adapted charter could, at some juncture, become a source of controversy. This was manifest in the 1994 confrontation between Libya and the Security Council over Tripoli's role in the bombing of a U.S. civilian aircraft, Pan Am 103, over Lockerbie, Scotland, in 1988. The council demanded the surrender of two suspects by Libya for possible trial in an American or British courtroom, but Libya parried, and sought a remedy from the International Court of Justice (ICJ) under the Montreal Convention, claiming that it had a treaty right to try its own nationals for their suspected involvement. In the course of a jurisdictional decision on the case, three ICJ judges intimated that the international court might have competence to review the legality of a Security Council Chapter VII resolution and even judge a resolution to be *ultra vires*, or exceeding the institution's authority.[34]

This would be a problematic development indeed, for the ability to renegotiate the text of the UN Charter is highly limited. The future of the United Nations as an organization that can meet some of the international community's security crises will depend on the prudent adaptation of its practice. The role of states, even the role of great powers, in effecting this adaptation may be the cost of preserving the charter as a founding document. The textual parsing of judges, who are not responsible for maintaining the public peace, may at times be an inadequate measure of legitimacy amid the security dilemmas of a brave new world. International law, ultimately, is made in large part by state practice. It is the moral responsibility of states toward their own populations and other peoples that may account for this assignment.

NOTES

1. See R. Wedgwood, "Gallant Delusions: What Is the International Community?" *Foreign Policy* (September–October 2002): 44.

2. United Nations High-Level Panel on Threats, Challenges, and Change, *A More Secure World: Our Shared Responsibility* (New York: United Nations, 2004), available at http://www.un.org/secureworld; International Commission on Intervention and State Sovereignty, *The Responsibility to Protect* (Ottawa: International Development Resource Centre, 2001), available at http://www.iciss.ca/report-en.asp; Government of Canada, *Towards a Rapid Reaction Capability for the United Nations*, Report of the Government of Canada, September 1995.

3. Olson noted that no particular actor has an incentive to fund a public good when, even as a scofflaw, he would enjoy the benefits of the public good. This can be applied to the problem of collective security and international order. *See* Mancur Olson Jr., *The Logic of Collective Action* (Cambridge, Mass.: Harvard University Press, 1971).

4. See Preamble, 1907 Hague Convention (IV) respecting the laws and customs of war on land, reprinted in A. Roberts and R. Guelf, *Documents on the Laws of War*, 2nd ed. (Oxford: Clarendon Press, 1989), 45 ("Until a more complete code of the laws of war has been issued, the High Contracting Parties deem it expedient to declare that, in cases not included in the Regulations adopted by them, the inhabitants and the belligerents remain under the protection and the rule of the principles of the law of nations, as they result from the usages established among civilized peoples, from the laws of humanity, and the dictates of the public conscience").

5. Cf. Mirjan Damaska, *The Faces of Justice and State Authority* (New Haven, Conn.: Yale University Press, 1986).

6. Declaration of Principles, Known as the Atlantic Charter, by the President of the United States of America and the Prime Minister of the United Kingdom, August 14, 1941, 55 Stat. 1603, E.A.S. No. 236, also in *American Journal of International Law* 35, no. 4, Supp. (1941): 191–192.

7. Declaration by United Nations: A Joint Declaration by the United States of America, the United Kingdom of Great Britain and Northern Ireland, the Union of Soviet Socialist Republics, China, Australia,

Belgium, Canada, Costa Rica, Cuba, Czechoslovakia, Dominican Republic, El Salvador, Greece, Guatemala, Haiti, Honduras, India, Luxembourg, Netherlands, New Zealand, Nicaragua, Norway, Panama, Poland, South Africa, Yugoslavia, January 1, 1942, 55 Stat. 1600, 204 L.N.T.S. 382, also in *American Journal of International Law* 36, no. 3, Supp. (1942): 191–192.

8. See, for example, Paul A. Rahe, "Prelude to Fulton: The Sinews of Peace Speech in Historical Context," in James W. Muller, ed., *Churchill's "Iron Curtain" Speech Fifty Years Later* (Columbia: University of Missouri Press, 1999), 49–67.

9. Identic Notes of the Government of the United States to the Governments of Australia, Belgium, Canada, Czechoslovakia, France, Germany, Great Britain, India, the Irish Free State, Italy, Japan, New Zealand, Poland, South Africa, June 23, 1928, reprinted in *American Journal of International Law* 22, no. 3, Supp. (1928): 109–115.

10. Article 27(3), UN Charter.

11. See S. D. Dailey and S. Daws, *The Procedure of the U.N. Security Council,* 3d ed. (Oxford: Oxford University Press, 1998), 250–257. The practice of accepting abstentions as concurrences began in 1946 with an abstention by the Soviet Union, to which other members of the Security Council did not object. See SC Res. 4 (29 April 1946), SCOR, 1st Sess., 39th mtg at 243. Also see decision of the International Court of Justice in the case entitled *Legal Consequences for States of the Continued Presence of South Africa in Namibia (South-West Africa) Notwithstanding Security Council Resolution 276, Advisory Opinion of 21 June 1971* (1971) International Court of Justice Reports 22.

12. See Gary Clyde Hufbauer, Jeffrey J. Schott, and Kimberly Ann Elliott. *Economic Sanctions Reconsidered: History and Current Policy,* 2nd ed. (Washington, D.C.: Institute for International Economics, 1990). Compare David Cortwright and George A. Lopez, *The Sanctions Decade: Assessing UN Strategies in the 1990s* (Boulder, Colo.: Lynne Rienner, 2000).

13. One should note, though, that collective commercial penalties are not always ruled out by international law in less draconian settings. Modern trade law allows "authorized retaliation" against economic sectors unconnected to a violation. A state that has suffered dumping or another violation of free trade agreements can impose penalties that target an entirely different sector of the opponent's economy. Citrus growers in the state of Florida know this fact all too well.

14. Report on the Chairman's Visit to Central and Southern Africa, May 1999, Security Council Committee Established Pursuant to Resolution 864 (1993) Concerning the Situation in Angola, annexed to UN Doc. S/1999/644, 4 June 1999.

15. Boutros Boutros-Ghali, *An Agenda for Peace: Preventive Diplomacy, Peacemaking and Peace-keeping* (Report of the secretary-general pursuant to the statement adopted by the Summit Meeting of the Security Council on 31 January 1992), A/47/277–S/24111, June 17, 1992; see also *A Supplement to the Agenda for Peace,* A/50/60–S/1995/1, January 3, 1995. Both are reprinted in Boutros Boutros-Ghali, *An Agenda for Peace* (New York: United Nations, 1995).

16. Accord Bruno Simma, ed., *The Charter of the United Nations: A Commentary* (Oxford: Oxford University Press, 1994), 234–235; Advisory Opinion of the International Court of Justice, Certain Expenses of the United Nations, 1962 ICJ Rep. 151, 163 (July 20, 1962).

17. See Remarks of Ambassador Danilo Turk, noting that the Security Council has "primary, but not exclusive responsibility for maintaining international peace and security," in United Nations Press Release, "Security Council Rejects Demand for Cessation of Use of Force against Federal Republic of Yugoslavia," UN Document SC/6659 (March 26, 1999).

18. See generally Ruth Wedgwood, "NATO's Campaign in Yugoslavia," *American Journal of International Law* 93 (1999): 828.

19. For a critique of the human rights problems under the transitional UN administration of Kosovo, including the absence of effective protection against interethnic violence, see Concluding Observations of the UN Human Rights Committee, UN Doc. CCPR/C/UNK/CO/1 (July 25, 2006), available at http://www.ohchr.org/english/bodies/hrc/hrcs87.htm.

20. See United Nations, "Secretary-General Presents His Annual Report to the General Assembly," press release SGSM7136, GA/9596 (September 20, 1999); see also Kofi Annan, "Two Concepts of Sovereignty," *Economist,* September 18, 1999.

21. As the secretary-general noted at greater length: "To those for whom the greatest threat to the future of international order is the use of force in the absence of a Security Council mandate, one might ask—not in the context of Kosovo—but in the context of Rwanda: If, in those dark days and hours leading up to the genocide, a coalition of States had been prepared to act in defence of the Tutsi population, but did not receive prompt Council authorization, should such a coalition have stood aside and allowed the horror to unfold?" See United Nations, "Secretary-General Presents His Annual Report to the General Assembly," press release SG/SM/7136, GA/9596 (September 20, 1999).

22. See R. Y. Jennings, "The Caroline and McLeod Cases," *American Journal of International Law* 32 (1938): 82, 85; and *Report of the Law Officers of the Crown*, dated February 21, 1838, Public Record Office in London, Foreign Office, vol. 83, 2207–2209.

23. Secretary-General Kofi Annan embraced a view close to the *Caroline* test, in his response to the High-Level Panel on Threats, Challenges, and Change. The secretary-general opined that "[i]mminent threats are fully covered by Article 51, which safeguards the inherent right of sovereign States to defend themselves against armed attack. Lawyers have long recognized that this covers an imminent attack as well as one that has already happened." See Kofi Annan, *In Larger Freedom: Towards Development, Security, and Human Rights for All* (New York: United Nations, 2005), par. 124, available at http://www.un .org/largerfreedom/contents.htm. The High-Level Panel adopted a similar view, stating that "a threatened State, according to long-established international law, can take military action as long as the threatened attack is imminent, no other means would deflect it and the action is proportionate." See United Nations High-Level Panel, *A More Secure World*, par. 188.

24. See generally John Lewis Gaddis, "The Post-War International System: Elements of Stability and Instability," in Øyvind Østerud, *Studies of War and Peace* (Oslo: Norwegian University Press, 1986), 125–160.

25. Compare the speech of President George W. Bush at West Point, June 1, 2002, available at http:// www.whitehouse.gov/news/release/2002/06/ 20020601-3.html: "For much of the last century, America's defense relied on the Cold War doctrines of deterrence and containment. In some cases, those strategies still apply. But new threats also require new thinking. Deterrence—the promise of massive retalia-

tion against nations—means nothing against shadowy terrorist networks with no nation or citizens to defend. Containment is not possible when unbalanced dictators with weapons of mass destruction can deliver those weapons on missiles or secretly provide them to terrorist allies."

26. United Nations Security Council Resolution 1373 (September 28, 2001).

27. United Nations High-Level Panel, *A More Secure World*, at para. 194.

28. Annan, *In Larger Freedom*, par. 125.

29. See Council on Foreign Relations, "A More Secure World: Who Needs to Do What?" (transcript of roundtable, Washington, D.C., December 16, 2004), available at http://www.cfr.org.

30. United Nations High-Level Panel, *A More Secure World*, par. 196.

31. But compare ibid., par. 190: "[I]f there are good arguments for preventive military action, with good evidence to support them, they should be put to the Security Council, which can authorize such action if it chooses to. If it does not so choose, there will be, by definition, time to pursue other strategies, including persuasion, negotiation, deterrence and containment —and to again visit the military option."

32. See Council on Foreign Relations, "A More Secure World: Who Needs to Do What?"

33. See *National Security Strategy of the United States of America* (Washington, D.C.: White House, 2002), available at http://www.whitehouse.gov/ncs/ nss.html: "In the 1990s we witnessed the emergence of a small number of rogue states that, while different in important ways, share a number of attributes. These states: brutalize their own people and squander their national resources for the personal gain of the rulers; display no regard for international law, threaten their neighbors, and callously violate international treaties to which they are party; are determined to acquire weapons of mass destruction, along with other advanced military technology, to be used as threats or offensively to achieve the aggressive designs of these regimes; sponsor terrorism around the globe; and reject basic human values and hate the United States and everything for which it stands."

Compare *National Security Strategy of the United States of America*, March 16, 2006, available at http://www.whitehouse.gov/nsc/nss/2006/intro.htm: "Our strong preference and common practice is to address proliferation concerns through international diplomacy, in concert with key allies and regional partners. If necessary, however, under long-standing principles of self defense, we do not rule out the use of force before attacks occur, even if uncertainty remains as to the time and place of the enemy's attack. When the consequences of an attack with WMD are potentially so devastating, we cannot afford to stand idly by as grave dangers materialize. This is the principle and logic of preemption. The place of preemption in our national security strategy remains the same."

34. Case concerning Questions of Interpretation and Application of the 1971 Montreal Convention Arising from the Aerial Incident at Lockerbie (*Libyan Arab Jamahiriya v. United Kingdom*), Judgment of 27 February 1998 (Preliminary Objections), Separate Opinion of Judge Kooijmans, at para. 17, and Joint Declaration of Judges Guillaume and Fleischhauer; compare Dissenting Opinion of Judge Sir Robert Jennings and Dissenting Opinion of President Stephen Schwebel.

PART VI

USES AND LIMITS OF GOVERNANCE IN CONFLICT MANAGEMENT

33

IS DEMOCRACY
THE ANSWER?

Marina Ottaway

SINCE THE END OF THE COLD WAR, IT has become axiomatic that democracy is the only political system able to heal the rifts of a divided society and help countries settle down after a civil war. Indeed, it has become axiomatic that democracy is the only acceptable political system, good for all countries under all circumstances. As a result, democracy promotion has become an important component of the relationship between the so-called international community—in practice the rich industrial democracies and the multilateral institutions they dominate—and the rest of the world. While in most countries democracy promotion is simply an attempt to encourage and facilitate transitions from authoritarianism, in postconflict countries, democracy promotion often takes on a strongly coercive quality. Since 1990 international interventions to end civil war, by either diplomatic or military means, have been followed by a process of coercive democratization. Countries where interventions take place are forced by the international community to adopt a democratic

system of government regardless of existing conditions and/or citizens' preference. They are quickly put through the formal steps expected to make democracy a reality, usually beginning with elections. This process of democratization supposedly complements any previous peace agreement, helping to stabilize the country and consolidate the peace.

A growing body of evidence suggests that coercive democratization is not a successful strategy in most postconflict situations. Democracy can be developed only in well-established states, capable of exercising authority over their entire territory. Democracy, and in particular the majoritarian democracy to which the international community appears committed, also requires a population that shares a common identity, not one deeply fragmented along lines of ethnicity and religion. Neither of these characteristics is common in countries emerging from civil war. Thus, the idea of coercive democratization as all-purpose solution in a postconflict situation needs to be discarded and a wider range of alternative solutions, particularly interim solutions, needs to be taken into consideration. To the extent that the international actors control the situation in postconflict countries, they should encourage them to opt for solutions that bring the country together —governments of national unity or consociational systems, for example—rather than pushing for the immediate adoption of competitive, and thus divisive, democratic systems.

There is no reason to challenge at the theoretical level the idea that democracy is a political system superior to all others. But democratization—the often conflictual, messy process of transformation from an authoritarian to a democratic system—and democracy—the stable political system that is the end point of successful democratization—are not the same thing. There is plenty of evidence that the benefits of democracy are not manifest in the early phases of a transformation process, particularly in countries where attempts at democratization take place in the aftermath of an internal conflict.

Well-established, mature democratic political systems are usually successful in handling the normal divisions and conflicting interests of a stable society by fostering compromise rather than confrontation. Democracy, as Ralf Dahrendorf has pointed out, is "government by conflict."[1] In other words, it is a political system that recognizes there can never be unanimity of interests and views in a society and therefore creates mechanisms to institutionalize conflict and manage it. Far from facilitating the resolution or regulation of existing conflicts, however, initial political openings often exacerbate divisions or trigger new confrontations. This is because democratization entails a redistribution of power among political actors and thus creates winners and losers. The change is highly threatening to incumbent rulers—not just to a few people at the top of the pyramid, but to a much broader group that benefited politically and economically from their relationship with the old political elite. Democratization can also be highly detrimental

to, and thus greatly feared by, members of minority groups who believe that a system based on majoritarianism would condemn them to permanent powerlessness and render them vulnerable to bias and discrimination. This belief is not unfounded. While it is true that well-established, strong democratic institutions can control the danger of unfettered majoritarianism, democratizing countries by definition do not have those strong institutions.

International interventions have multiplied rapidly from 1990 on. Most of these interventions have combined peace negotiations with the imposition of democratic political systems. Major interventions have taken place in Angola, Cambodia, Mozambique, Liberia, Sierra Leone, Bosnia, Haiti, Kosovo, East Timor (Timor-Leste), Afghanistan, and Iraq. Some of these interventions were carried out by the United Nations, some by regional organizations ranging from NATO in Europe to ECOWAS (the Economic Community of West African States) in Africa, some by individual countries acting on their own (the United States in Iraq) or on behalf of the international community (Australia in East Timor). But in all these cases coercive democratization was incorporated into the intervention as an instrument to seal the initial agreement and stabilize a turbulent peace.[2]

In many of these cases, the outcome of the intervention could not be evaluated completely at the time of this writing. Even partial evidence, however, makes it abundantly clear that coercive democratization is a highly problematic tool for consolidating peace. While in some countries there may not be any alternatives to coercive democratization, this is by no means an approach that should remain unquestioned or be implemented lightly.

DIFFICULT PROCESS, LIMITED ALTERNATIVES

Democratization is always difficult, but coercive democratization unfolds under particularly unfavorable circumstances. It is usually not the solution that the organized forces responsible for the conflict in the first place would have chosen if left to their own devices. None of the main parties in Cambodia and Angola—the countries where the international community first experimented with coercive democratization—really wanted democracy. In Angola, the ruling MPLA and its rival UNITA rearmed themselves while preparing for elections in 1992 and returned to war immediately afterward. In Cambodia, the Cambodian People's Party did not win the 1993 elections but nonetheless managed to retain power.[3] It is doubtful that former warlords competing in the 2005 elections in Afghanistan wanted democracy or even that President Hamid Karzai had democracy rather than the most basic control over the country as his primary goal. In Iraq, Sunnis are fearful of a democratic process, Shiites support elections (but not necessarily other aspects of democracy) as a means of gaining power, and Kurds will not settle for anything but autonomy no matter what the majority of Iraqis might want.

It is even doubtful that democracy as practiced in the modern state is truly the universal aspiration of ordinary citizens in countries emerging from conflict. While nobody likes the midnight knock on the door or the arbitrary acts of an authoritarian government, the formal democratic systems the international community seeks to impose are alien to the experience of people in most countries. And ordinary citizens in deeply divided countries are not always motivated to pursue the common good. They often share the nondemocratic aspirations of their leaders: while the ethnic conflicts that tore Bosnia apart were orchestrated by ultranationalist elites, they found plenty of willing followers ready to turn on their neighbors.

Even when the major parties accept the inevitability of the internationally imposed democratic system, they cannot make it happen on their own. Instead, the international community typically pays for postconflict elections and provides the logistical support and often the minimum level of security that makes the process possible. It helps write constitutions and election laws as well as organizing election commissions. In extreme cases, such as in Mozambique in 1994, it even de facto pays armed movements to turn themselves into political parties. The problem is that the generous support that is lavished on the first postconflict elections is seldom repeated, so that subsequent elections often deteriorate. Moreover, elections are not democracy, but just the tip of the iceberg of a process that continues to remain dependent on the donors' pressure and largesse. There is thus a strong element of artificiality and dependence in the course of coercive democratization.

Adding to this artificiality, coercive democratization is imposed on countries without considering whether they have met the preconditions that make democracy meaningful. Indeed, the international community operates on the tacit assumption that there are no preconditions and that any country can undergo democratization given sufficient political will domestically and technical support internationally. This insistence is in part a response to unproven and politically motivated claims that some populations are not yet ready for democracy because they are too ignorant, underdeveloped, or culturally unsuited for it.

But there are structural and institutional issues that cannot easily be dismissed. For populations to govern themselves democratically, they need as a prerequisite a workable state through which to do so. It is not enough for the state to be sovereign in the international system, that is, to be protected against interference from the outside. It is also crucial for the state to enjoy sovereignty internally, that is, for the government to be the supreme authority within the territory. But in severely divided societies emerging from, or immersed in, civil war, state sovereignty is contested. The state does not have political and military control of its own territory or the financial and human resources to administer it.

While the problems of postconflict coercive democratization are obvious, the alternatives are also problematic. International interventions in domestic conflict aim at preventing the outright victory of one side and promoting instead a negotiated agreement. This means that the new postconflict government must give all sides an equal chance to compete and share in the benefits of peace and reconstruction. A government formed in a democratic manner and subject to democratic rules of accountability will in theory provide the best chance for power sharing and evenhandedness. It would be an oxymoron for the international community to promote negotiations to end a conflict and then allow the establishment of an authoritarian government controlled by only one side. The problems of coercive democratization are many, but the alternatives are not obvious.

THE CHALLENGES OF COERCIVE DEMOCRATIZATION

The countries where the international community practices coercive democratization can be divided into two broad categories. The first includes countries that have the basic attributes of stateness that make democracy conceivable.[4] The Central European countries where the international community mounted the first, systematic attempts at engineering democracy through specially designed "democracy assistance" programs—for example, Poland, the Czech Republic, and Hungary—clearly were modern states with control over their territory, sufficient administrative capacity, and financial resources to support modern administrative and political processes. They also all had strong pro-democracy movements, meaning that there was little or no coercion in the process of democratization in such countries.

The experience in such countries, unusual because of the strength of the state and the vitality of the pro-democracy movements, put an imprint on the way in which the international community has thought of democracy promotion ever since. Democracy assistance targeted the perceived weaknesses of inexperienced civil society organizations and political parties, and it sought to encourage the development of an independent press and to strengthen the new democratic institutions. Democracy promoters were not concerned—indeed they did not have to be concerned—with the possible weaknesses of the state and how they might affect the prospects for transformation.

Countries where the weakness of the state does not preclude the possibility of democratic transformation exist in all parts of the world, and many are still not democratic. Many have made little progress toward democracy on their own, and some degree of coercion may become part of the process of transformation. Egypt is a prime example of such a country. It is a strong state, with full control over its territory and a well-developed—though by no means efficient—administrative apparatus. What is problematic in Egypt is not the state but the balance of power between a government that is capable of both repression and co-optation and opposition groups that are disorganized and incapable of reaching large constituencies.

The second and more problematic category of countries that can become targets of coercive democratization includes entities that do not meet, or barely meet, the basic attributes of stateness in terms of national identity, political and military control of territory, and administrative capacity. Most are postconflict countries—for example, Bosnia and Iraq, where stateness once existed but has been destroyed. Others are countries that never were real states. Afghanistan is an obvious example of a country that has never experienced stateness. The balance of factors that lead to weak stateness varies from country to country. Bosnia, for example, has the administrative capacity and financial resources to function as a state, but it is prevented from doing so by its ethnic divisions. Afghanistan has neither the administrative and financial resources nor the common identity.

Countries in this category face several major obstacles to democracy: not only an unfavorable balance of power between citizens and government, but also various forms of state weakness. Coercive democratization is particularly difficult in such cases. It entails rebuilding, or in some cases building for the first time, the country's administrative capacity. It also involves the redefinition of the identity of the state, a contested issue in countries emerging from internal conflict.

Redressing the Relation between Citizens and Governments

In more than a decade of democracy promotion the international community has developed ideas and tools suitable for countries that have the essential attributes of stateness but need to change the balance of power between citizens and governments. Democracy promoters have worked out an intellectual framework for parsing the process of democratization into its component parts: an initial period of liberalization that opens up political life by allowing political organizing, the formation of parties and organizations of civil society, and the operation of an independent media; a moment of transition marked by the holding of competitive elections; and finally a much longer period of consolidation, which, if successful, makes democracy irreversible—"the only game in town" in the words of Juan Linz and Alfred Stepan.[5]

Organizations involved in democracy promotions have also developed standard programs to make change happen: grant and training programs for civil society organizations, training programs for political parties and the media, tools for strengthening the independence of the judiciary by providing training and easier access to legal information, and tools for helping new parliaments become more effective by organizing committee systems and providing access to information. Very important, the international community has perfected the technical ability to organize elections in other countries even when political and security conditions are difficult—the elections held in Iraq in January 2005 despite the lack of security in the country were a triumph of the technical election expertise acquired by the international community.

The democratization programs the international community has implemented in stable states since the early 1990s bring about impressive results if success is measured in terms of formal indicators—number of multiparty elections carried out, number of NGOs formed, number of training sessions held for political parties, or judges, or journalists. Results look much more modest if measured in terms of how much political change they have brought about—the degree of press independence rather than the number of training sessions, or the impact of civil society organizations on politics and policies rather than the number of civil society organizations that donors have been able to summon into life by offering funding.[6]

One of the unfortunate outcomes of democracy assistance has been the rise of an increasing number of semiauthoritarian regimes: regimes that have the formal institutions and carry out the formal processes of democracy and even allow a modest amount of political space to their citizens but manipulate all processes successfully to avoid true competition, thus perpetuating their hold on power.[7] International pressure to democratize encourages many fundamentally authoritarian regimes to make cosmetic concessions to the democratic orthodoxy while at the same time protecting themselves from changes that would threaten their power. Many regimes, for example, organize multiparty elections because there is external pressure on them to do so, but at the same time they take steps to ensure that they will not face real competition. Or they will allow independent media to develop but force them to exercise self-censorship by harassing journalists or depriving offending publications of newsprint. Despite these and other problems, outside interventions have probably had at least some positive effect in recalibrating the balance of power between citizens and governments in reasonably well-functioning states.

Overcoming Ethnic and Religious Divisions

Both the political and technical problems of democracy promotion are magnified in countries that are deeply divided along lines of ethnicity or religion and not just lines of political ideology. The international community has learned some lessons from Bosnia about the dangers of democracy promotion in such countries and is learning more from Iraq. The major danger in such situations, as pointed out earlier, is that voters make their choices not on the basis of individual political preferences, but on the basis of ethnic or religious group identity. When citizens vote their identities in this way, they insert fixed choices into the democratic system, subverting it. A democratic system is based on the idea that citizens can and will change their views and preferences depending on issues and circumstances, thus that there will be no permanent majorities and minorities. This does not happen when people vote their identities. In such cases, majorities and minorities become fixed and the protection of minority rights becomes more problematic.

Unfortunately, it is relatively easy for the international community to impose democratic processes that lead to majority rule and to facilitate them with technical aid. Elections in particular are events outsiders can not only encourage but make happen. Yet outsiders are much less effective in imposing the other fundamental aspect of democracy: the protection of minority rights. Safeguarding the rights of all citizens is not an event, but an ongoing political task that outsiders can encourage but

enforce only by imposing political and administrative control—a financially and politically onerous undertaking. The international community made elections happen in Bosnia in 1998. Eight years later, it is still maintaining the occupation to protect the rights of all citizens, because all evidence points to the fact that such rights would be violated if there was an international withdrawal.[8]

At this point, the international community has few answers to the question of how to promote democracy in deeply divided societies. International presence to safeguard minority rights cannot be maintained indefinitely. Solutions based on group representation through power sharing on the basis of a fixed formula have their own problems, as the example of Lebanon shows. Since 1943, Lebanon has sought to address the problem of democracy and coexistence in a deeply divided society by developing a confessional system in which power is apportioned among all religious groups, theoretically in proportion to their share of the country's total population. Confessional systems like the Lebanese one, however, are rarely fair because once the system is adopted, it is very difficult to make adjustments when the demographics or political power structures change. Power sharing in Lebanon, admittedly an extreme case, is based on a formula first devised in 1943 using census data that were already a decade old at the time. The system worked reasonably well for thirty years, until the power balance in government became grossly disproportionate to the religious balance of society. Frustration and discontent erupted, and the country sank into a protracted and devastating civil war followed by a very tenuous peace. It is well known that the system is grossly unrepresentative, but revising it is an explosive issue that could once again sink the country into conflict. In addition, the confessional system prevents the development of a modern state with central authority and decision-making capabilities because political space is monopolized by power struggles among confessional groups, fragmentation of the state between groups prevents effective legislation and governance, and there is no independent domestic arbiter to force compromise and cooperation.[9]

The United States' position has long been that divided societies do not need special political systems and above all should avoid group representation because it deepens already troublesome divisions. Instead, divided countries, like all others, should apportion power not through an artificial agreement, but through the outcome of one person–one vote elections. In practice, the approach does not avoid the emergence of a confessional system. The example of Iraq is very clear: the interim constitution, or Transitional Administrative Law, did not call for power sharing among religious groups. But in three successive polls—the elections of January 2005, the referendum of October 15, 2005, and the elections of December 15, 2005—Iraqis voted their identities, de facto making the system into a confessional one.

Addressing Stateness

Although the international community does not have an answer to the difficult problem of how to promote political participation in divided societies without deepening or at least crystallizing the divisions, there is at least an awareness of the issue and much discussion about what can be done. The impact of state weakness on democracy promotion has received a lot less attention. In fact, democracy is seen as part of the solution to restoring functional states, and democratic political reform as an integral part of the package of steps the international community needs to take to help weak, failing, or failed states to be restored, if not to health, to some level of functionality.[10]

There is no reason to question this assumption in the long run. But there is also no evidence that a democratic transition in the short run can work in states that are still highly dysfunctional. The example of Afghanistan, an experiment in building democracy in an extremely weak state, illustrates the problem. In late 2005, Afghanistan was preparing for parliamentary elections. The official budget for the exercise, funded by the international community, was about $150 million—this included the cost of administering the election, not of maintaining security in the election period. The enormity of this $150 million budget can best be appreciated by comparing it with the total recurrent budget of Afghanistan, about $600 million, and the total revenue that Afghanistan can raise from taxes and customs duties, about $300 million.[11] In order to carry out elections that even begin to approximate international standards, Afghanistan is thus totally dependent on foreign funding, foreign technical assistance, and foreign security forces. And elections are only a small part of what is needed to make a democratic system work.

But cost is only one of the reasons to question whether it is advisable, or indeed possible, to impose coercive democratization on extremely weak states in the very early stages of reconstruction. Democracy is a system that allows citizens to choose their government and influence its policies. But is democracy a meaningful concept in countries where the government does not have enough control over its territory or administrative institutions to implement those policies? Is it a sustainable political system when the government does not even have the economic resources to develop such control? For example, is coercive democratization meaningful in the Democratic Republic of the Congo, where even the physical links between the capital and the rest of the country are problematic? Donors can come in with helicopters and all-terrain vehicles to make elections happen in 2006, but in the aftermath much of the country will still be outside the reach of ordinary administration. If that government does not control the territory, and does not have the administrative infrastructure and the financial capacity to implement policies, the way in which the government is chosen and formulates policies has severely limited meaning.

Afghanistan and the Democratic Republic of the Congo are not unique cases. The list of countries where the international community is trying to promote democracy although the existence of the state itself can be called into question has many entries—Sierra Leone, Liberia, and East Timor, for example. This raises the question of whether international efforts will only result in the formation of Potemkin democracies that are essentially unsustainable and will be dependent on foreign political, administrative, and financial support for a long time to come.

In conclusion, it is clear that coercive democratization is a multifaceted undertaking in most countries, but particularly in divided countries with weak institutions just emerging from conflict. The aspect of coercive democratization that receives the most attention is the attempt to change the relation between citizens and government by giving citizens the right to elect their leaders and to hold them accountable through new or strengthened governmental and nongovernmental institutions. Elections in particular receive a disproportionate amount of attention because they are a visible process and can easily be engineered from the outside with technical and financial assistance. But in weak, postconflict states, elections and efforts to develop new institutions are only a small part of what is needed to develop functioning democracies, and furthermore they should not be the first step. Democratization has preconditions. One is effective stateness, which is often weak in countries where the international community tries to impose democratization. Another is the existence of mechanisms to bridge the deep divisions normally found in postconflict countries. Without a minimum willingness to live together on the part of most citizens, coercive democratization becomes a source of conflict rather than reconciliation.

Sustainability of Coercive and Spontaneous Democratization

Coercive democratization, as defined in this paper, is the attempt to use outside pressure and support to bring about a democratic transformation in countries where the domestic balance of forces by itself would not lead to democracy. A major issue concerning coercive democratization is thus that of sustainability. We know from experience that international pressure, technical support, and financing can force a country to hold competitive elections reasonably successfully. But can pressure and support bring about lasting change? Can they be maintained long enough for domestic forces to develop and conditions to change, so that democracy can become self-supporting?

Democratization is not an irreversible process. Historically, many countries that started processes of democratization spontaneously, without outside intervention, failed in their attempt and reverted to authoritarian regimes.[12] Coalitions that support democratic change can fall apart. The disorder that often accompanies transitions from one political system to another can frighten citizens into turning away from democratic experiments and back to authoritarian leaders that promise order. Poorer countries are particularly prone to democratic reversals, as Adam Przeworski and colleagues show.[13]

Although the mechanisms that lead to democratic reversals are not always understood—why poor countries are more prone to reversals, for example—the historical evidence that many, perhaps even most, democratic transitions fail is quite clear. Out of the thirty-three countries that attempted democratic transitions during democracy's first wave, from 1828 to 1926, twenty-two failed. The same number, out of fifty-two countries, failed after democracy's second wave, from 1943 to 1962. The result of the more recent, still ongoing, third wave, which began in 1974, is unclear. As of 1990, only four of these sixty-five transitions had failed, but most of the countries undergoing political transformation were not yet consolidated democracies out of danger.[14] Przeworski et al. come up with similar numbers by examining the net transitions since 1950 to democracy on the one hand and dictatorship on the other; as of 1990, the score stood at fifty-nine transitions to democracy and forty-nine transitions to dictatorship.[15]

Countries that have undergone coercive democratization also often experience reversals. Most of the post–World War I coercive democratization experiments, for example, had failed long before World War II. Motivated by doctrines of self-determination and democracy after World War I, the Allies coerced many countries into embracing democratic systems. They forced Germany to become a democracy and split the Austro-Hungarian Empire into new, coercively democratized Eastern European and Balkan states. Yet among all of them, only Czechoslovakia actually functioned as a democracy during the interwar period. Indeed, the instability of these regimes was a significant contributing factor to the eruption of World War II.[16]

The colonial-era record in imposing democratization as part of the independence process has been just as poor. Democratic constitutions written by colonial powers in Africa, the Middle East, and Asia were revoked or simply ignored in most countries. Out of a total sixty-eight new countries formed after 1950, a mere twelve remained democracies by 1990.[17] The United States failed to impose democracy in the Philippines, as it did in most of the countries in which it intervened repeatedly in the early part of the twentieth century.[18] In fact, India remains a rare example of direct colonial success at coercive democratization—one of the few former colonies to have remained democratic without interruption from the day of its independence until now.[19]

The examples of coercive democratization in the countries defeated in World War II —Germany, Japan, Italy—are much more encouraging, although it is important to re-member that Germany and Italy were already carrying out their second attempt at democratization and that Germany and Japan were utterly defeated, the old regimes destroyed. Furthermore, in all three countries stateness was already well developed and the population was extremely homogeneous.

Concerning the attempts at coercive democratization in the post–Cold War period, the jury is still out because the experiences are too recent. There are a few clearly successful cases of democratization—the Czech Republic and Poland, for example, although these were spontaneous transformations where the international community helped strengthen government institutions and civil society organizations after the transition had already taken place. The countries where international pressure or intervention were crucial in fostering democratization, on the other hand, present a less encouraging picture, with semiauthoritarian regimes and reversals on all continents. Even in countries like Bosnia, Kosovo, East Timor, Sierra Leone, and Liberia, the deployment of international troops, international administrative control, and international aid have not succeeded so far in bringing about democratic change that can be expected to last beyond the international presence. Countries that have found a degree of stability after an international intervention, for example, Cambodia and Mozambique, have done so on the basis of political systems that fall short of democracy.

One of the problems of judging the likely outcome of coercive democratization is that the political process leading to change in countries exposed to foreign pressure is very different from that experienced by countries where change is spontaneous. Each historical experience at democratization has some unique characteristics, but all successful cases of spontaneous democratization share the length and slowness of the process, starting with the emergence of new political forces and coalitions and eventually culminating in the development of democratic political systems, often in stages.[20]

In a process of forced democratization, the initial period of development of new political forces and coalitions is reduced to months or years, new constitutions and laws are quickly written with outside technical advice, and elections are held as soon as the international community can organize them—two years from the time an agreement is reached has become the standard in postconflict situations.

Another important difference is that coercive democratization starts with a model of what a democratic system should look like, while political systems that emerge from a spontaneous process tend to display characteristics determined not by theories of good government but by the pragmatic decisions and compromises of political life. Furthermore, while all democratizing countries enact measures to protect human rights, countries undergoing spontaneous democratization defined human rights in ways that were determined by their traditions and the standards of the period and expanded them only slowly, over time. Countries undergoing coercive democratization are expected to immediately embrace the entire body of human rights accepted in the established democracies, regardless of their social norms and cultural values. Thus, the United States could see itself as a democracy even while accepting slavery and the inferior status of women, but the international community does not allow countries subject to coercive democratization to change gradually.

While it is far too early to judge the outcome of the many attempts at coercive democratization in postconflict societies that have taken place since the early 1990s, the failure rate will almost certainly be high. Many countries fail even when they attempt democratization spontaneously. They are even more likely to fail when the attempt is made under coercion before domestic conditions can trigger the process. The international community's long-term commitment to maintain a presence may help preserve stability and prevent a relapse into conflict, but there is no evidence yet to indicate that such long-term presence can transform a coerced process into a self-sustaining one.

THE UNITED STATES AND DEMOCRACY PROMOTION

The United States has been at the forefront of all recent attempts to promote democracy in other countries, including attempts at coercive democratization. European countries also are actively involved in promoting democracy and have participated in the efforts to coercively introduce democratic processes in postconflict situations, but they have been less outspoken than the United States on this issue and remain less likely to exercise strong overt pressure on incumbent governments to change.

The United States sees itself as a beacon for people with democratic aspirations around the world, but people around the world do not always see the United States in the same light. The range of perceptions about the United States and its commitment to democracy is broad. In some regions, the United States has a great deal of credibility when it talks of democracy; in others, it has virtually none.

In Eastern Europe and in the former Soviet Union, the United States initially enjoyed an enormous comparative advantage in the promotion of democracy. As the long-standing, uncompromising enemy of the Soviet Union and other socialist regimes, it symbolized the ideological alternative to socialism as well as a concrete model of how a successful democratic system works. It had been a source of moral support for anti-Soviet dissidents, and after the fall of the socialist regimes it became a source of financial and organizational support for struggling democratic organizations and institutions. In the 1990s, there was little opposition to or resentment of the U.S. role in the former socialist world. After the socialist regimes collapsed, there were initially no governments to object strongly to democracy promotion interventions, which were in any case mild and noncoercive. Aid aimed at strengthening organizations of civil society, struggling independent media, and new democratic institutions, not at imposing change on reluctant governments.

As attempted democratic transitions started faltering in many former socialist countries, however, the role of the United States became more coercive and as a result more controversial. Many new postsocialist governments erected the facade of democracy but tried in practice to eliminate competition and retain power even when they were losing support. Thus they did not welcome U.S. efforts to reverse the semi-authoritarian trend with forceful interventions. The United States' new coercive role first became apparent in Slovakia in 1999, when U.S. organizations for the first time helped train and fund Slovak NGOs for a massive effort to mobilize the opposition and vote the autocratic prime minister, Vladimir Meciar, out of power. The effort, presented as a nonpartisan effort to increase voter turnout and monitor the fairness of elections, succeeded in its real goal: ousting Meciar and his party.[21]

A similar operation was mounted a few months later in Croatia—although the U.S. role was less important there. It was replicated with a much higher profile in Serbia at the end of 2000, leading to the resignation of President Slobodan Milosevic.[22] It is not altogether clear to what extent U.S.-financed efforts contributed to the downfall of President Eduard Shevardnadze in Georgia in November 2003 or President Viktor Yanukovych in Ukraine in December 2004 (probably little in the latter case), but these events made U.S. democracy promotion very controversial among incumbent governments in the region.[23] Of course, the U.S. image among people seeking democratic change remained high.

In other parts of the world, the United States did not enjoy the same comparative advantage as it did in Eastern Europe and the former Soviet Union. In Latin America and to a lesser extent in Africa, Washington's new-

found enthusiasm for democracy was greeted with skepticism among liberals who remembered how the United States had supported numerous autocrats over the decades. Over time, however, U.S. credibility concerning democracy promotion has increased in these areas because Washington's policy has been reasonably consistent, aided by the fact that the United States does not have other overriding interests or face major security challenges that conflict with a democracy agenda.

The most difficult challenge to the United States' role in promoting democracy arose in the Middle East. The United States remained tolerant of Middle East autocrats long after it started promoting democracy in other regions, assuming that longtime U.S. allies like Saudi Arabia and Egypt would continue to maintain stability in their countries and protect U.S. interests. The evidence that most of the September 11 hijackers came from Saudi Arabia and Egypt destroyed this illusion, leading instead to the conclusion that autocratic regimes were contributing to the rise of terrorism because the democratic deficit caused frustration among their population. Whether or not the conclusion that democratic deficits directly cause terrorism was warranted, the United States embraced a new policy of democracy promotion in the Middle East.[24] The change in U.S. thinking was met with alarm and indignation by incumbent governments and with skepticism bordering on derision by most liberals. They simply refused to believe that U.S. policy would change and the fact that talk of democracy promotion in the Middle East coincided with the beginning of the Iraq war did little to reassure them. Coercive democratization looked more like regime change at gunpoint than a robust effort to put pressure on incumbent governments to open up politically and to help citizens organize more effectively.[25]

Outside the former Soviet sphere of influence, the U.S. role in democracy promotion has thus initially been met with caution or even outright hostility, including among those who seek political reform in their countries. Over time, skepticism has decreased in countries of Latin America and Africa where policy has been consistent, although it remains ready to flare up. Because the policy of democracy promotion in the Middle East is more recent, because the United States is a controversial actor as a result of its support for Israel and the war in Iraq, and because U.S. policies are less consistent owing to Washington's balancing act between its interest in democracy and its need for oil and the cooperation of Arab governments to control terrorism, Arab liberals continue to see more coercion than democracy in U.S. efforts to change Arab political systems.

NO SHORTCUTS TO DEMOCRACY

Coercive democratization as practiced since the early 1990s has not been a successful method to seal agreements and consolidate shaky peace in countries emerging from conflict. Democratization itself is a source of conflict, and in any case it cannot succeed in countries that still lack a minimal degree of stateness and where citizens have not developed, or even deliberately refuse to accept, a common national identity. In fact, coercive democratization is problematic even in stable countries, a reality that should make the international community more cautious in prescribing democracy as a universal solution for postconflict countries.

It is, however, difficult to formulate policies to replace coercive democratization in such countries. While the international community has a choice of whether to push a stable country toward a political transformation immediately or to wait for a more suitable opportunity, it does not have that choice in a postconflict situation where a new government needs to be set up immediately, not at some point in the future. Even if the former government still exists, it is part of the problem that triggered the conflict and must be replaced. International administration can be imposed for an interim period before a new

government is established, but this is costly and can itself become a source of conflict, as happened in Iraq. And installing a friendly dictator, a standard solution during the Cold War, is no longer seen as an option for ideological reasons. Pragmatically, furthermore, the "friendly dictator" option can be extremely effective in reestablishing stability in a country in the short run, but it often becomes a new source of conflict in the medium and long runs. Indeed, once the international community intervenes in a conflict, it really has no viable option but to work toward a democratic solution. The question is not whether this should be done, but how it can be done to minimize the problems discussed earlier.

Coercive democratization as practiced since the early 1990s has largely failed. Some of the countries where democratization has been attempted have stabilized, but not because a democratic process has consolidated a peace agreement. Mozambique is the most successful case, where democracy might eventually take hold despite the domination by Frelimo, the old liberation movement that led the country to independence in 1975 and has ruled ever since. Cambodia was stable at the time of this writing, but not democratic. Angola was no longer at war, but because the government finally won and UNITA disintegrated, not because of peace negotiations and democracy. East Timor remained relatively stable, aided by the fact that the incumbent party had encountered little competition, but there was growing international concern about the sustainability of the imposed democratic system. Liberia, Sierra Leone, and Haiti were neither stable nor democratic, although international presence kept those situations under control. Bosnia remained so divided and unsettled that the international community did not dare withdraw, even ten years after the signing of the peace agreement. Kosovo was equally unstable, with continuing ethnic tensions and no agreement as of the end of 2005 as to whether the territory should become an independent country or remain part of Serbia. In Afghanistan and Iraq a formal democratization imposed from the outside could not pave over the fact that the countries were still at war.

The first lesson to be derived from these experiences is that coercive democratization is at best a lengthy process with no certainty of a positive outcome. Interventions to stabilize peace through democratization must be designed as long-term, open-ended operations. This immediately raises the question of resources and sustainability. How often can the international community make an indefinite commitment of funding as well as of administrative and military personnel? How many countries can it cope with simultaneously? Can it make such a commitment to large countries where the scale of operations is daunting?

The second lesson is that some postconflict countries do not have the minimum preconditions of stateness and common identity to sustain a process of democratization.

Democracy presupposes the existence of a modern state. But Afghanistan is more a feudal state than a modern one, and the fealty of many warlords to the central and supposedly democratic government is open to question. In Sierra Leone and Liberia the administrative structures set up in colonial times, weak to begin with, have long since been disrupted. In none of these countries does the state enjoy anything even remotely resembling monopoly over the means of coercion. Under such conditions, elections and formal democratic institutions cannot be the starting point of democratization.

The third lesson, indeed a corollary of the first two, is that the international community needs to consider more seriously interim political solutions for postconflict countries. Democracy should remain as the long-term goal, but democracy is impossible in most postconflict countries in the short and even medium terms. What kind of interim arrangements can be developed? Suggestions made in recent years range from the moderate idea that

postconflict countries should be encouraged to set up national unity governments or governments of national reconciliation for a few years, to the far-reaching contention that they should surrender all or part of their sovereignty to the international community until they develop the capacity to maintain their own stability and govern themselves in a democratic way.

All suggestions are difficult to implement and fraught with problems. For example, while governments of national reconciliation tend to work well in countries that face a common external enemy, they are much more problematic when it is the former warring partners that are expected to unite and govern the country together. Limits to a country's sovereignty—in other words, the establishment of a partial or full protectorate—also raise a host of problems, including the danger of resistance against the intervening countries and organizations. Yet despite these difficulties, democracy cannot develop instantly in postconflict countries, so interim solutions suitable to the specific conditions of particular countries need to be explored.

Coercive democratization as implemented since the end of the Cold War does not offer a quick solution to the question of moving postconflict countries from turbulent peace to long-term stability. The dependent, Potemkin democracies that coercive democratization produces risk becoming more part of the problem of renewed confrontation than a solution to lingering conflicts.

NOTES

1. Ralf Dahrendorf, *Society and Democracy in Germany* (New York: Doubleday, 1967), 147.

2. Angola had five UN missions between 1988 and 2003 (UNAVEM I, UNAVEM II, UNAVEM III, MONUA, and UNMA) to monitor cease-fires, verify elections, assist in achieving peace and national reconciliation, and create an environment conducive to long-term stability, democratic development, and rehabilitation. Cambodia had two UN missions: UNAMIC maintained peace from 1991 to 1992 and

UNTAC acted as a transitional authority and held elections from 1992 to 1993. UNMOZ in Mozambique (1992–94) sought to implement peace and monitor the cease-fire and withdrawal of foreign forces in addition to providing transportation security, technical assistance, and electoral monitoring. Intervention in Liberia began in 1990 with ECOWAS's ECOMOG, a peace implementation monitoring group; the United Nations began UNOMIL in 1993 to implement agreements, maintain peace, and verify elections. Nigeria, ECOWAS, and two UN missions (UNOMSIL and UNAMSIL) intervened in Sierra Leone from 1997 to 1999 with little commitment and less success. After 2000, leadership by the United Kingdom was crucial in bringing international attention and security forces to the situation. The United Nations was present in Bosnia beginning in 1992, but no effective actions were taken until NATO sent in IFOR in 1995. Since that time NATO, UN, OSCE, and EU missions have run the country with broad mandates for administration, policing, elections, refugee return, and governance. Beginning in 1993 and lasting over a decade, UN, U.S., and OAS (Organization of American States) missions have intervened in Haiti, first to simply restore and later to rebuild the country's failed government. UNMIK in Kosovo began with a broad mandate: civil administration, coordination of humanitarian and disaster relief, promotion of self-government, determination of future status, and refugee return. What began as electoral consultation in East Timor transitioned to Australian-led peacemaking and then to UN-administered state building and democratization. The U.S.-led invasions of Afghanistan in 2001 and Iraq in 2003 were both followed by ambitious and ongoing programs of democratization.

Information was collected from Chester A. Crocker, Fen Osler Hampson, and Pamela Aall, eds., *Turbulent Peace: The Challenges of Managing International Conflict* (Washington, D.C.: United States Institute of Peace Press, 2001); International Commission on Intervention and State Sovereignty, *The Responsibility to Protect: Research, Bibliography, Background: Supplementary Volume to the Report of the International Commission on Intervention and State Sovereignty* (Ottawa: International Development Research Center, 2001); Stockholm International Peace Research Institute, *SIPRI Yearbook 2005: Armaments, Disarmament and International Security* (Oxford: Oxford University Press, 2005); and UNPBPU, *Lessons Learned from United Nations Peacekeeping Experiences in Sierra Leone,* Peace-

keeping Best Practices Unit, United Nations Department of Peacekeeping Operations, September 2003.

3. Frederick Z. Brown, "Cambodia's Rocky Venture in Democracy," and Marina Ottaway, "Angola's Failed Elections," in *Postconflict Elections, Democratization, and International Assistance,* ed. Krishna Kumar (Boulder, Colo.: Lynne Rienner, 1998), 87–110, 133–151.

4. J. P. Nettl clarified the concept of stateness, defining a state as (1) "a collectivity that summates a set of functions and structures in order to generalize their applicability," (2) "a unit in the field of international relations," (3) "an autonomous collectivity . . . in a functional sense a distinct *sector* or arena of society," and (4) "a sociocultural phenomenon." J. P. Nettl, "The State as a Conceptual Variable," *World Politics* 20, no. 4 (July 1968): 562, 563, 564, 565.

5. Juan J. Linz and Alfred Stepan, *Problems of Democratic Transition and Consolidation* (Baltimore: Johns Hopkins University Press, 1996), 5. For a discussion of the international community's approach to the democratization process, see Thomas Carothers et al., "Debating the Transition Paradigm," in *Critical Mission: Essays on Democracy Promotion,* by Thomas Carothers (Washington, D.C.: Carnegie Endowment for International Peace, 2004), 185–217.

6. Thomas Carothers, *Critical Mission: Essays on Democracy Promotion* (Washington, D.C.: Carnegie Endowment for International Peace, 2004), 99–106.

7. See Marina Ottaway, *Democracy Challenged: The Rise of Semi-authoritarianism* (Washington, D.C.: Carnegie Endowment for International Peace, 2002); and Daniel Brumberg, "The Trap of Liberalized Autocracy," *Journal of Democracy* 13, no. 4 (October 2002): 56.

8. The International Crisis Group has provided good ongoing coverage of the situation in Bosnia. See, in particular, International Crisis Group, *Bosnia's Nationalist Governments: Paddy Ashdown and the Paradoxes of State Building,* ICG Europe Report No. 146 (Sarajevo/Brussels: International Crisis Group, 2003); *No Early Exit: NATO's Continuing Challenge in Bosnia,* ICG Europe Report No. 110 (Sarajevo/Brussels: International Crisis Group, 2001); and *Is Dayton Failing? Bosnia Four Years after the Peace Agreement,* ICG Europe Report No. 80 (Sarajevo/Brussels: International Crisis Group, 1999).

9. For arguments espousing the benefits of power sharing, see Arend Lijphart, "Constitutional Design for Divided Societies," *Journal of Democracy* 15, no. 2 (April 2004); for typologies, strengths, and weaknesses of power-sharing systems, see Timothy D. Sisk, *Power Sharing and International Mediation in Ethnic Conflicts* (Washington, D.C.: United States Institute of Peace Press, 1996), 27–45; and for an explanation of the Lebanese system, see Julia Choucair, *Evaluating Lebanese Reform,* Carnegie Papers Middle East Series (Washington, D.C.: Carnegie Endowment for International Peace, 2006).

10. See Department for International Development, *Why We Need to Work More Effectively in Fragile States* (London: Department for International Development, 2005); U.S. Agency for International Development, *Fragile States Strategy* (Washington, D.C.: U.S. Agency for International Development, 2005); and Robert C. Orr, *Winning the Peace* (Washington, D.C.: CSIS Press, 2004).

11. These figures are derived from BBC News, *Q&A: Afghan Elections Guide,* September 16, 2005, http://news.bbc.co.uk/1/hi/world/south_asia/42515 80.stm; Jo Johnson, "Fears Challenge Vision of a Democratic Afghanistan," *Financial Times,* September 15, 2005; and Central Intelligence Agency, "Afghanistan," *CIA World Factbook,* 2005, http://www .odci.gov/cia/publications/factbook/geos/af.html.

12. Samuel P. Huntington, *The Third Wave: Democratization in the Late Twentieth Century* (Norman: University of Oklahoma Press, 1991), 15–26; and Adam Przeworski et al., *Democracy and Development: Political Institutions and Well-Being in the World, 1950–1990* (Cambridge: Cambridge University Press, 2000), 36–51.

13. Przeworski et al., *Democracy and Development.*

14. Huntington, *The Third Wave,* 14, 26.

15. Przeworski et al., *Democracy and Development,* 45.

16. Martin Kitchen, *Europe between the Wars: A Political History* (London: Longman, 1988), 102–130; G. John Ikenberry, *After Victory: Institutions, Strategic Restraint, and the Rebuilding of Order after Major Wars* (Princeton, N.J.: Princeton University Press, 2001), 117–162.

17. Przeworski et al., *Democracy and Development,* 39.

18. Minxin Pei and Sara Kasper, "Lessons from the Past: The American Record on Nation Building" (Washington, D.C.: Carnegie Endowment for International Peace, 2003).

19. Most other countries that can be included in this list are quite small, for example, Botswana, Trinidad and Tobago, and Jamaica. See Robert Pinkney, *Democracy in the Third World* (Boulder, Colo.: Lynne Rienner, 2003), 107.

20. See Barrington Moore, Jr., *Social Origins of Dictatorship and Democracy: Lord and Peasant in the Making of the Modern World* (Boston: Beacon Press, 1966); Dietrich Rueschemeyer et al., *Capitalist Development and Democracy* (Chicago: University of Chicago Press, 1992); and Theda Skocpol, *States and Social Revolutions: A Comparative Analysis of France, Russia, and China* (Cambridge: Cambridge University Press, 1979). In *Making Democracy Work: Civic Traditions in Modern Italy* (Princeton, N.J.: Princeton University Press, 1993), Robert Putnam furthermore attributes the success in developing strong and democratic regional administration in Northern Europe to changes that had taken place over a period of centuries.

21. Sarah E. Mendelson and John K. Glenn, *Democracy Assistance and NGO Strategies in Post-Communist Societies,* Working Paper No. 8 (Washington, D.C.: Carnegie Endowment for International Peace, 2000).

22. Misha Glenny, "Milosevic's Moment of Truth," and Steven Erlanger, "Milosevic Attacks Opponents on TV," *New York Times,* October 3, 2000; and Thomas Carothers, *Ousting Foreign Strongmen: Lessons from Serbia,* Policy Brief No. 5 (Washington, D.C.: Carnegie Endowment for International Peace, May 2001).

23. Scott Peterson, "Georgia's Partner in Democracy: US," *Christian Science Monitor,* November 26, 2003; and Adrian Karatnycky, "Ukraine's Orange Revolution," *Foreign Affairs* 84, no. 2 (March–April 2005).

24. For the issue's complications in U.S. foreign policy, see Thomas Carothers, "Promoting Democracy and Fighting Terror," *Foreign Affairs* 82, no. 1 (January–February 2003); for a thorough empirical and theoretical discussion, see Quan Li, "Does Democracy Promote or Reduce Transnational Terrorist Incidents?" *Journal of Conflict Resolution* 49, no. 2 (April 2005).

25. Marina Ottaway, *Promoting Democracy in the Middle East: The Problem of U.S. Credibility,* Carnegie Paper No. 35 (Washington, D.C.: Carnegie Endowment for International Peace, 2003).

34

IS STABILITY
THE ANSWER?

Kimberly Marten

MANY PEOPLE HAVE CRITICIZED THE administration of U.S. president George W. Bush for its perceived pursuit of a new American empire in Iraq. The policy of ousting a leader by force, and then using the Coalition Provisional Authority to replace Saddam Hussein's rule with a new governmental system more congenial to U.S. interests, bore an uncomfortable resemblance in some people's minds to the colonial occupations of a bygone era. As time went on, the insurgency, too, looked increasingly like the ones waged against imperial regimes in the past.

What few have recognized, however, is that the Bush administration's role in Iraq is in many ways not so different from the role that the international community—most often represented through peace enforcement missions approved by the United Nations Security Council—has played in a variety of countries since the mid-1990s. What set the invasion of Iraq apart was primarily its unilateralism (or at least the small size of the informal coalition of states that supported Washington). Unlike

other recent international interventions, the Iraq invasion lacked the approval either of the Security Council or of a major multilateral alliance like NATO. But in Bosnia, Kosovo, and East Timor, to name three examples, the international community, led by coalitions of powerful liberal democratic states, took actions that otherwise resembled what the United States and its allies did in Iraq: it pressured or forced existing governmental structures out of power (in two of those three cases, in the Balkans, by waging war) and put in their stead new political regimes under outside control, whose orientation was deemed more acceptable. Something similar has happened in Afghanistan, as well, where an initial U.S.-led intervention was supported explicitly by NATO and tacitly by the Security Council, and where a NATO peace enforcement mission under UN mandate is now supporting the regime of President Hamid Karzai.

Some might argue that in the cases of Bosnia, Kosovo, and East Timor, the overriding goal of the international community was humanitarianism, to prevent or stop the killing of innocent people. In contrast, the U.S. goal in Iraq was more self-interested, centered on a narrow definition of security interests that was not shared by many other nations and perhaps on gaining control over strategically located territory that is rich in oil. Yet the fact of the matter is that humanitarianism and self-interest are always intertwined when powerful states decide to act in today's world. The security and economic interests of NATO's Western European members were seen to be at stake in the Balkan civil wars, just as the security and economic interests of Australia were seen to be at stake in East Timor. Security against terrorism was certainly at stake in the intervention against the Taliban in Afghanistan, but this was intertwined with humanitarian outrage at the way the Taliban treated the Afghan population, especially women. Given the arbitrary brutality of Saddam Hussein's murderous regime, as well as the energy that the Bush administration put into trying to shape an Iraqi constitution based on principles of liberalism and democracy, it is also hard to argue that humanitarianism played no role in U.S. decision making in Iraq.

This chapter explores three lessons that have emerged as the international community has pursued peace enforcement missions since 1995:[1] (1) that its efforts at political and social transformation and control significantly resemble the imperialism practiced by liberal states at the turn of the twentieth century, (2) that states have rarely invested the political will or the resources necessary for these efforts to succeed, and (3) that given this set of facts, the most effective contribution that the international community can make to societies in conflict is to deploy robust peace operations designed to provide security for the affected populations and to reestablish the stability that allows normal life to resume, rather than to try to control the direction of political change in those societies.

Whether designed primarily for humanitarian purposes or in response to international security threats (this chapter makes no judgments about when intervention is warranted, only about how it should be oriented if it is undertaken), these operations need sufficient military force to deter spoilers of the peace process from attempting to reignite armed conflict among disaffected groups and to engage in counterinsurgency operations if deterrence should fail. They should be designed to protect civilians on the ground who might otherwise be targeted by organized violence. Since domestic police forces are usually either too weak or too corrupt to secure public order in the aftermath of war, the intervenors must also be prepared to take on the policelike duties of riot control, border control, and the protection of institutions and infrastructure that are necessary for societal functioning.

Outsiders cannot determine the political futures of failed or torn states, yet the attempt to do just that has been a primary driver of international military intervention both historically and today. This suggests the need for a fundamental reexamination of the utility and purposes of intervention as a policy tool. The chapter concludes with a discussion of how these lessons are relevant today for the United States in Iraq, as well as in any future cases that may arise.

BACKGROUND: PEACEKEEPING VERSUS PEACE ENFORCEMENT

Peace operations have changed drastically in recent years. Traditional peacekeeping, performed under Chapter VI of the United Nations Charter in a variety of cases since the mid-1950s, was far less complex and far less dangerous than the vast majority of peace operations taking place in the world today. The change began to happen in the mid-1990s, when the Security Council started to recognize that the peace operations being deployed to brutal civil wars differed fundamentally from the traditional peacekeeping missions the United Nations had taken on before. It was clear that a new approach was needed. The failure of traditional UN peacekeeping missions to stop mass killings in Rwanda in 1994 and in Bosnia in 1995 galvanized the move toward change.

Traditional peacekeeping did not involve the attempt at political transformation that is the hallmark of peace enforcement operations today. It involved intervening only with the full agreement of all the parties to a conflict, which were usually well-defined states rather than the diffuse and uncoordinated paramilitary groups that are so often involved in today's civil and transnational wars. Peacekeeping then was often requested by the involved parties because of the reputation for impartiality that UN-commanded forces had. During the Cold War, most militarized conflicts had at least some element of U.S.-Soviet competition attached to them, and the countries that chose to volunteer their troops for participation in peacekeeping missions were welcomed precisely because they stood apart from that divide and were disinterested in the political futures of the involved parties.

Peacekeepers then also had limited tasks. They were asked only to monitor cease-fires and act as confidence builders, as they stood between the forces of each side to ensure that fighting did not break out again. At most they collected the weapons of forces that were disarming voluntarily or oversaw mutual exchanges of prisoners of war. They were not asked to take on complex political activities. A few traditional peacekeeping operations are still ongoing today. For example, a traditional peacekeeping mission is still deployed on the relatively peaceful island of Cyprus, between the state of Cyprus that is recognized by the international community and dominated by ethnic Greeks and the territory claimed by Turkish Cypriots, where boundary and recognition issues remain unsettled. But a traditional-looking UN peacekeeping mission that was deployed between Ethiopia and Eritrea in 2000, called the United Nations Mission in Ethiopia

and Eritrea (UNMEE) turned out to be insufficient to provide long-term security for the two countries. In late 2005 Eritrea expelled UNMEE staff from eighteen Western countries from its territory and banned UNMEE helicopter overflights that were monitoring the border, raising fears that conflict between the two countries might resume.

In contrast to these traditional peacekeeping missions, recent peace enforcement missions in places including Bosnia, Kosovo, East Timor, and Afghanistan have been asked to become directly involved in the political futures of the countries where they are sent. The major disagreements provoking warfare are no longer centered on disputed borders and territorial divisions. Instead, most of today's wars are focused on the questions of who will control the political direction of the countries in question and how societal resources will be apportioned and used. This means that by definition peace operations are politicized. The fact that they support one future for the country—usually movement in the direction of liberal tolerance and democratic choice for all of the country's people—pits them against ethnic nationalist or other authoritarian figures, who often have a great deal of domestic popular support as well as control over the resources necessary to further their antiliberal agendas.

The situations on the ground today are much more violent, and the involved parties are much harder to identify accurately, since paramilitary or gang forces are involved in many of today's conflicts and can blend back into the social environments that spawned them. Hostile groups linked by family, ethnic, or trading ties flow back and forth across state borders that are virtually meaningless for the organized-crime operations they run. Cease-fires mean little when state leaders lack control over potential spoilers or can at least claim to lack control when it suits their political ends.

The success of peace missions in these brutal environments—ranging from the Balkans to Afghanistan, from Congo to Haiti, from

East Timor to Darfur—often requires that they be led by interested states that have the will and the resources to see them through difficult times. Without that kind of strong state support, outside intervention is often no match for the spoilers. Troops need to have trained shoulder to shoulder in order to be effective in dangerous and uncertain circumstances— something that has eased multilateral NATO operations in the Balkans and Afghanistan, for example, as well as the Australian-led intervention in East Timor—rather than being thrown together at the last minute as was traditionally the case in UN peacekeeping operations. They require advanced intelligence and communications equipment in addition to reliable weapons—things that only relatively wealthy and powerful states can provide and are usually willing to provide only when they have interests at stake. Peacekeepers must be prepared to turn at a moment's notice into counterinsurgency war fighters, as they and their missions come under attack from parties that do not want them there at all.

These missions also require troops who are trained and willing to act as police, since they must control mob rioting in the absence of local authorities and protect minority enclaves in areas of the world where the majority population would prefer ethnic cleansing or partition. Military forces are often asked to oversee the humane treatment of displaced people returning home after war to areas where they are no longer welcome and to stop the smuggling of guns, drugs, people, and tax-evading contraband over porous borders. The multitude of problems associated with today's peace operations have made it especially difficult to achieve intervention success in places where wealthy states have few security interests at stake and where the funding and staffing of robust missions have suffered as a result.

Today's peace missions often have explicitly political components. On some missions, soldiers are asked to help identify which villages are deserving of assistance and which should

be sidelined because they fail to cooperate with the intervention—something that happened frequently in the early years of the KFOR (NATO-led, UN Security Council–authorized) peace mission in Kosovo, for example. In Bosnia today, even when NATO soldiers have been replaced by European Union police forces, political judgment is still a critical component of the mission; EU assistance and Bosnia's possible EU accession are dependent on the behavior of local police and judicial forces, who might otherwise slip back into the corruption and ethnic intolerance of their recent past.

Sometimes peace forces are tasked with taking sides in potentially violent domestic political contests. This was the case, for example, in Bosnia and Herzegovina in 1997, when NATO troops stopped Serbian nationalist thugs from congregating at a rally in Banja Luka, where they were threatening to harm Biljana Plavsic, a pro-reform politician who had been ousted by hard-line ethnically Serbian authorities. It happened again in 2000, when NATO troops were asked to ensure that police stations in the Bosnian region of Mostar, where ethnic Croats were dominant, remained in the hands of those who were loyal to the new joint forces of the Bosnian state, rather than in the hands of those who took off their Bosnian uniforms and replaced them with the insignia of the Croatian Democratic Union (HDZ), the Croat nationalist party.[2] In Afghanistan, as part of the NATO-led International Security Assistance Force (ISAF) peace mission, British troops responsible for counternarcotics have worked with the government in Kabul to identify local warlords associated with the opium trade and have them kicked upstairs to prestigious positions in the capital to deprive them of easy contact with drug runners. (This often does not work, though, since the warlords simply leave political control in the hands of close family members.)[3] The UN Stabilization Mission in Haiti (MINUSTAH) has engaged in street battles against violent gangs who support ousted former president Jean-Bertrand

Aristide, leading to accusations that the peace enforcers are practicing political favoritism.

When all of this is added together, it means that, by definition, today's peace enforcers are a political force inside the involved regions, because their success represents the victory of some political actors—namely those favoring a liberal, tolerant, peaceful, and integrationist future—over others whose political and economic goals may actually better reflect those of the majority population. The international community has concluded that the only way to overcome these complex new conflicts, and to prevent open warfare from arising again when outside forces go home, is to institute political change in foreign societies. As a result, the job of the UN Security Council, NATO, and other international organizations and their member states has fundamentally shifted. No longer is it sufficient merely to stand between two parties that both want peace and both want the United Nations there. Instead, it is now perceived to be necessary to build new liberal democratic institutions in war-torn societies, in order to address the underlying causes of violence.

The United Nations, NATO, and other international organizations have believed that their presence and advice are necessary to help these societies design constitutions and judicial systems, electoral systems and parties, government bureaucracies and economic infrastructure, and media and education systems based on notions of tolerance and inclusiveness, so that everyone's needs will be met and no one will feel excluded or desperate. That is the only way to give populations a sense of ownership over the peace process, so that they see that their own interests are served by this new social and political ordering. The international community has become much more intimately involved with the evolution of domestic societies and politics than it ever was before, and soldiers have been tasked with supporting this process—especially soldiers from established liberal democracies, since it is usually those states (located in North America, Western and Central Europe, and Oceania) that have taken on the lead responsibilities in these missions.

Somehow the irony of this concept of ownership has been lost, as the affected population is told that it may only own the future if it changes the way it thinks and acts. In places ranging from Bosnia to Haiti, the international community (often represented by the United Nations but led by its wealthy Western members) has consistently attempted to guide postwar states and territories in the direction of becoming liberal democracies, even when those regions would not have moved in that direction if left to their own devices. The international community's intentions have been, for the most part, noble: to instill norms of ethnic, class, and political tolerance in societies torn apart by hatred; to discourage violence; to foster broad political participation across populations; and to empower individuals who would otherwise lack the opportunity to have their voices heard. Their stated end goal has usually been to pave the way for genuine self-determination, helping societies to emerge anew from arbitrary and violent authoritarian rule.

Often, however, the templates these intervenors employ to further self-determination contain internal contradictions. Sometimes these contradictions arise because democracy, as Fareed Zakaria has noted, can be illiberal.[4] The international community has sometimes privileged liberalism over democracy, when the two come into conflict. For example, in Bosnia and Herzegovina, a succession of leaders of the Office of the High Representative (appointed through a complex web of procedures that makes the term "international community" truly necessary, since neither the United Nations nor NATO nor any one institution had direct control)[5] faced the choice of either allowing democratically elected and legally appointed officials to engage in corrupt activities that support ethnically intolerant parties and policies or summarily evicting them from office, against the will of the majority who put them there. As time went on, these international officials increasingly chose the latter path, supported both by the deterrent of NATO or EU forces on the ground and by sanctions from a variety of international organizations providing aid and assistance to the country's fledgling economy. By 2005, ten years after the Dayton Peace Accords ended armed conflict in Bosnia, this had led to talk of ending the Office of the High Representative's purview, precisely because of the contradictions its presence raised. A commission led by former Italian prime minister Giuliano Amato argued that the OHR had "outlived its usefulness."[6]

While congratulating itself for protecting the rights of those—particularly the Bosniacs (Bosnian Muslims)—who would be threatened if the democratically chosen but ethnically intolerant political figures were allowed to remain in office, the international community has not sufficiently recognized that the message it is sending to this newly "democratic" state is that might still makes right in determining political outcomes. Those who believe in liberalism are winning because they have outside military and economic might behind them—and even if the Office of the High Representative disappears, a small number of U.S. forces are still on the ground in Bosnia, supporting EU police, and will likely remain for the foreseeable future.

Furthermore, EU economic pressure on behalf of liberal economic and political change will still hold sway, as the European Union holds out the dangling promise of eventual Bosnian membership in the institution—until, at least, the Bosnian population realizes that it is very unlikely to be admitted in any meaningful way to the European Union anytime soon. The European Union is designed as an institution to encourage free economic flows across the borders of European states, by breaking down legal and monetary differences that act as impediments. To extend that economic openness to a society as poverty-stricken and corrupt as Bosnia would be political suicide. It is difficult to believe that the Italian and German publics, for example, would accept the free flow of Bosnian labor across their borders, since a primary purpose of their states' aid policy toward Bosnia in the late 1990s was to stem the flow of Bosnian emigration. It is also unlikely that the European Union would accept Bosnian passport control procedures. The individuals who control the criminal economy of Bosnia—often the same people who are involved in the country's ugly ethnic nationalist politics—have no reason to step aside and assist the kind of revolutionary change that would be required for Bosnia to meet EU standards. If outside troops were to leave, it is unlikely that Bosnia would become a stable state. It is much more likely that ethnic nationalism would again come to the forefront with easy promises of a better future for its chosen populations.

Similarly in Kosovo in 2006, almost seven years after the war there ended, negotiations about the country's final status began, but it was still difficult to reach agreement within the international community about how the outcome should be determined. If popular will were allowed to express itself, Kosovo would surely become an independent state. In that case, the only way for outsiders to assure the well-being of any of the Serbian minority remaining in Kosovo once the 90 percent ethnic Albanian population had expressed its will would be to keep troops on the ground for the foreseeable future, leaving Kosovo's independence indefinitely conditional. The ultimate solution would probably be partition, forcing people to abandon their original homes permanently to ensure their own safety. On the one hand, many feared that in that case a precedent would be set, encouraging other maligned ethnic minorities around the world to engage in violent retribution and ethnic cleansing to free their territories from control by outsiders. Already by early 2006 Russia was arguing along that line, to support its own favored breakaway populations in the Georgian regions of Abkhazia and South Ossetia. (Moscow did not, however, extend the precedent to its own war-ravaged province of Chechnya.) On the other hand, though, if popular will continued to be suppressed in Kosovo, through what amounted to an international occupation force that lacked the respect of many of those it oversaw, it was feared that resentment of Westerners and their norms would continue to grow. As Simon Chesterman noted, Kosovars would continue to believe that the current, transitional political institutions would be overturned eventually, once the outsiders left, and would logically withhold the real social capital they might otherwise invest in building for the future.[7]

Sooner or later, the occupation force, too, is likely to end, if history follows its normal pattern; NATO will turn its attention elsewhere when the immediate danger of violence appears to have ended, as states try to respond to competing demands for intervention with limited troop resources. When it does end, there is no reason to expect anything but an illiberal and criminal free-for-all in Kosovo. The April 2004 pogrom against Serbs makes it clear that ethnic hatred still runs high among young ethnic Albanians, and organized-crime gangs control much of Kosovo's economy. In the absence of outside force, the spoilers would win the day.

In Afghanistan, the outside players seem to have taken the opposite tack from that taken in the Balkans, privileging democracy over liberalism in an attempt to secure reconciliation among competing factions. Great fanfare was made over the success of the parliamentary election of October 2005, even though it was marred by fraud and intimidation, and even though Human Rights Watch estimates that about 60 percent of those elected have ties to the armed militias that still control the political economy of the country, including the opium and heroin trade.[8] Local Afghan human rights groups are dismayed that many of those who are accused of war crimes are now MPs who will help determine the country's future path.[9] While the peace operation in Afghanistan may have succeeded in damping down the chances that civil war will break out, it has not brought a sense of lasting security to the population, and democracy on paper does not appear to be leading toward a liberal or stable future for the population.

THE IMPERIALISM OF LIBERAL DEMOCRATIC STATES

It is these kinds of attempts to control the political future of foreign societies that lead to the comparison between peace operations and imperialism, especially as it was practiced by liberal democratic states at the turn of the twentieth century. This means that the lessons of imperial failure have meaning for today's peace operations. The British, French, and American colonial empires (the latter including primarily the U.S. occupation of the Philippines, and also to a lesser or different degree such places as Hawaii, Cuba, and later Haiti) at that time in history were designed to exert control over foreign societies through the use of occupation forces. These imperial states were clearly motivated by self-interest, defined primarily in terms of the international security concerns of their day, much as the peace enforcers of the current era are. But they were also motivated by the desire to bring economic development and political enlightenment to the less fortunate peoples of the world who lacked their own advantages and who could not reach that level of development on their own. The security interests of the colonizing states were inextricably linked with a paternalistic, white man's burden, sort of humanitarianism. Interests and normative concerns reinforced each other, in an era when commerce and Christian charity were seen to be two sides of the same coin.

By the turn of the twentieth century, none of the liberal democratic imperial powers were gaining much economic profit from their colonies (with the exception of British India, which was self-sustaining).[10] Private trading companies gained from the commerce that went back and forth between capital and colony, but the colonizing states themselves were for the most part putting more resources into their colonies than they were getting out of them. Instead of profit, their interests were centered on security, which could come only through controlling foreign territory by occupying it. They believed that great-power war was looming on the distant horizon, and they wanted to ensure uninterrupted access to the raw materials that their colonies produced when it came. They also wanted to maintain distant seaports that would be useful for maritime dominance in future warfare.

This kind of control was not easy to maintain in the face of constant warfare in the colonies. In places where the colonial occupation was resented, it was fragile; peace and prosperity in the colonies depended on the goodwill of the colonized. This gave the imperial powers a strong incentive to convince the colonized populations not to fight against them. Instead, their goal was to win these populations over to the idea that empire served their own interests. They engaged in what resembled complex peace operations as a result, using limited and constrained military forces for police operations to maintain order in their colonies without turning the population against them. They also put real effort into economic development programs, in the belief that this would both help satisfy the populace and in the long run increase the ease of trade between center and periphery and make the colonies self-sustaining.[11]

In practice this didn't always work. There was too much distance between the capitals and the colonies, and directives that were aimed at limiting the use of force sometimes fell on deaf ears (as in the case of the horrific Amritsar massacre directed by British officers in India, or the brutal campaign against the Moros in the Philippines led by U.S. general Leonard Wood). Sometimes, as well, the "man on the spot" in the colonies was believed to have better information than his superiors back home, and officers intent on gaining battle glory and honors used this to their individual advantage, waging combat where it wasn't necessary in areas that their home governments would have preferred not to disturb.[12] Despite these lapses, the evidence indicates the intention of the leaders of liberal democratic states was to do good in their colonies, not to brutalize them.

Underpinning the effort was a set of philosophies that differed somewhat by empire but that were all directed at bringing the benefits of modern civilization to what were seen as backward peoples. In all three home states— Great Britain, France, and the United States —this included the elimination of slavery and other perceived social ills, such as polygamy. The French had their "civilizing mission," designed to bring French language and the achievements of French culture and technology to the colonies.[13] The British saw their colonies as trusteeships and spoke of readying them for eventual self-rule.[14] The Americans in the Philippines saw themselves as undoing the harm of Spanish despotism and over a period of several decades did lay the groundwork for at least halting democratic norms to emerge.[15] While there is an irresolvable scholarly debate about how sincere these humanistic intentions really were on the part of their leaders, there is no question that these motives were used to justify colonial occupations to the electorate at home. The majority of the British, French, and American populations were Christians who wanted to believe that they were doing their Christian duty in the colonies, and it is not surprising that colonial rule and commerce worked hand in hand with such explorer-missionaries as David Livingstone.[16]

PEACE OPERATIONS AND EMPIRE

There are obvious differences between empire as it was practiced by liberal democratic states and more recent peace operations. While the former operations were justified in terms of international law as it existed at that time, that law divided the world into the civilized states of Europe and North America and those that were not yet ready to be considered civilized. This was a far cry from today's universal UN jurisdiction. While the former operations did not turn much of a profit, they were nonetheless designed to secure resources in the colonies for the capitals. Today's operations are designed to distribute resources from the wealthy countries of the world to those in need. While the former operations were competitive, carving up territories into colonial spheres, today's operations are multilateral (even the United States was desperate to get foreign troops and funds to help with the occupation in Iraq), and the challenge is to convince a sufficient number of countries to contribute troops, not to stay out. And while the former operations were designed to be semipermanent, the goal of today's operations is to have local populations take responsibility for their own futures, so that the peace enforcers can go home.

That said, the parallels between colonialism as practiced by liberal democratic states and today's peace enforcement operations are striking. There is the same pattern of involvement primarily when and where perceived security interests are at stake. While the definition of insecurity has changed over time, to include disruptions caused by refugee movements, the threatened spread of ethnic violence over borders, and the harboring of terrorists, powerful states with capable armies and large resources tend to intervene abroad only when perceived self-interest is at stake. We saw the tragic results of this with the failure of anyone to intervene to stop genocide from happening in Rwanda in 1994 and later in the slow and weak response to targeted violence against civilians in Darfur. No powerful state believed it had an interest in intervening in those dangerous circumstances.

Beyond that continuing basic importance of state self-interest that ties today's peace operations to liberal imperialism, the two kinds of intervention share the same underlying sensibility that the developed world knows best which kind of political, social, and economic systems less fortunate societies should adopt. Even the military activities carried out on peace operations bear some resemblance to their colonial forebears. The British in particular were known for their success at combining military operations and policing in their colonies and at maintaining restraint in their use of force, for example, during riots.[17] It is not uncommon to hear British officers say that they do peace operations well because they learned from their colonial experiences, in places like Malaya and Northern Ireland.[18] Canadian and Australian officers, too, say that they learned from the regimental traditions handed down to them from the British Empire (the Australians participated alongside the British in Malaya), making them particularly good at the kinds of "hearts-and-minds" activities that are central to getting populations to believe that intervention is to their benefit. (In contrast, the U.S. Army has recent bad memories of hearts-and-minds campaigns gone wrong in Vietnam, something that slowed the military's initial institutional response to the necessities of counterinsurgency warfare in Iraq—even though U.S. forces also did hearts-and-minds work well in Manila a century ago.)

Given this historical trajectory, it is probably not accidental that the three permanent members of the UN Security Council that are most responsible for taking a leadership role in peace enforcement operations today are the United States, Great Britain, and France—the same countries that led liberal democratic imperial interventions of yesteryear. While these three are far from the only states that have played important roles in today's peace enforcement missions, their leadership has been crucial to gaining approval for every Security Council–approved peace mission on record. When these three countries are not sufficiently concerned about a potential security situation, no mission is approved, or at least sufficiently funded or overseen, and any response by the international community suffers as a result. When these three states are concerned, they lobby others to move forward. In contrast, China usually abstains from peace mission resolution votes unless the issue of Taiwan is somehow involved,[19] and Russia must often be persuaded by the other permanent members to come on board by granting it other favors. In 2005 it was widely perceived that foot dragging by China and Russia—two states that had strong commercial ties to the government in Sudan—helped explain why the Security Council was so slow to approve a robust peace enforcement mission for Darfur. Khartoum did not want strong outside military forces becoming involved in what it perceived to be a struggle over political resources in Sudan, and Moscow and Beijing were reluctant to anger Khartoum.

Current peace operations have an imperial heritage. In recognizing this, we should as well recognize the fact that imperial efforts often left in their wake unstable, illiberal, and violent political trajectories in the former colonies. While scholar Niall Ferguson may argue that the British Empire is responsible for the legacy of democratic and well-run India,[20] he cannot then escape the conclusion that Britain is also responsible for the coup-ridden, impoverished, and weak state of Pakistan. While the United States may have planted the seeds for democracy in the Philippines,[21] it must then also take responsibility for the brutal regime of Ferdinand Marcos. The legacy of the French Empire and the corrupt dictators it often left in place is no better. This should serve as a caution to those who believe they can control the future trajectories of foreign countries.

THE ABSENCE OF SUFFICIENT POLITICAL WILL

As in the case of the liberal empires of the past, today's peace operations suffer from inconsistencies. The good intentions of the intervenors are not always clearly reflected to those on the ground who must bear the consequences of their choices. Some of the inconsistencies in how today's liberal democratic lead states approach peace operations were outlined earlier, in the cases of political oversight in Bosnia and Kosovo. Institutions designed in principle to foster democracy instead make permanent trusteeship inevitable when peace agreements are imposed on populations whose natural inclinations would lead to nothing like the liberal integrationist states that wealthy Western countries prefer. In Afghanistan we have seen the reverse, where privileging elections as a panacea merely papers over the real sources of insecurity in society. In many ways it was a similar set of inconsistencies— the notion that the imperialists were preaching liberal self-determination in their schools and speeches while practicing political domination in their colonies—that led to the rise of anticolonialism and the eventual end of empire as the twentieth century wore on.

Even for those who might excuse today's philosophical inconsistencies on peace missions as an unavoidable consequence of revolutionary political change that is bound to be uneven and lengthy, there is another, practical set of inconsistencies that potentially undermines these operations' success. The liberal democratic states that lead today's peace missions are by definition subject to the varying preferences and changing wishes of their electorates. Democracies have difficulty maintaining long-term policy consistency within particular countries; they have even more difficulty when it comes to coordinating their policies with one another and with the variety of international organizations and NGOs that are now involved with peace operations.

This means that the political will even to bring security to foreign societies is often missing or inadequate.

Sometimes this is because the military forces on the ground are prevented from doing enough to make lasting peace a reality. Beyond the difficult and conflicting national policy choices that liberal democracies face, some also face political limits on how their military forces are used in peace operations. While British, Canadian, and Australian military forces may have few problems taking on police duties when it is necessary to do so in peace operations, U.S. military forces have sometimes been stopped from doing so, for example, by being pulled back midmission when they encounter rioting.[22] There is an entrenched belief in the Pentagon that the American public will not accept casualties on peace missions, a belief left over from the "Black Hawk Down" tragedy occurring in Somalia in fall 1993. The perception has been that to keep political backing for military action, especially in areas of the world that are not central to U.S. definitions of self-interest, it is necessary to limit the dangerous activities U.S. forces take on. Scholars, including Steven Kull, I. M. Destler, and James Burk, have cast doubt on the truth of this belief, demonstrating that the American public accepts casualties on peace operations when it understands the purpose of the mission (including a humanitarian purpose) and that this was true even in Somalia.[23] Yet the belief has been sufficiently entrenched that it limited U.S. tactics in Bosnia and Kosovo, for example, by keeping U.S. soldiers in "full battle rattle" gear, which makes them seem both frightening and frightened when they interact with local people on their patrols. In contrast, soldiers from many other countries take care to seem more approachable and refer to the U.S. troops with their Kevlar helmets and bulky flak jackets as "ninja turtles."

In Iraq, as many commentators began arguing that there was no clear U.S. interest in remaining on the ground, the Bush adminis-tration became convinced that the only way to maintain popular support for the intervention as casualties mounted was to declare that "victory" was within reach, using the term fifteen times in a speech delivered by the president at the U.S. Naval Academy in December 2005.[24] Bush relied on the work of scholars Peter D. Feaver and Christopher Gelpi, who made the argument (contested by other scholars) that public opinion was easier to rally when the prospect of victory was in sight. Bush seemed to believe that if only he told the American public enough times that victory was at hand, that would make it so. The number of American deaths in the Iraq insurgency was limited, in comparison to earlier wars, by the more sophisticated body armor that troops were given, yet the casualties (defined to include injuries as well as deaths) that did result were often horrific, as improvised explosive devices planted along roadsides caused a much higher percentage than in the recent past of lost limbs and serious head wounds. It is perhaps indicative of a certain inconsistency in American political beliefs that while peace operations have been controversial because of the casualty avoidance issue, in Iraq, an operation that the Bush administration considered central to U.S. national self-interest, insufficient resources were made available to buy the heavily armored vehicles that soldiers themselves believed were necessary to protect them.

The United States is far from the only liberal democracy that places limits on troop activities in peace operations. Both Spain and Germany, for example, are constitutionally prohibited from having military forces take on policing duties, either at home or abroad. While it is understandable, given the twentieth-century political histories of these countries, why their populations would want to limit the policing activities that military forces take on, these rules have had unfortunate and unforeseen consequences on peace operations. In Bosnia, it meant that Spanish troops assigned by NATO command to raid the Croat nationalist

Hercegovacka Bank during the disturbances of 2001 had to withdraw when they encountered rioters along the way. British troops were able to storm the bank successfully a few nights later, but the failed first attempt gave warning of NATO intentions, and when the bank was finally seized all of the suspect money and records of embezzlement on behalf of ethnic nationalists had been spirited away. In Afghanistan, it meant that German troops assigned to the town of Faizabad in September 2004 had to stand by helplessly as local people rioted against the Aga Khan Foundation, a respected NGO that was working in the area. The riots were started by rumors, completely false, that the international NGO was raping local women. The result was that several NGO facilities were burned to the ground, and unarmed Aga Khan employees had to rescue comrades who had been severely beaten by the crowd, bravely roaring up in civilian vehicles and pretending to have guns. Limits on the duties that military troops are allowed to perform can hence have real repercussions on mission effectiveness.

This will be an ongoing issue as NATO gradually expands its responsibilities in Afghanistan, taking over increasing numbers of the joint military-civilian provincial reconstruction team (PRT) locations (which are responsible for both humanitarian and security functions, and of which Faizabad is one) from U.S.-led Operation Enduring Freedom forces. While NATO commanders say that they understand these constitutional limit issues, and do their best to assign troops so that those working under constraints are least likely to face the need to take on policing roles, this obviously doesn't always work. No one expected Faizabad to be a dangerous location for German troops, given the absence of warlord fighting or ethnic tension there.

In practice, U.S. forces have done some policing duties quite well in places like Bosnia and Kosovo and are often proud of their accomplishments on patrols, for example, in terms of intercepting border smuggling operations. Other times, U.S. forces have seemed insensitive in their approach toward civilians in police-type operations, because of inadequate preparation and cultural awareness training. While the instances of this attitude that make the television news are usually so egregious that they constitute crimes punishable by court martial, such as the Abu Ghraib prison scandal in Iraq, others are more subtle and yet still detrimental to U.S. effectiveness. For example, U.S. helicopters bringing in forces to conduct predawn searches of Kosovar villages along the border with Macedonia in 2001 broadcast Wagner's "Ride of the Valkyries" theme to wake up the inhabitants[25]—the song that U.S. attack helicopters played as they strafed and napalmed a Vietnamese village in the 1979 Francis Ford Coppola movie *Apocalypse Now*, probably a familiar reference to at least some of Kosovo's inhabitants because the movie had just been reissued in a new DVD version that year. More recently, U.S. forces in Afghanistan have been criticized by local authorities for routinely breaking down the doors of residences to search for terrorist suspects and weapons—something that exposes pious Muslim women who are not properly attired to the eyes of male strangers and that often nets little anyway, since perpetrators manage to be tipped off in advance.

Yet properly trained and rewarded military forces can be good at doing police work when required. As noted, military organizations whose legacy includes engaging in colonial activities often argue that this heritage has been passed down in their training to this day, making them particularly well suited to these activities. For example, Canadian Forces (CF) patrolling Kabul and its environs in spring 2004 were adept at cultural outreach, even in circumstances that held potential danger. While Kabul was a relatively safe deployment in comparison to other places in Afghanistan, the peace mission remained a target, and Afghanistan was certainly unstable. For example, during the week that I visited the Canadian camp in May 2004, a rebel rocket hit the ISAF mission headquarters in downtown Kabul, injuring a German soldier.

In earlier incidents in 2004, two Canadian soldiers had been killed while on patrol in the area—one when his vehicle hit a freshly laid road mine and another when a suicide bomber threw himself across a jeep. Yet the Canadian commanders in Kabul insisted that the best force protection came from being open to the locals, to demonstrate that the foreign military forces were on their side. For example, Canadian jeeps stopped off at a refugee camp and soldiers removed their protective helmets, going inside a tent for about an hour to have tea with the elders.[26] Canadian soldiers also stopped frequently and spontaneously on their patrols to talk to local merchants, who complained that they had to sleep in their stores with guns at night to protect their goods from gangs who were in cahoots with the local police. While the CF lacked the resources to provide protection against these burglaries, they noted the locations where complaints were concentrated, so that the Afghan government could be advised about which districts needed a special concentration of police reform efforts. Canadian commanders believed that these tactics paid off when some locals notified them that mortars had been aimed at the Canadian camp from the basement of a nearby abandoned palace, allowing the CF to go in and collect the weapons before they were used. The locals appeared to want the CF to stay and were therefore passing along intelligence to prevent harm from being done to Canadian soldiers.

In late 2005, Canadian Forces were redeployed to the much more dangerous area of Kandahar, where Taliban attacks against the Western presence were more common and more Canadian troops were killed and wounded. Rather than being part of the NATO peace mission, as they were in Kabul in 2004, they were reassigned to the U.S.-led Operation Enduring Freedom campaign; among other tasks, they were given responsibility for leading the provincial reconstruction team in the area. PRT civilian leader Glyn Berry, a senior Canadian diplomat, was killed in a roadside bombing in January 2006, a tragic reminder of the risk involved in the Kandahar deployment. This deployment serves as a test of how well the attitudes of cultural awareness and openness that were inculcated in the CF in an earlier stint in Afghanistan will hold up in these more violent circumstances.

U.S. military commanders, as well as defense analysts, sometimes point out that civilian-friendly patrolling and other police actions demand a very different set of skills than war fighting. They argue that it isn't reasonable to expect that troops needed for combat can become peacekeepers at a moment's notice. Their war-fighting capabilities can be compromised if too much of their training is given over to the softer side of operations.[27] Yet while it would be ideal to leave policing to well-trained civilian police officers, the fact is that there are almost never enough of them available at a global level to go where they are needed in peace operations. At a minimum there is a "deployment gap" at the beginning of operations, as Michael Dziedzic has noted, since it takes time to get international police forces on the ground after the fighting stops.[28] But beyond this, there is simply a dearth of well-trained police officers at the global level who are available for foreign deployments, in either the quantity or quality that is necessary. Some states have hybrid forces, such as the French gendarmerie or the Italian carabinieri, which are designed to navigate the border between police and military activities, but their numbers are small and they alone cannot fill the need.

While some have argued that the United States military should create separate units of peacekeepers and war fighters,[29] this is unlikely to solve the problem. Soldiers must be capable of taking on public order missions at a moment's notice. This is something that the United States learned in Kosovo, when troops deployed in anticipation of ground warfare around Kosovo's borders were ordered to turn on a dime and become members of the KFOR peace mission, as Kosovars streamed back into the country unexpectedly quickly following the signing of peace accords. It was a lesson relearned in Iraq, when U.S.-led troops in inadequate numbers were the only public security forces available as Saddam Hussein's regime suddenly folded when Baghdad fell. Another approach is necessary, one that prepares soldiers for both combat and peace missions, especially in today's world, when international security so rarely revolves around the notion of professional state military organizations going to war against each other.

LESSONS IN IRAQ AND BEYOND

Indeed, this is something that senior U.S. officers are now seriously discussing, as the difficulties of operations in Iraq make it clear that winning traditional battles does not necessary lead to winning the war. Instead, counterinsurgency warfare has to take a lesson from the conduct of successful peace operations and integrate policing skills into the conduct of military operations in order to be successful. This became blatantly clear immediately after the fall of Saddam Hussein's regime, when U.S. forces did nothing to stop the looting that by some estimates caused more damage to Iraqi infrastructure than over a decade of UN sanctions did. Many observers believe that the failure to provide adequate security for the Iraqi population in the aftermath of the 2003 war was the key error that ignited popular displeasure at the U.S. presence, allowing the insurgency movement that followed to gain support it otherwise would not have had.

A debate about the future direction of U.S. forces, and whether and how to take account of the requirements of peace operations, had already begun to percolate several years ago,

according to journalist Dana Priest, although at that time those who emphasized the importance of peace missions remained in the minority.[30] Yet as Iraq unraveled it became clearer that something needed to change. Those in favor of altering training and preparation within the U.S. military started gaining ground. For example, a U.S. Army counterinsurgency operations field guide was updated and released in October 2004, for the first time since the Vietnam War. It was the result of close cooperation with the British military because of that organization's success in colonial and postcolonial operations,[31] indicating that the U.S. Army recognized the need to learn from its allies something new about its approach. While the contents of that guide have not been made public, it is likely that policing and other interactions with civilians are covered.

Then, in late 2005, Andrew F. Krepinevich, a respected Washington defense analyst with previous high-level Pentagon experience, published an article in *Foreign Affairs* arguing that the "center of gravity" in counterinsurgency operations is won by whoever has the support of the local population. In Iraq, he wrote, it was more important to provide security for ordinary people than to chase down insurgents who could never be completely eliminated as long as they had some sympathy among the locals.[32] By early November, commanding general George W. Casey had opened a new officer-training school for U.S. Army and Marines personnel inside Iraq, giving intensive one-week courses that centered on "building a strong relationship with the local Iraqis."[33] U.S. ambassador to Iraq Zalmay Khalilzad simultaneously announced that "area security" provision was a key new part of U.S. strategy in Iraq. The goal now would be to protect Iraqi cities and towns that had been cleared of insurgents, to ensure that people could lead normal lives and participate in politics without fear.[34]

While this is good news, it may be too late to make much of a difference in Iraq. The

United States did so much to squander the goodwill of the Iraqis that it may never be able to build a strong relationship with locals there. These mistakes ranged from the decision to completely disband the old Iraqi Army, leaving a large number of trained, armed Sunni men with no livelihood in the new political system dominated by their Shiite rivals, to the decision to try to keep U.S. control of the design details of the emerging Iraqi constitution.[35] Once again, the attempt to direct political change in a foreign society created a situation that provided no real stability to the country or its neighbors.

But these lessons may have a positive effect on the future decisions of both the United States and the international community more broadly. It can be hoped that the liberal democratic world will stop focusing on trying to replicate its own experiences and institutions elsewhere and instead focus on building security for populations who have been exhausted by warfare. When people are able to go about their daily lives in peace, they can choose their own political futures without fear. This requires that states with powerful militaries, which have the resources to lead robust peace missions, acquire the political will to maintain a security presence abroad over the long term—something the world has rarely seen. Yet only when people's security is assured is it possible for them to invest in the future. It is a sense of security that brings real ownership to peace processes, not political change that is forced from the outside.

Beyond the operational changes that are necessary for the military forces involved, what this chapter suggests is that a basic strategic rethinking about the goals and advisability of international intervention is in order. If outsiders believe they can control the direction of political developments in foreign societies, they will most likely be disappointed, and they will suffer from being tarred with the same brush as the colonial failures that preceded them. They will probably not have sufficient

political will to see the complexity of heavily politicized operations through for the length of time that is necessary. The inconsistencies inherent in the process of liberal democratization, as well as in their own visions (and constitutional and political limits) about how things should be done, will hobble their progress.

For these reasons, it is more sensible to focus on a different set of goals for intervention: stopping the killing, restoring the peace, and maintaining public security until the involved populations can sort out their own futures. While immense difficulties remain in resolving the tensions inherent in this process, and in determining the details of how it will be done, a new perspective may help bring fresh ideas to the policy table.

Notes

1. These lessons are drawn from Kimberly Zisk Marten, *Enforcing the Peace: Learning from the Imperial Past* (New York: Columbia University Press, 2004). The Afghanistan example was also discussed previously, in Marten, "In Building Nations, Establish Security, Then Democracy," *Chronicle of Higher Education*, March 18, 2005, B12–13.

2. All of these examples are documented and discussed in detail in Marten, *Enforcing the Peace*.

3. Ahmed Rashid, "Chief Ousted as British Troops Head for Afghan Drug Region," *Daily Telegraph* (London), December 23, 2005.

4. Fareed Zakaria, "The Rise of Illiberal Democracy," *Foreign Affairs* 76, no. 6 (November–December 1997): 22–43.

5. For a description of these procedures, see the official Web site of the Office of the High Representative: http://www.ohr.int/.

6. Nicholas Wood, "Can an Iron Fist Put Power in Bosnia's Hands?" *New York Times*, November 5, 2005.

7. Simon Chesterman, *Kosovo in Limbo: State-Building and "Substantial Autonomy,"* Project on Transitional Administrations Report (New York: International Peace Academy, 2001).

8. David Brunnstrom, "First Afghan Parliament in Decades to Meet Monday," Reuters, December 16, 2005.

9. Integrated Regional Information Network, "Rights Body Warns of Warlords' Success in Elections," IRIN News, UN Office for the Coordination of Humanitarian Affairs, October 18, 2005, http://www.irinnews.org.

10. In *Mammon and the Pursuit of Empire: The Political Economy of British Imperialism, 1860–1912* (New York: Cambridge University Press, 1986), Lance E. Davis and Robert A. Huttenback do the most careful job of disaggregating economic data to see where the profits were going. Others reaching similar conclusions include James J. Cooke, *New French Imperialism 1880–1910: The Third Republic and Colonial Expansion* (Hamden, Conn.: Archon Books, 1973); and Michael W. Doyle, *Empires* (Ithaca, N.Y.: Cornell University Press, 1986).

11. D. K. Fieldhouse, *Colonialism 1870–1945: An Introduction* (London: Weidenfeld and Nicolson, 1981); Crawford Young, *The African Colonial State in Comparative Perspective* (New Haven, Conn.: Yale University Press, 1994); and Alice L. Conklin, *A Mission to Civilize: The Republican Idea of Empire in France and West Africa, 1895-1930* (Stanford, Calif.: Stanford University Press, 1997).

12. For examples of this, see Lawrence James, *Imperial Rearguard: Wars of Empire, 1919–85* (New York: Brassey's, 1988); Douglas Porch, "Bugeaud, Galliéni, Lyautey: The Development of French Colonial Warfare," in *Makers of Modern Strategy from Machiavelli to the Nuclear Age*, ed. Peter Paret et al. (Princeton, N.J.: Princeton University Press, 1986); Moshe Gershovich, *French Military Rule in Morocco: Colonialism and Its Consequences* (London: Cass, 2000); Brian McAllister Linn, *Guardians of Empire: The U.S. Army and the Pacific, 1902–1940* (Chapel Hill: University of North Carolina Press, 1997); and Linn, "Cerberus' Dilemma: The U.S. Army and Internal Security in the Pacific, 1902–1940," in *Guardians of Empire: The Armed Forces of the Colonial Powers, c. 1700–1964*, ed. David Kilingray and David E. Omissi (New York: Manchester University Press, 1999).

13. Conklin, *A Mission to Civilize*.

14. Fieldhouse, *Colonialism 1870–1945*.

15. Tony Smith, *America's Mission: The United States and the Worldwide Struggle for Democracy in the Twentieth Century* (Princeton, N.J.: Princeton University Press, 1994), 37–59; Linn, *Guardians of Empire*, 5–50; and Linn, "Cerberus' Dilemma," 114–136.

16. Horst Gründer, "Christian Mission Activities in Africa in the Age of Imperialism and the Berlin Conference of 1884–1885," in *Bismarck, Europe, and Africa: The Berlin Africa Conference 1884–1885 and the Onset of Partition*, ed. Stig Förster, Wolfgang J. Mommsen, and Ronald Robinson (London: Oxford University Press, 1988), 85–103.

17. Anthony Clayton, "'Deceptive Might': Imperial Defense and Security, 1900–1968," in *The Oxford History of British Empire*, vol. 6, *The Twentieth Century*, ed. Judith M. Brown and Wm. Roger Louis (New York: Oxford, 1999); and Major General Charles W. Gwynn, *Imperial Policing* (London: Macmillan, 1934).

18. Rod Thornton, "The Role of Peace Support Operations Doctrine in the British Army," *International Peacekeeping* 7, no. 2 (Summer 2000): 41–63.

19. Nigel Thalakada, "China's Voting Pattern in the Security Council, 1990–1995," in *The Once and Future Security Council*, ed. Bruce Russett (New York: St. Martin's Press, 1997), 83–118.

20. Niall Ferguson, *Empire: The Rise and Demise of the British World Order* (New York: Basic Books, 2003).

21. Smith, *America's Mission*.

22. For examples, see Anthony D. Sinnott, "A Good Reputation Is the Best Force Protection," *Marine Corps Gazette* 84, no. 6 (June 2000): 45–46; and Carlotta Gall, "Serbs in Kosovo Stone U.S. Troops, Who Retreat," *New York Times*, February 21, 2000.

23. Steven Kull and I. M. Destler, *Misreading the Public: The Myth of a New Isolationism* (Washington, D.C.: Brookings Institution Press, 1999), 81–112; and James Burk, "Public Support for Peacekeeping in Lebanon and Somalia: Assessing the Casualties Hypothesis," *Political Science Quarterly* 114, no. 1 (Spring 1999): 53–78.

24. Scott Shane, "Bush's Speech on Iraq Echoes Analyst's Voice," *New York Times*, December 4, 2005.

25. Sergeant Gary Peterson, "Cordon and Search Keeps Kosovo Safe and Secure," *Falcon Flier*, August 1, 2001.

26. The author was embedded as a journalist with the Canadian Forces at Camp Julien in May 2004 and participated in these patrols.

27. For both sides of the issue, see John Hillen and Bill Nash, "Debate: Can Soldiers Be Peacekeepers and Warriors?" *NATO Review* 49, no. 2 (Summer 2001): 16–20; and Congressional Budget Office, *Making Peace While Staying Ready for War: The Challenges of U.S. Military Participation in Peace Operations,* 99-J-932-46 (Washington, D.C.: Congressional Budget Office, December 1999).

28. Michael J. Dziedzic, introduction to *Policing the New World Disorder: Peace Operations and Public Security,* ed. Robert B. Oakley, Michael J. Dziedzic, and Eliot M. Goldberg (Washington, D.C.: Defense University Press, 1998).

29. Thomas P. M. Barnett, *Blueprint for Action: A Future Worth Creating* (New York: Penguin, 2005).

30. Dana Priest, *The Mission: Waging War and Keeping Peace with America's Military* (New York: W. W. Norton, 2003).

31. Douglas Jehl and Thom Shanker, "For the First Time since Vietnam, the Army Prints a Guide to Fighting Insurgents," *New York Times,* November 13, 2004.

32. Andrew F. Krepinevich, "How to Win in Iraq," *Foreign Affairs* 84, no. 5 (September–October 2005): 87–104.

33. Eric Schmitt, "U.S. to Intensify Its Training in Iraq to Battle Insurgents," *New York Times,* November 2, 2005.

34. "New Bush Strategy in Iraq Will Aim to Shield Public from Insurgents," *Inside the Pentagon,* November 3, 2005.

35. Larry Diamond, *Squandered Victory: The American Occupation and Bungled Effort to Bring Democracy to Iraq* (New York: Henry Holt, 2005).

35

ECONOMIC FACTORS IN CIVIL WARS
POLICY CONSIDERATIONS

David M. Malone and Jake Sherman

THE ECONOMIC ASPECTS OF CONTEM-
porary internal conflicts have acquired
new relevance in policy circles. In the
past decade, globalization has enabled rival
factions, through licit and illicit commercial
networks, to better access international markets and thus finance civil wars. Few would
question the existence of economic motives
throughout the history of warfare, but until
recently there has been relatively little systematic research on the exact role of economically
motivated actions and processes in generating
and sustaining internal armed conflicts. This
attention has emerged in the context of research
and policy development work both on conflict
prevention and on peacebuilding.

The Canadian Foreign Ministry developed
a relatively early interest in the role of economic
factors in civil wars. This attention coincided
with the creation of a new Global Issues Bureau
in 1995, which, inter alia, sought to interlink
various policy areas believed relevant to contemporary conflict, including human rights,
humanitarian policy, combating international

crime and terrorism, and postconflict peacebuilding. Also, during the mid-1990s, Canadian foreign minister Lloyd Axworthy was
deeply engaged in developing a "human security" agenda focused on the protection of individuals rather than states. Thus, conditions
could not have been more favorable to undertake exploration of how private and group economic gain may have influenced such conflicts
as those of Bosnia, Angola, Liberia, Sri Lanka,
and Central America.

At the time, much of the academic and policy literature illuminating the economic "drivers" of contemporary civil wars was originating
in the United Kingdom in the fields of international relations and economics, sociology,
and anthropology. Interested scholars in the
United Kingdom had not undergone the drift
toward policy-irrelevant modeling and theo-
rizing of their American counterparts in some
fields.[1] United Kingdom–based nongovernmental organizations (NGOs) were also beginning to contribute important findings, notably
Global Witness's 1998 report calling attention

to the complicity of the diamond industry and key states in undermining UN sanctions regimes against the National Union for the Total Independence of Angola (UNITA) and the wider links between diamonds and the perpetuation of the Angola conflict.[2]

In 1999, the International Peace Academy; the Center for International Studies at Oxford University; the World Bank; and the governments of Canada and the United Kingdom organized a conference in London focusing on economic agendas in civil wars, and featuring Paul Collier, David Keen, Mark Duffield, and many other leading academics and practitioners. The overall aims in convening these researchers were, first, to improve the understanding of the political economy of armed conflict by examining the economic motivations and commercial agendas of elites from competing factions; second, to assess how globalization creates new opportunities for these elites to pursue their economic agendas through trade, investment, and migration ties, both legal and illegal, to neighboring states and to more distant industrial economies; and third, to examine the possible policy responses available to external actors, including governments, international organizations, NGOs, and the private sector, to shift the economic agendas of elites in civil wars from war toward peace.

In particular, the conference's organizers were keen to examine the kinds of trade-offs that would have to occur among elites, their internal supporters, and their external economic clients for a fundamental shift in incentives and disincentives to take place. It was thought that a proper understanding of these would be critical to the wider question of how best to ensure that the international community can effectively assist transitions from protracted war to lasting peace. There was no sense at the time of how ambitious—indeed, overreaching—these objectives were for one short conference. However, the conference proved instrumental in highlighting this important vector of policy research.[3] It yielded an enthusiastic response from the U.K. government, and word of its tentative conclusions soon spread to other players.[4]

A convergence of political factors, academic interests, and policy concerns helped to establish this research agenda. Its history is recounted here to underscore how policy-relevant research often gets started: A few interested individuals intrigued by scholarly findings apparently relevant to their professional portfolios, but often without any real knowledge of their own, are able to mobilize funding for further research and are eager to proselytize.

THE POLITICAL ECONOMY PERSPECTIVE

Most scholars writing about civil conflict since the Cold War have tended to concentrate on the *costs* of conflict and to treat civil war as a disruption of "normal" social, economic, and political interaction within a society.[5] "Peace" and "war" had been understood as separate and distinct categories, the latter being viewed as inherently "irrational" and dysfunctional.[6] In fact, this dichotomy between peace and war has a long tradition in Western thinking about war and has influenced the way international organizations, most notably the United Nations, approach contemporary civil wars. Yet combatants often have a vested interest in perpetuating conflict—violence often serves a range of political and economic goals, especially within weak or fragmented states.

These dynamics challenge many of the core assumptions that have informed thinking and guided policy with respect to civil wars in the 1990s and the 2000s. Indeed, the very notion of a "comprehensive political settlement," used to describe many of the peace agreements brokered by the United Nations during the past decade, suggests that the formal end of armed hostilities marks a definitive break with past patterns of conflict and violence. This has rarely been the case.

Contemporary conflicts in parts of Africa, Central America, the Balkans, and Southeast

Asia have all shown that an end to fighting does not mean that the underlying causes of conflict have been addressed. Grievances and conflicts of interest persist beyond the formal end of hostilities, and they continue to exert a strong influence on the politics and the process of "postconflict" peacebuilding.[7] Transitions from war to peace, as the experiences of the 1990s show, are more usefully seen as involving "a realignment of political interests and a readjustment of economic strategies rather than a clean break from violence to consent, from theft to production, or from repression to democracy."[8]

Economically motivated violence and the economic activities of belligerents may be powerful barriers to war termination. The cases of Sierra Leone, Somalia, Cambodia, and El Salvador all demonstrate that war—even when triggered by legitimate social, economic, and political grievances—over time may be transformed into an alternative system of profit and power that overwhelmingly favors certain groups at the expense of others. In many conflicts, violence is a means to control trade, appropriate land, exploit labor, extract benefits from humanitarian aid, and ensure continued control of economic privileges and assets. Thus, groups benefiting from violence—both during conflict and within war-torn societies emerging from conflict—may have substantial economic interests in preventing the advent of peace, democracy, and accountability for human rights abuses. Furthermore, the criminalization of economic relations in wartime frequently leaves lasting developmental distortions that, if left unattended, can fatally undermine subsequent efforts at postconflict reconstruction.

A further dimension of this issue is the effect of economic "globalization" on the ability of combatants, war profiteers, and other entrepreneurs to sustain and benefit from conflict. Increasingly, these actors have been able to tap into global networks of production and exchange, both licit and illicit, establishing ties to corporations, diaspora organizations, arms brokers, international organized crime, and corrupt governments reaching well beyond war zones to the world's capitals and major financial centers. For example, in Cambodia, the government and the Khmer Rouge (with the complicity of the Thai military) had few difficulties selling rubies and high-grade tropical timber on the world market; in Liberia, Charles Taylor was able to export large quantities of rubber and timber to Europe; and in Sierra Leone, warlords financed their military operations and accumulated personal wealth through the sale of diamonds on the world market.[9] The result has been to adversely influence the balance of incentives in favor of peace. Perhaps nowhere is this more evident than in Angola, where oil revenue— and illicit diamond–financed conflict resulted in the failure of two United Nations–brokered peace accords, atrocious loss of life, and crippling poverty for Angola's people —yet millions in profit for Angola's rival elites.[10] The corollary question for policymakers is therefore how to make peace more profitable than war.

EXISTING AND EMERGING POLICY RESPONSES

The types of economic activities and resource flows that fuel civil wars are diverse. Some are licit; others are clearly criminal. Some are necessary to civilian welfare (which may predate conflict, or be exacerbated by it); others are manifestly predatory. Although a number of these activities directly feed armed hostilities, most economic behavior contributes to conflict in more diffuse and indirect ways, with some also playing a vital role in the livelihoods of civilian populations. This complicated reality presents policymakers with the twofold challenge of accurately assessing the impact of discrete economic behaviors on conflict dynamics and of designing effective policy responses.

A range of policy instruments exists at the national, regional, and international levels to influence economic agendas in civil wars. Many of these were applied, with varying degrees of effectiveness, to a number of intrastate conflicts in the 1990s. These fall into several categories: the coercive (e.g., UN Security Council–mandated sanctions; intergovernmental agreements on money laundering); the exemplary (often focusing on basic human needs of civilian populations, such as food and health, e.g., corridors of peace negotiated for specific purposes); the financial (multilateral and bilateral assistance and potentially funding from certain key private-sector actors); and the rhetorical. At the time the London conference on economic agendas in civil wars was convened, little comprehensive work had been done to critically evaluate the role and possible limitations of these instruments. Recent work by the International Peace Academy (IPA), Fafo, the Overseas Development Institute, and other organizations is beginning to address this lacuna.[11]

Fortunately, policy development in this field need not be from scratch but is able to draw upon (at times) well-developed and successful initiatives in other areas. Economic sanctions and arms embargoes—increasingly in their "smart" or targeted version—remain the most widely used regulatory instrument wielded in conflict zones, but they are but one mechanism in a growing framework of possible responses. This framework has evolved rapidly during the past five years, though not necessarily in response to civil wars. These new initiatives include the suppression of money laundering, regulating the export of weapons, combating narcotics trafficking, targeting international organized crime, and minimizing the negative impact of private-sector activities. Much of this progress has been in response to advocacy campaigns by international NGOs, as well as the threat posed by transnational organized crime and international terrorism. Several key developments are highlighted below.

The certification of natural resource sectors implicated in financing armed conflict is an issue that has largely emerged out of attention

to sanctions violations, particularly in the case of diamonds. Of great concern was how to avoid an outright boycott of diamonds, which would have devastated the economies of "clean" producers while effectively denying "conflict diamonds" access to international markets. The Kimberley Process—a regulatory initiative of diamond-producing and -selling states, NGOs, and industry that was introduced by South Africa following Security Council and General Assembly resolutions—seeks to establish minimum common rules for rough diamond certification. The Kimberley Process relies on a "chain of warranties" intended to provide an audit trail linking each diamond to its mine of origin. An effective global certification regime will require implementation and compliance by relevant governments and industry actors alike, and it will have to simultaneously contend with corruption that would enable new laws to be circumvented. The lack of industry transparency—for example, the lack of consistent trade statistics—and the absence of guidelines for self-assessment and monitoring remain significant challenges to the Kimberley Process.

Moreover, it is far from certain that a regime such as the Kimberley Process can eliminate the illicit trade in diamonds, much of which occurs outside official channels, let alone the patronage and criminal networks it feeds, and thus prevent state failure. The "chain of warranties" idea is being applied on a more limited basis for the timber industry, identifying wood harvested from sustainable sources. Similar certification and warranty systems are used or are being considered to address other "conflict" commodities—notably timber.

A potentially more far-reaching issue is how to track the proceeds of criminal activity by leaderships in civil wars through thickets created internationally to conceal tax evasion and money laundering. Targeting the finances of combatants may be a cost-effective means of influencing the behavior of recalcitrant factions in civil conflicts. The required technology and expertise are already highly developed in the context of drug traffickers and terrorists and could be applied to belligerents.

The Organization for Economic Cooperation and Development's (OECD's) Financial Action Task Force on Money Laundering (FATF) is among the most effective instruments available in this arena. It comprises twenty-nine countries and has issued forty recommendations on accounting standards, mandatory reporting of suspicious or large financial transactions, elimination of anonymous accounts, and other measures. The FATF was initially a regional body, but its influence is increasingly global. The FATF was long faulted for failing to censure countries that routinely permitted—if not encouraged—the laundering of illicit profits through their domestic financial institutions. In 2000, the FATF issued a "blacklist" of fifteen "noncooperative" countries that were inadequately combating money laundering. In 2001, the FATF took the unprecedented step of demanding that Russia, the Philippines, and Nauru pass money-laundering legislation or face sanctions, including delaying the processing of international financial transactions and withholding loans from the International Monetary Fund and World Bank. This leverage creates a powerful incentive for compliance by nonmember countries.

The FATF's member states monitor and rank each other's efforts to combat financial crimes, but there is no similar system in place —at least at the international level—to rank or certify financial institutions. In response, Jonathan Winer, a former U.S. State Department official, recently proposed the creation of a global "white list" under which international commercial financial institutions would agree to principles of transparency, anti–money laundering, and external compliance monitoring. In exchange, such an institution would be added to the list and, pending a transition period, would be rewarded with preferential selection in the deposit and processing of financing from the World Bank, United Nations, and other public and multilateral agencies. Such an initiative not only creates a financial incentive for compliance but also supplements national regulatory efforts, particularly where governments have little direct means to enforce these standards.[12]

The cooperative relationship between international organized crime networks and local armed groups in all areas of illicit crime and the related increase in official corruption has been of growing concern to the international community as a whole. The United Nations has studied the subject at a number of important meetings, ultimately leading to the 2000 UN Convention against Transnational Organized Crime, the first legally binding UN treaty on the subject. The convention is a comprehensive and coordinated attempt to address the links between corruption and crime. By requiring member states to add four criminal offenses to their domestic laws—participation in an organized criminal group, money laundering, corruption, and obstruction of justice —it should strengthen national institutions in combating such crime. Nonetheless, regulatory approaches to organized crime have a history of failure—and a global approach faces enforcement on a global level.

Measures to combat international terrorism offer yet another potential legal and policy framework through which to control the finances sustaining civil war. The UN International Convention for the Suppression of the Financing of Terrorism, for example, requires states to criminalize the provision or collection of funds for acts defined as offenses by previous UN antiterrorism conventions, to provide legal assistance with investigations and extradition regardless of bank secrecy laws, and to cooperate with one another in investigations and extraditions when these offenses are committed.[13] The convention may have applications for the control of financing for civil wars, especially from diasporas located in OECD countries. Because of its broad definition of "terrorism," this convention applies to murders or physical violence perpetrated against noncombatants during war, though arguably only by nonstate actors and not acts of "state terror." The utility of these instruments as a means of conflict resolution and prevention has been less tested, though targeted financial sanctions and asset seizure have been applied against several rebel groups and governments with mixed results. The United Nations' Counter-Terrorism Committee, tasked with monitoring implementation of Security Council Resolution 1373 on combating international terrorism, likewise has important implications for policy work on illicit economic behavior in armed conflict, though admittedly it may be premature to consider any expansion of its mandate.

Finally, the international private sector—most obviously extractive industries (petroleum, mining, timber) but also the finance and insurance industries—play a critical, if mostly unintended, role in many conflict zones. Until recently, most firms have adopted a studiously "neutral" stance on civil strife, disclaiming any political agenda at all. Now, firms are increasingly aware—due in part to NGO advocacy—not only that their operations on the ground and in global markets may inevitably exacerbate conflicts but also that their profits and reputation may suffer as a result. Consequently, there are a growing number of voluntary, statutory, and (less frequently) legally binding "corporate social responsibility" initiatives that seek to minimize these negative aspects of private-sector behavior.

Under-Secretary General Kofi Annan, the United Nations has begun to address the role of private-sector actors in armed conflict, as well as their potential contribution to conflict prevention. The UN Global Compact—a voluntary initiative requiring participating companies to commit themselves to nine principles related to human rights, labor, and the environment—selected business and armed conflict as the theme of its first roundtable discussions. Nonetheless, as a voluntary initiative,

the compact lacks any monitoring of compliance or enforcement. Apart from their desire to be good corporate citizens, private-sector actors are unlikely to become good corporate citizens if it is not in their economic interest to do so. They are not inclined to modify their business practices if it will place them at a disadvantage vis-à-vis their competitors, particularly less reputable firms motivated solely by profits rather than broad social benefits.

A different approach, albeit one on a specific issue, is that of the United States' and United Kingdom's Voluntary Principles on Security and Human Rights, which are both a set of principles concerning use of private and public security forces and a tripartite dialogue on security and human rights with (an initial eight) companies in the extractive and energy sectors and several NGOs. The ongoing dialogue provides participants with the opportunity to review the principles and ensure their continuing relevance and efficacy. Through the participation of additional companies with similar concerns in other operating environments and their home governments, it is hoped the principles will set an emerging global standard on the use of private security. Ironically, the requirements for participation in the dialogue may exclude some non-U.S. or non-U.K. firms seeking to participate due to their questionable behavior in areas of armed conflict—the very environment in which firms are most in need of accountable security with clearly delineated responsibilities.

CHALLENGES FOR GOVERNMENT POLICY DEVELOPMENT

Different governments have had different reasons for coming to grips with issues concerning economic activities in conflict. Though some have done so reluctantly, others have done so more willingly. Yet even the best of intentions often fall victim to the types of trade-offs that policymakers must, as a practical matter, make to accommodate diverse, and often highly influential, constituencies. A case in point is Canada, a country deeply involved in mining activities, not only domestically—Canada is a diamond-mining and oil-producing country—but also abroad. Canadian companies are deeply engaged in mineral extraction in the Democratic Republic of the Congo, for example. For these reasons, individuals in the Canadian government are sensitive to natural resource issues. Several years ago, it became known that the Canadian oil company Talisman was involved in exploiting an oil field in central Sudan in partnership with companies from Malaysia and China. It was clear that the revenue derived from this drilling activity was contributing significantly to funding the Sudanese government's military campaign against rebels in the country's south, albeit unintentionally.

The Canadian foreign minister, Lloyd Axworthy, was deeply troubled by this relationship. As an initiator and energetic advocate of a "human security" agenda, he believed that the Canadian government could not permit the relationship between a Canadian oil company and a government engaged in war against its own people to continue unchallenged. He sought to convince the Canadian government that a halt should be put to Talisman's activities in Sudan. However, he was essentially stopped cold in his tracks. Talisman was a major employer in Calgary, and most political circles held that the Canadian government should be promoting job creation within the country rather than undermining it. Perhaps partly as a result of this experience, Axworthy was extremely supportive of research and policy development work on the issue of linkages between resources and internal armed conflict, hoping that such research might, in the future, inspire a different policy response from the government.

A second example involves the response of the British government to (previously tolerated) secrecy by its financial sector. Several individuals within the British Cabinet have been keen to tackle corporate misbehavior in conflict countries as well as the role of the U.K. financial sector in serving as a haven for ill-gotten gains deriving from such conflicts. It was a source of deep embarrassment to some in the British government when, following the death of the Nigerian dictator Sani Abacha, some of his expropriated wealth turned up in U.K. banks.[14] That governments and major international banks turned their attention to tracking down the fruits of Abacha's corruption only once he was safely dead (and some of his family safely in jail) was shocking to those advocating an "ethical" foreign policy. Others in the British government took the view that, while it was a worthy goal to try to "clean up" London's financial institutions, this should not be achieved at the risk of destroying it as a financial center to the benefit of rivals like Switzerland.

These opposing positions highlight the trade-offs that industry and, by extension, government face when deciding whether to adopt socially responsible policies. On the one hand, firms—in this case, British banks—face a reputational risk should they get caught on the wrong side of a politically sensitive issue, though many have survived what should have been crippling scandals (e.g., the Bank of New York). On the other hand, greater transparency, including disclosure of private trusts and shell accounts, risks a likely loss of market share to London's Swiss rivals. (British policy circles had long been worried that while the United Kingdom respects the decisions of the UN Security Council, including sanctions, Switzerland—which would not join the United Nations until September 2002—was not formally obligated to do so.) The protection of London's comparative advantage as the world's leading financial center was of real concern to many policymakers of all political stripes, and it influences British policy in a variety of fields.

These are but two examples of the types of quandaries that those in government, particularly at the cabinet level, actually face when attempting to undertake more ethical policies. These are not abstract issues for them; real interests—and real money—are at stake. Policymakers naturally feel a responsibility to watch over the interests of a variety of constituencies within their countries, while simultaneously wanting to pursue policies abroad that are as virtuous as possible.

ECONOMIC FACTORS AND THE UNITED NATIONS' WORK ON CONFLICT

The UN Secretariat and the Security Council became engaged in issues of illicit economic behavior during armed conflict in part serendipitously, largely through the Council's tendency during the 1990s to frequently invoke economic sanctions.[15] Early sanctions regimes, far from being successful, often achieved the opposite of their intended effect—humanitarian crises deepened, while dictatorial regimes became more entrenched and combatants continued their ability to wage war. Sanctions often lacked effective implementation and enforcement on the ground, enabling open circumvention by smugglers of arms, fuel, natural resources, and other commodities. Thus, the instrument was seen in Ottawa and other capitals as increasingly dysfunctional.

With its election to the Security Council for a term in 1999–2000, the Canadian government focused part of its efforts within the Council on sanctions reform. In January 1999, Canada took over the chairmanship of the Council's Angola Sanctions Committee. Canada's ambassador to the United Nations, Robert Fowler—knowing that sanctions against UNITA, the rebel group led by Jonas Savimbi, were widely flaunted within Africa and beyond—commissioned an in-depth independent study by a panel of experts on the taxonomy of sanctions busting in Angola. The panel sought to improve the effectiveness of sanctions —both minimizing their unintended consequences and improving their enforcement. The resulting report, which was quite earth shaking

by UN standards, named a number of African countries that were deeply engaged in sanctions busting. It also named Belgium, Ukraine, Israel, and some other countries in the industrial North that were in deep collusion with African partners in processing the proceeds of sanctions busting, arguably making most of the money out of the transactions. The United Nations subsequently established independent Panels of Experts on Sierra Leone and Liberian sanctions, and, in 2001, on the exploitation of natural resources in the Democratic Republic of the Congo (DRC).

The DRC report, initiated by France (which found the Angola report incomplete and objectionable, perhaps in part because most of the countries mentioned in connection with sanctions-busting Africa happened to be Francophone-African ones), was problematic because it contained many assertions, most of which rang true to those knowledgeable on the Great Lakes region, but very little hard proof. This is illustrative of the problems such an investigation faces. Indeed, the absence of hard data may not be surprising; individuals involved in the looting and their corresponding institutions in the North have a great deal to lose in both financial terms and in standing. Quite simply, lives are at stake—people are assassinated for much less than talking to Security Council investigators.

Consequently, the Security Council study group had tremendous difficulty getting their interlocutors to agree to be quoted in the DRC report, or to allow specifics to be quoted. Thus, the study proved highly atmospheric—and probably in its main lines absolutely true— but was also extremely difficult to act upon in the absence of more specific information. Furthermore, the study was mandated to focus on Uganda and Rwanda, which are involved in the conflict in the DRC, but to ignore the depredations within the Congo by Zimbabwe, Angola, and Namibia, which are involved in the conflict, at the request of the Congolese government. The report also ignored the looting by forces loyal to the Kabila government in Kinshasa, thus obscuring an important part of the overall picture. Therefore, the report was rightly criticized as unbalanced, and the study group was asked to report on the activities of these other actors as well.

By late 2001, there was discussion within the Security Council on the establishment of a Permanent Monitoring Mechanism to take over the functions of the independent ad hoc panels, though the exact form of the mechanism and under whose authority it will rest continued to be matters of considerable debate. Because the previous reports have challenged some of the Permanent Five Members of the Security Council's often vested interests within the continent, there has been an effort by some members of the Council to rein in the independence of any eventual mechanism, while still others were trying to broker an arrangement whereby independent investigations would be supported by a permanent institutional capacity within the Secretariat and thus would remain free from interference by the Council.

In the mid-1990s, none of the close observers of the Council would have predicted this evolution. The attention that the Council now places on sanctions busting, on natural resource exploitation, and increasingly on private-sector activity in conflict zones marks a recognition of the relevance of these issues to the maintenance of international peace and security. This attention will be the norm in the future, rather than the exception. Yet this progress also highlights a difficult question—when the international community actually possesses enough knowledge to take effective action to prevent such behavior, will the Security Council —particularly the Permanent Five Members —find a form of action that is helpful and that leads to positive results? Or, as often in sanctions cases, will it make decisions that are politically convenient in the short term but are counterproductive over time? This remains to be seen.

FUTURE PRIORITIES

Several final points of interest to policymakers are related to the future of policy development in this area—Paul Collier, Frances Stewart, Peter Wallensteen, and many other scholars having now been successful in capturing their attention. The first concerns the relationship between policymakers and academic research, which provides an important means of evaluating and refining—if not challenging—the practices and underlying assumptions of policymakers. The international policy community responsible for conflict prevention, conflict resolution, and peacebuilding is largely responsive to academic research. Sometimes, however, this research is both too complicated and abstract to be of ready use to the policy community. Econometric data in particular, as Andrew Mack has recently pointed out, is "largely incomprehensible to most policy makers."[16]

As a result, academic findings may inadvertently fall on a deaf audience, while policies continue to be formulated and prioritized without the benefit of important insights. Furthermore, contradictory findings—often with radically different policy implications—not only complicate the formulation of effective policies but also deepen the skepticism with which many within the United Nations regard the research community.[17] High-quality research findings may intrigue policymakers such that they begin thinking through the issues themselves. Generally, however, research must be made more accessible and its contradictions reconciled if it is to be of practical use.

Second, more thought needs to be given to designing incentives and disincentives for leaders to end conflict, or for preventing its outbreak. Civil wars often are triggered by power-hungry elites unconcerned about the tactics through which they seek and maintain power. Some time ago, IPA sponsored a retreat on conflict prevention involving UN Security Council members and some others. At one point, Nigeria's ambassador intervened, noting, with reference to a particular African country embroiled in conflict, in essence, that academic factors—by which he meant structural causes—"are all very nice, but where I sit, bad people are tremendously important." Not only in Africa, "bad people" have wreaked havoc in their own countries and in neighboring ones. In each of these cases, it would be difficult to assert that in the absence of those individuals the situation would be exactly the same. Policymakers are more sensitive to this factor than are academics, but research on how the agendas of such individuals can be favored or inhibited obviously remains important in policy terms. International actors involved in resolving armed conflict must reach a consensus on the types of behavior to proscribe, for this will influence whether to accommodate or co-opt rebel leaders through power sharing, or to pursue more coercive measures to isolate them.[18]

A third, related area for further research draws on the experience of policy actors in the 1990s in creating new instruments to prosecute crimes against humanity, war crimes, and genocide in order to establish if there are any "lessons learned" here for the international white-collar crime field. The 1990s saw tremendous progress on legal instruments to punish war criminals, but there was no parallel effort to address large-scale international white-collar crime. There was interest in international legal mechanisms to address economic crimes such as gross embezzlement and extortion by political and military actors, but not yet much energy behind this issue.

A related area requiring further systematic investigation involves defining what a regulatory system that actually worked in the OECD world would look like. In the industrial world, the OECD has been able to agree on measures to combat corruption as it affects companies headquartered in OECD countries. But OECD countries continue to do very poorly in combating white-collar crime related to these various conflicts and taking place within OECD countries. Existing regulatory frame-

works are very fragile and suffer huge gaps, overlapping in conceptual terms, but are often not mutually reinforcing for purposes of enforcement. In theory, they cover a great number of situations and contingencies, but as anyone who follows this policy field closely knows, the regulatory frameworks have essentially failed at every level. It is now possible to wonder whether an international legal regime could be constructed to address economic crimes by heads of state and other elites, including grand corruption and embezzlement. Any practical planning seems far off, and it may appear utopian to even think today of such a regime, but the International Criminal Court seemed totally utopian in 1990, and it entered into force in 2002, only twelve years later. IPA has initiated work along these lines.

Fourth, there is a strong consensus that the terms "civil war" and "internal conflict" do not sufficiently capture the key regional and global dimensions of most contemporary conflicts. In many cases, such as the former Yugoslavia, the Great Lakes region of Africa, and south central Asia, regional factors are crucial, not only to the onset of warfare but also to the character of the ensuing conflict and the challenges of peace implementation.[19] These regional dynamics range from direct efforts by regional actors, both official and private, to influence the political economy of armed conflicts (e.g., through explicit military alliances with one or another warring party or the provision of safe haven and supplies), to the spillover effects of states seeking to stem the flow of refugees and combatants across borders, to regional trade flows and other economic interactions. Better understanding is needed on the particular regional dimensions of war economies: how they affected the character and duration of conflict, and the challenges that these activities and their legacies pose for those seeking to promote peace through the control of economic behavior. Likewise, greater attention to the regulatory efforts undertaken by regional actors to stem the illicit extraction and trade in natural resources is needed, because these efforts may hold important lessons for international actors, including how to best coordinate with regional efforts and how regional interests, either official or private, may be complicit in and profit from this illicit activity, thereby rendering regulatory initiatives ineffective.

Fifth and finally, there is the question of addressing corporate roles in conflict situations. This is not a matter of codes of conduct—which may or may not work, and may, as many NGOs claim, be mainly window dressing for shabby corporate practices—or of external regulation per se. Rather, it is about refining existing knowledge of the way licit businesses' operations, regardless of their intentions, may contribute to the outbreak and duration of violent conflict. This includes, first, developing a better understanding of companies' strategies and motivations in situations of conflict; second, acknowledging the legitimate concerns of corporations in conflict zones; and third, soliciting their views in developing more effective responses, both voluntary and binding, available to them and to other stakeholders, including international policymakers, to minimize the former's direct or indirect contributory role in violent conflict.[20] Overcoming the possible loss of competitive advantage to less scrupulous rivals and the prospect of privately bearing the costs of supplying the public good of conflict prevention remain principal barriers to collective action. Likewise, the financial and insurance sectors must be given greater attention—both for their contributory role in illicit transactions, and as a potential source of leveraging corporate compliance.

CONCLUSIONS: SOME EARLY FINDINGS

At the outset of the IPA project on the political economy of conflict, a number of broad propositions ran through research on economic factors in civil wars. This included an assumption that global economic flows (trade, aid, and investment) affect the incidence, duration, intensity, and character of armed conflict; that economic factors are consequential to warring elites' decisions to pursue war and peace; that greed and not grievances is the chief driver of armed conflict; that countries with a high dependence on natural resources have a higher risk of conflict, and that resource wars have their own dynamics; and these that linkages are amenable to policy intervention. Five important findings emerged in the early stages of IPA's research, since completed. Some of these findings have necessitated refining or revising earlier propositions, and others have had policy implications unforeseen at the project's outset.

First, it is often difficult to separate "economic" factors from "political" factors (let alone those that are social or cultural). Both are sources of conflict, but the interplay and relative importance of these factors vary not only between conflicts but also among different actors within a specific conflict and over its duration. Thus, conflict may not be about greed or grievances but a combination of greed and grievances.[21] In some cases, the control of economic activities may be the principal motivation for the initiation or perpetuation of conflict, but this is not to say that wars are solely about greed. In fact, the existence of grievances, whether economic, political, or social, appears to be the most persuasive motivation for conflict. Poverty, social inequality, rapid economic decline, large numbers of young unemployed males, and radicalized identity politics may all, under the right conditions, provide the necessary catalyst for conflict, particularly when accompanied by repressive, illegal, or extralegal behavior on the part of governments. However, primarily political motivations for conflicts can then "mutate" into economic agendas: pillaging, seizing land, exploiting labor, and controlling trade. These economic motivations, however, appear more significant in sustaining, prolonging, and transforming conflict than in causing it.[22]

Second, it is important not to confuse what makes armed conflict feasible with what motivates it. Valuable natural resources are not in and of themselves a reliable indicator of where conflict is likely to occur. The presence of natural resources, particularly those that are easily lootable, does appear to make conflict more feasible when underlying grievances already exist, for they offer a ready means of financing rebellion.[23] This explains in part why, for example, not all diamond-producing countries experience conflict. Resources may also become a source of genuine grievances being mobilized on behalf of political agendas, as when state institutions responsible for their equitable management instead engage in private, criminal accumulation, or when there is a real or perceived maldistribution of revenues between regions of production and national capitals. Thus, formerly stable diamond-producing countries may become conflict prone if poor management and corruption gain the upper hand, as in Sierra Leone.

Third, as the civil wars of the 1990s demonstrated, exploitation of civilians to enrich powerful individuals and groups is carried out by both governments and rebel groups. Dichotomies between what constitutes "licit/legal" versus "illicit/criminal" behavior in civil wars (and, indeed, elsewhere) are more usefully seen as normative categories deriving from a notion of the state having a monopoly over interaction with global markets and over the legitimate use of force. Viewed as such, sovereignty does not legitimate corruption, predation, or repression on the part of the state, just as rebellion is not a priori a criminal endeavor, as when conducted in self-defense. Effective policy intervention requires a case-by-case examination of the link between opportunity and motive not only of armed groups but also of states, as well as of the wider socioeconomic and political context in which they both operate. This has important implications not only for international decisions on when and how to intervene in ongoing conflicts but also for

how to mitigate unintended negative humanitarian consequences.

Fourth, the policies of donor states, the United Nations, the International Monetary Fund, the World Bank, and multinational corporations should not be examined solely from the point of view of their role in conflict areas. A broader examination should be made of the impact of, for example, international economic policies (neoliberalism, structural adjustment, etc.) on state capacity and of patterns of consumption in the industrial North on the security and development of the developing South. Without more farsighted policies to address the underlying causes of conflict—such as those that support legitimate and inclusive governance and poverty reduction, resource management and market diversification, and legal and financial reform—the conflicts of the present will prove difficult to resolve, and the peace settlements of the future will be even more difficult to sustain.

Fifth, the changing nature of resource flows in war economies in the context of globalization, including the growing importance of private actors, has led to a need for a new generation of legal instruments and policies, including partnerships among donors, private companies, multilateral organizations, NGOs, and governments. Existing international and regional conventions, national legislation and bilateral agreements, codes of conduct, and market pressures already provide a well-developed legal and policy framework for addressing many of the resource flows that sustain armed conflict—including the suppression of money laundering, regulating the export of weapons, and targeting international organized crime. Generally, these initiatives are well developed and have the compliance of states and nonstate actors. Individually, some states, including Canada, have both the will and capacity to limit resource flows originating in or destined for conflict zones. But many countries, particularly those in the global South, lack adequate financial means or the enforcement capacity necessary for effective implementation. Likewise, multilateral organizations in Europe, Latin America, and parts of Africa have developed robust initiatives.

Yet even the most effective policy responses are ultimately likely to have diminishing returns, as both new illicit activities and networks fill the void and new means develop to evade detection. Where existing regulatory efforts have proven successful in particular areas—combating money laundering from narcotics, for example—this success has often not been translated into strategies for combating related activities—such as tracing proceeds from ill-gotten gains from looting or grand corruption.

Moreover, the existing regulatory framework is neither uniform in its application nor comprehensive in its reach, facilitating the ability of criminals to stay ahead of the law and confusing the efforts of legitimate actors to comply with it. The United Nations has an important role to play, not only in supporting national and regional efforts to control illicit economic behavior in civil wars—many of which efforts hold particular promise—but also in establishing norms for such behavior and in addressing the issues of structural prevention noted above. The United Nations is clearly moving in these directions, but more work remains to be done.

NOTES

This chapter originally appeared in Cynthia Arnson and I. William Zartman, *Rethinking the Economics of War: The Intersection of Need, Creed, and Greed* (Baltimore: Johns Hopkins University Press, 2005), pp. 234–255. © 2005 the Woodrow Wilson Center Press. Reprinted by permission of the Woodrow Wilson Center Press and the Johns Hopkins University Press.

1. Some of the most interesting insights emerged from the Adelphi Papers, the series of policy-oriented occasional papers published by the International Institute for Strategic Studies (IISS) in London, whereas several scholars at Oxford University proved to be in the vanguard of reflection on the political economy of contemporary wars. E.g., Mats Berdal, *Disarmament and Demobilisation after Civil Wars: Arms, Soldiers, and the Termination of Armed Conflict,* Adelphi Paper 303 (London: IISS, 1996); and David Keen, *The Economic Functions of Violence in Civil Wars,* Adelphi Paper 320 (London: IISS, 1998). Groundbreaking research in this field was either then or soon thereafter under way within the World Bank's Development Research Group and the UN University's World Institute for Development Economics Research, in partnership with Queen Elizabeth House at Oxford University. This work drew to some extent on earlier studies by Peter Wallensteen and Ted Gurr. Will Reno and David Keen were bringing to bear on the study of several conflicts in Africa important empirical findings and insights that were to prove vastly influential in ensuing years.

2. Global Witness, *A Rough Trade: The Role of Companies and Governments in the Angolan Conflict* (London: Global Witness, 1998).

3. The findings and views from the conference were eventually published in an edited volume: Mats Berdal and David Malone, eds., *Greed and Grievance: Economic Agendas in Civil Wars* (Boulder, Colo.: Lynne Rienner, 2000), which stressed policy relevance in its analysis and prescriptions.

4. That all of this proved increasingly of interest to policymakers is beyond doubt. Very soon, work in this area was passed on from the U.K. and Canadian governments to the International Peace Academy. The British and Canadian governments were joined in funding this work by Switzerland, Sweden, Norway, and the United Nations Foundation and Rockefeller Foundation.

5. E.g., Michael E. Brown and Richard N. Rosecrane, eds., *The Costs of Conflict: Prevention and Cure in the Global Arena,* Report of Carnegie Commission on Preventing Deadly Conflict, Carnegie Corporation of New York (Lanham, Md.: Rowman & Littlefield, 1999).

6. Cf. David Keen, "War and Peace: What's the Difference?" in *Managing Armed Conflicts in the 21st Century,* ed. Adekeye Adebajo and Chandra Lekha Sriram (Portland, Ore.: Frank Cass, 2001).

7. The challenges of peace implementation were the subject of a joint research project undertaken by the International Peace Academy and the Stanford University Center for International Security and Cooperation between 1997 and 2000. The project examined the sixteen peace agreements between 1980 and 1997 in which international actors were prominently involved. Its full findings were published in *Ending Civil Wars*, ed. S. Stedman, D. Rothchild, and E. Cousens (Boulder, Colo.: Lynne Rienner, 2002). See also Stephen J. Stedman, *Implementing Peace Agreements in Civil Wars: Lessons and Recommendations for Policy Makers*, IPA Policy Paper Series on Peace Implementation (New York: International Peace Academy, 2001).

8. Mats Berdal and David Keen, "Violence and Economic Agendas in Civil Wars: Some Policy Implications," *Millennium: Journal of International Studies* 26, no. 3 (1997): 798.

9. There is little to differentiate the behavior of the legitimate government of President Eduardo dos Santos in Luanda from that of the late Jonas Savimbi of UNITA in terms of their "warlordism," including in its predatory economic dimensions.

10. The death—in combat—of Jonas Savimbi opened up the possibility of a lasting cease-fire between the government and UNITA, but, as a Global Witness report indicated, the system of highly profitable and deliberate political and economic disorder that the war created remains the principal obstacle to reversing decades of destruction (Global Witness, "All the President's Men," March 2002).

11. P. Le Billon, J. Sherman, and M. Hartwell, "Policies and Practices for Regulating Resource Flows to Armed Conflicts," background paper prepared for the International Peace Academy conference on "Policies and Practices for Regulating Resource Flows to Armed Conflicts," Bellagio, Italy, May 21–23, 2002; Fafo, Economies of Conflict: Private Sector Activity in Armed Conflict project; the Overseas Development Institute is also undertaking research examining potential regulation of transnational corporations in situations of armed conflict.

12. Jonathan Winer, "How to Clean Up Dirty Money," *Financial Times Weekend*, March 23–24, 2002, 1.

13. UN International Convention for the Suppression of the Financing of Terrorism, December 1999, http://untreaty.un.org/English/Terrorism/Conv12.pdf.

14. The Abacha family agreed to restitute $1 billion to Nigeria from the late dictator's estate, nevertheless being allowed to keep at least $100 million, the source of which has not been fully elucidated.

15. From 1990 to 2000, the United Nations imposed sanctions six times more frequently than during the prior forty-five years of its history.

16. Andrew Mack, "Civil War," *Journal of Peace Research* 39, no. 5 (2002): 515–26.

17. E.g., Mack notes that with respect to the relationship between primary commodity dependence and the risk of armed conflict, Paul Collier and Anke Hoeffler have found a positive correlation, whereas Jim Fearon and David Laitin have found "slight or no evidence."

18. Michael Brown, ed., *The International Dimensions of Internal Conflict* (Cambridge, Mass.: MIT Press, 1996), 613–14.

19. The Center on International Cooperation at New York University is currently undertaking a study on regional conflict formations and strategies for conflict management and resolution; see http://www.nyu.edu/pages/cic/projects/projects.html.

20. Under the auspices of its Economic Agendas in Civil Wars project, IPA has begun a dialogue involving private sector actors. Though it will probably not lead to any published work, these discussions may help elucidate firms' strategies in conflict countries and thus lead to mutually beneficial and more effective initiatives for promoting peace and reconciliation in the countries involved.

21. On the basis of statistical models by Paul Collier, conflicts were thought more likely to be caused by "greed" than by "grievance." Proxies for greed were seen as good predictors for civil conflict; proxies for grievance less so. The former included an economy largely dependent on primary commodities (oil, minerals, timber, agricultural products), large numbers of (unemployed) young men, and low levels of education. Proxies for grievance included economic inequality, a lack of political rights, and government incompetence. Paul Collier and Anke Hoeffler, *Greed and Grievance in Civil War*, Policy Research Working Paper 2355 (Washington, D.C.: World Bank, 2000); updated 2001, and available at http://www.worldbank.org/research/conflict/papers/greedgrievance_23oct.pdf.

22. Indeed, fairly early on, Paul Collier and others accepted that factors of "greed" better explain the duration of conflict than its outbreak. One of the most rewarding aspects of IPA's work in this area has been the flexibility of Collier and some of his colleagues, notably Nicholas Sambanis, in taking on board perspectives, initially at least, in apparent conflict with their own findings. Consequently, and due also to progress in their own methodology, these have evolved considerably. Challenges remaining to be addressed are how statistical models drawing on national accounts can deal with the phenomenon of largely regional conflicts and how political factors can be integrated into statistical models—the proxies so far have been too rough to be of real use.

23. Related, different types of natural resources appear to have different effects on the intensity, duration, and incidence of conflict. Michael Ross, "Oil, Drugs and Diamonds: The Varying Roles of Natural Resources Vary in Civil War," in *The Political Economy of Armed Conflict: Beyond Greed and Grievance,* ed. Karen Ballentine and Jake Sherman (Boulder, Colo.: Lynne Rienner, 2003).

36

SHARING SOVEREIGNTY
NEW INSTITUTIONS
FOR COLLAPSED AND
FAILING STATES

Stephen D. Krasner

CONVENTIONAL SOVEREIGNTY ASSUMES a world of autonomous, internationally recognized, and well-governed states. Although frequently violated in practice, the fundamental rules of conventional sovereignty—recognition of juridically independent territorial entities and nonintervention in the internal affairs of other states—have rarely been challenged in principle. But these rules no longer work, and their inadequacies have had deleterious consequences for the strong as well as the weak. The policy tools that powerful and well-governed states have available to "fix" badly governed or collapsed states —principally governance assistance and transitional administration (whether formally authorized by the United Nations or engaged in by a coalition of the willing led by the United States)—are inadequate. In the future, better domestic governance in badly governed, failed, and occupied polities will require the transcendence of accepted rules, including the creation of shared sovereignty in specific areas. In some cases, decent governance may require some new form of trusteeship, almost certainly de facto rather than de jure.[1]

Many countries suffer under failed, weak, incompetent, or abusive national authority structures. The best that people living in such countries can hope for is marginal improvement in their material well-being; limited access to social services, including health care and education; and a moderate degree of individual physical security. At worst they will confront endemic violence, exploitative political leaders, falling life expectancy, declining per capita income, and even state-sponsored genocide. In the Democratic Republic of Congo (formerly Zaire), for example, civil wars that have persisted for more than two decades have resulted in millions of deaths. In Zimbabwe the policies of President Robert Mugabe, who was determined to stay in office regardless of the consequences for his country's citizens, led to an economic debacle that began in 2000 with falling per capita income, inflation above 500 percent, and the threat of mass starvation. In Colombia much of the territory is controlled by the Revolutionary Armed Forces of Colombia (FARC), a Marxist rebel group that derives most of its income from drug trafficking. In Rwanda more than 700,000 people were slaughtered in a matter of weeks in 1994 as a result of a government-organized genocide.

The consequences of failed and inadequate governance have not been limited to the societies directly affected. Poorly governed societies can generate conflicts that spill across international borders. Transnational criminal and terrorist networks can operate in territories not controlled by the internationally recognized government. Humanitarian disasters not only prick the conscience of political leaders in advanced democratic societies but also leave them with no policy options that are appealing to voters.

Challenges related to creating better governance also arise where national authority structures have collapsed because of external invasion and occupation rather than internal conflict. The availability of weapons of mass destruction and the presence of transnational terrorism have created a historically unprecedented situation in which polities with very limited material capability can threaten the security of much more powerful states. These polities can be conquered and occupied with relative ease, leaving the occupying power with the more challenging task of establishing an acceptable domestic governing structure. Afghanistan and Iraq are obvious cases in point.

Left to their own devices, collapsed and badly governed states will not fix themselves because they have limited administrative capacity, not least with regard to maintaining internal security.[2] Occupying powers cannot escape choices about what new governance structures will be created and sustained. To reduce international threats and improve the prospects for individuals in such polities, alternative institutional arrangements supported by external actors, such as de facto trusteeships and shared sovereignty, should be added to the list of policy options.

The current menu of policy instruments for dealing with collapsed and failing states is paltry, consisting primarily of transitional administration and foreign assistance to improve governance, both of which assume that in more or less short order, targeted states can function effectively on their own. Nationbuilding or state-building efforts are almost always described in terms of empowering local authorities to assume the responsibilities of conventional sovereignty. The role of external actors is understood to be limited with regard to time, if not scope, in the case of transitional administration exercising full executive authority. Even as the rules of conventional sovereignty are de facto violated if not de jure challenged, and it is evident that in many cases effective autonomous national government is far in the future, the language of diplomacy, the media, and the street portrays nothing other than a world of fully sovereign states.

The next section of this article describes the basic elements that constitute the conventional understanding of sovereignty and provides a taxonomy of alternative institutional forms. It is followed by a discussion of the ways in which conventional sovereignty has failed in some states, threatening the well-being of their own citizens and others. The inadequacy of the current repertoire of policy options for dealing with collapsed, occupied, and badly governed states—governance assistance and transitional administration—is then assessed. The possibilities for new institutional forms—notably shared sovereignty and some de facto form of trusteeship—are examined. Included is a discussion of why such arrangements might be accepted by political leaders in target as well as intervening states.

CONVENTIONAL SOVEREIGNTY AND SOME ALTERNATIVES

Conventional sovereignty has three elements: international legal sovereignty, Westphalian/ Vatellian sovereignty, and domestic sovereignty.[3]

·

The basic rule of international legal sovereignty is to recognize juridically independent territorial entities. These entities then have the right to freely decide which agreements or treaties they will enter into. In practice, this rule has been widely but not universally honored. Some entities that are not juridically independent have been recognized (e.g., Byelorussia and the Ukraine during the Cold War), and some entities that are juridically independent have not been recognized (e.g., the People's Republic of China from 1949 to the 1970s).

The fundamental rule of Westphalian/Vatellian sovereignty is to refrain from intervening in the internal affairs of other states. Each state has the right to determine its own domestic authority structures. In practice, Westphalian/Vatellian sovereignty has frequently been violated.

Domestic sovereignty does not involve a norm or a rule, but is rather a description of the nature of domestic authority structures and the extent to which they are able to control activities within a state's boundaries. Ideally, authority structures would ensure a society that is peaceful, protects human rights, has a consultative mechanism, and honors a rule of law based on a shared understanding of justice.

In the ideal sovereign state system, international legal sovereignty, Westphalian/Vatellian sovereignty, and domestic sovereignty are mutually supportive. Recognized authorities within territorial entities regulate behavior, enjoy independence from outside interference, and enter into mutually beneficial contractual relations (treaties) with other recognized entities. This is the conventional world of international politics in which state-to-state relations are what count. One of the most striking aspects of the contemporary world is the extent to which domestic sovereignty has faltered so badly in states that still enjoy international legal, and sometimes even Westphalian/Vatellian, sovereignty. Somalia, for instance, is still an internationally recognized entity, even though it has barely any national institutions; and external actors have not, in recent years, tried to do much about Somalia's domestic sovereignty, or the lack thereof.

Conventional sovereignty was not always the hegemonic structure for ordering political life. Obviously, the basic rules of medieval Europe or the pre-nineteenth-century Sinocentric world were very different. But even in the nineteenth century, by which time conventional sovereignty had become a well-recognized structure, there were also legitimated and accepted alternatives. Protectorates were one alternative to conventional sovereignty; the rulers of a protectorate relinquished control over foreign policy to a more powerful state but retained authority over domestic affairs. For instance, in 1899 the ruler of Kuwait signed an agreement that gave Britain control of most elements of his country's foreign policy because he needed external support against threats from both Iraq and members of his own family.[4] In nineteenth-century China the major powers established treaty ports where British, French, German, and Japanese authorities regulated commerce and exercised extraterritorial authority over their own citizens and sometimes Chinese as well.[5] Within the British Empire, Australia, Canada, and South Africa became dominions that enjoyed almost complete control over their domestic affairs, recognized the British ruler as the head of state, but to some extent deferred to Britain in matters of foreign policy. Finally, colonization was a legitimated practice in the nineteenth century that allowed powerful states to assume international legal sovereignty and regulate the domestic authority structures of far-flung territories.

Conventional sovereignty is currently the only fully legitimated institutional form, but unfortunately, it does not always work. Honoring Westphalian/Vatellian sovereignty (and sometimes international legal sovereignty as well) makes it impossible to secure decent and effective domestic sovereignty, because the autochthonous political incentives facing political leaders in many failed, failing, or occupied

Table 1. Alternative Institutional Arrangements

	International Legal Sovereignty		Westphalian/Vatellian Sovereignty			Duration of Rule Violation		
	No	*Yes*	*None*	*Some*	*Full*	*Short*	*Medium*	*Long*
Conventional sovereignty		X			X	n/a	n/a	n/a
Colony	X		X					X
Transitional administration with full foreign executive authority	X		X			X		
Trusteeship	X		X or	X			X	X
Shared sovereignty		X		X				X
Nineteenth-century protectorate	X			X				X

states are perverse. These leaders are better able to enhance their own power and wealth by making exclusionist ethnic appeals or undermining even the limited legal routinized administrative capacity that might otherwise be available.

To secure decent domestic governance in failed, failing, and occupied states, new institutional forms are needed that compromise Westphalian/Vatellian sovereignty for an indefinite period. Shared sovereignty, arrangements under which individuals chosen by international organizations, powerful states, or ad hoc entities would share authority with nationals over some aspects of domestic sovereignty, would be a useful addition to the policy repertoire. Ideally, shared sovereignty would be legitimated by a contract between national authorities and an external agent. In other cases, external interveners may conclude that the most attractive option would be the establishment of a de facto trusteeship or protectorate. Under such an arrangement, the Westphalian/Vatellian sovereignty of the target polity would be violated, executive authority would be vested primarily with external actors, and international

legal sovereignty would be suspended. There will not, however, be any effort to formalize through an international convention or treaty a general set of principles for such an option.[6] (For a summary of these different institutional possibilities, see table 1.)

FAILURES OF CONVENTIONAL SOVEREIGNTY

Failed, inadequate, incompetent, or abusive national authority structures have sabotaged the economic well-being, violated the basic human rights, and undermined the physical security of their countries' populations. In some cases, state authority has collapsed altogether for an extended period, although such instances are rare. Afghanistan in the early 1990s before the Taliban consolidated power, Liberia for much of the 1990s, and the Democratic Republic of Congo and Sierra Leone in the late 1990s are just a few of the examples. Governance challenges have also arisen in Afghanistan and Iraq, where authority structures collapsed as a result of external invasion rather than internal conflict. The occupying powers, most obviously the United States, were then confronted with the challenge of fashioning decent governance structures in both countries.

In some parts of the world, disorder (including civil war) has become endemic. For the period 1955 to 1998, the State Failure Task Force identified 136 occurrences of state failure in countries with populations larger than 500,000. The task force operationalized state failure as one of four kinds of internal political crisis: revolutionary war, ethnic war, "adverse regime change," or genocide. In 1955 fewer than 6 percent of the countries were in failure. In the early 1990s the figure had risen to almost 30 percent, falling to about 20 percent in 1998, the last year of the study. Adverse regime change was the most common form of state failure, followed by ethnic war, revolutionary war, and genocide.[7] The task force identified partial democracy, trade closure, and low levels of economic well-being as indicated by high infant mortality rates as the primary causes of state failure.[8] James Fearon and David Laitin show that internal strife is more likely in countries suffering from poverty, recent decolonization, high population, and mountainous terrain. These conditions allow even relatively small guerrilla bands to operate successfully because recognized governments do not have the administrative competence to engage in effective rural policing and counterinsurgency operations.[9]

States that experience failure or poor governance more generally are beset by many problems. In such states, infrastructure deteriorates; corruption is widespread; borders are unregulated; gross domestic product is declining or stagnant; crime is rampant; and the national currency is not widely accepted. Armed groups operate within the state's boundaries but outside the control of the government. The writ of the central government, the entity that exercises the prerogatives of international legal sovereignty (e.g., signing treaties and sending delegates to international meetings), may not extend to the whole country; in some cases, it

may not extend beyond the capital. Authority may be exercised by local entities in other parts of the country, or by no one at all.

Political leaders operating in an environment in which material and institutional resources are limited have often chosen policies that make a bad situation even worse. For some leaders, disorder and uncertainty are more attractive than order and stability because they are better able to extract resources from a disorderly society. Decisions affecting the distribution of wealth are based on personal connections rather than bureaucratic regulations or the rule of law. Leaders create multiple armed units that they can play off against each other. They find it more advantageous to take a bigger piece of a shrinking pie than a smaller piece of a growing pie.

The largest number of poorly governed states is found on the continent of Africa. Since the mid-1950s about a third of African states have been in failure.[10] In constant 1995 U.S. dollars, gross domestic product per capita for all of sub-Saharan Africa fell from $660 in 1980 to $587 in 1990 to $563 in 2000. Of the sub-Saharan states for which data are available from the World Bank, eighteen had increases in their per capita gross domestic product from 1990 to 2000, seven had decreases of less than 5 percent, and seventeen experienced decreases of more than 5 percent. With the exception of the former Soviet Union, no other area of the world fared so badly with regard to economic performance.[11]

Sierra Leone offers one example of state collapse. Government revenue declined from $250 million in the mid-1970s to $10 million in 1999. Most television service ended in 1987 when the minister of education sold the country's broadcasting tower. During the 1990s, civil strife resulted in at least 50,000 deaths and many more injuries and maimings. There was a military coup in 1992, an election in 1996, and another coup in 1997. A Nigerian-led West African peacekeeping force intervened in 1998 and restored the elected president to power, but it was unable to control rebel violence. A 1999 peace agreement brought Sankoh Foday, leader of the Revolutionary United Front (RUF), into the government as vice president and minister of mines. The RUF was infamous for cutting off the limbs of its victims. This agreement collapsed after 500 UN peacekeepers were kidnapped when they entered Sierra Leone's diamond area. Charles Taylor, then president of Liberia and currently under indictment for crimes against humanity by the Special Court for Sierra Leone, supported rebel groups in Sierra Leone in 2000 and 2001 because he wanted access to the country's diamond mines.[12] Order was finally restored in 2002 after the United Nations authorized a force that grew to 17,000 men. British units made a substantial contribution to finally defeating and disarming the rebel forces.[13] Describing Sierra Leone in the 1990s, William Reno writes, "The country's rulers intentionally made life for their subjects less secure and more materially poor. They became personally wealthy as a consequence of this disorder, and then sold chances to profit from disorder to those who could pay for them by providing services—as experts in violence, for example—and to those local and expatriate businessmen who traded their access to commercial networks."[14]

Thus, for many countries domestic sovereignty is not working, and the situation is not improving in any substantive way. Although the number and percentage of countries suffering from civil war declined during the 1990s, the per capita gross national income in current U.S. dollars of the least developed countries continued to drop, falling by 9 percent from 1990 to 2000, a period of robust growth for the world as a whole.[15]

WHY SOVEREIGNTY FAILURES MATTER

In the contemporary world, powerful states have not been able to ignore governance failures. Polities where domestic authority has collapsed or been inadequate have threatened the economic and security interests of these states. Humanitarian crises have engaged electorates in advanced democracies and created no-win situations for political leaders who are damned if they intervene and damned if they do not. And, most obviously, when a state has been invaded, the occupiers have been confronted with the problem of establishing effective domestic sovereignty.

The availability of weapons of mass destruction, the ease of movement across borders, and the emergence of terrorist networks have attenuated the relationship between the underlying capabilities of actors and the ability to kill large numbers of people. In the past, state and nonstate actors with limited resources could not threaten the security of states with substantial resources. The killing power of a nation's military depended on the underlying wealth of the country. Nonstate actors such as anarchist groups in the nineteenth century could throw bombs that might kill fifty or even several hundred people, but not more. This is no longer true. States with limited means can procure chemical and biological weapons. Nuclear weapons demand more resources, but they are not out of reach of even a dismally poor country such as North Korea. Weapons of mass destruction can be delivered in myriad ways, not only by missiles but also by commercial ships, trucks, planes, and even envelopes. Failed or weak states may provide terrorists with territory in which they can operate freely.

Moreover, political leaders who have effective control within their borders but limited resources to defend or deter an invasion present a tempting target if they adopt policies that threaten the core security interests of powerful states. For instance, throughout his rule Saddam Hussein sought and sometimes used weapons of mass destruction and, even when faced with invasion, failed to fully cooperate with UN inspectors. In Afghanistan the Taliban supported al Qaeda, which had already demonstrated that it could strike core targets in the United States. Neither Iraq nor Afghanistan could defend itself against, or deter, a U.S. attack. When the threat is high and invasion is easy, powerful states are likely to use military force to bring down a menacing regime. When, however, the old regime has collapsed, the occupiers confront the challenge of creating effective and decent domestic sovereignty.

Sovereignty failures may also present problems in the area of transnational criminality. Drug trafficking is difficult to control under any circumstances, but such activities are more likely to flourish where domestic sovereignty is inadequate. About 95 percent of illicit drug production takes place in areas of civil strife. Colombia, where the FARC controls a large part of the territory, has been one of the major sources of such drugs for the United States. In the late 1990s Afghanistan cultivated 75 percent of the world's opium poppies, and despite a ban by the Taliban at the end of its rule, production revived after the regime was overthrown because the new government in Kabul had only limited control over much of the country.[16] Transnational trafficking in persons is more likely in, although not limited to, countries where domestic authority and control are weak or ineffective. A 2004 State Department report lists ten countries—Bangladesh, Burma, Cuba, Ecuador, Equatorial Guinea, Guyana, North Korea, Sierra Leone, Sudan, and Venezuela—that have not met minimum efforts to control trafficking in persons. Most of the ten are failed or badly governed states.[17] In addition, it is more difficult to trace and punish the perpetrators of transnational financial fraud in countries where the police and judiciary do not function well.

Finally, gross violations of human rights present unpleasant political choices for democratic leaders in powerful states. There have been a number of humanitarian catastrophes in recent years, with the killings in Rwanda in the mid-1990s being one of the most appalling and most widely reported. Millions of people have died in other countries as well at the hands of their own government or rival political groups. These and other humanitarian disasters have engaged attentive elites. The Canadian ministry of foreign affairs, for instance, organized the International Commission on Intervention and State Sovereignty in 2000 in response to UN Secretary-General Kofi Annan's appeal for a new consensus on the right of humanitarian intervention. The commission, composed of twelve eminent persons, produced a widely circulated report entitled *The Responsibility to Protect*. The report defends the principle of humanitarian intervention when governments abuse or fail to protect their own citizens. Samantha Power's book *A Problem from Hell: America and the Age of Genocide*, which describes the failure of the United States to act either to prevent or to mitigate a number of genocides throughout the twentieth century, won a Pulitzer Prize in 2003.[18]

From an electoral perspective, American leaders cannot simply ignore humanitarian crises. Sowmya Anand and Jon Krosnick have shown that the U.S. electorate is made up of a number of distinct issue publics. Individuals in each of these publics are knowledgeable about their specific issue, including where presidential aspirants stand. Anand and Krosnick asked a random sample of the electorate questions about U.S. foreign policy before the 2000 elections such as, should the United States be "Helping poor countries provide food, clothing, and housing for their people? Helping resolve disputes between two other countries? Preventing governments of other countries from hurting [their] own citizens? Preventing people in other countries from killing each other?" On these four questions, between 7.3 percent and 9.6 percent of the electorate indicated that these issues were extremely important to them. These percentages are low compared with percentages on some other issues (e.g., 33.5 percent indicated that defending the United States against missile attack was very important), but the responses do indicate that there is a significant part of the U.S. electorate concerned with humanitarian issues in poorer countries.[19]

Humanitarian crises, then, present decision-makers in democratic countries with a no-win situation. If they fail to intervene and a humanitarian disaster occurs, they may lose the votes of citizens who are attentive to and care about the fate of particular countries, regions, ethnic groups, or principled issues in general. On the other hand, if a political leader does intervene, the costs in terms of soldiers killed will be readily apparent, but the number of lives saved can never be demonstrated with certainty.

THE EXISTING INSTITUTIONAL REPERTOIRE: GOVERNANCE ASSISTANCE AND TRANSITIONAL ADMINISTRATION

Political leaders in powerful and weak states have been reluctant to challenge the conventional norms of sovereignty. The policy options currently available to repair occupied or badly governed states—governance assistance and transitional administration—are consistent with these norms. They have made some limited contribution to improving governance in badly run and collapsed states, but policymakers would be better served if they had a wider repertoire of policy choices.

Governance Assistance

For the last decade international organizations, the United States, and other donor countries have devoted substantial resources to promoting better governance. U.S. foreign aid has been given to train judges, rewrite criminal codes, increase fiscal transparency, professionalize the police, encourage an open media, strengthen political parties, and monitor elections. In 2004 President George W. Bush's administration launched a new foreign aid initiative, the Millennium Challenge Account (MCA), which, if fully funded, will increase U.S. foreign assistance by 50 percent and provide these resources to a relatively small number of poor countries that have demonstrated good governance in the areas of promoting economic freedom, governing justly, and investing in people.[20]

Since the 1950s, international financial institutions have been involved in questions of policy and sometimes institutional reform in borrowing countries. The conditions attached to lending by the World Bank and the International Monetary Fund (IMF) have covered a wide range of issues such as aggregate credit expansion, subsidies, number of government employees, indexation of salaries, tariffs, tax rates, and institution building. International financial institutions have placed their own personnel in key bureaus.[21] In the mid-1990s the managing director of the IMF and the president of the World Bank committed themselves to a more aggressive attack on corruption in developing states.[22] In 1997 the World Bank subtitled its world development report *The State in a Changing World.* The report declares that the "clamor for greater government effectiveness has reached crisis proportions in many developing countries where the state has failed to deliver even such fundamental public goods as property rights, roads, and basic health and education."[23] Further, it lists basic tasks for the state, including establishing a foundation of law, protecting the environment, and shielding the vulnerable; chastises governments for spending too much on rich and middle-class students in universities while neglecting primary education; and urges these governments to manage ethnic and social differences.[24] Finally, and most ambitiously, the 1991 Agreement Establishing the European Bank for Reconstruction and Development explicitly includes a commitment to democracy as a condition of membership.[25]

Foreign assistance to improve governance in weak states does not usually contradict the rules of conventional sovereignty. Governments contract with external agencies (e.g., countries, multilateral organizations, and nongovernmental organizations [NGOs]) to provide training in various areas. Such contracting is a manifestation of international legal sovereignty and is consistent with Westphalian/Vatellian sovereignty, so long as the influence of external actors on domestic authority structures is limited to specific policies or improvements in the capabilities of government employees. When bargaining power is highly asymmetric, as may be the case in some conditionality agreements between international financial institutions and borrowing countries, Westphalian/Vatellian sovereignty can be compromised. External actors can influence not just policies but also institutional arrangements in target states. The borrowing country is better off with the agreement, conditions or no, than it would have been without it; otherwise it would not have signed. Nevertheless, political leaders may accept undesired and intrusive engagement from external actors because the alternative is loss of access to international capital markets.

The effectiveness of governance assistance will always be limited. Some leaders will find the exploitation of their own populations more advantageous than the introduction of reforms. The leverage of external actors will usually be constrained. International financial institutions are in the business of lending money; they cannot put too stringent restrictions on their loans lest their customers disappear. Many IMF agreements are renegotiated, sometimes several times. Small social democratic countries in Europe have been committed, because of the views of their electorates, to assisting the poor; they will be loath to allow their funding levels to drop below the generally recognized target of 0.7 percent of national income.[26] The wealthier countries also routinely provide humanitarian assistance, regardless of the quality of governance in a particular country.

Moreover, those providing governance assistance are likely to adopt formulas that reflect their own domestic experience and that may be ill suited to the environments of particular target countries. The United States, for instance, has emphasized elections and independent legislatures. Interest groups have been regarded as independent of the state, whereas in European social democratic countries, they are legitimated by and sometimes created by the state.[27]

Transitional Administration

Transitional administration is the one recognized alternative to conventional sovereignty that exists in the present international environment, but it is explicitly not meant as a challenge to the basic norms of sovereignty. The scope of transitional administration or peacekeeping and peacebuilding operations has ranged from the full assertion of executive authority by the UN for some period of time, East Timor being an example, to more modest efforts involving monitoring the implementation of peace agreements, as was the case in Guatemala in the 1990s. Transitional administration, usually authorized by the UN Security Council, has always been seen as a temporary, transitional measure designed to create the conditions under which conventional sovereignty can be restored. The U.S. occupation of Iraq has followed the same script, albeit without any UN endorsement of the occupation itself, although the Security Council did validate the restoration of international legal sovereignty in June 2004. Westphalian/Vatellian sovereignty and sometimes international legal sovereignty are violated in the short term so that they can be restored in the longer term; at least that is the standard explanation.

The record of peacebuilding efforts since World War II has been mixed. One recent study identified 124 cases of peacebuilding by the international community. Of these, 43 percent were judged to be successful based on the absence of hostilities. If progress toward democracy is added as a measure of success, only 35 percent were successful.[28]

More extensive peacekeeping operations, those that might accurately be called "transitional administration" because they involve the assertion of wide-ranging or full executive authority by the UN (or the United States), are difficult: the demands are high; advance planning, which must prejudge outcomes, is complicated, especially for the UN; and resources —economic, institutional, and military—are often limited. UN missions have run monetary systems, enforced laws, appointed officials, created central banks, decided property claims, regulated businesses, and operated public utilities. The resources to undertake these tasks have rarely been adequate. Each operation has been ad hoc; no cadres of bureaucrats, police, soldiers, or judges permanently committed to transitional administration exist; and there is a tension between devolving authority to local actors and having international actors assume responsibility for all governmental functions because, at least at the outset, this latter course is seen as being more efficient.[29]

Transitional administration is particularly problematic in situations where local actors disagree about basic objectives among themselves and with external actors. Under these circumstances, as opposed to situations in which local actors agree on goals but need external monitoring to provide reassurances about the behavior of their compatriots, the inherently temporary character of transitional administration increases the difficulty of creating stable institutions. If indigenous groups disagree about the distribution of power and the constitutional structure of the new state, then the optimal strategy for their political leaders is to strengthen their own position in anticipation of the departure of external actors. They do so by maximizing support among their followers rather than backing effective national institutions. Alternatively, local leaders who become dependent on external actors during a transitional administration, but who lack support within their own country, do not have an incentive to invest in the development of new institutional arrangements that would allow their external benefactors to leave at an earlier date.[30]

Multiple external actors with varying interests and little reason to coordinate their activities have exacerbated the problems associated with transitional administration. The bureaucratic and financial interests of international organizations are not necessarily complementary. NGOs need to raise money and make a mark. The command structures for security and civilian activities have been separated. The permanent members of the Security Council, to whom UN peacekeeping authorities are ultimately responsible, have not always had the same interests.[31]

Bosnia and Kosovo, two of the most well known peacekeeping endeavors, illustrate these problems. Neither Bosnia nor Kosovo appears to be a great success, despite the extensive involvement of not only UN organizations but also the major Western powers. The 1995 Dayton agreement created a complicated and possibly unworkable political structure. Because of antagonisms among the groups in Bosnia, the UN high representative, who has always been a West European, has made many decisions, large and small. For instance, in 1998 the high representative, Carlos Westendorp, mandated a license plate design that did not indicate where the driver was from. Had he not done this, many Bosnians would have been reluctant to leave their local districts.[32] In 2004 Paddy Ashdown, who had become the high representative two years earlier, dismissed sixty Bosnian Serb political leaders (including the interior minister and the speaker of the parliament) for failing to arrest Radovan Karadzib, twice indicted by the Hague war crimes tribunal.[33]

External actors, however, have not established a coherent administrative structure. The Security Council appoints the high representative for Bosnia and Herzegovina on the basis of a recommendation from the fifty-five-member Peace Implementation Council.[34] The high representative, however, has no authority over SFOR, the Stabilization Force. The commander of SFOR reports to NATO's commander in Europe, an American.[35] Nor has there been fully effective coordination among the many nonmilitary organizations operating in Bosnia and Herzegovina. The Organization for Security and Economic Cooperation in Europe (OSCE) deals with such issues as human rights, rule of law, security cooperation, and education reform. The European Union (EU) has provided, among other things, a special police organization whose members are working side by side with local officials. The UN High Commissioner for Refugees (UNHCR) is the lead agent for refugees and internally displaced persons. The UN Development Programme has administered more than $100 million in reconstruction funds. The World Bank has taken the lead in economic reconstruction. The International Committee of the Red Cross has dealt with missing persons. The policies of these different agencies have sometimes been at loggerheads. For instance, EU efforts to condition aid to Mostar, the largest city in Herzegovina, on cooperation between Croats and Serbs were frustrated by the issuance of a World Bank loan for the reconstruction of a hydroelectric plant that was granted without concern for political factors.[36]

The results of heavy-duty external engagement in Bosnia and Herzegovina have not been pretty. The economy has been kept afloat through outside assistance, amounting to 25 percent of Bosnia's gross national product in 2001. Over time the high representative has assumed more authority, but without an accountability mechanism that systematically engages local actors. Trafficking in drugs and persons has been common. Corruption is a constant problem. Unemployment is high. External investors have been cautious. The resettlement of refugees and internally displaced persons has been sporadic. Property laws have not been enforced. The legal system has not functioned well.[37]

UNHCR attempts to support moderate political voices have been ineffective. In some cases, external authorities have limited electoral statements in ways that have strained democratic principles by, for instance, prohibiting competing parties from advocating a separate status for one of the entities. Outside support of specific moderate candidates has sometimes backfired because voters have resented what they view as interference.[38]

The transitional administration in Bosnia is not likely to work because it is not in the interest of Bosnian political leaders to make it work. These leaders are committed to their ethnic constituents. A successful transition to a multiethnic democratic state would leave nationalist leaders with no base of support. Bosnia's indigenous leaders are acting on the assumption that at some point in the not-too-distant future SFOR, the high representative, and others will depart, leaving an environment in which they can become the ultimate winners.[39]

The situation in Kosovo is even more problematic. Whereas Bosnia ideally could become a well-functioning conventional sovereign entity, or at least a well-functioning member of the European Union, the final status of Kosovo remains unclear. At present, Kosovo is a de facto trusteeship; it has neither international legal nor Westphalian/Vatellian sovereignty. UN Security Council Resolution 1244, which established the transitional administration, reaffirms "the commitment of all Member States to the sovereignty and territorial integrity of the Federal Republic of Yugoslavia and the other States of the region" and, at the same time, calls for "substantial autonomy and meaningful self-administration for Kosovo."[40] Neighboring countries do not want an independent Kosovo or unification with Albania. The Kosovars have no desire to be closely integrated with the Federal Republic of Yugoslavia.

As in Bosnia, a multiplicity of external actors in Kosovo has made coordination difficult. The lead civilian agency, the United Nations Interim Administration Mission in Kosovo (UNMIK), is headed by the special representative of the secretary-general (SRSG). Many organizations have operated in Kosovo, and the SRSG does not have full authority over them. As in Bosnia the external security presence, in this case KFOR (Kosovo Force), has a separate command structure reporting to NATO. The UNHCR has been charged with overseeing humanitarian aid; the OSCE with building institutions; the EU with economic reconstruction; and the UN with many administrative tasks. International organizations involved in Kosovo have included the United Nations Children's Fund, the World Food Programme, the IMF, the World Bank, and the International Labour Organization. In addition to these official organizations, there are several hundred NGOs operating in the region.[41]

The outcome in Kosovo has, not surprisingly, been mixed. Neither official organizations nor NGOs have been able to cooperate to develop a common set of operational goals and strategies. When coordination has taken place, it has been at the tactical level. Actors concerned primarily with human rights have not seen eye to eye with those focused on security. The application of justice has been problematic: there are almost no Serb judges. Serbs have been dealt with harshly while ethnic Albanians have been treated more leniently, even when they have committed serious crimes well documented by UNMIK police. The SRSG decided in 2000 to introduce foreign judges even at the district level, but the threat of violence has constrained even international personnel.[42]

Transitional administration has been most effective when the level of violence in a country has been low, where there has been involvement by major powers, and where the contending parties within the country have reached a mutually acceptable agreement. The key role for the transitional administration is then to monitor the implementation of the agreement. For instance, in Namibia the contact group, comprising Canada, France, Germany, Great Britain, and the United States, was involved in UN discussions about the constitutional structure for an independent Namibia beginning in 1978. All of the major contending parties consented to the UN Transition Assistance Group (UNTAG) that was sent in 1989, allowing the lightly armed mission to play a neutral role between South Africa and Namibia. The strength of the major potential spoilers, hard-line whites, was undermined by the collapse of apartheid in South Africa. The major responsibility of UNTAG was to supervise the elections for the government that assumed power when Namibia secured international legal sovereignty.[43]

There were also successful missions in Central America in the 1990s. In both Guatemala and Nicaragua, government and rebel groups had reached a mutually acceptable settlement. Peacekeeping missions contributed to stability by supervising elections, helping to demobilize combatants, and training police.[44]

In sum, transitional administration has worked best for the easiest cases, those where the key actors have already reached a mutually acceptable agreement. In these situations, the transitional administration plays a monitoring role. It can be truly neutral among the contending parties. The mission does not have to be heavily armed. Transitional administration, however, is much more difficult in cases such as Bosnia, Kosovo, Afghanistan, and Iraq—that is, where local leaders have not reached agreement on what the ultimate outcome for their polity should be and where they must think about positioning themselves to win support from parochial constituencies when transitional administration, along with its large foreign military force, comes to an end.

NEW INSTITUTIONAL OPTIONS: DE FACTO TRUSTEESHIPS AND SHARED SOVEREIGNTY

Given the limitations of governance assistance and transitional administration, other options for dealing with countries where international legal sovereignty and Westphalian/Vatellian sovereignty are inconsistent with effective and responsible domestic sovereignty need to be explored. At least two such arrangements would add to the available tool kit of policy options. The first would be to revive the idea of trusteeship or protectorate, probably de facto rather than de jure. The second would be to explore possibilities for shared sovereignty in which national rulers would use their international legal sovereignty to legitimate institutions within their states in which authority was shared between internal and external actors.

De Facto Trusteeships

In a prescient article published in 1993, Gerald Helman and Steven Ratner argued that in extreme cases of state failure, the establishment of trusteeships under the auspices of the UN Security Council would be necessary. By the end of the 1990s, such suggestions had become more common. Analysts have noted that de facto trusteeships have become a fact of international life. In a monograph published in 2002, Richard Caplan argues, "An idea that once enjoyed limited academic currency at best—international trusteeship for failed states and contested territories—has become a reality in all but name." Martin Indyk, an assistant secretary of state during President Bill Clinton's administration, has argued that the most attractive path to permanent peace in the Middle East would be to establish a protectorate in Palestine, legitimated by the United Nations and with the United States playing a key role in security and other areas. Even if final status talks were completed, the trusteeship would remain in place until a responsible Palestinian government was established. [45]

Despite these recent observations, developing an alternative to conventional sovereignty, one that explicitly recognizes that international legal sovereignty will be withdrawn and that external actors will control many aspects of domestic sovereignty for an indefinite period of time, will not be easy. To date there has

been no effort, for instance, to produce a treaty or convention that would define and embody in international law a new form of trusteeship. Just the opposite. The rhetorical commitment of all significant actors, including the United States, has been to restore authority to local actors at the soonest possible moment, a stance exemplified by the decision to give what U.S. officials insisted was full sovereignty to Iraq in June 2004. [46]

Codifying a general set of principles and rules for some new kind of trusteeship or protectorate would involve deciding who would appoint the authority and oversee its activities: the UN Security Council? A regional organization such as the European Union? A coalition of the willing? A single state? A treaty or convention would have to define the possible scope of authority of the governing entity: all activities of the state including security and international affairs? Only matters related to the provision of public goods such as roads, but not those related to the private sphere such as marriage? Given that there would be no fixed date for ending a trusteeship or protectorate, how would the appropriate moment for transferring authority to local actors be determined? What intermediate steps would be taken? Could a trusteeship, for instance, be granted international legal recognition and sovereignty, while some aspects of domestic governance remained under the control of the trustee or conservator? [47]

The most substantial barrier to a general international treaty codifying a new form of trusteeship or protectorate is that it will not receive support from either the powerful, who would have to implement it, or the weak, who might be subject to it. There is widespread sentiment for the proposition that Westphalian/Vatellian sovereignty is not absolute and can be breached in cases of massive human rights violations. UN Secretary-General Annan expressed this view in 1999 to widespread international acclaim. [48] But arguing that Westphalian/Vatellian sovereignty is not absolute is quite different from codifying an explicit alternative that would deprive states of their international legal sovereignty as well as control over their domestic affairs.

An explicit and legitimated alternative to sovereignty would require, at minimum, agreement among the major powers. An arrangement supported by leading states that are not members of the OECD such as Brazil, China, India, Indonesia, Nigeria, and South Africa would be even better. Best of all would be an agreement endorsed by the Security Council and the General Assembly. There is no indication, however, that such widespread support would be given. None of the actors has a clear interest in doing so. The major powers, those with the capacity to create a trusteeship, want to be able to pick and choose not only where they intervene but also the policies they would follow. The endorsement of a new institutional arrangement would provide a new choice on the menu, but this option might make it difficult to engage in ad hoc arrangements better suited to specific circumstances. For states in the third world, any successor to the mandate system of the League of Nations, or the trusteeship system of the UN, would smell if not look too much like colonialism.[49]

Shared Sovereignty

Shared sovereignty would involve the engagement of external actors in some of the domestic authority structures of the target state for an indefinite period of time.[50] Such arrangements would be legitimated by agreements signed by recognized national authorities. National actors would use their international legal sovereignty to enter into agreements that would compromise their Westphalian/Vatellian sovereignty with the goal of improving domestic sovereignty. One core element of sovereignty —voluntary agreements—would be preserved, while another core element—the principle of autonomy—would be violated.

National leaders could establish shared sovereignty through either treaties or unilateral

commitments. To be effective, such arrangements would have to create self-enforcing equilibria involving either domestic players alone or some combination of domestic and international actors. Political elites in the target state would have to believe that they would be worse off if the shared sovereignty arrangement were violated.

For policy purposes, it would be best to refer to shared sovereignty as "partnerships." This would more easily let policymakers engage in organized hypocrisy, that is, saying one thing and doing another. Shared sovereignty or partnerships would allow political leaders to embrace sovereignty, because these arrangements would be legitimated by the target state's international legal sovereignty, even though they violate the core principle of Westphalian/Vatellian sovereignty: autonomy. Organized hypocrisy is not surprising in an environment such as the international system, where there are competing norms (e.g., human rights vs. Westphalian/Vatellian sovereignty), power differentials that allow strong actors to pursue policies that are inconsistent with recognized rules, and exceptional complexity that makes it impossible to write any set of rules that could provide optimal outcomes under all conditions. Shared sovereignty or partnerships would make no claim to being an explicit alternative to conventional sovereignty. It would allow actors to obfuscate the fact that their behavior would be inconsistent with their principles.

Historical Examples of Shared Sovereignty. Shared sovereignty agreements have been used in the past. There are several late-nineteenth-century shared sovereignty arrangements in which external actors assumed control over part of the revenue-generating stream of a state that had defaulted on its debt. The state wanted renewed access to international capital markets. The lenders wanted assurance that they would be repaid. Direct control over the collection of specific taxes provided greater confidence than other available measures.

For example, a shared sovereignty arrangement between external lenders and the Porte (the government of the Ottoman Empire) was constructed for some parts of the revenue system of the empire during the latter part of the nineteenth century. The empire entered international capital markets in the 1850s to fund military expenditures associated with the Crimean War. By 1875, after receiving more than a dozen new loans, the empire was unable to service its foreign debt. To again secure access to international capital markets, the Ottomans agreed in 1881 to create, through government decree, the Council of the Public Debt. The members of the council—two from France; one each from Austria, Germany, Italy, and the Ottoman Empire itself; and one from Britain and the Netherlands together—were selected by foreign creditors. Until the debt was liquidated, the Porte gave control of several major sources of revenue to the council and authorized it to take initiatives that would increase economic activity. The council promoted, for instance, the export of salt (the tax on which it controlled) to India and introduced new technologies for the silk and wine industries. It increased the confidence of foreign investors in the empire's railways by collecting revenues that the government had promised to foreign companies. In the decade before World War I, the council controlled about one-quarter of the empire's revenue. It was disbanded after the war.[51]

Unlike classic gunboat diplomacy, where the governments of foreign creditors took over control of customs houses to secure repayment of loans, in the case of the Ottoman Council of the Public Debt, the norm of international legal sovereignty was honored, at least in form. The council was established by an edict issued by the Ottoman Empire at the behest of foreign creditors. International legal sovereignty was honored; Westphalian/Vatellian sovereignty was ignored. This arrangement was durable because if the empire had revoked its decree, it would have lost access to international capital markets.

The relationship of the Soviet Union to the satellite states of Eastern Europe during the Cold War is another example of shared sovereignty. For more than forty years, Soviet penetration of domestic regimes, close oversight of officials, and policy direction from Moscow kept communist regimes in power. During the 1950s the Polish secret police, for instance, reported directly to Moscow. The militaries of the satellites were integrated into the Soviet command structure and unable to operate independently. The communist regimes that Moscow had put in place and sustained by violating Westphalian/Vatellian sovereignty dutifully signed off on the security arrangements that their overlord preferred. Except in a few instances, such as the invasion of Czechoslovakia in 1968, Soviet behavior was consistent with international legal sovereignty. The implicit and sometimes explicit use of force, however, was necessary to support these regimes because many of the citizens of the satellite states were alienated from their rulers.

The shared sovereignty arrangements established by the United States after World War II were more successful. Germany is the prime example. The Western allies wanted to internationally legitimate the Federal Republic of Germany (FRG or West Germany) but at the same time constrain its freedom of action. The Bonn agreements, signed in 1952 by the FRG, France, the United Kingdom, and the United States and revised in Paris in 1954, gave West Germany full authority over its internal and external affairs but with key exceptions in the security area. Not only did the FRG renounce its right to produce chemical, biological, and nuclear weapons; it also signed a status of forces agreement that gave the allies expansive powers. These included exclusive jurisdiction over the members of their armed forces and the right to patrol public areas, including roads, railways, and restaurants. Allied forces could take any measures necessary to ensure order and discipline.[52] West Germany's military was fully integrated into NATO.

Article 5(2) of the Convention on Relations gave the Western powers the right to declare a state of emergency until FRG officials obtained adequate powers enabling them to take effective action to protect the security of the foreign forces.[53] Without a clear definition of these adequate powers, the Western allies formally retained the right to resume their occupation of the Federal Republic until 1990, when the 1990 Treaty on the Final Settlement with Respect to Germany terminated the Bonn agreements.

The United States succeeded in the West German case because most Germans supported democracy, a market economy, and constraints on the FRG's security policies. Obviously the strength of this support reflected many factors, including the long-term economic success of the West relative to the Soviet bloc. Shared sovereignty arrangements for security in the FRG contributed to effective domestic governance by taking a potentially explosive issue off the table both within and, more important, without West Germany. Security dilemmas that might have strengthened undemocratic forces in the FRG never occurred because the Bonn government did not have exclusive control of the country's defense.

The Chad-Cameroon Pipeline and Shared Sovereignty. One recent arrangement that includes elements of shared sovereignty, albeit in watered-down form, is the program associated with the development of oil resources in Chad and the pipeline that carries this oil through Cameroon to the Atlantic. Both Chad and Cameroon have been badly governed. In the 1990s an oil company consortium led by Exxon wanted to develop Chad's oil, but it feared not only that the Chad and Cameroon governments might void any contract but also that they would be subject to public criticism and court action by human rights and environmental groups. Because of these fears, the oil companies insisted on the involvement of the World Bank as a minority partner,

an involvement that they hoped would lessen any chances of unilateral contract revisions and provide cover for, perhaps even improve, human rights and environmental performance.[54] The World Bank in turn insisted on a modest, in the end quite modest, degree of shared sovereignty.

Under pressure from World Bank officials, Chad enacted the Revenue Management Law in 1998. The law divides oil revenues into two categories: direct (dividends and royalties) and indirect (taxes, charges, and customs duties). Direct revenues are placed in a foreign escrow account, 10 percent of which is committed to future generations. Of the remaining 90 percent, 80 percent is to be used for social services (including health care and education), 15 percent for current government expenses, and 5 percent for the oil-exporting region. The law provided for the creation of the Oil Revenues Control and Monitoring Board, which is responsible for authorizing and monitoring disbursements from the escrow account. The board includes members from Chad's judiciary, civil society, and trade unions.[55]

In addition, in February 2001 the World Bank created an independent body known as the International Advisory Group, whose members it would appoint in consultation with national authorities. The group, which visits the area at least twice a year and has access to relevant information and officials, advises the governments of Chad and Cameroon and the World Bank about the misallocation or misuse of public funds, involvement of civil society, institution building, and governance more generally. The chair of the five-member group (which includes a former deputy minister in the Canadian government, a Dutch agricultural specialist, an American anthropologist, and an African NGO leader) is Mamadou Lamine Loum, a former Senegalese prime minister.[56]

The potential leverage of international actors before the project was put in place was significant. The project would provide Chad with a 50 percent increase in revenue. Chad and Cameroon could not have completed the project without the oil companies, and the companies would not have invested without the involvement of the World Bank. The bank, unlike the companies, had legitimacy, which allowed it to negotiate conditions related to Chad's domestic institutional structures.[57]

Nevertheless, despite the leverage enjoyed by the World Bank and the oil companies, the extent to which external actors have intruded on Chad's domestic governance is modest. The International Advisory Group is just advisory. Most of the members of the Chadian oversight committee are closely associated with the government. The allocation of funds to social services is not specified with regard to areas. If anything, the lesson of the Chad-Cameroon pipeline is that creating potent shared sovereignty institutions in weak states in the contemporary environment is difficult. More robust World Bank proposals for the project were dropped because of objections from some members of the bank's executive board, including those representing African states. In the case of the Chad-Cameroon oil development and pipeline project, adequate domestic governance would have been better assured by more intrusive engagement by external actors, including, for instance, a number of international representatives on the oversight committee, which must approve transfers from the escrow account.

In sum, like virtually every other institutional arrangement that can be imagined, shared sovereignty has been tried before: specific configurations of power and interest led stronger actors to introduce shared sovereignty arrangements, and weaker ones to accept them. In the late nineteenth century, lenders wanted assurance from defaulting states that if they provided new capital, they would be repaid. After World War II, both the United States and the Soviet Union used shared sovereignty to undergird their preferred domestic regimes in Western and Eastern Europe. Chad accepted

some constraints on its use of oil revenues because complete rejection of the World Bank's recommendations might have entirely scuttled the pipeline project.

Incentives for Shared Sovereignty. Shared sovereignty arrangements can work only if they create a self-enforcing equilibrium, which might include external as well as domestic players. There are at least four circumstances that might make shared sovereignty arrangements attractive for political decisionmakers, those who hold international legal sovereignty, in target states: avarice, postconflict occupation, desperation, and elections.

Natural Resources and Avarice. Rulers salivate at the wealth and power that natural resources, most notably oil, can bring them. Their bargaining position, however, depends on the acceptance of the precepts of conventional sovereignty: the state owns the oil and has the right to sign contracts and set rules governing its exploitation. Neither companies, nor consuming states, nor international organizations have challenged the property rights of the state. No one, at least no one in a position of authority, has suggested, for instance, that oil in badly governed states ought to be declared part of the common heritage of mankind and placed under the control of perhaps the World Bank.

For poorly governed countries, however, natural resources, especially oil, have been a curse that has feathered the nests of rulers and undermined democracy and economic growth. Oil concentrates resources in the hands of the state. The road to wealth and power for any ambitious individual leads through the offices of the central government, not through individual enterprise or productive economic activity. With oil wealth, the state can buy off dissenters and build military machines that can be used to repress those who cannot be bought off.[58]

Shared sovereignty arrangements for extractive industries would offer an alternative to conventional practices that would provide better governance in oil-abundant states, more benefits for their people, and fewer incentives for corruption and conflict. Such arrangements would depend on the willingness of wealthier democratic states to constrain the options available to political leaders in poorly governed resource-rich states. Conventional sovereignty would not be challenged in principle but would be compromised in practice. Political leaders in host countries would then be confronted with a choice between nothing and something, although much less than they might have at their private disposal under conventional practices.

A shared sovereignty arrangement for natural resources could work in the following way. An agreement between the host country and, say, the World Bank would create a trust. The trust would be domiciled in an advanced industrialized country with effective rule of law. All funds generated by the natural resources project would be placed in an international escrow account controlled by the trust. All disbursements from the account would have to be approved by a majority of the directors of the trust. Half of the board of directors of the trust would be appointed by the host government, the other half by the World Bank; the bank could name directors from any country but would not designate its own employees. Directors would have to believe that their success depended on the success of the trust.

The trust agreement would stipulate that a large part of these funds would be used for social welfare programs, although specific allocations for, say, health care or education would be left to the host government. The trust would refuse to dispense funds that did not conform with these commitments. The trust might even be charged with implementing programs using the resources of the escrow account if the government failed to act expeditiously.

The laws of the advanced democracy in which the trust was incorporated would hold accountable the directors of the trust. Legislation enacted by the country in which the trust was domiciled would back the firms' responsibility to pay revenues into the escrow account, and only the escrow account.

No doubt the leaders of oil-rich or other natural resource–rich countries would cringe at such arrangements. They would have much more difficulty putting billions of dollars in foreign bank accounts, as did Sani Abacha, the late Nigerian military dictator. It would be hard to spend half a billion dollars on a European vacation as did some members of the Saudi royal family in 2002. But if the major democracies passed legislation requiring that any imported oil be governed by a trust arrangement, avarice might induce political leaders in resource-rich countries to accept shared sovereignty, because without shared sovereignty they would get nothing.[59]

Postconflict Occupation. Postconflict occupation might also be conducive to creating shared sovereignty arrangements. When there is military intervention and occupation, local leaders have limited choice. In Afghanistan, Bosnia, East Timor, Iraq, and Kosovo, the local leaders have been dependent to some extent on external actors. They have had to accept the presence of nonnationals. Foreigners have been running many of the ministries in Bosnia. In Kosovo joint implementation for administrative structures has been the norm: there are twenty administrative departments and four independent agencies, all of which are codirected by a Kosovar and a senior UNMIK staff person.[60] In Afghanistan and Iraq, security has been provided in part by foreign forces.

Shared sovereignty contracts would make such arrangements permanent, not transitional. The presence of external actors would not be the result of a unilateral decision by an external administrator but rather of a contract between external and domestic actors who would be granted international legal sovereignty. Because the contract would have no termination date, local actors could no longer assume that they could simply wait for the foreigners to leave. Some local leaders might still decide that acting as a spoiler might maximize their interests, but others would see cooperation as more likely to enhance their long-term prospects.

Such arrangements could be successful in the long run only if they were supported by a winning coalition in the host country. Unlike oil trusts, external enforcement mechanisms would be difficult to create. External actors might bolster domestic agents committed to shared sovereignty or threaten to impose sanctions or cut foreign assistance if the agreement were violated, but there could not be an iron-clad guarantee of success.

Still, shared sovereignty arrangements would be more promising than constitution writing, which has been the center of attention in recent occupations. The problem with relying on a constitution or any other legal commitments made under pressure at a particular moment in time is that once the occupying power leaves, the incentives for domestic actors to honor their earlier commitments can radically change. Shared sovereignty, in contrast, could generate a self-enforcing equilibrium if it provided benefits to a large enough group of domestic actors.

Monetary policy is one area where shared sovereignty might work in a postconflict or even a more benign environment. Controlling inflation can be a daunting problem. A few countries, East Timor being one example, have simply resorted to using the U.S. dollar. Others have tried to engineer credible commitments through domestic institutions, such as independent central banks. Appointment of the governors of the central bank by both government and external actors could enhance the credibility of such arrangements. In this regard, the IMF might be the right partner. Nonnational governors could be of any nationality. They would not be IMF employees. The fund would sign a contract with the host country setting up shared sovereignty on a permanent basis or until both parties agreed to end the arrangement. If the national government unilaterally abrogated the arrangement,

it would be a clear signal to external actors that the government was abandoning the path of monetary responsibility. [61] If the central bank were successful in constraining inflation, the arrangement would generate support from domestic actors. Like oil trusts, one major attraction of such an agreement is that it would not be costly for the IMF or any other external actor.

Commercial courts might be another area where shared sovereignty could be productive. Again, the opportunities in this area would not be limited to postconflict situations. In a state where the rule of law has been sketchy, the international legal sovereign would conclude a contract with an external entity—for instance, a regional organization such as the EU or the Organization of American States —to establish a separate commercial court system. The judges in these courts would be appointed by both the national government and its external partner. The expectation would be that local business interests would find this court system attractive. It would provide a venue in which they could resolve disagreements more effectively than would be the case within existing national institutions. The presence of such a court system might even attract higher levels of foreign investment. Like oil trusts and central banks, such an arrangement would not involve substantial costs for the external actor. The national government, or even to some extent the litigants, could fund commercial courts.

Desperation. Aside from the avarice associated with natural resources and the pressures arising from occupation, desperation for external resources might also motivate national authorities to enter into shared sovereignty arrangements. For countries that have spiraled into the abyss because of civil war or misgovernance, and that do not have easily exploited natural resources, foreign assistance might be a major potential source of revenue. The bargaining leverage of political leaders under such circumstances would be limited. The ability of external actors to negotiate shared sovereignty arrangements would be high.

As in the case of occupation, the most promising spheres for shared sovereignty, such as monetary policy and commercial courts, would not require substantial resources from external actors but would generate adequate domestic support. In collapsed or near-collapsed states, however, external actors would have to provide resources at least for some period of time. This would open additional possibilities for shared sovereignty for activities funded by external donors. A committee composed of national officials and individuals appointed by the education ministries of major donor countries might make, for instance, decisions about educational curriculum. A system of health care facilities administered by external aid workers or NGOs could be created separate from the national ministry of health. Because donors are not likely to be willing to provide aid on a quasi-permanent basis, however, such arrangements could be sustained only if a large enough domestic coalition were willing to support them even after foreign funding had been withdrawn.

Elections. Finally, in badly governed illiberal democracies, elections might provide an incentive for shared sovereignty contracts. Political candidates might make such policies part of their electoral platform. Illiberal democracies are polities that hold competitive elections but are deficient with regard to rule of law, an active civil society, and a free press.[62] In illiberal democracies, government does not work very well. Public officials are disconnected from the citizenry. Individuals or parties might change, but policies remain more or less the same. Voters become cynical, and even potentially progressive political candidates have no way to make their campaign pledges credible. Shared sovereignty contracts could be an appealing political strategy for a dissident candidate. Such a political platform could win votes by signaling to the electorate that a politician would make a decisive break with the past by

engaging external actors in domestic decision-making processes.

The long-term credibility of a shared sovereignty arrangement concluded by a successful dissident candidate in an illiberal democracy would depend both on the extent to which such practices have been internationally legitimated and on their effectiveness. The more common shared sovereignty agreements are, the easier it would be for any one leader to defend his actions against opponents who might claim that he had compromised the state's sovereignty. The greater the improvement in governance associated with shared sovereignty arrangements, the greater the likelihood that they would be honored over the long term.

Thus some form of de facto protectorate and, more promising, shared sovereignty are policy tools that could be added to the meager selection of options currently available to deal with bad governance or to create effective institutions following military occupations. Legitimacy for shared sovereignty would be provided by the agreement of those exercising the target state's international legal sovereignty.

CONCLUSION

During the twentieth century, the norms of international legal sovereignty and Westphalian/Vatellian sovereignty became universally accepted. It has often been tacitly assumed that these norms would be accompanied by effective domestic sovereignty, that is, by governance structures that exercised competent and ideally constructive control over their countries' populations and territory. This assumption has proven false. Poor, even malevolent, governance is a widespread problem. Badly governed states have become a threat to the interests of much more powerful actors: weapons of mass destruction have broken the connection between resources and the ability to do grievous harm; genocides leave political leaders in democratic polities with uncomfortable choices; and transnational disease and crime are persistent challenges.

The policy tools available to external actors—governance assistance and transitional administration—are inadequate, even when foreign powers have militarily occupied a country. Governance assistance can have positive results in occupied or badly governed states, but the available evidence suggests that the impact is weak. Transitional administration, which aims to restore conventional sovereignty in a relatively short time frame, can be effective only if indigenous political leaders believe that they will be better off allying with external actors not only while these actors are present but also after they leave.

The menu of options to deal with failing and collapsed states could be expanded in at least two ways. First, major states or regional or international organizations could assume some form of de facto trusteeship or protectorate responsibility for specific countries, even if there is no general international convention defining such arrangements. In a trusteeship, international actors would assume control over local functions for an indefinite period of time. They might also eliminate the international legal sovereignty of the entity or control treaty-making powers in whole or in part (e.g., in specific areas such as security or trade). There would be no assumption of a withdrawal in the short or medium term.

Second, domestic sovereignty in collapsed or poorly governed states could be improved through shared sovereignty contracts. These contracts would create joint authority structures in specific areas. They would not involve a direct assault on sovereignty norms because they would be formally consistent with international legal sovereignty, even though they would violate Westphalian/Vatellian sovereignty. Natural resources trusts, whose directors were appointed by national and nonnational entities, would be one possibility; central banks whose boards of governors comprised citizens and noncitizens would be another.

Political leaders in target states might accept such arrangements to secure external resources, either payments for raw materials' exploitation or foreign assistance, to encourage the departure of occupying forces or to attract voters. To be durable, shared sovereignty institutions either would require external enforcement, something that would be possible for natural resources trusts, or would have to create adequate domestic support, which would depend on the results delivered.

For external signatories—international organizations, regional organizations, and states—the most attractive shared sovereignty arrangements would be ones that did not require any significant commitment of resources over the long term. Natural resources trusts and central bank administration would meet this condition. In cases of states recovering from collapse, or something near to it, where foreign aid is the incentive for national leaders to accept shared sovereignty, resources commitments by external actors would be unavoidable for the short and medium terms. Over the longer term, though, shared sovereignty institutions could survive only if the services they provided were funded from internal sources of revenue.

De facto trusteeships or protectorates and shared sovereignty hardly exhaust the possibilities for improving domestic sovereignty in poorly governed states. Leaders in some polities have already used private firms to carry out some activities that have traditionally been in the hands of state officials. Indonesia, for instance, used a Swiss firm to collect its customs for more than eleven years.[63] Other governments have hired private military companies (PMCs). Perhaps with stronger accountability mechanisms enforced by advanced industrial states, such as the ability to prosecute PMCs and their employees for abuses, the results might be more consistently salutary.[64]

There is no panacea for domestic sovereignty failures. Even with the best of intentions and substantial resources, external actors cannot quickly eliminate the causes of these failures: poverty, weak indigenous institutions, insecurity, and the raw materials curse. But the instruments currently available to policymakers to deal with places such as Congo, Liberia, and Iraq are woefully inadequate. De facto trusteeships, and especially shared sovereignty, would offer political leaders a better chance of bringing peace and prosperity to the populations of badly governed states and reduce the threat that such polities present to the wider international community.

NOTES

This article first appeared in *International Security* 29, no. 2 (Fall 2004): 85–120. © 2004 by the President and Fellows of Harvard College and the Massachusetts Institute of Technology. Reprinted with permission of MIT Press Journals.

The author would like to thank Jared Cohen, Larry Diamond, Karl Eikenberry, Donald Emmerson, Tarek Ghani, Robert Keohane, Amachai Magen, John McMillan, John Meyer, David Victor, Allen Weiner, and Amy Zegart, in addition to participants in seminars at Stanford, the University of California, Los Angeles, the University of Washington, the University of California, Berkeley, Panteion University, the University of Pennsylvania, and Harvard, as well as reviewers of this journal for their comments on earlier versions of this article.

1. For a discussion of the requirements for successful international engagement that complements many of the points made in this article, see James D. Fearon and David D. Laitin, "Neotrusteeship and the Problem of Weak States," *International Security*, Vol. 28, No. 4 (Spring 2004), pp. 5–43.

2. See ibid., especially pp. 36–37.

3. Although the principle of nonintervention is traditionally associated with the Peace of Westphalia of 1648, the doctrine was not explicitly articulated until a century later by the Swiss jurist Emmerich de Vattel in his *The Law of Nations or Principles of the Law of Nature Applied to the Conduct and Affairs of Nations and Sovereigns*, originally published in French in 1758.

4. Mary Ann Tetreault, "Autonomy, Necessity, and the Small State: Ruling Kuwait in the Twentieth Century," *International Organization*, Vol. 45, No. 4 (Autumn 1991), pp. 565–591.

5. In Shanghai, for instance, the British established a municipal council that regulated the activities of Chinese living within Shanghai as well as non-Chinese. See Jean Chesneaux, Marianne Bastid, and Marie-Claire Bergere, *China from the Opium Wars to the 1911 Revolution* (Hassocks, Sussex, U.K.: Harvester, 1977), pp. 61–68.

6. For two very similar analyses, see Robert O. Keohane, "Political Authority after Intervention: Gradations in Sovereignty," in J.L. Holzgrefe and Keohane, eds., *Humanitarian Intervention: Ethical, Legal, and Political Dilemmas* (Cambridge: Cambridge University Press, 2003), pp. 276–277; and Gerald B. Helman and Steven R. Ratner, "Saving Failed States," *Foreign Policy*, No. 89 (Winter 1993), pp. 3–21. Keohane argues that there should be gradations of sovereignty. Helman and Ratner suggest that there are three forms of what they call "guardianship": governance assistance, the delegation of government authority, and trusteeship. They also suggest the term "conservatorship" as an alternative to trusteeship.

7. The State Failure project was commissioned by the Central Intelligence Agency in 1994 and was carried out by a task force composed of individuals from universities and consulting companies. All of the data presented by the project are unclassified, and the findings of the project are those of the members of the task force, not the U.S. government or any of its agencies. The State Failure Task Force defines "adverse regime change" as "major, abrupt shifts in patterns of governance, including state collapse, periods of severe elite or regime instability, and shifts away from democracy toward authoritarian rule." There were fewer than twenty cases of state failure narrowly defined as the collapse of authority structures for several years. Jack A. Goldstone, Ted Robert Gurr, Barbara Harff, Marc A. Levy, Monty G. Marshall, Robert H. Bates, David L. Epstein, Colin H. Kahl, Pamela T. Surko, John C. Ulfelder Jr., and Alan N. Unger, *State Failure Task Force Report: Phase III Findings* (McLean, Va.: Science Applications International Corporation, September 30, 2000), pp. iv, v, 3–5.

8. Gary King and Langche Zeng criticize the methodology of the State Failure project even though they find that most of its conclusions, especially the empirical link between high infant mortality and partial democracy, are supported. King and Zeng,

"Improving Forecasts of State Failure," *World Politics*, Vol. 53, No. 4 (July 2001), pp. 623–658.

9. James D. Fearon and David D. Laitin, "Ethnicity, Insurgency, and Civil War," *American Political Science Review*, Vol. 97, No. 1 (March 2003), pp. 1–17; and Fearon and Laitin, "Neotrusteeship and the Problem of Weak States," pp. 36–37.

10. Goldstone et al., *State Failure Task Force Report*, p. 21.

11. These figures are derived from data found at World Bank, *WDI Online*, http://devdata.worldbank.org/dataonline.

12. The government of Sierra Leone and the United Nations agreed to establish the special court in August 2000. The court, which has both national and international judges, is charged with prosecuting those most responsible for the commission of serious crimes against international humanitarian and Sierra Leonean law. For the agreement between the government and the UN, see http://www.sc-sl.org/index.html.

13. William Reno, "Sierra Leone: Warfare in a Post-State Society," in Robert I. Rotberg, ed., *State Failure and State Weakness in a Time of Terror* (Washington, D.C.: Brookings, 2003), pp. 72–73, 88; and Somini Sengupta, "Liberian Leader Sets Date, and New Terms, for Exit?" *New York Times*, August 3, 2003, http://www.nytimes.com/; and http://www.infoplease.com/ce6/world/A086104.html.

14. Reno, "Sierra Leone," p. 75. For the argument that failed states are created by perverse rulers, see Robert I. Rotberg, "Failed States, Collapsed States, Weak States: Causes and Indicators," in Rotberg, *State Failure and State Weakness in a Time of Terror*, p. 14; and Michael Ignatieff, "State Failure and Nation-Building," in Holzgrefe and Keohane, *Humanitarian Intervention*, pp. 301–303.

15. Per capita income for the world as a whole increased by 28 percent for the period 1990–2000. Figures for per capita income gross derived from World Bank, *WDI Online*, http://devdata .worldbank.org/dataonline. Figures on civil war can be found in Fearon and Laitin, "Ethnicity, Insurgency, and Civil War," p. 77.

16. For a discussion of poppy policies under the Taliban, see UN Office on Drugs and Crime, "Afghanistan Ends Opium Poppy Cultivation," June 2001, http://www.unodc.org/unodc/en/news -letter_2001- 06–30_1_page002.html. So much opium was produced in 2004 that prices fell by 60 percent. See David Rhode, "Poppies Flood Afghanistan; Opium Tide May Yet Turn," *New York Times*, July 1, 2004, http://nytimes.com. For the relationship between civil war and drug production, see Paul Collier and Anke Hoeffler, "The Challenge of Reducing the Global Incidence of Civil War" (Oxford: Centre for the Study of African Economies, Department of Economics, Oxford University, rev., March 26, 2004), pp. 8–9.

17. U.S. Department of State, *Trafficking in Persons Report* (Washington, D.C.: U.S. Department of State, June 2004), http://www.state.gov/documents/organization/33614.pdf.

18. International Commission on Intervention and State Sovereignty, *The Responsibility to Protect* (Ottawa: International Development Research Centre, 2001), http://www.dfait-maeci.gc.ca/iciss-ciise/pdf/Commission-Report.pdf. See also Gareth Evans and Mohamed Sahnoun, "The Responsibility to Protect," *Foreign Affairs*, Vol. 81, No. 6 (November/December 2002), pp. 99–110.

19. Sowmya Anand and Jon A. Krosnick, "The Impact of Attitudes toward Foreign Policy Goals on Public Preferences among Presidential Candidates: A Study of Issue Publics and the Attentive Public in the 2000 U.S. Presidential Election," *Presidential Studies Quarterly*, Vol. 33, No. 1 (March 2003), Tables 2, 3.

20. For the White House description of the MCA, see http://www.whitehouse.gov/infocus/developingnations/millennium.html. For a list of the first set of countries to receive funding from the MCA, see MCA, press release, "The Millennium Challenge Corporation Names MCA Eligible Countries," May 6, 2004, http://www.usaid.gov/mca/Documents/PR_Eligible.pdf. For a discussion of the World Bank's governance assistance programs, see http://www.worldbank.org/wbi/governance/about.html. See also Arthur A. Goldsmith, "Foreign Aid and Statehood in Africa," *International Organization*, Vol. 55, No. 1 (Winter 2000), pp. 135–136.

21. International Monetary Fund, Fiscal Affairs Department, *Fund-Supported Programs, Fiscal Policy, and Income Distribution*, Occasional Paper No. 46 (Washington, D.C.: International Monetary Fund, 1986), p. 40; and Robin Broad, *Unequal Alliance: The World Bank, the International Monetary Fund, and the Philippines* (Berkeley: University of California Press, 1988), pp. 51–53, Table 12.

22. Paul Lewis, "Global Lenders Use Leverage to Combat Corruption," *New York Times,* late ed., August 11, 1997, p. 4; and James C. McKinley Jr., "Kenyan Who Charged 4 Officials with Graft Is Suspended," *New York Times,* late ed., July 31, 1998, p. 4.

23. World Bank, *World Development Report, 1997: The State in a Changing World* (Washington, D.C.: World Bank, 1997), p. 2.

24. Ibid., p. 4.

25. The first paragraph of the Agreement Establishing the European Bank for Reconstruction and Development, signed in Paris on May 29, 1990, states that contracting parties should be "committed to the fundamental principles of multiparty democracy, the rule of law, respect for human rights and market economics." See "Agreement Establishing the European Bank for Reconstruction and Development," http://www.ebrd.com/pubs/insti/basic/basic1.htm.

26. For a discussion of the ideational motivations for foreign aid, see David Lumsdaine, *Moral Vision in International Politics: The Foreign Aid Regime, 1949–89* (Princeton, N.J.: Princeton University Press, 1993).

27. For a critique of U.S. policies, see Thomas Carothers, *Aiding Democracy Abroad: The Learning Curve* (Washington, D.C.: Carnegie Endowment for International Peace, 1999).

28. Michael W. Doyle and Nicholas Sambanis, "International Peacebuilding: A Theoretical and Quantitative Analysis," *American Political Science Review,* Vol. 94, No. 4 (December 2000), pp. 779–802. For a second study with a different database but comparable findings, see George Downs and Stephen John Stedman, "Evaluating Issues in Peace Implementation," in Stedman, Donald Rothchild, and Elizabeth M. Cousens, eds., *Ending Civil Wars: The Implementation of Peace Agreements* (Boulder, Colo.: Lynne Rienner, 2002), pp. 50–52.

29. Richard Caplan, *A New Trusteeship? The International Administration of War-torn Territories* (London: International Institute for Strategic Studies, 2002), pp. 8–9, 50–51; United Nations, *Report of the Panel on United Nations Peace Operations* (Brahimi report) (New York: United Nations, 2000), pp. 7, 14. In June 2003 Secretary of Defense Donald Rumsfeld discussed the possibility of a standing international peacekeeping force under the leadership of the United States. Ester Schrader, "U.S. Looks at Organizing Global Peacekeeping Force," *Los Angeles Times,* June 27, 2003, p. A1.

30. Fearon and Laitin, "Neotrusteeship and the Problem of Weak States," p. 37. See also David M. Edelstein, "Occupational Hazards: Why Military Occupations Succeed or Fail," *International Security,* Vol. 29, No. 1 (Summer 2004), pp. 49–81.

31. Michael Ignatieff points to the possibly negative consequences of competition among NGOs. Ignatieff, "State Failure and Nation-Building," p. 27.

32. Elizabeth M. Cousens, "From Missed Opportunities to Overcompensation: Implementing the Dayton Agreement on Bosnia," in Stedman, Rothchild, and Cousens, *Ending Civil Wars,* p. 532; International Crisis Group, *Courting Disaster: The Misrule of Law in Bosnia & Herzegovina,* Balkans Report No. 127 (Sarajevo/Brussels: International Crisis Group, March 25, 2002), http://www.crisisweb.org/library/documents/report_archive/A400592_25032002.pdf, pp. 25, 33; Simon Chesterman, "Kosovo in Limbo: State-Building and 'Substantial Autonomy'" (New York: International Peace Academy, 2001), p. 1; and Caplan, *A New Trusteeship?* pp. 19, 39.

33. Nicholas Wood, "60 Bosnian Serbs Dismissed for Aid to War Crimes Figure," *New York Times,* late ed., July 1, 2004, p. 6.

34. The members and observers of the Peace Implementing Council can be found at http://www.ohr.int/ohr-info/gen-info/#pic.

35. See http://www.nato.int/sfor/index.htm and linked pages.

36. For a description of the activities of different organizations, see http://www.oscebih.org/mission/mandate.asp; UN Development Programme, "UNDP BiH —It's Not Just What We Do, but Also How We Do It!" http://www.undp.ba/osc.asp?idItem_2; UN High Commissioner for Refugees, "History," http://www.unhcr.ba/history/index.htm; and Office of the High Representative, http://www.ohr.int. See Cousens, "From Missed Opportunities to Overcompensation," p. 540; William O'Neill, *Kosovo: An Unfinished Peace* (Boulder, Colo.: Lynne Rienner, 2002), pp. 37–40; International Crisis Group, *Courting Disaster,* p. ii; and Caplan, *A New Trusteeship?* p. 24.

37. International Crisis Group, *Courting Disaster,* pp. 2, 4, 6, 17; and Gerald Knaus and Felix Martin, "Travails of the European Raj: Lessons from Bosnia and Herzegovina," *Journal of Democracy,* Vol. 14, No. 3 (July 2003), pp. 60–74.

38. Caplan, *A New Trusteeship?* pp. 55–56.

39. Ibid., p. 39.

40. Resolution 1244 (1000) can be found at http://www.nato.int/kosovo/docu/u990610a.htm.

41. Caplan, *A New Trusteeship?* p. 22.

42. O'Neill, *Kosovo,* pp. 84–91.

43. For Namibia, see Downs and Stedman, "Evaluating Issues in Peace Implementation," pp. 59–61; and Roland Paris, *At War's End? Building Peace after Civil Conflict* (Cambridge: Cambridge University Press, 2004), chap. 8.

44. Downs and Stedman, "Evaluating Issues in Peace Implementation," pp. 62–63; and Paris, *At War's End,* chap. 7.

45. Helman and Ratner, "Saving Failed States," pp. 3–21; Caplan, *A New Trusteeship?* p. 7; Ignatieff, "State Failure and Nation-Building," p. 308; and Martin Indyk, "A Trusteeship for Palestine?" *Foreign Affairs,* Vol. 82, No. 3 (May/June 2003), pp. 51–66.

46. At least one way to interpret the strategy of U.S. decisionmakers is to understand the June transfer as one that gives Iraq international legal sovereignty. With this international legal sovereignty, the new Iraqi government will be able to legitimate agreements with external agents. Given the dependence of the new government on the United States for security and revenue, such agreements will allow the United States to continue to pursue its core interests.

47. For a discussion of these and other issues, see Caplan, *A New Trusteeship?* p. 9.

48. Kofi Annan, "The Legitimacy to Intervene: International Action to Uphold Human Rights Requires a New Understanding of State and Individual Sovereignty," *Financial Times,* December 31, 1999.

49. Fearon and Laitin have suggested that "neotrusteeship" is the most appropriate term for arrangements that could cope with the postconflict security problems afflicting states suffering from weak administrative capacity, poverty, and rough terrain. Because such states are unlikely to be able to conduct effective policing and counterinsurgency operations on their own, maintaining security will require the engagement of external actors for an extended period of time. The authors do not, however, argue that neotrusteeship would involve a loss of international legal sovereignty. See Fearon and Laitin, "Neotrusteeship and the Problem of Weak States," especially pp. 24–41.

50. Robert Keohane has discussed a similar set of ideas using the concept of gradations of sovereignty. See Keohane, "Political Authority after Intervention," pp. 276–277.

51. Donald C. Blaisdell, *European Financial Control in the Ottoman Empire: A Study of the Establishment, Activities, and Significance of the Administration of the Ottoman Public Debt* (New York: Columbia University Press, 1929), pp. 90–120, 124–130; Herbert Feis, *Europe, the World's Banker, 1870–1914: An Account of European Foreign Investment and the Connection of World Finance with Diplomacy before World War I* (New York: W.W. Norton, 1965), pp. 332–341; Bernard Lewis, *The Middle East: A Brief History of the Last 2,000 Years* (New York: Scribner, 1995), pp. 298–299; and Roger Owen, *The Middle East in the World Economy, 1800–1914* (Cambridge: Cambridge University Press, 1981), p. 101.

52. "Revised NATO SOFA Supplementary Agreement," articles 19, 22, 28. The full text of the agreement is available at http://www.oxc.army.mil/others/Gca/files%5Cgermany.doc.

53. "Convention on Relations between the Three Powers and the Federal Republic of Germany," *American Journal of International Law,* Vol. 49, No. 3 (July 1955), pp. 57–69. For a detailed examination of the retained rights of the Western powers, see Joseph W. Bishop Jr., "The 'Contractual Agreements' with the Federal Republic of Germany," *American Journal of International Law,* Vol. 49, No. 2 (April 1955), pp. 125–147. For a general analysis of Germany's situation after World War II, see Peter J. Katzenstein, *Policy and Politics in West Germany: The Growth of a Semisovereign State* (Philadelphia: Temple University Press, 1987).

54. Royal Dutch Shell withdrew from the project in the mid-1990s because it feared being targeted for human rights violations, an accusation that had already been levied against the company because of its operations in Nigeria. See Ken Silverstein, "With War, Africa Oil Beckons," *Los Angeles Times,* March 21, 2003, p. 1.

55. Genoveva Hernandez Uriz, "To Lend or Not to Lend: Oil, Human Rights, and the World Bank's Internal Contradictions," *Harvard Human Rights Journal,* Vol. 14 (Spring 2001), p. 223; and World Bank, IBRD/IDA project information document, Chad-Cameroon Petroleum Development and Pipeline Project, June 23, 1999, http://www.worldbank.org/afr/ccproj/project/td44305.pdf.

56. World Bank, "Chad-Cameroon Pipeline and Related Projects: International Advisory Group Terms of Reference," http://www.worldbank.org/afr/ccproj/project/iag_tor_en.pdf; and World Bank, International Advisory Group on Chad-Cameroon Petroleum Development and Pipeline Project International Advisory Group, http://www.gic-iag.org/eiag.htm.

57. Uriz, "To Lend or Not to Lend," p. 198; and Paul Raeburn, "A Gusher for Everyone," *Business Week,* November 6, 2000, p. 60.

58. Michael Lewin Ross, "Does Oil Hinder Democracy?" *World Politics,* Vol. 53, No. 3 (April 2001), pp. 325–361.

59. This proposal assumes that oil could be exploited only by companies domiciled in advanced democratic polities interested in supporting good governance and that these countries cooperate with each other. Absent these conditions, the host country could play one oil company off against another and avoid the constraints that would come with a shared sovereignty trust.

60. Caplan, *A New Trusteeship?* p. 39.

61. The logic of this argument follows the case presented for the Bank of England by Douglass C. North and Barry R. Weingast; in this case, the creation of the bank served as a mechanism that provided information about the intentions of the ruler. See North and Weingast, "Constitutions and Commitment: The Evolution of Institutions Governing Public Choice in Seventeenth-Century England," *Journal of Economic History,* Vol. 49, No. 4 (December 1989), pp. 803–832.

62. A standard reference is Fareed Zakaria, *The Future of Freedom: Illiberal Democracy at Home and Abroad* (New York: W.W. Norton, 2003).

63. From April 1985 through March 1997, Indonesia relied on the Société Général de Surveillance to collect its customs duties through preshipment inspection of imports. The revenues collected were paid directly into government bank accounts, thus circumventing what had become an extremely corrupt and inefficient national customs service. See William E. James, "A Note on Pre-Shipment Inspection of Imports," Agency for International Development PPC/CDIE/DI report processing form, January 28, 2002, http://www.dec.org/pdf_docs/PNACQ680.pdf.

64. For a discussion of private military companies, see P.W. Singer, *Corporate Warriors: The Rise of the Privatized Military Industry* (Ithaca, N.Y.: Cornell University Press, 2003).

37

INTERVENTION AND THE NATION-BUILDING DEBATE

Fen Osler Hampson and David Mendeloff

IT SHOULD COME AS NO SURPRISE THAT there is so much disquiet about the purpose, legitimacy, goals, and effectiveness of "nation building"—international interventions directed not just at ending political violence but at restoring political order and laying the foundations for democracy in war-torn societies. The track record of such interventions is indeed a mixed one. In some cases—Bosnia, Croatia, Namibia, El Salvador, Mozambique, East Timor, and Sierra Leone—international interventions have helped to end violent conflicts, impose some political order, and, arguably, put societies on the road to democratic development. In others, such as Cambodia, violent conflict has all but ended and political order has been reestablished, but democracy has yet to take hold. And in other cases—Somalia, Haiti, the Democratic Republic of the Congo, Afghanistan, and Iraq—violence continues, and where nascent democratic institutions have been established, their long-term future remains in doubt. But it is not just the empirical record that generates

such intense debate; it is also the nature and purpose of the nation-building enterprise, which many critics fear is a futile exercise in social and political engineering in societies that are, at best, poor receptacles for democratic values and institutions.

This essay seeks to clarify this ongoing debate by exploring some of the key assumptions that underlie it. As we argue, the debate is not just one of how to interpret the historical record of post–Cold War nation building but also one that is informed by different philosophical assumptions about how to assess the conditions for political order and the appetite for democracy in societies that have hitherto had little exposure to democratic values and principles. Understanding this debate more clearly is critical to better assessing the merits of the nation-building enterprise.

Several key fault lines in this debate are readily apparent. First, some champions of nation building accept many of the rationalist assumptions of traditional liberalism of the Lockean or social contract variety, namely, that there is an inherent predisposition on the part of all people and societies, independent of culture or creed, to embrace "freedom and democracy"—the rule of law, liberal values such as human and civil rights, and the principles of representative government. Accordingly, the intervention challenge is to identify the right mix of external political and military pressure that will foster political stability and allow a new social contract based on democratic principles to emerge in a way that allows the local populace to rapidly take full ownership of their political fortunes. We refer to this approach to the nation-building challenge as the "fast-track democratization" school because it seeks to capitalize on the democratic appetites of the local populace to create new political institutions and to do so in a way that is most expedient and cost effective for the intervening authority.

Two independent critical perspectives take issue with this approach. We refer to these respectively as the "security first" and the "slow democratization" schools of nation building. "Security firsters" argue that establishing security and basic political stability should be the first—if not exclusive—objective of international interventions. Such interventions in an ideal world should leave in their wake viable states that have the capacity and instrumental authority independently to manage their internal security affairs because the alternative —a relapse into anarchy and violence—is a far worse outcome. Following Thomas Hobbes, intervention success is measured not by its ability to establish democracy but by its ability to maintain civil peace and security.[1] This is because anarchy is the normal state of affairs and liberal democratic predispositions are, at the best of times, weak, especially in war-torn failed states. Security firsters are relatively indifferent to the kind of political rule or character of statehood that arises from international interventions, or the normative implications of the means by which political order is created, because security takes priority above all

else. If, for example, authoritarian rule is the best way to secure a lasting or more durable peace, then it may be the preferred option. And if partition—an approach generally anathema to the international community—is the best way to end political violence among rival ethnic factions, then it should be pursued. Generally speaking, security firsters believe international actors should limit their focus to the problems of security management and not concern themselves with democracy promotion and advancement, which may be elusive at best and counterproductive at worst.

"Slow democratizers" adopt a more utilitarian approach to the nation-building enterprise. They accept the proposition that although the establishment (or, in some cases, the restoration) of democracy ought to be the ultimate goal of international interventions, following John Stuart Mill, democratic institutions must be adapted to the special cultural and historical circumstances of the societies in which they are to be built. There is no one-size-fits-all democratic model that can be transplanted throughout the world. Furthermore, to give people unrestricted freedom and to try suddenly to establish a radically new social order by, for example, holding free elections is a prescription for disaster. The tyranny of mob rule, particularly in ethnically and religiously divided societies, is just as much to be feared as the tyranny of repression.

According to this perspective, the minimum requirement for effective democratic nation building is the existence of sound administrative state institutions that have the capacity to provide public goods and services and promote a self-sustaining social and political order in which citizens can realize their individual potential—what Mill in earlier times referred to as a kind of democracy that fosters "self-development" and "individuality."[2] However, building such institutions is not the sort of thing that can be done quickly, easily, or "on the cheap," particularly if existing social and political conditions are not ripe for democracy.

Slow democratizers believe that the foundations for statehood must be laid before liberal democracy can be introduced into a society and that a rush job will only make things worse by precipitating a breakdown of social order and a renewed outbreak of violence.

In short, each of these perspectives on nation building rests on a different set of philosophical and theoretical assumptions about the foundations of political order and, by extension, the pace, scope, and ultimate objectives of nation-building efforts. For the fast-track democratizers, political order is rooted in individual liberty. Nation building, therefore, is synonymous with democratization—a transformation that can occur relatively quickly and easily as long as intervening states are committed to nurturing individuals' natural inclination for liberal democracy. For the security firsters, political order is rooted in the absence of anarchy, not democracy—which, in the short term, is highly destabilizing. Nation building, therefore, should be limited to short-term security provision, not ambitious social engineering. For slow democratizers, political order rests on the foundations of a functioning administrative state apparatus and, ultimately, a liberal social, economic, and political culture that supports the democratic enterprise. Nation building is a process that is directed at both state and society. Building a genuine liberal democracy is a slow, arduous, and extremely expensive process, requiring massive resources, manpower, and time commitments from intervening states.

This essay is structured as follows. The first three sections amplify the themes just mentioned by describing in greater detail the different schools of thought or approaches to nation building that are reflected in the intervention debate. We explore these different approaches in terms of their key philosophical and policy assumptions, recognizing at the outset that no single author readily falls into the different categories we have identified. However, we do believe that these categorizations are useful

insofar as they highlight some core assumptions and key points of difference in this debate. In the fourth section of the essay, we offer our own assessment of these perspectives and the challenges they pose to practitioners who are engaged in the conflict management and nation-building enterprise.

FAST-TRACK DEMOCRATIZERS

If the efforts of the current Bush administration to promote democracy in countries like Afghanistan and Iraq strike some critics as hopelessly naive or ill conceived, they must at the very least concede that these policies have a venerable provenance in traditional liberal democratic theory and the doctrine of natural rights—most closely associated with the writings of John Locke, Thomas Jefferson, and Jean-Jacques Rousseau.[3] In championing the virtues of popular sovereignty, early liberal theorists believed that all individuals are free and equal regardless of who they are or where they live. At the same time, they also believed that all people have an innate ability to exercise their rights and personal freedom in deciding how they are to be governed.

Locke and the Natural Democratic Impulse

In Locke's conception of the so-called state of nature, war is a temporary phenomenon and, given the opportunity to do so, men and women will look to ways to protect their natural rights and join themselves in a civil society where the rule of law prevails. And they will be willing to curtail some of their own freedoms in the process by creating governments and electing representatives who act on their behalf under a fiduciary arrangement. This is because people are rational and because "Reason," in Locke's words, "teaches all Mankind, who will but consult it, that being all equal and independent, no one ought to harm another in his Life, Health, Liberty or Possessions."[4] Locke's doctrine of natural rights and his views about the origins of self-government had enormous appeal among America's founding fathers, especially Thomas Jefferson.[5] Not only did many of these same principles find their way into the American Declaration of Independence, but U.S. presidents from George Washington to Woodrow Wilson, John F. Kennedy, and George W. Bush have continued to champion the virtues of democracy and self-determination in national and international affairs.[6]

According to traditional liberal social contract theorists, there is a natural inclination on the part of individuals to abandon the state of nature (and the violence that often accompanies it). The rule of law and representative government, which allow individuals to more fully exercise and enjoy their personal freedoms, are the natural and logical extensions of human reason. Ultimately, the only way to avoid anarchy and the outbreak of civil violence is through the rule of law and representative government. But because all individuals share the same basic civic inclinations and have a common desire to protect and advance their natural rights and freedoms, it does not take heroic efforts to create a society where these freedoms are protected and individuals elect their governments.

Nation Building: Democratization through Liberation

These assumptions about human rationality have been questioned by many political philosophers, including those of a more conservative persuasion, such as Edmund Burke, Alexis de Tocqueville, and John Stuart Mill, who had a decidedly more pessimistic view of human nature and the capacity of individuals in a democracy to make informed political choices.[7] However, traditional liberal views about the intrinsic, "rational" appeal of civil society, the rule of law, and democracy clearly continue to hold sway to the present day. Fast-track democratizers believe that international interventions should be directed at unleashing this

latent democratic potential even in the seemingly unwelcome environment of war-torn societies and failed or failing states. Nation building, in other words, should be a process of democratization through the liberation of societies from tyranny and oppression. This requires sufficient military force and diplomatic pressure to weaken (or, in some cases, overthrow) oppressive regimes and sufficient aid to build and strengthen legal and electoral institutions. This view, for example, is clearly articulated in what is perhaps the blueprint of the fast-track democratization approach—the Bush administration's 2002 *National Security Strategy*, which calls for the United States to stabilize failed states by helping to build "police forces, court systems, and legal codes, local and provincial government institutions, and electoral systems."[8] The Bush administration's intervention in Iraq starkly reveals the fast-track democratization approach. The administration's lack of emphasis on postwar planning followed clearly from the view that the democratization of Iraq would evolve naturally, and relatively quickly, in the wake of the Ba'ath Party's ouster.[9] Similarly, the belief that Iraq's "liberation" would spread democracy like toppling dominoes throughout the Middle East is also consistent with the assumptions of the fast-track democratization school.

Indeed, great powers (and their coalition partners) who have chosen to intervene in internal conflicts—with or without the explicit authorization of the United Nations Security Council—have explicitly promoted democratization as the best cure for the ills of "failed states." In these cases—Kosovo and Afghanistan, in addition to Iraq—although the initial intervention was prompted by a combination of humanitarian and/or national security considerations, subsequent efforts to restore political order were (and continue to be) intimately related to laying the foundations for democratic political processes through the promotion of elections and the development of legal institutions.

The assumptions of the fast-track democratization school are also implicit in United Nations–led interventions throughout the post–Cold War period. Indeed, the United Nations has been at the forefront of democratization efforts in recent years through its various and successive efforts at peacebuilding and conflict prevention in multiple conflict zones. The conceptual foundations for the United Nations' role in democracy promotion were first laid out in former UN secretary-general Boutros Boutros-Ghali's 1992 *Agenda for Peace*, which defined peacebuilding in rather politically neutral tones as a broad set of activities that "tend to consolidate the peace and advance a set of confidence and well-being among people." Although Boutros-Ghali did not directly equate the peacebuilding challenge with democracy promotion, it is quite clear that this is what he had in mind and how it has subsequently worked in practice. He argued that in addition to more traditional peacekeeping activities (assisting with the disarmament of combatants and weapons stocks, provision of public order, repatriation of refugees, etc.), the list of peacebuilding activities should include "monitoring elections, advancing efforts to promote human rights, reforming and strengthening governmental institutions and promoting formal and informal processes of political participation." And he went on to state that the "United Nations has an obligation to develop and provide . . . support for the transformation of deficient national structures and capabilities, and for strengthening democratic institutions."[10]

What accounts for this equating of nation building with democratization in war-torn states? At one level, it is an article of faith that even in the seemingly unfertile, rocky political terrain of failed states, the general populace harbors a deep-rooted appetite for a civil society where human rights are protected and guaranteed by the rule of law and democracy. Like traditional liberals who subscribed to the theory of the "social contract" and popular sovereignty, many policymakers and analysts believe that democracy and the rule of law have intrinsic appeal that is independent of culture, creed, or religion. At another level, this belief is reinforced by the recognition that democracy is the principal form of governance in the post–Cold War world. As Marc Plattner notes, "Although the third wave of democratic expansion may have crested, the international legitimacy of democracy has continued to soar. Both the international organizations and the great powers that have taken the lead in responding to most postconflict situations cannot easily evade their public commitment to democracy. These days one cannot imagine a U.S. president justifying—or U.S. public opinion accepting—a decision to hand over a jurisdiction under U.S. control to an unelected authoritarian ruler."[11] Finally, the widespread belief in the "democratic peace thesis"—that democracies are less conflict prone than other political regimes and much less likely to wage wars against one another—has given further impetus to the democratic imperative, especially with the collapse of communist regimes in East Europe and the former Soviet Union, which marked the end of the Cold War.[12] Indeed, this has been the most explicitly articulated assumption of the fast-track democratization school of nation building. It has become increasingly common to hear politicians and pundits, and not just those in the Bush administration, linking autocracy and tyranny to violence and terrorism, thereby justifying the imperative of democracy promotion.

Although traditional liberal theorists, such as Immanuel Kant, cautioned against democratic states waging wars to promote democracy on the grounds that this would threaten democracy itself—instead their best defense would be to form a defensive alliance of democratic states—today's fast-track democratizers harbor few such reservations.[13] This is because international norms are changing and sovereignty is increasingly viewed as "conditional," and when the governing authorities of states fail to protect the fundamental rights of their citizens, other states (and international actors) arguably have an obligation to intervene to defend those rights.[14] But a second reason has to do with U.S. power and the fact that the preeminent characteristic of the late twentieth and early twenty-first centuries is that the United States is the foremost—and largely unchallenged—military power in the international system.[15] In using its military power to defend its national interests and assert its primacy, the United States has also found itself taking the lead in exporting and promoting democracy in fractured, failed, and ailing states.

Marina Ottaway (see chapter 33) argues that countries that have been the subject of international interventions and "forced by the international community to adopt a democratic system of government regardless of existing conditions and/or citizens' preferences" are the objects of "coercive democratization." There are two elements to this coercive exercise of power: (1) the initial military intervention that places international forces in a country or territory in order to quell civil conflict and violence and/or eliminate authoritarian rule, and (2) subsequent efforts to organize popular elections, write a new constitution, and form political parties, often in the face of stiff opposition from traditional political authorities. However, from the point of view of fast-track democratizers, the term "coercive democratization" is a bit of a misnomer because there is nothing "coercive" about a process that gives to a people the basic political freedoms and rights that they purportedly already want and seek to enjoy. In the eyes of fast-track democratizers such interventions are ultimately a liberating and not a subjugating experience, although, as will be discussed, such hopes may be misplaced.

Nation Building: Democratization through Development

Although the focus of this essay is on the relationship between military intervention and nation building, we fully acknowledge that the democratization debate plays out on a much larger canvas. A new body of scholarship, which explores the relationship between democracy and economic development, argues that not only does the successful consolidation of democracy come from civil society and mass social movements but international development assistance has a crucial role to play in promoting the development of civil society and the formation of viable political institutions, which in turn enhances the prospects for economic development.[16] Under the right conditions, societies do not have to pass through the different phases or stages of political development, including authoritarian rule, to consolidate the democratic experience. In short, poor, underdeveloped societies can be stable, peaceful, and democratic.

However, for those countries that are wracked by internal strife and conflict, the question remains, How are they to make this transition? And when the international community intervenes militarily, how can it lay the foundations for political order and ultimately democracy in the face of chaos?

Democracy Promotion and International Commitments

Fast-track democratizers are not so naive as to believe that democratization interventions cannot go awry. Although kicking in the door can spark the universal desire for freedom and liberal democracy, fast-track democratizers acknowledge that this desire has to be nurtured through economic and social reconstruction and development. They recognize that the nation-building/democratization task is a supremely challenging one that must be undertaken with care as well as extraordinary levels of political commitment. As James Dobbins and his coauthors in a widely discussed and cited RAND report on the challenges of nation building argue, as the mission of U.S. military forces has changed from war fighting to postcombat stabilization and reconstruction missions, they have found themselves ill equipped and ill trained to carry out these tasks. However, by looking to the experiences of reconstruction and democratization that were successful, beginning with the post–World War II rehabilitation of Japan and Germany, as well as those carried out by the United Nations in places such as El Salvador, Mozambique, and Namibia, Dobbins and his coauthors argue that some important operational lessons emerge that, if properly absorbed, will reduce the costs and extent of commitments of future engagements, heightening the chances of intervention success.[17]

According to the RAND report, the most important "controllable" factor that explains the success of nation-building interventions is the amount of effort that went into the task, including the number of troops that were deployed, the amount of money that was spent, and the length of the operation. Second, multilateral nation-building undertakings generally tend to produce more thorough and successful political transformations than those that are carried out on a "unilateral" basis, but such operations are typically more complex and time-consuming even though they are less costly to their individual participants. Third, the bigger the size of the stabilization force relative to the local population, the lower the level of casualties. Finally, accountability for past injustices is an important component of democratization, but it is also highly controversial and divisive and can be undertaken only if there is a real long-term commitment to the operation.

But what the RAND report does not question is the assumption that democracy is transferable and that the foundations for human rights, rule of law, and representative government can be laid anywhere. The report argues that "[w]hat distinguishes Germany, Japan, Bosnia, and Kosovo on the one hand, from Somalia, Haiti, and Afghanistan on the other, are not their levels of economic development, Western culture, or national homo-

geneity. Rather, what distinguishes these two groups is the level of effort the international community has put into their democratic transformations."[18]

Michael Ignatieff offers a similar assessment of the prospects of nation building in countries such as Afghanistan that have had no real experience with democracy. Like other fast-track democratizers, he argues that democracy is a readily exportable, and transplantable, political commodity. Nation-building-cum-democratization, therefore, can succeed as long as international intervention is properly implemented. The export of democracy, Ignatieff argues, is a neo-imperial enterprise, and thus it can succeed only if there is a long-term, sustained international commitment to the processes of social, economic, and political reconstruction. Central to this is the development of the rule of law. The risk of failure arises only when this process is poorly implemented and undertaken on the cheap—what he refers to as "nation-building lite." Comparing the situation in Afghanistan with the earlier experience of the Balkans, he argues that "[t]he failure to grasp that democracy works only when it goes hand in hand with the rule of law has been the costliest mistake in the Balkans. . . . The right strategy, at least if the Balkans is anything to go by, is to build checks and balances from the start, by helping the Afghans to rewrite the criminal and civil code and train a new generation of lawyers, prosecutors, judges and criminal investigators. Without these legal foundations, no country can make the transition from a war economy to a peace economy."[19]

SECURITY FIRSTERS

Although the fast-track democratizer assertion that "democracy is readily exportable" continues to have its champions, it also has its critics. The perceived failure of the U.S. intervention in Iraq—as well as subsequent efforts to write a new constitution and hold elections—to quell acts of terrorism and civil violence in that country has prompted many observers to question whether the nation-building exercise is fundamentally flawed, especially if the outcome of all of these efforts is nothing short of a worsening descent into anarchy and interethnic violence and warfare, which international actors appear powerless to stop. Comparing the experience in Iraq with those of other international interventions in Kosovo, Afghanistan, and East Timor, where many of the same underlying problems of social order obtain, some observers have concluded that the overriding challenge for international authorities intervening in failed states is to restore political order through the provision of fundamental security, not through the practice of democracy. For those critics, the security firsters, nation building ought to entail only a minimal commitment of resources sufficient to secure a failed state from further political violence and restore the most basic components of a viable state—its monopoly on the legitimate use of force. As Larry Diamond writes, "In postconflict situations in which the state has collapsed, security trumps everything else: it is the central pedestal that supports all else. Without some minimum level of security, people cannot engage in trade and commerce, organize to rebuild their communities, or participate meaningfully in politics. Without security, a country has nothing but disorder, distrust, desparation—an utterly Hobbesian situation in which fear and raw force dominates. This is why violence-ridden societies tend to turn to almost any political force that promises to provide order, even if it is oppressive."[20]

In cases like Iraq, where societies are deeply divided by culture, ethnicity, or religion, the problem of political order is particularly acute. Nation building means, ultimately, the creation or re-creation of a common national identity as the foundation of common national political institutions. However, in divided societies that have experienced violent conflict,

oppression, or war, narrow clan-based, tribal, ethnic, or religious identities tend to harden, destroying any broader national identity that may have existed previously and raising the barriers to creating or re-creating one in the future.[21] Even if possible, manufacturing a new national identity, or reestablishing an old one, takes generations and very often a great deal of coercive power.[22] Further, the ability to build democracy in such societies, where mistrust and insecurity are acute, is particularly illusory. Efforts to impose political institutional arrangements, such as power sharing or federalism, in the absence of a common national identity have almost always failed.[23] According to security firsters, then, the benchmark for successful nation building in such cases should be basic physical security and social order, not the establishment of political institutions, let alone a new, collective, democratic political order.

Hobbes and the Problem of Insecurity

The problem of how to maintain order in the face of social unrest that threatens—or is preceded by—the outbreak of civil war is, of course, not a new one. Indeed, when Hobbes wrote his seminal treatise *Leviathan,* he, too, dealt with the subject of how societies could prevent civil wars from occurring (or reoccurring, as the case may be). Hobbes's answer to the problem was to construct a political order in which citizens would relinquish their own personal "sovereignty" to the state, or Leviathan —in exchange for a steadfast guarantee that their own physical security and right to go about their peaceful business would not be violated. However, the bargain was also intended to be a conditional one. Individuals reserved the right to take back their sovereignty from Leviathan if their physical security was threatened or could not be guaranteed. Hence, the individual's "right to revolution" was retained and with it the ongoing risk of civil war.[24] Security firsters are essentially modern-day Hobbesians.[25] States fail when social order collapses;

when the physical security of some or all citizens cannot be guaranteed by the state, they will look to alternative providers of that security. In cases of divided societies, this often means the armed militias of their clan or tribal, ethnic, or religious affiliates. In such cases, security dilemmas are intense, as groups arm themselves in response to one another. The result is frequently civil violence, oppression, and war. The challenge of nation building, therefore, is to dampen the security dilemma by providing security directly through military intervention, or encouraging national elites to provide it themselves through the provision of strategic military and political assistance.

Taming the Security Dilemma: International Security Guarantees

Adherents to the security first school argue that internationally provided security guarantees are critical to taming the security dilemma that often characterizes ethnically or religiously divided failed states.[26] In such deeply divided societies groups fundamentally mistrust one another and are therefore unwilling to sacrifice their ability to provide for their own physical security by disarming and demobilizing militias—a fundamental requirement of political order and national sovereignty. Thus, even if groups might desire peace and order, they are compelled to resist compromises required to create it; political order cannot be achieved through democracy, since this would give other groups a potential veto over one's own survival, politically or physically. Instability and violence continue. However, groups may be willing to demobilize, disarm, and even work together under a power-sharing arrangement if sufficient security can be provided by an outside power. These external security guarantees must contain two crucial elements: (1) they must be offered on sustainable terms by the intervening power or international authority in order to attenuate if not entirely eliminate the security dilemma, especially in those situations where interethnic suspicions and rivalries run

deep, and (2) they must be offered in a way that allows local authorities to secure their borders and control their own territory.

There is ample empirical evidence to support the assertion that security is the sine qua non of nation building. In a major study of what international actors can do to make parties in civil wars live up to their negotiated commitments, which often include a commitment to participate in elections and a democratic political process, Barbara Walter argues that third-party security guarantees, which protect different groups and ensure that promises are kept, are a key variable that explains the success of such undertakings. Walter distinguishes between "weak," "moderate," and "strong" security guarantees. Whereas weak guarantees involve only a political commitment to do something if the peace process breaks down, and moderate guarantees involve very modest troop deployments, strong guarantees typically consist of many thousands of troops who can provide an "unambiguous and indisputable demonstration of intent."[27]

Stephen Stedman also argues that the security situation in conflict and postconflict situations in failed states requires effective strategies of spoiler management—that is to say, strategies that deal with those extremist elements or groups in a conflict who have been radicalized, use violence to pursue their aims, are not interested in political compromise, and will, in fact, do anything to subvert the political process. Stedman argues that coercive strategies are generally required to deal with the "total spoiler" who sees the world in "all-or-nothing terms." This involves measures that root out and destroy the spoiler and his bases of political support, including the direct application of the use of force, targeted sanctions, and other kinds of penalties that raise the costs of noncooperation and noncompliance.[28]

Kimberly Marten (see chapter 34) likewise argues that effective security management is the paramount consideration in nation-building undertakings. Comparing recent peacekeeping and peace enforcement operations with those of occupying imperial powers in the colonial era, she argues that not only must "robust peace operations [be] designed to provide security for the affected populations," but "only when people's security is assured is it possible for them to invest in the future." And she also opines that "[i]t is a sense of security that brings real ownership to peace processes, *not political change that is forced from the outside* (emphasis added)."[29]

Challenges to Security Provision

Many security firsters point to at least three crucial issues of statecraft that arise in making security the paramount goal of nation building and the key to intervention "success." The first and most pressing issue is one that bedevils all peacekeeping and peace enforcement operations: to ensure that the intervening power or coalition has the political will, capacity, and staying power to see the job through, especially when confronted with mounting troop casualties and a worsening political and security situation. All democracies, weak or powerful, have shown that their publics have a limited appetite for prolonged military engagements abroad.

The second and related challenge is the ability and willingness of international actors to carry out the kinds of operations that are needed to bring security to lawless and conflict-ridden states. Nation builders are frequently presented with a dilemma, highlighted by the experience of the U.S.-led intervention in Iraq: Should an occupying power dismantle a country's existing security institutions that have a proven and demonstrated capacity to maintain social order but have maintained that order through illiberal methods? Or should they dismantle those institutions because of their illiberal practices and provide security until new institutions can be built? As Hobbesian logic dictates, and the Iraq case confirms, dismantling or destroying those institutions will generate a real security vacuum that is filled by violent criminal gangs and, eventually, insurgents. Further, this then thrusts the security burden on the shoulders of an occupying army that may be ill equipped or unwilling to carry out the kinds of policing duties that are required to maintain social order. As Simon Chesterman observes, "in many situations only the military is in a position to exercise comparable functions" to maintain local law and order.[30] On the other hand, leaving those institutions in place may guarantee social order, but at the expense of rule of law, domestic political legitimacy, and long-term democratic development.

This raises the third critical issue: avoiding a "Band-Aid" solution to the problem of insecurity in weak states. To focus on relatively short-term security and social order at the expense of long-term political development runs the risk of creating perpetually unstable states that may necessitate further intervention down the road. Fast-track democratizers, for example, would charge that neglecting democratic political development makes illusory any short-term security gains. As Francis Fukuyama argues, one of the mistakes of nation building is "to build a coercive state without the rules and norms needed to restrain it"—a consequence of an "outside power [who] gets tired of the project before it is complete."[31]

Order versus Democracy

Indeed, security firsters, in contrast to fast-track democratizers, generally tend to sidestep the question of what kinds of longer-term political arrangements will guarantee political order and authority in war-torn societies and failed states.[32] But because they measure nation-building success in terms of social order and security, they tolerate, and may even prefer, authoritarian regimes that impose strict limits on political participation in order to guarantee political order. In his classic study *Political Order and Changing Societies,* Samuel Huntington argues that military rule is necessary to control and restrict political participation, at least in the short run, for societies that are experiencing the rapid and extremely destabilizing consequences of modernization.[33] Some scholars have also argued that in special circumstances the military can be a positive force for the modernization and economic and political development of a country,[34] although this proposition is disputed by Eric Nordlinger and more recent studies that argue that "not only can poor countries democratize, poor democracies can develop quite effectively."[35] Like Hobbes, however, security firsters believe that political order is paramount and that social and political rights may have to be compromised, if only temporarily, in those societies making the tumultuous transition to modernity.

Other security firsters posit that political order, especially in ethnically divided societies or societies that are fractured along religious or cultural lines, can ultimately be secured only if state boundaries are redrawn in ways that formally acknowledge the national self-determination aspirations of different communities.[36] These arguments, though, have a Hobbesian cast because they are motivated almost exclusively by concerns about curtailing interethnic security dilemmas and ending political violence as opposed to traditional liberal or Wilsonian sensibilities about the need to respect communal rights and advance the principles of national-self determination.

SLOW DEMOCRATIZERS

Confronted with the obvious challenges of nation building in the modern world, some scholars argue that a much more measured and discriminatory approach has to be taken in exporting democracy to those cultures and societies where there is no previous tradition of liberal democracy. Slow democratizers share the fast trackers' belief in the salience of democracy in the nation-building process and their assumption about the link between illiberal and undemocratic states and political vio-

lence, war, and terrorism. Where they differ is over the means by which democracy can be created, the extent of international commitment and resources required to do so, and the ultimate measure of nation-building success. Slow democratizers reject the view that democracy is the sole endgame of nation building, or that nation building simply requires "liberating" oppressed populations from tyrannical rule and holding elections in order for democracy to flourish. On this they share the security firsters' skepticism that democracy can be readily exported. Democratization is a process of cultural, social, and political development that does not simply revolve around the exercise of the franchise and the holding of free elections. It also involves the establishment of a civic culture where citizens learn to become active and intelligent participants in society and the political life of their country. This process takes a great deal of time and the right local historical and political conditions.

Most critically, democracy can develop only in a society with a strong, well-functioning administrative state apparatus that is responsive to the needs and welfare of the general public. The provision of essential services and "public goods" is a critical element of "good governance," as is a proper understanding of the requirements for governance at both the national and local levels. Ultimately, for slow democratizers, the measure of successful nation building is the creation of a viable, functioning administrative state apparatus and not necessarily democracy itself. As Diamond asserts, "a country must first have a state before it can become a democracy."[37]

This much more qualified endorsement of the nation-building enterprise is also reflected in the writings of scholars like Simon Chesterman, Fareed Zakaria, Francis Fukuyama, Marina Ottaway, Roland Paris, Stephen Krasner, and students of comparative democratic political processes. Although their degree of skepticism, political assessments, and policy prescriptions differ in important ways, they all share in some measure the classical assumptions of traditional liberal utilitarianism about the social and cultural requirements for democracy and effective representative government, especially those of John Stuart Mill.

John Stuart Mill and the Logic of Slow Democratization

Like other utilitarian writers such as Jeremy Bentham and James Mill, John Stuart Mill believed that democracy is the best form of government because it allows individuals to pursue their self-interests and maximize their own personal happiness or welfare.[38] It was not so much the tyranny of authoritarian rule that worried Mill—what he called the "tyranny of the magistrate"—but the tyranny of majoritarian rule and "the tendency of society to impose, by other means than civil penalties, its own ideas and practices and rule of conduct on those who dissent from them." According to Mill, the unleashing of majoritarian rule in societies where there is no tradition of democracy —as in the extreme case of France under Jacobin rule—poses just as much a threat to personal liberty as authoritarian rule.[39] Of course, Mill is not alone in expressing this concern. Tocqueville expressed similar reservations about majoritarian rule, as did Alexander Hamilton, James Madison, and John Jay in *The Federalist Papers* (especially Number 10).[40] Nevertheless, Mill's essay *On Liberty* is considered to be the classic statement on the need for limited government, checks on majoritarian rule, and the educational and social underpinnings of democracy.

In stressing the importance of individuality and the exercise of personal freedom, Mill argued that there have to be political and legal guarantees for minority opinion and culture so that they are not trampled by the will of the majority. Mill was also one of the first writers to champion federalism as a form of government that would protect minority rights, especially in the British colony of Canada after the rebellion of the French minority in 1837. He

and other utilitarian philosophers also stressed the importance of professionalism in the administration of government through the development of a career-based public service that was immune to privilege and political pressure and would promote the general welfare of the citizenry.

Like Mill, many of today's critics of fast-track democratization believe that the social contract and automatic or sudden flowering of democracy are a myth. They also believe that efforts to transfer democracy to societies and cultures that have no real history or experience with it are doomed to failure and will unleash tyranny or mob rule where elites manipulate and exploit popular prejudices for their own selfish ends—what Zakaria has referred to as "illiberal democracy."[41] The consequences of illiberal democracy, according to some scholars, are grave. In the words of Edward Mansfield and Jack Snyder, "Without a coherent state grounded in a consensus on which citizens will exercise self-determination, unfettered electoral politics often gives rise to nationalism and violence at home and abroad. Absent these preconditions, democracy is deformed, and transitions toward democracy revert to autocracy or generate chaos. Pushing countries too soon into competitive electoral politics not only risks stoking war, sectarianism and terrorism, but it also makes the future consolidation of democracy more difficult."[42]

Nation Building and Democratic Development: Historical Conditions versus Foreign Commitments

Fukuyama's book *State-Building: Governance and World Order in the Twenty-first Century* offers a trenchant criticism of the modern nation-building enterprise in failed states. He argues that nation-building efforts in Afghanistan and Iraq have failed to recognize the real challenges of building from scratch new states that do not have viable political institutions and have had no real experience with democracy. Like Mill, Fukuyama believes that culture and history must be properly reckoned in state-building efforts because democracy is not readily transported to alien cultures. For fast-track democratizers, for example, nation-building success—that is, democratic political development—turns exclusively on the right kinds and proportions of foreign commitments. But for slow democratizers, like Fukuyama, the domestic conditions for democracy to develop are vastly more important.[43] The experience of Japan and Germany after World War II serves as a case in point. They are often held up by fast-track democratizers as cases of nation-building success that vindicate their model: with a sufficient "level of effort—measured in time, manpower, and money" —democracy can be readily established.[44] But Fukuyama argues that this is a misreading of the case. International commitments may have been necessary, but they were hardly sufficient to explain successful democratization. Far more significant was the extensive and highly competent administrative bureaucracy that was left virtually intact in both countries after the war. Administrative purges were much more limited than popularly believed.[45] The importance of the institutional preconditions for democracy relative to external commitments is starkly revealed when comparing those classic cases to recent nation-building interventions in places such as Bosnia and Kosovo. The resources committed to those two stalled nation-building efforts vastly outstrip those spent on the much more successful earlier projects.[46] By the end of the 1990s, per capita foreign aid to Bosnia alone was four times greater than aid to postwar Europe under the Marshall Plan.[47]

Nonetheless, resource commitments remain critically important to the slow democratization model of nation building. In the absence of existing state institutions, massive resource commitments are required to manufacture them. Like security firsters, slow democratizers place great emphasis on the historical and institutional environment that states find themselves in. But unlike their fellow critics of the fast-track school, slow democratizers do not see such factors as immutable and war-torn and divided societies as incapable of democratic development. Democracy *can* be created; it just requires patience, careful sequencing, and massive resource commitments.

State Building and Local-Capacity Building

The way in which state building is carried out is also a critical component of the slow democratization approach. According to Fukuyama, while some state-building functions may be more successful if they are carried out at the national level, most will have greater success if they rely on local capacities and political authority; it is important to strike the right balance in allocating political and administrative responsibilities between national and local authorities. But again, the determining factor will be the extent of local variation of each activity and a proper understanding of how those functions can be adapted successfully to local conditions. There is a substantial and growing body of scholarship on the appropriate requirements for constitutional and political institutional design that protect minority rights in multiethnic societies that are struggling toward democracy.[48] Many of these scholars also stress the importance of engaging local participants and adapting to local social and cultural norms in developing new institutions. As Diamond instructs, "ultimately the intervention cannot succeed—and the institutions it establishes cannot be viable—unless there is some sense of participation and ownership on the part of the people in the state being reconstructed."[49] Furthermore, as Ottaway (see chapter 33) points out, the citizenry has to be readied for democracy through training and development programs for civil society organizations and the media, and programs that strengthen the independence of key institutions such as the judiciary and parliament so that democracy is meaningful and the citizens can choose their government and influence its policies. International assistance has a key role to play in these functions.

Liberal Development and State Building: The Need for an "Akbar or Charlemagne"

Because slow democratizers measure the success of nation building in terms of the creation of viable state institutions, they are willing, like the security firsters, to trade stability and order for democratic freedoms, if only temporarily. It is a view that is consistent with Mill. Questioning the traditional liberal myth about the origins of the "social contract," Mill believed that democracy and representative government could take many different forms and would necessarily vary according to historical circumstance and culture. He also believed that not all societies are ready for democracy, because the democratic experience presupposes high levels of education, social awareness, and responsibility in the citizenry. In societies where these elements are lacking, people have to be readied for their civic duties and the democratic experience. Accordingly, Mill believed that "[d]espotism is a legitimate mode of government . . . provided the end be their improvement, and the means justified by actually effecting that end. Liberty, as a principle, has not application to any state of things anterior to the time when mankind have become capable of being improved by free and equal discussion. Until then, there is nothing for them but implicit obedience to an Akbar or a Charlemagne, if they are so fortunate as to find one."[50]

Like Mill, Fukuyama concedes that the modern-day functional equivalent of an Akbar or Charlemagne may be necessary to build up state institutions and capacity before democracy can be introduced. As Fukuyama succinctly states: "Before you have democracy you have to have government. Period. You have to have a functioning state that can, first of all, provide security and economic basics. It can be authoritarian and still develop. Most of East Asia has done well under authoritarian

governance. It is only over the longer term as a society grows more prosperous and there are greater social demands for participation that not having democracy becomes problematic from a development standpoint."[51]

But this model may not travel well to other regions, especially those that are poor. In the case of the Middle East, as Daniel Brumberg argues, "liberalized" autocracies, such as Egypt, Jordan, and Morocco, "depend on weak political parties and impotent legislatures," which have made it difficult to move toward genuine democracy.[52] Liberalized reforms have also tended to reinforce "Islamic power," and the resulting ideological confusion and growing civil strife have produced democratic transitions that lead "nowhere."

Like security firsters, then, slow democratizers are willing to tolerate authoritarian rule—or what Chesterman calls "benign autocracy"—but only as a means to an end.[53] Whereas security firsters stress the primacy of security and reestablishing law and order over long-term political development, slow democratizers will support autocracy as long as it effectively builds the state's organizational and public administrative capacities, provides key services, and meets the basic needs of the populace, thereby laying the foundation for eventual democratic development. For example, in his book *At War's End: Building Peace after Civil Conflict,* Paris has called for "institutionalization before liberalization" in states recovering from civil war: curtail economic liberalization and political freedoms in the short term, "in order to create conditions for a smoother and less hazardous transition to market democracy—and durable peace—in the long run."[54] Many peacebuilding/nation-building interventions have gone awry, he argues, because free elections, market reforms, and democracy were introduced far too early in societies that were ill equipped to make the transition from a war-torn state to democracy. "What is needed in the immediate postconflict period," he argues, "is not democratic ferment and economic upheaval, but political stability and the establishment of effective administration over the territory. Only when a working government authority has been re-established should peacebuilders initiate a series of gradual democratic and market-oriented reforms." Among his recommendations for a "smooth transition," Paris suggests delaying elections, designing electoral systems that "reward moderation," "promoting good civil society," controlling "hate speech," adopting "conflict-reducing economic policies," and rebuilding "effective state institutions."[55]

Jack Snyder and Karen Ballentine have similarly argued that the free and unfettered public debate that characterizes healthy political discourse in advanced democracies is a source of extreme volatility in multiethnic, war-torn fragile states.[56] Democratic freedom of expression is readily exploited by nationalist extremists, fueling communal conflict and violence and undermining long-term stability and liberalization. Like Paris, they call for a carefully sequenced approach to nation building: "Major efforts should be made to promote the institutionalization of norms of effective elite discourse, journalistic professionalism, and independent evaluative bodies, *before* the full opening of mass political participation. Whenever possible, market imperfections should be counteracted by decentralized institutions, not central regulatory directives, and by the promotion of norms of fair debate, not by restrictions on the content of speech. In some cases, however, certain kinds of restraints on speech may be necessary in multi-ethnic societies while these institutions are being built."[57]

International Trusteeships and Political Order

In cases of extreme state failure and collapse, where there is virtually no local administrative state capacity to speak of, slow democratizers argue that the required Akbar or Charlemagne may have to come in the form of an international authority who can build such capacity from scratch. Krasner, James Fearon and David Laitin, Paris, and others have argued that some form of international control over failed states is needed for nation building to succeed. Krasner has argued that the development of well-functioning polities and the promotion of democratic governance in failed or failing states may require short-term remedial actions to pool or share sovereignty where special administration and/or political entities are created with the joint consent of national political authorities and international actors or authorities. Successfully executed "shared sovereignty" arrangements will not only "provide security, social services, and opportunities for economically remunerative work"[58] but will also greatly enhance the prospects for building genuine democracy in the long run. More specifically, Paris has called for "a kind of temporary tutelary directorship" to "rebuild the governmental institutions of war-shattered states from scratch and, at least initially, exert direct control over these new institutions by staffing them primarily with foreign officials."[59] In cases of deeply divided societies emerging from war, Philip Roeder and Donald Rothchild call for a "Nation-State Stewardship" strategy: "If there is no victor in the domestic conflict and power sharing is the only governmental institution to which parties will agree, it is typically better for international stewards to rule directly (and possibly autocratically) for the interim."[60]

While there may be little choice but international trusteeship in the case of failed states, slow democratizers recognize that there is a serious dilemma with such an approach. As Fukuyama explains, "Outsiders are driven to supply sovereign-state functions because of the internal weakness of the countries in question. But stateness that is provided by outsiders often undermines the ability of domestic actors to create their own robust institutions. Too much state-building on the part of outsiders builds long-term dependence, and may ultimately come to seem illegitimate to the locals."[61] The response to this dilemma, however, generates another one. As Fearon and

Table 1. Approaches to Nation Building

Nation-Building School	Intervenor's Role	Supreme Value	Conditions for Success	Process Orientation
Fast-Track Democratization	Catalytic and transformative	Democracy and liberty	Supportive public opinion with the overthrow of authoritarian regime	Ends focused
Slow Democratization	Partial and instrumental	Liberty and security	State capacity and economic development, along with development of strong civil society institutions and supportive democratic political culture	Means focused
Security First	Limited to security assistance and stabilization	Security	Strong state security institutions	Preconditions focused

Laitin argue, "The more you invest in developing local capacities for self-government, the greater the risk that the external patron will ramp down its mission and leave, and the greater the number of potential local rivals empowered by the new security apparatus. Thus there can be a disincentive to actively or successfully develop indigenous state capabilities, leading to what President Bush's former special envoy to Afghanistan [and current ambassador to Iraq], Zalmay Khalilzad, has called 'security welfare states.'"[62]

ASSESSING THE DEBATE

As we have argued, today's nation-building debate has very old roots. It is a debate that has engaged political theorists from the seventeenth century onward and it is one that goes to the very heart of our understanding about the requirements for political order and democracy and the trade-offs that must be addressed in pursuing these two different goals. Whereas fast-track democratizers place their faith in the popular sovereign will and the enormous appetite for democracy that they believe

citizens everywhere share, security firsters and slow democratizers are much more skeptical about the prospects for democratic development in societies that have no experience with democracy and whose citizens are battle weary but not necessarily tutored in the norms, values, and beliefs of a liberal civic society. (For a summary of these different schools, see table 1.)

Each school draws different implications from its basic assumptions about the nature and character of democracy for international interventions in failing, fragile, or war-torn states. Fast-track democratizers believe that properly executed and timed international interventions can jump-start the democratic motor of a society. Such interventions need not be prolonged or unduly burdensome to the intervening authorities if they are done well. This is because the democratic impulse is so powerful—following the lines of traditional liberalism—that ultimately democracy will prevail. The policy challenge is to ensure that the right mix of military and political pressure, as well as appropriate inducements, is brought to bear on a society so the full potential of democracy is unleashed. Both security firsters and slow democratizers reject that view. Security firsters argue that fast-track democratizers underestimate the powerful effects of the security dilemma in war-torn states, which undermines social cohesion and thwarts the possibilities for any kind of meaningful or sustainable democratic political order. If not altogether eschewing democracy as a goal of nation building, security firsters stress the importance of managing the security dilemma through the interposition of military forces while looking to various state security–building measures in the long run. These measures include prolonged security guarantees and military assistance, support for authoritarian rule if that is the best way to quell violence and social unrest, and/or the formal partition of a territory. Slow democratizers are slightly more sanguine about democracy's prospects, suggesting a third way to go about nation building that involves adapting liberal institutions to local social and cultural conditions and developing transitional governance arrangements that promote democracy gradually. Slow democratizers also stress the importance of building and strengthening state institutions so that they can properly handle the stresses and strains of political mobilization that go with full-blown democracy.

There is something to be said for the fast trackers' belief in the inescapable power of the democratic imperative. As the high turnout levels in generally free and fair elections in war-torn Afghanistan and Iraq have shown, people will embrace democratic processes with enthusiasm, even under the most difficult and challenging circumstances. Those who doubt the democratic imperative need look no further than these two cases. But, as critics correctly point out, snap elections and hastily negotiated constitutions will not create democracy. Nor will they quell ongoing social unrest, terrorism, and violence as these and other cases sadly attest; in fact, they may very well contribute to those problems. In fledgling democracies the latent potential for violence and a rapid spiral downward into anarchy is enormous.

"Freedom" does not organically transform itself into a liberal democratic order.

Security firsters are obviously right to stress the importance of getting the security situation under control and to do it in ways that strengthen the security capacities of state institutions. But the objective of security firsters is to establish any form of political order that will stop the slide into chaos and violence. To paraphrase Marten, the job is to provide security while letting politics "sort themselves out."[63] Stopping the killing is an important and necessary task, but it is incomplete, especially when the sources of unrest and violence are rooted in particular forms of political order. Democracy may not be a panacea, but there is reason to believe that it provides the best chance for long-term stability and prosperity. Security firsters obviously pay insufficient attention to the longer-term challenge of securing the transition from political order to democracy.

It is only the slow democratizers who, like utilitarian liberal theorists, have pointed out the dilemmas of how to secure democracy even if it means making some short-term compromises.

Although we share the concerns of slow democratizers about the need to move carefully after the guns have fallen silent in promoting democratization, other qualifications must be added to their already cautious assessment of the conditions for democratic development. First, arguments about the need to strengthen civil society and promote democracy through a better-educated and -trained citizenry must also grapple with the question, Who has the legitimacy and capacity to do these things? International legitimacy, capacity, and political will do not necessarily go hand in hand. Some actors have legitimacy, but they may not have the requisite capacity or clout to do the job effectively or well. This is often the problem with small NGOs or small states that are involved in the democracy promotion and development business. On the other hand, powerful international actors, such as the United States government, may well have the capacity to get the job done, but because of how they are viewed by local actors they may not have the legitimacy or political authority to effectively assist with the democratization enterprise. Second, slow democratizers are insufficiently attuned to the realities of the electoral cycle in the intervening state(s), which frequently imposes unrealistic deadlines for getting things done, including the timing of elections in failed states. Even when politicians are all too aware of the importance of delaying elections and buying time so political parties can form and the local population can be readied for their civic obligations, they may not be able to set back the clock because they are hostage to their own domestic political pressures. Given these constraints, a measured and more leisurely approach to elections and the democratization process may not be viable. The real question then becomes how to manage and steer political processes to minimize political risk within these constraints, something that is not at all easy to do.

Finally, it is important to recognize the real and identifiable limits to developing various kinds of "shared sovereignty" arrangements no matter how sensible or appealing they may appear to be at first blush. Slow democratizers are willing to accept long periods of international trusteeship over failed states until a functioning, relatively autonomous democratic state can be built. However, as experience shows, the likely success of such imperial projects is exceptionally low. As Fearon and Laitin demonstrate, there are considerable obstacles to managing effective trusteeships, including burden sharing and coordination problems, ambiguity surrounding the accountability of trustees, and the challenges of transitioning back to sovereign, autonomous states.[64] In addition, there is the nagging problem of legitimacy: as security firsters point out, neotrusteeships are a form of quasi-imperial control; nation builders are foreign occupiers, and the power of nationalism is such that occupations tend initially to be tolerated, then gradually resented, and

eventually actively resisted. And then there is the obvious problem of capacity: there is only so much traffic that the international system can bear in establishing new international trusteeships—no matter how pressing the need. When great powers, such as the United States, are already overstretched in terms of their international commitments, it is not at all clear who else will assume responsibility for these operations or pick up the slack. Given the obvious difficulties—strategic as well as operational—of trusteeships, the challenge for theory and for public policy is to marry democratization with security in more effective ways by getting the sequence right and tailoring strategic goals to the actual context of the situation.[65]

A clear understanding of the democratization challenge should also pay greater heed to the utilitarian calculus of looking to the long-term consequences of interventions in failed states as well as for the intervenors themselves. If a rapid escalation of nation-building tasks is ultimately unsustainable because the local environment is simply too unstable and there is precious little public support or political will to advance in the face of adversity, then a more prudent course of action may be to avoid such interventions altogether until the requisite levels of international support, legitimacy, and political commitment can be found. If, owing to humanitarian catastrophe, the imperative to intervene is strong in the absence of such a commitment, then it may mean adopting the security first position—intervene to save lives and provide basic security, and explicitly avoid any "democratizing" ambitions. If the nation-building debate shows us anything, it is that the international community can succeed at ending wars and stopping killing; it is less effective, however, at the long-term institution building that will make states viable and peace self-sustaining. However, this presents an equally challenging dilemma. One reason why the security-first—only security matters—approach is problematic is that leaders of democratic states that sanction or participate in international interventions cannot remain indifferent to long-term political outcomes and the quality of local governance. This is because liberal democratic norms are firmly entrenched in today's world and the publics in those democratic states that are doing the intervening will not look favorably on costly military adventures that fail to produce democratic outcomes, even if those interventions could save lives. One need only look at the popular reaction to the initial U.S. intervention in Somalia in the early 1990s: by some estimates it saved hundreds of thousands of lives, yet it is widely considered a "failure."[66] Creating democratic states out of whole cloth is exceptionally costly, time-consuming, and very likely to fail. It is imperative, therefore, to minimize public expectations about the democratizing effects of nation-building interventions even though it may be terribly difficult to do.

NOTES

We are grateful for comments provided on an earlier draft of this paper by Pamela Aall, Chester Crocker, Kimberly Marten, Marina Ottaway, Dennis Sandole, and Jack Snyder.

1. Thomas Hobbes, *Leviathan*, ed. C. B. MacPherson (Hammondsworth, U.K.: Penguin Books, 1968).

2. John Stuart Mill, "On Liberty," in *The English Philosophers from Bacon to Mill*, ed. Edwin A. Burt (New York: Modern Library, 1939), 1011.

3. Unlike Locke, Rousseau was not a champion of the virtues of representative government: "Sovereignty," he states, "cannot be represented, for the same reason that it cannot be alienated; its essence is the general will, and will cannot be represented—either it is the general will or it is something else; there is no intermediate possibility." John Locke, *The Second Treatise of Government* (Indianapolis: Bobbs-Merrill, 1952); Thomas Jefferson, The Declaration of Independence of the United States, July 4, 1776; and Jean-Jacques Rousseau, *The Social Contract*, trans. Maurice Cranston (Hammondsworth, U.K.: Penguin Books, 1968), 141.

4. Locke, *The Second Treatise of Government*, 5.

5. As the Declaration of Independence of the United States, which was drafted by Thomas Jefferson, states: "We hold these truths to be self-evident, that all men are created equal, that they are endowed by their Creator with certain inalienable Rights, that among these are Life, Liberty and the pursuit of Happiness." Note that Locke's "health" and "possessions" are substituted by "Happiness."

6. See, for example, Robert Endicott Osgoode, *Ideals and Self-Interest in America's Foreign Relations* (Chicago: University of Chicago Press, 1974); and Roland Paris, "Wilson's Ghost: The Faulty Assumptions of Postconflict Peacebuilding," in *Turbulent Peace: The Challenges of Managing International Conflict*, ed. Chester A. Crocker, Fen Osler Hampson, and Pamela Aall (Washington, D.C.: United States Institute of Peace Press, 2001), 765–781.

7. Edmund Burke, *Reflections on the Revolution in France* (London: Penguin Books, 1978); Alexis de Tocqueville, *Democracy in America* (New York: Doubleday, 1969); and Mill, "On Liberty."

8. George W. Bush, *The National Security Strategy of the United States of America* (Washington, D.C.: White House, 2002), 31, http://www.whitehouse.gov/nsc/nss.html.

9. See, for example, Larry Diamond, "What Went Wrong and Right in Iraq," and Johanna Mendelson Forman, "Striking Out in Baghdad: How Postconflict Reconstruction Went Awry," in *Nation-Building: Beyond Afghanistan and Iraq* (Baltimore: Johns Hopkins University Press, 2006), 173–195, 196–217.

10. Boutros Boutros-Ghali, *An Agenda for Peace: Preventive Diplomacy, Peacemaking, and Peacekeeping* (New York: United Nations, 1992).

11. Marc F. Plattner, "Building Democracy after Conflict," *Journal of Democracy* 16, no. 1 (2005): 7–8.

12. Bruce Russett, *Grasping the Democratic Peace: Principles for a Post–Cold War World* (Princeton, N.J.: Princeton University Press, 1993).

13. Immanuel Kant, *Political Writings*, trans. H. B. Nisbet (Cambridge: Cambridge University Press, 1992). See also F. H. Hinsley, *Power and the Pursuit of Peace* (Cambridge: Cambridge University Press, 1963), 62–80.

14. International Commission on Intervention and State Sovereignty, *The Responsibility to Protect* (Ottawa: International Development Research Centre,

2001); and Ivo Daalder and James Steinberg, "Preventive War, a Useful Tool," *Los Angeles Times*, December 4, 2005, M3.

15. Michael Mandelbaum, *The Case for Goliath: How America Acts as the World's Government in the 21st Century* (New York: Public Affairs, 2005); and William C. Wohlforth, "The Stability of a Unipolar World," *International Security* 24, no. 1 (1999): 5–41.

16. Morton Halperin, Joseph T. Siegle, and Michael M. Weinstein, *The Democratic Advantage: How Democracies Promote Prosperity and Peace* (New York: Routledge, 2005).

17. James Dobbins et al., *America's Role in Nation-Building: From Germany to Iraq* (Santa Monica, Calif.: RAND Corporation, 2003).

18. Ibid., 161.

19. Michael Ignatieff, "Nation-Building Lite," *New York Times Magazine*, July 28, 2002, 26–31ff.

20. Larry Diamond, "What Went Wrong in Iraq," *Foreign Affairs* 83 (2004): 37.

21. Chaim D. Kaufmann, "Possible and Impossible Solutions to Ethnic Civil War," *International Security* 20, no. 4 (1996): 136–175; and Kaufmann, "When All Else Fails: Evaluating Population Transfers and Partition as Solutions to Ethnic Conflict," in *Civil Wars, Insecurity and Intervention*, ed. Barbara F. Walter and Jack Snyder (New York: Columbia University, 1999), 221–249; and Alexander B. Downes, "The Problem with Negotiated Settlements to Ethnic Civil Wars," *Security Studies* 13, no. 4 (2004): 230–279.

22. Daniel L. Byman, *Keeping the Peace: Lasting Solutions to Ethnic Conflicts* (Baltimore: Johns Hopkins University Press, 2002), 100–124.

23. On the failure of power sharing in divided societies to effectively build democracy, see Philip G. Roeder and Donald Rothchild, "Power Sharing as an Impediment to Peace and Democracy," in *Sustaining Peace: Powers and Democracy after Civil Wars*, ed. Philip G. Roeder and Donald Rothchild (Ithaca, N.Y.: Cornell University Press, 2005), 29–50. On the failure of internationally imposed federal systems in multiethnic states, see Nancy Bermeo, "The Import of Institutions," *Journal of Democracy* 13, no. 2 (2002): 96–110.

24. As Hobbes states, "The Obligation of Subjects to the Sovereign, is understood to last as long, and no longer, than the power lasteth, by which he is able to protect them. For the right men have by Nature to protect themselves, when none else can pro-

tect them, can by no covenant be relinquished. The Sovereignty is the Soule of the Commonwealth; which once departed from the Body, the members doe no more receive their motion from it." See Hobbes, *Leviathan*, chap. 21, par. 114, 272.

25. Some, like Kimberly Marten, are explicit about this. She writes, "What I mean by security is what . . . Hobbes meant when he talked about the role of the state, the so-called leviathan, in holding anarchy at bay." Kimberly Marten, *Enforcing the Peace: Learning from the Imperial Past* (New York: Columbia University Press, 2004), 157.

26. Barbara F. Walter, "The Critical Barrier to Civil War Settlement," *International Organization* 51, no. 3 (1997): 335–363; Walter, "Designing Transitions from Civil War: Demobilization, Democratization, and Commitments to Peace," *International Security* 24, no. 1 (1999): 127–155; and Walter, *Committing to Peace: The Successful Settlement of Civil Wars* (Princeton, N.J.: Princeton University Press, 2002).

27. Walter, "The Critical Barrier to Civil War Settlement," 374. See also Walter, *Committing to Peace*.

28. Stephen J. Stedman, "Spoiler Problems in Peace Processes," *International Security* 22, no. 2 (Fall 1997): 5–53.

29. See also Marten, *Enforcing the Peace*.

30. Simon Chesterman, *You the People: The United Nations, Transitional Administration, and State-Building* (New York: Oxford University Press, 2004), 123.

31. Francis Fukuyama, "'Stateness' First," *Journal of Democracy* 16, no. 1 (2005): 87–88.

32. An exception to this is Terrence Lyons, *Demilitarizing Politics: Elections on the Uncertain Road to Peace* (Boulder, Colo.: Lynne Rienner, 2005). Lyons argues that elections, if properly carried out, can help "demilitarize" the political environment by putting a country back on the road to peace.

33. Samuel P. Huntington, *Political Order and Changing Societies* (New Haven, Conn.: Yale University Press, 1968).

34. Morris Janowitz, *The Military in the Political Development of New Nations* (Chicago: University of Chicago Press, 1964); and W. Howard Wriggins, *The Ruler's Imperatives* (New York: Columbia University Press, 1969).

35. Eric A. Nordlinger, "Soldiers in Mufti: The Impact of Military Rule on Economic and Social Change in Non-Western States," *American Political*

Science Review 64, no. 4 (1970): 1131–1148; Nordlinger, *Soldiers in Politics* (Englewood Cliffs, N.J.: Prentice-Hall, 1977); and Halperin, Siegle, and Weinstein, *The Democratic Advantage*, 10.

36. See Kaufmann, "Possible and Impossible Solutions to Ethnic Civil War" and "When All Else Fails"; Charles A. Kupchan, "Independence for Kosovo," *Foreign Affairs* 84, no. 6 (2005): 14–21; Downes, "The Problem with Negotiated Settlements to Ethnic Civil Wars"; and Roeder and Rothchild, "Conclusions: Nation-State Stewardship and the Alternatives to Power Sharing," in *Sustainable Peace: Powers and Democracy after Civil War* (Ithaca, N.Y.: Cornell University Press, 2005), 337–338.

37. Diamond, "What Went Wrong in Iraq," 38.

38. Jeremy Bentham, "An Introduction to the Principles of Moral and Legislation," in *The English Philosophers from Bacon to Mill*, ed. Edwin A. Burt (New York: Modern Library, 1939), 791–856; and James Mill, "Government," in *The English Philosophers from Bacon to Mill*, ed. Edwin A. Burt (New York: Modern Library, 1939), 857–894. See also Dennis F. Thompson, *John Stuart Mill and Representative Government* (Princeton, N.J.: Princeton University Press, 1976).

39. Mill, "On Liberty," 952.

40. Alexander Hamilton, James Madison, and John Jay, *The Federalist Papers* (New York: Times Mirror, 1961), 77–84.

41. Fareed Zakaria, *The Future of Freedom: Illiberal Democracy at Home and Abroad* (New York: W. W. Norton, 2003).

42. Edward D. Mansfield and Jack Snyder, "Prone to Violence," *National Interest* 82 (Winter 2005–6), http://www.nationalinterest.org.

43. Francis Fukuyama, *State-Building: Governance and World Order in the Twenty-first Century* (Ithaca, N.Y.: Cornell University Press, 2004).

44. Dobbins et al., *America's Role in Nation-Building*, 165.

45. Fukuyama, *State-Building*, 38–39.

46. Justin Logan and Christopher Preble, "Failed States and Flawed Logic: The Case against a Standing Nation-Building Office," *Policy Analysis*, no. 560 (2006): 16, http://www.cato.org/pubs/pas/pa560/pdf.

47. Roeder and Rothchild, "Conclusions," 333.

48. Andrew Reynolds, ed., *The Architecture of Democracy: Constitutional Design, Conflict Management, and Democracy* (New York: Oxford University Press,

2002); and Philip G. Roeder and Donald Rothchild, eds., *Sustainable Peace: Power and Democracy after Civil Wars* (Ithaca, N.Y.: Cornell University Press).

49. Diamond, "What Went Wrong in Iraq," 21.

50. Mill, "On Liberty," 936.

51. Fukuyama, *State-Building*, 3.

52. Daniel Brumberg, "Liberalization versus Democracy," in *Uncharted Journey: Promoting Democracy in the Middle East*, ed. Thomas Carothers and Marina Ottaway (Washington, D.C.: Carnegie Endowment for International Peace), 15–36.

53. Chesterman, *You the People*.

54. Roland Paris, *At War's End: Building Peace after Civil Conflict* (Cambridge: Cambridge University Press, 2004), 188.

55. Ibid., 188–207.

56. Jack Snyder and Karen Ballentine, "Nationalism and the Marketplace of Ideas," *International Security* 21, no. 2 (1996): 5–40; and Snyder, *From Voting to Violence: Democratization and Nationalist Conflict* (New York: W. W. Norton, 2000).

57. Snyder and Ballentine, "Nationalism and the Marketplace of Ideas," 39–40.

58. Stephen D. Krasner, "The Case for Shared Sovereignty," *Journal of Democracy* 16, no. 1 (2005): 69. Also see James D. Fearon and David D. Laitin, "Neotrusteeship and the Problem of Weak States," *International Security* 28, no. 4 (2004): 5–43; Stephen D. Krasner, "Sharing Sovereignty: New Institutions for Collapsed and Failing States," *International Security* 29, no. 2 (2004): 85–120.

59. Paris, "Wilson's Ghost," 776, 777.

60. Roeder and Rothchild, "Conclusions," 333.

61. Fukuyama, "'Stateness' First," 85.

62. Fearon and Laitin, "Neotrusteeship and the Problem of Weak States," 37.

63. Marten, *Enforcing the Peace*, 156.

64. Fearon and Laitin, "Neotrusteeship and the Problem of Weak States." On these problems, see also Marten, *Enforcing the Peace*; Chesterman, *You the People*; and Richard Caplan, "Who Guards the Guardians? International Accountability in Bosnia," *International Peacekeeping* 12, no. 3 (2005): 463–476.

65. We are grateful to Jack Snyder for making this observation.

66. Chester A. Crocker, "The Lessons of Somalia: Not Everything Went Wrong," *Foreign Affairs* 74, no. 3 (1995): 2–10.

INDEX

LEASHING THE DOGS OF WAR

This book is set in Adobe Caslon. Hasten Design Studio designed the book's cover, and Helene Y. Redmond designed the interior. Pages were made up by Helene Y. Redmond. David Sweet and Karen Stough copyedited the text, which was proofread by Kimberly McCutcheon and EEI. The index was prepared by Jean Middleton. The book's editor was Nigel Quinney.